P9-DOC-703

COLLINS
PORTUGUESE
DICTIONARY

FULLY REVISED AND UPDATED—
AMERICAN ENGLISH USAGE

Contributors

John Whitlam
Vitoria Davies
Mike Harland
Lígia Xavier
Laura Neves

HARPER

An Imprint of HarperCollins*Publishers*

HARPER

An Imprint of HarperCollins*Publishers*
10 East 53rd Street
New York, New York 10022-5299

© William Collins Sons & Co. Ltd. 1990
© HarperCollins Publishers 2000, 2007
ISBN: 978-0-06-126050-6
ISBN-10: 0-06-126050-9

First Harper paperback printing: January 2008

10 9 8 7 6 5 4 3 2 1

ÍNDICE

CONTENTS

William Collins' dream of knowledge for all began with the publication of his first book in 1819. A self-educated mill worker, he not only enriched millions of lives, but also founded a flourishing publishing house. Today, staying true to this spirit, Collins books are packed with inspiration, innovation, and practical expertise. They place you at the centre of a world of possibility and give you exactly what you need to explore it.

Language is the key to this exploration, and at the heart of Collins Dictionaries is language as it is really used. New words, phrases, and meanings spring up every day, and all of them are captured and analysed by the Collins Word Web. Constantly updated, and with over 2.5 billion entries, this living language resource is unique to our dictionaries.

Words are tools for life. And a Collins Dictionary makes them work for you.

Collins. Do more

INTRODUÇÃO

Ficamos felizes com a sua decisão de comprar o Dicionário Inglês-Português Collins e esperamos que este lhe seja útil na escola, em casa, de férias ou no trabalho.

INTRODUCTION

We are delighted you have decided to buy the Collins Portuguese Dictionary and hope you will enjoy and benefit from using it at school, at home, on holiday or at work.

ABREVIATURAS

ABBREVIATIONS

abreviatura	*ab(b)r*	abbreviation
adjetivo	*adj*	adjective
administração	*Admin*	administration
advérbio, locução adverbial	*adv*	adverb, adverbial phrase
aeronáutica	*Aer*	flying, air travel
agricultura	*Agr*	agriculture
anatomia	*Anat*	anatomy
arquitetura	*Arq, Arch*	architecture
artigo definido	*art def*	definite article
artigo indefinido	*art indef*	indefinite article
uso atributivo do substantivo	*atr*	compound element
automobilismo	*Aut(o)*	the motor car and motoring
auxiliar	*aux*	auxiliary
aeronáutica	*Aviat*	flying, air travel
biologia	*Bio*	biology
botânica, flores	*Bot*	botany
português do Brasil	BR	Brazilian Portuguese
inglês britânico	BRIT	British English
química	*Chem*	chemistry
linguagem coloquial (!chulo)	*col(!)*	colloquial (offensive!)
comércio, finanças, bancos	*Com(m)*	commerce, finance, banking
comparativo	*compar*	comparative
computação	*Comput*	computing
conjunção	*conj*	conjunction
construção	*Constr*	building
uso atributivo do substantivo	*cpd*	compound element
cozinha	*Culin*	cookery
artigo definido	*def art*	definite article
economia	*Econ*	economics
educação, escola e universidade	*Educ*	schooling, schools and universities
eletricidade, eletrônica	*Elet, Elec*	electricity, electronics
especialmente	*esp*	especially
exclamação	*excl*	exclamation
feminino	f	feminine
ferrovia	*Ferro*	railways
uso figurado	*fig*	figurative use
física	*Fís*	physics
fotografia	*Foto*	photography

ABBREVIATIONS

ABBREVIATIONS

(verbo inglês) do qual a partícula é inseparável	*fus*	(phrasal verb) where the particle is inseparable
geralmente	*gen*	generally
geografia, geologia	*Geo*	geography, geology
geralmente	*ger*	generally
impessoal	*impess, impers*	impersonal
artigo indefinido	*indef art*	indefinite article
linguagem coloquial (!chulo)	*inf(!)*	colloquial (offensive!)
infinitivo	*infin*	infinitive
invariável	*inv*	invariable
irregular	*irreg*	irregular
jurídico	*Jur*	law
gramática, lingüística	*Ling*	grammar, linguistics
masculino	*m*	masculine
matemática	*Mat(h)*	mathematics
medicina	*Med*	medicine
ou masculino ou feminino, dependendo do sexo da pessoa	*m/f*	masculine/feminine
militar, exército	*Mil*	military matters
música	*Mús, Mus*	music
substantivo	*n*	noun
navegação, náutica	*Náut, Naut*	sailing, navigation
adjetivo ou substantivo numérico	*num*	numeral adjective or noun
	o.s.	oneself
pejorativo	*pej*	pejorative
fotografia	*Phot*	photography
física	*Phys*	physics
fisiologia	*Physio*	physiology
plural	*pl*	plural
política	*Pol*	politics
particípio passado	*pp*	past participle
preposição	*prep*	preposition
pronome	*pron*	pronoun
português de Portugal	*PT*	European Portuguese
pretérito	*pt*	past tense
química	*Quím*	chemistry
religião e cultos	*Rel*	religion, church services
	sb	somebody
educação, escola e universidade	*Sch*	schooling, schools and universities
singular	*sg*	singular

ABREVIATURAS

ABBREVIATIONS

	sth	something
sujeito (gramatical)	*su(b)j*	(grammatical) subject
subjuntivo, conjuntivo	*sub(jun)*	subjunctive
superlativo	*superl*	superlative
também	*tb*	also
técnica, tecnologia	*Tec(h)*	technical term, technology
telecomunicações	*Tel*	telecommunications
tipografia, imprensa	*Tip*	typography, printing
televisão	*TV*	television
tipografia, imprensa	*Typ*	typography, printing
inglês americano	*US*	American English
ver	*V*	see
verbo	*vb*	verb
verbo intransitivo	*vi*	intransitive verb
verbo reflexivo	*vr*	reflexive verb
verbo transitivo	*vt*	transitive verb
zoologia	*Zool*	zoology
marca registrada	®	registered trademark
equivalente cultural	≈	cultural equivalent

PORTUGUESE PRONUNCIATION

The rules given below refer to Portuguese as spoken in the city and surrounding region of Rio de Janeiro, Brazil.

CONSONANTS

c	[k] café	c before *a, o, u* is pronounced as in *c*at
ce, ci	[s] cego	c before *e* or *i*, as in re*c*eive
ç	[s] raça	ç is pronounced as in re*c*eive
ch	[ʃ] chave	ch is pronounced as in *sh*ock
d	[d] data	as in English EXCEPT
de, di	[dʒ] difícil cidade	d before an *i* sound or final unstressed *e* is pronounced as in ju*dge*
g	[g] gado	g before *a, o, u* as in *g*ap
ge, gi	[ʒ] gíria	g before *e* or *i*, as *s* in lei*s*ure
h	humano	h is always silent in Portuguese
j	[ʒ] jogo	j is pronounced as *s* in lei*s*ure
l	[l] limpo, janela	as in English EXCEPT
	[w] falta, total	l after a vowel tends to become *w*
lh	[ʎ] trabalho	lh is pronounced like the *lli* in mi*lli*on
m	[m] animal, massa	as in English EXCEPT
	[ãw] cantam	m at the end of a syllable preceded by a
	[ĩ] sim	vowel nasalizes the preceding vowel
n	[n] nadar, penal	as in English EXCEPT
	[ã] cansar	n at the end of a syllable, preceded by a
	[ẽ] alento	vowel and followed by a consonant, nasalizes the preceding vowel
nh	[ɲ] tamanho	nh is pronounced like the *ni* in o*ni*on
q	[k] queijo	qu before *i* or *e* is pronounced as in ki*ck*
q	[kw] quanto cinqüenta	qu before *a* or *o*, or *qü* before *e* or *i*, is pronounced as in *qu*een
-r-	[r] compra	r preceded by a consonant (except *n*) and followed by a vowel is pronounced with a single trill
r-, -r-	[x] rato, arpão	inital r, r followed by a consonant and rr pronounced similar to the Scottish *ch* in lo*ch*
rr	[x] borracha	
-r	[*] pintar, dizer	word-final r before a word beginning with a consonant or at the end of a sentence is pronounced [x]; before a word beginning with a vowel it is pronounced [r]. In colloquial speech this variable sound is often not pronounced at all.
s-	[s] sol	as in English EXCEPT

-s-	[z]	mesa	intervocalic *s* is pronounced as in ro*s*e
-s-	[ʒ]	rasgar, desmaio	*s* before *b, d, g, l, m, n, r,* and *v,* as in lei*s*ure
-s-, -s	[ʃ]	escada, livros	*s* before *c, f, p, qu, t* and finally, as in *s*ugar
-ss-	[s]	nosso	double *s* is always pronounced as in bo*ss*
t	[t]	todo	as in English EXCEPT
te, ti	[tʃ]	amante tipo	*t* followed by an *i* sound or final unstressed *e* is pronounced as *ch* in *ch*eer
x-	[ʃ]	xarope explorar	initial *x* or *x* before a consonant (except *c*) is pronounced as in *s*ugar
-xce-, -xci-	[s]	exceto excitar	*x* before *ce* or *ci* is unpronounced
ex-	[z]	exame	*x* in the prefix *ex* before a vowel is pronounced as *z* in squee*z*e
-x-	[ʃ]	relaxar	*x* in any other position may be pronounced
	[ks]	fixo	as in *s*ugar, a*x*e or *s*ail
	[s]	auxiliar	
z-, -z-	[z]	zangar	as in English EXCEPT
-z	[ʒ]	cartaz	final *z* is pronounced as in lei*s*ure

b, f, k, p, v, w are pronounced as in English.

VOWELS

a, á, à, â	[a]	mata	*a* is normally pronounced as in f*a*ther
ã	[ã]	irmã	*ã* is pronounced approximately as in s*u*ng
e	[e]	vejo	unstressed (except final) *e* is pronounced like *e* in th*ey*, stressed *e* is pronounced either as in th*ey* or as in b*e*t
-e	[i]	fome	final *e* is pronounced as in mon*ey*
é	[ɛ]	miséria	*é* is pronounced as in b*e*t
ê	[e]	pêlo	*ê* is pronounced as in th*ey*
i	[i]	vida	*i* is pronounced as in m*e*an
o	[o]	locomotiva	unstressed (except final) *o* is pronounced as in l*o*cal;
	[ɔ]	loja	stressed *o* is pronounced either as in
	[o]	globo	l*o*cal or as in r*o*ck
-o	[u]	livro	final *o* is pronounced as in f*oo*t
ó	[ɔ]	óleo	*ó* is pronounced as in r*o*ck
ô	[o]	colônia	*ô* is pronounced as in l*o*cal
u	[u]	luva	*u* is pronounced as in r*u*le; it is silent in *gue, gui, que* and *qui*

DIPHTHONGS

ãe	[ãj]	**mãe**	nasalized, approximately as in fl**y**ing
ai	[aj]	**vai**	as is r**i**de
ao, au	[aw]	**aos, auxílio**	as is sh**ou**t
ão	[ãw]	**vão**	nasalized, approximately as in r**ou**nd
ei	[ej]	**feira**	as is th**ey**
eu	[ew]	**deusa**	both elements pronounced
oi	[oj]	**boi**	as is t**oy**
ou	[o]	**cenoura**	as is l**o**cal
õe	[õj]	**aviões**	nasalized, approximately as in 'b**oi**ng!'

STRESS

The rules of stress in Portuguese are as follows:

(a)   when a word ends in *a, e, o, m* (except *im, um* and their plural forms) or *s*, the second last syllable is stressed;
camar*a*da; camar*a*das
p*a*rte; p*a*rtem

(b)   when a word ends in *i, u, im* (and plural), *um* (and plural), *n* or a consonant other than *m* or *s*, the stress falls on the last syllable:
ven*di*, al*gum*, al*guns*, fa*lar*

(c)   when the rules set out in (a) and (b) are not applicable, an acute or circumflex accent appears over the stressed vowel:
*ó*tica, *â*nimo, in*glês*

In the phonetic transcription, the symbol [^{1}] precedes the syllable on which the stress falls.

PRONÚNCIA INGLESA

VOGAIS

	Exemplo Inglês	Explicação
[a:]	father	Entre o a de padre e o o de nó; como em fada
[ʌ]	but, come	Aproximadamente como o primeiro a de cama
[æ]	man, cat	Som entre o a de lá e o e de pé
[ə]	father, ago	Som parecido com o e final pronuncia do em Portugal
[ə:]	bird, heard	Entre o e aberto e o o fechado
[ɛ]	get, bed	Como em pé
[ɪ]	it, big	Mais breve do que em si
[i:]	tea, see	Como em fino
[ɔ]	hot, wash	Como em pó
[ɔ:]	saw, all	Como o o de porte
[u]	put, book	Som breve e mais fechado do que em burro
[u:]	too, you	Som aberto como em juro

DITONGOS

	Exemplo Inglês	Explicação
[aɪ]	fly, high	Como em baile
[au]	how, house	Como em causa
[ɛə]	there, bear	Como o e de aeroporto
[eɪ]	day, obey	Como o ei de lei
[ɪə]	here, hear	Como ia de companhia
[əu]	go, note	[ə] seguido de um u breve
[ɔɪ]	boy, oil	Como em bóia
[uə]	poor, sure	Como ua em sua

CONSOANTES

	Exemplo Inglês	Explicação
[d]	mended	Como em dado, andar
[g]	get, big	Como em grande
[dʒ]	gin, judge	Como em idade
[ŋ]	sing	Como em cinco
[h]	house, he	h aspirado
[j]	young, yes	Como em iogurte
[k]	come, mock	Como em cama
[r]	red, tread	r como em para, mas pronunciado no céu da boca
[s]	sand, yes	Como em sala
[z]	rose, zebra	Como em zebra

[ʃ]	she, machine	Como em *ch*apéu
[tʃ]	chin, rich	Como *t* em *t*imbre
[w]	water, which	Como o *u* em á*gu*a
[ʒ]	vision	Como em *j*á
[θ]	think, myth	Sem equivalente, aproximadamente como um *s* pronunciado entre os dentes
[ð]	this, the	Sem equivalente, aproximadamente como um *z* pronunciado entre os dentes

b, f, l, m, n, p, t, v pronunciam-se como em português.

O signo [*] indica que o r final escrito pronuncia-se apenas em inglês britânico, exceto quando a palavra seguinte começa por uma vogal. O signo [¹] indica a sílaba acentuada.

EUROPEAN PORTUGUESE SPELLING

The spelling of European Portuguese differs significantly from that of Brazilian. The differences, which affect consonant groups and accents, follow general patterns but do not on the whole conform to fixed rules. Limited space makes it impossible to cover all European forms in the dictionary text, but major differences in spelling and vocabulary have been included. In addition, the following guide is intended as a broad outline of these differences.

The following changes in spelling are consistent:

- Brazilian *gü* and *qü* become European *gu* and *qu*, e.g. agüentar (BR), aguentar (PT); cinqüenta (BR), cinquenta (PT).
- Brazilian *-éia* becomes European *-eia*, e.g. idéia (BR), ideia (PT).
- European spelling links forms of the verb *haver de* with a hyphen, e.g. *hei de* (BR), *hei-de* (PT).
- The numbers dezesseis (BR), dezessete(BR), dezenove (BR) become dezasseis (PT), dezassete (PT), dezanove (PT).
- Adverbial forms of adjectives ending in *m* take double *m* in European spelling, single *m* in Brazilian, e.g. comumente (BR), comummente (PT).
- European spelling adds an acute accent to the final *a* in first person plural preterite forms of irregular *-ar* verbs to distinguish them from the present tense, e.g. amamos (BR), amámos (PT).
- Brazilian conosco becomes European connosco.

The following changes may take place, but are not consistent:

CONSONANT CHANGES
- Brazilian *c* and *ç* double to *cc* and *cç*, acionista (BR), accionista (PT), seção (BR), secção (PT).
- Brazilian *t* becomes *ct*, e.g. elétrico (BR), eléctrico (PT).
- European spelling adds *b* to certain words, e.g. súdito (BR), súbdito (PT), sutilizar (BR), subtilizar (PT).
- European spelling changes *ç*, *t* to *pç*, *pt* , e.g. exceção (BR), excepção (PT), ótimo (BR), óptimo (PT).
- Brazilian *-n-* becomes *-mn-*, e.g. anistia (BR), amnistia (PT).
- Brazilian *tr* becomes *t*, e.g. registro (BR), registo (PT).

ACCENTUATION CHANGES
- Brazilian *ôo* loses circumflex accent, e.g. vôo (BR), voo (PT).
- European spelling changes circumflex accent on *e* and *o* to acute, e.g. tênis (BR), ténis (PT), abdômen (BR), abdómen (PT).

1 Gerund. **2** Imperative. **3** Present. **4** Imperfect. **5** Preterite. **6** Future.
7 Present subjunctive. **8** Imperfect subjunctive. **9** Future subjunctive.
10 Past participle. **11** Pluperfect. **12** Personal infinitive.

etc indicates that the irregular root is used for all persons of the
tense, e.g. **ouvir 7** ouça ouça, ouças, ouça, ouçamos, ouçais, ouçam.

abrir 10 aberto
acudir 2 acode **3** acudo, acodes, acode, acodem
aderir 3 adiro **7** adira
advertir 3 advirto **7** advirta *etc*
agir 3 ajo **7** aja *etc*
agradecer 3 agradeço **7** agradeça *etc*
agredir 2 agride **3** agrido, agrides, agride, agridem **7** agrida *etc*
AMAR 1 amando **2** ama, amai **3** amo, amas, ama, amamos, amais, amam **4** amava, amavas, amava, amávamos, amavéis, amavam **5** amei, amaste, amou, amamos (*PT*: amámos), amastes, amaram
6 amarei, amarás, amará, amaremos, amareis, amarão **7** ame, ames, ame, amemos, ameis, amem **8** amasse, amasses, amasse, amássemos, amásseis, amassem **9** amar, amares, amar, ámarmos, amardes, amarem **10** amado **11** amara, amaras, amara, amáramos, amáreis, amaram **12** amar, amares, amar, amarmos, amardes, amarem
ansiar 2 anseia **3** anseio, anseias, anseia, anseiam **7** anseie *etc*
apreçar 7 aprece *etc*
arrancar 7 arranque *etc*
arruinar 2 arruína **3** arruíno, arruínas, arruína, arruínam **7** arruíne, arruínes, arruíne, arruínem
aspergir 3 aspirjo **7** aspirja *etc*
atribuir 3 atribuo, atribuis, atribui, atribuímos, atribuís, atribuem
averiguar 7 averigúe, averigúes, averigúe, averigúem
boiar 2 bóia, bóias, bóia, bóiam **7** bóie, bóies, bóie, bóiem
bulir 2 bole **3** bulo, boles, bole, bolem
caber 3 caibo **5** coube *etc* **7** caiba *etc* **8** coubesse *etc* **9** couber *etc*
cair 2 cai **3** caio, cais, cai, caímos, caís, caem **4** caía *etc* **5** caí, caíste **7** caia *etc* **8** caisse *etc*
cobrir 3 cubro **7** cubra *etc* **10** coberto
colorir 3 coluro **7** colura *etc*
compelir 3 compilo **7** compila *etc*
crer 2 crê **3** creio, crês, crê, cremos, credes, crêem **5** cri, creste, creu, cremos, crestes, creram **7** creia *etc*
cuspir 2 cospe **3** cuspo, cospes, cospe, cospem
dar 2 dá **3** dou, dás, dá, damos, dais, dão **5** dei, deste, deu, demos, destes, deram **7** dê, dês, dê, demos, deis, dêem **8** desse *etc* **9** der *etc* **11** dera *etc*
deduzir 2 deduz **3** deduzo, deduzes, deduz
denegrir 2 denigre **3** denigro, denigres, denigre, denigrem **7** denigre *etc*

despir 3 dispo 7 dispa *etc*
dizer 2 diz (dize) 3 digo, dizes, diz, dizemos, dizeis, dizem 5 disse *etc* 6 direi *etc* 7 diga *etc* 8 dissesse *etc* 9 disser *etc* 10 dito
doer 2 dói 3 dôo (BR), doo (PT), dóis, dói
dormir 3 durmo 7 durma *etc*
escrever 10 escrito
ESTAR 2 está 3 estou, estás, está, estamos, estais, estão 4 estava *etc* 5 estive, estiveste, esteve, estivemos, estivestes, estiveram 7 esteja *etc* 8 estivesse *etc* 9 estiver *etc* 11 estivera *etc*
extorquir 3 exturco 7 exturca *etc*
FAZER 3 faço 5 fiz, fizeste, fez, fizemos, fizestes, fizeram 6 farei *etc* 7 faça *etc* 8 fizesse *etc* 9 fizer *etc* 10 feito 11 fizera *etc*
ferir 3 firo 7 fira *etc*
fluir 3 fluo, fluis, flui, fluímos, fluís, fluem
fugir 2 foge 3 fujo, foges, foge, fogem 7 fuja *etc*
ganhar 10 ganho
gastar 10 gasto
gerir 3 giro 7 gira *etc*
haver 2 há 3 hei, hás, há, havemos, haveis, hão 4 havia *etc* 5 houve, houveste, houve, houvemos, houvestes, houveram 7 haja *etc* 8 houvesse *etc* 9 houver *etc* 11 houvera *etc*
ir 1 indo 2 vai 3 vou, vais, vai, vamos, ides, vão 4 ia *etc* 5 fui, foste, foi, fomos, fostes, foram 7 vá, vás, vá, vamos, vades, vão 8 fosse, fosses, fosse, fôssemos, fôsseis, fossem 9 for *etc* 10 ido 11 fora *etc*
ler 2 lê 3 leio, lês, lê, lemos, ledes, lêem 5 li, leste, leu, lemos, lestes, leram 7 leia *etc*
medir 3 meço, 7 meça *etc*
mentir 3 minto 7 minta *etc*

ouvir 3 ouço 7 ouça *etc*
pagar 10 pago
parar 2 pára 3 paro, paras, pára
parir 3 pairo 7 paira *etc*
pecar 7 peque *etc*
pedir 3 peço 7 peça *etc*
perder 3 perco 7 perca *etc*
poder 3 posso 5 pude, pudeste, pôde, pudemos, pudestes, puderam 7 possa *etc* 8 pudesse *etc* 9 puder *etc* 11 pudera *etc*
polir 2 pule 3 pulo, pules, pule, pulem 7 pula *etc*
pôr 1 pondo 2 põe 3 ponho, pões, põe, pomos, pondes, põem 4 punha *etc* 5 pus, puseste, pôs, pusemos, pusestes, puseram 6 porei *etc* 7 ponha *etc* 8 pusesse *etc* 9 puser *etc* 10 posto 11 pusera *etc*
preferir 3 prefiro 7 prefire *etc*
pervenir 2 previne 3 previno, prevines, previne, previnem 7 previna *etc*
prover 2 provê 3 provejo, provês, provê, provemos, provedes, provêem 5 provi, proveste, proveu, provemos, provestes, proveram 7 proveja *etc* 8 provesse *etc* 9 prover *etc*
querer 3 quero, queres, quer 5 quis, quiseste, quis, quisemos, quisestes, quiseram 7 queira *etc* 8 quisesse *etc* 9 quiser *etc* 11 quisera *etc*
refletir 3 reflito 7 reflita *etc*
repetir 3 repito 7 repita *etc*
requerer 3 requeiro, requeres, requer 7 requeira *etc*
reunir 2 reúne 3 reúno, reúnes, reúne, reúnem 7 reúna *etc*
rir 2 ri 3 rio, ris, ri, rimos, rides, ridem 5 ri, riste, riu, rimos, ristes, riram 7 ria *etc*
saber 3 sei, sabes, sabe, sabemos, sabeis, sabem

5 soube, soubeste, soube, soubemos, soubestes, souberam **7** saiba *etc* **8** soubesse *etc* **9** souber *etc* **11** soubera *etc*

seguir 3 sigo **7** siga *etc*

sentir 3 sinto **7** sinta *etc*

ser 2 sê **3** sou, és, é, somos, sois, são **4** era *etc* **5** fui, foste, foi, fomos, fostes, foram **7** seja *etc* **8** fosse *etc* **9** for *etc* **11** fora *etc*

servir 3 sirvo **7** sirva *etc*

subir 2 sobe **3** subo, sobes, sobe, sobem

suster 2 sustém **3** sustenho, sustens, sustém, sustendes, sustêm **5** sustive, sustiveste, susteve, sustivemos, sustivestes, sustiveram **7** sustenha *etc*

ter 2 tem **3** tenho, tens, tem, temos, tendes, têm **4** tinha *etc* **5** tive, tiveste, teve, tivemos, tivestes, tiveram **6** terei *etc* **7** tenha *etc* **8** tivesse *etc* **9** tiver *etc* **11** tivera *etc*

torcer 3 torço **7** torça *etc*

tossir 3 tusso **7** tussa *etc*

trair 2 trai **3** traio, trais, trai, traímos, traís, traem **7** traia *etc*

trazer 2 (traze) traz **3** trago, trazes, traz, **5** trouxe, trouxeste, trouxe, trouxemos, trouxestes, trouxeram **6** trarei *etc* **7** traga *etc* **8** trouxesse *etc* **9** trouxer *etc* **11** trouxera *etc*

UNIR 1 unindo **2** une, uni **3** uno, unes, une, unimos, unis, unem **4** unia, unias, uníamos, uníeis, uniam **5** uni, uniste, uniu, unimos, unistes, uniram

6 unirei, unirás, unirá, uniremos, unireis, unirão **7** una, unas, una, unamos, unais, unam **8** unisse, unisses, unisse, uníssemos, unísseis, unissem **9** unir, unires, unir, unirmos, unirdes, unirem **10** unido **11** unira, uniras, unira, uníramos, uníreis, uniram **12** unir, unires, unir, unirmos, unirdes, unirem

valer 3 valho **7** valha *etc*

ver 2 vê **3** vejo, vês, vê, vemos, vedes, vêem **4** via *etc* **5** vi, viste, viu, vimos, vistes, viram **7** veja *etc* **8** visse *etc* **9** vir *etc* **10** visto **11** vira

vir 1 vindo, **2** vem **3** venho, vens, vem, vimos, vindes, vêm **4** vinha *etc* **5** vim, vieste, veio, viemos, viestes, vieram **7** venha *etc* **8** viesse *etc* **9** vier *etc* **10** vindo **11** viera *etc*

VIVER 1 vivendo **2** vive, vivei **3** vivo, vives, vive, vivemos, viveis, vivem **4** vivia, vivias, vivia, vivíamos, vivíeis, viviam **5** vivi, viveste, viveu, vivemos, vivestes, viveram **6** viverei, viverás, viverá, viveremos, vivereis, viverão **7** viva, vivas, viva, vivamos, vivais, vivam **8** vivesse, vivesses, vivesse, vivêssemos, vivêsseis, vivessem **9** viver, viveres, viver, vivermos, viverdes, viverem **10** vivido **11** vivera, viveras, vivera, vivêramos, vivêreis, viveram **12** viver, viveres, viver, vivermos, viverdes, viverem

VERBOS IRREGULARES EM INGLÊS

PRESENT	PT	PP	PRESENT	PT	PP
arise	arose	arisen	fight	fought	fought
awake	awoke	awoken	find	found	found
be (am, is,	was, were	been	fling	flung	flung
are; being)			fly	flew	flown
bear	bore	born(e)	forbid	forbad(e)	forbidden
beat	beat	beaten	forecast	forecast	forecast
begin	began	begun	forget	forgot	forgotten
bend	bent	bent	forgive	forgave	forgiven
bet	bet,	bet,	freeze	froze	frozen
	betted	betted	get	got	got,
bid (at auction)	bid	bid			(US) goten
bind	bound	bound	give	gave	given
bite	bit	bitten	go (goes)	went	gone
bleed	bled	bled	grind	ground	ground
blow	blew	blown	grow	grew	grown
break	broke	broken	hang	hung	hung
breed	bred	bred	hang (execute)	hanged	hanged
bring	brought	brought	have	had	had
build	built	built	hear	heard	heard
burn	burnt,	burnt,	hide	hid	hidden
	burned	burned	hit	hit	hit
burst	burst	burst	hold	held	held
buy	bought	bought	hurt	hurt	hurt
can	could	(been able)	keep	kept	kept
cast	cast	cast	kneel	knelt,	knelt,
catch	caught	caught		kneeled	kneeled
choose	chose	chosen	know	knew	known
cling	clung	clung	lay	laid	laid
come	came	come	lead	led	led
cost	cost	cost	lean	leant,	leant,
creep	crept	crept		leaned	leaned
cut	cut	cut	leap	leapt,	leapt,
deal	dealt	dealt		leaped	leaped
dig	dug	dug	learn	learnt,	learnt,
do (does)	did	done		learned	learned
draw	drew	drawn	leave	left	left
dream	dreamed,	dreamed,	lend	lent	lent
	dreamt	dreamt	let	let	let
drink	drank	drunk	lie (lying)	lay	lain
drive	drove	driven	light	lit,	lit,
eat	ate	eaten		lighted	lighted
fall	fell	fallen	lose	lost	lost
feed	fed	fed	make	made	made
feel	felt	felt	may	might	–

PRESENT	PT	PP	PRESENT	PT	PP
mean	meant	meant	speak	spoke	spoken
meet	met	met	speed	sped,	sped,
mistake	mistook	mistaken		speeded	speeded
mow	mowed	mown,	spell	spelt,	spelt,
		mowed		spelled	spelled
must	(had to)	(had to)	spend	spent	spent
pay	paid	paid	spill	spilt,	spilt,
put	put	put		spilled	spilled
quit	quit,	quit,	spin	spun	spun
	quitted	quitted	spit	spat	spat
read	read	read	spoil	spoiled,	spoiled,
rid	rid	rid		spoilt	spoilt
ride	rode	ridden	spread	spread	spread
ring	rang	rung	spring	sprang	sprung
rise	rose	risen	stand	stood	stood
run	ran	run	steal	stole	stolen
saw	sawed	sawed,	stick	stuck	stuck
		sawn	sting	stung	stung
say	said	said	stink	stank	stunk
see	saw	seen	stride	strode	stridden
sell	sold	sold	strike	struck	struck
send	sent	sent	swear	swore	sworn
set	set	set	sweep	swept	swept
sew	sewed	sewn	swell	swelled	swollen,
shake	shook	shaken			swelled
shear	sheared	shorn,	swim	swam	swum
		sheared	swing	swung	swung
shed	shed	shed	take	took	taken
shine	shone	shone	teach	taught	taught
shoot	shot	shot	tear	tore	torn
show	showed	shown	tell	told	told
shrink	shrank	shrunk	think	thought	thought
shut	shut	shut	throw	threw	thrown
sing	sang	sung	thrust	thrust	thrust
sink	sank	sunk	tread	trod	trodden
sit	sat	sat	wake	woke,	woken,
sleep	slept	slept		waked	waked
slide	slid	slid	wear	wore	worn
sling	slung	slung	weave	wove	woven
slit	slit	slit	weep	wept	wept
smell	smelt,	smelt,	win	won	won
	smelled	smelled	wind	wound	wound
sow	sowed	sown,	wring	wrung	wrung
		sowed	write	wrote	written

DATAS

DATES

DIAS DA SEMANA
segunda(-feira)
terça(-feira)
quarta(-feira)
quinta(-feira)
sexta(-feira)
sábado
domingo

DAYS OF THE WEEK
Monday
Tuesday
Wednesday
Thursday
Friday
Saturday
Sunday

MESES
janeiro
fevereiro
março
abril
maio
junho
julho
agosto
setembro
outubro
novembro
dezembro

MONTHS
January
February
March
April
May
June
July
August
September
October
November
December

Note that the days of the week and the months start with a capital letter in Portugal and a small letter in Brazil.

VOCABULÁRIO ÚTIL
Que dia é hoje?
Hoje é dia 28.
Quando?
hoje
amanhã
ontem
hoje de manhã/à tarde
em duas semanas
daqui a uma semana
o mês passado/que vem

USEFUL VOCABULARY
What day is it today?
Today is the 28th.
When?
today
tomorrow
yesterday
this morning/afternoon
in two weeks *ou* a fortnight
in a week's time
last/next month

AS HORAS	THE TIME
QUE HORAS SÃO?	**WHAT TIME IS IT?**

É meio-dia / meia-noite.
_____

It's midday/midnight.

É uma e quinze.
É uma e um quarto (PT).
_____

It's one fifteen.

Faltam dez para as duas.
São duas menos dez (PT).
_____

It's ten to two.

São três e meia.
_____

It's half past three.

Faltam vinte para as oito.
São oito menos vinte (PT).
_____

It's twenty to eight.

São nove (horas) da
manhã / da noite.
_____

It's nine o'clock in the
morning/at night.

NÚMEROS

NUMBERS

NÚMEROS CARDINAIS

CARDINAL NUMBERS

Português		English
um (uma)	1	one
dois (duas)	2	two
três	3	three
quatro	4	four
cinco	5	five
seis	6	six
sete	7	seven
oito	8	eight
nove	9	nine
dez	10	ten
onze	11	eleven
doze	12	twelve
treze	13	thirteen
catorze	14	fourteen
quinze	15	fifteen
dezesseis (BR), dezasseis (PT)	16	sixteen
dezessete (BR), dezassete (PT)	17	seventeen
dezoito	18	eighteen
dezenove (BR), dezanove (PT)	19	nineteen
vinte	20	twenty
vinte e um (uma)	21	twenty-one
trinta	30	thirty
quarenta	40	forty
cinqüenta (BR), cinquenta (PT)	50	fifty
sessenta	60	sixty
setenta	70	seventy
oitenta	80	eighty
noventa	90	ninety
cem	100	a hundred
cento e um (uma)	101	a hundred and one
duzentos(-as)	200	two hundred
trezentos(-as)	300	three hundred
quinhentos(-as)	500	five hundred
mil	1.000/1,000	a thousand
um milhão	1.000.000/1,000,000	a million

FRAÇÕES ETC

zero vírgula cinco	0,5/0.5	
três vírgula quatro	3,4/3.4	
dez por cento	10%	
cem por cento	100%	

FRACTIONS ETC

zero point five
three point four
ten per cent
a hundred per cent

NÚMEROS ORDINAIS

primeiro	1°/1st
segundo	2°/2nd
terceiro	3°/3rd
quarto	4°/4th
quinto	5°/5th
sexto	6°/6th
sétimo	7°/7th
oitavo	8°/8th
nono	9°/9th
décimo	10°/10th
décimo primeiro	11°/11th
vigésimo	20°/20th
trigésimo	30°/30th
quadragésimo	40°/40th
qüinquagésimo(BR),	50°/50th
quinquagésimo(PT)	
centésimo	100°/100th
centésimo primeiro	101°/101st
milésimo	1000°/1000th

ORDINAL NUMBERS

first
second
third
fourth
fifth
sixth
seventh
eighth
ninth
tenth
eleventh
twentieth
thirtieth
fortieth
fiftieth

hundredth
hundred-and-first
thousandth

fazer algo

abnormal [æb'nɔːməl] *adj* anormal

aboard [ə'bɔːd] *adv* a bordo ▷ *prep* a
bordo de

abolish [ə'bɒlɪʃ] *vt* abolir

aborigine [æbə'rɪdʒɪnɪ] *n* aborígene *m/f*

abort [ə'bɔːt] *vt* (*Med*) abortar; (*plan*)
cancelar; **abortion** *n* aborto; **to have
an abortion** fazer um aborto, abortar

Ⓞ KEYWORD

about [ə'baut] *adv* **1** (*approximately*)
aproximadamente; **it takes about 10
hours** leva mais ou menos 10 horas;
it's just about finished está quase
terminado

2 (*referring to place*) por toda parte,
por todo lado; **to run/walk etc about**
correr/andar *etc* por todos os lados

3: **to be about to do sth** estar a ponto
de fazer algo

▷ *prep* **1** (*relating to*) acerca de, sobre;
what is it about? do que se trata?, é
sobre o quê?; **what** *or* **how about doing
this?** que tal se fizermos isso?

2 (*place*) em redor de, por

A [eɪ] *n* (*Mus*) lá *m*

Ⓞ KEYWORD

a [eɪ, ə] *indef art* (*before vowel or silent h*:
an) **1** um(a); **a book/girl** um livro/uma
menina; **an apple** uma maçã; **she's a
doctor** ela é médica

2 (*instead of the number "one"*) um(a); **a
year ago** há um ano, um ano atrás; **a
hundred/thousand etc pounds** cem/
mil *etc* libras

3 (*in expressing ratios, prices etc*): **3 a day/
week** 3 por dia/semana; **10 km an hour**
10 km por hora; **30p a kilo** 30p o quilo

aback [ə'bæk] *adv*: **to be taken ~** ficar
surpreendido, sobressaltar-se

abandon [ə'bændən] *vt* abandonar ▷ *n*:
with ~ com desenfreio

abbey ['æbɪ] *n* abadia, mosteiro

abbreviation *n* abreviatura

abdomen ['æbdəmən] *n* abdômen *m*

abduct [æb'dʌkt] *vt* seqüestrar

ability [ə'bɪlɪtɪ] *n* habilidade *f*,
capacidade *f*; (*talent*) talento

able ['eɪbl] *adj* capaz; (*skilled*) hábil,
competente; **to be ~ to do sth** poder

above [ə'bʌv] *adv* em *or* por cima, acima;
(*greater*) acima ▷ *prep* acima de, por cima
de; (*greater than: in rank*) acima de; (: *in
number*) mais de; **~ all** sobretudo

abroad [ə'brɔːd] *adv* (*be*) no estrangeiro;
(*go*) ao estrangeiro

abrupt [ə'brʌpt] *adj* (*sudden*) brusco;
(*curt*) ríspido

abscess ['æbsɪs] *n* abscesso (BR),
abcesso (PT)

absence ['æbsəns] *n* ausência

absent ['æbsənt] *adj* ausente; **absent-
minded** *adj* distraído

absolute ['æbsəluːt] *adj* absoluto;
absolutely [æbsə'luːtlɪ] *adv*
absolutamente

absorb [əb'zɔːb] *vt* absorver; (*business*)
incorporar; (*changes*) assimilar;
(*information*) digerir; **absorbent cotton**
(US) *n* algodão *m* hidrófilo

abstain [əb'steɪn] *vi*: **to ~ (from)** abster-
se (de)

abstract ['æbstrækt] *adj* abstrato

absurd [əb'sɜːd] *adj* absurdo

abuse [(*n*) ə'bjuːs, (*vb*) ə'bjuːz] *n* (*insults*)
insultos *mpl*; (*ill-treatment*) maus-tratos
mpl; (*misuse*) abuso ▷ *vt* insultar;
maltratar; abusar de; **abusive** [ə'bjuːsɪv]

adj ofensivo
abysmal [ə'bɪzməl] adj (ignorance)
profundo, total; (failure) péssimo
academic [ækə'dɛmɪk] adj acadêmico;
(pej: issue) teórico ▷ n universitário(-a)
academy [ə'kædəmɪ] n (learned body)
academia; ~ **of music** conservatório
accelerate [æk'sɛləreɪt] vt, vi acelerar;
accelerator n acelerador m
accent ['æksɛnt] n (written) acento;
(pronunciation) sotaque m; (fig: emphasis)
ênfase f
accept [ək'sɛpt] vt aceitar; (responsibility)
assumir; **acceptable** adj (offer) bem-
vindo; (risk) aceitável; **acceptance** n
aceitação f
access ['æksɛs] n acesso; **accessible**
[æk'sɛsəbl] adj acessível; (available)
disponível
accessory [æk'sɛsərɪ] n acessório; (Law):
~ **to** cúmplice m/f de
accident ['æksɪdənt] n acidente
m; (chance) casualidade f; **by ~**
(unintentionally) sem querer; (by
coincidence) por acaso; **accidental**
[æksɪ'dɛntl] adj acidental; **accidentally**
[æksɪ'dɛntəlɪ] adv sem querer
acclaim [ə'kleɪm] n aclamação f
accommodate [ə'kɔmədeɪt] vt alojar;
(subj: car, hotel, etc) acomodar; (oblige,
help) comprazer a; **accommodation**
[əkɔmə'deɪʃən] n alojamento;
accommodations (US) npl
= **accommodation**
accompany [ə'kʌmpənɪ] vt
acompanhar
accomplice [ə'kʌmplɪs] n cúmplice m/f
accomplish [ə'kʌmplɪʃ] vt
(task) concluir; (goal) alcançar;
accomplishment n realização f
accord [ə'kɔːd] n tratado ▷ vt
conceder; **of his own** ~ por sua
iniciativa; **accordance** [ə'kɔːdəns] n:
in accordance with de acordo com;
according: according to prep segundo,
conforme; **accordingly** adv por
conseguinte; (appropriately) do modo
devido
account [ə'kaunt] n conta; (report)
relato; **accounts** npl (books,
department) contabilidade f; **of no** ~ sem
importância; **on** ~ por conta; **on no** ~ de
modo nenhum; **on** ~ **of** por causa de; **to
take into** ~, **take** ~ **of** levar em conta;
account for vt fus (explain) explicar;
(represent) representar; **accountant** n

contador(a) m/f (BR), contabilista m/f
(PT); **account number** n número de
conta
accumulate [ə'kjuːmjuleɪt] vt
acumular ▷ vi acumular-se
accuracy ['ækjurəsɪ] n exatidão f,
precisão f
accurate ['ækjurɪt] adj (description)
correto; (person, device) preciso;
accurately adv com precisão
accusation [ækju'zeɪʃən] n (act)
incriminação f; (instance) acusação f
accuse [ə'kjuːz] vt acusar; **accused** n:
the accused o/a acusado/a
ace [eɪs] n ás m
ache [eɪk] n dor f ▷ vi (yearn): **to ~ to do
sth** ansiar por fazer algo; **my head ~s**
dói-me a cabeça
achieve [ə'tʃiːv] vt alcançar; (victory,
success) obter; **achievement** n
realização f; (success) proeza
acid ['æsɪd] adj ácido; (taste) azedo ▷ n
ácido
acknowledge [ək'nɔlɪdʒ] vt (fact)
reconhecer; (letter) acusar o
recebimento de (BR) ora recepção de (PT);
acknowledgement n notificação f de
recebimento
acne ['æknɪ] n acne f
acorn ['eɪkɔːn] n bolota
acoustic [ə'kuːstɪk] adj acústico
acquire [ə'kwaɪəʳ] vt adquirir
acquit [ə'kwɪt] vt absolver; **to ~ o.s. well**
desempenhar-se bem
acre ['eɪkəʳ] n acre m (= 4047m²)
across [ə'krɔs] prep (on the other side of)
no outro lado de; (crosswise) através
de ▷ adv: **to go** (or **walk**) ~ atravessar;
the lake is 12km ~ o lago tem 12km de
largura; ~ **from** em frente de
acrylic [ə'krɪlɪk] adj acrílico ▷ n acrílico
act [ækt] n ação f; (Theatre) ato; (in show)
número; (Law) lei f ▷ vi tomar ação;
(behave, have effect, Theatre) agir; (pretend)
fingir ▷ vt (part) representar; **in the ~ of**
no ato de; **to ~ as** servir de; **acting** adj
interino ▷ n: **to do some acting** fazer
teatro
action ['ækʃən] n ação f; (Mil) batalha,
combate m; (Law) ação judicial; **out of
~** (person) fora de combate; (thing) com
defeito; **to take** ~ tomar atitude; **action
replay** n (TV) replay m
activate ['æktɪveɪt] vt acionar
active ['æktɪv] adj ativo; (volcano) em
atividade; **actively** adv ativamente;

activity [æk'tɪvɪtɪ] *n* atividade *f*
actor ['æktə'] *n* ator *m*
actress ['æktrɪs] *n* atriz *f*
actual ['æktjuəl] *adj* real; (*emphatic use*) em si; **actually** *adv* realmente; (*in fact*) na verdade; (*even*) mesmo
acute [ə'kju:t] *adj* agudo; (*person*) perspicaz
ad [æd] *n abbr* = **advertisement**
A.D. *adv abbr* (= *Anno Domini*) d.C.
adamant ['ædəmənt] *adj* inflexível
adapt [ə'dæpt] *vt* adaptar ⊳ *vi*: **to ~ (to)** adaptar-se (a)
add [æd] *vt* acrescentar; (*figures: also:* **~ up**) somar ⊳ *vi*: **to ~ to** aumentar
addict ['ædɪkt] *n* viciado(-a); **drug ~** toxicômano(-a); **addicted** [ə'dɪktɪd] *adj*: **to be addicted to** ser viciado em; (*fig*) ser fanático por; **addiction** *n* dependência; **addictive** *adj* que causa dependência
addition [ə'dɪʃən] *n* adição *f*; (*thing added*) acréscimo; **in ~** além disso; **in ~ to** além de; **additional** *adj* adicional
additive ['ædɪtɪv] *n* aditivo
address [ə'drɛs] *n* endereço; (*speech*) discurso ⊳ *vt* (*letter*) endereçar; (*speak to*) dirigir-se a, dirigir a palavra a; **to ~ (o.s. to)** enfocar
adequate ['ædɪkwɪt] *adj* (*enough*) suficiente; (*satisfactory*) satisfatório
adhere [əd'hɪə'] *vi*: **to ~ to** aderir a; (*abide by*) ater-se a
adhesive [əd'hi:zɪv] *n* adesivo
adjective ['ædʒɛktɪv] *n* adjetivo
adjoining [ə'dʒɔɪnɪŋ] *adj* adjacente
adjourn [ə'dʒə:n] *vt* (*session*) suspender ⊳ *vi* ser suspenso
adjust [ə'dʒʌst] *vt* (*change*) ajustar; (*clothes*) arrumar; (*machine*) regular ⊳ *vi*: **to ~ (to)** adaptar-se (a); **adjustment** *n* ajuste *m*; (*of engine*) regulagem *f*; (*of prices, wages*) reajuste *m*; (*of person*) adaptação *f*
administer [əd'mɪnɪstə'] *vt* administrar; (*justice*) aplicar; (*drug*) ministrar; **administration** [ədmɪnɪs'treɪʃən] *n* administração *f*; (*management*) gerência; (*government*) governo; **administrative** [əd'mɪnɪstrətɪv] *adj* administrativo
admiral ['ædmərəl] *n* almirante *m*
admire [əd'maɪə'] *vt* (*respect*) respeitar; (*appreciate*) admirar
admission [əd'mɪʃən] *n* (*admittance*) entrada; (*fee*) ingresso; (*confession*) confissão *f*

admit [əd'mɪt] *vt* admitir; (*accept*) aceitar; (*confess*) confessar; **admit to** *vt fus* confessar; **admittance** *n* entrada; **admittedly** *adv* evidentemente
adolescent [ædəu'lɛsnt] *adj, n* adolescente *m/f*
adopt [ə'dɔpt] *vt* adotar; **adopted** *adj* adotivo; **adoption** *n* adoção *f*
adore [ə'dɔ:'] *vt* adorar
Adriatic (Sea) [eɪdrɪ'ætɪk-] *n* mar *m*
adrift [ə'drɪft] *adv* à deriva
adult ['ædʌlt] *n* adulto(-a) ⊳ *adj* adulto; (*literature, education*) para adultos
adultery [ə'dʌltərɪ] *n* adultério
advance [əd'vɑ:ns] *n* avanço; (*money*) adiantamento ⊳ *adj* antecipado ⊳ *vt* (*money*) adiantar ⊳ *vi* (*move*) avançar; (*progress*) progredir; **in ~** com antecedência; **to make ~s to sb** fazer propostas a alguém; **advanced** *adj* adiantado
advantage [əd'vɑ:ntɪdʒ] *n* (*gen, Tennis*) vantagem *f*; (*supremacy*) supremacia; **to take ~ of** aproveitar-se de, levar vantagem de
adventure [əd'vɛntʃə'] *n* façanha; (*excitement in life*) aventura
adverb ['ædvə:b] *n* advérbio
adverse ['ædvə:s] *adj* (*effect*) contrário; (*weather, publicity*) desfavorável
advert ['ædvə:t] *n abbr* = **advertisement**
advertise ['ædvətaɪz] *vi* anunciar ⊳ *vt* (*event, job*) anunciar; (*product*) fazer a propaganda de; **to ~ for** (*staff*) procurar; **advertisement** [əd'və:tɪsmənt] *n* (*classified*) anúncio; (*display, TV*) propaganda, anúncio; **advertising** *n* publicidade *f*
advice [əd'vaɪs] *n* conselhos *mpl*; (*notification*) aviso; **piece of ~** conselho; **to take legal ~** consultar um advogado
advise [əd'vaɪz] *vt* aconselhar; (*inform*): **to ~ sb of sth** avisar alguém de algo; **to ~ sb against sth/doing sth** desaconselhar algo a alguém/ aconselhar alguém a não fazer algo; **advisory** *adj* consultivo; **in an advisory capacity** na qualidade de assessor or consultor
advocate [(*vb*) 'ædvəkeɪt, (*n*) 'ædvəkɪt] *vt* defender; (*recommend*) advogar ⊳ *n* advogado(-a); (*supporter*) defensor(a) *m/f*
Aegean [i:'dʒi:ən] *n*: **the ~ (Sea)** o (mar) Egeu

aerial ['ɛərɪəl] n antena ▷ adj aéreo
aerobics [ɛə'rəʊbɪks] n ginástica
aeroplane ['ɛərəpleɪn] (BRIT) n avião m
aerosol ['ɛərəsɒl] n aerossol m
affair [ə'fɛə*] n (matter) assunto;
(business) negócio; (question) questão f;
(also: love ~) caso
affect [ə'fɛkt] vt afetar; (move) comover;
affected adj afetado
affection [ə'fɛkʃən] n afeto, afeição f;
affectionate adj afetuoso
afflict [ə'flɪkt] vt afligir
affluent adj rico; **the ~ society** a
sociedade de abundância
afford [ə'fɔːd] vt (provide) fornecer; (goods
etc) ter dinheiro suficiente para; (permit
o.s.): **I can't ~ the time/to take that
risk** não tenho tempo/não posso correr
esse risco
afraid [ə'freɪd] adj assustado; **to be ~
of/to** ter medo de; **I am ~ that** lamento
que; **I'm ~ so/not** receio que sim/não
Africa ['æfrɪkə] n África; **African** adj, n
africano(-a)
after ['ɑːftə*] prep depois de ▷ adv
depois ▷ conj depois que; **a quarter ~
two** (US) duas e quinze; **what/who are
you ~?** o que você quer?/quem procura?;
~ having done tendo feito; **he was
named ~ his grandfather** ele recebeu
o nome do avô; **to ask ~ sb** perguntar
por alguém; **~ all** afinal (de contas);
~ you! passe primeiro!; **aftermath**
n consequências fpl; **afternoon** n
tarde f; **after-shave (lotion)** n loção f
após-barba; **aftersun** n loção f pós-sol;
afterwards adv depois
again [ə'gɛn] adv (once more) outra vez;
(repeatedly) de novo; **to do sth ~** voltar a
fazer algo; **not ... ~!** ... de novo!; **~ and ~**
repetidas vezes
against [ə'gɛnst] prep contra; (compared
to) em contraste com
age [eɪdʒ] n idade f; (period) época ▷ vt,
vi envelhecer; **he's 20 years of ~** ele
tem 20 anos de idade; **to come of
~** atingir a maioridade; **it's been ~s
since I saw him** faz muito tempo que
eu não o vejo; **aged** ['eɪdʒɪd] adj idoso
▷ npl: **the aged** os idosos; **age group**
n faixa etária; **age limit** n idade f
mínima/máxima
agency ['eɪdʒənsɪ] n agência;
(government body) órgão m
agenda [ə'dʒɛndə] n ordem f do dia
agent ['eɪdʒənt] n agente m/f

aggravate ['ægrəveɪt] vt agravar;
(annoy) irritar
aggressive [ə'grɛsɪv] adj agressivo
AGM n abbr (= annual general meeting)
AGO f
ago [ə'gəʊ] adv: **2 days ~** há 2 dias (atrás);
not long ~ há pouco tempo; **how long
~?** há quanto tempo?
agony ['ægənɪ] n (pain) dor f; **to be in ~**
sofrer dores terríveis
agree [ə'griː] vt combinar ▷ vi
(correspond) corresponder; **to ~ (with)**
concordar (com); **to ~ to sth/to do
sth** consentir algo/aceitar fazer algo;
to ~ that concordar or admitir que;
agreeable adj agradável; (willing)
disposto; **agreed** adj combinado;
agreement n acordo; (Comm) contrato;
in agreement de acordo
agricultural [ægrɪ'kʌltʃərəl] adj (of
crops) agrícola; (of crops and cattle)
agropecuário
agriculture ['ægrɪkʌltʃə*] n (of
crops) agricultura; (of crops and cattle)
agropecuário
ahead [ə'hɛd] adv adiante; **go right** or
straight ~ siga em frente; **go ~!** (fig) vá
em frente!; **~ of** na frente de
aid [eɪd] n ajuda; (device) aparelho ▷ vt
ajudar; **in ~ of** em benefício de; **to ~ and
abet** (Law) ser cúmplice de
AIDS [eɪdz] n abbr (= acquired immune
deficiency syndrome) AIDS f (BR), SIDA f
(PT)
aim [eɪm] vt: **to ~ sth (at)** apontar algo
(para); (remark) dirigir algo (a) ▷ vi (also:
take ~) apontar ▷ n (skill) pontaria;
(objective) objetivo; **to ~ at** mirar; **to ~ to
do** pretender fazer
ain't [eɪnt] (inf) = am not; aren't; isn't
air [ɛə*] n ar m; (appearance) aparência,
aspeto; (tune) melodia ▷ vt arejar;
(grievances, ideas) discutir ▷ cpd aéreo;
to throw sth into the ~ jogar algo
para cima; **by ~** (travel) de avião; **on
the ~** (Radio, TV) no ar; **airbed** (BRIT) n
colchão m de ar; **air conditioning** n ar
condicionado; **aircraft** n inv aeronave f;
airfield n campo de aviação; **Air Force**
n Força Aérea, Aeronáutica; **air hostess**
(BRIT) n aeromoça (BR), hospedeira (PT);
airline n linha aérea; **airliner** n avião
m de passageiros; **airmail** n: **by airmail**
por via aérea; **airplane** (US) n avião m;
airport n aeroporto; **airsick** adj: **to
be airsick** enjoar (no avião); **airtight**

adj hermético; **airy** *adj* (room) arejado; (manner) leviano

aisle [aɪl] *n* (of church) nave f; (of theatre etc) corredor *m*

ajar [ə'dʒɑː'] *adj* entreaberto

alarm [ə'lɑːm] *n* alarme *m*; (anxiety) inquietação f ▷ *vt* alarmar; **alarm clock** *n* despertador *m*

album ['ælbəm] *n* (for stamps etc) álbum *m*; (record) elepê *m*

alcohol ['ælkəhɔl] *n* álcool *m*; **alcohol-free** *adj* sem álcool; **alcoholic** [ælkə'hɔlɪk] *adj* alcoólico ▷ *n* alcoólatra *m/f*

ale [eɪl] *n* cerveja

alert [ə'lət] *adj* atento; (to danger, opportunity) alerta ▷ *n* alerta ▷ *vt* alertar; **to be on the ~** estar alerta; (Mil) ficar de prontidão

Algarve [æl'gɑːv] *m*: **the ~** o Algarve

algebra ['ældʒɪbrə] *n* álgebra

Algeria [æl'dʒɪərɪə] *n* Argélia

alias ['eɪlɪəs] *adv* também chamado ▷ *n* (of criminal) alcunha; (of writer) pseudônimo

alibi ['ælɪbaɪ] *n* álibi *m*

alien ['eɪlɪən] *n* estrangeiro(-a); (from space) alienígena *m/f* ▷ *adj*: **~ to** alheio a

alight [ə'laɪt] *adj* em chamas; (eyes) aceso; (expression) intento ▷ *vi* (passenger) descer (de um veículo); (bird) pousar

alike [ə'laɪk] *adj* semelhante ▷ *adv* similarmente, igualmente; **to look ~** parecer-se

alive [ə'laɪv] *adj* vivo; (lively) alegre

⬤ **KEYWORD**

all [ɔːl] *adj* (sg) todo(-a); (pl) todos(-as); **all day/night** o dia inteiro/a noite inteira; **all five came** todos os cinco vieram; **all the books/food** todos os livros/toda a comida
▷ *pron* **1** tudo; **all of us/the boys went** todos nós fomos/todos os meninos foram; **is that all?** é só isso?; (in shop) mais alguma coisa?
2 (in phrases): **above all** sobretudo; **after all** afinal (de contas); **at all: not at all** (in answer to question) em absoluto, absolutamente não; **I'm not at all tired** não estou nada cansado; **anything at all will do** qualquer coisa serve; **all in all** ao todo
▷ *adv* todo, completamente; **all alone**

completamente só; **it's not as hard as all that** não é tão difícil assim; **all the more** ainda mais; **all the better** tanto melhor, melhor ainda; **all but** quase; **the score is 2 all** o escore é 2 a 2

allegiance [ə'liːdʒəns] *n* lealdade f

allergic [ə'ləːdʒɪk] *adj*: **~ (to)** alérgico (a)

allergy ['ælədʒɪ] *n* alergia f

alleviate [ə'liːvɪeɪt] *vt* (pain) aliviar; (difficulty) minorar

alley ['ælɪ] *n* viela

alliance [ə'laɪəns] *n* aliança

all-in (BRIT) *adj, adv* (charge) tudo incluído

allocate ['æləkeɪt] *vt* destinar

allot [ə'lɔt] *vt*: **to ~** designar para

all-out *adj* (effort etc) máximo ▷ *adv*: **all out** com toda a força

allow [ə'lau] *vt* permitir; (claim, goal) admitir; (sum, time) calcular; (concede): **to ~ that** reconhecer que; **to ~ sb to do** permitir a alguém fazer; **allow for** *vt fus* levar em conta; **allowance** [ə'lauəns] *n* ajuda de custo; (welfare payment) pensão f, auxílio; (Tax) abatimento; (pocket money) mesada; **to make allowances for** levar em consideração

all right *adv* (well) bem; (correctly) corretamente; (as answer) está bem!

ally [(n) 'ælaɪ, (vb) ə'laɪ] *n* aliado ▷ *vt*: **to ~ o.s. with** aliar-se com

almighty [ɔːl'maɪtɪ] *adj* onipotente; (row etc) a maior

almond ['ɑːmənd] *n* amêndoa

almost ['ɔːlməust] *adv* quase

alone [ə'ləun] *adj* só, sozinho; (unaided) sozinho ▷ *adv* só, somente, sozinho; **to leave sb ~** deixar alguém em paz; **to leave sth ~** não tocar em algo; **let ~ ...** sem falar em ...

along [ə'lɔŋ] *prep* por, ao longo de ▷ *adv*: **is he coming ~?** ele vem conosco?; **he was hopping/limping ~** ele ia pulando/coxeando; **~ with** junto com; **all ~** o tempo tudo; **alongside** *prep* ao lado de ▷ *adv* encostado

aloof [ə'luːf] *adj* afastado, altivo ▷ *adv*: **to stand ~** afastar-se

aloud [ə'laud] *adv* em voz alta

alphabet ['ælfəbɛt] *n* alfabeto

Alps [ælps] *npl*: **the ~** os Alpes

already [ɔːl'rɛdɪ] *adv* já

alright ['ɔːl'raɪt] (BRIT) *adv* = **all right**

also ['ɔːlsəu] *adv* também; (moreover) além disso

altar ['ɔltə'] *n* altar *m*

alter ['ɔːltə'] vt alterar ▷ vi modificar-se

alternate [(adj) ɔl'təːnɪt, (vb) 'ɔltəːneɪt] adj alternado; (us: alternative) alternativo ▷ vi alternar-se

alternative [ɔl'təːnətɪv] adj alternativo ▷ n alternativa; **alternatively** adv: **alternatively one could ...** por outro lado se podia ...

although [ɔːl'ðəu] conj embora; (given that) se bem que

altitude ['æltɪtjuːd] n altitude f

altogether [ɔːltə'geðə'] adv totalmente; (on the whole) no total

aluminium [ælju'mɪnɪəm] (us **aluminum**) n alumínio

always ['ɔːlweɪz] adv sempre

am [æm] vb see **be**

a.m. adv abbr (= ante meridiem) da manhã

amateur ['æmətə'] adj, n amador(a) m/f

amaze [ə'meɪz] vt pasmar; **to be ~d (at)** espantar-se (de or com); **amazement** n pasmo, espanto; **amazing** adj surpreendente; (fantastic) fantástico

Amazon ['æməzən] n Amazonas m

ambassador [æm'bæsədə'] n embaixador (embaixatriz) m/f

amber ['æmbə'] n âmbar m; **at ~** (BRIT: Aut) em amarelo

ambiguous [æm'bɪgjuəs] adj ambíguo

ambition [æm'bɪʃən] n ambição f; **ambitious** adj ambicioso

ambulance ['æmbjuləns] n ambulância

ambush ['æmbuʃ] n emboscada ▷ vt emboscar

amend [ə'mend] vt emendar; **to make ~s (for)** compensar

amenities [ə'miːnɪtɪz] npl atrações fpl, comodidades fpl

America [ə'mɛrɪkə] n (continent) América; (USA) Estados Unidos mpl; **American** adj americano; norte-americano, estadunidense ▷ n americano(-a); norte-americano(-a)

amicable ['æmɪkəbl] adj amigável

amid(st) [ə'mɪd(st)] prep em meio a

ammunition [æmju'nɪʃən] n munição f

among(st) [ə'mʌŋ(st)] prep entre, no meio de

amount [ə'maunt] n quantidade f; (of money etc) quantia ▷ vi: **to ~ to** (total) montar a; (be same as) equivaler a, significar

amp(ère) ['æmp(ɛə')] n ampère m

ample ['æmpl] adj amplo; (abundant) abundante; (enough) suficiente

amplifier ['æmplɪfaɪə'] n amplificador m

amuse [ə'mjuːz] vt divertir; (distract) distrair; **amusement** n diversão f; (pleasure) divertimento; (pastime) passatempo

an [æn, ən, n] indef art see **a**

anaesthetic [ænɪs'θɛtɪk] (us **anesthetic**) n anestésico

analyse ['ænəlaɪz] (us **analyze**) vt analisar; **analysis** [ə'næləsɪs] (pl **analyses**) n análise f; **analyst** ['ænəlɪst] n analista m/f; (psychoanalyst) psicanalista m/f

analyze ['ænəlaɪz] (us) vt = **analyse**

anarchy ['ænəkɪ] n anarquia

anatomy [ə'nætəmɪ] n anatomia

ancestor ['ænsɪstə'] n antepassado

anchor ['æŋkə'] n âncora ▷ vi (also: **to drop ~**) ancorar, fundear ▷ vt (fig): **to ~ sth to** firmar algo em; **to weigh ~** levantar âncoras

anchovy ['æntʃəvɪ] n enchova

ancient ['eɪnʃənt] adj antigo; (person, car) velho

and [ænd] conj e; **~ so on** e assim por diante; **try ~ come** tente vir; **he talked ~ talked** ele falou sem parar; **better ~ better** cada vez melhor

Andes ['ændiːz] npl: **the ~** os Andes

angel ['eɪndʒəl] n anjo

anger ['æŋgə'] n raiva

angina [æn'dʒaɪnə] n angina (de peito)

angle ['æŋgl] n ângulo; (viewpoint): **from their ~** do ponto de vista deles

Anglican ['æŋglɪkən] adj, n anglicano(-a)

angling ['æŋglɪŋ] n pesca à vara (BR) or à linha (PT)

angry ['æŋgrɪ] adj zangado; **to be ~ with sb/at sth** estar zangado com alguém/algo; **to get ~** zangar-se

anguish ['æŋgwɪʃ] n (physical) dor f, sofrimento; (mental) angústia

animal ['ænɪməl] n animal m, bicho ▷ adj animal

aniseed ['ænɪsiːd] n erva-doce f, anis f

ankle ['æŋkl] n tornozelo

annex [(n) 'ænɛks, (vb) ə'nɛks] n (also: BRIT: annexe: building) anexo ▷ vt anexar

anniversary [ænɪ'vəːsərɪ] n aniversário

announce [ə'nauns] vt anunciar; **announcement** n anúncio; (official) comunicação f; (in letter etc) aviso; **announcer** n (Radio, TV) locutor(a) m/f

annoy [ə'nɔɪ] vt aborrecer; **don't get ~ed!** não se aborreça!; **annoying** adj irritante

annual ['ænjuəl] *adj* anual ▷ *n* (Bot) anual *m*; (book) anuário
anonymous [æ'nɔnɪməs] *adj* anônimo
anorak ['ænəræk] *n* anoraque *m* (BR), anorak *m* (PT)
another [ə'nʌðəʳ] *adj*: ~ **book** (one more) outro livro, mais um livro; (a different one) um outro livro, um livro diferente ▷ *pron* outro; *see also* **one**
answer ['ɑ:nsəʳ] *n* resposta; (to problem) solução *f* ▷ *vi* responder ▷ *vt* (reply to) responder a; (problem) resolver; **in ~ to your letter** em resposta *or* respondendo à sua carta; **to ~ the phone** atender o telefone; **to ~ the bell** *or* **the door** atender à porta; **answer back** *vi* replicar, retrucar; **answer for** *vt fus* responder por, responsabilizar-se por; **answer to** *vt fus* (description) corresponder a; **answering machine** *n* secretária eletrônica
ant [ænt] *n* formiga
Antarctic [ænt'ɑ:ktɪk] *n*: **the ~** o Antártico
antenatal ['æntɪ'neɪtl] *adj* pré-natal
anthem ['ænθəm] *n*: **national ~** hino nacional
anticipate [æn'tɪsɪpeɪt] *vt* prever; (expect) esperar; (look forward to) aguardar, esperar; **anticipation** *n* expectativa; (eagerness) entusiasmo
anticlimax [æntɪ'klaɪmæks] *n* desapontamento
anticlockwise [æntɪ'klɔkwaɪz] (BRIT) *adv* em sentido anti-horário
antics ['æntɪks] *npl* bobices *fpl*; (of child) travessuras *fpl*
antifreeze ['æntɪfri:z] *n* anticongelante *m*
antihistamine [æntɪ'hɪstəmi:n] *n* anti-histamínico
antique [æn'ti:k] *n* antiguidade *f* ▷ *adj* antigo; **antique shop** *n* loja de antiguidades
antiseptic [æntɪ'sɛptɪk] *n* anti-séptico
antisocial [æntɪ'səʊʃəl] *adj* anti-social
antivirus [æntɪ'vaɪərəs] *adj* antivírus *inv*; **~ software** software *m* (de) antivírus, antivírus *m*
antlers ['æntləz] *npl* esgalhos *mpl*, chifres *mpl*
anxiety [æŋ'zaɪətɪ] *n* (worry) inquietude *f*; (Med) ansiedade *f*; (eagerness): **~ to do** ânsia de fazer
anxious ['æŋkʃəs] *adj* (worried) preocupado; (worrying) angustiante;

(keen): **~ to do** ansioso para fazer; **to be ~ that** desejar que

 KEYWORD

any ['ɛnɪ] *adj* **1** (in questions etc) algum(a); **have you any butter/children?** você tem manteiga/filhos?; **if there are any tickets left** se houver alguns bilhetes sobrando
2 (with negative) nenhum(a); **I haven't any money/books** não tenho dinheiro/livros
3 (no matter which) qualquer; **choose any book you like** escolha qualquer livro que quiser
4 (in phrases): **in any case** em todo o caso; **any day now** qualquer dia desses; **at any moment** a qualquer momento; **at any rate** de qualquer modo; **any time** a qualquer momento; (whenever) quando quer que seja
▷ *pron* **1** (in questions etc) algum(a); **have you got any?** tem algum?
2 (with negative) nenhum(a); **I haven't any (of them)** não tenho nenhum (deles)
3 (no matter which one(s)): **take any of those books (you like)** leve qualquer um desses livros (que você quiser)
▷ *adv* **1** (in questions etc) algo; **do you want any more soup/sandwiches?** quer mais sopa/sanduíches?; **are you feeling any better?** você está se sentindo melhor?
2 (with negative) nada; **I can't hear him any more** não consigo mais ouvi-lo

anybody ['ɛnɪbɔdɪ] *pron* = **anyone**
anyhow ['ɛnɪhaʊ] *adv* (at any rate) de qualquer modo, de qualquer maneira; (haphazard) de qualquer jeito; **I shall go ~** eu irei de qualquer jeito; **do it ~ you like** faça do jeito que você quiser; **she leaves things just ~** ela deixa as coisas de qualquer maneira
anyone ['ɛnɪwʌn] *pron* (in questions etc) alguém; (with negative) ninguém; (no matter who) quem quer que seja; **can you see ~?** você pode ver alguém?; **if ~ should phone ...** se alguém telefonar ...; **~ could do it** qualquer um (a)
anything ['ɛnɪθɪŋ] *pron* (in questions etc) alguma coisa; (with negative) nada; (no matter what) qualquer coisa; **can you see ~?** você pode ver alguma coisa?

anyway [ˈɛnɪweɪ] adv (at any rate) de qualquer modo; (besides) além disso; **I shall go ~** eu irei de qualquer jeito

anywhere [ˈɛnɪwɛəʳ] adv (in questions etc) em algum lugar; (with negative) em parte nenhuma; (no matter where) não importa onde, onde quer que seja; **can you see him ~?** você pode vê-lo em algum lugar?; **I can't see him ~** não o vejo em parte nenhuma; **~ in the world** em qualquer lugar do mundo

apart [əˈpɑːt] adv à parte, à distância; (separately) separado; (movement): **to move ~** distanciar-se; (aside): **... ~,** ... de lado, além de ...; **10 miles ~** separados por 10 milhas; **to take ~** desmontar; **~ from** com exceção de; (in addition to) além de

apartment [əˈpɑːtmənt] (us) n apartamento

ape [eɪp] n macaco ▷ vt macaquear, imitar

aperitif [əˈpɛrɪtɪv] n aperitivo

aperture [ˈæpətʃuəʳ] n orifício; (Phot) abertura

APEX n abbr (= advance purchase excursion) tarifa aérea com desconto, adquirida com antecedência

apologize [əˈpɒlədʒaɪz] vi: **to ~ (for sth to sb)** desculpar-se or pedir desculpas (por or de algo a alguém); **apology** n desculpas fpl

apostrophe [əˈpɒstrəfɪ] n apóstrofo

appalling adj horrível; (ignorance) terrível

apparatus [æpəˈreɪtəs] n aparelho; (in gym) aparelhos mpl; (organization) aparato

apparent [əˈpærənt] adj aparente; (obvious) claro, patente; **apparently** adv aparentemente, pelo(s) visto(s)

appeal [əˈpiːl] vi (Law) apelar, recorrer ▷ n (Law) recurso, apelação f; (request) pedido; (plea) súplica; (charm) atração f; **to ~ (to sb) for sth** (request) pedir algo (a alguém); (plead) suplicar algo (a alguém); **to ~ to** atrair; **appealing** adj atraente

appear [əˈpɪəʳ] vi aparecer; (Law) apresentar-se, comparecer; (publication) ser publicado; (seem) parecer; **to ~ in "Hamlet"** trabalhar em "Hamlet"; **to ~ on TV** (person, news item) sair na televisão; (programme) passar na televisão; **appearance** n aparecimento; (presence) comparecimento; (look) aparência

appendicitis [əpɛndɪˈsaɪtɪs] n

apendicite f

appendix [əˈpɛndɪks] (pl **appendices**) n apêndice m

appetite [ˈæpɪtaɪt] n apetite m; (fig) desejo; **appetizer** n (food) tira-gosto; (drink) aperitivo

applaud [əˈplɔːd] vi aplaudir ▷ vt aplaudir; (praise) admirar; **applause** n aplausos mpl

apple [ˈæpl] n maçã f

appliance [əˈplaɪəns] n aparelho; **electrical** or **domestic ~s** eletrodomésticos mpl

applicant [ˈæplɪkənt] n (for post) candidato(-a); (for benefit etc) requerente m/f

application [æplɪˈkeɪʃən] n aplicação f; (for a job, a grant etc) candidatura, requerimento; (hard work) esforço; **application form** n (formulário de) requerimento

apply [əˈplaɪ] vt (paint etc) usar; (law etc) pôr em prática ▷ vi: **to ~ to** (be suitable for) ser aplicável a; (be relevant to) valer para; (ask) pedir; **to ~ for** (permit, grant) solicitar, pedir; (job) candidatar-se a; **to ~ o.s. to** aplicar-se a, dedicar-se a

appoint [əˈpɔɪnt] vt (to post) nomear; **appointment** n (engagement) encontro marcado, compromisso; (at doctor's etc) hora marcada; (act) nomeação f; (post) cargo; **to make an appointment (with sb)** marcar um encontro (com alguém)

appraisal [əˈpreɪzl] n avaliação f

appreciate [əˈpriːʃɪeɪt] vt (like) apreciar, estimar; (be grateful for) agradecer a; (understand) compreender ▷ vi (Comm) valorizar-se; **appreciation** n a apreciação f, estima; (understanding) compreensão f; (gratitude) agradecimento; (Comm) valorização f

apprehensive adj apreensivo, receoso

apprentice [əˈprɛntɪs] n aprendiz m/f

approach [əˈprəutʃ] vi aproximar-se ▷ vt aproximar-se de; (ask, apply to) dirigir-se a; (subject, passer-by) abordar ▷ n aproximação f; (access) acesso; (to problem, situation) enfoque m

appropriate [(adj) əˈprəuprɪɪt, (vb) əˈprəuprɪeɪt] adj (apt) apropriado; (relevant) adequado ▷ vt apropriar-se de

approval [əˈpruːvəl] n aprovação f; **on ~** (Comm) a contento

approve [əˈpruːv] vt (publication, product) autorizar; (motion, decision) aprovar;

approve of vt fus aprovar

approximate [ə'prɒksɪmɪt] adj aproximado; **approximately** adv aproximadamente

apricot ['eɪprɪkɒt] n damasco

April ['eɪprəl] n abril m

apron ['eɪprən] n avental m

apt [æpt] adj (suitable) adequado; (appropriate) apropriado; (likely): ~ **to do** sujeito a fazer

Aquarius [ə'kwɛərɪəs] n Aquário

Arab ['ærəb] adj, n árabe m/f

Arabian [ə'reɪbɪən] adj árabe

Arabic ['ærəbɪk] adj árabe; (numerals) arábico ▷ n (Ling) árabe m

arbitrary ['ɑːbɪtrərɪ] adj arbitrário

arbitration [ɑːbɪ'treɪʃən] n arbitragem f

arcade [ɑː'keɪd] n arcos mpl; (passage with shops) galeria

arch [ɑːtʃ] n arco; (of foot) curvatura ▷ vt arquear, curvar

archaeology [ɑːkɪ'ɒlədʒɪ] (US **archeology**) n arqueologia

archbishop [ɑːtʃ'bɪʃəp] n arcebispo

archeology etc [ɑːkɪ'ɒlədʒɪ] (US) = **archaeology** etc

architect ['ɑːkɪtɛkt] n arquiteto(-a); **architecture** n arquitetura

Arctic ['ɑːktɪk] adj ártico ▷ n: **the ~** o Ártico

are [ɑːʳ] vb see **be**

area ['ɛərɪə] n (zone) zona, região f; (part of place) região; (in room, of knowledge, experience) área; (Math) superfície f, extensão f

area code (US) n (Tel) código de discagem (BR), indicativo (PT)

aren't [ɑːnt] = **are not**

Argentina [ɑːdʒən'tiːnə] n Argentina

arguably ['ɑːgjuəblɪ] adv possivelmente

argue ['ɑːgjuː] vi (quarrel) discutir; (reason) argumentar; **to ~ that** sustentar que

argument ['ɑːgjumənt] n (reasons) argumento; (quarrel) briga, discussão f

Aries ['ɛərɪz] n Áries m

arise [ə'raɪz] (pt **arose**, pp **~n**) vi (emerge) surgir

arithmetic [ə'rɪθmətɪk] n aritmética

arm [ɑːm] n braço; (of clothing) manga; (of organization etc) divisão f ▷ vt armar; **arms** npl (weapons) armas fpl; (Heraldry) brasão m; **~ in ~** de braços dados

arm: **armchair** n poltrona; **armed** adj armado

armour ['ɑːməʳ] (US **armor**) n armadura

armpit ['ɑːmpɪt] n sovaco

armrest ['ɑːmrɛst] n braço (de poltrona)

army ['ɑːmɪ] n exército

aroma [ə'rəumə] n aroma; **aromatherapy** n aromaterapia

arose [ə'rəuz] pt of **arise**

around [ə'raund] adv em volta; (in the area) perto ▷ prep em volta de; (near) perto de; (fig: about) cerca de

arouse [ə'rauz] vt despertar; (anger) provocar

arrange [ə'reɪndʒ] vt (organize) organizar; (put in order) arrumar; **to ~ to do sth** combinar em or ficar de fazer algo; **arrangement** n (agreement) acordo; (order, layout) disposição f; **arrangements** npl (plans) planos mpl; (preparations) preparativos mpl; **home deliveries by arrangement** entregas a domicílio por convênio; **I'll make all the necessary arrangements** eu vou tomar todas as providências necessárias

array [ə'reɪ] n: **~ of** variedade f de

arrears [ə'rɪəz] npl atrasos mpl; **to be in ~ with one's rent** atrasar o aluguel

arrest [ə'rɛst] vt prender, deter; (sb's attention) chamar, prender ▷ n detenção f, prisão f; **under ~** preso

arrival [ə'raɪvəl] n chegada; **new ~** recém-chegado; (baby) recém-nascido

arrive [ə'raɪv] vi chegar

arrogant ['ærəgənt] adj arrogante

arrow ['ærəu] n flecha; (sign) seta

arson ['ɑːsn] n incêndio premeditado

art [ɑːt] n arte f; (skill) habilidade f, jeito; **Arts** npl (Sch) letras fpl

artery ['ɑːtərɪ] n (Med) artéria; (fig) estrada principal

art gallery n museu m de belas artes; (small, private) galeria de arte

arthritis [ɑː'θraɪtɪs] n artrite f

artichoke ['ɑːtɪtʃəuk] n (also: **globe ~**) alcachofra; (also: **Jerusalem ~**) topinambo

article ['ɑːtɪkl] n artigo; **articles** npl (BRIT: Law: training) contrato de aprendizagem; **~s of clothing** peças fpl de vestuário

articulate [(adj) ɑː'tɪkjulɪt, (vb) ɑː'tɪkjuleɪt] adj (speech) bem articulado; (writing) bem escrito; (person) eloqüente ▷ vt expressar

artificial [ɑːtɪ'fɪʃəl] adj artificial; (manner) afetado

artist ['ɑːtɪst] n artista m/f; (Mus)

intérprete *m/f*; **artistic** [ɑːˈtɪstɪk] *adj* artístico

art school *n* ≈ escola de artes

 KEYWORD

as [æz, əz] *conj* **1** (*time*) quando; **as the years went by** no decorrer dos anos; **he came in as I was leaving** ele chegou quando eu estava saindo; **as from tomorrow** a partir de amanhã
2 (*in comparisons*) tão ... (como), tanto(s) ... (como); **as big as** tão grande como; **twice as big as** duas vezes maior que; **as much/many as** tanto/tantos como; **as much money/many books as** tanto dinheiro quanto/tantos livros quanto; **as soon as** logo que, assim que
3 (*since, because*) como
4 (*referring to manner, way*) como; **do as you wish** faça como quiser
5 (*concerning*): **as for** *or* **to that** quanto a isso
6: **as if** *or* **though** como se; **he looked as if he was ill** ele parecia doente ▷ *prep* (*in the capacity of*): **he works as a driver** ele trabalha como motorista; **he gave it to me as a present** ele me deu isso de presente; *see also* **long; such; well**

a.s.a.p. *abbr* = **as soon as possible**
asbestos [æzˈbɛstəs] *n* asbesto, amianto
ash [æʃ] *n* cinza; (*tree, wood*) freixo
ashamed [əˈʃeɪmd] *adj* envergonhado; **to be ~ of** ter vergonha de
ashore [əˈʃɔːʳ] *adv* em terra; **to go ~** descer à terra, desembarcar
ashtray [ˈæʃtreɪ] *n* cinzeiro
Asia [ˈeɪʃə] *n* Ásia; **Asian** *adj, n* asiático(-a)
aside [əˈsaɪd] *adv* à parte, de lado ▷ *n* aparte *m*
ask [ɑːsk] *vt* perguntar; (*invite*) convidar; **to ~ sb sth/to do sth** perguntar algo a alguém/pedir para alguém fazer algo; **to ~ (sb) a question** fazer uma pergunta (a alguém); **to ~ sb out to dinner** convidar alguém para jantar; **ask after** *vt fus* perguntar por; **ask for** *vt fus* pedir; **it's just asking for trouble** é procurar encrenca
asleep [əˈsliːp] *adj* dormindo; **to fall ~** dormir, adormecer
asparagus [əsˈpærəgəs] *n* aspargo (BR), espargo (PT)

aspect [ˈæspɛkt] *n* aspecto; (*direction in which a building etc faces*) direção *f*
aspire [əsˈpaɪəʳ] *vi*: **to ~ to** aspirar a
aspirin [ˈæsprɪn] *n* aspirina
ass [æs] *n* jumento, burro; (*inf*) imbecil *m/f*
assassinate [əˈsæsɪneɪt] *vt* assassinar
assault [əˈsɔːlt] *n* assalto; (*Mil, fig*) ataque *m* ▷ *vt* assaltar, atacar; (*sexually*) agredir, violar
assemble [əˈsɛmbl] *vt* (*people*) reunir; (*objects*) juntar; (*Tech*) montar ▷ *vi* reunir-se
assembly [əˈsɛmblɪ] *n* reunião *f*; (*institution*) assembléia
assert [əˈsəːt] *vt* afirmar
assess [əˈsɛs] *vt* avaliar; (*tax, damages*) calcular; **assessment** *n* avaliação *f*, cálculo
asset [ˈæsɛt] *n* vantagem *f*, trunfo; **assets** *npl* (*property, funds*) bens *mpl*
assign [əˈsaɪn] *vt* (*date*) fixar; **to ~ (to)** (*task*) designar (a); (*resources*) destinar (a); **assignment** *n* tarefa
assist [əˈsɪst] *vt* ajudar; **assistance** *n* ajuda, auxílio; **assistant** *n* assistente *m/f*, auxiliar *m/f*; (BRIT: *also*: **shop assistant**) vendedor(a) *m/f*
associate [(*adj, n*) əˈsəʊʃɪɪt, (*vb*) əˈsəʊʃɪeɪt] *adj* associado; (*professor etc*) adjunto ▷ *n* sócio(-a) ▷ *vi*: **to ~ with** associar-se com ▷ *vt* associar; **association** [əsəʊsɪˈeɪʃən] *n* associação *f*; (*link*) ligação *f*
assorted [əˈsɔːtɪd] *adj* sortido
assortment [əˈsɔːtmənt] *n* (*of shapes, colours*) sortimento; (*of books, people*) variedade *f*
assume [əˈsjuːm] *vt* (*suppose*) supor, presumir; (*responsibilities*) assumir; (*attitude, name*) adotar, tomar; **assumption** [əˈsʌmpʃən] *n* suposição *f*, presunção *f*
assurance [əˈʃuərəns] *n* garantia; (*confidence*) confiança; (*insurance*) seguro
assure [əˈʃuəʳ] *vt* assegurar; (*guarantee*) garantir
asthma [ˈæsmə] *n* asma
astonish [əˈstɒnɪʃ] *vt* assombrar, espantar; **astonishment** *n* assombro, espanto
astound [əˈstaund] *vt* pasmar, estarrecer
astray [əˈstreɪ] *adv*: **to go ~** extraviar-se; **to lead ~** desencaminhar
astrology [əsˈtrɒlədʒɪ] *n* astrologia

astronaut ['æstrənɔːt] n astronauta m/f
astronomy [əs'trɒnəmɪ] n astronomia
asylum [ə'saɪləm] n (refuge) asilo; (hospital) manicômio

⊙ **KEYWORD**

at [æt] prep **1** (referring to position) em; (referring to direction) a; **at the top** em cima; **at home** em casa; **to look at sth** olhar para algo
2 (referring to time): **at 4 o'clock** às quatro horas; **at night** à noite; **at Christmas** no Natal; **at times** às vezes
3 (referring to rates, speed etc): **at £1 a kilo** a uma libra o quilo; **two at a time** de dois em dois
4 (referring to manner): **at a stroke** de um golpe; **at peace** em paz
5 (referring to activity): **to be at work** estar no trabalho; **to play at cowboys** brincar de mocinho
6 (referring to cause): **to be shocked/ surprised/annoyed at sth** ficar chocado/surpreso/chateado com algo; **I went at his suggestion** eu fui por causa da sugestão dele
▷ n (symbol @) arroba

ate [eɪt] pt of **eat**
atheist ['eɪθɪɪst] n ateu (atéia) m/f
Athens ['æθɪnz] n Atenas
athlete ['æθliːt] n atleta m/f; **athletic** [æθ'letɪk] adj atlético; **athletics** n atletismo
Atlantic [ət'læntɪk] adj atlântico ▷ n: **the ~ (Ocean)** o (oceano) Atlântico
atlas ['ætləs] n atlas m inv
ATM n abbr (= automated telling machine) caixa m automático
atmosphere ['ætməsfɪəʳ] n atmosfera; (of place) ambiente m
atom ['ætəm] n átomo; **atomic** [ə'tɒmɪk] adj atômico
attach [ə'tætʃ] vt prender; (document) juntar, anexar; (importance etc) dar; **to be ~ed to sb/sth** (like) ter afeição por alguém/algo
attachment [ə'tætʃmənt] n (tool) acessório; (to e-mail) anexo; (love): **~ (to)** afeição f (por)
attack [ə'tæk] vt atacar; (subj: criminal) assaltar; (task etc) empreender ▷ n ataque m; (on sb's life) atentado; **heart ~** ataque cardíaco or de coração
attain [ə'teɪn] vt (also: **~ to**: happiness, results) alcançar, atingir; (: knowledge) obter
attempt [ə'tempt] n tentativa ▷ vt tentar; **to make an ~ on sb's life** atentar contra a vida de alguém
attend [ə'tend] vt (lectures) assistir a; (school) cursar; (church) ir a; (course) fazer; (patient) tratar; **attend to** vt fus (matter) encarregar-se de; (needs, customer) atender a; (patient) tratar de; **attendance** n comparecimento; (people present) assistência; **attendant** n servidor(a) m/f ▷ adj concomitante
attention [ə'tenʃən] n atenção f; (care) cuidados mpl ▷ excl (Mil) sentido!; **for the ~ of ...** (Admin) atenção ...
attic ['ætɪk] n sótão m
attitude ['ætɪtjuːd] n atitude f
attorney [ə'tɜːnɪ] n (us: lawyer) advogado(-a)
attract [ə'trækt] vt atrair, chamar; **attraction** n atração f; **attractive** adj atraente; (idea, offer) interessante
attribute [(n) 'ætrɪbjuːt, (vb) ə'trɪbjuːt] n atributo ▷ vt: **to ~ sth to** atribuir algo a
aubergine ['əubəʒiːn] n berinjela
auction ['ɔːkʃən] n (also: **sale by ~**) leilão m ▷ vt leiloar
audience ['ɔːdɪəns] n audiência; (at concert, theatre) platéia; (public) público
audit ['ɔːdɪt] vt fazer a auditoria de
audition [ɔː'dɪʃən] n audição f
August ['ɔːgəst] n agosto
aunt [ɑːnt] n tia; **auntie** n titia; **aunty** n titia
au pair ['əu'peəʳ] n (also: **~ girl**) au pair f
Australia [ɒs'treɪlɪə] n Austrália; **Australian** adj, n australiano(-a)
Austria ['ɒstrɪə] n Áustria; **Austrian** adj, n austríaco(-a)
authentic [ɔː'θentɪk] adj autêntico
author ['ɔːθə] n autor(a) m/f
authority [ɔː'θɒrɪtɪ] n autoridade f; (government body) jurisdição f; (permission) autorização f; **the authorities** npl (ruling body) as autoridades
authorize ['ɔːθəraɪz] vt autorizar
auto ['ɔːtəu] (us) n carro, automóvel m
autobiography [ɔːtəbaɪ'ɒgrəfɪ] n autobiografia
autograph ['ɔːtəgrɑːf] n autógrafo ▷ vt (photo etc) autografar
automatic [ɔːtə'mætɪk] adj automático ▷ n (gun) pistola automática; (washing machine) máquina de lavar roupa automática; (car) carro automático

automobile ['ɔːtəməbiːl] (US) n carro, automóvel m

autonomy [ɔːˈtɔnəmɪ] n autonomia

autumn ['ɔːtəm] n outono

auxiliary [ɔːgˈzɪlɪərɪ] adj, n auxiliar m/f

available [əˈveɪləbl] adj disponível; (time) livre

avalanche ['ævəlɑːnʃ] n avalanche f

Ave. abbr (= avenue) Av., Avda.

avenue ['ævənjuː] n avenida; (drive) caminho; (means) solução f

average ['ævərɪdʒ] n média ⊳ adj (mean) médio; (ordinary) regular ⊳ vt alcançar uma média de; **on ~** em média; **average out** vi: **to average out at** dar uma média de

avert [əˈvəːt] vt prevenir; (blow, one's eyes) desviar

avocado [ævəˈkɑːdəu] n (BRIT: also: ~ pear) abacate m

avoid [əˈvɔɪd] vt evitar

await [əˈweɪt] vt esperar, aguardar

awake [əˈweɪk] (pt awoke, pp awoken or ~d) adj acordado ⊳ vt, vi despertar, acordar; **~ to** atento a

award [əˈwɔːd] n prêmio, condecoração f; (Law) indenização f ⊳ vt outorgar, conceder; indenizar

aware [əˈwɛəʳ] adj: **~ of** (conscious) consciente de; (informed) informado de or sobre; **to become ~ of** reparar em, saber de; **awareness** n consciência

away [əˈweɪ] adv fora; (faraway) muito longe; **two kilometres ~** a dois quilômetros de distância; **the holiday was two weeks ~** faltavam duas semanas para as férias; **he's ~ for a week** está ausente uma semana; **to take ~** levar; **to work etc ~** trabalhar etc sem parar; **to fade ~** (colour) desbotar; (enthusiasm, sound) diminuir

awe [ɔː] n temor m respeitoso

awful ['ɔːfəl] adj terrível, horrível; (quantity): **an ~ lot of** um monte de; **awfully** adv (very) muito

awkward ['ɔːkwəd] adj (person, movement) desajeitado; (shape) incômodo; (problem) difícil; (situation) embaraçoso, delicado

awoke [əˈwəuk] pt of awake; **awoken** [əˈwəukən] pp of awake

axe [æks] (US **ax**) n machado ⊳ vt (project etc) abandonar; (jobs) reduzir

axle ['æksl] n (also: ~ **tree** Aut) eixo

b

B [biː] n (Mus) si m

baby ['beɪbɪ] n neném m/f, nenê m/f, bebê m/f; (US: inf) querido(-a); **baby carriage** (US) n carrinho de bebê; **baby-sit** (irreg) vi tomar conta da(s) criança(s); **baby-sitter** n baby-sitter m/f

bachelor ['bætʃələʳ] n solteiro; **B~ of Arts/Science** ≈ bacharel m em Letras/Ciências

back [bæk] n (of person) costas fpl; (of animal) lombo; (of hand) dorso; (of car, train) parte f traseira; (of house) fundos mpl; (of chair) encosto; (of page) verso; (of book) lombada; (of crowd) fundo; (Football) zagueiro (BR), defesa m (PT) ⊳ vt (candidate: also: ~ **up**) apoiar; (horse: at races) apostar em; (car) recuar ⊳ vi (car etc: also: ~ **up**) dar marcha-ré (BR), fazer marcha atrás (PT) ⊳ cpd (payment) atrasado; (Aut: seats, wheels) de trás ⊳ adv (not forward) para trás; (returned): **he's ~** ele voltou; (restitution): **throw the ball ~** devolva a bola; (again): **he called ~** chamou de novo; **he ran ~** recuou correndo; **back down** vi desistir; **back out** vi (of promise) voltar atrás, recuar; **back up** vt (support) apoiar; (Comput) tirar um backup de; **backache**

n dor *f* nas costas; **backbone** *n* coluna vertebral; (*fig*) esteio; **backfire** *vi* (*Aut*) engasgar; (*plan*) sair pela culatra; **background** *n* fundo; (*of events*) antecedentes *mpl*; (*basic knowledge*) bases *fpl*; (*experience*) conhecimentos *mpl*, experiência; **family background** antecedentes *mpl* familiares; **backing** *n* (*fig*) apoio; **backlog** *n*: **backlog of work** atrasos *mpl*; **backpack** *n* mochila; **back pay** *n* salário atrasado; **backstage** *adv* nos bastidores; **backstroke** *n* nado de costas; **backup** *adj* (*train, plane*) reserva *inv*; (*Comput*) de backup ▷ *n* (*support*) apoio; (*Comput: also:* **backup file**) backup *m*; **backward** *adj* (*movement*) para trás; (*person, country*) atrasado; **backwards** *adv* (*move, go*) para trás; (*read a list*) às avessas; (*fall*) de costas; **backyard** *n* quintal *m*

bacon ['beɪkən] *n* toucinho, bacon *m*

bacteria [bæk'tɪərɪə] *npl* bactérias *fpl*

bad [bæd] *adj* mau (má), ruim; (*child*) levado; (*mistake, injury*) grave; (*meat, food*) estragado; **his ~ leg** sua perna machucada; **to go ~** estragar-se

badge [bædʒ] *n* (*of school etc*) emblema *m*; (*policeman's*) crachá *m*

badger ['bædʒə'] *n* texugo

badly ['bædlɪ] *adv* mal; **~ wounded** gravemente ferido; **he needs it ~** faz-lhe grande falta; **to be ~ off (for money)** estar com pouco dinheiro

badminton ['bædmɪntən] *n* badminton *m*

bad-tempered [-'tɛmpəd] *adj* mal humorado; (*temporary*) de mau humor

bag [bæg] *n* saco, bolsa; (*handbag*) bolsa; (*satchel*) sacola; (*case*) mala; **~s of ...** (*inf: lots of*) ... de sobra; **baggage** *n* bagagem *f*; **baggy** *adj* folgado, largo; **bagpipes** *npl* gaita de foles

bail [beɪl] *n* (*payment*) fiança; (*release*) liberdade *f* sob fiança ▷ *vt* (*prisoner: gen: grant bail to*) libertar sob fiança; (*boat: also:* **~ out**) baldear a água de; **on ~** sob fiança; **bail out** *vt* (*prisoner*) afiançar

bait [beɪt] *n* isca, engodo; (*for criminal etc*) atrativo, chamariz *m* ▷ *vt* iscar, cevar; (*person*) apoquentar

bake [beɪk] *vt* cozinhar ao forno; (*Tech: clay etc*) cozer ▷ *vi* assar; **baked beans** *npl* feijão *m* cozido com molho de tomate; **baked potato** *n* batata assada com a casca; **baker** *n* padeiro(-a); **bakery** *n* (*for bread*) padaria; (*for cakes*)

confeitaria; **baking** *n* (*act*) cozimento; (*batch*) fornada ▷ *adj* (*inf: hot*) escaldante; **baking powder** *n* fermento em pó

balance ['bæləns] *n* equilíbrio; (*scales*) balança; (*Comm*) balanço; (*remainder*) resto, saldo ▷ *vt* equilibrar; (*budget*) nivelar; (*account*) fazer o balanço de; **~ of trade/payments** balança comercial/ balanço de pagamentos; **balanced** *adj* (*report*) objetivo; (*personality, diet*) equilibrado; **balance sheet** *n* balanço geral

balcony ['bælkənɪ] *n* varanda; (*closed*) galeria; (*in theatre*) balcão *m*

bald [bɔːld] *adj* calvo, careca; (*tyre*) careca

ball [bɔːl] *n* bola; (*of wool, string*) novelo; (*dance*) baile *m*; **to play ~ with sb** jogar bola com alguém; (*fig*) fazer o jogo de alguém

ballerina [bælə'riːnə] *n* bailarina

ballet ['bæleɪ] *n* balé *m*; **ballet dancer** *n* bailarino(-a)

balloon [bə'luːn] *n* balão *m*

ballot ['bælət] *n* votação *f*

ballpoint (pen) ['bɔːlpɔɪnt-] *n* (caneta) esferográfica

ban [bæn] *n* proibição *f*, interdição *f*; (*suspension*) exclusão *f* ▷ *vt* proibir, interditar; excluir

banana [bə'nɑːnə] *n* banana

band [bænd] *n* (*group*) orquestra; (*Mil*) banda; (*strip*) faixa, cinta; **band together** *vi* juntar-se, associar-se

bandage ['bændɪdʒ] *n* atadura (BR), ligadura (PT) ▷ *vt* enfaixar

bang [bæŋ] *n* estalo; (*of door*) estrondo; (*of gun, exhaust*) explosão *f*; (*blow*) pancada ▷ *excl* bum!, bumba! ▷ *vt* (*one's head etc*) bater; (*door*) fechar com violência ▷ *vi* produzir estrondo; (*door*) bater; (*fireworks*) soltar

bangs [bæŋz] (*US*) *npl* (*fringe*) franja

banish ['bænɪʃ] *vt* banir

banister(s) ['bænɪstə(z)] *n(pl)* corrimão *m*

bank [bæŋk] *n* banco; (*of river, lake*) margem *f*; (*of earth*) rampa, ladeira ▷ *vi* (*Aviat*) ladear-se; **bank on** *vt fus* contar com, apostar em; **bank account** *n* conta bancária; **bank card** *n* cartão *m* de garantia de cheques; **banker** *n* banqueiro(-a); **Bank holiday** (BRIT) *n* feriado nacional; **banking** *n* transações *fpl* bancárias; **banknote** *n* nota

(bancária)

bankrupt ['bæŋkrʌpt] *adj* falido, quebrado; **to go ~** falir

bank statement *n* extrato bancário

banner ['bænə'] *n* faixa

baptism ['bæptɪzəm] *n* batismo

bar [bɑː'] *n* barra; (*rod*) vara; (*of window etc*) grade *f*; (*fig: hindrance*) obstáculo; (*prohibition*) impedimento; (*pub*) bar *m*; (*counter: in pub*) balcão *m* ▷ *vt* (*road*) obstruir; (*person*) excluir; (*activity*) proibir ▷ *prep*: **~ none** sem exceção; **behind ~s** (*prisoner*) atrás das grades; **the B~** (*Law*) a advocacia

barbaric [bɑː'bærɪk] *adj* bárbaro

barbecue ['bɑːbɪkjuː] *n* churrasco

barbed wire ['bɑːbd-] *n* arame *m* farpado

barber ['bɑːbə'] *n* barbeiro, cabeleireiro

bar code *n* código de barras

bare [beə'] *adj* despido; (*head*) descoberto; (*trees*) sem vegetação; (*minimum*) básico ▷ *vt* mostrar; **barefoot** *adj*, *adv* descalço; **barely** *adv* apenas, mal

bargain ['bɑːgɪn] *n* negócio; (*agreement*) acordo; (*good buy*) pechincha ▷ *vi* (*haggle*) regatear; (*negotiate*) **to ~ (with sb)** pechinchar (com alguém); **into the ~** ainda por cima; **bargain for** *vt fus*: **he got more than he bargained for** ele conseguiu mais do que pediu

barge [bɑːdʒ] *n* barcaça; **barge in** *vi* irromper

bark [bɑːk] *n* (*of tree*) casca; (*of dog*) latido ▷ *vi* latir

barley ['bɑːlɪ] *n* cevada

barmaid ['bɑːmeɪd] *n* garçonete *f* (BR), empregada (de bar) (PT)

barman ['bɑːmən] (*irreg*) *n* garçom *m* (BR), empregado (de bar) (PT)

barn [bɑːn] *n* celeiro

barometer [bə'rɔmɪtə'] *n* barômetro

baron ['bærən] *n* barão *m*; (*of press*) magnata *m*; **baroness** ['bærənɪs] *n* baronesa

barracks ['bærəks] *npl* quartel *m*, caserna

barrage ['bærɑːʒ] *n* (*Mil*) fogo de barragem; (*dam*) barragem *f*; (*fig*): **a ~ of questions** uma saraivada de perguntas

barrel ['bærəl] *n* barril *m*; (*of gun*) cano

barren ['bærən] *adj* (*land*) árido

barricade [bærɪ'keɪd] *n* barricada

barrier ['bærɪə'] *n* barreira; (*fig: to progress etc*) obstáculo

barrister ['bærɪstə'] (BRIT) *n* advogado(-a), causídico(-a)

barrow ['bærəu] *n* (*wheelbarrow*) carrinho (de mão)

bartender ['bɑːtɛndə'] (US) *n* garçom *m* (BR), empregado (de bar) (PT)

base [beɪs] *n* base *f* ▷ *vt* (*opinion, belief*): **to ~ sth on** basear or fundamentar algo em ▷ *adj* (*thoughts*) sujo; **baseball** *n* beisebol *m*

basement ['beɪsmənt] *n* porão *m*

bases¹ ['beɪsɪz] *npl of* **base**

bases² ['beɪsiːz] *npl of* **basis**

bash [bæʃ] (*inf*) *vt* (*with fist*) dar soco or murro em; (*with object*) bater em

basic ['beɪsɪk] *adj* básico; (*facilities*) mínimo; **basically** *adv* basicamente; (*really*) no fundo; **basics** *npl*: **the basics** o essencial

basin ['beɪsn] *n* (*vessel, Geo*) bacia; (*also:* **wash~**) pia

basis ['beɪsɪs] (*pl* **bases**) *n* base *f*; **on a part-time ~** num esquema de meio-expediente; **on a trial ~** em experiência

basket ['bɑːskɪt] *n* cesto; (*with handle*) cesta; **basketball** *n* basquete(bol) *m*

bass [beɪs] *n* (*Mus*) baixo

bastard ['bɑːstəd] *n* bastardo(-a); (*inf!*) filho-da-puta *m* (!)

bat [bæt] *n* (*Zool*) morcego; (*for ball games*) bastão *m*; (BRIT: *for table tennis*) raquete *f* ▷ *vt*: **he didn't ~ an eyelid** ele nem pestanejou

batch [bætʃ] *n* (*of bread*) fornada; (*of papers*) monte *m*

bath [bɑːθ] *n* banho; (*bathtub*) banheira ▷ *vt* banhar; **to have a ~** tomar banho (de banheira); *see also* **baths**

bathe [beɪð] *vi* banhar-se; (US: *have a bath*) tomar um banho ▷ *vt* (*wound*) lavar; **bathing** *n* banho; **bathing costume** (US **bathing suit**) *n* (*woman's*) maiô *m* (BR), fato de banho (PT)

bathrobe ['bɑːθrəub] *n* roupão *m* de banho

bathroom ['bɑːθrum] *n* banheiro (BR), casa de banho (PT)

baths [bɑːðz] *npl* banhos *mpl* públicos

baton ['bætən] *n* (*Mus*) batuta; (*Athletics*) bastão *m*; (*truncheon*) cassetete *m*

batter ['bætə'] *vt* espancar; (*subj: wind, rain*) castigar ▷ *n* massa (mole); **battered** ['bætəd] *adj* (*hat, pan*) amassado, surrado

battery ['bætərɪ] *n* bateria; (*of torch*) pilha

battle ['bætl] *n* batalha; (*fig*) luta ▷ *vi*

lutar; **battlefield** n campo de batalha

bay [beɪ] n (Geo) baía; **to hold sb at ~** manter alguém à distância

bazaar [bəˈzɑː] n bazar m

B & B n abbr = **bed and breakfast**

BBC n abbr (= British Broadcasting Corporation) companhia britânica de rádio e televisão

B.C. adv abbr (= before Christ) a.C.

⊙ **KEYWORD**

be [biː] (pt was or were, pp been) aux vb **1** (with present participle: forming continuous tense) estar; **what are you doing?** o que você está fazendo (BR) or a fazer (PT)?; **it is raining** está chovendo (BR) or a chover (PT); **I've been waiting for you for hours** há horas que eu espero por você

2 (with pp: forming passives): **to be killed** ser morto; **the box had been opened** a caixa tinha sido aberta; **the thief was nowhere to be seen** ninguém viu o ladrão

3 (in tag questions): **it was fun, wasn't it?** foi divertido, não foi?; **she's back again, is she?** ela voltou novamente, é?

4 (+ to + infin): **the house is to be sold** a casa está à venda; **you're to be congratulated for all your work** você devia ser cumprimentado pelo seu trabalho; **he's not to open it** ele não pode abrir isso

▷ vb + complement **1** (gen): **I'm English** sou inglês; **I'm tired** estou cansado; **2 and 2 are 4** dois e dois são quatro; **be careful!** tome cuidado!; **be quiet!** fique quieto!, fique calado!; **be good!** seja bonzinho!

2 (of health) estar; **how are you?** como está?

3 (of age): **how old are you?** quantos anos você tem?; **I'm twenty (years old)** tenho vinte anos

4 (cost) ser; **how much was the meal?** quanto foi a refeição?; **that'll be £5.75, please** são £5.75, por favor

▷ vi **1** (exist, occur etc) existir, haver; **the best singer that ever was** o maior cantor de todos os tempos; **is there a God?** Deus existe?; **be that as it may ...** de qualquer forma ...; **so be it** que seja assim

2 (referring to place) estar; **I won't be here tomorrow** eu não estarei aqui amanhã;

Edinburgh is in Scotland Edinburgo é or fica na Escócia

3 (referring to movement) ir; **where have you been?** onde você foi?; **I've been in the garden** estava no quintal

▷ impers vb **1** (referring to time) ser; **it's 8 o'clock** são 8 horas; **it's the 28th of April** é 28 de abril

2 (referring to distance) ficar; **it's 10 km to the village** fica a 10 km do lugarejo

3 (referring to the weather) estar; **it's too hot/cold** está quente/frio demais

4 (emphatic): **it's only me** sou eu!; **it was Maria who paid the bill** foi Maria quem pagou a conta

beach [biːtʃ] n praia ▷ vt puxar para a terra or praia, encalhar

beacon [ˈbiːkən] n (lighthouse) farol m; (marker) baliza

bead [biːd] n (of necklace) conta; (of sweat) gota

beak [biːk] n bico

beam [biːm] n (Arch) viga; (of light) raio ▷ vi (smile) sorrir

bean [biːn] n feijão m; (of coffee) grão m; **runner/broad ~** vagem f/fava

bear [bɛəʳ] (pt bore, pp borne) n urso ▷ vt (carry, support) arcar com; (tolerate) suportar ▷ vi: **to ~ right/left** virar à direita/à esquerda; **bear out** vt (theory, suspicion) confirmar, corroborar; **bear up** vi agüentar, resistir

beard [bɪəd] n barba

bearing [ˈbɛərɪŋ] n porte m, comportamento; (connection) relação f; **bearings** npl (also: **ball ~s**) rolimã m; **to take a ~** fazer marcação

beast [biːst] n bicho; (inf) fera

beat [biːt] (pt ~, pp ~en) n (of heart) batida; (Mus) ritmo, compasso; (of policeman) ronda ▷ vt (hit) bater em; (eggs) bater; (defeat) vencer, derrotar ▷ vi (heart) bater; **to ~ it** (inf) cair fora; **off the ~en track** fora de mão; **beat off** vt repelir; **beat up** vt (inf: person) espancar; (eggs) bater; **beating** n (thrashing) surra

beautiful [ˈbjuːtɪful] adj belo, lindo, formoso; **beautifully** adv admiravelmente

beauty [ˈbjuːtɪ] n beleza; (person) beldade f, beleza

beaver [ˈbiːvəʳ] n castor m

because [bɪˈkɒz] conj porque; **~ of** por causa de

beckon [ˈbɛkən] vt (also: **~ to**) chamar

com sinais, acenar para

become [bɪ'kʌm] (*irreg: like* **come**) *vi* (+ *n*) virar, fazer-se, tornar-se; (+ *adj*) tornar-se, ficar

bed [bɛd] *n* cama; (*of flowers*) canteiro; (*of coal, clay*) camada, base *f*; (*of sea, lake*) fundo; (*of river*) leito; **to go to ~** ir dormir, deitar(-se); **bed and breakfast** *n* (*place*) pensão *f*; (*terms*) cama e café da manhã (BR) *or* pequeno almoço (PT); **bedclothes** *npl* roupa de cama; **bedding** *n* roupa de cama; **bedroom** *n* quarto, dormitório; **bedside** *n*: **at sb's bedside** à cabeceira de alguém; **bedsit(ter)** (BRIT) *n* conjugado; **bedspread** *n* colcha; **bedtime** *n* hora de ir para cama

❀ **BEDSIT**
❀
❀ Um **bedsit** é um quarto mobiliado
❀ cujo aluguel inclui uso de cozinha e
❀ banheiro comuns. Esse sistema de
❀ alojamento é muito comum na Grã-
❀ Bretanha entre estudantes, jovens
❀ profissionais liberais etc.

bee [biː] *n* abelha

beech [biːtʃ] *n* faia

beef [biːf] *n* carne *f* de vaca; **roast ~** rosbife *m*; **beefburger** *n* hambúrguer *m*

been [biːn] *pp of* **be**

beer [bɪə*ʳ*] *n* cerveja

beetle ['biːtl] *n* besouro

beetroot ['biːtruːt] (BRIT) *n* beterraba

before [bɪ'fɔː*ʳ*] *prep* (*of time*) antes de; (*of space*) diante de ▷ *conj* antes que ▷ *adv* antes, anteriormente; à frente, na dianteira; **~ going** antes de sair; **the week ~** a semana anterior; **I've never seen it ~** nunca vi isso antes; **beforehand** *adv* antes

beg [bɛg] *vi* mendigar, pedir esmola ▷ *vt* (*also: ~ for*) mendigar; **to ~ sb to do sth** implorar a alguém para fazer algo; *see also* **pardon**

began [bɪ'gæn] *pt of* **begin**

beggar ['bɛgə*ʳ*] *n* mendigo(-a)

begin [bɪ'gɪn] (*pt* **began**, *pp* **begun**) *vt*, *vi* começar, iniciar; **to ~ doing** *or* **to do sth** começar a fazer algo; **beginner** *n* principiante *m/f*; **beginning** *n* início, começo

behalf [bɪ'hɑːf] *n*: **on** *or* **in** (US) **~ of** (*as representative of*) em nome de; (*for benefit of*) no interesse de

behave [bɪ'heɪv] *vi* comportar-se;

(*well: also:* **~ o.s.**) comportar-se (bem); **behaviour** (US **behavior**) *n* comportamento

behind [bɪ'haɪnd] *prep* atrás de ▷ *adv* atrás; (*move*) para trás ▷ *n* traseiro; **to be ~ (schedule) with sth** estar atrasado *or* com atraso em algo; **~ the scenes** nos bastidores

beige [beɪʒ] *adj* bege

Beijing ['beɪ'ʒɪŋ] *m* Pequim

being ['biːɪŋ] *n* (*state*) existência; (*entity*) ser *m*

belated [bɪ'leɪtɪd] *adj* atrasado

belch [bɛltʃ] *vi* arrotar ▷ *vt* (*also:* **~ out**: *smoke etc*) vomitar

Belgian ['bɛldʒən] *adj*, *n* belga *m/f*

Belgium ['bɛldʒəm] *n* Bélgica

belief [bɪ'liːf] *n* (*opinion*) opinião *f*; (*trust, faith*) fé *f*

believe [bɪ'liːv] *vt*: **to ~ sth/sb** acreditar algo/em alguém ▷ *vi*: **to ~ in** (*God*) crer em; (*method, person*) acreditar em; **believer** *n* (*Rel*) crente *m/f*, fiel *m/f*; (*in idea*) partidário(-a)

bell [bɛl] *n* sino; (*small, doorbell*) campainha

bellow ['bɛləu] *vi* mugir; (*person*) bramar

belly ['bɛlɪ] *n* barriga, ventre *m*

belong [bɪ'lɔŋ] *vi*: **to ~ to** pertencer a; (*club etc*) ser sócio de; **the book ~s here** o livro fica guardado aqui; **belongings** *npl* pertences *mpl*

beloved [bɪ'lʌvɪd] *adj* querido, amado

below [bɪ'ləu] *prep* (*beneath*) embaixo de; (*less than*) abaixo de ▷ *adv* em baixo; **see ~** ver abaixo

belt [bɛlt] *n* cinto; (*of land*) faixa; (*Tech*) correia ▷ *vt* (*thrash*) surrar; **beltway** (US) *n* via circular

bemused [bɪ'mjuːzd] *adj* bestificado, estupidificado

bench [bɛntʃ] *n* banco; (*work bench*) bancada (de carpinteiro); (BRIT: *Pol*) assento num Parlamento; **the B~** (*Law: judge*) o magistrado; (*: judges*) os magistrados, o corpo de magistrados

bend [bɛnd] (*pt*, *pp* **bent**) *vt* (*leg, arm*) dobrar; (*pipe*) curvar ▷ *vi* dobrar-se, inclinar-se ▷ *n* curva; (*in pipe*) curvatura; **bend down** *vi* abaixar-se; **bend over** *vi* debruçar-se

beneath [bɪ'niːθ] *prep* abaixo de; (*unworthy of*) indigno de ▷ *adv* em baixo

beneficial [bɛnɪ'fɪʃəl] *adj*: **~ (to)** benéfico (a)

benefit ['bɛnɪfɪt] *n* benefício, vantagem

f: (*money*) subsídio, auxílio ▷ *vt* beneficiar ▷ *vi*: **~ from sth** beneficiar-se de algo

benign [bɪˈnaɪn] *adj* (*person, smile*) afável, bondoso; (*Med*) benigno

bent [bɛnt] *pt, pp of* **bend** ▷ *n* inclinação *f* ▷ *adj*: **to be ~ on** estar empenhado em

bereaved [bɪˈriːvd] *npl*: **the ~** os enlutados

beret [ˈbɛreɪ] *n* boina

Berlin [bəːˈlɪn] *n* Berlim

berry [ˈbɛrɪ] *n* baga

berth [bəːθ] *n* (*bed*) beliche *m*; (*cabin*) cabine *f*; (*on train*) leito; (*for ship*) ancoradouro ▷ *vi* (*in harbour*) atracar, encostar-se; (*at anchor*) ancorar

beside [bɪˈsaɪd] *prep* (*next to*) junto de, ao lado de, ao pé de; **to be ~ o.s. (with anger)** estar fora de si; **that's ~ the point** isso não tem nada a ver

besides [bɪˈsaɪdz] *adv* além disso; (*in any case*) de qualquer jeito ▷ *prep* (*as well as*) além de

best [bɛst] *adj* melhor ▷ *adv* (o) melhor; **the ~ part of** (*quantity*) a maior parte de; **at ~** na melhor das hipóteses; **to make the ~ of sth** tirar o maior partido possível de algo; **to do one's ~** fazer o possível; **to the ~ of my knowledge** que eu saiba; **to the ~ of my ability** o melhor que eu puder; **best man** *n* padrinho de casamento

bet [bɛt] (*pt, pp* **~** *or* **~ted**) *n* aposta ▷ *vt, vi* apostar

betray [bɪˈtreɪ] *vt* trair; (*denounce*) delatar

better [ˈbɛtəʳ] *adj, adv* melhor ▷ *vt* melhorar; (*go above*) superar ▷ *n*: **to get the ~ of** vencer; **you had ~ do it** é melhor você fazer isso; **he thought ~ of it** pensou melhor, mudou de opinião; **to get ~** melhorar; **better off** *adj* mais rico; (*fig*): **you'd be better off this way** seria melhor para você assim

betting [ˈbɛtɪŋ] *n* jogo; **betting shop** (*BRIT*) *n* agência de apostas

between [bɪˈtwiːn] *prep* no meio de, entre ▷ *adv* no meio

beverage [ˈbɛvərɪdʒ] *n* bebida

beware [bɪˈwɛəʳ] *vi*: **to ~ (of)** precaver-se (de), ter cuidado (com); **"~ of the dog"** "cuidado com o cachorro"

bewildered [bɪˈwɪldəd] *adj* atordeado; (*confused*) confuso

beyond [bɪˈjɔnd] *prep* (*in space*) além de; (*exceeding*) acima de, fora de; (*date*) mais tarde que; (*above*) acima de ▷ *adv* além; (*in time*) mais longe, mais adiante; **~**

doubt fora de qualquer dúvida; **to be ~ repair** não ter conserto

bias [ˈbaɪəs] *n* (*prejudice*) preconceito; **bias(s)ed** *adj* parcial

bib [bɪb] *n* babadouro, babador *m*

Bible [ˈbaɪbl] *n* Bíblia

bicycle [ˈbaɪsɪkl] *n* bicicleta

bid [bɪd] (*pt* **bade** *or* **~**, *pp* **~den** *or* **~**) *n* oferta; (*at auction*) lance *m*; (*attempt*) tentativa ▷ *vi* fazer lance ▷ *vt* oferecer; **to ~ sb good day** dar bom dia a alguém

big [bɪg] *adj* grande; (*bulky*) volumoso; **~ brother/sister** irmão/irmã mais velho/a

bigheaded [ˈbɪgˈhɛdɪd] *adj* convencido

bike [baɪk] *n* bicicleta

bikini [bɪˈkiːnɪ] *n* biquíni *m*

bilingual [baɪˈlɪŋgwəl] *adj* bilíngüe

bill [bɪl] *n* conta; (*invoice*) fatura; (*Pol*) projeto de lei; (*US: banknote*) bilhete *m*, nota; (*in restaurant*) conta, notinha; (*of bird*) bico; (*Theatre*) cartaz *m*; **to fit** *or* **fill the ~** (*fig*) servir; **billboard** *n* quadro para cartazes

billfold [ˈbɪlfəuld] (*US*) *n* carteira

billiards [ˈbɪlɪədz] *n* bilhar *m*

billion [ˈbɪlɪən] *n* (*BRIT*) trilhão *m*; (*US*) bilhão *m*

bin [bɪn] *n* caixa; (*BRIT: for rubbish*) lata de lixo

bind [baɪnd] (*pt, pp* **bound**) *vt* atar, amarrar; (*oblige*) obrigar; (*book*) encadernar ▷ *n* (*inf*) saco; (*nuisance*) chatice *f*

binge [bɪndʒ] (*inf*) *n*: **to go on a ~** tomar uma bebedeira

bingo [ˈbɪŋgəu] *n* bingo

binoculars [bɪˈnɔkjuləz] *npl* binóculo

bio... [baɪəu] *prefix* bio...; **biochemistry** *n* bioquímica; **biography** *n* biografia; **biology** *n* biologia; **biometric** *adj* biométrico

birch [bəːtʃ] *n* bétula

bird [bəːd] *n* ave *f*, pássaro; (*BRIT: inf: girl*) gatinha; **bird flu** *n* gripe *f* do frango

birth [bəːθ] *n* nascimento; **to give ~ to** dar à luz, parir; **birth certificate** *n* certidão *f* de nascimento; **birth control** *n* controle *m* de natalidade; (*methods*) métodos *mpl* anticoncepcionais; **birthday** *n* aniversário (*BR*), dia *m* de anos (*PT*) ▷ *cpd* de aniversário; *see also* **happy**

biscuit [ˈbɪskɪt] *n* (*BRIT*) bolacha, biscoito; (*US*) pão *m* doce

bishop [ˈbɪʃəp] *n* bispo; (*Chess*) peça de jogo de xadrez

bit [bɪt] *pt of* **bite** ▷ *n* pedaço, bocado; (*of horse*) freio; (*Comput*) bit *m*; **a ~ of** (*a little*) um pouco de; **~ by ~** pouco a pouco

bitch [bɪtʃ] *n* (*dog*) cadela, cachorra

bite [baɪt] (*pt* **bit**, *pp* **bitten**) *vt, vi* morder; (*insect etc*) picar ▷ *n* (*insect etc*) picada; (*mouthful*) bocado; **to ~ one's nails** roer as unhas; **let's have a ~ (to eat)** (*inf*) vamos fazer uma boquinha

bitter ['bɪtə'] *adj* amargo; (*wind, criticism*) cortante, penetrante; (*weather*) horrível ▷ *n* (BRIT: *beer*) cerveja amarga

black [blæk] *adj* preto; (*humour*) negro ▷ *n* (*colour*) cor *f* preta; (*person*): **B~** negro(-a), preto(-a) ▷ *vt* (BRIT: *Industry*) boicotar; **to give sb a ~ eye** esmurrar alguém e deixá-lo de olho roxo; **~ and blue** contuso, contundido; **to be in the ~** (*in credit*) estar com saldo credor; **blackberry** *n* amora silvestre; **blackbird** *n* melro; **blackboard** *n* quadro(-negro); **black coffee** *n* café *m* preto, bica (PT); **blackcurrant** *n* groselha negra; **blackmail** *n* chantagem *f* ▷ *vt* fazer chantagem a; **black market** *n* mercado *or* câmbio negro; **blackout** *n* blecaute *m*; (*fainting*) desmaio; (*of radio signal*) desvanecimento; **Black Sea** *n*: **the Black Sea** o mar Negro

bladder ['blædə'] *n* bexiga

blade [bleɪd] *n* lâmina; (*of oar*) pá *f*; **a ~ of grass** uma folha de relva

blame [bleɪm] *n* culpa ▷ *vt*: **to ~ sb for sth** culpar alguém por algo; **to be to ~** ter a culpa

bland [blænd] *adj* (*taste*) brando

blank [blæŋk] *adj* em branco; (*look*) sem expressão ▷ *n* (*of memory*): **to go ~** dar um branco; (*on form*) espaço em branco; (*cartridge*) bala de festim

blanket ['blæŋkɪt] *n* cobertor *m*

blast [blɑːst] *n* (*of wind*) rajada; (*of explosive*) explosão *f* ▷ *vt* fazer voar

blatant ['bleɪtənt] *adj* descarado

blaze [bleɪz] *n* (*fire*) fogo; (*fig: of colour*) esplendor *m*; (: *of glory, publicity*) explosão *f* ▷ *vi* (*fire*) arder; (*guns*) descarregar; (*eyes*) brilhar ▷ *vt*: **to ~ a trail** (*fig*) abrir (um) caminho

blazer ['bleɪzə'] *n* casaco esportivo, blazer *m*

bleach [bliːtʃ] *n* (*also*: **household ~**) água sanitária ▷ *vt* (*linen*) branquear

bleak [bliːk] *adj* (*countryside*) desolado; (*prospect*) desanimador(a), sombrio; (*weather*) ruim

bleed [bliːd] (*pt, pp* **bled**) *vi* sangrar

blemish ['blɛmɪʃ] *n* mancha; (*on reputation*) mácula

blend [blɛnd] *n* mistura ▷ *vt* misturar ▷ *vi* (*colours etc: also*: **~ in**) combinar-se, misturar-se; **blender** *n* liquidificador *m*

bless [blɛs] (*pt, pp* **~ed** *or* **blest**) *vt* abençoar; **~ you!** (*after sneeze*) saúde!; **blessing** *n* bênção *f*; (*godsend*) graça, dádiva; (*approval*) aprovação *f*

blew [bluː] *pt of* **blow**

blind [blaɪnd] *adj* cego ▷ *n* (*for window*) persiana; (: *also*: **Venetian ~**) veneziana ▷ *vt* cegar; (*dazzle*) deslumbrar; **the blind** *npl* (*people*) os cegos; **blind alley** *n* beco-sem-saída *m*; **blindfold** *n* venda ▷ *adj, adv* com os olhos vendados, às cegas ▷ *vt* vendar os olhos a

blink [blɪŋk] *vi* piscar

bliss [blɪs] *n* felicidade *f*

blister ['blɪstə'] *n* (*on skin*) bolha; (*in paint, rubber*) empola ▷ *vi* empolar-se

blizzard ['blɪzəd] *n* nevasca

bloated ['bləutɪd] *adj* (*swollen*) inchado; (*full*) empanturrado

blob [blɔb] *n* (*drop*) gota; (*indistinct shape*) ponto

block [blɔk] *n* (*of wood*) bloco; (*of stone*) laje *f*; (*in pipes*) entupimento; (*of buildings*) quarteirão *m* ▷ *vt* obstruir, bloquear; (*progress*) impedir; **~ of flats** (BRIT) prédio (de apartamentos); **mental ~** bloqueio; **blockade** [blɔˈkeɪd] *n* bloqueio; **blockage** *n* obstrução *f*; **blockbuster** *n* grande sucesso

blog [blɔg] (*inf*) *n* blog *m*, blogue *m*

blogger ['blɔgə'] (*inf*) *n* (*person*) blogueiro(-a)

bloke [bləuk] (BRIT: *inf*) *n* cara *m* (BR), gajo (PT)

blond(e) [blɔnd] *adj, n* louro(-a)

blood [blʌd] *n* sangue *m*; **blood donor** *n* doador(a) *m/f* de sangue; **blood group** *n* grupo sangüíneo; **blood poisoning** *n* toxemia; **blood pressure** *n* pressão *f* arterial *or* sangüínea; **bloodshed** *n* matança, carnificina; **bloodshot** *adj* (*eyes*) injetado; **bloodstream** *n* corrente *f* sangüínea; **blood test** *n* exame *m* de sangue; **blood vessel** *n* vaso sangüíneo; **bloody** *adj* sangrento; (*nose*) ensangüentado; (BRIT: *inf*): **this bloody ...** essa droga de ..., esse maldito ...; **bloody strong/good** forte/bom pra burro

bloom [bluːm] *n* flor *f* ▷ *vi* florescer

blossom ['blɔsəm] n flor f ▷ vi florescer; (fig): **to ~ into** (fig) tornar-se

blot [blɔt] n borrão m; (fig) mancha ▷ vt borrar; **blot out** (view) tapar; (memory) apagar

blouse [blauz] n blusa

blow [bləu] (pt **blew**, pp **~n**) n golpe m; (punch) soco ▷ vi soprar ▷ vt (subj: wind) soprar; (instrument) tocar; (fuse) queimar; **to ~ one's nose** assoar o nariz; **blow away** vt levar, arrancar ▷ vi ser levado pelo vento; **blow down** vt derrubar; **blow off** vt levar; **blow out** vi (candle) apagar; **blow over** vi (storm, crisis) passar; **blow up** vi explodir ▷ vt explodir; (tyre) encher; (Phot) ampliar; **blow-dry** n escova; **blow-out** n (of tyre) furo

blue [blu:] adj azul; (depressed) deprimido; **blues** n (Mus): **the ~s** o blues; **~ film/joke** filme/anedota picante; **out of the ~** (fig) de estalo, inesperadamente; **bluebell** n campainha

bluff [blʌf] vi blefar ▷ n blefe m; **to call sb's ~** pagar para ver alguém

blunder ['blʌndə'] n gafe f ▷ vi cometer or fazer uma gafe

blunt [blʌnt] adj (knife) cego; (pencil) rombudo; (person) franco, direto

blur [blə:'] n borrão m ▷ vt (vision) embaçar; (distinction) reduzir, diminuir

blush [blʌʃ] vi corar, ruborizar-se ▷ n rubor m, vermelhidão f

board [bɔ:d] n tábua; (cardboard) quadro; (notice board) quadro de avisos; (for chess etc) tabuleiro; (committee) junta, conselho; (in firm) diretoria, conselho administrativo; (Naut, Aviat): **on ~** a bordo ▷ vt embarcar em; **full ~** (BRIT) pensão f completa; **half ~** (BRIT) meia-pensão f; **~ and lodging** casa e comida; **to go by the ~** ficar abandonado, dançar (inf); **board up** vt entabuar; **boarding card** n = **boarding pass**; **boarding pass** (BRIT) n cartão m de embarque; **boarding school** n internato

boast [bəust] vi: **to ~ (about or of)** gabar-se (de), jactar-se (de)

boat [bəut] n (small) bote m; (big) navio

bob [bɔb] vi balouçar-se; **bob up** vi aparecer, surgir

body ['bɔdɪ] n corpo; (corpse) cadáver m; (of car) carroçaria; (fig: group) grupo; (: organization) organização f; (quantity) conjunto; (of wine) corpo; **body-building** n musculação f; **bodyguard** n guarda-

costas m inv; **bodywork** n lataria

bog [bɔg] n pântano, atoleiro ▷ vt: **to get ~ged down** (fig) atolar-se

bogus ['bəugəs] adj falso

boil [bɔɪl] vt ferver; (Culin) cozer, cozinhar ▷ vi ferver ▷ n (Med) furúnculo; **to come to the** (BRIT) or **a** (US) **~** começar a ferver; **boil down to** vt fus (fig) reduzir-se a; **boil over** vi transbordar; **boiled egg** n ovo cozido; **boiled potatoes** npl batatas fpl cozidas; **boiler** n caldeira; (for central heating) boiler m; **boiling point** n ponto de ebulição

bold [bəuld] adj corajoso; (pej) atrevido, insolente; (outline, colour) forte

Bolivia [bə'lɪvɪə] n Bolívia

bollard ['bɔləd] (BRIT) n (Aut) poste m de sinalização

bolt [bəult] n (lock) trinco, ferrolho; (with nut) parafuso, cavilha ▷ adv: **~ upright** direito como um fuso ▷ vt (door) fechar a ferrolho, trancar; (food) engolir às pressas ▷ vi fugir; (horse) disparar

bomb [bɔm] n bomba ▷ vt bombardear

bond [bɔnd] n (binding promise) compromisso; (link) vínculo, laço; (Finance) obrigação f; (Comm): **in ~** (goods) retido sob caução na alfândega

bone [bəun] n osso; (of fish) espinha ▷ vt desossar; tirar as espinhas de

bonfire ['bɔnfaɪə'] n fogueira

bonnet ['bɔnɪt] n toucado; (BRIT: of car) capô m

bonus ['bəunəs] n (payment) bônus m; (fig) gratificação f

boo [bu:] vt vaiar ▷ excl ruuh!, bu!

book [buk] n livro; (of stamps, tickets) talão m ▷ vt reservar; (driver) autuar; (football player) mostrar o cartão amarelo a; **books** npl (Comm) contas fpl, contabilidade f; **bookcase** n estante f (para livros); **booking office** (BRIT) n (Rail, Theatre) bilheteria (BR), bilheteira (PT); **book-keeping** n escrituração f, contabilidade f; **booklet** n livrinho, brochura; **bookshop** n, **bookstore** n livraria

boom [bu:m] n (noise) barulho, estrondo; (in sales) aumento rápido ▷ vi retumbar; (business) tomar surto

boost [bu:st] n estímulo ▷ vt estimular

boot [bu:t] n bota; (for football) chuteira; (BRIT: of car) porta-malas m (BR), porta-bagagem m (PT) ▷ vt (Comput) dar carga em; **to ~ ...** (in addition) ainda por cima ...

booth [bu:ð] n (at fair) barraca; (telephone

booth, voting booth) cabine f
booze [buːz] *(inf)* n bebida alcoólica
border ['bɔːdə'] n margem f; *(for flowers)*
borda; *(of a country)* fronteira; *(on cloth etc)* debrum m, remate m ▷ vt *(also: ~ on)* limitar-se com; **border on** vt fus *(fig)* chegar às raias de; **borderline** n fronteira
bore [bɔː'] *pt of* **bear** ▷ vt *(hole)* abrir; *(well)* cavar; *(person)* aborrecer ▷ n *(person)* chato(-a), maçante m/f; *(of gun)* calibre m; **to be ~d** estar entediado; **boredom** n tédio, aborrecimento; **boring** adj chato, maçante
born [bɔːn] adj: **to be ~** nascer
borne [bɔːn] pp *of* **bear**
borough ['bʌrə] n município
borrow ['bɔrəu] vt: **to ~ sth (from sb)** pedir algo emprestado a alguém
bosom ['buzəm] n peito
boss [bɔs] n *(employer)* patrão(-troa) m/f ▷ vt *(also: ~ about, ~ around)* mandar em; **bossy** adj mandão(-dona)
both [bəuθ] adj, pron ambos(-as), os dois *(as duas)* ▷ adv: **~ A and B** tanto A como B; **~ of us went, we ~ went** nós dois fomos, ambos fomos
bother ['bɔðə'] vt *(worry)* preocupar; *(disturb)* atrapalhar ▷ vi *(also: ~ o.s.)* preocupar-se ▷ n preocupação f; *(nuisance)* amolação f, inconveniente m
bottle ['bɔtl] n garrafa; *(of perfume, medicine)* frasco; *(baby's)* mamadeira (BR), biberão m (PT) ▷ vt engarrafar; **bottle up** vt conter, refrear
bottle bank n depósito de vidro para reciclagem, vidrão m (PT); **bottle-opener** n abridor m (de garrafas) (BR), abre-garrafas m inv (PT)
bottom ['bɔtəm] n fundo; *(buttocks)* traseiro; *(of page, list)* pé m; *(of class)* nível m mais baixo ▷ adj *(low)* inferior, mais baixo; *(last)* último
bought [bɔːt] pt, pp *of* **buy**
boulder ['bəuldə'] n pedregulho, matacão m
bounce [bauns] vi saltar, quicar; *(cheque)* ser devolvido ▷ vt fazer saltar ▷ n *(rebound)* salto; **bouncer** *(inf)* n leão-de-chácara m
bound [baund] pt, pp *of* **bind** ▷ n *(leap)* pulo, salto; *(gen pl: limit)* limite m ▷ vi *(leap)* pular, saltar ▷ vt *(border)* demarcar ▷ adj: **~ by** limitado por; **to be ~ to do sth** *(obliged)* ter a obrigação de fazer algo; *(likely)* na certa ir fazer algo; **~ for** com

destino a
boundary ['baundrɪ] n limite m, fronteira
bout [baut] n *(of malaria etc)* ataque m; *(of activity)* explosão f; *(Boxing etc)* combate m
bow¹ [bəu] n *(knot)* laço; *(weapon, Mus)* arco
bow² [bau] n *(of the body)* reverência; *(of the head)* inclinação f; *(Naut: also: ~s)* proa ▷ vi curvar-se, fazer uma reverência; *(yield)*: **to ~ to** or **before** ceder ante, submeter-se a
bowels ['bauəlz] npl intestinos mpl, tripas fpl; *(fig)* entranhas fpl
bowl [bəul] n tigela; *(ball)* bola ▷ vi *(Cricket)* arremessar a bola
bowler ['bəulə'] n *(Cricket)* lançador m (da bola); *(BRIT: also: ~ hat)* chapéu-coco m
bowling ['bəulɪŋ] n *(game)* boliche m; **bowling alley** n boliche m; **bowling green** n gramado (BR) or relvado (PT) para jogo de bolas
bowls [bəulz] n jogo de bolas
bow tie ['bəu-] n gravata-borboleta
box [bɔks] n caixa; *(Theatre)* camarote m ▷ vt encaixotar; *(Sport)* boxear contra ▷ vi *(Sport)* boxear; **boxer** n *(person)* boxeador m, pugilista m; **boxer shorts** npl samba-canção m (BR), boxers mpl (PT); **boxing** n *(Sport)* boxe m, pugilismo; **Boxing Day** *(BRIT)* n Dia de Santo Estêvão *(26 de dezembro)*; **box office** n bilheteria (BR), bilheteira (PT)
boy [bɔɪ] n *(young)* menino, garoto; *(older)* moço, rapaz m; *(son)* filho
boycott ['bɔɪkɔt] n boicote m, boicotagem f ▷ vt boicotar
boyfriend ['bɔɪfrɛnd] n namorado
bra [brɑː] n sutiã m (BR), soutien m (PT)
brace [breis] n *(on teeth)* aparelho; *(tool)* arco de pua ▷ vt retesar; **braces** npl *(BRIT)* suspensórios mpl; **to ~ o.s.** *(also fig)* preparar-se
bracelet ['breislɪt] n pulseira
bracket ['brækɪt] n *(Tech)* suporte m; *(group)* classe f, categoria; *(range)* faixa, parêntese m ▷ vt pôr entre parênteses; *(fig)* agrupar
brag [bræg] vi gabar-se, contar vantagem
braid [breid] n *(trimming)* galão m; *(of hair)* trança
brain [brein] n cérebro; **brains** npl *(Culin)* miolos mpl; *(intelligence)* inteligência, miolos

braise [breɪz] vt assar na panela

brake [breɪk] n freio (BR), travão m (PT)
▷ vt, vi frear (BR), travar (PT)

bran [bræn] n farelo

branch [brɑːntʃ] n ramo, galho; (Comm) sucursal f, filial f; **branch out** vi (fig) diversificar suas atividades; **to branch out into** estender suas atividades a

brand [brænd] n marca; (fig: type) tipo ▷ vt (cattle) marcar com ferro quente

brand-new adj novo em folha, novinho

brandy ['brændɪ] n conhaque m

brash [bræʃ] adj (forward) descarado

brass [brɑːs] n latão m; **the ~** (Mus) os metais; **brass band** n banda de música

brat [bræt] (pej) n pirralho(-a), fedelho(-a), malcriado(-a)

brave [breɪv] adj valente, corajoso ▷ vt (face up to) desafiar; **bravery** n coragem f, bravura

Brazil [brə'zɪl] n Brasil m; **Brazilian** adj, n brasileiro(-a)

breach [briːtʃ] vt abrir brecha em ▷ n (gap) brecha; (breaking): **~ of contract** inadimplência (BR), inadimplemento (PT); **~ of the peace** perturbação f da ordem pública

bread [brɛd] n pão m; **breadbin** (US **bread box**) n caixa de pão; **breadcrumbs** npl migalhas fpl; (Culin) farinha de rosca

breadth [brɛtθ] n largura; (fig) amplitude f

break [breɪk] (pt **broke**, pp **broken**) vt quebrar (BR), partir (PT); (promise) quebrar; (law) violar, transgredir; (record) bater ▷ vi quebrar-se, partir-se; (storm) começar subitamente; (weather) mudar; (dawn) amanhecer; (story, news) revelar ▷ n (gap) abertura; (fracture) fratura; (rest) descanso; (interval) intervalo; (at school) recreio; (chance) oportunidade f; **to ~ the news to sb** dar a notícia a alguém; **to ~ even** sair sem ganhar nem perder; **to ~ free** or **loose** soltar-se; **to ~ open** (door etc) arrombar; **break down** vt (figures, data) analisar ▷ vi (machine, Aut) enguiçar, pifar (inf); (Med) sofrer uma crise nervosa; (person: cry) desatar a chorar; (talks) fracassar; **break in** vt (horse etc) domar ▷ vi (burglar) forçar uma entrada; (interrupt) interromper; **break into** vt fus (house) arrombar; **break off** vi (speaker) parar-se, deter-se; (branch) partir; **break out** vi (war) estourar; (prisoner) libertar-se; **to break**

out in spots/a rash aparecer coberto de manchas/brotoejas; **break up** vi (ship) partir-se; (partnership) acabar; (marriage) desmanchar-se; **you're breaking up** (Tel) sua voz está falhando ▷ vt (rocks) partir; (biscuit etc) quebrar; (journey) romper; (fight) intervir em; **breakdown** n (Aut) enguiço, avaria; (in communications) interrupção f; (of marriage) fracasso, término; (Med: also: **nervous breakdown**) esgotamento nervoso; (of figures) discriminação f, desdobramento

breakfast ['brɛkfəst] n café m da manhã (BR), pequeno almoço (PT)

break: **break-in** n roubo com arrombamento; **breakthrough** n (fig) avanço, novo progresso

breast [brɛst] n (of woman) peito, seio; (chest, meat) peito; **breast-feed** (irreg: like **feed**) vt, vi amamentar; **breast-stroke** n nado de peito

breath [brɛθ] n fôlego, respiração f; **out of ~** ofegante, sem fôlego

breathe [briːð] vt, vi respirar; **breathe in** vt, vi inspirar; **breathe out** vt, vi expirar; **breathing** n respiração f

breathless ['brɛθlɪs] adj sem fôlego

breed [briːd] (pt, pp **bred**) vt (animals) criar; (plants) multiplicar ▷ vi criar, reproduzir ▷ n raça

breeze [briːz] n brisa, aragem f; **breezy** adj (person) despreocupado, animado; (weather) ventoso

brew [bruː] vt (tea) fazer; (beer) fermentar ▷ vi (storm, fig) armar-se; **brewery** n cervejaria

bribe [braɪb] n suborno ▷ vt subornar; **bribery** n suborno

brick [brɪk] n tijolo; **bricklayer** n pedreiro

bride [braɪd] n noiva; **bridegroom** n noivo; **bridesmaid** n dama de honra

bridge [brɪdʒ] n ponte f; (Naut) ponte de comando; (Cards) bridge m; (of nose) cavalete m ▷ vt transpor

bridle ['braɪdl] n cabeçada, freio

brief [briːf] adj breve ▷ n (Law) causa; (task) tarefa ▷ vt (inform) informar; **briefs** npl (for men) cueca (BR), cuecas fpl (PT); (for women) calcinha (BR), cuecas fpl (PT); **briefcase** n pasta; **briefly** adv (glance) rapidamente; (say) em poucas palavras

bright [braɪt] adj claro, brilhante; (weather) resplandecente; (person: clever) inteligente; (: lively) alegre, animado;

(colour) vivo; (future) promissor(a), favorável

brilliant ['brɪljənt] adj brilhante; (inf: great) sensacional

brim [brɪm] n borda; (of hat) aba

brine [braɪn] n (Culin) salmoura

bring [brɪŋ] (pt, pp **brought**) vt trazer; **bring about** vt ocasionar, produzir; **bring back** vt restabelecer; (return) devolver; **bring down** vt (price) abaixar; (government, plane) derrubar; **bring forward** vt adiantar; **bring off** vt (plan) levar a cabo; **bring out** vt (object) tirar; (meaning) salientar; (book etc) lançar; **bring round** vt fazer voltar a si; **bring up** vt (person) educar, criar; (carry up) subir; (question) introduzir; (food) vomitar

brisk [brɪsk] adj vigoroso; (tone, person) enérgico; (trade) ativo

bristle ['brɪsl] n (of animal) pêlo rijo; (of beard) pêlo de barba curta; (of brush) cerda ▷ vi (in anger) encolerizar-se

Britain ['brɪtən] n (also: **Great ~**) Grã-Bretanha

British ['brɪtɪʃ] adj britânico ▷ npl: the **~** os britânicos; **British Isles** npl: the **British Isles** as ilhas Britânicas

Briton ['brɪtən] n britânico(-a)

brittle ['brɪtl] adj quebradiço, frágil

broad [brɔːd] adj (street, range) amplo; (shoulders, smile) largo; (distinction) geral; (accent) carregado; **in ~ daylight** em plena luz do dia; **broadband** n banda larga; **broadcast** (pt, pp **broadcast**) n transmissão f ▷ vt, vi transmitir; **broaden** vt alargar ▷ vi alargar-se; **to broaden one's mind** abrir os horizontes; **broadly** adv em geral; **broad-minded** adj tolerante, liberal

broccoli ['brɔkəlɪ] n brócolis mpl

brochure ['brəʊʃʊəʳ] n folheto, brochura

broke [brəʊk] pt of **break** ▷ adj (inf) sem um vintém, duro; (: company): **to go ~** quebrar

broken ['brəʊkən] pp of **break** ▷ adj quebrado; **in ~ English** num inglês mascavado

broker ['brəʊkəʳ] n corretor(a) m/f

bronchitis [brɔŋ'kaɪtɪs] n bronquite f

bronze [brɔnz] n bronze m

brooch [brəʊtʃ] n broche m

brood [bruːd] n ninhada ▷ vi (person) cismar, remoer

broom [brum] n vassoura; (Bot) giesta-das-vassouras

Bros. abbr (Comm: = brothers) Irmãos

broth [brɔθ] n caldo

brothel ['brɔθl] n bordel m

brother ['brʌðəʳ] n irmão m; **brother-in-law** n cunhado

brought [brɔːt] pt, pp of **bring**

brow [braʊ] n (forehead) fronte f, testa; (rare: gen: eyebrow) sobrancelha; (of hill) cimo, cume m

brown [braʊn] adj marrom (BR), castanho (PT); (hair) castanho; (tanned) bronzeado, moreno ▷ n (colour) cor f marrom (BR) or castanha (PT) ▷ vt (Culin) dourar; **brown bread** n pão m integral; **Brownie** n (also: **Brownie Guide**) fadinha de bandeirante; **brown sugar** n açúcar m mascavo

browse [braʊz] vi (in shop) dar uma olhada; **to ~ through a book** folhear um livro

browser ['braʊzəʳ] n (Comput) browser m, navegador m

bruise [bruːz] n hematoma m, contusão f ▷ vt machucar

brunette [bruː'nɛt] n morena

brush [brʌʃ] n escova; (for painting, shaving) pincel m; (quarrel) bate-boca m ▷ vt varrer; (groom) escovar; (also: **~ against**) tocar ao passar, roçar; **brush aside** vt afastar, não fazer caso de; **brush up** vt retocar, revisar

Brussels ['brʌslz] n Bruxelas; **Brussels sprout** n couve-de-bruxelas f

brutal ['bruːtl] adj brutal

BSE n abbr: (= bovine spongiform encephalopathy) BSE f

bubble ['bʌbl] n bolha (BR), borbulha (PT) ▷ vi borbulhar; **bubble bath** n banho de espuma; **bubble gum** n chiclete m (de bola) (BR), pastilha elástica (PT)

buck [bʌk] n (rabbit) macho; (deer) cervo; (US: inf) dólar m ▷ vi corcovear; **to pass the ~** fazer o jogo de empurra; **buck up** vi (cheer up) animar-se, cobrar ânimo

bucket ['bʌkɪt] n balde m

buckle ['bʌkl] n fivela ▷ vt afivelar ▷ vi torcer-se, cambar-se

bud [bʌd] n broto; (of flower) botão m ▷ vi brotar, desabrochar

Buddhism ['budɪzəm] n budismo

buddy ['bʌdɪ] (US) n camarada m, companheiro

budge [bʌdʒ] vt mover ▷ vi mexer-se

budgerigar ['bʌdʒərɪgaːʳ] n periquito

budget ['bʌdʒɪt] n orçamento ▷ vi: **to ~ for sth** incluir algo no orçamento

budgie ['bʌdʒɪ] *n* = **budgerigar**

buff [bʌf] *adj* (*colour*) cor de camurça ▷ *n* (*inf: enthusiast*) aficionado(-a)

buffalo ['bʌfələu] (*pl ~ or ~es*) *n* (BRIT) búfalo; (*us: bison*) bisão *m*

buffer ['bʌfəʳ] *n* pára-choque *m*; (*Comput*) buffer *m*, memória intermediária

buffet¹ ['bufeɪ] (BRIT) *n* (*in station*) bar *m*; (*food*) bufê *m*; **buffet car** (BRIT) *n* vagão-restaurante *m*

buffet² ['bʌfɪt] *vt* fustigar

bug [bʌg] *n* (*esp us: insect*) bicho; (*fig: germ*) micróbio; (*spy device*) microfone *m* oculto, escuta clandestina; (*Comput: of program*) erro ▷ *vt* (*inf: annoy*) apoquentar, incomodar; (*room*) colocar microfones em; (*phone*) grampear

build [bɪld] (*pt, pp* **built**) *n* (*of person*) talhe *m*, estatura ▷ *vt* construir, edificar; **build up** *vt* acumular; **builder** *n* construtor(a) *m/f*, empreiteiro(-a); **building** *n* construção *f*; (*a building*) edifício, prédio; **building society** (BRIT) *n* sociedade *f* de crédito imobiliário, financiadora

built [bɪlt] *pt, pp of* **build** ▷ *adj*: **~-in** embutido

bulb [bʌlb] *n* (*Bot*) bulbo; (*Elec*) lâmpada

Bulgaria [bʌl'gɛərɪə] *n* Bulgária

bulge [bʌldʒ] *n* bojo, saliência ▷ *vi* inchar-se; (*pocket etc*) fazer bojo

bulk [bʌlk] *n* (*of building, object*) volume *m*; (*of person*) corpanzil *m*; **in ~** (*Comm*) a granel; **the ~ of** a maior parte de; **bulky** *adj* volumoso

bull [bul] *n* touro

bulldozer ['buldəuzəʳ] *n* buldôzer *m*, escavadora

bullet ['bulɪt] *n* bala

bulletin ['bulɪtɪn] *n* noticiário; (*journal*) boletim *m*

bullfight ['bulfaɪt] *n* tourada; **bullfighter** *n* toureiro; **bullfighting** *n* tauromaquia

bully ['bulɪ] *n* fanfarrão *m*, valentão *m* ▷ *vt* intimidar, tiranizar

bum [bʌm] *n* (*inf: backside*) bum-bum *m*; (*esp us: tramp*) vagabundo(-a), vadio(-a)

bumblebee ['bʌmblbi:] *n* mamangaba

bump [bʌmp] *n* (*blow*) batida; (*jolt*) sacudida; (*on head*) galo; (*on road*) elevação *f* ▷ *vt* bater contra, dar encontrão em ▷ *vi* dar sacudidas; **bump into** *vt fus* chocar-se com or contra, colidir com; (*inf: person*) dar com, topar com; **bumper** *n* (BRIT) pára-choque *m* ▷ *adj*: **bumper crop** supersafra

bumpy ['bʌmpɪ] *adj* (*road*) acidentado, cheio de altos e baixos

bun [bʌn] *n* pão *m* doce (BR), pãozinho (PT); (*in hair*) coque *m*

bunch [bʌntʃ] *n* (*of flowers*) ramo; (*of keys*) molho; (*of bananas*) cacho; (*of people*) grupo; **bunches** *npl* (*in hair*) cachos *mpl*

bundle ['bʌndl] *n* trouxa, embrulho; (*of sticks*) feixe *m*; (*of papers*) maço ▷ *vt* (*also: ~ up*) embrulhar, atar; (*put*): **to ~ sth/sb into** meter *or* enfiar algo/alguém correndo em

bungalow ['bʌŋgələu] *n* bangalô *m*, chalé *m*

bunion ['bʌnjən] *n* joanete *m*

bunk [bʌŋk] *n* beliche *m*; **bunk beds** *npl* beliche *m*, cama-beliche *f*

bunker ['bʌŋkəʳ] *n* (*coal store*) carvoeira; (*Mil*) abrigo, casamata; (*Golf*) bunker *m*

buoy [bɔɪ] *n* bóia; **buoy up** *vt* (*fig*) animar; **buoyant** *adj* flutuante; (*person*) alegre; (*Comm: market*) animado

burden ['bə:dn] *n* responsabilidade *f*, fardo; (*load*) carga ▷ *vt* sobrecarregar; (*trouble*): **to be a ~ to sb** ser um estorvo para alguém

bureau [bjuə'rəu] (*pl ~x*) *n* (BRIT: *desk*) secretária, escrivaninha; (*us: chest of drawers*) cômoda; (*office*) escritório, agência

bureaucracy [bjuə'rɔkrəsɪ] *n* burocracia

burglar ['bə:glə*ʳ*] *n* ladrão(ona) *m/f*; **burglar alarm** *n* alarma de roubo; **burglary** *n* roubo

burial ['bɛrɪəl] *n* enterro

burn [bə:n] (*pt, pp* **~ed** or **~t**) *vt* queimar; (*house*) incendiar ▷ *vi* queimar-se, arder; (*sting*) arder, picar ▷ *n* queimadura; **burn down** *vt* incendiar; **burning** *adj* ardente; (*hot: sand etc*) abrasador(a); (*ambition*) grande

burrow ['bʌrəu] *n* toca, lura ▷ *vi* fazer uma toca, cavar; (*rummage*) esquadrinhar

burst [bə:st] (*pt, pp* **~**) *vt* arrebentar; (*banks*) romper ▷ *vi* estourar; (*tyre*) furar ▷ *n* rajada; **to ~ into flames** incendiar-se de repente; **to ~ into tears** desatar a chorar; **to ~ out laughing** cair na gargalhada; **to be ~ing with** (*subj: room, container*) estar abarrotado de; (: *person: emotion*) estar tomado de; **a ~ of energy** uma explosão de energia; **burst into** *vt fus* (*room etc*) irromper em

bury ['bɛrɪ] *vt* enterrar; (*at funeral*) sepultar; **to ~ one's head in one's hands** cobrir o rosto com as mãos; **to**

~ **one's head in the sand** (fig) bancar avestruz; **to ~ the hatchet** (fig) fazer as pazes

bus [bʌs] n ônibus m inv (BR), autocarro (PT)

bush [buʃ] n arbusto, mata; (scrubland) sertão m; **to beat about the ~** ser evasivo

business ['bɪznɪs] n negócio; (trading) comércio, negócios mpl; (firm) empresa; (occupation) profissão f; **to be away on ~** estar fora a negócios; **it's my ~ to ...** encarrego-me de ...; **it's none of my ~** eu não tenho nada com isto; **he means ~** fala a sério; **businesslike** adj eficiente, metódico; **businessman** (irreg) n homem m de negócios; **business trip** n viagem f de negócios; **businesswoman** (irreg) n mulher f de negócios

busker ['bʌskəʳ] (BRIT) n artista m/f de rua

bust [bʌst] n (Anat) busto ▷ adj (inf: broken) quebrado; **to go ~** falir

busy ['bɪzɪ] adj (person) ocupado, atarefado; (place) movimentado; (US: Tel) ocupado (BR), impedido (PT) ▷ vt: **to ~ o.s. with** ocupar-se em or de

○ **KEYWORD**

but [bʌt] conj 1 (yet) mas, porém; **he's tired but Paul isn't** ele está cansado mas Paul não; **the trip was enjoyable but tiring** a viagem foi agradável porém cansativa

2 (however) mas; **I'd love to come, but I'm busy** eu adoraria vir, mas estou ocupado

3 (showing disagreement, surprise etc) mas; **but that's far too expensive!** mas isso é caro demais!

▷ prep (apart from, except) exceto, menos; **he was nothing but trouble** ele só deu problema; **no-one but him** só ele, ninguém a não ser ele; **but for** sem, se não fosse; **(I'll do) anything but that** (eu faria) qualquer coisa menos isso

▷ adv (just, only) apenas; **had I but known** se eu soubesse; **I can but try** a única coisa que eu posso fazer é tentar; **all but** quase

butcher ['butʃəʳ] n açougueiro (BR), homem m do talho (PT) ▷ vt (prisoners etc) chacinar, massacrar; (cattle etc for meat) abater e carnear; **butcher's (shop)** n açougue m (BR), talho (PT)

butler ['bʌtləʳ] n mordomo

butt [bʌt] n (cask) tonel m; (of gun) coronha; (of cigarette) toco (BR), ponta (PT); (BRIT: fig: target) alvo ▷ vt (subj: goat) marrar; (: person) dar uma cabeçada em; **butt in** vi (interrupt) interromper

butter ['bʌtəʳ] n manteiga ▷ vt untar com manteiga

butterfly ['bʌtəflaɪ] n borboleta; (Swimming: also: ~ **stroke**) nado borboleta

buttocks ['bʌtəks] npl nádegas fpl

button ['bʌtn] n botão m; (US: badge) emblema m ▷ vt (also: ~ **up**) abotoar ▷ vi ter botões

buy [baɪ] (pt, pp **bought**) vt comprar ▷ n compra; **to ~ sb sth/sth from sb** comprar algo para alguém/algo a alguém; **to ~ sb a drink** pagar um drinque para alguém; **buyer** n comprador(a) m/f

buzz [bʌz] n zumbido; (inf: phone call): **to give sb a ~** dar uma ligada para alguém ▷ vi zumbir; **buzzer** n cigarra, vibrador m

○ **KEYWORD**

by [baɪ] prep 1 (referring to cause, agent) por, de; **killed by lightning** morto por um raio; **a painting by Picasso** um quadro de Picasso

2 (referring to method, manner, means) de, com; **by bus/car/train** de ônibus/carro/trem; **to pay by cheque** pagar com cheque; **by moonlight/candlelight** sob o luar/à luz de vela; **by saving hard, he ...** economizando muito, ele ...

3 (via, through) por, via; **we came by Dover** viemos por ou via Dover

4 (close to) perto de, ao pé de; **a holiday by the sea** férias à beira-mar; **she sat by his bed** ela sentou-se ao lado de seu leito

5 (past) por; **she rushed by me** ela passou por mim correndo

6 (not later than): **by 4 o'clock** antes das quatro; **by this time tomorrow** esta mesma hora amanhã; **by the time I got here it was too late** quando eu cheguei aqui, já era tarde demais

7 (during): **by daylight** durante o dia

8 (amount) por; **by the kilometre** por quilômetro

9 (Math, measure) por; **it's broader by a metre** tem um metro a mais de largura

10 (according to) segundo, de acordo

com; **it's all right by me** por mim tudo bem

11: **(all) by oneself** *etc* (completamente) só, sozinho; **he did it (all) by himself** ele fêz tudo sozinho

12: **by the way** a propósito

▷ *adv* **1** *see* **go**; **pass** *etc*

2: **by and by** logo, mais tarde; **by and large** em geral

bye(-bye) ['baɪ('baɪ)] *excl* até logo (BR), tchau (BR), adeus (PT)

bypass ['baɪpɑːs] *n* via secundária, desvio; (*Med*) ponte *f* de safena ▷ *vt* evitar

byte [baɪt] *n* (*Comput*) byte *m*

C [siː] *n* (*Mus*) dó *m*

cab [kæb] *n* táxi *m*; (*of truck etc*) boléia; (*of train*) cabina de maquinista

cabaret ['kæbəreɪ] *n* cabaré *m*

cabbage ['kæbɪdʒ] *n* repolho (BR), couve *f* (PT)

cabin ['kæbɪn] *n* cabana; (*on ship*) camarote *m*; (*on plane*) cabina de passageiros

cabinet ['kæbɪnɪt] *n* (*Pol*) gabinete *m*; (*furniture*) armário; (*also*: **display ~**) armário com vitrina

cable ['keɪbl] *n* cabo; (*telegram*) cabograma *m* ▷ *vt* enviar cabograma para; **cable television** *n* televisão *f* a cabo

cactus ['kæktəs] (*pl* **cacti**) *n* cacto

café ['kæfeɪ] *n* café *m*

cage [keɪdʒ] *n* (*bird cage*) gaiola; (*for large animals*) jaula; (*of lift*) cabina

cagoule [kə'guːl] *n* casaco de náilon

Cairo ['kaɪərəu] *n* o Cairo

cake [keɪk] *n* (*large*) bolo; (*small*) doce *m*, bolinho; **~ of soap** sabonete *m*

calculate ['kælkjuleɪt] *vt* calcular; (*estimate*) avaliar; **calculation** *n* cálculo; **calculator** *n* calculador *m*, calculadora

calendar ['kæləndəʳ] *n* calendário; **~**

month/year mês m/ano civil
calf [kɑːf] (pl **calves**) n (of cow) bezerro, vitela; (of other animals) cria; (also: **~skin**) pele f ou couro de bezerro; (Anat) barriga-da-perna
calibre ['kælɪbə'] (US **caliber**) n (of person) capacidade f, calibre m
call [kɔːl] vt chamar; (label) qualificar, descrever; (Tel) telefonar a, ligar para; (witness) citar; (meeting) convocar ▷ vi chamar; (shout) gritar; (Tel) telefonar; (visit: also: **~ in**, **~ round**) dar um pulo ▷ n (shout) chamada; (also: **telephone ~**) chamada, telefonema m; (of bird) canto; **to be ~ed** chamar-se; **on ~** de plantão; **call back** vi (return) voltar, passar de novo; (Tel) ligar de volta; **call for** vt fus (demand) requerer, exigir; (fetch) ir buscar; **call off** vt (cancel) cancelar; **call on** vt fus (visit) visitar; (appeal to) pedir; **call out** vi gritar, bradar; **call up** vt (Mil) chamar às fileiras; (Tel) dar uma ligada; **callbox** (BRIT) n cabine f telefônica
call centre n (BRIT: Tel) central f de chamadas; **caller** n visita m/f; (Tel) chamador(a) m/f
callous ['kæləs] adj cruel, insensível
calm [kɑːm] adj calmo; (peaceful) tranqüilo; (weather) estável ▷ n calma ▷ vt acalmar; (fears, grief) abrandar; **calm down** vt acalmar, tranqüilizar ▷ vi acalmar-se
calorie ['kælərɪ] n caloria
calves [kɑːvz] npl of **calf**
Cambodia [kæm'bəudjə] n Camboja
camcorder ['kæmkɔːdə'] n filmadora, máquina de filmar
came [keɪm] pt of **come**
camel ['kæməl] n camelo
camera ['kæmərə] n máquina fotográfica; (Cinema, TV) câmera; **in ~** (Law) em câmara; **camera phone** n celular m com câmera
camouflage ['kæməflɑːʒ] n camuflagem f ▷ vt camuflar
camp [kæmp] n campo, acampamento; (Mil) acampamento; (for prisoners) campo; (faction) facção f ▷ vi acampar ▷ adj afeminado
campaign [kæm'peɪn] n (Mil, Pol etc) campanha ▷ vi fazer campanha
camper ['kæmpə'] n campista m/f; (vehicle) reboque m
camping ['kæmpɪŋ] n camping m (BR), campismo (PT); **to go ~** acampar
campsite ['kæmpsaɪt] n camping m (BR),

parque m de campismo (PT)
campus ['kæmpəs] n campus m, cidade f universitária
can¹ [kæn] n lata ▷ vt enlatar

○ **KEYWORD**

can² [kæn] (negative **cannot** or **can't**, pt, conditional **could**) aux vb 1 (be able to) poder; **you can do it if you try** se você tentar, você consegue fazê-lo; **I'll help you all I can** ajudarei você em tudo que eu puder; **she couldn't sleep that night** ela não conseguiu dormir aquela noite; **can you hear me?** você está me ouvindo?
2 (know how to) saber; **I can swim** sei nadar; **can you speak Portuguese?** você fala português?
3 (may): **could I have a word with you?** será que eu podia falar com você?
4 (expressing disbelief, puzzlement): **it CAN'T be true!** não pode ser verdade!; **what CAN he want?** o que é que ele quer?
5 (expressing possibility, suggestion etc): **he could be in the library** ele talvez esteja na biblioteca; **they could have forgotten** eles podiam ter esquecido

Canada ['kænədə] n Canadá m; **Canadian** [kə'neɪdɪən] adj, n canadense m/f
canal [kə'næl] n canal m
canary [kə'nɛərɪ] n canário
cancel ['kænsəl] vt cancelar; (contract) anular; (cross out) riscar, invalidar; **cancellation** [kænsə'leɪʃən] n cancelamento
cancer ['kænsə'] n câncer m (BR), cancro (PT); **C~** (Astrology) Câncer
candidate ['kændɪdeɪt] n candidato(-a)
candle ['kændl] n vela; (in church) círio; **candlestick** n (plain) castiçal m; (bigger, ornate) candelabro, lustre m
candy ['kændɪ] n (also: **sugar~**) açúcar m cristalizado; (US) bala (BR), rebuçado (PT)
cane [keɪn] n (Bot) cana; (stick) bengala ▷ vt (BRIT: Sch) castigar (com bengala)
canister ['kænɪstə'] n lata
cannabis ['kænəbɪs] n maconha
canned [kænd] adj (food) em lata, enlatado
cannon ['kænən] (pl inv or **~s**) n canhão m

cannot ['kænɔt] = **can not**

canoe [kə'nu:] n canoa

can't [ka:nt] = **can not**

canteen [kæn'ti:n] n cantina; (BRIT: of cutlery) jogo (de talheres)

canter ['kæntəʳ] vi ir a meio galope

canvas ['kænvəs] n (material) lona; (for painting) tela; (Naut) velas fpl

canvass ['kænvəs] vi (Pol): **to ~ for** fazer campanha por ▷ vt sondar

canyon ['kænjən] n canhão m, garganta, desfiladeiro

cap [kæp] n gorro; (of pen, bottle) tampa; (contraceptive: also: **Dutch ~**) diafragma m; (for toy gun) cartucho ▷ vt (outdo) superar; (put limit on) limitar

capable ['keɪpəbl] adj (of sth) capaz; (competent) competente, hábil

capacity [kə'pæsɪtɪ] n capacidade f; (of stadium etc) lotação f; (role) condição f, posição f

cape [keɪp] n capa; (Geo) cabo

caper ['keɪpəʳ] n (Culin: gen: capers) alcaparra; (prank) travessura

capital ['kæpɪtl] n (also: **~ city**) capital f; (money) capital m; (also: **~ letter**) maiúscula; **capitalism** n capitalismo; **capitalist** adj, n capitalista m/f; **capital punishment** n pena de morte

Capitol ['kæpɪtl] n: **the ~** o Capitólio; ver quadro

⦿ CAPITOL
⦿
⦿ O Capitólio (**Capitol**) é a sede do
⦿ Congresso dos Estados Unidos,
⦿ localizado no monte Capitólio (Capitol
⦿ Hill), em Washington.

Capricorn ['kæprɪkɔ:n] n Capricórnio

capsize [kæp'saɪz] vt, vi emborcar, virar

capsule ['kæpsju:l] n cápsula

captain ['kæptɪn] n capitão m

caption ['kæpʃən] n legenda

capture ['kæptʃəʳ] vt prender, aprisionar; (person) capturar; (place) tomar; (attention) atrair, chamar ▷ n captura; (of place) tomada

car [ka:ʳ] n carro, automóvel m; (Rail) vagão m

caramel ['kærəməl] n (sweet) caramelo; (burnt sugar) caramelado

caravan ['kærəvæn] n reboque m (BR), trailer m (BR), rulote f (PT); (in desert) caravana

carbohydrate [ka:bəu'haɪdreɪt] n

hidrato de carbono; (food) carboidrato

carbon ['ka:bən] n carbono; **carbon dioxide** n dióxido de carbono; **carbon monoxide** n monóxido de carbono

carburettor [ka:bju'rɛtəʳ] (US **carburetor**) n carburador m

card [ka:d] n (also: **playing ~**) carta; (visiting card) cartão m; (thin cardboard) cartolina; **cardboard** n cartão m, papelão m

cardigan ['ka:dɪgən] n casaco de lã, cardigã m

cardinal ['ka:dɪnl] adj cardeal; (Math) cardinal ▷ n (Rel) cardeal m

care [kɛəʳ] n cuidado; (worry) preocupação f; (charge) encargo, custódia ▷ vi: **to ~ about** (person, animal) preocupar-se com; (thing, idea) ter interesse em; **~ of** (on letter) aos cuidados de; **in sb's ~** a cargo de alguém; **to take ~ (to do)** ter o cuidado de (fazer); **to take ~ of** (person) cuidar de; (situation) encarregar-se de; **I don't ~** não me importa; **I couldn't ~ less** não dou a mínima; **care for** vt fus cuidar de; (like) gostar de

career [kə'rɪəʳ] n carreira ▷ vi (also: **~ along**) correr a toda velocidade

carefree ['kɛəfri:] adj despreocupado

careful ['kɛəful] adj (thorough) cuidadoso; (cautious) cauteloso; **(be) ~!** tenha cuidado!; **carefully** adv cuidadosamente; cautelosamente

careless ['kɛəlɪs] adj descuidado; (heedless) desatento

caretaker ['kɛəteɪkəʳ] n zelador(a) m/f

car-ferry n barca para carros (BR), barco de passagem (PT)

cargo ['ka:gəu] (pl **~es**) n carga

car hire (BRIT) n aluguel m (BR) or aluguer m (PT) de carros

Caribbean [kærɪ'bi:ən] n: **the ~ (Sea)** o Caribe

caring ['kɛərɪŋ] adj (person) bondoso; (society) humanitário

carnation [ka:'neɪʃən] n cravo

carnival ['ka:nɪvəl] n carnaval m; (US: funfair) parque m de diversões

carol ['kærəl] n: **(Christmas) ~** cântico de Natal

car park (BRIT) n estacionamento

carpenter ['ka:pɪntəʳ] n carpinteiro

carpet ['ka:pɪt] n tapete m ▷ vt atapetar

carriage ['kærɪdʒ] n carruagem f; (BRIT: Rail) vagão m; (of goods) transporte m; (: cost) porte m; **carriageway** (BRIT) n (*part of road*) pista

carrier ['kærɪəʳ] *n* transportador(a) *m/f*; (*company*) empresa de transportes, transportadora; (*Med*) portador(a) *m/f*; **carrier bag** (BRIT) *n* saco, sacola

carrot ['kærət] *n* cenoura

carry ['kærɪ] *vt* levar; (*transport*) transportar; (*involve: responsibilities etc*) implicar ▷ *vi* (*sound*) projetar-se; **to get carried away** (*fig*) exagerar; **carry on** *vi* seguir, continuar ▷ *vt* prosseguir, continuar; **carry out** (*orders*) cumprir; (*investigation*) levar a cabo, realizar

cart [kɑːt] *n* carroça, carreta ▷ *vt* transportar (em carroça)

carton ['kɑːtən] *n* (*box*) caixa (de papelão); (*of yogurt*) pote *m*; (*of milk*) caixa; (*packet*) pacote *m*

cartoon [kɑːˈtuːn] *n* (*drawing*) desenho; (BRIT: *comic strip*) história em quadrinhos (BR), banda desenhada (PT); (*film*) desenho animado

cartridge ['kɑːtrɪdʒ] *n* cartucho; (*of record player*) cápsula

carve [kɑːv] *vt* (*meat*) trinchar; (*wood, stone*) cinzelar, esculpir; (*initials, design*) gravar; **carve up** dividir, repartir; **carving** *n* (*object*) escultura; (*design*) talha, entalhe *m*

case [keɪs] *n* caso; (*for spectacles etc*) estojo; (*Law*) causa; (BRIT: *also*: **suit**~) mala; (*of wine etc*) caixa; **in ~ (of)** em caso (de); **in any ~** em todo o caso; **just in ~** (*conj*) se por acaso ▷ *adv* por via das dúvidas

cash [kæʃ] *n* dinheiro (em espécie) ▷ *vt* descontar; **to pay (in) ~** pagar em dinheiro; **~ on delivery** pagamento contra entrega; **cash card** (BRIT) *n* cartão *m* de saque; **cash desk** (BRIT) *n* caixa; **cash dispenser** *n* caixa automática *or* eletrônica

cashew [kæˈʃuː] *n* (*also*: **~ nut**) castanha de caju

cashier [kæˈʃɪəʳ] *n* caixa *m/f*

cash register *n* caixa registradora

casino [kəˈsiːnəu] *n* cassino

casket ['kɑːskɪt] *n* cofre *m*, porta-jóias *m inv*; (US: *coffin*) caixão *m*

casserole ['kæsərəul] *n* panela de ir ao forno; (*food*) ensopado (BR) no forno, guisado (PT) no forno

cassette [kæˈset] *n* fita-cassete *f*; **cassette player** *n* toca-fitas *m inv*

cast [kɑːst] (*pt, pp* ~) *vt* (*throw*) lançar, atirar; (*Theatre*): **to ~ sb as Hamlet** dar a

alguém o papel de Hamlet ▷ *n* (*Theatre*) elenco; (*also*: **plaster ~**) gesso; **to ~ one's vote** votar; **cast off** *vi* (*Naut*) soltar o cabo; (*Knitting*) rematar os pontos; **cast on** *vi* montar os pontos

caster sugar ['kɑːstəʳ-] (BRIT) *n* açúcar *m* branco refinado

castle ['kɑːsl] *n* castelo; (*Chess*) torre *f*

casual ['kæʒjul] *adj* (*by chance*) fortuito; (*work*) eventual; (*unconcerned*) despreocupado; (*clothes*) descontraído, informal

casualty ['kæʒjultɪ] *n* ferido(-a); (*dead*) morto(-a); (*of situation*) vítima; (*department*) pronto-socorro

cat [kæt] *n* gato

catalogue ['kætəlɔg] (US **catalog**) *n* catálogo ▷ *vt* catalogar

catarrh [kəˈtɑːʳ] *n* catarro

catastrophe [kəˈtæstrəfɪ] *n* catástrofe *f*

catch [kætʃ] (*pt, pp* **caught**) *vt* pegar (BR), apanhar (PT); (*fish*) pescar; (*arrest*) prender, deter; (*person: by surprise*) flagrar, surpreender; (*attention*) atrair; (*hear*) ouvir; (*also*: **~ up**) alcançar ▷ *vi* (*fire*) pegar; (*in branches etc*) ficar preso, prender-se ▷ *n* (*fish*) pesca; (*game*) manha, armadilha; (*of lock*) trinco, lingüeta; **to ~ fire** pegar fogo; (*building*) incendiar-se; **to ~ sight of** avistar; **catch on** *vi* (*understand*) entender (BR), perceber (PT); (*grow popular*) pegar; **catch up** *vi* equiparar-se ▷ *vt* (*also*: **catch up with**) alcançar; **catching** *adj* (*Med*) contagioso

category ['kætɪɡərɪ] *n* categoria

cater ['keɪtəʳ] *vi* preparar comida; **cater for** *vt fus* (*needs*) atender a; (*consumers*) satisfazer

caterpillar ['kætəpɪləʳ] *n* lagarta

cathedral [kəˈθiːdrəl] *n* catedral *f*

catholic ['kæθəlɪk] *adj* eclético; **Catholic** *adj, n* (*Rel*) católico(-a)

cattle ['kætl] *npl* gado

caught [kɔːt] *pt, pp of* **catch**

cauliflower ['kɔlɪflauəʳ] *n* couve-flor *f*

cause [kɔːz] *n* causa; (*reason*) motivo, razão *f* ▷ *vt* causar, provocar

caution ['kɔːʃən] *n* cautela, prudência; (*warning*) aviso ▷ *vt* acautelar, avisar

cautious ['kɔːʃəs] *adj* cauteloso, prudente, precavido

cave [keɪv] *n* caverna, gruta; **cave in** *vi* ceder

cc *abbr* (= *cubic centimetre*) cc

CD *n abbr* = **compact disc**; **compact**

disc player; CD burner; CD writer n gravador m de CD; **CD-ROM** n abbr (= compact disc read-only memory) CD-ROM m

cease [siːs] vt, vi cessar; **ceasefire** n cessar-fogo m

cedar ['siːdə'] n cedro

ceiling ['siːlɪŋ] n (also fig) teto

celebrate ['sɛlɪbreɪt] vt celebrar ▷ vi celebrar; (birthday, anniversary etc) festejar; (Rel: mass) rezar; **celebration** [sɛlɪ'breɪʃən] n (party) festa

celery ['sɛlərɪ] n aipo

cell [sɛl] n cela; (Bio) célula; (Elec) pilha, elemento

cellar ['sɛlə'] n porão m; (for wine) adega

cellphone ['sɛlfəun] n telefone m celular

cement [sə'mɛnt] n cimento

cemetery ['sɛmɪtrɪ] n cemitério

censor ['sɛnsə'] n censor(a) m/f ▷ vt censurar; **censorship** n censura

census ['sɛnsəs] n censo

cent [sɛnt] n cêntimo; see also **per**

centenary [sɛn'tiːnərɪ] n centenário

center ['sɛntə'] (US) = **centre**

centigrade ['sɛntɪgreɪd] adj centígrado

centimetre ['sɛntɪmiːtə'] (US **centimeter**) n centímetro

central ['sɛntrəl] adj central; **Central America** n América Central; **central heating** n aquecimento central

centre ['sɛntə'] (US **center**) n centro; (of room, circle etc) meio ▷ vt centrar

century ['sɛntjurɪ] n século; **20th ~** século vinte

ceramic [sɪ'ræmɪk] adj cerâmico

cereal ['siːrɪəl] n cereal m

ceremony ['sɛrɪmənɪ] n cerimônia; (ritual) rito; **to stand on ~** fazer cerimônia

certain ['səːtən] adj (sure) seguro; (person): **a ~ Mr Smith** um certo Sr. Smith; (particular): **~ days/places** certos dias/lugares; (some): **a ~ coldness/pleasure** uma certa frieza/um certo prazer; **for ~** com certeza; **certainly** adv certamente, com certeza; **certainty** n certeza

certificate [sə'tɪfɪkɪt] n certidão f

certify ['səːtɪfaɪ] vt certificar

cf. abbr (= compare) cf.

CFC n abbr (= chlorofluorocarbon) CFC m

chain [tʃeɪn] n corrente f; (of islands) grupo; (of mountains) cordilheira; (of shops) cadeia; (of events) série f ▷ vt (also: **~ up**) acorrentar

chair [tʃɛə'] n cadeira; (armchair) poltrona; (of university) cátedra; (of meeting) presidência, mesa ▷ vt (meeting) presidir; **chairlift** n teleférico; **chairman** (irreg) n presidente m

chalk [tʃɔːk] n (Geo) greda; (for writing) giz m

challenge ['tʃælɪndʒ] n desafio ▷ vt desafiar; (right) disputar, contestar; **challenging** adj desafiante; (tone) de desafio

chamber ['tʃeɪmbə'] n câmara; (BRIT: Law: gen pl) sala de audiências; **~ of commerce** câmara de comércio; **chambermaid** n arrumadeira (BR), empregada (PT)

champagne [ʃæm'peɪn] n champanhe m or f

champion ['tʃæmpɪən] n campeão(-peã) m/f; (of cause) defensor(a) m/f; **championship** n campeonato

chance [tʃɑːns] n (opportunity) oportunidade, ocasião f; (likelihood) chance f; (risk) risco ▷ vt arriscar ▷ adj fortuito, casual; **to take a ~** arriscar-se; **by ~** por acaso; **to ~ it** arriscar-se

chancellor ['tʃɑːnsələ'] n chanceler m; **C~ of the Exchequer** (BRIT) Ministro da Economia (Fazenda e Planejamento)

chandelier [ʃændə'lɪə'] n lustre m

change [tʃeɪndʒ] vt (alter) mudar; (wheel, money) trocar; (replace) substituir; (clothes, house) mudar de, trocar de; (nappy) mudar, trocar; (transform): **to ~ sb into** transformar alguém em ▷ vi mudar(-se); (change clothes) trocar-se; (trains) fazer baldeação (BR), mudar (PT); (be transformed): **to ~ into** transformar-se em ▷ n mudança; (exchange) troca; (difference) diferença; (of clothes) muda; (coins) trocado; **to ~ gear** (Aut) trocar de marcha; **to ~ one's mind** mudar de idéia; **for a ~** para variar; **changeable** adj (weather, mood) instável

channel ['tʃænl] n canal m; (of river) leito; (groove) ranhura; (fig: medium) meio, via ▷ vt canalizar; **the (English) C~** o Canal da Mancha

chant [tʃɑːnt] n canto; (Rel) cântico ▷ vt cantar; (slogan) entoar

chaos ['keɪɔs] n caos m

chap [tʃæp] n (BRIT: inf: man) sujeito (BR), tipo (PT)

chapel ['tʃæpəl] n capela

chapter ['tʃæptə'] n capítulo

character ['kærɪktəʳ] n caráter m; (in novel, film) personagem m/f; (letter) letra; **characteristic** [kærɪktə'rɪstɪk] adj característico

charcoal ['tʃɑːkəʊl] n carvão m de lenha; (Art) carvão m

charge [tʃɑːdʒ] n (Law) encargo, acusação f; (fee) preço, custo; (responsibility) encargo ▷ vt (battery) carregar; (Mil) atacar; (customer) cobrar dinheiro de; (Law): **to ~ sb (with)** acusar alguém (de) ▷ vi precipitar-se; **charges** npl: **bank ~s** taxas fpl cobradas pelo banco; **to reverse the ~s** (BRIT: Tel) ligar a cobrar; **how much do you ~?** quanto você cobra?; **to ~ an expense (up) to sb's account** pôr a despesa na conta de alguém; **to take ~ of** encarregar-se de, tomar conta de; **to be in ~ of** estar a cargo de or encarregado de; **charge card** n cartão m de crédito (emitido por uma loja)

charity ['tʃærɪtɪ] n caridade f; (organization) obra de caridade; (kindness) compaixão f; (money, gifts) donativo

charm [tʃɑːm] n (quality) charme m; (talisman) amuleto; (on bracelet) berloque m ▷ vt encantar, deliciar; **charming** adj encantador(a)

chart [tʃɑːt] n (graph) gráfico; (diagram) diagrama m; (map) carta de navegação ▷ vt traçar; **charts** npl (Mus) paradas fpl (de sucesso)

charter ['tʃɑːtəʳ] vt fretar ▷ n (document) carta, alvará m; **chartered accountant** (BRIT) n perito-contador (perita-contadora) m/f; **charter flight** n vôo charter or fretado

chase [tʃeɪs] vt perseguir; (also: **~ away**) enxotar ▷ n perseguição f, caça

chat [tʃæt] vi (also: **have a ~**) conversar, bater papo (BR), cavaquear (PT) ▷ n conversa, bate-papo m (BR), cavaqueira (PT); **chatroom** n sala de bate-papo; **chat show** (BRIT) n programa m de entrevistas

chatter ['tʃætəʳ] vi (person) tagarelar; (animal) emitir sons; (teeth) tiritar ▷ n tagarelice f; emissão f de sons; (of birds) chilro

chauvinist ['ʃəʊvɪnɪst] n chauvinista m/f; (also: **male ~**) machista m; (nationalist) chauvinista m/f

cheap [tʃiːp] adj barato; (poor quality) barato, de pouca qualidade; (behaviour) vulgar; (joke) de mau gosto ▷ adv barato; **cheaply** adv barato, por baixo preço

cheat [tʃiːt] vi trapacear; (at cards) roubar (BR), fazer batota (PT); (in exam) colar (BR), cabular (PT) ▷ vt: **to ~ sb (out of sth)** passar o conto do vigário em alguém ▷ n fraude f; (person) trapaceiro(-a)

check [tʃɛk] vt (examine) controlar; (facts) verificar; (halt) conter, impedir; (restrain) parar, refrear ▷ n controle m, inspeção f; (curb) freio; (us: bill) conta; (pattern: gen pl) xadrez m; (us) = **cheque** ▷ adj (pattern, cloth) xadrez inv; **check in** vi (in hotel) registrar-se; (in airport) apresentar-se ▷ vt (luggage) entregar; **check out** vi pagar a conta e sair; **check up** vi: **to check up on sth** verificar algo; **to check up on sb** investigar alguém; **checkers** (us) n (jogo de) damas fpl; **check-in (desk)** n check-in m; **checking account** (us) n conta corrente; **checkout** n caixa; **checkpoint** n (ponto de) controle m; **checkroom** (us) n depósito de bagagem; **checkup** n (Med) check-up m

cheek [tʃiːk] n bochecha; (impudence) folga, descaramento; **cheekbone** n maçã f do rosto; **cheeky** adj insolente, descarado

cheer [tʃɪəʳ] vt dar vivas a, aplaudir; (gladden) alegrar, animar ▷ vi gritar com entusiasmo ▷ n (gen pl) gritos mpl de entusiasmo; **cheers** npl (of crowd) aplausos mpl; **~s!** saúde!; **cheer up** vi animar-se, alegrar-se ▷ vt alegrar, animar; **cheerful** adj alegre; **cheerio** (BRIT) excl tchau (BR), adeus (PT)

cheese [tʃiːz] n queijo

chef [ʃɛf] n cozinheiro-chefe (cozinheira-chefe) m/f

chemical ['kɛmɪkəl] adj químico ▷ n produto químico

chemist ['kɛmɪst] n (BRIT: pharmacist) farmacêutico(-a); (scientist) químico(-a); **chemistry** n química; **chemist's (shop)** (BRIT) n farmácia

cheque [tʃɛk] (BRIT) n cheque m; **chequebook** n talão m (BR) or livro (PT) de cheques; **cheque card** (BRIT) n cartão m (de garantia) de cheques

cherry ['tʃɛrɪ] n cereja; (also: **~ tree**) cerejeira

chess [tʃɛs] n xadrez m

chest [tʃɛst] n (Anat) peito; (box) caixa, cofre m; **~ of drawers** cômoda

chestnut ['tʃɛsnʌt] n castanha

chew [tʃuː] vt mastigar; **chewing gum** n chiclete m (BR), pastilha elástica (PT)

chic [ʃiːk] adj elegante

chick [tʃɪk] n pinto; (inf: girl) broto

chicken ['tʃɪkɪn] n galinha; (food) galinha, frango; (inf: coward) covarde m/f, galinha; **chicken out** (inf) vi agalinhar-se; **chickenpox** n catapora (BR), varicela (PT)

chief [tʃiːf] n (of tribe) cacique m, morubixaba m; (of organization) chefe m/f ▷ adj principal; **chiefly** adv principalmente

child [tʃaɪld] (pl ~ren) n criança; (offspring) filho(-a); **childbirth** n parto; **childhood** n infância; **childish** adj infantil; **child minder** (BRIT) n cuidadora de crianças; **children** ['tʃɪldrən] npl of **child**

Chile ['tʃɪlɪ] n Chile m

chill [tʃɪl] n frio, friagem f; (Med) resfriamento ▷ vt (Culin) semi-congelar; (person) congelar

chilli ['tʃɪlɪ] (US **chili**) n pimentão m picante

chilly ['tʃɪlɪ] adj frio; (person) friorento

chimpanzee [tʃɪmpæn'ziː] n chimpanzé m

chin [tʃɪn] n queixo

China ['tʃaɪnə] n China

china ['tʃaɪnə] n porcelana; (crockery) louça fina

Chinese [tʃaɪ'niːz] adj chinês(-esa) ▷ n inv chinês(-esa) m/f; (Ling) chinês m

chip [tʃɪp] n (gen pl: Culin) batata frita; (: US: also: **potato ~**) batatinha frita; (of wood) lasca; (of glass, stone) lasca, pedaço; (Comput: also: **micro~**) chip m ▷ vt (cup, plate) lascar; **chip in** (inf) vi interromper; (contribute) compartilhar as despesas

chiropodist [kɪ'rɔpədɪst] (BRIT) n pedicuro(-a)

chisel ['tʃɪzl] n (for wood) formão m; (for stone) cinzel m

chives [tʃaɪvz] npl cebolinha

chocolate ['tʃɔklɪt] n chocolate m

choice [tʃɔɪs] n (selection) seleção f; (option) escolha; (preference) preferência ▷ adj seleto, escolhido

choir ['kwaɪə⁺] n coro

choke [tʃəuk] vi sufocar-se; (on food) engasgar ▷ vt estrangular; (block) obstruir ▷ n (Aut) afogador m (BR), ar m (PT)

cholesterol [kə'lɛstərɔl] n colesterol m

choose [tʃuːz] (pt **chose**, pp **chosen**) vt escolher; **to ~ to do** optar por fazer

chop [tʃɔp] vt (wood) cortar, talhar; (Culin: also: **~ up**) cortar em pedaços; (meat) picar ▷ n golpe m; (Culin) costeleta; **chops** npl (inf: jaws) beiços mpl

chopsticks ['tʃɔpstɪks] npl pauzinhos mpl, palitos mpl

chord [kɔːd] n (Mus) acorde m

chore [tʃɔː⁺] n tarefa; (routine task) trabalho de rotina

chorus ['kɔːrəs] n (group) coro; (song) coral m; (refrain) estribilho

chose [tʃəuz] pt of **choose**; **chosen** pp of **choose**

Christ [kraɪst] n Cristo

christen ['krɪsn] vt batizar; (nickname) apelidar

Christian ['krɪstɪən] adj, n cristão(-tã) m/f; **Christianity** [krɪstɪ'ænɪtɪ] n cristianismo; **Christian name** n prenome m, nome m de batismo

Christmas ['krɪsməs] n Natal m; **Happy** or **Merry ~!** Feliz Natal!; **Christmas card** n cartão m de Natal; **Christmas cracker** n buscapé-surpresa m; ver quadro; **Christmas Day** n dia m de Natal; **Christmas Eve** n véspera de Natal; **Christmas tree** n árvore f de Natal

⊛ **CHRISTMAS CRACKER**
⊛
⊛ Um cilindro de papelão que ao ser
⊛ aberto faz estourar uma bombinha.
⊛ Contém um presente surpresa e um
⊛ chapéu de papel que cada convidado
⊛ coloca na cabeça durante a ceia de
⊛ Natal.

chronic ['krɔnɪk] adj crônico; (fig: drunkenness) inveterado

chubby ['tʃʌbɪ] adj roliço, gorducho

chuck [tʃʌk] vt jogar (BR), deitar (PT); (BRIT: also: **~ up, ~ in**: job) largar; (: person) acabar com; **chuck out** vt (thing) jogar (BR) or deitar (PT) fora; (person) expulsar

chuckle ['tʃʌkl] vi rir

chum [tʃʌm] n camarada m/f

church [tʃəːtʃ] n igreja; **churchyard** n adro, cemitério

churn [tʃəːn] n (for butter) batedeira; (also: **milk ~**) lata, vasilha; **churn out** vt produzir em série

chute [ʃuːt] n rampa; (also: **rubbish ~**) despejador m

CIA (US) n abbr (= Central Intelligence Agency) CIA f

CID (BRIT) n abbr = **Criminal Investigation Department**

cider ['saɪdə'] n sidra

cigar [sɪ'gɑː'] n charuto

cigarette [sɪgə'rɛt] n cigarro

cinema ['sɪnəmə] n cinema m

cinnamon ['sɪnəmən] n canela

circle ['sə:kl] n círculo; (in cinema) balcão m ▷ vi dar voltas ▷ vt (surround) rodear, cercar; (move round) dar a volta de

circuit ['sə:kɪt] n circuito; (lap) volta; (track) pista

circular ['sə:kjulə'] adj circular ▷ n (carta) circular f

circulate ['sə:kjuleɪt] vt, vi circular; **circulation** [sə:kju'leɪʃən] n circulação f; (of newspaper, book etc) tiragem f

circumstances ['sə:kəmstənsɪz] npl circunstâncias fpl; (conditions) condições fpl; (financial condition) situação f econômica

circus ['sə:kəs] n circo

citizen ['sɪtɪzn] n (of country) cidadão(-dã) m/f; (of town) habitante m/f; **citizenship** n cidadania

city ['sɪtɪ] n cidade f; **the C~** centro financeiro de Londres

civic ['sɪvɪk] adj cívico, municipal

civil ['sɪvɪl] adj civil; (polite) delicado, cortês; **civilian** [sɪ'vɪlɪən] adj, n civil m/f

civilized ['sɪvɪlaɪzd] adj civilizado; **civil servant** n funcionário público (funcionária pública); **Civil Service** n administração f pública; **civil war** n guerra civil

claim [kleɪm] vt exigir, reclamar; (rights etc) reivindicar; (responsibility, credit) assumir; (assert): **to ~ that/to be** afirmar que/ser ▷ vi (for insurance) reclamar ▷ n reclamação f; (assertion) afirmação f; (wage claim etc) reivindicação f

clam [klæm] n molusco

clamp [klæmp] n grampo ▷ vt (two things together) grampear; (put: one thing on another) prender; **clamp down on** vt fus suprimir, proibir

clan [klæn] n clã m

clap [klæp] vi bater palmas, aplaudir

clarinet [klærɪ'nɛt] n clarinete m

clarity ['klærɪtɪ] n clareza

clash [klæʃ] n (fight) confronto; (disagreement) desavença; (of beliefs) divergência; (of colours, styles) choque m; (of dates) coincidência; (noise) estrondo ▷ vi (gangs, beliefs) chocar-se; (disagree) entrar em conflito, ter uma desavença; (colours) não combinar; (dates) coincidir; (weapons, cymbals etc) estrefitar

clasp [klɑːsp] n fecho; (embrace) abraço ▷ vt prender; abraçar

class [klɑːs] n classe f; (lesson) aula; (type) tipo ▷ vt classificar

classic ['klæsɪk] adj clássico ▷ n clássico; **classical** adj clássico

classmate ['klɑːsmeɪt] n colega m/f de aula

classroom ['klɑːsrum] n sala de aula

clatter ['klætə'] n ruído, barulho; (of hooves) tropel m ▷ vi fazer barulho or ruído

clause [klɔːz] n cláusula; (Ling) oração f

claw [klɔː] n (of animal) pata; (of bird of prey) garra; (of lobster) pinça; **claw at** vt fus arranhar; (tear) rasgar

clay [kleɪ] n argila

clean [kliːn] adj limpo; (story) inocente ▷ vt limpar; (hands etc) lavar; **clean out** vt limpar; **clean up** vt limpar, assear; **cleaner** n faxineiro(-a); (product) limpador m; **cleaner's** n (also: **dry cleaner's**) tinturaria; **cleaning** n limpeza

clear [klɪə'] adj claro; (footprint, photograph) nítido; (obvious) evidente; (glass, water) transparente; (road, way) limpo, livre; (conscience) tranqüilo; (skin) macio ▷ vt (space) abrir; (room) esvaziar; (Law: suspect) absolver; (fence) saltar, transpor; (cheque) compensar ▷ vi (weather) abrir; (sky) clarear; (fog etc) dissipar-se ▷ adv: **~ of** a salvo de; **to ~ the table** tirar a mesa; **clear up** vt limpar; (mystery) resolver, esclarecer; **clearance** n remoção f; (permission) permissão f; **clear-cut** adj bem definido, nítido; **clearing** n (in wood) clareira; **clearly** adv distintamente; (obviously) claramente; (coherently) coerentemente; **clearway** (BRIT) n estrada onde não se pode estacionar

clench [klɛntʃ] vt apertar, cerrar; (teeth) trincar

clerk [klɑːk, (US) klə:rk] n auxiliar m/f de escritório; (US: sales person) balconista m/f

clever ['klɛvə'] adj inteligente; (deft) hábil; (arrangement) engenhoso

click [klɪk] vt (tongue) estalar; (heels) bater, livre; (Comput) clicar em ▷ vi (make sound) estalar; (Comput) clicar

client ['klaɪənt] n cliente m/f
cliff [klɪf] n penhasco
climate ['klaɪmɪt] n clima m
climax ['klaɪmæks] n clímax m, ponto
culminante; (sexual) clímax
climb [klaɪm] vi subir; (plant) trepar;
(plane) ganhar altitude; (prices etc)
escalar ▷ vt (stairs) subir; (tree) trepar
em; (hill) escalar ▷ n subida; (of prices
etc) escalada; **climber** n alpinista
m/f; (plant) trepadeira; **climbing** n
alpinismo
clinch [klɪntʃ] vt (deal) fechar; (argument)
decidir, resolver
cling [klɪŋ] (pt, pp **clung**) vi: **to ~ to** pegar-
se a, aderir a; (support, idea) agarrar-se a;
(clothes) ajustar-se a
clinic ['klɪnɪk] n clínica
clip [klɪp] n (for hair) grampo (BR), gancho
(PT); (also: **paper ~**) mola, clipe m; (TV,
Cinema) clipe ▷ vt (cut) aparar; (fasten)
grampear
cloak [kləuk] n capa, manto ▷ vt (fig)
encobrir; **cloakroom** n vestiário; (BRIT:
WC) sanitários mpl (BR), lavatórios mpl
(PT)
clock [klɔk] n relógio; **clock in** or **on**
(BRIT) vi assinar o ponto na entrada;
clock off or **out** (BRIT) vi assinar o ponto
na saída; **clockwise** adv em sentido
horário; **clockwork** n mecanismo de
relógio ▷ adj de corda
clog [klɔg] n tamanco ▷ vt entupir ▷ vi
(also: **~ up**) entupir-se
close¹ [kləus] adj: **~ (to)** próximo (a);
(friend) íntimo; (examination) minucioso;
(watch) atento; (contest) apertado;
(weather) abafado ▷ adv perto; **~ to**
perto de; **~ by**, **~ at hand** perto, pertinho; **~ at hand**
= **close by**; **to have a ~ shave** (fig) livrar-
se por um triz
close² [kləuz] vt fechar; (end) encerrar
▷ vi fechar; (end) concluir-se, terminar-se
▷ n (end) fim m, conclusão f, terminação
f; **close down** vi fechar definitivamente;
closed adj fechado
closely ['kləuslɪ] adv (watch) de perto;
(connected, related) intimamente;
(resemble) muito
closet ['klɔzɪt] n (cupboard) armário
close-up [kləus-] n close m, close-up m
closure ['kləuʒəʳ] n fechamento
clot [klɔt] n (gen: blood clot) coágulo; (inf:
idiot) imbecil m/f ▷ vi coagular-se
cloth [klɔθ] n (material) tecido, fazenda;
(rag) pano

clothes [kləuðz] npl roupa
clothing ['kləuðɪŋ] n = **clothes**
cloud [klaud] n nuvem f; **cloudy** adj
nublado; (liquid) turvo
clove [kləuv] n cravo; **~ of garlic** dente
m de alho
clown [klaun] n palhaço ▷ vi (also: **~
about**, **~ around**) fazer palhaçadas
club [klʌb] n (society) clube m; (weapon)
cacete m; (also: **golf ~**) taco ▷ vt
esbordoar ▷ vi: **to ~ together** cotizar-se;
clubs npl (Cards) paus mpl
clue [kluː] n indício, pista; (in crossword)
definição f; **I haven't a ~** não faço idéia
clumsy ['klʌmzɪ] adj (person)
desajeitado; (movement) deselegante,
mal-feito; (attempt) inábil
clung [klʌŋ] pt, pp of **cling**
cluster ['klʌstəʳ] n grupo; (of flowers)
ramo ▷ vi agrupar-se, apinhar-se
clutch [klʌtʃ] n (grip, grasp) garra; (Aut)
embreagem f (BR), embraiagem f (PT) ▷ vt
empunhar, pegar em
Co. abbr = **county**; (= company) Cia.
c/o abbr (= care of) a/c
coach [kəutʃ] n (bus) ônibus m (BR),
autocarro (PT); (horse-drawn) carruagem
f, coche m; (of train) vagão m; (Sport)
treinador(a) m/f, instrutor(a) m/f; (tutor)
professor(a) m/f particular ▷ vt (Sport)
treinar; (student) preparar, ensinar;
coach trip n passeio de ônibus (BR) or
autocarro (PT)
coal [kəul] n carvão m
coalition [kəuə'lɪʃən] n (Pol) coalizão f
coarse [kɔːs] adj grosso, áspero; (vulgar)
grosseiro, ordinário
coast [kəust] n costa, litoral m ▷ vi (Aut)
ir em ponto morto; **coastal** adj costeiro;
coastguard n (person) guarda m que
policia a costa; (service) guarda costeira;
coastline n litoral m
coat [kəut] n (overcoat) sobretudo; (of
animal) pelo; (of paint) demão f, camada
▷ vt cobrir, revestir; **coat hanger** n
cabide m; **coating** n camada
coax [kəuks] vt persuadir com meiguice
cobweb ['kɔbwɛb] n teia de aranha
cocaine [kə'keɪn] n cocaína
cock [kɔk] n (rooster) galo; (male bird)
macho ▷ vt (gun) engatilhar; **cockerel** n
frango, galo pequeno
cockney ['kɔknɪ] n londrino(-a) (nativo
dos bairros populares do leste de Londres)
cockpit ['kɔkpɪt] n (in aircraft) cabina; (in
racing car) compartimento do piloto

cockroach ['kɔkrəutʃ] n barata
cocktail ['kɔkteɪl] n coquetel m (BR),
cocktail m (PT)
cocoa ['kəukəu] n cacau m; (drink)
chocolate m
coconut ['kəukənʌt] n coco
cod [kɔd] n inv bacalhau m
code [kəud] n cifra; (dialling code, post
code) código; ~ **of practice** deontologia
coffee ['kɔfɪ] n café m; **coffee bar** (BRIT) n
café m, lanchonete f; **coffee bean** n grão
m de café; **coffeepot** n cafeteira; **coffee
table** n mesinha de centro
coffin ['kɔfɪn] n caixão m
coil [kɔɪl] n rolo; (Elec) bobina;
(contraceptive) DIU m ▷ vt enrolar
coin [kɔɪn] n moeda ▷ vt (word) cunhar,
criar
coincide [kəuɪn'saɪd] vi coincidir;
coincidence [kəu'ɪnsɪdəns] n
coincidência
coke [kəuk] n (coal) coque m
colander ['kɔləndər] n coador m,
passador m
cold [kəuld] adj frio ▷ n frio; (Med)
resfriado (BR), constipação f (PT); **it's ~**
está frio; **to be** or **feel ~** (person) estar
com frio; (object) estar frio; **to catch ~**
resfriar-se (BR), apanhar constipação
(PT); **to catch a ~** apanhar um resfriado
(BR) or uma constipação (PT); **in ~ blood**
a sangue frio; **cold sore** n herpes m
labial
coleslaw ['kəulslɔ:] n salada de repolho
cru
collapse [kə'læps] vi cair, tombar;
(building) desabar; (resistance,
government) sucumbir; (Med) desmaiar
▷ n desabamento, desmoronamento; (of
government) queda; (Med) colapso
collar ['kɔlər] n (of shirt) colarinho; (of
coat etc) gola; (for dog) coleira; (Tech) aro,
colar m; **collarbone** n clavícula
colleague ['kɔli:g] n colega m/f
collect [kə'lɛkt] vt (as a hobby) colecionar;
(gather) recolher; (wages, debts) cobrar;
(donations, subscriptions) colher; (mail)
coletar; (BRIT: call for) (ir) buscar, vir
apanhar ▷ vi (people) reunir-se ▷ adv: **to
call ~** (us: Tel) ligar a cobrar; **collection** n
coleção f; (of people) grupo; (of donations)
arrecadação f; (of post, for charity)
coleta; (of writings) coletânea; **collector**
n colecionador(a) m/f; (of taxes etc)
cobrador(a) m/f
college ['kɔlɪdʒ] n (of university)

faculdade f; (of technology, agriculture)
escola de nível superior

COLLEGE

Além de "universidade", **college**
também se refere a um centro de
educação superior para jovens que
terminaram a educação obrigatória,
secondary school. Alguns oferecem
cursos de especialização em matérias
técnicas, artísticas ou comerciais,
outros oferecem disciplinas
universitárias.

collide [kə'laɪd] vi: **to ~ (with)** colidir
(com)
collision [kə'lɪʒən] n colisão f
Colombia [kə'lɔmbɪə] n Colômbia
colon ['kəulən] n (sign) dois pontos;
(Med) cólon m
colonel ['kɜ:nl] n coronel m
colony ['kɔlənɪ] n colônia
colour ['kʌlər] (us **color**) n cor f ▷ vt
colorir; (with crayons) colorir, pintar; (dye)
tingir; (fig: account) falsear ▷ vi (blush)
corar; **colours** npl (of party, club) cores
fpl; **in ~** (photograph etc) a cores; **colour
in** vt (drawing) colorir; **colour-blind**
adj daltônico; **coloured** adj colorido;
(person) de cor; **colour film** n filme m a
cores; **colourful** adj colorido; (account)
vívido; (personality) vivo, animado;
colouring ['kʌlərɪŋ] n colorido;
(complexion) tez f; (in food) colorante m;
colour television n televisão f a cores
column ['kɔləm] n coluna; (of smoke)
faixa; (of people) fila
coma ['kəumə] n coma
comb [kəum] n pente m; (ornamental)
crista ▷ vt pentear; (area) vasculhar
combat ['kɔmbæt] n combate m ▷ vt
combater
combination [kɔmbɪ'neɪʃən] n
combinação f; (of safe) segredo
combine [(vb) kəm'baɪn, (n) 'kɔmbaɪn]
vt combinar; (qualities) reunir ▷ vi
combinar-se ▷ n (Econ) associação f

O KEYWORD

come [kʌm] (pt **came**, pp **come**) vi
1 (movement towards) vir; **come with
me** vem comigo; **to come running** vir
correndo
2 (arrive) chegar; **she's come here to**

work ela veio aqui para trabalhar; **to come home** chegar em casa
3 (*reach*): **to come to** chegar a; **the bill came to £40** a conta deu £40; **her hair came to her waist** o cabelo dela batia na cintura
4 (*occur*): **an idea came to me** uma idéia me ocorreu
5 (*be, become*) ficar; **to come loose/ undone** soltar-se/desfazer-se; **I've come to like him** passei a gostar dele
come about *vi* suceder, acontecer
come across *vt fus* (*person*) topar com; (*thing*) encontrar
come away *vi* (*leave*) ir-se embora; (*become detached*) desprender-se, soltar-se
come back *vi* (*return*) voltar
come by *vt fus* (*acquire*) conseguir
come down *vi* (*price*) baixar; (*tree*) cair; (*building*) desmoronar-se
come forward *vi* apresentar-se
come from *vt fus* (*subj: person*) ser de; (*: thing*) originar-se de
come in *vi* entrar; (*on deal*) participar; (*be involved*) estar envolvido
come in for *vt fus* (*criticism*) merecer
come into *vt fus* (*money*) herdar; (*fashion*) ser; (*be involved*) estar envolvido em
come off *vi* (*button*) desprender-se, soltar-se; (*attempt*) dar certo
come on *vi* (*pupil, work, project*) avançar; (*lights, electricity*) ser ligado; **come on!** vamos!, vai!
come out *vi* (*fact*) vir à tona; (*book*) ser publicado; (*stain, sun*) sair
come round *vi* voltar a si
come to *vi* voltar a si
come up *vi* (*sun*) nascer; (*in conversation*) surgir; (*event*) acontecer
come up against *vt fus* (*resistance, difficulties*) tropeçar com, esbarrar em
come up with *vt fus* (*idea*) propor, sugerir; (*money*) contribuir
come upon *vt fus* encontrar, achar

comedian [kə'miːdɪən] *n* cômico, humorista *m*
comedy ['kɔmɪdɪ] *n* comédia
comfort ['kʌmfət] *n* (*well-being*) bem-estar *m*; (*relief*) alívio ▷ *vt* consolar, confortar; **comforts** *npl* (*of home etc*) conforto; **comfortable** *adj* confortável; (*financially*) tranqüilo; (*walk, climb etc*) fácil
comic ['kɔmɪk] *adj* (*also:* **~al**) cômico ▷ *n* (*person*) humorista *m/f*; (BRIT: *magazine*) revista em quadrinhos (BR), revista de banda desenhada (PT), gibi *m* (BR: INF)
comma ['kɔmə] *n* vírgula
command [kə'mɑːnd] *n* ordem *f*, mandado; (*control*) controle *m*; (Mil: *authority*) comando; (*mastery*) domínio ▷ *vt* mandar; **commander** *n* (Mil) comandante *m/f*
commemorate [kə'mɛməreɪt] *vt* (*with monument*) comemorar; (*with celebration*) celebrar
commence [kə'mɛns] *vt, vi* começar, iniciar
commend [kə'mɛnd] *vt* elogiar, louvar; (*recommend*) recomendar
comment ['kɔmɛnt] *n* comentário ▷ *vi*: **to ~ (on)** comentar (sobre); **"no ~"** "sem comentário"; **commentary** ['kɔməntərɪ] *n* comentário; **commentator** ['kɔmənteɪtə'] *n* comentarista *m/f*
commerce ['kɔmə:s] *n* comércio
commercial [kə'mə:ʃəl] *adj* comercial ▷ *n* anúncio, comercial *m*
commission [kə'mɪʃən] *n* comissão *f*; (*order*) empreitada, encomenda ▷ *vt* (*work of art*) encomendar; **out of ~** com defeito; **commissioner** *n* comissário(-a)
commit [kə'mɪt] *vt* cometer; (*resources*) alocar; (*to sb's care*) entregar; **to ~ o.s. (to do)** comprometer-se (a fazer); **to ~ suicide** suicidar-se; **commitment** *n* compromisso; (*political etc*) engajamento; (*undertaking*) promessa
committee [kə'mɪtɪ] *n* comitê *m*
commodity [kə'mɔdɪtɪ] *n* mercadoria
common ['kɔmən] *adj* comum; (*vulgar*) vulgar ▷ *n* área verde aberta ao público; **Commons** *npl* (BRIT: Pol): **the (House of) C~s** a Câmara dos Comuns; **in ~** em comum; **commonly** *adv* geralmente; **commonplace** *adj* vulgar; **common sense** *n* bom senso; **Commonwealth** *n*: **the Commonwealth** a Comunidade Britânica
communal ['kɔmjuːnl] *adj* comum
commune [(*n*) 'kɔmjuːn; (*vb*) kə'mjuːn] *n* (*group*) comuna ▷ *vi*: **to ~ with** comunicar-se com
communicate [kə'mjuːnɪkeɪt] *vt* comunicar ▷ *vi*: **to ~ (with)** comunicar-se (com); **communication** [kəmjuː-nɪ'keɪʃən] *n* comunicação *f*; (*letter, call*) mensagem *f*
communion [kə'mjuːnɪən] *n* (*also:* **Holy C~**) comunhão *f*

communism ['kɔmjunɪzəm] n
comunismo; **communist** adj, n
comunista m/f
community [kə'mjuːnɪtɪ] n comunidade
f; **community centre** n centro social
commute [kə'mjuːt] vi viajar
diariamente ▷ vt comutar; **commuter** n
viajante m/f habitual
compact [(adj) kəm'pækt, (n) 'kɔmpækt]
adj compacto ▷ n (also: **powder ~**)
estojo; **compact disc** n disco laser,
CD m; **compact disc player** n som cd m
companion [kəm'pænɪən] n
companheiro(-a)
company ['kʌmpənɪ] n companhia;
(Comm) sociedade f, companhia; **to keep
sb ~** fazer companhia a alguém
comparative [kəm'pærətɪv] adj (study)
comparativo; (peace, safety) relativo;
(stranger) meio; **comparatively** adj
relativamente
compare [kəm'pεəʳ] vt comparar ▷ vi: **to
~ with** comparar-se com; **comparison**
[kəm'pærɪsn] n comparação f
compartment [kəm'pɑːtmənt] n
compartimento; (of wallet) divisão f
compass ['kʌmpəs] n bússola;
compasses npl compasso
compassion [kəm'pæʃən] n compaixão f
compatible [kəm'pætɪbl] adj compatível
compel [kəm'pεl] vt obrigar
compensate ['kɔmpənseɪt] vt indenizar
▷ vi: **to ~ for** compensar; **compensation**
[kɔmpən'seɪʃən] n compensação f;
(damages) indenização f
compete [kəm'piːt] vi (take part)
competir; (vie): **to ~ (with)** competir
(com), fazer competição (com)
competent ['kɔmpɪtənt] adj
competente
competition [kɔmpɪ'tɪʃən] n (contest)
concurso; (Econ) concorrência; (rivalry)
competição f
competitive [kəm'pεtɪtɪv] adj
competitivo; (person) competidor(a)
competitor [kəm'pεtɪtəʳ] n (rival)
competidor(a) m/f; (participant, Econ)
concorrente m/f
complain [kəm'pleɪn] vi queixar-se; **to
~ of** (pain) queixar-se de; **complaint** n
(objection) objeção f; (criticism) queixa;
(Med) achaque m, doença
complement ['kɔmplɪmənt] n
complemento; (esp ship's crew) tripulação
f ▷ vt complementar
complete [kəm'pliːt] adj completo;

(finished) acabado ▷ vt (finish: building,
task) acabar; (: set, group) completar;
(a form) preencher; **completely** adv
completamente; **completion** n
conclusão f, término; (of contract etc)
realização f
complex ['kɔmplεks] adj complexo ▷ n
complexo; (of buildings) conjunto
complexion [kəm'plεkʃən] n (of face)
cor f, tez f
complicate ['kɔmplɪkeɪt] vt complicar;
complicated adj complicado;
complication [kɔmplɪ'keɪʃən] n
problema m; (Med) complicação f
compliment [(n) 'kɔmplɪmənt, (vb)
'kɔmplɪmənt] n (praise) elogio ▷ vt
elogiar; **compliments** npl (regards)
cumprimentos mpl; **to pay sb a ~**
elogiar alguém; **complimentary**
[kɔmplɪ'mεntərɪ] adj lisonjeiro; (free)
gratuito
comply [kəm'plaɪ] vi: **to ~ with** cumprir
com
component [kəm'pəunənt] adj
componente ▷ n (part) peça
compose [kəm'pəuz] vt compor;
to be ~d of compor-se de; **to ~ o.s.**
tranqüilizar-se; **composer** n (Mus)
compositor(a) m/f; **composition**
[kɔmpə'zɪʃən] n composição f
compound ['kɔmpaund] n (Chem, Ling)
composto; (enclosure) recinto ▷ adj
composto
comprehensive [kɔmprɪ'hεnsɪv]
adj abrangente; (Insurance) total;
comprehensive (school) (BRIT) n escola
secundária de amplo programa

❀ **COMPREHENSIVE SCHOOL**
❀
❀ Criadas na década de 1960 pelo
❀ governo trabalhista da época,
❀ as **comprehensive schools**
❀ são estabelecimentos de ensino
❀ secundário polivalentes concebidos
❀ para acolher todos os alunos
❀ sem distinção e lhes oferecer
❀ oportunidades iguais, em oposição
❀ ao sistema seletivo das grammar
❀ schools. A maioria dos estudantes
❀ britânicos freqüenta atualmente
❀ uma **comprehensive school**, mas as
❀ grammar schools não desapareceram
❀ de todo.

compress [(vb) kəm'prεs, (n) 'kɔmprεs]

vt comprimir; (*text, information etc*) reduzir ▷ n (*Med*) compressa

comprise [kəm'praɪz] vt (*also:* **be ~d of**) compreender, constar de; (*constitute*) constituir

compromise ['kɒmprəmaɪz] n meio-termo ▷ vt comprometer ▷ vi chegar a um meio-termo

compulsive [kəm'pʌlsɪv] adj compulsório

compulsory [kəm'pʌlsərɪ] adj obrigatório; (*retirement*) compulsório

computer [kəm'pju:tər] n computador m; **computer game** n vídeo game m; **computerize** vt informatizar, computadorizar; **computing** n computação f; (*science*) informática

conceal [kən'si:l] vt ocultar; (*information*) omitir

conceited adj vaidoso

conceive [kən'si:v] vt conceber ▷ vi conceber, engravidar

concentrate ['kɒnsəntreɪt] vi concentrar-se ▷ vt concentrar; **concentration** n concentração f

concept ['kɒnsɛpt] n conceito

concern [kən'sə:n] n (*Comm*) empresa; (*anxiety*) preocupação f ▷ vt preocupar; (*involve*) envolver; (*relate to*) dizer respeito a; **to be ~ed (about)** preocupar-se (com); **concerning** prep sobre, a respeito de, acerca de

concert ['kɒnsət] n concerto

concession [kən'sɛʃən] n concessão f; **tax ~** redução no imposto

conclude [kən'klu:d] vt (*finish*) acabar, concluir; (*treaty etc*) firmar; (*agreement*) chegar a; (*decide*) decidir

conclusion [kən'klu:ʒən] n conclusão f

concrete ['kɒnkri:t] n concreto (BR), betão m (PT) ▷ adj concreto

concussion [kən'kʌʃən] n (*Med*) concussão f cerebral

condemn [kən'dɛm] vt denunciar; (*prisoner, building*) condenar

condensation [kɒndɛn'seɪʃən] n condensação f

condense [kən'dɛns] vi condensar-se ▷ vt condensar

condition [kən'dɪʃən] n condição f; (*Med: illness*) doença ▷ vt condicionar; **conditions** npl (*circumstances*) circunstâncias fpl; **on ~ that** com a condição (de) que; **conditioner** n (*for hair*) condicionador m; (*for fabrics*) amaciante m

condom ['kɒndɔm] n preservativo, camisinha, camisa-de-Venus f

condominium [kɒndə'mɪnɪəm] (us) n (*building*) edifício

condone [kən'dəun] vt admitir, aceitar

conduct [(n) 'kɒndʌkt, (vb) kən'dʌkt] n conduta, comportamento ▷ vt (*research etc*) fazer; (*heat, electricity*) conduzir; (*Mus*) reger; **to ~ o.s.** comportar-se; **conducted tour** n viagem f organizada; **conductor** n (*of orchestra*) regente m/f; (*on bus*) cobrador(a) m/f; (*us: Rail*) revisor(a) m/f; (*Elec*) condutor m

cone [kəun] n cone m; (*Bot*) pinha; (*for ice-cream*) casquinha; (*on road*) cone colorido para sinalizar obras

confectionery n (*sweetmeats*) doces mpl; (*sweets*) balas fpl

confer [kən'fə:r] vt: **to ~ sth on** conferir algo a; (*advantage*) conceder algo a ▷ vi conferenciar

conference ['kɒnfərns] n congresso

confess [kən'fɛs] vt confessar ▷ vi (*admit*) admitir; **confession** n admissão f; (*Rel*) confissão f

confide [kən'faɪd] vi: **to ~ in** confiar em, fiar-se em

confidence ['kɒnfɪdns] n confiança; (*faith*) fé f; (*secret*) confidência; **in ~** em confidência; **confident** adj confiante, convicto; (*positive*) seguro; **confidential** [kɒnfɪ'dɛnʃəl] adj confidencial

confine [kən'faɪn] vt (*shut up*) encarcerar; (*limit*): **to ~ (to)** confinar (a); **confined** adj (*space*) reduzido

confirm [kən'fə:m] vt confirmar; **confirmation** [kɒnfə'meɪʃən] n confirmação f; (*Rel*) crisma

confiscate ['kɒnfɪskeɪt] vt confiscar

conflict [(n) 'kɒnflɪkt, (vb) kən'flɪkt] n (*disagreement*) divergência; (*of interests, loyalties etc*) conflito; (*fighting*) combate m ▷ vi estar em conflito; (*opinions*) divergir

conform [kən'fɔ:m] vi conformar-se; **to ~ to** ajustar-se a, acomodar-se a

confront [kən'frʌnt] vt (*problems*) enfrentar; (*enemy, danger*) defrontar-se com; **confrontation** [kɒnfrən'teɪʃən] n confrontação f

confuse [kən'fju:z] vt (*perplex*) desconcertar; (*mix up*) confundir, misturar; (*complicate*) complicar; **confused** adj confuso; **confusing** adj confuso; **confusion** [kən'fju:ʒən] n (*mix-up*) mal-entendido; (*perplexity*)

perplexidade f; (disorder) confusão f
congestion [kən'dʒestʃən] n (Med)
congestão f; (traffic) congestionamento
congratulate [kən'grætjuleɪt]
vt parabenizar; **congratulations**
[kəngrætju'leɪʃənz] npl parabéns mpl
congress ['kɔŋgrɛs] n congresso; (us):
C~ Congresso; **congressman** (us: irreg)
n deputado

❋ **CONGRESS**
❋
❋ O Congresso é o Parlamento dos
❋ Estados Unidos. Consiste na House
❋ of Representatives e no Senado Senate.
❋ Os representantes e senadores são
❋ eleitos por sufrágio universal direto.
❋ O Congresso se reúne no Capitol, em
❋ Washington.

conjure ['kʌndʒəʳ] vi fazer truques;
conjure up vt (ghost, spirit) fazer
aparecer, invocar; (memories) evocar
connect [kə'nɛkt] vt (Elec, Tel) ligar; (fig:
associate) associar; (join): **to ~ sth (to)**
juntar or unir algo (a) ▷ vi: **to ~ with**
(train) conectar com; **to be ~ed with**
estar relacionado com; **I'm trying to ~
you** (Tel) estou tentando completar a
ligação; **connection** n ligação f; (Elec,
Rail, fig) conexão f; (Tel) ligação f
conquer ['kɔŋkəʳ] vt conquistar; (enemy)
vencer; (feelings) superar; **conquest**
['kɔŋkwɛst] n conquista
conscience ['kɔnʃəns] n consciência
conscientious [kɔnʃɪ'ɛnʃəs] adj
consciencioso
conscious ['kɔnʃəs] adj consciente;
(deliberate) intencional; **consciousness**
n consciência; (Med): **to lose/regain
consciousness** perder/recuperar os
sentidos
consent [kən'sɛnt] n consentimento
▷ vi: **to ~ to** consentir em
consequence ['kɔnsɪkwəns] n
conseqüência; (significance): **of ~ de**
importância; **consequently** adv por
conseguinte
conservation [kɔnsə'veɪʃən] n
conservação f; (of the environment)
preservação f
conservative [kən'sə:vətɪv] adj
conservador(a); (cautious) moderado;
(BRIT: Pol): C~ conservador(a) ▷ n (BRIT:
Pol) conservador(a) m/f
conservatory [kən'sə:vətrɪ] n (Mus)

conservatório; (greenhouse) estufa
consider [kən'sɪdəʳ] vt considerar; (take
into account) levar em consideração;
(study) estudar, examinar; **to ~ doing sth**
pensar em fazer algo
considerable [kən'sɪdərəbl] adj
considerável; (sum) importante
considerate [kən'sɪdərɪt] adj atencioso;
consideration [kənsɪdə'reɪʃən] n
consideração f; (deliberation) deliberação
f; (factor) fator m
considering [kən'sɪdərɪŋ] prep em
vista de
consist [kən'sɪst] vi: **to ~ of** (comprise)
consistir em
consistency [kən'sɪstənsɪ] n coerência;
(thickness) consistência
consistent [kən'sɪstənt] adj (person)
coerente, estável; (idea) sólido
consolation [kɔnsə'leɪʃən] n conforto
console [(vb) kən'səul, (n) 'kɔnsəul] vt
confortar ▷ n consolo
consonant ['kɔnsənənt] n consoante f
conspicuous [kən'spɪkjuəs] adj
conspícuo
conspiracy [kən'spɪrəsɪ] n conspiração
f, trama
constable ['kʌnstəbl] (BRIT) n policial
m/f(BR), polícia m/f(PT); **chief ~ chefe**
m/f de polícia
constant ['kɔnstənt] adj constante
constipated ['kɔnstɪpeɪtəd] adj com
prisão de ventre
constipation [kɔnstɪ'peɪʃən] n prisão f
de ventre
constituency [kən'stɪtjuənsɪ] n (Pol)
distrito eleitoral; (people) eleitorado
constitution [kɔnstɪ'tjuːʃən] n
constituição f; (health) compleição f
constraint [kən'streɪnt] n coação f,
pressão f; (restriction) limitação f
construct [kən'strʌkt] vt construir;
construction n construção f; (structure)
estrutura
consul ['kɔnsl] n cônsul m/f; **consulate**
['kɔnsjulɪt] n consulado
consult [kən'sʌlt] vt consultar;
consultant n (Med) (médico(-a))
especialista m/f; (other specialist)
assessor(a) m/f, consultor(a) m/f;
consulting room (BRIT) n consultório
consume [kən'sjuːm] vt (eat) comer;
(drink) beber; (fire etc, Comm) consumir;
consumer n consumidor(a) m/f
consumption [kən'sʌmpʃən] n
consumação f; (buying, amount) consumo

cont. *abbr* = **continued**

contact ['kɔntækt] *n* contato ▷ *vt* entrar or pôr-se em contato com; **contact lenses** *npl* lentes *fpl* de contato

contagious [kən'teɪdʒəs] *adj* contagioso; (*fig: laughter etc*) contagiante

contain [kən'teɪn] *vt* conter; **to ~ o.s.** conter-se; **container** *n* recipiente *m*; (*for shipping etc*) container *m*, cofre *m* de carga

contaminate [kən'tæmɪneɪt] *vt* contaminar

cont'd *abbr* = **continued**

contemplate ['kɔntəmpleɪt] *vt* (*idea*) considerar; (*person etc*) contemplar

contemporary [kən'tɛmpərərɪ] *adj* (*account*) contemporâneo; (*design*) moderno ▷ *n* contemporâneo(-a)

contempt [kən'tɛmpt] *n* desprezo; **~ of court** (*Law*) desacato à autoridade do tribunal

contend [kən'tɛnd] *vt* (*assert*): **to ~ that** afirmar que ▷ *vi*: **to ~ with** (*struggle*) lutar com; (*difficulty*) enfrentar; (*compete*): **to ~ for** competir por

content [(*adj, vb*) kən'tɛnt, (*n*) 'kɔntɛnt] *adj* (*happy*) contente; (*satisfied*) satisfeito ▷ *vt* contentar, satisfazer ▷ *n* conteúdo; (*fat content, moisture content etc*) quantidade *f*; **contents** *npl* (*of packet, book*) conteúdo; **contented** *adj* contente, satisfeito

contest [(*n*) 'kɔntɛst, (*vb*) kən'tɛst] *n* contenda; (*competition*) concurso ▷ *vt* (*legal case*) defender; (*Pol*) ser candidato a; (*competition*) disputar; (*statement*) contestar; **contestant** [kən'tɛstənt] *n* competidor(a) *m/f*; (*in fight*) adversário(-a)

context ['kɔntɛkst] *n* contexto

continent ['kɔntɪnənt] *n* continente *m*; **the C~** (BRIT) o continente europeu; **continental** [kɔntɪ'nɛntl] *adj* continental; **continental quilt** (BRIT) *n* edredom *m*

continual [kən'tɪnjuəl] *adj* contínuo

continue [kən'tɪnjuː] *vi* prosseguir, continuar ▷ *vt* continuar; (*start again*) recomeçar, retomar; **continuous** [kən'tɪnjuəs] *adj* contínuo

contour ['kɔntuəʳ] *n* contorno; (*also: ~ line*) curva de nível

contraceptive [kɔntrə'sɛptɪv] *adj* anticoncepcional ▷ *n* anticoncepcional *f*

contract [(*n*) 'kɔntrækt, (*vb*) kən'trækt] *n* contrato ▷ *vi* (*become smaller*) contrair-se, encolher-se; (*Comm*): **to ~ to do sth** comprometer-se por contrato a fazer algo ▷ *vt* contrair

contradict [kɔntrə'dɪkt] *vt* contradizer, desmentir

contrary¹ ['kɔntrərɪ] *adj* contrário ▷ *n* contrário; **on the ~** muito pelo contrário; **unless you hear to the ~** salvo aviso contrário

contrary² [kən'trɛərɪ] *adj* teimoso

contrast [(*n*) 'kɔntrɑːst, (*vb*) kən'trɑːst] *n* contraste *m* ▷ *vt* comparar; **in ~ to** em contraste com, ao contrário de

contribute [kən'trɪbjuːt] *vt* contribuir ▷ *vi* dar; **to ~ to** (*charity*) contribuir para; (*newspaper*) escrever para; (*discussion*) participar de; **contribution** [kɔntrɪ'bjuːʃən] *n* (*donation*) doação *f*; (BRIT: *for social security*) contribuição *f*; (*to debate*) intervenção *f*; (*to journal*) colaboração *f*; **contributor** [kən'trɪbjutəʳ] *n* (*to appeal*) contribuinte *m/f*; (*to newspaper*) colaborador(a) *m/f*

control [kən'trəul] *vt* controlar; (*machinery*) regular; (*temper*) dominar ▷ *n* controle *m*; (*of car*) direção *f* (BR), condução *f* (PT); (*check*) freio, controle; **controls** *npl* (*of vehicle*) instrumentos *mpl* de controle; (*on radio, television etc*) controle; (*governmental*) medidas *fpl* de controle; **to be in ~ of** ter o controle de; (*in charge of*) ser responsável por

controversial [kɔntrə'vəːʃl] *adj* controvertido, polêmico

controversy ['kɔntrəvəːsɪ] *n* controvérsia, polêmica

convenience [kən'viːnɪəns] *n* (*easiness*) facilidade *f*; (*suitability*) conveniência; (*advantage*) vantagem *f*, conveniência; **at your ~** quando lhe convier; **all modern ~s** (*also*: BRIT: **all mod cons**) com todos os confortos

convenient [kən'viːnɪənt] *adj* conveniente

convent ['kɔnvənt] *n* convento

convention [kən'vɛnʃən] *n* (*custom*) costume *m*; (*agreement*) convenção *f*; (*meeting*) assembléia; **conventional** *adj* convencional

conversation [kɔnvə'seɪʃən] *n* conversação *f*, conversa

convert [(*vb*) kən'vəːt, (*n*) 'kɔnvəːt] *vt* converter ▷ *n* convertido(-a); **convertible** [kən'vəːtəbl] *n* conversível *m*

convey [kən'veɪ] *vt* transportar, levar;

(*thanks*) expressar; (*information*) exprimir;
conveyor belt n correia transportadora
convict [(*vb*) kən'vɪkt, (*n*) 'kɒnvɪkt] vt
condenar ▷ n presidiário(-a); **conviction**
n condenação f; (*belief*) convicção f;
(*certainty*) certeza
convince [kən'vɪns] vt (*assure*)
assegurar; (*persuade*) convencer;
convincing adj convincente
cook [kuk] vt cozinhar; (*meal*) preparar
▷ vi cozinhar ▷ n cozinheiro(-a);
cookbook n livro de receitas; **cooker** n
fogão m; **cookery** n culinária; **cookery
book** (*BRIT*) n = **cookbook**; **cookie** (*US*) n
bolacha, biscoito; **cooking** n cozinha
cool [ku:l] adj fresco; (*calm*) calmo;
(*unfriendly*) frio ▷ vt resfriar ▷ vi esfriar
cop [kɒp] (*inf*) n polícia m/f, policial m/f
(*BR*), tira m (*inf*)
cope [kəup] vi: **to ~ with** poder com,
arcar com; (*problem*) estar à altura de
copper ['kɒpəʳ] n (*metal*) cobre m; (*BRIT:
inf: policeman/woman*) polícia m/f, policial
m/f (*BR*); **coppers** npl (*coins*) moedas fpl
de pouco valor
copy ['kɒpɪ] n duplicata; (*of book etc*)
exemplar m ▷ vt copiar; (*imitate*) imitar;
copyright n direitos mpl autorais,
copirraite m
coral ['kɒrəl] n coral m
cord [kɔ:d] n corda; (*Elec*) fio, cabo;
(*fabric*) veludo cotelê
corduroy ['kɔ:dərɔɪ] n veludo cotelê
core [kɔ:ʳ] n centro; (*of fruit*) caroço; (*of
problem*) âmago ▷ vt descaroçar
cork [kɔ:k] n rolha; (*tree*) cortiça;
corkscrew n saca-rolhas m inv
corn [kɔ:n] n (*BRIT*) trigo; (*US: maize*)
milho; (*on foot*) calo; **~ on the cob** (*Culin*)
espiga de milho
corned beef ['kɔ:nd-] n carne f de boi
enlatada
corner ['kɔ:nəʳ] n (*outside*) esquina;
(*inside*) canto; (*in road*) curva; (*Football,
Boxing*) córner m ▷ vt (*trap*) encurralar;
(*Comm*) açambarcar, monopolizar ▷ vi
fazer uma curva
cornflakes ['kɔ:nfleɪks] npl flocos mpl
de milho
cornflour ['kɔ:nflauəʳ] (*BRIT*) n farinha
de milho, maisena®
cornstarch ['kɔ:nstɑ:tʃ] (*US*) n
= **cornflour**
Cornwall ['kɔ:nwəl] n Cornualha
coronary ['kɒrənərɪ] n: **~ (thrombosis)**
trombose f (coronária)

coronation [kɒrə'neɪʃən] n coroação f
coroner ['kɒrənəʳ] n magistrado que
investiga mortes suspeitas
corporal ['kɔ:pərl] n cabo ▷ adj: **~
punishment** castigo corporal
corporate ['kɔ:pərɪt] adj coletivo;
(*finance*) corporativo; (*image*) de empresa
corporation [kɔ:pə'reɪʃən] n (*of town*)
município, junta; (*Comm*) sociedade f
corps [kɔ:ʳ] (*pl* **~**) n (*Mil*) unidade f;
(*diplomatic*) corpo; **the press ~** a
imprensa
corpse [kɔ:ps] n cadáver m
correct [kə'rɛkt] adj exato; (*proper*)
correto ▷ vt corrigir; **correction** n
correção f
correspond [kɒrɪs'pɒnd] vi (*write*): **to
~ (with)** corresponder-se (com); (*be
equal to*): **to ~ to** corresponder a; (*be in
accordance*): **to ~ (with)** corresponder a;
correspondence n correspondência;
correspondent n correspondente m/f
corridor ['kɒrɪdɔ:ʳ] n corredor m
corrode [kə'rəud] vt corroer ▷ vi corroer-
se
corrupt [kə'rʌpt] adj corrupto; (*Comput*)
corrupto, danificado ▷ vt corromper;
corromper, danificar; **corruption** n
corrupção f; corrupção, danificação f
Corsica ['kɔ:sɪkə] n Córsega
cosmetic [kɒz'mɛtɪk] n cosmético ▷ adj
(*fig*) simbólico, artificial
cost [kɒst] (*pt, pp* **~**) n (*price*) preço ▷ vt
custar; **costs** npl (*Comm: overheads*)
custos mpl; (*Law*) custas fpl; **at all ~s**
custe o que custar
co-star [kəu-] n co-estrela m/f
Costa Rica ['kɒstə'ri:kə] n Costa Rica
costly ['kɒstlɪ] adj caro
costume ['kɒstju:m] n traje m; (*BRIT:
also:* **swimming ~**: *woman's*) maiô m (*BR*),
fato de banho (*PT*); (: *man's*) calção m (*de
banho*) (*BR*), calções mpl de banho (*PT*)
cosy ['kəuzɪ] (*US* **cozy**) adj aconchegante;
(*person*) confortável
cot [kɒt] n (*BRIT*) cama (de criança),
berço; (*US*) cama de lona
cottage ['kɒtɪdʒ] n casa de campo;
cottage cheese n ricota (*BR*), queijo
creme (*PT*)
cotton ['kɒtn] n algodão m; (*thread*) fio,
linha; **cotton on** (*inf*) vi: **to cotton on
(to sth)** sacar (algo); **cotton candy** (*US*)
n algodão m doce; **cotton wool** (*BRIT*) n
algodão m (hidrófilo)
couch [kautʃ] n sofá m; (*doctor's*) cama;

(psychiatrist's) divã m

cough [kɔf] vi tossir ▷ n tosse f

could [kud] pt, conditional of **can²**

couldn't ['kudnt] = **could not**

council ['kaunsl] n conselho; **city** or **town ~** câmara municipal; **council estate** (BRIT) n conjunto habitacional; **council house** (BRIT) n casa popular; **councillor** n vereador(a) m/f

counsellor (US **counselor**) n conselheiro(-a); (US: Law) advogado(-a)

count [kaunt] vt contar; (include) incluir ▷ vi contar ▷ n (of votes etc) contagem f; (of pollen, alcohol) nível m; (nobleman) conde m; **count on** vt fus (expect) esperar; (depend on) contar com; **countdown** n contagem f regressiva

counter ['kauntəʳ] n (in shop) balcão m; (in post office etc) guichê m; (in games) ficha ▷ vt contrariar ▷ adv: **~ to** ao contrário de

counterfeit ['kauntəfɪt] n falsificação f ▷ vt falsificar ▷ adj falso, falsificado

counterpart ['kauntəpɑ:t] n (of person) homólogo(-a); (of company etc) equivalente m/f

countess ['kauntɪs] n condessa

countless ['kauntlɪs] adj inumerável

country ['kʌntrɪ] n país m; (nation) nação f; (native land) terra; (as opposed to town) campo; (region) região f, terra; **countryside** n campo

county ['kauntɪ] n condado

coup [ku:] n golpe m de mestre; (also: **~ d'état**) golpe (de estado)

couple ['kʌpl] n (of things, people) par m; (married couple) casal m; **a ~ of** um par de; (a few) alguns (algumas)

coupon ['ku:pɔn] n cupom m (BR), cupão m (PT); (voucher) vale m

courage ['kʌrɪdʒ] n coragem f

courier ['kurɪəʳ] n correio; (for tourists) guia m/f, agente m/f de turismo

course [kɔ:s] n (direction) direção f; (process) desenvolvimento; (of river, Sch) curso; (of ship) rumo; (Golf) campo; (part of meal) prato; **~ of treatment** tratamento; **of ~** naturalmente; (certainly) certamente; **of ~!** claro!, lógico!

court [kɔ:t] n (royal) corte f; (Law) tribunal m; (Tennis etc) quadra ▷ vt (woman) cortejar, namorar; **to take ~ to** demandar, levar a julgamento

courtesy ['kə:təsɪ] n cortesia; **(by) ~ of** com permissão de

court-house (US) n palácio de justiça

courtroom ['kɔ:trum] n sala de tribunal

courtyard ['kɔ:tjɑ:d] n pátio

cousin ['kʌzn] n primo(a) m/f; **first ~** primo irmão (prima irmã)

cover ['kʌvəʳ] vt cobrir; (with lid) tapar; (chairs etc) revestir; (distance) percorrer; (include) abranger; (protect) abrigar; (issues) tratar ▷ n (lid) tampa; (for chair etc) capa; (for bed) cobertor m; (of book, magazine) capa; (shelter) abrigo; (Insurance: also: of spy) cobertura; **to take ~** abrigar-se; **under ~** (indoors) abrigado; **under separate ~** (Comm) em separado; **cover up** vi: **to cover up for sb** cobrir alguém; **coverage** n cobertura; **cover charge** n couvert m

cover-up n encobrimento (dos fatos)

cow [kau] n vaca ▷ vt intimidar

coward ['kauəd] n covarde m/f; **cowardly** adj covarde

cowboy ['kaubɔɪ] n vaqueiro

cozy ['kauzɪ] (US) adj = **cosy**

crab [kræb] n caranguejo

crack [kræk] n rachadura; (gap) brecha; (noise) estalo; (drug) crack m ▷ vt quebrar; (nut) partir, descascar; (wall) rachar; (whip etc) estalar; (joke) soltar; (mystery) resolver; (code) decifrar ▷ adj (expert) de primeira classe; **crack down on** vt fus (crime) ser linha dura com; **crack up** vi (Psych) sofrer um colapso nervoso; **cracker** n (biscuit) biscoito; (Christmas cracker) busca-pé-surpresa m

crackle ['krækl] vi crepitar

cradle ['kreɪdl] n berço

craft [krɑ:ft] n (skill) arte f; (trade) ofício; (boat: pl inv) barco; (plane: pl inv) avião; **craftsman** (irreg) n artífice m, artesão m; **craftsmanship** n qualidade f

cram [kræm] vt (fill): **to ~ sth with** encher or abarrotar algo de; (put): **to ~ sth into** enfiar algo em ▷ vi (for exams) estudar na última hora

cramp [kræmp] n (Med) cãibra; **cramped** adj apertado, confinado

cranberry ['krænbərɪ] n oxicoco

crane [kreɪn] n (Tech) guindaste m; (bird) grou m

crash [kræʃ] n (noise) estrondo; (of car) batida; (of plane) desastre m de avião; (Comm) falência, quebra; (Stock Exchange) craque m ▷ vt (car) colidir; (plane) espatifar ▷ vi bater; cair, espatifar-se; (cars) colidir, bater; (Comm) falir, quebrar; **crash course** n curso intensivo

crate [kreɪt] n caixote m; (for bottles) engradado

crave [kreɪv] vt, vi: **to ~ for** ansiar por

crawl [krɔ:l] vi arrastar-se; (child) engatinhar; (insect) andar; (vehicle) arrastar-se a passo de tartaruga ▷ n (Swimming) crawl m

crayfish ['kreɪfɪʃ] n inv (freshwater) camarão-d'água-doce m; (saltwater) lagostim m

crayon ['kreɪən] n lápis m de cera, crayon m

craze [kreɪz] n (fashion) moda

crazy ['kreɪzɪ] adj louco, maluco, doido

creak [kri:k] vi chiar, ranger

cream [kri:m] n (of milk) nata; (artificial cream, cosmetic) creme m; (élite): **the ~ of** a fina flor de ▷ adj (colour) creme inv; **cream cheese** n ricota (BR), queijo creme (PT); **creamy** adj (colour) creme inv; (taste) cremoso

crease [kri:s] n (fold) dobra, vinco; (in trousers) vinco; (wrinkle) ruga ▷ vt (wrinkle) amassar, amarrotar ▷ vi amassar-se, amarrotar-se

create [kri:'eɪt] vt criar; (produce) produzir

creature ['kri:tʃəʳ] n (animal) animal m, bicho; (living thing) criatura

credit ['krɛdɪt] n crédito; (merit) mérito ▷ vt (also: **give ~ to**) acreditar; (Comm) creditar; **credits** npl (Cinema, TV) crédito; **to ~ sb with sth** (fig) atribuir algo a alguém; **to be in ~** ter fundos; **credit card** n cartão m de crédito

creek [kri:k] n enseada; (US) riacho

creep [kri:p] (pt, pp **crept**) vi (animal) rastejar; (person) deslizar(-se)

cremate [krɪ'meɪt] vt cremar; **crematorium** (pl **crematoria**) n crematório

crept [krɛpt] pt, pp of **creep**

crescent ['krɛsnt] n meia-lua; (street) rua semicircular

cress [krɛs] n agrião m

crest [krɛst] n (of bird) crista; (of hill) cimo, topo; (of coat of arms) timbre m

crew [kru:] n (of ship) tripulação f; (Cinema) equipe f

crib [krɪb] n manjedoura, presépio; (US: cot) berço ▷ vt (inf) colar

cricket ['krɪkɪt] n (insect) grilo; (game) criquete m, cricket m

crime [kraɪm] n (no pl: illegal activities) crime m; (offence) delito; (fig) pecado, maldade f; **criminal** ['krɪmɪnl] n

criminoso ▷ adj criminal; (morally wrong) imoral

crimson ['krɪmzn] adj carmesim inv

cringe [krɪndʒ] vi encolher-se

cripple ['krɪpl] n aleijado(-a) ▷ vt aleijar

crisis ['kraɪsɪs] (pl **crises**) n crise f

crisp [krɪsp] adj fresco; (bacon etc) torrado; (manner) seco; **crisps** (BRIT) npl batatinhas fpl fritas

criterion [kraɪ'tɪərɪən] (pl **criteria**) n critério

critic ['krɪtɪk] n crítico(-a); **critical** adj crítico; (illness) grave; **to be critical of sth/sb** criticar algo/alguém; **criticism** ['krɪtɪsɪzəm] n crítica; **criticize** ['krɪtɪsaɪz] vt criticar

Croatia [krəʊ'eɪʃə] n Croácia

crockery ['krɔkərɪ] n louça

crocodile ['krɔkədaɪl] n crocodilo

crocus ['krəʊkəs] n açafrão-da-primavera m

crook [kruk] n (inf: criminal) vigarista m/f; (of shepherd) cajado; **crooked** ['krukɪd] adj torto; (dishonest) desonesto

crop [krɔp] n (produce) colheita; (amount produced) safra; (riding crop) chicotinho ▷ vt cortar; **crop up** vi surgir

cross [krɔs] n cruz f; (hybrid) cruzamento ▷ vt cruzar; (street) atravessar; (thwart) contrariar ▷ adj zangado, mal-humorado; **cross out** vt riscar; **cross over** vi atravessar; **crossing** n (sea passage) travessia; (also: **pedestrian crossing**) faixa (para pedestres) (BR), passadeira (PT); **crossroads** n cruzamento; **crosswalk** (US) n faixa (para pedestres) (BR), passadeira (PT); **crossword** n palavras fpl cruzadas

crouch [krautʃ] vi agachar-se

crow [krəʊ] n (bird) corvo; (of cock) canto, cocoricó m ▷ vi (cock) cantar, cocoricar

crowd [kraud] n multidão f ▷ vt (fill) apinhar ▷ vi (gather): **to ~ round** reunir-se; (cram): **to ~ in** apinhar-se em; **crowded** adj (full) lotado; (densely populated) superlotado

crown [kraun] n coroa; (of head, hill) topo ▷ vt coroar; (fig) rematar; **crown jewels** npl jóias fpl reais

crucial ['kru:ʃl] adj (decision) vital; (vote) decisivo

crucifix ['kru:sɪfɪks] n crucifixo

crude [kru:d] adj (materials) bruto; (fig: basic) tosco; (: vulgar) grosseiro

cruel ['kruəl] adj cruel

cruise [kru:z] n cruzeiro ▷ vi (ship) fazer

um cruzeiro; (*car*): **to ~ at … km/h** ir a … km por hora

crumb [krʌm] *n* (*of bread*) migalha; (*of cake*) farelo

crumble ['krʌmbl] *vt* esfarelar ▷ *vi* (*building*) desmoronar-se; (*plaster, earth*) esfacelar-se; (*fig*) desintegrar-se

crumpet ['krʌmpɪt] *n bolo leve*

crumple ['krʌmpl] *vt* (*paper*) amassar; (*material*) amarrotar

crunch [krʌntʃ] *vt* (*food etc*) mastigar; (*underfoot*) esmagar ▷ *n* (*fig*): **the ~** o momento decisivo; **crunchy** *adj* crocante

crush [krʌʃ] *n* (*crowd*) aglomeração *f*; (*love*): **to have a ~ on sb** ter um rabicho por alguém; (*drink*): **lemon ~** limonada ▷ *vt* (*press*) esmagar; (*squeeze*) espremer; (*paper*) amassar; (*cloth*) enrugar; (*army, opposition*) aniquilar; (*hopes*) destruir; (*person*) arrasar

crust [krʌst] *n* (*of bread*) casca; (*of snow*) crosta; (*of earth*) camada

crutch [krʌtʃ] *n* muleta

cry [kraɪ] *vi* chorar; (*shout: also*: **~ out**) gritar ▷ *n* grito; (*of bird*) pio; (*of animal*) voz *f*; **cry off** *vi* desistir

crystal ['krɪstl] *n* cristal *m*

cub [kʌb] *n* filhote *m*; (*also*: **~ scout**) lobinho

Cuba ['kju:bə] *n* Cuba

cube [kju:b] *n* cubo ▷ *vt* (*Math*) elevar ao cubo; **cubic** *adj* cúbico

cubicle ['kju:bɪkl] *n* cubículo

cuckoo ['kuku:] *n* cuco

cucumber ['kju:kʌmbəʳ] *n* pepino

cuddle ['kʌdl] *vt* abraçar ▷ *vi* abraçar-se

cue [kju:] *n* (*Snooker*) taco; (*Theatre etc*) deixa

cuff [kʌf] *n* (*of shirt, coat etc*) punho; (*US: on trousers*) bainha; (*blow*) bofetada; **off the ~** de improviso

cul-de-sac ['kʌldəsæk] *n* beco sem saída

cull [kʌl] *vt* (*story, idea*) escolher, selecionar ▷ *n* matança seletiva

culminate ['kʌlmɪneɪt] *vi*: **to ~ in** terminar em

culprit ['kʌlprɪt] *n* culpado(-a)

cult [kʌlt] *n* culto

cultivate ['kʌltɪveɪt] *vt* cultivar

cultural ['kʌltʃərəl] *adj* cultural

culture ['kʌltʃəʳ] *n* cultura

cunning ['kʌnɪŋ] *n* astúcia ▷ *adj* astuto, malandro; (*device, idea*) engenhoso

cup [kʌp] *n* xícara (BR), chávena (PT); (*prize, of bra*) taça

cupboard ['kʌbəd] *n* armário

curator [kjuə'reɪtəʳ] *n* diretor(a) *m/f*

curb [kə:b] *vt* refrear ▷ *n* freio; (*US: kerb*) meio-fio (BR), borda do passeio (PT)

curdle ['kə:dl] *vi* coalhar

cure [kjuəʳ] *vt* curar ▷ *n* (*Med*) tratamento, cura; (*solution*) remédio

curfew ['kə:fju:] *n* toque *m* de recolher

curious ['kjuəriəs] *adj* curioso; (*nosy*) abelhudo; (*unusual*) estranho

curl [kə:l] *n* (*of hair*) cacho ▷ *vt* (*loosely*) frisar; (: *tightly*) encrespar ▷ *vi* (*hair*) encaracolar; **curl up** *vi* encaracolar-se; **curler** *n* rolo, bobe *m*; **curly** *adj* cacheado, crespo

currant ['kʌrnt] *n* passa de corinto; (*blackcurrant, redcurrant*) groselha

currency ['kʌrnsɪ] *n* moeda; **to gain ~** (*fig*) consagrar-se

current ['kʌrnt] *n* corrente *f* ▷ *adj* corrente; (*present*) atual; **current account** (BRIT) *n* conta corrente; **current affairs** *npl* atualidades *fpl*; **currently** *adv* atualmente

curriculum [kə'rɪkjuləm] (*pl* **~s** or **curricula**) *n* programa *m* de estudos; **curriculum vitae** *n* curriculum vitae *m*, currículo

curry ['kʌrɪ] *n* caril *m* ▷ *vt*: **to ~ favour with** captar simpatia de

curse [kə:s] *vi* xingar (BR), praguejar (PT) ▷ *vt* (*swear at*) xingar (BR); (*bemoan*) amaldiçoar ▷ *n* maldição *f*; (*swearword*) palavrão *m* (BR), baixo calão *m* (PT); (*problem*) castigo

cursor ['kə:səʳ] *n* (*Comput*) cursor *m*

curt [kə:t] *adj* seco, brusco

curtain ['kə:tn] *n* cortina; (*Theatre*) pano

curve [kə:v] *n* curva ▷ *vi* encurvar-se, torcer-se; (*road*) fazer (uma) curva

cushion ['kuʃən] *n* almofada; (*of air*) colchão *m* ▷ *vt* amortecer

custard ['kʌstəd] *n* nata, creme *m*

custody ['kʌstədɪ] *n* custódia; **to take into ~** deter

custom ['kʌstəm] *n* (*tradition*) tradição *f*; (*convention*) costume *m*; (*habit*) hábito; (*Comm*) clientela; **customer** *n* cliente *m/f*; **customized** *adj* (*car etc*) feito sob encomenda

customs ['kʌstəmz] *npl* alfândega; **customs officer** *n* inspetor(a) *m/f* da alfândega, aduaneiro(-a)

cut [kʌt] (*pt, pp* **~**) *vt* cortar; (*reduce*) reduzir ▷ *vi* cortar ▷ *n* corte *m*; (*in spending*) redução *f*; (*of garment*) talho; **cut down** vt (tree) derrubar; (consumption) reduzir; **cut off** vt (piece, Tel) cortar; (person, village) isolar; (supply) suspender; **cut out** vt (shape) recortar; (activity etc) suprimir; (remove) remover; **cut up** vt cortar em pedaços

cute [kju:t] adj bonitinho, gracinha

cutlery ['kʌtlərɪ] n talheres mpl

cutlet ['kʌtlɪt] n costeleta; (vegetable cutlet, nut cutlet) medalhão m

cut: cut-price (US **cut-rate**) adj a preço reduzido; **cutting** adj cortante ▷ n (BRIT: from newspaper) recorte m; (from plant) muda

CV n abbr = **curriculum vitae**

cybercafé ['saɪbəkæfeɪ] n cibercafé m

cyberspace ['saɪbəspeɪs] n ciberespaço

cycle ['saɪkl] n ciclo; (bicycle) bicicleta ▷ vi andar de bicicleta

cycling ['saɪklɪŋ] n ciclismo

cyclist ['saɪklɪst] n ciclista m/f

cylinder ['sɪlɪndəʳ] n cilindro; (of gas) bujão m

Cyprus ['saɪprəs] n Chipre f

cyst [sɪst] n cisto; **cystitis** n cistite f

czar [zɑ:ʳ] n czar m

Czech [tʃɛk] adj tcheco ▷ n tcheco(-a); (Ling) tcheco; **Czech Republic** n: **the Czech Republic** a República Tcheca

d

D [di:] n (Mus) ré m

dab [dæb] vt (eyes, wound) tocar (de leve); (paint, cream) aplicar de leve

dad [dæd] (inf) n papai m

daddy ['dædɪ] n = **dad**

daffodil ['dæfədɪl] n narciso-dos-prados m

daft [dɑ:ft] adj bobo, besta

dagger ['dægəʳ] n punhal m, adaga

daily ['deɪlɪ] adj diário ▷ n (paper) jornal m, diário ▷ adv diariamente

dairy ['dɛərɪ] n leiteria

daisy ['deɪzɪ] n margarida

dam [dæm] n represa, barragem f ▷ vt represar

damage ['dæmɪdʒ] n (harm) prejuízo; (dents etc) avaria ▷ vt danificar; (harm) prejudicar; **damages** npl (Law) indenização f por perdas e danos

damn [dæm] vt condenar; (curse) maldizer ▷ n (inf): **I don't give a ~** não dou a mínima, estou me lixando ▷ adj (inf: also: **~ed**) danado, maldito; **~ (it)!** (que) droga!

damp [dæmp] adj úmido ▷ n umidade f ▷ vt (also: **~en**: cloth, rag) umedecer; (: enthusiasm etc) jogar água fria em

dance [dɑ:ns] n dança; (party etc) baile

m ▷ *vi* dançar; **dancer** *n* dançarino(-a); (*professional*) bailarino(-a); **dancing** *n* dança

dandelion ['dændɪlaɪən] *n* dente-de-leão *m*

dandruff ['dændrəf] *n* caspa

Dane [deɪn] *n* dinamarquês(-esa) *m/f*

danger ['deɪndʒə'] *n* perigo; (*risk*) risco; **"~!"** (*on sign*) "perigo!"; **to be in ~ of** correr o risco de; **in ~** em perigo; **dangerous** *adj* perigoso

dangle ['dæŋgl] *vt* balançar ▷ *vi* pender balançando

Danish ['deɪnɪʃ] *adj* dinamarquês(-esa) ▷ *n* (*Ling*) dinamarquês *m*

dare [dɛə'] *vt*: **to ~ sb to do sth** desafiar alguém a fazer algo ▷ *vi*: **to ~ (to) do sth** atrever-se a fazer algo, ousar fazer algo; **I ~ say** (*I suppose*) acho provável que; **daring** *adj* audacioso; (*bold*) ousado ▷ *n* coragem *f*, destemor *m*

dark [dɑːk] *adj* escuro; (*complexion*) moreno ▷ *n* escuro; **to be in the ~ about** (*fig*) estar no escuro sobre; **after ~** depois de escurecer; **darken** *vt* escurecer; (*colour*) fazer mais escuro ▷ *vi* escurecer-se; **darkness** *n* escuridão *f*; **darkroom** *n* câmara escura

darling ['dɑːlɪŋ] *adj, n* querido(-a)

dart [dɑːt] *n* dardo; (*in sewing*) alinhavo ▷ *vi* precipitar-se, correr para; **to ~ away/along** ir-se/seguir precipitadamente; **darts** *n* (*game*) jogo de dardos

dash [dæʃ] *n* (*sign*) hífen *m*; (: *long*) travessão *m*; (*quantity*) pontinha ▷ *vt* arremessar; (*hopes*) frustrar ▷ *vi* correr para, ir depressa; **dash away** *vi* sair apressado; **dash off** *vi* = **dash away**

dashboard ['dæʃbɔːd] *n* painel *m* de instrumentos

data ['deɪtə] *npl* dados *mpl*; **database** *n* banco de dados; **data processing** *n* processamento de dados

date [deɪt] *n* data; (*with friend*) encontro; (*fruit*) tâmara ▷ *vt* datar; (*person*) namorar; **to ~** até agora; **out of ~** fora de moda; (*expired*) desatualizado; **up to ~** moderno; **dated** ['deɪtɪd] *adj* antiquado

daughter ['dɔːtə'] *n* filha; **daughter-in-law** (*pl* **daughters-in-law**) *n* nora

daunting ['dɔːntɪŋ] *adj* desanimador(a)

dawn [dɔːn] *n* alvorada, amanhecer *m*; (*of period, situation*) surgimento, início ▷ *vi* (*day*) amanhecer; (*fig*): **it ~ed on him that ...** começou a perceber que ...

day [deɪ] *n* dia *m*; (*working day*) jornada, dia útil; (*heyday*) apogeu *m*; **the ~ before** a véspera; **the ~ before yesterday** anteontem; **the ~ after tomorrow** depois de amanhã; **by ~** de dia; **daydream** *vi* devanear; **daylight** *n* luz *f* (do dia); **day return** (BRIT) *n* bilhete *m* de ida e volta no mesmo dia; **daytime** *n* dia *m*; **day-to-day** *adj* cotidiano

dazzle ['dæzl] *vt* (*bewitch*) deslumbrar; (*blind*) ofuscar

dead [dɛd] *adj* morto; (*numb*) dormente; (*telephone*) cortado; (*Elec*) sem corrente ▷ *adv* completamente; (*exactly*) absolutamente ▷ *npl*: **the ~** os mortos; **to shoot sb ~** matar alguém a tiro; **~ tired** morto de cansado; **to stop ~** estacar (*pain*) anestesiar; **dead end** *n* beco sem saída; **deadline** *n* prazo final; **deadly** *adj* mortal, fatal; (*accuracy, insult*) devastador(a); (*weapon*) mortífero

deaf [dɛf] *adj* surdo; **deafen** *vt* ensurdecer

deal [diːl] (*pt, pp* **~t**) *n* (*agreement*) acordo ▷ *vt* (*cards, blows*) dar; **a good** *or* **great ~ (of)** bastante, muito; **deal in** *vt fus* (*Comm*) negociar em *or* com; **deal with** *vt fus* (*people*) tratar com; (*problem*) ocupar-se de; (*subject*) tratar de; **dealer** *n* negociante *m/f*; **dealings** *npl* transações *fpl*

dean [diːn] *n* (*Rel*) decano; (*Sch*: BRIT) reitor(a) *m/f*; (: US) orientador(a) *m/f* de estudos

dear [dɪə'] *adj* querido, caro; (*expensive*) caro ▷ *n*: **my ~** meu querido (minha querida) ▷ *excl*: **~ me!** ai, meu Deus!; **D~ Sir/Madam** (*in letter*) Ilmo. Senhor/Exma. Senhora (BR), Exmo. Senhor/Exma. Senhora (PT); **D~ Mr/Mrs X** Caro Sr. X/Cara Sra. X; **dearly** *adv* (*love*) ternamente; (*pay*) caro

death [dɛθ] *n* morte *f*; (*Admin*) óbito; **death penalty** *n* pena de morte

debate [dɪ'beɪt] *n* debate *m* ▷ *vt* debater

debit ['dɛbɪt] *n* débito ▷ *vt*: **to ~ a sum to sb** *or* **to sb's account** lançar uma quantia ao débito de alguém *or* à conta de alguém; *see also* **direct debit**

debt [dɛt] *n* dívida; (*state*) endividamento; **to be in ~** ter dívidas, estar endividado

decade ['dɛkeɪd] *n* década

decaffeinated [dɪ'kæfɪneɪtɪd] *adj* descafeinado

decay [dɪ'keɪ] *n* ruína; (*also*: **tooth ~**)

cárie f ▷ vi (rot) apodrecer-se
deceased [dɪ'si:st] n falecido(-a)
deceit [dɪ'si:t] n engano; (duplicity) fraude f
deceive [dɪ'si:v] vt enganar
December [dɪ'sɛmbəʳ] n dezembro
decent ['di:sənt] adj (proper) decente; (kind, honest) honesto, amável
deception [dɪ'sɛpʃən] n engano; (deceitful act) fraude f; **deceptive** adj enganador(a)
decide [dɪ'saɪd] vt (person) convencer; (question) resolver ▷ vi decidir; **to ~ on sth** decidir-se por algo
decimal ['dɛsɪməl] adj decimal ▷ n decimal m
decision [dɪ'sɪʒən] n (choice) escolha; (act of choosing) decisão f; (decisiveness) resolução f
decisive [dɪ'saɪsɪv] adj (action) decisivo; (person) decidido
deck [dɛk] n (Naut) convés m; (of bus): **top ~** andar m de cima; (of cards) baralho; **record ~** toca-discos m inv; **deckchair** n cadeira de lona, espreguiçadeira
declare [dɪ'klɛəʳ] vt (intention) revelar; (result) divulgar; (income, at customs) declarar
decline [dɪ'klaɪn] n declínio; (lessening) diminuição f, baixa ▷ vt recusar ▷ vi diminuir
decorate ['dɛkəreɪt] vt (adorn) adornar; (paint) pintar; (paper) decorar com papel; **decoration** [dɛkə'reɪʃən] n enfeite m; (act) decoração f; (medal) condecoração f; **decorator** n (painter) pintor(a) m/f
decrease [(n) 'di:kri:s, (vb) di:'kri:s] n: **~ (in)** diminuição f (de) ▷ vt reduzir ▷ vi diminuir
decree [dɪ'kri:] n decreto
dedicate ['dɛdɪkeɪt] vt dedicar; **dedication** [dɛdɪ'keɪʃən] n dedicação f; (in book) dedicatória; (on radio) mensagem f
deduce [dɪ'dju:s] vt deduzir
deduct [dɪ'dʌkt] vt deduzir; **deduction** n (deducting) redução f; (amount) subtração f; (deducing) dedução f
deed [di:d] n feito; (Law) escritura, título
deep [di:p] adj profundo; (voice) baixo, grave; (breath) fundo; (colour) forte, carregado ▷ adv: **the spectators stood 20 ~** os espectadores formaram-se em 20 fileiras; **to be 4 metres ~** ter 4 metros de profundidade; **deepen** vt aprofundar ▷ vi aumentar

deer [dɪəʳ] n inv veado, cervo
default [dɪ'fɔ:lt] n (Comput: also: **~ value**) valor m de default; **by ~** (win) por desistência
defeat [dɪ'fi:t] n derrota; (failure) malogro ▷ vt derrotar, vencer
defect [(n) 'di:fɛkt, (vb) dɪ'fɛkt] n defeito ▷ vi: **to ~ to the enemy** desertar para se juntar ao inimigo; **defective** [dɪ'fɛktɪv] adj defeituoso
defence [dɪ'fɛns] (US **defense**) n defesa, justificação f
defend [dɪ'fɛnd] vt defender; (Law) contestar; **defendant** n acusado(-a); (in civil case) réu (ré) m/f; **defender** n defensor(a) m/f; (Sport) defesa
defer [dɪ'fə:ʳ] vt (postpone) adiar
defiance [dɪ'faɪəns] n desafio, rebeldia; **in ~ of** a despeito de
defiant [dɪ'faɪənt] adj desafiador(a)
deficiency [dɪ'fɪʃənsɪ] n (lack) deficiência, falta; (defect) defeito
deficit ['dɛfɪsɪt] n déficit m
define [dɪ'faɪn] vt definir
definite ['dɛfɪnɪt] adj (fixed) definitivo; (clear, obvious) claro, categórico; (certain) certo; **he was ~ about it** ele foi categórico; **definitely** adv sem dúvida
deflate [di:'fleɪt] vt esvaziar
deflect [dɪ'flɛkt] vt desviar
defraud [dɪ'frɔ:d] vt: **to ~ sb (of sth)** trapacear alguém (por causa de algo)
defrost [di:'frɔst] vt descongelar
defuse [di:'fju:z] vt tirar o estopim or a espoleta de; (situation) neutralizar
defy [dɪ'faɪ] vt desafiar; (resist) opor-se a
degree [dɪ'gri:] n grau m; (Sch) diploma m, título; **~ in maths** formatura em matemática; **by ~s** (gradually) pouco a pouco; **to some ~, to a certain ~** até certo ponto
dehydrated [di:haɪ'dreɪtɪd] adj desidratado; (eggs, milk) em pó
delay [dɪ'leɪ] vt (decision etc) retardar, atrasar; (train, person) atrasar ▷ vi hesitar ▷ n demora; (postponement) adiamento; **to be ~ed** estar atrasado; **without ~** sem demora or atraso
delegate [(n) 'dɛlɪgɪt, (vb) 'dɛlɪgeɪt] n delegado(-a) ▷ vt (person) autorizar; (task) delegar
delete [dɪ'li:t] vt eliminar, riscar; (Comput) deletar
deliberate [(adj) dɪ'lɪbərɪt, (vb) dɪ'lɪbəreɪt] adj (intentional) intencional; (slow) pausado, lento ▷ vi considerar;

deliberately [dɪ'lɪbərɪtlɪ] adv (on purpose) de propósito

delicacy ['dɛlɪkəsɪ] n delicadeza; (of problem) dificuldade f; (food) iguaria

delicate ['dɛlɪkɪt] adj delicado; (health) frágil

delicatessen [dɛlɪkə'tɛsn] n delicatessen m

delicious [dɪ'lɪʃəs] adj delicioso; (food) saboroso

delight [dɪ'laɪt] n prazer m, deleite m; (person) encanto; (experience) delícia ▷ vt encantar, deleitar; **to take (a) ~ in** deleitar-se com; **delighted** adj: **delighted (at** or **with)** encantado (com); **delightful** adj encantador(a), delicioso

delinquent [dɪ'lɪŋkwənt] adj, n delinqüente m/f

deliver [dɪ'lɪvə'] vt (distribute) distribuir; (hand over) entregar; (message) comunicar; (speech) proferir; (Med) partejar; **delivery** n distribuição f; (of speaker) enunciação f; (Med) parto; **to take delivery of** receber

delusion [dɪ'lu:ʒən] n ilusão f

demand [dɪ'mɑ:nd] vt exigir; (rights) reivindicar, reclamar ▷ n exigência; (claim) reivindicação f; (Econ) procura; **to be in ~** estar em demanda; **on ~** à vista; **demanding** adj (boss) exigente; (work) absorvente

demise [dɪ'maɪz] n falecimento

demo ['dɛməu] (inf) n abbr (= demonstration) passeata

democracy [dɪ'mɔkrəsɪ] n democracia; **democrat** ['dɛməkræt] n democrata m/f; **democratic** [dɛmə'krætɪk] adj democrático

demolish [dɪ'mɔlɪʃ] vt demolir, derrubar; (argument) refutar, contestar

demonstrate ['dɛmənstreɪt] vt demonstrar ▷ vi: **to ~ (for/against)** manifestar-se (a favor de/contra); **demonstration** [dɛmən'streɪʃən] n (Pol) manifestação f; (: march) passeata; (proof) demonstração f; (exhibition) exibição f; **demonstrator** n manifestante m/f

demote [dɪ'məut] vt rebaixar de posto

den [dɛn] n (of animal) covil m; (of thieves) antro, esconderijo; (room) aposento privado, cantinho

denial [dɪ'naɪəl] n refutação f; (refusal) negativa

denim ['dɛnɪm] n brim m, zuarte m; **denims** npl jeans m (BR), jeans mpl (PT)

Denmark ['dɛnmɑ:k] n Dinamarca

denomination [dɪnɔmɪ'neɪʃən] n valor m, denominação f; (Rel) confissão f, seita

denounce [dɪ'nauns] vt denunciar

dense [dɛns] adj denso, espesso; (inf: stupid) estúpido, bronco

density ['dɛnsɪtɪ] n densidade f; **single/double ~ disk** (Comput) disco de densidade simples/dupla

dent [dɛnt] n amolgadura, depressão f ▷ vt amolgar, dentar

dental ['dɛntl] adj (treatment) dentário; (hygiene) dental

dentist ['dɛntɪst] n dentista m/f

dentures ['dɛntʃəz] npl dentadura

deny [dɪ'naɪ] vt negar; (refuse) recusar

deodorant [di:'əudərənt] n desodorante m (BR), desodorizante m (PT)

depart [dɪ'pɑ:t] vi ir-se, partir; (train etc) sair; **to ~ from** (fig: differ from) afastar-se de

department [dɪ'pɑ:tmənt] n (Sch) departamento; (Comm) seção f; (Pol) repartição f; **department store** n magazine m (BR), grande armazém m (PT)

departure [dɪ'pɑ:tʃə'] n partida, ida; (of train etc) saída; (of employee) saída; **a new ~** uma nova orientação; **departure lounge** n sala de embarque

depend [dɪ'pɛnd] vi: **to ~ (up)on** depender de; (rely on) contar com; **it ~s** depende; **~ing on the result ...** dependendo do resultado ...; **dependant** n dependente m/f; **dependent** adj: **to be dependent (on)** depender (de), ser dependente (de) ▷ n = **dependant**

depict [dɪ'pɪkt] vt (in picture) retratar, representar; (describe) descrever

deport [dɪ'pɔ:t] vt deportar

deposit [dɪ'pɔzɪt] n (Comm, Geo) depósito; (Chem) sedimento; (of ore, oil) jazida; (down payment) sinal m ▷ vt depositar; (luggage) guardar; **deposit account** n conta de depósito a prazo

depot ['dɛpəu] n (storehouse) depósito, armazém m; (for vehicles) garagem f, parque m; (US) estação f

depress [dɪ'prɛs] vt deprimir; (wages) reduzir; (press down) apertar; **depressed** adj deprimido; (area) em depressão; **depressing** adj deprimente; **depression** n depressão f; (hollow) achatamento

deprive [dɪ'praɪv] vt: **to ~ sb of** privar alguém de; **deprived** adj carente

depth [dɛpθ] n profundidade f; (of feeling) intensidade f; **in the ~s of despair** no

auge do desespero; **to be out of one's ~**
(BRIT: *swimmer*) estar sem pé; (*fig*) estar
voando
deputy ['dɛpjutɪ] *adj*: **~ chairman**
vice-presidente(-a) *m/f* ▷ *n* (*assistant*)
adjunto(-a); (*Pol: MP*) deputado(-a); **~
head** (BRIT: *Sch*) diretor adjunto (diretora
adjunta) *m/f*
derail [dɪ'reɪl] *vt*: **to be ~ed** descarrilhar
derelict ['dɛrɪlɪkt] *adj* abandonado
derive [dɪ'raɪv] *vt*: **to ~ (from)** obter or
tirar (de) ▷ *vi*: **to ~ from** derivar-se de
descend [dɪ'sɛnd] *vt, vi* descer; **to ~
from**: **to ~ to** descambar em;
descent *n* descida; (*origin*) descendência
describe [dɪs'kraɪb] *vt* descrever;
description [dɪs'krɪpʃən] *n* descrição *f*;
(*sort*) classe *f*, espécie *f*
desert [(*n*) 'dɛzət, (*vb*) dɪ'zə:t] *n* deserto
▷ *vt* (*place*) desertar; (*partner, family*)
abandonar ▷ *vi* (*Mil*) desertar
deserve [dɪ'zə:v] *vt* merecer
design [dɪ'zaɪn] *n* (*sketch*) desenho,
esboço; (*layout, shape*) plano, projeto;
(*pattern*) desenho, padrão *m*; (*art*) design
m; (*intention*) propósito, intenção *f* ▷ *vt*
(*plan*) projetar
designer [dɪ'zaɪnəʳ] *n* (*Art*) artista
m/f gráfico(-a); (*Tech*) desenhista *m/f*,
projetista *m/f*; (*fashion designer*) estilista
m/f
desire [dɪ'zaɪəʳ] *n* anseio; (*sexual*) desejo
▷ *vt* querer, desejar, cobiçar
desk [dɛsk] *n* (*in office*) mesa, secretária;
(*for pupil*) carteira *f*; (*at airport*) balcão
m; (*in hotel*) recepção *f*; (BRIT: *in shop*,
restaurant) caixa
despair [dɪs'pɛəʳ] *n* desesperança ▷ *vi*: **to
~ of** desesperar-se de
despatch [dɪs'pætʃ] *n, vt* = **dispatch**
desperate ['dɛspərɪt] *adj* desesperado;
(*situation*) desesperador(a); (*fugitive*)
violento; **to be ~ for sth/to do** estar
louco por algo/para fazer; **desperately**
adv desesperadamente; (*very: unhappy*)
terrivelmente; (: *ill*) gravemente;
desperation [dɛspə'reɪʃən] *n*
desespero, desesperança; **in (sheer)
desperation** desesperado
despise [dɪs'paɪz] *vt* desprezar
despite [dɪs'paɪt] *prep* apesar de, a
despeito de
dessert [dɪ'zə:t] *n* sobremesa
destination [dɛstɪ'neɪʃən] *n* destino
destined ['dɛstɪnd] *adj*: **to be ~ to do sth**
estar destinado a fazer algo; **~ for** com

destino a
destiny ['dɛstɪnɪ] *n* destino
destroy [dɪs'trɔɪ] *vt* destruir; (*animal*)
sacrificar; **destruction** *n* destruição *f*
detach [dɪ'tætʃ] *vt* separar;
(*unstick*) desprender; **detached** *adj*
(*attitude*) imparcial, objetivo; (*house*)
independente, isolado
detail ['di:teɪl] *n* detalhe *m*; (*trifle*)
bobagem *f* ▷ *vt* detalhar; **in ~**
pormenorizado, em detalhe
detain [dɪ'teɪn] *vt* deter; (*in captivity*)
prender; (*in hospital*) hospitalizar
detect [dɪ'tɛkt] *vt* perceber; (*Med, Police*)
identificar; (*Mil, Radar, Tech*) detectar;
detection *n* descoberta; **detective**
n detetive *m/f*; **detective story** *n*
romance *m* policial
detention [dɪ'tɛnʃən] *n* detenção *f*,
prisão *f*; (*Sch*) castigo
deter [dɪ'tə:ʳ] *vt* (*discourage*) desanimar;
(*dissuade*) dissuadir
detergent [dɪ'tə:dʒənt] *n* detergente *m*
deteriorate [dɪ'tɪərɪəreɪt] *vi* deteriorar-
se
determine [dɪ'tə:mɪn] *vt* descobrir;
(*limits*) demarcar; **determined** *adj*
(*person*) resoluto; **determined to do**
decidido a fazer
detour ['di:tuəʳ] *n* desvio
detract [dɪ'trækt] *vi*: **to ~ from** diminuir
detrimental [dɛtrɪ'mɛntl] *adj*: **~ (to)**
prejudicial (a)
develop [dɪ'vɛləp] *vt* desenvolver; (*Phot*)
revelar; (*disease*) contrair; (*resources*)
explotar ▷ *vi* (*advance*) progredir; (*evolve*)
evoluir; (*appear*) aparecer; **development**
[dɪ'vɛləpməntd] *n* desenvolvimento;
(*advance*) progresso; (*of land*)
urbanização *f*
device [dɪ'vaɪs] *n* aparelho, dispositivo
devil ['dɛvl] *n* diabo
devious ['di:vɪəs] *adj* (*person*) malandro,
esperto
devise [dɪ'vaɪz] *vt* (*plan*) criar; (*machine*)
inventar
devote [dɪ'vəut] *vt*: **to ~ sth to**
dedicar algo a; **devoted** [dɪ'vəutɪd]
adj (*friendship*) leal; (*partner*) fiel; **to be
devoted to** estar devotado a; **the book
is devoted to politics** o livro trata de
política; **devotion** *n* devoção *f*; (*to duty*)
dedicação *f*
devour [dɪ'vauəʳ] *vt* devorar
devout [dɪ'vaut] *adj* devoto
dew [dju:] *n* orvalho

diabetes [daɪəˈbiːtiːz] n diabete f
diagnosis [daɪəgˈnəʊsɪs] (pl **diagnoses**) n diagnóstico
diagonal [daɪˈægənl] adj diagonal ▷ n diagonal f
diagram [ˈdaɪəgræm] n diagrama m, esquema m
dial [ˈdaɪəl] n disco ▷ vt (number) discar (BR), marcar (PT)
dialect [ˈdaɪəlɛkt] n dialeto
dialling code [ˈdaɪəlɪŋ-] (us **dial code**) n código de discagem
dialling tone [ˈdaɪəlɪŋ-] (us **dial tone**) n sinal m de discagem (BR) or de marcar (PT)
dialogue [ˈdaɪəlɔg] (us **dialog**) n diálogo; (conversation) conversa
diameter [daɪˈæmɪtəʳ] n diâmetro
diamond [ˈdaɪəmənd] n diamante m; (shape) losango, rombo; **diamonds** npl (Cards) ouros mpl
diarrhoea [daɪəˈriːə] (us **diarrhea**) n diarréia
diary [ˈdaɪərɪ] n (daily account) diário; (engagements book) agenda
dice [daɪs] n inv dado ▷ vt (Culin) cortar em cubos
dictate [dɪkˈteɪt] vt ditar; **dictation** n (of letter) ditado; (of orders) ordem f
dictator [dɪkˈteɪtəʳ] n ditador(a) m/f
dictionary [ˈdɪkʃənrɪ] n dicionário
did [dɪd] pt of **do**
didn't [ˈdɪdnt] = **did not**
die [daɪ] vi morrer; (fig: fade) murchar; **to be dying for sth/to do sth** estar louco por algo/para fazer algo; **die away** vi (sound, light) extinguir-se lentamente; **die down** vi (fire) apagar-se; (wind) abrandar; (excitement) diminuir; **die out** vi desaparecer
diesel [ˈdiːzl] n diesel m; (also: **~ oil**) óleo diesel
diet [ˈdaɪət] n dieta; (restricted food) regime m ▷ vi (also: **be on a ~**) estar de dieta, fazer regime
differ [ˈdɪfəʳ] vi (be different): **to ~ from sth** ser diferente de algo, diferenciar-se de algo; (disagree): **to ~ (about)** discordar (sobre); **difference** n diferença; (disagreement) divergência; **different** adj diferente; **differentiate** [dɪfəˈrɛnʃɪeɪt] vi: **to differentiate (between)** distinguir (entre)
difficult [ˈdɪfɪkəlt] adj difícil; **difficulty** n dificuldade f
dig [dɪg] (pt, pp **dug**) vt cavar ▷ n (prod) pontada; (archaeological) excavação f;

(remark) alfinetada; **to ~ one's nails into sth** cravar as unhas em algo; **dig into** vt fus (savings) gastar; **dig up** vt (plant) arrancar; (information) trazer à tona
digest [(vb) daɪˈdʒɛst, (n) ˈdaɪdʒɛst] vt (food) digerir; (facts) assimilar ▷ n sumário; **digestion** [dɪˈdʒɛstʃən] n digestão f
digit [ˈdɪdʒɪt] n (Math) dígito; (finger) dedo
digital adj digital; **digital camera** n câmara digital; **digital TV** n televisão f digital
dignified [ˈdɪgnɪfaɪd] adj digno
dignity [ˈdɪgnɪtɪ] n dignidade f
dilemma [daɪˈlɛmə] n dilema m
dilute [daɪˈluːt] vt diluir
dim [dɪm] adj fraco; (outline) indistinto; (room) escuro; (inf: person) burro ▷ vt diminuir; (us: Aut) baixar
dime [daɪm] (us) n dez centavos
dimension [dɪˈmɛnʃən] n dimensão f; (measurement) medida; (also: **~s**: scale, size) tamanho
diminish [dɪˈmɪnɪʃ] vi diminuir
din [dɪn] n zoeira
dine [daɪn] vi jantar; **diner** n comensal m/f; (us: eating place) lanchonete f
dinghy [ˈdɪŋgɪ] n dingue m; (also: **rubber ~**) bote m; (also: **sailing ~**) bote de borracha
dingy [ˈdɪndʒɪ] adj (room) sombrio, lúgubre; (clothes, curtains etc) sujo
dining car [ˈdaɪnɪŋ-] (BRIT) n (Rail) vagão-restaurante m
dining room [ˈdaɪnɪŋ-] n sala de jantar
dinner [ˈdɪnəʳ] n (evening meal) jantar m; (lunch) almoço; (banquet) banquete m; **dinner jacket** n smoking m; **dinner party** n jantar m; **dinner time** n (midday) hora de almoçar; (evening) hora de jantar
dip [dɪp] n (slope) inclinação f; (in sea) mergulho; (Culin) pasta para servir com salgadinhos ▷ vt (in water) mergulhar; (ladle) meter; (BRIT: Aut: lights) baixar ▷ vi descer subitamente
diploma [dɪˈpləʊmə] n diploma m
diplomat [ˈdɪpləmæt] n diplomata m/f
dipstick [ˈdɪpstɪk] (us **diprod**) n (Aut) vareta medidora
dire [daɪəʳ] adj terrível
direct [daɪˈrɛkt] adj direto; (route) reto; (manner) franco, sincero ▷ vt dirigir; (order): **to ~ sb to do sth** ordenar alguém para fazer algo ▷ adv direto; **can you ~ me to ...?** pode me indicar o caminho

a ...?; **direction** n (way) indicação f; (TV, Radio, Cinema) direção f; **directions** npl (instructions) instruções fpl; **directions for use** modo de usar; **directly** adv diretamente; (at once) imediatamente; **director** n diretor(a) m/f

directory [dɪˈrɛktərɪ] n (Tel) lista (telefônica); (also Comm) anuário comercial; (Comput) diretório; **directory enquiries** (us **directory assistance**) n informações fpl

dirt [dɜːt] n sujeira (BR), sujidade (PT); **dirty** adj sujo; (joke) indecente ▷ vt sujar

disability [dɪsəˈbɪlɪtɪ] n incapacidade f

disabled [dɪsˈeɪbld] adj deficiente ▷ npl: **the ~** os deficientes

disadvantage [dɪsədˈvɑːntɪdʒ] n desvantagem f; (prejudice) inconveniente m

disagree [dɪsəˈɡriː] vi (differ) diferir; (be against, think otherwise): **to ~ (with)** não concordar (com), discordar (de); **disagreeable** adj desagradável; **disagreement** n desacordo; (quarrel) desavença

disappear [dɪsəˈpɪər] vi desaparecer, sumir; (custom etc) acabar; **disappearance** n desaparecimento, desaparição f

disappoint [dɪsəˈpɔɪnt] vt decepcionar; **disappointed** adj desiludido; **disappointment** n decepção f; (cause) desapontamento

disapproval [dɪsəˈpruːvəl] n desaprovação f

disapprove [dɪsəˈpruːv] vi: **to ~ of** desaprovar

disarmament n desarmamento

disaster [dɪˈzɑːstər] n (accident) desastre m; (natural) catástrofe f

disbelief [dɪsbəˈliːf] n incredulidade f

disc [dɪsk] n disco; (Comput) = **disk**

discard [dɪsˈkɑːd] vt (old things) desfazer-se de; (fig) descartar

discharge [(vb) dɪsˈtʃɑːdʒ, (n) ˈdɪstʃɑːdʒ] vt (duties) cumprir, desempenhar; (patient) dar alta a; (employee) despedir; (soldier) dar baixa em, dispensar; (defendant) pôr em liberdade; (waste etc) descarregar, despejar ▷ n (Elec, Chem) descarga; (dismissal) despedida; (of duty) desempenho; (of debt) quitação f; (from hospital) alta; (from army) baixa; (Law) absolvição f; (Med) secreção f

discipline [ˈdɪsɪplɪn] n disciplina ▷ vt disciplinar; (punish) punir

disc jockey n (on radio) radialista m/f; (in disco) discotecário(-a)

disclose [dɪsˈkləuz] vt revelar

disco [ˈdɪskəu] n abbr discoteca

discomfort [dɪsˈkʌmfət] n (unease) inquietação f; (physical) desconforto

disconnect [dɪskəˈnɛkt] vt desligar; (pipe, tap) desmembrar

discontent [dɪskənˈtɛnt] n descontentamento

discontinue [dɪskənˈtɪnjuː] vt interromper; (payments) suspender; **"~d"** (Comm) "fora de linha"

discount [(n) ˈdɪskaunt, (vb) dɪsˈkaunt] n desconto ▷ vt descontar; (idea) ignorar

discourage [dɪsˈkʌrɪdʒ] vt (dishearten) desanimar; (advise against): **to ~ sth/sb from doing** desaconselhar algo/alguém a fazer

discover [dɪsˈkʌvər] vt descobrir; (missing person) encontrar; (mistake) achar; **discovery** n descoberta

discredit [dɪsˈkrɛdɪt] vt desacreditar; (claim) desmerecer

discreet [dɪˈskriːt] adj discreto; (careful) cauteloso

discrepancy [dɪˈskrɛpənsɪ] n diferença

discretion [dɪˈskrɛʃən] n discrição f; **at the ~ of** ao arbítrio de

discriminate [dɪsˈkrɪmɪneɪt] vi: **to ~ between** fazer distinção entre; **to ~ against** discriminar contra; **discrimination** [dɪskrɪmɪˈneɪʃən] n (discernment) discernimento; (bias) discriminação f

discuss [dɪsˈkʌs] vt discutir; (analyse) analisar; **discussion** n discussão f; (debate) debate m

disease [dɪˈziːz] n doença

disembark [dɪsɪmˈbɑːk] vt, vi desembarcar

disgrace [dɪsˈɡreɪs] n ignomínia; (shame) desonra ▷ vt (family) envergonhar; (name, country) desonrar; **disgraceful** adj vergonhoso; (behaviour) escandaloso

disgruntled [dɪsˈɡrʌntld] adj descontente

disguise [dɪsˈɡaɪz] n disfarce m ▷ vt: **to ~ (as)** disfarçar (de); **in ~** disfarçado

disgust [dɪsˈɡʌst] n repugnância ▷ vt repugnar a, dar nojo em; **disgusting** adj repugnante; (unacceptable) inaceitável

dish [dɪʃ] n prato; (serving dish) travessa; **to do** or **wash the ~es** lavar os pratos or a louça; **dish out** vt repartir; **dish up** vt servir; **dishcloth** n pano de prato or

de louça
dishonest [dɪs'ɔnɪst] *adj* (*person*)
desonesto; (*means*) fraudulento
dishwasher ['dɪʃwɔʃə*r*] *n* máquina de
lavar louça *or* pratos
disillusion [dɪsɪ'luːʒən] *vt* desiludir
disinfectant [dɪsɪn'fɛktənt] *n*
desinfetante *m*
disintegrate [dɪs'ɪntɪgreɪt] *vi*
desintegrar-se
disk [dɪsk] *n* (*Comput*) disco; **single-/
double-sided ~** disquete de face
simples/dupla; **disk drive** *n* unidade *f* de
disco; **diskette** [dɪs'kɛt] (*us*) *n* = **disk**
dislike [dɪs'laɪk] *n* (*feeling*) desagrado;
(*gen pl: object of dislike*) antipatia, aversão
f ▷ *vt* antipatizar com, não gostar de
dislocate ['dɪsləkeɪt] *vt* deslocar
disloyal [dɪs'lɔɪəl] *adj* desleal
dismal ['dɪzml] *adj* (*depressing*)
deprimente; (*very bad*) horrível
dismantle [dɪs'mæntl] *vt* desmontar,
desmantelar
dismay [dɪs'meɪ] *n* consternação *f* ▷ *vt*
consternar
dismiss [dɪs'mɪs] *vt* (*worker*) despedir;
(*pupils*) dispensar; (*soldiers*) dar baixa
a; (*Law, possibility*) rejeitar; **dismissal**
n demissão *f*; **disobedient** *adj*
desobediente
disobey [dɪsə'beɪ] *vt* desobedecer a;
(*rules*) transgredir
disorder [dɪs'ɔːdə*r*] *n* desordem *f*; (*rioting*)
distúrbios *mpl*, tumulto; (*Med*) distúrbio
disown [dɪs'əun] *vt* repudiar; (*child*)
rejeitar
dispatch [dɪs'pætʃ] *vt* (*send: parcel etc*)
expedir; (*: messenger*) enviar ▷ *n* (*sending*)
remessa, urgência; (*Press*) comunicado,
(*Mil*) parte *f*
dispel [dɪs'pɛl] *vt* dissipar
dispense [dɪs'pɛns] *vt* (*medicine*)
preparar (e vender); **dispense with** *vt*
fus prescindir de; **dispenser** *n* (*device*)
distribuidor *m* automático
disperse [dɪs'pəːs] *vt* espalhar; (*crowd*)
dispersar ▷ *vi* dispersar-se
display [dɪs'pleɪ] *n* (*in shop*) mostra;
(*exhibition*) exposição *f*; (*Comput,
Tech: information*) apresentação *f*
visual; (*: device*) display *m*; (*of feeling*)
manifestação *f* ▷ *vt* mostrar;
(*ostentatiously*) ostentar
displease [dɪs'pliːz] *vt* (*offend*) ofender;
(*annoy*) aborrecer
disposable [dɪs'pəuzəbl] *adj*

disposal [dɪs'pəuzl] *n* (*of rubbish*)
destruição *f*; (*of property etc*) venda,
traspasse *m*; **at sb's ~** à disposição de
alguém; **disposition** [dɪspə'zɪʃən] *n*
disposição *f*; (*temperament*) índole *f*
dispute [dɪs'pjuːt] *n* (*domestic*) briga;
(*also:* **industrial ~**) conflito, disputa ▷ *vt*
(*fact, statement*) questionar; (*ownership*)
contestar
disqualify [dɪs'kwɔlɪfaɪ] *vt* (*Sport*)
desclassificar; **to ~ sb for sth/from
doing sth** desqualificar alguém para
algo/de fazer algo
disregard [dɪsrɪ'gaːd] *vt* ignorar
disrupt [dɪs'rʌpt] *vt* (*plans*) desfazer;
(*conversation*) perturbar, interromper
dissect [dɪ'sɛkt] *vt* dissecar
dissent [dɪ'sɛnt] *n* dissensão *f*
dissertation [dɪsə'teɪʃən] *n* (*also: Sch*)
dissertação *f*, tese *f*
dissolve [dɪ'zɔlv] *vt* dissolver ▷ *vi*
dissolver-se; **to ~ in(to) tears** debulhar-
se em lágrimas
distance ['dɪstns] *n* distância; **in the ~**
ao longe
distant ['dɪstnt] *adj* distante; (*manner*)
afastado, reservado
distil [dɪs'tɪl] (*us* **distill**) *vt* destilar;
distillery *n* destilaria
distinct [dɪs'tɪŋkt] *adj* distinto; (*clear*)
claro; (*unmistakable*) nítido; **as ~ from**
em oposição a; **distinction** *n* diferença;
(*honour*) honra; (*in exam*) distinção *f*
distinguish [dɪs'tɪŋgwɪʃ] *vt* (*differentiate*)
diferenciar; (*identify*) identificar; **to ~
o.s.** distinguir-se; **distinguished** *adj*
(*eminent*) eminente; (*in appearance*)
distinto
distort [dɪs'tɔːt] *vt* distorcer
distract [dɪs'trækt] *vt* distrair; (*attention*)
desviar; **distracted** *adj* distraído;
(*anxious*) aturdido; **distraction** *n*
distração *f*; (*confusion*) aturdimento,
perplexidade *f*; (*amusement*) divertimento
distraught [dɪs'trɔːt] *adj* desesperado
distress [dɪs'trɛs] *n* angústia ▷ *vt* afligir;
distressing *adj* angustiante
distribute [dɪs'trɪbjuːt] *vt* distribuir;
(*share out*) repartir, dividir; **distribution**
[dɪstrɪ'bjuːʃən] *n* distribuição *f*; (*of
profits*) repartição *f*; **distributor** *n* (*Aut*)
distribuidor *m*; (*Comm*) distribuidor(a)
m/f
district ['dɪstrɪkt] *n* (*of country*) região *f*;
(*of town*) zona; (*Admin*) distrito; **district**

attorney (US) n promotor público
(promotora pública) m/f
distrust [dɪsˈtrʌst] n desconfiança ▷ vt
desconfiar de
disturb [dɪsˈtəːb] vt (disorganize)
perturbar; (upset) incomodar; (interrupt)
atrapalhar; **disturbance** n (upheaval)
convulsão f; (political, violent) distúrbio;
(of mind) transtorno; **disturbed**
adj perturbado; (childhood) infeliz;
to be emotionally disturbed ter
problemas emocionais; **disturbing** adj
perturbador(a)
ditch [dɪtʃ] n fosso; (irrigation ditch) rego
▷ vt (inf: partner) abandonar; (: car, plan
etc) desfazer-se de
ditto [ˈdɪtəu] adv idem
dive [daɪv] n (from board) salto;
(underwater) mergulho ▷ vi mergulhar;
to ~ into (bag, drawer) enfiar a mão
em; (shop, car) enfiar-se em; **diver** n
mergulhador(a) m/f
diversion n (BRIT: Aut) desvio;
(distraction) diversão f; (of funds) desvio
divert [daɪˈvəːt] vt desviar
divide [dɪˈvaɪd] vt (Math) dividir;
(separate) separar; (share out) repartir
▷ vi dividir-se; (road) bifurcar-se; **divided
highway** (US) n pista dupla
divine [dɪˈvaɪn] adj (also fig) divino
diving [ˈdaɪvɪŋ] n salto; (underwater)
mergulho; **diving board** n trampolim m
division [dɪˈvɪʒən] n divisão f; (sharing
out) repartição f; (disagreement) discórdia;
(Football) grupo
divorce [dɪˈvɔːs] n divórcio ▷ vt divorciar-
se de; (dissociate) dissociar; **divorced** adj
divorciado; **divorcee** n divorciado(-a)
DIY n abbr = **do-it-yourself**
dizzy [ˈdɪzɪ] adj tonto
DJ n abbr = **disc jockey**

○ **KEYWORD**

do [duː] (pt **did**, pp **done**) vb aux
1 (in negative constructions): **I don't
understand** eu não compreendo
2 (to form questions): **didn't you know?**
você não sabia?; **what do you think?** o
que você acha?
3 (for emphasis, in polite expressions): **she
does seem rather late** ela está muito
atrasada; **do sit down/help yourself**
sente-se/sirva-se; **do take care!** tome
cuidado!
4 (used to avoid repeating vb): **she swims**

better than I do ela nada melhor que
eu; **do you agree? - yes, I do/no, I don't**
você concorda? - sim, concordo/não,
não concordo; **she lives in Glasgow - so
do I** ela mora em Glasgow - eu também;
who broke it? - I did quem quebrou isso?
- (fui) eu
5 (in question tags): **you like him,
don't you?** você gosta dele, não é?; **he
laughed, didn't he?** ele riu, não foi?
▷ vt **1** (gen: carry out, perform etc) fazer;
what are you doing tonight? o que
você vai fazer hoje à noite?; **to do the
washing-up/cooking** lavar a louça/
cozinhar; **to do one's teeth/nails**
escovar os dentes/fazer as unhas; **to do
one's hair** (comb) pentear-se; (style) fazer
um penteado; **we're doing Othello
at school** (studying) nós estamos
estudando Otelo na escola; (performing)
nós vamos encenar Otelo na escola
2 (Aut etc): **the car was doing 100** o
carro estava a 100 por hora; **we've done
200 km already** nós já fizemos 200 km;
he can do 100 in that car ele consegue
dar 100 nesse carro
▷ vi **1** (act, behave) fazer; **do as I do** faça
como eu faço
2 (get on, fare) ir; **how do you do?** como
você está indo?
3 (suit) servir; **will it do?** serve?
4 (be sufficient) bastar; **will £10 do?** £10
dá?; **that'll do** é suficiente; **that'll do!** (in
annoyance) basta!, chega!; **to make do
(with)** contentar-se (com)
▷ n (inf: party etc) festa; **it was rather a
do** foi uma festança
do away with vt fus (kill) matar; (law etc)
abolir; (withdraw) retirar
do up vt (laces) atar; (zip) fechar; (dress,
skirt) abotoar; (renovate: room, house)
arrumar, renovar
do with vt fus (need): **I could do with a
drink/some help** eu bem que gostaria
de tomar alguma coisa/eu bem que
precisaria de uma ajuda; (be connected)
ter a ver com; **what has it got to do
with you?** o que é que isso tem a ver com
você?
do without vi: **if you're late for tea
then you'll do without** se você chegar
atrasado ficará sem almoço
▷ vt fus passar sem

dock [dɔk] n (Naut) doca; (Law) banco
(dos réus) ▷ vi (Naut: enter dock) entrar

no estaleiro; (*Space*) unir-se no espaço; **docks** *npl* docas *fpl*

doctor ['dɒktə'] *n* médico(-a); (*PhD etc*) doutor(a) *m/f* ▷ *vt* (*drink etc*) falsificar

document ['dɒkjumənt] *n* documento; **documentary** [dɒkju'mɛntəri] *adj* documental ▷ *n* documentário

dodge [dɒdʒ] *n* (*trick*) trapaça ▷ *vt* esquivar-se de, evitar; (*tax*) sonegar; (*blow*) furtar-se a

does [dʌz] *vb see* **do**; **doesn't** = **does not**

dog [dɒg] *n* cachorro, cão *m* ▷ *vt* (*subj: person*) seguir; (: *bad luck*) perseguir

do-it-yourself *n* sistema *m* faça-você-mesmo

dole [dəʊl] (*BRIT*) *n* (*payment*) subsídio de desemprego; **on the ~** desempregado; **dole out** *vt* distribuir

doll [dɒl] *n* boneca; (*US: inf: woman*) mulher *f* jovem e bonita

dollar ['dɒlə'] *n* dólar *m*

dolphin ['dɒlfɪn] *n* golfinho

dome [dəʊm] *n* (*Arch*) cúpula

domestic [də'mɛstɪk] *adj* doméstico; (*national*) nacional

dominate ['dɒmɪneɪt] *vt* dominar

domino ['dɒmɪnəʊ] (*pl ~es*) *n* peça de dominó; **dominoes** *n* (*game*) dominó *m*

donate [də'neɪt] *vt*: **to ~ (to)** doar (para)

done [dʌn] *pp of* **do**

donkey ['dɒŋkɪ] *n* burro

donor ['dəʊnə'] *n* doador(a) *m/f*; **donor card** *n* cartão *m* de doador

don't [dəʊnt] = **do not**

doodle ['duːdl] *vi* rabiscar

doom [duːm] *n* (*fate*) destino ▷ *vt*: **to be ~ed to failure** estar destinado *or* fadado ao fracasso

door [dɔː'] *n* porta; **doorbell** *n* campainha; **doorstep** *n* degrau *m* da porta, soleira; **doorway** *n* vão *m* da porta, entrada

dope [dəʊp] *n* (*inf: person*) imbecil *m/f*; (: *drug*) maconha ▷ *vt* (*horse etc*) dopar

dormitory ['dɔːmɪtrɪ] *n* dormitório; (*US*) residência universitária

dose [dəʊs] *n* dose *f*

dot [dɒt] *n* ponto; (*speck*) marca pequena ▷ *vt*: **~ted with** salpicado de; **on the ~** em ponto

dotcom [dɒt'kɒm] *n* empresa pontocom

double ['dʌbl] *adj* duplo ▷ *adv* (*twice*): **to cost ~ (sth)** custar o dobro (de algo) ▷ *n* (*person*) duplo(-a) ▷ *vt* dobrar ▷ *vi* dobrar; **at the ~** (*BRIT*), **on the ~** em passo acelerado; **double bass**

n contrabaixo; **double bed** *n* cama de casal; **double-click** ['dʌbl'klɪk] *vi* (*Comput*) dar um clique duplo; **doubledecker** *n* ônibus *m* (*BR*) *or* autocarro (*PT*) de dois andares; **double room** *n* quarto de casal

doubt [daʊt] *n* dúvida ▷ *vt* duvidar; (*suspect*) desconfiar de; **to ~ if** *or* **whether** duvidar que; **doubtful** *adj* duvidoso; **doubtless** *adv* sem dúvida

dough [dəʊ] *n* massa; **doughnut** (*US* **donut**) *n* sonho (*BR*), bola de Berlim (*PT*)

dove [dʌv] *n* pomba

down [daʊn] *n* (*feathers*) penugem *f* ▷ *adv* (*downwards*) para baixo; (*on the ground*) por terra ▷ *prep* (*towards lower level*) embaixo de; (*movement along*) ao longo de ▷ *vt* (*inf: drink*) tomar de um gole só; **~ with X!** abaixo X!; **down-and-out** *n* (*tramp*) vagabundo(-a); **downfall** *n* queda, ruína; **downhill** *adv*: **to go downhill** descer, ir morro abaixo; (*fig: business*) degringolar

Downing Street ['daʊnɪŋ-] (*BRIT*) *n ver* quadro

◈ **DOWNING STREET**
◈
◈ **Downing Street** é a rua de
◈ Westminster (Londres) onde estão
◈ localizadas as residências oficiais
◈ do Primeiro-ministro (número 10)
◈ e do Ministro da Fazenda (número
◈ 11). O termo **Downing Street** é
◈ freqüentemente utilizado para
◈ designar o governo britânico.

down: **download** [daʊn'ləʊd] *vt* (*Comput*) fazer o download de, baixar; **downright** *adj* (*lie*) patente; (*refusal*) categórico; **downstairs** *adv* (*below*) (lá) em baixo; (*downwards*) para baixo; **down-to-earth** *adj* prático, realista; **downtown** *adv* no centro da cidade; **down under** *adv* na Austrália (*or* Nova Zelândia); **downward** *adj*, *adv* para baixo; **downwards** *adv* = **downward**

doze [dəʊz] *vi* dormitar; **doze off** *vi* cochilar

dozen ['dʌzn] *n* dúzia; **a ~ books** uma dúzia de livros; **~s of** milhares de

drab [dræb] *adj* sombrio

draft [drɑːft] *n* (*first copy*) rascunho; (*Pol: of bill*) projeto de lei; (*bank draft*) saque *m*, letra; (*US: call-up*) recrutamento ▷ *vt* (*plan*) esboçar; (*speech, letter*) rascunhar;

see also **draught**

drag [dræg] *vt* arrastar; (*river*) dragar
▷ *vi* arrastar-se ▷ *n* (*inf*) chatice *f* (BR),
maçada (PT); (*women's clothing*): **in ~** em
travesti; **drag on** *vi* arrastar-se

dragon ['drægən] *n* dragão *m*

dragonfly ['drægənflaɪ] *n* libélula

drain [dreɪn] *n* bueiro; (*source of loss*)
sorvedouro ▷ *vt* (*glass*) esvaziar; (*land,
marshes*) drenar; (*vegetables*) coar ▷ *vi*
(*water*) escorrer, escoar-se; **drainage**
n (*act*) drenagem *f*; (*system*) esgoto;
drainpipe *n* cano de esgoto

drama ['drɑːmə] *n* (*art*) teatro; (*play*)
drama *m*; **dramatic** [drə'mætɪk] *adj*
dramático; (*theatrical*) teatral

drank [dræŋk] *pt of* **drink**

drape [dreɪp] *vt* ornar, cobrir

drastic ['dræstɪk] *adj* drástico

draught [drɑːft] (*us* **draft**) *n* (*of air*)
corrente *f*; (*Naut*) calado; (*beer*) chope *m*;
on ~ (*beer*) de barril; **draughts** (BRIT) *n*
(jogo de) damas *fpl*

draw [drɔː] (*pt* **drew**, *pp* **~n**) *vt* desenhar;
(*cart*) puxar; (*curtain*) fechar; (*gun*) sacar;
(*attract*) atrair; (*money*) tirar; (: *from
bank*) sacar ▷ *vi* empatar ▷ *n* empate *m*;
(*lottery*) sorteio; **to ~ near** aproximar-
se; **draw out** *vt* (*money*) sacar; **draw
up** *vi* (*stop*) parar(-se) ▷ *vt* (*chair etc*)
puxar; (*document*) redigir; **drawback**
n inconveniente *m*, desvantagem *f*;
drawer *n* gaveta; **drawing** *n* desenho;
drawing pin (BRIT) *n* tachinha (BR),
pionés *m* (PT); **drawing room** *n* sala de
visitas

drawn [drɔːn] *pp of* **draw**

dread [dred] *n* medo, pavor *m* ▷ *vt* temer,
recear, ter medo de; **dreadful** *adj* terrível

dream [driːm] (*pt, pp* **~ed** *or* **~t**) *n* sonho
▷ *vt, vi* sonhar

dreary ['drɪərɪ] *adj* (*talk, time*) monótono;
(*weather*) sombrio

drench [drentʃ] *vt* encharcar

dress [dres] *n* vestido; (*no pl: clothing*)
traje *m* ▷ *vt* vestir; (*wound*) fazer curativo
em ▷ *vi* vestir-se; **to get ~ed** vestir-se;
dress up *vi* vestir-se com elegância; (*in
fancy dress*) fantasiar-se; **dress circle**
(BRIT) *n* balcão *m* nobre; **dresser** *n*
(BRIT: *cupboard*) aparador *m*; (*us: chest of
drawers*) cômoda de espelho; **dressing** *n*
(*Med*) curativo; (*Culin*) molho; **dressing
gown** (BRIT) *n* roupão *m*; (*woman's*)
peignoir *m*; **dressing room** *n* (*Theatre*)
camarim *m*; (*Sport*) vestiário; **dressing

table** *n* penteadeira (BR), toucador *m*
(PT); **dressmaker** *n* costureiro(-a)

drew [druː] *pt of* **draw**

dribble ['drɪbl] *vi* (*baby*) babar ▷ *vt* (*ball*)
driblar

dried [draɪd] *adj* (*fruit, beans*) seco; (*eggs,
milk*) em pó

drier ['draɪə] *n* = **dryer**

drift [drɪft] *n* (*of current etc*) força; (*of
snow*) monte *m*; (*meaning*) sentido ▷ *vi*
(*boat*) derivar; (*sand, snow*) amontoar-se

drill [drɪl] *n* furadeira; (*of dentist*) broca;
(*for mining etc*) broca, furadeira; (*Mil*)
exercícios *mpl* militares ▷ *vt* furar,
brocar; (*Mil*) exercitar ▷ *vi* (*for oil*)
perfurar

drink [drɪŋk] (*pt* **drank**, *pp* **drunk**) *n*
bebida; (*sip*) gole *m* ▷ *vt, vi* beber; **a ~
of water** um copo d'água; **drinker** *n*
bebedor(a) *m/f*; **drinking water** *n* água
potável

drip [drɪp] *n* gotejar *m*; (*one drip*) gota,
pingo; (*Med*) gota a gota *m* ▷ *vi* gotejar;
(*tap*) pingar

drive [draɪv] (*pt* **drove**, *pp* **~n**) *n* passeio
(de automóvel); (*journey*) trajeto,
percurso; (*also*: **~way**) entrada; (*energy*)
energia, vigor *m*; (*campaign*) campanha;
(*Comput: also*: **disk ~**) unidade *f* de disco
▷ *vt* (*car*) dirigir (BR), guiar (PT); (*push*)
empurrar; (*Tech: motor*) acionar; (*nail
etc*) cravar ▷ *vi* (*Aut: at controls*) dirigir
(BR), guiar (PT); (: *travel*) ir de carro; **left-/
right-hand ~** direção à esquerda/direita;
to ~ sb mad deixar alguém louco

driver ['draɪvə] *n* motorista *m/f*; (*Rail*)
maquinista *m*; **driver's license** (US)
n carteira de motorista (BR), carta de
condução (PT)

driveway ['draɪvweɪ] *n* entrada

driving ['draɪvɪŋ] *n* direção *f* (BR),
condução *f* (PT); **driving instructor** *n*
instrutor(a) *m/f* de auto-escola (BR) or
de condução (PT); **driving licence** (BRIT)
n carteira de motorista (BR), carta de
condução (PT); **driving test** *n* exame *m*
de motorista

drizzle ['drɪzl] *n* chuvisco

droop [druːp] *vi* pender

drop [drɒp] *n* (*of water*) gota; (*lessening*)
diminuição *f*; (*fall: distance*) declive *m* ▷ *vt*
(*allow to fall*) deixar cair; (*voice, eyes, price*)
baixar; (*set down from car*) deixar (saltar/
descer); (*omit*) omitir ▷ *vi* cair; (*wind*)
parar; **drops** *npl* (*Med*) gotas *fpl*; **drop off**
vi (*sleep*) cochilar ▷ *vt* (*passenger*) deixar

(saltar/descer); **drop out** vi (withdraw) retirar-se; **drop-out** n pessoa que abandona o trabalho, os estudos etc

drought [draut] n seca

drove [drəuv] pt of **drive**

drown [draun] vt afogar; (also: ~ **out**: sound) encobrir ▷ vi afogar-se

drowsy ['drauzɪ] adj sonolento

drug [drʌg] n remédio, medicamento; (narcotic) droga ▷ vt drogar; **to be on ~s** estar viciado em drogas; (Med) estar sob medicação; **drug addict** n toxicômano(-a); **druggist** (US) n farmacêutico(-a); **drugstore** (US) n drogaria

drum [drʌm] n tambor m; (for oil, petrol) tambor, barril m; **drums** npl (kit) bateria; **drummer** n baterista m/f

drunk [drʌŋk] pp of **drink** ▷ adj bêbado ▷ n (also: ~ard) bêbado(-a); **drunken** adj (laughter) de bêbado; (party) cheio de bêbado; (person) bêbado

dry [draɪ] adj seco; (day) sem chuva; (humour) irônico ▷ vt secar, enxugar; (tears) limpar ▷ vi secar; **dry up** vi secar completamente; **dry-cleaner's** n tinturaria; **dryer** n secador m; (US: spin-dryer) secadora

DSS (BRIT) n abbr (= Department of Social Security) ≈ INAMPS m

DTP n abbr (= desktop publishing) DTP m

dual ['djuəl] adj dual, duplo; **dual carriageway** (BRIT) n pista dupla

dubious ['dju:bɪəs] adj duvidoso; (reputation, company) suspeitoso

duck [dʌk] n pato ▷ vi abaixar-se repentinamente

due [dju:] adj (proper) devido; (expected) esperado ▷ n: **to give sb his (or her) ~** ser justo com alguém ▷ adv: ~ **north** exatamente ao norte; **dues** npl (for club, union) quota; (in harbour) direitos mpl; **in ~ course** no devido tempo; (eventually) no final; ~ **to** devido a

duet [dju:'ɛt] n dueto

dug [dʌg] pt, pp of **dig**

duke [dju:k] n duque m

dull [dʌl] adj (light) sombrio; (wit) lento; (boring) enfadonho; (sound, pain) surdo; (weather) nublado, carregado ▷ vt (pain) aliviar; (mind, senses) entorpecer

dumb [dʌm] adj mudo; (pej: stupid) estúpido

dummy ['dʌmɪ] n (tailor's model) manequim m; (mock-up) modelo; (BRIT: for baby) chupeta ▷ adj falso

dump [dʌmp] n (also: **rubbish ~**) depósito de lixo; (inf: place) chiqueiro ▷ vt (put down) depositar, descarregar; (get rid of) desfazer-se de; (Comput) tirar um dump de

dumpling ['dʌmplɪŋ] n bolinho cozido

dungarees [dʌŋgə'ri:z] npl macacão m (BR), fato macaco (PT)

dungeon ['dʌndʒən] n calabouço

duplex ['dju:plɛks] (US) n casa geminada; (also: ~ **apartment**) duplex m

duplicate [(n) 'dju:plɪkət, (vb) 'dju:plɪkeɪt] n (of document) duplicata; (of key) cópia ▷ vt duplicar; (photocopy) multigrafar; (repeat) reproduzir

durable ['djuərəbl] adj durável; (clothes, metal) resistente

during ['djuərɪŋ] prep durante

dusk [dʌsk] n crepúsculo, anoitecer m

dust [dʌst] n pó m, poeira ▷ vt (furniture) tirar o pó de; (cake etc): **to ~ with** polvilhar com; **dustbin** n (BRIT) lata de lixo; **duster** n pano de pó; **dustman** (BRIT: irreg) n lixeiro, gari m (BR: INF); **dusty** adj empoeirado

Dutch [dʌtʃ] adj holandês(-esa) ▷ n (Ling) holandês m ▷ adv: **let's go ~** (inf) cada um paga o seu, vamos rachar; **the Dutch** npl (people) os holandeses; **Dutchman** (irreg) n holandês m; **Dutchwoman** (irreg) n holandesa

duty ['dju:tɪ] n dever m; (tax) taxa; **on ~** de serviço; **off ~** de folga; **duty-free** adj livre de impostos

duvet ['du:veɪ] (BRIT) n edredom m (BR), edredão m (PT)

DVD n abbr (= digital versatile or video disc) DVD m; **DVD burner, DVD writer** n gravador m de DVD

dwarf [dwɔ:f] (pl **dwarves**) n anão (anã) m/f ▷ vt ananicar

dwindle ['dwɪndl] vi diminuir

dye [daɪ] n tintura, tinta ▷ vt tingir

dynamite ['daɪnəmaɪt] n dinamite f

dyslexia [dɪs'lɛksɪə] n dislexia

e

E [i:] n (Mus) mi m

each [i:tʃ] adj cada inv ▷ pron cada um(a); **~ other** um ao outro; **they hate ~ other** (eles) se odeiam

eager ['i:gəʳ] adj ávido; **to be ~ for/to do sth** ansiar por/por fazer algo

eagle ['i:gl] n águia

ear [ɪəʳ] n (external) orelha; (inner, fig) ouvido; (of corn) espiga; **earache** n dor f de ouvidos; **eardrum** n tímpano

earl [ə:l] (BRIT) n conde m

earlier ['ə:lɪəʳ] adj mais adiantado; (edition) anterior ▷ adv mais cedo

early ['ə:lɪ] adv cedo; (before time) com antecedência ▷ adj cedo; (sooner than expected) prematuro; (reply) pronto; (Christians, settlers) primeiro; (man) primitivo; (life, work) juvenil; **in the ~ or ~ in the spring/19th century** no princípio da primavera/do século dezenove

earmark ['ɪəmɑ:k] vt: **to ~ sth for** reservar or destinar algo para

earn [ə:n] vt ganhar; (Comm: interest) render; (praise) merecer

earnest ['ə:nɪst] adj (wish) intenso; (manner) sério; **in ~** a sério

earnings ['ə:nɪŋz] npl (personal) vencimentos mpl, salário, ordenado; (of company) lucro

ear: earphones npl fones mpl de ouvido; **earring** n brinco

earth [ə:θ] n terra; (BRIT: Elec) fio terra ▷ vt (BRIT: Elec) ligar à terra; **earthquake** n terremoto (BR), terramoto (PT)

ease [i:z] n facilidade f; (relaxed state) sossego; (comfort) conforto ▷ vt facilitar; (pain, tension) aliviar; (help pass): **to ~ sth in/out** meter/tirar algo com cuidado; **at ~!** (Mil) descansar!; **ease off** vi acalmar-se; (wind) baixar; (rain) moderar-se; **ease up** vi = **ease off**

easily ['i:zɪlɪ] adv facilmente, fácil (inf)

east [i:st] n leste m ▷ adj (region) leste; (wind) do leste ▷ adv para o leste; **the E~** o Oriente; (Pol) o leste

Easter ['i:stəʳ] n Páscoa; **Easter egg** n ovo de Páscoa

eastern ['i:stən] adj do leste, oriental

easy ['i:zɪ] adj fácil; (comfortable) folgado, cômodo; (relaxed) natural, complacente; (victim, prey) desprotegido ▷ adv: **to take it** or **things ~** (not worry) levar as coisas com calma; (go slowly) ir devagar; (rest) descansar; **easy-going** adj pacato, fácil

eat [i:t] (pt **ate**, pp **~en**) vt, vi comer; **eat away** vt corroer; **eat away at** vt fus corroer; **eat into** vt fus = **eat away at**

eavesdrop ['i:vzdrɔp] vi: **to ~ (on)** escutar às escondidas

eccentric [ɪk'sɛntrɪk] adj, n excêntrico(-a)

echo ['ɛkəu] (pl **~es**) n eco ▷ vt ecoar, repetir ▷ vi ressoar, repetir

eclipse [ɪ'klɪps] n eclipse m

ecology [ɪ'kɔlədʒɪ] n ecologia

e-commerce n abbr (= electronic commerce) comércio eletrônico

economic [i:kə'nɔmɪk] adj econômico; (business etc) rentável; **economical** adj econômico; **economics** n economia ▷ npl aspectos mpl econômicos

economize [ɪ'kɔnəmaɪz] vi economizar, fazer economias

economy [ɪ'kɔnəmɪ] n economia; **economy class** n (Aviat) classe f econômica

ecstasy ['ɛkstəsɪ] n êxtase m; **ecstatic** [ɛks'tætɪk] adj extasiado

eczema ['ɛksɪmə] n eczema m

edge [ɛdʒ] n (of knife etc) fio; (of table, chair etc) borda; (of lake etc) margem f ▷ vt (trim) embainhar; **on ~** (fig) = **edgy**; **to ~ away from** afastar-se pouco a pouco de; **edgy** adj nervoso, inquieto

edible ['ɛdɪbl] adj comestível
Edinburgh ['ɛdɪnbərə] n Edimburgo
edit ['ɛdɪt] vt editar; (be editor of) dirigir; (cut) cortar, redigir; (Comput, TV) editar; (Cinema) montar; **edition** [ɪ'dɪʃən] n edição f; **editor** n redator(a) m/f; (of newspaper) diretor(a) m/f; (of column) editor(a) m/f; (of book) organizador(a) m/f; **editorial** [ɛdɪ'tɔ:rɪəl] adj editorial
educate ['ɛdjukeɪt] vt educar
education [ɛdju'keɪʃən] n educação f; (schooling) ensino; (teaching) pedagogia; **educational** adj (policy, experience) educacional; (toy etc) educativo
eel [i:l] n enguia
eerie ['ɪərɪ] adj (strange) estranho; (mysterious) misterioso
effect [ɪ'fɛkt] n efeito ▷ vt (repairs) fazer; (savings) efetuar; **to take ~** (law) entrar em vigor; (drug) fazer efeito; **in ~** na realidade; **effective** [ɪ'fɛktɪv] adj eficaz; (actual) efetivo
efficiency [ɪ'fɪʃənsɪ] n eficiência
efficient [ɪ'fɪʃənt] adj eficiente; (machine) rentável
effort ['ɛfət] n esforço; **effortless** adj fácil
e.g. adv abbr (= exempli gratia) p. ex.
egg [ɛg] n ovo; **hard-boiled/soft-boiled ~** ovo duro/mole; **egg on** vt incitar; **eggcup** n oveiro; **eggplant** (esp us) n beringela; **eggshell** n casca de ovo
ego ['i:gəu] n ego
Egypt ['i:dʒɪpt] n Egito; **Egyptian** [ɪ'dʒɪpʃən] adj, n egípcio(-a)
eight [eɪt] num oito; **eighteen** [eɪ'ti:n] num dezoito; **eighth** [eɪtθ] num oitavo; **eighty** ['eɪtɪ] num oitenta
Eire ['ɛərə] n (República da) Irlanda
either ['aɪðə'] adj (one or other) um ou outro; (each) cada; (both) ambos ▷ pron: **~ (of them)** qualquer (dos dois) ▷ adv: **no, I don't ~** eu também não ▷ conj: **~ yes or no** ou sim ou não
eject [ɪ'dʒɛkt] vt expulsar
elaborate [(adj) ɪ'læbərɪt, (vb) ɪ'læbəreɪt] adj complicado ▷ vt (expand) expandir; (refine) aperfeiçoar ▷ vi: **to ~ on** acrescentar detalhes a
elastic [ɪ'læstɪk] adj elástico; (adaptable) flexível, adaptável ▷ n elástico; **elastic band** (BRIT) n elástico
elbow ['ɛlbəu] n cotovelo
elder ['ɛldə'] adj mais velho ▷ n (tree) sabugueiro; (person) o mais velho (a mais velha); **elderly** adj idoso, de idade ▷ npl: **the elderly** as pessoas de idade, os idosos
eldest ['ɛldɪst] adj mais velho ▷ n o mais velho (a mais velha)
elect [ɪ'lɛkt] vt eleger ▷ adj: **the president ~** o presidente eleito; **to ~ to do** (choose) optar por fazer; **election** n (voting) votação f; (installation) eleição f; **electorate** n eleitorado
electric [ɪ'lɛktrɪk] adj elétrico; **electrical** adj elétrico; **electric fire** lareira elétrica
electrician [ɪlɛk'trɪʃən] n eletricista m/f
electricity [ɪlɛk'trɪsɪtɪ] n eletricidade f
electrify [ɪ'lɛktrɪfaɪ] vt (fence, Rail) eletrificar; (audience) eletrizar
electronic [ɪlɛk'trɔnɪk] adj eletrônico; **electronic mail** n correio eletrônico; **electronics** n eletrônica
elegant ['ɛlɪgənt] adj (person, building) elegante; (idea) refinado
element ['ɛlɪmənt] n elemento; **elementary** [ɛlɪ'mɛntərɪ] adj (gen) elementar; (primitive) rudimentar; (school, education) primário; **elementary school** (us) n escola primária; ver quadro

🌑 **ELEMENTARY SCHOOL**
🌑
🌑 Nos Estados Unidos e no Canadá,
🌑 uma **elementary school** (também
🌑 chamada de grade school ou grammar
🌑 school nos Estados Unidos) é uma
🌑 escola pública onde os alunos passam
🌑 de seis a oito dos primeiros anos
🌑 escolares.

elephant ['ɛlɪfənt] n elefante(-a) m/f
elevator ['ɛlɪveɪtə'] (us) n elevador m
eleven [ɪ'lɛvn] num onze; **eleventh** num décimo-primeiro
eligible ['ɛlɪdʒəbl] adj elegível, apto; **to be ~ for sth** (job etc) ter qualificações para algo
elm [ɛlm] n olmo
eloquent ['ɛləkwənt] adj eloqüente
El Salvador [ɛl'sælvədɔ:'] n El Salvador
else [ɛls] adv outro, mais; **something ~** outra coisa; **nobody ~ spoke** ninguém mais falou; **elsewhere** adv (be) em outro lugar (BR), noutro sítio (PT); (go) para outro lugar (BR), a outro sítio (PT)
elusive [ɪ'lu:sɪv] adj esquivo; (quality) indescritível
e-mail ['i:meɪl] n e-mail m, correio eletrônico ▷ vt (person) enviar um e-mail a; **e-mail account** n conta de e-mail,

conta de correio eletrônico; **e-mail address** n e-mail m, endereço eletrônico
embark [ɪm'bɑːk] vi embarcar ▷ vt embarcar; **to ~ on** (fig) empreender, começar
embarrass [ɪm'bærəs] vt constranger; (politician) embaraçar; **embarrassed** adj desconfortável; **embarrassing** adj embaraçoso, constrangedor(a); **embarrassment** n embaraço, constrangimento
embassy ['ɛmbəsɪ] n embaixada
embrace [ɪm'breɪs] vt abraçar, dar um abraço em; (include) abarcar, abranger ▷ vi abraçar-se ▷ n abraço
embroider [ɪm'brɔɪdə'] vt bordar; **embroidery** n bordado
emerald ['ɛmərəld] n esmeralda
emerge [ɪ'mɜːdʒ] vi sair; (from sleep) acordar; (fact, idea) emergir
emergency [ɪ'mɜːdʒənsɪ] n emergência; **in an ~** em caso de urgência; **emergency exit** n saída de emergência; **emergency landing** n aterrissagem forçada (BR), aterragem forçosa (PT)
emigrate ['ɛmɪgreɪt] vi emigrar
eminent ['ɛmɪnənt] adj eminente
emit [ɪ'mɪt] vt (smoke) soltar; (smell) exalar; (sound) produzir
emotion [ɪ'məuʃən] n emoção f; **emotional** adj (needs) emocional; (person) sentimental, emotivo; (scene) comovente; (tone) emocionante
emperor ['ɛmpərə'] n imperador m
emphasis ['ɛmfəsɪs] (pl **emphases**) n ênfase f
emphasize ['ɛmfəsaɪz] vt (word, point) enfatizar, acentuar; (feature) salientar
empire ['ɛmpaɪə'] n império
employ [ɪm'plɔɪ] vt empregar; (tool) utilizar; **employee** n empregado(-a); **employer** n empregador(a) m/f, patrão(-troa) m/f; **employment** n (gen) emprego; (work) trabalho
empress ['ɛmprɪs] n imperatriz f
emptiness ['ɛmptɪnɪs] n vazio, vácuo
empty ['ɛmptɪ] adj vazio; (place) deserto; (house) desocupado; (threat) vão (vã) ▷ vt esvaziar; (place) evacuar ▷ vi esvaziar-se; (place) ficar deserto; **empty-handed** adj de mãos vazias
emulsion [ɪ'mʌlʃən] n emulsão f; (also: ~ paint) tinta plástica
enable [ɪ'neɪbl] vt: **to ~ sb to do sth** (allow) permitir que alguém faça algo; (make possible) tornar possível que

alguém faça algo
enamel [ɪ'næməl] n esmalte m
enclose [ɪn'kləuz] vt (land) cercar; (with letter) anexar (BR), enviar junto (PT); **please find ~d** segue junto
enclosure [ɪn'kləuʒə'] n cercado
encore [ɔŋ'kɔː'] excl bis!, outra! ▷ n bis m
encounter [ɪn'kauntə'] n encontro ▷ vt encontrar, topar com; (difficulty) enfrentar
encourage [ɪn'kʌrɪdʒ] vt (activity) encorajar; (growth) estimular; (person): **to ~ sb to do sth** animar alguém a fazer algo; **encouragement** n estímulo
encyclop(a)edia [ɛnsaɪkləu'piːdɪə] n enciclopédia
end [ɛnd] n fim m; (of table, rope etc) ponta; (of street, town) final m ▷ vt acabar, terminar; (also: **bring to an ~**, **put an ~ to**) acabar com, pôr fim a ▷ vi terminar, acabar; **in the ~** ao fim, por fim, finalmente; **on ~** na ponta; **to stand on ~** (hair) arrepiar-se; **for hours on ~** por horas a fio; **end up** vi: **to end up in** terminar em; (place) ir parar em
endanger [ɪn'deɪndʒə'] vt pôr em risco
endearing [ɪn'dɪərɪŋ] adj simpático, atrativo
endeavour [ɪn'dɛvə'] (US **endeavor**) n esforço; (attempt) tentativa ▷ vi: **to ~ to do** esforçar-se para fazer; (try) tentar fazer
ending ['ɛndɪŋ] n fim m, conclusão f; (of book) desenlace m; (Ling) terminação f
endless ['ɛndlɪs] adj interminável; (possibilities) infinito
endorse [ɪn'dɔːs] vt (cheque) endossar; (approve) aprovar; **endorsement** n (BRIT: on driving licence) descrição f das multas; (approval) aval m
endure [ɪn'djuə'] vt (bear) agüentar, suportar ▷ vi (last) durar
enemy ['ɛnəmɪ] adj, n inimigo(-a)
energy ['ɛnədʒɪ] n energia
enforce [ɪn'fɔːs] vt (Law) fazer cumprir
engage [ɪn'geɪdʒ] vt (attention) chamar; (interest) atrair; (lawyer) contratar; (clutch) engrenar ▷ vi engrenar; **to ~ in** dedicar-se a, ocupar-se com; **to ~ sb in conversation** travar conversa com alguém; **engaged** adj (BRIT: phone) ocupado (BR), impedido (PT); (: toilet) ocupado; (betrothed) noivo; **to get engaged** ficar noivo; **engaged tone** (BRIT) n (Tel) sinal m de ocupado (BR) or de impedido (PT); **engagement** n

encontro; (*booking*) contrato; (*to marry*) noivado; **engagement ring** n aliança de noivado

engine ['ɛndʒɪn] n (*Aut*) motor m; (*Rail*) locomotiva

engineer [ɛndʒɪ'nɪəʳ] n engenheiro(-a); (*US: Rail*) maquinista m/f; (*BRIT: for repairs*) técnico(-a); (*on ship*) engenheiro(-a) naval; **engineering** n engenharia

England ['ɪŋglənd] n Inglaterra

English ['ɪŋglɪʃ] adj inglês (inglesa) ▷ n (*Ling*) inglês m; **the English** npl (*people*) os ingleses; **English Channel** n: **the English Channel** o Canal da Mancha

engraving [ɪn'greɪvɪŋ] n gravura

enhance [ɪn'hɑːns] vt (*gen*) ressaltar, salientar; (*enjoyment*) aumentar; (*beauty*) realçar; (*reputation*) melhorar; (*add to*) aumentar

enjoy [ɪn'dʒɔɪ] vt gostar de; (*health, privilege*) desfrutar de; **to ~ o.s.** divertir-se; **enjoyable** adj agradável; **enjoyment** n prazer m

enlarge [ɪn'lɑːdʒ] vt aumentar; (*Phot*) ampliar ▷ vi: **to ~ on** (*subject*) desenvolver, estender-se sobre

enlist [ɪn'lɪst] vt alistar; (*support*) conseguir, aliciar ▷ vi alistar-se

enormous [ɪ'nɔːməs] adj enorme

enough [ɪ'nʌf] adj: **~ time/books** tempo suficiente/livros suficientes ▷ pron: **have you got ~?** você tem o suficiente? ▷ adv: **big ~** suficientemente grande; **~!** basta!, chega!; **that's ~, thanks** chega, obrigado; **I've had ~ of him** estou farto dele; **which, funnily** or **oddly ~ ...** o que, por estranho que pareça ...

enquire [ɪn'kwaɪəʳ] vt, vi = **inquire**

enrage [ɪn'reɪdʒ] vt enfurecer, enraivecer

enrol [ɪn'rəul] (*US* **enroll**) vt inscrever; (*Sch*) matricular ▷ vi inscrever-se; matricular-se; **enrolment** n inscrição f; (*Sch*) matrícula

ensure [ɪn'ʃuəʳ] vt assegurar

entail [ɪn'teɪl] vt implicar

enter ['ɛntəʳ] vt entrar em; (*club*) ficar or fazer-se sócio de; (*army*) alistar-se em; (*competition*) inscrever-se em; (*sb for a competition*) inscrever; (*write down*) completar; (*Comput*) entrar com ▷ vi entrar; **enter for** vt fus inscrever-se em; **enter into** vt fus estabelecer; (*plans*) fazer parte de; (*debate*) entrar em; (*agreement*) chegar a, firmar

enterprise ['ɛntəpraɪz] n empresa;

(*undertaking*) empreendimento; (*initiative*) iniciativa; **enterprising** adj empreendedor(a)

entertain [ɛntə'teɪn] vt divertir, entreter; (*guest*) receber (em casa); (*idea*) estudar; **entertainer** n artista m/f; **entertaining** adj divertido; **entertainment** n (*amusement*) entretenimento, diversão f; (*show*) espetáculo

enthusiasm [ɪn'θuːzɪæzəm] n entusiasmo

enthusiast [ɪn'θuːzɪæst] n entusiasta m/f; **enthusiastic** [ɪnθuːzɪ'æstɪk] adj entusiasmado; **to be enthusiastic about** entusiasmar-se por

entire [ɪn'taɪəʳ] adj inteiro; **entirely** adv totalmente, completamente

entitle [ɪn'taɪtl] vt: **to ~ sb to sth** dar a alguém direito a algo; **entitled** [ɪn'taɪtld] adj (*book etc*) intitulado; **to be entitled to do** ter direito de fazer

entrance [(n) 'ɛntrns, (vb) ɪn'trɑːns] n entrada; (*arrival*) chegada ▷ vt encantar, fascinar; **to gain ~ to** (*university etc*) ser admitido em; **entrance examination** n exame m de admissão; **entrance fee** n jóia

entrant ['ɛntrənt] n participante m/f; (*BRIT: in exam*) candidato(-a)

entrepreneur [ɔntrəprə'nəːʳ] n empresário(-a)

entrust [ɪn'trʌst] vt: **to ~ sth to sb** confiar algo a alguém

entry ['ɛntrɪ] n entrada; (*in competition*) participante m/f; (*in register*) registro, assentamento; (*in account*) lançamento; (*in dictionary*) verbete m; (*arrival*) chegada; **"no ~"** "entrada proibida"; (*Aut*) "contramão" (*BR*), "entrada proibida" (*PT*); **entry phone** (*BRIT*) n interfone m (*em apartamento*)

envelope ['ɛnvələup] n envelope m

envious ['ɛnvɪəs] adj invejoso; (*look*) de inveja

environment [ɪn'vaɪrnmənt] n meio ambiente m; **environmental** [ɪnvaɪrn'mɛntl] adj ambiental; **environmentally friendly** adj (*products, industry*) não agressivo ao meio ambiente

envisage [ɪn'vɪzɪdʒ] vt prever

envoy ['ɛnvɔɪ] n enviado(-a)

envy ['ɛnvɪ] n inveja ▷ vt ter inveja de; **to ~ sb sth** invejar alguém por algo, cobiçar algo de alguém

epic ['ɛpɪk] n epopéia ▷ adj épico

epidemic [ɛpɪ'dɛmɪk] n epidemia
epilepsy ['ɛpɪlɛpsɪ] n epilepsia
episode ['ɛpɪsəʊd] n episódio
equal ['iːkwl] adj igual; (treatment)
equitativo, equivalente ▷ n igual m/f ▷ vt
ser igual a; **to be ~ to** (task) estar à altura
de; **equality** [iː'kwɔlɪtɪ] n igualdade f;
equalize vi igualar; (Sport) empatar;
equally adv igualmente; (share etc) por
igual
equator [ɪ'kweɪtəʳ] n equador m
equip [ɪ'kwɪp] vt equipar; (person) prover,
munir; **to be well ~ped** estar bem
preparado or equipado; **equipment** n
equipamento; (machines) equipamentos
mpl, aparelhagem f
equivalent [ɪ'kwɪvələnt] adj: ~ **(to)**
equivalente (a) ▷ n equivalente m
era ['ɪərə] n era, época
erase [ɪ'reɪz] vt apagar; **eraser** n
borracha (de apagar)
erect [ɪ'rɛkt] adj (posture) ereto; (tail, ears)
levantado ▷ vt erigir, levantar; (assemble)
montar; **erection** n construção f;
(of tent, Physio) ereção f; (assembly)
montagem f
erode [ɪ'rəʊd] vt (Geo) causar erosão em;
(confidence) minar
erotic [ɪ'rɔtɪk] adj erótico
errand ['ɛrnd] n recado, mensagem f
erratic [ɪ'rætɪk] adj imprevisível
error ['ɛrəʳ] n erro
erupt [ɪ'rʌpt] vi entrar em erupção; (fig)
explodir, estourar; **eruption** n erupção
f; explosão f
escalate ['ɛskəleɪt] vi intensificar-se
escalator ['ɛskəleɪtəʳ] n escada rolante
escape [ɪ'skeɪp] n fuga; (of gas)
escapatória ▷ vi escapar; (flee) fugir,
evadir-se; (leak) vazar, escapar ▷ vt fugir
de; (elude): **his name ~s me** o nome dele
me foge à memória; **to ~ from** (place)
escapar de; (person) escapulir de
escort [(n) 'ɛskɔːt, (vb) ɪs'kɔːt] n
acompanhante m/f; (Mil) escolta ▷ vt
acompanhar
especially [ɪ'spɛʃlɪ] adv (above all)
sobretudo; (particularly) em particular
espionage ['ɛspɪənɑːʒ] n espionagem f
essay ['ɛseɪ] n ensaio
essence ['ɛsns] n essência
essential [ɪ'sɛnʃl] adj (necessary)
indispensável; (basic) essencial ▷ n
elemento essencial
establish [ɪ'stæblɪʃ] vt estabelecer;
(facts) verificar; (proof) demonstrar;

(reputation) firmar; **establishment** n
estabelecimento; **the Establishment** a
classe dirigente
estate [ɪ'steɪt] n (land) fazenda (BR),
propriedade f (PT); (Law) herança; (Pol)
estado; (BRIT: also: **housing ~**) conjunto
habitacional; **estate agent** (BRIT) n
corretor(a) m/f de imóveis (BR), agente
m/f imobiliário(-a) (PT); **estate car** (BRIT)
n perua (BR), canadiana (PT)
estimate [(n) 'ɛstɪmət, (vb) 'ɛstɪmeɪt]
n (assessment) avaliação f; (calculation)
cálculo; (Comm) orçamento ▷ vt estimar,
avaliar, calcular
etc. abbr (= et cetera) etc.
eternal [ɪ'təːnl] adj eterno
eternity [ɪ'təːnɪtɪ] n eternidade f
ethical ['ɛθɪkl] adj ético
ethics ['ɛθɪks] n ética ▷ npl moral f
Ethiopia [iːθɪ'əʊpɪə] n Etiópia
ethnic ['ɛθnɪk] adj étnico; (culture)
folclórico
e-ticket ['iːtɪkɪt] m bilhete m eletrônico
etiquette ['ɛtɪkɛt] n etiqueta
EU abbr (= European Union) UE f
euro ['jʊərəʊ] n (currency) euro m
Europe ['jʊərəp] n Europa; **European**
[jʊərə'piːən] adj, n europeu(-péia);
European Union n: **the European
Union** a União Européia
evacuate [ɪ'vækjueɪt] vt evacuar
evade [ɪ'veɪd] vt (person) evitar; (question,
duties) evadir; (tax) sonegar
evaporate [ɪ'væpəreɪt] vi evaporar-se
eve [iːv] n: **on the ~ of** na véspera de
even ['iːvn] adj (level) plano; (smooth)
liso; (equal) igual; (number) par ▷ adv até,
mesmo; (showing surprise) até (mesmo);
(introducing a comparison) ainda; ~ **if**
mesmo que; ~ **though** mesmo que,
embora; ~ **more** ainda mais; ~ **so** mesmo
assim; **not ~** nem; **to get ~ with sb**
ficar quite com alguém; **even out** vi
nivelar-se
evening ['iːvnɪŋ] n (early) tarde f; (late)
noite f; (event) noitada; **in the ~** à noite;
evening class n aula noturna
event [ɪ'vɛnt] n acontecimento;
(Sport) prova; **in the ~ of** no caso de;
eventful adj movimentado, cheio de
acontecimentos; (game etc) cheio de
emoção, agitado
eventual [ɪ'vɛntʃuəl] adj final;
eventually adv finalmente; (in time)
por fim
ever ['ɛvəʳ] adv (always) sempre; (at

any time) em qualquer momento; (*in question*): **why ~ not?** por que não?; **the best ~** o melhor que já se viu; **have you ~ seen it?** você alguma vez já viu isto?; **better than ~** melhor que nunca; **~ since** *adv* desde então ▷ *conj* depois que; **evergreen** *n* sempre-verde *f*

⚙ **KEYWORD**

every ['εvrι] *adj* **1** (*each*) cada; **every one of them** cada um deles; **every shop in the town was closed** todas as lojas da cidade estavam fechadas
2 (*all possible*) todo(-a); **I have every confidence in her** tenho absoluta confiança nela; **we wish you every success** desejamo-lhe o maior sucesso; **he's every bit as clever as his brother** ele é tão inteligente quanto o irmão
3 (*showing recurrence*) todo(-a); **every other car had been broken into** cada dois carros foram arrombados; **she visits me every other/third day** ele me visita cada dois/três dias; **every now and then** de vez em quando

everybody ['εvrιbɒdι] *pron* todos, todo mundo (BR), toda a gente (PT)
everyday ['εvrιdeι] *adj* (*daily*) diário; (*usual*) corrente; (*common*) comum
everyone ['εvrιwʌn] *pron* = **everybody**
everything ['εvrιθιŋ] *pron* tudo
everywhere ['εvrιwεəʳ] *adv* (*be*) em todo lugar (BR), em toda a parte (PT); (*go*) a todo lugar (BR), a toda a parte (PT); (*wherever*): **~ you go you meet ...** aonde quer que se vá, encontra-se ...
evict [ι'vιkt] *vt* despejar
evidence ['εvιdəns] *n* (*proof*) prova(s) *f(pl)*; (*of witness*) testemunho, depoimento; (*indication*) sinal *m*; **to give ~** testemunhar, prestar depoimento
evident ['εvιdənt] *adj* evidente; **evidently** *adv* evidentemente; (*apparently*) aparentemente
evil ['i:vl] *adj* mau (má) ▷ *n* mal *m*, maldade *f*
evoke [ι'vəuk] *vt* evocar
evolution [i:və'lu:ʃən] *n* evolução *f*; (*development*) desenvolvimento
evolve [ι'vɒlv] *vt* desenvolver ▷ *vi* desenvolver-se
exact [ιg'zækt] *adj* exato; (*person*) meticuloso ▷ *vt*: **to ~ sth (from)** exigir algo (de); **exactly** *adv* exatamente;

(*indicating agreement*) isso mesmo
exaggerate [ιg'zædʒəreιt] *vt*, *vi* exagerar; **exaggeration** [ιgzædʒə'reιʃən] *n* exagero
exam [ιg'zæm] *n abbr* = **examination**
examination [ιgzæmι'neιʃən] *n* exame *m*; (*inquiry*) investigação *f*
examine [ιg'zæmιn] *vt* examinar; (*inspect*) inspecionar; **examiner** *n* examinador(a) *m/f*
example [ιg'zɑ:mpl] *n* exemplo; **for ~** por exemplo
excavate ['εkskəveιt] *vt* escavar
exceed [ιk'si:d] *vt* exceder; (*number*) ser superior a; (*speed limit*) ultrapassar; (*limits*) ir além de; (*powers*) exceder-se em; (*hopes*) superar; **exceedingly** *adv* extremamente
excellent ['εksələnt] *adj* excelente
except [ιk'sεpt] *prep* (*also*: **~ for, ~ing**) exceto, a não ser ▷ *vt* excluir; **~ if/when** a menos que, a não ser que; **exception** *n* exceção *f*; **to take exception to** ressentir-se de
excerpt ['εksə:pt] *n* trecho
excess [ιk'sεs] *n* excesso; **excess baggage** *n* excesso de bagagem; **excessive** *adj* excessivo
exchange [ιks'tʃeιndʒ] *n* troca; (*of teachers, students*) intercâmbio; (*also*: **telephone ~**) estação *f* telefônica (BR), central *f* telefónica (PT) ▷ *vt*: **to ~ (for)** trocar (por); **exchange rate** *n* (taxa de) câmbio
excite [ιk'saιt] *vt* excitar; **to get ~d** entusiasmar-se; **excitement** *n* emoções *fpl*; (*agitation*) agitação *f*; **exciting** *adj* emocionante, empolgante
exclaim [ιk'skleιm] *vi* exclamar; **exclamation** [εksklə'meιʃən] *n* exclamação *f*; **exclamation mark** *n* ponto de exclamação (BR) or de admiração (PT)
exclude [ιk'sklu:d] *vt* excluir
exclusive [ιk'sklu:sιv] *adj* exclusivo; **~ of tax** sem incluir os impostos
excruciating [ιk'skru:ʃιeιtιŋ] *adj* doloroso, martirizante
excursion [ιk'skə:ʃən] *n* excursão *f*
excuse [(*n*) ιks'kju:s, (*vb*) ιks'kju:z] *n* desculpa ▷ *vt* desculpar, perdoar; **to ~ sb from doing sth** dispensar alguém de fazer algo; **~ me!** desculpe!; **if you will ~ me ...** com a sua licença ...
execute ['εksιkju:t] *vt* (*plan*) realizar; (*order*) cumprir; (*person, movement*)

executar; **execution** n realização f;
(killing) execução f
executive [ɪgˈzɛkjutɪv] adj, n
executivo(-a)
exempt [ɪgˈzɛmpt] adj isento ▷ vt: **to ~
sb from** dispensar or isentar alguém de
exercise [ˈɛksəsaɪz] n exercício ▷ vt
exercer; (right) valer-se de; (dog) levar
para passear; (mind) ocupar ▷ vi (also: **to
take ~**) fazer exercício; **exercise book**
n caderno
exert [ɪgˈzəːt] vt exercer; **to ~ o.s.**
esforçar-se, empenhar-se; **exertion** n
esforço
exhale [ɛksˈheɪl] vt expirar; (air) exalar;
(smoke) emitir ▷ vi expirar
exhaust [ɪgˈzɔːst] n (Auto: also: ~
pipe) escape m, exaustor m; (fumes)
escapamento (de gás) ▷ vt esgotar;
exhaustion n exaustão f
exhibit [ɪgˈzɪbɪt] n (Art) obra exposta;
(Law) objeto exposto ▷ vt (courage)
manifestar, mostrar; (quality, emotion)
demonstrar; (paintings) expor;
exhibition [ɛksɪˈbɪʃən] n exposição f; (of
talent etc) mostra
exhilarating [ɪgˈzɪləreɪtɪŋ] adj
estimulante, tônico
exile [ˈɛksaɪl] n exílio; (person) exilado(-a)
▷ vt desterrar, exilar
exist [ɪgˈzɪst] vi existir; (live) viver;
existence n existência; vida; **existing**
adj atual
exit [ˈɛksɪt] n saída ▷ vi (Comput, Theatre)
sair
exotic [ɪgˈzɔtɪk] adj exótico
expand [ɪkˈspænd] vt aumentar ▷ vi
aumentar; (gas etc) expandir-se; (metal)
dilatar-se
expansion [ɪkˈspænʃən] n (of town)
desenvolvimento; (of trade) expansão f;
(of population) aumento
expect [ɪkˈspɛkt] vt esperar; (suppose)
supor; (require) exigir ▷ vi: **to be
~ing** estar grávida; **expectation**
[ɛkspɛkˈteɪʃən] n esperança; (belief)
expectativa
expedition [ɛkspəˈdɪʃən] n expedição f
expel [ɪkˈspɛl] vt expelir; (from place,
school) expulsar
expense [ɪkˈspɛns] n gasto, despesa;
(expenditure) despesas fpl; **expenses** npl
(costs) despesas fpl; **at the ~ of** à custa
de; **expense account** n relatório de
despesas
expensive [ɪkˈspɛnsɪv] adj caro

experience [ɪkˈspɪərɪəns] n experiência
▷ vt (situation) enfrentar; (feeling) sentir;
experienced adj experiente
experiment [ɪkˈspɛrɪmənt] n
experimento, experiência ▷ vi: **to ~
(with/on)** fazer experiências (com/em)
expert [ˈɛkspəːt] adj hábil, perito ▷ n
especialista m/f; **expertise** [ɛkspəːˈtiːz]
n perícia
expire [ɪkˈspaɪər] vi expirar; (run
out) vencer; **expiry** n expiração f,
vencimento
explain [ɪkˈspleɪn] vt explicar; (clarify)
esclarecer
explicit [ɪkˈsplɪsɪt] adj explícito
explode [ɪkˈspləud] vi estourar, explodir
exploit [(n) ˈɛksplɔɪt, (vb) ɪksˈplɔɪt] n
façanha ▷ vt explorar; **exploitation**
[ɛksplɔɪˈteɪʃən] n exploração f
explore [ɪkˈsplɔːr] vt explorar; (fig)
examinar, pesquisar; **explorer** n
explorador(a) m/f
explosion [ɪkˈspləuʒən] n explosão f
explosive [ɪkˈspləusɪv] adj explosivo ▷ n
explosivo
export [(vb) ɛksˈpɔːt, (n) ˈɛkspɔːt] vt
exportar ▷ n exportação f ▷ cpd de
exportação; **exporter** n exportador(a)
m/f
expose [ɪkˈspəuz] vt expor; (unmask)
desmascarar; **exposed** adj (house etc)
desabrigado
exposure [ɪkˈspəuʒər] n exposição f;
(publicity) publicidade f; (Phot) revelação
f; **to die from ~** (Med) morrer de frio
express [ɪkˈsprɛs] adj expresso, explícito;
(BRIT: letter etc) urgente ▷ n rápido
▷ vt exprimir, expressar; (quantity)
representar; **expression** n expressão f;
expressway (US) n rodovia (BR), auto-
estrada (PT)
extend [ɪkˈstɛnd] vt (visit, street)
prolongar; (building) aumentar; (offer)
fazer; (hand) estender
extension [ɪkˈstɛnʃən] n (Elec) extensão
f; (building) acréscimo, expansão f; (of
time) prorrogação f; (of rights) ampliação
f; (Tel) ramal m (BR), extensão f (PT); (of
deadline) prolongamento, prorrogação f
extensive [ɪkˈstɛnsɪv] adj extenso;
(damage) considerável; (coverage) amplo;
(broad) vasto, amplo
extent [ɪkˈstɛnt] n (breadth) extensão
f; (of damage etc) dimensão f; (scope)
alcance m; **to some ~** até certo ponto
exterior [ɛkˈstɪərɪər] adj externo ▷ n

exterior m; (appearance) aspecto

external [εk'stə:nl] adj externo

extinct [ɪk'stɪŋkt] adj extinto

extinguish [ɪk'stɪŋgwɪʃ] vt extinguir

extra ['εkstrə] adj adicional ▷ adv
adicionalmente ▷ n (luxury) luxo;
(surcharge) extra m, suplemento; (Cinema,
Theatre) figurante m/f

extract [(vb) ɪks'trækt, (n) 'εkstrækt] vt
tirar, extrair; (tooth) arrancar; (mineral)
extrair; (money) extorquir; (promise)
conseguir, obter ▷ n extrato

extradite ['εkstrədaɪt] vt (from country)
extraditar; (to country) obter a extradição
de

extraordinary [ɪk'strɔ:dnrɪ] adj
extraordinário; (odd) estranho

extravagance [ɪk'strævəgəns]
n extravagância; (no pl: spending)
esbanjamento

extravagant [ɪk'strævəgənt] adj (lavish)
extravagante; (wasteful) gastador(a),
esbanjador(a)

extreme [ɪk'stri:m] adj extremo ▷ n
extremo; **extremely** adv muito,
extremamente

extrovert ['εkstrəvə:t] n
extrovertido(-a)

eye [aɪ] n olho; (of needle) buraco ▷ vt
olhar, observar; **to keep an ~ on**
vigiar, ficar de olho em; **eyebrow** n
sobrancelha; **eyedrops** npl gotas fpl
para os olhos; **eyelash** n cílio; **eyelid**
n pálpebra; **eyeliner** n delineador m;
eyeshadow n sombra de olhos;
eyesight n vista, visão f

fabric ['fæbrɪk] n tecido, pano

face [feɪs] n cara, rosto; (grimace) careta;
(of clock) mostrador m; (side) superfície f;
(of building) frente f, fachada ▷ vt (facts)
enfrentar; (direction) dar para; **~ down** de
bruços; (card) virado para baixo; **to lose
~** perder o prestígio; **to save ~** salvar as
aparências; **to make** or **pull a ~** fazer
careta; **in the ~ of** diante de, à vista de;
on the ~ of it a julgar pelas aparências,
à primeira vista; **face up to** vt fus
enfrentar; **face cloth** (BRIT) n toalhinha
de rosto

facilities [fə'sɪlɪtɪz] npl facilidades fpl,
instalações fpl; **credit ~** crediário

fact [fækt] n fato; **in ~** realmente, na
verdade

factor ['fæktəʳ] n fator m

factory ['fæktərɪ] n fábrica

factual ['fæktjuəl] adj real, fatual

faculty ['fækəltɪ] n faculdade f; (US)
corpo docente

fad [fæd] (inf) n mania, modismo

fade [feɪd] vi desbotar; (sound, hope)
desvanecer-se; (light) apagar-se; (flower)
murchar

fag [fæg] (BRIT: inf) n cigarro

fail [feɪl] vt (candidate) reprovar; (exam)

não passar em, ser reprovado em; (*subj: leader*) fracassar; (: *courage*): **his courage ~ed him** faltou-lhe coragem; (: *memory*) falhar ▷ *vi* fracassar; (*brakes*) falhar; (*health*) deteriorar; (*light*) desaparecer; **to ~ to do sth** deixar de fazer algo; (*be unable*) não conseguir fazer algo; **without ~** sem falta; **failing** *n* defeito ▷ *prep* na ora à falta de; **failing that** senão; **failure** *n* fracasso; (*mechanical*) falha

faint [feint] *adj* fraco; (*recollection*) vago; (*mark*) indistinto; (*smell*) leve ▷ *n* desmaio ▷ *vi* desmaiar; **to feel ~** sentir tonteira

fair [fɛəʳ] *adj* justo; (*hair*) louro; (*complexion*) branco; (*weather*) bom; (*good enough*) razoável; (*sizeable*) considerável ▷ *adv*: **to play ~** fazer jogo limpo ▷ *n* (*also*: **trade ~**) feira; (*BRIT*: *funfair*) parque *m* de diversões; **fairly** *adv* (*justly*) com justiça; (*quite*) bastante

fairy ['fɛərɪ] *n* fada

faith [feɪθ] *n* fé *f*; (*trust*) confiança; (*denomination*) seita; **faithful** *adj* fiel; (*account*) exato; **faithfully** *adv* fielmente; **yours faithfully** (*BRIT*: *in letters*) atenciosamente

fake [feɪk] *n* (*painting etc*) falsificação *f*; (*person*) impostor(a) *m/f* ▷ *adj* falso ▷ *vt* fingir; (*painting etc*) falsificar

falcon ['fɔːlkən] *n* falcão *m*

fall [fɔːl] (*pt* **fell**, *pp* **~en**) *n* queda; (*US*: *autumn*) outono ▷ *vi* cair; (*price*) baixar; (*country*) render-se; **falls** *npl* (*waterfall*) cascata, queda d'água; **to ~ flat** cair de cara no chão; (*plan*) falhar; (*joke*) não agradar; **fall back** *vi* retroceder; **fall back on** *vt fus* recorrer a; **fall behind** *vi* ficar para trás; **fall down** *vi* (*person*) cair; (*building*) desabar; **fall for** *vt fus* (*trick*) cair em; (*person*) enamorar-se de; **fall in** *vi* ruir; (*Mil*) alinhar-se; **fall off** *vi* cair; (*diminish*) declinar, diminuir; **fall out** *vi* cair; (*friends etc*) brigar; **fall through** *vi* furar

fallout ['fɔːlaut] *n* chuva radioativa

false [fɔːls] *adj* falso; **under ~ pretences** por meios fraudulentos; **false teeth** (*BRIT*) *npl* dentadura postiça

fame [feɪm] *n* fama

familiar [fə'mɪlɪəʳ] *adj* (*well-known*) conhecido; (*tone*) familiar, íntimo; **to be ~ with** (*subject*) estar familiarizado com

family ['fæmɪlɪ] *n* família

famine ['fæmɪn] *n* fome *f*

famous ['feɪməs] *adj* famoso, célebre

fan [fæn] *n* (*hand-held*) leque *m*; (*Elec*) ventilador *m*; (*person*) fã *m/f* (*BR*), fan *m/f* (*PT*) ▷ *vt* abanar; (*fire, quarrel*) atiçar; **fan out** *vi* espalhar-se

fanatic [fə'nætɪk] *n* fanático(-a)

fan belt *n* correia do ventilador (*BR*) ou da ventoinha (*PT*)

fancy ['fænsɪ] *n* capricho; (*imagination*) imaginação *f*; (*fantasy*) fantasia ▷ *adj* ornamental; (*clothes*) extravagante; (*food*) elaborado; (*luxury*) luxoso ▷ *vt* desejar, querer; (*imagine*) imaginar; (*think*) acreditar, achar; **to take a ~ to** tomar gosto por; **he fancies her** (*inf*) ele está a fim dela; **fancy dress** *n* fantasia

fantastic [fæn'tæstɪk] *adj* fantástico

fantasy ['fæntəsɪ] *n* (*dream*) sonho; (*unreality*) fantasia; (*imagination*) imaginação *f*

far [fɑːʳ] *adj* (*distant*) distante ▷ *adv* muito; (*also*: **~ away**, **~ off**) longe; **at the ~ side/end** do lado/extremo mais afastado; **~ better** muito melhor; **~ from** longe de; **by ~** de longe; **go as ~ as the farm** vá até à (*BR*) ou à (*PT*) fazenda; **as ~ as I know** que eu saiba; **how ~?** até onde?; (*fig*) até que ponto?

farce [fɑːs] *n* farsa

fare [fɛəʳ] *n* (*on trains, buses*) preço (da passagem); (*in taxi: cost*) tarifa; (*food*) comida; **half/full ~** meia/inteira passagem

Far East *n*: **the ~** o Extremo Oriente

farewell [fɛə'wɛl] *excl* adeus ▷ *n* despedida

farm [fɑːm] *n* fazenda (*BR*), quinta (*PT*) ▷ *vt* cultivar; **farmer** *n* fazendeiro(-a), agricultor *m*; **farmhouse** *n* casa da fazenda (*BR*) ou da quinta (*PT*); **farming** *n* agricultura; (*tilling*) cultura; (*of animals*) criação *f*; **farmyard** *n* curral *m*

far-reaching [-'riːtʃɪŋ] *adj* de grande alcance, abrangente

farther ['fɑːðəʳ] *adv* mais longe ▷ *adj* mais distante, mais afastado

farthest ['fɑːðɪst] *superl of* **far**

fascinate ['fæsɪneɪt] *vt* fascinar

fashion ['fæʃən] *n* moda; (*fashion industry*) indústria da moda; (*manner*) maneira ▷ *vt* modelar, dar feitio a; **in ~** na moda; **fashionable** *adj* da moda, elegante; **fashion show** *n* desfile *m* de modas

fast [fɑːst] *adj* rápido; (*dye, colour*) firme, permanente; (*clock*): **to be ~** estar adiantado ▷ *adv* rápido, rapidamente,

depressa; (*stuck, held*) firmemente ▷ *n*
jejum *m* ▷ *vi* jejuar; **~ asleep** dormindo
profundamente

fasten ['fɑːsn] *vt* fixar, prender; (*coat*)
fechar; (*belt*) apertar ▷ *vi* prender-se,
fixar-se

fast food *n* fast food *f*

fat [fæt] *adj* gordo; (*book*) grosso; (*wallet*)
recheado; (*profit*) grande ▷ *n* gordura;
(*lard*) banha, gordura

fatal ['feɪtl] *adj* fatal; (*injury*) mortal

fate [feɪt] *n* destino; (*of person*) sorte *f*

father ['fɑːðə^r] *n* pai *m*; **father-in-law**
n sogro

fatigue [fə'tiːg] *n* fadiga, cansaço

fatty ['fætɪ] *adj* (*food*) gorduroso ▷ *n* (*inf*)
gorducho(-a)

fault [fɔːlt] *n* (*blame*) culpa; (*defect*)
defeito; (*Geo*) falha; (*Tennis*) falta, bola
fora ▷ *vt* criticar; **to find ~ with** criticar,
queixar-se de; **at ~** culpado; **faulty** *adj*
defeituoso

favour ['feɪvə^r] (*US* **favor**) *n* favor *m* ▷ *vt*
favorecer; (*assist*) auxiliar; **to do sb a ~**
fazer favor a alguém; **to find ~ with** cair
nas boas graças de; **in ~ of** em favor de;
favourite ['feɪvrɪt] *adj* predileto ▷ *n*
favorito(-a)

fawn [fɔːn] *n* cervo novo, cervato ▷ *adj*
(*also:* **~-coloured**) castanho-claro *inv*
▷ *vi*: **to ~ (up)on** bajular

fax [fæks] *n* fax *m*, fac-símile *m* ▷ *vt*
enviar por fax or fac-símile

FBI *n abbr* (= *Federal Bureau of Investigation*)
FBI *m*

fear [fɪə^r] *n* medo ▷ *vt* ter medo de,
temer; **for ~ of** com medo de; **fearful** *adj*
medonho, temível; (*cowardly*) medroso;
(*awful*) terrível

feasible ['fiːzəbl] *adj* viável

feast [fiːst] *n* banquete *m*; (*Rel: also:* **~
day**) festa ▷ *vi* banquetear-se

feat [fiːt] *n* façanha, feito

feather ['feðə^r] *n* pena, pluma

feature ['fiːtʃə^r] *n* característica; (*article*)
reportagem *f* ▷ *vt* (*subj: film*) apresentar
▷ *vi*: **to ~ in** figurar em; **features** *npl* (*of
face*) feições *fpl*; **feature film** *n* longa-
metragem *m*

February ['fɛbruərɪ] *n* fevereiro

fed [fɛd] *pt, pp of* **feed**

federal ['fɛdərəl] *adj* federal

fed up *adj*: **to be ~** estar (de saco) cheio
(*BR*), estar farto (*PT*)

fee [fiː] *n* taxa (*BR*), propina (*PT*); (*of
school*) matrícula; (*of doctor, lawyer*)

honorários *mpl*

feeble ['fiːbl] *adj* fraco; (*attempt*) ineficaz

feed [fiːd] (*pt, pp* **fed**) *n* (*of baby*) alimento
infantil; (*of animal*) ração *f*; (*on printer*)
mecanismo alimentador ▷ *vt* alimentar;
(*baby*) amamentar; (*animal*) dar de comer
a; (*data*): **to ~ into** introduzir em; **feed
on** *vt fus* alimentar-se de; **feedback** *m*
reação *f*

feel [fiːl] (*pt, pp* **felt**) *n* sensação *f*; (*sense*)
tato; (*impression*) impressão *f* ▷ *vt* tocar,
apalpar; (*anger, pain etc*) sentir; (*think*)
achar, acreditar; **to ~ hungry/cold** estar
com fome/frio (*BR*), ter fome/frio (*PT*);
to ~ lonely/better sentir-se só/melhor;
I don't ~ well não estou me sentindo
bem; **it ~s soft** é macio; **to ~ like** querer;
to ~ about or **around** tatear; **feeling**
n sensação *f*; (*emotion*) sentimento;
(*impression*) impressão *f*

feet [fiːt] *npl of* **foot**

fell [fɛl] *pt of* **fall** ▷ *vt* (*tree*) lançar por
terra, derrubar

fellow ['fɛləu] *n* camarada *m/f*; (*inf: man*)
cara *m* (*BR*), tipo (*PT*); (*of learned society*)
membro ▷ *cpd*: **~ students** colegas *m/fpl*
de curso; **fellowship** *n* amizade *f*; (*grant*)
bolsa de estudo; (*society*) associação *f*

felony ['fɛlənɪ] *n* crime *m*

felt [fɛlt] *pt, pp of* **feel** ▷ *n* feltro

female ['fiːmeɪl] *n* (*Zool*) fêmea; (*pej:
woman*) mulher *f* ▷ *adj* fêmeo(-a); (*sex,
character*) feminino; (*vote*) das mulheres;
(*child*) do sexo feminino

feminine ['fɛmɪnɪn] *adj* feminino

feminist ['fɛmɪnɪst] *n* feminista *m/f*

fence [fɛns] *n* cerca ▷ *vt* (*also:* **~ in**) cercar
▷ *vi* esgrimir; **fencing** *n* (*sport*) esgrima

fend [fɛnd] *vi*: **~ for o.s.** defender-se,
virar-se; **fend off** *vt* defender-se de

ferment [(*vb*) fə'mɛnt, (*n*) 'fɜːmɛnt] *vi*
fermentar ▷ *n* (*fig*) agitação *f*

fern [fɜːn] *n* samambaia (*BR*), feto (*PT*)

ferocious [fə'rəuʃəs] *adj* feroz

ferret ['fɛrɪt] *n* furão *m*; **ferret out** *vt*
(*information*) desenterrar, descobrir

ferry ['fɛrɪ] *n* (*small*) barco (de travessia);
(*large: also:* **~boat**) balsa ▷ *vt* transportar

fertile ['fɜːtaɪl] *adj* fértil; (*Bio*) fecundo;
fertilizer ['fɜːtɪlaɪzə^r] *n* adubo,
fertilizante *m*

festival ['fɛstɪvəl] *n* (*Rel*) festa; (*Art, Mus*)
festival *m*

festive ['fɛstɪv] *adj* festivo; **the ~ season**
(*BRIT: Christmas*) a época do Natal

fetch [fɛtʃ] *vt* ir buscar, trazer; (*sell for*)

alcançar
fête [feɪt] n festa
feud [fju:d] n disputa, rixa
fever ['fi:vəʳ] n febre f; **feverish** adj febril
few [fju:] adj, pron poucos(-as); **a ~** ...
alguns (algumas) ...; **fewer** ['fju:əʳ] adj
menos; **fewest** ['fju:ɪst] adj o menor
número de
fib [fɪb] n lorota
fickle ['fɪkl] adj inconstante; (weather)
instável
fiction ['fɪkʃən] n ficção f; **fictional** adj
de ficção
fiddle ['fɪdl] n (Mus) violino; (swindle)
trapaça ▷ vt (BRIT: accounts) falsificar;
fiddle with vt fus brincar com
fidget ['fɪdʒɪt] vi estar irrequieto,
mexer-se
field [fi:ld] n campo; (fig) área, esfera,
especialidade f
fierce [fɪəs] adj feroz; (wind) violento;
(heat) intenso
fifteen [fɪf'ti:n] num quinze
fifth [fɪfθ] num quinto
fifty ['fɪftɪ] num cinqüenta; **fifty-fifty**
adv: **to share** or **go fifty-fifty with sb**
dividir meio a meio com alguém, rachar
com alguém ▷ adj: **to have a fifty-fifty
chance** ter 50% de chance
fig [fɪg] n figo
fight [faɪt] (pt, pp **fought**) n briga; (Mil)
combate m; (struggle: against illness etc)
luta ▷ vt lutar contra; (cancer, alcoholism)
combater; (election) competir ▷ vi lutar,
brigar, bater-se
figure ['fɪgəʳ] n (Drawing, Math) figura,
desenho; (number) número, cifra; (outline)
forma; (person) personagem m ▷ vt (esp
us) imaginar ▷ vi figurar; **figure out** vt
compreender
file [faɪl] n (tool) lixa; (dossier) dossiê m,
pasta; (folder) pasta; (Comput) arquivo;
(row) fila, coluna ▷ vt (wood, nails) lixar;
(papers) arquivar; (Law: claim) apresentar,
dar entrada em ▷ vi: **to ~ in/out** entrar/
sair em fila
fill [fɪl] vt: **to ~ with** encher com; (vacancy)
preencher; (need) satisfazer ▷ n: **to eat
one's ~** encher-se or fartar-se de comer;
fill in vt (form) preencher; (hole) tapar;
(time) encher; **fill up** vt encher ▷ vi (Aut)
abastecer o carro
fillet ['fɪlɪt] n filete m, filé m; **fillet steak**
n filé m
filling ['fɪlɪŋ] n (Culin) recheio; (for tooth)
obturação f (BR), chumbo (PT); **filling**

station n posto de gasolina
film [fɪlm] n filme m; (of liquid) camada,
veu m ▷ vt rodar, filmar ▷ vi filmar; **film
star** n astro/estrela do cinema
filter ['fɪltəʳ] n filtro ▷ vt filtrar
filth [fɪlθ] n sujeira (BR), sujidade f (PT);
filthy adj sujo; (language) indecente,
obsceno
fin [fɪn] n barbatana
final ['faɪnl] adj final, último; (ultimate)
maior; (definitive) definitivo ▷ n (Sport)
final f; **finals** npl (Sch) exames mpl
finais; **finale** [fɪ'nɑ:lɪ] n final m; **finalize**
vt concluir, completar; **finally** adv
finalmente, por fim
finance [faɪ'næns] n fundos mpl; (money
management) finanças fpl ▷ vt financiar;
finances npl (personal finances) finanças;
financial [faɪ'nænʃəl] adj financeiro
find [faɪnd] (pt, pp **found**) vt encontrar,
achar; (discover) descobrir ▷ n achado,
descoberta; **to ~ sb guilty** (Law) declarar
alguém culpado; **find out** vt descobrir;
(person) desmascarar ▷ vi: **to find out
about** (by chance) saber de; **findings**
npl (Law) veredito, decisão f; (of report)
constatações fpl
fine [faɪn] adj fino; (excellent) excelente;
(subtle) sutil ▷ adv muito bem ▷ n (Law)
multa ▷ vt (Law) multar; **to be ~** (person)
estar bem; (weather) estar bom; **fine arts**
npl belas artes fpl
finger ['fɪŋgəʳ] n dedo ▷ vt manusear;
fingernail n unha; **fingerprint** n
impressão f digital; **fingertip** n ponta
do dedo
finish ['fɪnɪʃ] n fim m; (Sport) chegada; (on
wood etc) acabamento ▷ vt, vi terminar,
acabar; **to ~ doing sth** terminar de fazer
algo; **to ~ third** chegar no terceiro lugar;
finish off vt terminar; (kill) liquidar;
finish up vt acabar ▷ vi ir parar
Finland ['fɪnlənd] n Finlândia
Finn [fɪn] n finlandês(-esa) m/f; **Finnish**
adj finlandês(-esa) ▷ n (Ling) finlandês m
fir [fəːʳ] n abeto
fire ['faɪəʳ] n fogo; (accidental) incêndio;
(gas fire, electric fire) aquecedor m ▷ vt
(gun) disparar; (arrow) atirar; (interest)
estimular; (dismiss) despedir ▷ vi
disparar; **on ~** em chamas; **fire alarm** n
alarme m de incêndio; **firearm** n arma de
fogo; **fire brigade** (us **fire department**)
n (corpo de) bombeiros mpl; **fire engine**
n carro de bombeiro; **fire escape** n
escada de incêndio; **fire extinguisher**

n extintor *m* de incêndio; **fireman** (*irreg*)
n bombeiro; **fireplace** *n* lareira; **fire
station** *n* posto de bombeiros; **firewall**
n (*Comput*) firewall *m*; **firewood** *n* lenha;
fireworks *npl* fogos *mpl* de artifício
firm [fəːm] *adj* firme ▷ *n* firma
first [fəːst] *adj* primeiro ▷ *adv* (*before
others*) primeiro; (*listing reasons*) em
primeiro lugar ▷ *n* (*in race*) primeiro(-a);
(*Aut*) primeira; (*BRIT*: *Sch*) menção *f*
honrosa; **at ~** no início; **~ of all** antes
de tudo, antes de mais nada; **first aid** *n*
primeiros socorros *mpl*; **first-aid kit** *n*
estojo de primeiros socorros; **first-class**
adj de primeira classe; **first-hand** *adj* de
primeira mão; **first lady** (*US*) *n* primeira
dama; **firstly** *adv* primeiramente, em
primeiro lugar; **first name** *n* primeiro
nome *m*; **first-rate** *adj* de primeira
categoria
fish [fɪʃ] *n inv* peixe *m* ▷ *vt*, *vi* pescar; **to
go ~ing** ir pescar; **fisherman** (*irreg*) *n*
pescador *m*; **fishing boat** *n* barco de
pesca; **fishing line** *n* linha de pesca;
fishmonger's (shop) *n* peixaria; **fishy**
(*inf*) *adj* (*tale*) suspeito
fist [fɪst] *n* punho
fit [fɪt] *adj* em (boa) forma; (*suitable*)
adequado, apropriado ▷ *vt* (*subj*:
clothes) caber em; (*put in*) colocar; (*equip*)
equipar; (*suit*) assentar a ▷ *vi* (*clothes*)
servir; (*parts*) ajustar-se; (*in space*) caber
▷ *n* (*Med*) ataque *m*; (*of anger*) acesso; **~
to** bom para; **~ for** adequado para; **by
~s and starts** espasmodicamente; **fit
in** *vi* encaixar-se; (*person*) dar-se bem
(com todos); **fitness** *n* (*Med*) saúde *f*,
boa forma; **fitting** *adj* apropriado ▷ *n*
(*of dress*) prova; **fittings** *npl* (*in building*)
instalações *fpl*, acessórios *mpl*
five [faɪv] *num* cinco; **fiver** (*inf*) *n* (*BRIT*)
nota de cinco libras; (*US*) nota de cinco
dólares
fix [fɪks] *vt* (*secure*) fixar, colocar; (*arrange*)
arranjar; (*mend*) consertar; (*meal, drink*)
preparar ▷ *n*: **to be in a ~** estar em
apuros; **fix up** *vt* (*meeting*) marcar; **to
fix sb up with sth** arranjar algo para
alguém; **fixed** *adj* (*prices, smile*) fixo;
fixture *n* (*furniture*) móvel *m* fixo; (*Sport*)
desafio, encontro
fizzy ['fɪzɪ] *adj* com gás, gasoso
flag [flæg] *n* bandeira; (*for signalling*)
bandeirola; (*flagstone*) laje *f* ▷ *vi* acabar-
se, descair; **flag down** *vt*: **to flag sb
down** fazer sinais a alguém para que

pare
flagpole ['flægpəʊl] *n* mastro de
bandeira
flair [flɛəʳ] *n* (*talent*) talento; (*style*)
habilidade *f*
flake [fleɪk] *n* (*of rust, paint*) lasca; (*of
snow, soap powder*) floco ▷ *vi* (*also*: **~ off**)
lascar, descamar-se
flamboyant [flæm'bɔɪənt] *adj* (*dress*)
espalhafatoso; (*person*) extravagante
flame [fleɪm] *n* chama
flammable ['flæməbl] *adj* inflamável
flan [flæn] (*BRIT*) *n* torta
flannel ['flænl] *n* (*BRIT*: *also*: **face ~**)
toalhinha de rosto; (*fabric*) flanela;
flannels *npl* calça (*BR*) *or* calças *fpl* (*PT*)
de flanela
flap [flæp] *n* (*of pocket*) aba; (*of envelope*)
dobra ▷ *vt* (*arms*) oscilar; (*wings*) bater
▷ *vi* (*sail, flag*) ondular; (*inf*: *also*: **be in a ~**)
estar atarantado
flare [flɛəʳ] *n* fogacho, chama; (*Mil*)
artifício de sinalização; (*in skirt etc*)
folga; **flare up** *vi* chamejar; (*fig*: *person*)
encolerizar-se; (: *violence*) irromper
flash [flæʃ] *n* (*of lightning*) clarão *m*;
(*also*: **news ~**) notícias *fpl* de última
hora; (*Phot*) flash *m* ▷ *vt* piscar; (*news,
message*) transmitir; (*look, smile*) brilhar
▷ *vi* brilhar; (*light on ambulance, eyes etc*)
piscar; **in a ~** num instante; **to ~ by** or
past passar como um raio; **flashlight** *n*
lanterna de bolso
flat [flæt] *adj* plano; (*battery*)
descarregado; (*tyre*) vazio; (*beer*) choco;
(*denial*) categórico; (*Mus*) abemolado;
(: *voice*) desafinado; (*rate*) único; (*fee*) fixo
▷ *n* (*BRIT*: *apartment*) apartamento; (*Mus*)
bemol *m*; (*Aut*) pneu *m* furado; **~ out**
(*work*) a toque de caixa; **flatten** *vt* (*also*:
flatten out) aplanar; (*demolish*) arrasar
flatter ['flætəʳ] *vt* lisonjear; **flattering**
adj lisonjeiro; (*clothes etc*) favorecedor(a)
flaunt [flɔːnt] *vt* ostentar, pavonear
flavour ['fleɪvəʳ] (*US* **flavor**) *n* sabor
m ▷ *vt* condimentar, aromatizar;
strawberry-~ed com sabor de morango
flaw [flɔː] *n* defeito; (*in character*) falha;
flawless *adj* impecável
flea [fliː] *n* pulga
flee [fliː] (*pt, pp* **fled**) *vt* fugir de ▷ *vi* fugir
fleece [fliːs] *n* tosão *m*; (*wool*) lã *f*; (*coat*)
velo ▷ *vt* (*inf*) espoliar
fleet [fliːt] *n* (*of lorries etc*) frota; (*of ships*)
esquadra
fleeting ['fliːtɪŋ] *adj* (*glimpse, happiness*)

fugaz; (visit) passageiro

Flemish ['flɛmɪʃ] adj flamengo

flesh [flɛʃ] n carne f; (of fruit) polpa

flew [fluː] pt of **fly**

flex [flɛks] n fio ▷ vt (muscles) flexionar; **flexible** adj flexível

flick [flɪk] n pancada leve; (with finger) peteleco, piparote m; (with whip) chicotada ▷ vt dar um peteleco; (towel) dar uma lambada; (whip) dar uma chicotada; (switch) apertar; **flick through** vt fus folhear

flicker ['flɪkəʳ] vi tremular; (eyelids) tremer

flight [flaɪt] n vôo m; (escape) fuga; (of steps) lance m; **flight attendant** (us) n comissário(-a) de bordo

flimsy ['flɪmzɪ] adj (thin) delgado, franzino; (shoes) ordinário; (clothes) de tecido fino; (building) barato; (weak) débil; (excuse) fraco

flinch [flɪntʃ] vi encolher-se; **to ~ from sth/from doing sth** vacilar diante de algo/em fazer algo

fling [flɪŋ] (pt, pp **flung**) vt lançar

flint [flɪnt] n pederneira; (in lighter) pedra

flipper ['flɪpəʳ] n (of animal) nadadeira; (for swimmer) pé-de-pato, nadadeira

flirt [fləːt] vi flertar ▷ n namorador(a) m/f, paquerador(a) m/f

float [fləʊt] n bóia; (in procession) carro alegórico; (sum of money) caixa ▷ vi flutuar; (swimmer) boiar

flock [flɔk] n rebanho; (of birds) bando ▷ vi: **to ~ to** afluir a

flood [flʌd] n enchente f, inundação f; (of letters, imports etc) enxurrada ▷ vt inundar, alagar ▷ vi (place) alagar; (people, goods): **to ~ into** inundar; **flooding** n inundação f; **floodlight** n refletor m, holofote m

floor [flɔːʳ] n chão m; (storey) andar m; (of sea) fundo ▷ vt (fig: confuse) confundir, pasmar; (subj: blow) derrubar; (: question, remark) aturdir; **ground ~** (BRIT) or **first ~** (US) andar térreo (BR), rés-do-chão (PT); **first ~** (BRIT) or **second ~** (US) primeiro andar; **floorboard** n tábua de assoalho; **floor show** n show m

flop [flɔp] n fracasso ▷ vi fracassar; (into chair) cair pesadamente

floppy ['flɔpɪ] adj frouxo, mole; **floppy (disk)** n disquete m

florist ['flɔrɪst] n florista m/f; **florist's (shop)** n floricultura

flour ['flaʊəʳ] n farinha

flourish ['flʌrɪʃ] vi florescer ▷ vt brandir, menear ▷ n gesto floreado

flow [fləʊ] n fluxo; (of river, Elec) corrente f; (of blood) circulação f ▷ vi correr; (traffic) fluir; (blood, Elec) circular; (clothes, hair) ondular

flower ['flaʊəʳ] n flor f ▷ vi florescer, florir; **flower bed** n canteiro; **flowerpot** n vaso

flown [fləʊn] pp of **fly**

flu [fluː] n gripe f

fluctuate ['flʌktjueɪt] vi flutuar; (temperature) variar

fluent ['fluːənt] adj fluente; **he speaks ~ French, he's ~ in French** ele fala francês fluentemente

fluff [flʌf] n felpa, penugem f; **fluffy** adj macio, fofo; (toy) de pelúcia

fluid ['fluːɪd] adj fluido ▷ n fluido

fluke [fluːk] (inf) n sorte f

flung [flʌŋ] pt, pp of **fling**

fluoride ['fluəraɪd] n fluoreto

flurry ['flʌrɪ] n (of snow) lufada; **~ of activity** muita atividade

flush [flʌʃ] n (on face) rubor m; (fig) resplendor m ▷ vt lavar com água ▷ vi ruborizar-se ▷ adj: **~ with** rente com; **to ~ the toilet** dar descarga; **flush out** vt levantar

flute [fluːt] n flauta

flutter ['flʌtəʳ] n agitação f; (of wings) bater m ▷ vi esvoaçar

fly [flaɪ] (pt **flew**, pp **flown**) n mosca; (on trousers: also: **flies**) braguilha ▷ vt (plane) pilotar; (passengers, cargo) transportar (de avião); (distances) percorrer ▷ vi voar; (passengers) ir de avião; (escape) fugir; (flag) hastear-se; **fly away** or **off** vi voar; **flying** n aviação f ▷ adj: **flying visit** visita de médico; **with flying colours** brilhantemente; **flying saucer** n disco voador; **flyover** (BRIT) n viaduto

foal [fəʊl] n potro

foam [fəʊm] n espuma; (also: **~ rubber**) espuma de borracha ▷ vi espumar

focus ['fəʊkəs] (pl **~es**) n foco ▷ vt enfocar ▷ vi: **to ~ on** enfocar, focalizar; **in/out of ~** em foco/fora de foco

fog [fɔg] n nevoeiro; **foggy** adj: **it's foggy** está nevoento

foil [fɔɪl] vt frustrar ▷ n folha metálica; (also: **kitchen ~**) folha or papel m de alumínio; (complement) contraste m, complemento; (Fencing) florete m

fold [fəʊld] n dobra, vinco, prega; (of skin) ruga; (Agr) redil m, curral m ▷ vt

dobrar; (arms) cruzar; **fold up** vi dobrar;
(business) abrir falência ▷ vt dobrar;
folder n pasta; **folding** adj dobrável
folk [fəuk] npl gente f ▷ cpd popular,
folclórico; **folks** npl (family) família,
parentes mpl; (parents) pais mpl; **folklore**
['fəuklɔːʳ] n folclore m
follow ['fɔləu] vt seguir; (event, story)
acompanhar ▷ vi seguir; (person, period of
time) acompanhar; (result) resultar; **to ~
suit** fazer o mesmo; **follow up** vt (letter)
responder a; (offer) levar adiante; (case)
acompanhar; **follower** n seguidor(a)
m/f; **following** adj seguinte ▷ n
adeptos mpl
fond [fɔnd] adj carinhoso; (hopes)
absurdo, descabido; **to be ~ of** gostar de
food [fuːd] n comida; **food mixer**
n batedeira; **food poisoning** n
intoxicação f alimentar; **food processor**
n multiprocessador m de cozinha
fool [fuːl] n tolo(-a); (Culin) purê m de
frutas com creme ▷ vt enganar ▷ vi (gen:
fool around) brincar; **foolish** adj burro;
(careless) imprudente; **foolproof** adj
infalível
foot [fut] (pl feet) n pé m; (of animal)
pata; (measure) pé (304 mm; 12 inches)
▷ vt (bill) pagar; **on ~** a pé; **footage** n
(Cinema: length) ≈ metragem f; (: material)
seqüências fpl; **football** n bola; (game:
BRIT) futebol m; (: US) futebol norte-
americano; **football player** n (BRIT:
also: **footballer**) jogador m de futebol;
footbridge n passarela; **foothold** n
apoio para o pé; **footing** n (fig) posição
f; **to lose one's footing** escorregar;
footnote n nota ao pé da página, nota
de rodapé; **footpath** n caminho, atalho;
footprint n pegada; **footstep** n passo;
footwear n calçados mpl

KEYWORD

for [fɔːʳ] prep **1** (indicating destination,
direction) para; **he went for the paper**
foi pegar o jornal; **is this for me?** é para
mim?; **it's time for lunch** é hora de
almoçar
2 (indicating purpose) para; **what's it for?**
para quê serve?; **to pray for peace** orar
pela paz
3 (on behalf of, representing) por; **he works
for the government/a local firm** ele
trabalha para o governo/uma firma
local; **G for George** G de George

4 (because of) por; **for this reason** por
esta razão; **for fear of being criticised**
com medo de ser criticado
5 (with regard to) para; **it's cold for July**
está frio para julho
6 (in exchange for) por; **it was sold for £5**
foi vendido por £5
7 (in favour of) a favor de; **are you for
or against us?** você está a favor de ou
contra nós?; **I'm all for it** concordo
plenamente, tem todo o meu apoio;
vote for X vote em X
8 (referring to distance): **there are
roadworks for 5 km** há obras na estrada
por 5 quilômetros; **we walked for miles**
andamos quilômetros
9 (referring to time): **she will be away for
a month** ela ficará fora um mês; **I have
known her for years** eu a conheço há
anos; **can you do it for tomorrow?** você
pode fazer isso para amanhã?
10 (with infinite clause): **it is not for me
to decide** não cabe a mim decidir; **it
would be best for you to leave** seria
melhor que você fosse embora; **there
is still time for you to do it** ainda há
tempo para você fazer isso; **for this to be
possible ...** para que isso seja possível ...
11 (in spite of) apesar de
▷ conj (since, as: rather formal) pois,
porque

forbid [fə'bɪd] (pt forbad(e), pp ~den) vt
proibir; **to ~ sb to do sth** proibir alguém
de fazer algo
force [fɔːs] n força ▷ vt forçar; **the
Forces** npl (BRIT) as Forças Armadas; **in ~**
em vigor; **forceful** adj enérgico, vigoroso
ford [fɔːd] n vau m
fore [fɔːʳ] n: **to come to the ~** salientar-se
forearm ['fɔːrɑːm] n antebraço
forecast ['fɔːkɑːst] (irreg: like cast) n
previsão f; (also: **weather ~**) previsão do
tempo ▷ vt prognosticar, prever
forefinger ['fɔːfɪŋgəʳ] n (dedo)
indicador m
foreground ['fɔːgraund] n primeiro
plano
forehead ['fɔrɪd] n testa
foreign ['fɔrɪn] adj estrangeiro; (trade)
exterior; (object, matter) estranho;
foreigner n estrangeiro(-a); **foreign
exchange** n câmbio; **Foreign Office**
(BRIT) n Ministério das Relações
Exteriores
foreman ['fɔːmən] (irreg) n capataz m; (in

construction) contramestre *m*
foremost ['fɔːməust] *adj* principal ▷ *adv*:
first and ~ antes de mais nada
forensic [fə'rɛnsɪk] *adj* forense; **~
medicine** medicina legal
foresee [fɔː'siː] (*irreg: like* **see**) *vt* prever;
foreseeable *adj* previsível
forest ['fɔrɪst] *n* floresta
forestry ['fɔrɪstrɪ] *n* silvicultura
forever [fə'rɛvə'] *adv* para sempre
foreword ['fɔːwəːd] *n* prefácio
forfeit ['fɔːfɪt] *vt* perder (direito a)
forgave [fə'geɪv] *pt of* **forgive**
forge [fɔːdʒ] *n* ferraria ▷ *vt* falsificar;
(*metal*) forjar; **forge ahead** *vi*
avançar constantemente; **forger**
n falsificador(a) *m/f*; **forgery** *n*
falsificação *f*
forget [fə'gɛt] (*pt* **forgot**, *pp* **forgotten**)
vt, *vi* esquecer; **forgetful** *adj* esquecido
forgive [fə'gɪv] (*pt* **forgave**, *pp* **~n**) *vt*
perdoar; **to ~ sb for sth** perdoar algo a
alguém, perdoar alguém de algo
fork [fɔːk] *n* (*for eating*) garfo; (*for
gardening*) forquilha; (*of roads etc*)
bifurcação *f* ▷ *vi* bifurcar-se; **fork out**
(*inf*) *vt* (*pay*) desembolsar, morrer em
forlorn [fə'lɔːn] *adj* desolado; (*attempt*)
desesperado; (*hope*) último
form [fɔːm] *n* forma; (*type*) tipo; (*Sch*)
série *f*; (*questionnaire*) formulário ▷ *vt*
formar; (*organization*) criar; **to ~ a queue**
(*BRIT*) fazer fila; **in top ~** em plena forma
formal ['fɔːməl] *adj* (*offer*) oficial; (*person*)
cerimonioso; (*occasion, education*) formal;
(*dress*) a rigor (*BR*), de cerimónia (*PT*);
(*garden*) simétrico
format ['fɔːmæt] *n* formato ▷ *vt*
(*Comput*) formatar
former ['fɔːmə'] *adj* anterior; (*earlier*)
antigo; **the ~ ... the latter ...** aquele ...
este ...; **formerly** *adv* anteriormente
formidable ['fɔːmɪdəbl] *adj* terrível,
temível
formula ['fɔːmjulə] (*pl* **~s** *or* **~e**) *n*
fórmula
fort [fɔːt] *n* forte *m*
fortify ['fɔːtɪfaɪ] *vt* (*city*) fortificar;
(*person*) fortalecer
fortnight ['fɔːtnaɪt] (*BRIT*) *n* quinzena,
quinze dias *mpl*; **fortnightly** *adj*
quinzenal ▷ *adv* quinzenalmente
fortunate ['fɔːtʃənɪt] *adj* (*event*) feliz;
(*person*): **to be ~** ter sorte; **it is ~ that ...**
é uma sorte que ...; **fortunately** *adv*
felizmente

fortune ['fɔːtʃən] *n* sorte *f*; (*wealth*)
fortuna; **fortune-teller** *n* adivinho(-a)
forty ['fɔːtɪ] *num* quarenta
forward ['fɔːwəd] *adj* (*movement*) para
a frente; (*position*) avançado; (*in time*)
futuro; (*not shy*) imodesto, presunçoso
▷ *n* (*Sport*) atacante *m* ▷ *vt* (*letter*)
remeter; (*goods, parcel*) expedir; (*career*)
promover; (*plans*) ativar; **to move ~**
avançar; **forward(s)** *adv* para a frente
foster ['fɔstə'] *vt* adotar (por um tempo
limitado); (*activity*) promover; **foster
child** (*irreg*) *n* filho adotivo (por um
tempo limitado)
fought [fɔːt] *pt*, *pp of* **fight**
foul [faul] *adj* horrível; (*language*)
obsceno ▷ *n* (*Sport*) falta ▷ *vt* sujar; **foul
play** *n* (*Law*) crime *m*
found [faund] *pt*, *pp of* **find** ▷ *vt*
(*establish*) fundar; **foundation**
[faun'deɪʃən] *n* (*act, organization*)
fundação *f*; (*base*) base *f*; (*also:*
foundation cream) creme *m*
base; **foundations** *npl* (*of building*)
alicerces *mpl*
founder ['faundə'] *n* fundador(a) *m/f*
▷ *vi* naufragar
fountain ['fauntɪn] *n* chafariz *m*;
fountain pen *n* caneta-tinteiro *f*
four [fɔː'] *num* quatro; **on all ~s** de
quatro; **fourteen** *num* catorze; **fourth**
num quarto
fowl [faul] *n* ave *f* (doméstica)
fox [fɔks] *n* raposa ▷ *vt* deixar perplexo
foyer ['fɔɪeɪ] *n* saguão *m*
fraction ['frækʃən] *n* fração *f*
fracture ['fræktʃə'] *n* fratura ▷ *vt*
fraturar
fragile ['frædʒaɪl] *adj* frágil
fragment ['frægmənt] *n* fragmento
frail [freɪl] *adj* (*person*) fraco; (*structure*)
frágil
frame [freɪm] *n* (*of building*) estrutura;
(*body*) corpo; (*of picture, door*) moldura;
(*of spectacles: also:* **~s**) armação *f*, aro
▷ *vt* (*picture*) emoldurar; **framework** *n*
armação *f*
France [frɑːns] *n* França
frank [fræŋk] *adj* franco ▷ *vt* (*letter*)
franquear; **frankly** *adv* francamente;
(*candidly*) abertamente
frantic ['fræntɪk] *adj* frenético; (*person*)
fora de si
fraud [frɔːd] *n* fraude *f*; (*person*)
impostor(a) *m/f*
fraught [frɔːt] *adj* tenso; **~ with** repleto

de
fray [freɪ] n guerra ▷ vi esfiapar-se;
tempers were ~ed estavam com os
nervos em frangalhos
freak [friːk] n (person) anormal m/f;
(event) anomalia
freckle ['frɛkl] n sarda
free [friː] adj livre; (seat) desocupado;
(costing nothing) gratis, gratuito ▷ vt pôr
em liberdade; (jammed object) soltar; **~
(of charge)** grátis, de graça; **freedom**
n liberdade f; **freelance** adj autônomo;
freely adv livremente; **free-range** n
(egg) caseiro; **freeway** (US) n auto-
estrada; **free will** n livre arbítrio; **of
one's own free will** por sua própria
vontade
freeze [friːz] (pt **froze**, pp **frozen**) vi
gelar-se, congelar-se ▷ vt congelar ▷ n
geada; (on arms, wages) congelamento;
freezer n congelador m, freezer m (BR);
freezing adj: **freezing (cold)** (weather)
glacial; (water) gelado; **3 degrees below
freezing** 3 graus abaixo de zero; **freezing
point** n ponto de congelamento
freight [freɪt] n (goods) carga; (money
charged) frete m; **freight train** (US) n
trem m de carga
French [frɛntʃ] adj francês(-esa) ▷ n
(Ling) francês m; **the French** npl (people)
os franceses; **French bean** (BRIT) n
feijão m comum; **French fried potatoes**
(US **French fries**) npl batatas fpl
fritas; **Frenchman** (irreg) n francês m;
Frenchwoman (irreg) n francesa
frenzy ['frɛnzɪ] n frenesi m
frequent [(adj) 'friːkwənt, (vt) frɪ'kwɛnt]
adj freqüente ▷ vt freqüentar;
frequently adv freqüentemente, a
miúdo
fresh [frɛʃ] adj fresco; (new) novo; (cheeky)
atrevido; **freshen** vi (wind, air) tornar-
se mais forte; **freshen up** vi (person)
lavar-se, refrescar-se; **freshly** adv
recentemente, há pouco
fret [frɛt] vi afligir-se
friction ['frɪkʃən] n fricção f; (between
people) atrito
Friday ['fraɪdɪ] n sexta-feira f
fridge [frɪdʒ] (BRIT) n geladeira (BR),
frigorífico (PT)
fried [fraɪd] adj frito; **~ egg** ovo estrelado
or frito
friend [frɛnd] n amigo(-a); **friendly** adj
simpático; (match) amistoso; **friendship**
n amizade f

fright [fraɪt] n terror m; (scare) pavor
m; **to take ~** assustar-se; **frighten**
vt assustar; **frightened** adj: **to be
frightened of** ter medo de; **frightening**
adj assustador(a); **frightful** adj terrível,
horrível
frill [frɪl] n babado
fringe [frɪndʒ] n franja; (on shawl etc)
beira, orla; (edge: of forest etc) margem f
fritter ['frɪtə*] n bolinho frito; **fritter
away** vt desperdiçar
frivolous ['frɪvələs] adj frívolo; (activity)
fútil
fro [frəu] adj see **to**
frock [frɔk] n vestido
frog [frɔg] n rã f; **frogman** (irreg) n
homem-rã m

⭕ **KEYWORD**

from [frɔm] prep **1** (indicating starting
place) de; **where do you come from?** de
onde você é?; **from London to Glasgow**
de Londres para Glasgow; **to escape
from sth/sb** escapar de algo/alguém
2 (indicating origin etc) de; **a letter/
telephone call from my sister** uma
carta/um telefonema de minha irmã;
tell him from me that ... diga a ele que
da minha parte ...; **to drink from the
bottle** beber na garrafa
3 (indicating time): **from one o'clock to** or
until or **till two** da uma hora até às duas;
from January (on) a partir de janeiro
4 (indicating distance): **we're still a
long way from home** ainda estamos
muito longe de casa
5 (indicating price, number etc) de; **prices
range from £10 to £50** os preços vão de
£10 a £50
6 (indicating difference) de; **he can't tell
red from green** ele não pode diferenciar
vermelho do verde
7 (because of/on the basis of): **from what
he says** pelo que ele diz; **to act from
conviction** agir por convicção; **weak
from hunger** fraco de fome

front [frʌnt] n frente f; (of vehicle) parte
f dianteira; (of house, fig) fachada; (also:
sea ~) orla marítima ▷ adj da frente; **in ~
(of)** em frente (de); **front door** n porta
principal; **frontier** ['frʌntɪə*] n fronteira;
front page n primeira página
frost [frɔst] n geada; (also: **hoar~**) gelo;
frostbite n ulceração f produzida pelo

frio; **frosty** adj (window) coberto de geada; (welcome) glacial

froth [frɔθ] n espuma

frown [fraun] vi franzir as sobrancelhas, amarrar a cara

froze [frəuz] pt of **freeze**

frozen ['frəuzn] pp of **freeze**

fruit [fru:t] n inv fruta; (fig: pl fruits) fruto; **fruit juice** n suco (BR) or sumo (PT) de frutas; **fruit machine** (BRIT) n caça-níqueis m inv (BR), máquina de jogo (PT); **fruit salad** n salada de frutas

frustrate [frʌs'treɪt] vt frustrar

fry [fraɪ] (pt, pp **fried**) vt fritar; see also **small**; **frying pan** n frigideira

fudge [fʌdʒ] n (Culin) ≈ doce m de leite

fuel [fjuəl] n (for heating) combustível m; (for propelling) carburante m; **fuel tank** n depósito de combustível

fulfil [ful'fɪl] (US **fulfill**) vt (function) cumprir; (condition) satisfazer; (wish, desire) realizar

full [ful] adj cheio; (use, volume) máximo; (complete) completo; (information) detalhado; (price) integral; (skirt) folgado ▷ adv: ~ **well** perfeitamente; **I'm ~ (up)** estou satisfeito; ~ **employment** pleno emprego; **a ~ two hours** duas horas completas; **at ~ speed** a toda a velocidade; **in ~** integralmente; **full stop** n ponto (final); **full-time** adj, adv (work) de tempo completo or integral; **fully** adv completamente; (at least) pelo menos

fumble ['fʌmbl] vi: **to ~ with** vt fus atrapalhar-se com

fume [fju:m] vi fumegar; (be angry) estar com raiva; **fumes** npl gases mpl

fun [fʌn] n divertimento; **to have ~** divertir-se; **for ~** de brincadeira; **to make ~ of** fazer troça de, zombar de

function ['fʌŋkʃən] n função f; (reception, dinner) recepção f ▷ vi funcionar

fund [fʌnd] n fundo; (source, store) fonte f; **funds** npl (money) fundos mpl

fundamental [fʌndə'mɛntl] adj fundamental

funeral ['fju:nərəl] n (burial) enterro

funfair ['fʌnfɛər] (BRIT) n parque m de diversões

fungus ['fʌŋgəs] (pl **fungi**) n fungo; (mould) bolor m, mofo

funnel ['fʌnl] n funil m; (of ship) chaminé m

funny ['fʌnɪ] adj engraçado, divertido; (strange) esquisito, estranho

fur [fə:r] n pele f; (BRIT: in kettle etc)

depósito, crosta

furious ['fjuərɪəs] adj furioso; (effort) incrível

furnish ['fə:nɪʃ] vt mobiliar (BR), mobilar (PT); (supply): **to ~ sb with sth** fornecer algo a alguém; **furnishings** npl mobília

furniture ['fə:nɪtʃər] n mobília, móveis mpl; **piece of ~** móvel m

furry ['fə:rɪ] adj peludo

further ['fə:ðər] adj novo, adicional ▷ adv mais longe; (more) mais; (moreover) além disso ▷ vt promover; **further education** (BRIT) n educação f superior; **furthermore** adv além disso

furthest ['fə:ðɪst] superl of **far**

fury ['fjuərɪ] n fúria

fuse [fju:z] n fusível m; (for bomb etc) espoleta, mecha ▷ vt fundir; (fig) unir ▷ vi (metal) fundir-se; unir-se; **to ~ the lights** (BRIT) (Elec) queimar as luzes; **fuse box** n caixa de fusíveis

fuss [fʌs] n estardalhaço; (complaining) escândalo; **to make a ~** criar caso; **to make a ~ of sb** papariçar alguém; **fussy** adj (person) exigente; (dress, style) espalhafatoso

future ['fju:tʃər] adj futuro ▷ n futuro; **in ~** no futuro

fuze [fju:z] (US) = **fuse**

fuzzy ['fʌzɪ] adj (Phot) indistinto; (hair) frisado, encrespado

for anything topar qualquer parada; **big ~** caça grossa

gang [gæŋ] n bando, grupo; (of criminals) gangue f; (of workmen) turma ▷ vi: **to ~ up on sb** conspirar contra alguém

gangster ['gæŋstər] n gângster m, bandido

gap [gæp] n brecha, fenda; (in trees, traffic) abertura; (in time) intervalo; (difference) diferença

gape [geɪp] vi (person) estar or ficar boquiaberto; (hole) abrir-se

garage ['gærɑːʒ] n garagem f; (for car repairs) oficina (mecânica)

garbage ['gɑːbɪdʒ] n (US) lixo; (inf: nonsense) disparates mpl; **garbage can** (US) n lata de lixo

garden ['gɑːdn] n jardim m; **gardens** npl (public park) jardim público, parque m; **gardener** n jardineiro(-a); **gardening** n jardinagem f

garlic ['gɑːlɪk] n alho

garment ['gɑːmənt] n peça de roupa

garrison ['gærɪsn] n guarnição f

gas [gæs] n gás m; (US: gasoline) gasolina ▷ vt asfixiar com gás; **gas cooker** (BRIT) n fogão m a gás; **gas cylinder** n bujão m de gás; **gas fire** (BRIT) n aquecedor m a gás

gasket ['gæskɪt] n (Aut) junta, gaxeta

gasoline ['gæsəliːn] (US) n gasolina

gasp [gɑːsp] n arfada ▷ vi arfar; **gasp out** vt dizer com voz entrecortada

gas station (US) n posto de gasolina

gate [geɪt] n portão m; **gatecrash** (BRIT) vt entrar de penetra em; **gateway** n portão m, passagem f

gather ['gæðər] vt colher; (assemble) reunir; (Sewing) franzir; (understand) compreender ▷ vi reunir-se; **to ~ speed** acelerar-se; **gathering** n reunião f, assembléia

gauge [geɪdʒ] n (instrument) medidor m ▷ vt (fig: character) avaliar

gave [geɪv] pt of **give**

gay [geɪ] adj (homosexual) gay; (old-fashioned: cheerful) alegre; (colour) vistoso; (music) vivo

gaze [geɪz] n olhar m fixo ▷ vi: **to ~ at sth** fitar algo

GB abbr = **Great Britain**

gear [gɪər] n equipamento m; (Tech) engrenagem f; (Aut) velocidade f, marcha (BR), mudança (PT) ▷ vt (fig: adapt): **to ~ sth to** preparar algo para; **top** (BRIT) or **high** (US)/**low ~** quarta/primeira

---

G [dʒiː] n (Mus) sol m

gadget ['gædʒɪt] n aparelho, engenhoca

Gaelic ['geɪlɪk] adj gaélico(-a) ▷ n (Ling) gaélico

gag [gæg] n (on mouth) mordaça; (joke) piada ▷ vt amordaçar

gain [geɪn] n ganho; (profit) lucro ▷ vt ganhar ▷ vi (watch) adiantar-se; (benefit): **to ~ from sth** tirar proveito de algo; **to ~ on sb** aproximar-se de alguém; **to ~ 3lbs (in weight)** engordar 3 libras

gal. abbr = **gallon**

gale [geɪl] n ventania; **~ force 10** vento de força 10

gallery ['gælərɪ] n (in theatre etc) galeria; (also: **art ~**: public) museu m; (: private) galeria (de arte)

gallon ['gæln] n galão m (= 8 pints; BRIT = 4.5l; US = 3.8l)

gallop ['gæləp] n galope m ▷ vi galopar

gallstone ['gɔːlstəun] n cálculo biliar

gamble ['gæmbl] n risco ▷ vt apostar ▷ vi jogar, arriscar; **gambler** n jogador(a) m/f; **gambling** n jogo

game [geɪm] n jogo; (match) partida; (esp Tennis) jogada; (strategy) plano, esquema m; (Hunting) caça ▷ adj (willing): **to be ~**

(marcha); **in ~** engrenado

geese [giːs] npl of **goose**

gel [dʒɛl] n gel m

gem [dʒɛm] n jóia, gema

Gemini ['dʒɛmɪnaɪ] n Gêminis m, Gêmeos mpl

gender ['dʒɛndər] n gênero

general ['dʒɛnərl] n general m ▷ adj geral; **in ~** em geral; **generally** adv geralmente; **general anaesthetic** n anestesia geral; **general practitioner** n clínico(-a) geral

generate ['dʒɛnəreɪt] vt gerar; **generator** n gerador m

generous ['dʒɛnərəs] adj generoso; (measure etc) abundante

Geneva [dʒɪ'niːvə] n Genebra

genitals ['dʒɛnɪtlz] npl órgãos mpl genitais

genius ['dʒiːnɪəs] n gênio

gentle ['dʒɛntl] adj (touch) leve, suave; (landscape) suave; (animal) manso

gentleman ['dʒɛntlmən] (irreg) n senhor m; (social position) fidalgo; (well-bred man) cavalheiro

gently ['dʒɛntlɪ] adv suavemente

gents [dʒɛnts] n banheiro de homens (BR), casa de banho dos homens (PT)

genuine ['dʒɛnjuɪn] adj autêntico; (person) sincero

geography [dʒɪ'ɔgrəfɪ] n geografia

geology [dʒɪ'ɔlədʒɪ] n geologia

geometry [dʒɪ'ɔmətrɪ] n geometria

geranium [dʒɪ'reɪnjəm] n gerânio

geriatric [dʒɛrɪ'ætrɪk] adj geriátrico

germ [dʒəːm] n micróbio, bacilo

German ['dʒəːmən] adj alemão(-mã) ▷ n alemão(-mã) m/f; (Ling) alemão m; **German measles** n rubéola

Germany ['dʒəːmənɪ] n Alemanha

gesture ['dʒɛstjər] n gesto

Ⓞ KEYWORD

get [gɛt] (pt, pp **got**, pp **gotten** (US)) vi
1 (become, be) ficar, tornar-se; **to get old/tired/cold** envelhecer/cansar-se/resfriar-se; **to get annoyed/bored** aborrecer-se/amuar-se; **to get drunk** embebedar-se; **to get dirty** sujar-se; **to get killed/married** ser morto/casar-se; **when do I get paid?** quando eu recebo?, quando eu vou ser pago?; **it's getting late** está ficando tarde
2 (go): **to get to/from** ir para/de; **to get home** chegar em casa

3 (begin) começar a; **to get to know sb** começar a conhecer alguém; **let's get going** or **started** vamos lá!
▷ modal aux vb: **you've got to do it** você tem que fazê-lo
▷ vt 1: **to get sth done** (do) fazer algo; (have done) mandar fazer algo; **to get one's hair cut** cortar o cabelo; **to get the car going** or **to go** fazer o carro andar; **to get sb to do sth** convencer alguém a fazer algo; **to get sth/sb ready** preparar algo/arrumar alguém
2 (obtain) ter; (find) achar; (fetch) buscar; **to get sth for sb** arranjar algo para alguém; (fetch) ir buscar algo para alguém; **get me Mr Jones, please** (Tel) pode chamar o Sr Jones por favor; **can I get you a drink?** você está servido?
3 (receive: present, letter) receber; (acquire: reputation, prize) ganhar
4 (catch) agarrar; (hit: target etc) pegar; **to get sb by the arm/throat** agarrar alguém pelo braço/pela garganta; **get him!** pega ele!
5 (take, move) levar; **to get sth to sb** levar algo para alguém; **I can't get it in/out/through** não consigo enfiá-lo/tirá-lo/passá-lo; **do you think we'll get it through the door?** você acha que conseguiremos passar isto na porta?
6 (plane, bus etc) pegar, tomar
7 (understand) entender; (hear) ouvir; **I've got it** entendi; **I don't get your meaning** não entendo o que você quer dizer
8 (have, possess): **to have got** ter

get about vi (news) espalhar-se

get along vi (agree) entender-se; (depart) ir embora; (manage) = **get by**

get around = **get round**

get at vt fus (attack, criticize) atacar; (reach) alcançar; **what are you getting at?** o que você está querendo dizer?

get away vi (leave) partir; (escape) escapar

get away with vt fus conseguir fazer impunemente

get back vi (return) regressar, voltar ▷ vt receber de volta, recobrar

get by vi (pass) passar; (manage) virar-se

get down vi descer ▷ vt fus abaixar ▷ vt (object) abaixar, descer; (depress: person) deprimir

get down to vt fus (work) pôr-se a (fazer)

get in vi entrar; (train) chegar; (arrive

home) voltar para casa
get into vt fus entrar em; (*vehicle*) subir em; (*clothes*) pôr, vestir, enfiar; **to get into bed/a rage** meter-se na cama/ficar com raiva
get off vi (*from train etc*) saltar (BR), descer (PT); (*depart*) sair; (*escape*) escapar ▷ vt (*remove: clothes, stain*) tirar; (*send off*) mandar
▷ vt fus (*train, bus*) saltar de (BR), sair de (PT)
get on vi (*at exam etc*): **how are you getting on?** como vai?; (*agree*): **to get on (with)** entender-se (com)
▷ vt fus (*train etc*) subir em (BR), subir para (PT); (*horse*) montar em
get out vi (*of place, vehicle*) sair
▷ vt (*take out*) tirar
get out of vt fus (*duty etc*) escapar de
get over vt fus (*illness*) restabelecer-se de
get round vt fus rodear; (*fig: person*) convencer
get through vi (*Tel*) completar a ligação
get through to vt fus (*Tel*) comunicar-se com
get together vi (*people*) reunir-se
▷ vt reunir
get up vi levantar-se
▷ vt fus levantar
get up to vt fus (*reach*) chegar a; (*BRIT: prank etc*) fazer

getaway ['gɛtəweɪ] n fuga, escape m
ghastly ['gɑːstlɪ] adj horrível; (*building*) medonho; (*appearance*) horripilante; (*pale*) pálido
ghost [gəʊst] n fantasma m
giant ['dʒaɪənt] n gigante m ▷ adj gigantesco, gigante
gift [gɪft] n presente m, dádiva; (*ability*) dom m, talento; **gifted** adj bem-dotado
gigantic [dʒaɪˈgæntɪk] adj gigantesco
giggle ['gɪgl] vi dar risadinha boba
gills [gɪlz] npl (*of fish*) guelras fpl, brânquias fpl
gilt [gɪlt] adj dourado ▷ n dourado
gimmick ['gɪmɪk] n truque m or macete m (*publicitário*)
gin [dʒɪn] n gim m, genebra
ginger ['dʒɪndʒə^r] n gengibre m
gipsy ['dʒɪpsɪ] n cigano
giraffe [dʒɪˈrɑːf] n girafa
girl [gəːl] n (*small*) menina (BR), rapariga (PT); (*young woman*) jovem f, moça; (*daughter*) filha; **girlfriend** n (*of girl*)

amiga; (*of boy*) namorada
gist [dʒɪst] n essencial m

◯ **KEYWORD**

give [gɪv] (*pt* **gave**, *pp* **given**) vt **1** (*hand over*) dar; **to give sb sth, give sth to sb** dar algo a alguém
2 (*used with n to replace a vb*): **to give a cry/sigh/push** etc dar um grito/suspiro/empurrão etc; **to give a speech/a lecture** fazer um discurso/uma palestra
3 (*tell, deliver: news, advice, message etc*) dar; **to give the right/wrong answer** dar a resposta certa/errada
4 (*supply, provide: opportunity, job etc*) dar; (*bestow: title, right*) conceder; **the sun gives warmth and light** o sol fornece calor e luz
5 (*dedicate: time, one's life/attention*) dedicar; **she gave it all her attention** ela dedicou toda sua atenção a isto
6 (*organize*): **to give a party/dinner** etc dar uma festa/jantar etc
▷ vi **1** (*also: break, collapse*) dar folga; **his legs gave beneath him** suas pernas bambearam; **the roof/floor gave as I stepped on it** o telhado/chão desabou quando eu pisei nele
2 (*stretch: fabric*) dar de si
give away vt (*money, opportunity*) dar; (*secret, information*) revelar
give back vt devolver
give in vi (*yield*) ceder
▷ vt (*essay etc*) entregar
give off vt (*heat, smoke*) soltar
give out vt (*distribute*) distribuir; (*make known*) divulgar
give up vi (*surrender*) desistir, dar-se por vencido
▷ vt (*job, boyfriend, habit*) renunciar a; (*idea, hope*) abandonar; **to give up smoking** deixar de fumar; **to give o.s. up** entregar-se
give way vi (*yield*) ceder; (*break, collapse: rope*) arrebentar; (*: ladder*) quebrar; (BRIT: Aut) dar a preferência (BR), dar prioridade (PT)

glacier ['glæsɪə^r] n glaciar m, geleira
glad [glæd] adj contente
gladly ['glædlɪ] adv com muito prazer
glamorous ['glæmərəs] adj encantador(a), glamouroso
glamour ['glæmə^r] n encanto, glamour m

glance [glɑːns] n relance m, vista de olhos ▷ vi: **to ~ at** olhar (de relance); **glance off** vt fus (bullet) ricochetear de

gland [glænd] n glândula

glare [glɛəʳ] n (of anger) olhar m furioso; (of light) luminosidade f; (of publicity) foco ▷ vi brilhar; **to ~ at** olhar furiosamente para; **glaring** adj (mistake) notório

glass [glɑːs] n vidro, cristal m; (for drinking) copo; **glasses** npl (spectacles) óculos mpl

glaze [gleɪz] vt (door) envidraçar; (pottery) vitrificar ▷ n verniz m

gleam [gliːm] vi brilhar

glide [glaɪd] vi deslizar; (Aviat, birds) planar; **glider** n (Aviat) planador m

glimmer ['glɪməʳ] n luz f trêmula; (of interest, hope) lampejo

glimpse [glɪmps] n vista rápida, vislumbre m ▷ vt vislumbrar, ver de relance

glint [glɪnt] vi cintilar

glisten ['glɪsn] vi brilhar

glitter ['glɪtəʳ] vi reluzir, brilhar

global ['gləubl] adj mundial; **globalization** [gləubəlaɪ'zeɪʃən] n globalização f; **global warming** n aquecimento global

globe [gləub] n globo, esfera

gloom [gluːm] n escuridão f; (sadness) tristeza; **gloomy** adj escuro; triste

glorious ['glɔːrɪəs] adj (weather) magnífico; (future) glorioso

glory ['glɔːrɪ] n glória

gloss [glɔs] n (shine) brilho; (also: ~ paint) pintura brilhante, esmalte m; **gloss over** vt fus encobrir

glossary ['glɔsərɪ] n glossário

glossy ['glɔsɪ] adj lustroso

glove [glʌv] n luva

glow [gləu] vi (shine) brilhar; (fire) arder

glucose ['gluːkəus] n glicose f

glue [gluː] n cola ▷ vt colar

GM adj abbr (= genetically modified) geneticamente modificado

gnaw [nɔː] vt roer

⊙ **KEYWORD**

go [gəu] (pt **went**, pp **gone**, pl **goes**) vi **1** ir; (travel, move) viajar; **a car went by** um carro passou; **he has gone to Aberdeen** ele foi para Aberdeen **2** (depart) partir, ir-se **3** (attend) ir; **she went to university in Rio** ela fez universidade no Rio; **he**

goes to the local church ele freqüenta a igreja local **4** (take part in an activity) ir; **to go for a walk** ir passear **5** (work) funcionar; **the bell went just then** a campainha acabou de tocar **6** (become): **to go pale/mouldy** ficar pálido/mofado **7** (be sold): **to go for £10** ser vendido por £10 **8** (fit, suit): **to go with** acompanhar, combinar com **9** (be about to, intend to): **he's going to do it** ele vai fazê-lo; **are you going to come?** você vem? **10** (time) passar **11** (event, activity) ser; **how did it go?** como foi? **12** (be given): **the job is to go to someone else** o emprego vai ser dado para outra pessoa **13** (break) romper-se; **the fuse went** o fusível queimou; **the leg of the chair went** a perna da cadeira quebrou **14** (be placed): **where does this cup go?** onde é que põe esta xícara?; **the milk goes in the fridge** pode guardar o leite na geladeira ▷ n **1** (try): **to have a go (at)** tentar a sorte (com) **2** (turn) vez f **3** (move): **to be on the go** ter muito para fazer **go about** vi (also: go around: rumour) espalhar-se ▷ vt fus: **how do I go about this?** como é que eu faço isto? **go ahead** vi (make progress) progredir; (get going) ir em frente **go along** vi ir ▷ vt fus ladear; **to go along with** concordar com **go away** vi (leave) ir-se, ir embora **go back** vi (return) voltar; (go again) ir de novo **go back on** vt fus (promise) faltar com **go by** vi (years, time) passar ▷ vt fus (book, rule) guiar-se por **go down** vi (descend) descer, baixar; (ship) afundar; (sun) pôr-se ▷ vt fus (stairs, ladder) descer **go for** vt fus (fetch) ir buscar; (like) gostar de; (attack) atacar **go in** vi (enter) entrar **go in for** vt fus (competition) inscrever-se em; (like) gostar de

go into vt fus (enter) entrar em; (investigate) investigar; (embark on) embarcar em

go off vi (leave) ir-se; (food) estragar, apodrecer; (bomb, gun) explodir; (event) realizar-se ▷ vt fus (person, food etc) deixar de gostar de

go on vi (continue) seguir, continuar; (happen) acontecer, ocorrer

go out vi sair; (for entertainment): **are you going out tonight?** você vai sair hoje à noite?; (couple): **they went out for 3 years** eles namoraram 3 anos; (fire, light) apagar-se

go over vi (ship) soçobrar ▷ vt fus (check) revisar

go round vi (news, rumour) circular

go through vt fus (town etc) atravessar; (search through) vasculhar; (examine) percorrer de cabo a rabo

go up vi subir; (price) aumentar

go without vt fus passar sem

go-ahead adj empreendedor(a) ▷ n luz f verde

goal [gəul] n meta, alvo; (Sport) gol m (BR), golo (PT); **goalkeeper** n goleiro(-a) (BR), guarda-redes m/f inv (PT)

goat [gəut] n cabra

gobble ['gɔbl] vt (also: ~ **down**, ~ **up**) engolir rapidamente, devorar

god [gɔd] n deus m; **G~** Deus; **godchild** n afilhado(-a); **goddess** n deusa; **godfather** n padrinho; **godmother** n madrinha

goggles ['gɔglz] npl óculos mpl de proteção

going ['gəuɪŋ] n (conditions) estado do terreno ▷ adj: **the ~ rate** tarifa corrente or em vigor

gold [gəuld] n ouro ▷ adj de ouro; **golden** adj (made of gold) de ouro; (gold in colour) dourado; **goldfish** n inv peixe-dourado m; **gold-plated** adj plaquê inv

golf [gɔlf] n golfe m; **golf ball** n bola de golfe; (on typewriter) esfera; **golf club** n clube m de golfe; (stick) taco; **golf course** n campo de golfe; **golfer** n jogador(a) m/f, golfista m/f

gone [gɔn] pp of **go**

gong [gɔŋ] n gongo

good [gud] adj bom (boa); (kind) bom, bondoso; (well-behaved) educado ▷ n bem m; **goods** npl (Comm) mercadorias fpl; **~!** bom!; **to be ~ at** ser bom em; **to be ~ for** servir para; **it's ~ for you** faz-lhe bem; **a ~ deal (of)** muito; **a ~ many** muitos; **to make ~** reparar; **it's no ~ complaining** não adianta se queixar; **for ~** para sempre, definitivamente; **~ morning/afternoon/evening!** bom dia/boa tarde/boa noite!; **~ night!** boa noite!; **goodbye** excl até logo (BR), adeus (PT); **to say goodbye** despedir-se; **Good Friday** n Sexta-Feira Santa; **good-looking** adj bonito; **good-natured** adj (person) de bom gênio; (pet) de boa índole; **goodwill** n boa vontade f

google ['gugl] vi, vt pesquisar no Google®

goose [gu:s] (pl **geese**) n ganso

gooseberry ['guzbəri] n groselha; **to play ~** (BRIT) ficar de vela

gorge [gɔ:dʒ] n desfiladeiro ▷ vt: **to ~ o.s. (on)** empanturrar-se (de)

gorgeous ['gɔ:dʒəs] adj magnífico, maravilhoso; (person) lindo

gorilla [gə'rɪlə] n gorila m

gospel ['gɔspl] n evangelho

gossip ['gɔsɪp] n (scandal) fofocas fpl (BR), mexericos mpl (PT); (chat) conversa; (scandalmonger) fofoqueiro(-a) (BR), mexeriqueiro(-a) (PT) ▷ vi (chat) bater (um) papo (BR), cavaquear (PT)

got [gɔt] pt, pp of **get**

gotten ['gɔtn] (US) pp of **get**

govern ['gʌvən] vt governar; (event) controlar

government ['gʌvnmənt] n governo

governor ['gʌvənəʳ] n governador(a) m/f; (of school, hospital, jail) diretor(a) m/f

gown [gaun] n vestido; (of teacher, judge) toga

GP n abbr (Med) = **general practitioner**

grab [græb] vt agarrar ▷ vi: **to ~ at** tentar agarrar

grace [greɪs] n (Rel) graça; (gracefulness) elegância, fineza ▷ vt (honour) honrar; (adorn) adornar; **5 days' ~** um prazo de 5 dias; **graceful** adj elegante, gracioso; **gracious** ['greɪʃəs] adj gracioso, afável

grade [greɪd] n (quality) classe f, qualidade f; (degree) grau m; (US: Sch) série f, classe ▷ vt classificar; **grade crossing** (US) n passagem f de nível; **grade school** (US) n escola primária

gradient ['greɪdɪənt] n declive m

gradual ['grædjuəl] adj gradual, gradativo; **gradually** adv gradualmente, gradativamente, pouco a pouco

graduate [(n) 'grædjuɪt, (vb) 'grædjueɪt]

n graduado, licenciado; (US) diplomado do colégio ▷ *vi* formar-se, licenciar-se; **graduation** [grædju'eɪʃən] *n* formatura

graffiti [grə'fi:tɪ] *n*, *npl* pichações *fpl*

graft [grɑ:ft] *n* (Agr, Med) enxerto; (BRIT: inf) trabalho pesado; (bribery) suborno ▷ *vt* enxertar

grain [greɪn] *n* grão *m*; (no pl: cereals) cereais *mpl*; (in wood) veio, fibra

gram [græm] *n* grama *m*

grammar ['græmə'] *n* gramática; **grammar school** *n* (BRIT) ≈ liceu

gramme [græm] *n* = **gram**

grand [grænd] *adj* esplêndido; (inf: wonderful) ótimo, formidável; **granddad** *n* vovô *m*; **granddaughter** *n* neta; **grandfather** *n* avô *m*; **grandma** *n* avó *f*, vovó *f*; **grandmother** *n* avó *f*; **grandpa** *n* = **granddad**; **grandparents** *npl* avós *mpl*; **grand piano** *n* piano de cauda; **grandson** *n* neto

granite ['grænɪt] *n* granito

granny ['grænɪ] (inf) *n* avó *f*, vovó *f*

grant [grɑ:nt] *vt* (concede) conceder; (a request etc) anuir a; (admit) admitir ▷ *n* (Sch) bolsa; (Admin) subvenção *f*, subsídio; **to take sth for ~ed** dar algo por certo

grape [greɪp] *n* uva

grapefruit ['greɪpfru:t] (pl inv or ~s) *n* toranja, grapefruit *m* (BR)

graph [grɑ:f] *n* gráfico; **graphic** ['græfɪk] *adj* gráfico; **graphics** *n* (art) artes *fpl* gráficas ▷ *npl* (drawings) desenhos *mpl*

grasp [grɑ:sp] *vt* agarrar, segurar; (understand) compreender, entender ▷ *n* aperto de mão; (understanding) compreensão *f*

grass [grɑ:s] *n* grama (BR), relva (PT); **grasshopper** *n* gafanhoto

grate [greɪt] *n* (fireplace) lareira ▷ *vi* ranger ▷ *vt* (Culin) ralar

grateful ['greɪtful] *adj* agradecido, grato

grater ['greɪtə'] *n* ralador *m*

gratitude ['grætɪtju:d] *n* agradecimento

grave [greɪv] *n* cova, sepultura ▷ *adj* sério; (mistake) grave

gravestone ['greɪvstəun] *n* lápide *f*

graveyard ['greɪvjɑ:d] *n* cemitério

gravity ['grævɪtɪ] *n* (Phys) gravidade *f*; (seriousness) seriedade *f*, gravidade

gravy ['greɪvɪ] *n* molho (de carne)

gray [greɪ] (US) *adj* = **grey**

graze [greɪz] *vi* pastar ▷ *vt* (touch lightly) roçar; (scrape) raspar ▷ *n* (Med) esfoladura, arranhadura

grease [gri:s] *n* (fat) gordura; (lubricant) graxa, lubrificante *m* ▷ *vt* untar, lubrificar, engraxar; **greasy** *adj* gordurento, gorduroso; (skin, hair) oleoso

great [greɪt] *adj* grande; (inf) genial; (pain, heat) forte; (important) importante; **Great Britain** *n* Grã-Bretanha; **great-grandfather** *n* bisavô *m*; **great-grandmother** *n* bisavó *f*; **greatly** *adv* imensamente, muito

◈ **GREAT BRITAIN**
◈
◈ A Grã-Bretanha, **Great Britain** ou
◈ **Britain** em inglês, designa a maior das
◈ ilhas britânicas e, portanto, engloba
◈ a Escócia e o País de Gales. Junto com
◈ a Irlanda, a ilha de Man e as ilhas
◈ Anglo-normandas, a Grã-Bretanha
◈ forma as ilhas Britânicas, ou British
◈ Isles. Reino Unido, em inglês United
◈ Kingdom ou UK, é o nome oficial da
◈ entidade política que compreende a
◈ Grã-Bretanha e a Irlanda do Norte.

Greece [gri:s] *n* Grécia

greed [gri:d] *n* (also: **~iness**) avidez *f*, cobiça; **greedy** *adj* avarento; (for food) guloso

Greek [gri:k] *adj* grego ▷ *n* grego(-a); (Ling) grego

green [gri:n] *adj* verde; (inexperienced) inexperiente, ingênuo ▷ *n* verde *m*; (stretch of grass) gramado (BR), relvado (PT); (on golf course) green *m*; **greens** *npl* (vegetables) verduras *fpl*; **greenhouse** *n* estufa

Greenland ['gri:nlənd] *n* Groenlândia

greet [gri:t] *vt* acolher; (news) receber; **greeting** *n* acolhimento; **greeting(s) card** *n* cartão *m* comemorativo

grew [gru:] *pt of* **grow**

grey [greɪ] (US **gray**) *adj* cinzento; (dismal) sombrio; **grey-haired** *adj* grisalho; **greyhound** *n* galgo

grid [grɪd] *n* grade *f*; (Elec) rede *f*

grief [gri:f] *n* dor *f*, pesar *m*

grievance ['gri:vəns] *n* motivo de queixa, agravo

grieve [gri:v] *vi* sofrer ▷ *vt* dar pena a, afligir; **to ~ for** chorar por

grill [grɪl] *n* (on cooker) grelha; (also: **mixed ~**) prato de grelhados ▷ *vt* (BRIT) grelhar; (inf: question) interrogar cerradamente

grille [grɪl] *n* grade *f*; (Aut) grelha

grim [grɪm] *adj* desagradável; (*unattractive*) feio; (*stern*) severo

grime [graɪm] *n* sujeira (BR), sujidade f (PT)

grin [grɪn] *n* sorriso largo ▷ *vi*: **to ~ (at)** dar um sorriso largo (para)

grind [graɪnd] (*pt, pp* **ground**) *vt* triturar; (*coffee etc*) moer; (*make sharp*) afiar; (*US: meat*) picar ▷ *n* (*work*) trabalho (repetitivo e maçante)

grip [grɪp] *n* (*of person*) aperto de mão; (*of animal*) força; (*handle*) punho; (*of tyre, shoe*) aderência; (*holdall*) valise f ▷ *vt* agarrar; (*attention*) prender; **to come to ~s with** arcar com

gripping ['grɪpɪŋ] *adj* absorvente, emocionante

grit [grɪt] *n* areia, grão m de areia; (*courage*) coragem f ▷ *vt* (*road*) pôr areia em; **to ~ one's teeth** cerrar os dentes

groan [grəun] *n* gemido ▷ *vi* gemer

grocer ['grəusəʳ] *n* dono(-a) de mercearia; **groceries** *npl* comestíveis *mpl*; **grocer's (shop)** *n* mercearia

groin [grɔɪn] *n* virilha

groom [gru:m] *n* cavalariço; (*also*: **bride~**) noivo ▷ *vt* (*horse*) tratar; (*fig*): **to ~ sb for sth** preparar alguém para algo; **well-~ed** bem-posto

groove [gru:v] *n* ranhura, entalhe m

grope [grəup] *vi*: **to ~ for** procurar às cegas

gross [grəus] *adj* (*flagrant*) grave; (*vulgar*) vulgar; (: *building*) de mau-gosto; (*Comm*) bruto

ground [graund] *pt, pp of* **grind** ▷ *n* terra, chão m; (*Sport*) campo; (*land*) terreno; (*reason: gen pl*) motivo, razão f; (*US: also*: **~wire**) (ligação f à) terra, fio-terra m ▷ *vt* (*plane*) manter em terra; (*US: Elec*) ligar à terra; **grounds** *npl* (*of coffee etc*) borra; (*gardens etc*) jardins *mpl*, parque m; **on the ~** no chão; **to the ~** por terra; **groundsheet** (BRIT) *n* capa impermeável; **groundwork** *n* base f, preparação f

group [gru:p] *n* grupo; (*also*: **pop ~**) conjunto ▷ *vt* (*also*: **~ together**) agrupar ▷ *vi* (*also*: **~ together**) agrupar-se

grouse [graus] *n inv* (*bird*) tetraz m, galo-silvestre m ▷ *vi* (*complain*) queixar-se, resmungar

grovel ['grɔvl] *vi* (*fig*): **to ~ (before)** abaixar-se (diante de)

grow [grəu] (*pt* **grew**, *pp* **~n**) *vi* crescer; (*increase*) aumentar; (*develop*): **to ~ (out of/from)** originar-se; (*become*): **to ~ rich/weak** enriquecer(-se)/enfraquecer-se ▷ *vt* plantar, cultivar; (*beard*) deixar crescer; **grow up** *vi* crescer, fazer-se homem/mulher

growl [graul] *vi* rosnar

grown [grəun] *pp of* **grow**

grown-up *n* adulto(-a), pessoa mais velha

growth [grəuθ] *n* crescimento; (*increase*) aumento; (*Med*) abcesso, tumor m

grub [grʌb] *n* larva, lagarta; (*inf: food*) comida, rango (BR)

grubby ['grʌbɪ] *adj* encardido

grudge [grʌdʒ] *n* motivo de rancor ▷ *vt*: **to ~ sb sth** dar algo a alguém de má vontade, invejar algo a alguém; **to bear sb a ~ for sth** guardar rancor de alguém por algo

gruelling ['gruəlɪŋ] (*US* **grueling**) *adj* duro, árduo

gruesome ['gru:səm] *adj* horrível

grumble ['grʌmbl] *vi* resmungar, bufar

grumpy ['grʌmpɪ] *adj* rabugento

grunt [grʌnt] *vi* grunhir

guarantee [gærən'ti:] *n* garantia ▷ *vt* garantir

guard [gɑ:d] *n* guarda; (*one person*) guarda m; (BRIT: *Rail*) guarda-freio; (*on machine*) dispositivo de segurança; (*also*: **fire~**) guarda-fogo ▷ *vt* (*protect*): **to ~ (against)** proteger (contra); (*prisoner*) vigiar; **to be on one's ~** estar prevenido; **guard against** *vt fus* prevenir-se contra; **guardian** *n* protetor(a) m/f; (*of minor*) tutor(a) m/f

Guatemala [gwɔtə'mɑːlə] *n* Guatemala

guerrilla [gə'rɪlə] *n* guerrilheiro(-a)

guess [ges] *vt, vi* (*estimate*) avaliar, conjeturar; (*answer*) adivinhar; (*US*) achar, supor ▷ *n* suposição f, conjetura; **to take** *or* **have a ~** adivinhar, chutar (*inf*)

guest [gest] *n* convidado(-a); (*in hotel*) hóspede m/f

guidance ['gaɪdəns] *n* conselhos *mpl*

guide [gaɪd] *n* (*person*) guia m/f; (*book, fig*) guia m; (BRIT: *also*: **girl ~**) escoteira ▷ *vt* guiar; **guidebook** *n* guia m; **guide dog** *n* cão m de guia; **guidelines** *npl* (*advice*) orientação f

guilt [gɪlt] *n* culpa; **guilty** *adj* culpado

guinea pig *n* porquinho-da-Índia m, cobaia; (*fig*) cobaia

guitar [gɪ'tɑːʳ] *n* violão m

gulf [gʌlf] *n* golfo; (*abyss: also fig*) abismo

gull [gʌl] n gaivota

gulp [gʌlp] vi engolir em seco ▷ vt (also: **~ down**) engolir

gum [gʌm] n (Anat) gengiva; (glue) goma; (also: **~ drop**) bala de goma; (also: **chewing-~**) chiclete m (BR), pastilha elástica (PT) ▷ vt colar

gun [gʌn] n (gen) arma (de fogo); (revolver) revólver m; (small) pistola; (rifle) espingarda; (cannon) canhão m; **gunfire** n tiroteio; **gunman** (irreg) n pistoleiro; **gunpoint** n: **at gunpoint** sob a ameaça de uma arma; **gunpowder** n pólvora; **gunshot** n tiro (de arma de fogo)

gust [gʌst] n (of wind) rajada

gut [gʌt] n intestino, tripa; **guts** npl (Anat) entranhas fpl; (inf: courage) coragem f, raça (inf)

gutter ['gʌtə'] n (of roof) calha; (in street) sarjeta

guy [gaɪ] n (also: **~rope**) corda; (inf: man) cara m (BR), tipo (PT); **Guy Fawkes' Night** n ver quadro

gym [dʒɪm] n (also: **~nasium**) ginásio; (also: **~nastics**) ginástica

gymnast ['dʒɪmnæst] n ginasta m/f

gymnastics [dʒɪm'næstɪks] n ginástica

gynaecologist [gaɪnɪ'kɔlədʒɪst] (US **gynecologist**) n ginecologista m/f

gypsy ['dʒɪpsɪ] n = **gipsy**

h

haberdashery ['hæbə'dæʃərɪ] (BRIT) n armarinho

habit ['hæbɪt] n hábito, costume m; (addiction) vício; (Rel) hábito

hack [hæk] vt (cut) cortar; (chop) talhar ▷ n (pej: writer) escrevinhador(a) m/f; **hacker** n (Comput) pirata m (de dados de computador)

had [hæd] pt, pp of **have**

haddock ['hædək] (pl **inv** or **~s**) n hadoque m (BR), eglefim m (PT)

hadn't ['hædnt] = **had not**

haemorrhage ['hɛmərɪdʒ] (US **hemorrhage**) n hemorragia

haemorrhoids ['hɛmərɔɪdz] (US **hemorrhoids**) npl hemorróidas fpl

haggle ['hægl] vi pechinchar, regatear

hail [heɪl] n granizo; (of objects) chuva; (of criticism) torrente f ▷ vt (greet) cumprimentar; (taxi) chamar; (person, event) saudar ▷ vi chover granizo; **hailstone** n pedra de granizo

hair [hɛə'] n (of human) cabelo; (of animal) pêlo; **to do one's ~** pentear-se; **hairbrush** n escova de cabelo; **haircut** n corte m de cabelo; **hairdo** n penteado; **hairdresser** n cabeleireiro(-a); **hairdresser's** n cabeleireiro; **hair dryer**

n secador *m* de cabelo; **hair gel** *n* gel *m* para o cabelo; **hair spray** *n* laquê *m* (BR), laca (PT); **hairstyle** *n* penteado; **hairy** *adj* cabeludo, peludo; (*inf: situation*) perigoso

hake [heɪk] (*pl inv or* ~**s**) *n* abrótea

half [hɑːf] (*pl* **halves**) *n* metade *f*; (*Rail, bus, of beer etc*) meia ▷ *adj* meio ▷ *adv* meio, pela metade; **~ a pound** meia libra; **two and a ~** dois e meio; **~ a dozen** meia-dúzia; **to cut sth in ~** cortar algo ao meio; **~ asleep/empty/closed** meio adormecido/vazio/fechado; **half-hearted** *adj* irresoluto, indiferente; **half-hour** *n* meia hora; **half-price** *adj, adv* pela metade do preço; **half term** (BRIT) *n* (*Sch*) dias de folga no meio do semestre; **half-time** *n* meio tempo; **halfway** *adv* a meio caminho; (*in time*) no meio

hall [hɔːl] *n* (*for concerts*) sala; (*entrance way*) hall *m*, entrada

hallmark ['hɔːlmɑːk] *n* (*also fig*) marca

hall of residence (BRIT): (*pl* **halls of residence**) *n* residência universitária

Hallowe'en ['hæləʊ'iːn] *n* Dia *m* das Bruxas (*31 de outubro*)

⊛ **HALLOWE'EN**

⊛ Segundo a tradição, **Hallowe'en**
⊛ é a noite dos fantasmas e dos
⊛ bruxos. Na Escócia e nos Estados
⊛ Unidos, sobretudo (bem menos na
⊛ Inglaterra), as crianças, para festejar
⊛ o **Hallowe'en**, se fantasiam e batem
⊛ de porta em porta pedindo prendas
⊛ (chocolates, maçãs etc).

hallway ['hɔːlweɪ] *n* hall *m*, entrada

halo ['heɪləʊ] *n* (*of saint etc*) auréola

halt [hɔːlt] *n* parada (BR), paragem *f* (PT) ▷ *vi* parar ▷ *vt* deter; (*process*) interromper

halve [hɑːv] *vt* (*divide*) dividir ao meio; (*reduce by half*) reduzir à metade

halves [hɑːvz] *npl of* **half**

ham [hæm] *n* presunto, fiambre *m* (PT)

hamburger ['hæmbəːgəʳ] *n* hambúrguer *m*

hammer ['hæməʳ] *n* martelo ▷ *vt* martelar ▷ *vi* (*on door*) bater insistentemente

hammock ['hæmək] *n* rede *f*

hamper ['hæmpəʳ] *vt* dificultar, atrapalhar ▷ *n* cesto

hamster ['hæmstəʳ] *n* hamster *m*

hand [hænd] *n* mão *f*; (*of clock*) ponteiro; (*writing*) letra; (*of cards*) cartas *fpl*; (*worker*) trabalhador *m* ▷ *vt* dar, passar; **to give** *or* **lend sb a ~** dar uma mãozinha a alguém, dar uma ajuda a alguém; **at ~** à mão, disponível; **in ~** livre; (*situation*) sob controle; **to be on ~** (*person*) estar disponível; (*emergency services*) estar num estado de prontidão; **on the one ~ ..., on the other ~ ...** por um lado ..., por outro (lado) ...; **hand in** *vt* entregar; **hand out** *vt* distribuir; **hand over** *vt* entregar; (*responsibility*) transferir; **handbag** *n* bolsa; **handbook** *n* manual *m*; **handbrake** *n* freio (BR) *or* travão *m* (PT) de mão; **handcuffs** *npl* algemas *fpl*; **handful** *n* punhado; (*of people*) grupo

handicap ['hændɪkæp] *n* (*Med*) incapacidade *f*; (*disadvantage*) desvantagem *f*; (*Sport*) handicap *m* ▷ *vt* prejudicar; **mentally/physically ~ped** deficiente menta/físico

handkerchief ['hæŋkətʃɪf] *n* lenço

handle ['hændl] *n* (*of door etc*) maçaneta; (*of cup etc*) asa; (*of knife etc*) cabo; (*for winding*) manivela ▷ *vt* manusear; (*deal with*) tratar de; (*treat: people*) lidar com; **"~ with care"** "cuidado - frágil"; **to fly off the ~** perder as estribeiras; **handlebar(s)** *n(pl)* guidom *m* (BR), guidão *m* (PT)

hand: **handmade** *adj* feito à mão; **handout** *n* (*money, food*) doação *f*; (*leaflet*) folheto; (*at lecture*) apostila; **hands-free kit** *or* **set** *n* viva-voz *m*

handsome ['hænsəm] *adj* bonito, elegante; (*profit*) considerável

handwriting ['hændraɪtɪŋ] *n* letra, caligrafia

handy ['hændɪ] *adj* (*close at hand*) à mão; (*useful*) útil; (*skilful*) habilidoso, hábil

hang [hæŋ] (*pt, pp* **hung**) *vt* pendurar; (*criminal: pt, pp* **hanged**) enforcar ▷ *vi* estar pendurado; (*hair, drapery*) cair ▷ *n* (*inf*): **to get the ~ of sth** pegar o jeito de algo; **hang about** *or* **around** *vi* vadiar, vagabundear; **hang on** *vi* (*wait*) esperar; **hang up** *vt* (*coat*) pendurar ▷ *vi* (*Tel*) desligar; **to hang up on sb** bater o telefone na cara de alguém

hanger ['hæŋəʳ] *n* cabide *m*

hang-gliding *n* vôo livre

hangover ['hæŋəʊvəʳ] *n* ressaca

happen ['hæpən] *vi* acontecer; **to ~ to do sth** fazer algo por acaso; **as it ~s ...** acontece que ...

happily ['hæpɪlɪ] *adv* (*luckily*) felizmente;

(*cheerfully*) alegremente
happiness ['hæpɪnɪs] *n* felicidade *f*
happy ['hæpɪ] *adj* feliz; (*cheerful*)
contente; **to be ~ to do** (*willing*) estar
disposto a fazer; **~ birthday!** feliz
aniversário
harass ['hærəs] *vt* importunar;
harassment *n* perseguição *f*
harbour ['hɑːbəʳ] (*us* **harbor**) *n* porto
▷ *vt* (*hope etc*) abrigar; (*hide*) esconder
hard [hɑːd] *adj* duro; (*difficult*) difícil;
(*work*) árduo; (*person*) severo, cruel;
(*facts*) verdadeiro ▷ *adv* (*work*)
muito, diligentemente; (*think, try*)
seriamente; **to look ~ at** olhar firme
or fixamente para; **no ~ feelings!** sem
ressentimentos!; **to be ~ of hearing**
ser surdo; **to be ~ done by** ser tratado
injustamente; **hardback** *n* livro de capa
dura; **hard disk** *n* (*Comput*) disco rígido;
harden *vt* endurecer; (*steel*) temperar;
(*fig*) tornar insensível ▷ *vi* endurecer-se
hardly ['hɑːdlɪ] *adv* (*scarcely*) apenas; (*no
sooner*) mal; **~ ever/anywhere** quase
nunca/em lugar nenhum
hardship ['hɑːdʃɪp] *n* privação *f*; **hard
shoulder** *n* acostamento *m*
hardware ['hɑːdwɛəʳ] *n* ferragens *fpl*;
(*Comput*) hardware *m*
hard-working *adj* trabalhador(a);
(*student*) aplicado
hardy ['hɑːdɪ] *adj* forte; (*plant*) resistente
hare [hɛəʳ] *n* lebre *f*
harm [hɑːm] *n* mal *m*; (*damage*) dano
▷ *vt* (*person*) fazer mal a, prejudicar;
(*thing*) danificar; **out of ~'s way** a
salvo; **harmful** *adj* prejudicial, nocivo;
harmless *adj* inofensivo
harmony ['hɑːmənɪ] *n* harmonia
harness ['hɑːnɪs] *n* (*for horse*) arreios *mpl*;
(*for child*) correia; (*safety harness*) correia
de segurança ▷ *vt* (*horse*) arrear, pôr
arreios em; (*resources*) aproveitar
harp [hɑːp] *n* harpa ▷ *vi*: **to ~ on about**
bater sempre na mesma tecla sobre
harsh [hɑːʃ] *adj* (*life*) duro; (*sound*)
desarmonioso; (*light*) forte
harvest ['hɑːvɪst] *n* colheita ▷ *vt* colher
has [hæz] *vb see* **have**
hasn't ['hæznt] = **has not**
hassle ['hæsl] (*inf*) *n* complicação *f*
haste [heɪst] *n* pressa; **hasten** ['heɪsn]
vt acelerar ▷ *vi*: **to hasten to do sth**
apressar-se em fazer algo; **hastily** *adv*
depressa; **hasty** *adj* apressado; (*rash*)

precipitado
hat [hæt] *n* chapéu *m*
hatch [hætʃ] *n* (*Naut: also:* **~way**)
escotilha; (*also:* **service ~**) comunicação
f entre a cozinha e a sala de jantar ▷ *vi*
sair do ovo, chocar
hate [heɪt] *vt* odiar, detestar ▷ *n* ódio;
hatred ['heɪtrɪd] *n* ódio
haul [hɔːl] *vt* puxar ▷ *n* (*of fish*) redada;
(*of stolen goods etc*) pilhagem *f*, presa
haunt [hɔːnt] *vt* (*subj: ghost*) assombrar;
(: *problem, memory*) perseguir ▷ *n* reduto;
(*haunted house*) casa mal-assombrada

◯ **KEYWORD**

have [hæv] (*pt, pp* **had**) *aux vb* **1** (*gen*) ter;
to have gone/eaten ter ido/comido;
he has been kind/promoted ele foi
bondoso/promovido; **having finished**
or **when he had finished, he left**
quando ele terminou, foi embora
2 (*in tag questions*): **you've done it,
haven't you?** você fez isto, não fez?;
he hasn't done it, has he? ele não fez
isto, fez?
3 (*in short questions and answers*): **you've
made a mistake - no I haven't/so
I have** você fez um erro - não, eu não
fiz/sim, eu fiz; **I've been there before,
have you?** eu já estive lá, e você?
▷ *modal aux vb* (*be obliged*): **to have (got)
to do sth** ter que fazer algo; **I haven't
got** *or* **I don't have to wear glasses** eu
não preciso usar óculos
▷ *vt* **1** (*possess*) ter; **he has (got) blue
eyes/dark hair** ele tem olhos azuis/
cabelo escuro
2 (*referring to meals etc*): **to have
breakfast** tomar café (*BR*), tomar o
pequeno almoço (*PT*); **to have lunch/
dinner** almoçar/jantar; **to have a
drink/a cigarette** tomar um drinque/
fumar um cigarro
3 (*receive, obtain etc*): **may I have your
address?** pode me dar seu endereço?;
you can have it for 5 pounds você pode
levá-lo por 5 libras; **to have a baby** dar à
luz (*BR*), ter um nenê *or* bebê (*PT*)
4 (*maintain, allow*): **he will have it that
he is right** ele vai insistir que ele está
certo; **I won't have it/this nonsense!**
não vou agüentar isso/este absurdo!; **we
can't have that** não podemos permitir
isto
5: **to have sth done** mandar fazer algo;

to have one's hair cut ir cortar o cabelo; **to have sb do sth** mandar alguém fazer algo

6 (*experience, suffer*): **to have a cold** estar resfriado (BR) or constipado (PT); **to have flu** estar com gripe; **she had her bag stolen** ela teve sua bolsa roubada; **to have an operation** fazer uma operação

7 (+ *n: take, hold etc*): **to have a swim/ walk/bath/rest** ir nadar/passear/tomar um banho/descansar; **let's have a look** vamos dar uma olhada; **to have a party** fazer uma festa

8 (*inf: dupe*): **he's been had** ele comprou gato por lebre

have out vt: **to have it out with sb** (*settle a problem*) explicar-se com alguém

haven ['heɪvn] n porto; (*fig*) abrigo, refúgio

haven't ['hævnt] = **have not**

havoc ['hævək] n destruição f; **to play ~ with** (*fig*) estragar

hawk [hɔːk] n falcão m

hay [heɪ] n feno; **hay fever** n febre f do feno; **haystack** n palheiro

hazard ['hæzəd] n perigo, risco ▷ vt aventurar, arriscar; **hazard warning lights** npl (Aut) pisca-alerta m

haze [heɪz] n névoa

hazelnut ['heɪzlnʌt] n avelã f

hazy ['heɪzɪ] adj nublado; (*idea*) confuso

he [hiː] pron ele; **he who ...** quem ..., aquele que ...

head [hɛd] n cabeça; (*of table*) cabeceira; (*of queue*) frente f; (*of organization*) chefe m/f; (*of school*) diretor(a) m/f ▷ vt (*list*) encabeçar; (*group*) liderar; (*ball*) cabecear; **~s or tails** cara ou coroa; **~ first** de cabeça; **~ over heels** de pernas para o ar; **~ over heels in love** apaixonadíssimo; **head for** vt fus dirigir-se a; (*disaster*) estar procurando; **headache** n dor f de cabeça; **heading** n título, cabeçalho; **headlamp** (BRIT) n = **headlight**; **headlight** n farol m; **headline** n manchete f; **head office** n matriz f; **headphones** npl fones mpl de ouvido; **headquarters** npl sede f; (Mil) quartel m general; **headroom** n (*in car*) espaço (para a cabeça); (*under bridge*) vão m livre; **headscarf** (*irreg*) n lenço de cabeça

heal [hiːl] vt curar ▷ vi cicatrizar

health [hɛlθ] n saúde f; **good ~!** saúde!; **healthy** adj (*person*) saudável; (*air, walk*)

sadio; (*economy*) próspero, forte

heap [hiːp] n pilha, montão m ▷ vt: **to ~ sth with** encher algo de; **~s (of)** (*inf*) um monte (de); **to ~ sth on** empilhar algo em

hear [hɪəʳ] (*pt, pp* **~d** [hɜːd]) vt ouvir; (*listen to*) escutar; (*news*) saber; **to ~ about** ouvir falar de; **to ~ from sb** ter notícias de alguém; **hearing** n (*sense*) audição f; (*Law*) audiência; **hearing aid** n aparelho para a surdez

hearse [hɜːs] n carro fúnebre

heart [hɑːt] n coração m; (*of problem, city*) centro; **hearts** npl (*Cards*) copas fpl; **to lose/take ~** perder o ânimo/criar coragem; **at ~** no fundo; **by ~** (*learn, know*) de cor; **heart attack** n ataque m de coração; **heartbeat** n batida do coração; **heartbroken** adj: **to be heartbroken** estar inconsolável; **heartburn** n azia

hearty ['hɑːtɪ] adj (*person*) energético; (*laugh*) animado; (*appetite*) bom (boa); (*welcome*) sincero; (*dislike*) absoluto

heat [hiːt] n calor m; (*excitement*) ardor m; (Sport: *also*: **qualifying ~**) (*prova*) eliminatória ▷ vt esquentar; (*room, house*) aquecer; **heat up** vi aquecer-se, esquentar ▷ vt esquentar; **heated** adj aquecido; (*fig*) acalorado; **heater** n aquecedor m

heather ['hɛðəʳ] n urze f

heating ['hiːtɪŋ] n aquecimento, calefação f

heaven ['hɛvn] n céu m, paraíso; **heavenly** adj celestial; (Rel) divino

heavily ['hɛvɪlɪ] adv pesadamente; (*drink, smoke*) excessivamente; (*sleep, depend*) profundamente

heavy ['hɛvɪ] adj pesado; (*work*) duro; (*responsibility*) grande; (*rain, meal*) forte; (*drinker, smoker*) inveterado; (*weather*) carregado

Hebrew ['hiːbruː] adj hebreu (hebréia) ▷ n (Ling) hebraico

Hebrides ['hɛbrɪdiːz] npl: **the ~** as (ilhas) Hébridas

hectic ['hɛktɪk] adj agitado

he'd [hiːd] = **he would**; **he had**

hedge [hɛdʒ] n cerca viva, sebe f ▷ vi dar evasivas ▷ vt: **to ~ one's bets** (*fig*) resguardar-se

hedgehog ['hɛdʒhɔg] n ouriço

heed [hiːd] vt (*also*: **take ~ of**) prestar atenção a

heel [hiːl] n (*of shoe*) salto; (*of foot*)

calcanhar m ▷ vt (shoe) pôr salto em
hefty ['hɛftɪ] adj (person) robusto; (parcel) pesado; (profit) alto
height [haɪt] n (of person) estatura; (of building, tree) altura; (altitude, of plane) altitude f; (high ground) monte m; (fig: of power) auge m; (: of luxury) máximo; (: of stupidity) cúmulo; **heighten** vt elevar; (fig) aumentar
heir [ɛəʳ] n herdeiro; **heiress** n herdeira
held [hɛld] pt, pp of **hold**
helicopter ['hɛlɪkɒptəʳ] n helicóptero
hell [hɛl] n inferno; ~! (inf) droga!
he'll [hiːl] = **he will; he shall**
hello [hə'ləʊ] excl oi! (BR), olá! (PT); (surprise) ora essa!
helmet ['hɛlmɪt] n capacete m
help [hɛlp] n ajuda; (charwoman) faxineira ▷ vt ajudar; ~! socorro!; ~ **yourself** sirva-se; **he can't ~ it** não tem culpa; **helper** n ajudante m/f; **helpful** adj prestativo; (advice) útil; **helping** n porção f; **helpless** adj (incapable) incapaz; (defenceless) indefeso
hem [hɛm] n bainha ▷ vt embainhar; **hem in** vt cercar, encurralar
hemorrhage ['hɛmərɪdʒ] (US) n = **haemorrhage**
hemorrhoids ['hɛmərɔɪdz] (US) npl = **haemorrhoids**
hen [hɛn] n galinha; (female bird) fêmea
hence [hɛns] adv daí, portanto; **2 years** ~ daqui a 2 anos
her [həːʳ] pron (direct) a; (indirect) lhe; (stressed, after prep) ela ▷ adj seu (sua), dela; see also **me; my**
herb [həːb] n erva
herd [həːd] n rebanho
here [hɪəʳ] adv aqui; (at this point) nesse ponto; ~! (present) presente!; ~ **is/are** aqui está/estão; ~ **she is!** aqui está ela!
heritage ['hɛrɪtɪdʒ] n patrimônio
hernia ['həːnɪə] n hérnia
hero ['hɪərəʊ] (pl ~**es**) n herói m; (of book, film) protagonista m
heroin ['hɛrəʊɪn] n heroína
heroine ['hɛrəʊɪn] n heroína; (of book, film) protagonista
heron ['hɛrən] n garça
herring ['hɛrɪŋ] (pl inv or ~**s**) n arenque m
hers [həːz] pron (o) seu ((a) sua), (o(-a)) dela; see also **mine¹**
herself [həː'sɛlf] pron (reflexive) se; (emphatic) ela mesma; (after prep) si (mesma); see also **oneself**
he's [hiːz] = **he is; he has**

hesitant ['hɛzɪtənt] adj hesitante, indeciso
hesitate ['hɛzɪteɪt] vi hesitar; **hesitation** [hɛzɪ'teɪʃən] n hesitação f, indecisão f
heterosexual ['hɛtərəʊ'sɛksjuəl] adj heterossexual
heyday ['heɪdeɪ] n: **the ~ of** o auge or apogeu de
hi [haɪ] excl oi!
hibernate ['haɪbəneɪt] vi hibernar
hiccough ['hɪkʌp] vi soluçar ▷ npl: ~**s, to have (the) ~s** estar com soluço
hiccup ['hɪkʌp] = **hiccough**
hide [haɪd] (pt **hid**, pp **hidden**) n (skin) pele f ▷ vt esconder, ocultar; (view) obscurecer ▷ vi: **to ~ (from sb)** esconder-se or ocultar-se (de alguém)
hideous ['hɪdɪəs] adj horrível
hiding ['haɪdɪŋ] n (beating) surra; **to be in ~** (concealed) estar escondido
hi-fi ['haɪfaɪ] n alta-fidelidade f; (system) som m ▷ adj de alta-fidelidade
high [haɪ] adj alto; (number) grande; (price) alto, elevado; (wind) forte; (voice) agudo; (opinion) ótimo; (principles) nobre ▷ adv alto, a grande altura; **it is 20 m** ~ tem 20 m de altura; ~ **in the air** nas alturas; **highchair** n cadeira alta (para criança); **higher education** n ensino superior; **high jump** n (Sport) salto em altura; **the Highlands** npl a Alta Escócia; **highlight** n (fig) ponto alto; (in hair) mecha ▷ vt realçar, ressaltar; **highly** adv: **highly paid** muito bem pago; (a lot): **to speak/think highly of** falar elogiosamente de/pensar muito bem de; **high-rise** adj alto; **high school** n (BRIT) escola secundária; (US) científico; **high street** n (BRIT) rua principal; **highway** (US) n estrada; (main road) rodovia

🏵 **HIGH SCHOOL**
🏵
🏵 Uma **high school** é um
🏵 estabelecimento de ensino
🏵 secundário. Nos Estados Unidos,
🏵 existem a Junior High School, que
🏵 equivale aproximadamente aos dois
🏵 últimos anos do primeiro grau, e a
🏵 Senior High School, que corresponde
🏵 ao segundo grau. Na Grã-Bretanha,
🏵 esse termo às vezes é utilizado para as
🏵 escolas secundárias.

hijack ['haɪdʒæk] vt seqüestrar; **hijacker**

n seqüestrador(a) *m/f* (de avião)
hike [haɪk] *vi* caminhar ▷ *n* caminhada,
excursão *f* a pé; **hiker** *n* caminhante *m/f*,
andarilho(-a)
hilarious [hɪˈlɛərɪəs] *adj* hilariante
hill [hɪl] *n* colina; (*high*) montanha; (*slope*)
ladeira, rampa; **hillside** *n* vertente *f*;
hilly *adj* montanhoso
him [hɪm] *pron* (*direct*) o; (*indirect*) lhe;
(*stressed, after prep*) ele; *see also* **me**;
himself *pron* (*reflexive*) se; (*emphatic*) ele
mesmo; (*after prep*) si (mesmo); *see also*
oneself
hinder [ˈhɪndəʳ] *vt* retardar
hindsight [ˈhaɪndsaɪt] *n*: **with ~** em
retrospecto
Hindu [ˈhɪnduː] *adj* hindu
hinge [hɪndʒ] *n* dobradiça ▷ *vi* (*fig*): **to ~
on** depender de
hint [hɪnt] *n* (*suggestion*) insinuação *f*;
(*advice*) palpite *m*, dica; (*sign*) sinal *m* ▷ *vt*:
to ~ that insinuar que ▷ *vi*: **to ~ at** fazer
alusão a
hip [hɪp] *n* quadril *m*
hippopotamus [hɪpəˈpɔtəməs] (*pl* **~es**
or **hippopotami**) *n* hipopótamo
hire [ˈhaɪəʳ] *vt* (*BRIT: car, equipment*)
alugar; (*worker*) contratar ▷ *n* aluguel *m*
(*BR*), aluguer *m* (*PT*); **for ~** aluga-se; (*taxi*)
livre; **hire purchase** (*BRIT*) *n* compra a
prazo
his [hɪz] *pron* o seu (a sua), (o (a)) dele
▷ *adj* seu (sua), dele; *see also* **my; mine**¹
hiss [hɪs] *vi* (*snake, fat*) assoviar; (*gas*)
silvar; (*boo*) vaiar
historic(al) [hɪˈstɔrɪk(l)] *adj* histórico
history [ˈhɪstərɪ] *n* história
hit [hɪt] (*pt, pp* **~**) *vt* bater em; (*target*)
acertar, alcançar; (*car*) bater em, colidir
com; (*fig: affect*) atingir ▷ *n* golpe *m*;
(*success*) sucesso; (*Internet visit*) visita; **to
~ it off with sb** dar-se bem com alguém
hitch [hɪtʃ] *vt* (*fasten*) atar, amarrar; (*also:*
~ up) levantar ▷ *n* (*difficulty*) dificuldade
f; **to ~ a lift** pegar carona (*BR*), arranjar
uma boleia (*PT*)
hitch-hike *vi* pegar carona (*BR*), andar à
boleia (*PT*); **hitch-hiker** *n* pessoa que pega
carona (*BR*) *or* anda à boleia (*PT*)
hi-tech *adj* tecnologicamente avançado
▷ *n* alta tecnologia
HIV *abbr*: **~-negative/-positive** *adj* HIV
negativo/positivo
hive [haɪv] *n* colméia; **hive off** (*inf*) *vt*
transferir
hoard [hɔːd] *n* provisão *f*; (*of money*)

tesouro ▷ *vt* acumular
hoarse [hɔːs] *adj* rouco
hoax [həuks] *n* trote *m*
hob [hɔb] *n* parte de cima do fogão
hobble [ˈhɔbl] *vi* mancar
hobby [ˈhɔbɪ] *n* hobby *m*, passatempo
predileto
hobo [ˈhəubəu] (*US*) *n* vagabundo
hockey [ˈhɔkɪ] *n* hóquei *m*
hog [hɔg] *n* porco ▷ *vt* (*fig*) monopolizar;
to go the whole ~ ir até o fim
hoist [hɔɪst] *vt* içar
hold [həuld] (*pt, pp* **held**) *vt* segurar;
(*contain*) conter; (*have*) ter; (*record
etc: meeting*) realizar; (*detain*) deter;
(*consider*): **to ~ sb responsible (for
sth)** responsabilizar alguém (por algo);
(*keep in certain position*): **to ~ one's
head up** manter a cabeça erigida ▷ *vi*
(*withstand pressure*) resistir; (*be valid*)
ser válido ▷ *n* (*grasp*) pressão *f*; (*fig*)
influência, domínio; (*of ship*) porão *m*;
(*of plane*) compartimento para cargo;
(*control*) controle *m*; **~ the line!** (*Tel*) não
desligue!; **to ~ one's own** (*fig*) virar-se,
sair-se bem; **to catch** *or* **get (a) ~ of**
agarrar, pegar; **hold back** *vt* reter;
(*secret*) manter, guardar; **hold down**
vt (*person*) segurar; (*job*) manter; **hold
off** *vt* (*enemy*) afastar, repelir; **hold on**
vi agarrar-se; (*wait*) esperar; **hold on!**
espera aí!; (*Tel*) não desligue!; **hold on to**
vt fus agarrar-se a; (*keep*) guardar, ficar
com; **hold out** *vt* (*hand*) estender; (*hope*)
ter ▷ *vi* (*resist*) resistir; **hold up** *vt* (*raise*)
levantar; (*support*) apoiar; (*delay*) atrasar;
(*rob*) assaltar; **holdall** (*BRIT*) *n* bolsa de
viagem; **holder** *n* (*container*) recipiente
m; (*of ticket*) portador(a) *m/f*; (*of record*)
detentor(a) *m/f*; (*of office, title*) titular
m/f; **hold-up** *n* (*robbery*) assalto; (*delay*)
demora; (*BRIT: in traffic*) engarrafamento
hole [həul] *n* buraco; (*small: in sock etc*)
furo ▷ *vt* esburacar
holiday [ˈhɔlədɪ] *n* (*BRIT: vacation*) férias
fpl; (*day off*) dia *m* de folga; (*public holiday*)
feriado; **on ~** de férias; **holiday camp**
(*BRIT*) *n* colônia de férias; **holiday-
maker** (*BRIT*) *n* pessoa (que está) de
férias; **holiday resort** *n* local *m* de férias
Holland [ˈhɔlənd] *n* Holanda
hollow [ˈhɔləu] *adj* oco, vazio; (*cheeks*)
côncavo; (*eyes*) fundo; (*sound*) surdo;
(*laugh, claim*) falso ▷ *n* (*in ground*)
cavidade *f*, depressão *f* ▷ *vt*: **to ~ out**
escavar

holly ['hɒlɪ] n azevinho
holy ['həʊlɪ] adj sagrado; (person) santo, bento
home [həʊm] n casa, lar m; (country) pátria; (institution) asilo ▷ cpd caseiro, doméstico; (Econ, Pol) nacional, interno; (Sport: team) de casa; (: game) no próprio campo ▷ adv (direction) para casa; (right in: nail etc) até o fundo; **at ~** em casa; **make yourself at ~** fique à vontade; **home address** n endereço residencial; **homeland** n terra (natal); **homeless** adj sem casa, desabrigado; **homely** adj (simple) simples inv; **home-made** adj caseiro; **Home Office** n (BRIT) Ministério do Interior; **home page** n (Comput) home page f, página inicial; **Home Secretary** (BRIT) n Ministro(-a) do Interior; **homesick** adj: **to be homesick** estar com saudades (do lar); **home town** n cidade f natal; **homework** n dever m de casa
homoeopathic [həʊmɪəʊ'pæθɪk] (US **homeopathic**) adj homeopático
homosexual [hɒməʊ'sɛksjʊəl] adj, n homossexual m/f
Honduras [hɒn'djʊərəs] n Honduras f (no article)
honest ['ɒnɪst] adj (truthful) franco; (trustworthy) honesto; (sincere) sincero; **honestly** adv honestamente; **honesty** n honestidade f, sinceridade f
honey ['hʌnɪ] n mel m; **honeymoon** n lua-de-mel f; (trip) viagem f de lua-de-mel
honorary ['ɒnərərɪ] adj (unpaid) não remunerado; (duty, title) honorário
honour ['ɒnə'] (US **honor**) vt honrar ▷ n honra; **honourable** adj honrado
hood [hʊd] n capuz m; (of cooker) tampa; (BRIT: Aut) capota; (US: Aut) capô m
hoof [huːf] (pl **hooves**) n casco, pata
hook [hʊk] n gancho; (on dress) gancho, colchete m; (for fishing) anzol m ▷ vt prender com gancho (or colchete); (fish) fisgar
hooligan ['huːlɪgən] n desordeiro(-a), bagunceiro(-a)
hoop [huːp] n arco
hooray [huː'reɪ] excl = **hurrah**
hoot [huːt] vi (Aut) buzinar; (siren) tocar; (owl) piar
hooves [huːvz] npl of **hoof**
hop [hɒp] vi saltar, pular; (on one foot) pular num pé só
hope [həʊp] vt, vi esperar ▷ n esperança; **I ~ so/not** espero que sim/não; **hopeful**

adj (person) otimista, esperançoso; (situation) promissor(a); **hopefully** adv esperançosamente; **hopefully, they'll come back** é de esperar or esperamos que voltem; **hopeless** adj desesperado, irremediável; (useless) inútil
horizon [hə'raɪzn] n horizonte m; **horizontal** [hɒrɪ'zɒntl] adj horizontal
horn [hɔːn] n corno, chifre m; (material) chifre; (Mus) trompa; (Aut) buzina
horoscope ['hɒrəskəʊp] n horóscopo
horrendous [hə'rɛndəs] adj horrendo
horrible ['hɒrɪbl] adj horrível; (terrifying) terrível
horrid ['hɒrɪd] adj horrível
horror ['hɒrə'] n horror m; **horror film** n filme m de terror
horse [hɔːs] n cavalo; **horseback**: **on horseback** adj, adv a cavalo; **horse chestnut** n castanha-da-índia; **horsepower** n cavalo-vapor m; **horse-racing** n corridas fpl de cavalo; turfe m
hose [həʊz] n (also: **~pipe**) mangueira
hospital ['hɒspɪtl] n hospital m
hospitality [hɒspɪ'tælɪtɪ] n hospitalidade f
host [həʊst] n anfitrião m; (TV, Radio) apresentador(a) m/f; (Rel) hóstia; (large number): **a ~ of** uma multidão de
hostage ['hɒstɪdʒ] n refém m/f
hostel ['hɒstl] n albergue m, abrigo; (also: **youth ~**) albergue da juventude
hostess ['həʊstɪs] n anfitriã f; (BRIT: air hostess) aeromoça (BR), hospedeira de bordo (PT); (TV, Radio) apresentadora
hostile ['hɒstaɪl] adj hostil
hostility [hɒ'stɪlɪtɪ] n hostilidade f
hot [hɒt] adj quente; (as opposed to only warm) muito quente; (spicy) picante; (fierce) ardente; **to be ~** (person) estar com calor; (thing, weather) estar quente; **hot dog** n cachorro-quente m
hotel [həʊ'tɛl] n hotel m
hound [haʊnd] vt acossar, perseguir ▷ n cão m de caça, sabujo
hour ['aʊə'] n hora; **hourly** adj de hora em hora; (rate) por hora
house [(n) haʊs, (vb) haʊz] n (gen, firm) casa; (Pol) câmara; (Theatre) assistência, lotação f ▷ vt (person) alojar; (collection) abrigar; **on the ~** (fig) por conta da casa; **household** n família; (house) casa; **housekeeper** n governanta; **housekeeping** n (work) trabalhos mpl domésticos; (money) economia doméstica; **housewife** (irreg) n dona

de casa; **housework** n trabalhos mpl domésticos; **housing** n (provision) alojamento; (houses) residências fpl; **housing development** (BRIT **housing estate**) n conjunto residencial

hover ['hɔvəʳ] vi pairar; **hovercraft** n aerobarco

O KEYWORD

how [hau] adv **1** (in what way) como; **how was the film?** que tal o filme?; **how are you?** como vai?
2 (to what degree) quanto; **how much milk/many people?** quanto de leite/quantas pessoas?; **how long have you been here?** quanto tempo você está aqui?; **how old are you?** quantos anos você tem?; **how tall is he?** qual é a altura dele?; **how lovely/awful!** que ótimo/terrível!

however [hau'ɛvəʳ] adv de qualquer modo; (+ adj) por mais ... que; (in questions) como ▷ conj no entanto, contudo

howl [haul] vi uivar
H.P. (BRIT) n abbr = **hire purchase**
h.p. abbr (Aut: = horsepower) CV
HQ n abbr (= headquarters) QG m
HTML n abbr (= Hypertext Mark-up Language) HTML f
huddle ['hʌdl] vi: **to ~ together** aconchegar-se
huff [hʌf] n: **in a ~** com raiva
hug [hʌg] vt abraçar; (thing) agarrar, prender
huge [hjuːdʒ] adj enorme, imenso
hull [hʌl] n (of ship) casco
hum [hʌm] vt cantarolar ▷ vi cantarolar; (insect, machine etc) zumbir
human ['hjuːmən] adj humano ▷ n (also: **~ being**) ser m humano
humane [hjuː'meɪn] adj humano
humanitarian [hjuːmænɪ'tɛərɪən] adj humanitário
humanity [hjuː'mænɪtɪ] n humanidade f
humble ['hʌmbl] adj humilde ▷ vt humilhar
humid ['hjuːmɪd] adj úmido
humiliate [hjuː'mɪlɪeɪt] vt humilhar
humorous ['hjuːmərəs] adj humorístico; (person) engraçado
humour ['hjuːməʳ] (us **humor**) n humorismo, senso de humor; (mood)

humor m ▷ vt fazer a vontade de
hump [hʌmp] n (in ground) elevação f; (camel's) corcova, giba; (deformity) corcunda
hunch [hʌntʃ] n (premonition) pressentimento, palpite m
hundred ['hʌndrəd] num cem; (before lower numbers) cento; **~s of people** centenas de pessoas
hung [hʌŋ] pt, pp of **hang**
Hungary ['hʌŋgərɪ] n Hungria
hunger ['hʌŋgəʳ] n fome f ▷ vi: **to ~ for** (desire) desejar ardentemente
hungry ['hʌŋgrɪ] adj faminto, esfomeado; (keen): **~ for** (fig) ávido de, ansioso por; **to be ~** estar com fome
hunt [hʌnt] vt buscar; (criminal, fugitive) perseguir; (Sport, for food) caçar ▷ vi caçar; (search): **to ~ (for)** procurar (por) ▷ n caça, caçada; **hunter** n caçador(a) m/f; **hunting** n caça
hurdle ['həːdl] n (Sport) barreira; (fig) obstáculo
hurl [həːl] vt arremessar, lançar; (abuse) gritar
hurrah [hu'rɑː] excl oba!, viva!
hurray [hu'reɪ] excl = **hurrah**
hurricane ['hʌrɪkən] n furacão m
hurry ['hʌrɪ] n pressa ▷ vi (also: **~ up**) apressar-se ▷ vt (also: **~ up**: person) apressar; (: work) acelerar; **to be in a ~** estar com pressa
hurt [həːt] (pt, pp **~**) vt machucar; (injure) ferir; (fig) magoar ▷ vi doer
husband ['hʌzbənd] n marido, esposo
hush [hʌʃ] n silêncio, quietude f ▷ vt silenciar, fazer calar; **~!** silêncio!, psiu!; **hush up** vt abafar, encobrir
husky ['hʌskɪ] adj rouco ▷ n cão m esquimó
hut [hʌt] n cabana, choupana; (shed) alpendre m
hyacinth ['haɪəsɪnθ] n jacinto
hydrofoil ['haɪdrəfɔɪl] n hidrofoil m, aliscafo
hydrogen ['haɪdrədʒən] n hidrogênio
hygiene ['haɪdʒiːn] n higiene f
hymn [hɪm] n hino
hype [haɪp] (inf) n tititi m, falatório
hypermarket ['haɪpəmɑːkɪt] (BRIT) n hipermercado
hyphen ['haɪfn] n hífen m
hypnotize vt hipnotizar
hypocrite ['hɪpəkrɪt] n hipócrita m/f; **hypocritical** adj hipócrita
hysterical [hɪ'stʃrɪkl] adj histérico;

(funny) hilariante; **hysterics** *npl (nervous)* crise *f* histérica; *(laughter)* ataque *m* de riso; **to be in** *or* **have hysterics** *(anger, panic)* ter uma crise histérica; *(laughter)* ter um ataque de riso

I [aɪ] *pron* eu
ice [aɪs] *n* gelo; *(ice cream)* sorvete *m* ▷ *vt (cake)* cobrir com glacê ▷ *vi (also:* **~ over, ~ up)** gelar; **iceberg** *n* iceberg *m*; **ice cream** *n* sorvete *m (BR)*, gelado *(PT)*; **ice cube** *n* pedra de gelo; **ice hockey** *n* hóquei *m* sobre o gelo
Iceland ['aɪslənd] *n* Islândia
ice: ice lolly *(BRIT) n* picolé *m*; **ice rink** *n* pista de gelo, rinque *m*
icing ['aɪsɪŋ] *n (Culin)* glacê *m*; **icing sugar** *(BRIT) n* açúcar *m* glacê
icon ['aɪkɔn] *n (gen, Comput)* ícone *m*
icy ['aɪsɪ] *adj* gelado
I'd [aɪd] = **I would**; **I had**
idea [aɪ'dɪə] *n* idéia
ideal [aɪ'dɪəl] *n* ideal *m* ▷ *adj* ideal
identical [aɪ'dɛntɪkl] *adj* idêntico
identification [aɪdentɪfɪ'keɪʃən] *n* identificação *f*; **means of ~** documentos pessoais
identify [aɪ'dɛntɪfaɪ] *vt* identificar
identity [aɪ'dɛntɪtɪ] *n* identidade *f*; **identity card** *n* carteira de identidade
idiom ['ɪdɪəm] *n* expressão *f* idiomática; *(style)* idioma *m*, linguagem *f*
idiot ['ɪdɪət] *n* idiota *m/f*
idle ['aɪdl] *adj* ocioso; *(lazy)* preguiçoso;

(*unemployed*) desempregado;
(*question, conversation*) fútil; (*pleasure*)
descontraído ▷ *vi* (*machine*) funcionar
com a transmissão desligada; **idle away**
vt: **to idle away the time** perder or
desperdiçar tempo
idol ['aɪdl] *n* ídolo
i.e. *abbr* (= *id est: that is*) i.e., isto é

 KEYWORD

if [ɪf] *conj* **1** (*conditional use*) se; **if
necessary** se necessário; **if I were you**
se eu fôsse você
2 (*whenever*) quando
3 (*although*): **(even) if** mesmo que
4 (*whether*) se
5: **if so/not** sendo assim/do contrário; **if
only** se pelo menos; *see also* **as**

ignition [ɪg'nɪʃən] *n* (*Aut*) ignição *f*; **to
switch on/off the ~** ligar/desligar o
motor
ignorant ['ɪgnərənt] *adj* ignorante; **to
be ~ of** ignorar
ignore [ɪg'nɔːʳ] *vt* (*person*) não fazer caso
de; (*fact*) não levar em consideração,
ignorar
I'll [aɪl] = **I will; I shall**
ill [ɪl] *adj* doente; (*harmful: effects*) nocivo
▷ *n* mal *m* ▷ *adv*: **to speak/think ~ of sb**
falar/pensar mal de alguém; **to be taken
~** ficar doente
illegal [ɪ'liːgl] *adj* ilegal
illegible [ɪ'ledʒɪbl] *adj* ilegível
illegitimate [ɪlɪ'dʒɪtɪmət] *adj* ilegítimo
illiterate [ɪ'lɪtərət] *adj* analfabeto
illness ['ɪlnɪs] *n* doença
illuminate [ɪ'luːmɪneɪt] *vt* iluminar,
clarear
illusion [ɪ'luːʒən] *n* ilusão *f*
illustrate ['ɪləstreɪt] *vt* ilustrar; (*point*)
exemplificar; **illustration** [ɪlə'streɪʃən]
n ilustração *f*; (*example*) exemplo;
(*explanation*) esclarecimento
I'm [aɪm] = **I am**
image ['ɪmɪdʒ] *n* imagem *f*
imaginary [ɪ'mædʒɪnərɪ] *adj*
imaginário
imagination [ɪmædʒɪ'neɪʃən]
n imaginação *f*; (*inventiveness*)
inventividade *f*
imagine [ɪ'mædʒɪn] *vt* imaginar
imbalance [ɪm'bæləns] *n*
desigualdade *f*
imitate ['ɪmɪteɪt] *vt* imitar; **imitation**

[ɪmɪ'teɪʃən] *n* imitação *f*; (*copy*) cópia;
(*mimicry*) mímica
immaculate [ɪ'mækjulət] *adj*
impecável; (*Rel*) imaculado
immature [ɪmə'tjuəʳ] *adj* imaturo; (*fruit*)
verde; (*cheese*) fresco
immediate [ɪ'miːdɪət] *adj* imediato;
(*pressing*) urgente, premente;
(*neighbourhood, family*) próximo;
immediately *adv* imediatamente;
(*directly*) diretamente; **immediately
next to** bem junto a
immense [ɪ'mɛns] *adj* imenso;
(*importance*) enorme
immerse [ɪ'məːs] *vt* submergir; **to be ~d
in** (*fig*) estar absorto em
immigrant ['ɪmɪgrənt] *n* imigrante
m/f
immigration [ɪmɪ'greɪʃən] *n*
imigração *f*
imminent ['ɪmɪnənt] *adj* iminente
immoral [ɪ'mɔrl] *adj* imoral
immortal [ɪ'mɔːtl] *adj* imortal
immune [ɪ'mjuːn] *adj*: **~ to** imune a,
imunizado contra
impact ['ɪmpækt] *n* impacto (BR),
impacte *m* (PT)
impair [ɪm'pɛəʳ] *vt* prejudicar
impartial [ɪm'pɑːʃl] *adj* imparcial
impatience [ɪm'peɪʃəns] *n*
impaciência
impatient [ɪm'peɪʃənt] *adj* impaciente;
to get *or* **grow ~** impacientar-se
impeccable [ɪm'pɛkəbl] *adj* impecável
impending [ɪm'pendɪŋ] *adj* iminente,
próximo
imperative [ɪm'pɛrətɪv] *adj* (*tone*)
imperioso, obrigatório; (*need*) vital;
(*necessary*) indispensável ▷ *n* (*Ling*)
imperativo
imperfect [ɪm'pəːfɪkt] *adj* imperfeito;
(*goods etc*) defeituoso ▷ *n* (*Ling: also:* **~
tense**) imperfeito
imperial [ɪm'pɪərɪəl] *adj* imperial
impersonal [ɪm'pəːsənl] *adj* impessoal
impersonate [ɪm'pəːsəneɪt] *vt* fazer-se
passar por, personificar; (*Theatre*) imitar
implement [(*n*) 'ɪmplɪmənt, (*vb*)
'ɪmplɪment] *n* instrumento,
ferramenta; (*for cooking*) utensílio ▷ *vt*
efetivar
implicit [ɪm'plɪsɪt] *adj* implícito;
(*complete*) absoluto
imply [ɪm'plaɪ] *vt* (*mean*) significar; (*hint*)
dar a entender que
impolite [ɪmpə'laɪt] *adj* indelicado,

mal-educado

import [(vb) ɪm'pɔːt, (n) 'ɪmpɔːt] vt
importar ▷ n importação f; (article)
mercadoria importada

importance [ɪm'pɔːtəns] n importância

important [ɪm'pɔːtənt] adj importante;
it's not ~ não tem importância, não
importa

impose [ɪm'pəuz] vt impor ▷ vi: **to ~
on sb** abusar de alguém; **imposing** adj
imponente

impossible [ɪm'pɔsɪbl] adj impossível;
(situation) inviável; (person) insuportável

impotent ['ɪmpətənt] adj impotente

impoverished [ɪm'pɔvərɪʃt] adj
empobrecido; (land) esgotado

impractical [ɪm'præktɪkl] adj pouco
prático

impress [ɪm'prɛs] vt impressionar;
(mark) imprimir; **to ~ sth on sb** inculcar
algo em alguém

impression [ɪm'prɛʃən] n impressão f;
(imitation) caricatura; **to be under the ~
that** estar com a impressão de que

impressive [ɪm'prɛsɪv] adj
impressionante

imprison [ɪm'prɪzn] vt encarcerar

improbable [ɪm'prɔbəbl] adj
improvável; (story) inverossímil (BR),
inverosímil (PT)

improper [ɪm'prɔpə*] adj (unsuitable)
impróprio; (dishonest) desonesto

improve [ɪm'pruːv] vt melhorar
▷ vi melhorar; (pupils) progredir;
improvement n melhora, progresso

improvise ['ɪmprəvaɪz] vt, vi improvisar

impulse ['ɪmpʌls] n impulso; **on ~** sem
pensar, num impulso

⭕ **KEYWORD**

in [ɪn] prep **1** (indicating place, position)
em; **in the house/garden** na casa/no
jardim; **I have it in my hand** eu estou
assegurando isto; **in here/there** aqui
dentro/lá dentro

2 (with place names: of town, country,
region) em; **in London/Rio** em Londres/
no Rio; **in England/Japan/the United
States** na Inglaterra/no Japão/nos
Estados Unidos

3 (indicating time: during) em; **in spring/
autumn** na primavera/no outono; **in
1988** em 1988; **in May** em maio; **I'll see
you in July** até julho; **in the morning** de
manhã; **at 4 o'clock in the afternoon**

às 4 da tarde

4 (indicating time: in the space of) em;
I did it in 3 hours/days fiz isto em 3
horas/dias; **in 2 weeks** or **in 2 weeks'
time** daqui a 2 semanas

5 (indicating manner etc): **in a loud/soft
voice** em voz alta/numa voz sauve;
written in pencil/ink escrito a lápis/à
caneta; **in English/Portuguese** em
inglês/português; **the boy in the blue
shirt** o menino de camisa azul

6 (indicating circumstances): **in the sun** ao
or sob o sol; **in the rain** na chuva; **a rise
in prices** um aumento nos preços

7 (indicating mood, state): **in tears** aos
prantos; **in anger/despair** com raiva/
desesperado; **in good condition** em
boas condições

8 (with ratios, numbers): **1 in 10** 1 em 10,
1 em cada 10; **20 pence in the pound**
vinte pênis numa libra; **they lined up in
twos** eles se alinharam dois a dois

9 (referring to people, works) em

10 (indicating profession etc): **to be in
teaching/publishing** ser professor/
trabalhar numa editora

11 (after superl): **the best pupil in the
class** o melhor aluno da classe; **the
biggest/smallest in Europe** o maior/
menor na Europa

12 (with present participle): **in saying this**
ao dizer isto

▷ adv: **to be in** (person: at home) estar
em casa; (: at work) estar no trabalho;
(fashion) estar na moda; (ship, plane,
train): **it's in** chegou; **is he in?** ele
está?; **to ask sb in** convidar alguém
para entrar; **to run/limp** etc **in** entrar
correndo/mancando etc

▷ n: **the ins and outs** (of proposal,
situation etc) os cantos e recantos, os
pormenores

in. abbr = **inch(es)**

inability [ɪnə'bɪlɪtɪ] n: **~ (to do)**
incapacidade f (de fazer)

inaccurate [ɪn'ækjurət] adj inexato,
impreciso

inadequate [ɪn'ædɪkwət] adj
insuficiente; (person) impróprio

inadvertently [ɪnəd'vəːtntlɪ] adv
inadvertidamente, sem querer

inappropriate [ɪnə'prəuprɪət]
adj inadequado; (word, expression)
impróprio

incapable [ɪn'keɪpəbl] adj incapaz

incense [(*n*) 'ɪnsɛns, (*vb*) ɪn'sɛns]
n incenso ▷ *vt* (*anger*) exasperar,
enraivecer

incentive [ɪn'sɛntɪv] *n* incentivo

inch [ɪntʃ] *n* polegada (= 25 *mm*; 12 *in a
foot*); **to be within an ~ of** estar a um
passo de; **he didn't give an ~** ele não
cedeu nem um milímetro; **inch forward**
vi avançar palmo a palmo

incident ['ɪnsɪdnt] *n* incidente *m*,
evento

inclination [ɪnklɪ'neɪʃən] *n* (*tendency*)
tendência; (*disposition*) inclinação *f*

incline [(*n*) 'ɪnklaɪn, (*vb*) ɪn'klaɪn] *n*
inclinação *f*, ladeira ▷ *vt* curvar, inclinar
▷ *vi* inclinar-se; **to be ~d to** tender a, ser
propenso a

include [ɪn'kluːd] *vt* incluir

including [ɪn'kluːdɪŋ] *prep* inclusive

inclusive [ɪn'kluːsɪv] *adj* incluído,
incluso; **~ of** incluindo

income ['ɪnkʌm] *n* (*earnings*) renda,
rendimentos *mpl*; (*unearned*) renda;
income tax *n* imposto de renda (BR),
imposto complementar (PT)

incoming ['ɪnkʌmɪŋ] *adj* (*flight*) de
chegada; (*mail*) de entrada; (*government*)
novo; (*tide*) enchente

incompetent [ɪn'kɔmpɪtənt] *adj*
incompetente

incomplete [ɪnkəm'pliːt] *adj*
incompleto; (*unfinished*) por terminar

inconsistent [ɪnkən'sɪstnt] *adj*
inconsistente; **~ with** incompatível com

inconvenience [ɪnkən'viːnjəns] *n*
(*quality*) inconveniência; (*problem*)
inconveniente *m* ▷ *vt* incomodar

inconvenient [ɪnkən'viːnjənt] *adj*
inconveniente, incômodo; (*time, place*)
inoportuno

incorporate [ɪn'kɔːpəreɪt] *vt* incorporar;
(*contain*) compreender

incorrect [ɪnkə'rɛkt] *adj* incorreto

increase [(*n*) 'ɪnkriːs, (*vb*) ɪn'kriːs] *n*
aumento ▷ *vi, vt* aumentar

incredible [ɪn'krɛdɪbl] *adj* inacreditável;
(*enormous*) incrível

incur [ɪn'kəː'] *vt* incorrer em; (*expenses*)
contrair

indecent [ɪn'diːsnt] *adj* indecente

indeed [ɪn'diːd] *adv* de fato; (*certainly*)
certamente; (*furthermore*) aliás; **yes ~!**
claro que sim!

indefinitely *adv* indefinidamente

independence [ɪndɪ'pɛndns] *n*
independência; **Independence Day** *n*

Dia *m* de Independência; *ver quadro*

independent [ɪndɪ'pɛndnt] *adj*
independente; (*inquiry*) imparcial

index ['ɪndɛks] (*pl* **~es**) *n* (*in book*) índice
m; (*in library etc*) catálogo; (*pl* **indices**:
ratio, sign) índice *m*, expoente *m*

India ['ɪndɪə] *n* Índia; **Indian** *adj, n* (*from
India*) indiano(-a); (*American, Brazilian*)
índio(-a)

indicate ['ɪndɪkeɪt] *vt* (*show*) sugerir;
(*point to, mention*) indicar; **indication**
[ɪndɪ'keɪʃən] *n* indício, sinal *m*;
indicative [ɪn'dɪkətɪv] *adj*: **indicative
of** sintomático de ▷ *n* (*Ling*) indicativo;
indicator *n* indicador *m*; (*Aut*) pisca-
pisca *m*

indices ['ɪndɪsiːz] *npl of* **index**

indifferent [ɪn'dɪfrənt] *adj* indiferente;
(*quality*) medíocre

indigenous [ɪn'dɪdʒɪnəs] *adj* indígena,
nativo

indigestion [ɪndɪ'dʒɛstʃən] *n*
indigestão *f*

indignant [ɪn'dɪgnənt] *adj*: **to be ~
about sth/with sb** estar indignado com
algo/alguém, indignar-se de algo/
alguém

indirect [ɪndɪ'rɛkt] *adj* indireto

individual [ɪndɪ'vɪdjuəl] *n* indivíduo
▷ *adj* individual; (*personal*) pessoal;
(*characteristic*) particular

Indonesia [ɪndəˈniːzɪə] *n* Indonésia

indoor ['ɪndɔː'] *adj* (*inner*) interno,
interior; (*inside*) dentro de casa; (*plant*)
para dentro de casa; (*swimming pool*)
coberto; (*games, sport*) de salão; **indoors**
adv em lugar fechado

induce [ɪn'djuːs] *vt* (*Med*) induzir; (*bring
about*) causar, produzir

indulge [ɪn'dʌldʒ] *vt* (*desire*) satisfazer;
(*whim*) condescender com; (*person*)
comprazer; (*child*) fazer a vontade de
▷ *vi*: **to ~ in** entregar-se a, satisfazer-se

com; **indulgent** adj indulgente
industrial [ɪnˈdʌstrɪəl] adj industrial
industry [ˈɪndəstrɪ] n indústria;
(diligence) aplicação f, diligência
inefficient [ɪnɪˈfɪʃənt] adj ineficiente
inequality [ɪnɪˈkwɔlɪtɪ] n
desigualdade f
inevitable [ɪnˈɛvɪtəbl] adj inevitável;
inevitably adv inevitavelmente
inexpensive [ɪnɪkˈspɛnsɪv] adj barato,
econômico
inexperienced [ɪnɪkˈspɪərɪənst] adj
inexperiente
infamous [ˈɪnfəməs] adj infame,
abominável
infant [ˈɪnfənt] n (baby) bebê m; (young
child) criança
infant school (BRIT) n pré-escola
infect [ɪnˈfɛkt] vt (person) contagiar;
(food) contaminar; **infection** n
infecção f; **infectious** adj contagioso;
(fig) infeccioso
infer [ɪnˈfəːʳ] vt deduzir, inferir
inferior [ɪnˈfɪərɪəʳ] adj inferior; (goods)
de qualidade inferior ▷ n inferior m/f; (in
rank) subalterno(-a)
infertile [ɪnˈfəːtaɪl] adj infértil; (person,
animal) estéril
infinite [ˈɪnfɪnɪt] adj infinito
infirmary n enfermaria, hospital m
inflamed [ɪnˈfleɪmd] adj inflamado
inflammation [ɪnfləˈmeɪʃən] n
inflamação f
inflatable [ɪnˈfleɪtəbl] adj inflável
inflate [ɪnˈfleɪt] vt (tyre, balloon) inflar,
encher; (price) inflar; **inflation** n (Econ)
inflação f
inflict [ɪnˈflɪkt] vt: **to ~ on** infligir em
influence [ˈɪnfluəns] n influência
▷ vt influir em, influenciar; **under the
~ of alcohol** sob o efeito do álcool;
influential [ɪnfluˈɛnʃl] adj influente
influenza [ɪnfluˈɛnzə] n gripe f
inform [ɪnˈfɔːm] vt informar ▷ vi: **to ~ on
sb** delatar alguém
informal [ɪnˈfɔːml] adj informal; (visit,
discussion) extra-oficial
information [ɪnfəˈmeɪʃən] n
informação f, informações fpl;
(knowledge) conhecimento; **a piece of ~**
uma informação
informative [ɪnˈfɔːmətɪv] adj
informativo
infuriating [ɪnˈfjuərɪeɪtɪŋ] adj de dar
raiva, enfurecedor(a)
ingenious [ɪnˈdʒiːnjəs] adj engenhoso

ingredient [ɪnˈgriːdɪənt] n ingrediente
m; (of situation) fator m
inhabit [ɪnˈhæbɪt] vt habitar;
inhabitant n habitante m/f
inhale [ɪnˈheɪl] vt inalar ▷ vi (in smoking)
tragar
inherent [ɪnˈhɪərənt] adj: **~ in** or **to**
inerente a
inherit [ɪnˈhɛrɪt] vt herdar; **inheritance**
n herança
inhibit [ɪnˈhɪbɪt] vt inibir; **inhibition**
[ɪnhɪˈbɪʃən] n inibição f
initial [ɪˈnɪʃl] adj inicial ▷ n inicial f ▷ vt
marcar com iniciais; **initials** npl (of name)
iniciais fpl; **initially** adv inicialmente,
no início
initiate [ɪˈnɪʃɪeɪt] vt (start) iniciar,
começar; (person) iniciar; **to ~ sb into a
secret** revelar um segredo a alguém
initiative [ɪˈnɪʃətɪv] n iniciativa
inject [ɪnˈdʒɛkt] vt (liquid, fig: money)
injetar; (person) dar uma injeção em;
injection n injeção f
injure [ˈɪndʒəʳ] vt ferir; (reputation etc)
prejudicar; (feelings) ofender; **injured**
adj ferido; (feelings) ofendido, magoado;
injury n ferida
injustice [ɪnˈdʒʌstɪs] n injustiça
ink [ɪŋk] n tinta
inland [(adj) ˈɪnlənd, (adv) ɪnˈlænd] adj
interior, interno ▷ adv para o interior;
Inland Revenue (BRIT) n ≈ fisco,
≈ receita federal (BR)
inmate [ˈɪnmeɪt] n (in prison)
presidiário(-a); (in asylum) internado(-a)
inn [ɪn] n hospedaria, taberna
inner [ˈɪnəʳ] adj (place) interno; (feeling)
interior; **inner city** n aglomeração f
urbana, metrópole f
innocent [ˈɪnəsnt] adj inocente
in-patient n paciente m/f interno(-a)
input [ˈɪnput] n entrada; (resources)
investimento
inquest [ˈɪnkwɛst] n inquérito judicial
inquire [ɪnˈkwaɪəʳ] vi pedir informação
▷ vt perguntar; **inquire about** vt fus
pedir informações sobre; **inquire into**
vt fus investigar, indagar; **inquiry** n
pergunta; (Law) investigação f, inquérito
ins. abbr = **inches**
insane [ɪnˈseɪn] adj louco, doido; (Med)
demente, insano; **insanity** [ɪnˈsænɪtɪ] n
loucura; insanidade f, demência
inscrutable [ɪnˈskruːtəbl] adj
inescrutável, impenetrável
insect [ˈɪnsɛkt] n inseto

insecure [ɪnsɪ'kjuəʳ] *adj* inseguro

insensitive [ɪn'sɛnsɪtɪv] *adj* insensível

insert [ɪn'səːt] *vt* (*between things*) intercalar; (*into sth*) introduzir, inserir

inside ['ɪn'saɪd] *n* interior *m* ▷ *adj* interior, interno ▷ *adv* (*be*) dentro; (*go*) para dentro ▷ *prep* dentro de; (*of time*): **~ 10 minutes** em menos de 10 minutos; **insides** *npl* (*inf*) entranhas *fpl*; **inside out** *adv* às avessas; (*know*) muito bem; **to turn sth inside out** virar algo pelo avesso

insight ['ɪnsaɪt] *n* insight *m*

insignificant [ɪnsɪg'nɪfɪknt] *adj* insignificante

insincere [ɪnsɪn'sɪəʳ] *adj* insincero

insist [ɪn'sɪst] *vi* insistir; **to ~ on doing** insistir em fazer; **to ~ that** insistir que; (*claim*) cismar que; **insistent** *adj* insistente, pertinaz; (*continual*) persistente

insomnia [ɪn'sɔmnɪə] *n* insônia

inspect [ɪn'spɛkt] *vt* inspecionar; (*building*) vistoriar; (ʙʀɪᴛ: *tickets*) fiscalizar; (*troops*) passar revista em; **inspection** *n* inspeção *f*; vistoria; fiscalização *f*; **inspector** *n* inspetor(a) *m/f*; (ʙʀɪᴛ: *on buses, trains*) fiscal *m*

inspire [ɪn'spaɪəʳ] *vt* inspirar

install [ɪn'stɔːl] *vt* instalar; (*official*) nomear; **installation** [ɪnstə'leɪʃən] *n* instalação *f*

installment [ɪn'stɔːlmənt] (*US* **installment**) *n* (*of money*) prestação *f*; (*of story*) fascículo; (*of TV serial etc*) capítulo; **in ~s** (*pay*) a prestações; (*receive*) em várias vezes

instance ['ɪnstəns] *n* exemplo; **for ~** por exemplo; **in the first ~** em primeiro lugar

instant ['ɪnstənt] *n* instante *m*, momento ▷ *adj* imediato; (*coffee*) instantâneo; **instantly** *adv* imediatamente; **instant messaging** *n* mensagens *fpl* instantâneas, sistema *m* de mensagens instantâneas

instead [ɪn'stɛd] *adv* em vez disso; **~ of** em vez de, em lugar de

instinct ['ɪnstɪŋkt] *n* instinto

institute ['ɪnstɪtjuːt] *n* instituto; (*professional body*) associação *f* ▷ *vt* (*inquiry*) começar, iniciar; (*proceedings*) instituir, estabelecer

institution [ɪnstɪ'tjuːʃən] *n* instituição *f*; (*organization*) instituto; (*Med: home*) asilo; (*asylum*) manicômio; (*custom*) costume *m*

instruct [ɪn'strʌkt] *vt*: **to ~ sb in sth** instruir alguém em *or* sobre algo; **to ~ sb to do sth** dar instruções a alguém para fazer algo; **instruction** *n* (*teaching*) instrução *f*; **instructions** *npl* (*orders*) ordens *fpl*; **instructions (for use)** modo de usar; **instructor** *n* instrutor(a) *m/f*

instrument ['ɪnstrumənt] *n* instrumento

insufficient [ɪnsə'fɪʃənt] *adj* insuficiente

insulate ['ɪnsjuleɪt] *vt* isolar; (*protect*) segregar; **insulation** [ɪnsju'leɪʃən] *n* isolamento

insulin ['ɪnsjulɪn] *n* insulina

insult [(*n*) 'ɪnsʌlt, (*vb*) ɪn'sʌlt] *n* ofensa ▷ *vt* insultar, ofender

insurance [ɪn'ʃuərəns] *n* seguro; **fire/ life ~** seguro contra incêndio/de vida

insure [ɪn'ʃuəʳ] *vt* segurar

intact [ɪn'tækt] *adj* intacto, íntegro; (*unharmed*) ileso, são e salvo

intake ['ɪnteɪk] *n* (*of food*) quantidade *f* ingerida; (ʙʀɪᴛ: *Sch*): **an ~ of 200 a year** 200 matriculados por ano

integral ['ɪntɪgrəl] *adj* (*part*) integrante, essencial

integrate ['ɪntɪgreɪt] *vt* integrar ▷ *vi* integrar-se

intellect ['ɪntəlɛkt] *n* intelecto; **intellectual** [ɪntə'lɛktjuəl] *adj*, *n* intelectual *m/f*

intelligence [ɪn'tɛlɪdʒəns] *n* inteligência; (*Mil etc*) informações *fpl*

intelligent [ɪn'tɛlɪdʒənt] *adj* inteligente

intend [ɪn'tɛnd] *vt* (*gift etc*): **to ~ sth for** destinar algo a; **to ~ to do sth** tencionar *or* pretender fazer algo; (*plan*) planejar fazer algo

intense [ɪn'tɛns] *adj* intenso; (*person*) muito emotivo

intensive [ɪn'tɛnsɪv] *adj* intensivo; **intensive care unit** *n* unidade *f* de tratamento intensivo

intent [ɪn'tɛnt] *n* intenção *f* ▷ *adj*: **to be ~ on doing sth** estar resolvido a fazer algo; **to all ~s and purposes** para todos os efeitos

intention [ɪn'tɛnʃən] *n* intenção *f*, propósito; **intentional** *adj* intencional, propositado

interact [ɪntər'ækt] *vi* interagir; **interactive** *adj* (*Comput*) interactivo

interchange ['ɪntətʃeɪndʒ] *n* intercâmbio; (*exchange*) troca, permuta; (*on motorway*) trevo

intercourse ['ıntəkɔːs] n: **sexual ~** relações fpl sexuais

interest ['ıntrıst] n interesse m; (Comm: sum) juros mpl; (: in company) participação f ▷ vt interessar; **to be ~ed in** interessar-se por, estar interessado em; **interesting** adj interessante

interface ['ıntəfeıs] n (Comput) interface f

interfere [ıntə'fıəʳ] vi: **to ~ in** interferir or intrometer-se em; **to ~ with** (objects) mexer em; (hinder) impedir; (plans) interferir em

interference [ıntə'fıərəns] n intromissão f; (Radio, TV) interferência

interior [ın'tıərıəʳ] n interior m ▷ adj interno; (ministry) do interior

intermediate [ıntə'miːdıət] adj intermediário

intermission [ıntə'mıʃən] n intervalo

intern [(vb) ın'təːn, (n) 'ıntəːn] vt internar ▷ n (us) médico-interno (médica-interna)

internal [ın'təːnl] adj interno

international [ıntə'næʃənl] adj internacional ▷ n (BRIT: Sport: game) jogo internacional

Internet ['ıntənet] n: **the ~** a internet; **Internet café** n cibercafé m; **Internet Service Provider** n provedor m de acesso à Internet

interpret [ın'təːprıt] vt interpretar; (translate) traduzir ▷ vi interpretar; **interpreter** n intérprete m/f

interrogate [ın'tεrəugeıt] vt interrogar; **interrogation** [ıntεrəu'geıʃən] n interrogatório

interrupt [ıntə'rʌpt] vt, vi interromper; **interruption** n interrupção f

interval ['ıntəvl] n intervalo

intervene [ıntə'viːn] vi intervir; (event) ocorrer; (time) decorrer

interview ['ıntəvjuː] n entrevista ▷ vt entrevistar; **interviewer** n entrevistador(a) m/f

intimate [(adj) 'ıntımət, (vb) 'ıntımeıt] adj íntimo; (knowledge) profundo ▷ vt insinuar, sugerir

into ['ıntu] prep em; **she burst ~ tears** ela desatou a chorar; **come ~ the house** venha para dentro; **research ~ cancer** pesquisa sobre o câncer; **he worked late ~ the night** ele trabalhou até altas horas; **he was shocked ~ silence** ele ficou mudo de choque; **~ 3 pieces/French** em 3 pedaços/para o francês

intolerant [ın'tɔlərənt] adj: **~ (of)** intolerante (com or para com)

intranet ['ıntrənet] n intranet f

intricate ['ıntrıkət] adj complexo, complicado

intrigue [ın'triːg] n intriga ▷ vt intrigar; (fascinate) fascinar; **intriguing** adj curioso

introduce [ıntrə'djuːs] vt introduzir; **to ~ sb (to sb)** apresentar alguém (a alguém); **to ~ sb to** (pastime, technique) iniciar alguém em; **introduction** n introdução f; (of person) apresentação f; **introductory** adj introdutório

intrude [ın'truːd] vi: **to ~ (on)** intrometer-se (em); **intruder** n intruso(-a)

inundate ['ınʌndeıt] vt: **to ~ with** inundar de

invade [ın'veıd] vt invadir

invalid [(n) 'ınvəlıd, (adj) ın'vælıd] n inválido(-a) ▷ adj inválido, nulo

invaluable [ın'væljuəbl] adj valioso, inestimável

invariably [ın'vεərıəblı] adv invariavelmente

invent [ın'vεnt] vt inventar; **invention** n invenção f; (inventiveness) engenho; (lie) ficção f, mentira; **inventor** n inventor(a) m/f

inventory ['ınvəntrı] n inventário, relação f

invest [ın'vεst] vt investir ▷ vi: **to ~ in** investir em; (acquire) comprar

investigate [ın'vεstıgeıt] vt investigar; **investigation** [ınvεstı'geıʃən] n investigação f

investment [ın'vεstmənt] n investimento

invisible [ın'vızıbl] adj invisível

invitation [ınvı'teıʃən] n convite m

invite [ın'vaıt] vt convidar; (opinions etc) incitar; **inviting** adj convidativo

invoice ['ınvɔıs] n fatura ▷ vt faturar

involve [ın'vɔlv] vt (entail) implicar; (require) exigir; (concern) envolver; **to ~ sb (in)** envolver alguém (em); **involved** adj (complex) complexo; **to be involved in** estar envolvido em; **involvement** n envolvimento

inward ['ınwəd] adj (movement) interior, interno; (thought, feeling) íntimo; **inward(s)** adv para dentro

IQ n abbr (= intelligence quotient) QI m

IRA n abbr (= Irish Republican Army) IRA m

Iran [ı'rɑːn] n Irã m (BR), Irão m (PT)

Iraq [ɪˈrɑːk] n Iraque m
Ireland [ˈaɪələnd] n Irlanda
iris [ˈaɪrɪs] (pl ~es) n íris f
Irish [ˈaɪrɪʃ] adj irlandês(-esa) ▷ npl:
the ~ os irlandeses; **Irishman** (irreg) n
irlandês m; **Irish Sea** n: **the Irish Sea**
o mar da Irlanda; **Irishwoman** (irreg) n
irlandesa
iron [ˈaɪən] n ferro; (for clothes) ferro de
passar roupa ▷ adj de ferro ▷ vt (clothes)
passar; **iron out** vt (problem) resolver
ironic(al) [aɪˈrɒnɪk(l)] adj irônico
ironing [ˈaɪənɪŋ] n (activity) passar m
roupa; (clothes) roupa passada; **ironing
board** n tábua de passar roupa
irony [ˈaɪrənɪ] n ironia
irrational [ɪˈræʃənl] adj irracional
irregular [ɪˈregjuləʳ] adj irregular;
(surface) desigual
irrelevant [ɪˈreləvənt] adj irrelevante
irresistible [ɪrɪˈzɪstɪbl] adj irresistível
irresponsible [ɪrɪˈspɒnsɪbl] adj
irresponsável
irrigation [ɪrɪˈgeɪʃən] n irrigação f
irritate [ˈɪrɪteɪt] vt irritar; **irritating**
adj irritante; **irritation** [ɪrɪˈteɪʃən] n
irritação f
is [ɪz] vb see **be**
Islam [ˈɪzlɑːm] n islamismo
island [ˈaɪlənd] n ilha; **islander** n ilhéu
(ilhoa) m/f
isle [aɪl] n ilhota, ilha
isn't [ˈɪznt] = **is not**
ISP n abbr = **Internet Service Provider**
Israel [ˈɪzreɪl] n Israel m (no article);
Israeli [ɪzˈreɪlɪ] adj, n israelense m/f
issue [ˈɪʃjuː] n questão f, tema m; (of
book) edição f; (of stamps) emissão f ▷ vt
(statement) fazer; (rations, equipment)
distribuir; (orders) dar; **at ~** em debate;
to take ~ with sb (over sth) discordar
de alguém (sobre algo); **to make an ~ of
sth** criar caso com algo

⊙ **KEYWORD**

it [ɪt] pron **1** (specific: subject) ele (ela);
(: direct object) o (a); (: indirect object) lhe;
it's on the table está em cima da mesa; **I
can't find it** não consigo achá-lo; **give it
to me** dê-mo; **about/from it** sobre/de
isto; **did you go to it?** (party, concert etc)
você foi?
2 (impers) isto, isso; (after prep) ele, ela;
it's raining está chovendo (BR) or a
chover (PT); **it's six o'clock/the 10th**

of August são seis horas/hoje é (dia) 10
de agosto; **who is it? - it's me** quem é?
- sou eu

Italian [ɪˈtæljən] adj italiano ▷ n
italiano(-a); (Ling) italiano
italics [ɪˈtælɪks] npl itálico
Italy [ˈɪtəlɪ] n Itália
itch [ɪtʃ] n comichão f, coceira ▷ vi
(person) estar com or sentir comichão or
coceira; (part of body) comichar, coçar;
I'm ~ing to do sth estou louco para fazer
algo; **itchy** adj que coça; **to be itchy**
= **to itch**
it'd [ˈɪtd] = **it would**; **it had**
item [ˈaɪtəm] n item m; (on agenda)
assunto; (in programme) número; (also:
news ~) notícia
itinerary [aɪˈtɪnərərɪ] n itinerário
it'll [ˈɪtl] = **it will**; **it shall**
its [ɪts] adj seu (sua), dele (dela) ▷ pron o
seu (a sua), o dele (a dela)
it's [ɪts] = **it is**; **it has**
itself [ɪtˈsɛlf] pron (reflexive) si mesmo(-a);
(emphatic) ele mesmo (ela mesma)
ITV (BRIT) n abbr (= Independent Television)
canal de televisão comercial
I've [aɪv] = **I have**
ivory [ˈaɪvərɪ] n marfim m
ivy [ˈaɪvɪ] n hera

j

jab [dʒæb] vt cutucar ▷ n cotovelada, murro; (*Med: inf*) injeção f; **to ~ sth into sth** cravar algo em algo

jack [dʒæk] n (*Aut*) macaco; (*Cards*) valete m; **jack up** vt (*Aut*) levantar com macaco

jacket ['dʒækɪt] n jaqueta, casaco curto, forro; (*of book*) sobrecapa; **jacket potato** n batata assada com a casca

jackpot ['dʒækpɔt] n bolada, sorte f grande

jagged ['dʒægɪd] adj dentado, denteado

jail [dʒeɪl] n prisão f, cadeia ▷ vt encarcerar

jam [dʒæm] n geléia; (*also:* **traffic ~**) engarrafamento; (*inf*) apuro ▷ vt obstruir, atravancar; (*mechanism*) emperrar; (*Radio*) bloquear, interferir ▷ vi (*mechanism, drawer etc*) emperrar; **to ~ sth into sth** forçar algo dentro de algo

Jamaica [dʒə'meɪkə] n Jamaica

janitor ['dʒænɪtər] n zelador m

January ['dʒænjuərɪ] n janeiro

Japan [dʒə'pæn] n Japão m; **Japanese** [dʒæpə'niːz] adj japonês(-esa) ▷ n inv japonês(-esa) m/f; (*Ling*) japonês m

jar [dʒɑːr] n jarro ▷ vi (*sound*) ranger, chiar; (*colours*) destoar

jargon ['dʒɑːgən] n jargão m

javelin ['dʒævlɪn] n dardo de arremesso

jaw [dʒɔː] n mandíbula, maxilar m

jazz [dʒæz] n jazz m; **jazz up** vt animar, avivar

jealous ['dʒɛləs] adj ciumento; **jealousy** n ciúmes mpl

jeans [dʒiːnz] npl jeans m (pl PT)

jelly ['dʒɛlɪ] n gelatina; (*jam*) geléia; **jellyfish** ['dʒɛlɪfɪʃ] n inv água-viva

jerk [dʒəːk] n solavanco, sacudida; (*wrench*) puxão m; (*inf: idiot*) babaca m ▷ vt sacudir ▷ vi dar um solavanco

jersey ['dʒəːzɪ] n suéter m or f (BR), camisola (PT); (*fabric*) jérsei m, malha

Jesus ['dʒiːzəs] n Jesus m

jet [dʒɛt] n (*of gas, liquid*) jato; (*Aviat*) avião m a jato; (*stone*) azeviche m; **jet lag** n cansaço devido à diferença de fuso horário

jetty ['dʒɛtɪ] n quebra-mar m, cais m

Jew [dʒuː] n judeu(-dia) m/f

jewel ['dʒuːəl] n jóia; **jeweller** (US **jeweler**) n joalheiro(-a); **jeweller's (shop)** n joalheria; **jewellery** (US **jewelry**) n jóias fpl

Jewish ['dʒuːɪʃ] adj judeu (judia)

jigsaw ['dʒɪgsɔː] n (*also:* **~ puzzle**) quebra-cabeça m

job [dʒɔb] n trabalho; (*task*) tarefa; (*duty*) dever m; (*post*) emprego; **it's not my ~** não faz parte das minhas funções; **it's a good ~ that ...** ainda bem que ...; **just the ~!** justo o que queria!; **jobless** adj desempregado

jockey ['dʒɔkɪ] n jóquei m ▷ vi: **to ~ for position** manobrar para conseguir uma posição

jog [dʒɔg] vt empurrar, sacudir ▷ vi fazer jogging or cooper; **jog along** vi ir levando; **jogging** n jogging m

join [dʒɔɪn] vt (*things*) juntar, unir; (*queue*) entrar em; (*become member of*) associar-se a; (*meet*) encontrar-se com; (*accompany*) juntar-se a ▷ vi (*roads, rivers*) confluir ▷ n junção f; **join in** vi participar ▷ vt fus participar em; **join up** vi unir-se; (*Mil*) alistar-se

joint [dʒɔɪnt] n (*Tech*) junta, união f; (*wood*) encaixe m; (*Anat*) articulação f; (BRIT: *Culin*) quarto; (*inf: place*) espelunca; (: *of marijuana*) baseado ▷ adj comum; (*combined*) conjunto; (*committee*) misto

joke [dʒəuk] n piada; (*also:* **practical ~**) brincadeira, peça ▷ vi brincar; **to play a ~ on** pregar uma peça em; **joker** n (*Cards*) curingão m

jolly ['dʒɔlı] adj (merry) alegre; (enjoyable) divertido ▷ adv (BRIT: inf) muito, extremamente

jolt [dʒəult] n (shake) sacudida, solavanco; (shock) susto ▷ vt sacudir; (emotionally) abalar

Jordan ['dʒɔːdən] n Jordânia; (river) Jordão m

journal ['dʒəːnl] n jornal m; (magazine) revista; (diary) diário; **journalism** n jornalismo; **journalist** n jornalista m/f

journey ['dʒəːnı] n viagem f; (distance covered) trajeto

joy [dʒɔı] n alegria

judge [dʒʌdʒ] n juiz (juíza m/f); (in competition) árbitro; (fig: expert) especialista m/f, conhecedor(a) m/f ▷ vt julgar; (competition) arbitrar; (estimate) avaliar; (consider) considerar

judo ['dʒuːdəu] n judô m

jug [dʒʌg] n jarro

juggle ['dʒʌgl] vi fazer malabarismos; **juggler** n malabarista m/f

juice [dʒuːs] n suco (BR), sumo (PT); **juicy** adj suculento

July [dʒuːˈlaı] n julho

jumble ['dʒʌmbl] n confusão f, mixórdia ▷ vt (also: ~ up: mix up) misturar; **jumble sale** (BRIT) n bazar m; ver quadro

⚫ **JUMBLE SALE**
⚫
⚫ As **jumble sales** têm lugar dentro
⚫ de igrejas, salões de festa e escolas,
⚫ onde são vendidos diversos tipos
⚫ de mercadorias, em geral baratas e
⚫ sobretudo de segunda mão, a fim de
⚫ coletar dinheiro para uma obra de
⚫ caridade, uma escola ou uma igreja.

jump [dʒʌmp] vi saltar, pular; (start) sobressaltar-se; (increase) disparar ▷ vt pular, saltar ▷ n pulo, salto; (increase) alta; (fence) obstáculo; **to ~ the queue** (BRIT) furar a fila (BR), pôr-se à frente (PT)

jumper ['dʒʌmpəʳ] n (BRIT: pullover) suéter m (BR), camisola (PT); (US: pinafore dress) avental m; **jumper cables** (US) npl = **jump leads**

jump leads (BRIT) npl cabos mpl para ligar a bateria

Jun. abbr = **junior**

junction ['dʒʌŋkʃən] (BRIT) n (of roads) cruzamento; (Rail) entroncamento

June [dʒuːn] n junho

jungle ['dʒʌŋgl] n selva, mato

junior ['dʒuːnıəʳ] adj (in age) mais novo or moço; (position) subalterno ▷ n jovem m/f

junk [dʒʌŋk] n (cheap goods) tranqueira, velharias fpl; (rubbish) lixo; **junk food** n comida pronta de baixo valor nutritivo; **junk mail** n correspondência não-solicitada

jury ['dʒuərı] n júri m

just [dʒʌst] adj justo ▷ adv (exactly) justamente, exatamente; (only) apenas, somente; **he's ~ done it/left** ele acabou (BR) or acaba (PT) de fazê-lo/ir; **~ right** perfeito; **~ two o'clock** duas (horas) em ponto; **she's ~ as clever as you** ela é tão inteligente como você; **it's ~ as well that ...** ainda bem que ...; **~ as he was leaving** no momento em que ele saía; **~ before/enough** justo antes/o suficiente; **~ here** bem aqui; **he ~ missed** falhou por pouco; **~ listen** escute aqui!

justice ['dʒʌstıs] n justiça; (us: judge) juiz (juíza) m/f; **to do ~ to** (fig) apreciar devidamente

justify ['dʒʌstıfaı] vt justificar

jut [dʒʌt] vi (also: ~ out) sobressair

juvenile ['dʒuːvənaıl] adj juvenil; (court) de menores; (books) para adolescentes; (humour, mentality) infantil ▷ n menor m/f de idade

k

K *abbr* (= *kilobyte*) K ▷ *n abbr* (= *one thousand*) mil

kangaroo [kæŋgə'ru:] *n* canguru *m*

karate [kə'rɑ:tɪ] *n* karatê *m*

kebab [kə'bæb] *n* churrasquinho, espetinho

keen [ki:n] *adj* (*interest, desire*) grande, vivo; (*eye, intelligence*) penetrante; (*competition*) acirrado, intenso; (*edge*) afiado; (*eager*) entusiasmado; **to be ~ to do** *or* **on doing sth** sentir muita vontade de fazer algo; **to be ~ on sth/sb** gostar de algo/alguém

keep [ki:p] (*pt, pp* **kept**) *vt* guardar, ficar com; (*house etc*) cuidar; (*detain*) deter; (*shop etc*) tomar conta de; (*preserve*) conservar; (*accounts, family*) manter; (*promise*) cumprir; (*chickens, bees etc*) criar; (*prevent*): **to ~ sb from doing sth** impedir alguém de fazer algo ▷ *vi* (*food*) conservar-se; (*remain*) ficar ▷ *n* (*of castle*) torre *f* de menagem; (*food etc*): **to earn one's ~** ganhar a vida; (*inf*): **for ~s** para sempre; **to ~ doing sth** continuar fazendo algo; **to ~ sb happy** manter alguém satisfeito; **to ~ a place tidy** manter um lugar limpo; **keep on** *vi*: **to keep on doing** continuar fazendo; **to**

keep on (about sth) falar sem parar sobre algo; **keep out** *vt* impedir de entrar; **"keep out"** "entrada proibida"; **keep up** *vt* manter ▷ *vi* não atrasar-se, acompanhar; **to keep up with** (*pace*) acompanhar; (*level*) manter-se ao nível de; **keeper** *n* guarda *m*, guardião(-diã) *m/f*

kennel ['kɛnl] *n* casa de cachorro; **kennels** *n* (*establishment*) canil *m*

kerb [kə:b] (*BRIT*) *n* meio-fio (*BR*), borda do passeio (*PT*)

kettle ['kɛtl] *n* chaleira

key [ki:] *n* chave *f*; (*Mus*) clave *f*; (*of piano, typewriter*) tecla ▷ *cpd* (*issue etc*) chave ▷ *vt* (*also*: ~ **in**) colocar; **keyboard** *n* teclado; **keyhole** *n* buraco da fechadura; **keyring** *n* chaveiro

khaki ['kɑ:kɪ] *adj* cáqui

kick [kɪk] *vt* dar um pontapé em; (*ball*) chutar; (*inf: habit*) conseguir superar ▷ *vi* (*horse*) dar coices ▷ *n* (*from person*) pontapé *m*; (*from animal*) coice *m*, patada; (*to ball*) chute *m*; (*inf: thrill*): **he does it for ~s** faz isso para curtir; **kick off** *vi* (*Sport*) dar o chute inicial

kid [kɪd] *n* (*inf: child*) criança; (*animal*) cabrito; (*leather*) pelica ▷ *vi* (*inf*) brincar

kidnap ['kɪdnæp] *vt* seqüestrar

kidney ['kɪdnɪ] *n* rim *m*

kill [kɪl] *vt* matar; (*murder*) assassinar ▷ *n* ato de matar; **killer** *n* assassino(-a); **killing** *n* assassinato; **to make a killing** (*inf*) faturar uma boa nota

kiln [kɪln] *n* forno

kilo ['ki:ləu] *n* quilo; **kilobyte** *n* quilobyte *m*; **kilogram(me)** *n* quilograma *m*; **kilometre** (*US* **kilometer**) *n* quilômetro; **kilowatt** *n* quilowatt *m*

kilt [kɪlt] *n* saiote *m* escocês

kin [kɪn] *n* see **next**

kind [kaɪnd] *adj* (*friendly*) gentil; (*generous*) generoso; (*good*) bom (boa), bondoso, amável; (*voice*) suave ▷ *n* espécie *f*, classe *f*; (*species*) gênero; **in ~** (*Comm*) em espécie

kindergarten ['kɪndəgɑ:tn] *n* jardim *m* de infância

kindly ['kaɪndlɪ] *adj* bom (boa), bondoso; (*gentle*) gentil, carinhoso ▷ *adv* bondosamente, amavelmente; **will you ~ ...** você pode fazer o favor de ...

kindness ['kaɪndnɪs] *n* bondade *f*, gentileza

king [kɪŋ] *n* rei *m*; **kingdom** *n* reino; **kingfisher** *n* martim-pescador *m*

kiosk ['kiːɔsk] n banca (BR), quiosque m
(PT); (BRIT: Tel) cabine f
kipper ['kɪpə'] n arenque defumado
kiss [kɪs] n beijo ▷ vt beijar; **to ~ (each
other)** beijar-se; **kiss of life** (BRIT) n
respiração f artificial
kit [kɪt] n (for sport etc) kit m; (equipment)
equipamento; (tools) caixa de
ferramentas; (for assembly) kit m para
montar
kitchen ['kɪtʃɪn] n cozinha
kite [kaɪt] n (toy) papagaio, pipa
kitten ['kɪtn] n gatinho
kitty ['kɪtɪ] n fundo comum, vaquinha
km abbr (= kilometre) km
knack [næk] n jeito
knee [niː] n joelho; **kneecap** n rótula
kneel [niːl] (pt, pp **knelt**) vi (also: **~ down**)
ajoelhar-se
knew [njuː] pt of **know**
knickers ['nɪkəz] (BRIT) npl calcinha (BR),
cuecas fpl (PT)
knife [naɪf] (pl **knives**) n faca ▷ vt
esfaquear
knight [naɪt] n cavaleiro; (Chess) cavalo
knit [nɪt] vt tricotar; (brows) franzir ▷ vi
tricotar (BR), fazer malha (PT); (bones)
consolidar-se; **knitting** n tricô m;
knitting needle n agulha de tricô (BR)
or de malha (PT); **knitwear** n roupa de
malha
knives [naɪvz] npl of **knife**
knob [nɔb] n (of door) maçaneta; (of stick)
castão m; (on TV etc) botão m
knock [nɔk] vt bater em; (bump into)
colidir com; (inf) criticar, malhar ▷ n
pancada, golpe m; (on door) batida ▷ vi:
to ~ at or **on the door** bater à porta;
knock down vt derrubar; (pedestrian)
atropelar; **knock off** vi (inf: finish)
terminar ▷ vt (inf: steal) abafar; (from
price): **to knock off £10** fazer um
desconto de £10; **knock out** vt pôr
nocaute, nocautear; (defeat) eliminar;
knock over vt derrubar; (pedestrian)
atropelar
knot [nɔt] n nó m ▷ vt dar nó em
know [nəu] (pt **knew**, pp **~n**) vt saber;
(person, author, place) conhecer; **to ~
how to swim** saber nadar; **to ~ about**
or **of sth** saber de algo; **know-how** n
know-how m, experiência; **knowingly**
adv (purposely) de propósito; (spitefully)
maliciosamente
knowledge ['nɔlɪdʒ] n conhecimento;
(learning) saber m, conhecimentos mpl;

knowledgeable adj entendido, versado
knuckle ['nʌkl] n nó m
Koran [kɔ'rɑːn] n: **the ~** o Alcorão
Korea [kə'rɪə] n Coréia
kosher ['kəuʃə'] adj kosher inv
Kosovo ['kɒsəvəu] n Kosovo m

L *abbr* (BRIT: Aut) = **learner**

lab [læb] *n abbr* = **laboratory**

label ['leɪbl] *n* etiqueta, rótulo ▷ *vt* etiquetar, rotular

labor *etc* ['leɪbə'] (US) = **labour** *etc*

laboratory [lə'bɒrətərɪ] *n* laboratório

labour ['leɪbə'] (US **labor**) *n* trabalho; (workforce) mão-de-obra *f*; (Med): **to be in ~** estar em trabalho de parto ▷ *vi* trabalhar ▷ *vt* insistir em; **the L~ Party** (BRIT) o Partido Trabalhista; **labourer** *n* operário; **farm labourer** trabalhador *m* rural, peão *m*

lace [leɪs] *n* renda; (of shoe etc) cadarço ▷ *vt* (shoe) amarrar

lack [læk] *n* falta ▷ *vt* (money, confidence) faltar; (intelligence) carecer de; **through or for ~ of** por falta de; **to be ~ing** faltar; **to be ~ing in** carecer de

lacquer ['lækə'] *n* laca; (hair lacquer) fixador *m*

lad [læd] *n* menino, rapaz *m*, moço

ladder ['lædə'] *n* escada *f* de mão; (BRIT: in tights) defeito (em forma de escada)

ladle ['leɪdl] *n* concha (de sopa)

lady ['leɪdɪ] *n* senhora; (distinguished, noble) dama; (in address): **ladies and gentlemen ...** senhoras e senhores ...;

young ~ senhorita; **"ladies' (toilets)"** "senhoras"; **ladybird** (US **ladybug**) *n* joaninha

lag [læg] *n* atraso, retardamento ▷ *vi* (also: **~ behind**) ficar para trás ▷ *vt* (pipes) revestir com isolante térmico

lager ['lɑ:gə'] *n* cerveja leve e clara

lagoon [lə'gu:n] *n* lagoa

laid [leɪd] *pt, pp of* **lay**

lain [leɪn] *pp of* **lie**

lake [leɪk] *n* lago

lamb [læm] *n* cordeiro

lame [leɪm] *adj* coxo, manco; (excuse, argument) pouco convincente, fraco

lament [lə'mɛnt] *n* lamento, queixa ▷ *vt* lamentar-se de

lamp [læmp] *n* lâmpada; **lamppost** (BRIT) *n* poste *m*; **lampshade** *n* abajur *m*, quebra-luz *m*

land [lænd] *n* terra; (country) país *m*; (piece of land) terreno; (estate) terras *fpl*, propriedades *fpl* ▷ *vi* (from ship) desembarcar; (Aviat) pousar, aterrissar (BR), aterrar (PT); (fig: arrive) cair, terminar ▷ *vt* desembarcar; **to ~ sb with sth** (inf) sobrecarregar alguém com algo; **land up** *vi* ir parar; **landing** *n* (Aviat) pouso, aterrissagem *f* (BR), aterragem *f* (PT); (of staircase) patamar *m*; **landlady** *n* senhoria; (of pub) dona, proprietária; **landlord** *n* senhorio, locador *m*; (of pub) dono, proprietário; **landmark** *n* lugar *m* conhecido; (fig) marco; **landowner** *n* latifundiário(-a)

landscape ['lændskeɪp] *n* paisagem *f*

landslide ['lændslaɪd] *n* (Geo) desmoronamento, desabamento; (fig: Pol) vitória esmagadora

lane [leɪn] *n* caminho, estrada estreita; (Aut) pista; (in race) raia

language ['læŋgwɪdʒ] *n* língua; (way one speaks) linguagem *f*; **bad ~** palavrões *mpl*; **language laboratory** *n* laboratório de línguas; **language school** *n* escola de línguas

lantern ['læntn] *n* lanterna

lap [læp] *n* (of track) volta; (of person) colo ▷ *vt* (also: **~ up**) lamber ▷ *vi* (waves) marulhar; **lap up** *vt* (fig) receber com sofreguidão

lapel [lə'pɛl] *n* lapela

lapse [læps] *n* lapso; (bad behaviour) deslize *m* ▷ *vi* (law) prescrever; **to ~ into bad habits** adquirir maus hábitos

laptop (computer) ['læptɔp-] *n*

laptop m
lard [lɑːd] n banha de porco
larder ['lɑːdəʳ] n despensa
large [lɑːdʒ] adj grande; **at ~** (free) em liberdade; (generally) em geral; **largely** adv em grande parte; (introducing reason) principalmente; **large-scale** adj (map) em grande escala; (fig) importante, de grande alcance
lark [lɑːk] n (bird) cotovia; (joke) brincadeira, peça; **lark about** vi divertir-se, brincar
laryngitis [lærɪnˈdʒaɪtɪs] n laringite f
laser ['leɪzəʳ] n laser m; **laser printer** n impressora a laser
lash [læʃ] n (blow) chicotada; (also: **eye~**) pestana, cílio ▷ vt chicotear, açoitar; (subj: rain, wind) castigar; (tie) atar; **lash out** vi: **to lash out at sb** atacar alguém violentamente; (criticize) atacar alguém verbalmente
lass [læs] (BRIT) n moça
last [lɑːst] adj último; (final) derradeiro ▷ adv em último lugar ▷ vi durar; (continue) continuar; **~ night/week** ontem à noite/na semana passada; **at ~** finalmente; **~ but one** penúltimo; **lastly** adv por fim, por último; (finally) finalmente; **last-minute** adj de última hora
latch [lætʃ] n trinco, fecho, tranca
late [leɪt] adj (not on time) atrasado; (far on in day etc) tardio; (former) antigo, ex-, anterior; (dead) falecido ▷ adv tarde; (behind time, schedule) atrasado; **of ~** recentemente; **in ~ May** no final de maio; **latecomer** n retardatário(-a); **lately** adv ultimamente; **later** ['leɪtəʳ] adj (date etc) posterior; (version etc) mais recente ▷ adv mais tarde, depois; **later on** mais tarde; **latest** ['leɪtɪst] adj último; **at the latest** no mais tardar
lather ['lɑːðəʳ] n espuma (de sabão) ▷ vt ensaboar
Latin ['lætɪn] n (Ling) latim m ▷ adj latino; **Latin America** n América Latina; **Latin American** adj, n latino-americano(-a)
latitude ['lætɪtjuːd] n latitude f
latter ['lætəʳ] adj último; (of two) segundo ▷ n: **the ~** o último, este
laugh [lɑːf] n riso, risada ▷ vi rir, dar risada (or gargalhada); **(to do sth) for a ~** (fazer algo) só de curtição; **laugh at** vt fus rir de; **laugh off** vt disfarçar sorrindo; **laughter** n riso, risada

launch [lɔːntʃ] n (boat) lancha; (Comm, of rocket etc) lançamento ▷ vt lançar; **launch into** vt fus lançar-se a
laundry ['lɔːndrɪ] n lavanderia; (clothes) roupa para lavar
lava ['lɑːvə] n lava
lavatory ['lævətərɪ] n privada (BR), casa de banho (PT)
lavender ['lævəndəʳ] n lavanda
lavish ['lævɪʃ] adj (amount) generoso; (person): **~ with** pródigo em, generoso com ▷ vt: **to ~ sth on sb** encher or cobrir alguém de algo
law [lɔː] n lei f; (rule) regra; (Sch) direito; **lawful** adj legal, lícito
lawn [lɔːn] n gramado (BR), relvado (PT); **lawnmower** n cortador m de grama (BR) or de relva (PT)
lawsuit ['lɔːsuːt] n ação f judicial, processo
lawyer ['lɔːjəʳ] n advogado(-a); (for sales, wills etc) notário(-a), tabelião(-liã) m/f
lax [læks] adj (discipline) relaxado; (person) negligente
laxative ['læksətɪv] n laxante m
lay [leɪ] (pt, pp **laid**) pt of **lie** ▷ adj leigo ▷ vt colocar; (eggs, table) pôr; **lay aside** or **by** vt pôr de lado; **lay down** vt depositar; (rules etc) impor, estabelecer; **to lay down the law** (pej) impor regras; **to lay down one's life** sacrificar voluntariamente a vida; **lay off** vt (workers) demitir; **lay on** vt (meal etc) prover; **lay out** vt (spread out) dispor em ordem; **lay-by** (BRIT) n acostamento
layer ['leɪəʳ] n camada
layman ['leɪmən] (irreg) n leigo
layout ['leɪaʊt] n (of garden, building) desenho; (of writing) leiaute m
lazy ['leɪzɪ] adj preguiçoso; (movement) lento
lb. abbr = **pound** (weight)
lead¹ [liːd] (pt, pp **led**) n (front position) dianteira; (Sport) liderança; (fig) vantagem f; (clue) pista; (Elec) fio; (for dog) correia; (in play, film) papel m principal ▷ vt levar; (be leader of) chefiar; (start, guide: activity) encabeçar ▷ vi encabeçar; **to be in the ~** (Sport: in race) estar na frente; (: in match) estar ganhando; **to ~ the way** assumir a direção; **lead away** vt levar; **lead back** vt levar de volta; **lead on** vt (tease) provocar; **lead to** vt fus levar a, conduzir a; **lead up to** vt fus conduzir a

lead² [lɛd] n chumbo; (in pencil) grafite f
leader ['li:dər] n líder m/f; **leadership** n
liderança; (quality) poder m de liderança
lead-free [lɛd-] adj sem chumbo
leading ['li:dɪŋ] adj principal; (role)
de destaque; (first, front) primeiro,
dianteiro
lead singer [li:d-] n cantor(a) m/f
leaf [li:f] (pl **leaves**) n folha ▷ vi: **to ~
through** (book) folhear; **to turn over a
new ~** mudar de vida, partir para outra
(inf)
leaflet ['li:flɪt] n folheto
league [li:g] n liga; **to be in ~ with** estar
de comum acordo com
leak [li:k] n (of liquid, gas) escape m,
vazamento; (hole) buraco, rombo;
(in roof) goteira; (fig: of information)
vazamento ▷ vi (ship) fazer água; (shoe)
deixar entrar água; (roof) gotejar; (pipe,
container, liquid) vazar; (gas) escapar ▷ vt
(news) vazar
lean [li:n] (pt, pp **-ed** or **-t**) adj magro
▷ vt: **to ~ sth on** encostar or apoiar
algo em ▷ vi inclinar-se; **to ~ against**
encostar-se or apoiar-se contra; **to ~
on** encostar-se or apoiar-se em; **lean
forward/back** vi inclinar-se para
frente/para trás; **lean out** vi inclinar-
se; **lean over** vi debruçar-se ▷ vt fus
debruçar-se sobre
leap [li:p] (pt, pp **-ed** or **-t**) n salto, pulo
▷ vi saltar; **leap year** n ano bissexto
learn [lə:n] (pt, pp **-ed** or **-t**) vt aprender;
(by heart) decorar ▷ vi aprender; **to
~ about sth** (Sch: hear, read) saber de
algo; **learner** n principiante m/f; (BRIT:
also: **learner driver**) aprendiz m/f de
motorista
lease [li:s] n arrendamento ▷ vt
arrendar
leash [li:ʃ] n correia
least [li:st] adj: **the ~ +** n o/a menor;
(smallest amount of) a menor quantidade
de ▷ adv: **the ~ +** adj o/a menos; **at ~**
pelo menos; **not in the ~** de maneira
nenhuma
leather ['lɛðər] n couro
leave [li:v] (pt, pp **left**) vt deixar; (go away
from) abandonar ▷ vi ir-se, sair; (train)
sair ▷ n licença; **to ~ sth to sb** deixar
algo para alguém; **to be left** sobrar;
leave behind vt deixar para trás; (forget)
esquecer; **leave out** vt omitir
leaves [li:vz] npl of **leaf**
Lebanon ['lɛbənən] n Líbano

lecture ['lɛktʃər] n conferência, palestra;
(Sch) aula ▷ vi dar aulas, lecionar ▷ vt
(scold) passar um sermão em; **lecturer**
(BRIT) n (at university) professor(a) m/f
led [lɛd] pt, pp of **lead¹**
ledge [lɛdʒ] n (of window) peitoril m; (of
mountain) saliência, proeminência
leek [li:k] n alho-poró m
left [lɛft] pt, pp of **leave** ▷ adj esquerdo
▷ n esquerda ▷ adv à esquerda; **on the
~** à esquerda; **to the ~** para a esquerda;
the L ~ (Pol) a Esquerda; **left-handed** adj
canhoto; **left-luggage (office)** (BRIT)
n depósito de bagagem; **left-wing** adj
(Pol) de esquerda, esquerdista
leg [lɛg] n perna; (of animal) pata;
(Culin: of meat) perna; (of journey) etapa;
1st/2nd ~ (Sport) primeiro/segundo
turno
legacy ['lɛgəsɪ] n legado; (fig) herança
legal ['li:gl] adj legal
legend ['lɛdʒənd] n lenda; (person) mito
leggings ['lɛgɪŋz] npl legging f
legislation [lɛdʒɪs'leɪʃən] n legislação f
legitimate [lɪ'dʒɪtɪmət] adj legítimo
leisure ['lɛʒər] n lazer m; **at ~**
desocupado, livre
lemon ['lɛmən] n limão(-galego) m;
lemonade [lɛmə'neɪd] n limonada;
lemon tea n chá m de limão
lend [lɛnd] (pt, pp **lent**) vt emprestar
length [lɛŋθ] n comprimento, extensão
f; (amount of time) duração f; **at ~** (at
last) finalmente, afinal; (lengthily) por
extenso; **lengthen** vt encompridar,
alongar ▷ vi encompridar-se;
lengthways adv longitudinalmente, ao
comprido; **lengthy** adj comprido, longo;
(meeting) prolongado
lens [lɛnz] n (of spectacles) lente f; (of
camera) objetiva
Lent [lɛnt] n Quaresma
lent [lɛnt] pt, pp of **lend**
lentil ['lɛntl] n lentilha
Leo ['li:əu] n Leão m
leotard ['li:ətɑ:d] n collant m
lesbian ['lɛzbɪən] n lésbica
less [lɛs] adj, pron, adv menos
▷ prep: **~ tax/10% discount** menos
imposto/10% de desconto; **~ than
ever** menos do que nunca; **~ and ~**
cada vez menos; **the ~ he works ...**
quanto menos trabalha ...
lessen ['lɛsn] vi diminuir, minguar ▷ vt
diminuir, reduzir
lesser ['lɛsər] adj menor; **to a ~ extent**

nem tanto

lesson ['lɛsn] n aula; (*example, warning*) lição f; **to teach sb a ~** (*fig*) dar uma lição em alguém

let [lɛt] (*pt, pp* ~) vt (*allow*) deixar; (*BRIT: lease*) alugar; **to ~ sb know sth** avisar alguém de algo; **~'s go!** vamos!; **"to ~"** "aluga-se"; **let down** vt (*tyre*) esvaziar; (*disappoint*) desapontar; **let go** vt, vi soltar; **let in** vt deixar entrar; (*visitor etc*) fazer entrar; **let off** vt (*culprit*) perdoar; (*firework etc*) soltar; **let on** vi revelar; **let out** vt deixar sair; (*scream*) soltar; **let up** vi cessar, afrouxar

lethal ['li:θl] adj letal

letter ['lɛtə'] n (*of alphabet*) letra; (*correspondence*) carta; **letterbox** (*BRIT*) n caixa do correio

lettuce ['lɛtɪs] n alface f

leukaemia [lu:'ki:mɪə] (*US* **leukemia**) n leucemia

level ['lɛvl] adj (*flat*) plano ▷ adv: **to draw ~ with** alcançar ▷ n nível m; (*height*) altura ▷ vt aplanar; **to be ~ with** estar no mesmo nível que; **on the ~** em nível; **"A" ~s** (*BRIT*) ≈ vestibular m; **"O" ~s** *exames optativos feitos após o término do 10 Grau*; (*fig: honest*) sincero; **level off** or **out** vi (*prices etc*) estabilizar-se; **level crossing** (*BRIT*) n passagem f de nível

lever ['li:və'] n alavanca; (*fig*) estratagema m; **leverage** n força de uma alavanca; (*fig: influence*) influência

liability [laɪə'bɪlətɪ] n responsabilidade f; (*handicap*) desvantagem f; **liabilities** npl (*Comm*) exigibilidades fpl, obrigações fpl

liable ['laɪəbl] adj (*subject*): **~ to** sujeito a; (*responsible*): **~ for** responsável por; (*likely*): **~ to do** capaz de fazer

liaise [li:'eɪz] vi: **to ~ (with)** cooperar (com)

liar ['laɪə'] n mentiroso(-a)

libel ['laɪbl] n difamação f ▷ vt caluniar, difamar

liberal ['lɪbərl] adj liberal; (*generous*) generoso

liberation n liberação f, libertação f

liberty ['lɪbətɪ] n liberdade f; (*criminal*): **to be at ~** estar livre; **to be at ~ to do** ser livre de fazer

Libra ['li:brə] n Libra, Balança

librarian [laɪ'brɛərɪən] n bibliotecário(-a)

library ['laɪbrərɪ] n biblioteca

Libya ['lɪbɪə] n Líbia

licence ['laɪsns] (*US* **license**) n (*gen, Comm*) licença; (*Aut*) carta de motorista (*BR*), carta de condução (*PT*)

license ['laɪsns] n (*US*) = **licence** ▷ vt autorizar, dar licença a; **licensed** adj (*car*) autorizado oficialmente; (*for alcohol*) autorizado para vender bebidas alcoólicas; **license plate** (*US*) n (*Aut*) placa (de identificação) (*do carro*)

lick [lɪk] vt lamber; (*inf: defeat*) arrasar, surrar; **to ~ one's lips** (*also fig*) lamber os beiços

lid [lɪd] n tampa; (*eyelid*) pálpebra

lie [laɪ] (*pt* **lay**, *pp* **lain**) vi (*act*) deitar-se; (*state*) estar deitado; (*object: be situated*) estar, encontrar-se; (*fig: problem, cause*) residir; (*in race, league*) ocupar; (*tell lies: pt, pp* **lied**) mentir ▷ n mentira; **to ~ low** (*fig*) esconder-se; **lie about** or **around** vi (*things*) estar espalhado; (*people*) vadiar; **lie-in** (*BRIT*) n: **to have a lie-in** dormir até tarde

lieutenant [lɛf'tɛnənt, (*US*) lu:'tɛnənt] n (*Mil*) tenente m

life [laɪf] (*pl* **lives**) n vida; **to come to ~** animar-se; **lifeboat** n barco salva-vidas; **lifeguard** n (*guarda m/f*) salva-vidas m/f inv; **life jacket** n colete m salva-vidas; **lifelike** adj natural; (*realistic*) realista; **life preserver** (*US*) n = **lifebelt**; **life jacket**; **life sentence** n pena de prisão perpétua; **lifetime** n vida

lift [lɪft] vt levantar ▷ vi (*fog*) dispersar-se, dissipar-se ▷ n (*BRIT: elevator*) elevador m; **to give sb a ~** (*BRIT*) dar uma carona para alguém (*BR*), dar uma boleia a alguém (*PT*); **lift-off** n decolagem f

light [laɪt] (*pt, pp* **lit**) n luz f; (*Aut: headlight*) farol m; (*: rear light*) luz traseira; (*for cigarette etc*): **have you got a ~?** tem fogo? ▷ vt acender; (*room*) iluminar ▷ adj (*colour, room*) claro; (*not heavy, fig*) leve; (*rain, traffic*) fraco; (*movement*) delicado; **lights** npl (*Aut*) sinal m de trânsito; **to come to ~** vir à tona; **in the ~ of** à luz de; **light up** vi iluminar-se ▷ vt iluminar; **light bulb** n lâmpada; **lighten** vt tornar mais leve; **lighter** n (*also: cigarette lighter*) isqueiro, acendedor m; **light-hearted** adj alegre, despreocupado; **lighthouse** n farol m; **lighting** n iluminação f; **lightly** adv ligeiramente; **to get off**

lightly conseguir se safar, livrar a cara (inf)

lightning ['laɪtnɪŋ] n relâmpago, raio; **lightweight** adj (suit) leve; (Boxing) peso-leve

like [laɪk] vt gostar de ▷ prep como; (such as) tal qual ▷ adj parecido, semelhante ▷ n: **the ~ coisas** fpl parecidas; **his ~s and dislikes** seus gostos e aversões; **I would ~, I'd ~** (eu) gostaria de; **to be** or **look ~ sb/sth** parecer-se com alguém/algo, parecer alguém/algo; **do it ~ this** faça isso assim; **it is nothing ~ ...** não se parece nada com ...; **likeable** adj simpático, agradável

likelihood ['laɪklɪhud] n probabilidade f

likely ['laɪklɪ] adj provável; **he's ~ to leave** é provável que ele se vá; **not ~!** (inf) nem morto!

likewise ['laɪkwaɪz] adv igualmente; **to do ~** fazer o mesmo

liking ['laɪkɪŋ] n afeição f, simpatia; **to be to sb's ~** ser ao gosto de alguém

lilac ['laɪlək] n lilás m

lily ['lɪlɪ] n lírio, açucena

limb [lɪm] n membro

limbo ['lɪmbəu] n: **to be in ~** (fig) viver na expectativa

lime [laɪm] n (tree) limeira; (fruit) limão m; (also: **~ juice**) suco (BR) or sumo (PT) de limão; (Geo) cal f

limelight ['laɪmlaɪt] n: **to be in the ~** ser o centro das atenções

limestone ['laɪmstəun] n pedra calcária

limit ['lɪmɪt] n limite m ▷ vt limitar; **limited** adj limitado; **to be limited to** limitar-se a

limp [lɪmp] n: **to have a ~** mancar, ser coxo ▷ vi mancar ▷ adj frouxo

line [laɪn] n linha; (rope) corda; (wire) fio; (row) fila, fileira; (on face) ruga ▷ vt (road, room) encarreirar; (container, clothing) forrar; **to ~ the streets** ladear as ruas; **in ~ with** de acordo com; **line up** vi enfileirar-se ▷ vt enfileirar; (set up, have ready) preparar, arranjar

linen ['lɪnɪn] n artigos de cama e mesa; (cloth) linho

liner ['laɪnər] n navio de linha regular; (also: **bin ~**) saco para lata de lixo

linger ['lɪŋgər] vi demorar-se, retardar-se; (smell, tradition) persistir

lining ['laɪnɪŋ] n forro; (Anat) parede f

link [lɪŋk] n (of a chain) elo; (connection)
conexão f ▷ vt vincular, unir; (associate) **to ~ with** or **to** unir a; **links** npl (Golf) campo de golfe; **link up** vt acoplar ▷ vi unir-se

lion ['laɪən] n leão m; **lioness** n leoa

lip [lɪp] n lábio; **lipread** (irreg) vi ler os lábios; **lip salve** n pomada para os lábios; **lipstick** n batom m

liqueur [lɪ'kjuər] n licor m

liquid ['lɪkwɪd] adj líquido ▷ n líquido

liquor ['lɪkər] n licor m, bebida alcoólica

liquor store (US) n loja que vende bebidas alcoólicas

Lisbon ['lɪzbən] n Lisboa

lisp [lɪsp] n ceceio ▷ vi cecear, falar com a língua presa

list [lɪst] n lista ▷ vt (write down) fazer uma lista or relação de; (enumerate) enumerar

listen ['lɪsn] vi escutar, ouvir; **to ~ to** escutar; **listener** n ouvinte m/f

lit [lɪt] pt, pp of **light**

liter ['liːtər] (US) n = **litre**

literacy ['lɪtərəsɪ] n capacidade f de ler e escrever, alfabetização f

literal ['lɪtərl] adj literal

literary ['lɪtərərɪ] adj literário

literate ['lɪtərət] adj alfabetizado, instruído; (educated) culto, letrado

literature ['lɪtərɪtʃər] n literatura; (brochures etc) folhetos mpl

litre ['liːtər] (US **liter**) n litro

litter ['lɪtər] n (rubbish) lixo; (young animals) ninhada; **litter bin** (BRIT) n lata de lixo

little ['lɪtl] adj (small) pequeno; (not much) pouco ▷ often translated by suffix: eg: **~ house** casinha ▷ adv pouco; **a ~** um pouco (de); **for a ~ while** por um instante; **as ~ as possible** o menos possível; **~ by ~** pouco a pouco

live [(vb) lɪv, (adj) laɪv] vi viver; (reside) morar ▷ adj vivo; (wire) eletrizado; (broadcast) ao vivo; (shell) carregado; **~ ammunition** munição de guerra; **live down** vt redimir; **live on** vt fus viver de, alimentar-se de; **to live on £50 a week** viver com £50 por semana; **live together** vi viver juntos; **live up to** vt fus (fulfil) cumprir

livelihood ['laɪvlɪhud] n meio de vida, subsistência

lively ['laɪvlɪ] adj vivo

liven up ['laɪvn-] vt animar ▷ vi animar-se

liver ['lɪvər] n fígado

lives [laɪvz] *npl of* **life**
living ['lɪvɪŋ] *adj* vivo ▷ *n*: **to earn** *or* **make a ~** ganhar a vida; **living room** *n* sala de estar
lizard ['lɪzəd] *n* lagarto
load [ləud] *n* carga; *(weight)* peso ▷ *vt* *(gen, Comput)* carregar; **a ~ of, ~s of** *(fig)* um monte de, uma porção de; **loaded** *adj (question)* intencionado; *(inf: rich)* cheio da nota; *(vehicle)*: **to be loaded with** estar carregado de
loaf [ləuf] *(pl* **loaves***) n* pão-de-forma *m*
loan [ləun] *n* empréstimo ▷ *vt* emprestar; **on ~** emprestado
loathe [ləuð] *vt* detestar, odiar
loaves [ləuvz] *npl of* **loaf**
lobby ['lɔbɪ] *n* vestíbulo, saguão *m*; *(Pol: pressure group)* grupo de pressão, lobby *m* ▷ *vt* pressionar
lobster ['lɔbstə'] *n* lagostim *m*; *(large)* lagosta
local ['ləukl] *adj* local ▷ *n (pub)* bar *m* (local); **the locals** *npl (local inhabitants)* os moradores locais; **local anaesthetic** *n* anestesia local
locate [ləu'keɪt] *vt (find)* localizar, situar; *(situate)*: **to be ~d in** estar localizado em
location [ləu'keɪʃən] *n* local *m*, posição *f*; **on ~** *(Cinema)* em externas
loch [lɔx] *n* lago
lock [lɔk] *n (of door, box)* fechadura; *(of canal)* eclusa; *(of hair)* anel *m*, mecha ▷ *vt* *(with key)* trancar ▷ *vi (door etc)* fechar-se à chave; *(wheels)* travar-se; **lock in** *vt* trancar dentro; **lock out** *vt* trancar do lado de fora; **lock up** *vt (criminal, mental patient)* prender; *(house)* trancar ▷ *vi* fechar tudo
locker ['lɔkə'] *n* compartimento com chave
locksmith ['lɔksmɪθ] *n* serralheiro(-a)
lodge [lɔdʒ] *n* casa do guarda, guarita; *(hunting lodge)* pavilhão *m* de caça ▷ *vi (person)*: **to ~ (with)** alojar-se (na casa de) ▷ *vt (complaint)* apresentar; **lodger** *n* inquilino(-a), hóspede *m/f*
loft [lɔft] *n* sótão *m*
log [lɔg] *n (of wood)* tora; *(book)* = **logbook** ▷ *vt* registrar
logbook ['lɔgbuk] *n (Naut)* diário de bordo; *(Aviat)* diário de vôo; *(of car)* documentação *f* (do carro)
logic ['lɔdʒɪk] *n* lógica; **logical** *adj* lógico
lollipop ['lɔlɪpɔp] *n* pirulito (BR), chupa-chupa *m* (PT); **lollipop lady/man** (BRIT)

n ver quadro

London ['lʌndən] *n* Londres; **Londoner** *n* londrino(-a)
lone [ləun] *adj (person)* solitário; *(thing)* único
loneliness ['ləunlɪnɪs] *n* solidão *f*, isolamento
lonely ['ləunlɪ] *adj (person)* só; *(place)* solitário, isolado
long [lɔŋ] *adj* longo; *(road, hair, table)* comprido ▷ *adv* muito tempo ▷ *vi*: **to ~ for sth** ansiar *or* suspirar por algo; **how ~ is the street?** qual é a extensão da rua?; **how ~ is the lesson?** quanto dura a lição?; **all night ~** a noite inteira; **he no ~er comes** ele não vem mais; **~ before/after** muito antes/depois; **before ~** (+ *future*) dentro de pouco; (+ *past*) pouco tempo depois; **at ~ last** por fim, no final; **so** *or* **as ~ as** contanto que; **long-distance** *adj (travel)* de longa distância; *(call)* interurbano; **longing** *n* desejo, anseio
longitude ['lɔŋgɪtjuːd] *n* longitude *f*
long: long jump *n* salto em distância; **long-sighted** *adj* presbita; **long-standing** *adj* de muito tempo; **long-term** *adj* a longo prazo
loo [luː] *(BRIT: inf)* *n* banheiro (BR), casa de banho (PT)
look [luk] *vi* olhar; *(seem)* parecer; *(building etc)*: **to ~ south/(out) onto the sea** dar para o sul/o mar ▷ *n* olhar *m*; *(glance)* olhada, vista de olhos; *(appearance)* aparência, aspecto; **looks** *npl (good looks)* físico, aparência; **~ (here)!** *(annoyance)* escuta aqui!; **~!** *(surprise)* olha!; **look after** *vt fus* cuidar de; *(deal with)* lidar com; **look at** *vt fus* olhar (para); *(read quickly)* ler rapidamente; *(consider)* considerar; **look back** *vi*: **to look back on** *(remember)*

recordar, rever; **look down on** vt fus
(fig) desdenhar, desprezar; **look for** vt
fus procurar; **look forward to** vt fus
aguardar com prazer, ansiar por; (in
letter): **we look forward to hearing
from you** no aguardo de suas notícias;
look into vt fus investigar; **look on** vi
assistir; **look out** vi (beware): **to look
out (for)** tomar cuidado (com); **look out
for** vt fus (await) esperar; **look round** vi
virar a cabeça, voltar-se; **look through**
vt fus (papers, book) examinar; **look to**
vt fus (rely on) contar com; **look up** vi
levantar os olhos; (improve) melhorar ▷ vt
(word) procurar
loop [luːp] n laço ▷ vt: **to ~ sth round sth**
prender algo em torno de algo
loose [luːs] adj solto; (not tight) frouxo
▷ n: **to be on the ~** estar solto; **loosely**
adv frouxamente, folgadamente; **loosen**
vt (free) soltar; (slacken) afrouxar
loot [luːt] n saque m, despojo ▷ vt
saquear, pilhar
lord [lɔːd] n senhor m; **L~ Smith** Lord
Smith; **the L~** (Rel) o Senhor; **good L~!**
Deus meu!; **the (House of) L~s** (BRIT) a
Câmara dos Lordes
lorry [ˈlɔrɪ] (BRIT) n caminhão m (BR),
camião m (PT); **lorry driver** (BRIT) n
caminhoneiro (BR), camionista m/f (PT)
lose [luːz] (pt, pp lost) vt, vi perder;
to ~ (time) (clock) atrasar-se; **loser**
n perdedor(a) m/f; (inf: failure)
derrotado(-a), fracassado(-a)
loss [lɔs] n perda; (Comm): **to make a
~** sair com prejuízo; **heavy ~es** (Mil)
grandes perdas; **to be at a ~** estar
perplexo
lost [lɔst] pt, pp of lose ▷ adj perdido;
~ and found (US) (seção f de) perdidos
e achados mpl; **lost property** (BRIT) n
(objetos mpl) perdidos e achados mpl
lot [lɔt] n (set of things) porção f; (at
auctions) lote m; **the ~** tudo, todos(-as); **a
~** muito, bastante; **a ~ of, ~s of** muito(s);
I read a ~ leio bastante; **to draw ~s** tirar
à sorte
lotion [ˈləʊʃən] n loção f
lottery [ˈlɔtərɪ] n loteria
loud [laud] adj (voice) alto; (shout)
forte; (noise) barulhento; (support,
condemnation) veemente; (gaudy)
berrante ▷ adv alto; **out ~** em voz alta;
loudly adv ruidosamente; (aloud) em voz
alta; **loudspeaker** n alto-falante m
lounge [laundʒ] n sala f de estar; (of

airport) salão m; (BRIT: also: **~ bar**) bar m
social ▷ vi recostar-se, espreguiçar-se;
lounge about vi ficar à-toa; **lounge
around** vi = **lounge about**
lousy [ˈlauzɪ] (inf) adj ruim, péssimo; (ill):
to feel ~ sentir-se mal
love [lʌv] n amor m ▷ vt amar; (care
for) gostar; (activity): **to ~ to do** gostar
(muito); **~ (from) Anne** (on letter) um
abraço or um beijo, Anne; **I ~ you** eu
te amo; **I ~ coffee** adoro o café; **"15
~"** (Tennis) "15 a zero"; **to be in ~ with**
estar apaixonado por; **to fall in ~ with**
apaixonar-se por; **to make ~** fazer amor;
love affair n aventura (amorosa), caso
(de amor); **love life** n vida sentimental
lovely [ˈlʌvlɪ] adj encantador(a),
delicioso; (beautiful) lindo, belo; (holiday)
muito agradável, maravilhoso
lover [ˈlʌvəʳ] n amante m/f
loving [ˈlʌvɪŋ] adj carinhoso, afetuoso;
(actions) dedicado
low [ləu] adj baixo; (depressed) deprimido;
(ill) doente ▷ adv baixo ▷ n (Meteorology)
área de baixa pressão; **to be ~ on**
(supplies) ter pouco; **to reach a new** or
an all-time ~ cair para o seu nível mais
baixo; **low-alcohol** adj de baixo teor
alcoólico; **low-calorie** adj de baixas
calorias; **lower** adj mais baixo; (less
important) inferior ▷ vt abaixar; (reduce)
reduzir, diminuir; **low-fat** adj magro
loyal [ˈlɔɪəl] adj leal; **loyalty** n lealdade f;
loyalty card n (BRIT) cartão m de
fidelidade
L-plates [ˈɛlpleɪts] (BRIT) npl placas fpl de
aprendiz de motorista

● **L-PLATES**
●
● As **L-plates** são placas quadradas com
● um "L" vermelho que são colocadas na
● parte de trás do carro para mostrar
● que a pessoa ao volante ainda não
● tem carteira de motorista. Até à
● obtenção da carteira, o motorista
● aprendiz possui uma permissão
● provisória e não tem direito de dirigir
● sem um motorista qualificado ao
● lado. Os motoristas aprendizes não
● podem dirigir em estradas mesmo que
● estejam acompanhados.

Ltd (BRIT) abbr (= limited (liability)
company) SA
luck [lʌk] n sorte f; **bad ~** azar m; **good ~!**

boa sorte!; **bad** or **hard** or **tough ~!** que
azar!; **luckily** adv por sorte, felizmente;
lucky adj (person) sortudo; (situation)
afortunado; (object) de sorte
ludicrous ['lu:dɪkrəs] adj ridículo
luggage ['lʌgɪdʒ] n bagagem f; **luggage
rack** n porta-bagagem m, bagageiro
lukewarm ['lu:kwɔ:m] adj morno,
tépido; (fig) indiferente
lull [lʌl] n pausa, interrupção f ▷ vt: **to
~ sb to sleep** acalentar alguém; **to be
~ed into a false sense of security** ser
acalmado com uma falsa sensação de
segurança
lullaby ['lʌləbaɪ] n canção f de ninar
lumber ['lʌmbəʳ] n (junk) trastes mpl
velhos; (wood) madeira serrada, tábua
▷ vt: **to ~ sb with sth/sb** empurrar algo/
alguém para cima de alguém
luminous ['lu:mɪnəs] adj luminoso
lump [lʌmp] n torrão m; (fragment)
pedaço; (on body) galo, caroço; (also:
sugar ~) cubo de açúcar ▷ vt: **to ~
together** amontoar; **a ~ sum** uma
quantia global; **lumpy** adj encaroçado
lunatic ['lu:nətɪk] adj louco(-a)
lunch [lʌntʃ] n almoço
lung [lʌŋ] n pulmão m
lure [luəʳ] n isca ▷ vt atrair, seduzir
lurk [lə:k] vi (hide) esconder-se; (wait)
estar à espreita
lush [lʌʃ] adj exuberante
lust [lʌst] n luxúria; (greed) cobiça; **lust
after** or **for** vt fus cobiçar
Luxembourg ['lʌksəmbə:g] n
Luxemburgo
luxurious [lʌg'zjuərɪəs] adj luxuoso
luxury ['lʌkʃərɪ] n luxo ▷ cpd de luxo
lying ['laɪɪŋ] n mentira(s) f(pl) ▷ adj
mentiroso, falso
lyrics ['lɪrɪks] npl (of song) letra

M.A. abbr (Sch) = **Master of Arts**
mac [mæk] (BRIT) n capa impermeável
macaroni [mækə'rəʊnɪ] n macarrão m
machine [mə'ʃi:n] n máquina ▷ vt
(dress etc) costurar à máquina; (Tech)
usinar; **machine gun** n metralhadora;
machinery n maquinaria; (fig) máquina
mackerel ['mækrl] n inv cavala
mackintosh ['mækɪntɔʃ] (BRIT) n capa
impermeável
mad [mæd] adj louco; (foolish) tolo;
(angry) furioso, brabo; (keen): **to be ~
about** ser louco por
madam ['mædəm] n senhora, madame f
made [meɪd] pt, pp of **make**
made-to-measure (BRIT) adj feito sob
medida
madly ['mædlɪ] adv loucamente; **~ in
love** louco de amor
madman ['mædmən] (irreg) n louco
madness ['mædnɪs] n loucura;
(foolishness) tolice f
magazine [mægə'zi:n] n (Press) revista;
(Radio, TV) programa m de atualidades
maggot ['mægət] n larva de inseto
magic ['mædʒɪk] n magia, mágica ▷ adj
mágico; **magical** adj mágico; **magician**
[mə'dʒɪʃən] n mago(-a); (entertainer)

mágico(-a)

magistrate ['mædʒɪstreɪt] n
magistrado(-a), juiz (juíza) m/f

magnet ['mægnɪt] n ímã m; **magnetic**
[mæg'nɛtɪk] adj magnético

magnificent [mæg'nɪfɪsnt] adj
magnífico

magnify ['mægnɪfaɪ] vt aumentar;
magnifying glass n lupa, lente f de
aumento

magpie ['mægpaɪ] n pega

mahogany [mə'hɔgənɪ] n mogno,
acaju m

maid [meɪd] n empregada; **old ~** (pej)
solteirona

maiden name n nome m de solteira

mail [meɪl] n correio; (letters) cartas
fpl ▷ vt pôr no correio; **mailbox** (us) n
caixa do correio; **mailing list** n lista de
clientes, mailing list m

main [meɪn] adj principal ▷ n (pipe) cano
or esgoto principal; **the mains** npl (Elec,
gas, water) a rede; **in the ~** na maior
parte; **mainland** n: **the mainland** o
continente; **mainly** adv principalmente;
main road n estrada principal;
mainstream n corrente f principal

maintain [meɪn'teɪn] vt manter; (keep
up) conservar (em bom estado); (affirm)
sustentar, afirmar; **maintenance**
['meɪntənəns] n manutenção f;
(alimony) alimentos mpl, pensão f
alimentícia

maize [meɪz] n milho

majesty ['mædʒɪstɪ] n majestade f

major ['meɪdʒə'] n (Mil) major m
▷ adj (main) principal; (considerable)
importante; (Mus) maior

Majorca [mə'jɔ:kə] n Maiorca

majority [mə'dʒɔrɪtɪ] n maioria

make [meɪk] (pt, pp **made**) vt fazer;
(manufacture) fabricar, produzir; (cause
to be): **to ~ sb sad** entristecer alguém,
fazer alguém ficar triste; (force): **to ~ sb
do sth** fazer com que alguém faça algo;
(equal): **2 and 2 ~ 4** dois e dois são quatro
▷ n marca; **to ~ a profit/loss** ter um
lucro/uma perda; **to ~ it** (arrive) chegar;
(succeed) ter sucesso; **what time do
you ~ it?** que horas você tem?; **to ~ do
with** contentar-se com; **make for** vt fus
(place) dirigir-se a; **make out** vt (decipher)
decifrar; (understand) compreender;
(see) divisar, avistar; (cheque) preencher;
make up vt (constitute) constituir;
(invent) inventar; (parcel) embrulhar ▷ vi

reconciliar-se; (with cosmetics) maquilar-
se (BR), maquilhar-se (PT); **make up for**
vt fus compensar; **maker** n (of film etc)
criador m; (manufacturer) fabricante m/f;
makeshift adj provisório; **make-up** n
maquilagem f (BR), maquilhagem f (PT)

malaria [mə'lɛərɪə] n malária

Malaysia [mə'leɪzɪə] n Malaísia (BR),
Malásia (PT)

male [meɪl] n macho ▷ adj masculino;
(child etc) do sexo masculino

malignant [mə'lɪgnənt] adj (Med)
maligno

mall [mɔ:l] n (also: **shopping ~**)
shopping m

mallet ['mælɪt] n maço, marreta

malt [mɔ:lt] n malte m

Malta ['mɔ:ltə] n Malta

mammal ['mæml] n mamífero

mammoth ['mæməθ] n mamute m ▷ adj
gigantesco, imenso

man [mæn] (pl **men**) n homem m ▷ vt
(Naut) tripular; (Mil) guarnecer; (machine)
operar; **an old ~** um velho; **~ and wife**
marido e mulher

manage ['mænɪdʒ] vi arranjar-se,
virar-se ▷ vt (be in charge of) dirigir,
administrar; (business) gerenciar;
(ship, person) controlar; **manageable**
adj manejável; (task etc) viável;
management n administração f,
direção f, gerência; **manager** n gerente
m/f; (Sport) técnico(-a); **manageress**
[mænɪdʒə'rɛs] n gerente f; **managerial**
[mænɪ'dʒɪərɪəl] adj administrativo,
gerencial; **managing director** n
diretor(a) m/f, diretor-gerente (diretora-
gerente) m/f

mandarin ['mændərɪn] n (fruit)
tangerina; (person) mandarim m

mandatory ['mændətərɪ] adj
obrigatório

mane [meɪn] n (of horse) crina; (of lion)
juba

maneuver [mə'nu:və'] (us)
= **manoeuvre**

mango ['mæŋgəu] (pl **~es**) n manga

manhole ['mænhəul] n poço de
inspeção

manhood ['mænhud] n (age) idade f
adulta; (masculinity) virilidade f

mania ['meɪnɪə] n mania; **maniac**
['meɪnɪæk] n maníaco(-a); (fig) louco(-a)

manic ['mænɪk] adj maníaco

manicure ['mænɪkjuə'] n manicure f
(BR), manicura (PT)

manifest ['mænɪfɛst] vt manifestar, mostrar ▷ adj manifesto, evidente

manipulate [mə'nɪpjuleɪt] vt manipular

mankind [mæn'kaɪnd] n humanidade f, raça humana

man-made adj sintético, artificial

manner ['mænəʳ] n modo, maneira; (behaviour) conduta, comportamento; (type): **all ~ of things** todos os tipos de coisa; **manners** npl (conduct) boas maneiras fpl, educação f; **bad ~s** falta de educação; **all ~ of** todo tipo de

manoeuvre [mə'nu:vəʳ] (us **maneuver**) vt manobrar; (manipulate) manipular ▷ vi manobrar ▷ n manobra

manpower ['mænpauəʳ] n potencial m humano, mão-de-obra f

mansion ['mænʃən] n mansão f, palacete m

manslaughter ['mænslɔ:təʳ] n homicídio involuntário

mantelpiece ['mæntlpi:s] n consolo da lareira

manual ['mænjuəl] adj manual ▷ n manual m

manufacture [mænju'fæktʃəʳ] vt manufaturar, fabricar ▷ n fabricação f; **manufacturer** n fabricante m/f

manure [mə'njuəʳ] n estrume m, adubo m

manuscript ['mænjuskrɪpt] n manuscrito

many ['mɛnɪ] adj, pron muitos(-as); **a great ~** muitíssimos; **~ a time** muitas vezes

map [mæp] n mapa m; **map out** vt traçar

maple ['meɪpl] n bordo

mar [mɑ:ʳ] vt estragar

marathon ['mærəθən] n maratona

marble ['mɑ:bl] n mármore m; (toy) bola de gude

March [mɑ:tʃ] n março

march [mɑ:tʃ] vi marchar; (demonstrators) desfilar ▷ n marcha; passeata

mare [mɛəʳ] n égua

margarine [mɑ:dʒə'ri:n] n margarina

margin ['mɑ:dʒɪn] n margem f; **marginal** adj marginal; **marginal seat** (Pol) cadeira ganha por pequena maioria

marigold ['mærɪgəuld] n malmequer m

marijuana [mærɪ'wɑ:nə] n maconha

marine [mə'ri:n] adj marinho; (engineer) naval ▷ n fuzileiro naval

marital ['mærɪtl] adj matrimonial, marital; **~ status** estado civil

marjoram ['mɑ:dʒərəm] n manjerona

mark [mɑ:k] n marca, sinal m; (imprint) impressão f; (stain) mancha; (Brit: Sch) nota; (currency) marco ▷ vt marcar; (stain) manchar; (indicate) indicar; (commemorate) comemorar; (Brit: Sch) dar nota em; (: correct) corrigir; **to ~ time** marcar passo; **marker** n (sign) marcador m, marca; (bookmark) marcador

market ['mɑ:kɪt] n mercado ▷ vt (Comm) comercializar; **marketing** n marketing m; **marketplace** n mercado; **market research** n pesquisa de mercado

marmalade ['mɑ:məleɪd] n geléia de laranja

maroon [mə'ru:n] vt: **to be ~ed** ficar abandonado (numa ilha) ▷ adj de cor castanho-avermelhado, vinho inv

marquee [mɑ:'ki:] n toldo, tenda

marriage ['mærɪdʒ] n casamento

married ['mærɪd] adj casado; (life, love) conjugal

marrow ['mærəu] n medula; (vegetable) abóbora

marry ['mærɪ] vt casar(-se) com; (subj: father, priest etc) casar, unir ▷ vi (also: **get married**) casar(-se)

Mars [mɑ:z] n Marte m

marsh [mɑ:ʃ] n pântano; (salt marsh) marisma

marshal ['mɑ:ʃl] n (Mil: also: **field ~**) marechal m; (at sports meeting etc) oficial m ▷ vt (thoughts, support) organizar; (soldiers) formar

martyr ['mɑ:təʳ] n mártir m/f

marvel ['mɑ:vl] n maravilha ▷ vi: **to ~ (at)** maravilhar-se (de or com); **marvellous** (us **marvelous**) adj maravilhoso

Marxist ['mɑ:ksɪst] adj, n marxista m/f

mascara [mæs'kɑ:rə] n rímel® m

masculine ['mæskjulɪn] adj masculino

mash [mæʃ] vt (Culin) fazer um purê de; (crush) amassar

mask [mɑ:sk] n máscara ▷ vt (face) encobrir; (feelings) esconder, ocultar

mason ['meɪsn] n (also: **stone ~**) pedreiro(-a); (also: **free~**) maçom m; **masonry** n alvenaria

mass [mæs] n quantidade f; (people) multidão f; (Phys) massa; (Rel) missa; (great quantity) montão m ▷ cpd de massa ▷ vi reunir-se; (Mil) concentrar-se; **the masses** npl (ordinary people) as massas;

~es of (inf) montes de

massacre ['mæsəkə'] n massacre m, carnificina

massage ['mæsɑ:ʒ] n massagem f

massive ['mæsɪv] adj (large) enorme; (support) massivo

mass media npl meios mpl de comunicação de massa, mídia

mast [mɑ:st] n (Naut) mastro; (Radio etc) antena

master ['mɑ:stə'] n mestre m; (fig: of situation) dono; (in secondary school) professor m; (title for boys): **M~ X** o menino X ▷ vt controlar; (learn) conhecer a fundo; **mastermind** n (fig) cabeça ▷ vt dirigir, planejar; **masterpiece** n obra-prima

mat [mæt] n esteira; (also: **door~**) capacho; (also: **table~**) descanso ▷ adj fosco, sem brilho

match [mætʃ] n fósforo; (game) jogo, partida; (equal) igual m/f ▷ vt (also: **~ up**) casar, emparelhar; (go well with) combinar com; (equal) igualar; (correspond to) corresponder a ▷ vi combinar; (couple) formar um bom casal; **matchbox** n caixa de fósforos; **matching** adj que combina com

mate [meɪt] n (inf) colega m/f; (assistant) ajudante m/f; (animal) macho/fêmea; (in merchant navy) imediato ▷ vi acasalar-se

material [mə'tɪərɪəl] n (substance) matéria; (equipment) material m; (cloth) pano, tecido; (data) dados mpl ▷ adj material; **materials** npl (equipment) material

maternal [mə'tə:nl] adj maternal

maternity [mə'tə:nɪtɪ] n maternidade f

mathematical [mæθə'mætɪkl] adj matemático

mathematics [mæθə'mætɪks] n matemática

maths [mæθs] (us **math**) n matemática

matron ['meɪtrən] n (in hospital) enfermeira-chefe f; (in school) inspetora

matter ['mætə'] n questão f, assunto; (Phys) matéria; (substance) substância; (reading matter etc) material m; (Med: pus) pus m ▷ vi importar; **matters** npl (affairs) questões fpl; **it doesn't ~** não importa; (I don't mind) tanto faz; **what's the ~?** o que (é que) há?, qual é o problema?; **no ~ what** aconteça o que acontecer; **as a ~ of course** por rotina; **as a ~ of fact** na realidade, de fato

mattress ['mætrɪs] n colchão m

mature [mə'tjuə'] adj maduro; (cheese, wine) amadurecido ▷ vi amadurecer

maul [mɔ:l] vt machucar, maltratar

mauve [məuv] adj cor de malva inv

maximum ['mæksɪməm] (pl **maxima** or **~s**) adj máximo ▷ n máximo

May [meɪ] n maio

may [meɪ] (pt, conditional **might**) aux vb (indicating possibility): **he ~ come** pode ser que ele venha, é capaz de vir; (be allowed to): **~ I smoke?** posso fumar?; (wishes): **~ God bless you!** que Deus lhe abençoe

maybe ['meɪbi:] adv talvez; **~ not** talvez não

mayhem ['meɪhɛm] n caos m

mayonnaise [meɪə'neɪz] n maionese f

mayor [mɛə'] n prefeito (BR), presidente m do município (PT); **mayoress** n prefeita (BR), presidenta do município (PT)

maze [meɪz] n labirinto

me [mi:] pron me; (stressed, after prep) mim; **he heard me** ele me ouviu; **it's me** sou eu; **he gave me the money** ele deu o dinheiro para mim; **give it to me** dê-mo; **with me** comigo; **without me** sem mim

meadow ['mɛdəu] n prado, campina

meagre ['mi:gə'] (us **meager**) adj escasso

meal [mi:l] n refeição f; (flour) farinha; **mealtime** n hora da refeição

mean [mi:n] (pt, pp **~t**) adj (with money) sovina, avarento, pão-duro inv (BR); (unkind) mesquinho; (shabby) malcuidado, dilapidado; (average) médio ▷ vt (signify) significar, querer dizer; (refer to): **I thought you ~t her** eu pensei que você estivesse se referindo a ela; (intend): **to ~ to do sth** pretender or tencionar fazer algo ▷ n meio, meio termo; **means** npl (way, money) meio; **do you ~ it?** você está falando sério?; **by ~s of** por meio de, mediante; **by all ~s!** claro que sim!, pois não

meaning ['mi:nɪŋ] n sentido, significado; **meaningful** adj significativo; (relationship) sério; **meaningless** adj sem sentido

meant [mɛnt] pt, pp of **mean**

meantime ['mi:ntaɪm] adv (also: **in the ~**) entretanto, enquanto isso

meanwhile ['mi:nwaɪl] adv = **meantime**

measles ['mi:zlz] n sarampo

measure ['mɛʒəʳ] vt, vi medir ▷ n
medida; (ruler: also: **tape ~**) fita métrica;
measurements npl (size) medidas fpl
meat [mi:t] n carne f; **cold ~s** (BRIT) frios;
meatball n almôndega
Mecca ['mɛkə] n Meca; (fig): **a ~ (for)** a
meca (de)
mechanic [mɪ'kænɪk] n mecânico;
mechanical adj mecânico
mechanism ['mɛkənɪzəm] n
mecanismo
medal ['mɛdl] n medalha
meddle ['mɛdl] vi: **to ~ in** meter-se em,
intrometer-se em; **to ~ with sth** mexer
em algo
media ['mi:dɪə] npl meios mpl de
comunicação, mídia
mediaeval [mɛdɪ'i:vl] adj = **medieval**
mediate ['mi:dɪeɪt] vi mediar
medical ['mɛdɪkl] adj médico ▷ n
(examination) exame m médico
medication [mɛdɪ'keɪʃən] n medicação f
medicine ['mɛdsɪn] n medicina; (drug)
remédio, medicamento
medieval [mɛdɪ'i:vl] adj medieval
mediocre [mi:dɪ'əʊkəʳ] adj medíocre
meditate ['mɛdɪteɪt] vi meditar
Mediterranean [mɛdɪtə'reɪnɪən] adj
mediterrâneo; **the ~ (Sea)** o (mar)
Mediterrâneo
medium ['mi:dɪəm] (pl **media** or **~s**) adj
médio ▷ n (means) meio; (pl **mediums**:
person) médium m/f
meek [mi:k] adj manso, dócil
meet [mi:t] (pt, pp **met**) vt encontrar;
(accidentally) topar com, dar de cara
com; (by arrangement) encontrar-
se com, ir ao encontro de; (for the
first time) conhecer; (go and fetch) ir
buscar; (opponent, problem) enfrentar;
(obligations) cumprir; (need) satisfazer
▷ vi encontrar-se; (for talks) reunir-se;
(join) unir-se; (get to know) conhecer-
se; **meet with** vt fus reunir-se com;
(difficulty) encontrar; **meeting** n
encontro; (session: of club etc) reunião f;
(assembly) assembléia; (Sport) corrida
megabyte ['mɛgəbaɪt] n (Comput)
megabyte m
megaphone ['mɛgəfəʊn] n megafone m
megapixel ['mɛgəpiksl] n megapixel m
melancholy ['mɛlənkəlɪ] n melancolia
▷ adj melancólico
melody ['mɛlədɪ] n melodia
melon ['mɛlən] n melão m
melt [mɛlt] vi (metal) fundir-se; (snow)

derreter ▷ vt derreter; **melt down** vt
fundir
member ['mɛmbəʳ] n membro(-a);
(of club) sócio(-a); (Anat) membro; **M~
of Parliament** (BRIT) deputado(-a);
membership n (state) adesão
f; (members) número de sócios;
membership card n carteira de sócio
memento [mə'mɛntəu] n lembrança
memo ['mɛməu] n memorando, nota
memorandum [mɛmə'rændəm] (pl
memoranda) n memorando
memorial [mɪ'mɔ:rɪəl] n monumento
comemorativo ▷ adj comemorativo;
Memorial Day (US) n ver quadro

❊ **MEMORIAL DAY**
❊
❊ **Memorial Day** é um feriado nos
❊ Estados Unidos, a última segunda-
❊ feira de maio na maior parte dos
❊ estados, em memória aos soldados
❊ americanos mortos em combate.

memorize ['mɛməraɪz] vt decorar,
aprender de cor
memory ['mɛmərɪ] n memória;
(recollection) lembrança; **memory card** n
placa de memória
men [mɛn] npl of **man**
menace ['mɛnəs] n ameaça; (nuisance)
droga ▷ vt ameaçar
mend [mɛnd] vt consertar, reparar;
(darn) remendar ▷ n: **to be on the ~** estar
melhorando
meningitis [mɛnɪn'dʒaɪtɪs] n
meningite f
menopause ['mɛnəupɔ:z] n menopausa
menstruation [mɛnstru'eɪʃən] n
menstruação f
mental ['mɛntl] adj mental; **mentality**
[mɛn'tælɪtɪ] n mentalidade f
mention ['mɛnʃən] n menção f ▷ vt
(speak of) falar de; **don't ~ it!** não tem de
quê!, de nada!
menu ['mɛnju:] n (set menu, Comput)
menu m; (printed) cardápio (BR), ementa
(PT)
MEP n abbr = Member of the European
Parliament
mercenary ['mə:sɪnərɪ] adj mercenário
▷ n mercenário
merchandise ['mə:tʃəndaɪz] n
mercadorias fpl
merchant ['mə:tʃənt] n comerciante m/f
merciless ['mə:sɪlɪs] adj desumano,

inclemente
mercury ['mə:kjurı] n mercúrio
mercy ['mə:sı] n piedade f; (Rel) misericórdia; **at the ~ of** à mercê de
mere [mıə^r] adj mero, simples inv; **merely** adv simplesmente, somente, apenas
merge [mə:dʒ] vt unir ▷ vi unir-se; (Comm) fundir-se; **merger** n fusão f
meringue [mə'ræŋ] n suspiro, merengue m
merit ['mɛrıt] n mérito; (advantage) vantagem f ▷ vt merecer
mermaid ['mə:meıd] n sereia
merry ['mɛrı] adj alegre; **M~ Christmas!** Feliz Natal!; **merry-go-round** n carrossel m
mesh [mɛʃ] n malha
mess [mɛs] n confusão f; (in room) bagunça; (Mil) rancho; **to be in a ~** ser uma bagunça, estar numa bagunça; **mess about** (inf) vi perder tempo; (pass the time) vadiar; **mess about with** (inf) vt fus mexer com; **mess around** (inf) vi = **mess about**; **mess around with** (inf) vt fus = **mess about with**; **mess up** vt (spoil) estragar; (dirty) sujar
message ['mɛsıdʒ] n recado, mensagem f
messenger ['mɛsındʒə^r] n mensageiro(-a)
messy ['mɛsı] adj (dirty) sujo; (untidy) desarrumado
met [mɛt] pt, pp of **meet**
metal ['mɛtl] n metal m
meteorology [mi:tıə'rɔlədʒı] n meteorologia
meter ['mi:tə^r] n (instrument) medidor m; (also: **parking ~**) parcômetro; (US: unit) = **metre**
method ['mɛθəd] n método; **methodical** [mı'θɔdıkl] adj metódico
metre ['mi:tə^r] (US **meter**) n metro
metric ['mɛtrık] adj métrico
metropolitan [mɛtrə'pɔlıtən] adj metropolitano
Mexico ['mɛksıkəu] n México
mice [maıs] npl of **mouse**
micro... [maıkrəu] prefix micro...; **microchip** n microchip m; **microphone** n microfone m; **microscope** n microscópio; **microwave** n (also: **microwave oven**) forno microondas
mid [mıd] adj: **~ May/afternoon** meados de maio/meio da tarde; **in ~ air** em pleno ar; **midday** n meio-dia m

middle ['mıdl] n meio; (waist) cintura ▷ adj meio; (quantity, size) médio, mediano; **middle-aged** adj de meia-idade; **Middle Ages** npl: **the Middle Ages** a Idade Média; **Middle East** n: **the Middle East** o Oriente Médio; **middle name** n segundo nome m
midge [mıdʒ] n mosquito
midget ['mıdʒıt] n anão (anã) m/f
midnight ['mıdnaıt] n meia-noite f
midst [mıdst] n: **in the ~ of** no meio de, entre
midsummer [mıd'sʌmə^r] n: **a ~ day** um dia em pleno verão
midway [mıd'weı] adj, adv: **~ (between)** no meio do caminho (entre)
midweek [mıd'wi:k] adv no meio da semana
midwife ['mıdwaıf] (pl **midwives**) n parteira
might [maıt] vb see **may** ▷ n poder m, força; **mighty** adj poderoso, forte
migraine ['mi:greın] n enxaqueca
migrant ['maıgrənt] adj migratório; (worker) emigrante
migrate [maı'greıt] vi emigrar; (birds) arribar
mike [maık] n abbr = **microphone**
mild [maıld] adj (character) pacífico; (climate) temperado; (taste) suave; (illness) leve, benigno; (interest) pequeno
mile [maıl] n milha (1609 m); **mileage** n número de milhas; (Aut) ≈ quilometragem f
milestone ['maılstəun] n marco miliário
military ['mılıtərı] adj militar
milk [mılk] n leite m ▷ vt (cow) ordenhar; (fig) explorar, chupar; **milk chocolate** n chocolate m de leite; **milkman** (irreg) n leiteiro; **milky** adj leitoso
mill [mıl] n (windmill etc) moinho; (coffee mill) moedor m de café; (factory) moinho, engenho ▷ vt moer ▷ vi (also: **~ about**) aglomerar-se, remoinhar
millimetre (US **millimeter**) n milímetro
million ['mıljən] n milhão m; **a ~ times** um milhão de vezes; **millionaire** n milionário(-a)
mime [maım] n mimo; (actor) mímico(-a), comediante m/f ▷ vt imitar ▷ vi fazer mímica
mimic ['mımık] n mímico(-a), imitador(a) m/f ▷ vt imitar, parodiar
min. abbr = **minute**; (= minimum) min.

mince [mɪns] vt moer ▷ vi (*in walking*) andar com afetação ▷ n (*BRIT: Culin*) carne f moída; **mincemeat** n recheio de sebo e frutas picadas; (*us: meat*) carne f moída; **mince pie** n pastel com recheio de sebo e frutas picadas

mind [maɪnd] n mente f; (*intellect*) intelecto; (*opinion*) **to my ~** a meu ver; (*sanity*): **to be out of one's ~** estar fora de si ▷ vt (*attend to, look after*) tomar conta de, cuidar de; (*be careful of*) ter cuidado com; (*object to*): **I don't ~ the noise** o barulho não me incomoda; **it is on my ~** não me sai da cabeça; **to keep** *or* **bear sth in ~** levar algo em consideração, não esquecer-se de algo; **to make up one's ~** decidir-se; **I don't ~** (*it doesn't worry me*) eu nem ligo; (*it's all the same to me*) para mim tanto faz; **~ you, ...** se bem que ...; **never ~!** não faz mal, não importa!; (*don't worry*) não se preocupe!; **"~ the step"** "cuidado com o degrau"; **mindless** adj (*violence*) insensato; (*job*) monótono

mine¹ [maɪn] pron (o) meu m, (a) minha f; **a friend of ~** um amigo meu

mine² [maɪn] n mina ▷ vt (*coal*) extrair, explorar; (*ship, beach*) minar

miner ['maɪnəʳ] n mineiro

mineral ['mɪnərəl] adj mineral ▷ n mineral m; **minerals** npl (*BRIT: soft drinks*) refrigerantes mpl; **mineral water** n água mineral

mingle ['mɪŋgl] vi: **to ~ with** misturar-se com

miniature ['mɪnətʃəʳ] adj em miniatura ▷ n miniatura

minibus ['mɪnɪbʌs] n microônibus m

minimal ['mɪnɪml] adj mínimo

minimum ['mɪnɪməm] (*pl* **minima**) adj mínimo ▷ n mínimo

mining ['maɪnɪŋ] n exploração f de minas

miniskirt ['mɪnɪskəːt] n minissaia

minister ['mɪnɪstəʳ] n (*BRIT: Pol*) ministro(-a); (*Rel*) pastor m ▷ vi: **to ~ to sb** prestar assistência a alguém; **to ~ to sb's needs** atender às necessidades de alguém

ministry ['mɪnɪstrɪ] n (*BRIT: Pol*) ministério; (*Rel*): **to go into the ~** ingressar no sacerdócio

minor ['maɪnəʳ] adj menor; (*unimportant*) de pouca importância; (*Mus*) menor ▷ n (*Law*) menor m/f de idade

minority [maɪˈnɔrɪtɪ] n minoria

mint [mɪnt] n (*plant*) hortelã f; (*sweet*) bala de hortelã ▷ vt (*coins*) cunhar; **the (Royal** (*BRIT*) *or* **US** (*US*)) **M~** ≈ a Casa da Moeda; **in ~ condition** em perfeito estado

minus ['maɪnəs] n (*also:* **~ sign**) sinal m de subtração ▷ prep menos

minute¹ [maɪˈnjuːt] adj miúdo, diminuto; (*search*) minucioso

minute² ['mɪnɪt] n minuto; **minutes** npl (*of meeting*) atas fpl; **at the last ~** no último momento

miracle ['mɪrəkl] n milagre m

mirage ['mɪrɑːʒ] n miragem f

mirror ['mɪrəʳ] n espelho; (*in car*) retrovisor m

misbehave [mɪsbɪˈheɪv] vi comportar-se mal

miscarriage ['mɪskærɪdʒ] n (*Med*) aborto (espontâneo); (*failure*): **~ of justice** erro judicial

miscellaneous [mɪsɪˈleɪnɪəs] adj (*items, expenses*) diverso; (*selection*) variado

mischief ['mɪstʃɪf] n (*naughtiness*) travessura; (*fun*) diabrura; (*maliciousness*) malícia; **mischievous** ['mɪstʃɪvəs] adj (*naughty*) travesso; (*playful*) traquino

misconception [mɪskənˈsɛpʃən] n concepção f errada, conceito errado

misconduct [mɪsˈkɔndʌkt] n comportamento impróprio; **professional ~** má conduta profissional

miser ['maɪzəʳ] n avaro(-a), sovina m/f

miserable ['mɪzərəbl] adj triste; (*wretched*) miserável; (*weather, person*) deprimente; (*contemptible: offer*) desprezível; (*: failure*) humilhante

misery ['mɪzərɪ] n (*unhappiness*) tristeza; (*wretchedness*) miséria

misfortune [mɪsˈfɔːtʃən] n desgraça, infortúnio

misguided [mɪsˈgaɪdɪd] adj enganado

mishap ['mɪshæp] n desgraça, contratempo

misinterpret [mɪsɪnˈtəːprɪt] vt interpretar mal

misjudge [mɪsˈdʒʌdʒ] vt fazer um juízo errado de, julgar mal

mislay [mɪsˈleɪ] (*irreg*) vt extraviar, perder

mislead [mɪsˈliːd] (*irreg*) vt induzir em erro, enganar; **misleading** adj enganoso, errôneo

misplace [mɪsˈpleɪs] vt extraviar, perder

misprint ['mɪsprɪnt] n erro tipográfico

Miss [mɪs] n Senhorita (BR), a menina (PT)
miss [mɪs] vt (train, class, opportunity) perder; (fail to hit) errar, não acertar em; (fail to see): **you can't ~ it** e impossível não ver; (regret the absence of): **I ~ him** sinto a falta dele ▷ vi falhar ▷ n (shot) tiro perdido or errado; **miss out** (BRIT) vt omitir
missile ['mɪsaɪl] n míssil m; (object thrown) projétil m
missing ['mɪsɪŋ] adj (pupil) ausente; (thing) perdido; (removed) que está faltando; (Mil) desaparecido; **to be ~** estar desaparecido; **to go ~** desaparecer
mission ['mɪʃən] n missão f; (official representatives) delegação f
mist [mɪst] n (light) neblina; (heavy) névoa; (at sea) bruma ▷ vi (eyes: also: ~ over) enevoar-se; (BRIT: also: ~ over, ~ up: windows) embaçar
mistake [mɪs'teɪk] (irreg) n erro, engano ▷ vt entender or interpretar mal; **by ~** por engano; **to make a ~** fazer um erro; **to ~ A for B** confundir A com B; **mistaken** pp of **mistake** ▷ adj errado; **to be mistaken** enganar-se, equivocar-se
mister ['mɪstəᵊ] (inf) n senhor m; see **Mr**
mistletoe ['mɪsltəu] n visco
mistook [mɪs'tuk] pt of **mistake**
mistress ['mɪstrɪs] n (lover) amante f; (of house) dona (da casa); (BRIT: in school) professora, mestra; (of situation) dona; see **Mrs**
mistrust [mɪs'trʌst] vt desconfiar de
misty ['mɪstɪ] adj (day) nublado; (glasses etc) embaçado
misunderstand [mɪsʌndə'stænd] (irreg) vt, vi entender or interpretar mal; **misunderstanding** n mal-entendido; (disagreement) desentendimento
misuse [(n) mɪs'juːs, (vb) mɪs'juːz] n uso impróprio; (of power) abuso; (of funds) desvio ▷ vt abusar de; desviar
mix [mɪks] vt misturar; (combine) combinar ▷ vi (people) entrosar-se ▷ n mistura; (combination) combinação f; **mix up** vt (confuse: things) misturar; (: people) confundir; **mixed** adj misto; **mixed-up** adj confuso; **mixer** n (for food) batedeira; (person) pessoa sociável; **mixture** n mistura; (Med) preparado; **mix-up** n trapalhada, confusão f
mm abbr (= millimetre) mm
moan [məun] n gemido ▷ vi gemer; (inf: complain): **to ~ (about)** queixar-se (de), bufar (sobre) (inf)

moat [məut] n fosso
mob [mɔb] n multidão f ▷ vt cercar
mobile ['məubaɪl] adj móvel ▷ n móvel m; **mobile phone** n telefone m celular
mock [mɔk] vt ridicularizar; (laugh at) zombar de, gozar de ▷ adj falso, fingido; (exam etc) simulado; **mockery** n zombaria; **to make a mockery of** ridicularizar
mode [məud] n modo; (of transport) meio
model ['mɔdl] n modelo; (Arch) maqueta; (person: for fashion, Art) modelo m/f ▷ adj exemplar ▷ vt modelar ▷ vi servir de modelo; (in fashion) trabalhar como modelo; **to ~ o.s. on** mirar-se em
modem ['məudɛm] n modem m
moderate [(adj) 'mɔdərət, (vb) 'mɔdəreɪt] adj moderado ▷ vi moderar-se, acalmar-se ▷ vt moderar
modern ['mɔdən] adj moderno; **modernize** vt modernizar, atualizar
modest ['mɔdɪst] adj modesto; **modesty** n modéstia
modify ['mɔdɪfaɪ] vt modificar
moist [mɔɪst] adj úmido (BR), húmido (PT), molhado; **moisture** n umidade f (BR), humidade f (PT); **moisturizer** n creme m hidratante
mole [məul] n (animal) toupeira; (spot) sinal m, lunar m; (spy) espião(-piã) m/f
molest [məu'lɛst] vt molestar; (attack sexually) atacar sexualmente
molten ['məultən] adj fundido; (lava) liquefeito
mom [mɔm] (US) n = **mum**
moment ['məumənt] n momento; **at the ~** neste momento; **momentary** adj momentâneo; **momentous** [məu'mɛntəs] adj importantíssimo
momentum [məu'mɛntəm] n momento; (fig) ímpeto; **to gather ~** ganhar ímpeto
mommy ['mɔmɪ] (US) n = **mummy**
Monaco ['mɔnəkəu] n Mônaco (no article)
monarch ['mɔnək] n monarca m/f; **monarchy** n monarquia
monastery ['mɔnəstərɪ] n mosteiro, convento
Monday ['mʌndɪ] n segunda-feira
monetary ['mʌnɪtərɪ] adj monetário
money ['mʌnɪ] n dinheiro; (currency) moeda; **to make ~** ganhar dinheiro;

money order n vale m (postal)
mongrel ['mʌŋgrəl] n (dog) vira-lata m
monitor ['mɒnɪtə*] n (TV, Comput)
terminal m (de vídeo) ▷ vt (heartbeat,
pulse) controlar; (broadcasts, progress)
monitorar
monk [mʌŋk] n monge m
monkey ['mʌŋkɪ] n macaco
monopoly [mə'nɔpəlɪ] n monopólio
monotonous [mə'nɔtənəs] adj
monótono
monsoon [mɒn'suːn] n monção f
monster ['mɒnstə*] n monstro
month [mʌnθ] n mês m; **monthly** adj
mensal ▷ adv mensalmente
monument ['mɒnjumənt] n
monumento
mood [muːd] n humor m; (of crowd)
atmosfera; **to be in a good/bad ~**
estar de bom/mau humor; **moody** adj
(variable) caprichoso, de veneta; (sullen)
rabugento
moon [muːn] n lua; **moonlight** n luar m
▷ vi ter dois empregos, ter um bico
moor [muə*] n charneca ▷ vt (ship)
amarrar ▷ vi fundear, atracar
moose [muːs] n inv alce m
mop [mɒp] n esfregão m; (for dishes)
esponja com cabeça; (of hair) grenha ▷ vt
esfregar; **mop up** vt limpar
mope [məup] vi estar or andar deprimido
or desanimado
moped ['məuped] n moto f pequena (BR),
motorizada (PT)
moral ['mɔrl] adj moral ▷ n moral f;
morals npl (principles) moralidade f,
costumes mpl
morale [mɔ'rɑːl] n moral f, estado de
espírito
morality [mə'rælɪtɪ] n moralidade f;
(correctness) retidão f, probidade f

Ⓞ **KEYWORD**

more [mɔː*] adj **1** (greater in number etc)
mais; **more people/work/letters than
we expected** mais pessoas/trabalho/
cartas do que esperávamos
2 (additional) mais; **do you want (some)
more tea?** você quer mais chá?; **I have
no** or **I don't have any more money**
não tenho mais dinheiro
▷ pron **1** (greater amount) mais; **more
than 10** mais de 10; **it cost more than
we expected** custou mais do que
esperávamos

2 (further or additional amount) mais;
is there any more? tem ainda mais?;
there's no more não tem mais
▷ adv mais; **more dangerous/difficult
etc than** mais perigoso/difícil etc do que;
more easily (than) mais fácil (do que);
more and more cada vez mais; **more
or less** mais ou menos; **more than ever**
mais do que nunca

moreover [mɔː'rəuvə*] adv além do
mais, além disso
morning ['mɔːnɪŋ] n manhã f; (early
morning) madrugada ▷ cpd da manhã; **in
the ~** de manhã; **7 o'clock in the ~** (as) 7
da manhã; **morning sickness** n náusea
matinal
Morocco [mə'rɔkəu] n Marrocos m
moron ['mɔːrɒn] (inf) n débil mental m/f,
idiota m/f
Morse [mɔːs] n (also: **~ code**) código
Morse
mortar ['mɔːtə*] n (cannon) morteiro;
(Constr) argamassa; (dish) pilão m,
almofariz m
mortgage ['mɔːgɪdʒ] n hipoteca ▷ vt
hipotecar
mortuary ['mɔːtjuərɪ] n necrotério
mosaic [məu'zeɪɪk] n mosaico
Moscow ['mɒskəu] n Moscou (BR),
Moscovo (PT)
Moslem ['mɔzləm] adj, n = **Muslim**
mosque [mɔsk] n mesquita
mosquito [mɔs'kiːtəu] (pl **~es**) n
mosquito
moss [mɔs] n musgo

Ⓞ **KEYWORD**

most [məust] adj **1** (almost all: people,
things etc) a maior parte de, a maioria
de; **most people** a maioria das pessoas
2 (largest, greatest: interest) máximo;
(money): **who has (the) most money?**
quem é que tem mais dinheiro?; **he
derived the most pleasure from
her visit** ele teve o maior prazer em
recebê-la
▷ pron (greatest quantity, number) a maior
parte, a maioria; **most of it/them**
a maioria dele/deles; **most of the
money** a maior parte do dinheiro; **do
the most you can** faça o máximo que
você puder; **I saw the most** vi mais; **to
make the most of sth** aproveitar algo
ao máximo; **at the (very) most** quando

muito, no máximo
▷ adv (+ vb) o mais; (+ adj): **the most
intelligent/expensive** etc o mais
inteligente/caro etc; (+ adv: carefully,
easily etc) o mais; (very: polite, interesting
etc) muito; **a most interesting book**
um livro interessantíssimo

mostly ['məustlɪ] adv principalmente,
na maior parte
MOT (BRIT) n abbr (= Ministry of Transport):
the ~ (test) vistoria anual dos veículos
automotores
motel [məu'tɛl] n motel m
moth [mɔθ] n mariposa; (clothes moth)
traça
mother ['mʌðəʳ] n mãe f ▷ adj materno
▷ vt (care for) cuidar de (como uma mãe);
motherhood n maternidade f; **mother-
in-law** n sogra; **mother-of-pearl** n
madrepérola; **mother-to-be** n futura
mamãe f; **mother tongue** n língua
materna
motion ['məuʃən] n movimento;
(gesture) gesto, sinal m; (at meeting)
moção f ▷ vt, vi: **to ~ (to) sb to do sth**
fazer sinal a alguém para que faça algo;
motionless adj imóvel; **motion picture**
n filme m (cinematográfico)
motive ['məutɪv] n motivo
motor ['məutəʳ] n motor m; (BRIT:
inf: vehicle) carro, automóvel m
▷ cpd (industry) de automóvel;
motorbike n moto(cicleta) f, motoca
(inf); **motorboat** n barco a motor;
motorcar (BRIT) n carro, automóvel m;
motorcycle n motocicleta; **motorist**
n motorista m/f; **motor racing** (BRIT)
n corrida de carros, automobilismo;
motorway (BRIT) n rodovia (BR),
autoestrada (PT)
motto ['mɔtəu] (pl ~es) n lema m
mound [maund] n (of earth) monte m; (of
blankets, leaves etc) pilha, montanha
mount [maunt] n monte m ▷ vt (horse
etc) montar em, subir a; (stairs) subir;
(exhibition) montar; (picture) emoldurar
▷ vi (increase) aumentar; **mount up** vi
aumentar
mountain ['mauntɪn] n montanha
▷ cpd de montanha; **mountain bike**
n mountain bike f; **mountaineer**
[mauntɪ'nɪəʳ] n alpinista m/f,
montanhista m/f; **mountaineering**
n alpinismo; **mountainous** adj
montanhoso

mourn [mɔ:n] vt chorar, lamentar ▷ vi:
to ~ for chorar or lamentar a morte de;
mourning n luto; **in mourning** de luto
mouse [maus] (pl mice) n camundongo
(BR), rato (PT); (Comput) mouse m; **mouse
mat, mouse pad** n (Comput) mouse
pad m
mousse [mu:s] n musse f; (for hair)
mousse f
moustache [məs'tɑ:ʃ] (US **mustache**) n
bigode m
mouth [mauθ] n boca; (of cave, hole)
entrada; (of river) desembocadura;
mouthful n bocado; **mouth organ** n
gaita; **mouthwash** n colutório
move [mu:v] n movimento; (in game)
lance m, jogada; (: turn to play) turno, vez
f; (of house, job) mudança ▷ vt (change
position of) mudar; (: in game) jogar;
(emotionally) comover; (Pol: resolution
etc) propor ▷ vi mexer-se, mover-se;
(traffic) circular; (also: ~ **house**) mudar-
se; (develop: situation) desenvolver; **to ~
sb to do sth** convencer alguém a fazer
algo; **to get a ~ on** apressar-se; **move
about** or **around** vi (fidget) mexer-se;
(travel) deslocar-se; **move along** vi
avançar; **move away** vi afastar-se;
move back vi voltar; **move forward** vi
avançar; **move in** vi (to a house) instalar-
se (numa casa); **move on** vi ir andando;
move out vi sair (de uma casa); **move
over** vi afastar-se; **move up** vi ser
promovido
movement ['mu:vmənt] n movimento;
(gesture) gesto; (of goods) transporte m;
(in attitude) mudança
movie ['mu:vɪ] n filme m; **to go to the ~s**
ir ao cinema
moving ['mu:vɪŋ] adj (emotional)
comovente; (that moves) móvel
mow [məu] (pt ~ed, pp ~ed or ~n) vt
(grass) cortar; (corn) ceifar; **mow down**
vt (massacre) chacinar; **mower** n ceifeira;
(also: **lawnmower**) cortador m de grama
(BR) or de relva (PT)
Mozambique [məuzəm'bi:k] n
Moçambique m (no article)
MP n abbr = **Member of Parliament**
MP3 player n tocador m MP3
mph abbr = miles per hour (60 mph = 96
km/h)
Mr ['mɪstəʳ] (US **Mr.**) n: **Mr Smith** (o) Sr.
Smith
Mrs ['mɪsɪz] (US **Mrs.**) n: ~ **Smith** (a) Sra.
Smith

Ms [mɪz] (us **Ms.**) n (= Miss or Mrs): **Ms X**
(a) Sa X

● **MS**
●
● **Ms** é um título utilizado em lugar de
● Mrs (senhora) ou de Miss (senhorita)
● para evitar a distinção tradicional
● entre mulheres casadas e solteiras. É
● aceito, portanto, como o equivalente
● de Mr (senhor) para os homens.
● Muitas vezes reprovado por ter
● surgido como manifestação de um
● feminismo exacerbado, é uma forma
● de tratamento muito comum hoje
● em dia.

MSc n abbr = Master of Science

⊙ **KEYWORD**

much [mʌtʃ] adj muito; **how much
money/time do you need?** quanto
dinheiro/tempo você precisa?; **he's
done so much work for the charity** ele
trabalhou muito para a obra de caridade;
as much as tanto como
▷ pron muito; **much has been gained
from our discussions** nossas discussões
foram muito proveitosas; **how much
does it cost? - too much** quanto custa
isso? - caro demais
▷ adv **1** (greatly) muito; **thank you very
much** muito obrigado(-a); **we are very
much looking forward to your visit**
estamos aguardando a sua visita com
muita ansiedade; **he is very much the
gentleman/politician** ele é muito
cavalheiro/político; **as much as** tanto
como; **as much as you** tanto quanto
você
2 (by far) de longe; **I'm much better now**
estou bem melhor agora
3 (almost) quase; **how are you feeling?
- much the same** como você está (se
sentindo)? - do mesmo jeito

muck [mʌk] n (dirt) sujeira (BR), sujidade f
(PT); **muck about** or **around** (inf) vi fazer
besteiras; **muck up** (inf) vt estragar
mud [mʌd] n lama
muddle ['mʌdl] n confusão f, bagunça;
(mix-up) trapalhada ▷ vt (also: **~ up**:
person, story) confundir; (: things)
misturar; **muddle through** vi virar-se
muddy ['mʌdɪ] adj (road) lamacento

mudguard ['mʌdgɑ:d] n pára-lama m
muesli ['mju:zlɪ] muesli m
muffin ['mʌfɪn] n bolinho redondo e chato
mug [mʌg] n (cup) caneca; (: for beer)
caneco, canecão; (inf: face) careta;
(: fool) bobo(-a) ▷ vt (assault) assaltar;
mugging n assalto
muggy ['mʌgɪ] adj abafado
mule [mju:l] n mula
multimedia [mʌltɪ'mi:dɪə] adj
multimídia
multiple ['mʌltɪpl] adj múltiplo ▷ n
múltiplo; **multiple sclerosis**
[-sklɪ'rəusɪs] n esclerose f múltipla
multiply ['mʌltɪplaɪ] vt multiplicar ▷ vi
multiplicar-se
multistorey ['mʌltɪ'stɔ:rɪ] (BRIT) adj de
vários andares
mum [mʌm] (BRIT: inf) n mamãe f ▷ adj:
to keep ~ ficar calado
mumble ['mʌmbl] vt, vi resmungar,
murmurar
mummy ['mʌmɪ] n (BRIT: mother)
mamãe f; (embalmed) múmia
mumps [mʌmps] n caxumba
municipal [mju:'nɪsɪpl] adj municipal
murder ['mə:də*] n assassinato ▷ vt
assassinar; **murderer** n assassino
murky ['mə:kɪ] adj escuro; (water) turvo
murmur ['mə:mə*] n murmúrio ▷ vt, vi
murmurar
muscle ['mʌsl] n músculo; (fig: strength)
força (muscular); **muscle in** vi imiscuir-
se, impor-se; **muscular** adj muscular;
(person) musculoso
museum [mju:'zɪəm] n museu m
mushroom ['mʌʃrum] n cogumelo ▷ vi
crescer da noite para o dia, pipocar
music ['mju:zɪk] n música; **musical** adj
musical; (harmonious) melodioso ▷ n
musical m; **musician** [mju:'zɪʃən] n
músico(-a)
Muslim ['mʌzlɪm] adj, n muçulmano(-a)
mussel ['mʌsl] n mexilhão m
must [mʌst] aux vb (obligation): **I ~ do it**
tenho que or devo fazer isso; (probability):
he ~ be there by now ele já deve estar
lá; (suggestion, invitation): **you ~ come
and see me soon** você tem que vir me
ver em breve; (indicating sth unwelcome):
why ~ he behave so badly? por que
ele tem que se comportar tão mal? ▷ n
necessidade f; **it's a ~** é imprescindível
mustache ['mʌstæʃ] (us) n
= moustache
mustard ['mʌstəd] n mostarda

mustn't ['mʌsnt] = **must not**

mute [mjuːt] adj mudo

mutiny ['mjuːtɪnɪ] n motim m, rebelião f

mutter ['mʌtəʳ] vt, vi resmungar, murmurar

mutton ['mʌtn] n carne f de carneiro

mutual ['mjuːtʃʊəl] adj mútuo; (shared) comum

muzzle ['mʌzl] n (of animal) focinho; (guard: for dog) focinheira; (of gun) boca ▷ vt pôr focinheira em

my [maɪ] adj meu (minha); **this is my house/car/brother** esta é a minha casa/meu carro/meu irmão; **I've washed my hair/cut my finger** lavei meu cabelo/cortei meu dedo

myself [maɪ'sɛlf] pron (reflexive) me; (emphatic) eu mesmo; (after prep) mim mesmo; see also **oneself**

mysterious [mɪs'tɪərɪəs] adj misterioso

mystery ['mɪstərɪ] n mistério

mystify ['mɪstɪfaɪ] vt mistificar

myth [mɪθ] n mito; **mythology** [mɪ'θɔlədʒɪ] n mitologia

nag [næg] vt ralhar, apoquentar

nail [neɪl] n (human) unha; (metal) prego ▷ vt pregar; **to ~ sb down to a date/price** conseguir que alguém se defina sobre a data/o preço; **nailbrush** n escova de unhas; **nailfile** n lixa de unhas; **nail polish** n esmalte m (BR) or verniz m (PT) de unhas; **nail polish remover** n removedor m de esmalte (BR) or verniz (PT); **nail scissors** npl tesourinha de unhas; **nail varnish** (BRIT) n = **nail polish**

naïve [naɪ'iːv] adj ingênuo

naked ['neɪkɪd] adj nu (nua)

name [neɪm] n nome m; (surname) sobrenome m; (reputation) reputação f, fama ▷ vt (child) pôr nome em; (criminal) apontar; (price) fixar; (date) marcar; **what's your ~?** qual é o seu nome?, como (você) se chama?; **by ~** de nome; **in the ~ of** em nome de; **namely** adv a saber, isto é

nanny ['nænɪ] n babá f

nap [næp] n (sleep) soneca ▷ vi: **to be caught ~ping** ser pego de surpresa

napkin ['næpkɪn] n (also: **table ~**) guardanapo

nappy ['næpɪ] (BRIT) n fralda

narrative ['nærətɪv] n narrativa

narrow ['nærəu] adj estreito; (fig: majority) pequeno; (: ideas) tacanho ▷ vi (road) estreitar-se; (difference) diminuir; **to have a ~ escape** escapar por um triz; **to ~ sth down to** restringir or reduzir algo a; **narrowly** adv (miss) por pouco; **narrow-minded** adj de visão limitada, bitolado

nasty ['nɑ:stɪ] adj (remark) desagradável; (: person) mau, ruim; (malicious) maldoso; (rude) grosseiro, obsceno; (taste, smell) repugnante, asqueroso; (wound etc) grave, sério

nation ['neɪʃən] n nação f

national ['næʃənl] adj, n nacional m/f; **national anthem** n hino nacional; **National Health Service** (BRIT) n ≈ Instituto Nacional de Assistência Médica e Previdência Social, ≈ INAMPS m; **nationality** [næʃə'nælɪtɪ] n nacionalidade f; **nationalize** vt nacionalizar; **national park** n parque m nacional; **National Trust** (BRIT) n ver quadro

⬧ **NATIONAL TRUST**
⬧
⬧ O **National Trust** é uma instituição
⬧ independente, sem fins lucrativos,
⬧ cuja missão é proteger e valorizar
⬧ os monumentos e a paisagem da
⬧ Grã-Bretanha devido a seu interesse
⬧ histórico ou beleza natural.

nationwide ['neɪʃənwaɪd] adj de âmbito or a nível nacional ▷ adv em todo o país

native ['neɪtɪv] n natural m/f, (in colonies) indígena m/f, nativo(-a) ▷ adj (indigenous) indígena; (of one's birth) natal; (language) materno; (innate) inato, natural; **a ~ speaker of Portuguese** uma pessoa de língua (materna) portuguesa

NATO ['neɪtəu] n abbr (= North Atlantic Treaty Organization) OTAN f

natural ['nætʃrəl] adj natural; **naturally** adv naturalmente; (of course) claro, evidentemente

nature ['neɪtʃə'] n natureza f, (character) caráter m, índole f

naughty ['nɔ:tɪ] adj travesso, levado

nausea ['nɔ:sɪə] n náusea

naval ['neɪvl] adj naval

nave [neɪv] n nave f

navel ['neɪvl] n umbigo

navigate ['nævɪgeɪt] vi navegar; (Aut) ler o mapa; **navigation** [nævɪ'geɪʃən] n (action) navegação f, (science) náutica

navy ['neɪvɪ] n marinha (de guerra)

Nazi ['nɑ:tsɪ] n nazista m/f (BR), nazi m/f (PT)

NB abbr (= nota bene) NB

near [nɪə'] adj (place) vizinho; (time) próximo; (relation) íntimo ▷ adv perto ▷ prep (also: ~ **to**: space) perto de; (: time) perto de, quase ▷ vt aproximar-se de; **nearby** [nɪə'baɪ] adj próximo, vizinho ▷ adv à mão, perto; **nearly** adv quase; **I nearly fell** quase que caí; **near-sighted** adj míope

neat [ni:t] adj (place) arrumado, em ordem; (person) asseado, arrumado; (work) organizado; (plan) engenhoso, bem bolado; (spirits) puro; **neatly** adv caprichosamente, com capricho; (skilfully) habilmente

necessarily ['nɛsɪsrɪlɪ] adv necessariamente

necessary ['nɛsɪsrɪ] adj necessário

necessity [nɪ'sɛsɪtɪ] n (thing needed) necessidade f, requisito; (compelling circumstances) necessidade; **necessities** npl (essentials) artigos mpl de primeira necessidade

neck [nɛk] n (Anat) pescoço; (of garment) gola; (of bottle) gargalo ▷ vi (inf) ficar de agarramento; **~ and ~** emparelhados

necklace ['nɛklɪs] n colar m

necktie ['nɛktaɪ] (esp US) n gravata

need [ni:d] n (lack) falta, carência; (necessity) necessidade f, (thing) requisito, necessidade ▷ vt precisar de; **I ~ to do it** preciso fazê-lo

needle ['ni:dl] n agulha ▷ vt (inf) provocar, alfinetar

needless ['ni:dlɪs] adj inútil, desnecessário; **~ to say ...** desnecessário dizer que ...

needlework ['ni:dlwə:k] n (item(s)) trabalho de agulha; (activity) costura

needn't ['ni:dnt] = **need not**

needy ['ni:dɪ] adj necessitado, carente

negative ['nɛgətɪv] adj negativo ▷ n (Phot) negativo; (Ling) negativa

neglect [nɪ'glɛkt] vt (one's duty) negligenciar, não cumprir com; (child) descuidar, esquecer-se de ▷ n (of child) descuido, desatenção f, (of house etc) abandono; (of duty) negligência

negotiate [nɪ'gəuʃɪeɪt] vi: **to ~ (with)** negociar (com) ▷ vt (treaty, transaction) negociar; (*obstacle*) contornar; (*bend in road*) fazer; **negotiation** [nɪgəʊʃɪ'eɪʃən] *n* negociação *f*

neighbour ['neɪbə'] (*us* **neighbor**) *n* vizinho(-a); **neighbourhood** *n* (*place*) vizinhança, bairro; (*people*) vizinhos *mpl*; **neighbouring** *adj* vizinho

neither ['naɪðə'] *conj*: **I didn't move and ~ did he** não me movi nem ele ▷ *adj*, *pron* nenhum (dos dois), nem um nem outro ▷ *adv*: **~ good nor bad** nem bom nem mau; **~ story is true** nenhuma das estórias é verdade

neon ['niːɔn] *n* neônio, néon *m*

nephew ['nɛvjuː] *n* sobrinho

nerve [nɜːv] *n* (*Anat*) nervo; (*courage*) coragem *f*; (*impudence*) descaramento, atrevimento; **to have a fit of ~s** ter uma crise nervosa

nervous ['nɜːvəs] *adj* (*Anat*) nervoso; (*anxious*) apreensivo; (*timid*) tímido, acanhado; **nervous breakdown** *n* crise *f* nervosa

nest [nɛst] *vi* aninhar-se ▷ *n* (*of bird*) ninho; (*of wasp*) vespeiro

net [nɛt] *n* rede *f*; (*fabric*) filó *m*; (*fig*) sistema *m* ▷ *adj* (*Comm*) líquido ▷ *vt* pegar na rede; (*money: subj: person*) faturar; (: *deal, sale*) render; **the N~** (*Internet*) a Rede; **netball** *n* espécie de basquetebol

Netherlands ['nɛðələndz] *npl*: **the ~** os Países Baixos

nett [nɛt] *adj* = **net**

nettle ['nɛtl] *n* urtiga

network ['nɛtwɜːk] *n* rede *f*; **there's no ~ coverage here** (*Tel*) aqui não tem cobertura

neurotic [njuə'rɔtɪk] *adj*, *n* neurótico(-a)

neuter ['njuːtə'] *adj* neutro ▷ *vt* (*cat etc*) castrar, capar

neutral ['njuːtrəl] *adj* neutro ▷ *n* (*Aut*) ponto morto

never ['nɛvə'] *adv* nunca; *see also* **mind**; **never-ending** *adj* sem fim, interminável; **nevertheless** *adv* todavia, contudo

new [njuː] *adj* novo; **newborn** *adj* recém-nascido; **newcomer** *n* recém-chegado(-a), novato(-a); **newly** *adv* recém, novamente

news [njuːz] *n* notícias *fpl*; (*Radio, TV*) noticiário; **a piece of ~** uma notícia; **newsagent** (*BRIT*) *n* jornaleiro(-a); **newscaster** *n* locutor(a) *m/f*; **newsletter** *n* boletim *m* informativo;

newspaper *n* jornal *m*; **newsreader** *n* = **newscaster**

newt [njuːt] *n* tritão *m*

New Year *n* ano novo; **New Year's Day** *n* dia *m* de ano novo; **New Year's Eve** *n* véspera de ano novo

New Zealand [-'ziːlənd] *n* Nova Zelândia; **New Zealander** *n* neozelandês(-esa) *m/f*

next [nɛkst] *adj* (*in space*) próximo, vizinho; (*in time*) seguinte, próximo ▷ *adv* depois; depois, logo; **~ time** na próxima vez; **~ year** o ano que vem; **~ to** ao lado de; **~ to nothing** quase nada; **next door** *adv* na casa do lado ▷ *adj* vizinho; **next-of-kin** *n* parentes *mpl* mais próximos

NHS *n abbr* = **National Health Service**

nibble ['nɪbl] *vt* mordiscar, beliscar

Nicaragua [nɪkə'rægjuə] *n* Nicarágua

nice [naɪs] *adj* (*likeable*) simpático; (*kind*) amável, atencioso; (*pleasant*) agradável; (*attractive*) bonito; **nicely** *adv* agradavelmente, bem

nick [nɪk] *n* (*wound*) corte *m*; (*cut, indentation*) entalhe *m*, incisão *f* ▷ *vt* (*inf: steal*) furtar, arrochar; **in the ~ of time** na hora H, no momento exato

nickel ['nɪkl] *n* níquel *m*; (*us*) moeda de 5 centavos

nickname ['nɪkneɪm] *n* apelido (*BR*), alcunha (*PT*) ▷ *vt* apelidar de (*BR*), alcunhar de (*PT*)

niece [niːs] *n* sobrinha

Nigeria [naɪ'dʒɪərɪə] *n* Nigéria

night [naɪt] *n* noite *f*; **at** *or* **by ~** à *or* de noite; **the ~ before last** anteontem à noite; **nightclub** *n* boate *f*

nightlife ['naɪtlaɪf] *n* vida noturna

nightly ['naɪtlɪ] *adj* noturno, de noite ▷ *adv* todas as noites, cada noite

nightmare ['naɪtmɛə'] *n* pesadelo

night-time *n* noite *f*

nil [nɪl] *n* nada; (*BRIT: Sport*) zero

nine [naɪn] *num* nove; **nineteen** ['naɪn'tiːn] *num* dezenove (*BR*), dezanove (*PT*); **ninety** ['naɪntɪ] *num* noventa; **ninth** [naɪnθ] *num* nono

nip [nɪp] *vt* (*pinch*) beliscar; (*bite*) morder

nipple ['nɪpl] *n* (*Anat*) bico do seio, mamilo

nitrogen ['naɪtrədʒən] *n* nitrogênio

⊙ **KEYWORD**

no [nəʊ] (*pl* **noes**) *adv* (*opposite of "yes"*) não; **are you coming? - no (I'm not)** você vem? - não (eu não)

▷ *adj* (*not any*) nenhum(a), não ... algum(a); **I have no more money/ time/books** não tenho mais dinheiro/ tempo/livros; **"no entry"** "entrada proibida"; **"no smoking"** é proibido fumar"
▷ *n* não *m*, negativa

nobility [nəu'bɪlɪtɪ] *n* nobreza
noble ['nəubl] *adj* (*person*) nobre; (*title*) de nobreza
nobody ['nəubədɪ] *pron* ninguém
nod [nɔd] *vi* (*greeting*) cumprimentar com a cabeça; (*in agreement*) acenar (que sim) com a cabeça; (*doze*) cochilar, dormitar
▷ *vt*: **to ~ one's head** inclinar a cabeça
▷ *n* inclinação *f* da cabeça; **nod off** *vi* cochilar
noise [nɔɪz] *n* barulho; **noisy** *adj* barulhento
nominate ['nɔmɪneɪt] *vt* (*propose*) propor; (*appoint*) nomear; **nominee** [nɔmɪ'ni:] *n* pessoa nomeada, candidato(-a)
none [nʌn] *pron* (*person*) ninguém; (*thing*) nenhum(a), nada; **~ of you** nenhum de vocês; **I've ~ left** não tenho mais
nonetheless [nʌnðə'les] *adv* no entanto, apesar disso, contudo
non-fiction *n* literatura de não-ficção
nonsense ['nɔnsəns] *n* disparate *m*, besteira, absurdo; **~!** bobagem!, que nada!
non: **non-smoker** *n* não-fumante *m/f*; **non-stick** *adj* tefal®, não-aderente
noodles ['nu:dlz] *npl* talharim *m*
noon [nu:n] *n* meio-dia *m*
no-one *pron* = **nobody**
nor [nɔːʳ] *conj* = **neither** ▷ *adv see* **neither**
norm [nɔːm] *n* (*convention*) norma; (*requirement*) regra
normal ['nɔːml] *adj* normal
north [nɔːθ] *n* norte *m* ▷ *adj* do norte, setentrional ▷ *adv* ao or para o norte; **North America** *n* América do Norte; **north-east** *n* nordeste *m*; **northern** ['nɔːðən] *adj* do norte, setentrional; **Northern Ireland** *n* Irlanda do Norte; **North Pole** *n*: **the North Pole** o Pólo Norte; **North Sea** *n*: **the North Sea** o Mar do Norte; **north-west** *n* noroeste *m*
Norway ['nɔːweɪ] *n* Noruega; **Norwegian** [nɔː'wi:dʒən] *adj* norueguês(-esa) ▷ *n* norueguês(-esa) *m/f*; (*Ling*) norueguês *m*
nose [nəuz] *n* (*Anat*) nariz *m*; (*Zool*)

focinho; (*sense of smell: of person*) olfato; (: *of animal*) faro; **nose about** *vi* bisbilhotar; **nose around** *vi* = **nose about**; **nosebleed** *n* hemorragia nasal; **nosey** (*inf*) *adj* = **nosy**
nostalgia [nɔs'tældʒɪə] *n* nostalgia
nostril ['nɔstrɪl] *n* narina
nosy ['nəuzɪ] (*inf*) *adj* intrometido, abelhudo
not [nɔt] *adv* não; **he is ~ or isn't here** ele não está aqui; **it's too late, isn't it?** é muito tarde, não?; **he asked me ~ to do it** ele me pediu para não fazer isto; **~ yet/ now** ainda/agora não; *see also* **all; only**
notably ['nəutəblɪ] *adv* (*particularly*) particularmente; (*markedly*) notavelmente
notch [nɔtʃ] *n* (*in wood*) entalhe *m*; (*in blade*) corte *m*
note [nəut] *n* (*Mus, banknote*) nota; (*letter*) nota, bilhete *m*; (*record*) nota, anotação *f*; (*tone*) tom *m* ▷ *vt* (*observe*) observar, reparar em; (*also*: **~ down**) anotar, tomar nota de; **notebook** *n* caderno; **notepad** *n* bloco de anotações; **notepaper** *n* papel *m* de carta
nothing ['nʌθɪŋ] *n* nada; (*zero*) zero; **he does ~** ele não faz nada; **~ new/much** nada de novo/quase nada; **~ for ~** de graça, grátis; (*in vain*) em vão, por nada
notice ['nəutɪs] *n* (*sign*) aviso, anúncio; (*warning*) aviso; (*dismissal*) demissão *f*; (*of leaving*) aviso prévio; (*period of time*) prazo ▷ *vt* reparar em, notar; **at short ~** de repente, em cima da hora; **until further ~** até nova ordem; **to hand in one's ~** demitir, pedir a demissão; **to take ~ of** prestar atenção a, fazer caso de; **to bring sth to sb's ~** levar algo ao conhecimento de alguém; **noticeable** *adj* evidente, visível; **notice board** (BRIT) *n* quadro de avisos
notify ['nəutɪfaɪ] *vt*: **to ~ sb of sth** avisar alguém de algo
notion ['nəuʃən] *n* noção *f*, idéia
nought [nɔːt] *n* zero
noun [naun] *n* substantivo
nourish ['nʌrɪʃ] *vt* nutrir, alimentar; (*fig*) fomentar, alentar; **nourishment** *n* alimento, nutrimento
novel ['nɔvl] *n* romance *m* ▷ *adj* novo, recente; **novelist** *n* romancista *m/f*; **novelty** *n* novidade *f*
November [nəu'vɛmbəʳ] *n* novembro
now [nau] *adv* agora; (*these days*) atualmente, hoje em dia ▷ *conj*: **~ (that)**

agora que; **right ~** agora mesmo; **by ~**
já; **just ~** atualmente; **~ and then, ~ and
again** de vez em quando; **from ~ on** de
agora em diante; **nowadays** adv hoje
em dia

nowhere ['nəuwɛəʳ] adv (go) a lugar
nenhum; (be) em nenhum lugar

nozzle ['nɔzl] n bocal m

nuclear ['njuːklɪəʳ] adj nuclear

nucleus ['njuːklɪəs] (pl **nuclei**) n núcleo

nude [njuːd] adj nu (nua) ▷ n (Art) nu m;
in the ~ nu, pelado

nudge [nʌdʒ] vt acotovelar, cutucar (BR)

nudist ['njuːdɪst] n nudista m/f

nuisance ['njuːsns] n amolação f,
aborrecimento; (person) chato; **what a ~!**
que saco! (BR), que chatice! (PT)

numb [nʌm] adj: **~ with cold** duro de frio;
~ with fear paralisado de medo

number ['nʌmbəʳ] n número; (numeral)
algarismo ▷ vt (pages etc) numerar;
(amount to) montar a; **a ~ of** vários,
muitos; **to be ~ed among** figurar entre;
they were ten in ~ eram em número de
dez; **number plate** (BRIT) n placa (do
carro)

numerous ['njuːmərəs] adj numeroso

nun [nʌn] n freira

nurse [nəːs] n enfermeiro(-a); (also:
~maid) ama-seca, babá f ▷ vt (patient)
cuidar de, tratar de

nursery ['nəːsərɪ] n (institution) creche
f; (room) quarto das crianças; (for plants)
viveiro; **nursery rhyme** n poesia
infantil; **nursery school** n escola
maternal

nursing ['nəːsɪŋ] n (profession)
enfermagem f; (care) cuidado,
assistência; **nursing home** n sanatório,
clínica de repouso

nut [nʌt] n (Tech) porca; (Bot) noz f

nutmeg ['nʌtmɛg] n noz-moscada

nutritious [njuːˈtrɪʃəs] adj nutritivo

nuts [nʌts] (inf) adj: **he's ~** ele é doido

nylon ['naɪlɔn] n náilon m (BR), nylon m
(PT) ▷ adj de náilon

O

oak [əuk] n carvalho ▷ adj de carvalho

OAP (BRIT) n abbr = **old-age pensioner**

oar [ɔːʳ] n remo

oasis [əuˈeɪsɪs] (pl **oases**) n oásis m inv

oath [əuθ] n juramento; (swear word)
palavrão m

oatmeal ['əutmiːl] n farinha or mingau
m de aveia

oats [əuts] n aveia

obedient [əˈbiːdɪənt] adj obediente

obey [əˈbeɪ] vt obedecer a; (instructions,
regulations) cumprir

obituary [əˈbɪtjuərɪ] n necrológio

object [(n) ˈɔbdʒɪkt, (vb) əbˈdʒɛkt] n
objeto; (purpose) objetivo ▷ vi: **to ~ to**
(attitude) desaprovar, objetar a; (proposal)
opor-se a; **I ~!** protesto!; **he ~ed that ...**
ele objetou que ...; **expense is no ~**
o preço não é problema; **objection**
[əbˈdʒɛkʃən] n objeção f; **I have no
objection to ...** não tenho nada
contra ...; **objective** n objetivo

obligation [ɔblɪˈgeɪʃən] n obrigação f;
without ~ sem compromisso

obligatory [əˈblɪgətərɪ] adj obrigatório

oblige [əˈblaɪdʒ] vt (do a favour for)
obsequiar, fazer um favor a; (force)
obrigar, forçar; **to be ~d to sb for doing**

sth ficar agradecido por alguém fazer algo

oblong ['ɔblɔŋ] *adj* oblongo, retangular ▷ *n* retângulo

obnoxious [əb'nɔkʃəs] *adj* odioso, detestável; (*smell*) enjoativo

oboe ['əubəu] *n* oboé *m*

obscene [əb'siːn] *adj* obsceno

obscure [əb'skjuəʳ] *adj* obscuro, desconhecido; (*difficult to understand*) pouco claro ▷ *vt* ocultar, escurecer; (*hide: sun etc*) esconder

observant [əb'zəːvnt] *adj* observador(a)

observation [ɔbzə'veɪʃən] *n* observação *f*; (*Med*) exame *m*

observatory [əb'zəːvətrɪ] *n* observatório

observe [əb'zəːv] *vt* observar; (*rule*) cumprir; **observer** *n* observador(a) *m/f*

obsess [əb'ses] *vt* obsedar, obcecar

obsolete ['ɔbsəliːt] *adj* obsoleto

obstacle ['ɔbstəkl] *n* obstáculo; (*hindrance*) estorvo, impedimento

obstinate ['ɔbstɪnɪt] *adj* obstinado

obstruct [əb'strʌkt] *vt* obstruir; (*block: hinder*) estorvar

obtain [əb'teɪn] *vt* obter; (*achieve*) conseguir

obvious ['ɔbvɪəs] *adj* óbvio; **obviously** *adv* evidentemente; **obviously not!** (é) claro que não!

occasion [ə'keɪʒən] *n* ocasião *f*; (*event*) acontecimento; **occasional** *adj* de vez em quando; **occasionally** *adv* de vez em quando

occupation [ɔkju'peɪʃən] *n* ocupação *f*; (*job*) profissão *f*

occupy ['ɔkjupaɪ] *vt* ocupar; (*house*) morar em; **to ~ o.s. in doing** ocupar-se de fazer

occur [ə'kəːʳ] *vi* ocorrer; (*phenomenon*) acontecer; **to ~ to sb** ocorrer a alguém; **occurrence** *n* ocorrência, acontecimento; (*existence*) existência

ocean ['əuʃən] *n* oceano

o'clock [ə'klɔk] *adv*: **it is 5 o'clock** são cinco horas

October [ɔk'təubəʳ] *n* outubro

octopus ['ɔktəpəs] *n* polvo

odd [ɔd] *adj* (*strange*) estranho, esquisito; (*number*) ímpar; (*sock etc*) desemparelhado; **60-~** 60 e tantos; **at ~ times** às vezes, de vez em quando; **to be the ~ one out** ficar sobrando, ser a exceção; **oddly** *adv* curiosamente; *see also* **enough**; **odds** *npl* (*in betting*) pontos

mpl de vantagem; **it makes no odds** dá no mesmo; **at odds** brigados(-as), de mal

odour ['əudəʳ] (*us* **odor**) *n* odor *m*, cheiro; (*unpleasant*) fedor *m*

⬤ **KEYWORD**

of [ɔv, əv] *prep* **1** (*gen*) de; **a friend of ours** um amigo nosso; **a boy of 10** um menino de 10 anos; **that was very kind of you** foi muito gentil da sua parte

2 (*expressing quantity, amount, dates etc*) de; **how much of this do you need?** de quanto você precisa?; **3 of them** 3 deles; **3 of us went** 3 de nós foram; **the 5th of July** dia 5 de julho

3 (*from, out of*) de; **made of wood** feito de madeira

⬤ **KEYWORD**

off [ɔf] *adv* **1** (*distance, time*): **it's a long way off** fica bem longe; **the game is 3 days off** o jogo é daqui a 3 dias

2 (*departure*): **I'm off** estou de partida; **to go off to Paris/Italy** ir para Paris/a Itália; **I must be off** devo ir-me

3 (*removal*): **to take off one's hat/ coat/clothes** tirar o chapéu/o casaco/a roupa; **the button came off** o botão caiu; **10% off** (*Comm*) 10% de abatimento or desconto

4 (*not at work*): **to have a day off** tirar um dia de folga; (*: sick*): **to be off sick** estar ausente por motivo de saúde ▷ *adj* **1** (*not turned on: machine, water, gas*) desligado; (*: light*) apagado; (*: tap*) fechado

2 (*cancelled*) cancelado

3 (*BRIT: not fresh: food*) passado; (*: milk*) talhado, anulado

4: **on the off chance** (*just in case*) ao acaso; **today I had an off day** (*not as good as usual*) hoje não foi o meu dia ▷ *prep* **1** (*indicating motion, removal, etc*) de; **the button came off my coat** o botão do meu casaco caiu

2 (*distant from*) de; **5 km off (the road)** a 5 km (da estrada); **off the coast** em frente à costa

3: **to be off meat** (*no longer eat it*) não comer mais carne; (*no longer like it*) enjoar de carne

offence [ə'fɛns] (*us* **offense**) *n* (*crime*) delito; **to take ~ at** ofender-se com, melindrar-se com

offend [ə'fɛnd] vt ofender; **offender** n delinqüente m/f

offensive [ə'fɛnsɪv] adj (weapon, remark) ofensivo; (smell etc) repugnante ▷ n (Mil) ofensiva

offer ['ɔfə'] n oferta; (proposal) proposta ▷ vt oferecer; (opportunity) proporcionar; **"on ~"** (Comm) "em oferta"

office ['ɔfɪs] n (place) escritório; (room) gabinete m; (position) cargo, função f; **to take ~** tomar posse; **doctor's ~** (US) consultório; **office block** (US **office building**) n conjunto de escritórios

officer ['ɔfɪsə'] n (Mil etc) oficial m/f; (of organization) diretor(a) m/f; (also: **police ~**) agente m/f policial or de polícia

office worker n empregado(-a) or funcionário(-a) de escritório

official [ə'fɪʃl] adj oficial ▷ n oficial m/f; (civil servant) funcionário público (funcionária pública)

off: off-licence (BRIT) n loja que vende bebidas alcoólicas; **off line** adj, adv (Comput) fora de linha; **off-peak** adj (heating etc) de período de pouco consumo; (ticket, train) de período de pouco movimento; **off-putting** (BRIT) adj desconcertante; **off-season** adj, adv fora de estação or temporada

⬤ **OFF-LICENCE**
⬤
⬤ Uma loja **off-licence** vende bebidas
⬤ alcoólicas (para viagem) nos horários
⬤ em que os pubs estão fechados.
⬤ Nesses estabelecimentos também se
⬤ pode comprar bebidas não-alcoólicas,
⬤ cigarros, batatas fritas, balas,
⬤ chocolates etc.

offset ['ɔfsɛt] (irreg) vt compensar, contrabalançar

offshore [ɔf'ɔ:'] adj (breeze) de terra; (fishing) costeiro; **~ oilfield** campo petrolífero ao largo

offside ['ɔf'saɪd] adj (Sport) impedido; (Aut) do lado do motorista

offspring ['ɔfsprɪŋ] n descendência, prole f

often ['ɔfn] adv muitas vezes, freqüentemente; **how ~ do you go?** quantas vezes você vai?

oil [ɔɪl] n (Culin) azeite m; (petroleum) petróleo; (for heating) óleo ▷ vt (machine) lubrificar; **oil painting** n pintura a óleo;

oil rig n torre f de perfuração; **oil slick** n mancha negra; **oil tanker** n (ship) petroleiro; (truck) carro-tanque m de petróleo; **oil well** n poço petrolífero; **oily** adj oleoso; (food) gorduroso

ointment ['ɔɪntmənt] n pomada

O.K. ['əu'keɪ] excl está bem, está bom, tá (bem or bom) (inf) ▷ adj bom; (correct) certo ▷ vt aprovar

old [əuld] adj velho; (former) antigo, anterior; **how ~ are you?** quantos anos você tem?; **he's 10 years ~** ele tem 10 anos; **~er brother** irmão mais velho; **old age** n velhice f; **old-age pensioner** (BRIT) n aposentado(-a) (BR), reformado(-a) (PT); **old-fashioned** adj fora de moda; (person) antiquado; (values) absoleto, retrógrado

olive ['ɔlɪv] n (fruit) azeitona; (tree) oliveira ▷ adj (also: **~-green**) verde-oliva inv; **olive oil** n azeite m de oliva

Olympic [əu'lɪmpɪk] adj olímpico

omelet(te) ['ɔmlɪt] n omelete f (BR), omeleta (PT)

omen ['əumən] n presságio, agouro

ominous ['ɔmɪnəs] adj preocupante

omit [əu'mɪt] vt omitir

⬤ **KEYWORD**

on [ɔn] prep **1** (indicating position) sobre, em (cima de); **on the wall** na parede; **on the left** à esquerda
2 (indicating means, method, condition etc): **on foot** a pé; **on the train/plane** no trem/avião; **on the telephone/radio** no telefone/rádio; **on television** na televisão; **to be on drugs** (addicted) ser viciado em drogas; (Med) estar sob medicação; **to be on holiday** estar de férias
3 (referring to time): **on Friday** na sexta-feira; **a week on Friday** sem ser esta sexta-feira, a outra; **on arrival** ao chegar; **on seeing this** ao ver isto
4 (about, concerning) sobre
▷ adv **1** (referring to dress, covering): **to have one's coat on** estar de casaco; **what's she got on?** o que ela está usando?; **she put her boots on** ela calçou as botas; **he put his gloves/hat on** ele colocou as luvas/o chapéu; **screw the lid on tightly** atarraxar bem a tampa
2 (further, continuously): **to walk/drive on** continuar andando/dirigindo; **to go on** continuar (em frente); **to read on**

continuar a ler
▷ *adj* **1** (*functioning, in operation: machine*) em funcionamento; (*light*) aceso; (*radio*) ligado; (*tap*) aberto; (*brakes: of car etc*): **to be on** estar freado; (*meeting*): **is the meeting still on?** (*in progress*) a reunião ainda está sendo realizada?; (*not cancelled*) ainda vai haver reunião?; **there's a good film on at the cinema** tem um bom filme passando no cinema **2**: **that's not on!** (*inf: of behaviour*) isso não se faz!

once [wʌns] *adv* uma vez; (*formerly*) outrora ▷ *conj* depois que; **~ he had left/it was done** depois que ele saiu/foi feito; **at ~** imediatamente; (*simultaneously*) de uma vez, ao mesmo tempo; **~ more** mais uma vez; **~ and for all** uma vez por todas; **~ upon a time** era uma vez
oncoming [ˈɔnkʌmɪŋ] *adj* (*traffic*) que vem de frente

🔵 **KEYWORD**

one [wʌn] *num* um(a); **one hundred and fifty** cento e cinqüenta; **one by one** um por um
▷ *adj* **1** (*sole*) único; **the one book which ...** o único livro que ...
2 (*same*) mesmo; **they came in the one car** eles vieram no mesmo carro
▷ *pron* **1** um(a); **this one** este (esta); **that one** esse (essa), aquele (aquela); **I've already got one/a red one** eu já tenho um/um vermelho
2: **one another** um ao outro; **do you two ever see one another?** vocês dois se vêem de vez em quando?
3 (*impers*): **one never knows** nunca se sabe; **to cut one's finger** cortar o dedo; **one needs to eat** é preciso comer

oneself [wʌnˈsɛlf] *pron* (*reflexive*) se; (*after prep, emphatic*) si (mesmo(-a)); **by ~** sozinho(-a); **to hurt ~** ferir-se; **to keep sth for ~** guardar algo para si mesmo; **to talk to ~** falar consigo mesmo
one: **one-sided** *adj* (*argument*) parcial; **one-way** *adj* (*street, traffic*) de mão única (BR), de sentido único (PT)
ongoing [ˈɔngəʊɪŋ] *adj* (*project*) em andamento; (*situation*) existente
onion [ˈʌnjən] *n* cebola
on line *adj* (Comput) on-line, em linha
▷ *adv* em linha

onlooker [ˈɔnlukəʳ] *n* espectador(a) *m/f*
only [ˈəʊnlɪ] *adv* somente, apenas ▷ *adj* único, só ▷ *conj* só que, porém; **an ~ child** um filho único; **not ~ ... but also ...** não só ... mas também ...
onset [ˈɔnsɛt] *n* começo
onto [ˈɔntu] *prep* = **on to**
onward(s) [ˈɔnwəd(z)] *adv* (*move*) para diante, para a frente; **from this time onward(s)** de (ag)ora em diante
ooze [uːz] *vi* ressumar, filtrar-se
opaque [əʊˈpeɪk] *adj* opaco, fosco
open [ˈəʊpn] *adj* aberto; (*car*) descoberto; (*road*) livre; (*fig: frank*) aberto, franco; (*meeting*) aberto, sem restrições ▷ *vt* abrir ▷ *vi* abrir(-se); (*book etc*) começar; **in the ~ (air)** ao ar livre; **open on to** *vt fus* (*subj: room, door*) dar para; **open up** *vt* abrir; (*blocked road*) desobstruir ▷ *vi* (Comm) abrir; **opening** *adj* de abertura ▷ *n* abertura; (*start*) início; (*opportunity*) oportunidade *f*; **openly** *adv* abertamente; **open-minded** *adj* aberto, imparcial; **open-necked** *adj* aberto no colo; **open-plan** *adj* sem paredes divisórias; **Open University** (BRIT) *n* ver quadro

▒ **OPEN UNIVERSITY**
▒
▒ Fundada em 1969, a **Open University**
▒ oferece um tipo de ensino que
▒ compreende cursos (alguns blocos
▒ da programação da TV e do rádio são
▒ reservados para esse fim), deveres que
▒ são enviados pelo aluno ao diretor
▒ ou diretora de estudos e uma estada
▒ obrigatória numa universidade de
▒ verão. É preciso cumprir um certo
▒ número de unidades ao longo de um
▒ período determinado e obter a média
▒ em um certo número delas para
▒ receber o diploma almejado.

opera [ˈɔpərə] *n* ópera
operate [ˈɔpəreɪt] *vt* fazer funcionar, pôr em funcionamento ▷ *vi* funcionar; (*Med*): **to ~ on sb** operar alguém
operation [ɔpəˈreɪʃən] *n* operação *f*; (*of machine*) funcionamento; **to be in ~** (*system*) estar em vigor
operator [ˈɔpəreɪtəʳ] *n* (*of machine*) operador(a) *m/f*, manipulador(a) *m/f*; (Tel) telefonista *m/f*
opinion [əˈpɪnɪən] *n* opinião *f*; **in my ~** na minha opinião, a meu ver

opponent [ə'pəunənt] n oponente m/f;
(Mil, Sport) adversário(-a)
opportunity [ɔpə'tjuːnɪtɪ] n
oportunidade f; **to take the ~ of doing**
aproveitar a oportunidade para fazer
oppose [ə'pəuz] vt opor-se a; **to be ~d to**
sth opor-se a algo, estar contra algo; **as**
~d to em oposição a
opposite ['ɔpəzɪt] adj oposto; (house etc)
em frente ▷ adv (lá) em frente ▷ prep
em frente de, defronte de ▷ n oposto,
contrário
opposition [ɔpə'zɪʃən] n oposição f
opt [ɔpt] vi: **to ~ for** optar por; **to ~ to do**
optar por fazer; **opt out** vi: **to opt out of**
doing sth optar por não fazer algo
optician [ɔp'tɪʃən] n oculista m/f
optimist ['ɔptɪmɪst] n otimista f;
optimistic [ɔptɪ'mɪstɪk] adj otimista
option ['ɔpʃən] n opção f; **optional** adj
opcional, facultativo
or [ɔːʳ] conj ou; (with negative): **he hasn't**
seen or heard anything ele não viu nem
ouviu nada; **or else** senão
oral ['ɔːrəl] adj oral ▷ n (exame m) oral f
orange ['ɔrɪndʒ] n (fruit) laranja ▷ adj cor
de laranja inv, alaranjado
orbit ['ɔːbɪt] n órbita ▷ vt orbitar
orchard ['ɔːtʃəd] n pomar m
orchestra ['ɔːkɪstrə] n orquestra; (US:
seating) platéia
orchid ['ɔːkɪd] n orquídea
ordeal [ɔː'diːl] n experiência penosa,
provação f
order ['ɔːdəʳ] n ordem f; (Comm)
encomenda; (good order) bom estado
▷ vt (also: **put in ~**) pôr em ordem,
arrumar; (in restaurant) pedir; (Comm)
encomendar; (command) mandar,
ordenar; **in (working) ~** em bom estado;
in ~ to do/that para fazer/que (+ sub);
on ~ (Comm) encomendado; **out of ~**
com defeito, enguiçado; **order form** n
impresso para encomendas; **orderly**
n (Mil) ordenança m; (Med) servente
m/f ▷ adj (room) arrumado, ordenado;
(person) metódico
ordinary ['ɔːdnrɪ] adj comum, usual;
(pej) ordinário, medíocre; **out of the ~**
fora do comum, extraordinário
ore [ɔːʳ] n minério
organ ['ɔːgən] n órgão m; **organic**
[ɔː'gænɪk] adj orgânico
organization [ɔːgənaɪ'zeɪʃən] n
organização f
organize ['ɔːgənaɪz] vt organizar

orgasm ['ɔːgæzəm] n orgasmo
origin ['ɔrɪdʒɪn] n origem f
original [ə'rɪdʒɪnl] adj original ▷ n
original m
originate [ə'rɪdʒɪneɪt] vi: **to ~ from**
originar-se de, surgir de; **to ~ in** ter
origem em
Orkneys ['ɔːknɪz] npl: **the ~** (also: **the**
Orkney Islands) as ilhas Órcadas
ornament ['ɔːnəmənt] n ornamento;
(on dress) enfeite m; **ornamental**
[ɔːnə'mɛntl] adj decorativo, ornamental
ornate [ɔː'neɪt] adj enfeitado, requintado
orphan ['ɔːfn] n órfão (órfã) m/f
orthopaedic [ɔːθə'piːdɪk] (US
orthopedic) adj ortopédico
ostrich ['ɔstrɪtʃ] n avestruz m/f
other ['ʌðəʳ] adj outro ▷ pron: **the ~**
(one) o outro (a outra) ▷ adv (usually in
negatives): **~ than** (apart from) a não ser;
(anything but) exceto; **~s** (other people)
outros; **otherwise** adv (in a different way)
de outra maneira; (apart from that) do
contrário, caso contrário ▷ conj (if not)
senão
otter ['ɔtəʳ] n lontra
ouch [autʃ] excl ai!
ought [ɔːt] (pt ~) aux vb: **I ~ to do it** eu
deveria fazê-lo; **he ~ to win** (probability)
ele deve ganhar
ounce [auns] n onça (= 28.35g; 16 in a
pound)
our ['auəʳ] adj nosso; see also **my**; **ours**
pron (o) nosso ((a) nossa) etc; see also
mine; **ourselves** [auə'sɛlvz] pron pl
(reflexive, after prep) nós; (emphatic) nós
mesmos(-as); see also **oneself**
oust [aust] vt expulsar

⭕ **KEYWORD**

out [aut] adv **1** (not in) fora; **(to stand)**
out in the rain/snow (estar em pé) na
chuva/neve; **out loud** em voz alta
2 (not at home, absent) fora (de casa); **Mr**
Green is out at the moment Sr. Green
não está no momento; **to have a day/**
night out passar o dia fora/sair à noite
3 (indicating distance): **the boat was 10**
km out o barco estava a 10 km da costa
4 (Sport): **the ball is/has gone out** a
bola caiu fora; **out!** (Tennis etc) fora!
▷ adj **1**: **to be out** (unconscious) estar
inconsciente; (out of game) estar fora; (out
of fashion) estar fora de moda
2 (have appeared: news, secret) do

conhecimento público; (: *flowers*): **the flowers are out** as flores desabrocham **3** (*extinguished: light, fire*) apagado; **before the week was out** (*finished*) antes da semana acabar **4**: **to be out to do sth** (*intend*) pretender fazer algo; **to be out in one's calculations** (*wrong*) enganar-se nos cálculos
▷ *prep*: **out of 1** (*outside, beyond*): **out of** fora de; **to go out of the house** sair da casa; **to look out of the window** olhar pela janela **2** (*cause, motive*) por **3** (*origin*): **to drink sth out of a cup** beber algo na xícara **4** (*from among*): **1 out of every 3** 1 entre 3 **5** (*without*) sem; **to be out of milk/sugar/petrol** *etc* não ter leite/açúcar/gasolina *etc*

outback ['autbæk] *n* (*in Australia*): **the ~** o interior
outbreak ['autbreik] *n* (*of war*) deflagração *f*; (*of disease*) surto; (*of violence etc*) explosão *f*
outburst ['autbə:st] *n* explosão *f*
outcast ['autkɑ:st] *n* pária *m/f*
outcome ['autkʌm] *n* resultado
outcry ['autkrai] *n* clamor *m* (de protesto)
outdated [aut'deitid] *adj* antiquado, fora de moda
outdoor [aut'dɔ:ʳ] *adj* ao ar livre; (*clothes*) de sair; **outdoors** *adv* ao ar livre
outer ['autəʳ] *adj* exterior, externo; **outer space** *n* espaço (exterior)
outfit ['autfit] *n* roupa, traje *m*
outgoing ['autgəuiŋ] *adj* de saída; (*character*) extrovertido, sociável; **outgoings** (BRIT) *npl* despesas *fpl*
outing ['autiŋ] *n* excursão *f*
outlaw ['autlɔ:] *n* fora-da-lei *m/f* ▷ *vt* (*person*) declarar fora da lei; (*practice*) declarar ilegal
outlay ['autlei] *n* despesas *fpl*
outlet ['autlet] *n* saída, escape *m*; (*of pipe*) desagüe *m*, escoadouro; (*us: Elec*) tomada; (*also*: **retail ~**) posto de venda
outline ['autlain] *n* (*shape*) contorno, perfil *m*; (*of plan*) traçado; (*sketch*) esboço, linhas *fpl* gerais ▷ *vt* (*theory, plan*) traçar, delinear
outlook ['autluk] *n* (*attitude*) ponto de vista; (*fig: prospects*) perspectiva; (: *for weather*) previsão *f*

outnumber [aut'nʌmbəʳ] *vt* exceder em número
out-of-date *adj* (*passport, ticket*) sem validade; (*clothes*) fora de moda
out-of-the-way *adj* remoto, afastado
outpatient ['autpeiʃənt] *n* paciente *m/f* externo(-a) or de ambulatório
outpost ['autpəust] *n* posto avançado
output ['autput] *n* (*volume m de*) produção *f*; (*Comput*) saída ▷ *vt* (*Comput*) liberar
outrage ['autreidʒ] *n* escândalo; (*atrocity*) atrocidade *f* ▷ *vt* ultrajar; **outrageous** [aut'reidʒəs] *adj* ultrajante, escandaloso
outright [(*adv*) aut'rait, (*adj*) 'autrait] *adv* (*kill, win*) completamente; (*ask, refuse*) abertamente ▷ *adj* completo; franco
outset ['autset] *n* início, princípio
outside [aut'said] *n* exterior *m* ▷ *adj* exterior, externo ▷ *adv* (*lá*) fora ▷ *prep* fora de; (*beyond*) além (dos limites) de; **at the ~** (*fig*) no máximo; **outsider** *n* (*stranger*) estranho(-a), forasteiro(-a)
outsize ['autsaiz] *adj* (*clothes*) de tamanho extra-grande or especial
outskirts ['autskə:ts] *npl* arredores *mpl*, subúrbios *mpl*
outspoken [aut'spəukən] *adj* franco, sem rodeios
outstanding [aut'stændiŋ] *adj* excepcional; (*work, debt*) pendente
outward ['autwəd] *adj* externo; (*journey*) de ida
outweigh [aut'wei] *vt* ter mais valor do que
oval ['əuvl] *adj* ovalado ▷ *n* oval *m*
Oval Office *n* ver quadro

🔸 OVAL OFFICE
🔸
🔸 O Salão Oval (**Oval Office**) é o
🔸 escritório particular do presidente
🔸 dos Estados Unidos na Casa Branca,
🔸 assim chamado devido a sua forma
🔸 oval. Por extensão, o termo se refere à
🔸 presidência em si.

ovary ['əuvəri] *n* ovário
oven ['ʌvn] *n* forno

 KEYWORD

over ['əuvəʳ] *adv* **1** (*across: walk, jump, fly etc*) por cima; **to cross over to the other side of the road** atravessar para o outro lado da rua; **over here** por aqui, cá; **over there** por ali, lá; **to ask sb over** (*to one's home*) convidar alguém

2 : **to fall over** cair; **to knock over** derrubar; **to turn over** virar; **to bend over** curvar-se, debruçar-se

3 (*finished*): **to be over** estar acabado

4 (*excessively*: clever, rich, fat etc) muito, demais; **she's not over intelligent** ela não é superdotada

5 (*remaining*: money, food etc): **there are 3 over** tem 3 sobrando/sobraram 3

6: **all over** (*everywhere*) por todos os lados

7: **over and over** (*again*) repetidamente ▷ *prep* **1** (*on top of*) sobre; (*above*) acima de **2** (*on the other side of*) no outro lado de; **he jumped over the wall** ele pulou o muro

3 (*more than*) mais de; **over and above** além de

4 (*during*) durante

overall [(*adj, n*) 'əuvərɔːl, (*adv*) əuvər'ɔːl] *adj* (*length*) total; (*study*) global ▷ *adv* (*view*) globalmente; (*measure, paint*) totalmente ▷ *n* (*also*: **~s**) macacão *m* (BR), (fato) macaco (PT)

overboard ['əuvəbɔːd] *adv* (Naut) ao mar

overcast ['əuvəkɑːst] *adj* nublado, fechado

overcharge [əuvə'tʃɑːdʒ] *vt*: **to ~ sb** cobrar em excesso a alguém

overcoat ['əuvəkəut] *n* sobretudo

overcome [əuvə'kʌm] (*irreg*) *vt* vencer, dominar; (*difficulty*) superar

overcrowded [əuvə'kraudɪd] *adj* superlotado

overdo [əuvə'duː] (*irreg*) *vt* exagerar; (*overcook*) cozinhar demais; **to ~ it** (*work too hard*) exceder-se

overdose ['əuvədəus] *n* overdose *f*, dose *f* excessiva

overdraft ['əuvədrɑːft] *n* saldo negativo

overdrawn [əuvə'drɔːn] *adj* (*account*) sem fundos, a descoberto

overdue [əuvə'djuː] *adj* atrasado; (*change*) tardio

overestimate [əuvər'ɛstɪmeɪt] *vt* sobrestimar

overflow [(*vb*) əuvə'fləu, (*n*) 'əuvəfləu] *vi* transbordar ▷ *n* (*also*: **~ pipe**) tubo de descarga, ladrão *m*

overgrown [əuvə'grəun] *adj* (*garden*) coberto de vegetação

overhaul [(*vb*) əuvə'hɔːl, (*n*) 'əuvəhɔːl] *vt* revisar ▷ *n* revisão *f*

overhead [(*adv*) əuvə'hɛd, (*adj, n*) 'əuvəhɛd] *adv* por cima, em cima; (*in the sky*) no céu ▷ *adj* (*lighting*) superior; (*railway*) suspenso ▷ *n* (US) = **overheads**; **overheads** *npl* (*expenses*) despesas *fpl* gerais

overhear [əuvə'hɪər] (*irreg*) *vt* ouvir por acaso

overheat [əuvə'hiːt] *vi* (*engine*) aquecer demais

overland ['əuvəlænd] *adj, adv* por terra

overlap [əuvə'læp] *vi* (*edges*) sobrepor-se em parte; (*fig*) coincidir

overload [əuvə'ləud] *vt* sobrecarregar

overlook [əuvə'luk] *vt* (*have view on*) dar para; (*miss*) omitir; (*forgive*) fazer vista grossa a

overnight [(*adv*) əuvə'naɪt, (*adj*) 'əuvənaɪt] *adv* durante a noite; (*fig*) da noite para o dia ▷ *adj* de uma (*or* de) noite; **to stay ~** passar a noite, pernoitar

overpass ['əuvəpɑːs] (*esp* US) *n* viaduto

overpower [əuvə'pauər] *vt* dominar, subjugar; (*fig*) assolar

overrule [əuvə'ruːl] *vt* (*decision*) anular; (*claim*) indeferir

overrun [əuvə'rʌn] (*irreg*) *vt* (*country etc*) invadir; (*time limit*) ultrapassar, exceder

overseas [əuvə'siːz] *adv* (*abroad*) no estrangeiro, no exterior ▷ *adj* (*trade*) exterior; (*visitor*) estrangeiro

overshadow [əuvə'ʃædəu] *vt* ofuscar

oversight ['əuvəsaɪt] *n* descuido

oversleep [əuvə'sliːp] (*irreg*) *vi* dormir além da hora

overt [əu'vəːt] *adj* aberto, indissimulado

overtake [əuvə'teɪk] (*irreg*) *vt* ultrapassar

overthrow [əuvə'θrəu] (*irreg*) *vt* (*government*) derrubar

overtime ['əuvətaɪm] *n* horas *fpl* extras

overturn [əuvə'təːn] *vt* virar; (*system*) derrubar; (*decision*) anular ▷ *vi* (*car etc*) capotar

overweight [əuvə'weɪt] *adj* gordo demais, com excesso de peso

overwhelm [əuvə'wɛlm] *vt* esmagar, assolar; **overwhelming** *adj* (*victory, defeat*) esmagador(a); (*heat*) sufocante; (*desire*) irresistível

owe [əu] *vt*: **to ~ sb sth, to ~ sth to sb** dever algo a alguém; **owing to** *prep* devido a, por causa de

owl [aul] *n* coruja

own [əun] *adj* próprio ▷ *vt* possuir, ter;

a room of my ~ meu próprio quarto;
to get one's ~ **back** ir à forra; **on one's**
~ sozinho; **own up** *vi*: **to own up to**
sth confessar algo; **owner** *n* dono(-a),
proprietário(-a); **ownership** *n* posse *f*
ox [ɔks] (*pl* **oxen**) *n* boi *m*
oxygen ['ɔksɪdʒən] *n* oxigênio
oyster ['ɔɪstə^r] *n* ostra
oz. *abbr* = **ounce(s)**
ozone ['əuzəun] *n* ozônio

p [piː] *abbr* (= *page*) p; (*BRIT*) = **penny;**
pence
p.a. *abbr* (= *per annum*) p.a.
pace [peɪs] *n* passo; (*speed*) velocidade
f ▷ *vi*: **to ~ up and down** andar de
um lado para o outro; **to keep ~ with**
acompanhar o passo de; **pacemaker** *n*
(*Med*) marcapasso *m*
Pacific [pə'sɪfɪk] *n*: **the ~ (Ocean)** o
(Oceano) Pacífico
pack [pæk] *n* pacote *m*, embrulho; (*US*:
of cigarettes) maço; (*of hounds*) matilha;
(*of thieves*) bando, quadrilha; (*of cards*)
baralho; (*backpack*) mochila ▷ *vt* encher;
(*in suitcase*) arrumar (na mala); (*cram*):
to ~ into entupir de, entulhar com; **to ~**
(one's bags) fazer as malas; **to ~ sb off**
despedir alguém; **~ it in!** pára com isso!
package ['pækɪdʒ] *n* pacote *m*; (*bulky*)
embrulho, fardo; (*also*: **~ deal**) acordo
global, pacote; **package tour** (*BRIT*) *n*
excursão *f* organizada
packed lunch [pækt-] (*BRIT*) *n* merenda
packet ['pækɪt] *n* pacote *m*; (*of cigarettes*)
maço; (*of washing powder etc*) caixa
packing ['pækɪŋ] *n* embalagem *f*; (*act*)
empacotamento
pad [pæd] *n* (*of paper*) bloco; (*to prevent*

friction) acolchoado; *(inf: home)* casa ▷ *vt* acolchoar, enchumaçar

paddle ['pædl] *n* remo curto; *(us: for table tennis)* raquete *f* ▷ *vt* remar ▷ *vi* patinhar; **paddling pool** *(BRIT)* *n* lago de recreação

paddock ['pædək] *n* cercado; *(at race course)* paddock *m*

padlock ['pædlɔk] *n* cadeado

page [peɪdʒ] *n* página; *(also: ~ boy)* mensageiro ▷ *vt* mandar chamar

pager ['peɪdʒər], **paging device** ['peɪdʒɪŋ-] *n* bip *m*

paid [peɪd] *pt, pp of* **pay** ▷ *adj (work)* remunerado; *(holiday)* pago; *(official)* assalariado; **to put ~ to** *(BRIT)* acabar com

pain [peɪn] *n* dor *f*; **to be in ~** sofrer *or* sentir dor; **to take ~s to do sth** dar-se ao trabalho de fazer algo; **painful** *adj* doloroso; *(laborious)* penoso; *(unpleasant)* desagradável; **painkiller** *n* analgésico; **painstaking** ['peɪnzteɪkɪŋ] *adj (work)* esmerado; *(person)* meticuloso

paint [peɪnt] *n* pintura ▷ *vt* pintar; **paintbrush** *n (artist's)* pincel *m*; *(decorator's)* broxa; **painter** *n (artist)* pintor(a) *m/f*; *(decorator)* pintor(a); **painting** *n* pintura; *(picture)* tela, quadro

pair [pɛər] *n* par *m*; **a ~ of scissors** uma tesoura; **a ~ of trousers** uma calça *(BR)*, umas calças *(PT)*

pajamas [pɪ'dʒɑːməz] *(us) npl* pijama *m*

Pakistan [pɑːkɪ'stɑːn] *n* Paquistão *m*; **Pakistani** *adj, n* paquistanês(-esa) *m/f*

pal [pæl] *(inf) n* camarada *m/f*, colega *m/f*

palace ['pæləs] *n* palácio

pale [peɪl] *adj* pálido; *(colour)* claro; *(light)* fraco ▷ *vi* empalidecer ▷ *n*: **to be beyond the ~** passar dos limites

Palestine ['pælɪstaɪn] *n* Palestina; **Palestinian** [pælɪs'tɪnɪən] *adj, n* palestino(-a)

palm [pɑːm] *n (of hand)* palma; *(also: ~ tree)* palmeira ▷ *vt*: **to ~ sth off on sb** *(inf)* impingir algo a alguém

pamper ['pæmpər] *vt* paparicar, mimar

pamphlet ['pæmflət] *n* panfleto

pan [pæn] *n (also: **sauce~**)* panela *(BR)*, caçarola *(PT)*; *(also: **frying ~**)* frigideira

Panama ['pænəmɑː] *n* Panamá *m*

pancake ['pænkeɪk] *n* panqueca

panda ['pændə] *n* panda *m/f*

pane [peɪn] *n* vidraça, vidro

panel ['pænl] *n (of wood, Radio, TV)* painel *m*

panic ['pænɪk] *n* pânico ▷ *vi* entrar em pânico

pansy ['pænzɪ] *n (Bot)* amor-perfeito; *(inf: pej)* bicha *(BR)*, maricas *m (PT)*

pant [pænt] *vi* arquejar, ofegar

panther ['pænθər] *n* pantera

panties ['pæntɪz] *npl* calcinha *(BR)*, cuecas *fpl (PT)*

pantomime ['pæntəmaɪm] *(BRIT) n* pantomima

⚜ **PANTOMIME**
⚜
⚜ Uma **pantomime**, também chamada
⚜ simplesmente de *panto*, é um gênero
⚜ de comédia em que o personagem
⚜ principal em geral é um rapaz e na
⚜ qual há sempre uma **dame**, isto é,
⚜ uma mulher idosa representada por
⚜ um homem, e um vilão. Na maior
⚜ parte das vezes, a história é baseada
⚜ em um conto de fadas, como "A gata
⚜ borralheira" ou "O gato de botas", e
⚜ a platéia é encorajada a participar
⚜ prevenindo os heróis dos perigos que
⚜ estão por vir. Esse tipo de espetáculo,
⚜ voltado sobretudo para as crianças,
⚜ visa também ao público adulto por
⚜ meio de diversas brincadeiras que
⚜ fazem alusão aos fatos atuais.

pants [pænts] *npl (BRIT: underwear: woman's)* calcinha *(BR)*, cuecas *fpl (PT)*; *(: man's)* cueca *(BR)*, cuecas *(PT)*; *(us: trousers)* calça *(BR)*, calças *fpl (PT)*

paper ['peɪpər] *n* papel *m*; *(also: **news~**)* jornal *m*; *(also: **wall~**)* papel de parede; *(study, article)* artigo, dissertação *f*; *(exam)* exame *m*, prova ▷ *adj* de papel ▷ *vt (room)* revestir (com papel de parede); **papers** *npl (also: **identity ~s**)* documentos *mpl*; **paperback** *n* livro de capa mole; **paper bag** *n* saco de papel; **paper clip** *n* clipe *m*; **paperwork** *n* trabalho burocrático; *(pej)* papelada

par [pɑːr] *n* paridade *f*, igualdade *f*; *(Golf)* média *f*; **on a ~ with** em pé de igualdade com

parachute ['pærəʃuːt] *n* pára-quedas *m inv*

parade [pə'reɪd] *n* desfile *m* ▷ *vt (show off)* exibir ▷ *vi (Mil)* passar revista

paradise ['pærədaɪs] *n* paraíso

paraffin ['pærəfɪn] *(BRIT) n*: **~ (oil)** querosene *m*

paragraph ['pærəgrɑːf] *n* parágrafo

Paraguay ['pærəgwaɪ] n Paraguai m

parallel ['pærəlɛl] adj (lines etc) paralelo; (fig) correspondente ▷ n paralela; correspondência

paralysis [pə'rælɪsɪs] (pl **paralyses**) n paralisia

paranoid ['pærənɔɪd] adj paranóico

parcel ['pɑːsl] n pacote m ▷ vt (also: ~ **up**) embrulhar, empacotar

pardon ['pɑːdn] n (Law) indulto ▷ vt perdoar; ~ **me!, I beg your** ~ (apologizing) desculpe(-me); **(I beg your)** ~? (BRIT), ~ **me?** (US) (not hearing) como?, como disse?

parent ['pɛərənt] n (father) pai m; (mother) mãe f; **parents** npl (mother and father) pais mpl

Paris ['pærɪs] n Paris

parish ['pærɪʃ] n paróquia, freguesia

park [pɑːk] n parque m ▷ vt, vi estacionar

parking ['pɑːkɪŋ] n estacionamento; **"no ~"** "estacionamento proibido"; **parking lot** (US) n (parque m de) estacionamento; **parking meter** n parquímetro; **parking ticket** n multa por estacionamento proibido

parliament ['pɑːləmənt] (BRIT) n parlamento

parole [pə'rəul] n: **on** ~ em liberdade condicional, sob promessa

parrot ['pærət] n papagaio

parsley ['pɑːslɪ] n salsa

parsnip ['pɑːsnɪp] n cherivia, pastinaga

parson ['pɑːsn] n padre m, clérigo; (in Church of England) pastor m

part [pɑːt] n parte f; (of machine) peça; (Theatre etc) papel m; (of serial) capítulo; (US: in hair) risca, repartido ▷ adv = **partly** ▷ vt dividir; (hair) repartir ▷ vi (people) separar-se; (crowd) dispersar-se; **to take ~ in** participar de, tomar parte em; **to take sb's** ~ defender alguém; **for my ~** pela minha parte; **for the most** ~ na maior parte; **to take sth in good** ~ não se ofender com algo; **part with** vt fus ceder, entregar; (money) pagar

partial ['pɑːʃl] adj parcial; **to be ~ to** gostar de, ser apreciador(a) de

participate [pɑː'tɪsɪpeɪt] vi: **to ~ in** participar de

particle ['pɑːtɪkl] n partícula; (of dust) grão m

particular [pə'tɪkjulər] adj (special) especial; (specific) específico; (fussy) exigente, minucioso; **particulars** npl detalhes mpl; (personal details) dados mpl pessoais; **in ~** em particular; **particularly**

adv em particular, especialmente

parting ['pɑːtɪŋ] n (act) separação f; (farewell) despedida; (BRIT: in hair) risca, repartido ▷ adj de despedida

partition [pɑː'tɪʃən] n (Pol) divisão f; (wall) tabique m, divisória

partly ['pɑːtlɪ] adv em parte

partner ['pɑːtnər] n (Comm) sócio(-a); (Sport) parceiro(-a); (at dance) par m; (spouse) cônjuge m/f; **partnership** n associação f, parceria; (Comm) sociedade f

partridge ['pɑːtrɪdʒ] n perdiz f

part-time adj, adv de meio expediente

party ['pɑːtɪ] n (Pol) partido; (celebration) festa; (group) grupo; (Law) parte f interessada, litigante m/f ▷ cpd (Pol) do partido, partidário

pass [pɑːs] vt passar; (exam) passar em; (place) passar por; (overtake) ultrapassar; (approve) aprovar ▷ vi passar; (Sch) ser aprovado, passar ▷ n (permit) passe m; (membership card) carteira; (in mountains) desfiladeiro; (Sport) passe m; (Sch): **to get a ~ in** ser aprovado em; **to make a ~ at sb** tomar liberdade com alguém; **pass away** vi falecer; **pass by** vi passar ▷ vt passar por cima de; **pass for** vt fus passar por; **pass on** vt (news, illness) transmitir; (object) passar para; **pass out** vi desmaiar; **pass up** vt deixar passar; **passable** adj (road) transitável; (work) aceitável

passage ['pæsɪdʒ] n (also: ~**way**: indoors) corredor m; (: outdoors) passagem f; (Anat) via; (act of passing) trânsito; (in book) passagem, trecho; (by boat) travessia

passenger ['pæsɪndʒər] n passageiro(-a)

passer-by ['pɑːsə'-] (pl **passers-by**) n transeunte m/f

passion ['pæʃən] n paixão f; **passionate** adj apaixonado

passive ['pæsɪv] adj passivo

passport ['pɑːspɔːt] n passaporte m

password ['pɑːswɜːd] n senha, contra-senha

past [pɑːst] prep (in front of) por; (beyond) mais além de; (later than) depois de ▷ adj passado; (president etc) ex-, anterior ▷ n passado; **he's ~ forty** ele tem mais de quarenta anos; **ten/quarter ~ four** quatro e dez/quinze; **for the ~ few/3 days** nos últimos/3 dias

pasta ['pæstə] n massa

paste [peɪst] n pasta; (glue) grude m, cola

▷ vt grudar; **tomato ~** massa de tomate

pasteurized ['pæstəraɪzd] adj pasteurizado

pastime ['pɑːstaɪm] n passatempo

pastry ['peɪstrɪ] n massa; (cake) bolo

pasture ['pɑːstʃəʳ] n pasto

pasty [(n) 'pæstɪ, (adj) 'peɪstɪ] n empadão m de carne ▷ adj (complexion) pálido

pat [pæt] vt dar palmadinhas em; (dog etc) fazer festa em

patch [pætʃ] n retalho; (eye patch) tapa-olho m, tampão m; (area) aréa pequena; (mend) remendo ▷ vt remendar; **(to go through) a bad ~** (passar por) um mau pedaço; **patch up** vt consertar provisoriamente; (quarrel) resolver; **patchy** adj (colour) desigual; (information) incompleto

pâté ['pæteɪ] n patê m

patent ['peɪtnt] n patente f ▷ vt patentear ▷ adj patente, evidente

paternal [pə'təːnl] adj paternal; (relation) paterno

path [pɑːθ] n caminho; (trail, track) trilha, senda; (trajectory) trajetória

pathetic [pə'θetɪk] adj (pitiful) patético, digno de pena; (very bad) péssimo

pathway ['pɑːθweɪ] n caminho, trilha

patience ['peɪʃns] n paciência

patient ['peɪʃnt] adj, n paciente m/f

patio ['pætɪəʊ] n pátio

patrol [pə'trəʊl] n patrulha ▷ vt patrulhar; **patrol car** n carro de patrulha

patron ['peɪtrən] n (customer) cliente m/f, freguês(-esa) m/f; (of charity) benfeitor(a) m/f; **~ of the arts** mecenas m

pattern ['pætən] n (Sewing) molde m; (design) desenho

pause [pɔːz] n pausa ▷ vi fazer uma pausa

pave [peɪv] vt pavimentar; **to ~ the way for** preparar o terreno para

pavement ['peɪvmənt] (BRIT) n calçada (BR), passeio (PT)

pavilion [pə'vɪlɪən] n (Sport) barraca

paving ['peɪvɪŋ] n pavimento, calçamento

paw [pɔː] n pata; (of cat) garra

pawn [pɔːn] n (Chess) peão m; (fig) títere m ▷ vt empenhar; **pawnbroker** n agiota m/f

pay [peɪ] (pt, pp **paid**) n salário; (of manual worker) paga ▷ vt pagar; (debt) liquidar, saldar; (visit) fazer ▷ vi valer a pena, render; **to ~ attention (to)** prestar atenção (a); **to ~ one's respects to sb**

fazer uma visita de cortesia a alguém; **pay back** vt (money) devolver; (person) pagar; **pay for** vt fus pagar a; (fig) recompensar; **pay in** vt depositar; **pay off** vt (debts) saldar, liquidar; (creditor) pagar, reembolsar ▷ vi (plan) valer a pena; **pay up** vi pagar; **payable** adj pagável; (cheque) **payable to** nominal em favor de; **payment** n pagamento; **monthly payment** pagamento mensal; **pay packet** (BRIT) n envelope m de pagamento; **pay phone** n telefone m público; **payroll** n folha de pagamento; **pay television** n televisão f por assinatura

PC n abbr (= personal computer) PC m

PDA n abbr (= personal digital assistant) PDA m (assistente digital pessoal)

pea [piː] n ervilha

peace [piːs] n paz f; (calm) tranqüilidade f, quietude f; **peaceful** adj (person) tranqüilo, pacífico; (place, time) tranqüilo, sossegado

peach [piːtʃ] n pêssego

peacock ['piːkɔk] n pavão m

peak [piːk] n (of mountain: top) cume m; (of cap) pala, viseira; (fig) apogeu m

peanut ['piːnʌt] n amendoim m; **peanut butter** n manteiga de amendoim

pear [pɛəʳ] n pêra

pearl [pəːl] n pérola

peasant ['pɛznt] n camponês(-esa) m/f

peat [piːt] n turfa

pebble ['pɛbl] n seixo, calhau m

peck [pɛk] vt (also: ~ at) bicar, dar bicadas em ▷ n bicada; (kiss) beijoca; **peckish** (BRIT: inf) adj: **I feel peckish** estou a fim de comer alguma coisa

peculiar [pɪ'kjuːlɪəʳ] adj (strange) estranho, esquisito; (belonging to): **~ to** próprio de

pedal ['pɛdl] n pedal m ▷ vi pedalar

pedestrian [pɪ'dɛstrɪən] n pedestre m/f(BR), peão m (PT) ▷ adj (fig) prosaico; **pedestrian crossing** (BRIT) n passagem f para pedestres (BR), passadeira (PT)

pedigree ['pɛdɪgriː] n raça; (fig) genealogia ▷ cpd (animal) de raça

pee [piː] (inf) vi fazer xixi, mijar

peek [piːk] vi: **to ~ at** espiar, espreitar

peel [piːl] n casca ▷ vt descascar ▷ vi (paint, skin) descascar; (wallpaper) desprender-se

peep [piːp] n (BRIT: look) espiadela; (sound) pio ▷ vi espreitar; **peep out** (BRIT) vi mostrar-se, surgir

peer [pɪər] vi: **to ~ at** perscrutar, fitar
▷ n (noble) par m/f; (equal) igual m/f;
(contemporary) contemporâneo(-a)
peg [pɛg] n (for coat etc) cabide m; (BRIT:
also: **clothes ~**) pregador m
pelican ['pɛlɪkən] n pelicano
pelt [pɛlt] vt: **to ~ sb with sth** atirar
algo em alguém ▷ vi (rain: also: **~ down**)
chover a cântaros; (inf: run) correr ▷ n
pele f (não curtida)
pelvis ['pɛlvɪs] n pelvis f, bacia
pen [pɛn] n caneta; (for sheep etc) redil m,
cercado
penalty ['pɛnltɪ] n pena, penalidade f;
(fine) multa; (Sport) punição f
pence [pɛns] (BRIT) npl of **penny**
pencil ['pɛnsl] n lápis m; **pencil case**
n lapiseira, porta-lápis m inv; **pencil
sharpener** n apontador m (de lápis) (BR),
apara-lápis m inv (PT)
pendant ['pɛndnt] n pingente m
pending ['pɛndɪŋ] prep, adj pendente
penetrate ['pɛnɪtreɪt] vt penetrar
penfriend ['pɛnfrɛnd] (BRIT) n = **penpal**
penguin ['pɛŋgwɪn] n pingüim m
peninsula [pə'nɪnsjulə] n península
penis ['piːnɪs] n pênis m
penitentiary [pɛnɪ'tɛnʃərɪ] (US) n
penitenciária, presídio
penknife ['pɛnnaɪf] (irreg) n canivete m
penniless ['pɛnɪlɪs] adj sem dinheiro,
sem um tostão
penny ['pɛnɪ] (pl **pennies** or (BRIT)
pence) n pêni m; (US) cêntimo
penpal ['pɛnpæl] n amigo(-a) por
correspondência, correspondente m/f
pension ['pɛnʃən] n pensão f; (old-
age pension) aposentadoria, pensão
do governo; **pensioner** (BRIT) n
aposentado(-a) (BR), reformado(-a) (PT)
Pentagon ['pɛntəgə] n: **the ~** o
Pentágono; ver quadro

◈ **PENTAGON**
◈
◈ O Pentágono **Pentagon** é o nome
◈ dado aos escritórios do Ministério da
◈ Defesa americano, localizados em
◈ Arlington, no estado da Virgínia, por
◈ causa da forma pentagonal do edifício
◈ onde se encontram. Por extensão,
◈ o termo é utilizado também para se
◈ referir ao ministério.

penthouse ['pɛnthaus] n cobertura
people ['piːpl] npl gente f, pessoas fpl;
(inhabitants) habitantes m/fpl; (citizens)
povo; (Pol) **the ~** o povo ▷ n (nation, race)
povo; **several ~ came** vieram várias
pessoas; **~ say that ...** dizem que ...
pepper ['pɛpər] n pimenta; (vegetable)
pimentão m ▷ vt apimentar; (fig): **to ~
with** salpicar de; **peppermint** n (sweet)
bala de hortelã
per [pəːr] prep por
perceive [pə'siːv] vt perceber; (notice)
notar; (realize) compreender
per cent n por cento
percentage [pə'sɛntɪdʒ] n porcentagem
f, percentagem f
perch [pəːtʃ] (pl **~es**) n (for bird) poleiro;
(pl: inv or **perches**: fish) perca ▷ vi: **to ~
(on)** (bird) empoleirar-se (em); (person)
encarapitar-se (em)
perfect [(adj, n) 'pəːfɪkt, (vb) pə'fɛkt]
adj perfeito; (utter) completo ▷ n (also:
~ tense) perfeito ▷ vt aperfeiçoar;
perfectly adv perfeitamente
perform [pə'fɔːm] vt (carry out) realizar,
fazer; (piece of music) interpretar ▷ vi
(well, badly) interpretar; **performance** n
desempenho; (of play, by artist) atuação
f; (of car) performance f; **performer** n
(actor) artista m/f, ator (atriz) m/f; (Mus)
intérprete m/f
perfume ['pəːfjuːm] n perfume m
perhaps [pə'hæps] adv talvez
perimeter [pə'rɪmɪtər] n perímetro
period ['pɪərɪəd] n período; (Sch)
aula; (full stop) ponto final; (Med)
menstruação f, regra ▷ adj (costume,
furniture) da época
perish ['pɛrɪʃ] vi perecer; (decay)
deteriorar-se
perjury ['pəːdʒərɪ] n (Law) perjúrio, falso
testemunho
perk [pəːk] (inf) n mordomia, regalia;
perk up vi (cheer up) animar-se
perm [pəːm] n permanente f
permanent ['pəːmənənt] adj
permanente
permission [pə'mɪʃən] n permissão f;
(authorization) autorização f
permit [(n) 'pəːmɪt, (vb) pə'mɪt] n
licença; (to enter) passe m ▷ vt permitir;
(authorize) autorizar
perplex [pə'plɛks] vt deixar perplexo
persecute ['pəːsɪkjuːt] vt importunar
persevere [pəːsɪ'vɪər] vi perseverar
Persian ['pəːʃən] adj persa ▷ n (Ling)
persa m; **the ~ Gulf** o golfo Pérsico
persist [pə'sɪst] vi: **to ~ (in)** persistir

(em); **persistent** [pə'sɪstənt] *adj*
persistente; (*determined*) teimoso
person ['pɜːsn] *n* pessoa; **in ~** em
pessoa; **personal** *adj* pessoal; (*private*)
particular; (*visit*) em pessoa, pessoal;
personal assistant *n* secretário(-a)
particular; **personal computer** *n*
computador *m* pessoal; **personality**
[pɜːsə'nælɪtɪ] *n* personalidade *f*;
personal organizer *n* agenda
personnel [pɜːsə'nɛl] *n* pessoal *m*
perspective [pə'spɛktɪv] *n* perspectiva
perspiration [pɜːspɪ'reɪʃən] *n*
transpiração *f*
persuade [pə'sweɪd] *vt*: **to ~ sb to do
sth** persuadir alguém a fazer algo
Peru [pə'ruː] *n* Peru *m*
pervert [(*n*) 'pɜːvɜːt, (*vb*) pə'vɜːt] *n*
pervertido(-a) ▷ *vt* perverter, corromper;
(*truth*) distorcer
pessimist ['pɛsɪmɪst] *n* pessimista *m/f*;
pessimistic [pɛsɪ'mɪstɪk] *adj* pessimista
pest [pɛst] *n* (*insect*) inseto nocivo; (*fig*)
peste *f*
pester ['pɛstə'] *vt* incomodar
pet [pɛt] *n* animal *m* de estimação
▷ *cpd* predileto ▷ *vt* acariciar ▷ *vi* (*inf*)
acariciar-se; **teacher's ~** (*favourite*)
preferido(-a) do professor
petal ['pɛtl] *n* pétala
petite [pə'tiːt] *adj* delicado, mignon
petition [pə'tɪʃən] *n* petição *f*; (*list of
signatures*) abaixo-assinado
petrified ['pɛtrɪfaɪd] *adj* (*fig*) petrificado,
paralisado
petrol ['pɛtrəl] (BRIT) *n* gasolina; **two/
four-star ~** gasolina de duas/quatro
estrelas
petroleum [pə'trəulɪəm] *n* petróleo
petrol: **petrol pump** (BRIT) *n* bomba de
gasolina; **petrol station** (BRIT) *n* posto
(BR) or bomba (PT) de gasolina; **petrol
tank** (BRIT) *n* tanque *m* de gasolina
petticoat ['pɛtɪkəut] *n* anágua
petty ['pɛtɪ] *adj* (*mean*) mesquinho;
(*unimportant*) insignificante
pew [pjuː] *n* banco (de igreja)
pewter ['pjuːtə'] *n* peltre *m*
phantom ['fæntəm] *n* fantasma *m*
pharmacy ['fɑːməsɪ] *n* farmácia
phase [feɪz] *n* fase *f* ▷ *vt*: **to ~ in/out**
introduzir/retirar por etapas
PhD *n abbr* = **Doctor of Philosophy**
pheasant ['fɛznt] *n* faisão *m*
phenomenon [fə'nɔmɪnən] (*pl*
phenomena) *n* fenômeno

philosophical [fɪlə'sɔfɪkl] *adj* filosófico;
(*fig*) calmo, sereno
philosophy [fɪ'lɔsəfɪ] *n* filosofia
phishing ['fɪʃɪŋ] *n* phishing *m*; **~ attack**
golpe *m* de phishing
phobia ['fəubjə] *n* fobia
phone [fəun] *n* telefone *m* ▷ *vt* telefonar
para, ligar para; **to be on the ~** ter
telefone; (*be calling*) estar no telefone;
phone back *vt, vi* ligar de volta; **phone
up** *vt* telefonar para ▷ *vi* telefonar;
phone book *n* lista telefônica; **phone
box** (BRIT) *n* cabine *f* telefônica; **phone
call** *n* telefonema *m*, ligada; **phone
card** *n* cartão para uso em telefone público;
phone number *n* número de telefone
phonetics [fə'nɛtɪks] *n* fonética
phoney ['fəunɪ] *adj* falso; (*person*) fingido
photo ['fəutəu] *n* foto *f*
photo... ['fəutəu] *prefix* foto...;
photocopier *n* fotocopiadora *f*;
photocopy *n* fotocópia, xerox® *m* ▷ *vt*
fotocopiar, xerocar
photograph ['fəutəgrɑːf] *n* fotografia
▷ *vt* fotografar; **photographer**
[fə'tɔgrəfə'] *n* fotógrafo(-a);
photography [fə'tɔgrəfɪ] *n* fotografia
phrase [freɪz] *n* frase *f* ▷ *vt* expressar;
phrase book *n* livro de expressões
idiomáticas (para turistas)
physical ['fɪzɪkl] *adj* físico
physician [fɪ'zɪʃən] *n* médico(-a)
physics ['fɪzɪks] *n* física
physiotherapy [fɪzɪəu'θɛrəpɪ] *n*
fisioterapia
physique [fɪ'ziːk] *n* físico
pianist ['piːənɪst] *n* pianista *m/f*
piano [pɪ'ænəu] *n* piano
pick [pɪk] *n* (*tool: also*: **~axe**) picareta
▷ *vt* (*select*) escolher, selecionar; (*gather*)
colher; (*remove*) tirar; (*lock*) forçar; **take
your ~** escolha o que quiser; **the ~ of**
o melhor de; **to ~ one's nose** colocar
o dedo no nariz; **to ~ one's teeth**
palitar os dentes; **to ~ a quarrel with
sb** comprar uma briga com alguém;
pick at *vt fus* (*food*) beliscar; **pick on**
vt fus (*person: criticize*) criticar; (*: treat
badly*) azucrinar, aporrinhar; **pick out**
vt escolher; (*distinguish*) distinguir; **pick
up** *vi* (*improve*) melhorar ▷ *vt* (*from floor,
Aut*) apanhar; (*Police*) prender; (*collect*)
buscar; (*for sexual encounter*) paquerar;
(*learn*) aprender; (*Radio*) pegar; **to pick
up speed** acelerar; **to pick o.s. up**
levantar-se

pickle ['pɪkl] n (also: **~s**: as condiment) picles mpl; (fig: mess) apuro ▷ vt (in vinegar) conservar em vinagre; (in salt) conservar em sal e água

pickpocket ['pɪkpɔkɪt] n batedor(a) m/f de carteira (BR), carteirista m/f (PT)

picnic ['pɪknɪk] n piquenique m

picture ['pɪktʃəʳ] n (also: **~ dress**) avental m ▷ vt imaginar-se; **the pictures** npl (BRIT: inf) o cinema; **picture messaging** n picture messaging m

pie [paɪ] n (vegetable) pastelão m; (fruit) torta; (meat) empadão m

piece [piːs] n pedaço; (portion) fatia; (item): **a ~ of clothing/furniture/advice** uma roupa/um móvel/um conselho ▷ vt: **to ~ together** juntar; **to take to ~s** desmontar

pie chart n gráfico de setores

pier [pɪəʳ] n cais m; (jetty) embarcadouro, molhe m

pierce [pɪəs] vt furar, perfurar

pig [pɪg] n porco; (fig) porcalhão(-lhona) m/f; (pej: unkind person) grosseiro(-a); (: greedy person) ganancioso(-a)

pigeon ['pɪdʒən] n pombo

piggy bank ['pɪgɪ-] n cofre em forma de porquinho

pigsty ['pɪgstaɪ] n chiqueiro

pigtail ['pɪgteɪl] n rabo-de-cavalo, trança

pike [paɪk] n (pl inv or **~s**) (fish) lúcio

pilchard ['pɪltʃəd] n sardinha

pile [paɪl] n (heap) monte m; (of carpet) pêlo; (of cloth) lado felpudo ▷ vt (also: **~ up**) empilhar ▷ vi (also: **~ up**: objects) empilhar-se; (: problems, work) acumular-se; **pile into** vt fus (car) apinhar-se

piles [paɪlz] npl hemorróidas fpl

pile-up n (Aut) engavetamento

pilgrim ['pɪlgrɪm] n peregrino(-a)

pill [pɪl] n pílula; **the ~** a pílula

pillar ['pɪləʳ] n pilar m; **pillar box** (BRIT) n caixa coletora (do correio) (BR), marco do correio (PT)

pillow ['pɪləu] n travesseiro (BR), almofada (PT); **pillowcase** n fronha

pilot ['paɪlət] n piloto(-a) ▷ cpd (scheme etc) piloto inv ▷ vt pilotar; **pilot light** n piloto

pimple ['pɪmpl] n espinha

PIN [pɪn] n abbr (= personal identification number) número de identificação pessoal, senha

pin [pɪn] n alfinete m ▷ vt alfinetar; **~s and needles** comichão f, sensação f de formigamento; **to ~ sth on sb** (fig) culpar alguém de algo; **pin down** vt (fig): **to pin sb down** conseguir que alguém se defina or tome atitude

pinafore ['pɪnəfɔːʳ] n (also: **~ dress**) avental m

pinch [pɪntʃ] n (of salt etc) pitada ▷ vt beliscar; (inf: steal) afanar; **at a ~** em último caso

pine [paɪn] n pinho ▷ vi: **to ~ for** ansiar por; **pine away** vi consumir-se, definhar

pineapple ['paɪnæpl] n abacaxi m (BR), ananás m (PT)

pink [pɪŋk] adj cor de rosa inv ▷ n (colour) cor f de rosa; (Bot) cravo, cravina

pinpoint ['pɪnpɔɪnt] vt (discover) descobrir; (explain) identificar; (locate) localizar com precisão

pint [paɪnt] n quartilho (BRIT: = 568cc; US: = 473cc)

pioneer [paɪə'nɪəʳ] n pioneiro(-a)

pious ['paɪəs] adj pio, devoto

pip [pɪp] n (seed) caroço, semente f; **the pips** npl (BRIT: time signal on radio) ≈ o toque de seis segundos

pipe [paɪp] n cano; (for smoking) cachimbo ▷ vt canalizar, encanar; **pipes** npl (also: **bag~s**) gaita de foles; **pipe down** (inf) vi calar o bico, meter a viola no saco; **pipeline** n (for oil) oleoduto; (for gas) gaseoduto

pirate ['paɪərət] n pirata m ▷ vt piratear

Pisces ['paɪsiːz] n Pisces m, Peixes mpl

pistol ['pɪstl] n pistola

piston ['pɪstən] n pistão m, êmbolo

pit [pɪt] n cova, fossa; (quarry, hole in surface of sth) buraco; (also: **coal ~**) mina de carvão ▷ vt: **to ~ one's wits against sb** competir em conhecimento or inteligência contra alguém; **pits** npl (Aut) box m

pitch [pɪtʃ] n (Mus) tom m; (fig: degree) intensidade f; (BRIT: Sport) campo; (tar) piche m, breu m ▷ vt (throw) arremessar, lançar; (tent) armar ▷ vi (fall forwards) cair (para frente); **pitch-black** adj escuro como o breu

pitfall ['pɪtfɔːl] n perigo (imprevisto), armadilha

pitiful ['pɪtɪful] adj comovente, tocante

pity ['pɪtɪ] n compaixão f, piedade f ▷ vt ter pena de, compadecer-se de

pixel ['pɪksl] *n* pixel *m*
pizza ['pi:tsə] *n* pizza
placard ['plækɑ:d] *n* placar *m*; (*in march etc*) cartaz *m*
place [pleɪs] *n* lugar *m*; (*position*) posição *f*; (*post*) posto; (*role*) papel *m*; (*home*): **at/to his ~** na/para a casa dele ▷ *vt* pôr, colocar; (*identify*) identificar, situar; **to take ~** realizar-se; (*occur*) ocorrer; **out of ~** (*not suitable*) fora de lugar, deslocado; **in the first ~** em primeiro lugar; **to change ~s with sb** trocar de lugar com alguém; **to be ~d** (*in race, exam*) classificar-se
plague [pleɪg] *n* (*Med*) peste *f*; (*fig*) praga ▷ *vt* atormentar, importunar
plaice [pleɪs] *n inv* solha
plain [pleɪn] *adj* (*unpatterned*) liso; (*clear*) claro, evidente; (*simple*) simples *inv*, despretensioso; (*not handsome*) sem atrativos ▷ *adv* claramente, com franqueza ▷ *n* planície *f*, campina; **plain chocolate** *n* chocolate *m* amargo; **plainly** *adv* claramente, obviamente; (*hear, see*) facilmente; (*state*) francamente
plaintiff ['pleɪntɪf] *n* querelante *m/f*, queixoso(-a)
plait [plæt] *n* trança, dobra
plan [plæn] *n* plano; (*scheme*) projeto; (*schedule*) programa *m* ▷ *vt* planejar (*BR*), planear (*PT*) ▷ *vi* fazer planos; **to ~ to do** pretender fazer
plane [pleɪn] *n* (*Aviat*) avião *m*; (*also*: **~ tree**) plátano; (*fig: level*) nível *m*; (*tool*) plaina; (*Math*) plano
planet ['plænɪt] *n* planeta *m*
plank [plæŋk] *n* tábua
planning ['plænɪŋ] *n* planejamento (*BR*), planeamento (*PT*); **family ~** planejamento *or* planeamento familiar
plant [plɑ:nt] *n* planta; (*machinery*) maquinaria; (*factory*) usina, fábrica ▷ *vt* plantar; (*field*) semear; (*bomb*) colocar, pôr
plaster ['plɑ:stər] *n* (*for walls*) reboco; (*also*: **~ of Paris**) gesso; (*BRIT: also*: **sticking ~**) esparadrapo, band-aid *m* ▷ *vt* rebocar; (*cover*): **to ~ with** encher *or* cobrir de
plastic ['plæstɪk] *n* plástico ▷ *adj* de plástico; **plastic bag** *n* sacola de plástico; **plastic surgery** *n* cirurgia plástica
plate [pleɪt] *n* prato, chapa; (*dental*) chapa; (*in book*) gravura; **gold/silver ~** placa de ouro/prata
plateau ['plætəu] (*pl* **~s** *or* **~x**) *n* planalto

platform ['plætfɔ:m] *n* (*Rail*) plataforma (*BR*), cais *m* (*PT*); (*at meeting*) tribuna; (*raised structure: for landing etc*) plataforma; (*BRIT: of bus*) plataforma; (*Pol*) programa *m* partidário
platinum ['plætɪnəm] *n* platina
plausible ['plɔ:zɪbl] *adj* plausível; (*person*) convincente
play [pleɪ] *n* (*Theatre*) obra, peça ▷ *vt* jogar; (*team*) jogar contra; (*music*) tocar; (*role*) fazer o papel de ▷ *vi* (*music*) tocar; (*frolic*) brincar; **to ~ safe** não se arriscar, não correr riscos; **play down** *vt* minimizar; **play up** *vi* (*person*) dar trabalho; (*TV, car*) estar com defeito; **player** *n* jogador(a) *m/f*; (*Theatre*) ator (atriz) *m/f*; (*Mus*) músico(-a); **playful** *adj* brincalhão(-lhona); **playground** *n* (*in park*) playground *m*; (*in school*) pátio de recreio; **playgroup** *n* espécie de jardim de infância; **playing card** *n* carta de baralho; **playing field** *n* campo de esportes (*BR*) *or* jogos (*PT*); **playtime** *n* (*Sch*) recreio; **playwright** *n* dramaturgo(-a)
plea [pli:] *n* (*request*) apelo, petição *f*; (*Law*) defesa
plead [pli:d] *vt* (*Law*) defender, advogar; (*give as excuse*) alegar ▷ *vi* (*Law*) declarar-se; (*beg*): **to ~ with sb** suplicar *or* rogar a alguém
pleasant ['plɛznt] *adj* agradável; (*person*) simpático
please [pli:z] *excl* por favor ▷ *vt* agradar a, dar prazer a ▷ *vi* agradar, dar prazer; (*think fit*): **do as you ~** faça o que *or* como quiser; **~ yourself!** (*inf*) como você quiser!, você que sabe!; **pleased** *adj* (*happy*): **pleased (with)** satisfeito (com); **pleased to meet you** prazer (em conhecê-lo)
pleasure ['plɛʒər] *n* prazer *m*; **"it's a ~"** "não tem de quê"
pleat [pli:t] *n* prega
pledge [plɛdʒ] *n* (*promise*) promessa ▷ *vt* prometer; **to ~ support for sb** empenhar-se a apoiar alguém
plentiful ['plɛntɪful] *adj* abundante
plenty ['plɛntɪ] *n*: **~ of** (*food, money*) bastante; (*jobs, people*) muitos(-as)
pliers ['plaɪəz] *npl* alicate *m*
plod [plɔd] *vi* caminhar pesadamente; (*fig*) trabalhar laboriosamente
plonk [plɔŋk] (*inf*) *n* (*BRIT: wine*) zurrapa ▷ *vt*: **to ~ sth down** deixar cair algo (pesadamente)

plot [plɔt] n (scheme) conspiração f,
complô m; (of story, play) enredo, trama;
(of land) lote m ▷ vt (conspire) tramar,
planejar (BR), planear (PT); (Aviat, Naut,
Math) plotar ▷ vi conspirar; **a vegetable
~** (BRIT) uma horta
plough [plau] (US **plow**) n arado ▷ vt
arar; **to ~ money into** investir dinheiro
em; **plough through** vt fus abrir
caminho por; **ploughman's lunch** (BRIT)
n lanche de pão, queijo e picles
ploy [plɔɪ] n estratagema m
pluck [plʌk] vt (fruit) colher; (musical
instrument) dedilhar; (bird) depenar
▷ n coragem f, punho m; **to ~ one's
eyebrows** fazer as sobrancelhas; **to ~ up
courage** criar coragem
plug [plʌg] n (Elec) tomada (BR),
ficha (PT); (in sink) tampa; (Aut: also:
spark(ing) ~) vela (de ignição) ▷ vt (hole)
tapar; (inf: advertise) fazer propaganda
de; **plug in** vt (Elec) ligar
plum [plʌm] n (fruit) ameixa ▷ cpd (inf): **a
~ job** um emprego jóia
plumber ['plʌməʳ] n bombeiro(-a) (BR),
encanador(a) m/f(BR), canalizador(a)
m/f(PT)
plumbing ['plʌmɪŋ] n (trade) ofício de
encanador; (piping) encanamento
plummet ['plʌmɪt] vi: **to ~ (down)** (bird,
aircraft) cair rapidamente; (price) baixar
rapidamente
plump [plʌmp] adj roliço, rechonchudo
▷ vi: **to ~ for** (inf: choose) escolher, optar
por; **plump up** vt (cushion) afofar
plunge [plʌndʒ] n (dive) salto; (fig) queda
▷ vt (hand, knife) enfiar, meter ▷ vi (fall,
fig) cair; (dive) mergulhar; **to take the ~**
topar a parada
plural ['pluərl] adj plural ▷ n plural m
plus [plʌs] n (also: **~ sign**) sinal m de
adição ▷ prep mais; **ten/twenty ~**
dez/vinte e tantos
ply [plaɪ] n (of wool) fio ▷ vt (a trade)
exercer ▷ vi (ship) ir e vir; **to ~ sb with
drink/questions** bombardear alguém
com bebidas/perguntas; **plywood** n
madeira compensada
p.m. adv abbr (= post meridiem) da tarde,
da noite
PMT n abbr (= premenstrual tension) TPM f,
tensão f pré-menstrual
pneumatic drill n perfuratriz f
poach [pəutʃ] vt (cook: fish) escaldar;
(: eggs) fazer pochê (BR), escalfar (PT);
(steal) furtar ▷ vi caçar (or pescar) em

propriedade alheia
pocket ['pɔkɪt] n bolso; (fig: small area)
pedaço ▷ vt meter no bolso; (steal)
embolsar; **to be out of ~** (BRIT) perder,
ter prejuízo; **pocketbook** (US) n carteira;
pocket money n dinheiro para despesas
miúdas; (for child) mesada
pod [pɔd] n vagem f
podcast ['pɔdkɑ:st] n pocast m;
podcasting ['pɔdkɑ:stɪŋ] n
podcasting m
podiatrist [pɔ'di:ətrɪst] (US) n
pedicuro(-a)
poem ['pəuɪm] n poema m
poet ['pəuɪt] n poeta (poetisa) m/f;
poetic [pəu'etɪk] adj poético; **poetry**
['pəuɪtrɪ] n poesia
point [pɔɪnt] n ponto; (of needle etc)
ponta; (purpose) finalidade f, (significant
part) ponto principal; (position) lugar m,
posição f; (moment) momento; (stage)
estágio; (Elec: also: **power ~**) tomada;
(also: **decimal ~**): **2 ~ 3 (2.3)** dois vírgula
três ▷ vt mostrar; (gun etc): **to ~ sth
at sb** apontar algo para alguém ▷ vi:
to ~ at apontar para; **points** npl (Aut)
platinado, contato; (Rail) agulhas fpl; **to
be on the ~ of doing sth** estar prestes a
or a ponto de fazer algo; **to make a ~ of**
fazer questão de, insistir em; **to get the
~** perceber; **to miss the ~** compreender
mal; **to come to the ~** ir ao assunto;
there's no ~ (in doing) não há razão
(para fazer); **point out** vt (in debate etc)
ressaltar; **point to** vt fus (fig) indicar;
point-blank adv categoricamente; (also:
at point-blank range) à queima-roupa;
pointed adj (stick etc) pontudo; (remark)
mordaz; **pointer** n (on chart) indicador
m; (on machine) ponteiro; (fig) dica;
pointless adj (useless) inútil; (senseless)
sem sentido; **point of view** n ponto de
vista
poison ['pɔɪzn] n veneno ▷ vt envenenar;
poisonous adj venenoso; (fumes etc)
tóxico
poke [pəuk] vt cutucar; (put): **to ~ sth
in(to)** enfiar or meter algo em; **poke
about** vi escarafunchar, espionar
poker ['pəukəʳ] n atiçador m (de brasas);
(Cards) pôquer m
Poland ['pəulənd] n Polônia
polar ['pəuləʳ] adj polar; **polar bear** n
urso polar
Pole [pəul] n polonês(-esa) m/f
pole [pəul] n vara; (Geo) pólo; (telegraph

pole) poste *m*; (*flagpole*) mastro; **pole bean** (*US*) *n* feijão-trepador *m*; **pole vault** *n* salto com vara

police [pə'liːs] *n* polícia ▷ *vt* policiar; **police car** *n* rádio-patrulha *f*; **policeman** (*irreg*) *n* policial *m* (*BR*), polícia *m* (*PT*); **police station** *n* delegacia (de polícia) (*BR*), esquadra (*PT*); **policewoman** (*irreg*) *n* policial *f* (feminina) (*BR*), mulher *f* polícia (*PT*)

policy ['pɔlɪsɪ] *n* política; (*also:* **insurance ~**) apólice *f*

polio ['pəʊlɪəʊ] *n* polio(mielite) *f*

Polish ['pəʊlɪʃ] *adj* polonês(-esa) ▷ *n* (*Ling*) polonês *m*

polish ['pɔlɪʃ] *n* (*for shoes*) graxa; (*for floor*) cera (para encerar); (*shine*) brilho; (*fig*) refinamento, requinte *m* ▷ *vt* (*shoes*) engraxar; (*make shiny*) lustrar, dar brilho a; **polish off** *vt* (*work*) dar os arremates a; (*food*) raspar

polite [pə'laɪt] *adj* educado; **politeness** *n* gentileza, cortesia

political [pə'lɪtɪkl] *adj* político

politician [pɔlɪ'tɪʃən] *n* político(-a)

politics ['pɔlɪtɪks] *n*, *npl* política

poll [pəʊl] *n* (*votes*) votação *f*; (*also:* **opinion ~**) pesquisa, sondagem *f* ▷ *vt* (*votes*) receber, obter

pollen ['pɔlən] *n* pólen *m*

pollute [pə'luːt] *vt* poluir; **pollution** *n* poluição *f*

polyester [pɔlɪ'estə'] *n* poliéster *m*

polystyrene [pɔlɪ'staɪriːn] *n* isopor® *m*

polythene ['pɔlɪθiːn] *n* politeno

pomegranate ['pɔmɪgrænɪt] *n* romã *f*

pond [pɔnd] *n* (*natural*) lago pequeno; (*artificial*) tanque *m*

ponder ['pɔndə'] *vt*, *vi* ponderar, meditar (sobre)

pony ['pəʊnɪ] *n* pônei *m*; **ponytail** *n* rabo-de-cavalo; **pony trekking** (*BRIT*) *n* excursão *f* em pônei

poodle ['puːdl] *n* cão-d'água *m*

pool [puːl] *n* (*puddle*) poça, charco; (*pond*) lago; (*also:* **swimming ~**) piscina; (*fig: of light*) feixe *m*; (*: of liquid*) poça; (*Sport*) sinuca ▷ *vt* juntar; **pools** *npl* (*football pools*) loteria esportiva (*BR*), totobola (*PT*); **typing** (*BRIT*) *or* **secretary** (*US*) ~ seção *f* de datilografia

poor [pʊə'] *adj* pobre; (*bad*) inferior, mau ▷ *npl*: **the ~os** pobres; **~ in** (*resources etc*) deficiente em; **poorly** *adj* adoentado, indisposto ▷ *adv* mal

pop [pɔp] *n* (*sound*) estalo, estouro;

(*Mus*) pop *m*; (*US: inf: father*) papai *m*; (*inf: fizzy drink*) bebida gasosa ▷ *vt*: **to ~ sth into/onto** *etc* (*put*) pôr em/sobre *etc* ▷ *vi* estourar; (*cork*) saltar; **pop in** *vi* dar um pulo; **pop out** *vi* dar uma saída; **pop up** *vi* surgir, aparecer inesperadamente; **popcorn** *n* pipoca

pope [pəʊp] *n* papa *m*

poplar ['pɔplə'] *n* álamo, choupo

poppy ['pɔpɪ] *n* papoula

popular ['pɔpjʊlə'] *adj* popular; (*person*) querido

population [pɔpjʊ'leɪʃən] *n* população *f*

porcelain ['pɔːslɪn] *n* porcelana

porch [pɔːtʃ] *n* pórtico; (*US: verandah*) varanda

pore [pɔː'] *n* poro ▷ *vi*: **to ~ over** examinar minuciosamente

pork [pɔːk] *n* carne *f* de porco

pornography [pɔː'nɔgrəfɪ] *n* pornografia

porridge ['pɔrɪdʒ] *n* mingau *m* (de aveia)

port [pɔːt] *n* (*harbour*) porto; (*Naut: left side*) bombordo; (*wine*) vinho do Porto; **~ of call** porto de escala

portable ['pɔːtəbl] *adj* portátil

porter ['pɔːtə'] *n* (*for luggage*) carregador *m*; (*doorkeeper*) porteiro

portfolio [pɔːt'fəʊlɪəʊ] *n* (*case*) pasta; (*Pol*) pasta ministerial; (*Finance*) carteira de ações ou títulos; (*of artist*) pasta, portfólio

portion ['pɔːʃən] *n* porção *f*, quinhão *m*; (*of food*) ração *f*

portrait ['pɔːtreɪt] *n* retrato

portray [pɔː'treɪ] *vt* retratar; (*act*) interpretar

Portugal ['pɔːtjʊgl] *n* Portugal *m* (*no article*)

Portuguese [pɔːtjʊ'giːz] *adj* português(-esa) ▷ *n inv* português(-esa) *m/f*; (*Ling*) português *m*

pose [pəʊz] *n* postura, pose *f* ▷ *vi* (*pretend*): **to ~ as** fazer-se passar por ▷ *vt* (*question*) fazer; (*problem*) causar; **to ~ for** (*painting*) posar para

posh [pɔʃ] (*inf*) *adj* fino, chique; (*upper-class*) de classe alta

position [pə'zɪʃən] *n* posição *f*; (*job*) cargo; (*situation*) situação *f* ▷ *vt* colocar, situar

positive ['pɔzɪtɪv] *adj* positivo; (*certain*) certo; (*definite*) definitivo

possess [pə'zes] *vt* possuir; **possession** *n* posse *f*, possessão *f*; **possessions** *npl* (*belongings*) pertences *mpl*; **to take**

possession of sth tomar posse de algo
possibility [pɔsɪ'bɪlɪtɪ] n possibilidade f;
(of sth happening) probabilidade f
possible ['pɔsɪbl] adj possível; **possibly**
adv pode ser, talvez; (surprise): **what
could they possibly want with me?**
o que eles podem querer comigo?;
(emphasizing effort): **they did everything
they possibly could** eles fizeram tudo
o que podiam; **I cannot possibly come**
estou impossibilitado de vir
post [pəust] n (BRIT: mail) correio;
(job) cargo, posto; (pole) poste m; (Mil)
nomeação f ▷ vt (BRIT: send by post) pôr
no correio; (: appoint): **to ~ to** destinar
a; **postage** n porte m, franquia; **postal
order** n vale m postal; **postbox** (BRIT) n
caixa de correio; **postcard** n cartão m
postal; **postcode** (BRIT) n código postal,
≈ CEP m (BR)
poster ['pəustə'] n cartaz m; (as
decoration) pôster m
postman ['pəustmən] (irreg) n carteiro
postmark ['pəustmɑːk] n carimbo do
correio
post office n (building) agência do
correio, correio; (organization) ≈ Empresa
Nacional dos Correios e Telégrafos (BR),
≈ Correios, Telégrafos e Telefones (PT)
postpone [pəs'pəun] vt adiar
posture ['pɔstʃə'] n postura; (fig) atitude f
pot [pɔt] n (for cooking) panela; (for
flowers) vaso; (container, teapot, coffeepot)
pote m; (inf: marijuana) maconha ▷ vt
(plant) plantar em vaso; **to go to ~** (inf)
arruinar-se, degringolar
potato [pə'teɪtəu] (pl **~es**) n batata;
potato peeler n descascador m de
batatas
potent ['pəutnt] adj poderoso; (drink)
forte; (man) potente
potential [pə'tɛnʃl] adj potencial ▷ n
potencial m
pothole ['pɔthəul] n (in road) buraco;
(BRIT: underground) caldeirão m, cova
potter ['pɔtə'] n (artistic) ceramista
m/f; (artisan) oleiro(-a) ▷ vi (BRIT):
to ~ around, ~ about ocupar-se
com pequenos trabalhos; **pottery** n
cerâmica; (factory) olaria
potty ['pɔtɪ] adj (inf: mad) maluco, doido
▷ n penico
pouch [pautʃ] n (Zool) bolsa; (for tobacco)
tabaqueira
poultry ['pəultrɪ] n aves fpl domésticas;
(meat) carne f de aves domésticas

pounce [pauns] vi: **to ~ on** lançar-se
sobre; (person) agarrar em; (fig: mistake
etc) apontar
pound [paund] n libra (weight = 453g,
16 ounces; money = 100 pence) ▷ vt (beat)
socar, esmurrar; (crush) triturar ▷ vi
(heart) bater
pour [pɔː'] vt despejar; (drink) servir ▷ vi
correr, jorrar; **pour away** vt esvaziar,
decantar; **pour in** vi (people) entrar
numa enxurrada; (information) chegar
numa enxurrada; **pour off** vt esvaziar,
decantar; **pour out** vi (people) sair
aos borbotões ▷ vt (drink) servir; (fig)
extravasar; **pouring** ['pɔːrɪŋ] adj:
pouring rain chuva torrencial
pout [paut] vi fazer beicinho or biquinho
poverty ['pɔvətɪ] n pobreza, miséria
powder ['paudə'] n pó m; (face powder)
pó-de-arroz m ▷ vt (face) empoar, passar
pó em; **powdered milk** n leite m em pó
power ['pauə'] n poder m; (of explosion,
engine) força, potência; (ability) poder,
poderio; (electricity) força; **to be in ~** estar
no poder; **power cut** (BRIT) n corte m
de energia, blecaute m (BR); **powerful**
adj poderoso; (engine) potente; (body)
vigoroso; (blow) violento; (argument)
convincente; (emotion) intenso;
powerless adj impotente; **power point**
(BRIT) n tomada; **power station** n
central f elétrica
PR n abbr = public relations
practical ['præktɪkl] adj prático;
practical joke n brincadeira, peça
practice ['præktɪs] n (habit, Rel) costume
m, hábito; (exercise) prática; (of profession)
exercício; (training) treinamento; (Med)
consultório; (Law) escritório ▷ vt, vi (US)
= **practise**; **in ~** na prática; **out of ~**
destreinado
practise ['præktɪs] (US **practice**) vt
praticar; (profession) exercer; (sport)
treinar ▷ vi (doctor) ter consultório;
(lawyer) ter escritório; (train) treinar,
praticar
practitioner [præk'tɪʃənə'] n (Med)
médico(-a)
prairie ['preərɪ] n campina, pradaria
praise [preɪz] n louvor m; (admiration)
elogio ▷ vt elogiar, louvar
pram [præm] (BRIT) n carrinho de bebê
prank [præŋk] n travessura, peça
prawn [prɔːn] n pitu m; (small)
camarão m
pray [preɪ] vi: **to ~ for/that** rezar por/

para que; **prayer** [prɛəʳ] n (activity) reza; (words) oração f, prece f
preach [priːtʃ] vt pregar ▷ vi pregar; (pej) catequizar
precede [prɪˈsiːd] vt preceder
precedent [ˈprɛsɪdənt] n precedente m
preceding [prɪˈsiːdɪŋ] adj anterior
precinct [ˈpriːsɪŋkt] n (us: district) distrito policial; **precincts** npl (of large building) arredores mpl; **pedestrian ~** (BRIT) zona para pedestres (BR) or peões (PT); **shopping ~** (BRIT) zona comercial
precious [ˈprɛʃəs] adj precioso
precise [prɪˈsaɪs] adj exato, preciso; (plans) detalhado
predecessor [ˈpriːdɪsɛsəʳ] n predecessor(a) m/f, antepassado(-a)
predicament [prɪˈdɪkəmənt] n situação f difícil, apuro
predict [prɪˈdɪkt] vt prever, predizer, prognosticar; **predictable** adj previsível
predominantly [prɪˈdɔmɪnəntlɪ] adv predominantemente, na maioria
preface [ˈprɛfəs] n prefácio
prefect [ˈpriːfɛkt] n (BRIT: Sch) monitor(a) m/f, tutor(a) m/f; (in Brazil) prefeito(-a)
prefer [prɪˈfəːʳ] vt preferir; **preferably** [ˈprɛfrəblɪ] adv de preferência
prefix [ˈpriːfɪks] n prefixo
pregnancy [ˈprɛgnənsɪ] n gravidez f; (animal) prenhez f
pregnant [ˈprɛgnənt] adj grávida; (animal) prenha
prehistoric [priːhɪsˈtɔrɪk] adj pré-histórico
prejudice [ˈprɛdʒudɪs] n preconceito; **prejudiced** adj cheio de preconceitos; **to be prejudiced against sb/sth** estar com prevenção contra alguém/algo
premature [ˈprɛmətʃuəʳ] adj prematuro
première [ˈprɛmɪɛəʳ] n estréia
premium [ˈpriːmɪəm] n prêmio; **to be at a ~** ser caro
premonition [prɛməˈnɪʃən] n presságio, pressentimento
preoccupied [priːˈɔkjupaɪd] adj preocupado
prepaid [priːˈpeɪd] adj com porte pago
preparation [prɛpəˈreɪʃən] n preparação f; **preparations** npl (arrangements) preparativos mpl
prepare [prɪˈpɛəʳ] vt preparar ▷ vi: **to ~ for** preparar-se or aprontar-se para; **~d to** disposto a; **~d for** pronto para
preposition [prɛpəˈzɪʃən] n preposição f

prerequisite [priːˈrɛkwɪzɪt] n pré-requisito, condição f prévia
prescribe [prɪˈskraɪb] vt prescrever; (Med) receitar
prescription [prɪˈskrɪpʃən] n receita
presence [ˈprɛzns] n presença; (spirit) espectro
present [(adj, n) ˈprɛznt, (vb) prɪˈzɛnt] adj presente; (current) atual ▷ n presente m; (actuality): **the ~** o presente ▷ vt (give): **to ~ sth to sb, to ~ sb with sth** entregar algo a alguém; (information, programme, threat) apresentar; (describe) descrever; **at ~** no momento, agora; **to give sb a ~** presentear alguém; **presentation** [prɛznˈteɪʃən] n apresentação f; (ceremony) entrega; (of plan etc) exposição f; **present-day** adj atual, de hoje; **presenter** n apresentador(a) m/f; **presently** adv (after) logo após; (soon) logo, em breve; (now) atualmente
preservative [prɪˈzəːvətɪv] n conservante m
preserve [prɪˈzəːv] vt (situation) conservar, manter; (building, manuscript) preservar; (food) pôr em conserva ▷ n (often pl: jam) geléia; (: fruit) compota, conserva
president [ˈprɛzɪdənt] n presidente(-a) m/f; **presidential** [prɛzɪˈdɛnʃl] adj presidencial
press [prɛs] n (printer's) imprensa, prelo; (newspapers) imprensa; (of switch) pressão f ▷ vt apertar; (clothes: iron) passar; (put pressure on: person) assediar; (insist): **to ~ sth on sb** insistir para que alguém aceite algo ▷ vi (squeeze) apertar; (pressurize): **to ~ for** pressionar por; **we are ~ed for time/money** estamos com pouco tempo/dinheiro; **press on** vi continuar; **pressing** adj urgente; **press stud** (BRIT) n botão m de pressão; **press-up** (BRIT) n flexão f
pressure [ˈprɛʃəʳ] n pressão f; **to put ~ on sb (to do sth)** pressionar alguém (a fazer algo); **pressure cooker** n panela de pressão
prestige [prɛsˈtiːʒ] n prestígio
presume [prɪˈzjuːm] vt supor
pretence [prɪˈtɛns] (us **pretense**) n pretensão f; **under false ~s** por meios fraudulentos
pretend [prɪˈtɛnd] vt, vi fingir
pretense [prɪˈtɛns] (us) n = **pretence**
pretty [ˈprɪtɪ] adj bonito ▷ adv (quite) bastante

prevail [prɪ'veɪl] vi triunfar; (be current)
imperar
prevalent ['prɛvələnt] adj (common)
predominante
prevent [prɪ'vɛnt] vt impedir
preview ['pri:vju:] n pré-estréia
previous ['pri:vɪəs] adj (earlier) anterior;
previously adv (before) previamente; (in
the past) anteriormente
prey [preɪ] n presa ▷ vi: **to ~ on** (feed
on) alimentar-se de; **it was ~ing on his
mind** preocupava-o, atormentava-o
price [praɪs] n preço ▷ vt fixar o preço de;
priceless adj inestimável; (inf: amusing)
impagável
prick [prɪk] n picada ▷ vt picar; (make
hole in) furar; **to ~ up one's ears** aguçar
os ouvidos
pride [praɪd] n orgulho; (pej) soberba
▷ vt: **to ~ o.s. on** orgulhar-se de
priest [pri:st] n (Christian) padre m; (non-
Christian) sacerdote m
primarily ['praɪmərɪlɪ] adv
principalmente
primary ['praɪmərɪ] adj primário; (first
in importance) principal ▷ n (us: election)
eleição f primária; **primary school** (BRIT)
n escola primária

※ **PRIMARY SCHOOL**
※
※ As **primary schools** da Grã-Bretanha
※ acolhem crianças de 5 a 11 anos.
※ Assinalam o início do ciclo escolar
※ obrigatório e são compostas de duas
※ partes: a pré-escola (infant school) e o
※ primário (junior school).

prime [praɪm] adj primeiro, principal;
(excellent) de primeira ▷ vt (wood)
imprimar; (fig) aprontar, preparar ▷ n:
in the ~ of life na primavera da vida;
~ example exemplo típico; **prime
minister** n primeiro-ministro (primeira-
ministra)
primitive ['prɪmɪtɪv] adj primitivo;
(crude) rudimentar
primrose ['prɪmrəuz] n prímula,
primavera
prince [prɪns] n príncipe m
princess [prɪn'sɛs] n princesa
principal ['prɪnsɪpl] adj principal ▷ n (of
school, college) diretor(a) m/f
principle ['prɪnsɪpl] n princípio; **in ~** em
princípio; **on ~** por princípio
print [prɪnt] n (letters) letra de forma;

(fabric) estampado; (Art) estampa,
gravura; (Phot) cópia; (footprint) pegada;
(fingerprint) impressão f digital ▷ vt
imprimir; (write in capitals) escrever em
letra de imprensa; **out of ~** esgotado;
printer n (person) impressor(a) m/f;
(firm) gráfica; (machine) impressora;
printout n (Comput) cópia impressa
prior ['praɪəʳ] adj anterior, prévio; (more
important) prioritário; **~ to doing** antes
de fazer
priority [praɪ'ɔrɪtɪ] n prioridade f
prison ['prɪzn] n prisão f ▷ cpd
carcerário; **prisoner** n (in prison)
preso(-a), presidiário(-a); (under arrest)
detido(-a)
privacy ['prɪvəsɪ] n isolamento, solidão f,
privacidade f
private ['praɪvɪt] adj privado; (personal)
particular; (confidential) confidencial,
reservado; (personal: belongings) pessoal;
(: thoughts, plans) secreto, íntimo;
(place) isolado; (quiet: person) reservado;
(intimate) íntimo ▷ n soldado raso; **"~"**
(on envelope) "confidencial"; (on door)
"privativo"; **in ~** em particular; **privatize**
vt privatizar
privilege ['prɪvɪlɪdʒ] n privilégio
prize [praɪz] n prêmio ▷ adj de primeira
classe ▷ vt valorizar; **prizewinner** n
premiado(-a)
pro [prəu] n (Sport) profissional m/f ▷ prep
a favor de; **the ~s and cons** os prós e os
contras
probability [prɔbə'bɪlɪtɪ] n
probabilidade f
probable ['prɔbəbl] adj provável;
(plausible) verossímil
probation [prə'beɪʃən] n: **on ~** (employee)
em estágio probatório; (Law) em
liberdade condicional
probe [prəub] n (Med, Space) sonda;
(enquiry) pesquisa ▷ vt investigar,
esquadrinhar
problem ['prɔbləm] n problema m
procedure [prə'si:dʒəʳ] n procedimento;
(method) método, processo
proceed [prə'si:d] vi (do afterwards): **to ~
to do sth** passar a fazer algo; (continue):
to ~ (with) continuar or prosseguir
(com); (activity) continuar; (go) ir em
direção a, dirigir-se a; **proceedings** npl
evento, acontecimento; (Law) processo;
proceeds ['prəusi:dz] npl produto,
proventos mpl
process ['prəusɛs] n processo ▷ vt

processar; **procession** [prə'sɛʃən] n desfile m, procissão f; **funeral procession** cortejo fúnebre

proclaim [prə'kleɪm] vt anunciar

prod [prɔd] vt empurrar; (with finger, stick) cutucar ▷ n empurrão m; cotovelada; espetada

produce [(n) 'prɔdjuːs, (vb) prə'djuːs] n (Agr) produtos mpl agrícolas ▷ vt produzir; (cause) provocar; (evidence, argument) apresentar, mostrar; (show) apresentar, exibir; (Theatre) pôr em cena or em cartaz; **producer** n (Theatre) diretor(a) m/f; (Agr, Cinema, of record) produtor(a) m/f; (country) produtor m

product ['prɔdʌkt] n produto

production [prə'dʌkʃən] n produção f; (of electricity) geração f; (Theatre) encenação f

profession [prə'fɛʃən] n profissão f; (people) classe f; **professional** n profissional m/f ▷ adj profissional; (work) de profissional

professor [prə'fɛsəʳ] n (BRIT) catedrático(-a); (US, CANADA) professor(a) m/f

profile ['prəufaɪl] n perfil m

profit ['prɔfɪt] n (Comm) lucro ▷ vi: **to ~ by** or **from** (benefit) aproveitar-se de, tirar proveito de; **profitable** adj (Econ) lucrativo, rendoso

profound [prə'faund] adj profundo

programme ['prəugræm] (US **program**) n programa m ▷ vt programar; **programming** (US **programing**) n (Comput) programação f

progress [(n) 'prəugrɛs, (vb) prə'grɛs] n progresso ▷ vi progredir, avançar; **in ~** em andamento; **progressive** [prə'grɛsɪv] adj progressivo; (person) progressista

prohibit [prə'hɪbɪt] vt proibir

project [(n) 'prɔdʒɛkt, (vb) prə'dʒɛkt] n projeto; (Sch: research) pesquisa ▷ vt projetar; (figure) estimar ▷ vi (stick out) ressaltar, sobressair

projection [prə'dʒɛkʃən] n projeção f; (overhang) saliência

projector [prə'dʒɛktəʳ] n projetor m

prolong [prə'lɔŋ] vt prolongar

prom [prɔm] n abbr = **promenade**; **promenade concert**; (US: ball) baile m de estudantes

promenade [prɔmə'nɑːd] n (by sea) passeio (à orla marítima); **promenade concert** (BRIT) n concerto (de música clássica); ver quadro

prominent ['prɔmɪnənt] adj (standing out) proeminente; (important) eminente, notório

promise ['prɔmɪs] n promessa; (hope) esperança ▷ vt, vi prometer; **promising** adj promissor(a), promotedor(a)

promote [prə'məut] vt promover; (product) promover, fazer propaganda de; **promotion** n promoção f

prompt [prɔmpt] adj pronto, rápido ▷ adv (exactly) em ponto, pontualmente ▷ n (Comput) sinal m de orientação, prompt m ▷ vt (urge) incitar, impelir; (cause) provocar, ocasionar; **to ~ sb to do sth** induzir alguém a fazer algo; **promptly** adv imediatamente; (exactly) pontualmente

prone [prəun] adj (lying) de bruços; **~ to** propenso a, predisposto a

pronoun ['prəunaun] n pronome m

pronounce [prə'nauns] vt pronunciar; (verdict, opinion) declarar

pronunciation [prənʌnsɪ'eɪʃən] n pronúncia

proof [pruːf] n prova ▷ adj: **~ against** à prova de

prop [prɔp] n suporte m, escora; (fig) amparo, apoio ▷ vt (also: **~ up**) apoiar, escorar; (lean): **to ~ sth against** apoiar algo contra

propaganda [prɔpə'gændə] n propaganda

proper ['prɔpəʳ] adj (correct) correto; (socially acceptable) respeitável, digno;

(*authentic*) genuíno, autêntico; (*referring to place*): **the village ~** a cidadezinha propriamente dita; **properly** adv (*eat, study*) bem; (*behave*) decentemente

property ['prɔpətɪ] n propriedade f; (*goods*) posses fpl, bens mpl; (*buildings*) imóveis mpl

prophet ['prɔfɪt] n profeta m/f

proportion [prə'pɔːʃən] n proporção f; **proportional** adj proporcional

proposal [prə'pəuzl] n proposta; (*of marriage*) pedido

propose [prə'pəuz] vt propor; (*toast*) erguer ▷ vi propor casamento; **to ~ to do** propor-se fazer

proposition [prɔpə'zɪʃən] n proposta, proposição f; (*offer*) oferta

proprietor [prə'praɪətəʳ] n proprietário(-a), dono(-a)

prose [prəuz] n prosa

prosecute ['prɔsɪkjuːt] vt processar; **prosecution** [prɔsɪ'kjuːʃən] n acusação f; (*accusing side*) autor m da demanda

prospect [(*n*) 'prɔspɛkt, (*vb*) prə'spɛkt] n (*chance*) probabilidade f; (*outlook*) perspectiva ▷ vi: **to ~ (for)** prospectar (por); **prospects** fpl (*for work etc*) perspectivas fpl

prospectus [prə'spɛktəs] n prospecto, programa m

prostitute ['prɔstɪtjuːt] n prostituta; **male ~** prostituto

protect [prə'tɛkt] vt proteger; **protection** n proteção f; **protective** adj protetor(a)

protein ['prəutiːn] n proteína

protest [(*n*) 'prəutɛst, (*vb*) prə'tɛst] n protesto ▷ vi protestar ▷ vt insistir

Protestant ['prɔtɪstənt] adj, n protestante m/f

protester [prə'tɛstəʳ] n manifestante m/f

proud [praud] adj orgulhoso; (*pej*) vaidoso, soberbo

prove [pruːv] vt comprovar ▷ vi: **to ~ (to be) correct** etc vir a ser correto etc; **to ~ o.s.** pôr-se à prova

proverb ['prɔvəːb] n provérbio

provide [prə'vaɪd] vt fornecer, proporcionar; **to ~ sb with sth** fornecer alguém de algo, fornecer algo a alguém; **provide for** vt fus (*person*) prover à subsistência de

providing [prə'vaɪdɪŋ] conj: **~ (that)** contanto que (+ sub)

province ['prɔvɪns] n província; (*fig*)

esfera; **provincial** [prə'vɪnʃəl] adj provincial; (*pej*) provinciano

provision [prə'vɪʒən] n (*supplying*) abastecimento; (*in contract*) cláusula, condição f; **provisions** npl (*food*) mantimentos mpl; **provisional** adj provisório, interino; (*agreement, licence*) provisório

provocative [prə'vɔkətɪv] adj provocante; (*sexually*) excitante

provoke [prə'vəuk] vt provocar; (*cause*) causar

prowl [praul] vi (*also*: **~ about, ~ around**) rondar, andar à espreita ▷ n: **on the ~** de ronda, rondando

proxy ['prɔksɪ] n: **by ~** por procuração

prudent ['pruːdənt] adj prudente

prune [pruːn] n ameixa seca ▷ vt podar

pry [praɪ] vi: **to ~ (into)** intrometer-se (em)

PS n abbr (= *postscript*) PS m

pseudonym n pseudônimo

psychiatrist [saɪ'kaɪətrɪst] n psiquiatra m/f

psychic ['saɪkɪk] adj psíquico; (*also*: **~al**: *person*) sensível a forças psíquicas

psychologist [saɪ'kɔlədʒɪst] n psicólogo(-a)

psychology [saɪ'kɔlədʒɪ] n psicologia

PTO abbr (= *please turn over*) v.v., vire

pub [pʌb] n abbr (= *public house*) pub m, bar m, botequim m

◉ **PUB**

◉ Um **pub** geralmente consiste em duas
◉ salas: uma (*the lounge*) é bastante
◉ confortável, com poltronas e bancos
◉ estofados, enquanto a outra (*the public*
◉ *bar*) é simplesmente um bar onde a
◉ consumação é em geral mais barata.
◉ O *public bar* é muitas vezes também
◉ um salão de jogos, dos quais os mais
◉ comuns são os dardos, dominó e
◉ bilhar. Atualmente muitos pubs
◉ servem refeições, sobretudo na hora
◉ do almoço, e essa é a única hora em
◉ que a entrada de crianças é permitida,
◉ desde que estejam acompanhadas por
◉ adultos. Em geral os pubs funcionam
◉ das 11 às 23 horas, mas isso pode variar
◉ de acordo com sua permissão de
◉ funcionamento; alguns pubs fecham
◉ à tarde.

public ['pʌblɪk] adj público ▷ n público;

in ~ em público; **to make** ~ tornar público; **public convenience** (BRIT) n banheiro público; **public holiday** n feriado; **public house** (BRIT) n pub m, bar m, taberna

publicity [pʌb'lisiti] n publicidade f

publicize ['pʌblisaiz] vt divulgar

public school n (BRIT) escola particular; (US) escola pública

public transport (US **public transportation**) n transporte m coletivo

publish ['pʌbliʃ] vt publicar; **publisher** n editor(a) m/f; (company) editora; **publishing** n a indústria editorial

pudding ['pudiŋ] n (BRIT: dessert) sobremesa; (cake) pudim m, doce m; **black** (BRIT) or **blood** (US) ~ morcela

puddle ['pʌdl] n poça

puff [pʌf] n sopro; (of cigarette) baforada; (of air, smoke) lufada ▷ vt: **to** ~ **one's pipe** tirar baforadas do cachimbo ▷ vi (pant) arquejar; **puff out** (cheeks) encher; **puff pastry** (US **puff paste**) n massa folhada

pull [pul] n (tug): **to give sth a** ~ dar um puxão em algo ▷ vt puxar; (trigger) apertar; (curtain, blind) fechar ▷ vi puxar, dar um puxão; **to** ~ **to pieces** picar em pedacinhos; **to** ~ **one's punches** não usar toda a força; **to** ~ **one's weight** fazer a sua parte; **to** ~ **o.s. together** recompor-se; **to** ~ **sb's leg** (fig) brincar com alguém, sacanear alguém (inf); **pull apart** vt (break) romper; **pull down** vt (building) demolir, derrubar; **pull in** vi (Aut: at the kerb) encostar; (Rail) chegar (na plataforma); **pull off** vt tirar; (fig: deal etc) acertar; **pull out** vi (Aut: from kerb) sair; (Rail) partir ▷ vt tirar, arrancar; **pull over** vi (Aut) encostar; **pull through** vi (Med) sobreviver; **pull up** vi (stop) deter-se, parar ▷ vt levantar; (uproot) desarraigar, arrancar

pulley ['puli] n roldana

pullover ['puləuvəʳ] n pulôver m

pulp [pʌlp] n (of fruit) polpa

pulse [pʌls] n (Anat) pulso; (of music, engine) cadência; (Bot) legume m

pump [pʌmp] n bomba; (shoe) sapatilha (de dança) ▷ vt bombear; **pump up** vt encher

pumpkin ['pʌmpkin] n abóbora

pun [pʌn] n jogo de palavras, trocadilho

punch [pʌntʃ] n (blow) soco, murro; (tool) punção m; (drink) ponche m ▷ vt (hit): **to**

~ **sb/sth** esmurrar or socar alguém/algo

punctual ['pʌŋktjuəl] adj pontual

punish ['pʌniʃ] vt punir, castigar; **punishment** n castigo, punição f

punk [pʌŋk] n (also: ~ **rocker**) punk m/f; (also: ~ **rock**) punk m; (US: inf: hoodlum) pinta-brava m

pupil ['pju:pl] n aluno(-a); (of eye) pupila

puppet ['pʌpit] n marionete f, títere m; (fig) fantoche m

puppy ['pʌpi] n cachorro, cachorrinho (BR)

purchase ['pə:tʃis] n compra ▷ vt comprar

pure [pjuəʳ] adj puro

purple ['pə:pl] adj roxo, purpúreo

purpose ['pə:pəs] n propósito, objetivo; **on** ~ de propósito

purse [pə:s] n (BRIT) carteira; (US) bolsa ▷ vt enrugar, franzir

pursue [pə'sju:] vt perseguir; (fig: activity) exercer; (: interest, plan) dedicar-se a; (: result) lutar por

pursuit [pə'sju:t] n caça; (fig) busca; (pastime) passatempo

push [puʃ] n empurrão m; (of button) aperto ▷ vt empurrar; (button) apertar; (promote) promover ▷ vi empurrar; (press) apertar; (fig): **to** ~ **for** reivindicar; **push aside** vt afastar com a mão; **push off** (inf) vi dar o fora; **push on** vi prosseguir; **push through** vi abrir caminho ▷ vt (measure) forçar a aceitação de; **push up** vt forçar a alta de; **pushchair** (BRIT) n carrinho; **pusher** n (also: **drug pusher**) traficante m/f or passador(a) m/f de drogas; **push-up** (US) n flexão f

put [put] (pt, pp ~) vt pôr, colocar; (put into) meter; (person: in institution etc) internar; (say) dizer, expressar; (case) expor; (question) fazer; (estimate) avaliar, calcular; (write, type etc) colocar; **put about** vt (rumour) espalhar; **put across** vt (ideas) comunicar; **put away** vt guardar; **put back** vt (replace) repor; (postpone) adiar; (delay) atrasar; **put by** vt (money etc) poupar, pôr de lado; **put down** vt pôr em; (animal) sacrificar; (in writing) anotar, inscrever; (revolt etc) sufocar; (attribute: case, view): **to put sth down to** atribuir algo a; **put forward** vt apresentar, propor; **put in** vt (application, complaint) apresentar; (time, effort) investir, gastar; **put off** vt adiar, protelar; (discourage) desencorajar; **put**

on vt (clothes, make-up, dinner) pôr; (light) acender; (play) encenar; (weight) ganhar; (brake) aplicar; (record, video, kettle) ligar; (accent, manner) assumir; **put out** vt (take out) colocar fora; (fire, cigarette, light) apagar; (one's hand) estender; (inf: person): **to be put out** estar aborrecido; **put through** vt (call) transferir; (plan) ser aprovado; **put up** vt (raise) levantar, erguer; (hang) prender; (build) construir, edificar; (tent) armar; (increase) aumentar; (accommodate) hospedar; **put up with** vt fus suportar, agüentar

puzzle ['pʌzl] n charada; (jigsaw) quebra-cabeça m; (also: **crossword ~**) palavras cruzadas fpl; (mystery) mistério ▷ vt desconcertar, confundir ▷ vi: **to ~ over sth** tentar entender algo; **puzzling** adj intrigante, confuso

pyjamas [pɪ'dʒɑːməz] (US **pajamas**) npl pijama m or f

pylon ['paɪlən] n pilono, poste m, torre f

pyramid ['pɪrəmɪd] n pirâmide f

Pyrenees [pɪrə'niːz] npl: **the ~** os Pirineus

q

quack [kwæk] n grasnido; (pej: doctor) curandeiro(-a), charlatão(-tã) m/f

quaint [kweɪnt] adj (ideas) curioso, esquisito; (village etc) pitoresco

quake [kweɪk] vi (with fear) tremer ▷ n abbr = **earthquake**

qualification [kwɔlɪfɪ'keɪʃən] n (skill, quality) qualificação f; (reservation) restrição f, ressalva; (modification) modificação f; (often pl: degree, training) título, qualificação

qualified ['kwɔlɪfaɪd] adj (trained) habilitado, qualificado; (professionally) diplomado; (fit): **~ to** apto para, capaz de; (limited) limitado

qualify ['kwɔlɪfaɪ] vt (modify) modificar ▷ vi: **to ~ (as)** (pass examination(s)) formar-se or diplomar-se (em); **to ~ (for)** reunir os requisitos (para)

quality ['kwɔlɪtɪ] n qualidade f; **quality (news)papers** npl ver quadro

❖ **QUALITY (NEWS)PAPERS**
❖
❖ Os **quality (news)papers** (ou **quality**
❖ **press**) englobam os jornais "sérios",
❖ diários ou semanais, em oposição
❖ aos jornais populares (tabloid press).

- Esses jornais visam a um público que
- procura informações detalhadas sobre
- uma grande variedade de assuntos
- e que está disposto a dedicar um
- bom tempo à leitura. Geralmente os
- **quality newspapers** são publicados
- em formato grande.

quantity ['kwɒntɪtɪ] n quantidade f

quarantine ['kwɒrntiːn] n quarentena

quarrel ['kwɒrl] n (argument) discussão f
▷ vi: **to ~ (with)** brigar (com)

quarry ['kwɒrɪ] n (for stone) pedreira;
(animal) presa, caça

quart [kwɔːt] n quarto de galão (1.136 l)

quarter ['kwɔːtəʳ] n quarto, quarta
parte f; (of year) trimestre m; (district)
bairro; (US: 25 cents) (moeda de) 25
centavos mpl de dólar ▷ vt dividir em
quatro; (Mil: lodge) aquartelar; **quarters**
npl (Mil) quartel m; (living quarters)
alojamento; **a ~ of an hour** um quarto
de hora; **quarter final** n quarta de
final; **quarterly** adj trimestral ▷ adv
trimestralmente

quay [kiː] n (also: **~side**) cais m

queasy ['kwiːzɪ] adj (sickly) enjoado

queen [kwiːn] n rainha; (also: **~ bee**)
abelha-mestra, rainha; (Cards etc) dama

queer [kwɪəʳ] adj (odd) esquisito,
estranho ▷ n (inf: homosexual) bicha m
(BR), maricas m inv (PT)

quench [kwɛntʃ] vt: **to ~ one's thirst**
matar a sede

query ['kwɪərɪ] n pergunta ▷ vt
questionar

quest [kwɛst] n busca

question ['kwɛstʃən] n pergunta;
(doubt) dúvida; (issue) questão f; (in
text) problema m ▷ vt (doubt) duvidar;
(interrogate) interrogar, inquirir; **beyond
~** sem dúvida; **out of the ~** fora de
cogitação, impossível; **questionable** adj
discutível; (doubtful) duvidoso; **question
mark** n ponto de interrogação;
questionnaire [kwɛstʃə'nɛəʳ] n
questionário

queue [kjuː] (BRIT) n fila (BR), bicha (PT)
▷ vi (also: **~ up**) fazer fila (BR) or bicha (PT)

quick [kwɪk] adj rápido; (agile) ágil; (mind)
sagaz, despachado ▷ n: **to cut sb to
the ~** ferir alguém; **be ~!** ande depressa!,
vai rápido!; **quickly** adv rapidamente,
depressa

quid [kwɪd] (BRIT: inf) n inv libra

quiet ['kwaɪət] adj (voice, music) baixo;

(peaceful: place) tranqüilo; (person: calm)
calmo; (not noisy: place) silencioso;
(: person) calado; (silent) silencioso;
(ceremony) discreto ▷ n (peacefulness)
sossego; (silence) quietude f ▷ vt, vi (US)
= **quieten**; **quieten** (also: **quieten
down**) vi (grow calm) acalmar-se; (grow
silent) calar-se ▷ vt tranqüilizar; fazer
calar; **quietly** adv silenciosamente;
(talk) baixo

quilt [kwɪlt] n acolchoado, colcha;
(continental) ~ (BRIT) edredom m (BR),
edredão m (PT)

quit [kwɪt] (pt, pp ~ or ~**ted**) vt (smoking
etc) parar; (job) deixar; (premises)
desocupar ▷ vi desistir; (resign) demitir-
se, deixar o emprego

quite [kwaɪt] adv (rather) bastante;
(entirely) completamente, totalmente;
that's not ~ big enough não é
suficientemente grande; **~ a few of
them** um bom número deles; **~ (so)!**
exatamente!, isso mesmo!

quiver ['kwɪvəʳ] vi estremecer

quiz [kwɪz] n concurso (de cultura geral)
▷ vt interrogar

quota ['kwəʊtə] n cota, quota

quotation [kwəʊ'teɪʃən] n citação f;
(estimate) orçamento; **quotation marks**
npl aspas fpl

quote [kwəʊt] n citação f; (estimate)
orçamento ▷ vt citar; (price) propor;
(figure, example) citar, dar; **quotes** npl
aspas fpl

r

rabbi ['ræbaɪ] n rabino
rabbit ['ræbɪt] n coelho
rabies ['reɪbiːz] n raiva
RAC (BRIT) n abbr (= Royal Automobile Club) ≈ TCB m (BR), ≈ ACP m (PT)
race [reɪs] n corrida; (species) raça ▷ vt (horse) fazer correr ▷ vi (compete) competir; (run) correr; (pulse) bater rapidamente; **race car** (US) n = **racing car**; **racecourse** n hipódromo; **racehorse** n cavalo de corridas; **racetrack** n pista de corridas; (for cars) autódromo
racing ['reɪsɪŋ] n corrida; **racing car** (BRIT) n carro de corrida; **racing driver** (BRIT) n piloto(-a) de corrida
racism ['reɪsɪzəm] n racismo; **racist** (pej) adj, n racista m/f
rack [ræk] n (also: **luggage ~**) bagageiro; (shelf) estante f; (also: **roof ~**) xalmas fpl, porta-bagagem m; (dish rack) secador m de prato ▷ vt: **~ed by** (pain, anxiety) tomado por; **to ~ one's brains** quebrar a cabeça
racket ['rækɪt] n (for tennis) raquete f (BR), raqueta (PT); (noise) barulheira, zoeira; (swindle) negócio ilegal, fraude f
racquet ['rækɪt] n raquete f (BR),

raqueta (PT)
radiation [reɪdɪ'eɪʃən] n radiação f
radiator ['reɪdɪeɪtəʳ] n radiador m
radical ['rædɪkl] adj radical
radio ['reɪdɪəu] n rádio ▷ vt: **to ~ sb** comunicar-se por rádio com alguém
radio... [reɪdɪəu] prefix radio...
radioactive ['reɪdɪəu'æktɪv] adj radioativo
radio station n emissora, estação f de rádio
radish ['rædɪʃ] n rabanete m
raffle ['ræfl] n rifa
raft [rɑːft] n balsa
rag [ræg] n trapo; (torn cloth) farrapo; (pej: newspaper) jornaleco; (University) atividades estudantis beneficentes; **rags** npl (torn clothes) trapos mpl, farrapos mpl
rage [reɪdʒ] n (fury) raiva, furor m ▷ vi (person) estar furioso; (storm) assolar; (debate) continuar calorosamente; **it's all the ~** é a última moda
ragged ['rægɪd] adj (edge) irregular, desigual; (clothes) puído, gasto; (appearance) esfarrapado, andrajoso
raid [reɪd] n (Mil) incursão f; (criminal) assalto; (attack) ataque m; (by police) batida ▷ vt invadir, atacar; assaltar; atacar; fazer uma batida em
rail [reɪl] n (on stair) corrimão m; (on bridge) parapeito, antepara; (of ship) amurada; **rails** npl (for train) trilhos mpl; **by ~** de trem (BR), por caminho de ferro (PT); **railing(s)** n(pl) grade f; **railroad** (US) n = **railway**; **railway** n estrada (BR) or caminho (PT) de ferro; **railway line** (BRIT) n linha de trem (BR) or de comboio (PT); **railway station** (BRIT) n estação f ferroviária (BR) or de caminho de ferro (PT)
rain [reɪn] n chuva ▷ vi chover; **it's ~ing** está chovendo (BR), está a chover (PT); **rainbow** n arco-íris m inv; **raincoat** n impermeável m, capa de chuva; **raindrop** n gota de chuva; **rainfall** n chuva; (measurement) pluviosidade f; **rainforest** n floresta tropical; **rainy** adj chuvoso; **a rainy day** um dia de chuva
raise [reɪz] n aumento ▷ vt (lift) levantar; (salary, production) aumentar; (morale, standards) melhorar; (doubts) suscitar, despertar; (cattle, family) criar; (crop) cultivar, plantar; (army) recrutar, alistar; (funds) angariar; (loan) levantar, obter; **to ~ one's voice** levantar a voz
raisin ['reɪzn] n passa, uva seca
rake [reɪk] n ancinho ▷ vt (garden)

revolver or limpar com o ancinho; (with machine gun) varrer

rally ['rælɪ] n (Pol etc) comício; (Aut) rally m, rali m; (Tennis) rebatida ▷ vt reunir ▷ vi reorganizar-se; (sick person, Stock Exchange) recuperar-se; **rally round** vt fus dar apoio a

RAM [ræm] n abbr (Comput: = random access memory) RAM f

ram [ræm] n carneiro ▷ vt (push) cravar; (crash into) colidir com

ramble ['ræmbl] n caminhada, excursão f a pé ▷ vi caminhar; (talk: also: ~ on) divagar; **rambler** n caminhante m/f; (Bot) roseira trepadeira; **rambling** adj (speech) desconexo, incoerente; (house) cheio de recantos; (plant) rastejante

ramp [ræmp] n (incline) rampa; **on/off ~** (us: Aut) entrada (para a rodovia)/saída da rodovia

rampage [ræm'peɪdʒ] n: **to be on the ~** alvoroçar-se

ran [ræn] pt of **run**

ranch [rɑ:ntʃ] n rancho, fazenda, estância

random ['rændəm] adj ao acaso, casual, fortuito; (Comput, Math) aleatório ▷ n: **at ~** a esmo, aleatoriamente

rang [ræŋ] pt of **ring**

range [reɪndʒ] n (of mountains) cadeia, cordilheira; (of missile) alcance m; (of voice) extensão f; (series) série f; (of products) gama, sortimento; (Mil: also: **shooting ~**) estande m; (also: **kitchen ~**) fogão m ▷ vt (place) colocar; (arrange) arrumar, ordenar ▷ vi: **to ~ over** (extend) estender-se por; **to ~ from ... to ...** variar de ... a ..., oscilar entre ... e ...

rank [ræŋk] n (row) fila, fileira; (Mil) posto; (status) categoria, posição f; (BRIT: also: **taxi ~**) ponto de táxi ▷ vi: **to ~ among** figurar entre ▷ adj fétido, malcheiroso; **the ~ and file** (fig) a gente comum

ransom ['rænsəm] n resgate m; **to hold sb to ~** (fig) encostar alguém contra a parede

rant [rænt] vi arengar

rap [ræp] vt bater de leve ▷ n: **~ (music)** rap m

rape [reɪp] n estupro; (Bot) colza ▷ vt violentar, estuprar

rapid ['ræpɪd] adj rápido

rapids ['ræpɪdz] npl (Geo) cachoeira

rapist ['reɪpɪst] n estuprador m

rapport [ræ'pɔ:ʳ] n harmonia, afinidade f

rare [rɛəʳ] adj raro; (Culin: steak) mal passado

rascal ['rɑ:skl] n maroto, malandro

rash [ræʃ] adj impetuoso, precipitado ▷ n (Med) exantema m, erupção f cutânea; (of events) série f, torrente f

rasher ['ræʃəʳ] n fatia fina

raspberry ['rɑ:zbərɪ] n framboesa

rat [ræt] n rato (BR), ratazana (PT)

rate [reɪt] n (ratio) razão f; (price) preço, taxa; (: of hotel) diária; (of interest, change) taxa; (speed) velocidade f ▷ vt (value) taxar; (estimate) avaliar; **rates** npl (BRIT) imposto predial e territorial; (fees) pagamento; **to ~ sb/sth as** considerar alguém/algo como

rather ['rɑ:ðəʳ] adv (somewhat) um tanto, meio; (: to some extent) até certo ponto; (more accurately): **or ~** ou melhor; **it's ~ expensive** (quite) é meio caro; (too) é caro demais; **there's ~ a lot** há bastante or muito; **I would ~ go** preferiria or preferia ir; **or ~** ou melhor

ratio ['reɪʃɪəu] n razão f, proporção f

ration ['ræʃən] n ração f ▷ vt racionar; **rations** npl (Mil) mantimentos mpl, víveres mpl

rational ['ræʃənl] adj lógico; (person) sensato, razoável

rat race n: **the ~** a competição acirrada na vida moderna

rattle ['rætl] n (of door) batida; (of train etc) chocalhada; (of coins) chocalhar m; (object: for baby) chocalho; ▷ vi (small objects) tamborilar; **there's ~ a lot** há bastante ▷ vt sacudir, fazer bater; (unnerve) perturbar

rave [reɪv] vi (in anger) encolerizar-se; (Med) delirar; (with enthusiasm): **to ~ about** vibrar com

raven ['reɪvən] n corvo

ravine [rə'vi:n] n ravina, barranco

raw [rɔ:] adj (uncooked) cru(a); (not processed) bruto; (sore) vivo; (inexperienced) inexperiente, novato; (weather) muito frio

ray [reɪ] n raio; **~ of hope** fio de esperança

razor ['reɪzəʳ] n (open) navalha; (safety razor) aparelho de barbear; (electric) aparelho de barbear elétrico; **razor blade** n gilete m (BR), lâmina de barbear (PT)

Rd abbr = **road**

re [ri:] prep referente a

reach [ri:tʃ] n alcance m; (of river etc) extensão f ▷ vt alcançar; (arrive at:

place) chegar em; (*: agreement*) chegar
a; (*by telephone*) conseguir falar com
▷ *vi* (*stretch out*) esticar-se; **within ~**
ao alcance (da mão); **out of ~** fora de
alcance; **reach out** *vt* (*hand*) esticar ▷ *vi*:
to reach out for sth estender *or* esticar a
mão para pegar (em) algo
react [riːˈækt] *vi* reagir; **reaction**
n reação *f*; **reactions** *npl* (*reflexes*)
reflexos *mpl*
reactor [riːˈæktəʳ] *n* (*also*: **nuclear ~**)
reator *m* nuclear
read [riːd, (*pt, pp*) rɛd] (*pt, pp* **~**) *vi* ler ▷ *vt*
ler; (*understand*) compreender; (*study*)
estudar; **read out** *vt* ler em voz alta;
reader *n* leitor(a) *m/f*; (*book*) livro de
leituras *n*; (BRIT: *at university*) professor(a)
m/f adjunto(-a)
readily [ˈrɛdɪlɪ] *adv* (*willingly*) de boa
vontade; (*easily*) facilmente; (*quickly*) sem
demora, prontamente
reading [ˈriːdɪŋ] *n* leitura; (*on instrument*)
indicação *f*, registro (BR), registo (PT)
ready [ˈrɛdɪ] *adj* pronto, preparado;
(*willing*) disposto; (*available*) disponível
▷ *n*: **at the ~** (*Mil*) pronto para atirar;
to get ~ *vi* preparar-se ▷ *vt* preparar;
ready-made *adj* (*já*) feito; (*clothes*)
pronto
real [rɪəl] *adj* real; (*genuine*) verdadeiro,
autêntico; **in ~ terms** em termos reais;
real estate *n* bens *mpl* imobiliários or de
raiz; **realistic** [rɪəˈlɪstɪk] *adj* realista
reality [riːˈælɪtɪ] *n* realidade *f*; **reality TV**
n reality TV *f*
realization [rɪəlaɪˈzeɪʃən] *n*
(*fulfilment*) realização *f*; (*understanding*)
compreensão *f*; (*Comm*) conversão *f* em
dinheiro, realização
realize [ˈrɪəlaɪz] *vt* (*understand*) perceber;
(*fulfil, Comm*) realizar
really [ˈrɪəlɪ] *adv* (*for emphasis*) realmente;
(*actually*): **what ~ happened?** o que
aconteceu na verdade?; **~?** (*interest*)
é mesmo?; (*surprise*) verdade!; **~!**
(*annoyance*) realmente!
realm [rɛlm] *n* reino; (*fig*) esfera, domínio
realtor [ˈrɪəltəʳ] (US) *n* corretor(a) *m/f* de
imóveis (BR), agente *m/f* imobiliário(-a)
(PT)
reappear [riːəˈpɪəʳ] *vi* reaparecer
rear [rɪəʳ] *adj* traseiro, de trás ▷ *n* traseira
▷ *vt* criar ▷ *vi* (*also*: **~ up**) empinar-se
reason [ˈriːzn] *n* (*cause*) razão *f*; (*ability*)
raciocínio; (*sense*) bom-senso ▷ *vi*: **to
~ with sb** argumentar com alguém,

persuadir alguém; **it stands to ~ that**
é razoável *or* lógico que; **reasonable**
adj (*fair*) razoável; (*sensible*) sensato;
reasonably *adv* razoavelmente;
sensatamente; **reasoning** *n* raciocínio
reassurance [riːəˈʃuərəns] *n* garantia
reassure [riːəˈʃuəʳ] *vt* tranquilizar; **to ~
sb of** reafirmar a confiança de alguém
acerca de
rebate [ˈriːbeɪt] *n* devolução *f*
rebel [(*n*) ˈrɛbl, (*vb*) rɪˈbɛl] *n* rebelde *m/f*
▷ *vi* rebelar-se; **rebellious** [rɪˈbɛljəs] *adj*
insurreto; (*behaviour*) rebelde
recall [(*vb*) rɪˈkɔːl, (*n*) ˈriːkɔl] *vt* recordar,
lembrar; (*parliament*) reunir de volta;
(*ambassador*) chamar de volta ▷ *n*
(*memory*) recordação *f*, lembrança; (*of
ambassador*) chamada (de volta)
receipt [rɪˈsiːt] *n* recibo; (*act*)
recebimento (BR), recepção *f* (PT);
receipts *npl* (*Comm*) receitas *fpl*
receive [rɪˈsiːv] *vt* receber; (*guest*)
acolher; (*wound, criticism*) sofrer;
receiver *n* (*Tel*) fone *m* (BR), auscultador
m (PT); (*Radio, TV*) receptor *m*; (*of stolen
goods*) receptador(a) *m/f*; (*Comm*)
curador(a) *m/f* síndico(-a) de massa
falida
recent [ˈriːsnt] *adj* recente; **recently**
adv recentemente; (*in recent times*)
ultimamente
reception [rɪˈsɛpʃən] *n* recepção *f*;
(*welcome*) acolhida; **reception desk** *n*
(mesa de) recepção *f*; **receptionist** *n*
recepcionista *m/f*
recession [rɪˈsɛʃən] *n* recessão *f*
recipe [ˈrɛsɪpɪ] *n* receita
recipient [rɪˈsɪpɪənt] *n* recipiente
m/f, recebedor(a) *m/f*; (*of letter*)
destinatário(-a)
recite [rɪˈsaɪt] *vt* recitar
reckless [ˈrɛkləs] *adj* (*driver*) imprudente;
(*speed*) imprudente, excessivo; (*spending*)
irresponsável
reckon [ˈrɛkən] *vt* (*calculate*) calcular,
contar; (*think*): **I ~ that ...** acho que ...;
reckon on *vt fus* contar com
reclaim [rɪˈkleɪm] *vt* (*demand back*)
reivindicar; (*land: from sea*) aterrar; (*waste
materials*) reaproveitar
recline [rɪˈklaɪn] *vi* reclinar-se
recognition [rɛkəɡˈnɪʃən] *n*
reconhecimento
recognize [ˈrɛkəɡnaɪz] *vt* reconhecer
recommend [rɛkəˈmɛnd] *vt*
recomendar

reconcile ['rεkənsaɪl] vt reconciliar; (*facts*) conciliar, harmonizar; **to ~ o.s. to sth** resignar-se a or conformar-se com algo

reconsider [ri:kən'sɪdər] vt reconsiderar

reconstruct [ri:kən'strʌkt] vt reconstruir; (*event*) reconstituir

record [(n, adj)'rεkɔ:d, (vb) rɪ'kɔ:d] n (*Mus*) disco; (*of meeting etc*) ata, minuta; (*Comput, of attendance*) registro (BR), registo (PT); (*written*) história; (*also:* **criminal ~**) antecedentes mpl; (*Sport*) recorde m ▷ vt (*write down*) anotar; (*temperature, speed*) registrar (BR), registar (PT); (*Mus: song etc*) gravar ▷ adj: **in ~ time** num tempo recorde; **off the ~** adj confidencial ▷ adv confidencialmente; **recorder** n (*Mus*) flauta; **recording** n (*Mus*) gravação f; **record player** n toca-discos m inv (BR), gira-discos m inv (PT)

recover [rɪ'kʌvər] vt recuperar ▷ vi (*from illness*) recuperar-se; (*from shock*) refazer-se; **recovery** n recuperação f; (*Med*) recuperação, melhora

recreation [rεkrɪ'eɪʃən] n recreio

recruit [rɪ'kru:t] n recruta m/f; (*in company*) novato(-a) ▷ vt recrutar

rectangle ['rεktæŋgl] n retângulo

rector ['rεktər] n (*Rel*) pároco

recur [rɪ'kə:r] vi repetir-se, ocorrer outra vez; (*symptoms*) reaparecer

recyclable [ri:'saɪkləbl] adj reciclável

recycle [ri:'saɪkl] vt reciclar; **recycling** n reciclagem f

red [rεd] n vermelho; (*Pol: pej*) vermelho(-a) ▷ adj vermelho; (*hair*) ruivo; (*wine*) tinto; **to be in the ~** não ter fundos; **Red Cross** n Cruz f Vermelha

redeem [rɪ'di:m] vt (*Rel*) redimir; (*sth in pawn*) tirar do prego; (*loan, fig: situation*) salvar

red: red-haired adj ruivo; **redhead** n ruivo(-a); **red-hot** adj incandescente

red-light district n zona (de meretrício)

reduce [rɪ'dju:s] vt reduzir; (*lower*) rebaixar; **"~ speed now"** (*Aut*) "diminua a velocidade"; **to ~ sb to** (*silence, begging*) levar alguém a; (*tears*) reduzir alguém a; **reduction** [rɪ'dʌkʃən] n redução f; (*of price*) abatimento

redundancy [rɪ'dʌndənsɪ] (BRIT) n (*dismissal*) demissão f; (*unemployment*) desemprego

redundant [rɪ'dʌndnt] adj (BRIT: *worker*) desempregado; (*detail, object*) redundante, supérfluo; **to be made ~** ficar desempregado or sem trabalho

reed [ri:d] n (*Bot*) junco; (*Mus: of clarinet etc*) palheta

reef [ri:f] n (*at sea*) recife m

reel [ri:l] n carretel m, bobina; (*of film*) rolo, filme m; (*on fishing-rod*) carretilha; (*dance*) dança típica da Escócia ▷ vi (*sway*) cambalear, oscilar; **reel in** vt puxar enrolando a linha

ref [rεf] (*inf*) n abbr = **referee**

refectory [rɪ'fεktərɪ] n refeitório

refer [rɪ'fə:r] vt (*matter, problem*): **to ~ sth to** submeter algo à apreciação de; (*person, patient*): **to ~ sb to** encaminhar alguém a ▷ vi: **to ~ to** referir-se or aludir a; (*consult*) recorrer a

referee [rεfə'ri:] n árbitro(-a); (BRIT: *for job application*) referência f ▷ vt apitar

reference ['rεfrəns] n referência; (*mention*) menção f; **with ~ to** com relação a; (*Comm: in letter*) com referência a

refill [(vb) ri:'fɪl, (n) 'ri:fɪl] vt reencher; (*lighter etc*) reabastecer ▷ n (*for pen*) carga nova

refine [rɪ'faɪn] vt refinar; **refined** adj refinado, culto

reflect [rɪ'flεkt] vt refletir ▷ vi (*think*) refletir, meditar; **it ~s badly/well on him** isso repercute mal/bem para ele; **reflection** n reflexo; (*thought, act*) reflexão f; (*criticism*): **reflection on** crítica de; **on reflection** pensando bem

reflex ['ri:flεks] adj reflexo ▷ n reflexo

reform [rɪ'fɔ:m] n reforma ▷ vt reformar

refrain [rɪ'freɪn] vi: **to ~ from doing** abster-se de fazer ▷ n estribilho, refrão m

refresh [rɪ'frεʃ] vt refrescar; **refreshing** adj refrescante; (*sleep*) repousante; **refreshments** npl bebidas fpl (não-alcoólicas) e guloseimas

refrigerator [rɪ'frɪdʒəreɪtər] n refrigerador m, geladeira (BR), frigorífico (PT)

refuel [ri:'fjʊəl] vi reabastecer

refuge ['rεfju:dʒ] n refúgio; **to take ~ in** refugiar-se em

refugee [rεfju'dʒi:] n refugiado(-a)

refund [(n) 'ri:fʌnd, (vb) rɪ'fʌnd] n reembolso ▷ vt devolver, reembolsar

refurbish [ri:'fə:bɪʃ] vt renovar

refusal [rɪ'fju:zəl] n recusa, negativa; **first ~** primeira opção

refuse[1] [rɪ'fju:z] vt recusar; (*order*) recusar-se a ▷ vi recusar-se, negar-se; (*horse*) recusar-se a pular a cerca

refuse² [ˈrɛfjuːs] n refugo, lixo
regain [rɪˈɡeɪn] vt recuperar, recobrar
regard [rɪˈɡɑːd] n (gaze) olhar m firme;
(attention) atenção f; (esteem) estima,
consideração f ▷ vt (consider) considerar;
to give one's ~s to dar lembranças a;
"with kindest ~s" "cordialmente"; **as ~s,
with ~ to** com relação a, com respeito a,
quanto a; **regarding** prep com relação
a; **regardless** adv apesar de tudo;
regardless of apesar de
regiment [ˈrɛdʒɪmənt] n regimento
region [ˈriːdʒən] n região f; **in the ~ of**
(fig) por volta de, ao redor de; **regional**
adj regional
register [ˈrɛdʒɪstəʳ] n registro (BR),
registo (PT); (Sch) chamada ▷ vt registrar
(BR), registar (PT); (subj: instrument)
marcar, indicar ▷ vi (at hotel) registrar-
se (BR), registar-se (PT); (for work)
candidatar-se; (as student) inscrever-se;
(make impression) causar impressão;
registered adj (letter, parcel) registrado
(BR), registado (PT)
registrar [ˈrɛdʒɪstrɑːʳ] n oficial m/f de
registro (BR) or registo (PT), escrivão(-vã)
m/f; (in college) funcionário(-a)
administrativo(-a) sênior; (in hospital)
médico(-a) sênior
registration [rɛdʒɪsˈtreɪʃən] n (act)
registro (BR), registo (PT); (Aut: also: ~
number) número da placa
regret [rɪˈɡrɛt] n desgosto, pesar m ▷ vt
lamentar; (repent of) arrepender-se de
regular [ˈrɛɡjuləʳ] adj regular; (frequent)
freqüente; (usual) habitual; (soldier) de
linha ▷ n habitual m/f; **regularly** adv
regularmente; (shaped) simetricamente;
(often) freqüentemente
regulate [ˈrɛɡjuleɪt] vt (speed) regular;
(spending) controlar; (Tech) regular,
ajustar; **regulation** [rɛɡjuˈleɪʃən] n
(rule) regra, regulamento; (adjustment)
ajuste m

rehearsal [rɪˈhəːsəl] n ensaio
rehearse [rɪˈhəːs] vt ensaiar
reign [reɪn] n reinado; (fig) domínio ▷ vi
reinar; imperar
reimburse [riːɪmˈbəːs] vt reembolsar
rein [reɪn] n (for horse) rédea
reindeer [ˈreɪndɪəʳ] n inv rena
reinforce [riːɪnˈfɔːs] vt reforçar
reinstate [riːɪnˈsteɪt] vt (worker)
readmitir; (tax, law) reintroduzir
reject [(n) ˈriːdʒɛkt, (vb) rɪˈdʒɛkt] n
(Comm) artigo defeituoso ▷ vt rejeitar;

(offer of help) recusar; (goods) refugar;
rejection n rejeição f; recusa
rejoice [rɪˈdʒɔɪs] vi: **to ~ at** or **over**
regozijar-se or alegrar-se de
relate [rɪˈleɪt] vt (tell) contar, relatar;
(connect): **to ~ sth to** relacionar algo com
▷ vi: **to ~ to** relacionar-se com; **~d to**
ligado a, relacionado a
relation [rɪˈleɪʃən] n (person) parente m/f;
(link) relação f; **relations** npl (dealings)
relações fpl; (relatives) parentes mpl;
relationship n relacionamento;
(between two things) relação f; (also:
family relationship) parentesco
relative [ˈrɛlətɪv] n parente m/f ▷ adj
relativo; **relatively** adv relativamente
relax [rɪˈlæks] vi (unwind) descontrair-
se; (muscle) relaxar-se ▷ vt (grip)
afrouxar; (control) relaxar; (mind, person)
descansar; **relaxation** [riːlækˈseɪʃən]
n (rest) descanso; (of muscle, control)
relaxamento; (of grip) afrouxamento;
(recreation) lazer m; **relaxed** adj relaxado;
(tranquil) descontraído
relay [ˈriːleɪ, (vb) rɪˈleɪ] n (race)
(corrida de) revezamento ▷ vt (message)
retransmitir
release [rɪˈliːs] n (from prison) libertação
f; (from obligation) liberação f; (of gas)
escape m; (of water) despejo; (of film,
book etc) lançamento ▷ vt (prisoner) pôr
em liberdade; (book, film) lançar; (report,
news) publicar; (gas etc) soltar; (free: from
wreckage etc) soltar; (Tech: catch, spring
etc) desengatar, desapertar
relegate [ˈrɛləɡeɪt] vt relegar; (Sport): **to
be ~d** ser rebaixado
relent [rɪˈlɛnt] vi (yield) ceder; **relentless**
adj (unceasing) contínuo; (determined)
implacável
relevant [ˈrɛləvənt] adj pertinente; **~ to**
relacionado com
reliable [rɪˈlaɪəbl] adj (person, firm: digno)
de confiança, confiável, sério; (method,
machine) seguro; (news) fidedigno
relic [ˈrɛlɪk] n (Rel) relíquia; (of the past)
vestígio
relief [rɪˈliːf] n alívio; (help, supplies)
ajuda, socorro; (Art, Geo) relevo
relieve [rɪˈliːv] vt (pain, fear) aliviar; (bring
help to) ajudar, socorrer; (take over from:
gen) substituir, revezar; (: guard) render;
to ~ sb of sth (load) tirar algo de alguém;
(duties) destituir alguém de algo; **to ~
o.s.** fazer as necessidades
religion [rɪˈlɪdʒən] n religião f; **religious**

adj religioso

relish ['rɛlɪʃ] *n* (Culin) condimento, tempero; (*enjoyment*) entusiasmo ▷ *vt* (*food etc*) saborear; (*thought*) ver com satisfação

reluctant [rɪ'lʌktənt] *adj* relutante; **reluctantly** *adv* relutantemente, de má vontade

rely on [rɪ'laɪ-] *vt fus* confiar em, contar com; (*be dependent on*) depender de

remain [rɪ'meɪn] *vi* (*survive*) sobreviver; (*stay*) ficar, permanecer; (*be left*) sobrar; (*continue*) continuar; **remainder** *n* resto, restante *m*; **remaining** *adj* restante; **remains** *npl* (*of body*) restos *mpl*; (*of meal*) sobras *fpl*; (*of building*) ruínas *fpl*

remand [rɪ'mɑːnd] *n*: **on ~** sob prisão preventiva ▷ *vt*: **to be ~ed in custody** continuar sob prisão preventiva, manter sob custódia

remark [rɪ'mɑːk] *n* observação *f*, comentário ▷ *vt* comentar; **remarkable** *adj* (*outstanding*) extraordinário

remarry [riː'mærɪ] *vi* casar-se de novo

remedy ['rɛmədɪ] *n*: **~ (for)** remédio (contra *ora*) ▷ *vt* remediar

remember [rɪ'mɛmbəʳ] *vt* lembrar-se de, lembrar; (*bear in mind*) ter em mente; (*send greetings*): **~ me to her** dê lembranças a ela

remembrance [rɪ'mɛmbrəns] *n* (*memory*) memória; (*souvenir*) lembrança, recordação *f*; **Remembrance Sunday** or **Day** *n* Dia *m* do Armistício; *ver quadro*

❀ **REMEMBRANCE SUNDAY**
❀
❀ **Remembrance Sunday** ou
❀ **Remembrance Day** é o domingo
❀ mais próximo do dia 11 de novembro,
❀ dia em que a Primeira Guerra Mundial
❀ terminou oficialmente e no qual se
❀ homenageia as vítimas das duas
❀ guerras mundiais. Nessa ocasião são
❀ observados dois minutos de silêncio
❀ às 11 horas, horário da assinatura do
❀ armistício com a Alemanha em 1918.
❀ Nos dias anteriores, papoulas de
❀ papel são vendidas por associações
❀ de caridade e a renda é revertida aos
❀ ex-combatentes e suas famílias.

remind [rɪ'maɪnd] *vt*: **to ~ sb to do sth** lembrar a alguém que tem de fazer algo; **to ~ sb of sth** lembrar algo a alguém, lembrar alguém de algo; **reminder** *n*

lembrança; (*letter*) carta de advertência

remnant ['rɛmnənt] *n* resto; (*of cloth*) retalho; **remnants** *npl* (*Comm*) retalhos *mpl*

remorse [rɪ'mɔːs] *n* remorso

remote [rɪ'məut] *adj* remoto; (*person*) reservado, afastado; **remote control** *n* controle *m* remoto; **remotely** *adv* remotamente; (*slightly*) levemente

removal [rɪ'muːvəl] *n* (*taking away*) remoção *f*; (*BRIT: from house*) mudança; (*from office: sacking*) afastamento, demissão *f*; (*Med*) extração *f*; **removal van** (*BRIT*) *n* caminhão *m* (*BR*) or camião *m* (*PT*) de mudanças

remove [rɪ'muːv] *vt* tirar, retirar; (*clothing*) tirar; (*stain*) remover; (*employee*) afastar, demitir; (*name from list, obstacle*) eliminar, remover; (*doubt, abuse*) afastar; (*Med*) extrair, extirpar

render ['rɛndəʳ] *vt* (*thanks*) trazer; (*service*) prestar; (*make*) fazer, tornar

rendezvous ['rɔndɪvuː] *n* encontro; (*place*) ponto de encontro

renew [rɪ'njuː] *vt* retomar, recomeçar; (*loan etc*) prorrogar; (*negotiations*) reatar

renovate ['rɛnəveɪt] *vt* renovar; (*house*) reformar

rent [rɛnt] *n* aluguel *m* (*BR*), aluguer *m* (*PT*) ▷ *vt* (*also*: **~ out**) alugar; **rental** *n* (*for television, car*) aluguel *m* (*BR*), aluguer *m* (*PT*)

rep [rɛp] *n abbr* (*Comm*) = **representative**; (*Theatre*) = **repertory**

repair [rɪ'pɛəʳ] *n* reparação *f*, conserto ▷ *vt* consertar; **in good/bad ~** em bom/mau estado; **repair kit** *n* caixa de ferramentas

repay [riː'peɪ] (*irreg*) *vt* (*money*) reembolsar, restituir; (*person*) pagar de volta; (*debt*) saldar, liquidar; (*sb's efforts*) corresponder, retribuir; (*favour*) retribuir; **repayment** *n* reembolso; (*of debt*) pagamento

repeat [rɪ'piːt] *n* (*Radio, TV*) repetição *f* ▷ *vt* repetir; (*Comm: order*) renovar ▷ *vi* repetir-se

repetitive [rɪ'pɛtɪtɪv] *adj* repetitivo

replace [rɪ'pleɪs] *vt* (*put back*) repor, devolver; (*take the place of*) substituir; **replacement** *n* (*substitution*) substituição *f*; (*substitute*) substituto(-a)

replay ['riːpleɪ] *n* (*of match*) partida decisiva; (*TV: also*: **action ~**) replay *m*

replica ['rɛplɪkə] *n* réplica, cópia, reprodução *f*

reply [rɪ'plaɪ] n resposta ▷ vi responder

report [rɪ'pɔːt] n relatório; (Press etc) reportagem f; (BRIT: also: **school ~**) boletim m escolar; (of gun) estampido, detonação f ▷ vt informar sobre; (Press etc) fazer uma reportagem sobre; (bring to notice) comunicar, anunciar ▷ vi (make a report): **to ~ (on)** apresentar um relatório (sobre); (present o.s.): **to ~ (to sb)** apresentar-se (a alguém); (be responsible to): **to ~ to sb** obedecer as ordens de alguém; **report card** (US, Scottish) n boletim m escolar; **reportedly** adv: **she is reportedly living in Spain** dizem que ela mora na Espanha; **reporter** n repórter m/f

represent [rɛprɪ'zɛnt] vt representar; (constitute) constituir; (Comm) ser representante de; **representation** [rɛprɪzɛn'teɪʃən] n representação f; (picture, statue) representação, retrato; (petition) petição f; **representations** npl (protest) reclamação f, protesto; **representative** [rɛprɪ'zɛntətɪv] n representante m/f; (US: Pol) deputado(-a) ▷ adj: **representative (of)** representativo (de)

repress [rɪ'prɛs] vt reprimir; **repression** n repressão f

reproduce [riːprə'djuːs] vt reproduzir ▷ vi reproduzir-se

reptile ['rɛptaɪl] n réptil m

republic [rɪ'pʌblɪk] n república; **republican** adj, n republicano(-a); (US: Pol): **Republican** membro(-a) do Partido Republicano

reputable ['rɛpjutəbl] adj (make etc) bem conceituado, de confiança; (person) honrado, respeitável

reputation [rɛpju'teɪʃən] n reputação f

request [rɪ'kwɛst] n pedido; (formal) petição f ▷ vt: **to ~ sth of** or **from sb** pedir algo a alguém; (formally) solicitar algo a alguém; **request stop** (BRIT) n (for bus) parada não obrigatória

require [rɪ'kwaɪəʳ] vt (need: subj: person) precisar de, necessitar; (: thing, situation) requerer, exigir; (want) pedir; (order): **to ~ sb to do sth/sth of sb** exigir que alguém faça algo/algo de alguém; **requirement** n (need) necessidade f; (want) pedido

rescue ['rɛskjuː] n salvamento, resgate m ▷ vt: **to ~ (from)** resgatar (de); (save, fig) salvar (de)

research [rɪ'səːtʃ] n pesquisa ▷ vt pesquisar

resemblance [rɪ'zɛmbləns] n semelhança

resemble [rɪ'zɛmbl] vt parecer-se com

resent [rɪ'zɛnt] vt (attitude) ressentir-se de; (person) estar ressentido com; **resentful** adj ressentido

reservation [rɛzə'veɪʃən] n reserva

reserve [rɪ'zəːv] n reserva; (Sport) suplente m/f, reserva m/f (BR) ▷ vt reservar; **reserves** npl (Mil) (tropas fpl da) reserva; (Comm) reserva; **in ~** de reserva; **reserved** adj reservado

residence ['rɛzɪdəns] n residência; (formal: home) domicílio; **residence permit** (BRIT) n autorização f de residência

resident ['rɛzɪdənt] n (of country, town) habitante m/f; (in hotel) hóspede m/f ▷ adj (population) permanente; (doctor) interno, residente; **residential** [rɛzɪ'dɛnʃəl] adj residencial

residue ['rɛzɪdjuː] n resto

resign [rɪ'zaɪn] vt renunciar a, demitir-se de ▷ vi: **to ~ (from)** demitir-se (de); **to ~ o.s. to** resignar-se a; **resignation** [rɛzɪg'neɪʃən] n demissão f; (state of mind) resignação f

resist [rɪ'zɪst] vt resistir a

resolution [rɛzə'luːʃən] n resolução f; (of problem) solução f

resolve [rɪ'zɔlv] n resolução f ▷ vt resolver ▷ vi: **to ~ to do** resolver-se a fazer

resort [rɪ'zɔːt] n local m turístico, estação f de veraneio; (recourse) recurso ▷ vi: **to ~ to** recorrer a; **in the last ~** em último caso, em última instância

resource [rɪ'sɔːs] n (raw material) recurso natural; **resources** npl (coal, money, energy) recursos mpl; **resourceful** adj engenhoso, habilidoso

respect [rɪs'pɛkt] n respeito ▷ vt respeitar; **respects** npl (greetings) cumprimentos mpl; **respectable** adj respeitável; (large) considerável; (result, player) razoável; **respectful** adj respeitoso

respond [rɪs'pɔnd] vi (answer) responder; (react) reagir; **response** n resposta; reação f

responsibility [rɪspɔnsɪ'bɪlɪtɪ] n responsabilidade f; (duty) dever m

responsible [rɪs'pɔnsɪbl] adj sério, responsável; (job) de responsabilidade; (liable): **~ (for)** responsável (por)

responsive [rɪs'pɔnsɪv] adj receptivo

rest [rɛst] *n* descanso, repouso; (*pause*) pausa, intervalo; (*support*) apoio; (*remainder*) resto; (*Mus*) pausa ▷ *vi* descansar; (*stop*) parar; (*be supported*): **to ~ on** apoiar-se em ▷ *vt* descansar; (*lean*): **to ~ sth on/against** apoiar algo em *or* sobre/contra; **the ~ of them** os outros; **it ~s with him to do it** cabe a ele fazê-lo

restaurant ['rɛstərɔn] *n* restaurante *m*; **restaurant car** (*BRIT*) *n* vagão-restaurante *m*

restless ['rɛstlɪs] *adj* desassossegado, irrequieto

restore [rɪ'stɔːʳ] *vt* (*building, order*) restaurar; (*sth stolen*) restituir; (*health*) restabelecer

restrain [rɪs'treɪn] *vt* (*feeling*) reprimir; (*growth, inflation*) refrear; (*person*): **to ~ (from doing)** impedir (de fazer); **restraint** *n* (*restriction*) restrição *f*; (*moderation*) moderação *f*, comedimento; (*of style*) sobriedade *f*

restrict [rɪs'trɪkt] *vt* restringir, limitar; (*people, animals*) confinar; (*activities*) limitar; **restriction** *n* restrição *f*, limitação *f*

rest room (*US*) *n* banheiro (*BR*), lavabo (*PT*)

result [rɪ'zʌlt] *n* resultado ▷ *vi*: **to ~ in** resultar em; **as a ~ of** como resultado *or* conseqüência de

resume [rɪ'zjuːm] *vt* (*work, journey*) retomar, recomeçar ▷ *vi* recomeçar

résumé ['reɪzjuːmeɪ] *n* (*summary*) resumo; (*US: curriculum vitae*) curriculum vitae *m*, currículo

resuscitate [rɪ'sʌsɪteɪt] *vt* (*Med*) ressuscitar, reanimar

retail ['riːteɪl] *adj* a varejo (*BR*), a retalho (*PT*) ▷ *adv* a varejo (*BR*), a retalho (*PT*); **retailer** *n* varejista *m/f* (*BR*), retalhista *m/f* (*PT*)

retain [rɪ'teɪn] *vt* (*keep*) reter, conservar

retire [rɪ'taɪəʳ] *vi* aposentar-se; (*withdraw*) retirar-se; (*go to bed*) deitar-se; **retired** *adj* aposentado (*BR*), reformado (*PT*); **retirement** *n* aposentadoria (*BR*), reforma (*PT*)

retort [rɪ'tɔːt] *vi* replicar, retrucar

retreat [rɪ'triːt] *n* (*place*) retiro; (*act*) retirada ▷ *vi* retirar-se

retrieve [rɪ'triːv] *vt* (*sth lost*) reaver, recuperar; (*situation, honour*) salvar; (*error, loss*) reparar

retrospect ['rɛtrəspɛkt] *n*: **in ~** retrospectivamente, em retrospecto;

retrospective [rɛtrə'spɛktɪv] *adj* retrospectivo; (*law*) retroativo

return [rɪ'tɜːn] *n* regresso, volta; (*of sth stolen etc*) devolução *f*; (*Finance: from land, shares*) rendimento ▷ *cpd* (*journey*) de volta; (*BRIT*: *ticket*) de ida e volta; (*match*) de revanche ▷ *vi* voltar, regressar; (*symptoms*) voltar; (*regain*): **to ~ to** (*consciousness*) recobrar; (*power*) retornar a ▷ *vt* devolver; (*favour etc*) retribuir; (*verdict*) proferir, anunciar; (*Pol: candidate*) eleger; **returns** *npl* (*Comm*) receita; **in ~ (for)** em troca (de); **many happy ~s (of the day)!** parabéns!; **by ~ (of post)** por volta do correio

reunion [riː'juːnɪən] *n* (*family*) reunião *f*; (*two people, class*) reencontro

reunite [riːju:'naɪt] *vt* reunir; (*reconcile*) reconciliar

revamp ['riː'væmp] *vt* dar um jeito em

reveal [rɪ'viːl] *vt* revelar; (*make visible*) mostrar; **revealing** *adj* revelador(a)

revel ['rɛvl] *vi*: **to ~ in sth/in doing sth** deleitar-se com algo/em fazer algo

revenge [rɪ'vɛndʒ] *n* vingança, desforra; **to take ~ on** vingar-se de

revenue ['rɛvənju:] *n* receita, renda

reversal [rɪ'vəːsl] *n* (*of order*) reversão *f*; (*of direction*) mudança em sentido contrário; (*of decision*) revogação *f*; (*of roles*) inversão *f*

reverse [rɪ'vəːs] *n* (*opposite*) contrário; (*of cloth*) avesso; (*of coin*) reverso; (*of paper*) dorso; (*Aut: also: ~ gear*) marcha à ré (*BR*), marcha atrás (*PT*); (*setback*) revés *m*, derrota ▷ *adj* (*order*) inverso, oposto; (*direction*) contrário; (*process*) inverso ▷ *vt* inverter; (*position*) mudar; (*process, decision*) revogar; (*car*) dar marcha-ré em ▷ *vi* (*BRIT: Aut*) dar (marcha à) ré (*BR*), fazer marcha atrás (*PT*); **reverse-charge call** (*BRIT*) *n* (*Tel*) ligação *f* a cobrar

revert [rɪ'vəːt] *vi*: **to ~ to** voltar a; (*Law*) reverter a

review [rɪ'vju:] *n* (*magazine, Mil*) revista; (*of book, film*) crítica, resenha; (*examination*) recapitulação *f*, exame *m* ▷ *vt* rever, examinar; (*Mil*) passar em revista; (*book, film*) fazer a crítica *or* resenha de

revise [rɪ'vaɪz] *vt* (*manuscript*) corrigir; (*opinion, procedure*) alterar; (*price*) revisar; **revision** [rɪ'vɪʒən] *n* correção *f*; (*for exam*) revisão *f*

revival [rɪ'vaɪvəl] *n* (*recovery*) restabelecimento; (*of interest*)

renascença, renascimento; (*Theatre*)
reestréia; (*of faith*) despertar *m*
revive [rɪ'vaɪv] *vt* (*person*) reanimar,
ressuscitar; (*economy*) recuperar; (*custom*)
restabelecer, restaurar; (*hope, courage*)
despertar; (*play*) reapresentar ▷ *vi*
(*person: from faint*) voltar a si, recuperar os
sentidos; (: *from ill-health*) recuperar-se;
(*activity, economy*) reativar; (*hope, interest*)
renascer
revolt [rɪ'vəult] *n* revolta, rebelião *f*,
insurreição *f* ▷ *vi* revoltar-se ▷ *vt* causar
aversão a, repugnar; **revolting** *adj*
revoltante, repulsivo
revolution [rɛvə'luːʃən] *n* revolução *f*; (*of
wheel, earth*) rotação *f*
revolve [rɪ'vɒlv] *vi* girar
revolver [rɪ'vɒlvəʳ] *n* revólver *m*
reward [rɪ'wɔːd] *n* recompensa ▷ *vt*:
to ~ (for) recompensar *or* premiar
(por); **rewarding** *adj* (*fig*) gratificante,
compensador(a)
rewind [riː'waɪnd] (*irreg*) *vt* (*tape*) voltar
para trás
rewritable [riː'raɪtəbl] *adj* regravável
rheumatism ['ruːmətɪzəm] *n*
reumatismo
rhinoceros [raɪ'nɒsərəs] *n*
rinoceronte *m*
rhubarb ['ruːbɑːb] *n* ruibarbo
rhyme [raɪm] *n* rima; (*verse*) verso(s)
m(pl) rimado(s), poesia
rhythm ['rɪðm] *n* ritmo
rib [rɪb] *n* (*Anat*) costela ▷ *vt* (*mock*)
zombar de, encarnar em
ribbon ['rɪbən] *n* fita; **in ~s** (*torn*) em
tirinhas, esfarrapado
rice [raɪs] *n* arroz *m*; **rice pudding** *n*
arroz *m* doce
rich [rɪtʃ] *adj* rico; (*clothes*) valioso; (*soil*)
fértil; (*food*) suculento, forte; (*colour*)
intenso; (*voice*) suave, cheio ▷ *npl*: **the ~**
os ricos; **riches** *npl* (*wealth*) riquezas *fpl*
rid [rɪd] (*pt, pp* **~**) *vt*: **to ~ sb of sth** livrar
alguém de algo; **to get ~ of** livrar-se de;
(*sth no longer required*) desfazer-se de
riddle ['rɪdl] *n* (*conundrum*) adivinhação *f*;
(*mystery*) enigma *m*, charada ▷ *vt*: **to be
~d with** estar cheio de
ride [raɪd] (*pt* **rode**, *pp* **ridden**) *n* (*gen*)
passeio; (*on horse*) passeio a cavalo;
(*distance covered*) percurso, trajeto ▷ *vi*
(*as sport*) montar; (*go somewhere: on horse,
bicycle*) ir (a cavalo, de bicicleta); (*journey:
on bicycle, motorcycle, bus*) viajar ▷ *vt* (*a
horse*) montar a; (*bicycle, motorcycle*)

andar de; (*distance*) percorrer; **to ~ at
anchor** (*Naut*) estar ancorado; **to take
sb for a ~** (*fig*) enganar alguém; **rider**
n (*on horse: male*) cavaleiro; (: *female*)
amazona; (*on bicycle*) ciclista *m/f*; (*on
motorcycle*) motociclista *m/f*
ridge [rɪdʒ] *n* (*of hill*) cume *m*, topo; (*of
roof*) cumeeira; (*wrinkle*) ruga
ridicule ['rɪdɪkjuːl] *n* escárnio, zombaria,
mofa ▷ *vt* ridicularizar, zombar de;
ridiculous *adj* ridículo
riding ['raɪdɪŋ] *n* equitação *f*
rife [raɪf] *adj*: **to be ~** ser comum; **to be ~
with** estar repleto de, abundar em
rifle ['raɪfl] *n* rifle *m*, fuzil *m* ▷ *vt* saquear;
rifle through *vt fus* vasculhar
rift [rɪft] *n* fenda, fratura; (*in
clouds*) brecha; (*fig: between friends*)
desentendimento; (: *in party*)
rompimento, divergência
rig [rɪg] *n* (*also*: **oil ~**) torre *f* de perfuração
▷ *vt* adulterar *or* falsificar os resultados
de; **rig out** (BRIT) *vt*: **to rig out as/in**
ataviar *or* vestir como/com; **rig up** *vt*
instalar, montar, improvisar
right [raɪt] *adj* certo, correto; (*suitable*)
adequado, conveniente; (: *decision*)
certo; (*just*) justo; (*morally good*) bom;
(*not left*) direito ▷ *n* direito; (*not left*)
direita ▷ *adv* bem, corretamente; (*fairly*)
adequadamente, justamente; (*not on
the left*) à direita; (*exactly*): **~ now** agora
mesmo ▷ *vt* colocar em pé; (*correct*)
corrigir, indireitar ▷ *excl* bom!; **to be ~**
(*person*) ter razão; (*answer, clock*) estar
certo; **by ~s** por direito; **on the ~** à
direita; **to be in the ~** ter razão; **~ away**
imediatamente, logo, já; **~ in the middle**
bem no meio; **rightful** *adj* (*heir*) legítimo;
(*place*) justo, legítimo; **right-handed**
adj destro; **rightly** *adv* (*with reason*) com
razão; **right of way** *n* prioridade *f* de
passagem; (*Aut*) preferência; **right-wing**
adj de direita
rigid ['rɪdʒɪd] *adj* rígido; (*principle*)
inflexível
rim [rɪm] *n* borda, beira; (*of spectacles,
wheel*) aro
rind [raɪnd] *n* (*of bacon*) pele *f*; (*of lemon
etc*) casca; (*of cheese*) crosta, casca
ring [rɪŋ] (*pt* **rang**, *pp* **rung**) *n* (*of metal*)
aro; (*on finger*) anel *m*; (*of people, objects*)
círculo, grupo; (*for boxing*) ringue *m*;
(*of circus*) pista, picadeiro; (*bullring*)
picadeiro, arena; (*of light, smoke*) círculo;
(*of small bell*) toque *m*; (*of large bell*)

badalada, repique m ▷ vi (on telephone) telefonar; (bell) tocar; (also: ~ **out**) soar; (ears) zumbir ▷ vt (BRIT: Tel) telefonar a, ligar para; (bell etc) badalar; (doorbell) tocar; **to give sb a ~** (BRIT: Tel) dar uma ligada or ligar para alguém; **ring back** (BRIT) vi (Tel) telefonar or ligar de volta ▷ vt telefonar or ligar de volta para; **ring off** (BRIT) vi (Tel) desligar; **ring up** (BRIT) vt (Tel) telefonar a, ligar para; **ringing tone** (BRIT) n (Tel) sinal m de chamada; **ringleader** n cabeça m/f, cérebro; **ring road** (BRIT) n estrada periférica or perimetral; **ringtone** n (on cellphone) toque m (de celular)

rink [rɪŋk] n (also: **ice ~**) pista de patinação, rinque m

rinse [rɪns] n enxaguada ▷ vt enxaguar; (also: ~ **out**: mouth) bochechar

riot ['raɪət] n distúrbio, motim m, desordem f; (of colour) festival m, profusão f ▷ vi provocar distúrbios, amotinar-se; **to run ~** desenfrear-se

rip [rɪp] n rasgão m ▷ vt rasgar ▷ vi rasgar-se

ripe [raɪp] adj maduro

ripple ['rɪpl] n ondulação f, encrespação f; (of laughter etc) onda ▷ vi encrespar-se

rise [raɪz] (pt **rose**, pp **~n**) n elevação f, ladeira; (hill) colina, rampa; (in wages: BRIT) aumento; (in prices, temperature) subida; (to power etc) ascensão f ▷ vi levantar-se, erguer-se; (prices, waters) subir; (sun) nascer; (from bed etc) levantar(-se); (sound) aumentar, erguer-se; (also: ~ **up**: rebel) erguer-se; (: rebel) sublevar-se; (in rank) ascender, subir; **to give ~ to** ocasionar, dar origem a; **to ~ to the occasion** mostrar-se à altura da situação; **rising** adj (prices) em alta; (number) crescente, cada vez maior; (tide) montante; (sun, moon) nascente

risk [rɪsk] n risco, perigo; (Insurance) risco ▷ vt pôr em risco; (chance) arriscar, aventurar; **to take** or **run the ~ of doing** correr o risco de fazer; **at ~** em perigo; **at one's own ~** por sua própria conta e risco; **risky** adj perigoso

rite [raɪt] n rito; **last ~s** últimos sacramentos

ritual ['rɪtjuəl] adj ritual ▷ n ritual m; (of initiation) rito

rival ['raɪvl] adj, n rival m/f; (in business) concorrente m/f ▷ vt competir com; **rivalry** ['raɪvlrɪ] n rivalidade f

river ['rɪvər] n rio ▷ cpd (port, traffic)

fluvial; **up/down ~** rio acima/abaixo; **riverbank** n margem f (do rio)

road [rəud] n via; (motorway etc) estrada (de rodagem); (in town) rua ▷ cpd rodoviário; **roadblock** n barricada; **road map** n mapa m rodoviário; **road rage** n conduta agressiva dos motoristas no trânsito; **roadside** n beira da estrada; **roadsign** n placa de sinalização

roam [rəum] vi vagar, perambular, errar

roar [rɔːʳ] n (of animal) rugido, urro; (of crowd) bramido; (of vehicle, storm) estrondo; (of laughter) barulho m ▷ vi (animal, engine) rugir; (person, crowd) bradar; **to ~ with laughter** dar gargalhadas

roast [rəust] n carne f assada, assado ▷ vt assar; (coffee) torrar; **roast beef** n rosbife m

rob [rɔb] vt roubar; (bank) assaltar; **to ~ sb of sth** roubar algo de alguém; (fig: deprive) despojar alguém de algo; **robber** n ladrão (ladra) m/f; **robbery** n roubo

robe [rəub] n toga, beca; (also: **bath ~**) roupão m (de banho)

robin ['rɔbɪn] n pisco-de-peito-ruivo (BR), pintarroxo (PT)

robot ['rəubɔt] n robô m

robust [rəu'bʌst] adj robusto, forte; (appetite) sadio; (economy) forte

rock [rɔk] n rocha; (boulder) penhasco, rochedo; (US: small stone) cascalho; (BRIT: sweet) pirulito ▷ vt (swing gently: cradle) balançar, oscilar; (: child) embalar, acalentar; (shake) sacudir ▷ vi (object) balançar-se; (person) embalar-se, ir the ~s (drink) com gelo; (marriage etc) arruinado, em dificuldades; **rock and roll** n rock-and-roll m

rocket ['rɔkɪt] n foguete m

rocky ['rɔkɪ] adj rochoso, bambo, instável; (marriage) instável

rod [rɔd] n vara, varinha; (also: **fishing ~**) vara de pescar

rode [rəud] pt of **ride**

rodent ['rəudnt] n roedor m

rogue [rəug] n velhaco, maroto

role [rəul] n papel m

roll [rəul] n rolo; (of banknotes) maço; (also: **bread ~**) pãozinho; (register) rol m, lista; (of drums etc) rufar m ▷ vt rolar; (also: ~ **up**: string) enrolar; (: sleeves) arregaçar; (cigarette) enrolar; (eyes) virar; (also: ~ **out**: pastry) esticar; (lawn, road etc) aplanar ▷ vi rolar; (drum) rufar; (vehicle: also: ~ **along**) rodar; (ship)

balançar, jogar; **roll about** or **around**
vi ficar rolando; **roll by** vi (time) passar;
roll in vi (mail, cash) chegar em grande
quantidade; **roll over** vi dar uma volta;
roll up vi (inf) pintar, chegar, aparecer
▷ vt enrolar; **roller** n (in machine) rolo,
cilindro; (wheel) roda, roldana; (for lawn,
road) rolo compressor; (for hair) rolo;
roller coaster n montanha-russa; **roller
skates** npl patins mpl de roda
rolling pin n rolo de pastel
ROM [rɔm] n abbr (Comput: = read-only
memory) ROM m
Roman ['rəumən] adj, n romano(-a);
Roman Catholic adj, n católico(-a)
(romano(-a))
romance [rə'mæns] n aventura
amorosa, romance m; (book) história de
amor; (charm) romantismo
Romania [ruː'meɪnɪə] n Romênia;
Romanian adj romeno ▷ n romeno(-a);
(Ling) romeno
romantic [rə'mæntɪk] adj romântico
Rome [rəum] n Roma
roof [ruːf] n (of house) telhado; (of car)
capota, teto ▷ vt telhar, cobrir com
telhas; **the ~ of the mouth** o céu da
boca; **roof rack** n (Aut) bagageiro
rook [ruk] n (bird) gralha; (Chess) torre f
room [ruːm] n (in house) quarto,
aposento; (also: **bed~**) quarto,
dormitório; (in school etc) sala; (space)
espaço, lugar m; (scope: for improvement
etc) espaço; **rooms** npl (lodging)
alojamento; **"~s to let"** (BRIT), **"~s
for rent"** (US) "alugam-se quartos
or apartamentos"; **roommate** n
companheiro(-a) de quarto; **room
service** n serviço de quarto; **roomy** adj
espaçoso; (garment) folgado
rooster ['ruːstə'] n galo
root [ruːt] n raiz f; (fig) origem f ▷ vi
enraizar, arraigar; **roots** npl (family
origins) raízes fpl; **root about** vi (fig): **to
root about in** (drawer) vasculhar; (house)
esquadrinhar; **root for** vt fus torcer por;
root out vt extirpar
rope [rəup] n corda; (Naut) cabo ▷ vt (tie)
amarrar; (climbers: also: **~ together**)
amarrar or atar com uma corda; (area:
also: **~ off**) isolar; **to know the ~s** (fig)
estar por dentro (do assunto); **rope in** vt
(fig): **to rope sb in** persuadir alguém a
tomar parte
rose [rəuz] pt of **rise** ▷ n rosa; (also:
~bush) roseira; (on watering can) crivo

rosé ['rəuzeɪ] n rosado, rosé m
rosemary ['rəuzmərɪ] n alecrim m
rosy ['rəuzɪ] adj rosado, rosáceo; (cheeks)
rosado; (situation) cor-de-rosa inv; **a ~
future** um futuro promissor
rot [rɔt] n (decay) putrefação f, podridão f;
(fig: pej) besteira ▷ vt, vi apodrecer
rota ['rəutə] n lista de tarefas, escala de
serviço
rotate [rəu'teɪt] vt fazer girar, dar voltas
em; (jobs) alternar, revezar ▷ vi girar, dar
voltas
rotten ['rɔtn] adj podre; (wood)
carcomido; (fig) corrupto; (inf: bad)
péssimo; **to feel ~** (ill) sentir-se podre
rough [rʌf] adj (skin, surface) áspero;
(terrain) acidentado; (road) desigual;
(voice) áspero, rouco; (person, manner)
violento; (: brusque) ríspido;
(weather) tempestuoso; (treatment)
brutal, mau (má); (sea) agitado; (district)
violento; (plan) preliminar; (work)
grosseiro; (guess) aproximado ▷ n
(Golf): **in the ~** na grama crescida; **to
sleep ~** (BRIT) dormir na rua; **roughly**
adv bruscamente; (make) toscamente;
(approximately) aproximadamente
roulette [ruː'lɛt] n roleta
round [raund] adj redondo ▷ n
(BRIT: of toast) rodela; (of policeman)
ronda; (of milkman) trajeto; (of doctor)
visitas fpl; (game: of cards etc) partida;
(of ammunition) cartucho; (Boxing)
round e m, assalto; (of talks) ciclo ▷ vt
virar, dobrar ▷ prep (surrounding):
~ his neck/the table em volta de
seu pescoço/ao redor da mesa; (in
a circular movement): **to move ~ the
room/~ the world** mover-se pelo
quarto/dar a volta ao mundo; (in
various directions) por; (approximately):
~ about aproximadamente ▷ adv: **all
~** por todos os lados; **the long way ~** o
caminho mais comprido; **all the year
~** durante todo o ano; **it's just ~ the
corner** (fig) está pertinho; **~ the clock**
ininterrupto; **to go ~ the back** passar
por detrás; **to go ~ a house** visitar uma
casa; **enough to go ~** suficiente para
todos; **a ~ of applause** uma salva de
palmas; **a ~ of drinks** uma rodada de
bebidas; **~ of sandwiches** sanduíche
m (BR), sandes f inv (PT); **round off** vt
terminar, completar; **round up** vt
(cattle) encurralar; (people) reunir; (price,
figure) arredondar; **roundabout** n (BRIT:

Aut) rotatória; (: *at fair*) carrossel *m* ▷ *adj* indireto; **round trip** *n* viagem *f* de ida e volta

rouse [rauz] *vt* (*wake up*) despertar, acordar; (*stir up*) suscitar

route [ru:t] *n* caminho, rota; (*of bus*) trajeto; (*of shipping*) rumo, rota; (*of procession*) rota

routine [ru:'ti:n] *adj* (*work*) rotineiro; (*procedure*) de rotina ▷ *n* rotina; (*Theatre*) número

row[1] [rəu] *n* (*line*) fila, fileira; (*in theatre, boat*) fileira; (*Knitting*) carreira, fileira ▷ *vi, vt* remar; **in a ~** (*fig*) a fio, seguido

row[2] [rau] *n* barulho, balbúrdia; (*dispute*) discussão *f*, briga; (*scolding*) repreensão *f* ▷ *vi* brigar

rowboat ['rəubəut] (*US*) *n* barco a remo

rowing ['rəuɪŋ] *n* remo; **rowing boat** (*BRIT*) *n* barco a remo

royal ['rɔɪəl] *adj* real

Royal Academy (of Arts) (*BRIT*) *n* ver quadro

⬤ **ROYAL ACADEMY**
⬤
⬤ A **Royal Academy**, ou **Royal**
⬤ **Academy of Arts**, fundada em 1768
⬤ por George III para desenvolver a
⬤ pintura, a escultura e a arquitetura,
⬤ situa-se em Burlington House,
⬤ Piccadilly. A cada verão há uma
⬤ exposição de obras de artistas
⬤ contemporâneos. A **Royal Academy**
⬤ também oferece cursos de pintura,
⬤ escultura e arquitetura.

royalty *n* família real, realeza; (*payment: to author*) direitos *mpl* autorais

rpm *abbr* (= *revolutions per minute*) rpm

rub [rʌb] *vt* friccionar; (*part of body*) esfregar ▷ *n*: **to give sth a ~** dar uma esfregada em algo; **to ~ sb up** (*BRIT*) or **~ sb** (*US*) **the wrong way** irritar alguém; **rub off** *vi* sair esfregando; **rub off on** *vt fus* transmitir-se para, influir sobre; **rub out** *vt* apagar

rubber ['rʌbə'] *n* borracha; (*BRIT: eraser*) borracha; **rubber band** *n* elástico, tira elástica

rubbish ['rʌbɪʃ] *n* (*waste*) refugo; (*from household, in street*) lixo; (*junk*) coisas *fpl* sem valor; (*fig: pej: nonsense*) disparates *mpl*, asneiras *fpl*; **rubbish bin** (*BRIT*) *n* lata de lixo; **rubbish dump** *n* (*in town*) depósito (de lixo)

rubble ['rʌbl] *n* (*debris*) entulho; (*Constr*) escombros *mpl*

ruby ['ru:bɪ] *n* rubi *m*

rucksack ['rʌksæk] *n* mochila

rudder ['rʌdə'] *n* leme *m*; (*of plane*) leme de direção

rude [ru:d] *adj* (*person*) grosso, mal-educado; (*word, manners*) grosseiro; (*shocking*) obsceno, chocante

rug [rʌg] *n* tapete *m*; (*BRIT: for knees*) manta (de viagem)

rugby ['rʌgbɪ] *n* (*also: ~ football*) rúgbi *m* (*BR*), râguebi *m* (*PT*)

rugged ['rʌgɪd] *adj* (*landscape*) acidentado, irregular; (*features*) marcado; (*character*) severo, austero

ruin ['ru:ɪn] *n* ruína; (*of plans*) destruição *f*; (*downfall*) queda; (*bankruptcy*) bancarrota ▷ *vt* destruir; (*future, person*) arruinar; (*spoil*) estragar; **ruins** *npl* (*of building*) ruínas *fpl*

rule [ru:l] *n* (*norm*) regra; (*regulation*) regulamento; (*government*) governo, domínio; (*ruler*) régua ▷ *vt* governar ▷ *vi* governar; (*monarch*) reger; (*Law*): **to ~ in favour of/against** decidir oficialmente a favor de/contra; **as a ~** por via de regra, geralmente; **rule out** *vt* excluir; **ruler** *n* (*sovereign*) soberano(-a); (*for measuring*) régua; **ruling** *adj* (*party*) dominante; (*class*) dirigente ▷ *n* (*Law*) parecer *m*, decisão *f*

rum [rʌm] *n* rum *m*

rumble ['rʌmbl] *n* ruído surdo, barulho; (*of thunder*) estrondo, ribombo ▷ *vi* ribombar, ressoar; (*stomach*) roncar; (*pipe*) fazer barulho; (*thunder*) ribombar

rumour ['ru:mə'] (*US* **rumor**) *n* rumor *m*, boato ▷ *vt*: **it is ~ed that ...** corre o boato de que ...

rump steak *n* alcatra

run [rʌn] (*pt* **ran**, *pp* **~**) *n* corrida; (*in car*) passeio (de carro); (*distance travelled*) trajeto, percurso; (*journey*) viagem *f*; (*series*) série *f*; (*Theatre*) temporada; (*Ski*) pista; (*in stockings*) fio puxado ▷ *vt* (*race*) correr; (*operate: business*) dirigir; (: *competition, course*) organizar; (: *hotel, house*) administrar; (*water*) deixar correr; (*bath*) encher; (*Press: feature*) publicar; (*Comput*) rodar; (*hand, finger*) passar ▷ *vi* correr; (*work: machine*) funcionar; (*bus, train: operate*) circular; (: *travel*) ir; (*continue: play*) continuar em cartaz; (: *contract*) ser válido; (*river, bath*) fluir, correr; (*colours*) desbotar; (*in election*) candidatar-se; (*nose*) escorrer; **there was a ~ on** houve muita procura de; **in the long ~** no final das contas, mais cedo ou mais tarde; **on the ~** em fuga, foragido; **run about** *or* **around** *vi* correr por todos os lados; **run across** *vt fus* encontrar por acaso, topar com, dar com; **run away** *vi* fugir; **run down** *vt* (*Aut*) atropelar; (*production*) reduzir; (*criticize*) criticar; **to be run down** estar enfraquecido *or* exausto; **run in** (BRIT) *vt* (*car*) rodar; **run into** *vt fus* (*meet: person*) dar com, topar com; (: *trouble*) esbarrar em; (*collide with*) bater em; **run off** *vi* fugir; **run out** *vi* (*person*) sair correndo; (*liquid*) escorrer, esgotar-se; (*lease, passport*) caducar, vencer; (*money*) acabar; **run out of** *vt fus* ficar sem; **run over** *vt* (*Aut*) atropelar ▷ *vt fus* (*revise*) recapitular; **run through** *vt fus* (*instructions, play*) recapitular; **run up** *vt* (*debt*) acumular ▷ *vi:* **to run up against** esbarrar em; **runaway** *adj* (*horse*) desembestado; (*truck*) desgovernado; (*person*) fugitivo

rung [rʌŋ] *pp of* **ring** ▷ *n* (*of ladder*) degrau *m*

runner ['rʌnə'] *n* (*in race*) corredor(a) *m/f*; (*horse*) corredor *m*; (*on sledge*) patim *m*, lâmina; (*for drawer*) corrediça; **runner bean** (BRIT) *n* (*Bot*) vagem *f* (BR), feijão *m* verde (PT); **runner-up** *n* segundo(-a) colocado(-a)

running ['rʌnɪŋ] *n* (*sport*) corrida; (*of business*) direção *f* ▷ *adj* (*water*) corrente; (*commentary*) contínuo, seguido; **6 days ~** 6 dias seguidos *or* consecutivos; **to be in/out of the ~ for sth** disputar algo/estar fora da disputa por algo

runny ['rʌnɪ] *adj* aguado; (*egg*) mole; **to have a ~ nose** estar com coriza, estar com o nariz escorrendo

run-up *n:* **~ to sth** (*election etc*) período que antecede algo

runway ['rʌnweɪ] *n* (*Aviat*) pista (de decolagem *or* de pouso)

rupture ['rʌptʃə'] *n* (*Med*) hérnia

rural ['ruərl] *adj* rural

rush [rʌʃ] *n* (*hurry*) pressa; (*Comm*) grande procura *or* demanda; (*Bot*) junco; (*current*) torrente *f*; (*of emotion*) ímpeto ▷ *vt* apressar ▷ *vi* apressar-se, precipitar-se; **rush hour** *n* rush *m* (BR), hora de ponta (PT)

Russia ['rʌʃə] *n* Rússia; **Russian** *adj* russo ▷ *n* russo(-a); (*Ling*) russo

rust [rʌst] *n* ferrugem *f* ▷ *vi* enferrujar

rusty ['rʌstɪ] *adj* enferrujado

ruthless ['ru:θlɪs] *adj* implacável, sem piedade

rye [raɪ] *n* centeio

S

Sabbath ['sæbəθ] *n* (*Christian*) domingo; (*Jewish*) sábado
sabotage ['sæbətɑːʒ] *n* sabotagem *f* ▷ *vt* sabotar
saccharin(e) ['sækərɪn] *n* sacarina
sachet ['sæʃeɪ] *n* sachê *m*
sack [sæk] *n* (*bag*) saco, saca ▷ *vt* (*dismiss*) despedir; (*plunder*) saquear; **to get the ~** ser demitido
sacred ['seɪkrɪd] *adj* sagrado
sacrifice ['sækrɪfaɪs] *n* sacrifício ▷ *vt* sacrificar
sad [sæd] *adj* triste; (*deplorable*) deplorável, triste
saddle ['sædl] *n* sela; (*of cycle*) selim *m* ▷ *vt* selar; **to ~ sb with sth** (*inf: task, bill*) pôr algo nas costas de alguém; (*: responsibility*) sobrecarregar alguém com algo
sadistic [sə'dɪstɪk] *adj* sádico
sadly ['sædlɪ] *adv* tristemente; (*regrettably*) infelizmente; (*mistaken, neglected*) gravemente; **~ lacking (in)** muito carente (de)
sadness ['sædnɪs] *n* tristeza
safe [seɪf] *adj* seguro; (*out of danger*) fora de perigo; (*unharmed*) ileso, incólume ▷ *n* cofre *m*, caixa-forte *f*; **~ from** protegido de; **~ and sound** são e salvo; **(just) to be on the ~ side** por via das dúvidas; **safely** *adv* com segurança, a salvo; (*without mishap*) sem perigo
safety ['seɪftɪ] *n* segurança; **safety belt** *n* cinto de segurança; **safety pin** *n* alfinete *m* de segurança
sag [sæg] *vi* (*breasts*) cair; (*roof*) afundar; (*hem*) desmanchar
sage [seɪdʒ] *n* salva; (*man*) sábio
Sagittarius [sædʒɪ'tɛərɪəs] *n* Sagitário
Sahara [sə'hɑːrə] *n*: **the ~ (Desert)** o Saara
said [sɛd] *pt, pp of* **say**
sail [seɪl] *n* (*on boat*) vela; (*trip*): **to go for a ~** dar um passeio de barco a vela ▷ *vt* (*boat*) governar ▷ *vi* (*travel: ship*) navegar, velejar; (*: passenger*) ir de barco; (*Sport*) velejar; (*set off*) zarpar; **they ~ed into Rio de Janeiro** entraram no porto do Rio de Janeiro; **sail through** *vt fus* (*fig*) fazer com facilidade; **sailboat** (*US*) *n* barco a vela; **sailing** *n* (*Sport*) navegação *f* a vela, vela; **to go sailing** ir velejar
sailor ['seɪlə*r*] *n* marinheiro, marujo
saint [seɪnt] *n* santo(-a)
sake [seɪk] *n*: **for the ~ of** por (causa de), em consideração a; **for sb's/sth's ~** pelo bem de alguém/algo
salad ['sæləd] *n* salada; **salad cream** (*BRIT*) *n* maionese *f*; **salad dressing** *n* tempero *or* molho da salada
salami [sə'lɑːmɪ] *n* salame *m*
salary ['sælərɪ] *n* salário
sale [seɪl] *n* venda; (*at reduced prices*) liquidação *f*, saldo; (*auction*) leilão *m*; **sales** *npl* (*total amount sold*) vendas *fpl*; **"for ~"** "vende-se"; **on ~** à venda; **on ~ or return** em consignação; **sales assistant** (*US* **sales clerk**) *n* vendedor(a) *m/f*
salmon ['sæmən] *n inv* salmão *m*
salon ['sælɔn] *n* (*hairdressing salon*) salão *m* (de cabeleireiro); (*beauty salon*) salão (de beleza)
saloon [sə'luːn] *n* (*US*) bar *m*, botequim *m*; (*BRIT: Aut*) sedã *m*; (*ship's lounge*) salão *m*
salt [sɔːlt] *n* sal *m* ▷ *vt* salgar; **saltwater** *adj* de água salgada; **salty** *adj* salgado
salute [sə'luːt] *n* (*greeting*) saudação *f*; (*of guns*) salva; (*Mil*) continência ▷ *vt* saudar; (*Mil*) fazer continência a
salvage ['sælvɪdʒ] *n* (*saving*) salvamento, recuperação *f*; (*things saved*) salvados *mpl* ▷ *vt* salvar
same [seɪm] *adj* mesmo ▷ *pron*: **the ~**

o mesmo (a mesma); **the ~ book as** o mesmo livro que; **all** *or* **just the ~** apesar de tudo, mesmo assim; **the ~ to you!** igualmente!

sample ['sɑːmpl] *n* amostra ▷ *vt* (*food, wine*) provar, experimentar

sanction ['sæŋkʃən] *n* sanção *f* ▷ *vt* sancionar

sanctuary ['sæŋktjuərɪ] *n* (*holy place*) santuário; (*refuge*) refúgio, asilo; (*for animals*) reserva

sand [sænd] *n* areia; (*beach: also:* **~s**) praia ▷ *vt* (*also:* **~ down**) lixar

sandal ['sændl] *n* sandália

sand: **sandbox** (*us*) *n* caixa de areia; **sandcastle** *n* castelo de areia; **sandpaper** *n* lixa; **sandpit** *n* (*for children*) caixa de areia; **sandstone** *n* arenito, grés *m*

sandwich ['sændwɪtʃ] *n* sanduíche *m* (*BR*), sandes *f inv* (*PT*) ▷ *vt*: **~ed between** encaixado entre

sandy ['sændɪ] *adj* arenoso; (*colour*) vermelho amarelado

sane [seɪn] *adj* são (sã) do juízo; (*sensible*) ajuizado, sensato

sang [sæŋ] *pt of* **sing**

sanity ['sænɪtɪ] *n* sanidade *f*, equilíbrio mental; (*common sense*) juízo, sensatez *f*

sank [sæŋk] *pt of* **sink**

Santa Claus [sæntə'klɔːz] *n* Papai Noel *m*

sap [sæp] *n* (*of plants*) seiva ▷ *vt* (*strength*) esgotar, minar

sapphire ['sæfaɪər] *n* safira

sarcasm ['sɑːkæzm] *n* sarcasmo

sardine [sɑː'diːn] *n* sardinha

Sardinia [sɑː'dɪnɪə] *n* Sardenha

sat [sæt] *pt, pp of* **sit**

satchel ['sætʃl] *n* sacola

satellite ['sætəlaɪt] *n* satélite *m*; **satellite dish** *n* antena parabólica; **satellite television** *n* televisão *f* via satélite

satin ['sætɪn] *n* cetim *m* ▷ *adj* acetinado

satire ['sætaɪər] *n* sátira

satisfaction [sætɪs'fækʃən] *n* satisfação *f*; (*refund, apology etc*) compensação *f*; **satisfactory** *adj* satisfatório

satisfy ['sætɪsfaɪ] *vt* satisfazer; (*convince*) convencer, persuadir

Saturday ['sætədɪ] *n* sábado

sauce [sɔːs] *n* molho; (*sweet*) calda; **saucepan** *n* panela (*BR*), caçarola (*PT*)

saucer ['sɔːsər] *n* pires *m inv*

Saudi ['saudɪ]: **~ Arabia** *n* Arábia Saudita;

Saudi (Arabian) *adj* saudita

sauna ['sɔːnə] *n* sauna

sausage ['sɔsɪdʒ] *n* salsicha, lingüiça; (*cold meat*) frios *mpl*; **sausage roll** *n* folheado de salsicha

savage ['sævɪdʒ] *adj* (*cruel, fierce*) cruel, feroz; (*primitive*) selvagem ▷ *n* selvagem *m/f*

save [seɪv] *vt* (*rescue, Comput*) salvar; (*money*) poupar, economizar; (*time*) ganhar; (*Sport*) impedir; (*avoid: trouble*) evitar; (*keep: seat*) guardar ▷ *vi* (*also:* **~ up**) poupar ▷ *n* (*Sport*) salvamento ▷ *prep* salvo, exceto

saw [sɔː] (*pt* **~ed**, *pp* **~ed** *or* **~n**) *pt of* **see** ▷ *n* (*tool*) serra ▷ *vt* serrar; **sawdust** *n* serragem *f*, pó *m* de serra

saxophone ['sæksəfəun] *n* saxofone *m*

say [seɪ] (*pt, pp* **said**) *n*: **to have one's ~** exprimir sua opinião, vender seu peixe (*inf*) ▷ *vt* dizer, falar; **to have a** *or* **some ~ in sth** opinar sobre algo, ter que ver com algo; **could you ~ that again?** poderia repetir?; **that is to ~** ou seja; **saying** *n* ditado, provérbio

scab [skæb] *n* casca, crosta (de ferida); (*pej*) fura-greve *m/f inv*

scald [skɔːld] *n* escaldadura ▷ *vt* escaldar, queimar

scale [skeɪl] *n* escala; (*of fish*) escama; (*of salaries, fees etc*) tabela ▷ *vt* (*mountain*) escalar; **scales** *npl* (*for weighing*) balança; **~ of charges** tarifa, lista de preços; **scale down** *vt* reduzir

scallop ['skɔləp] *n* (*Zool*) vieira, venera; (*Sewing*) barra, arremate *m*

scalp [skælp] *n* couro cabeludo ▷ *vt* escalpar

scampi ['skæmpɪ] *npl* camarões *mpl* fritos

scan [skæn] *vt* (*examine*) esquadrinhar, perscrutar; (*glance at quickly*) passar uma vista de olhos por; (*TV, Radar*) explorar ▷ *n* (*Med*) exame *m*

scandal ['skændl] *n* escândalo; (*gossip*) fofocas *fpl*; (*fig: disgrace*) vergonha

Scandinavian [skændɪ'neɪvɪən] *adj* escandinavo

scanner ['skænər] *n* (*Med, Comput*) scanner *m*

scapegoat ['skeɪpgəut] *n* bode *m* expiatório

scar [skɑː] *n* cicatriz *f* ▷ *vt* marcar (com uma cicatriz)

scarce [skɛəs] *adj* escasso, raro; **to make o.s. ~** (*inf*) dar o fora, cair fora; **scarcely**

adv mal, quase não; (*barely*) apenas

scare [skɛəʳ] *n* susto; (*panic*) pânico ▷ *vt* assustar; **to ~ sb stiff** deixar alguém morrendo de medo; **bomb ~** alarme de bomba; **scare away** *vt* espantar; **scare off** *vt* = **scare away**; **scarecrow** *n* espantalho; **scared** *adj*: **to be scared** estar assustado or com medo

scarf [skɑːf] (*pl* ~**s** *or* **scarves**) *n* cachecol *m*; (*square*) lenço (de cabeça)

scarlet ['skɑːlɪt] *adj* escarlate

scary ['skɛərɪ] (*inf*) *adj* assustador(a)

scatter ['skætəʳ] *vt* espalhar; (*put to flight*) dispersar ▷ *vi* espalhar-se

scene [siːn] *n* (*Theatre, fig*) cena; (*of crime, accident*) cenário; (*sight*) vista, panorama *m*; (*fuss*) escândalo; **scenery** ['siːnərɪ] *n* (*Theatre*) cenário; (*landscape*) paisagem *f*; **scenic** *adj* pitoresco

scent [sɛnt] *n* perfume *m*; (*smell*) aroma; (*track, fig*) pista, rastro

schedule ['ʃɛdjuːl, (US)'skɛdjuːl] *n* (*of trains*) horário; (*of events*) programa *m*; (*list*) lista ▷ *vt* (*timetable*) planejar; (*visit*) marcar (a hora de); **on ~** na hora, sem atraso; **to be ahead of/behind ~** estar adiantado/atrasado

scheme [skiːm] *n* (*plan*) maquinação *f*; (*pension scheme*) projeto; (*arrangement*) arranjo ▷ *vi* conspirar

scholar ['skɔləʳ] *n* aluno(-a), estudante *m/f*; (*learned person*) sábio(-a), erudito(-a); **scholarship** *n* erudição *f*; (*grant*) bolsa de estudos

school [skuːl] *n* escola; (*secondary school*) colégio; (*US: university*) universidade *f* ▷ *cpd* escolar; **schoolboy** *n* aluno; **schoolchildren** *npl* alunos *mpl*; **schoolgirl** *n* aluna; **schoolteacher** *n* professor(a) *m/f*

science ['saɪəns] *n* ciência; **science fiction** *n* ficção *f* científica; **scientific** [saɪən'tɪfɪk] *adj* científico; **scientist** *n* cientista *m/f*

scissors ['sɪzəz] *npl* tesoura; **a pair of ~** uma tesoura

scold [skəuld] *vt* ralhar

scone [skɔn] *n* bolinho de trigo

scoop [skuːp] *n* colherona; (*for flour etc*) pá *f*; (*Press*) furo (jornalístico); **scoop out** *vt* escavar; **scoop up** *vt* recolher

scooter ['skuːtəʳ] *n* (*also:* **motor ~**) lambreta; (*toy*) patinete *m*

scope [skəup] *n* liberdade *f* de ação; (*of undertaking*) âmbito; (*of person*) competência; (*opportunity*)

oportunidade *f*

score [skɔːʳ] *n* (*points etc*) escore *m*, contagem *f*; (*Mus*) partitura; (*twenty*) vintena *f* ▷ *vt* (*goal, point*) fazer; (*mark*) marcar, entalhar; (*success*) alcançar ▷ *vi* (*in game*) marcar; (*Football*) marcar or fazer um gol; (*keep score*) marcar o escore; **on that ~** a esse respeito, por esse motivo; **~s of** (*fig*) um monte de; **to ~ 6 out of 10** conseguir um escore de 6 num total de 10; **score out** *vt* riscar; **scoreboard** *n* marcador *m*, placar *m*

scorn [skɔːn] *n* desprezo ▷ *vt* desprezar, rejeitar

Scorpio ['skɔːpɪəu] *n* Escorpião *m*

Scot [skɔt] *n* escocês(-esa) *m/f*

Scotch [skɔtʃ] *n* uísque *m* (BR) *or* whisky *m* (PT) escocês

Scotland ['skɔtlənd] *n* Escócia; **Scots** *adj* escocês(-esa); **Scotsman** (*irreg*) *n* escocês *m*; **Scotswoman** (*irreg*) *n* escocesa; **Scottish** *adj* escocês(-esa)

scout [skaut] *n* (*Mil*) explorador *m*, batedor *m*; (*also:* **boy ~**) escoteiro; **girl ~** (*US*) escoteira; **scout around** *vi* explorar

scowl [skaul] *vi* franzir a testa; **to ~ at sb** olhar de cara feia para alguém

scramble ['skræmbl] *n* (*climb*) escalada (difícil); (*struggle*) luta ▷ *vi*: **to ~ out/ through** conseguir sair com dificuldade; **to ~ for** lutar por; **scrambled eggs** *npl* ovos *mpl* mexidos

scrap [skræp] *n* (*of paper*) pedacinho; (*of material*) fragmento; (*fig: of truth*) mínimo; (*fight*) rixa, luta; (*also:* **~ iron**) ferro velho, sucata ▷ *vt* sucatar, jogar no ferro velho; (*fig*) descartar, abolir ▷ *vi* brigar; **scraps** *npl* (*leftovers*) sobras *fpl*, restos *mpl*; **scrapbook** *n* álbum *m* de recortes

scrape [skreɪp] *n* (*fig*): **to get into a ~** meter-se numa enrascada ▷ *vt* raspar; (*scrape against: hand, car*) arranhar, roçar ▷ *vi*: **to ~ through** (*in exam*) passar raspando; **scrape together** *vt* (*money*) juntar com dificuldade

scrap paper *n* papel *m* de rascunho

scratch [skrætʃ] *n* arranhão *m*; (*from claw*) arranhadura ▷ *cpd*: **~ team** time *m* improvisado, escrete *m* ▷ *vt* (*rub*) coçar; (*with claw, nail*) arranhar, unhar; (*damage*) arranhar ▷ *vi* coçar(-se); **to start from ~** partir do zero; **to be up to ~** estar à altura (das circunstâncias)

scream [skriːm] *n* grito ▷ *vi* gritar

screen [skriːn] *n* (*Cinema, TV, Comput*)

tela (BR), écran m (PT); (movable) biombo; (fig) cortina ▷ vt (conceal) esconder, tapar; (from the wind etc) proteger; (film) projetar; (candidates etc) examinar; **screenplay** n roteiro

screensaver ['skri:nseɪvə'] n protetor m de tela

screw [skru:] n parafuso ▷ vt aparafusar; (also: ~ **in**) apertar, atarraxar; **to ~ up one's eyes** franzir os olhos; **screw up** vt (paper etc) amassar; **screwdriver** n chave f de fenda or de parafuso

scribble ['skrɪbl] n garrancho ▷ vt escrevinhar ▷ vi rabiscar

script [skrɪpt] n (Cinema etc) roteiro, script m; (writing) escrita, caligrafia

scroll [skrəʊl] n rolo de pergaminho

scrub [skrʌb] n mato, cerrado ▷ vt esfregar; (inf) cancelar, eliminar

scruffy ['skrʌfɪ] adj desmazelado

scrutiny ['skru:tɪnɪ] n escrutínio, exame m cuidadoso

sculptor ['skʌlptə'] n escultor(a) m/f

sculpture ['skʌlptʃə'] n escultura

scum [skʌm] n (on liquid) espuma; (pej: people) ralé f, gentinha

scurry ['skʌrɪ] vi sair correndo; **scurry off** vi sair correndo, dar no pé

sea [si:] n mar m ▷ cpd do mar, marino; **on the ~** (boat) no mar; (town) junto ao mar; **to go by ~** viajar por mar; **out to** or **at ~** em alto mar; **to be all at ~** (fig) estar confuso or desorientado; **seafood** n mariscos mpl; **seagull** n gaivota

seal [si:l] n (animal) foca; (stamp) selo ▷ vt fechar; **seal off** vt fechar

sea level n nível m do mar

seam [si:m] n costura; (where edges meet) junta; (of coal) veio, filão m

search [sə:tʃ] n busca, procura; (Comput) procura; (inspection) exame m, investigação f ▷ vt (look in) procurar em; (examine) examinar; (person) revistar ▷ vi: **to ~ for** procurar; **in ~ of** à procura de; **search through** vt fus dar busca em; **search engine** n (on Internet) ferramenta f de busca; **search party** n equipe f de salvamento

sea: **seashore** n praia, beira-mar f, litoral m; **seasick** adj: **to be seasick** enjoar; **seaside** n praia; **seaside resort** n balneário

season ['si:zn] n (of year) estação f; (sporting etc) temporada; (of films etc) série f ▷ vt (food) temperar; **to be in/out of ~** (fruit) estar na época/fora de época;

season ticket n bilhete m de temporada

seat [si:t] n (in bus, train: place) assento; (chair) cadeira; (Pol) lugar m, cadeira; (buttocks) traseiro, nádegas fpl; (of trousers) fundilhos mpl ▷ vt sentar; (have room for) ter capacidade para; **to be ~ed** estar sentado; **seat belt** n cinto de segurança

sea: **sea water** n água do mar; **seaweed** n alga marinha

sec. abbr (= second) seg.

secluded [sɪ'klu:dɪd] adj (place) afastado; (life) solitário

second¹ [sɪ'kɔnd] (BRIT) vt (employee) transferir temporariamente

second² ['sɛkənd] adj segundo ▷ adv (in race etc) em segundo lugar ▷ n segundo; (Aut: also: ~ **gear**) segunda; (Comm) artigo defeituoso; (BRIT: Sch: degree) qualificação boa mas sem distinção ▷ vt (motion) apoiar, secundar; **secondary** adj secundário; **secondary school** n escola secundária, colégio; **second-class** adv em segunda classe; **secondhand** adj de (BR) or em (PT) segunda mão, usado; **second hand** n (on clock) ponteiro de segundos; **secondly** adv em segundo lugar; **second-rate** adj de segunda categoria; **second thoughts** (US **second thought**) npl: **to have second thoughts (about doing sth)** pensar duas vezes (antes de fazer algo); **on second thoughts** pensando bem

⚅ **SECONDARY SCHOOL**
⚅
⚅ Uma **secondary school** é um
⚅ estabelecimento de ensino para
⚅ alunos de 11 a 18 anos, alguns dos quais
⚅ interrompem os estudos aos 16 anos. A
⚅ maior parte dessas escolas é formada
⚅ por comprehensive schools , mas
⚅ algumas secondary schools ainda têm
⚅ sistemas rigorosos de seleção.

secrecy ['si:krəsɪ] n sigilo

secret ['si:krɪt] adj secreto ▷ n segredo

secretary ['sɛkrətərɪ] n secretário(-a); (BRIT: Pol): **S~ of State** Ministro(-a) de Estado

secretive ['si:krətɪv] adj sigiloso, reservado

section ['sɛkʃən] n seção f; (part) parte f, porção f; (of document) parágrafo, artigo; (of opinion) setor m; **cross-~** corte m transversal

sector ['sɛktə'] n setor m
secular ['sɛkjulə'] adj (priest) secular;
(music, society) leigo
secure [sɪ'kjuə'] adj (safe) seguro; (firmly
fixed) firme, rígido ▷ vt (fix) prender; (get)
conseguir, obter; **security** n segurança;
(for loan) fiança, garantia; **security
guard** n guarda m
sedate [sɪ'deɪt] adj calmo ▷ vt sedar,
tratar com calmantes; **sedative** n
calmante m, sedativo
seduce [sɪ'dju:s] vt seduzir; **seductive**
adj sedutor(a)
see [si:] (pt saw, pp ~n) vt ver; (understand)
entender; (accompany): **to ~ sb to the
door** acompanhar or levar alguém até
a porta ▷ vi ver; (find out) achar ▷ n sé f,
sede f; **to ~ that** (ensure) assegurar que;
~ you soon! até logo!; **see about** vt fus
tratar de; **see off** vt despedir-se de; **see
through** vt fus enxergar através de ▷ vt
levar a cabo; **see to** vt fus providenciar
seed [si:d] n semente f; (sperm) esperma
m; (fig: gen pl) germe m; (Tennis) pré-
selecionado(-a); **to go to ~** produzir
sementes; (fig) deteriorar-se
seeing ['si:ɪŋ] conj: **~ (that)** visto (que),
considerando (que)
seek [si:k] (pt, pp sought) vt procurar;
(post) solicitar
seem [si:m] vi parecer; **there ~s to be ...**
parece que há ...
seen [si:n] pp of see
seesaw ['si:sɔ:] n gangorra, balanço
segment ['sɛgmənt] n segmento; (of
orange) gomo
seize [si:z] vt agarrar, pegar; (power,
hostage) apoderar-se de, confiscar;
(territory) tomar posse de; (opportunity)
aproveitar; **seize up** vi (Tech) gripar;
seize (up)on vt fus valer-se de; **seizure**
n (Med) ataque m, acesso; (Law, of power)
confisco, embargo
seldom ['sɛldəm] adv raramente
select [sɪ'lɛkt] adj seleto, fino ▷ vt
escolher, selecionar; (Sport) selecionar,
escalar; **selection** n seleção f, escolha;
(Comm) sortimento
self [sɛlf] (pl selves) pron see **herself;
himself; itself; myself; oneself;
ourselves; themselves; yourself** ▷ n:
the ~ o eu; **self-assured** adj seguro de
si; **self-catering** (BRIT) adj (flat) com
cozinha; (holiday) em casa alugada;
self-centred (US **self-centered**)
adj egocêntrico; **self-confidence** n

autoconfiança, confiança em si; **self-
conscious** adj inibido, constrangido;
self-control n autocontrole m,
autodomínio; **self-defence** (US **self-
defense**) n legítima defesa, autodefesa;
in self-defence em legítima defesa; **self-
employed** adj autônomo; **self-interest**
n egoísmo; **selfish** adj egoísta; **self-pity**
n pena de si mesmo; **self-respect** n
amor m próprio; **self-service** adj de
auto-serviço
sell [sɛl] (pt, pp sold) vt vender; (fig): **to
~ sb an idea** convencer alguém de uma
idéia ▷ vi vender-se; **to ~ at** or **for £10**
vender a or por £10; **sell off** vt liquidar;
sell out vi vender todo o estoque
▷ vt: **the tickets are all sold out**
todos os ingressos já foram vendidos;
sell-by date n vencimento; **seller** n
vendedor(a) m/f
selves [sɛlvz] pl of self
semi... [sɛmɪ] prefix semi...,
meio...; **semicircle** n semicírculo;
semidetached (house) (BRIT) n (casa)
geminada
seminar ['sɛmɪnɑ:'] n seminário
senate ['sɛnɪt] n senado; **senator** n
senador(a) m/f
send [sɛnd] (pt, pp sent) vt mandar,
enviar; (dispatch) expedir, remeter;
(transmit) transmitir; **send away**
vt (letter, goods) expedir, mandar;
(unwelcome visitor) mandar embora; **send
away for** vt fus encomendar, pedir pelo
correio; **send back** vt devolver, mandar
de volta; **send for** vt fus mandar buscar;
(by post) encomendar, pedir pelo correio;
send off vt (goods) despachar, expedir;
(BRIT: Sport: player) expulsar; **send out** vt
(invitation) distribuir; (signal) emitir; **send
up** vt (person, price) fazer subir; (BRIT:
parody) parodiar; **sender** n remetente
m/f; **send-off** n: **a good send-off** uma
boa despedida
senior ['si:nɪə'] adj (older) mais velho or
idoso; (on staff) mais antigo; (of higher
rank) superior; **senior citizen** n idoso(-a)
sensation [sɛn'seɪʃən] n sensação f;
sensational adj sensacional; (headlines,
result) sensacionalista
sense [sɛns] n sentido; (feeling) sensação
f; (good sense) bom senso ▷ vt sentir,
perceber; **it makes ~** faz sentido;
senseless adj insensato, estúpido;
(unconscious) sem sentidos, inconsciente;
sensible adj sensato, de bom senso;

(*reasonable: price*) razoável; (: *advice, decision*) sensato

sensitive ['sɛnsɪtɪv] *adj* sensível; (*fig: touchy*) suscetível

sensual ['sɛnsjuəl] *adj* sensual

sensuous ['sɛnsjuəs] *adj* sensual

sent [sɛnt] *pt, pp of* **send**

sentence ['sɛntəns] *n* (*Ling*) frase *f*, oração *f*; (*Law*) sentença ▷ *vt*: **to ~ sb to death/to 5 years** condenar alguém à morte/a 5 anos de prisão

sentiment ['sɛntɪmənt] *n* sentimento; (*opinion: also pl*) opinião *f*; **sentimental** [sɛntɪ'mɛntl] *adj* sentimental

separate [(*adj*)'sɛprɪt, (*vb*)'sɛpəreɪt] *adj* separado; (*distinct*) diferente ▷ *vt* separar; (*part*) dividir ▷ *vi* separar-se; **separately** *adv* separadamente

September [sɛp'tɛmbə'] *n* setembro

septic ['sɛptɪk] *adj* sético; (*wound*) infeccionado

sequel ['si:kwl] *n* conseqüência, resultado; (*of film, story*) continuação *f*

sequence ['si:kwəns] *n* série *f*, seqüência; (*Cinema*) série

sequin ['si:kwɪn] *n* lantejoula, paetê *m*

sergeant ['sɑ:dʒənt] *n* sargento

serial ['sɪərɪəl] *n* seriado; **serial number** *n* número de série

series ['sɪərɪːz] *n inv* série *f*

serious ['sɪərɪəs] *adj* sério; (*matter*) importante; (*illness*) grave; **seriously** *adv* a sério, com seriedade; (*hurt*) gravemente

sermon ['sə:mən] *n* sermão *m*

servant ['sə:vənt] *n* empregado(-a); (*fig*) servidor(a) *m/f*

serve [sə:v] *vt* servir; (*customer*) atender; (*subj: train*) passar por; (*apprenticeship*) fazer; (*prison term*) cumprir ▷ *vi* (*at table*) servir-se; (*Tennis*) sacar; (*be useful*): **to ~ as/for/to do** servir como/para/para fazer ▷ *n* (*Tennis*) saque *m*; **it ~s him right** é bem feito para ele; **serve out** *vt* (*food*) servir; **serve up** *vt* = **serve out**

service ['sə:vɪs] *n* serviço; (*Rel*) culto; (*Aut*) revisão *f*; (*Tennis*) saque *m*; (*also*: **dinner ~**) aparelho de jantar ▷ *vt* (*car, washing machine*) fazer a revisão de, revisar; **the Services** *npl* (*army, navy etc*) as Forças Armadas; **to be of ~ to sb** ser útil a alguém; **service area** *n* (*on motorway*) posto de gasolina com bar, restaurante *etc*; **service charge** (*BRIT*) *n* serviço; **serviceman** (*irreg*) *n* militar *m*; **service station** *n* posto de gasolina

(*BR*), estação *f* de serviço (*PT*)

serviette [sə:vi'ɛt] (*BRIT*) *n* guardanapo

session ['sɛʃən] *n* sessão *f*; **to be in ~** estar reunido em sessão

set [sɛt] (*pt, pp ~*) *n* (*of things*) jogo; (*radio set, TV set*) aparelho; (*of utensils*) bateria de cozinha; (*of cutlery*) talher *m*; (*of books*) coleção *f*; (*of people*) grupo; (*Tennis*) set *m*; (*Theatre, Cinema*) cenário; (*Hairdressing*) penteado; (*Math*) conjunto ▷ *adj* fixo; (*ready*) pronto ▷ *vt* pôr, colocar; (*table*) pôr; (*price*) fixar; (*rules etc*) estabelecer, decidir; (*record*) estabelecer; (*time*) marcar; (*adjust*) ajustar; (*task, exam*) passar ▷ *vi* (*sun*) pôr-se; (*jam, jelly, concrete*) endurecer, solidificar-se; **to be ~ on doing sth** estar decidido a fazer algo; **to ~ to music** musicar, pôr música em; **to ~ on fire** botar fogo em, incendiar; **to ~ free** libertar; **to ~ sth going** pôr algo em movimento; **set about** *vt fus* começar com; **set aside** *vt* deixar de lado; **set back** *vt* (*cost*): **it set me back £5** me deu um prejuízo de £5; (*in time*): **to set sb back (by)** atrasar alguém (em); **set off** *vi* partir, ir indo ▷ *vt* (*bomb*) fazer explodir; (*alarm*) disparar; (*chain of events*) iniciar; (*show up well*) ressaltar; **set out** *vi* partir ▷ *vt* (*arrange*) colocar, dispor; (*state*) expor, explicar; **to set out to do sth** pretender fazer algo; **set up** *vt* fundar, estabelecer; **setback** *n* revés *m*, contratempo; **set menu** *n* refeição *f* a preço fixo

settee [sɛ'ti:] *n* sofá *m*

setting ['sɛtɪŋ] *n* (*background*) cenário; (*position*) posição *f*; (*of sun*) pôr(-do-sol) *m*; (*of jewel*) engaste *m*

settle ['sɛtl] *vt* (*argument, matter*) resolver, esclarecer; (*accounts*) ajustar, liquidar; (*Med: calm*) acalmar, tranqüilizar ▷ *vi* (*dust etc*) assentar; (*calm down: children*) acalmar-se; (*also*: **~ down**) instalar-se, estabilizar-se; **to ~ for sth** optar por algo; **to ~ on sth** optar por algo; **settle in** *vi* instalar-se; **settle up** *vi*: **to settle up with sb** ajustar as contas com alguém; **settlement** *n* (*payment*) liquidação *f*; (*agreement*) acordo, convênio; (*village etc*) povoado, povoação *f*

setup ['sɛtʌp] *n* (*organization*) organização *f*; (*situation*) situação *f*

seven ['sɛvn] *num* sete; **seventeen** *num* dezessete; **seventh** *num* sétimo; **seventy** *num* setenta

sever ['sɛvə'] vt cortar; (relations) romper
several ['sɛvərl] adj, pron vários(-as); ~ **of us** vários de nós
severe [sɪ'vɪə'] adj severo; (serious) grave; (hard) duro; (pain) intenso; (dress) austero
sew [səu] (pt ~**ed**, pp ~**n**) vt coser, costurar; **sew up** vt coser, costurar
sewage ['su:ɪdʒ] n detritos mpl
sewer ['su:ə'] n (cano do) esgoto, bueiro
sewing ['səuɪŋ] n costura; **sewing machine** n máquina de costura
sewn [səun] pp of **sew**
sex [sɛks] n sexo; **sexist** adj sexista
sexual ['sɛksjuəl] adj sexual
sexy ['sɛksɪ] adj sexy
shabby ['ʃæbɪ] adj (person) esfarrapado, maltrapilho; (clothes) usado, surrado; (behaviour) indigno
shack [ʃæk] n choupana, barraca
shade [ʃeɪd] n sombra; (for lamp) quebra-luz m; (of colour) tom m, tonalidade f; (small quantity): **a ~ (more/too large)** um pouquinho (mais/grande) ▷ vt dar sombra a; (eyes) sombrear; **in the ~** à sombra
shadow ['ʃædəu] n sombra ▷ vt (follow) seguir de perto (sem ser visto)
shady ['ʃeɪdɪ] adj à sombra; (fig: dishonest: person) suspeito, duvidoso; (: deal) desonesto
shaft [ʃɑ:ft] n (of arrow, spear) haste f; (Aut, Tech) eixo, manivela; (of mine, of lift) poço; (of light) raio
shake [ʃeɪk] (pt shook, pp ~**n**) vt sacudir; (building, confidence) abalar; (surprise) surpreender ▷ vi tremer; **to ~ hands with sb** apertar a mão de alguém; **to ~ one's head** (in refusal etc) dizer não com a cabeça; (in dismay) sacudir a cabeça; **shake off** vt sacudir; (fig) livrar-se de; **shake up** vt sacudir; (fig) reorganizar; **shaky** adj (hand, voice) trêmulo; (table) instável; (building) abalado
shall [ʃæl] aux vb: **I ~ go** irei; ~ **I open the door?** posso abrir a porta?; **I'll get some, ~ I?** eu vou pegar algum, está bem?
shallow ['ʃæləu] adj raso; (breathing) fraco; (fig) superficial
sham [ʃæm] n fraude f, fingimento ▷ vt fingir, simular
shambles ['ʃæmblz] n confusão f
shame [ʃeɪm] n vergonha ▷ vt envergonhar; **it is a ~ (that/to do)** é (uma) pena (que/fazer); **what a ~!** que pena!; **shameful** adj vergonhoso; **shameless** adj sem vergonha, descarado

shampoo [ʃæm'pu:] n xampu m (BR), champô m (PT) ▷ vt lavar o cabelo (com xampu or champô)
shandy ['ʃændɪ] n mistura de cerveja com refresco gaseificado
shan't [ʃɑ:nt] = **shall not**
shape [ʃeɪp] n forma ▷ vt (form) moldar; (sb's ideas) formar; (sb's life) definir, determinar; **to take ~** tomar forma; **shape up** vi (events) desenrolar-se; (person) tomar jeito
share [ʃɛə'] n parte f; (contribution) cota; (Comm) ação f ▷ vt dividir; (have in common) compartilhar; **share out** vi distribuir; **shareholder** n acionista m/f
shark [ʃɑ:k] n tubarão m
sharp [ʃɑ:p] adj (razor, knife) afiado; (point, features) pontiagudo; (outline) definido, bem marcado; (pain, voice) agudo; (taste) acre; (Mus) desafinado; (contrast) marcado; (quick-witted) perspicaz; (dishonest) desonesto ▷ n (Mus) sustenido ▷ adv: **at 2 o'clock ~** às 2 (horas) em ponto; **sharpen** vt afiar; (pencil) apontar, fazer a ponta de; (fig) aguçar; **sharpener** n (also: **pencil sharpener**) apontador m (BR), apara-lápis m inv (PT); **sharply** adv (abruptly) bruscamente; (clearly) claramente; (harshly) severamente
shatter ['ʃætə'] vt despedaçar, estilhaçar; (fig: ruin) destruir, acabar com; (: upset) arrasar ▷ vi despedaçar-se, estilhaçar-se
shave [ʃeɪv] vt barbear, fazer a barba de ▷ vi fazer a barba, barbear-se ▷ n: **to have a ~** fazer a barba; **shaver** n (also: **electric shaver**) barbeador m elétrico; **shaving cream** n creme m de barbear; **shaving foam** n espuma de barbear
shawl [ʃɔ:l] n xale m
she [ʃi:] pron ela ▷ prefix: ~**-elephant** etc elefante etc fêmea
sheath [ʃi:θ] n bainha; (contraceptive) camisa-de-vênus f, camisinha
shed [ʃed] (pt, pp ~) n alpendre m, galpão m ▷ vt (skin) mudar; (load) perder; (tears, blood) derramar; (workers) despedir
she'd [ʃi:d] = **she had; she would**
sheep [ʃi:p] n inv ovelha; **sheepdog** n cão m pastor; **sheepskin** n pele f de carneiro, pelego
sheer [ʃɪə'] adj (utter) puro, completo; (steep) íngreme, empinado; (almost transparent) fino, translúcido ▷ adv a pique

sheet [ʃiːt] n (on bed) lençol m; (of paper) folha; (of glass, metal) lâmina, chapa; (of ice) camada

sheik(h) [ʃeɪk] n xeque m

shelf [ʃɛlf] (pl **shelves**) n prateleira

shell [ʃɛl] n (on beach) concha; (of egg, nut etc) casca; (explosive) obus m; (of building) armação f, esqueleto ▷ vt (peas) descascar; (Mil) bombardear

she'll [ʃiːl] = **she will; she shall**

shellfish [ʃɛlfɪʃ] n inv crustáceo; (pl: as food) frutos mpl do mar, mariscos mpl

shelter [ʃɛltə] n (building) abrigo; (protection) refúgio ▷ vt (protect) proteger; (give lodging to) abrigar ▷ vi abrigar-se, refugiar-se

shepherd [ʃɛpəd] n pastor m ▷ vt guiar, conduzir; **shepherd's pie** (BRIT) n empadão m de carne e batata

sheriff [ʃɛrɪf] (US) n xerife m

sherry [ʃɛrɪ] n (vinho de) Xerez m

she's [ʃiːz] = **she is; she has**

Shetland [ʃɛtlənd] n (also: **the ~s, the ~ Isles**) as ilhas Shetland

shield [ʃiːld] n escudo; (Sport) escudo, brasão m; (protection) proteção f ▷ vt: **to ~ (from)** proteger (contra)

shift [ʃɪft] n mudança; (of work) turno; (of workers) turma ▷ vt transferir; (remove) tirar ▷ vi mudar

shin [ʃɪn] n canela (da perna)

shine [ʃaɪn] (pt, pp **shone**) n brilho, lustre m ▷ vi brilhar ▷ vt (glasses) polir; (shoes: pt, pp **shined**) lustrar; **to ~ a torch on sth** apontar uma lanterna para algo

shingles [ʃ] n (Med) herpes-zoster m

shiny [ʃaɪnɪ] adj brilhante, lustroso

ship [ʃɪp] n barco ▷ vt (goods) embarcar; (send) transportar or mandar (por via marítima); **shipment** n carregamento; **shipping** n (ships) navios mpl; (cargo) transporte m de mercadorias (por via marítima); (traffic) navegação f; **shipwreck** n (event) malogro; (ship) naufrágio ▷ vt: **to be shipwrecked** naufragar; **shipyard** n estaleiro

shirt [ʃəːt] n (man's) camisa; (woman's) blusa; **in ~ sleeves** em manga de camisa

shiver [ʃɪvə] n tremor m, arrepio ▷ vi tremer, estremecer, tiritar

shock [ʃɔk] n (impact) choque m; (Elec) descarga; (emotional) comoção f, abalo; (start) susto, sobressalto; (Med) trauma m ▷ vt dar um susto em, chocar; (offend) escandalizar; **shocking** adj chocante, lamentável; (outrageous) revoltante,

chocante

shoe [ʃuː] (pt, pp **shod**) n sapato; (for horse) ferradura ▷ vt (horse) ferrar; **shoelace** n cadarço, cordão m (de sapato); **shoe polish** n graxa de sapato; **shoeshop** n sapataria

shone [ʃɔn] pt, pp of **shine**

shook [ʃuk] pt of **shake**

shoot [ʃuːt] (pt, pp **shot**) n (on branch, seedling) broto ▷ vt disparar; (kill) matar à bala, balear; (wound) ferir à bala, balear; (execute) fuzilar; (film) filmar, rodar ▷ vi: **to ~ (at)** atirar (em); (Football) chutar; **shoot down** vt (plane) derrubar, abater; **shoot in/out** vi entrar/sair correndo; **shoot up** vi (fig) subir vertiginosamente

shop [ʃɔp] n loja; (workshop) oficina ▷ vi (also: **go ~ping**) ir fazer compras; **shop assistant** (BRIT) n vendedor(a) m/f; **shopkeeper** n lojista m/f; **shoplifting** n furto (em lojas); **shopping** n (goods) compras fpl; **shopping bag** n bolsa (de compras); **shopping centre** (US **shopping center**) n shopping (center) m; **shop window** n vitrine f (BR), montra (PT)

shore [ʃɔː] n (of sea) costa, praia; (of lake) margem f ▷ vt: **to ~ (up)** reforçar, escorar; **on ~** em terra

short [ʃɔːt] adj curto; (in time) breve, de curta duração; (person) baixo; (curt) seco, brusco; (insufficient) insuficiente, em falta; **to be ~ of sth** estar em falta de algo; **in ~** em resumo; **~ of doing ...** a não ser fazer ...; **everything ~ of ...** tudo a não ser ...; **it is ~ for** é a abreviatura de; **to cut ~** (speech, visit) encurtar; **to fall ~ of** não ser à altura de; **to run ~ of sth** ficar sem algo; **to stop ~** parar de repente; **to stop ~ of** chegar quase a; **shortage** n escassez f, falta; **shortbread** n biscoito amanteigado; **shortcoming** n defeito, imperfeição f, falha; **short(crust) pastry** (BRIT) n massa amanteigada; **shortcut** n atalho; **shorten** vt encurtar; (visit) abreviar; **shorthand** (BRIT) n estenografia; **shortly** adv em breve, dentro em pouco; **shorts** npl: **(a pair of) shorts** um calção (BR), um short (BR), uns calções (PT); **short-sighted** (BRIT) adj míope; (fig) imprevidente; **short story** n conto; **short-tempered** adj irritadiço; **short-term** adj a curto prazo

shot [ʃɔt] pt, pp of **shoot** ▷ n (of gun) tiro; (pellets) chumbo; (try, Football) tentativa;

(*injection*) injeção f; (*Phot*) fotografia; **to be a good/bad ~** (*person*) ter boa/má pontaria; **like a ~** como um relâmpago, de repente; **shotgun** n espingarda

should [ʃʊd] *aux vb*: **I ~ go now** devo ir embora agora; **he ~ be there now** ele já deve ter chegado; **I ~ go if I were you** se eu fosse você eu iria; **I ~ like to** eu gostaria de

shoulder [ˈʃəʊldəʳ] n ombro ▷ vt (*fig*) arcar com; **shoulder blade** n omoplata f

shouldn't [ˈʃʊdnt] = **should not**

shout [ʃaʊt] n grito ▷ vt gritar ▷ vi (*also*: **~ out**) gritar, berrar; **shout down** vt fazer calar com gritos

shove [ʃʌv] vt empurrar; (*inf*: *put*): **to ~ sth in** botar algo em; **shove off** (*inf*) vi dar o fora

shovel [ˈʃʌvl] n pá f; (*mechanical*) escavadeira ▷ vt cavar com pá

show [ʃəʊ] (*pt* **~ed**, *pp* **~n**) n (*of emotion*) demonstração f; (*semblance*) aparência; (*exhibition*) exibição f; (*Theatre*) espetáculo, representação f; (*Cinema*) sessão f ▷ vt mostrar; (*courage etc*) demonstrar, dar prova de; (*exhibit*) exibir, expor; (*depict*) ilustrar; (*film*) exibir ▷ vi mostrar-se; (*appear*) aparecer; **to be on ~** estar em exposição; **show in** vt mandar entrar; **show off** vi (*pej*) mostrar-se, exibir-se ▷ vt (*display*) exibir, mostrar; **show out** vt levar até à porta; **show up** vi (*stand out*) destacar-se; (*inf*: *turn up*) aparecer, pintar ▷ vt descobrir; **show business** n o mundo do espetáculo

shower [ˈʃaʊəʳ] n (*rain*) pancada de chuva; (*of stones etc*) chuva, enxurrada; (*also*: **~ bath**) chuveiro ▷ vi tomar banho (de chuveiro) ▷ vt: **to ~ sb with** (*gifts etc*) cumular alguém de; **to have** or **take a ~** tomar banho (de chuveiro)

showing [ˈʃəʊɪŋ] n (*of film*) projeção f, exibição f

show jumping [-ˈdʒʌmpɪŋ] n hipismo

shown [ʃəʊn] *pp* of **show**

show: **show-off** (*inf*) n (*person*) exibicionista m/f, faroleiro(-a); **showpiece** n (*of exhibition etc*) obra mais importante; **showroom** n sala de exposição

shrank [ʃræŋk] *pt* of **shrink**

shred [ʃred] n (*gen pl*) tira, pedaço ▷ vt rasgar em tiras, retalhar; (*Culin*) desfiar, picar

shrewd [ʃruːd] *adj* perspicaz

shriek [ʃriːk] n grito ▷ vi gritar, berrar

shrimp [ʃrɪmp] n camarão m

shrine [ʃraɪn] n santuário

shrink [ʃrɪŋk] (*pt* **shrank**, *pp* **shrunk**) vi encolher; (*be reduced*) reduzir-se; (*also*: **~ away**) encolher-se ▷ vt (*cloth*) fazer encolher ▷ n (*inf*: *pej*) psicanalista m/f; **to ~ from doing sth** não se atrever a fazer algo

shrivel [ˈʃrɪvl] vt (*also*: **~ up**: *dry*) secar; (: *crease*) enrugar ▷ vi secar-se; enrugar-se, murchar

Shrove Tuesday [ʃrəʊv-] n terça-feira gorda

shrub [ʃrʌb] n arbusto

shrug [ʃrʌg] n encolhimento dos ombros ▷ vt, vi: **to ~ (one's shoulders)** encolher os ombros, dar de ombros (BR); **shrug off** vt negar a importância de

shrunk [ʃrʌŋk] *pp* of **shrink**

shudder [ˈʃʌdəʳ] n estremecimento, tremor m ▷ vi estremecer, tremer de medo

shuffle [ˈʃʌfl] vt (*cards*) embaralhar ▷ vi: **to ~ (one's feet)** arrastar os pés

shun [ʃʌn] vt evitar, afastar-se de

shut [ʃʌt] (*pt*, *pp* **~**) vt fechar ▷ vi fechar(-se); **shut down** vt, vi fechar; **shut off** vt cortar, interromper; **shut up** vi (*inf*: *keep quiet*) calar-se, calar a boca ▷ vt (*close*) fechar; (*silence*) calar; **shutter** n veneziana; (*Phot*) obturador m

shuttle [ˈʃʌtl] n (*plane*: *also*: **~ service**) ponte f aérea; (*space shuttle*) ônibus m espacial

shuttlecock [ˈʃʌtlkɔk] n peteca

shy [ʃaɪ] *adj* tímido; (*reserved*) reservado

sick [sɪk] *adj* (*ill*) doente; (*nauseated*) enjoado; (*humour*) negro; (*vomiting*): **to be ~** vomitar; **to feel ~** estar enjoado; **to be ~ of** (*fig*) estar cheio or farto de; **sickening** *adj* (*fig*) repugnante

sick: **sick leave** n licença por doença; **sickly** *adj* doentio; (*causing nausea*) nauseante; **sickness** n doença, indisposição f; (*vomiting*) náusea, enjôo

side [saɪd] n lado; (*of body*) flanco; (*of lake*) margem f; (*aspect*) aspecto; (*team*) time m (BR), equipa (PT); (*of hill*) declive m ▷ cpd (*door*, *entrance*) lateral ▷ vi: **to ~ with sb** tomar o partido de alguém; **by the ~ of** ao lado de; **~ by ~** lado a lado, juntos; **from ~ to ~** para lá e para cá; **to take ~s with** pôr-se ao lado de; **sideboard** n aparador m; **sideboards** *npl* (BRIT) = **sideburns**; **sideburns** *npl* suiças *fpl*, costeletas *fpl*; **side effect** *n* efeito colateral; **sidelight** *n* (Aut) luz *f* lateral; **sidetrack** *vt* (fig) desviar (do seu propósito); **sidewalk** (us) *n* calçada; **sideways** *adv* de lado

siege [siːdʒ] *n* sítio, assédio

sieve [sɪv] *n* peneira ▷ *vt* peneirar

sift [sɪft] *vt* peneirar; (fig) esquadrinhar, analisar minuciosamente

sigh [saɪ] *n* suspiro ▷ *vi* suspirar

sight [saɪt] *n* (faculty) vista, visão *f*; (spectacle) espetáculo; (on gun) mira ▷ *vt* avistar; **in** ~ à vista; **on** ~ (shoot) no local; **out of** ~ longe dos olhos; **sightseeing** *n* turismo; **to go sightseeing** fazer turismo, passear

sign [saɪn] *n* (with hand) sinal *m*, aceno; (indication) indício; (notice) letreiro, tabuleta; (written) signo ▷ *vt* assinar; **to ~ sth over to sb** assinar a transferência de algo para alguém; **sign on** *vi* (Mil) alistar-se; (BRIT: as unemployed) cadastrar-se para receber auxílio-desemprego; (for course) inscrever-se ▷ *vt* (Mil) alistar; (employee) efetivar; **sign up** *vi* (Mil) alistar-se; (for course) inscrever-se ▷ *vt* recrutar

signal [ˈsɪgnl] *n* sinal *m*, aviso ▷ *vi* (also: Aut) sinalizar, dar sinal ▷ *vt* (person) fazer sinais para; (message) transmitir

signature [ˈsɪgnətʃəʳ] *n* assinatura

significance [sɪgˈnɪfɪkəns] *n* importância; **significant** *adj* significativo; (important) importante

sign language *n* mímica, linguagem *f* através de sinais

silence [ˈsaɪləns] *n* silêncio ▷ *vt* silenciar, impor silêncio a

silent [ˈsaɪlənt] *adj* silencioso; (not speaking) calado; (film) mudo; **to remain** ~ manter-se em silêncio

silhouette [sɪluːˈɛt] *n* silhueta

silicon chip [ˈsɪlɪkən-] *n* placa or chip *m* de silício

silk [sɪlk] *n* seda ▷ *adj* de seda

silly [ˈsɪlɪ] *adj* (person) bobo, idiota, imbecil; (idea) absurdo, ridículo

silver [ˈsɪlvəʳ] *n* prata; (money) moedas *fpl*; (also: ~ware) prataria ▷ *adj* de prata; **silver-plated** *adj* prateado, banhado a prata

similar [ˈsɪmɪləʳ] *adj*: ~ **to** parecido com, semelhante a

simmer [ˈsɪməʳ] *vi* cozer em fogo lento, ferver lentamente

simple [ˈsɪmpl] *adj* simples *inv*; (foolish)

ingênuo; **simply** *adv* de maneira simples; (merely) simplesmente

simultaneous [sɪməlˈteɪnɪəs] *adj* simultâneo

sin [sɪn] *n* pecado ▷ *vi* pecar

since [sɪns] *adv* desde então, depois ▷ *prep* desde ▷ *conj* (time) desde que; (because) porque, visto que, já que; ~ **then** desde então; **(ever)** ~ desde que

sincere [sɪnˈsɪəʳ] *adj* sincero; **sincerely** *adv*: **yours sincerely** (at end of letter) atenciosamente

sing [sɪŋ] (pt **sang**, pp **sung**) *vt*, *vi* cantar

Singapore [sɪŋgəˈpɔː] *n* Cingapura (no article)

singer [ˈsɪŋəʳ] *n* cantor(a) *m/f*

singing [ˈsɪŋɪŋ] *n* canto; (songs) canções *fpl*

single [ˈsɪŋgl] *adj* único, só; (unmarried) solteiro; (not double) simples *inv* ▷ *n* (BRIT: also: ~ **ticket**) passagem *f* de ida; (record) compacto; **single out** *vt* (choose) escolher; (distinguish) distinguir; **single file** *n*: **in single file** em fila indiana; **single-handed** *adv* sem ajuda, sozinho; **single-minded** *adj* determinado; **single room** *n* quarto individual

singular [ˈsɪŋgjuləʳ] *adj* (odd) esquisito; (outstanding) extraordinário, excepcional; (Ling) singular ▷ *n* (Ling) singular *m*

sinister [ˈsɪnɪstəʳ] *adj* sinistro

sink [sɪŋk] (pt **sank**, pp **sunk**) *n* pia ▷ *vt* (ship) afundar; (foundations) escavar ▷ *vi* afundar-se; (heart) partir; (spirits) ficar deprimido; (also: ~ **back**, ~ **down**) cair or mergulhar gradativamente; **to ~ sth into** enterrar algo em; **sink in** *vi* (fig) penetrar

sinus [ˈsaɪnəs] *n* (Anat) seio paranasal

sip [sɪp] *n* gole *m* ▷ *vt* sorver, bebericar

sir [səʳ] *n* senhor *m*; **S~ John Smith** Sir John Smith; **yes,** ~ sim, senhor

siren [ˈsaɪərn] *n* sirena

sirloin [ˈsəːlɔɪn] *n* lombo de vaca

sister [ˈsɪstəʳ] *n* irmã *f*; (BRIT: nurse) enfermeira-chefe *f*; (nun) freira; **sister-in-law** *n* cunhada

sit [sɪt] (pt, pp **sat**) *vi* sentar-se; (be sitting) estar sentado; (assembly) reunir-se; (for painter) posar ▷ *vt* (exam) prestar; **sit down** *vi* sentar-se; **sit in on** *vt fus* assistir a; **sit up** *vi* (after lying) levantar-se; (straight) endireitar-se; (not go to bed) aguardar acordado, velar

sitcom [ˈsɪtkɔm] *n abbr* (= situation

comedy) comédia de costumes
site [saɪt] *n* local *m*, sítio; (*also*: **building ~**) lote *m* (de terreno) ▷ *vt* situar, localizar
sitting ['sɪtɪŋ] *n* (*in canteen*) turno; **sitting room** *n* sala de estar
situation [sɪtju'eɪʃən] *n* situação *f*; (*job*) posição *f*; (*location*) local *m*; "**~s vacant**" (BRIT) "empregos oferecem-se"
six [sɪks] *num* seis; **sixteen** *num* dezesseis; **sixth** *num* sexto; **sixty** *num* sessenta
size [saɪz] *n* tamanho; (*extent*) extensão *f*; (*of clothing*) tamanho, medida; (*of shoes*) número; **size up** *vt* avaliar, formar uma opinião sobre; **sizeable** *adj* considerável, importante
sizzle ['sɪzl] *vi* chiar
skate [skeɪt] *n* patim *m*; (*fish*: *pl inv*) arraia ▷ *vi* patinar; **skateboard** *n* skate *m*, patim-tábua *m*; **skating** *n* patinação *f*; **skating rink** *n* rinque *m* de patinação
skeleton ['skɛlɪtn] *n* esqueleto; (*Tech*) armação *f*; (*outline*) esquema *m*, esboço
sketch [skɛtʃ] *n* (*drawing*) desenho; (*outline*) esboço, croqui *m*; (*Theatre*) quadro, esquete *m* ▷ *vt* desenhar, esboçar; (*ideas*: *also*: **~ out**) esboçar
skewer ['skjuːəʳ] *n* espetinho
ski [skiː] *n* esqui *m* ▷ *vi* esquiar; **ski boot** *n* bota de esquiar
skid [skɪd] *n* derrapagem *f* ▷ *vi* deslizar; (*Aut*) derrapar
ski: **skier** *n* esquiador(a) *m/f*; **skiing** *n* esqui *m*
skilful ['skɪlful] (US **skillful**) *adj* habilidoso, jeitoso
ski lift *n* ski lift *m*
skill [skɪl] *n* habilidade *f*, perícia; (*for work*) técnica; **skilled** *adj* hábil, perito; (*worker*) especializado, qualificado
skim [skɪm] *vt* (*milk*) desnatar; (*glide over*) roçar ▷ *vi*: **to ~ through** (*book*) folhear; **skimmed milk** *n* leite *m* desnatado
skin [skɪn] *n* pele *f*; (*of fruit, vegetable*) casca ▷ *vt* (*fruit etc*) descascar; (*animal*) tirar a pele de; **skinny** *adj* magro, descarnado
skip [skɪp] *n* salto, pulo; (*BRIT*: *container*) balde *m* ▷ *vi* saltar; (*with rope*) pular corda ▷ *vt* (*pass over*) omitir, saltar; (*miss*) deixar de
skipper ['skɪpəʳ] *n* capitão *m*
skipping rope ['skɪpɪŋ-] (*BRIT*) *n* corda (de pular)
skirt [skəːt] *n* saia ▷ *vt* orlar, circundar
skirting board (*BRIT*) *n* rodapé *m*

skull [skʌl] *n* caveira; (*Anat*) crânio
skunk [skʌŋk] *n* gambá *m*
sky [skaɪ] *n* céu *m*; **skyscraper** *n* arranha-céu *m*
slab [slæb] *n* (*stone*) bloco; (*flat*) laje *f*; (*of cake*) fatia grossa
slack [slæk] *adj* (*loose*) frouxo; (*slow*) lerdo; (*careless*) descuidado, desmazelado; **slacks** *npl* (*trousers*) calça (BR), calças *fpl* (PT)
slam [slæm] *vt* (*door*) bater or fechar (com violência); (*throw*) atirar violentamente; (*criticize*) malhar, criticar ▷ *vi* fechar-se (com violência)
slander ['slɑːndəʳ] *n* calúnia, difamação *f*
slang [slæŋ] *n* gíria; (*jargon*) jargão *m*
slant [slɑːnt] *n* declive *m*, inclinação *f*; (*fig*) ponto de vista
slap [slæp] *n* tapa *m* or *f* ▷ *vt* dar um(a) tapa em; (*paint etc*): **to ~ sth on sth** passar algo em algo descuidadamente ▷ *adv* diretamente, exatamente
slash [slæʃ] *vt* cortar, talhar; (*fig: prices*) cortar
slate [sleɪt] *n* ardósia ▷ *vt* (*fig: criticize*) criticar duramente, arrasar
slaughter ['slɔːtəʳ] *n* (*of animals*) matança; (*of people*) carnificina ▷ *vt* abater; matar, massacrar; **slaughterhouse** *n* matadouro
slave [sleɪv] *n* escravo(-a) ▷ *vi* (*also*: **~ away**) trabalhar como escravo; **slavery** *n* escravidão *f*
slay [sleɪ] (*pt* **slew**, *pp* **slain**) *vt* (*literary*) matar
sleazy ['sliːzɪ] *adj* sórdido
sledge [slɛdʒ] *n* trenó *m*
sleek [sliːk] *adj* (*hair, fur*) macio, lustroso; (*car, boat*) aerodinâmico
sleep [sliːp] (*pt*, *pp* **slept**) *n* sono ▷ *vi* dormir; **to go to ~** dormir, adormecer; **sleep around** *vi* ser promíscuo sexualmente; **sleep in** *vi* (*oversleep*) dormir demais; **sleeper** *n* (*Rail*: *train*) vagão-leitos *m* (BR), carruagem-camas *f* (PT); **sleeping bag** *n* saco de dormir; **sleeping car** *n* vagão-leitos *m* (BR), carruagem-camas *f* (PT); **sleeping pill** *n* pílula para dormir; **sleepy** *adj* sonolento; (*fig*) morto
sleet [sliːt] *n* chuva com neve or granizo
sleeve [sliːv] *n* manga; (*of record*) capa
sleigh [sleɪ] *n* trenó *m*
slender ['slɛndəʳ] *adj* esbelto, delgado; (*means*) escasso, insuficiente
slept [slɛpt] *pt*, *pp* of **sleep**

slice [slaɪs] n (of meat, bread) fatia; (of lemon) rodela; (utensil) pá f or espátula de bolo ▷ vt cortar em fatias

slick [slɪk] adj (skilful) jeitoso, ágil, engenhoso; (clever) esperto, astuto ▷ n (also: **oil ~**) mancha de óleo

slide [slaɪd] (pt, pp **slid**) n deslizamento, escorregão m; (in playground) escorregador m; (Phot) slide m; (BRIT: also: **hair ~**) passador m ▷ vt deslizar ▷ vi escorregar; **sliding** adj (door) corrediço

slight [slaɪt] adj (slim) fraco, franzino; (frail) delicado; (small) pequeno; (trivial) insignificante ▷ n desfeita, desconsideração f; **not in the ~est** em absoluto, de maneira alguma; **slightly** adv ligeiramente, um pouco

slim [slɪm] adj esbelto, delgado; (chance) pequeno ▷ vi emagrecer

slimming ['slɪmɪŋ] n emagrecimento

sling [slɪŋ] (pt, pp **slung**) n (Med) tipóia; (for baby) bebêbag m; (weapon) estilingue m, funda ▷ vt atirar, arremessar, lançar

slip [slɪp] n (fall) escorregão m; (mistake) erro, lapso; (underskirt) combinação f; (of paper) tira ▷ vt deslizar ▷ vi (slide) deslizar; (lose balance) escorregar; (decline) decair; (move smoothly): **to ~ into/out of** entrar furtivamente em/sair furtivamente de; **to ~ sth on/off** enfiar/tirar algo; **to give sb the ~** esgueirar-se de alguém; **a ~ of the tongue** um lapso da língua; **slip away** vi escapulir; **slip in** vt meter ▷ vi (errors) surgir; **slip out** vi (go out) sair (um momento); **slip up** vi cometer um erro

slipper ['slɪpə*] n chinelo

slippery ['slɪpərɪ] adj escorregadio

slip-up n equívoco, mancada

slit [slɪt] (pt, pp ~) n fenda; (cut) corte m ▷ vt (cut) rachar, cortar; (open) abrir

slog [slɔg] (BRIT) vi mourejar ▷ n: **it was a ~** deu um trabalho louco

slogan ['sləugən] n lema m, slogan m

slope [sləup] n ladeira; (side of mountain) encosta, vertente f; (ski slope) pista; (slant) inclinação f, declive m ▷ vi: **to ~ down** estar em declive; **to ~ up** inclinar-se; **sloping** adj inclinado, em declive; (handwriting) torto

sloppy ['slɔpɪ] adj (work) descuidado; (appearance) relaxado

slot [slɔt] n (in machine) fenda ▷ vt: **to ~ into** encaixar em

slow [sləu] adj lento; (not clever) bronco, de raciocínio lento; (watch): **to be ~** atrasar ▷ adv lentamente, devagar ▷ vt, vi ir (mais) devagar; **"~"** (road sign) "devagar"; **slowly** adv lentamente, devagar; **slow motion** n: **in slow motion** em câmara lenta

slug [slʌg] n lesma; **sluggish** adj vagaroso; (business) lento

slum [slʌm] n (area) favela; (house) cortiço, barraco

slump [slʌmp] n (economic) depressão f; (Comm) baixa, queda ▷ vi (person) cair; (prices) baixar repentinamente

slung [slʌŋ] pt, pp of **sling**

slur [slə:*] n calúnia ▷ vt pronunciar indistintamente

slush [slʌʃ] n neve f meio derretida

sly [slaɪ] adj (person) astuto; (smile, remark) malicioso, velhaco

smack [smæk] n palmada ▷ vt bater; (child) dar uma palmada em; (on face) dar um tabefe em ▷ vi: **to ~ of** cheirar a, saber a

small [smɔ:l] adj pequeno; **small change** n trocado

smart [smɑ:t] adj elegante; (clever) inteligente, astuto; (quick) vivo, esperto ▷ vi sofrer

smash [smæʃ] n (also: **~-up**) colisão f, choque m; (smash hit) sucesso de bilheteira ▷ vt (break) escangalhar, despedaçar; (car etc) bater com; (Sport: record) quebrar ▷ vi despedaçar-se; (against wall etc) espatifar-se; **smashing** (inf) adj excelente

smear [smɪə*] n mancha, nódoa; (Med) esfregaço ▷ vt untar; (to make dirty) lambuzar

smell [smɛl] (pt, pp **smelt** or ~ed) n cheiro; (sense) olfato ▷ vt cheirar ▷ vi (food etc) cheirar; (pej) cheirar mal; **to ~ of** cheirar a; **smelly** (pej) adj fedorento, malcheiroso

smile [smaɪl] n sorriso ▷ vi sorrir

smirk [smə:k] (pej) n sorriso falso or afetado

smog [smɔg] n nevoeiro com fumaça (BR) or fumo (PT)

smoke [sməuk] n fumaça (BR), fumo (PT) ▷ vi fumar; (chimney) fumegar ▷ vt (cigarettes) fumar; **smoked** adj (bacon) defumado; (glass) fumée; **smoker** n (person) fumante m/f; (Rail) vagão m para fumantes; **smoking** n: **"no smoking"** (sign) "proibido fumar"; **smoky** adj enfumaçado; (taste) defumado

smooth [smu:ð] adj liso, macio; (sauce)

cremoso; (sea) tranqüilo, calmo; (flavour, movement) suave; (person: pej) meloso ▷ vt (also: ~ out) alisar; (: difficulties) aplainar

smother ['smʌðə'] vt (fire) abafar; (person) sufocar; (emotions) reprimir

SMS n abbr (= short message service) SMS m

smudge [smʌdʒ] n mancha ▷ vt manchar, sujar

smug [smʌg] (pej) adj convencido

smuggle ['smʌgl] vt contrabandear; **smuggling** n contrabando

snack [snæk] n lanche m (BR), merenda (PT); **snack bar** n lanchonete f (BR), snackbar m (PT)

snag [snæg] n dificuldade f, obstáculo

snail [sneɪl] n caracol m

snake [sneɪk] n cobra

snap [snæp] n (sound) estalo; (photograph) foto f ▷ adj repentino ▷ vt quebrar; (fingers) estalar ▷ vi quebrar; (fig: person) retrucar asperamente; **to ~ shut** fechar com um estalo; **snap at** vt fus (subj: dog) tentar morder; **snap off** vt (break) partir; **snap up** vt arrebatar, comprar rapidamente; **snapshot** n foto f (instantânea)

snarl [snɑːl] vi grunhir

snatch [snætʃ] n (small piece) trecho ▷ vt agarrar; (fig: look) roubar

sneak [sniːk] (pt ~ed (US)) snuck vi: **to ~ in/out** entrar/sair furtivamente ▷ n (inf) dedo-duro; **to ~ up on sb** chegar de mausinho perto de alguém; **sneakers** npl tênis m (BR), sapatos mpl de treino (PT)

sneer [snɪə'] vi rir-se com desdém; (mock): **to ~ at** zombar de, desprezar

sneeze [sniːz] n espirro ▷ vi espirrar

sniff [snɪf] n fungada; (of dog) farejada; (of person) fungadela ▷ vi fungar ▷ vt fungar, farejar; (glue, drug) cheirar

snigger ['snɪgə'] vi rir-se com dissimulação

snip [snɪp] n tesourada; (BRIT: inf) pechincha ▷ vt cortar com tesoura

sniper ['snaɪpə'] n franco-atirador(a) m/f

snob [snɔb] n esnobe m/f

snooker ['snuːkə'] n sinuca

snoop [snuːp] vi: **to ~ about** bisbilhotar

snooze [snuːz] n soneca ▷ vi tirar uma soneca, dormir

snore [snɔː'] vi roncar ▷ n ronco

snorkel ['snɔːkl] n tubo snorkel

snort [snɔːt] n bufo, bufido ▷ vi bufar

snow [snəu] n neve f ▷ vi nevar; **snowball** n bola de neve ▷ vi (fig) aumentar (como bola de neve);

snowdrift n monte m de neve (formado pelo vento); **snowman** (irreg) n boneco de neve; **snowplough** (US **snowplow**) n máquina limpa-neve, removedor m de neve; **snowstorm** n nevasca, tempestade f de neve

snub [snʌb] vt desdenhar, menosprezar ▷ n repulsa

snug [snʌg] adj (sheltered) abrigado, protegido; (fitted) justo, cômodo

KEYWORD

so [səu] adv **1** (thus, likewise) assim, deste modo; **so saying he walked away** falou isto e foi embora; **if so** se for assim, se assim é; **I didn't do it - you did so** não fiz isso - você fez!; **so do I, so am I** etc eu também; **so it is!** é verdade!; **I hope/think so** espero/acho que sim; **so far** até aqui

2 (in comparisons etc: to such a degree) tão; **so big/quickly (that)** tão grande/ rápido (que)

3: **so much** adj, adv tanto; **I've got so much work** tenho tanto trabalho; **so many** tantos(-as); **there are so many people to see** tem tanta gente para ver

4 (phrases): **10 or so** 10 mais ou menos; **so long!** (inf: goodbye) tchau!

▷ conj **1** (expressing purpose): **so as to** do para fazer; **we hurried so as not to be late** nós apressamos para não chegarmos atrasados; **so (that)** para que, a fim de que

2 (result) de modo que; **he didn't arrive so I left** como ele não chegou, eu fui embora; **so I was right after all** então eu estava certo no final das contas

soak [səuk] vt embeber, ensopar; (put in water) pôr de molho ▷ vi estar de molho, impregnar-se; **soak in** vi infiltrar; **soak up** vt absorver

soap [səup] n sabão m; **soap opera** n novela; **soap powder** n sabão m em pó

soar [sɔː'] vi (on wings) elevar-se em vôo; (rocket, temperature) subir; (building etc) levantar-se; (price, production) disparar

sob [sɔb] n soluço ▷ vi soluçar

sober ['səubə'] adj (serious) sério; (not drunk) sóbrio; (colour, style) discreto; **sober up** vi ficar sóbrio

so-called [-kɔːld] adj chamado

soccer ['sɔkə'] n futebol m

social ['səuʃl] adj social ▷ n reunião f

social; **socialism** n socialismo; **socialist**
adj, n socialista m/f; **socialize** vi: **to
socialize (with)** socializar (com); **social
security** (BRIT) n previdência social;
social work n assistência social, serviço
social; **social worker** n assistente m/f
social

society [sə'saɪətɪ] n sociedade f; (club)
associação f; (also: **high ~**) alta sociedade

sociology [səʊsɪ'ɒlədʒɪ] n sociologia

sock [sɒk] n meia (BR), peúga (PT)

socket ['sɒkɪt] n bocal m, encaixe m;
(BRIT: Elec) tomada

soda ['səʊdə] n (Chem) soda; (also: **~
water**) água com gás; (US: also: **~ pop**)
soda

sofa ['səʊfə] n sofá m

soft [sɒft] adj mole; (voice, music, light)
suave; (kind) meigo, bondoso; **soft
drink** n refrigerante m; **soften** vt
amolecer, amaciar; (effect) abrandar;
(expression) suavizar ▷ vi amolecer-se;
(voice, expression) suavizar-se; **softly** adv
suavemente; (gently) delicadamente;
software n (Comput) software m

soggy ['sɒgɪ] adj ensopado, encharcado

soil [sɔɪl] n terra, solo; (territory) território
▷ vt sujar, manchar

solar ['səʊləʳ] adj solar

sold [səʊld] pt, pp of **sell** ▷ adj: **~ out**
(Comm) esgotado

soldier ['səʊldʒəʳ] n soldado; (army man)
militar m

sole [səʊl] n (of foot, shoe) sola; (fish: pl inv)
solha, linguado ▷ adj único

solicitor [sə'lɪsɪtəʳ] (BRIT) n (for wills
etc) tabelião(-lioa) m/f; (in court)
= advogado(-a)

solid ['sɒlɪd] adj sólido; (gold etc) maciço;
(person) sério ▷ n sólido; **solids** npl (food)
comida sólida

solitary ['sɒlɪtərɪ] adj solitário, só; (walk)
só; (isolated) isolado, retirado; (single)
único

solo ['səʊləʊ] n, adv solo; **soloist** n
solista m/f

solution [sə'lu:ʃən] n solução f

solve [sɒlv] vt resolver, solucionar

solvent ['sɒlvənt] adj (Comm) solvente
▷ n (Chem) solvente m

◯ KEYWORD

some [sʌm] adj **1** (a certain number or
amount): **some tea/water/biscuits** um
pouco de chá/água/uns biscoitos; **some**

children came algumas crianças vieram
2 (certain: in contrasts) algum(a); **some
people say that …** algumas pessoas
dizem que …
3 (unspecified) um pouco de; **some
woman was asking for you** uma
mulher estava perguntando por você;
some day um dia
▷ pron **1** (a certain number) alguns
(algumas); **I've got some** (books etc)
tenho alguns; **some went for a taxi and
some walked** alguns foram pegar um
táxi e outros foram andando
2 (a certain amount) um pouco; **I've got
some** (milk etc) tenho um pouco
▷ adv: **some 10 people** umas 10 pessoas

some: **somebody** ['sʌmbədɪ] pron
= **someone**; **somehow** ['sʌmhaʊ] adv
de alguma maneira; (for some reason)
por uma razão ou outra; **someone**
['sʌmwʌn] pron alguém; **someplace**
['sʌmpleɪs] (US) adv = **somewhere**

something ['sʌmθɪŋ] pron alguma
coisa, algo (BR)

sometime ['sʌmtaɪm] adv (in future)
algum dia, em outra oportunidade;
(in past): **~ last month** durante o mês
passado

sometimes ['sʌmtaɪmz] adv às vezes, de
vez em quando

somewhat ['sʌmwɒt] adv um tanto

somewhere ['sʌmweəʳ] adv (be) em
algum lugar; (go) para algum lugar; **~
else** em outro lugar; para outro lugar

son [sʌn] n filho

song [sɒŋ] n canção f; (of bird) canto

son-in-law ['sʌnɪnlɔ:] n genro

soon [su:n] adv logo, brevemente;
(a short time after) logo após; (early)
cedo; **~ afterwards** pouco depois; see
also **as**; **sooner** adv antes, mais cedo;
(preference): **I would sooner do that**
preferia fazer isso; **sooner or later** mais
cedo ou mais tarde

soothe [su:ð] vt acalmar, sossegar; (pain)
aliviar, suavizar

soprano [sə'prɑ:nəʊ] n soprano m/f

sore [sɔ:ʳ] adj dolorido ▷ n chaga, ferida

sorrow ['sɒrəʊ] n tristeza, mágoa, dor f;
sorrows npl (causes of grief) tristezas fpl

sorry ['sɒrɪ] adj (regretful) arrependido;
(condition, excuse) lamentável; **~!**
desculpe!, perdão!, sinto muito!; **to feel
~ for sb** sentir pena de alguém

sort [sɔ:t] n tipo ▷ vt (also: **~ out**: papers)

classificar; (: *problems*) solucionar, resolver

SOS *n abbr* (= *save our souls*) S.O.S. *m*

so-so *adv* mais ou menos, regular

sought [sɔ:t] *pt, pp of* **seek**

soul [səʊl] *n* alma; (*person*) criatura

sound [saʊnd] *adj* (*healthy*) saudável, sadio; (*safe, not damaged*) sólido, completo; (*secure*) seguro; (*reliable*) confiável; (*sensible*) sensato ▷ *adv:* ~ **asleep** dormindo profundamente ▷ *n* (*noise*) som *m*, ruído, barulho; (*volume: on TV etc*) volume *m*; (*Geo*) estreito, braço (de mar) ▷ *vt* (*alarm*) soar ▷ *vi* soar, tocar; (*fig: seem*) parecer; **to ~ like** parecer; **sound out** *vi* sondar; **soundtrack** *n* trilha sonora

soup [su:p] *n* sopa; **in the ~** (*fig*) numa encrenca

sour ['saʊə^r] *adj* azedo, ácido; (*milk*) talhado; (*fig*) mal-humorado, rabugento; **it's ~ grapes!** (*fig*) é despeito!

source [sɔ:s] *n* fonte *f*

south [saʊθ] *n* sul *m* ▷ *adj* do sul, meridional ▷ *adv* ao or para o sul; **South Africa** *n* África do Sul; **South African** *adj, n* sul-africano(-a); **South America** *n* América do Sul; **South American** *adj, n* sul-americano(-a); **south-east** *n* sudeste *m*; **southern** ['sʌðən] *adj* (*to the south*) para o sul, em direção do sul; (*from the south*) do sul, sulista; **the southern hemisphere** o Hemisfério Sul; **South Pole** *n* Pólo Sul; **southward(s)** *adv* para o sul; **south-west** *n* sudoeste *m*

souvenir [su:və'nɪə^r] *n* lembrança

sovereign ['sɔvrɪn] *n* soberano(-a)

sow[1] [saʊ] *n* porca

sow[2] [səʊ] (*pt* **~ed**, *pp* **~n**) *vt* semear; (*fig: spread*) disseminar, espalhar

soya ['sɔɪə] (*US* **soy**) *n:* ~ **bean** semente *f* de soja; ~ **sauce** molho de soja

spa [spa:] *n* (*town*) estância hidromineral; (*US: also:* **health ~**) estância balnear

space [speɪs] *n* (*gen*) espaço; (*room*) lugar *m*; (*cpd*) espacial ▷ *vt* (*also:* ~ **out**) espaçar; **spacecraft** *n* nave *f* espacial; **spaceship** *n* = **spacecraft**; **spacious** ['speɪʃəs] *adj* espaçoso

spade [speɪd] *n* pá *f*; **spades** *npl* (*Cards*) espadas *fpl*

Spain [speɪn] *n* Espanha

spam [spæm] (*junk e-mail*) *n* spam *m*

span [spæn] *n* (*also:* **wing~**) envergadura; (*of arch*) vão *m*; (*in time*)

lapso, espaço ▷ *vt* estender-se sobre, atravessar; (*fig*) abarcar

Spaniard ['spænjəd] *n* espanhol(a) *m/f*

Spanish ['spænɪʃ] *adj* espanhol(a) ▷ *n* (*Ling*) espanhol *m*, castelhano; **the Spanish** *npl* os espanhóis

spanner ['spænə^r] (*BRIT*) *n* chave *f* inglesa

spare [spɛə^r] *adj* vago, desocupado; (*surplus*) de sobra, a mais ▷ *n* = **spare part** ▷ *vt* dispensar, passar sem; (*make available*) dispor de; (*refrain from hurting*) perdoar, poupar; **to ~** de sobra; **spare part** *n* peça sobressalente; **spare time** *n* tempo livre; **spare wheel** *n* estepe *m*

spark [spa:k] *n* chispa, faísca; (*fig*) centelha

sparkle ['spa:kl] *n* cintilação *f*, brilho ▷ *vi* (*shine*) brilhar, faiscar; **sparkling** *adj* (*mineral water*) gasoso; (*wine*) espumante; (*conversation*) animado; (*performance*) brilhante

sparrow ['spærəʊ] *n* pardal *m*

sparse [spa:s] *adj* escasso; (*hair*) ralo

spasm ['spæzəm] *n* (*Med*) espasmo

spat [spæt] *pt, pp of* **spit**

speak [spi:k] (*pt* **spoke**, *pp* **spoken**) *vt* (*language*) falar; (*truth*) dizer ▷ *vi* falar; (*make a speech*) discursar; ~ **up!** fale alto!; **speaker** *n* (*in public*) orador(a) *m/f*; (*also:* **loudspeaker**) alto-falante *m*; (*Pol*): **the Speaker** o Presidente da Câmara

spear [spɪə^r] *n* lança ▷ *vt* lancear, arpoar

special ['spɛʃl] *adj* especial; (*edition etc*) extra; (*delivery*) rápido; **specialist** *n* especialista *m/f*; **speciality** [spɛʃɪ'ælɪtɪ] *n* especialidade *f*; **specialize** *vi:* **to specialize (in)** especializar-se (em); **specially** *adv* especialmente; **specialty** ['spɛʃəltɪ] (*esp US*) *n* = **speciality**

species ['spi:ʃi:z] *n inv* espécie *f*

specific [spə'sɪfɪk] *adj* específico

specimen ['spɛsɪmən] *n* espécime *m*, amostra; (*for testing, Med*) espécime

speck [spɛk] *n* mancha, pinta

spectacle ['spɛktəkl] *n* espetáculo; **spectacles** *npl* (*glasses*) óculos *mpl*; **spectacular** [spɛk'tækjulə^r] *adj* espetacular ▷ *n* (*Cinema etc*) superprodução *f*

spectator [spɛk'teɪtə^r] *n* espectador(a) *m/f*

spectrum ['spɛktrəm] (*pl* **spectra**) *n* espectro

speech [spi:tʃ] *n* (*faculty, Theatre*) fala; (*formal talk*) discurso; **speechless** *adj* estupefato, emudecido

speed [spi:d] (*pt, pp* **sped**) *n* velocidade *f*; (*rate*) rapidez *f*; (*haste*) pressa; (*promptness*) prontidão *f*; **at full** *or* **top ~ a** toda a velocidade; **speed up** (*pt, pp* **speeded up**) *vt, vi* acelerar; **speedboat** *n* lancha; **speeding** *n* (*Aut*) excesso de velocidade; **speed limit** *n* limite *m* de velocidade, velocidade *f* máxima; **speedometer** [spɪˈdɔmɪtəʳ] *n* velocímetro; **speedy** *adj* veloz, rápido; (*prompt*) pronto, imediato

spell [spɛl] (*pt, pp* **~ed**; BRIT **spelt**) *n* (*also*: **magic ~**) encanto, feitiço; (*period of time*) período, temporada ▷ *vt* (*also*: **~ out**) soletrar; (*fig*) pressagiar, ser sinal de; **to cast a ~ on sb** enfeitiçar alguém; **he can't ~** não sabe escrever bem, comete erros de ortografia

spend [spɛnd] (*pt, pp* **spent**) *vt* (*money*) gastar; (*time*) passar

sperm [spə:m] *n* esperma

sphere [sfɪəʳ] *n* esfera

spice [spaɪs] *n* especiaria ▷ *vt* condimentar

spicy [ˈspaɪsɪ] *adj* condimentado

spider [ˈspaɪdəʳ] *n* aranha

spike [spaɪk] *n* (*point*) ponta, espigão *m*; (*Bot*) espiga

spill [spɪl] (*pt, pp* **spilt** *or* **~ed**) *vt* entornar, derramar ▷ *vi* derramar-se; **spill over** *vi* transbordar

spin [spɪn] (*pt* **spun** *or* **span**, *pp* **spun**) *n* (*Aviat*) parafuso; (*trip in car*) volta *or* passeio de carro; (*ball*): **to put ~ on** fazer rolar ▷ *vt* (*wool etc*) fiar, tecer ▷ *vi* girar, rodar; (*make thread*) tecer; **spin out** *vt* prolongar; (*money*) fazer render

spinach [ˈspɪnɪtʃ] *n* espinafre *m*

spinal cord *n* espinha dorsal

spin-dryer (BRIT) *n* secadora

spine [spaɪn] *n* espinha dorsal; (*thorn*) espinho

spiral [ˈspaɪərl] *n* espiral *f* ▷ *vi* (*prices*) disparar

spire [spaɪəʳ] *n* flecha, agulha

spirit [ˈspɪrɪt] *n* (*soul*) alma; (*ghost*) fantasma *m*; (*courage*) coragem *f*, ânimo; (*frame of mind*) estado de espírito; (*sense*) sentido; **spirits** *npl* (*drink*) álcool *m*; **in good ~s** alegre, de bom humor; **spiritual** *adj* espiritual ▷ *n* (*also*: **Negro spiritual**) canto religioso dos negros

spit [spɪt] (*pt, pp* **spat**) *n* (*for roasting*) espeto; (*saliva*) saliva ▷ *vi* cuspir; (*sound*) escarrar; (*rain*) chuviscar

spite [spaɪt] *n* rancor *m*, ressentimento ▷ *vt* contrariar; **in ~ of** apesar de, a despeito de; **spiteful** *adj* maldoso, malévolo

splash [splæʃ] *n* (*sound*) borrifo, respingo; (*of colour*) mancha ▷ *vt*: **to ~ (with)** salpicar (de) ▷ *vi* (*also*: **~ about**) borrifar, respingar

splendid [ˈsplɛndɪd] *adj* esplêndido; (*impressive*) impressionante

splinter [ˈsplɪntəʳ] *n* (*of wood, glass*) lasca; (*in finger*) farpa ▷ *vi* lascar-se, estilhaçar-se, despedaçar-se

split [splɪt] (*pt, pp* **~**) *n* fenda, brecha; (*fig: division*) rompimento; (*: difference*) diferença; (*Pol*) divisão *f* ▷ *vt* partir, fender; (*party, work*) dividir; (*profits*) repartir ▷ *vi* (*divide*) dividir-se, repartir-se; **split up** *vi* (*couple*) separar-se, acabar; (*meeting*) terminar

spoil [spɔɪl] (*pt, pp* **~t** *or* **~ed**) *vt* (*damage*) danificar; (*mar*) estragar, arruinar; (*child*) mimar

spoke [spəuk] *pt of* **speak** ▷ *n* raio

spoken [ˈspəukn] *pp of* **speak**

spokesman [ˈspəuksmən] (*irreg*) *n* porta-voz *m*

spokeswoman [ˈspəukswumən] (*irreg*) *n* porta-voz *f*

sponge [spʌndʒ] *n* esponja; (*cake*) pão-de-ló *m* ▷ *vt* lavar com esponja ▷ *vi*: **to ~ on sb** viver às custas de alguém; **sponge bag** (BRIT) *n* bolsa de toalete

sponsor [ˈspɔnsəʳ] *n* patrocinador(a) *m/f* ▷ *vt* patrocinar; apadrinhar; fiar; (*applicant, proposal*) apoiar, defender; **sponsorship** *n* patrocínio

spontaneous [spɔnˈteɪnɪəs] *adj* espontâneo

spooky [ˈspu:kɪ] (*inf*) *adj* arrepiante

spoon [spu:n] *n* colher *f*; **spoonful** *n* colherada

sport [spɔ:t] *n* esporte *m* (BR), desporto (PT); (*person*) bom perdedor (boa perdedora) *m/f* ▷ *vt* (*wear*) exibir; **sport jacket** (US) *n* = **sports jacket**; **sports car** *n* carro esporte (BR), carro de sport (PT); **sports jacket** (BRIT) *n* casaco esportivo (BR) or desportivo (PT); **sportsman** (*irreg*) *n* esportista *m* (BR), desportista *m* (PT); **sports utilty vehicle** *n* veículo com tração nas quatro rodas, veículo 4x4; **sportswear** *n* roupa esportiva (BR) or desportiva (PT) or desporto (PT); **sportswoman** (*irreg*) *n* esportista (BR), desportista (PT); **sporty** *adj* esportivo (BR), desportivo (PT)

spot [spɔt] n (mark) marca; (place) lugar m, local m; (dot: on pattern) mancha, ponto; (on skin) espinha; (Radio, TV) hora; (small amount): **a ~ of** um pouquinho de ▷ vt notar; **on the ~** na hora; (there) ali mesmo; (in difficulty) em apuros; **spotless** adj sem mancha, imaculado; **spotlight** n holofote m, refletor m

spouse [spauz] n cônjuge m/f

sprain [spreɪn] n distensão f, torcedura ▷ vt torcer

sprang [spræŋ] pt of **spring**

sprawl [sprɔːl] vi esparramar-se

spray [spreɪ] n borrifo; (container) spray m, atomizador m; (garden spray) vaporizador m; (of flowers) ramalhete m ▷ vt pulverizar; (crops) borrifar, regar

spread [sprɛd] (pt, pp ~) n extensão f; (distribution) expansão f, difusão f; (Culin) pasta; (inf: food) banquete m ▷ vt espalhar; (butter) untar, passar; (wings, sails) abrir, desdobrar; (workload, wealth) distribuir; (scatter) disseminar ▷ vi (news, stain) espalhar-se; (disease) alastrar-se; **spread out** vi dispersar-se; **spreadsheet** n (Comput) planilha

spree [spriː] n: **to go on a ~** cair na farra

spring [sprɪŋ] (pt **sprang**, pp **sprung**) n salto, pulo; (coiled metal) mola; (season) primavera; (of water) fonte f; **spring up** vi aparecer de repente

sprinkle ['sprɪŋkl] vt (liquid) salpicar; (salt, sugar) borrifar; **to ~ water on, ~ with water** salpicar de água

sprint [sprɪnt] n corrida de pequena distância ▷ vi correr a toda velocidade

sprung [sprʌŋ] pp of **spring**

spun [spʌn] pt, pp of **spin**

spur [spəː'] n espora; (fig) estímulo ▷ vt (also: ~ **on**) incitar, estimular; **on the ~ of the moment** de improviso, de repente

spurt [spəːt] n (of energy) acesso; (of blood etc) jorro ▷ vi jorrar

spy [spaɪ] n espião (espiã) m/f ▷ vi: **to ~ on** espiar, espionar ▷ vt enxergar, avistar

sq. abbr (Math etc) = **square**

squabble ['skwɔbl] vi brigar, discutir

squad [skwɔd] n (Mil, Police) pelotão m, esquadra; (Football) seleção f

squadron ['skwɔdrən] n (Mil) esquadrão m; (Aviat) esquadrilha; (Naut) esquadra

squander ['skwɔndə'] vt esbanjar, dissipar; (chances) desperdiçar

square [skwɛə'] n quadrado; (in town) praça; (inf: person) quadrado(-a), careta m/f ▷ adj quadrado; (inf: ideas, tastes)

careta, antiquado ▷ vt (arrange) ajustar, acertar; (Math) elevar ao quadrado; (reconcile) conciliar; **all ~** igual, quite; **a ~ meal** uma refeição substancial; **2 metres ~** um quadrado de dois metros de lado; **2 ~ metres** 2 metros quadrados

squash [skwɔʃ] n (BRIT: drink): **lemon/orange ~** limonada/laranjada concentrada; (Sport) squash m; (US: vegetable) abóbora ▷ vt esmagar

squat [skwɔt] adj atarracado ▷ vi (also: ~ **down**) agachar-se, acocorar-se; **squatter** n posseiro(-a)

squeak [skwiːk] vi (door) ranger; (mouse) guinchar

squeal [skwiːl] vi guinchar, gritar agudamente

squeeze [skwiːz] n (gen, of hand) aperto; (Econ) arrocho ▷ vt comprimir, socar; (hand, arm) apertar; **squeeze out** vt espremer; (fig) extorquir

squid [skwɪd] (pl **inv** or ~s) n lula

squint [skwɪnt] vi olhar or ser vesgo ▷ n (Med) estrabismo

squirm [skwəːm] vi retorcer-se

squirrel ['skwɪrəl] n esquilo

squirt [skwəːt] vi, vt jorrar, esguichar

Sr abbr = **senior**

St abbr (= saint) S.; = **street**

stab [stæb] n (with knife etc) punhalada; (of pain) pontada; (inf: try): **to have a ~ at (doing) sth** tentar (fazer) algo ▷ vt apunhalar

stable ['steɪbl] adj estável ▷ n estábulo, cavalariça

stack [stæk] n montão m, pilha ▷ vt amontoar, empilhar

stadium ['steɪdɪəm] (pl **stadia** or ~s) n estádio

staff [stɑːf] n (work force) pessoal m, quadro; (BRIT: Sch: also: **teaching ~**) corpo docente ▷ vt prover de pessoal

stag [stæg] n veado, cervo

stage [steɪdʒ] n palco, cena; (point) etapa, fase f; (platform) plataforma, estrado; (profession): **the ~** o palco, o teatro ▷ vt pôr em cena, representar; (demonstration) montar, organizar; **in ~s** por etapas

stagger ['stægə'] vi cambalear ▷ vt (amaze) surpreender, chocar; (hours, holidays) escalonar; **staggering** adj (amazing) surpreendente, chocante

stain [steɪn] n mancha; (colouring) tinta, tintura ▷ vt manchar; (wood) tingir

stair [stɛə'] n (step) degrau m; **stairs**

npl (*flight of steps*) escada; **staircase**
n escadaria, escada; **stairway** n
= **staircase**

stake [steɪk] n estaca, poste m; (*Comm:
interest*) interesse m, participação f;
(*Betting: gen pl*) aposta ▷ vt apostar;
(*claim*) reivindicar; **to be at ~** estar em
jogo

stale [steɪl] adj (*bread*) dormido; (*food*)
estragado; (*air*) viciado; (*smell*) mofado;
(*beer*) velho

stalk [stɔːk] n talo, haste f ▷ vt caçar
de tocaia; **to ~ in/out** entrar/sair
silenciosamente; **to ~ off** andar com
arrogância

stall [stɔːl] n (BRIT: *in market*) barraca;
(*in stable*) baia ▷ vt (Aut) fazer morrer;
(*fig: delay*) impedir, atrasar ▷ vi morrer;
esquivar-se, ganhar tempo; **stalls** npl
(BRIT: *in cinema, theatre*) platéia

stamina ['stæmɪnə] n resistência

stammer ['stæməʳ] n gagueira ▷ vi
gaguejar, balbuciar

stamp [stæmp] n selo; (*rubber stamp*)
carimbo, timbre m; (*mark, also fig*) marca,
impressão f ▷ vi (*also:* **~ one's foot**)
bater com o pé ▷ vt (*letter*) selar; (*mark*)
marcar; (*with rubber stamp*) carimbar

stampede [stæm'piːd] n debandada,
estouro (da boiada)

stance [stæns] n postura, posição f

stand [stænd] (*pt, pp* **stood**) n posição
f, postura; (*for taxis*) ponto; (*also:* **hall
~**) pedestal m; (*also:* **music ~**) estante
f; (*Sport*) tribuna, palanque m; (*stall*)
barraca ▷ vi (*be*) estar, encontrar-se;
(*be on foot*) estar em pé; (*rise*) levantar-
se; (*remain: decision, offer*) estar de pé;
(*in election*) candidatar-se ▷ vt (*place*)
pôr, colocar; (*tolerate*) agüentar,
suportar; (*cost*) pagar; **to make a ~**
resistir; (*fig*) ater-se a um princípio; **to
~ for parliament** (BRIT) apresentar-se
como candidato ao parlamento; **stand
by** vi estar a postos ▷ vt fus (*opinion*)
aferrar-se a; (*person*) ficar ao lado de;
stand down vi retirar-se; **stand for**
vt fus (*signify*) significar; (*represent*)
representar; (*tolerate*) tolerar, permitir;
stand in for vt fus substituir; **stand
out** vi (*be prominent*) destacar-se; **stand
up** vi levantar-se; **stand up for** vt fus
defender; **stand up to** vt fus enfrentar

standard ['stændəd] n padrão m,
critério; (*flag*) estandarte m; (*level*) nível
m ▷ adj padronizado, regular, normal;

standards npl (*morals*) valores mpl
morais; **standard of living** n padrão m
de vida (BR), nível m de vida (PT)

stand-by adj de reserva ▷ n: **to be on
~** estar de sobreaviso or de prontidão;
stand-by ticket n bilhete m de stand-by

standing ['stændɪŋ] adj (*on foot*) em pé;
(*permanent*) permanente ▷ n posição f,
reputação f; **of many years' ~** de muitos
anos

standpoint ['stændpɔɪnt] n ponto de
vista

standstill ['stændstɪl] n: **at a ~**
paralisado, parado; **to come to a ~** (*car*)
parar; (*factory, traffic*) ficar paralisado

stank [stæŋk] pt of **stink**

staple ['steɪpl] n (*for papers*) grampo ▷ adj
(*food etc*) básico ▷ vt grampear

star [stɑːʳ] n estrela; (*celebrity*) astro/
estrela ▷ vi: **to ~ in** ser a estrela em,
estrelar ▷ vt (*Cinema*) ser estrelado por;
the stars npl (*horoscope*) o horóscopo

starboard ['stɑːbəd] n estibordo

starch [stɑːtʃ] n (*in food*) amido, fécula;
(*for clothes*) goma

stardom ['stɑːdəm] n estrelato

stare [stɛəʳ] n olhar m fixo ▷ vi: **to ~ at**
olhar fixamente, fitar

stark [stɑːk] adj severo, áspero ▷ adv: **~
naked** completamente nu, em pêlo

start [stɑːt] n princípio, começo;
(*departure*) partida; (*sudden movement*)
sobressalto, susto; (*advantage*)
vantagem f ▷ vt começar, iniciar;
(*cause*) causar; (*found*) fundar; (*engine*)
ligar ▷ vi começar, iniciar; (*with fright*)
sobressaltar-se, assustar-se; (*train etc*)
sair; **start off** vi começar, principiar;
(*leave*) sair, pôr-se a caminho; **start up** vi
começar; (*car*) pegar, pôr-se em marcha
▷ vt começar; (*car*) ligar; **starter** n (Aut)
arranque m; (*Sport: official*) juiz (juíza)
m/f da partida; (BRIT: *Culin*) entrada;
starting point n ponto de partida

startle ['stɑːtl] vt assustar, aterrar;
startling adj surpreendente

starvation [stɑː'veɪʃən] n fome f

starve [stɑːv] vi passar fome; (*to death*)
morrer de fome ▷ vt fazer passar fome;
(*fig*) privar

state [steɪt] n estado ▷ vt afirmar,
declarar; **the States** npl (Geo) os Estados
Unidos; **to be in a ~** estar agitado;
statement n declaração f; **statesman**
(*irreg*) n estadista m

static ['stætɪk] n (Radio, TV) interferência

▷ adj estático

station ['steɪʃən] n estação f; (Police) delegacia; (Radio) emissora ▷ vt colocar

stationary ['steɪʃnərɪ] adj estacionário

station wagon (US) n perua (BR), canadiana (PT)

statistic [stə'tɪstɪk] n estatística; **statistics** [stə'tɪstɪks] n (science) estatística

statue ['stætju:] n estátua

status ['steɪtəs] n posição f; (classification) categoria; (importance) status m

staunch [stɔ:ntʃ] adj fiel

stay [steɪ] n estadia, estada ▷ vi ficar; (as guest) hospedar-se; (spend some time) demorar-se; **to ~ put** não se mexer; **to ~ the night** pernoitar; **stay behind** vi ficar atrás; **stay in** vi ficar em casa; **stay on** vi ficar; **stay out** vi ficar fora de casa; **stay up** vi (at night) velar, ficar acordado

steadily ['stɛdɪlɪ] adv (firmly) firmemente; (unceasingly) sem parar, constantemente; (walk) regularmente

steady ['stɛdɪ] adj (job, boyfriend) constante; (speed) fixo; (regular) regular; (person, character) sensato; (calm) calmo, sereno ▷ vt (stabilize) estabilizar; (nerves) acalmar

steak [steɪk] n filé m; (beef) bife m

steal [sti:l] (pt **stole**, pp **stolen**) vt roubar ▷ vi mover-se furtivamente

steam [sti:m] n vapor m ▷ vt (Culin) cozinhar no vapor ▷ vi fumegar; **steamy** adj vaporoso; (room) cheio de vapor, úmido (BR), húmido (PT); (heat, atmosphere) vaporoso

steel [sti:l] n aço ▷ adj de aço

steep [sti:p] adj íngreme; (increase) acentuado; (price) exorbitante ▷ vt (food) colocar de molho; (cloth) ensopar, encharcar

steeple ['sti:pl] n campanário, torre f

steer [stɪə'] vt (person) guiar; (vehicle) dirigir ▷ vi conduzir; **steering** n (Aut) direção f; **steering wheel** n volante m

stem [stɛm] n (of plant) caule m, haste f; (of glass) pé m ▷ vt deter, reter; (blood) estancar; **stem from** vt fus originar-se de

step [stɛp] n passo; (stair) degrau m ▷ vi: **to ~ forward** dar um passo a frente/ atrás; **steps** npl (BRIT) = **stepladder**; **to be in ~ (with)** (fig) manter a paridade (com); **to be out of ~ (with)** (fig) estar em disparidade (com); **step down** vi (fig)

renunciar; **step on** vt fus pisar; **step up** vt aumentar; **stepbrother** n meio-irmão m; **stepdaughter** n enteada; **stepfather** n padrasto; **stepladder** (BRIT) n escada portátil or de abrir; **stepmother** n madrasta; **stepsister** n meia-irmã f; **stepson** n enteado

stereo ['stɛrɪəu] n estéreo; (record player) (aparelho de) som m ▷ adj (also: ~phonic) estereofônico

sterile ['stɛraɪl] adj esterelizado; (barren) estéril; **sterilize** ['stɛrɪlaɪz] vt esterilizar

sterling ['stə:lɪŋ] adj esterlino; (silver) de lei ▷ n (currency) libra esterlina; **one pound ~** uma libra esterlina

stern [stə:n] adj severo, austero ▷ n (Naut) popa, ré f

stew [stju:] n guisado, ensopado ▷ vt guisar, ensopar; (fruit) cozinhar

steward ['stju:əd] n (Aviat) comissário de bordo; **stewardess** n aeromoça (BR), hospedeira de bordo (PT)

stick [stɪk] (pt, pp **stuck**) n pau m; (as weapon) cacete m; (walking stick) bengala, cajado ▷ vt (glue) colar; (thrust): **to ~ sth into** cravar or enfiar algo em; (inf: put) meter; (: tolerate) agüentar, suportar ▷ vi (become attached) colar-se; (be unmoveable) emperrar; (in mind etc) gravar-se; **stick out** vi estar saliente, projetar-se; **stick up** vi estar saliente, projetar-se; **stick up for** vt fus defender; **sticker** n adesivo; **sticking plaster** n esparadrapo

sticky ['stɪkɪ] adj pegajoso; (label) adesivo; (fig) delicado

stiff [stɪf] adj (strong) forte; (hard) duro; (difficult) difícil; (moving with difficulty: person) teso; (: door, zip) empenado; (formal) formal ▷ adv (bored, worried) extremamente

stigma ['stɪgmə] n estigma m

stiletto [stɪ'lɛtəu] (BRIT) n (also: ~ heel) salto alto e fino

still [stɪl] adj parado ▷ adv (up to this time) ainda; (even, yet) ainda; (nonetheless) entretanto, contudo

stimulate ['stɪmjuleɪt] vt estimular

stimulus ['stɪmjuləs] (pl **stimuli**) n estímulo, incentivo

sting [stɪŋ] (pt, pp **stung**) n (wound) picada; (pain) ardência; (of insect) ferrão m ▷ vt arguilhar ▷ vi (insect, animal) picar; (eyes, ointment) queimar

stink [stɪŋk] (pt **stank**, pp **stunk**) n fedor m, catinga ▷ vi feder, cheirar mal

stir [stəːʳ] n (fig) comoção f, rebuliço ▷ vt mexer; (fig) comover ▷ vi mover-se, remexer-se; **stir up** vt excitar; (trouble) provocar

stitch [stɪtʃ] n (Sewing, Knitting, Med) ponto; (pain) pontada ▷ vt costurar; (Med) dar pontos em, suturar

stock [stɔk] n suprimento; (Comm: reserves) estoque m, provisão f; (: selection) sortimento; (Agr) gado; (Culin) caldo; (lineage) estirpe f, linhagem f; (Finance) valores mpl, títulos mpl ▷ adj (reply etc) de sempre, costumeiro ▷ vt ter em estoque, estocar; **in/out of ~** em estoque/esgotado; **to take ~ of** (fig) fazer um balanço de; **~s and shares** valores e títulos mobiliários; **stock up** vi: **to stock up (with)** abastecer-se (de); **stockbroker** n corretor(a) m/f; **stock cube** (BRIT) n cubo de caldo; **stock exchange** n Bolsa de Valores

stocking [ˈstɔkɪŋ] n meia

stock market (BRIT) n Bolsa, mercado de valores

stole [stəul] pt of **steal** ▷ n estola

stolen [ˈstəuln] pp of **steal**

stomach [ˈstʌmək] n (Anat) estômago; (belly) barriga, ventre m ▷ vt suportar, tolerar

stone [stəun] n pedra; (pebble) pedrinha; (in fruit) caroço; (Med) pedra, cálculo; (BRIT: weight) = 6.348kg; 14 pounds ▷ adj de pedra ▷ vt apedrejar; (fruit) tirar o(s) caroço(s) de

stood [stud] pt, pp of **stand**

stool [stuːl] n tamborete m, banco

stoop [stuːp] vi (also: **have a ~**) ser corcunda; (also: **~ down**) debruçar-se, curvar-se

stop [stɔp] n parada, interrupção f; (for bus etc) parada (BR), ponto (BR), paragem f (PT); (also: **full ~**) ponto ▷ vt parar, deter; (break off) interromper; (cheque) sustar, suspender; (also: **put a ~ to**) impedir ▷ vi parar, deter-se; (watch, noise) parar; (end) acabar; **to ~ doing sth** deixar de fazer algo; **stop dead** vi parar de repente; **stop off** vi dar uma parada; **stop up** vt tapar; **stopover** n parada rápida; (Aviat) escala

storage [ˈstɔːrɪdʒ] n armazenagem f

store [stɔːʳ] n (stock) suprimento; (depot) armazém m; (reserve) estoque m; (BRIT: large shop) loja de departamentos; (US: shop) loja ▷ vt armazenar; **stores** npl (provisions) víveres mpl, provisões fpl;

who knows what is in **~ for us?** quem sabe o que nos espera?; **store up** vt acumular

storey [ˈstɔːrɪ] (US **story**) n andar m

storm [stɔːm] n tempestade f; (fig) tumulto ▷ vi (fig) enfurecer-se ▷ vt tomar de assalto, assaltar; **stormy** adj tempestuoso

story [ˈstɔːrɪ] n história, estória; (lie) mentira; (US) = **storey**

stout [staut] adj sólido, forte; (fat) gordo, corpulento; (resolute) decidido, resoluto ▷ n cerveja preta

stove [stəuv] n (for cooking) fogão m; (for heating) estufa, fogareiro

straight [streɪt] adj reto; (back) esticado; (hair) liso; (honest) honesto; (simple) simples inv ▷ adv reto; (drink) puro; **to put** or **get sth ~** esclarecer algo; **~ away**, **~ off** imediatamente; **straighten** vt arrumar; **straighten out** vt endireitar; (fig) esclarecer; **to straighten things out** arrumar as coisas; **straightforward** adj (simple) simples inv, direto; (honest) honesto, franco

strain [streɪn] n tensão f; (Tech) esforço; (Med: back strain) distensão f; (: tension) luxação f; (breed) raça, estirpe f ▷ vt forçar, torcer, distender; (stretch) puxar, estirar; (Culin) coar; **strains** npl (Mus) acordes mpl; **strained** adj distendido; (laugh) forçado; (relations) tenso; **strainer** n coador m; (sieve) peneira

strait [streɪt] n estreito; **straits** npl (fig): **to be in dire straits** estar em apuros

strand [strænd] n (of thread, hair) fio; (of rope) tira; **stranded** adj preso

strange [streɪndʒ] adj (not known) desconhecido; (odd) estranho, esquisito; **strangely** adv estranhamente; **stranger** n desconhecido(-a); (from another area) forasteiro(-a)

strangle [ˈstræŋgl] vt estrangular; (fig) sufocar

strap [stræp] n correia; (of slip, dress) alça

strategic [strəˈtiːdʒɪk] adj estratégico

strategy [ˈstrætɪdʒɪ] n estratégia

straw [strɔː] n palha; (drinking straw) canudo; **that's the last ~!** essa foi a última gota!

strawberry [ˈstrɔːbərɪ] n morango

stray [streɪ] adj (animal) extraviado; (bullet) perdido; (scattered) espalhado ▷ vi perder-se

streak [striːk] n listra, traço; (in hair) mecha ▷ vt listrar ▷ vi: **to ~ past** passar como um raio

stream [striːm] *n* riacho, córrego; (*of people, vehicles*) fluxo; (*of smoke*) rastro; (*of questions etc*) torrente *f* ▷ *vt* (*Sch*) classificar ▷ *vi* correr, fluir; **to ~ in/out** entrar/sair em massa

street [striːt] *n* rua; **streetcar** (*US*) *n* bonde *m* (*BR*), eléctrico (*PT*); **street plan** *n* mapa *m*

strength [strɛŋθ] *n* força; (*of girder etc*) firmeza, resistência; (*fig*) poder *m*; **strengthen** *vt* fortificar; (*fig*) fortalecer

strenuous ['strɛnjuəs] *adj* enérgico; (*determined*) tenaz

stress [strɛs] *n* pressão *f*; (*mental strain*) tensão *f*, stress *m*; (*emphasis*) ênfase *f*; (*Tech*) tensão ▷ *vt* realçar, dar ênfase a; (*syllable*) acentuar

stretch [strɛtʃ] *n* (*of sand etc*) trecho, extensão *f* ▷ *vi* espreguiçar-se; (*extend*): **to ~ to** *or* **as far as** estender-se até ▷ *vt* estirar, esticar; (*fig: subj: job, task*) exigir o máximo de; **stretch out** *vi* esticar-se ▷ *vt* (*arm etc*) estirar; (*spread*) estirar

stretcher ['strɛtʃəʳ] *n* maca, padiola

strict [strɪkt] *adj* (*person*) severo, rigoroso; (*meaning*) exato, estrito

stride [straɪd] (*pt* **strode**, *pp* **stridden**) *n* passo largo ▷ *vi* andar a passos largos

strike [straɪk] (*pt*, *pp* **struck**) *n* greve *f*; (*of oil etc*) descoberta; (*attack*) ataque *m* ▷ *vt* bater em; (*fig*): **the thought** *or* **it ~s me that ...** me ocorre que ...; (*oil etc*) descobrir; (*deal*) fechar, acertar ▷ *vi* estar em greve; (*attack: soldiers, illness*) atacar; (*: disaster*) assolar; (*clock*) bater; **on ~** em greve; **to ~ a match** acender um fósforo; **strike down** *vt* derrubar; **strike up** *vt* (*Mus*) começar a tocar; (*conversation, friendship*) travar; **striker** *n* grevista *m/f*; (*Sport*) atacante *m/f*; **striking** *adj* impressionante

string [strɪŋ] (*pt*, *pp* **strung**) *n* (*cord*) barbante *m* (*BR*), cordel *m* (*PT*); (*of beads*) cordão *m*; (*of onions*) réstia; (*Mus*) corda ▷ *vt*: **to ~ out** esticar; **the strings** *npl* (*Mus*) os instrumentos de corda; **to ~ together** (*words*) unir; (*ideas*) concatenar; **to get a job by pulling ~s** (*fig*) usar pistolão

strip [strɪp] *n* tira; (*of land*) faixa; (*of metal*) lâmina, tira ▷ *vt* despir; (*also: ~ down: machine*) desmontar ▷ *vi* despir-se

stripe [straɪp] *n* listra; (*Mil*) galão *m*; **striped** *adj* listrado, com listras

strive [straɪv] (*pt* **strove**, *pp* **~n**) *vi*: **to**

~ for sth/to do sth esforçar-se por *or* batalhar para algo/para fazer algo

strode [strəud] *pt of* **stride**

stroke [strəuk] *n* (*blow*) golpe *m*; (*Med*) derrame *m* cerebral; (*of paintbrush*) pincelada; (*Swimming: style*) nado ▷ *vt* acariciar, afagar; **at a ~** de repente, de golpe

stroll [strəul] *n* volta, passeio ▷ *vi* passear, dar uma volta; **stroller** (*US*) *n* carrinho (de criança)

strong [strɔŋ] *adj* forte; (*imagination*) fértil; (*personality*) forte, dominante; (*nerves*) de aço; **they are 50 ~** são 50; **stronghold** *n* fortaleza; (*fig*) baluarte *m*; **strongly** *adv* firmemente; (*defend*) vigorosamente; (*believe*) profundamente

strove [strəuv] *pt of* **strive**

struck [strʌk] *pt*, *pp of* **strike**

structure ['strʌktʃəʳ] *n* estrutura; (*building*) construção *f*

struggle ['strʌgl] *n* luta, contenda ▷ *vi* (*fight*) lutar; (*try hard*) batalhar

strung [strʌŋ] *pt*, *pp of* **string**

stub [stʌb] *n* (*of ticket etc*) canhoto; (*of cigarette*) toco, ponta; **to ~ one's toe** dar uma topada; **stub out** *vt* apagar

stubble ['stʌbl] *n* restolho; (*on chin*) barba por fazer

stubborn ['stʌbən] *adj* teimoso, cabeçudo, obstinado

stuck [stʌk] *pt*, *pp of* **stick** ▷ *adj* (*jammed*) emperrado

stud [stʌd] *n* (*shirt stud*) botão *m*; (*earring*) tarraxa, rosca; (*of boot*) cravo; (*also: ~ farm*) fazenda de cavalos; (*also: ~ horse*) garanhão *m* ▷ *vt* (*fig*): **~ded with** salpicado de

student ['stjuːdənt] *n* estudante *m/f* ▷ *adj* estudantil; **student driver** (*US*) *n* aprendiz *m/f*

studio ['stjuːdɪəu] *n* estúdio; (*sculptor's*) ateliê *m*

study ['stʌdɪ] *n* estudo; (*room*) sala de leitura *or* estudo ▷ *vt* estudar; (*examine*) examinar, investigar ▷ *vi* estudar; **studies** *npl* (*subjects*) estudos *mpl*, matérias *fpl*

stuff [stʌf] *n* (*substance*) troço; (*things*) troços *mpl*, coisas *fpl* ▷ *vt* (*Culin*) rechear; (*animals*) empalhar; (*inf: push*) enfiar; **~ed toy** brinquedo de pelúcia; **stuffing** *n* recheio; **stuffy** *adj* (*room*) abafado, mal ventilado; (*person*) rabujento, melindroso

stumble ['stʌmbl] *vi* tropeçar; **to ~ across** *or* **on** (*fig*) topar com

stump [stʌmp] n (of tree) toco; (of limb) coto ▷ vt: **to be ~ed** ficar perplexo

stun [stʌn] vt (subj: blow) aturdir; (: news) pasmar

stung [stʌŋ] pt, pp of **sting**

stunk [stʌŋk] pp of **stink**

stunning ['stʌnɪŋ] adj (news) atordoante; (appearance) maravilhoso

stunt [stʌnt] n façanha sensacional; (publicity stunt) truque m publicitário

stupid ['stjuːpɪd] adj estúpido, idiota

sturdy ['stɜːdɪ] adj (person) robusto, firme; (thing) sólido

stutter ['stʌtəʳ] n gagueira, gaguez f ▷ vi gaguejar

style [staɪl] n estilo; (elegance) elegância; **stylish** adj elegante, chique

subconscious adj do subconsciente

subject [(n) 'sʌbdʒɪkt, (vb) səb'dʒɛkt] n (of king) súdito(-a); (theme) assunto; (Sch) matéria; (Ling) sujeito ▷ vt: **to ~ sb to sth** submeter alguém a algo; **to be ~ to** estar sujeito a; **subjective** [səb'dʒɛktɪv] adj subjetivo; **subject matter** n assunto; (content) conteúdo

submarine ['sʌbməriːn] n submarino

submission [səb'mɪʃən] n submissão f; (to committee) petição f; (of plan) apresentação f, exposição f

submit [səb'mɪt] vt submeter ▷ vi submeter-se

subordinate [sə'bɔːdɪnət] adj, n subordinado(-a)

subscribe [səb'skraɪb] vi subscrever; **to ~ to** (opinion) concordar com; (fund) contribuir para; (newspaper) assinar; **subscription** [səb'skrɪpʃən] n assinatura

subsequent ['sʌbsɪkwənt] adj subseqüente, posterior; **subsequently** adv posteriormente, depois

subside [səb'saɪd] vi (feeling, wind) acalmar-se; (flood) baixar

subsidiary [səb'sɪdɪərɪ] adj secundário ▷ n (also: **~ company**) subsidiária

subsidize ['sʌbsɪdaɪz] vt subsidiar

subsidy ['sʌbsɪdɪ] n subsídio

substance ['sʌbstəns] n substância

substantial [səb'stænʃl] adj (solid) sólido; (reward, meal) substancial

substitute ['sʌbstɪtjuːt] n (thing) substituto(-a); (person) suplente m/f ▷ vt: **to ~ A for B** substituir B por A

subtle ['sʌtl] adj sutil

subtract [səb'trækt] vt subtrair, deduzir

suburb ['sʌbəːb] n subúrbio; **suburban**

[səˈbəːbən] adj suburbano; (train etc) de subúrbio

subway ['sʌbweɪ] n (BRIT) passagem f subterrânea; (US) metrô m (BR), metro(-politano) (PT)

succeed [sək'siːd] vi (person) ser bem sucedido, ter êxito; (plan) sair bem ▷ vt suceder a; **to ~ in doing** conseguir fazer

success [sək'sɛs] n êxito; (hit, person) sucesso; **successful** adj (venture) bem sucedido; (writer) de sucesso, bem sucedido; **to be successful (in doing)** conseguir (fazer); **successfully** adv com sucesso, com êxito

succession [sək'sɛʃən] n sucessão f, série f; (to throne) sucessão

such [sʌtʃ] adj tal, semelhante; (of that kind: sg): **~ a book** um livro parecido, tal livro; (: pl): **~ books** tais livros; (so much): **~ courage** tanta coragem ▷ adv tão; **~ a long trip** uma viagem tão longa; **~ a lot of** tanto; **~ as** tal como; **as ~** como tal; **such-and-such** adj tal e qual

suck [sʌk] vt chupar; (breast) mamar

sudden ['sʌdn] adj (rapid) repentino, súbito; (unexpected) imprevisto; **all of a ~** inesperadamente; **suddenly** adv inesperadamente

sue [suː] vt processar

suede [sweɪd] n camurça

suffer ['sʌfəʳ] vt sofrer; (bear) agüentar, suportar ▷ vi sofrer, padecer; **to ~ from** sofrer de, estar com; **suffering** n sofrimento

sufficient [sə'fɪʃənt] adj suficiente, bastante

suffocate ['sʌfəkeɪt] vi sufocar(-se), asfixiar(-se)

sugar ['ʃugəʳ] n açúcar m ▷ vt pôr açúcar em, açucarar

suggest [sə'dʒɛst] vt sugerir; (indicate) indicar; **suggestion** n sugestão f; indicação f

suicide ['suɪsaɪd] n suicídio; (person) suicida m/f; see also **commit**; **suicide attack** n ataque m suicida, atentado suicida; **suicide bomber** n homem-bomba m, mulher-bomba f, terrorista m/f suicida; **suicide bombing** n bombardeio suicida

suit [suːt] n (man's) terno (BR), fato (PT); (woman's) conjunto; (Law) processo; (Cards) naipe m ▷ vt convir a; (clothes) ficar bem a; (adapt): **to ~ sth to** adaptar or acomodar algo a; **they are well ~ed** fazem um bom par; **suitable** adj conveniente; (*appropriate*) apropriado

suitcase ['su:tkeɪs] *n* mala

suite [swi:t] *n* (*of rooms*) conjunto de salas; (*Mus*) suite *f*; (*furniture*) conjunto

sulfur ['sʌlfəʳ] (*us*) *n* = **sulphur**

sulk [sʌlk] *vi* ficar emburrado, fazer beicinho *or* biquinho (*inf*)

sulphur ['sʌlfəʳ] (*us* **sulfur**) *n* enxofre *m*

sultana [sʌl'tɑ:nə] *n* passa branca

sum [sʌm] *n* soma; (*calculation*) cálculo; **sum up** *vt*, *vi* resumir

summarize ['sʌməraɪz] *vt* resumir

summary ['sʌmərɪ] *n* resumo

summer ['sʌməʳ] *n* verão *m* ▷ *adj* de verão; **in ~** no verão; **summertime** *n* (*season*) verão *m*

summit ['sʌmɪt] *n* topo, cume *m*; (*also:* **~ conference**) (conferência de) cúpula

summon ['sʌmən] *vt* (*person*) mandar chamar; (*meeting*) convocar; (*Law: witness*) convocar; **summon up** *vt* concentrar

sun [sʌn] *n* sol *m*; **sunbathe** *vi* tomar sol; **sunblock** *n* bloqueador *m* solar; **sunburn** *n* queimadura do sol

Sunday ['sʌndɪ] *n* domingo

sunflower ['sʌnflauəʳ] *n* girassol *m*

sung [sʌŋ] *pp of* **sing**

sunglasses ['sʌnglɑ:sɪz] *npl* óculos *mpl* de sol

sunk [sʌŋk] *pp of* **sink**

sun: sunlight *n* (luz *f* do) sol *m*; **sunny** *adj* cheio de sol; (*day*) ensolarado, de sol; **sunrise** *n* nascer *m* do sol; **sun roof** *n* (*Aut*) teto solar; **sunscreen** *n* protetor *m* solar; **sunset** *n* pôr *m* do sol; **sunshade** *n* pára-sol *m*; **sunshine** *n* (luz *f* do) sol *m*; **sunstroke** *n* insolação *f*; **suntan** *n* bronzeado; **suntan lotion** *n* loção *f* de bronzear

super ['su:pəʳ] (*inf*) *adj* bacana (*BR*), muito giro (*PT*)

superb [su:'pə:b] *adj* excelente

superintendent [su:pərɪn'tendənt] *n* superintendente *m/f*; (*Police*) chefe *m/f* de polícia

superior [su'pɪərɪəʳ] *adj* superior; (*smug*) desdenhoso ▷ *n* superior *m*

supermarket ['su:pəmɑ:kɪt] *n* supermercado

supernatural [su:pə'nætʃərəl] *adj* sobrenatural ▷ *n*: **the ~** o sobrenatural

superpower ['su:pəpauəʳ] *n* (*Pol*) superpotência

superstitious [su:pə'stɪʃəs] *adj* supersticioso

supervise ['su:pəvaɪz] *vt* supervisar, supervisionar; **supervision** [su:pə'vɪʒən] *n* supervisão *f*; **supervisor** *n* supervisor(a) *m/f*; (*academic*) orientador(a) *m/f*

supper ['sʌpəʳ] *n* jantar *m*; (*late evening*) ceia

supple ['sʌpl] *adj* flexível

supplement [(*n*) 'sʌplɪmənt, (*vb*) sʌplɪ'ment] *n* suplemento ▷ *vt* suprir, completar

supplier [sə'plaɪəʳ] *n* abastecedor(a) *m/f*, fornecedor(a) *m/f*

supply [sə'plaɪ] *vt* (*provide*): **to ~ sth (to sb)** fornecer algo (para alguém); (*equip*): **to ~ (with)** suprir (de) ▷ *n* fornecimento, provisão *f*; (*stock*) estoque *m*; (*supplying*) abastecimento

support [sə'pɔ:t] *n* (*moral, financial etc*) apoio; (*Tech*) suporte *m* ▷ *vt* apoiar; (*financially*) manter; (*Tech: hold up*) sustentar; (*theory etc*) defender; **supporter** *n* (*Pol etc*) partidário(-a); (*Sport*) torcedor(a) *m/f*

suppose [sə'pəuz] *vt* supor; (*imagine*) imaginar; (*duty*): **to be ~d to do sth** dever fazer algo; **supposedly** [sə'pəuzɪdlɪ] *adv* supostamente, pretensamente; **supposing** *conj* caso, supondo-se que

suppress [sə'prɛs] *vt* (*information*) suprimir; (*feelings, revolt*) reprimir; (*yawn*) conter

supreme [su'pri:m] *adj* supremo

surcharge ['sə:tʃɑ:dʒ] *n* sobretaxa

sure [ʃuəʳ] *adj* seguro; (*definite*) certo; (*aim*) certeiro; **to make ~ of sth/that** assegurar-se de algo/que; **~!** claro que sim!; **~ enough** efetivamente; (*certainly: us: also:* **sure**) certamente

surf [sə:f] *n* (*waves*) ondas *fpl*, arrebentação *f*

surface ['sə:fɪs] *n* superfície *f* ▷ *vt* (*road*) revestir ▷ *vi* vir à superfície *or* à tona; (*fig: news, feeling*) vir à tona

surfboard ['sə:fbɔ:d] *n* prancha de surfe

surfer ['sə:fəʳ] *n* (*in sea*) surfista *m/f*; **web** *or* **net ~** internauta *m/f*

surfing ['sə:fɪŋ] *n* surfe *m*

surge [sə:dʒ] *n* onda ▷ *vi* (*sea*) encapelar-se; (*people, vehicles*) precipitar-se; (*feeling*) aumentar repentinamente

surgeon ['sə:dʒən] *n* cirurgião(-giã) *m/f*

surgery ['sə:dʒərɪ] *n* cirurgia; (*BRIT: room*) consultório; (: *also:* **~ hours**) horas *fpl* de consulta

surname ['sə:neɪm] n sobrenome m (BR), apelido (PT)
surplus ['sə:pləs] n excedente m; (Comm) superávit m ▷ adj excedente, de sobra
surprise [sə'praɪz] n surpresa ▷ vt surpreender; **surprising** adj surpreendente
surrender [sə'rɛndə'] n rendição f, entrega ▷ vi render-se, entregar-se
surround [sə'raund] vt circundar, rodear; (Mil etc) cercar; **surrounding** adj circundante, adjacente; **surroundings** npl arredores mpl, cercanias fpl
surveillance [sə:'veɪləns] n vigilância
survey [(n) 'sə:veɪ, (vb) sə:'veɪ] n inspeção f; (of habits etc) pesquisa; (of land) levantamento; (of house) inspeção f ▷ vt observar, contemplar; (land) fazer um levantamento de; **surveyor** n (of land) agrimensor(a) m/f; (of building) inspetor(a) m/f
survival [sə'vaɪvl] n sobrevivência; (relic) remanescente m
survive [sə'vaɪv] vi sobreviver; (custom etc) perdurar ▷ vt sobreviver a; **survivor** n sobrevivente m/f
suspect [(adj, n) 'sʌspɛkt, (vb) səs'pɛkt] adj, n suspeito(-a) ▷ vt suspeitar, desconfiar
suspend [səs'pɛnd] vt suspender; **suspenders** npl (BRIT) ligas fpl; (US) suspensórios mpl
suspense [səs'pɛns] n incerteza, ansiedade f; (in film etc) suspense m; **to keep sb in ~** manter alguém em suspense or na expectativa
suspension [səs'pɛnʃən] n suspensão f; (of driving licence) cassação f
suspicion [səs'pɪʃən] n suspeita; **suspicious** adj (suspecting) suspeitoso; (causing suspicion) suspeito
sustain [səs'teɪn] vt sustentar; (suffer) sofrer
SUV n abbr (= sports utility vehicle) SUV m
swallow ['swɔləu] n (bird) andorinha ▷ vt engolir, tragar; (fig: story) engolir; (pride) pôr de lado; (one's words) retirar; **swallow up** vt (savings etc) consumir
swam [swæm] pt of **swim**
swamp [swɔmp] n pântano, brejo ▷ vt atolar, inundar; (fig) assoberbar
swan [swɔn] n cisne m
swap [swɔp] n troca, permuta ▷ vt: **to ~ (for)** trocar (por); (replace (with)) substituir (por)
swarm [swɔ:m] n (of bees) enxame m;

(of people) multidão f ▷ vi enxamear; aglomerar-se; (place): **to be ~ing with** estar apinhado de
sway [sweɪ] vi balançar-se, oscilar ▷ vt (influence) influenciar
swear [swɛə'] (pt swore, pp sworn) vi (curse) xingar ▷ vt (promise) jurar; **swearword** n palavrão m
sweat [swɛt] n suor m ▷ vi suar
sweater n suéter m or f (BR), camisola (PT)
sweaty adj suado
Swede [swi:d] n sueco(-a)
swede [swi:d] n tipo de nabo
Sweden ['swi:dən] n Suécia; **Swedish** adj sueco ▷ n (Ling) sueco
sweep [swi:p] (pt, pp swept) n (act) varredura; (also: chimney ~) limpador m de chaminés ▷ vt varrer; (with arm) empurrar; (subj: current) arrastar; (: fashion, craze) espalhar-se por ▷ vi varrer; **sweep away** vt varrer; **sweep past** vi passar rapidamente; **sweep up** vi varrer
sweet [swi:t] n (candy) bala (BR), rebuçado (PT); (BRIT: pudding) sobremesa ▷ adj doce; (fig: air) fresco; (: water, smell) doce; (: sound) suave; (: kind) meigo; (baby, kitten) bonitinho; **sweetheart** n namorado(-a)
swell [swɛl] (pt ~ed, pp swollen or ~ed) n (of sea) vaga, onda ▷ adj (US: inf: excellent) bacana ▷ vi (increase) aumentar; (get stronger) intensificar-se; (also: ~ up) inchar-se; **swelling** n (Med) inchaço f
swept [swɛpt] pt, pp of **sweep**
swerve [swə:v] vi desviar-se
swift [swɪft] n (bird) andorinhão m ▷ adj rápido
swim [swɪm] (pt swam, pp swum) n: **to go for a ~** ir nadar ▷ vi nadar; (head, room) rodar ▷ vt atravessar a nado; (distance) percorrer (a nado); **swimmer** n nadador(a) m/f; **swimming** n natação f; **swimming costume** (BRIT) n (woman's) maiô m (BR), fato de banho (PT); (man's) calção m de banho (BR), calções mpl de banho (PT); **swimming pool** n piscina; **swimming trunks** npl sunga (BR), calções mpl de banho (PT); **swimsuit** n maiô m (BR), fato de banho (PT)
swing [swɪŋ] (pt, pp swung) n (in playground) balanço; (movement) balanceio, oscilação f; (in opinion) mudança, virada; (rhythm) ritmo ▷ vt balançar; (also: ~ round) girar, rodar ▷ vi oscilar; (on swing) balançar; (also: ~

round) voltar-se bruscamente; **to be in full ~** estar a todo vapor

swirl [swəːl] *vi* redemoinhar

Swiss [swɪs] *adj, n inv* suíço(-a)

switch [swɪtʃ] *n* (*for light, radio etc*) interruptor *m*; (*change*) mudança ▷ *vt* (*change*) trocar; **switch off** *vt* apagar; (*engine*) desligar; **switch on** *vt* acender; ligar; **switchboard** *n* (*Tel*) mesa telefônica

Switzerland ['swɪtsələnd] *n* Suíça

swollen ['swəulən] *pp of* **swell**

swoop [swuːp] *n* (*by police etc*) batida ▷ *vi* (*also:* **~ down**) precipitar-se, cair

swop [swɔp] *n, vt* = **swap**

sword [sɔːd] *n* espada

swore [swɔːʳ] *pt of* **swear**

sworn [swɔːn] *pp of* **swear** ▷ *adj* (*statement*) sob juramento; (*enemy*) declarado

swum [swʌm] *pp of* **swim**

swung [swʌŋ] *pt, pp of* **swing**

syllable ['sɪləbl] *n* sílaba

syllabus ['sɪləbəs] *n* programa *m* de estudos

symbol ['sɪmbl] *n* símbolo

sympathetic [sɪmpə'θɛtɪk] *adj* (*understanding*) compreensivo; (*likeable*) agradável; (*supportive*): **~ to(wards)** solidário com

sympathize ['sɪmpəθaɪz] *vi*: **to ~ with** (*person*) compadecer-se de; (*sb's feelings*) compreender; (*cause*) simpatizar com

sympathy ['sɪmpəθɪ] *n* compaixão *f*; **sympathies** *npl* (*tendencies*) simpatia; **in ~** em acordo; (*strike*) em solidariedade; **with our deepest ~** com nossos mais profundos pêsames

symphony ['sɪmfənɪ] *n* sinfonia

symptom ['sɪmptəm] *n* sintoma *m*; (*sign*) indício

syndicate ['sɪndɪkɪt] *n* sindicato; (*of newspapers*) cadeia

synthetic [sɪn'θɛtɪk] *adj* sintético

Syria ['sɪrɪə] *n* Síria

syringe [sɪ'rɪndʒ] *n* seringa

syrup ['sɪrəp] *n* xarope *m*; (*also:* **golden ~**) melaço

system ['sɪstəm] *n* sistema *m*; (*method*) método; (*Anat*) organismo; **systematic** [sɪstə'mætɪk] *adj* sistemático

tab [tæb] *n* lingüeta, aba; (*label*) etiqueta; **to keep ~s on** (*fig*) vigiar

ta [tɑː] (*BRIT: inf*) *excl* obrigado(-a)

table ['teɪbl] *n* mesa ▷ *vt* (*motion etc*) apresentar; **to lay** *or* **set the ~** pôr a mesa; **~ of contents** índice *m*, sumário; **tablecloth** *n* toalha de mesa; **tablemat** *n* descanso; **table salt** *n* sal *m* fino; **tablespoon** *n* colher *f* de sopa; (*also:* **tablespoonful**: *as measurement*) colherada

tablet ['tæblɪt] *n* (*Med*) comprimido; (*of stone*) lápide *f*

table tennis *n* pingue-pongue *m*, tênis *m* de mesa

table wine *n* vinho de mesa

tabloid ['tæblɔɪd] *n* tablóide *m*; **tabloid press** *n* ver quadro

⊛ **TABLOID PRESS**
⊛
⊛ O termo **tabloid press** refere-se
⊛ aos jornais populares de formato
⊛ meio jornal que apresentam muitas
⊛ fotografias e adotam um estilo
⊛ bastante conciso. O público-alvo
⊛ desses jornais é composto por
⊛ leitores que se interessam pelos fatos

● do dia que contenham um certo
● toque de escândalo; veja **quality**
● **(news)papers**.

tack [tæk] n (nail) tachinha, percevejo
▷ vt prender com tachinha; (stitch)
alinhavar ▷ vi virar de bordo

tackle ['tækl] n (gear) equipamento;
(also: **fishing ~**) apetrechos mpl; (for
lifting) guincho; (Football) ato de tirar a
bola de adversário ▷ vt (difficulty) atacar;
(challenge: person) desafiar; (grapple with)
atracar-se com; (Football) tirar a bola de

tacky ['tækɪ] adj pegajoso, grudento;
(inf: tasteless) cafona

tact [tækt] n tato, diplomacia; **tactful**
adj diplomático

tactics ['tæktɪks] n, npl tática

tactless ['tæktlɪs] adj sem diplomacia

tag [tæg] n (label) etiqueta; **tag along**
vi seguir

tail [teɪl] n rabo; (of comet, plane) cauda;
(of shirt, coat) aba ▷ vt (follow) seguir bem
de perto; **tail away** or **off** vi diminuir
gradualmente

tailor ['teɪlə^r] n alfaiate m

take [teɪk] (pt **took**, pp **~n**) vt tomar;
(photo, holiday) tirar; (grab) pegar (em);
(prize) ganhar; (effort, courage) requerer,
exigir; (tolerate) agüentar; (accompany,
bring: person) acompanhar, trazer;
(: thing) trazer, carregar; (exam) fazer;
(passengers etc): **it ~s 50 people** cabem
50 pessoas; **to ~ sth from** (drawer etc)
tirar algo de; (person) pegar algo de; **I ~
it that ...** suponho que ...; **take after**
vt fus parecer-se com; **take apart** vt
desmontar; **take away** vt (extract)
tirar; (carry off) levar; (subtract) subtrair;
take back vt (return) devolver; (one's
words) retirar; **take down** vt (building)
demolir; (dismantle) desmontar; (letter
etc) tomar por escrito; **take in** vt (deceive)
enganar; (understand) compreender;
(include) abranger; (lodger) receber; **take
off** vi (Aviat) decolar; (go away) ir-se
▷ vt (remove) tirar; **take on** vt (work)
empreender; (employee) empregar;
(opponent) desafiar; **take out** vt tirar;
(extract) extrair; (invite) acompanhar;
take over vt (business) assumir; (country)
tomar posse de ▷ vi: **to take over
from sb** suceder a alguém; **take to** vt
fus (person) simpatizar com; (activity)
afeiçoar-se a; **to take to doing sth** criar
o hábito de fazer algo; **take up** vt (dress)

encurtar; (time, space) ocupar; (hobby
etc) dedicar-se a; (offer) aceitar; **to take
sb up on a suggestion/offer** aceitar a
oferta/sugestão de alguém sobre algo;
takeaway (BRIT) adj (food) para levar;
takeoff n (Aviat) decolagem f; **takeover**
n (Comm) aquisição f de controle;
takings npl (Comm) receita, renda

talc [tælk] n (also: **~um powder**) talco

tale [teɪl] n (story) conto; (account)
narrativa; **to tell ~s** (fig: lie) dizer
mentiras

talent ['tælənt] n talento; **talented** adj
talentoso

talk [tɔːk] n conversa, fala; (gossip)
mexerico, fofocas fpl; (conversation)
conversa, conversação f ▷ vi falar;
talks npl (Pol etc) negociações fpl; **to ~
about** falar sobre; **to ~ sb into/out of
doing sth** convencer alguém a fazer
algo/dissuadir alguém de fazer algo; **to
~ shop** falar sobre negócios/questões
profissionais; **talk over** vt discutir

tall [tɔːl] adj alto; **to be 6 feet ~** medir 6
pés, ter 6 pés de altura

tame [teɪm] adj domesticado; (fig: story,
style) sem graça, insípido

tamper ['tæmpə^r] vi: **to ~ with** mexer em

tampon ['tæmpən] n tampão m

tan [tæn] n (also: **sun~**) bronzeado ▷ vi
bronzear-se ▷ adj (colour) bronzeado,
marrom claro

tangerine [tændʒə'riːn] n tangerina,
mexerica

tangle ['tæŋgl] n emaranhado; **to get
in(to) a ~** meter-se num rolo

tank [tæŋk] n depósito, tanque m; (for
fish) aquário; (Mil) tanque m

tanker ['tæŋkə^r] n (ship) navio-tanque m;
(truck) caminhão-tanque m

tantrum ['tæntrəm] n chilique m, acesso
(de raiva)

tap [tæp] n (on sink etc) torneira; (gentle
blow) palmadinha; (gas tap) chave f
▷ vt dar palmadinha em, bater de leve;
(resources) utilizar, explorar; (telephone)
grampear; **on ~** disponível

tape [teɪp] n fita; (also: **magnetic ~**) fita
magnética; (sticky tape) fita adesiva ▷ vt
(record) gravar (em fita); (stick with tape)
colar; **tape measure** n fita métrica,
trena

tar [tɑː] n alcatrão m

target ['tɑːgɪt] n alvo

tariff ['tærɪf] n tarifa

tarmac ['tɑːmæk] n (BRIT: on road)

macadame *m*; (*Aviat*) pista
tarpaulin [tɑː'pɔːlɪn] *n* lona alcatroada
tart [tɑːt] *n* (*Culin*) torta; (*BRIT: inf: pej: woman*) piranha ▷ *adj* (*flavour*) ácido, azedo; **tart up** (*inf*) *vt* arrumar, dar um jeito em; **to tart o.s. up** arrumar-se; (*pej*) empetecar-se
tartan ['tɑːtn] *n* tartan *m* (*pano escocês axadrezado*) ▷ *adj* axadrezado
tartar ['tɑːtə'] *n* (*on teeth*) tártaro
taste [teɪst] *n* gosto; (*also:* **after~**) gosto residual; (*sample, fig*) amostra, idéia ▷ *vt* provar; (*test*) experimentar ▷ *vi:* **to ~ of** or **like** ter gosto or sabor de; **you can ~ the garlic (in it)** sente-se o gosto de alho; **in good/bad ~** de bom/mau gosto; **tasteful** *adj* de bom gosto; **tasteless** *adj* insípido, insosso; (*remark*) de mau gosto; **tasty** *adj* saboroso, delicioso
tatters ['tætəz] *npl:* **in ~** (*clothes*) em farrapos; (*papers etc*) em pedaços
tattoo [tə'tuː] *n* tatuagem *f*; (*spectacle*) espetáculo militar ▷ *vt* tatuar
taught [tɔːt] *pt, pp of* **teach**
taunt [tɔːnt] *n* zombaria, escárnio ▷ *vt* zombar de, mofar de
Taurus ['tɔːrəs] *n* Touro
taut [tɔːt] *adj* esticado
tax [tæks] *n* imposto ▷ *vt* tributar; (*fig: test*) sobrecarregar; (: *patience*) esgotar; **tax-free** *adj* isento de impostos
taxi ['tæksɪ] *n* táxi *m* ▷ *vi* (*Aviat*) taxiar; **taxi driver** *n* motorista *m/f* de táxi; **taxi rank** (*BRIT*) *n* ponto de táxi; **taxi stand** *n* = **taxi rank**
tax: **tax payer** *n* contribuinte *m/f*; **tax return** *n* declaração *f* de rendimentos
TB *abbr of* **tuberculosis**
tea [tiː] *n* chá *m*; (*BRIT: meal*) refeição *f* à noite; **high ~** (*BRIT*) ajantarado; **tea bag** *n* saquinho (*BR*) or carteira (*PT*) de chá; **tea break** (*BRIT*) *n* pausa (para o chá)
teach [tiːtʃ] (*pt, pp* **taught**) *vt:* **to ~ sb sth, ~ sth to sb** ensinar algo a alguém; (*in school*) lecionar ▷ *vi* ensinar; (*be a teacher*) lecionar; **teacher** *n* professor(a) *m/f*; **teaching** *n* ensino; (*as profession*) magistério
teacup ['tiːkʌp] *n* xícara (*BR*) or chávena (*PT*) de chá
team [tiːm] *n* (*Sport*) time *m* (*BR*), equipa (*PT*); (*group*) equipe *f* (*BR*), equipa (*PT*); (*of animals*) parelha
teapot ['tiːpɔt] *n* bule *m* de chá
tear¹ [tɛə'] (*pt* **tore**, *pp* **torn**) *n* rasgão *m*

▷ *vt* rasgar ▷ *vi* rasgar-se; **tear along** *vi* (*rush*) precipitar-se; **tear up** *vt* rasgar
tear² [tɪə'] *n* lágrima; **in ~s** chorando, em lágrimas; **tearful** *adj* choroso; **tear gas** *n* gás *m* lacrimogênio
tearoom ['tiːruːm] *n* salão *m* de chá
tease [tiːz] *vt* implicar com
teaspoon ['tiːspuːn] *n* colher *f* de chá; (*also:* **~ful**: *as measurement*) (conteúdo de) colher de chá
teatime ['tiːtaɪm] *n* hora do chá
tea towel (*BRIT*) *n* pano de prato
technical ['tɛknɪkl] *adj* técnico
technician [tɛk'nɪʃn] *n* técnico(-a)
technique [tɛk'niːk] *n* técnica
technology [tɛk'nɔlədʒɪ] *n* tecnologia
teddy (bear) ['tɛdɪ-] *n* ursinho de pelúcia
tedious ['tiːdɪəs] *adj* maçante, chato
teenage ['tiːneɪdʒ] *adj* (*fashions etc*) de or para adolescentes; **teenager** *n* adolescente *m/f*, jovem *m/f*
teens [tiːnz] *npl:* **to be in one's ~** estar entre os 13 e 19 anos, estar na adolescência
teeth [tiːθ] *npl of* **tooth**
teetotal ['tiː'təutl] *adj* abstêmio
teleconferencing ['tɛlɪkɔnfərənsɪŋ] *n* teleconferência *f*
telegram ['tɛlɪgræm] *n* telegrama *m*
telephone ['tɛlɪfəun] *n* telefone *m* ▷ *vt* (*person*) telefonar para; (*message*) telefonar; **to be on the ~** (*BRIT*), **to have a ~** (*subscriber*) ter telefone; **to be on the ~** (*be speaking*) estar falando no telefone; **telephone booth** (*BRIT* **telephone box**) *n* cabine *f* telefônica; **telephone call** *n* telefonema *m*; **telephone directory** *n* lista telefônica, catálogo (*BR*); **telephone number** *n* (número de) telefone *m*
telesales ['tɛlɪseɪlz] *npl* televendas *fpl*
telescope ['tɛlɪskəup] *n* telescópio
television ['tɛlɪvɪʒən] *n* televisão *f*; **on ~** na televisão
tell [tɛl] (*pt, pp* **told**) *vt* dizer; (*relate: story*) contar; (*distinguish*): **to ~ sth from** distinguir algo de ▷ *vi* (*have effect*) ter efeito; (*talk*): **to ~ (of)** falar (de or em); **to ~ sb to do sth** dizer para alguém fazer algo; **tell off** *vt* repreender
telly ['tɛlɪ] (*BRIT: inf*) *n abbr* = **television**
temp [tɛmp] (*BRIT: inf*) *abbr* = **temporary** ▷ *n* temporário(-a) ▷ *vi* trabalhar como temporário(-a)
temper ['tɛmpə'] *n* (*nature*)

temperamento; (*mood*) humor *m*; (*fit of anger*) cólera ▷ *vt* (*moderate*) moderar; **to be in a ~** estar de mau humor; **to lose one's ~** perder a paciência *or* a calma, ficar zangado

temperament ['tɛmprəmənt] *n* temperamento; **temperamental** [tɛmprə'mɛntl] *adj* temperamental

temperature ['tɛmprətʃə'] *n* temperatura; **to have** *or* **run a ~** ter febre

temple ['tɛmpl] *n* (*building*) templo; (*Anat*) têmpora

temporary ['tɛmpərərɪ] *adj* temporário; (*passing*) transitório

tempt [tɛmpt] *vt* tentar; **tempting** *adj* tentador(a)

ten [tɛn] *num* dez

tenant ['tɛnənt] *n* inquilino(-a), locatário(-a)

tend [tɛnd] *vt* (*sick etc*) cuidar de ▷ *vi*: **to ~ to do sth** tender a fazer algo

tendency ['tɛndənsɪ] *n* tendência

tender ['tɛndə'] *adj* terno; (*age*) tenro; (*sore*) sensível, dolorido; (*meat*) macio ▷ *n* (*Comm*: *offer*) oferta, proposta; (*money*): **legal ~** moeda corrente *or* legal ▷ *vt* oferecer; **to ~ one's resignation** pedir demissão

tennis ['tɛnɪs] *n* tênis *m*; **tennis ball** *n* bola de tênis; **tennis court** *n* quadra de tênis; **tennis player** *n* jogador(a) *m/f* de tênis; **tennis racket** *n* raquete *f* de tênis

tenor ['tɛnə'] *n* (*Mus*) tenor *m*

tense [tɛns] *adj* tenso; (*muscle*) rígido, teso ▷ *n* (*Ling*) tempo

tension ['tɛnʃən] *n* tensão *f*

tent [tɛnt] *n* tenda, barraca

tentative ['tɛntətɪv] *adj* provisório, tentativo; (*person*) hesitante, indeciso

tenth [tɛnθ] *num* décimo

tent peg *n* estaca

tent pole *n* pau *m*

tepid ['tɛpɪd] *adj* tépido, morno

term [tə:m] *n* (*expression*) termo, expressão *f*; (*period*) período; (*Sch*) trimestre *m* ▷ *vt* denominar; **terms** *npl* (*conditions*) condições *fpl*; (*Comm*) cláusulas *fpl*, termos *mpl*; **in the short/long ~** a curto/longo prazo; **to be on good ~s with sb** dar-se bem com alguém; **to come to ~s with** aceitar

terminal ['tə:mɪnl] *adj* incurável ▷ *n* (*Elec*) borne *m*; (*BRIT*: *also*: **air ~**) terminal *m*; (*also Comput*) terminal *m*; (*BRIT*: *also*: **coach ~**) estação *f* rodoviária

terminate ['tə:mɪneɪt] *vt* terminar; **to ~ a pregnancy** fazer um aborto

terminus ['tə:mɪnəs] (*pl* **termini**) *n* terminal *m*

terrace ['tɛrəs] *n* terraço; (*BRIT*: *houses*) lance *m* de casas; **the terraces** *npl* (*BRIT*: *Sport*) a arquibancada (*BR*), a geral (*PT*); **terraced** *adj* (*house*) ladeado por outras casas; (*garden*) em dois níveis

terrain [tɛ'reɪn] *n* terreno

terrible ['tɛrɪbl] *adj* terrível, horroroso; (*conditions*) precário; (*inf*: *awful*) terrível; **terribly** *adv* terrivelmente; (*very badly*) pessimamente

terrific [tə'rɪfɪk] *adj* terrível, magnífico; (*wonderful*) maravilhoso, sensacional

terrify ['tɛrɪfaɪ] *vt* apavorar

territory ['tɛrɪtərɪ] *n* território

terror ['tɛrə'] *n* terror *m*; **terrorist** *n* terrorista *m/f*

test [tɛst] *n* (*trial, check*) prova, ensaio; (*of courage etc, Chem*) prova; (*Med*) exame *m*; (*exam*) teste *m*, prova; (*also*: **driving ~**) exame de motorista ▷ *vt* testar, pôr à prova

testicle ['tɛstɪkl] *n* testículo

testify ['tɛstɪfaɪ] *vi* (*Law*) depor, testemunhar; **to ~ to sth** atestar algo, testemunhar algo

testimony ['tɛstɪmənɪ] *n* (*Law*) testemunho, depoimento; **to be (a) ~ to** ser uma prova de

test: **test match** *n* (*Cricket, Rugby*) jogo internacional; **test tube** *n* proveta, tubo de ensaio

tetanus ['tɛtənəs] *n* tétano

text [tɛkst] *n* texto; (*text message*) mensagem *f* de texto, torpedo (*inf*) ▷ *vt* mandar uma mensagem de texto *ou* (*inf*) um torpedo a; **textbook** *n* livro didático; (*Sch*) livro escolar; **text message** *n* mensagem *f* de texto, torpedo (*inf*)

texture ['tɛkstʃə'] *n* textura

Thailand ['taɪlænd] *n* Tailândia

Thames [tɛmz] *n*: **the ~** o Tâmisa (*BR*), o Tamisa (*PT*)

than [ðæn, ðən] *conj* (*in comparisons*) do que; **more ~ 10** mais de 10; **I have more/less ~ you** tenho mais/menos do que você; **she has more apples ~ pears** ela tem mais maçãs do que peras; **she is older ~ you think** ela é mais velha do que você pensa

thank [θæŋk] *vt* agradecer; **~ you (very much)** muito obrigado(-a); **thanks** *npl*

agradecimentos *mpl* ▷ *excl* obrigado(-a)!;
Thanksgiving (Day) *n* Dia *m* de Ação
de Graças

❉ **THANKSGIVING DAY**
❉
❉ O feriado de Ação de graças
❉ **Thanksgiving Day** nos Estados
❉ Unidos, quarta quinta-feira do
❉ mês de novembro, é o dia em que
❉ se comemora a boa colheita feita
❉ pelos peregrinos originários da Grã-
❉ Bretanha em 1621; tradicionalmente,
❉ é um dia em que se agradece a Deus
❉ e se organiza um grande banquete.
❉ Uma festa semelhante é celebrada no
❉ Canadá na segunda segunda-feira de
❉ outubro.

○ KEYWORD

that [ðæt, ðət] (*pl* **those**) *adj*
(*demonstrative*) esse (essa); (*more remote*)
aquele (aquela); **that man/woman/**
book aquele homem/aquela mulher/
aquele livro; **that one** esse (essa)
▷ *pron* **1** (*demonstrative*) esse (essa),
aquele (aquela); (*neuter*) isso, aquilo;
who's/what's that? quem é?/o que é
isso?; **is that you?** é você?; **I prefer this**
to that eu prefiro isto a aquilo; **that's**
what he said foi isso o que ele disse;
that is (to say) isto é, quer dizer
2 (*relative: direct: thing, person*) que;
(: *person*) quem; (*relative: indirect: thing*,
person) o qual (a qual) *sg*, os quais (as
quais) *pl*; (: *person*) quem; **the book**
(that) I read o livro que eu li; **the box**
(that) I put it in a caixa na qual eu botei-
o; **the man (that) I spoke to** o homem
com quem *or* o qual falei
3 (*relative: of time*): **on the day that he**
came no dia em que ele veio
▷ *conj* que; **she suggested that I phone**
you ela sugeriu que eu telefonasse para
você
▷ *adv* (*demonstrative*): **I can't work**
that much não posso trabalhar tanto;
I didn't realize it was that bad não
pensei que fôsse tão ruim; **that high**
dessa altura, até essa altura

thatched [θætʃt] *adj* (*roof*) de sapê; **~**
cottage chalé *m* com telhado de sapê *or*
de colmo
thaw [θɔ:] *n* degelo ▷ *vi* (*ice*) derreter-
se; (*food*) descongelar-se ▷ *vt* (*food*)
descongelar

○ KEYWORD

the [ði:, ðə] *def art* **1** (*gen: sg*) o (a); (: *pl*) os
(as); **the books/children** os livros/as
crianças; **she put it on the table** ela
colocou-o na mesa; **he took it from the**
drawer ele tirou isto da gaveta; **to play**
the piano/violin tocar piano/violino;
I'm going to the cinema vou ao cinema
2 (+ *adj to form n*): **the rich and the poor**
os ricos e os pobres; **to attempt the**
impossible tentar o impossível
3 (*in titles*): **Richard the Second** Ricardo
II; **Peter the Great** Pedro o Grande
4 (*in comparisons: + adv*): **the more he**
works the more he earns quanto mais
ele trabalha, mais ele ganha

theatre ['θɪətə^r] (*US* **theater**) *n* teatro;
(*Med: also*: **operating ~**) sala de operação
theft [θɛft] *n* roubo
their [ðɛə^r] *adj* seu (sua), deles (delas);
theirs *pron* (o) seu ((a) sua); *see also*
mine²
them [ðɛm, ðəm] *pron* (*direct*) os (as);
(*indirect*) lhes; (*stressed, after prep*) a eles
(a elas)
theme [θi:m] *n* tema *m*; **theme park** *n*
parque de diversões em torno de um único
tema
themselves [ðəm'sɛlvz] *pron* eles
mesmos (elas mesmas), se; (*after prep*) si
(mesmos(-as))
then [ðɛn] *adv* (*at that time*) então; (*next*)
em seguida; (*later*) logo, depois; (*and also*)
além disso ▷ *conj* (*therefore*) então, nesse
caso, portanto ▷ *adj*: **the ~ president** o
então presidente; **by ~** (*past*) até então;
(*future*) até lá; **from ~ on** a partir de então
theology [θɪ'ɔlədʒɪ] *n* teologia
theory ['θɪərɪ] *n* teoria; **in ~** em teoria,
teoricamente
therapy ['θɛrəpɪ] *n* terapia

○ KEYWORD

there [ðɛə^r] *adv* **1**: **there is, there are**
há, tem; **there are 3 of them** há 3 deles;
there is no-one here/no bread left não
tem ninguém aqui/não tem mais pão;
there has been an accident houve um
acidente
2 (*referring to place*) aí, ali, lá; **put it**

in/on/up/down there põe isto lá dentro/cima/em cima/embaixo; **I want that book there** quero aquele livro lá; **there he is!** lá está ele!
3: **there, there!** (esp to child) calma!

thereabouts ['ðɛərəbauts] adv por aí; (amount) aproximadamente

thereafter [ðɛərˈɑːftəʳ] adv depois disso

thereby ['ðɛəbaɪ] adv assim, deste modo

therefore ['ðɛəfɔː] adv portanto

there's [ðɛəz] = **there is; there has**

thermal ['θəːml] adj térmico

thermometer [θəˈmɔmɪtəʳ] n termômetro

thermostat ['θəːməustæt] n termostato

these [ðiːz] pl adj, pron estes (estas)

thesis ['θiːsɪs] (pl **theses**) n tese f

they [ðeɪ] pl pron eles (elas); **~ say that ...** (it is said that) diz-se que ..., dizem que ...; **they'd** = **they had; they would; they'll** = **they shall; they will; they've** = **they have**

thick [θɪk] adj espesso; (mud, fog, forest) denso; (sauce) grosso; (stupid) burro ⊳ n: **in the ~ of the battle** em plena batalha; **it's 20 cm ~** tem 20 cm de espessura; **thicken** vi (fog) adensar-se; (plot etc) complicar-se ⊳ vt engrossar; **thickness** n espessura, grossura

thief [θiːf] (pl **thieves**) n ladrão (ladra) m/f

thigh [θaɪ] n coxa

thin [θɪn] adj magro; (slice) fino; (light) leve; (hair) ralo; (crowd) pequeno; (soup, sauce) aguado ⊳ vt (also: **~ down**) diluir

thing [θɪŋ] n coisa; (object) negócio; (matter) assunto, negócio; (mania) mania; **things** npl (belongings) pertences mpl; **to have a ~ about sb/sth** ser vidrado em alguém/algo; **the best ~ would be to ...** o melhor seria ...; **how are ~s?** como vai?, tudo bem?; **she's got a ~ about ...** ela detesta ...; **poor ~!** coitadinho(-a)!

think [θɪŋk] (pt, pp **thought**) vi pensar; (believe) achar ⊳ vt pensar, achar; (imagine) imaginar; **what did you ~ of them?** o que você achou deles?; **to ~ about sth/sb** pensar em algo/alguém; **I'll ~ about it** vou pensar sobre isso; **to ~ of doing sth** pensar em fazer algo; **I ~ so/not** acho que sim/não; **to ~ well of sb** fazer bom juízo de alguém; **think over** vt refletir sobre, meditar sobre;

think up vt inventar, bolar

third [θəːd] adj terceiro ⊳ n terceiro(-a); (fraction) terço; (Aut) terceira; (Sch: degree) terceira categoria; **thirdly** adv em terceiro lugar; **third party insurance** n seguro contra terceiros; **Third World** n: **the Third World** o Terceiro Mundo

thirst [θəːst] n sede f; **thirsty** adj (person) sedento, com sede; (work) que dá sede; **to be thirsty** estar com sede

thirteen ['θəːˈtiːn] num treze

thirty ['θəːtɪ] num trinta

 KEYWORD

this [ðɪs] (pl **these**) adj (demonstrative) este (esta); **this man/woman/book** este homem/esta mulher/este livro; **these people/children/records** estas pessoas/crianças/estes discos; **this one** este aqui
⊳ pron (demonstrative) este (esta); (neuter) isto; **who/what is this?** quem é esse?/o que é isso?; **this is where I live** é aqui que eu moro; **this is Mr Brown** este é o Sr Brown; (on phone) aqui é o Sr Brown
⊳ adv (demonstrative): **this high/long** desta altura/deste comprimento; **we can't stop now we've gone this far** não podemos parar agora que fomos tão longe

thistle ['θɪsl] n cardo

thorn [θɔːn] n espinho

thorough ['θʌrə] adj (search) minucioso; (knowledge, research, person) metódico, profundo; **thoroughly** adv minuciosamente; (search) profundamente; (wash) completamente; (very) muito

those [ðəuz] pl pron, adj esses (essas)

though [ðəu] conj embora, se bem que
⊳ adv no entanto

thought [θɔːt] pt, pp of **think** ⊳ n pensamento; (idea) idéia; (opinion) opinião f; (reflection) reflexão f; **thoughtful** adj pensativo; (serious) sério; (considerate) atencioso; **thoughtless** adj desatencioso; (words) inconseqüente

thousand ['θauzənd] num mil; **two ~** dois mil; **~s (of)** milhares mpl (de); **thousandth** num milésimo

thrash [θræʃ] vt surrar, malhar; (defeat) derrotar; **thrash about** vi debater-se; **thrash out** vt discutir exaustivamente

thread [θrɛd] n fio, linha; (of screw) rosca
▷ vt (needle) enfiar

threat [θrɛt] n ameaça; **threaten** vi
ameaçar ▷ vt: **to threaten sb with
sth/to do** ameaçar alguém com algo/de
fazer

three [θriː] num três; **three-
dimensional** adj tridimensional, em três
dimensões; **three-piece suit** n terno (3
peças) (BR), fato de 3 peças (PT)

threshold ['θrɛʃhəʊld] n limiar m

threw [θruː] pt of **throw**

thrill [θrɪl] n emoção f; (shudder)
estremecimento ▷ vt emocionar,
vibrar; **to be ~ed** (with gift etc) estar
emocionado; **thriller** n romance m
(or filme m) de suspense; **thrilling** adj
emocionante

throat [θrəʊt] n garganta; **to have a
sore ~** estar com dor de garganta

throb [θrɔb] n (of heart) batida; (of engine)
vibração f; (of pain) latejo ▷ vi (heart)
bater, palpitar; (pain) dar pontadas;
(engine) vibrar

throne [θrəʊn] n trono

through [θruː] prep por, através de; (time)
durante; (by means of) por meio de, por
intermédio de; (owing to) devido a ▷ adj
(ticket, train) direto ▷ adv através; **to put
sb ~ to sb** (Tel) ligar alguém com alguém;
to be ~ (Tel) estar na linha; (have finished)
acabar; **"no - road"** "rua sem saída"; **I'm
halfway ~ the book** estou na metade
do livro; **throughout** prep (place) por
todo(-a) o(-a); (time) durante todo(-a)
o(-a) ▷ adv por or em todas as partes

throw [θrəʊ] (pt **threw**, pp ~**n**) n
arremesso, tiro; (Sport) lançamento ▷ vt
jogar, atirar; lançar; (rider) derrubar;
(fig) desconcertar; **to ~ a party** dar uma
festa; **throw away** vt (dispose of) jogar
fora; (waste) desperdiçar; **throw off** vt
desfazer-se de; (habit, cold) livrar-se;
throw out vt expulsar; (rubbish) jogar
fora; (idea) rejeitar; **throw up** vi vomitar,
botar para fora

thru [θruː] (us) prep, adj, adv = **through**

thrush [θrʌʃ] n (Zool) tordo

thrust [θrʌst] (pt, pp ~) n impulso; (Tech)
empuxo ▷ vt empurrar

thud [θʌd] n baque m, som m surdo

thug [θʌg] n facínora m/f

thumb [θʌm] n (Anat) polegar m; **to ~
a lift** pegar carona (BR), arranjar uma
boléia (PT); **thumb through** vt fus
folhear; **thumbtack** (us) n percevejo,
tachinha

thump [θʌmp] n murro, pancada;
(sound) baque m ▷ vt dar um murro em
▷ vi bater

thunder ['θʌndəʳ] n trovão m ▷ vi
trovejar; (train etc): **to ~ past** passar
como um raio; **thunderstorm** n
tempestade f com trovoada, temporal m

Thursday ['θəːzdɪ] n quinta-feira

thyme [taɪm] n tomilho

tick [tɪk] n (of clock) tique-taque m;
(mark) tique m, marca; (Zool) carrapato;
(BRIT: inf): **in a ~** num instante ▷ vi fazer
tique-taque ▷ vt marcar, ticar; **tick off** vt
assinalar, ticar; (person) dar uma bronca
em; **tick over** (BRIT) vi (engine) funcionar
em marcha lenta; (fig) ir indo

ticket ['tɪkɪt] n (for bus, plane) passagem
f; (for theatre, raffle) bilhete m; (for cinema)
entrada; (in shop: on goods) etiqueta;
(parking ticket: fine) multa; (for library)
cartão m; **to get a (parking) ~** (Aut)
ganhar uma multa (por estacionamento
ilegal); **ticket collector** n revisor(a) m/f;
ticket office n bilheteria (BR), bilheteira
(PT)

tickle ['tɪkl] vt fazer cócegas em ▷ vi
fazer cócegas; **ticklish** adj coceguento;
(problem) delicado

tide [taɪd] n maré f; (fig) curso; **high/low
~** maré alta/baixa; **the ~ of public
opinion** a corrente da opinião pública;
tide over vt ajudar num período difícil

tidy ['taɪdɪ] adj (room) arrumado; (dress,
work) limpo; (person) bem arrumado ▷ vt
(also: ~ **up**) pôr em ordem, arrumar

tie [taɪ] n (string etc) fita, corda; (BRIT: also:
neck~) gravata; (fig: link) vínculo, laço;
(Sport: draw) empate m ▷ vt amarrar
▷ vi (Sport) empatar; **to ~ in a bow**
dar um laço em; **to ~ a knot in sth** dar
um nó em algo; **tie down** vt amarrar;
(fig: restrict) limitar, restringir; (to date,
price etc) obrigar; **tie up** vt embrulhar;
(dog) prender; (boat, prisoner) amarrar;
(arrangements) concluir; **to be tied up**
estar ocupado

tier [tɪəʳ] n fileira; (of cake) camada

tiger ['taɪgəʳ] n tigre m

tight [taɪt] adj (rope) esticado, firme;
(money) escasso; (clothes, shoes) justo;
(bend) fechado; (budget, programme)
rigoroso; (inf: drunk) bêbado
▷ adv (squeeze) bem forte; (shut)
hermeticamente; **tighten** vt (rope)
esticar; (screw, grip) apertar; (security)

aumentar ▷ vi esticar-se; apertar-se;
tightly adv firmemente
tile [taɪl] n (on roof) telha; (on floor)
ladrilho; (on wall) azulejo, ladrilho
till [tɪl] n caixa (registradora) ▷ vt (land)
cultivar ▷ prep, conj = **until**
tilt [tɪlt] vt inclinar ▷ vi inclinar-se
timber ['tɪmbəʳ] n (material) madeira;
(trees) mata, floresta
time [taɪm] n tempo; (epoch: often
pl) época; (by clock) hora; (moment)
momento; (occasion) vez f; (Mus)
compasso ▷ vt calcular or medir o tempo
de; (visit etc) escolher o momento para; **a
long ~** muito tempo; **4 at a ~** quatro de
uma vez; **for the ~ being** por enquanto;
from ~ to ~ de vez em quando; **at ~s**
às vezes; **in ~** (soon enough) a tempo;
(after some time) com o tempo; (Mus) no
compasso; **in a week's ~** dentro de uma
semana; **in no ~** num abrir e fechar de
olhos; **any ~** a qualquer hora; **on ~** na
hora; **5 ~s 5 is 25** 5 vezes 5 são 25; **what
~ is it?** que horas são?; **to have a good
~** divertir-se; **timely** adj oportuno;
timetable n horário; **time zone** n fuso
horário
timid ['tɪmɪd] adj tímido
timing ['taɪmɪŋ] n escolha do momento;
(Sport) cronometragem f; **the ~ of his
resignation** o momento que escolheu
para se demitir
tin [tɪn] n estanho; (also: **~ plate**) folha-
de-flandres f; (BRIT: can) lata
tingle ['tɪŋgl] vi formigar
tinned [tɪnd] (BRIT) adj (food) em lata, em
conserva
tin opener (BRIT) n abridor m de latas
(BR), abre-latas m inv (PT)
tinsel ['tɪnsl] n ouropel m
tint [tɪnt] n matiz m; (for hair) tintura,
tinta; **tinted** adj (hair) pintado;
(spectacles, glass) fumê inv
tiny ['taɪnɪ] adj pequenininho, minúsculo
tip [tɪp] n ponta; (gratuity) gorjeta; (BRIT:
for rubbish) depósito; (advice) dica ▷ vt dar
uma gorjeta a; (tilt) inclinar; (overturn:
also: **~ over**) virar, emborcar; (empty: also:
~ out) esvaziar, entornar
tiptoe ['tɪptəu] n: **on ~** na ponta dos pés
tire ['taɪəʳ] n (US) = **tyre** ▷ vt cansar ▷ vi
cansar-se; (become bored) chatear-se;
tired adj cansado; **to be tired of sth**
estar farto or cheio de algo; **tiring** adj
cansativo
tissue ['tɪʃuː] n tecido; (paper handkerchief)

lenço de papel; **tissue paper** n papel m
de seda
tit [tɪt] n (bird) passarinho; **to give ~ for
tat** pagar na mesma moeda
title ['taɪtl] n título
TM n abbr = **trademark**

○ **KEYWORD**

to [tuː, tə] prep **1** (direction) a, para;
(towards) para; **to go to France/
London/school/the station** ir à
França/a Londres/ao colégio/à estação;
to go to Lígia's/the doctor's ir à
casa de Lígia/ao médico; **the road to
Edinburgh** a estrada para Edinburgo; **to
the left/right** à esquerda/direita
2 (as far as) até; **to count to 10** contar
até 10; **from 40 to 50 people** de 40 a 50
pessoas
3 (with expressions of time): **a quarter
to 5** quinze para as 5 (BR), 5 menos um
quarto (PT)
4 (for, or) de, para; **the key to the front
door** a chave da porta da frente; **a letter
to his wife** uma carta para a sua mulher
5 (expressing indirect object): **to give sth
to sb** dar algo a alguém; **to talk to sb**
falar com alguém; **I sold it to a friend**
vendi isto para um amigo; **to cause
damage to sth** causar danos em algo
6 (in relation to) para; **3 goals to 2** 3 a 2; **8
apples to the kilo** 8 maçãs por quilo
7 (purpose, result) para; **to come to sb's
aid** prestar ajuda a alguém; **to sentence
sb to death** condenar alguém à morte;
to my surprise para minha surpresa
▷ with vb **1** (simple infin): **to go/eat**
ir/comer
2 (following another vb): **to want/try to
do** querer/tentar fazer; **to start to do**
começar a fazer
3 (with vb omitted): **I don't want to** eu
não quero; **you ought to** você deve
4 (purpose, result) para
5 (equivalent to relative clause) para, a;
I have things to do eu tenho coisas
para fazer; **the main thing is to try** o
principal é tentar
6 (after adj etc) para; **ready to go** pronto
para ir; **too old/young to ...** muito
velho/jovem para ...
▷ adv: **pull/push the door to** puxar/
empurrar a porta

toad [təud] n sapo

toadstool ['təudstu:l] n chapéu-de-cobra m, cogumelo venenoso
toast [təust] n (Culin) torradas fpl; (drink, speech) brinde m ▷ vt torrar; brindar; **toaster** n torradeira
tobacco [tə'bækəu] n tabaco, fumo (BR)
today [tə'deɪ] adv, n hoje m
toddler ['tɒdləʳ] n criança que começa a andar
toe [təu] n dedo do pé; (of shoe) bico ▷ vt: **to ~ the line** (fig) conformar-se, cumprir as obrigações
toffee ['tɒfɪ] n puxa-puxa m (BR), caramelo (PT)
together [tə'gɛðəʳ] adv juntos; (at same time) ao mesmo tempo; **~ with** junto com
toilet ['tɔɪlət] n privada, vaso sanitário; (BRIT: lavatory) banheiro (BR), casa de banho (PT) ▷ cpd de toalete; **toilet paper** n papel m higiênico; **toiletries** npl artigos mpl de toalete; **toilet roll** n rolo de papel higiênico
token ['təukən] n (sign) sinal m, símbolo, prova; (souvenir) lembrança; (substitute coin) ficha ▷ adj simbólico; **book/record ~** (BRIT) vale para comprar livros/discos
told [təuld] pt, pp of **tell**
tolerant ['tɒlərənt] adj: **~ of** tolerante com
tolerate ['tɒləreɪt] vt suportar; (Med, Tech) tolerar
toll [təul] n (of casualties) número de baixas; (charge) pedágio (BR), portagem f (PT) ▷ vi dobrar, tanger
tomato [tə'mɑːtəu] (pl ~es) n tomate m
tomb [tu:m] n tumba
tombstone ['tu:mstəun] n lápide f
tomorrow [tə'mɒrəu] adv, n amanhã m; **the day after ~** depois de amanhã; **~ morning** amanhã de manhã
ton [tʌn] n tonelada (BRIT = 1016KG; US = 907KG); **~s of** (inf) um monte de
tone [təun] n tom m ▷ vi harmonizar; **tone down** vt (colour, criticism) suavizar; (sound) baixar; (Mus) entoar; **tone up** vt (muscles) tonificar
tongs [tɒnz] npl (for coal) tenaz f; (for hair) ferros mpl de frisar cabelo
tongue [tʌn] n língua; **~ in cheek** ironicamente
tonic ['tɒnɪk] n (Med) tônico; (also: **~ water**) (água) tônica
tonight [tə'naɪt] adv, n esta noite, hoje à noite
tonsil ['tɒnsəl] n amígdala; **tonsillitis** [tɒnsɪ'laɪtɪs] n amigdalite f
too [tu:] adv (excessively) demais, muito; (also) também; **~ much** (adv) demais; (adj) demasiado; **~ many** demasiados(-as)
took [tuk] pt of **take**
tool [tu:l] n ferramenta
tooth [tu:θ] (pl **teeth**) n (Anat, Tech) dente m; (molar) molar m; **toothache** n dor f de dente; **to have toothache** estar com dor de dente; **toothbrush** n escova de dentes; **toothpaste** n pasta de dentes, creme m dental; **toothpick** n palito
top [tɒp] n (of mountain) cume m, cimo; (of tree) topo; (of head) cocuruto; (of cupboard, table) superfície f, topo; (of box, jar, bottle) tampa; (of ladder, page) topo; (toy) pião m; (blouse etc) top m, blusa ▷ adj (shelf, step) mais alto; (marks) máximo; (in rank) principal, superior ▷ vt exceder; (be first in) estar à cabeça de; **on ~ of** sobre, em cima de; (in addition to) além de; **from ~ to toe** (BRIT) da cabeça aos pés; **from ~ to bottom** de cima abaixo; **top up** (US **top off**) vt completar; (phone) recarregar; **top-up card** n (for mobile phone) cartão de recarga (para celular); **top floor** n último andar m
topic ['tɒpɪk] n tópico, assunto; **topical** adj atual
topless adj (bather etc) topless inv, sem a parte superior do biquíni
topple ['tɒpl] vt derrubar ▷ vi cair para frente
torch [tɔːtʃ] (BRIT: electric) lanterna
tore [tɔːʳ] pt of **tear**
torment [(n) 'tɔːmɛnt, (vb) tɔː'mɛnt] n tormento, suplício ▷ vt atormentar; (fig: annoy) chatear, aborrecer
torn [tɔːn] pp of **tear**
tornado [tɔː'neɪdəu] (pl ~es) n tornado
torrent ['tɒrənt] n torrente f
tortoise ['tɔːtəs] n tartaruga
torture ['tɔːtʃəʳ] n tortura ▷ vt torturar; (fig) atormentar
Tory ['tɔːrɪ] (BRIT) adj, n (Pol) conservador(a) m/f
toss [tɒs] vt atirar, arremessar; (head) lançar para trás ▷ vi: **to ~ and turn in bed** virar de um lado para o outro na cama; **to ~ a coin** tirar cara ou coroa; **to ~ up for sth** (BRIT) jogar cara ou coroa por algo
total ['təutl] adj total ▷ n total m, soma ▷ vt (add up) somar; (amount to) montar a

touch [tʌtʃ] n (*sense*) toque m; (*contact*) contato ▷ vt tocar (em); (*tamper with*) mexer com; (*make contact with*) fazer contato com; (*emotionally*) comover; **a ~ of** (*fig*) um traço de; **to get in ~ with sb** entrar em contato com alguém; **to lose ~** perder o contato; **touch on** vt fus (*topic*) tocar em, fazer menção de; **touch up** vt (*paint*) retocar; **touchdown** n aterrissagem f (BR), aterragem f (PT); (*on sea*) amerissagem f (BR), amaragem f (PT); (US: *Football*) touchdown m; **touching** adj comovedor(a)

tough [tʌf] adj duro; (*difficult*) difícil; (*resistant*) resistente; (*person: physically*) forte; (: *mentally*) tenaz; (*firm*) firme, inflexível

tour ['tuəʳ] n viagem f, excursão f; (*also:* **package ~**) excursão organizada; (*of town, museum*) visita; (*by artist*) turnê f ▷ vt (*country, city*) excursionar por; (*factory*) visitar

tourism ['tuərɪzm] n turismo

tourist ['tuərɪst] n turista m/f ▷ cpd turístico; **tourist office** n (*in country*) escritório de turismo; (*in embassy etc*) departamento de turismo

tournament ['tuənəmənt] n torneio

tow [təu] vt rebocar; **"on ~"** (BRIT), **"in ~"** (US) (*Aut*) "rebocado"

toward(s) [tə'wɔːd(z)] prep em direção a; (*of attitude*) para com; (*of purpose*) para; **toward(s) noon/the end of the year** perto do meio-dia/do fim do ano

towel ['tauəl] n toalha; **towelling** n (*fabric*) tecido para toalhas

tower ['tauəʳ] n torre f; **tower block** (BRIT) n prédio alto, espigão m, cortiço (BR)

town [taun] n cidade f; **to go to ~** ir à cidade; (*fig*) fazer com entusiasmo, mandar brasa (BR); **town centre** n centro (da cidade); **town hall** n prefeitura (BR), concelho (PT)

toy [tɔɪ] n brinquedo; **toy with** vt fus brincar com; (*idea*) contemplar

trace [treɪs] n (*sign*) sinal m; (*small amount*) traço ▷ vt (*draw*) traçar, esboçar; (*follow*) seguir a pista de; (*locate*) encontrar

track [træk] n (*mark*) pegada, vestígio; (*path: gen*) caminho, vereda; (: *of bullet etc*) trajetória; (: *of suspect, animal*) pista, rasto; (*Rail*) trilhos (BR), carris mpl (PT); (*on tape*) trilha; (*Sport*) pista; (*on record*) faixa ▷ vt seguir a pista de; **to keep ~**

of não perder de vista; (*fig*) manter-se informado sobre; **track down** vt (*prey*) seguir a pista de; (*sth lost*) procurar e encontrar

tractor ['træktəʳ] n trator m

trade [treɪd] n comércio; (*skill, job*) ofício ▷ vi negociar, comerciar ▷ vt: **to ~ sth (for sth)** trocar algo (por algo); **trade in** vt dar como parte do pagamento; **trademark** n marca registrada; **trader** n comerciante m/f; **tradesman** (*irreg*) n lojista m; **trade union** n sindicato

tradition [trə'dɪʃən] n tradição f; **traditional** adj tradicional

traffic ['træfɪk] n trânsito; (*air traffic etc*) tráfego; (*illegal*) tráfico ▷ vi: **to ~ in** (*pej: liquor, drugs*) traficar com, fazer tráfico com; **traffic circle** (US) n rotatória; **traffic jam** n engarrafamento, congestionamento; **traffic lights** npl sinal m luminoso; **traffic warden** n guarda m/f de trânsito

tragedy ['trædʒədɪ] n tragédia

tragic ['trædʒɪk] adj trágico

trail [treɪl] n (*tracks*) rasto, pista; (*path*) caminho, trilha; (*of smoke, dust*) rasto ▷ vt (*drag*) arrastar; (*follow*) seguir a pista de ▷ vi arrastar-se; (*hang loosely*) pender; (*in game, contest*) ficar para trás; **trail behind** vi atrasar-se; **trailer** n (*Aut*) reboque m; (US: *caravan*) trailer m (BR), rulote f (PT); (*Cinema*) trailer

train [treɪn] n trem m (BR), comboio (PT); (*of dress*) cauda ▷ vt formar; (*teach skills to*) instruir; (*Sport*) treinar; (*dog*) adestrar, amestrar; (*point: gun etc*): **to ~ on** apontar para ▷ vi (*learn a skill*) instruir; (*Sport*) treinar; (*be educated*) ser treinado; **to lose one's ~ of thought** perder o fio; **trainee** [treɪ'niː] n estagiário(-a); **trainer** n (*Sport*) treinador(a) m/f; (*of animals*) adestrador(a) m/f; **trains** npl (*shoes*) tênis m; **training** n instrução f; (*Sport, for occupation*) treinamento; (*professional*) formação f

trait [treɪt] n traço

traitor ['treɪtəʳ] n traidor(a) m/f

tram [træm] (BRIT) n (*also:* **~car**) bonde m (BR), eléctrico (PT)

tramp [træmp] n (*person*) vagabundo(-a); (*inf. pej: woman*) piranha ▷ vi caminhar pesadamente

trample ['træmpl] vt: **to ~ (underfoot)** calcar aos pés

trampoline ['træmpəliːn] n trampolim m

tranquil ['træŋkwɪl] *adj* tranqüilo;
  tranquillizer *n* (*Med*) tranqüilizante *m*
transfer [(*n*) 'trænsfə', (*vb*) træns'fə:']
  n transferência; (*picture, design*)
  decalcomania ▷ *vt* transferir; **to ~ the
  charges** (BRIT: *Tel*) ligar a cobrar
transform [træns'fɔ:m] *vt* transformar
transfusion [træns'fju:ʒən] *n* (*also*:
  blood ~) transfusão *f* (de sangue)
transit ['trænzɪt] *n*: **in ~** em trânsito, de
  passagem
translate [trænz'leɪt] *vt* traduzir;
  translation *n* tradução *f*; **translator** *n*
  tradutor(a) *m/f*
transmission [trænz'mɪʃən] *n*
  transmissão *f*
transmit [trænz'mɪt] *vt* transmitir
transparent [træns'pærnt] *adj*
  transparente
transplant [(*vb*) træns'plɑ:nt, (*n*)
  'trænsplɑ:nt] *vt* transplantar ▷ *n* (*Med*)
  transplante *m*
transport [(*n*) 'trænspɔ:t, (*vb*)
  træns'pɔ:t] *n* transporte *m* ▷ *vt*
  transportar; (*carry*) acarretar;
  transportation ['trænspɔ:'teɪʃən] *n*
  transporte *m*
trap [træp] *n* (*snare*) armadilha, cilada;
  (*trick*) cilada; (*carriage*) aranha, charrete
  f ▷ *vt* pegar em armadilha; (*person: trick*)
  armar; (: *in bad marriage*) prender; (: *in
  fire*): **to be ~ped** ficar preso; (*immobilize*)
  bloquear
trash [træʃ] *n* (*pej: nonsense*) besteiras *fpl*;
  (US: *rubbish*) lixo; **trash can** (US) *n* lata
  de lixo
trauma ['trɔ:mə] *n* trauma *m*
travel ['trævl] *n* viagem *f* ▷ *vi* viajar;
  (*sound*) propagar-se; (*news*) levar;
  (*wine*): **this wine ~s well** este vinho
  não sofre alteração ao ser transportado
  ▷ *vt* percorrer; **travels** *npl* (*journeys*)
  viagens *fpl*; **travel agent** *n* agente
  m/f de viagens; **traveller** (US **traveler**)
  n viajante *m/f*; (*Comm*) caixeiro(-a)
  viajante; **traveller's cheque** (US
  traveler's check) *n* cheque *m* de
  viagem; **travelling** (US **traveling**) *n* as
  viagens, viajar *m* ▷ *adj* (*circus, exhibition*)
  itinerante; (*salesman*) viajante ▷ *cpd* de
  viagem; **travel sickness** *n* enjôo
tray [treɪ] *n* bandeja; (*on desk*) cesta
treacherous ['trɛtʃərəs] *adj* traiçoeiro;
  (*ground, tide*) perigoso
treacle ['tri:kl] *n* melado
tread [trɛd] (*pt* **trod**, *pp* **trodden**) *n* (*step*)

passo, pisada; (*sound*) passada; (*of stair*)
  piso; (*of tyre*) banda de rodagem ▷ *vi*
  pisar; **tread on** *vt fus* pisar (em)
treasure ['trɛʒə'] *n* tesouro; (*person*) jóia
  ▷ *vt* (*value*) apreciar, estimar; **treasures**
  npl (*art treasures etc*) preciosidades *fpl*
treasurer ['trɛʒərə'] *n* tesoureiro(-a)
treasury ['trɛʒərɪ] *n* tesouraria
treat [tri:t] *n* regalo, deleite *m* ▷ *vt*
  tratar; **to ~ sb to sth** convidar alguém
  para algo
treatment ['tri:tmənt] *n* tratamento
treaty ['tri:tɪ] *n* tratado, acordo
treble ['trɛbl] *adj* tríplice ▷ *vt* triplicar
  ▷ *vi* triplicar(-se)
tree [tri:] *n* árvore *f*
trek [trɛk] *n* (*long journey*) jornada; (*walk*)
  caminhada
tremble ['trɛmbl] *vi* tremer
tremendous [trɪ'mɛndəs] *adj*
  tremendo; (*enormous*) enorme; (*excellent*)
  sensacional, fantástico
trench [trɛntʃ] *n* trincheira
trend [trɛnd] *n* (*tendency*) tendência;
  (*of events*) curso; (*fashion*) modismo,
  tendência; **trendy** *adj* (*idea*) de acordo
  com a tendência atual; (*clothes*) da
  última moda
trespass ['trɛspəs] *vi*: **to ~ on** invadir;
  "no ~ing" "entrada proibida"
trial ['traɪəl] *n* (*Law*) processo; (*test: of
  machine etc*) prova, teste *m*; **trials** *npl*
  (*unpleasant experiences*) dissabores *mpl*;
  by ~ and error por tentativas; **to be on
  ~** ser julgado; **trial period** *n* período de
  experiência
triangle ['traɪæŋgl] *n* (*Math, Mus*)
  triângulo
tribe [traɪb] *n* tribo *f*
tribunal [traɪ'bju:nl] *n* tribunal *m*
tribute ['trɪbju:t] *n* homenagem *f*;
  to pay ~ to prestar homenagem a,
  homenagear
trick [trɪk] *n* truque *m*; (*joke*) peça,
  brincadeira; (*skill, knack*) habilidade *f*;
  (*Cards*) vaza ▷ *vt* enganar; **to play a ~
  on sb** pregar uma peça em alguém; **that
  should do the ~** (*inf*) isso deveria dar
  resultado
trickle ['trɪkl] *n* (*of water etc*) fio (de água)
  ▷ *vi* gotejar, pingar
tricky ['trɪkɪ] *adj* difícil, complicado
trifle ['traɪfl] *n* bobagem *f*, besteira;
  (*Culin*) tipo de bolo com fruta e creme ▷ *adv*:
  a ~ long um pouquinho longo
trigger ['trɪgə'] *n* (*of gun*) gatilho; **trigger**

off vt desencadear

trim [trɪm] adj (figure) elegante; (house) arrumado; (garden) bem cuidado ▷ n (haircut) aparada; (on car) estofamento ▷ vt aparar, cortar; (decorate): **to ~ (with)** enfeitar (com); (Naut: sail) ajustar

trip [trɪp] n viagem f; (outing) excursão f; (stumble) tropeção m ▷ vi tropeçar; (go lightly) andar com passos ligeiros; **on a ~** de viagem; **trip up** vi tropeçar ▷ vt passar uma rasteira em

triple ['trɪpl] adj triplo, tríplice; **triplets** npl trigêmeos(-as) m/fpl

tripod ['traɪpɒd] n tripé m

triumph ['traɪʌmf] n (satisfaction) satisfação f; (great achievement) triunfo ▷ vi: **to ~ (over)** triunfar (sobre)

trivial ['trɪvɪəl] adj insignificante; (commonplace) trivial

trod [trɒd] pt of **tread**; **trodden** pp of **tread**

trolley ['trɒlɪ] n carrinho; (table on wheels) mesa volante

trombone [trɒm'bəʊn] n trombone m

troop [truːp] n bando, grupo ▷ vi: **to ~ in/out** entrar/sair em bando; **troops** npl (Mil) tropas fpl; **~ing the colour** (BRIT) saudação da bandeira

trophy ['trəʊfɪ] n troféu m

tropic ['trɒpɪk] n trópico; **tropical** adj tropical

trot [trɒt] n trote m; (fast pace) passo rápido ▷ vi trotar; (person) andar rapidamente; **on the ~** (fig: inf) a fio

trouble ['trʌbl] n problema(s) m (pl), dificuldade(s) f (pl); (worry) preocupação f; (effort) incômodo, trabalho; (Pol) distúrbios mpl; (Med): **stomach** etc **~ problemas** mpl gástricos etc ▷ vt perturbar; (worry) preocupar, incomodar ▷ vi: **to ~ to do sth** incomodar-se or preocupar-se de fazer algo; **troubles** npl (Pol etc) distúrbios mpl; **to be in ~** estar num aperto; (ship, climber etc) estar em dificuldade; **what's the ~?** qual é o problema?; **troubled** adj preocupado; (epoch, life) agitado; **troublemaker** n criador(a)-de-casos m/f; (child) encrenqueiro(-a); **troublesome** adj importuno; (child, cough) incômodo

trough [trɒf] n (also: **drinking ~**) bebedouro, cocho; (also: **feeding ~**) gamela; (depression) depressão f

trousers ['traʊzəz] npl calça (BR), calças fpl (PT)

trout [traʊt] n inv truta

truant ['truːənt] (BRIT) n: **to play ~** matar aula (BR), fazer gazeta (PT)

truce [truːs] n trégua, armistício

truck [trʌk] n caminhão m (BR), camião m (PT); (Rail) vagão m; **truck driver** n caminhoneiro(-a) (BR), camionista m/f (PT)

true [truː] adj verdadeiro; (accurate) exato; (genuine) autêntico; (faithful) fiel, leal; **to come ~** realizar-se, tornar-se realidade

truly ['truːlɪ] adv realmente; (truthfully) verdadeiramente; (faithfully) fielmente; **yours ~** (in letter) atenciosamente

trumpet ['trʌmpɪt] n trombeta

trunk [trʌŋk] n tronco; (of elephant) tromba; (case) baú m; (US: Aut) mala (BR), porta-bagagens m (PT); **trunks** npl (also: **swimming ~s**) sunga (BR), calções mpl de banho (PT)

trust [trʌst] n confiança; (responsibility) responsabilidade f; (Law) fideicomisso ▷ vt (rely on) confiar em; (entrust): **to ~ sth to sb** confiar algo a alguém; (hope): **to ~ (that)** esperar que; **to take sth on ~** aceitar algo sem verificação prévia; **trusted** adj de confiança; **trustworthy** adj digno de confiança

truth [truːθ] n verdade f; **truthful** adj (person) sincero, honesto

try [traɪ] n tentativa; (Rugby) ensaio ▷ vt (Law) julgar; (test: sth new) provar, pôr à prova; (strain) cansar ▷ vi tentar; **to have a ~** fazer uma tentativa; **to ~ to do sth** tentar fazer algo; **try on** vt (clothes) experimentar, provar; **trying** adj exasperante

T-shirt n camiseta (BR), T-shirt f (PT)

tub [tʌb] n tina; (bath) banheira

tube [tjuːb] n tubo; (pipe) cano; (BRIT: underground) metrô m (BR), metro(-politano) (PT); (for tyre) câmara-de-ar f

tuck [tʌk] vt (put) enfiar, meter; **tuck away** vt esconder; **to be tucked away** estar escondido; **tuck in** vt enfiar para dentro; (child) aconchegar ▷ vi (eat) comer com apetite; **tuck up** vt (child) aconchegar

Tuesday ['tjuːzdɪ] n terça-feira

tug [tʌg] n (ship) rebocador m ▷ vt puxar

tuition [tjuː'ɪʃən] n ensino; (private tuition) aulas fpl particulares; (US: fees) taxas fpl escolares

tulip ['tjuːlɪp] n tulipa

tumble ['tʌmbl] n (fall) queda ▷ vi cair, tombar; **to ~ to sth** (inf) sacar algo

tumbler ['tʌmblə'] n copo
tummy ['tʌmɪ] (inf) n (belly) barriga;
(stomach) estômago
tumour ['tju:mə'] (US **tumor**) n tumor m
tuna ['tju:nə] n inv (also: ~ **fish**) atum m
tune [tju:n] n melodia ▷ vt (Mus) afinar;
(Radio, TV) sintonizar; (Aut) regular; **to be
in/out of ~** (instrument) estar afinado/
desafinado; (singer) cantar afinado/
desafinar; **to be in/out of ~ with** (fig)
harmonizar-se com/destoar de; **tune in**
vi (Radio, TV): **to tune in (to)** sintonizar
(com); **tune up** vi (musician) afinar (seu
instrumento)
tunic ['tju:nɪk] n túnica
Tunisia [tju:'nɪzɪə] n Tunísia
tunnel ['tʌnl] n túnel m; (in mine) galeria
▷ vi abrir um túnel (or uma galeria)
turbulence ['tə:bjuləns] n (Aviat)
turbulência
turf [tə:f] n torrão m ▷ vt relvar, gramar;
turf out (inf) vt (person) pôr no olho da
rua
Turk [tə:k] n turco(-a)
Turkey ['tə:kɪ] n Turquia
turkey ['tə:kɪ] n peru(a) m/f
Turkish ['tə:kɪʃ] adj turco(-a) ▷ n (Ling)
turco
turmoil ['tə:mɔɪl] n tumulto, distúrbio,
agitação f; **in ~** agitado, tumultuado
turn [tə:n] n volta, turno; (in road) curva;
(of mind, events) propensão f, tendência;
(Theatre) número; (Med) choque m ▷ vt
dar volta a, fazer girar; (collar) virar;
(change): **to ~ sth into** converter algo
em ▷ vi virar; (person: look back) voltar-se;
(reverse direction) mudar de direção;
(milk) azedar; (become) tornar-se, virar;
to ~ nasty engrossar; **to ~ forty** fazer
quarenta anos; **a good ~** um favor; **it
gave me quite a ~** me deu um susto
enorme; **"no left ~"** (Aut) "proibido virar
à esquerda"; **it's your ~** é a sua vez; **in ~**
por sua vez; **to take ~s (at)** revezar (em);
turn away vi virar a cabeça ▷ vt recusar;
turn back vi voltar atrás ▷ vt voltar
para trás; (clock) atrasar; **turn down**
vt (refuse) recusar; (reduce) baixar; (fold)
dobrar, virar para baixo; **turn in** vi (inf:
go to bed) ir dormir ▷ vt (fold) dobrar para
dentro; **turn off** vi (from road) sair
do caminho ▷ vt (light, radio etc) apagar;
(engine) desligar; **turn on** vt (light)
acender; (engine, radio) ligar; (tap) abrir;
turn out vt (light, gas) apagar; (produce)
produzir ▷ vi (troops) ser mobilizado;

to turn out to be ... revelar-se (ser) ...,
resultar (ser) ..., vir a ser ...; **turn over** vi
(person) virar-se ▷ vt (object) virar; **turn
round** vi voltar-se, virar-se; **turn up**
vi (person) aparecer, pintar; (lost object)
aparecer ▷ vt (collar) subir; (radio etc)
aumentar; **turning** n (in road) via lateral
turnip ['tə:nɪp] n nabo
turnout ['tə:naut] n assistência; (in
election) comparecimento às urnas
turnover ['tə:nəuvə'] n (Comm: amount of
money) volume m de negócios; (: of goods)
movimento; (of staff) rotatividade f
turn-up (BRIT) n (on trousers) volta, dobra
turquoise ['tə:kwɔɪz] n (stone) turquesa
▷ adj azul-turquesa inv
turtle ['tə:tl] n tartaruga, cágado
tusk [tʌsk] n defesa (de elefante)
tutor ['tju:tə'] n professor(a) m/f; (private
tutor) professor(a) m/f particular;
tutorial [tju:'tɔ:rɪəl] n (Sch) seminário
tuxedo [tʌk'si:dəu] (US) n smoking m
TV n abbr (= television) TV f
tweed [twi:d] n tweed m, pano grosso de lã
tweezers ['twi:zəz] npl pinça (pequena)
twelfth [twelfθ] num décimo segundo
twelve [twelv] num doze; **at ~ (o'clock)**
(midday) ao meio-dia; (midnight) à meia-
noite
twentieth ['twentɪɪθ] num vigésimo
twenty ['twentɪ] num vinte
twice [twaɪs] adv duas vezes; **~ as much**
duas vezes mais
twig [twɪg] n graveto, varinha ▷ vi (inf)
sacar
twilight ['twaɪlaɪt] n crepúsculo, meia-
luz f
twin [twɪn] adj gêmeo; (beds) separado
▷ n gêmeo ▷ vt irmanar; **twin(-bedded)
room** n quarto com duas camas
twinkle ['twɪŋkl] vi cintilar; (eyes)
pestanejar
twist [twɪst] n torção f; (in road, coil)
curva; (in flex) virada; (in story) mudança
imprevista ▷ vt torcer, retorcer; (ankle)
torcer; (weave) entrelaçar; (roll around)
enrolar; (fig) deturpar ▷ vi serpentear
twit [twɪt] (inf) n idiota m/f, bobo(-a)
twitch [twɪtʃ] n puxão m; (nervous) tique
m nervoso ▷ vi contrair-se
two [tu:] num dois; **to put ~ and ~
together** (fig) tirar conclusões; **two-
way** adj: **two-way traffic** trânsito em
mão dupla
type [taɪp] n (category) tipo, espécie
f; (model) modelo; (Typ) tipo, letra

▷ vt (letter etc) datilografar, bater (à máquina); **typewriter** n máquina de escrever

typhoid ['taɪfɔɪd] n febre f tifóide
typical ['tɪpɪkl] adj típico
typing ['taɪpɪŋ] n datilografia
typist ['taɪpɪst] n datilógrafo(-a) m/f
tyre ['taɪə'] (us **tire**) n pneu m

UFO ['juːfəʊ] n abbr (= unidentified flying object) óvni m
Uganda [juːˈgændə] n Uganda (no article)
ugly ['ʌglɪ] adj feio; (dangerous) perigoso
UK n abbr = **United Kingdom**
ulcer ['ʌlsə'] n úlcera; **mouth ~** afta
ultimate ['ʌltɪmət] adj último, final; (authority) máximo; **ultimately** adv (in the end) no final, por último; (fundamentally) no fundo
ultrasound ['ʌltrəsaʊnd] n (Med) ultra-som m
umbrella [ʌmˈbrɛlə] n guarda-chuva m; (for sun) guarda-sol m, barraca (da praia)
umpire ['ʌmpaɪə'] n árbitro ▷ vt arbitrar
UN n abbr (= United Nations) ONU f
unable [ʌnˈeɪbl] adj: **to be ~ to do sth** não poder fazer algo
unanimous [juːˈnænɪməs] adj unânime
unarmed [ʌnˈɑːmd] adj (without a weapon) desarmado; (defenceless) indefeso
unattended [ʌnəˈtɛndɪd] adj (car, luggage) abandonado
unattractive [ʌnəˈtræktɪv] adj sem atrativos; (building, appearance, idea) pouco atraente

unavoidable [ʌnə'vɔɪdəbl] adj inevitável
unaware [ʌnə'wɛəʳ] adj: **to be ~ of** ignorar, não perceber
unawares [ʌnə'wɛəz] adv improvisadamente, de surpresa
unbearable [ʌn'bɛərəbl] adj insuportável
unbeatable [ʌn'bi:təbl] adj (team) invencível; (price) sem igual
unbelievable [ʌnbɪ'li:vəbl] adj inacreditável; (amazing) incrível
unborn [ʌn'bɔ:n] adj por nascer
unbutton [ʌn'bʌtn] vt desabotoar
uncalled-for [ʌn'kɔ:ld-] adj desnecessário, gratuito
uncanny [ʌn'kænɪ] adj estranho; (knack) excepcional
uncertain [ʌn'sə:tn] adj incerto; (character) indeciso; (unsure): **~ about** inseguro sobre; **in no ~ terms** em termos precisos; **uncertainty** n incerteza; (also: **doubts**) dúvidas fpl
uncle ['ʌŋkl] n tio
uncomfortable [ʌn'kʌmfətəbl] adj incômodo; (uneasy) pouco à vontade; (situation) desagradável
uncommon [ʌn'kɔmən] adj raro, incomum, excepcional
unconditional [ʌnkən'dɪʃənl] adj incondicional
unconscious [ʌn'kɔnʃəs] adj sem sentidos, desacordado; (unaware): **~ of** inconsciente de ▷ n: **the ~** o inconsciente
uncontrollable [ʌnkən'trəuləbl] adj (temper) ingovernável; (child, animal, laughter) incontrolável
unconventional [ʌnkən'vɛnʃənl] adj inconvencional
uncover [ʌn'kʌvəʳ] vt descobrir; (take lid off) destapar, destampar
undecided [ʌndɪ'saɪdɪd] adj indeciso; (question) não respondido, pendente
under ['ʌndəʳ] prep embaixo de (BR), debaixo de (PT); (fig) sob; (less than) menos de; (according to) segundo, de acordo com ▷ adv embaixo; (movement) por baixo; **~ there** ali embaixo; **~ repair** em conserto; **undercover** adj secreto, clandestino; **underdog** n o mais fraco; **underdone** adj (Culin) mal passado; **underestimate** vt subestimar; **undergo** (irreg) vt sofrer; (test) passar por; (operation, treatment) ser submetido a; **undergraduate** n universitário(-a); **underground** n (BRIT) metrô m (BR), metro(-politano) (PT); (Pol) organização

f clandestina ▷ adj subterrâneo; (fig) clandestino ▷ adv (work) embaixo da terra; (fig) na clandestinidade; **undergrowth** n vegetação f rasteira; **underline** vt sublinhar; **undermine** vt minar, solapar; **underneath** adv embaixo, debaixo, por baixo ▷ prep embaixo de (BR), debaixo de (PT); **underpaid** adj mal pago; **underpants** (BRIT) npl cueca(s) f(pl) (BR), cuecas fpl (PT); **underpass** (BRIT) n passagem f inferior; **underprivileged** adj menos favorecido
understand [ʌndə'stænd] (irreg) vt entender, compreender ▷ vi: **to ~ that** acreditar que; **understandable** adj compreensível; **understanding** adj compreensivo ▷ n compreensão f; (knowledge) entendimento; (agreement) acordo
understatement [ʌndə'steɪtmənt] n (quality) subestimação f; (euphemism) eufemismo; **it's an ~ to say that ...** é uma subestimação dizer que ...
understood [ʌndə'stud] pt, pp of **understand** ▷ adj entendido; (implied) subentendido, implícito
undertake [ʌndə'teɪk] (irreg: like **take**) vt incumbir-se de, encarregar-se de; **to ~ to do sth** comprometer-se a fazer algo
undertaking ['ʌndəteɪkɪŋ] n empreendimento; (promise) promessa
underwater [ʌndə'wɔ:təʳ] adv sob a água ▷ adj subaquático
underwear ['ʌndəwɛəʳ] n roupa de baixo, roupa íntima
underworld ['ʌndəwə:ld] n (of crime) submundo
undo [ʌn'du:] (irreg: like **do**) vt (unfasten) desatar; (spoil) desmanchar
undress [ʌn'drɛs] vi despir-se, tirar a roupa
unearth [ʌn'ə:θ] vt desenterrar; (fig) revelar
uneasy [ʌn'i:zɪ] adj (person) preocupado; (feeling) incômodo; (peace, truce) desconfortável
uneducated [ʌn'ɛdjukeɪtɪd] adj inculto, sem instrução, não escolarizado
unemployed [ʌnɪm'plɔɪd] adj desempregado ▷ npl: **the ~** os desempregados
unemployment [ʌnɪm'plɔɪmənt] n desemprego
uneven [ʌn'i:vn] adj desigual; (road etc) irregular, acidentado

unexpected [ʌnɪk'spɛktɪd]
adj inesperado; **unexpectedly**
[ʌnɪks'pɛktɪdlɪ] *adv* inesperadamente
unfair [ʌn'fɛəʳ] *adj*: ~ **(to)** injusto (com)
unfaithful [ʌn'feɪθful] *adj* infiel
unfamiliar [ʌnfə'mɪlɪəʳ] *adj* pouco
familiar, desconhecido; **to be ~ with sth**
não estar familiarizado com algo
unfashionable [ʌn'fæʃnəbl] *adj* fora
da moda
unfasten [ʌn'fɑːsn] *vt* desatar; (*open*)
abrir
unfavourable [ʌn'feɪvərəbl] (*us*
unfavorable) *adj* desfavorável
unfinished [ʌn'fɪnɪʃt] *adj* incompleto,
inacabado
unfit [ʌn'fɪt] *adj* sem preparo físico;
(*incompetent*): ~ **(for)** incompetente
(para), incapaz (de); ~ **for work** inapto
para trabalhar
unfold [ʌn'fəuld] *vt* desdobrar ▷ *vi*
(*situation*) desdobrar-se
unfortunate [ʌn'fɔːtʃənət] *adj* infeliz;
(*event, remark*) inoportuno
unfriendly [ʌn'frɛndlɪ] *adj* antipático
unhappiness [ʌn'hæpɪnɪs] *n*
infelicidade *f*
unhappy [ʌn'hæpɪ] *adj* triste;
(*unfortunate*) desventurado; (*childhood*)
infeliz; (*dissatisfied*): ~ **with** descontente
com, insatisfeito com
unhealthy [ʌn'hɛlθɪ] *adj* insalubre;
(*person*) doentio; (*fig*) anormal
unheard-of [ʌn'həːd-] *adj* insólito
unhurt [ʌn'həːt] *adj* ileso
uniform ['juːnɪfɔːm] *n* uniforme *m* ▷ *adj*
uniforme
uninhabited [ʌnɪn'hæbɪtɪd] *adj*
inabitado
unintentional [ʌnɪn'tɛnʃənəl] *adj*
involuntário, não intencional
union ['juːnjən] *n* união *f*; (*also:* **trade**
~) sindicato (de trabalhadores) ▷ *cpd*
sindical; **Union Jack** *n* bandeira
britânica
unique [juː'niːk] *adj* único, sem igual
unit ['juːnɪt] *n* unidade *f*; (*of furniture etc*)
seção *f*; (*team, squad*) equipe *f*; **kitchen ~**
armário de cozinha
unite [juː'naɪt] *vt* unir ▷ *vi* unir-se;
united *adj* unido; (*effort*) conjunto;
United Kingdom *n* Reino Unido;
United Nations (Organization) *n*
(Organização *f* das) Nações *fpl* Unidas;
United States (of America) *n* Estados
Unidos *mpl* (da América)

universal [juːnɪ'vəːsl] *adj* universal
universe ['juːnɪvəːs] *n* universo
university [juːnɪ'vəːsɪtɪ] *n* universidade *f*
unjust [ʌn'dʒʌst] *adj* injusto
unkind [ʌn'kaɪnd] *adj* maldoso;
(*comment etc*) cruel
unknown [ʌn'nəun] *adj* desconhecido
unlawful [ʌn'lɔːful] *adj* ilegal
unleaded [ʌn'lɛdɪd] *adj* (*petrol, fuel*) sem
chumbo
unleash [ʌn'liːʃ] *vt* (*fig*) desencadear
unless [ʌn'lɛs] *conj* a menos que, a não
ser que; ~ **he comes** a menos que ele
venha
unlike [ʌn'laɪk] *adj* diferente ▷ *prep*
diferentemente de, ao contrário de
unlikely [ʌn'laɪklɪ] *adj* (*not likely*)
improvável; (*unexpected*) inesperado
unlisted [ʌn'lɪstɪd] (*us*) *adj* (*Tel*) que não
consta na lista telefônica
unload [ʌn'ləud] *vt* descarregar
unlock [ʌn'lɔk] *vt* destrancar
unlucky [ʌn'lʌkɪ] *adj* infeliz; (*object,
number*) de mau agouro; **to be ~** ser
azarado, ter azar
unmarried [ʌn'mærɪd] *adj* solteiro
unmistak(e)able [ʌnmɪs'teɪkəbl] *adj*
inconfundível
unnatural [ʌn'nætʃrəl] *adj* antinatural,
artificial; (*manner*) afetado; (*habit*)
depravado
unnecessary [ʌn'nɛsəsərɪ] *adj*
desnecessário, inútil
UNO ['juːnəu] *n abbr* (= *United Nations
Organization*) ONU *f*
unofficial [ʌnə'fɪʃl] *adj* não-oficial,
informal; (*strike*) desautorizado
unpack [ʌn'pæk] *vi* desembrulhar ▷ *vt*
desfazer
unpleasant [ʌn'plɛznt] *adj*
desagradável; (*person, manner*) antipático
unplug [ʌn'plʌg] *vt* desligar
unpopular [ʌn'pɔpjuləʳ] *adj* impopular
unprecedented [ʌn'prɛsɪdəntɪd] *adj*
sem precedentes
unpredictable [ʌnprɪ'dɪktəbl] *adj*
imprevisível
unravel [ʌn'rævl] *vt* desemaranhar;
(*mystery*) desvendar
unreal [ʌn'rɪəl] *adj* irreal, ilusório;
(*extraordinary*) extraordinário
unrealistic [ʌnrɪə'lɪstɪk] *adj* pouco
realista
unreasonable [ʌn'riːznəbl] *adj*
insensato; (*demand*) absurdo
unrelated [ʌnrɪ'leɪtɪd] *adj* sem relação;

(family) sem parentesco

unreliable [ʌnrɪˈlaɪəbl] *adj (person)* indigno de confiança; *(machine)* incerto, perigoso

unrest [ʌnˈrɛst] *n* inquietação *f*, desassossego; *(Pol)* distúrbios *mpl*

unroll [ʌnˈrəʊl] *vt* desenrolar

unruly [ʌnˈruːlɪ] *adj* indisciplinado; *(hair)* desalinhado

unsafe [ʌnˈseɪf] *adj* perigoso

unsatisfactory [ʌnsætɪsˈfæktərɪ] *adj* insatisfatório

unscrew [ʌnˈskruː] *vt* desparafusar

unsettled [ʌnˈsɛtld] *adj (weather)* instável; *(person)* inquieto

unsightly [ʌnˈsaɪtlɪ] *adj* feio, disforme

unskilled [ʌnˈskɪld] *adj* não-especializado

unstable [ʌnˈsteɪbl] *adj* em falso; *(mentally)* instável

unsteady [ʌnˈstɛdɪ] *adj* trêmulo; *(ladder)* em falso

unsuccessful [ʌnsəkˈsɛsful] *adj (attempt)* frustrado, vão (vã); *(writer, proposal)* sem êxito; **to be ~** *(in attempting sth)* ser mal sucedido, não conseguir; *(application)* ser recusado

unsuitable [ʌnˈsuːtəbl] *adj* inadequado; *(time)* inconveniente

unsure [ʌnˈʃuəʳ] *adj* inseguro, incerto; **to be ~ of o.s.** não ser seguro de si

untidy [ʌnˈtaɪdɪ] *adj (room)* desarrumado, desleixado; *(appearance)* desmazelado, desalinhado

untie [ʌnˈtaɪ] *vt* desatar, desfazer; *(dog, prisoner)* soltar

until [ənˈtɪl] *prep* até ▷ *conj* até que; **~ he comes** até que ele venha; **~ now** até agora; **~ then** até então

unused¹ [ʌnˈjuːzd] *adj* novo, sem uso

unused² [ʌnˈjuːst] *adj*: **to be ~ to sth/to doing sth** não estar acostumado com algo/a fazer algo

unusual [ʌnˈjuːʒuəl] *adj (strange)* estranho; *(rare)* incomum; *(exceptional)* extraordinário

unveil [ʌnˈveɪl] *vt* desvelar, descobrir

unwanted [ʌnˈwɔntɪd] *adj* não desejado, indesejável

unwell [ʌnˈwɛl] *adj*: **to be ~** estar doente; **to feel ~** estar indisposto

unwilling [ʌnˈwɪlɪŋ] *adj*: **to be ~ to do sth** relutar em fazer algo, não querer fazer algo

unwind [ʌnˈwaɪnd] *(irreg)* *vt* desenrolar ▷ *vi (relax)* relaxar-se

unwise [ʌnˈwaɪz] *adj* imprudente

unwrap [ʌnˈræp] *vt* desembrulhar

O KEYWORD

up [ʌp] *prep*: **to go/be up sth** subir algo/estar em cima de algo; **we climbed/walked up the hill** nós subimos/andamos até em cima da colina; **they live further up the street** eles moram mais adiante nesta rua
▷ *adv* **1** *(upwards, higher)* em cima, para cima; **up in the sky/the mountains** lá no céu/nas montanhas; **up there** lá em cima; **up above** em cima
2: **to be up** *(out of bed)* estar de pé; *(prices, level)* estar elevado; *(building, tent)* estar erguido
3: **up to** *(as far as)* até; **up to now** até agora
4: **to be up to** *(depending on)*: **it is up to you** você é quem sabe, você decide
5: **to be up to** *(equal to)* estar à altura de; **he's not up to it** *(job, task etc)* ele não é capaz de fazê-lo; **his work is not up to the required standard** seu trabalho não atende aos padrões exigidos
6: **to be up to** *(inf: be doing)* estar fazendo *(BR)* or a fazer *(PT)*; **what is he up to?** o que ele está querendo?, o que ele está tramando?
▷ *n*: **ups and downs** altos *mpl* e baixos *mpl*

upbringing [ˈʌpbrɪŋɪŋ] *n* educação *f*, criação *f*

update [ʌpˈdeɪt] *vt* atualizar, pôr em dia

upgrade [ʌpˈɡreɪd] *vt (person)* promover; *(job)* melhorar; *(house)* reformar

upheaval [ʌpˈhiːvl] *n* transtorno; *(unrest)* convulsão *f*

uphill [ʌpˈhɪl] *adj* ladeira acima; *(fig: task)* trabalhoso, árduo ▷ *adv*: **to go ~** ir morro acima; *(face, look)* para cima

upon [əˈpɔn] *prep* sobre

upper [ˈʌpəʳ] *adj* superior, de cima ▷ *n (of shoe)* gáspea, parte *f* superior; **upper-class** *adj* de classe alta

upright [ˈʌpraɪt] *adj* vertical; *(straight)* reto; *(fig)* honesto

uprising [ˈʌpraɪzɪŋ] *n* revolta, rebelião *f*, sublevação *f*

uproar [ˈʌprɔːʳ] *n* tumulto, algazarra

upset [*(n)* ˈʌpsɛt, *(vb, adj)* ʌpˈsɛt] *(irreg: like **set**)* *n (to plan etc)* revés *m*, reviravolta; *(stomach upset)* indisposição *f* ▷ *vt (glass* *etc*) virar; (*plan*) perturbar; (*person*: *annoy*) aborrecer ▷ *adj* aflito; (*stomach*) indisposto

upside down ['ʌpsaɪd-] *adv* de cabeça para baixo; **to turn a place ~** (*fig*) deixar um lugar de cabeça para baixo

upstairs [ʌp'steəz] *adv* (*be*) em cima; (*go*) lá em cima ▷ *adj* (*room*) de cima ▷ *n* andar *m* de cima

up-to-date *adj* (*person*) moderno, atualizado; (*information*) atualizado

upward ['ʌpwəd] *adj* ascendente, para cima; **upward(s)** *adv* para cima; (*more than*): **upward(s) of** para cima de

urban ['əːbən] *adj* urbano, da cidade

urge [əːdʒ] *n* desejo ▷ *vt*: **to ~ sb to do sth** incitar alguém a fazer algo

urgent ['əːdʒənt] *adj* urgente; (*tone, plea*) insistente

urinal ['juərɪnl] (BRIT) *n* (*vessel*) urinol *m*; (*building*) mictório

urine ['juərɪn] *n* urina

URL *n abbr* (= *uniform resource locator*) URL *m*

Uruguay ['juərəgwaɪ] *n* Uruguai *m*

us [ʌs] *pron* nos; (*after prep*) nós; *see also* **me**

US(A) *n abbr* (= *United States (of America)*) EUA *mpl*

use [(*n*) juːs, (*vb*) juːz] *n* uso, emprego; (*usefulness*) utilidade *f* ▷ *vt* usar, utilizar; (*phrase*) empregar; **in ~** em uso; **out of ~** fora de uso; **to be of ~** ser útil; **it's no ~** (*pointless*) é inútil; (*not useful*) não serve; **to be ~d to** estar acostumado a; **she ~d to do it** ela costumava fazê-lo; **use up** *vt* esgotar, consumir; (*money*) gastar; **used** [juːzd] *adj* usado; **useful** ['juːsful] *adj* útil; **useless** ['juːslɪs] *adj* inútil; (*person*) incapaz; **user** ['juːzəʳ] *n* usuário(-a) (BR), utente *m/f* (PT); **user-friendly** *adj* de fácil utilização

usual ['juːʒuəl] *adj* usual, habitual; **as ~** como de hábito, como sempre; **usually** ['juːʒuəlɪ] *adv* normalmente

utensil [juː'tɛnsl] *n* utensílio

utmost ['ʌtməust] *adj* maior ▷ *n*: **to do one's ~** fazer todo o possível

utter ['ʌtəʳ] *adj* total ▷ *vt* (*sounds*) emitir; (*words*) proferir, pronunciar; **utterly** *adv* completamente, totalmente

U-turn *n* retorno

vacancy ['veɪkənsɪ] *n* (BRIT: *job*) vaga; (*room*) quarto livre

vacant ['veɪkənt] *adj* desocupado, livre; (*expression*) distraído

vacate [və'keɪt] *vt* (*house*) desocupar; (*job*) deixar

vacation [və'keɪʃən] (*esp* US) *n* férias *fpl*

vacuum ['vækjum] *n* vácuo *m*; **vacuum cleaner** *n* aspirador *m* de pó

vagina [və'dʒaɪnə] *n* vagina

vague [veɪg] *adj* vago; (*blurred: memory*) fraco

vain [veɪn] *adj* vaidoso; (*useless*) vão (vã), inútil; **in ~** em vão

valentine ['væləntaɪn] *n* (*also*: **~ card**) cartão *m* do Dia dos Namorados; (*person*) namorado

valid ['vælɪd] *adj* válido

valley ['vælɪ] *n* vale *m*

valuable ['væljuəbl] *adj* (*jewel*) de valor; (*time*) valioso; (*help*) precioso; **valuables** *npl* objetos *mpl* de valor

value ['væljuː] *n* valor *m*; (*importance*) importância ▷ *vt* (*fix price of*) avaliar; (*appreciate*) valorizar, estimar; **values** *npl* (*principles*) valores *mpl*

valve [vælv] *n* válvula

van [væn] *n* (*Aut*) camionete *f* (BR),

camioneta (PT)

vandal ['vændl] n vândalo(-a);
vandalize vt destruir, depredar

vanilla [və'nɪlə] n baunilha

vanish ['vænɪʃ] vi desaparecer, sumir

vanity ['vænɪtɪ] n vaidade f

vapour ['veɪpəʳ] (us **vapor**) n vapor m

variety [və'raɪətɪ] n variedade f,
diversidade f; (type, quantity) variedade

various ['vɛərɪəs] adj vários(-as),
diversos(-as); (several) vários(-as)

varnish ['vɑ:nɪʃ] n verniz m; (nail varnish)
esmalte m ▷ vt envernizar, pintar (com
esmalte)

vary ['vɛərɪ] vt mudar ▷ vi variar; (become
different): **to ~ with** variar de acordo com

vase [vɑ:z] n vaso

vast [vɑ:st] adj enorme

VAT [væt] (BRIT) n abbr (= value added tax)
≈ ICM m (BR), IVA m (PT)

vault [vɔ:lt] n (of roof) abóbada; (tomb)
sepulcro; (in bank) caixa-forte f ▷ vt (also:
~ over) saltar (por cima de)

VCR n abbr = **video cassette recorder**

VDU n abbr = **visual display unit**

veal [vi:l] n carne f de vitela

vegan ['vi:gən] n vegetalista m/f

vegetable ['vɛdʒtəbl] n (Bot) vegetal m;
(edible plant) legume m, hortaliça ▷ adj
vegetal

vegetarian [vɛdʒɪ'tɛərɪən] adj, n
vegetariano(-a)

vehicle ['vi:ɪkl] n veículo

veil [veɪl] n véu m ▷ vt velar

vein [veɪn] n veia; (of ore etc) filão m; (on
leaf) nervura

velvet ['vɛlvɪt] n veludo ▷ adj aveludado

vending machine ['vɛndɪŋ-] n
vendedor m automático

Venezuela [vɛnɛ'zweɪlə] n Venezuela

vengeance ['vɛndʒəns] n vingança;
with a ~ (fig) para valer

venison ['vɛnɪsn] n carne f de veado

venom ['vɛnəm] n veneno; (bitterness)
malevolência

vent [vɛnt] n (in jacket) abertura; (also:
air ~) respiradouro ▷ vt (fig: feelings)
desabafar, descarregar

venture ['vɛntʃəʳ] n empreendimento
▷ vt (opinion) arriscar ▷ vi arriscar-se;
business ~ empreendimento comercial

venue ['vɛnju:] n local m

verb [və:b] n verbo

verdict ['və:dɪkt] n veredicto, decisão f;
(fig) opinião f, parecer m

verge [və:dʒ] n beira, margem f; (on road)

acostamento (BR), berma (PT); **"soft
~s"** (BRIT: Aut) "acostamento mole"; **to
be on the ~ of doing sth** estar a ponto
or à beira de fazer algo; **verge on** vt fus
beirar em

versatile ['və:sətaɪl] adj (person) versátil;
(machine, tool etc) polivalente

verse [və:s] n verso, poesia; (stanza)
estrofe f; (in bible) versículo

version ['və:ʃən] n versão f

versus ['və:səs] prep contra, versus

vertical ['və:tɪkl] adj vertical

very ['vɛrɪ] adv muito ▷ adj: **the ~ book
which** o mesmo livro que; **the ~ last** o
último (de todos), bem o último; **at the ~
least** no mínimo; **~ much** muitíssimo

vessel ['vɛsl] n (Naut) navio, barco;
(container) vaso, vasilha

vest [vɛst] n (BRIT) camiseta (BR),
camisola interior (PT); (us: waistcoat)
colete m

vet [vɛt] n abbr (= veterinary surgeon)
veterinário(-a) ▷ vt examinar

veteran ['vɛtərn] n (also: **war ~**)
veterano de guerra

veto ['vi:təu] n (pl **~es**) veto ▷ vt vetar

via ['vaɪə] prep por, via

vibrate [vaɪ'breɪt] vi vibrar

vicar ['vɪkəʳ] n vigário

vice [vaɪs] n (evil) vício; (Tech) torno
mecânico

vice- [vaɪs] prefix vice-

vice versa ['vaɪsɪ'və:sə] adv vice-versa

vicinity [vɪ'sɪnɪtɪ] n: **in the ~ of** nas
proximidades de

vicious ['vɪʃəs] adj violento; (cruel) cruel

victim ['vɪktɪm] n vítima f

victor ['vɪktəʳ] n vencedor(a) m/f

Victorian [vɪk'tɔ:rɪən] adj vitoriano

victory ['vɪktərɪ] n vitória

video ['vɪdɪəu] n (video film) vídeo; (also:
~ cassette) videocassete m; (also: **~
cassette recorder**) videocassete m;
videophone n videofone m

Vienna [vɪ'ɛnə] n Viena

Vietnam ['vjɛt'næm] n Vietnã m;
Vietnamese [vjɛtnə'mi:z] adj
vietnamita ▷ n inv vietnamita m/f; (Ling)
vietnamita m

view [vju:] n vista; (outlook) perspectiva;
(opinion) opinião f, parecer m ▷ vt olhar;
in full ~ (of) à plena vista (de); **in my ~**
na minha opinião; **in ~ of the weather/the
fact that** em vista do tempo/do fato
de que; **viewer** n telespectador(a)
m/f; **viewpoint** n ponto de vista; (place)

lugar m

vigorous ['vɪgərəs] adj vigoroso; (plant) vigoso

vile [vaɪl] adj vil, infame; (smell) repugnante, repulsivo; (temper) violento

villa ['vɪlə] n (country house) casa de campo; (suburban house) vila, quinta

village ['vɪlɪdʒ] n aldeia, povoado; **villager** n aldeão (aldeã) m/f

villain ['vɪlən] n (scoundrel) patife m; (in novel etc) vilão m; (BRIT: criminal) marginal m/f

vine [vaɪn] n planta trepadeira

vinegar ['vɪnɪgəʳ] n vinagre m

vineyard ['vɪnjɑːd] n vinha, vinhedo

vintage ['vɪntɪdʒ] n vindima; (year) safra, colheita ▷ cpd (comedy) de época; (performance) clássico; **the 1970 ~** a safra de 1970

viola [vɪ'əʊlə] n viola

violate ['vaɪəleɪt] vt violar

violence ['vaɪələns] n violência; (strength) força

violent ['vaɪələnt] adj violento; (intense) intenso

violet ['vaɪələt] adj violeta ▷ n violeta

violin [vaɪə'lɪn] n violino

VIP n abbr (= very important person) VIP m/f

virgin ['vəːdʒɪn] n virgem m/f ▷ adj virgem

Virgo ['vəːgəʊ] n Virgem f

virtually ['vəːtjʊəlɪ] adv praticamente

virtue ['vəːtjuː] n virtude f; (advantage) vantagem f; **by ~ of** em virtude de

virus ['vaɪərəs] n vírus m

visa ['viːzə] n visto

visible ['vɪzəbl] adj visível

vision ['vɪʒən] n (sight) vista, visão f; (foresight, in dream) visão f

visit ['vɪzɪt] n visita ▷ vt (person: us: also: **~ with**) visitar, fazer uma visita a; (place) ir a, ir conhecer; **visiting hours** npl horário de visita; **visitor** n visitante m/f; (to one's house) visita; (tourist) turista m/f

visual ['vɪzjʊəl] adj visual; **visualize** vt visualizar

vital ['vaɪtl] adj essencial, indispensável; (important) de importância vital; (crucial) crucial; (person) vivo; (of life) vital

vitamin ['vɪtəmɪn] n vitamina

vivid ['vɪvɪd] adj (account) vívido; (light) claro, brilhante; (imagination, colour) vivo

V-neck n: **~ jumper, ~ pullover** suéter f com decote em V

vocabulary [vəʊ'kæbjʊlərɪ] n vocabulário

vocal ['vəʊkl] adj vocal; (noisy) clamoroso; (articulate) claro, eloqüente

vodka ['vɔdkə] n vodca

vogue [vəʊg] n voga, moda; **to be in ~** estar na moda

voice [vɔɪs] n voz f ▷ vt expressar; **voice mail** n (Tel) correio m de voz

void [vɔɪd] n vazio; (hole) oco ▷ adj nulo; (empty): **~ of** destituido de

volatile ['vɔlətaɪl] adj volátil; (situation, person) imprevisível

volcano [vɔl'keɪnəʊ] (pl **~es**) n vulcão m

volt [vəʊlt] n volt m

volume ['vɔljuːm] n volume m; (of tank) capacidade f

voluntarily ['vɔləntrɪlɪ] adv livremente, voluntariamente

voluntary ['vɔləntərɪ] adj voluntário; (unpaid) (a título) gratuito

volunteer [vɔlən'tɪəʳ] n voluntário(-a) ▷ vt oferecer voluntariamente ▷ vi (Mil) alistar-se voluntariamente; **to ~ to do** oferecer-se voluntariamente para fazer

vomit ['vɔmɪt] n vômito ▷ vt, vi vomitar

vote [vəʊt] n voto; (votes cast) votação f; (right to vote) direito de votar ▷ vt: **to be ~d chairman etc** ser eleito presidente etc; (propose): **to ~ that** propor que; (in election) votar ▷ vi votar; **voter** n votante m/f, eleitor(a) m/f

voucher ['vaʊtʃəʳ] n (also: **luncheon ~**) vale-refeição m; (with petrol etc) vale m; (gift voucher) vale m para presente

vow [vaʊ] n voto ▷ vt: **to ~ to do/that** prometer solenemente fazer/que

vowel ['vaʊəl] n vogal f

voyage ['vɔɪɪdʒ] n viagem f

vulgar ['vʌlgəʳ] adj grosseiro, ordinário; (in bad taste) vulgar, baixo

vulture ['vʌltʃəʳ] n abutre m, urubu m

W

wade [weɪd] vi: **to ~ through** andar em; (fig: a book) ler com dificuldade

wafer ['weɪfər] n (biscuit) bolacha

waffle ['wɔfl] n (Culin) waffle m; (empty talk) lengalenga ▷ vi encher linguiça

wag [wæg] vt (tail) sacudir; (finger) menear ▷ vi abanar

wage [weɪdʒ] n (also: ~s) salário, ordenado ▷ vt: **to ~ war** empreender or fazer guerra

wag(g)on ['wægən] n (horse-drawn) carroça; (BRIT: Rail) vagão m

wail [weɪl] n lamento, gemido ▷ vi lamentar-se, gemer; (siren) tocar

waist [weɪst] n cintura; **waistcoat** n colete m

wait [weɪt] n espera ▷ vi esperar; **I can't ~ to** (fig) estou morrendo de vontade de; **to ~ for sb/sth** esperar por alguém/ algo; **wait behind** vi ficar para trás; **wait on** vt fus servir; **waiter** n garçom m (BR), empregado (PT); **waiting list** n lista de espera; **waiting room** n sala de espera; **waitress** n garçonete f (BR), empregada (PT)

waive [weɪv] vt abrir mão de

wake [weɪk] (pt **woke** or **~d**, pp **woken** or **~d**) vt (also: ~ **up**) acordar ▷ vi acordar

▷ n (for dead person) velório; (Naut) esteira

Wales [weɪlz] n País m de Gales

walk [wɔːk] n passeio; (hike) excursão f a pé, caminhada; (gait) passo, modo de andar; (in park etc) alameda, passeio ▷ vi andar; (for pleasure, exercise) passear ▷ vt (distance) percorrer a pé, andar; (dog) levar para passear; **it's 10 minutes' ~ from here** daqui são 10 minutos a pé; **people from all ~s of life** pessoas de todos os níveis; **walk out** vi sair; (audience) retirar-se (em protesto); (strike) entrar em greve; **walk out on** vt fus abandonar; **walkie-talkie** n transmissor-receptor m portátil, walkie-talkie m; **walking** n o andar; **walking shoes** npl sapatos mpl para caminhar; **walking stick** n bengala; **walkway** n passeio, passadiço

wall [wɔːl] n parede f; (exterior) muro m; (city wall etc) muralha

wallet ['wɔlɪt] n carteira

wallpaper ['wɔːlpeɪpər] n papel m de parede ▷ vt colocar papel de parede em

walnut ['wɔːlnʌt] n noz f; (tree, wood) nogueira

walrus ['wɔːlrəs] (pl inv or **~es**) n morsa, vaca marinha

waltz [wɔːlts] n valsa ▷ vi valsar

wand [wɔnd] n (also: **magic ~**) varinha de condão

wander ['wɔndər] vi (person) vagar, perambular; (thoughts) divagar ▷ vt perambular

want [wɔnt] vt querer; (demand) exigir; (need) precisar de, necessitar; **wanted** adj (criminal etc) procurado (pela polícia); **"cook wanted"** (in advertisement) "precisa-se cozinheiro"

war [wɔːr] n guerra; **to make ~ (on)** fazer guerra (contra)

ward [wɔːd] n (in hospital) ala; (Pol) distrito eleitoral; (Law: child) tutelado(-a), pupilo(-a); **ward off** vt desviar, aparar; (attack) repelir

warden ['wɔːdn] n (BRIT: of institution) diretor(a) m/f; (of park, youth hostel) administrador(a) m/f; (BRIT: also: **traffic ~**) guarda m/f

wardrobe ['wɔːdrəub] n guarda-roupa m; (Cinema, Theatre) figurinos mpl

warehouse ['wɛəhaus] n armazém m, depósito

warfare ['wɔːfɛər] n guerra, combate m

warhead ['wɔːhɛd] n ogiva

warm [wɔːm] *adj* quente; (*thanks, welcome*) caloroso; **it's ~** está quente; **I'm ~** estou com calor; **warm up** *vt*, *vi* esquentar; **warmly** *adv* (*applaud, welcome*) calorosamente; (*dress*): **to dress warmly** vestir-se com roupas de inverno; **warmth** *n* calor *m*; (*friendliness*) calor humano

warn [wɔːn] *vt* prevenir, avisar; **to ~ sb that/of/(not) to do** prevenir alguém de que/de/para (não) fazer

warning ['wɔːnɪŋ] *n* advertência; (*in writing*) aviso; (*signal*) sinal *m*

warrant ['wɔrnt] *n* (*voucher*) comprovante *m*; (*Law: to arrest*) mandado de prisão; (: *to search*) mandado de busca; **warranty** *n* garantia

warrior ['wɔrɪə'] *n* guerreiro(-a)

Warsaw ['wɔːsɔː] *n* Varsóvia

warship ['wɔːʃɪp] *n* navio de guerra

wart [wɔːt] *n* verruga

wartime ['wɔːtaɪm] *n*: **in ~** em tempo de guerra

wary ['wɛərɪ] *adj* cauteloso, precavido

was [wɔz] *pt of* **be**

wash [wɔʃ] *vt* lavar ▷ *vi* lavar-se; (*subj: washing machine*) lavar; (*sea etc*): **to ~ over/against sth** bater contra/chocar-se contra algo; (*clothes*): **this shirt ~es well** esta camisa resiste bem à lavagem ▷ *n* (*clothes etc*) lavagem *f*; (*washing programme*) programa *m* de lavagem; (*of ship*) esteira; **to have a ~** lavar-se; **wash away** *vt* (*stain*) tirar ao lavar; (*subj: river etc*) levar, arrastar; **wash off** *vt* tirar lavando ▷ *vi* sair ao lavar; **wash up** *vi* (BRIT) lavar a louça; (US) lavar-se; **washbasin** *n* pia (BR), lavatório (PT); **washing** *n* (*dirty*) roupa suja; (*clean*) roupa lavada; **washing machine** *n* máquina de lavar roupa, lavadora; **washing powder** (BRIT) *n* sabão *m* em pó; **washing-up** *n*: **to do the washing-up** lavar a louça; **washing-up liquid** *n* detergente *m*; **washroom** (US) *n* banheiro (BR), casa de banho (PT)

wasn't ['wɔznt] = **was not**

wasp [wɔsp] *n* vespa

waste [weɪst] *n* desperdício, esbanjamento; (*of time*) perda; (*also:* **household ~**) detritos *mpl* domésticos; (*rubbish*) lixo ▷ *adj* (*material*) de refugo; (*left over*) de sobra; (*land*) baldio ▷ *vt* (*squander*) esbanjar, desperdiçar; (*time, opportunity*) perder; **wastes** *npl* (*land*) ermos *mpl*; **to lay ~** devastar; **waste**

away *vi* definhar

watch [wɔtʃ] *n* (*clock*) relógio; (*also:* **wrist~**) relógio de pulso; (*act of watching*) vigia; (*guard: Mil*) sentinela; (*Naut: spell of duty*) quarto ▷ *vt* (*look at*) observar, olhar; (*programme, match*) assistir a; (*television*) ver; (*spy on, guard*) vigiar; (*be careful of*) tomar cuidado com ▷ *vi* ver, olhar; (*keep guard*) montar guarda; **watch out** *vi* ter cuidado; **watchdog** *n* cão *m* de guarda; (*fig*) vigia *m/f*

water ['wɔːtə'] *n* água ▷ *vt* (*plant*) regar ▷ *vi* (*eyes*) lacrimejar; (*mouth*) salivar; **in British ~s** nas águas territoriais britânicas; **water down** *vt* (*milk*) aguar; (*fig*) diluir; **watercolour** (US **watercolor**) *n* aquarela; **waterfall** *n* cascata, cachoeira; **watering can** *n* regador *m*; **watermelon** *n* melancia; **waterproof** *adj* impermeável; **water-skiing** *n* esqui *m* aquático

watt [wɔt] *n* watt *m*

wave [weɪv] *n* onda; (*of hand*) aceno, sinal *m*; (*in hair*) onda, ondulação *f* ▷ *vi* acenar com a mão; (*flag, grass*) tremular ▷ *vt* (*hand*) acenar; (*handkerchief*) acenar com; (*weapon*) brandir; **wavelength** *n* comprimento de onda; **to be on the same wavelength as** ter os mesmos gostos e atitudes que

waver ['weɪvə'] *vi* vacilar; (*voice, eyes, love*) hesitar

wavy ['weɪvɪ] *adj* (*hair*) ondulado; (*line*) ondulante

wax [wæks] *n* cera ▷ *vt* encerar; (*car*) polir ▷ *vi* (*moon*) crescer

way [weɪ] *n* caminho; (*distance*) percurso; (*direction*) direção *f*, sentido; (*manner*) maneira, modo; (*habit*) costume *m*; **which ~? — this ~** por onde? - por aqui; **on the ~ (to)** a caminho (de); **to be on one's ~** estar a caminho; **to be in the ~** atrapalhar; **to go out of one's ~ to do sth** dar-se ao trabalho de fazer algo; **to lose one's ~** perder-se; **to be under ~** estar em andamento; **in a ~** de certo modo, até certo ponto; **in some ~s** a certos respeitos; **by the ~** a propósito; **"~ in"** (BRIT) "entrada"; **"~ out"** (BRIT) "saída"; **the ~ back** (BRIT. *Aut*) "dê a preferência"; **no ~!** (*inf*) de jeito nenhum!

WC ['dʌblju:'si:] *n abbr* (= *water closet*) privada

we [wi:] pl pron nós

weak [wi:k] adj fraco, débil; (morally, currency) fraco; (excuse) pouco convincente; (tea) aguado, ralo; **weaken** vi enfraquecer(-se); (give way) ceder; (influence, power) diminuir ▷ vt enfraquecer; **weakness** n fraqueza; (fault) ponto fraco; **to have a weakness for** ter uma queda por

wealth [wɛlθ] n riqueza; (of details) abundância; **wealthy** adj rico, abastado; (country) rico

weapon ['wɛpən] n arma; **weapons of mass destruction** npl armas de destruição em massa

wear [wɛəʳ] (pt **wore**, pp **worn**) n (use) uso; (deterioration) desgaste m; (clothing) roupa infantil/de esporte ▷ vt (clothes) usar; (shoes) usar, calçar; (put on) vestir; (damage: through use) desgastar ▷ vi (last) durar; (rub through etc) gastar-se; **town/evening** ~ traje m de passeio/de noite; **wear away** vt gastar ▷ vi desgastar-se; **wear down** vt gastar; (strength) esgotar; **wear off** vi (pain etc) passar; **wear out** vt desgastar; (person, strength) esgotar

weary ['wɪərɪ] adj cansado; (dispirited) deprimido ▷ vi: **to ~ of** cansar-se de

weasel ['wi:zl] n (Zool) doninha

weather ['wɛðəʳ] n tempo ▷ vt (storm, crisis) resistir a; **under the ~** (fig: ill) doente; **weather forecast** n previsão f do tempo

weave [wi:v] (pt **wove**, pp **woven**) vt tecer

web [wɛb] n (of spider) teia; (on foot) membrana; (network) rede f; **the (World Wide) W~** a (World Wide) Web; **web address** n endereço de site; **webcam** ['wɛbkæm] n webcam f; **weblog** n weblog m; **webpage** n página (da) web; **website** ['wɛbsaɪt] n site m, website m

wed [wɛd] (pt, pp **~ded**) vt casar ▷ vi casar-se

we'd [wi:d] = **we had; we would**

wedding ['wɛdɪŋ] n casamento, núpcias fpl; **silver/golden ~** (anniversary) bodas fpl de prata/de ouro; **wedding dress** n vestido de noiva; **wedding ring** n anel m or aliança de casamento

wedge [wɛdʒ] n (of wood etc) cunha, calço; (of cake) fatia ▷ vt (pack tightly) apinhar; (door) pôr calço em

Wednesday ['wɛdnzdɪ] n quarta-feira

wee [wi:] (Scottish) adj pequeno, pequenino

weed [wi:d] n erva daninha ▷ vt capinar; **weedkiller** n herbicida m

week [wi:k] n semana; **a ~ today** daqui a uma semana; **a ~ on Tuesday** sem ser essa terça-feira, a próxima; **weekday** n dia m de semana; (Comm) dia útil; **weekend** n fim m de semana; **weekly** adv semanalmente ▷ adj semanal ▷ n semanário

weep [wi:p] (pt, pp **wept**) vi (person) chorar

weigh [weɪ] vt, vi pesar; **to ~ anchor** levantar ferro; **weigh down** vt sobrecarregar; (fig: with worry) deprimir, acabrunhar; **weigh up** vt ponderar, avaliar

weight [weɪt] n peso; **to lose/put on ~** emagrecer/engordar

weird [wɪəd] adj esquisito, estranho

welcome ['wɛlkəm] adj bem-vindo ▷ n acolhimento, recepção f ▷ vt dar as boas-vindas a; (be glad of) saudar; **you're ~** (after thanks) de nada

weld [wɛld] n solda ▷ vt soldar, unir

welfare ['wɛlfɛəʳ] n bem-estar m; (social aid) assistência social; **welfare state** n país auto-financiador da sua assistência social

well [wɛl] n poço ▷ adv bem ▷ adj: **to be ~** estar bem (de saúde) ▷ excl bem!, então!; **as ~** também; **as ~ as** assim como; **~ done!** muito bem!; **get ~ soon!** melhoras!; **to do ~** ir or sair-se bem; (business) ir bem; **well up** vi brotar

we'll [wi:l] = **we will; we shall**

well: **well-behaved** adj bem comportado; **well-built** adj robusto; **well-dressed** adj bem vestido

wellingtons ['wɛlɪŋtənz] n (also: **wellington boots**) botas de borracha até os joelhos

well: **well-known** adj conhecido; **well-off** adj próspero, rico

Welsh [wɛlʃ] adj galês (galesa) ▷ n (Ling) galês m; **the Welsh** npl (people) os galeses; **Welshman** (irreg) n galês m; **Welshwoman** (irreg) n galesa

went [wɛnt] pt of **go**

wept [wɛpt] pt, pp of **weep**

were [wəːʳ] pt of **be**

we're [wɪəʳ] = **we are**

weren't [wəːnt] = **were not**

west [wɛst] n oeste m ▷ adj ocidental, do

oeste ▷ *adv* para o oeste *or* ao oeste; **the W~** (*Pol*) o Oeste, o Ocidente; **western** *adj* ocidental ▷ *n* (*Cinema*) western *m*, bangue-bangue (BR: INF); **West Indian** *adj*, *n* antilhano(-a); **West Indies** *npl* Antilhas *fpl*

wet [wɛt] *adj* molhado; (*damp*) úmido; (*wet through*) encharcado; (*rainy*) chuvoso ▷ *n* (*BRIT: Pol*) político de tendência moderada; **to get ~** molhar-se; **"~ paint"** "tinta fresca"; **wetsuit** *n* roupa de mergulho

we've [wiːv] = **we have**

whale [weɪl] *n* (*Zool*) baleia

wharf [wɔːf] (*pl* **wharves**) *n* cais *m inv*

🔘 **KEYWORD**

what [wɔt] *adj* **1** (*in direct/indirect questions*) que, qual; **what size is it?** que tamanho é este?; **what colour/ shape is it?** qual é a cor/o formato?; **he asked me what books I needed** ele me perguntou de quais os livros eu precisava

2 (*in exclamations*) quê!, como!; **what a mess!** que bagunça!

▷ *pron* **1** (*interrogative*) que, o que; **what are you doing?** o que é que você está fazendo?; **what is it called?** como se chama?; **what about me?** e eu?; **what about doing ...?** que tal fazer ...?

2 (*relative*) o que; **I saw what you did/was on the table** eu vi o que você fez/estava na mesa; **he asked me what she had said** ele me perguntou o que ela tinha dito

▷ *excl* (*disbelieving*): **what, no coffee!** o que, não tem café!

whatever [wɔt'ɛvəʳ] *adj*: **~ book** qualquer livro ▷ *pron*: **do ~ is necessary/ you want** faça tudo o que for preciso/o que você quiser; **~ happens** aconteça o que acontecer; **no reason ~ or whatsoever** nenhuma razão seja qual for *or* em absoluto; **nothing ~** nada em absoluto

whatsoever [wɔtsəu'ɛvəʳ] *adj* = **whatever**

wheat [wiːt] *n* trigo

wheel [wiːl] *n* roda; (*also:* **steering ~**) volante *m*; (*Naut*) roda do leme ▷ *vt* (*pram etc*) empurrar ▷ *vi* (*birds*) dar voltas; (*also:* **~ round**) girar, dar voltas, virar-se; **wheelbarrow** *n* carrinho de mão;

wheelchair *n* cadeira de rodas; **wheel clamp** *n* (*Aut*) grampo *com que se imobiliza carros estacionados ilegalmente*

wheeze [wiːz] *vi* respirar ruidosamente

🔘 **KEYWORD**

when [wɛn] *adv* quando

▷ *conj* **1** (*at, during, after the time that*) quando; **when you've read it, tell me what you think** depois que você tiver lido isto, diga-me o que acha; **that was when I needed you** foi quando eu precisei de você

2 (*on, at which*) quando, em que; **on the day when I met him** no dia em que o conheci; **one day when it was raining** um dia quando estava chovendo

3 (*whereas*) ao passo que; **you said I was wrong when in fact I was right** você disse que eu estava errado quando, na verdade, eu estava certo

whenever [wɛn'ɛvəʳ] *conj* quando, quando quer que; (*every time that*) sempre que ▷ *adv* quando você quiser

where [wɛəʳ] *adv* onde ▷ *conj* onde, aonde; **this is ~ ...** aqui é onde ...; **whereabouts** ['wɛərəbauts] *adv* (por) onde ▷ *n*: **nobody knows his whereabouts** ninguém sabe o seu paradeiro; **whereas** [wɛər'æz] *conj* uma vez que, ao passo que; **whereby** *adv* (*formal*) pelo qual (*or* pela qual *etc*); **wherever** [wɛər'ɛvəʳ] *conj* onde quer que ▷ *adv* (*interrogative*) onde?

whether ['wɛðəʳ] *conj* se; **I don't know ~ to accept or not** não sei se aceito ou não; **~ you go or not** quer você vá quer não; **it's doubtful ~ ...** não é certo que ...

🔘 **KEYWORD**

which [wɪtʃ] *adj* **1** (*interrogative: direct, indirect*) que, qual; **which picture do you want?** que quadro você quer?; **which books are yours?** quais são os seus livros?; **which one?** qual?

2: **in which case** em cujo caso; **by which time** momento em que

▷ *pron* **1** (*interrogative*) qual; **which (of these) are yours?** quais (destes) são seus?

2 (*relative*) que, o que, o qual *etc*; **the apple which you ate** a maçã que você comeu; **the chair on which you are**

sitting a cadeira na qual você está sentado; **he said he knew, which is true** ele disse que sabia, o que é verdade; **after which** depois do que

whichever [wɪtʃˈɛvəʳ] adj: **take ~ book you prefer** pegue o livro que preferir; **~ book you take** qualquer livro que você pegue

while [waɪl] n tempo, momento ▷ conj enquanto, ao mesmo tempo que; (as long as) contanto que; (although) embora; **for a ~** durante algum tempo; **while away** vt (time) encher

whim [wɪm] n capricho, veneta

whine [waɪn] n (of pain) gemido; (of engine, siren) zunido ▷ vi gemer; zunir; (fig) lamuriar-se

whip [wɪp] n açoite m; (for riding) chicote m; (Pol) líder m/f da bancada ▷ vt chicotear; (snatch) apanhar de repente; (cream, eggs) bater; (move quickly): **to ~ sth out/off/away** etc arrancar algo; **whipped cream** n (creme) m chantilly m

whirl [wəːl] vt fazer girar ▷ vi (dancers) rodopiar; (leaves, water etc) redemoinhar

whisk [wɪsk] n (Culin) batedeira ▷ vt bater; **to ~ sb away** or **off** levar alguém rapidamente

whiskers [ˈwɪskəz] npl (of animal) bigodes mpl; (of man) suíças fpl

whisky [ˈwɪskɪ] (US, IRELAND **whiskey**) n uísque m (BR), whisky m (PT)

whisper [ˈwɪspəʳ] n sussurro, murmúrio ▷ vt, vi sussurrar

whistle [ˈwɪsl] n (sound) assobio; (object) apito ▷ vt, vi assobiar

white [waɪt] adj branco; (pale) pálido ▷ n branco; (of egg) clara; **white coffee** n café m com leite

White House n: **the ~** a Casa Branca

whitewash n (paint) cal f ▷ vt caiar; (fig) encobrir

whiting [ˈwaɪtɪŋ] n inv pescada

Whitsun [ˈwɪtsn] n Pentecostes m

whizz [wɪz] vi: **to ~ past** or **by** passar a toda velocidade

○ **KEYWORD**

who [huː] pron **1** (interrogative) quem?; **who is it?** quem é?
2 (relative) que, o qual etc, quem; **my cousin, who lives in New York** meu primo que mora em Nova Iorque; **the man who spoke to me** o homem que falou comigo

whole [həul] adj (complete) todo, inteiro; (not broken) intacto ▷ n (all): **the ~ of the time** o tempo todo; (entire unit) conjunto; **on the ~, as a ~** como um todo, no conjunto; **wholemeal** (BRIT) adj integral; **wholesale** n venda por atacado ▷ adj por atacado; (destruction) em grande escala ▷ adv por atacado; **wholewheat** adj = **wholemeal**; **wholly** [ˈhəulɪ] adv totalmente, completamente

○ **KEYWORD**

whom [huːm] pron **1** (interrogative) quem?; **to whom did you give it?** para quem você deu isto?
2 (relative) que, quem; **the man whom I saw/to whom I spoke** o homem que eu vi/com quem eu falei

○ **KEYWORD**

whose [huːz] adj **1** (possessive: interrogative): **whose book is this?**, **whose is this book?** de quem é este livro?; **I don't know whose it is** eu não sei de quem é isto
2 (possessive: relative): **the man whose son you rescued** o homem cujo filho você salvou; **the woman whose car was stolen** a mulher de quem o carro foi roubado
▷ pron de quem

○ **KEYWORD**

why [waɪ] adv por que (BR), porque (PT); (at end of sentence) por quê (BR), porquê (PT)
▷ conj por que; **that's not why I'm here** não é por isso que estou aqui; **the reason why** a razão por que

▷ *excl* (*expressing surprise, shock, annoyance*) ora essa!; (*explaining*) bem!; **why, it's you!** ora, é você!

wicked ['wɪkɪd] *adj* perverso; (*smile*) malicioso

wicket ['wɪkɪt] *n* (*Cricket*) arco

wide [waɪd] *adj* largo; (*area, publicity, knowledge*) amplo ▷ *adv*: **to open ~** abrir totalmente; **to shoot ~** atirar longe do alvo; **widely** *adv* extremamente; (*travelled*) muito; (*believed, known*) amplamente; **widen** *vt* alargar; (*one's experience*) aumentar ▷ *vi* alargar-se; **wide open** *adj* (*eyes*) arregalado; (*door*) escancarado; **widespread** *adj* (*belief etc*) difundido, comum

widow ['wɪdəu] *n* viúva; **widower** *n* viúvo

width [wɪdθ] *n* largura

wield [wi:ld] *vt* (*sword*) brandir, empunhar; (*power*) exercer

wife [waɪf] (*pl* **wives**) *n* mulher *f*, esposa

wig [wɪg] *n* peruca

wild [waɪld] *adj* (*animal*) selvagem; (*plant*) silvestre; (*rough*) violento, furioso; (*idea*) disparatado, extravagante; (*person*) insensato; **wilderness** ['wɪldənɪs] *n* ermo; **wildlife** *n* animais *mpl* selvagens; **wildly** *adv* (*behave*) freneticamente; (*hit, guess*) irrefletidamente; (*happy*) extremamente

 KEYWORD

will [wɪl] (*vt*): (*pt, pp* **willed**) *aux vb*
1 (*forming future tense*): **I will finish it tomorrow** vou acabar isto amanhã; **I will have finished it by tomorrow** até amanhã eu terei terminado isto; **will you do it? - yes I will/no I won't** você vai fazer isto? - sim, vou/não eu não vou
2 (*in conjectures, predictions*): **he will come** ele virá; **he will** *or* **he'll be there by now** nesta altura ele está lá; **that will be the postman** deve ser o carteiro; **this medicine will/won't help you** este remédio vai/não vai fazer efeito em você
3 (*in commands, requests, offers*): **will you be quiet!** fique quieto, por favor!; **will you come?** você vem?; **will you help me?** você pode me ajudar?; **will you have a cup of tea?** você vai querer uma xícara de chá *or* um chá?; **I won't put up with it** eu não vou tolerar isto

▷ *vt*: **to will sb to do sth** desejar que alguém faça algo; **he willed himself to go on** reuniu grande força de vontade para continuar
▷ *n* (*volition*) vontade *f*; (*testament*) testamento

willing ['wɪlɪŋ] *adj* disposto, pronto; (*enthusiastic*) entusiasmado; **willingly** *adv* de bom grado, de boa vontade

willow ['wɪləu] *n* salgueiro

willpower ['wɪlpauəʳ] *n* força de vontade

wilt [wɪlt] *vi* (*flower*) murchar; (*plant*) morrer

win [wɪn] (*pt, pp* **won**) *n* vitória ▷ *vt* ganhar, vencer; (*obtain*) conseguir, obter; (*support*) alcançar ▷ *vi* ganhar; **win over** *vt* conquistar; **win round** (*BRIT*) *vt* = **win over**

wince [wɪns] *vi* encolher-se, estremecer

wind¹ [wɪnd] *n* vento; (*Med*) gases *mpl*, flatulência; (*breath*) fôlego ▷ *vt* (*take breath away from*) deixar sem fôlego

wind² [waɪnd] (*pt, pp* **wound**) *vt* enrolar, bobinar; (*wrap*) envolver; (*clock, toy*) dar corda a ▷ *vi* (*road, river*) serpentear; **wind up** *vt* (*clock*) dar corda em; (*debate*) rematar, concluir

windfall ['wɪndfɔ:l] *n* golpe *m* de sorte

winding ['waɪndɪŋ] *adj* (*road*) sinuoso, tortuoso; (*staircase*) de caracol, em espiral

windmill ['wɪndmɪl] *n* moinho de vento

window ['wɪndəu] *n* janela; (*in shop etc*) vitrine *f* (*BR*), montra (*PT*); **window box** *n* jardineira (no peitoril da janela); **window cleaner** *n* limpador(a) *m/f* de janelas; **window-shopping** *n*: **to go window-shopping** ir ver vitrines

windscreen ['wɪndskri:n] (*BRIT*) *n* pára-brisa *m*; **windscreen wiper** (*BRIT*) *n* limpador *m* de pára-brisa

windshield *etc* ['wɪndʃi:ld] (*US*) *n* = **windscreen** *etc*

windy ['wɪndɪ] *adj* com muito vento, batido pelo vento; **it's ~** está ventando (*BR*), faz vento (*PT*)

wine [waɪn] *n* vinho; **wine bar** *n* bar *m* (para degustação de vinhos); **wine glass** *n* cálice *m* (de vinho); **wine list** *n* lista de vinhos

wing [wɪŋ] *n* asa; (*of building*) ala; (*Aut*) aleta, pára-lamas *m inv*; **wings** *npl* (*Theatre*) bastidores *mpl*

wink [wɪŋk] n piscadela ▷ vi piscar o olho; (light etc) piscar

winner ['wɪnə'] n vencedor(a) m/f

winning ['wɪnɪŋ] adj (team) vencedor(a); (goal) decisivo; (smile) sedutor(a)

winter ['wɪntə'] n inverno; **winter sports** npl esportes mpl (BR) or desportos mpl (PT) de inverno

wipe [waɪp] n: **to give sth a ~** limpar algo com um pano ▷ vt limpar; (rub) esfregar; (erase: tape) apagar; **wipe off** vt remover esfregando; **wipe out** vt (debt) liquidar; (memory) apagar; (destroy) exterminar; **wipe up** vt limpar

wire ['waɪə'] n arame m; (Elec) fio (elétrico); (telegram) telegrama m ▷ vt (house) instalar a rede elétrica em; (also: ~ up) conectar; (telegram) telegrafar para

wiring ['waɪərɪŋ] n instalação f elétrica

wisdom ['wɪzdəm] n prudência; (of action, remark) bom-senso, sabedoria; **wisdom tooth** n dente m do siso

wise [waɪz] adj prudente; (action, remark) sensato

wish [wɪʃ] n desejo ▷ vt (want) querer; **best ~es** (on birthday etc) parabéns mpl, felicidades fpl; **with best ~es** (in letter) cumprimentos; **to ~ sb goodbye** despedir-se de alguém; **he ~ed me well** me desejou boa sorte; **to ~ to do/sb to do sth** querer fazer/que alguém faça algo; **to ~ for** desejar

wistful ['wɪstful] adj melancólico

wit [wɪt] n (wittiness) presença de espírito, engenho; (intelligence: also: ~s) entendimento; (person) espirituoso(-a)

witch [wɪtʃ] n bruxa

◉ **KEYWORD**

with [wɪð, wɪθ] prep **1** (accompanying, in the company of) com; **I was with him** eu estava com ele; **to stay overnight with friends** dormir na casa de amigos; **we'll take the children with us** vamos levar as crianças conosco; **I'll be with you in a minute** vou vê-lo num minuto; **I'm with you** (I understand) compreendo; **to be with it** (inf) estar por dentro; (aware) estar a par da situação; (: up-to-date) estar atualizado com

2 (descriptive) com, de; **a room with a view** um quarto com vista; **the man with the grey hat/blue eyes** o homem do chapéu cinza/de olhos azuis

3 (indicating manner, means, cause) com,

de; **with tears in her eyes** com os olhos cheios de lágrimas; **to fill sth with water** encher algo de água

withdraw [wɪð'drɔː] (irreg) vt tirar, remover; (offer) retirar ▷ vi retirar-se; **to ~ money (from the bank)** retirar dinheiro (do banco); **withdrawal** n retirada; **withdrawal symptoms** npl síndrome f de abstinência; **withdrawn** adj (person) reservado, introvertido

wither ['wɪðə'] vi murchar

withhold [wɪð'həuld] (irreg: like **hold**) vt (money) reter; (permission) negar; (information)

within [wɪð'ɪn] prep dentro de ▷ adv dentro; **~ reach (of)** ao alcance (de); **~ sight (of)** à vista (de); **~ the week** antes do fim da semana; **~ a mile of** a uma milha de

without [wɪð'aut] prep sem; **~ anybody knowing** sem ninguém saber; **to go ~ sth** passar sem algo

withstand [wɪð'stænd] (irreg: like **stand**) vt resistir a

witness ['wɪtnɪs] n testemunha ▷ vt testemunhar, presenciar; (document) legalizar; **to bear ~ to sth** (fig) testemunhar algo

witty ['wɪtɪ] adj espirituoso

wives [waɪvz] npl of **wife**

wizard ['wɪzəd] n feiticeiro, mago

wk abbr = **week**

wobble ['wɔbl] vi oscilar; (chair) balançar

woe [wəu] n dor f, mágoa

woke [wəuk] pt of **wake**; **woken** pp of **wake**

wolf [wulf] (pl **wolves**) n lobo

woman ['wumən] (pl **women**) n mulher f; **~ doctor** médica

womb [wuːm] n (Anat) matriz f, útero

women ['wɪmɪn] npl of **woman**

won [wʌn] pt, pp of **win**

wonder ['wʌndə'] n maravilha, prodígio; (feeling) espanto ▷ vi perguntar-se a si mesmo; **to ~ at** admirar-se de; **to ~ about** pensar sobre or em; **it's no ~ that** não é de admirar que; **wonderful** adj maravilhoso; (miraculous) impressionante

won't [wəunt] = **will not**

wood [wud] n (timber) madeira; (forest) floresta, bosque m; **wooden** adj de madeira; (fig) inexpressivo; **woodwind** n (Mus) instrumentos mpl de sopro de madeira; **woodwork** n carpintaria

wool [wul] n lã f; **to pull the ~ over
sb's eyes** (fig) enganar alguém, vender
a alguém gato por lebre; **woollen** adj
de lã; **woolly** (US **wooly**) adj de lã; (fig)
confuso

word [wə:d] n palavra; (news) notícia
▷ vt redigir; **in other ~s** em outras
palavras, ou seja; **to break/keep one's
~** faltar à palavra/cumprir a promessa;
to have ~s with sb discutir com alguém;
wording n fraseado; **word processing**
n processamento de textos; **word
processor** n processador m de textos

wore [wɔ:ʳ] pt of **wear**

work [wə:k] n trabalho; (job) emprego,
trabalho; (Art, Literature) obra ▷ vi
trabalhar; (mechanism) funcionar;
(medicine etc) surtir efeito, ser eficaz
▷ vt (clay) moldar; (wood) talhar; (mine
etc) explorar; (machine) fazer trabalhar,
manejar; (effect, miracle) causar; **to ~
loose** (part) soltar-se; (knot) afrouxar-se;
work on vt fus trabalhar em, dedicar-se
a; (person: influence) tentar convencer;
(principle) basear-se em; **work out** vi
dar certo, surtir efeito ▷ vt (problem)
resolver; (plan) elaborar, formular; **it
works out at £100** monta or soma
a £100; **worker** n trabalhador(a)
m/f, operário(-a); **working class** n
proletariado, classe f operária ▷ adj:
working-class do proletariado, da
classe operária; **workman** (irreg) n
operário, trabalhador m; **worksheet** n
folha de exercícios; **workshop** n oficina;
(practical session) aula prática

world [wə:ld] n mundo ▷ cpd mundial;
to think the ~ of sb (fig) ter alguém em
alto conceito

worm [wə:m] n (also: **earth~**) minhoca,
lombriga

worn [wɔ:n] pp of **wear** ▷ adj gasto;
worn-out adj (object) gasto; (person)
esgotado, exausto

worry ['wʌrɪ] n preocupação f ▷ vt
preocupar, inquietar ▷ vi preocupar-se,
afligir-se

worse [wə:s] adj, adv pior ▷ n o pior; **a
change for the ~** uma mudança para
pior, uma piora; **worsen** vt, vi piorar;
worse off adj com menos dinheiro; (fig):
you'll be worse off this way assim você
ficará pior que nunca

worship ['wə:ʃɪp] n adoração f ▷ vt
adorar, venerar; (person, thing) adorar;
Your W~ (BRIT: to mayor) vossa

Excelência; (: to judge) senhor Juiz

worst [wə:st] adj (o(-a)) pior ▷ adv pior
▷ n o pior; **at ~** na pior das hipóteses

worth [wə:θ] n valor m, mérito ▷ adj: **to
be ~** valer; **it's ~ it** vale a pena; **to be ~
one's while (to do)** valer a pena (fazer);
worthless adj (person) imprestável;
(thing) inútil; **worthwhile** adj (activity)
que vale a pena; (cause) de mérito,
louvável

worthy ['wə:ðɪ] adj (person)
merecedor(a), respeitável; (motive) justo;
~ of digno de

○ **KEYWORD**

would [wud] aux vb **1** (conditional tense): **if
you asked him, he would do it** se você
pedisse, ele faria isto; **if you had asked
him, he would have done it** se você
tivesse pedido, ele teria feito isto
2 (in offers, invitations, requests): **would
you like a biscuit?** você quer um
biscoito?; **would you ask him to come
in?** pode pedir a ele para entrar?; **would
you close the door, please?** quer fechar
a porta por favor?
3 (in indirect speech): **I said I would do it**
eu disse que eu faria isto
4 (emphatic): **you WOULD say that,
wouldn't you?** é lógico que você vai
dizer isso
5 (insistence): **she wouldn't behave** não
houve feito dela se comportar
6 (conjecture): **it would have been
midnight** devia ser meia-noite; **it would
seem so** parece que sim
7 (indicating habit): **he would go on
Mondays** costumava ir às segundas-
feiras

wouldn't ['wudnt] = **would not**

wound¹ [waund] pt, pp of **wind²**

wound² [wu:nd] n ferida ▷ vt ferir

wove [wəuv] pt of **weave**; **woven** pp of
weave

wrap [ræp] n (stole) xale m; (cape)
capa ▷ vt (cover) envolver; (also: **~ up**)
embrulhar; (wind: tape etc) amarrar;
wrapper n invólucro; (BRIT: of book)
capa; **wrapping paper** n papel m de
embrulho; (fancy) papel de presente

wreath [ri:θ] n coroa

wreck [rɛk] n (vehicle) destroços mpl;
(ship) restos mpl do naufrágio; (pej:
person) ruína, caco ▷ vt destruir,

danificar; (fig) arruinar, arrasar;
wreckage n (of car, plane) destroços
mpl; (of ship) restos mpl; (of building)
escombros mpl
wren [rɛn] n (Zool) carriça
wrench [rɛntʃ] n (Tech) chave f inglesa;
(tug) puxão m; (fig) separação f penosa
▷ vt torcer com força; **to ~ sth from sb**
arrancar algo de alguém
wrestle ['rɛsl] vi: **to ~ (with sb)** lutar
(com or contra alguém); **wrestler** n
lutador m; **wrestling** n luta (livre)
wretched ['rɛtʃɪd] adj desventurado,
infeliz; (inf) maldito
wriggle ['rɪgl] vi (also: ~ **about**) retorcer-
se, contorcer-se
wring [rɪŋ] (pt, pp **wrung**) vt (clothes,
neck) torcer; (hands) apertar; (fig): **to ~**
sth out of sb arrancar algo de alguém
wrinkle ['rɪŋkl] n (on skin) ruga; (on paper)
prega ▷ vt franzir ▷ vi enrugar-se
wrist [rɪst] n pulso
write [raɪt] (pt **wrote**, pp **written**) vt
escrever; (cheque, prescription) passar
▷ vi escrever; **to ~ to sb** escrever para
alguém; **write down** vt (note) anotar;
(put on paper) pôr no papel; **write off**
vt cancelar; **write out** vt escrever por
extenso; (cheque etc) passar; **write up** vt
redigir; **write-off** n perda total; **writer** n
escritor(a) m/f
writing ['raɪtɪŋ] n escrita; (handwriting)
caligrafia, letra; (of author) obra; **in ~** por
escrito
wrong [rɔŋ] adj (bad) errado, mau;
(unfair) injusto; (incorrect) errado,
equivocado; (inappropriate) impróprio
▷ adv mal, errado ▷ n injustiça ▷ vt
ser injusto com; **you are ~ to do it**
você se engana ao fazê-lo; **you are ~**
about that, you've got it ~ você está
enganado sobre isso; **to be in the ~** não
ter razão; **what's ~?** o que é que há?; **to**
go ~ (person) desencaminhar-se; (plan)
dar errado; (machine) sofrer uma avaria;
wrongly ['rɔŋlɪ] adv errado
wrote [rəʊt] pt of **write**
wrung [rʌŋ] pt, pp of **wring**
WWW n abbr = **World Wide Web; the ~**
a WWW

X

Xmas ['ɛksməs] n abbr = **Christmas**
X-ray [ɛks'reɪ] n radiografia ▷ vt
radiografar, tirar uma chapa de

y

yacht [jɔt] n iate m
yachting n iatismo
yard [jɑːd] n pátio, quintal m; (measure) jarda (914 mm; 3 feet)
yarn [jɑːn] n fio; (tale) história inverossímil
yawn [jɔːn] n bocejo ▷ vi bocejar
yeah [jɛə] (inf) adv é
year [jɪəʳ] n ano; **to be 8 ~s old** ter 8 anos; **an eight-~-old child** uma criança de oito anos (de idade); **yearly** adj anual ▷ adv anualmente
yearn [jəːn] vi: **to ~ to do/for sth** ansiar fazer/por algo
yeast [jiːst] n levedura, fermento
yell [jɛl] n grito, berro ▷ vi gritar, berrar
yellow [ˈjɛləu] adj amarelo
yes [jɛs] adv, n sim m
yesterday [ˈjɛstədɪ] adv, n ontem m
yet [jɛt] adv ainda ▷ conj porém, no entanto; **the best ~** o melhor até agora; **as ~** até agora, ainda
yew [juː] n teixo
yield [jiːld] n (Agr) colheita; (Comm) rendimento ▷ vt produzir; (profit) render; (surrender) ceder ▷ vi render-se, ceder; (us: Aut) ceder
yog(h)urt [ˈjəugət] n iogurte m

yolk [jəuk] n gema (do ovo)

 KEYWORD

you [juː] pron **1** (subj: sg) tu, você; (: pl) vós, vocês; **you French enjoy your food** vocês franceses gostam de comer; **you and I will go** nós iremos
2 (direct object: sg) te, o (a); (: pl) vos, os (as); (indirect object: sg) te, lhe; (: pl) vos, lhes; **I know you** eu lhe conheço; **I gave it to you** dei isto para você
3 (stressed) você; **I told you to do it** eu disse para você fazer isto
4 (after prep, in comparisons: sg) ti, você; (: pl) vós, vocês; (polite form: sg) o senhor (a senhora); (: pl) os senhores (as senhoras); **it's for you** é para você; **with you** contigo, com você; convosco, com vocês; com o senhor etc
5 (impers: one): **you never know** nunca se sabe; **apples do you good** as maçãs fazem bem à saúde

you'd [juːd] = **you had; you would**
you'll [juːl] = **you will; you shall**
young [jʌŋ] adj jovem ▷ npl (of animal) filhotes mpl, crias fpl; (people): **the ~** a juventude, os jovens; **younger** [ˈjʌŋgəʳ] adj mais novo
your [jɔːʳ] pron teu (tua), seu (sua); (pl) vosso, seu (sua); (formal) do senhor (da senhora); see also **my**
you're [juəʳ] = **you are**
yours [jɔːz] pron teu (tua), seu (sua); (pl) vosso, seu (sua); (formal) do senhor (da senhora); **~ sincerely** or **faithfully** atenciosamente; see also **mine¹**
yourself [jɔːˈsɛlf] pron (emphatic) tu mesmo, você mesmo; (object, reflexive) te, se; (after prep) ti mesmo, si mesmo; (formal) o senhor mesmo (a senhora mesma); **yourselves** pl, pron vós mesmos, vocês mesmos; vos, se; vós mesmos, vôces mesmos; os senhores mesmos (as senhoras mesmas); see also **oneself**
youth [juːθ] n mocidade f, juventude f; (young man) jovem m; **youth club** n associação f de juventude; **youthful** adj juvenil; **youth hostel** n albergue m da juventude
you've [juːv] = **you have**

Z

zebra ['ziːbrə] *n* zebra; **zebra crossing**
(BRIT) *n* faixa (para pedestres) (BR),
passadeira (PT)
zero ['zɪərəu] *n* zero
zest [zest] *n* vivacidade *f*, entusiasmo; (*of
lemon etc*) zesto
zigzag ['zɪgzæg] *n* ziguezague *m* ▷ *vi*
ziguezaguear
zinc [zɪŋk] *n* zinco
zip [zɪp] *n* (*also:* **~ fastener**) fecho ecler
(BR) *or* éclair (PT) ▷ *vt* (*also:* **~ up**) fechar
o fecho ecler de, subir o fecho ecler de;
zip code (US) *n* código postal; **zip file** *n*
arquivo zipado; **zipper** (US) *n* = **zip**
zodiac ['zəudɪæk] *n* zodíaco
zone [zəun] *n* zona
zoo [zuː] *n* (jardim *m*) zoológico
zoom [zuːm] *vi:* **to ~ past** passar
zunindo; **zoom lens** *n* zoom *m*, zum *m*
zucchini [zuːˈkiːnɪ] (US) *n(pl)* abobrinha

I recognized him immediately; **ele
ficou muito nervoso ao falar com o
professor** he became very nervous while
he was talking to the teacher
10 (PT: + infin: gerúndio): **a correr**
running; **estou a trabalhar** I'm working

a

PALAVRA CHAVE

a [a] (a + o(s) = ao(s); a + a(s) = à(s); a +
aquele/a(s) = àquele/a(s)) art def the; ver
tb **o**
▷ pron (ela) her; (você) you; (coisa) it; ver
tb **o**
▷ prep **1** (direção) to; **à direita/esquerda**
to ou on the right/left
2 (distância): **está a 15 km daqui** it's 15
km from here
3 (posição): **ao lado de** beside, at the
side of
4 (tempo) at; **a que horas?** at what
time?; **às 5 horas** at 5 o'clock; **à noite** at
night; **aos 15 anos** at 15 years of age
5 (maneira): **à francesa** in the French
way; **a cavalo/pé** on horseback/foot
6 (meio, instrumento): **à força** by force; **a
mão** by hand; **a lápis** in pencil; **fogão a
gás** gas stove
7 (razão): **a R$1 o quilo** at R$1 a kilo; **a
mais de 100 km/h** at over 100 km/h
8 (depois de certos verbos): **começou a
nevar** it started snowing ou to snow;
passar a fazer to become
9 (+ infin): **ao vê-lo, o reconheci
imediatamente** when I saw him,

à [a] = **a + a**
(a) abr (= assinado) signed
aba ['aba] f (de chapéu) brim; (de casaco)
tail; (de montanha) foot
abacate [aba'katʃi] m avocado (pear)
abacaxi [abaka'ʃi] (BR) m pineapple
abafado, -a [aba'fadu, a] adj (ar)
stuffy; (tempo) humid, close; (ocupado)
(extremely) busy; (angustiado) anxious
abaixar [abaj'ʃaʳ] vt to lower; (luz, som) to
turn down; **~-se** vr to stoop
abaixo [a'bajʃu] adv down ▷ prep: **~ de**
below; **~ o governo!** down with the
government!; **morro ~** downhill; **rio
~** downstream; **mais ~** further down;
~ e acima up and down; **~ assinado**
undersigned; **abaixo-assinado**
[-asi'nadu] (pl **abaixo-assinados**) m
petition
abalado, -a [aba'ladu, a] adj (objeto)
unstable, unsteady; (fig: pessoa) shaken
abalar [aba'laʳ] vt to shake; (fig: comover)
to affect ▷ vi to shake; **~-se** vr to be
moved
abalo [a'balu] m (comoção) shock; (ação)
shaking; **~ sísmico** earth tremor
abanar [aba'naʳ] vt to shake; (rabo) to
wag; (com leque) to fan
abandonar [abãdo'naʳ] vt to leave;
(idéia) to reject; (esperança) to give up;
(descuidar) to neglect
abarrotado, -a [abaxo'tadu, a] adj
(gaveta) crammed full; (lugar) packed
abastecer [abaʃte'seʳ] vt to supply;
(motor) to fuel; (Auto) to fill up; (Aer) to
refuel; **~-se** vr: **~-se de** to stock up with
abastecimento [abaʃtesi'mẽtu] m
supply; (comestíveis) provisions pl;
(ato) supplying; **abastecimentos** mpl
(suprimentos) supplies
abater [aba'teʳ] vt (gado) to slaughter;
(preço) to reduce; (desalentar) to upset;
abatido, -a [aba'tʃidu, a] adj depressed,
downcast; **abatimento** [abatʃi'mẽtu] m
(fraqueza) weakness; (de preço) reduction;
(prostração) depression; **fazer um
abatimento em** to give a discount on
abdômen [ab'domẽ] m abdomen
á-bê-cê [abe'se] m alphabet

abecedário [abese'darju] *m* alphabet, ABC

abelha [a'beʎa] *f* bee

abelhudo, -a [abe'ʎudu, a] *adj* nosy

abençoar [abẽ'swaˡ] *vt* to bless

aberto, -a [a'bɛxtu, a] *pp de* **abrir** ▷ *adj* open; (*céu*) clear; (*sinal*) green; (*torneira*) running; **a torneira estava aberta** the tap was on

abestalhado, -a [abeʃta'ʎadu, a] *adj* stupid

abismado, -a [abiʒ'madu, a] *adj* astonished

ABL *abr f* = **Academia Brasileira de Letras**

abnegado, -a [abne'gadu, a] *adj* self-sacrificing

abnegar [abne'gaˡ] *vt* to renounce

abóbada [a'bɔbada] *f* vault; (*telhado*) arched roof

abobalhado, -a [aboba'ʎadu, a] *adj* (*criança*) simple

abóbora [a'bɔbora] *f* pumpkin

abobrinha [abo'briɲa] *f* courgette (BRIT), zucchini (US)

abolir [abo'liˡ] *vt* to abolish

aborrecer [aboxe'seˡ] *vt* (*chatear*) to annoy; (*maçar*) to bore; **~-se** *vr* to get upset; to get bored; **aborrecido, -a** [aboxe'sidu, a] *adj* annoyed; boring; **aborrecimento** [aboxesi'mẽtu] *m* annoyance; boredom

abortar [abox'taˡ] *vi* (Med) to have a miscarriage; (: *de propósito*) to have an abortion; **aborto** [a'bɔxtu] *m* miscarriage; abortion; **fazer/ter um aborto** to have an abortion/a miscarriage

abotoadura [abotwa'dura] *f* cufflink

abotoar [abo'twaˡ] *vt* to button up ▷ *vi* (Bot) to bud

abraçar [abra'saˡ] *vt* to hug; (*causa*) to embrace; **~-se** *vr* to embrace; **ele abraçou-se a mim** he embraced me; **abraço** [a'brasu] *m* embrace, hug; **com um abraço** (*em carta*) with best wishes

abre-garrafas ['abri-] (PT) *m inv* bottle opener

abre-latas ['abri-] (PT) *m inv* tin (BRIT) *ou* can opener

abreviar [abre'vjaˡ] *vt* to abbreviate; (*texto*) to abridge; **abreviatura** [abrevja'tura] *f* abbreviation

abridor [abri'doˡ] (BR) *m*: **~ (de lata)** tin (BRIT) *ou* can opener; **~ de garrafa** bottle opener

abrigar [abri'gaˡ] *vt* to shelter; (*proteger*) to protect; **~-se** *vr* to take shelter

abrigo [a'brigu] *m* shelter, cover; **~ anti-aéreo** air-raid shelter; **~ anti-nuclear** fall-out shelter

abril [a'briw] (PT **Abril**) *m* April; **25 de Abril** (PT) *see boxed note*

✿ 25 DE ABRIL

On 25 April 1974 in Portugal, the MAF (Armed Forces Movement) instigated the bloodless revolution that was to topple the 48-year-old dictatorship presided over until 1968 by António de Oliveira Salazar. The red carnation has come to symbolize the coup, as it is said that the Armed Forces took to the streets with carnations in the barrels of their rifles. 25 April is now a public holiday in Portugal.

abrir [a'briˡ] *vt* to open; (*fechadura*) to unlock; (*vestuário*) to unfasten; (*torneira*) to turn on; (*exceção*) to make ▷ *vi* to open; (*sinal*) to turn green; **~-se** *vr*: **~-se com alguém** to confide in sb

abrupto, -a [a'bruptu, a] *adj* abrupt; (*repentino*) sudden

absolutamente [absoluta'mẽtʃi] *adv* absolutely; (*em resposta*) absolutely not, not at all

absoluto, -a [abso'lutu, a] *adj* absolute; **em ~** absolutely not, not at all

absorto, -a [ab'soxtu, a] *pp de* **absorver** ▷ *adj* absorbed, engrossed

absorvente [absox'vẽtʃi] *adj* (*papel etc*) absorbent; (*livro etc*) absorbing

absorver [absox'veˡ] *vt* to absorb; **~-se** *vr*: **~-se em** to concentrate on

abstêmio, -a [abʃ'temju, a] *adj* abstemious; (*álcool*) teetotal ▷ *m/f* abstainer; teetotaller (BRIT), teetotaler (US)

abster-se [ab'ʃtexsi] (*irreg: como* **ter**) *vr*: **~ de** to abstain *ou* refrain from

abstinência [abʃtʃi'nẽsja] *f* abstinence; (*jejum*) fasting

abstracto, -a [abʃ'tratu, a] (PT) *adj* = **abstrato**

abstrato, -a [abʃ'tratu, a] *adj* abstract

absurdo, -a [abi'suxdu, a] *adj* absurd ▷ *m* nonsense

abundante [abũ'dãtʃi] *adj* abundant; **abundar** [abũ'daˡ] *vi* to abound

abusar [abu'zaˡ] *vi* to go too far; **~ de** to

abuse

abuso [a'buzu] *m* abuse; (*Jur*) indecent assault

a.C. *abr* (= *antes de Cristo*) B.C.

a/c *abr* (= *aos cuidados de*) c/o

acabado, -a [aka'badu, a] *adj* finished; (*esgotado*) worn out

acabamento [akaba'mētu] *m* finish

acabar [aka'ba'] *vt* to finish, complete; (*consumir*) to use up; (*rematar*) to finish off ▷ *vi* to finish, end; **~-se** *vr* to be over; (*prazo*) to expire; (*esgotar-se*) to run out; **~ com** to put an end to; **~ de chegar** to have just arrived; **~ por fazer** to end up (by) doing; **acabou-se!** it's all over!; (*basta!*) that's enough!

academia [akade'mia] *f* academy; **Academia Brasileira de Letras** *see boxed note*; **acadêmico, -a** [aka'demiku, a] *adj, m/f* academic

⊛ **ACADEMIA BRASILEIRA DE LETRAS**
⊛
⊛ Founded in 1896 in Rio de Janeiro, on
⊛ the initiative of the author Machado
⊛ de Assis, the **Academia Brasileira de**
⊛ **Letras**, or ABL, aims to preserve and
⊛ develop the Portuguese language and
⊛ Brazilian literature. Machado de Assis
⊛ was its president until 1908. It is made
⊛ up of forty life members known as
⊛ the *imortais*. The Academia's activities
⊛ include publication of reference
⊛ books, promotion of literary prizes,
⊛ and running a library, museum and
⊛ archive.

açafrão [asa'frãw] *m* saffron

acalmar [akaw'ma'] *vt* to calm ▷ *vi* (*vento etc*) to abate; **~-se** *vr* to calm down

acampamento [akãpa'mētu] *m* camping; (*Mil*) camp, encampment

acampar [akã'pa'] *vi* to camp

acanhado, -a [aka'ɲadu, a] *adj* shy

acanhamento [akaɲa'mētu] *m* shyness

acanhar-se [aka'ɲaxsi] *vr* to be shy

ação [a'sãw] (*pl* -**ões**) *f* action; (*ato*) act, deed; (*Mil*) battle; (*enredo*) plot; (*Jur*) lawsuit; (*Com*) share; **~ ordinária/ preferencial** (*Com*) ordinary/preference share

acarajé [akara'ʒɛ] *m* (*Culin*) beans fried in palm oil

acarretar [akaxe'ta'] *vt* to result in, bring about

acaso [a'kazu] *m* chance; **ao ~** at random; **por ~** by chance

acatar [aka'ta'] *vt* to respect; (*lei*) to obey

acção [a'sãw] (*PT*) *f* = **ação**

accionar *etc* [asjo'na'] (*PT*) = **acionar** *etc*

aceitação [asejta'sãw] *f* acceptance; (*aprovação*) approval

aceitar [asej'ta'] *vt* to accept; (*aprovar*) to approve; **aceitável** [asej'tavew] (*pl* -**eis**) *adj* acceptable; **aceito, -a** [a'sejtu, a] *pp de* **aceitar**

acelerador [aselera'do'] *m* accelerator

acelerar [asele'ra'] *vt* (*Auto*): **~ o carro** to accelerate; (*ritmo, negociações*) to speed up ▷ *vi* to accelerate; **~ o passo** to go faster

acenar [ase'na'] *vi* (*com a mão*) to wave; (*com a cabeça: afirmativo*) to nod; (: *negativo*) to shake one's head

acender [asē'de'] *vt* (*cigarro, fogo*) to light; (*luz*) to switch on; (*fig*) to excite, inflame

acento [a'sētu] *m* accent; (*de intensidade*) stress; **acentuar** [asē'twa'] *vt* to accent; (*salientar*) to stress, emphasize

acepção [asep'sãw] (*pl* -**ões**) *f* (*de uma palavra*) sense

acerca [a'sexka]: **~ de** *prep* about, concerning

acertado, -a [asex'tadu, a] *adj* right, correct; (*sensato*) sensible

acertar [asex'ta'] *vt* (*ajustar*) to put right; (*relógio*) to set; (*alvo*) to hit; (*acordo*) to reach; (*pergunta*) to get right ▷ *vi* to get it right, be right; **~ o caminho** to find the right way; **~ com** to hit upon

aceso, -a [a'sezu, a] *pp de* **acender** ▷ *adj*: **a luz estava acesa/o fogo estava ~** the light was on/the fire was alight; (*excitado*) excited; (*furioso*) furious

acessar [ase'sa'] *vt* (*Comput*) to access

acessível [ase'sivew] (*pl* -**eis**) *adj* accessible; (*pessoa*) approachable

acesso [a'sɛsu] *m* access; (*Med*) fit, attack

acessório, -a [ase'sɔrju, a] *adj* (*máquina, equipamento*) backup; (*Educ*): **matéria acessória** subsidiary subject ▷ *m* accessory

achado, -a [a'ʃadu, a] *m* find, discovery; (*pechincha*) bargain; (*sorte*) godsend

achar [a'ʃa'] *vt* (*descobrir*) to find; (*pensar*) to think; **~-se** *vr* to think (that) one is; (*encontrar-se*) to be; **~ de fazer** (*resolver*) to decide to do; **o que é que você acha disso?** what do you think of that?; **acho que sim** I think so

achatar [aʃa'ta'] *vt* to squash, flatten

acidentado, -a [asidẽ'tadu, a] *adj*
(*terreno*) rough; (*estrada*) bumpy; (*viagem*)
eventful; (*vida*) difficult ▷ *m/f* injured
person

acidental [asidẽ'taw] (*pl* **-ais**) *adj*
accidental

acidente [asi'dẽtʃi] *m* accident; **por ~** by
accident

acidez [asi'deʒ] *f* acidity

ácido, -a ['asidu, a] *adj* acid; (*azedo*) sour
▷ *m* acid

acima [a'sima] *adv* above; (*para cima*)
up ▷ *prep*: **~ de** above; (*além de*) beyond;
mais ~ higher up; **rio ~** up river; **passar**
rua ~ to go up the street; **~ de 1000** more
than 1000

acionar [asjo'naʳ] *vt* to set in motion;
(*máquina*) to operate; (*Jur*) to sue

acionista [asjo'niʃta] *m/f* shareholder

acirrado, -a [asi'xadu, a] *adj* (*luta*,
competição) tough

acirrar [asi'xaʳ] *vt* to incite, stir up

aclamar [akla'maʳ] *vt* to acclaim;
(*aplaudir*) to applaud

aço ['asu] *m* steel

acocorar-se [akoko'raxsi] *vr* to squat,
crouch

acode *etc* [a'kɔdʒi] *vb ver* **acudir**

ações [a'sõjʃ] *fpl de* **ação**

acolá [ako'la] *adv* over there

acolchoado [akow'ʃwadu] *m* quilt

acolhedor, a [akoʎe'doʳ, a] *adj*
welcoming; (*hospitaleiro*) hospitable

acolher [ako'ʎeʳ] *vt* to welcome;
(*abrigar*) to shelter; (*aceitar*) to accept;
~-se *vr* to shelter; **acolhida** [ako'ʎida] *f*
(*recepção*) reception, welcome; (*refúgio*)
refuge; **acolhimento** [akoʎi'mẽtu] *m*
= **acolhida**

acomodação [akomoda'sãw] (*pl* **-ões**) *f*
accommodation; (*arranjo*) arrangement;
(*adaptação*) adaptation

acomodar [akomo'daʳ] *vt* to
accommodate; (*arrumar*) to arrange;
(*adaptar*) to adapt

acompanhamento [akõpaɲa'mẽtu] *m*
attendance; (*cortejo*) procession; (*Mús*)
accompaniment; (*Culin*) side dish

acompanhante [akõpa'ɲãtʃi] *m/f*
companion; (*Mús*) accompanist

acompanhar [akõpa'ɲaʳ] *vt* to
accompany

aconchegante [akõʃe'gãtʃi] *adj* cosy
(*BRIT*), cozy (*US*)

aconselhar [akõse'ʎaʳ] *vt* to advise; **~-se**
vr: **~-se com** to consult

acontecer [akõte'seʳ] *vi* to happen;
acontecimento [akõtesi'mẽtu] *m*
event

acordar [akox'daʳ] *vt* to wake (up);
(*concordar*) to agree (on) ▷ *vi* to wake up

acorde [a'kɔrdʒi] *m* chord

acordo [a'koxdu] *m* agreement;
"de ~!" "agreed!"; **de ~ com** (*pessoa*)
in agreement with; (*conforme*) in
accordance with; **estar de ~** to agree

Açores [a'soriʃ] *mpl*: **os ~** the Azores;
açoriano, -a [aso'rjanu, a] *adj, m/f*
Azorean

acossar [ako'saʳ] *vt* (*perseguir*) to pursue;
(*atormentar*) to harass

acostamento [akoʃta'mẽtu] *m* hard
shoulder (*BRIT*), berm (*US*)

acostumado, -a [akoʃtu'madu, a] *adj*
usual, customary; **estar ~ a algo** to be
used to sth

acostumar [akoʃtu'maʳ] *vt* to accustom;
~-se *vr*: **~-se a** to get used to

açougue [a'sogi] *m* butcher's (shop);
açougueiro [aso'gejru] *m* butcher

acovardar-se [akovax'daxsi] *vr*
(*desanimar*) to lose courage; (*amedrontar-
se*) to flinch, cower

acreditado, -a [akredʒi'tadu, a] *adj*
accredited

acreditar [akredʒi'taʳ] *vt* to believe;
(*Com*) to credit; (*afiançar*) to guarantee
▷ *vi*: **~ em** to believe in

acrescentar [akresẽ'taʳ] *vt* to add

activo, -a *etc* [a'tivu, a] (*PT*) = **ativo** *etc*

acto ['atu] (*PT*) *m* = **ato**

actor [a'toʳ] (*PT*) *m* = **ator**

actriz [a'triʒ] (*PT*) *f* = **atriz**

actual *etc* [a'twaw] (*PT*) = **atual** *etc*

actuar *etc* [a'twaʳ] (*PT*) = **atuar** *etc*

açúcar [a'sukaʳ] *m* sugar; **açucareiro**
[asuka'rejru] *m* sugar bowl

açude [a'sudʒi] *m* dam

acudir [aku'dʒiʳ] *vt* (*ir em socorro*) to help,
assist ▷ *vi* (*responder*) to reply, respond; **~**
a to come to the aid of

acumular [akumu'laʳ] *vt* to accumulate;
(*reunir*) to collect; (*funções*) to combine

acusação [akuza'sãw] (*pl* **-ões**) *f*
accusation, charge; (*Jur*) prosecution

acusar [aku'zaʳ] *vt* to accuse; (*revelar*)
to reveal; (*culpar*) to blame; **~ o**
recebimento de to acknowledge receipt
of

acústico, -a [a'kuʃtʃiku, a] *adj* acoustic

adaptar [adap'taʳ] *vt* to adapt;
(*acomodar*) to fit; **~-se** *vr*: **~-se a** to

adapt to

adega [a'dɛga] f cellar

ademais [adʒi'majʃ] adv besides, moreover

adentro [a'dẽtru] adv inside, in; **mata ~** into the woods

adequado, -a [ade'kwadu, a] adj appropriate

adereço [ade'resu] m adornment; **adereços** mpl (Teatro) stage props

aderente [ade'rẽtʃi] adj adhesive, sticky ▷ m/f supporter

aderir [ade'ri'] vi to adhere

adesão [ade'zãw] f adhesion; (patrocínio) support

adesivo, -a [ade'zivu, a] adj adhesive, sticky ▷ m adhesive tape; (Med) sticking plaster

adestrar [adeʃ'tra'] vt to train; (cavalo) to break in

adeus [a'dewʃ] excl goodbye!

adiantado, -a [adʒjã'tadu, a] adj advanced; (relógio) fast; **chegar ~** to arrive ahead of time; **pagar ~** to pay in advance

adiantamento [adʒjãta'mẽtu] m progress; (dinheiro) advance (payment)

adiantar [adʒjã'ta'] vt (dinheiro, trabalho) to advance; (relógio) to put forward; **não adianta reclamar** there's no point complaining

adiante [a'dʒjãtʃi] adv (na frente) in front; (para a frente) forward; **mais ~** further on; (no futuro) later on

adiar [a'dʒja'] vt to postpone, put off; (sessão) to adjourn

adição [adʒi'sãw] (pl **-ões**) f addition; (Mat) sum; **adicionar** [adʒisjo'na'] vt to add

adido, -a [a'dʒidu, a] m/f attaché

adiro etc [a'diru] vb ver **aderir**

adivinhar [adʒivi'ɲa'] vt to guess; (ler a sorte) to foretell ▷ vi to guess; **~ o pensamento de alguém** to read sb's mind; **adivinho, -a** [adʒi'viɲu, a] m/f fortune-teller

adjetivo [adʒe'tʃivu] m adjective

adjudicar [adʒudʒi'ka'] vt to award, grant

administração [adʒiminiʃtra'sãw] (pl **-ões**) f administration; (direção) management; (comissão) board

administrador, a [adʒiminiʃtra'do', a] m/f administrator; (diretor) director; (gerente) manager

administrar [adʒiminiʃ'tra'] vt to

administer, manage; (governar) to govern

admiração [adʒimira'sãw] f wonder; (estima) admiration; **ponto de ~** (PT) exclamation mark

admirado, -a [adʒimi'radu, a] adj astonished, surprised

admirar [adʒimi'ra'] vt to admire; **~-se** vr: **~-se de** to be surprised at; **admirável** [adʒimi'ravew] (pl **-eis**) adj amazing

admissão [adʒimi'sãw] (pl **-ões**) f admission; (consentimento para entrar) admittance; (de escola) intake

admitir [adʒimi'tʃi'] vt to admit; (permitir) to allow; (funcionário) to take on

adoção [ado'sãw] f adoption

adoçar [ado'sa'] vt to sweeten

adoecer [adoe'se'] vi: **~ (de ou com)** to fall ill (with) ▷ vt to make ill

adoidado, -a [adoj'dadu, a] adj crazy

adolescente [adole'sẽtʃi] adj, m/f adolescent

adoptar etc [ado'ta'] (PT) = **adotar** etc

adorar [ado'ra'] vt to adore; (venerar) to worship

adormecer [adoxme'se'] vi to fall asleep; (entorpecer-se) to go numb; **adormecido, -a** [adoxme'sidu, a] adj sleeping ▷ m/f sleeper

adorno [a'doxnu] m adornment

adotar [ado'ta'] vt to adopt; **adotivo, -a** [ado'tʃivu, a] adj (filho) adopted

adquirir [adʒiki'ri'] vt to acquire

Adriático, -a [a'drjatʃiku, a] adj: **o (mar) ~** the Adriatic

adro ['adru] m (church) forecourt; (em volta da igreja) churchyard

adulação [adula'sãw] f flattery

adulterar [aduwte'ra'] vt to adulterate; (contas) to falsify ▷ vi to commit adultery

adultério [aduw'tɛrju] m adultery

adulto, -a [a'duwtu, a] adj, m/f adult

advento [ad'vẽtu] m advent; **o A~** Advent

advérbio [ad'vɛxbju] m adverb

adverso, -a [adʒi'vɛxsu, a] adj adverse; (oposto): **~ a** opposed to

advertência [adʒivex'tẽsja] f warning

advertir [adʒivex'tʃi'] vt to warn; (repreender) to reprimand; (chamar a atenção a) to draw attention to

advogado, -a [adʒivo'gadu, a] m/f lawyer

advogar [adʒivo'ga'] vt to advocate; (Jur) to plead ▷ vi to practise (BRIT) ou practice (US) law

aéreo, -a [a'erju, a] adj air atr

aerobarco [aero'baxku] *m* hovercraft
aeromoço, -a [aero'mosu, a] (BR) *m/f*
steward/air hostess
aeronáutica [aero'nawtʃika] *f* air force;
(*ciência*) aeronautics *sg*
aeronave [aero'navi] *f* aircraft
aeroporto [aero'poxtu] *m* airport
aerossol [aero'sɔw] (*pl* **-óis**) *m* aerosol
afã [a'fã] *m* (*entusiasmo*) enthusiasm;
(*diligência*) diligence; (*ânsia*) eagerness;
(*esforço*) effort
afagar [afa'gaʀ] *vt* to caress; (*cabelo*) to
stroke
afastado, -a [afaʃ'tadu, a] *adj* (*distante*)
remote; (*isolado*) secluded; **manter-se ~**
to keep to o.s
afastamento [afaʃta'mẽtu] *m* removal;
(*distância*) distance; (*de pessoal*) lay-off
afastar [afaʃ'taʀ] *vt* to remove; (*separar*)
to separate; (*idéia*) to put out of one's
mind; (*pessoal*) to lay off; **~-se** *vr* to move
away
afável [a'favew] (*pl* **-eis**) *adj* friendly
afazeres [afa'zeriʃ] *mpl* business *sg*;
(*dever*) duties, tasks; **~ domésticos**
household chores
afectar *etc* [afek'taʀ] (PT) = **afetar** *etc*
afeição [afej'sãw] *f* affection, fondness;
(*dedicação*) devotion; **afeiçoado, -a**
[afej'swadu, a] *adj*: **afeiçoado a**
(*amoroso*) fond of; (*devotado*) devoted to;
afeiçoar-se [afej'swaxsi] *vr*: **afeiçoar-
se a** to take a liking to
afeito, -a [a'fejtu, a] *adj*: **~ a** accustomed
to, used to
aferrado, -a [afe'xadu, a] *adj* obstinate,
stubborn
afetar [afe'taʀ] *vt* to affect; (*fingir*) to
feign
afetivo, -a [afe'tʃivu, a] *adj* affectionate;
(*problema*) emotional
afeto [a'fɛtu] *m* affection; **afetuoso, -a**
[afe'twozu, ɔza] *adj* affectionate
afiado, -a [a'fjadu, a] *adj* sharp; (*pessoa*)
well-trained
afiar [a'fjaʀ] *vt* to sharpen
aficionado, -a [afisjo'nadu, a] *m/f*
enthusiast
afilhado, -a [afi'ʎadu, a] *m/f* godson/
goddaughter
afim [a'fĩ] (*pl* **-ns**) *adj* (*semelhante*) similar;
(*consangüíneo*) related ▷ *m/f* relative,
relation
afinado, -a [afi'nadu, a] *adj* in tune
afinal [afi'naw] *adv* at last, finally; **~ (de
contas)** after all

afinar [afi'naʀ] *vt* (*Mús*) to tune
afinco [a'fĩku] *m* tenacity, persistence
afins [a'fĩʃ] *pl de* **afim**
afirmação [afixma'sãw] (*pl* **-ões**) *f*
affirmation; (*declaração*) statement
afirmar [afix'maʀ] *vt*, *vi* to affirm, assert;
(*declarar*) to declare
afirmativo, -a [afixma'tʃivu, a] *adj*
affirmative
afixar [afik'saʀ] *vt* (*cartazes*) to stick, post
aflição [afli'sãw] *f* affliction; (*ansiedade*)
anxiety; (*angústia*) anguish
afligir [afli'ʒiʀ] *vt* to distress; (*atormentar*)
to torment; (*inquietar*) to worry; **~-se**
vr: **~-se com** to worry about; **aflito, -a**
[a'flitu, a] *pp de* **afligir** ▷ *adj* distressed,
anxious
afluência [a'flwẽsja] *f* affluence;
(*corrente copiosa*) flow; (*de pessoas*)
stream; **afluente** [a'flwẽtʃi] *adj* copious;
(*rico*) affluent ▷ *m* tributary
afobação [afoba'sãw] *f* fluster;
(*ansiedade*) panic
afobado, -a [afo'badu, a] *adj* flustered;
(*ansioso*) panicky, nervous
afobar [afo'baʀ] *vt* to fluster; (*deixar
ansioso*) to make nervous *ou* panicky ▷ *vi*
to get flustered; to panic, get nervous;
~-se *vr* to get flustered
afogar [afo'gaʀ] *vt* to drown ▷ *vi* (*Auto*) to
flood; **~-se** *vr* to drown
afoito, -a [a'fojtu, a] *adj* bold, daring
afortunado, -a [afoxtu'nadu, a] *adj*
fortunate, lucky
África ['afrika] *f*: **a ~** Africa; **a ~ do Sul**
South Africa; **africano, -a** [afri'kanu, a]
adj, *m/f* African
afro-brasileiro, -a ['afru-] (*pl* **~s**) *adj*
Afro-Brazilian
afronta [a'frõta] *f* insult, affront;
afrontar [afrõ'taʀ] *vt* to insult; (*ofender*)
to offend
afrouxar [afro'ʃaʀ] *vt* (*desapertar*) to
slacken; (*soltar*) to loosen ▷ *vi* to come
loose
afta ['afta] *f* (mouth) ulcer
afugentar [afuʒẽ'taʀ] *vt* to drive away,
put to flight
afundar [afũ'daʀ] *vt* to sink; (*cavidade*) to
deepen; **~-se** *vr* to sink
agachar-se [aga'ʃaxsi] *vr* (*acaçapar-se*) to
crouch, squat; (*curvar-se*) to stoop
agarrar [aga'xaʀ] *vt* to seize, grasp; **~-se**
vr: **~-se a** to cling to, hold on to
agasalhar [agaza'ʎaʀ] *vt* to dress
warmly, wrap up; **~-se** *vr* to wrap o.s. up

agasalho [aga'zaʎu] *m* (*casaco*) coat; (*suéter*) sweater

ágeis ['aʒejʃ] *pl de* **ágil**

agência [a'ʒẽsja] *f* agency; (*escritório*) office; **~ de correio** (*BR*) post office; **~ de viagens** travel agency

agenda [a'ʒẽda] *f* diary; **~ eletrônica** personal organiser

agente [a'ʒẽtʃi] *m/f* agent; (*de polícia*) policeman/woman

ágil ['aʒiw] (*pl* **-eis**) *adj* agile

agir [a'ʒiʳ] *vi* to act

agitação [aʒita'sãw] (*pl* **-ões**) *f* agitation; (*perturbação*) disturbance; (*inquietação*) restlessness

agitado, -a [aʒi'tadu, a] *adj* agitated, disturbed; (*inquieto*) restless

agitar [aʒi'taʳ] *vt* to agitate, disturb; (*sacudir*) to shake; (*cauda*) to wag; (*mexer*) to stir; **~-se** *vr* to get upset; (*mar*) to get rough

aglomeração [aglomera'sãw] (*pl* **-ões**) *f* gathering; (*multidão*) crowd

aglomerar [aglome'raʳ] *vt* to heap up, pile up; **~-se** *vr* (*multidão*) to crowd together

agonia [ago'nia] *f* agony, anguish; (*ânsia da morte*) death throes *pl*; **agonizante** [agoni'zãtʃi] *adj* dying ▷ *m/f* dying person; **agonizar** [agoni'zaʳ] *vi* to be dying; (*afligir-se*) to agonize

agora [a'gɔra] *adv* now; **~ mesmo** right now; (*há pouco*) a moment ago; **até ~** so far, up to now; **por ~** for now

agosto [a'goʃtu] (*PT* **Agosto**) *m* August

agouro [a'goru] *m* omen

agraciar [agra'sjaʳ] *vt* to decorate

agradar [agra'daʳ] *vt* to please; (*fazer agrados a*) to be nice to ▷ *vi* to be pleasing; (*satisfazer*) to go down well

agradável [agra'davew] (*pl* **-eis**) *adj* pleasant

agradecer [agrade'seʳ] *vt*: **~ algo a alguém, ~ a alguém por algo** to thank sb for sth; **agradecido, -a** [agrade'sidu, a] *adj* grateful; **mal agradecido** ungrateful; **agradecimento** [agradesi'mẽtu] *m* gratitude; **agradecimentos** *mpl* (*gratidão*) thanks

agrado [a'gradu] *m*: **fazer um ~ a alguém** (*afagar*) to be affectionate with sb; (*ser agradável*) to be nice to sb

agrário, -a [a'grarju, a] *adj* agrarian; **reforma agrária** land reform

agravante [agra'vãtʃi] *adj* aggravating ▷ *f* aggravating circumstance

agravar [agra'vaʳ] *vt* to aggravate, make worse; **~-se** *vr* (*piorar*) to get worse

agredir [agre'dʒiʳ] *vt* to attack; (*insultar*) to insult

agregar [agre'gaʳ] *vt* (*juntar*) to collect; (*acrescentar*) to add

agressão [agre'sãw] (*pl* **-ões**) *f* aggression; (*ataque*) attack; (*assalto*) assault

agressivo, -a [agre'sivu, a] *adj* aggressive

agressões [agre'sõjʃ] *fpl de* **agressão**

agreste [a'grɛʃtʃi] *adj* rural, rustic; (*terreno*) wild

agrião [a'grjãw] *m* watercress

agrícola [a'grikola] *adj* agricultural

agricultor [agrikuw'toʳ] *m* farmer

agricultura [agrikuw'tura] *f* agriculture, farming

agrido *etc* [a'gridu] *vb ver* **agredir**

agridoce [agri'dosi] *adj* bittersweet

agronegócio [agrone'gɔsju] *m* agribusiness

agronomia [agrono'mia] *f* agronomy

agropecuária [agrope'kwarja] *f* farming, agriculture

agrupar [agru'paʳ] *vt* to group; **~-se** *vr* to group together

agrura [a'grura] *f* bitterness

água ['agwa] *f* water; **águas** *fpl* (*mar*) waters; (*chuvas*) rain *sg*; (*maré*) tides; **~ abaixo/acima** downstream/ upstream; **dar ~ na boca** (*comida*) to be mouthwatering; **estar na ~** (*bêbado*) to be drunk; **fazer ~** (*Náut*) to leak; **~ benta/corrente/doce** holy/running/ fresh water; **~ dura/leve** hard/soft water; **~ mineral** mineral water; **~ oxigenada** peroxide; **~ salgada** salt water; **~ sanitária** household bleach

água-de-coco *f* coconut milk

água-de-colônia (*pl* **águas-de-colônia**) *f* eau-de-cologne

aguado, -a [a'gwadu, a] *adj* watery

aguardar [agwax'daʳ] *vt* to wait for; (*contar com*) to expect ▷ *vi* to wait

aguardente [agwax'dẽtʃi] *m kind of* brandy

aguçado, -a [agu'sadu, a] *adj* pointed; (*espírito, sentidos*) acute

agudo, -a [a'gudu, a] *adj* sharp, shrill; (*intenso*) acute

agüentar [agwẽ'taʳ] *vt* (*muro etc*) to hold up; (*dor, injustiças*) to stand, put up with; (*peso*) to withstand ▷ *vi* to last; **~-se** *vr* to remain, hold on; **~ fazer algo**

to manage to do sth; **não ~ de** not to be able to stand

águia ['agja] f eagle; (fig) genius

agulha [a'guʎa] f (de coser, tricô) needle; (Náut) compass; (Ferro) points pl (BRIT), switch (US); **trabalho de ~** needlework

ai [aj] excl (suspiro) oh!; (de dor) ouch! ▷ m (suspiro) sigh; (gemido) groan; **ai de mim** poor me!

aí [a'i] adv there; (então) then; **por aí** (em lugar indeterminado) somewhere over there, thereabouts; **espera aí!** wait!, hang on a minute!; **está aí!** (col) right!; **e aí?** and then what?

AIDS ['ajdʒs] abr f AIDS

ainda [a'ĩda] adv still; (mesmo) even; **~ agora** just now; **~ assim** even so, nevertheless; **~ bem** just as well; **~ por cima** on top of all that, in addition; **~ não** not yet; **~ que** even if; **maior ~** even bigger

aipo ['ajpu] m celery

ajeitar [aʒej'ta'] vt (roupa, cabelo) to adjust; (emprego) to arrange; **~-se** vr to adapt

ajo etc ['aʒu] vb ver **agir**

ajoelhar [aʒwe'ʎa'] vi to kneel (down); **~-se** vr to kneel down

ajuda [a'ʒuda] f help; (subsídio) grant, subsidy; **dar ~ a alguém** to lend ou give sb a hand; **~ de custo** allowance; **ajudante** [aʒu'dãtʃi] m/f assistant, helper; (Mil) adjutant

ajudar [aʒu'da'] vt to help

ajuizado, -a [aʒwi'zadu, a] adj (sensato) sensible; (sábio) wise; (prudente) discreet

ajuntamento [aʒũta'mẽtu] m gathering

ajustagem [aʒuʃ'taʒẽ] (BR): (pl -ns) f (Tec) adjustment

ajustamento [aʒuʃta'mẽtu] m adjustment; (de contas) settlement

ajustar [aʒuʃ'ta'] vt to adjust; (conta, disputa) to settle; (acomodar) to fit; (roupa) to take in; (preço) to agree on; **~-se a** vr: to conform to; (adaptar-se) to adapt to

ajuste [a'ʒuʃtʃi] m (acordo) agreement; (de contas) settlement; (adaptação) adjustment

ala ['ala] f wing; (fileira) row; (passagem) aisle

alagar [ala'ga'] vt, vi to flood

alameda [ala'meda] f (avenida) avenue; (arvoredo) grove

alarde [a'laxdʒi] m ostentation; (jactância) boasting; **fazer ~ de** to boast about; **alardear** [alax'dʒja'] vt to show off; (gabar-se de) to boast of ▷ vi to show off; to boast; **alardear-se** vr to boast

alargar [alax'ga'] vt to extend; (fazer mais largo) to widen, broaden; (afrouxar) to loosen, slacken

alarma [a'laxma] f alarm; (susto) panic; (tumulto) tumult; (vozearia) outcry; **dar o sinal de ~** to raise the alarm; **~ de roubo** burglar alarm; **alarmante** [alax'mãtʃi] adj alarming; **alarmar** [alax'ma'] vt to alarm; **alarmar-se** vr to be alarmed

alarme [a'laxmi] m = **alarma**

alastrar [alaʃ'tra'] vt to scatter; (disseminar) to spread; **~-se** vr (epidemia, rumor) to spread

alavanca [ala'vãka] f lever; (pé-de-cabra) crowbar; **~ de mudanças** gear lever

albergue [aw'bɛxgi] m (estalagem) inn; (refúgio) hospice, shelter; **~ noturno** hotel; **~ para jovens** youth hostel

álbum ['awbũ] (pl -ns) m album; **~ de recortes** scrapbook

alça ['awsa] f strap; (asa) handle; (de fusil) sight

alcachofra [awka'ʃofra] f artichoke

alcançar [awkã'sa'] vt to reach; (estender) to hand, pass; (obter) to obtain, get; (atingir) to attain; (compreender) to understand; (desfalcar): **~ uma firma em $1 milhão** to embezzle $1 million from a firm

alcance [aw'kãsi] m reach; (competência) power; (compreensão) understanding; (de tiro, visão) range; **ao ~** within reach ou range of; **ao ~ da voz** within earshot; **de grande ~** far-reaching; **fora do ~ da mão** out of reach; **fora do ~ de alguém** beyond sb's grasp

alcaparra [awka'paxa] f caper

alcatrão [awka'trãw] m tar

álcool ['awkow] m alcohol; **alcoólatra** [aw'kɔlatra] m/f alcoholic; **alcoólico, -a** [aw'kɔliku, a] adj, m/f alcoholic

Alcorão [awko'rãw] m Koran

alcova [aw'kova] f bedroom

alcunha [aw'kuɲa] f nickname

aldeão, -eã [aw'dʒjãw, jã] (pl aldeões/ -s) m/f villager

aldeia [aw'deja] f village

aldeões [aw'dʒjõjʃ] mpl de **aldeão**

alecrim [ale'krĩ] m rosemary

alegar [ale'ga'] vt to allege; (Jur) to plead

alegoria [alego'ria] f allegory

alegórico, -a [ale'gɔriku, a] adj

allegorical; **carro ~** float
alegrar [ale'gra^r] vt to cheer (up),
gladden; (ambiente) to brighten up;
(animar) to liven (up); **~-se** vr to cheer up
alegre [a'lεgri] adj cheerful; (contente)
happy, glad; (cores) bright; (embriagado)
merry, tight; **alegria** [ale'gria] f joy,
happiness
aleijado, -a [alej'ʒadu, a] adj crippled
▷ m/f cripple
aleijar [alej'ʒa^r] vt to maim
além [a'lẽj] adv (lá ao longe) over there;
(mais adiante) further on ▷ m: **o ~** the
hereafter ▷ prep: **~ de** beyond; (no outro
lado de) on the other side of; (para mais de)
over; (ademais de) apart from, besides; **~
disso** moreover; **mais ~** further
alemã [ale'mã] f de **alemão**
alemães [ale'mãjʃ] mpl de **alemão**
Alemanha [ale'mãɲa] f: **a ~** Germany
alemão, -mã [ale'mãw, 'mã] (pl
alemães/-s) adj, m/f German ▷ m (Ling)
German
alento [a'lẽtu] m (fôlego) breath; (ânimo)
courage; **dar ~** to encourage; **tomar ~** to
draw breath
alergia [alex'ʒia] f: **~ (a)** allergy (to); (fig)
aversion (to); **alérgico, -a** [a'lεxʒiku,
a] adj: **alérgico (a)** allergic (to); **ele é
alérgico a João/à política** he can't
stand João/politics
alerta [a'lεxta] adj alert ▷ adv on the
alert ▷ m alert
alfabetizar [awfabetʃi'za^r] vt to teach
to read and write; **~-se** vr to learn to read
and write
alfabeto [awfa'betu] m alphabet
alface [aw'fasi] f lettuce
alfaiate [awfa'jatʃi] m tailor
alfândega [aw'fãdʒiga] f customs
pl, customs house; **alfandegário, -a**
[awfãde'garju, a] m/f customs officer
alfazema [awfa'zema] f lavender
alfinete [awfi'netʃi] m pin; **~ de
segurança** safety pin
alga ['awga] f seaweed
Algarve [aw'gaxvi] m: **o ~** the Algarve
algazarra [awga'zaxa] f uproar, racket
álgebra ['awʒebra] f algebra
algemas [aw'ʒemaʃ] fpl handcuffs
algo ['awgu] adv somewhat, rather
▷ pron something; (qualquer coisa)
anything
algodão [awgo'dãw] m cotton; **~
(hidrófilo)** cotton wool (BRIT), absorbent
cotton (US)

alguém [aw'gẽj] pron someone,
somebody; (em frases interrogativas ou
negativas) anyone, anybody
algum, a [aw'gũ, 'guma] (pl **alguns/-s**)
adj some; (em frases interrogativas ou
negativas) any ▷ pron one; (no plural)
some; (negativa): **de modo ~** in no way;
coisa ~a nothing; **~ dia** one day; **~
tempo** for a while; **~a coisa** something;
~a vez sometime
alheio, -a [a'ʎeju, a] adj (de outrem)
someone else's; (estranho) alien;
(estrangeiro) foreign; (impróprio) irrelevant
alho ['aʎu] m garlic
ali [a'li] adv there; **~** up to there; **por
~** around there; (direção) that way; **~ por
(tempo)** round about; **de ~ por diante**
from then on; **~ dentro** in there
aliado, -a [a'ljadu, a] adj allied ▷ m/f ally
aliança [a'ljãsa] f alliance; (anel) wedding
ring
aliar [a'lja^r] vt to ally; **~-se** vr to form an
alliance
aliás [a'ljajʃ] adv (a propósito) as a matter
of fact; (ou seja) rather, that is; (contudo)
nevertheless; (diga-se de passagem)
incidentally
álibi ['alibi] m alibi
alicate [ali'katʃi] m pliers pl; **~ de unhas**
nail clippers pl
alienação [aljena'sãw] f alienation; (de
bens) transfer (of property); **~ mental**
insanity
alienado, -a [alje'nadu, a] adj alienated;
(demente) insane; (bens) transferred ▷ m/f
lunatic
alienar [alje'na^r] vt (afastar) to alienate;
(bens) to transfer
alimentação [alimẽta'sãw] f (alimentos)
food; (ação) feeding; (nutrição)
nourishment; (Elet) supply
alimentar [alimẽ'ta^r] vt to feed; (fig) to
nurture ▷ adj (produto) food atr; (hábitos)
eating atr; **~-se** vr: **~-se de** to feed on
alimento [ali'mẽtu] m food; (nutrição)
nourishment
alisar [ali'za^r] vt to smooth; (cabelo) to
straighten; (acariciar) to stroke
aliviar [ali'vja^r] vt to relieve
alívio [a'livju] m relief
alma ['awma] f soul; (entusiasmo)
enthusiasm; (caráter) character
almejar [awme'ʒa^r] vt to long for, yearn
for
almirante [awmi'rãtʃi] m admiral
almoçar [awmo'sa^r] vi to have lunch

▷ *vt*: **~ peixe** to have fish for lunch

almoço [aw'mosu] *m* lunch; **pequeno ~** (PT) breakfast

almofada [awmo'fada] *f* cushion; (PT: *travesseiro*) pillow

almoxarifado [awmoʃari'fadu] *m* storeroom

alô [a'lo] (BR) *excl* (*Tel*) hullo

alocar [alo'kaʳ] *vt* to allocate

alojamento [aloʒa'mẽtu] *m* accommodation (BRIT), accommodations *pl* (US); (*habitação*) housing

alojar [alo'ʒaʳ] *vt* (*hóspede: numa pensão*) to accommodate; (: *numa casa*) to put up; (*sem teto, refugiado*) to house; (*Mil*) to billet; **~-se** *vr* to stay

alongar [alõ'gaʳ] *vt* to lengthen; (*braço*) to stretch out; (*prazo, contrato*) to extend; (*reunião, sofrimento*) to prolong; **~-se** *vr* (*sobre um assunto*) to dwell

aloprado, -a [alo'pradu, a] (*col*) *adj* nutty

alpendre [aw'pẽdri] *m* (*telheiro*) shed; (*pórtico*) porch

Alpes ['awpiʃ] *mpl*: **os ~** the Alps

alpinismo [awpi'niʒmu] *m* mountaineering, climbing; **alpinista** [awpi'niʃta] *m/f* mountaineer, climber

alta ['awta] *f* (*de preços*) rise; (*de hospital*) discharge

altar [aw'taʳ] *m* altar

alterado, -a [awte'radu, a] *adj* bad-tempered, irritated

alterar [awte'raʳ] *vt* to alter; (*falsificar*) to falsify; **~-se** *vr* to change; (*enfurecer-se*) to get angry, lose one's temper

alternar [awtex'naʳ] *vt, vi* to alternate; **~-se** *vr* to alternate; (*por turnos*) to take turns

alternativa [awtexna'tʃiva] *f* alternative

alternativo, -a [awtexna'tʃivu, a] *adj* alternative; (*Elet*) alternating

alteza [aw'teza] *f* highness

altitude [awtʃi'tudʒi] *f* altitude

alto, -a ['awtu, a] *adj* high; (*pessoa*) tall; (*som*) high, sharp; (*voz*) loud; (*Geo*) upper ▷ *adv* (*falar*) loudly, loud; (*voar*) high ▷ *excl* halt! ▷ *m* top, summit; **do ~** from above; **por ~** superficially; **alta fidelidade** high fidelity, hi-fi; **na alta noite** at dead of night

alto-falante (*pl* **~s**) *m* loudspeaker

altura [aw'tura] *f* height; (*momento*) point, juncture; (*altitude*) altitude; (*de um*

som) pitch; **em que ~ do Rio Branco fica a livraria?** whereabouts in Rio Branco is the bookshop?; **nesta ~** at this juncture; **estar à ~ de** (*ser capaz de*) to be up to; **ter 1.80 metros de ~** to be 1.80 metres (BRIT) *ou* meters (US) tall

alucinado, -a [alusi'nadu, a] *adj* crazy

alucinante [alusi'nãtʃi] *adj* crazy

alugar [alu'gaʳ] *vt* (*tomar de aluguel*) to rent, hire; (*dar de aluguel*) to let, rent out; **~-se** *vr* to let; **aluguel** [alu'gɛw] (*pl* **-éis**) (BR) *m* rent; (*ação*) renting; **aluguel de carro** car hire (BRIT) *ou* rental (US); **aluguer** [alu'gɛʳ] (PT) *m* = **aluguel**

alumínio [alu'minju] *m* aluminium (BRIT), aluminum (US)

aluno, -a [a'lunu, a] *m/f* pupil, student

alvejar [awve'ʒaʳ] *vt* (*tomar como alvo*) to aim at; (*branquear*) to bleach

alvenaria [awvena'ria] *f* masonry; **de ~** brick *atr*, brick-built

alvéolo [aw'vɛolu] *m* cavity

alvo, -a ['awvu, a] *adj* white ▷ *m* target

alvorada [awvo'rada] *f* dawn

alvorecer [awvore'seʳ] *vi* to dawn

alvoroço [awvo'rosu] *m* commotion; (*entusiasmo*) enthusiasm

amabilidade [amabili'dadʒi] *f* kindness; (*simpatia*) friendliness

amaciante [ama'sjatʃi] *m*: **~ (de roupa)** fabric conditioner

amaciar [ama'sjaʳ] *vt* (*tornar macio*) to soften; (*carro*) to run in

amado, -a [a'madu, a] *m/f* beloved, sweetheart

amador, a [ama'doʳ, a] *adj, m/f* amateur

amadurecer [amadure'seʳ] *vt, vi* (*frutos*) to ripen; (*fig*) to mature

âmago ['amagu] *m* (*centro*) heart, core; (*medula*) pith; (*essência*) essence

amalgamar [amawga'maʳ] *vt* to amalgamate; (*combinar*) to fuse (BRIT), fuze (US), blend

amalucado, -a [amalu'kadu, a] *adj* crazy, whacky

amamentar [amamẽ'taʳ] *vt, vi* to breast-feed

amanhã [ama'ɲã] *adv, m* tomorrow

amanhecer [amaɲe'seʳ] *vi* (*alvorecer*) to dawn; (*encontrar-se pela manhã*): **amanhecemos em Paris** we were in Paris at daybreak ▷ *m* dawn; **ao ~** at daybreak

amansar [amã'saʳ] *vt* (*animais*) to tame; (*cavalos*) to break in; (*aplacar*) to placate

amante [a'mãtʃi] *m/f* lover

amar [a'ma^r] vt to love; **eu te amo** I love you

amarelo, -a [ama'rɛlu, a] adj yellow ▷ m yellow

amargar [amax'ga^r] vt to make bitter; (fig) to embitter

amargo, -a [a'maxgu, a] adj bitter; **amargura** [amax'gura] f bitterness

amarrar [ama'xa^r] vt to tie (up); (Náut) to moor; **~ a cara** to frown, scowl

amarrotar [amaxo'ta^r] vt to crease

amassar [ama'sa^r] vt (pão) to knead; (misturar) to mix; (papel) to screw up; (roupa) to crease; (carro) to dent

amável [a'mavew] (pl -eis) adj kind

Amazonas [ama'zonaʃ] m: **o ~** the Amazon

Amazônia [ama'zonja] f: **a ~** the Amazon region

✿ **AMAZÔNIA**

✿
✿ **Amazônia** is the region formed by
✿ the basin of the river Amazon (the
✿ river with the largest volume of water
✿ in the world) and its tributaries.
✿ With a total area of almost 7 million
✿ square kilometres, it stretches from
✿ the Atlantic to the Andes. Most of
✿ **Amazônia** is in Brazilian territory,
✿ although it also extends into Peru,
✿ Colombia, Venezuela and Bolivia. It
✿ contains the richest biodiversity and
✿ largest area of tropical rainforest in
✿ the world.

ambição [ambi'sãw] (pl -ões) f ambition; **ambicionar** [ãbisjo'na^r] vt to aspire to; **ambicioso, -a** [ãbi'sjozu, ɔza] adj ambitious

ambidestro, -a [ãbi'deʃtru, a] adj ambidextrous

ambientar [ãbjē'ta^r] vt (filme etc) to set; (adaptar): **~ alguém a algo** to get sb used to sth; **~-se** vr to fit in

ambiente [ã'bjētʃi] m atmosphere; (meio, Comput) environment; **meio ~** environment; **temperatura ~** room temperature

ambíguo, -a [ã'bigwu, a] adj ambiguous

âmbito ['ãbitu] m extent; (campo de ação) scope, range

ambos, -as ['ãbuʃ, aʃ] adj pl both

ambulância [ãbu'lãsja] f ambulance

ambulante [ãbu'lãtʃi] adj walking; (errante) wandering; (biblioteca) mobile

ambulatório [ãbula'tɔrju] m outpatient department

ameaça [ame'asa] f threat; **ameaçar** [amea'sa^r] vt to threaten

amedrontar [amedrõ'ta^r] vt to scare, intimidate; **~-se** vr to be frightened

ameixa [a'mejʃa] f plum; (passa) prune

amém [a'mēj] excl amen

amêndoa [a'mēdwa] f almond; **amendoeira** [amē'dwejra] f almond tree

amendoim [amēdo'ĩ] (pl -ns) m peanut

amenidade [ameni'dadʒi] f wellbeing; **amenidades** fpl (assuntos superficiais) small talk sg

amenizar [ameni'za^r] vt (abrandar) to soften; (tornar agradável) to make pleasant; (facilitar) to ease

ameno, -a [a'mɛnu, a] adj pleasant; (clima) mild

América [a'mɛrika] f: **a ~** America; **a ~ do Norte/do Sul** North/South America; **a ~ Central/Latina** Central/Latin America; **americano, -a** [ameri'kanu, a] adj, m/f American

amestrar [ameʃ'tra^r] vt to train

amianto [a'mjãtu] m asbestos

amido [a'midu] m starch

amigável [ami'gavew] (pl -eis) adj amicable, friendly

amígdala [a'migdala] f tonsil; **amigdalite** [amigda'litʃi] f tonsillitis

amigo, -a [a'migu, a] adj friendly ▷ m/f friend; **ser ~ de** to be friends with

amistoso, -a [amiʃ'tozu, ɔza] adj friendly, cordial ▷ m (jogo) friendly

amiúde [a'mjudʒi] adv often, frequently

amizade [ami'zadʒi] f (relação) friendship; (simpatia) friendliness

amnistia [amniʃ'tia] (PT) f = **anistia**

amolação [amola'sãw] (pl -ões) f bother, annoyance

amolar [amo'la^r] vt to sharpen; (aborrecer) to annoy, bother ▷ vi to be annoying

amolecer [amole'se^r] vt to soften ▷ vi to soften; (abrandar-se) to relent

amônia [a'monja] f ammonia

amoníaco [amo'niaku] m ammonia

amontoar [amõ'twa^r] vt to pile up, accumulate; **~ riquezas** to amass a fortune

amor [a'mo^r] m love; **por ~ de** for the sake of; **fazer ~** to make love

amora [a'mɔra] f: **~ silvestre** blackberry

amordaçar [amoxda'sa^r] vt to gag

amoroso, -a [amo'rozu, ɔza] *adj* loving, affectionate

amor-perfeito (*pl* **amores-perfeitos**) *m* pansy

amortização [amoxtʃiza'sãw] *f* payment in instalments (BRIT) *ou* installments (US)

amortizar [amoxtʃi'za'] *vt* to pay in instalments (BRIT) *ou* installments (US)

amostra [a'mɔʃtra] *f* sample

amparar [ãpa'ra'] *vt* to support; (*ajudar*) to help, assist; **~-se** *vr*: **~-se em** to lean on

amparo [ã'paru] *m* support; help, assistance

ampliação [amplja'sãw] (*pl* **-ões**) *f* enlargement; (*extensão*) extension

ampliar [ã'plja'] *vt* to enlarge; (*conhecimento*) to broaden

amplificador [ãplifika'do'] *m* amplifier

amplificar [ãplifi'ka'] *vt* to amplify

amplitude [ãpli'tudʒi] *f* (*espaço*) spaciousness; (*fig: extensão*) extent

amplo, -a ['ãplu, a] *adj* (*sala*) spacious; (*conhecimento, sentido*) broad; (*possibilidade*) ample

amputar [ãpu'ta'] *vt* to amputate

Amsterdã [amiʃtex'dã] (BR) *n* Amsterdam

Amsterdão [amiʃtex'dãw] (PT) *n* = **Amsterdã**

amuado, -a [a'mwadu, a] *adj* sulky

anã [a'nã] *f de* **anão**

anais [a'najʃ] *mpl* annals

analfabeto, -a [anawfa'bɛtu, a] *adj, m/f* illiterate

analgésico [anaw'ʒɛziku] *m* painkiller, analgesic

analisar [anali'za'] *vt* to analyse; **análise** [a'nalizi] *f* analysis; **analista** [ana'liʃta] *m/f* analyst

ananás [ana'naʃ] (*pl* **ananases**) *m* (BR) variety of pineapple; (PT) pineapple

anão, -anã [a'nãw, a'nã] (*pl* **anões/-s**) *m/f* dwarf

anarquia [anax'kia] *f* anarchy; **anarquista** [anax'kiʃta] *m/f* anarchist

anatomia [anato'mia] *f* anatomy

anca ['ãka] *f* (*de pessoa*) hip; (*de animal*) rump

ancião, -anciã [ã'sjãw, ã'sjã] (*pl* **anciões/-s**) *adj* old ▷ *m/f* old man/ woman; (*de uma tribo*) elder

anciões [ã'sjõjʃ] *mpl de* **ancião**

âncora ['ãkora] *f* anchor; **ancorar** [ãko'ra'] *vt, vi* to anchor

andaime [ã'dajmi] *m* (*Arq*) scaffolding

andamento [ãda'mẽtu] *m* (*progresso*) progress; (*rumo*) course; (*Mús*) tempo; **em ~** in progress

andar [ã'da'] *vi* to walk; (*máquina*) to work; (*progredir*) to progress; (*estar*): **ela anda triste** she's been sad lately ▷ *m* gait; (*pavimento*) floor, storey (BRIT), story (US); **anda!** hurry up!; **~ a cavalo** to ride; **~ de trem/avião/bicicleta** to travel by train/fly/ride a bike

Andes ['ãdʒiʃ] *mpl*: **os ~** the Andes

andorinha [ãdo'riɲa] *f* (*pássaro*) swallow

anedota [ane'dɔta] *f* anecdote

anel [a'nɛw] (*pl* **-éis**) *m* ring; (*elo*) link; (*de cabelo*) curl; **~ de casamento** wedding ring

anestesia [aneʃte'zia] *f* anaesthesia (BRIT), anesthesia (US); (*anestésico*) anaesthetic (BRIT), anesthetic (US)

anexar [anek'sa'] *vt* to annex; (*juntar*) to attach; (*documento*) to enclose; **anexo, -a** [a'nɛksu, a] *adj* attached ▷ *m* annexe; (*em carta*) enclosure; (*em e-mail*) attachment; **segue em anexo** please find enclosed

anfitrião, -triã [ãfi'trjãw, 'trjã] (*pl* **anfitriões/-s**) *m/f* host/hostess

angina [ã'ʒina] *f*: **~ do peito** angina (pectoris)

Angola [ã'gola] *f* Angola

angu [ã'gu] *m* corn-meal purée

ângulo ['ãgulu] *m* angle; (*canto*) corner

angústia [ã'guʃtʃia] *f* anguish, distress

animado, -a [ani'madu, a] *adj* lively; (*alegre*) cheerful; **~ com** enthusiastic about

animador, a [anima'do', a] *adj* encouraging ▷ *m/f* (BR: TV) presenter

animal [ani'maw] (*pl* **-ais**) *adj, m* animal; **~ de estimação** pet (animal)

animar [ani'ma'] *vt* to liven up; (*encorajar*) to encourage; **~-se** *vr* to cheer up; (*festa etc*) to liven up; **~-se a** to bring o.s. to

ânimo ['animu] *m* (*coragem*) courage; **~!** cheer up!; **perder o ~** to lose heart; **recobrar o ~** to pluck up courage; (*alegrar-se*) to cheer up

aninhar [ani'ɲa'] *vt* to nestle; **~-se** *vr* to nestle

anis [a'niʃ] *m* aniseed

anistia [aniʃ'tʃia] *f* amnesty

aniversário [anivex'sarju] *m* anniversary; (*de nascimento*) birthday; (: *festa*) birthday party

anjo ['ãʒu] *m* angel; **~ da guarda** guardian angel

ano ['anu] *m* year; **Feliz A~ Novo!** Happy New Year!; **o ~ que vem** next year; **por** per annum; **fazer ~s** to have a birthday; **ter dez ~s** to be ten (years old); **dia de ~s** (PT) birthday; **~ letivo** academic year; (*da escola*) school year

anões [a'nõjʃ] *mpl de* **anão**

anoitecer [anojte'se'] *vi* to grow dark ▷ *m* nightfall

anomalia [anoma'lia] *f* anomaly

anônimo, -a [a'nonimu, a] *adj* anonymous

anoraque [ano'raki] *m* anorak

anormal [anox'maw] (*pl* **-ais**) *adj* abnormal; (*excepcional*) handicapped; **anormalidade** [anoxmali'dadʒi] *f* abnormality

anotação [anota'sãw] (*pl* **-ões**) *f* annotation; (*nota*) note

anotar [ano'ta'] *vt* to annotate; (*tomar nota*) to note down

anseio *etc* [ã'seju] *vb ver* **ansiar**

ânsia ['ãsja] *f* anxiety; (*desejo*): **~ (de)** longing (for); **ter ~s (de vômito)** to feel sick

ansiar [ã'sja'] *vi*: **~ por** (*desejar*) to yearn for; **~ por fazer** to long to do

ansiedade [ãsje'dadʒi] *f* anxiety; (*desejo*) eagerness

ansioso, -a [ã'sjozu, ɔza] *adj* anxious; (*desejoso*) eager

Antártico [ã'taxtʃiku] *m*: **o ~** the Antarctic

ante ['ãtʃi] *prep* (*na presença de*) before; (*em vista de*) in view of, faced with

antecedência [ãtese'dẽsja] *f*: **com ~** in advance; **3 dias de ~** three days' notice

antecedente [ãtese'dẽtʃi] *adj* preceding ▷ *m* antecedent; **antecedentes** *mpl* (*registro*) record *sg*; (*passado*) background *sg*

anteceder [ãtese'de'] *vt* to precede

antecipação [ãtesipa'sãw] *f* anticipation; **com um mês de ~** a month in advance; **~ de pagamento** advance (payment)

antecipadamente [ãtesipada'mẽtʃi] *adv* in advance, beforehand

antecipado, -a [ãtesi'padu, a] *adj* (*pagamento*) (in) advance

antecipar [ãtesi'pa'] *vt* to anticipate, forestall; (*adiantar*) to bring forward

antemão [ante'mãw]: **de ~** *adv* beforehand

antena [ã'tena] *f* (*Bio*) antenna, feeler; (*Radio, TV*) aerial

anteontem [ãtʃi'õtẽ] *adv* the day before yesterday

antepassado [ãtʃipa'sadu] *m* ancestor

anterior [ãte'rjo'] *adj* previous; (*antigo*) former; (*de posição*) front

antes ['ãtʃiʃ] *adv* before; (*antigamente*) formerly; (*ao contrário*) rather ▷ *prep*: **~ de** before; **o quanto ~** as soon as possible; **~ de partir** before leaving; **~ de tudo** above all; **~ que** before

anti- [ãtʃi] *prefixo* anti-

antiácido, -a [ã'tʃjasidu, a] *adj* antacid ▷ *m* antacid

antibiótico, -a [ãtʃi'bjɔtʃiku, a] *adj* antibiotic ▷ *m* antibiotic

anticaspa [ãtʃi'kaʃpa] *adj inv*: **xampu ~** dandruff shampoo

anticlímax [ãtʃi'klimaks] *m* anticlimax

anticoncepcional [ãtʃikõsepsjo'naw] (*pl* **-ais**) *adj, m* contraceptive

antidepressivo [ãtʃidepre'sivu] *m* antidepressant

antigamente [ãtʃiga'mẽtʃi] *adv* formerly; (*no passado*) in the past

antiglobalização [ãtʃiglobaliza'sãw] *f* antiglobalization

antigo, -a [ã'tʃigu, a] *adj* old; (*histórico*) ancient; (*de estilo*) antique; (*chefe etc*) former

antiguidade [ãtʃigi'dadʒi] *f* antiquity, ancient times *pl*; (*de emprego*) seniority; **antiguidades** *fpl* (*monumentos*) ancient monuments; (*artigos*) antiques

anti-horário, -a *adj* anticlockwise

antilhano, -a [ãtʃi'ʎanu, a] *adj, m/f* West Indian

Antilhas [ã'tʃiʎaʃ] *fpl*: **as ~** the West Indies

antipatia [ãtʃipa'tʃia] *f* dislike; **antipático, -a** [ãtʃi'patʃiku, a] *adj* unpleasant, unfriendly

antipatizar [ãtʃipatʃi'za'] *vi*: **~ com alguém** to dislike sb

antiquado, -a [ãtʃi'kwadu, a] *adj* antiquated; (*fora de moda*) out of date, old-fashioned

antiquário, -a [ãtʃi'kwarju, a] *m/f* antique dealer ▷ *m* (*loja*) antique shop

anti-semita *adj* anti-Semitic

anti-séptico, -a *adj* antiseptic ▷ *m* antiseptic

anti-social (*pl* **-ais**) *adj* antisocial

antivírus [ãtʃi'viruʃ] *m inv* (*Comput*) antivirus

antologia [ãtolo'ʒia] f anthology

anual [a'nwaw] (pl **-ais**) adj annual, yearly

anulação [anula'sãw] (pl **-ões**) f cancellation; (de contrato, casamento) annulment

anunciante [anũ'sjãtʃi] m (Com) advertiser

anunciar [anũ'sjaʳ] vt to announce; (Com) to advertise

anúncio [a'nũsju] m announcement; (Com) advertisement; (cartaz) notice; **~s classificados** small ou classified ads

ânus ['anuʃ] m inv anus

anzol [ã'zɔw] (pl **-óis**) m fish-hook

ao [aw] = a + o

aonde [a'õdʒi] adv where; **~ quer que** wherever

aos [awʃ] = a + os

Ap. abr = **apartamento**

apagado, -a [apa'gadu, a] adj: **o fogo estava ~/a luz estava apagada** the fire was out/the light was off

apagar [apa'gaʳ] vt to put out; (luz elétrica) to switch off; (vela) to blow out; (com borracha) to rub out, erase; **~-se** vr to go out

apaixonado, -a [apajʃo'nadu, a] adj (discurso) impassioned; (pessoa): **ele está ~ por ela** he is in love with her; **ele é ~ por tênis** he's mad about tennis

apaixonar-se [apajʃo'naxsi] vr: **~ por** to fall in love with

apalpar [apaw'paʳ] vt to touch, feel; (Med) to examine

apanhado [apa'ɲadu] m (de flores) bunch; (resumo) summary

apanhar [apa'ɲaʳ] vt to catch; (algo à mão, do chão) to pick up; (surra, táxi) to get; (flores, frutas) to pick; (agarrar) to grab ▷ vi to get a beating; **~ sol/chuva** to sunbathe/get soaked

aparador [apara'doʳ] m sideboard

apara-lápis [apara'lapiʃ] (PT) m inv pencil sharpener

aparar [apa'raʳ] vt (cabelo) to trim; (lápis) to sharpen; (algo arremessado) to catch

aparato [apa'ratu] m pomp; (coleção) array

aparecer [apare'seʳ] vi to appear; (apresentar-se) to turn up; (ser publicado) to be published; **~ em casa de alguém** to call on sb; **aparecimento** [aparesi'mẽtu] m appearance; (publicação) publication

aparelho [apa'reʎu] m apparatus; (equipamento) equipment; (Pesca) tackle; (máquina) machine; (BR: fone) telephone; **~ de barbear** electric shaver; **~ de chá** tea set; **~ de rádio/TV** radio/TV set; **~ doméstico** domestic appliance

aparência [apa'rẽsja] f appearance; **na ~** apparently; **sob a ~ de** under the guise of; **ter ~ de** to look like, seem

aparentar [aparẽ'taʳ] vt (fingir) to feign; (parecer) to look; **não aparenta a sua idade** he doesn't look his age

aparente [apa'rẽtʃi] adj apparent

aparição [apari'sãw] (pl **-ões**) f (visão) apparition; (fantasma) ghost

apartamento [apaxta'mẽtu] m apartment, flat (BRIT)

apartar [apax'taʳ] vt to separate; **~-se** vr to separate

apatia [apa'tʃia] f apathy

apático, -a [a'patʃiku, a] adj apathetic

apavorado, -a [apavo'radu, a] adj terrified

apavorante [apavo'rãtʃi] adj terrifying

apavorar [apavo'raʳ] vt to terrify ▷ vi to be terrifying; **~-se** vr to be terrified

apear-se [a'pjaxsi] vr: **~ de** (cavalo) to dismount from

apegado, -a [ape'gadu, a] adj: **ser ~ a** (gostar de) to be attached to

apegar-se [ape'gaxsi] vr: **~ a** (afeiçoar-se) to become attached to

apego [a'pegu] m (afeição) attachment

apelar [ape'laʳ] vi to appeal; **~ da sentença** (Jur) to appeal against the sentence; **~ para** to appeal to; **~ para a ignorância/violência** to resort to abuse/violence

apelido [ape'lidu] m (BR: alcunha) nickname; (PT: nome de família) surname

apelo [a'pelu] m appeal

apenas [a'penaʃ] adv only

apendicite [apẽdʒi'sitʃi] f appendicitis

aperfeiçoar [apexfej'swaʳ] vt to perfect; (melhorar) to improve

apertado, -a [apex'tadu, a] adj tight; (estreito) narrow; (sem dinheiro) hard-up; (vida) hard

apertar [apex'taʳ] vt (agarrar) to hold tight; (roupa) to take in; (esponja) to squeeze; (botão) to press; (despesas) to limit; (vigilância) to step up; (coração) to break; (fig: pessoa) to put pressure on ▷ vi (sapatos) to pinch; (chuva, frio) to get worse; (estrada) to narrow; **~ em** (insistir) to insist on; **~ a mão de alguém** to shake hands with sb

aperto [a'pɛxtu] *m* pressure; (*situação difícil*) spot of bother, jam; **um ~ de mãos** a handshake

apesar [ape'zaʳ]: **~ de** *prep* in spite of, despite; **~ disso** nevertheless; **~ de que** even though

apetecer [apete'seʳ] *vi* (*comida*) to be appetizing

apetite [ape'tʃitʃi] *m* appetite; **bom ~!** enjoy your meal!

apetrechos [ape'trɛʃuʃ] *mpl* gear *sg*; (*Pesca*) tackle *sg*

apinhado, -a [api'ɲadu, a] *adj* crowded

apitar [api'taʳ] *vi* to whistle; **apito** [a'pitu] *m* whistle

aplacar [apla'kaʳ] *vt* to placate ▷ *vi* to calm down; **~-se** *vr* to calm down

aplaudir [aplaw'dʒiʳ] *vt* to applaud

aplauso [a'plawzu] *m* applause; (*apoio*) support; (*elogio*) praise; (*aprovação*) approval; **aplausos** applause *sg*

aplicação [aplika'sãw] (*pl* **-ões**) *f* application; (*esforço*) effort; (*da lei*) enforcement; (*de dinheiro*) investment

aplicado, -a [apli'kadu, a] *adj* hard-working

aplicar [apli'kaʳ] *vt* to apply; (*lei*) to enforce; (*dinheiro*) to invest; **~-se** *vr*: **~-se a** to devote o.s. to

apoderar-se [apode'raxsi] *vr*: **~ de** to seize, take possession of

apodrecer [apodre'seʳ] *vt* to rot; (*dente*) to decay ▷ *vi* to rot; to decay

apogeu [apo'ʒew] *m* (*fig*) height, peak

apoiar [apo'jaʳ] *vt* to support; (*basear*) to base; (*moção*) to second; **~-se** *vr*: **~-se em** to rest on

apoio [a'poju] *m* support; (*financeiro*) backing

apólice [a'pɔlisi] *f* (*certificado*) policy, certificate; (*ação*) share, bond; **~ de seguro** insurance policy

apontamento [apõta'mẽtu] *m* (*nota*) note

apontar [apõ'taʳ] *vt* (*fusil*) to aim; (*erro*) to point out; (*com o dedo*) to point at ou to; (*razão*) to put forward ▷ *vi* to begin to appear; (*brotar*) to sprout; (*com o dedo*) to point; **~ para** to point to; (*com arma*) to aim at

após [a'pɔjʃ] *prep* after

aposentado, -a [apozẽ'tadu, a] *adj* retired ▷ *m/f* retired person, pensioner; **ser ~** to be retired; **aposentadoria** [apozẽtado'ria] *f* retirement; (*dinheiro*) pension

aposentar [apozẽ'taʳ] *vt* to retire; **~-se** *vr* to retire

aposento [apo'zẽtu] *m* room

apossar-se [apo'saxsi] *vr*: **~ de** to take possession of, seize

apostar [apoʃ'taʳ] *vt* to bet ▷ *vi*: **~ em** to bet on

apóstrofo [a'pɔʃtrofu] *m* apostrophe

apreciar [apre'sjaʳ] *vt* to appreciate; (*gostar de*) to enjoy

apreço [a'presu] *m* esteem, regard; (*consideração*) consideration; **em ~** in question

apreender [aprjẽ'deʳ] *vt* to apprehend; (*tomar*) to seize; (*entender*) to grasp

apreensão [aprjẽ'sãw] (*pl* **-ões**) *f* (*percepção*) perception; (*tomada*) seizure; (*receio*) apprehension

apreensivo, -a [aprjẽ'sivu, a] *adj* apprehensive

apreensões [aprjẽ'sõjʃ] *fpl de* **apreensão**

apregoar [apre'gwaʳ] *vt* to proclaim, announce; (*mercadorias*) to cry

aprender [aprẽ'deʳ] *vt, vi* to learn; **~ a ler** to learn to read; **~ de cor** to learn by heart

aprendizagem [aprẽdʒi'zaʒẽ] *f* (*num ofício*) apprenticeship; (*numa profissão*) training; (*escolar*) learning

apresentação [aprezẽta'sãw] (*pl* **-ões**) *f* presentation; (*de peça, filme*) performance; (*de pessoas*) introduction; (*porte pessoal*) appearance

apresentador, a [aprezẽta'doʳ, a] *m/f* presenter

apresentar [aprezẽ'taʳ] *vt* to present; (*pessoas*) to introduce; **~-se** *vr* to introduce o.s.; (*problema*) to present itself; (*à polícia etc*) to report; **quero ~-lhe** may I introduce you to

apressado, -a [apre'sadu, a] *adj* hurried, hasty; **estar ~** to be in a hurry

apressar [apre'saʳ] *vt* to hurry; **~-se** *vr* to hurry (up)

aprisionar [aprizjo'naʳ] *vt* (*cativar*) to capture; (*encarcerar*) to imprison

aprontar [aprõ'taʳ] *vt* to get ready, prepare; **~-se** *vr* to get ready

apropriado, -a [apro'prjadu, a] *adj* appropriate, suitable

aprovado, -a [apro'vadu, a] *adj* approved; **ser ~ num exame** to pass an exam

aprovar [apro'vaʳ] *vt* to approve of; (*exame*) to pass ▷ *vi* to make the grade

aproveitador, a [aprovejta'do^r, a] m/f
opportunist
aproveitamento [aprovejta'mẽtu] m
use, utilization; (nos estudos) progress
aproveitar [aprovej'ta^r] vt to
take advantage of; (utilizar) to use;
(oportunidade) to take ▷ vi to make the
most of it; (PT) to be of use; **aproveite!**
enjoy yourself!
aproximação [aprosima'sãw] (pl -ões)
f approximation; (chegada) approach;
(proximidade) nearness
aproximar [aprosi'ma^r] vt to bring near;
(aliar) to bring together; **~-se** vr: **~-se de**
to approach
aptidão [aptʃi'dãw] f aptitude; (jeito)
knack; **~ física** physical fitness
apto, -a ['aptu, a] adj apt; (capaz) capable
apto. abr = **apartamento**
apunhalar [apuɲa'la^r] vt to stab
apurado, -a [apu'radu, a] adj refined
apurar [apu'ra^r] vt to perfect; (averiguar)
to investigate; (dinheiro) to raise, get;
(votos) to count; **~-se** vr to dress up
aquarela [akwa'rɛla] f watercolour
(BRIT), watercolor (US)
aquário [a'kwarju] m aquarium; **A~**
(Astrologia) Aquarius
aquático, -a [a'kwatʃiku, a] adj aquatic,
water atr
aquecer [ake'se^r] vt to heat ▷ vi to heat
up; **~-se** vr to heat up; **aquecido, -a**
[ake'sidu, a] adj heated; **aquecimento**
[akesi'mẽtu] m heating; **aquecimento
central** central heating; **aquecimento
global** global warming
aquele, -ela [a'keli, ɛla] adj (sg) that; (pl)
those ▷ pron (sg) that one; (pl) those
àquele, -ela [a'keli, ɛla] = a + **aquele/
ela**
aquém [a'kẽj] adv on this side; **~ de** on
this side of
aqui [a'ki] adv here; **eis ~** here is/are; **~
mesmo** right here; **até ~** up to here; **por
~** hereabouts; (nesta direção) this way
aquilo [a'kilu] pron that; **~ que** what
àquilo [a'kilu] = a + **aquilo**
aquisição [akizi'sãw] (pl -ões) f
acquisition
ar [a^r] m air; (aspecto) look; (brisa) breeze;
(PT: Auto) choke; **ares** mpl (atitude) airs;
(clima) climate sg; **ao ar livre** in the open
air; **no ar** (TV, Rádio) on air; (fig: planos) up
in the air; **dar-se ares** to put on airs; **ar
condicionado** (aparelho) air conditioner;
(sistema) air conditioning

árabe ['arabi] adj, m/f Arab ▷ m (Ling)
Arabic
Arábia [a'rabja] f: **a ~ Saudita** Saudi
Arabia
arame [a'rami] m wire
aranha [a'raɲa] f spider
arara [a'rara] f macaw
arbitragem [axbi'traʒẽ] f arbitration
arbitrar [axbi'tra^r] vt to arbitrate;
(Esporte) to referee
arbitrário, -a [axbi'trarju, a] adj
arbitrary
arbítrio [ax'bitrju] m decision; **ao ~ de**
at the discretion of
árbitro ['axbitru] m (juiz) arbiter; (Jur)
arbitrator; (Futebol) referee; (Tênis etc)
umpire
arbusto [ax'buʃtu] m shrub, bush
arca ['axka] f chest, trunk; **~ de Noé**
Noah's Ark
arcar [ax'ka^r] vt: **~ com** (responsabilidades)
to shoulder; (despesas) to handle;
(conseqüencias) to take
arcebispo [arse'biʃpu] m archbishop
arco ['axku] m (Arq) arch; (Mil, Mús) bow;
(Elet, Mat) arc
arco-íris m inv rainbow
arder [ax'de^r] vi to burn; (pele, olhos) to
sting; **~ de raiva** to seethe (with rage)
ardiloso, -a [axdʒi'lozu, ɔza] adj
cunning
ardor [ax'do^r] m ardour (BRIT), ardor (US);
ardoroso, -a [axdo'rozu, ɔza] adj ardent
árduo, -a ['axdwu, a] adj arduous; (difícil)
hard, difficult
área ['arja] f area; (Esporte) penalty area;
(fig) field; **~ (de serviço)** balcony (for
hanging washing etc)
areia [a'reja] f sand; **~ movediça**
quicksand
arejar [are'ʒa^r] vt to air ▷ vi to get some
air; (descansar) to have a breather; **~-se** vr
to get some air; to have a break
arena [a'rɛna] f arena; (de circo) ring
Argélia [ax'ʒɛlja] f: **a ~** Algeria
Argentina [axʒẽ'tʃina] f: **a ~** Argentina
argila [ax'ʒila] f clay
argola [ax'gola] f ring; **argolas** fpl
(brincos) hooped earrings; **~ (de porta)**
door-knocker
argumentação [axgumẽta'sãw] f line
of argument
argumentar [axgumẽ'ta^r] vt, vi to argue
argumento [axgu'mẽtu] m argument;
(de obra) theme
aridez [ari'deʒ] f dryness; (esterilidade)

barrenness; (*falta de interesse*) dullness

árido, -a ['aridu, a] *adj* arid, dry; (*estéril*) barren; (*maçante*) dull

Áries ['arif] *f* Aries

aritmética [aritʃ'mɛtʃika] *f* arithmetic

arma ['axma] *f* weapon; **armas** *fpl* (*nucleares etc*) arms; (*brasão*) coat *sg* of arms; **passar pelas ~s** to shoot, execute; **~ convencional/nuclear** conventional/nuclear weapon; **~ de fogo** firearm; **~s de destruição em massa** weapons of mass destruction

armação [axma'sãw] (*pl* **-ões**) *f* (*armadura*) frame; (*Pesca*) tackle; (*Náut*) rigging; (*de óculos*) frames *pl*

armado, -a [ax'madu, a] *adj* armed

armar [ax'maʳ] *vt* to arm; (*montar*) to assemble; (*barraca*) to pitch; (*um aparelho*) to set up; (*armadilha*) to set; (*Náut*) to fit out; **~-se** *vr* to arm o.s.; **~ uma briga com** to pick a quarrel with

armarinho [axma'riɲu] *m* haberdashery (BRIT), notions *pl* (US)

armário [ax'marju] *m* cupboard; (*de roupa*) wardrobe

armazém [axma'zẽj] (*pl* **-ns**) *m* (*depósito*) warehouse; (*loja*) grocery store;

armazenar [axmaze'naʳ] *vt* to store; (*provisões*) to stock

aro ['aru] *m* (*argola*) ring; (*de óculos, roda*) rim; (*de porta*) frame

aroma [a'rɔma] *m* aroma; **aromático, -a** [aro'matʃiku, a] *adj* (*comida*) aromatic; (*perfume*) fragrant

arpão [ax'pãw] (*pl* **-ões**) *m* harpoon

arqueiro, -a [ax'kejru, a] *m/f* archer; (*goleiro*) goalkeeper

arqueologia [axkjolo'ʒia] *f* archaeology (BRIT), archeology (US); **arqueólogo, -a** [ax'kjɔlogu, a] *m/f* archaeologist (BRIT), archeologist (US)

arquiteto, -a [axki'tɛtu, a] (*PT* **-ect-**) *m/f* architect; **arquitetônico, -a** [axkite'toniku, a] (*PT* **-ectó-**) *adj* architectural; **arquitetura** [axkite'tura] (*PT* **-ect-**) *f* architecture

arquivar [axki'vaʳ] *vt* to file; (*projeto*) to shelve

arquivo [ax'kivu] *m* (*ger, Comput*) file; (*lugar*) archive; (*de empresa*) files *pl*; (*móvel*) filing cabinet; **~ zipado** (*Comput*) zip file

arraial [axa'jaw] (*pl* **-ais** (*PT*)) *m* (*festa*) fair

arrancada [axã'kada] *f* (*movimento, puxão*) jerk; **dar uma ~ em** (*puxar*) to

jerk; **dar uma ~** (*em carro*) to pull away (suddenly)

arrancar [axã'kaʳ] *vt* to pull out; (*botão etc*) to pull off; (*arrebatar*) to snatch (away); (*fig: confissão*) to extract ▷ *vi* to start (off); **~-se** *vr* to leave; (*fugir*) to run off

arranha-céu [a'xaɲa-] (*pl* **~s**) *m* skyscraper

arranhão [axa'ɲãw] (*pl* **-ões**) *m* scratch

arranhar [axa'ɲaʳ] *vt* to scratch

arranjar [axã'ʒaʳ] *vt* to arrange; (*emprego etc: emprego, namorado*) to get, find, to find; (*doença*) to get, catch; (*questão*) to settle; **~-se** *vr* to manage; (*conseguir emprego*) to get a job; **~-se sem** to do without

arranjo [a'xãʒu] *m* arrangement

arrasar [axa'zaʳ] *vt* to devastate; (*demolir*) to demolish; (*estragar*) to ruin; **~-se** *vr* to be devastated; (*destruir-se*) to destroy o.s.; (*arruinar-se*) to lose everything

arrastão [axaʃ'tãw] (*pl* **-ões**) *m* tug; (*rede*) dragnet

arrastar [axaʃ'taʳ] *vt* to drag; (*atrair*) to draw ▷ *vi* to trail; **~-se** *vr* to crawl; (*tempo, processo*) to drag (on)

arrebatado, -a [axeba'tadu, a] *adj* rash, impetuous

arrebatar [axeba'taʳ] *vt* to snatch (away); (*levar*) to carry off; (*enlevar*) to entrance; (*enfurecer*) to enrage; **~-se** *vr* to be entranced

arrebentado, -a [axebẽ'tadu, a] *adj* broken; (*estafado*) worn out

arrebentar [axebẽ'taʳ] *vt* to break; (*porta*) to break down; (*corda*) to snap ▷ *vi* to break; (*corda*) to snap; (*guerra*) to break out

arrebitado, -a [axebi'tadu, a] *adj* turned-up; (*nariz*) snub

arrecadar [axeka'daʳ] *vt* (*impostos etc*) to collect

arredondado, -a [axedõ'dadu, a] *adj* round, rounded

arredondar [axedõ'daʳ] *vt* to round (off); (*conta*) to round up

arredores [axe'dɔriʃ] *mpl* suburbs; (*cercanias*) outskirts

arrefecer [axefe'seʳ] *vt* to cool; (*febre*) to lower; (*desanimar*) to discourage ▷ *vi* to cool (off); to get discouraged

ar-refrigerado [-xefriʒe'radu] *m* air conditioning

arregaçar [axega'saʳ] *vt* to roll up

arregalado, -a [axega'ladu, a] *adj* (*olhos*) wide

arregalar [axega'la'] *vt*: **~ os olhos** to stare in amazement

arrematar [axema'ta'] *vt* (*dizer concluindo*) to conclude; (*comprar*) to buy by auction; (*vender*) to sell by auction; (*Costura*) to finish off

arremessar [axeme'sa'] *vt* to throw, hurl; **arremesso** [axe'mesu] *m* throw

arremeter [axeme'te'] *vi* to lunge; **~ contra** (*acometer*) to attack, assail

arrendar [axē'da'] *vt* to lease

arrepender-se [axepē'dexsi] *vr* to repent; (*mudar de opinião*) to change one's mind; **~ de** to regret, be sorry for; **arrependido, -a** [axepē'dʒidu, a] *adj* (*pessoa*) sorry; **arrependimento** [axepēdʒi'mētu] *m* regret; (*Rel, de crime*) repentance

arrepiar [axe'pja'] *vt* (*amedrontar*) to horrify; (*cabelo*) to cause to stand on end; **~-se** *vr* to shiver; (*cabelo*) to stand on end; **(ser) de ~ os cabelos** (to be) hair-raising

arrepio [axe'piu] *m* shiver; (*de frio*) chill; **isso me dá ~s** it gives me the creeps

arriar [a'xja'] *vt* to lower; (*depor*) to lay down ▷ *vi* to drop; (*vergar*) to sag; (*desistir*) to give up; (*fig*) to collapse

arriscado, -a [axiʃ'kadu, a] *adj* risky; (*audacioso*) daring

arriscar [axiʃ'ka'] *vt* to risk; (*pôr em perigo*) to endanger, jeopardize; **~-se** *vr* to take a risk; **~-se a fazer** to risk doing

arrogante [axo'gātʃi] *adj* arrogant

arrojado, -a [axo'ʒadu, a] *adj* (*design*) bold; (*temerário*) rash; (*ousado*) daring

arrolar [axo'la'] *vt* to list

arrombar [axõ'ba'] *vt* (*porta*) to break down; (*cofre*) to crack

arrotar [axo'ta'] *vi* to belch ▷ *vt* (*alardear*) to boast of

arroz [a'xoʒ] *m* rice; **~ doce** rice pudding

arruinar [axwi'na'] *vt* to ruin; (*destruir*) to destroy; **~-se** *vr* to be ruined; (*perder a saúde*) to ruin one's health

arrumação [axuma'sãw] *f* arrangement; (*de um quarto etc*) tidying up; (*de malas*) packing

arrumadeira [axuma'dejra] *f* cleaning lady; (*num hotel*) chambermaid

arrumar [axu'ma'] *vt* to put in order, arrange; (*quarto etc*) to tidy up; (*malas*) to pack; (*emprego*) to get; (*vestir*) to dress up; (*desculpa*) to make up, find; (*vida*) to sort

out; **~-se** *vr* (*aprontar-se*) to get dressed, get ready; (*na vida*) to sort o.s. out; (*virar-se*) to manage

arte ['axtʃi] *f* art; (*habilidade*) skill; (*ofício*) trade, craft

artefato [axtʃi'fatu] (*PT* **-act-**) *m* (manufactured) article

artéria [ax'terja] *f* (*Anat*) artery

artesão, -sã [axte'zãw, zã] (*pl* **~s/-s**) *m/f* artisan, craftsman/woman

ártico, -a ['axtʃiku, a] *adj* Arctic ▷ *m*: **o Ártico** the Arctic

artificial [axtʃifi'sjaw] (*pl* **-ais**) *adj* artificial

artifício [axtʃi'fisju] *m* stratagem, trick

artigo [ax'tʃigu] *m* article; (*Com*) item; **artigos** *mpl* (*produtos*) goods

artista [ax'tʃiʃta] *m/f* artist; **artístico, -a** [ax'tʃiʃtʃiku, a] *adj* artistic

artrite [ax'tritʃi] *f* (*Med*) arthritis

árvore ['axvori] *f* tree; (*Tec*) shaft; **~ de Natal** Christmas tree

as [aʃ] *art def ver* **a**

ás [ajʃ] *m* ace

às [ajʃ] = **a + as**

asa ['aza] *f* wing; (*de xícara etc*) handle

ascendência [asē'dēsja] *f* (*antepassados*) ancestry; (*domínio*) ascendancy, sway; **ascendente** [asē'dētʃi] *adj* rising, upward

ascender [asē'de'] *vi* to rise, ascend

ascensão [asē'sãw] (*pl* **-ões**) *f* ascent; (*Rel*): **dia da A~** Ascension Day

asco ['aʃku] *m* loathing, revulsion; **dar ~ a** to revolt, disgust

asfalto [aʃ'fawtu] *m* asphalt

asfixia [aʃfik'sia] *f* asphyxia, suffocation

Ásia ['azja] *f*: **a ~** Asia

asiático, -a [a'zjatʃiku, a] *adj, m/f* Asian

asilo [a'zilu] *m* (*refúgio*) refuge; (*estabelecimento*) home; **~ político** political asylum

asma ['aʒma] *f* asthma

asneira [aʒ'nejra] *f* (*tolice*) stupidity; (*ato, dito*) stupid thing

asno ['aʒnu] *m* donkey; (*fig*) ass

aspas ['aʃpaʃ] *fpl* inverted commas

aspecto [aʃ'pɛktu] *m* aspect; (*aparência*) look, appearance; (*característica*) feature; (*ponto de vista*) point of view

aspereza [aʃpe'reza] *f* roughness; (*severidade*) harshness; (*rudeza*) rudeness

áspero, -a ['aʃperu, a] *adj* rough; (*severo*) harsh; (*rude*) rude

aspiração [aʃpira'sãw] (*pl* **-ões**) *f* aspiration; (*inalação*) inhalation

aspirador [aʃpira'doʳ] *m*: **~ (de pó)** vacuum cleaner; **passar o ~ (em)** to vacuum

aspirante [aʃpi'rãtʃi] *adj* aspiring ▷ *m/f* candidate

aspirar [aʃpi'raʳ] *vt* to breathe in; (*bombear*) to suck up ▷ *vi* to breathe; (*soprar*) to blow; (*desejar*): **~ a algo** to aspire to sth

aspirina [aʃpi'rina] *f* aspirin

asqueroso, -a [aʃke'rozu, ɔza] *adj* disgusting, revolting

assado, -a [a'sadu, a] *adj* roasted; (*Culin*) roast ▷ *m* roast; **carne assada** roast beef

assaltante [asaw'tãtʃi] *m/f* assailant; (*de banco*) robber; (*de casa*) burglar; (*na rua*) mugger

assaltar [asaw'taʳ] *vt* to attack; (*casa*) to break into; (*banco*) to rob; (*pessoa na rua*) to mug; **assalto** [a'sawtu] *m* attack; raid, robbery; burglary, break-in; mugging; (*Boxe*) round

assar [a'saʳ] *vt* to roast; (*na grelha*) to grill

assassinar [asasi'naʳ] *vt* to murder, kill; (*Pol*) to assassinate; **assassinato** [asasi'natu] *m* murder, killing; assassination; **assassino, -a** [asa'sinu, a] *m/f* murderer; assassin

assaz [a'saʒ] *adv* (*suficientemente*) sufficiently; (*muito*) rather

assediar [ase'dʒjaʳ] *vt* (*sitiar*) to besiege; (*importunar*) to pester; **assédio** [a'sɛdʒu] *m* siege; (*insistência*) insistence

assegurar [asegu'raʳ] *vt* to secure; (*garantir*) to ensure; (*afirmar*) to assure; **~-se** *vr*: **~-se de** to make sure of

asseio [a'seju] *m* cleanliness

assembléia [asē'blɛja] *f* assembly; (*reunião*) meeting; **~ geral (ordinária)** annual general meeting

assentar [asē'taʳ] *vt* (*fazer sentar*) to seat; (*colocar*) to place; (*estabelecer*) to establish; (*decidir*) to decide upon ▷ *vi* (*pó etc*) to settle; **~-se** *vr* to sit down; **~ em** *ou* **a** (*roupa*) to suit

assentir [asē'tʃiʳ] *vi*: **~ (em)** to agree (to)

assento [a'sētu] *m* seat; (*base*) base

assíduo, -a [a'sidwu, a] *adj* (*aluno*) who attends regularly; (*diligente*) assiduous; (*constante*) constant; **ser ~ num lugar** to be a regular visitor to a place

assim [a'sī] *adv* (*deste modo*) like this, in this way, thus; (*portanto*) therefore; (*igualmente*) likewise; **~ ~** so-so; **~ mesmo** in any case; **e ~ por diante** and so on; **~**

como as well as; **como ~?** how do you mean?; **~ que** (*logo que*) as soon as

assimilar [asimi'laʳ] *vt* to assimilate; (*apreender*) to take in; (*assemelhar*) to compare

assinante [asi'nãtʃi] *m/f* (*de jornal etc*) subscriber

assinar [asi'naʳ] *vt* to sign

assinatura [asina'tura] *f* (*nome*) signature; (*de jornal etc*) subscription; (*Teatro*) season ticket

assinto *etc* [a'sĩtu] *vb ver* **assentir**

assistência [asiʃ'tēsja] *f* (*presença*) presence; (*público*) audience; (*auxílio*) aid; **~ social** social work

assistente [asiʃ'tētʃi] *adj* assistant ▷ *m/f* spectator, onlooker; (*ajudante*) assistant; **~ social** social worker

assistir [asiʃ'tʃiʳ] *vt, vi*: **~ (a)** (*Med*) to attend (to); **~ a** to assist; (*TV, filme, jogo*) to watch; (*reunião*) to attend

assoar [aso'aʳ] *vt*: **~ o nariz** to blow one's nose; **~-se** *vr* (*PT*) to blow one's nose

assobiar [aso'bjaʳ] *vi* to whistle

assobio [aso'biu] *m* whistle

associação [asosja'sãw] (*pl* **-ões**) *f* association; (*organização*) society; (*parceria*) partnership

associado, -a [aso'sjadu, a] *adj* associate ▷ *m/f* associate, member; (*Com*) associate; (*sócio*) partner

associar [aso'sjaʳ] *vt* to associate; **~-se** *vr*: **~-se a** to associate with

assombração [asõbra'sãw] (*pl* **-ões**) *f* ghost

assombro [a'sõbru] *m* amazement, astonishment; (*maravilha*) marvel; **assombroso, -a** [asõ'brozu, ɔza] *adj* astonishing, amazing

assoviar [aso'vjaʳ] *vt* = **assobiar**

assovio [aso'viu] *m* = **assobio**

assumir [asu'miʳ] *vt* to assume, take on; (*reconhecer*) to accept

assunto [a'sũtu] *m* subject, matter; (*enredo*) plot

assustador, a [asuʃta'doʳ, a] *adj* (*alarmante*) startling; (*amedrontador*) frightening

assustar [asuʃ'taʳ] *vt* to frighten; (*alarmar*) to startle; **~-se** *vr* to be frightened

asteca [aʃ'tɛka] *adj, m/f* Aztec

astrologia [aʃtrolo'ʒia] *f* astrology

astronauta [aʃtro'nawta] *m/f* astronaut

astronave [aʃtro'navi] *f* spaceship

astronomia [aʃtrono'mia] *f* astronomy

astúcia [aʃ'tusja] f cunning

ata ['ata] f (de reunião) minutes pl

atacado [ata'kadu] m: **por ~** wholesale

atacante [ata'kãtʃi] adj attacking ▷ m/f attacker, assailant ▷ m (Futebol) forward

atacar [ata'kaʳ] vt to attack; (problema etc) to tackle

atado, -a [a'tadu, a] adj (desajeitado) clumsy, awkward; (perplexo) puzzled

atalho [a'taʎu] m (caminho) short cut

ataque [a'taki] m attack; **~ aéreo** air raid; **~ suicida** suicide attack

atar [a'taʳ] vt to tie (up), fasten; **não ~ nem desatar** (pessoa) to waver; (negócio) to be in the air

atarefado, -a [atare'fadu, a] adj busy

atarracado, -a [ataxa'kadu, a] adj stocky

até [a'tɛ] prep (PT: + a: lugar) up to, as far as; (tempo etc) until, till ▷ adv (tb: **~ mesmo**) even; **~ certo ponto** to a certain extent; **~ em cima** to the top; **~ já** see you soon; **~ logo** bye!; **~ onde** as far as; **~ que** until; **~ que enfim!** at last!

atear [ate'aʳ] vt (fogo) to kindle; (fig) to incite, inflame; **~-se** vr to blaze; (paixões) to flare up

atéia [a'tɛja] f de **ateu**

atemorizar [atemori'zaʳ] vt to frighten; (intimidar) to intimidate

Atenas [a'tenaʃ] n Athens

atenção [atẽ'sãw] (pl -ões) f attention; (cortesia) courtesy; (bondade) kindness; **~!** be careful!; **chamar a ~** to attract attention; **atencioso, -a** [atẽ'sjozu, ɔza] adj considerate

atender [atẽ'deʳ] vt: **~ (a)** to attend to; (receber) to receive; (deferir) to grant; (telefone etc) to answer; (paciente) to see ▷ vi to answer; (dar atenção) to pay attention; **atendimento** [atẽdʒi'mẽtu] m service; (recepção) reception; **horário de atendimento** opening hours; (em consultório) surgery (BRIT) ou office (US) hours

atentado [atẽ'tadu] m attack; (crime) crime; (contra a vida de alguém) attempt on sb's life; **~ suicida** suicide attack

atento, -a [a'tẽtu, a] adj attentive; **estar ~ a** to be aware ou mindful of

atenuante [ate'nwãtʃi] adj extenuating ▷ m extenuating circumstance

atenuar [ate'nwaʳ] vt to reduce, lessen

aterragem [ate'xaʒẽj] (PT): (pl -ns) f (Aer) landing

aterrar [ate'xaʳ] (PT) vi (Aer) to land

aterrissagem [atexi'saʒẽ] (BR): (pl -ns) f (Aer) landing

aterrissar [atexi'saʳ] (BR) vi (Aer) to land

aterrorizante [atexori'zãtʃi] adj terrifying

aterrorizar [atexori'zaʳ] vt to terrorize

atestado [ateʃ'tadu] m certificate; (prova) proof; (Jur) testimony

ateu, -atéia [a'tew, a'tɛja] adj, m/f atheist

atinar [atʃi'naʳ] vt (acertar) to guess correctly ▷ vi: **~ com** (solução) to find; **~ em** to notice; **~ a fazer algo** to succeed in doing sth

atingir [atʃĩ'ʒiʳ] vt to reach; (acertar) to hit; (afetar) to affect; (objetivo) to achieve; (compreender) to grasp

atirador, a [atʃira'doʳ, a] m/f marksman/woman; **~ de tocaia** sniper

atirar [atʃi'raʳ] vt to throw, fling ▷ vi (arma) to shoot; **~-se** vr: **~-se a** to hurl o.s. at

atitude [atʃi'tudʒi] f attitude; (postura) posture

atividade [atʃivi'dadʒi] f activity

ativo, -a [a'tʃivu, a] adj active ▷ m (Com) assets pl

atlântico, -a [at'lãtʃiku, a] adj Atlantic ▷ m: **o (Oceano) A~** the Atlantic (Ocean)

atlas ['atlaʃ] m inv atlas

atleta [at'lɛta] m/f athlete; **atlético, -a** [at'lɛtʃiku, a] adj athletic; **atletismo** [atle'tʃiʒmu] m athletics sg

atmosfera [atmoʃ'fera] f atmosphere

ato ['atu] m act, action; (cerimônia) ceremony; (Teatro) act; **em ~ contínuo** straight after; **no ~** on the spot; **no mesmo ~** at the same time

à-toa adj (insignificante) insignificant; (simples) simple, easy ▷ adv ver **toa**

atômico, -a [a'tomiku, a] adj atomic

átomo ['atomu] m atom

atônito, -a [a'tonitu, a] adj astonished, amazed

ator [a'toʳ] m actor

atordoado, -a [atox'dwadu, a] adj dazed

atordoar [atox'dwaʳ] vt to daze, stun

atormentar [atoxmẽ'taʳ] vt to torment

atração [atra'sãw] (pl -ões) f attraction

atracar [atra'kaʳ] vt, vi (Náut) to moor; **~-se** vr to grapple

atrações [atra'sõjʃ] fpl de **atração**

atractivo, -a [atra'tivu, a] (PT) adj = **atrativo**

atraente [atra'ẽtʃi] adj attractive

atrair [atra'i^r] vt to attract; (*fascinar*) to fascinate

atrapalhar [atrapa'ʎa^r] vt to confuse; (*perturbar*) to disturb; (*dificultar*) to hinder ▷ vi to be a nuisance

atrás [a'trajʃ] adv behind; (*no fundo*) at the back ▷ prep: **~ de** behind; (*no tempo*) after; **dois meses ~** two months ago

atrasado, -a [atra'zadu, a] adj late; (*país etc*) backward; (*relógio etc*) slow; (*pagamento*) overdue; **atrasados** [atra'zaduʃ] mpl (*Com*) arrears

atrasar [atra'za^r] vt to delay; (*progresso, desenvolvimento: progresso*) to hold back; (*relógio*) to put back; (*pagamento*) to be late with ▷ vi (*relógio etc*) to be slow; (*avião, pessoa*) to be late; **~-se** vr to be late; (*num trabalho*) to fall behind; (*num pagamento*) to get into arrears

atraso [a'trazu] m delay; (*de país etc*) backwardness; **atrasos** mpl (*Com*) arrears; **com 20 minutos de ~** 20 minutes late

atrativo, -a [atra'tʃivu, a] adj attractive ▷ m attraction; (*incentivo*) incentive; **atrativos** mpl (*encantos*) charms

através [atra'vɛʃ] adv across; **~ de** across; (*pelo centro de*) through

atravessar [atrave'sa^r] vt to cross; (*pôr ao través*) to put ou lay across; (*traspassar*) to pass through

atrever-se [atre'vexsi] vr: **~ a** to dare to; **atrevido, -a** [atre'vidu, a] adj cheeky; (*corajoso*) bold; **atrevimento** [atrevi'mẽtu] m cheek; boldness

atribuir [atri'bwi^r] vt: **~ algo a** to attribute sth to; (*prêmios, regalias*) to confer sth on

atributo [atri'butu] m attribute

átrio ['atrju] m hall; (*pátio*) courtyard

atrito [a'tritu] m (*fricção*) friction; (*desentendimento*) disagreement

atriz [a'triʃ] f actress

atropelamento [atropela'mẽtu] m (*de pedestre*) road accident

atropelar [atrope'la^r] vt to knock down, run over; (*empurrar*) to jostle

atuação [atwa'sãw] (*pl* -ões) f acting; (*de ator etc*) performance

atual [a'twaw] (*pl* -ais) adj current; (*pessoa, carro*) modern; **atualidade** [atwali'dadʒi] f present (time); **atualidades** fpl (*notícias*) news sg; **atualizar** [atwali'za^r] vt to update; **atualmente** [atwaw'mẽtʃi] adv at present, currently; (*hoje em dia*) nowadays

atuante [a'twãtʃi] adj active

atuar [a'twa^r] vi to act; **~ para** to contribute to; **~ sobre** to influence

atum [a'tũ] (*pl* -ns) m tuna (fish)

aturdido, -a [atux'dʒidu, a] adj stunned; (*com barulho*) deafened; (*com confusão, movimento*) bewildered

audácia [aw'dasja] f boldness; (*insolência*) insolence; **audacioso, -a** [awda'sjozu, ɔza] adj daring; insolent

audição [awdʒi'sãw] (*pl* -ões) f audition

audiência [aw'dʒjẽsja] f audience; (*de tribunal*) session, hearing

auditar [awdʒi'ta^r] vt to audit

auditor, a [awdʒi'to^r, a] m/f auditor; (*juiz*) judge; (*ouvinte*) listener

auditoria [awdʒito'ria] f: **fazer a ~ de** to audit

auditório [awdʒi'tɔrju] m audience; (*recinto*) auditorium

auge ['awʒi] m height, peak

aula ['awla] f (*PT: sala*) classroom; (*lição*) lesson, class; **dar ~** to teach

aumentar [awmẽ'ta^r] vt to increase; (*salários, preços: salários*) to raise; (*sala, casa*) to expand, extend; (*suj: lente*) to magnify; (*acrescentar*) to add ▷ vi to increase; (*preço, salário: preço*) to rise, go up

aumento [aw'mẽtu] m increase; rise; (*ampliação*) enlargement; (*crescimento*) growth

ausência [aw'zẽsja] f absence

ausentar-se [awzẽ'taxsi] vr (*ir-se*) to go away; (*afastar-se*) to stay away

ausente [aw'zẽtʃi] adj absent

austral [awʃ'traw] (*pl* -ais) adj southern

Austrália [awʃ'tralja] f: **a ~** Australia; **australiano, -a** [awʃtra'ljanu, a] adj, m/f Australian

Áustria ['awʃtrja] f: **a ~** Austria; **austríaco, -a** [awʃ'triaku, a] adj, m/f Austrian

autêntico, -a [aw'tẽtʃiku, a] adj authentic; (*pessoa*) genuine; (*verdadeiro*) true, real

auto ['awtu] m car; **autos** mpl (*Jur: processo*) legal proceedings; (*documentos*) legal papers

autobiografia [awtobjogra'fia] f autobiography

autobronzeador [awtobrõza'do^r] adj self-tanning

autocarro [awto'kaxu] (*PT*) m bus

autodefesa [awtode'feza] f self-defence

(BRIT), self-defense (US)

autódromo [aw'tɔdromu] *m* race track

auto-estrada *f* motorway (BRIT), expressway (US)

autografar [awtogra'fa^r] *vt* to autograph

autógrafo [aw'tɔgrafu] *m* autograph

automático, -a [awto'matʃiku, a] *adj* automatic

automobilismo [awtomobi'liʒmu] *m* motoring; (*Esporte*) motor car racing

automóvel [awto'mɔvew] (*pl* -**eis**) *m* motor car (BRIT), automobile (US)

autonomia [awtono'mia] *f* autonomy

autor, a [aw'to^r, a] *m/f* author; (*de um crime*) perpetrator; (*Jur*) plaintiff

autoral [awto'raw] (*pl* -**ais**) *adj*: **direitos autorais** copyright *sg*

autoridade [awtori'dadʒi] *f* authority

autorização [awtoriza'sãw] (*pl* -**ões**) *f* permission, authorization; **dar ~ a alguém para** to authorize sb to

autorizar [awtori'za^r] *vt* to authorize

auto-serviço *m* self-service

auxiliar [awsi'lja^r] *adj* auxiliary ▷ *m/f* assistant ▷ *vt* to help; **auxílio** [aw'silju] *m* help, assistance

Av *abr* (= *avenida*) Ave

aval [a'vaw] (*pl* -**ais**) *m* guarantee

avalancha [ava'lãʃa] *f* avalanche

avaliar [ava'lja^r] *vt* to value; (*apreciar*) to assess

avançado, -a [avã'sadu, a] *adj* advanced; (*idéias, pessoa*) progressive

avançar [avã'sa^r] *vt* to move forward ▷ *vi* to advance; **avanço** [a'vãsu] *m* advancement; (*progresso*) progress

avaria [ava'ria] *f* (*Tec*) breakdown; **avariado, -a** [ava'rjadu, a] *adj* (*máquina*) out of order; (*carro*) broken down; **avariar** [ava'rja^r] *vt* to damage ▷ *vi* to suffer damage; (*Tec*) to break down

ave ['avi] *f* bird

aveia [a'veja] *f* oats *pl*

avelã [ave'lã] *f* hazelnut

avenida [ave'nida] *f* avenue

avental [avẽ'taw] (*pl* -**ais**) *m* apron; (*vestido*) pinafore dress (BRIT), jumper (US)

averiguar [averi'gwa^r] *vt* to investigate; (*verificar*) to verify

avermelhado, -a [avexme'ʎadu, a] *adj* reddish

avesso, -a [a'vesu, a] *adj* (*lado*) opposite, reverse ▷ *m* wrong side, reverse; **ao ~** inside out; **às avessas** (*inverso*) upside

down; (*oposto*) the wrong way round

avestruz [aveʃ'truʒ] *m* ostrich

aviação [avja'sãw] *f* aviation, flying

aviador, a [avja'do^r, a] *m/f* aviator, airman/woman

avião [a'vjãw] (*pl* -**ões**) *m* aeroplane; **~ a jato** jet; **ávido, -a** ['avidu, a] *adj* greedy; eager

aviões [a'vjõjʃ] *mpl de* **avião**

avisar [avi'za^r] *vt* to warn; (*informar*) to tell, let know; **aviso** [a'vizu] *m* (*comunicação*) notice

avistar [aviʃ'ta^r] *vt* to catch sight of

avô, avó [a'vo, a'vɔ] *m/f* grandfather/mother; **avós** *mpl* grandparents

avulso, -a [a'vuwsu, a] *adj* separate, detached

axila [ak'sila] *f* armpit

azar [a'za^r] *m* bad luck; **~!** too bad, bad luck!; **estar com ~, ter ~** to be unlucky; **azarento, -a** [aza'rẽtu, a] *adj* unlucky

azedar [aze'da^r] *vt* to turn sour ▷ *vi* to turn sour; (*leite*) to go off; **azedo, -a** [a'zedu, a] *adj* sour; off; (*fig*) grumpy

azeite [a'zejtʃi] *m* oil; (*de oliva*) olive oil

azeitona [azej'tɔna] *f* olive

azia [a'zia] *f* heartburn

azougue [a'zogi] *m* (*Quím*) mercury

azul [a'zuw] (*pl* -**uis**) *adj* blue

azulejo [azu'leʒu] *m* (glazed) tile

azul-marinho *adj inv* navy blue

azul-turquesa *adj inv* turquoise

b

baba ['baba] f dribble

babá [ba'ba] f nanny

babaca [ba'baka] (col) adj stupid ▷ m/f idiot

babado [ba'badu] m frill; (col) piece of gossip

babador [baba'do'] m bib

babar [ba'ba'] vi to dribble; **~-se** vr to dribble

baby-sitter ['bejbisite'] (pl **~s**) m/f baby-sitter

bacalhau [baka'ʎaw] m (dried) cod

bacana [ba'kana] (col) adj great

bacharel [baʃa'rɛw] (pl **-éis**) m graduate

bacia [ba'sia] f basin; (Anat) pelvis

backup [ba'kapi] (pl **~s**) m (Comput) back-up; **tirar um ~ de** to back up

bactéria [bak'tɛrja] f germ, bacterium; **bactérias** npl bacteria pl

badalar [bada'la'] vt, vi to ring

baderna [ba'dɛxna] f commotion

bafo ['bafu] m (bad) breath

bagaço [ba'gasu] m (de frutos) pulp; (PT: cachaça) brandy; **estar/ficar um ~** (fig: pessoa) to be/get run down

bagageiro [baga'ʒejru] m (Auto) roofrack; (PT) porter

bagagem [ba'gaʒẽ] f luggage; (fig)

baggage; **recebimento de ~** (Aer) baggage reclaim

bagulho [ba'guʎu] m (objeto) piece of junk

bagunça [ba'gũsa] f mess, shambles sg; **bagunçado, -a** [bagũ'sadu, a] adj in a mess; **bagunçar** [bagũ'sa'] vt to mess up; **bagunceiro, -a** [bagũ'sejru, a] adj messy

baía [ba'ia] f bay

bailado [baj'ladu] m dance; (balé) ballet

bailarino, -a [bajla'rinu, a] m/f ballet dancer

baile ['bajli] m dance; (formal) ball; **~ à fantasia** fancy-dress ball

bainha [ba'iɲa] f (de arma) sheath; (de costura) hem

bairro ['bajxu] m district

baixa ['bajʃa] f decrease; (de preço: redução) reduction; (: queda) fall; (em vendas) drop; (em combate) casualty; (do serviço) discharge

baixar [baj'ʃa'] vt to lower; (ordem) to issue; (lei) to pass; (Comput) to download ▷ vi to go (ou come) down; (temperatura, preço) to drop, fall

baixinho [baj'ʃiɲu] adv (falar) softly, quietly; (em segredo) secretly

baixo, -a ['bajʃu, a] adj low; (pessoa) short, small; (rio) shallow; (linguagem) common; (olhos, cabeça) lowered; (atitude) mean; (metal) base ▷ adv low; (em posição baixa) low down; (falar) softly ▷ m (Mús) bass; **em ~** below; (em casa) downstairs; **em voz baixa** in a quiet voice; **para ~** down, downwards; (em casa) downstairs; **por ~ de** under, underneath; **baixo-astral** (col) m: **estar num baixo-astral** to be on a downer

bala ['bala] f bullet; (BR: doce) sweet

balança [ba'lãsa] f scales pl; **B~** (Astrologia) Libra; **~ comercial** balance of trade; **~ de pagamentos** balance of payments

balançar [balã'sa'] vt to swing; (pesar) to weigh (up) ▷ vi to swing; (carro, avião) to shake; (em cadeira) to rock; **~-se** vr to swing; **balanço** [ba'lãsu] m (movimento) swaying; (brinquedo) swing; (de carro, avião) shaking; (Com: registro) balance (sheet); (: verificação) audit; **fazer um balanço de** (fig) to take stock of

balão [ba'lãw] (pl **-ões**) m balloon

balbúrdia [baw'buxdʒja] f uproar, bedlam

balcão [baw'kãw] (pl **-ões**) m balcony;

(de loja) counter; *(Teatro)* circle; ~
de informações information desk;
balconista [bawko'niʃta] *m/f* shop
assistant
balde ['bawdʒi] *m* bucket, pail
balé [ba'lɛ] *m* ballet
baleia [ba'leja] *f* whale
baliza [ba'liza] *f (estaca)* post; *(bóia)*
buoy; *(luminosa)* beacon; *(Esporte)* goal
balneário [baw'njarju] *m* bathing
resort
balões [ba'lõjʃ] *mpl de* **balão**
baloiço [ba'lojsu] *(PT) m (de criança)*
swing; *(ação)* swinging
balsa ['bawsa] *f* raft; *(barca)* ferry
bamba ['bãba] *adj, m/f* expert
bambo, -a ['bãbu, a] *adj* slack, loose
banana [ba'nana] *f* banana; **bananeira**
[bana'nejra] *f* banana tree
banca ['bãka] *f* bench; *(escritório)*
office; *(em jogo)* bank; ~ **(de jornais)**
newsstand; **bancada** [bã'kada] *f (banco,
Pol)* bench; *(de cozinha)* worktop
bancar [bã'kaʳ] *vt* to finance ▷ *vi (fingir)*:
~ **que** to pretend that; **bancário, -a**
[bã'karju, a] *adj* bank *atr* ▷ *m/f* bank
employee
bancarrota [bãka'xota] *f* bankruptcy; **ir
à ~** to go bankrupt
banco ['bãku] *m (assento)* bench; *(Com)*
bank; ~ **de areia** sandbank; ~ **de dados**
(Comput) database
banda ['bãda] *f* band; *(lado)* side; *(cinto)*
sash; **de ~** sideways; **pôr de ~** to put
aside; ~ **desenhada** *(PT)* cartoon; ~ **larga**
(Tel) broadband
bandeira [bã'dejra] *f* flag; *(estandarte)*
banner; **bandeirinha** [bãdej'riɲa] *m*
(Esporte) linesman
bandeja [bã'deʒa] *f* tray
bandido [bã'dʒidu, a] *m* bandit
bando ['bãdu] *m* band; *(grupo)* group; *(de
malfeitores)* gang; *(de ovelhas)* flock; *(de
gado)* herd; *(de livros etc)* pile
banha ['baɲa] *f* fat; *(de porco)* lard
banhar [ba'ɲaʳ] *vt* to wet; *(mergulhar)* to
dip; *(lavar)* to wash; ~**-se** *vr* to bathe
banheira [ba'ɲejra] *f* bath
banheiro [ba'ɲejru] *m* bathroom
banho ['baɲu] *m* bath; *(mergulho)* dip;
tomar ~ to have a bath; *(de chuveiro)* to
have a shower; ~ **de chuveiro** shower; ~
de sol sunbathing
banir [ba'niʳ] *vt* to banish
banqueiro, -a [bã'kejru, a] *m/f* banker
banquete [bã'ketʃi] *m* banquet

baptismo *etc* [ba'tiʒmu] *(PT)* = **batismo**
etc
bar [baʳ] *m* bar
baralho [ba'raʎu] *m* pack of cards
barata [ba'rata] *f* cockroach
barateiro, -a [bara'tejru, a] *adj* cheap
barato, -a [ba'ratu, a] *adj* cheap ▷ *adv*
cheaply
barba ['baxba] *f* beard; **fazer a ~** to shave
bárbaro, -a ['baxbaru, a] *adj* barbaric;
(dor, calor) terrible; *(maravilhoso)* great
barbeador [baxbja'doʳ] *m* razor; *(tb: ~
elétrico)* shaver
barbear [bax'bjaʳ] *vt* to shave; ~**-se** *vr* to
shave; **barbearia** [baxbja'ria] *f* barber's
(shop)
barbeiro [bax'bejru] *m* barber; *(loja)*
barber's
barca ['baxka] *f* barge; *(de travessia)* ferry
barco ['baxku] *m* boat; ~ **a motor**
motorboat; ~ **a remo** rowing boat; ~ **a
vela** sailing boat
barganha [bax'gaɲa] *f* bargain;
barganhar [baxga'ɲaʳ] *vt, vi* to
negotiate
barman [bax'mã] *(pl* **-men)** *m* barman
barra ['baxa] *f* bar; *(faixa)* strip; *(traço)*
stroke; *(alavanca)* lever
barraca [ba'xaka] *f (tenda)* tent; *(de
feira)* stall; *(de madeira)* hut; *(de praia)*
sunshade; **barracão** [baxa'kãw] *(pl* **-ões)**
m shed; **barraco** [ba'xaku] *m* shack,
shanty
barragem [ba'xaʒẽ] *(pl* **-ns)** *f* dam;
(impedimento) barrier
barrar [ba'xaʳ] *vt* to bar
barreira [ba'xejra] *f* barrier; *(cerca)* fence;
(Esporte) hurdle
barricada [baxi'kada] *f* barricade
barriga [ba'xiga] *f* belly; **estar de
~** to be pregnant; ~ **da perna** calf;
barrigudo, -a [baxi'gudu, a] *adj*
paunchy, pot-bellied
barril [ba'xiw] *(pl* **-is)** *m* barrel, cask
barro ['baxu] *m* clay; *(lama)* mud
barulhento, -a [baruʎẽtu, a] *adj* noisy
barulho [ba'ruʎu] *m (ruído)* noise;
(tumulto) din
base ['bazi] *f* base; *(fig)* basis; **sem ~**
groundless; **com ~ em** based on; **na ~ de**
by means of
basear [ba'zjaʳ] *vt* to base; ~**-se** *vr*: ~**-se
em** to be based on
básico, -a ['baziku, a] *adj* basic
basquete [baʃ'ketʃi] *m* = **basquetebol**
basquetebol [baʃkete'bɔw] *m*

basketball

basta ['baʃta] m: **dar um ~ em** to call a halt to

bastante [baʃˈtãtʃi] adj (suficiente) enough; (muito) quite a lot (of) ▷ adv enough; a lot

bastão [baʃˈtãw] (pl -ões) m stick

bastar [baʃˈtaʳ] vi to be enough, be sufficient; **~-se** vr to be self-sufficient; **basta!** (that's) enough!; **~ para** to be enough to

bastardo, -a [baʃˈtaxdu, a] adj, m/f bastard

bastões [baʃˈtõjʃ] mpl de **bastão**

bata ['bata] f (de mulher) smock; (de médico) overall

batalha [baˈtaʎa] f battle; **batalhador, a** [bataʎaˈdoʳ, a] adj struggling ▷ m/f fighter; **batalhão** [bataˈʎãw] (pl -ões) m battalion; **batalhar** [bataˈʎaʳ] vi to battle, fight; (esforçar-se) to make an effort, try hard ▷ vt (emprego) to go after

batata [baˈtata] f potato; **~ doce** sweet potato; **~s fritas** chips pl (BRIT), French fries pl (US); (de pacote) crisps pl (BRIT), (potato) chips pl (US)

bate-boca ['batʃi-] (pl -s) m row, quarrel

batedeira [bateˈdejra] f beater; (de manteiga) churn; **~ elétrica** mixer

batente [baˈtẽtʃi] m doorpost

bate-papo ['batʃi-] (pl -s (BR)) m chat

bater [baˈteʳ] vt to beat, strike; (pé) to stamp; (foto) to take; (porta) to slam; (asas) to flap; (recorde) to break; (roupa) to wear all the time ▷ vi to beat; (sino) to ring; (janela) to bang; (coração) to beat; (sol) to beat down; **~-se** vr: **~-se para fazer/por** to fight to do/for; **~ (à porta)** to knock (at the door); **~ à maquina** to type; **~ em** to hit; **~ com o carro** to crash one's car; **~ com a cabeça** to bang one's head; **~ com o pé (em)** to kick

bateria [bateˈria] f battery; (Mús) drums pl; **~ de cozinha** kitchen utensils pl; **baterista** [bateˈriʃta] m/f drummer

batida [baˈtʃida] f beat; (da porta) slam; (à porta) knock; (da polícia) raid; (Auto) crash; (bebida) cocktail of cachaça, fruit and sugar

batido, -a [baˈtʃidu, a] adj beaten; (roupa) worn ▷ m: **~ de leite** (PT) milkshake

batina [baˈtʃina] f (Rel) cassock

batismo [baˈtʃiʒmu] m baptism, christening

batizar [batʃiˈzaʳ] vt to baptize, christen

batom [baˈtõ] (pl -ns) m lipstick

batucada [batuˈkada] f dance percussion group

batucar [batuˈkaʳ] vt, vi to drum

baú [baˈu] m trunk

baunilha [bawˈniʎa] f vanilla

bazar [baˈzaʳ] m bazaar; (loja) shop

bêbado, -a ['bebadu, a] adj, m/f drunk

bebê [beˈbe] m baby

bebedeira [bebeˈdejra] f drunkenness; **tomar uma ~** to get drunk

bêbedo, -a ['bebedu, a] adj, m/f = bêbado

bebedouro [bebeˈdouru] m drinking fountain

beber [beˈbeʳ] vt to drink; (absorver) to soak up ▷ vi to drink; **bebida** [beˈbida] f drink

beça ['bɛsa] (col) f: **à ~** (com vb): **ele comeu à ~** he ate a lot; (com n): **ela tinha livros à ~** she had a lot of books

beco ['beku] m alley, lane; **~ sem saída** cul-de-sac

bege ['bɛʒi] adj inv beige

beija-flor [bejʒa-ˈflɔʳ] (pl -es) m hummingbird

beijar [bejˈʒaʳ] vt to kiss; **~-se** vr to kiss (one another); **beijo** ['bejʒu] m kiss; **dar beijos em alguém** to kiss sb

beira ['bejra] f edge; (de rio) bank; (orla) border; **à ~ de** on the edge of; (ao lado de) beside, by; (fig) on the verge of; **~ do telhado** eaves pl; **beira-mar** f seaside

belas-artes fpl fine arts

beldade [bewˈdadʒi] f beauty

beleza [beˈleza] f beauty; **que ~!** how lovely!

belga ['bɛwga] adj, m/f Belgian

Bélgica ['bɛwʒika] f: **a ~** Belgium

beliche [beˈliʃi] m bunk

beliscão [beliʃˈkãw] (pl -ões) m pinch; **beliscar** [beliʃˈkaʳ] vt to pinch, nip; (comida) to nibble

Belize [beˈlizi] m Belize

belo, -a ['bɛlu, a] adj beautiful

⬤ **PALAVRA CHAVE**

bem [bẽj] adv **1** (de maneira satisfatória, correta etc) well; **trabalha/come bem** she works/eats well; **respondeu bem** he answered correctly; **me sinto/não me sinto bem** I feel fine/I don't feel very well; **tudo bem? - tudo bem** how's it going? - fine

2 (*valor intensivo*) very; **um quarto bem quente** a nice warm room; **bem se vê que ...** it's clear that ...
3 (*bastante*) quite, fairly; **a casa é bem grande** the house is quite big
4 (*exatamente*): **bem ali** right there; **não é bem assim** it's not quite like that
5 (*estar bem*): **estou muito bem aqui** I feel very happy here; **está bem! vou fazê-lo** oh all right, I'll do it!
6 (*de bom grado*): **eu bem que iria mas ...** I'd gladly go but ...
7 (*cheirar*) good, nice
▷ *m* **1** (*bem-estar*) good; **estou dizendo isso para o seu bem** I'm telling you for your own good; **o bem e o mal** good and evil
2 (*posses*): **bens** goods, property *sg*; **bens de consumo** consumer goods; **bens de família** family possessions; **bens móveis/imóveis** moveable property *sg*/real estate *sg*
▷ *excl* **1** (*aprovação*): **bem!** OK!; **muito bem!** well done!
2 (*desaprovação*): **bem feito!** it serves you right!
▷ *adj inv* (*tom depreciativo*): **gente bem** posh people
▷ *conj* **1**: **nem bem** as soon as, no sooner than; **nem bem ela chegou começou a dar ordens** as soon as she arrived she started to give orders, no sooner had she arrived than she started to give orders
2: **se bem que** though; **gostaria de ir se bem que não tenho dinheiro** I'd like to go even though I've got no money
3: **bem como** as well as; **o livro bem como a peça foram escritos por ele** the book as well as the play was written by him

bem-conceituado, -a [bẽjkõsejˈtwadu, a] *adj* highly regarded
bem-disposto, -a [bẽjdʒiʃˈpoʃtu, ˈpɔʃta] *adj* well, in good form
bem-me-quer (*pl* **~es**) *m* daisy
bem-vindo, -a *adj* welcome
bênção [ˈbẽsãw] (*pl* **~s**) *f* blessing
beneficência [benefiˈsẽsja] *f* kindness; (*caridade*) charity
beneficiar [benefiˈsjaʳ] *vt* to benefit; (*melhorar*) to improve; **~-se** *vr* to benefit
benefício [beneˈfisju] *m* benefit; (*vantagem*) profit; (*favor*) favour (*BRIT*), favor (*US*); **em ~ de** in aid of; **benéfico, -a**

[beˈnɛfiku, a] *adj* beneficial; (*generoso*) generous
bengala [bẽˈgala] *f* walking stick
benigno, -a [beˈnignu, a] *adj* kind; (*agradável*) pleasant; (*Med*) benign
bens [bẽjʃ] *mpl de* **bem**
bento, -a [ˈbẽtu, a] *pp de* **benzer** ▷ *adj* blessed; (*água*) holy
benzer [bẽˈzeʳ] *vt* to bless; **~-se** *vr* to cross o.s
berço [ˈbexsu] *m* cradle; (*cama*) cot; (*origem*) birthplace
Berlim [bexˈlĩ] *n* Berlin
berma [ˈbɛxma] (*PT*) *f* hard shoulder (*BRIT*), berm (*US*)
berrar [beˈxaʳ] *vi* to bellow; (*criança*) to bawl; **berreiro** [beˈxejru] *m*: **abrir o berreiro** to burst out crying; **berro** [ˈbexu] *m* yell
besta [ˈbeʃta] *adj* stupid; (*convencido*) full of oneself; **~ de carga** beast of burden; **besteira** [beʃˈtejra] *f* foolishness; **dizer besteiras** to talk nonsense; **fazer uma besteira** to do something silly; **bestial** [beʃˈtʃjaw] (*pl* **-ais**) *adj* bestial; (*repugnante*) repulsive
best-seller [ˈbɛstˈsɛleʳ] (*pl* **~s**) *m* best seller
betão [beˈtãw] (*PT*) *m* concrete
beterraba [beteˈxaba] *f* beetroot
bexiga [beˈʃiga] *f* bladder
bezerro, -a [beˈzexu, a] *m/f* calf
BI *abr m* (*PT: bilhete de identidade*) identity card; *see boxed note*

⬡ **BI**
⬡
⬡ All Portuguese citizens are required
⬡ to carry an identity card, known as
⬡ the **BI** or *bilhete de identidade*. The
⬡ photocard, which gives the holder's
⬡ name, date of birth, marital status,
⬡ height and a fingerprint, can be
⬡ used instead of a passport for travel
⬡ within the European Union. Failure
⬡ to produce a valid identity card when
⬡ stopped by the police can result in
⬡ a fine.

Bíblia [ˈbiblja] *f* Bible
bibliografia [bibljograˈfia] *f* bibliography
biblioteca [bibljoˈtɛka] *f* library; (*estante*) bookcase; **bibliotecário, -a** [bibljoteˈkarju, a] *m/f* librarian
bica [ˈbika] *f* tap; (*PT*) black coffee,

expresso

bicha ['biʃa] f (lombriga) worm; (BR: col, pej: homossexual) queer; (PT: fila) queue

bicho ['biʃu] m animal; (inseto) insect, bug

bicicleta [bisi'klɛta] f bicycle; (col) bike; **andar de ~** to cycle; **~ do exército** exercise bike

bico ['biku] m (de ave) beak; (ponta) point; (de chaleira) spout; (boca) mouth; (de pena) nib; (do peito) nipple; (de gás) jet; (col: emprego) casual job; (chupeta) dummy; **calar o ~** to shut up

bidê [bi'de] m bidet

bife ['bifi] m (beef) steak; **~ a cavalo** steak with fried eggs; **~ à milanesa** beef escalope; **~ de panela** beef stew

bifurcação [bifuxka'sãw] (pl -ões) f fork

bifurcar-se [bifux'kaxsi] vr to fork, divide

bigode [bi'gɔdʒi] m moustache

bijuteria [biʒute'ria] f (costume) jewellery (BRIT) ou jewelry (US)

bilhão [bi'ʎãw] (pl -ões) m billion

bilhar [bi'ʎaʳ] m (jogo) billiards sg

bilhete [bi'ʎetʃi] m ticket; (cartinha) note; **~ de ida** single (BRIT) ou one-way ticket; **~ de ida e volta** return (BRIT) ou round-trip (US) ticket; **~ eletrônico** e-ticket; **bilheteira** [biʎe'tejra] (PT) f **= bilheteria**; **bilheteiro, -a** [biʎe'tejru, a] m/f ticket seller; **bilheteria** [biʎete'ria] f ticket office

bilhões [bi'ʎõjʃ] mpl de **bilhão**

bilíngüe [bi'lĩgwi] adj bilingual

binóculo [bi'nɔkulu] m binoculars pl; (para teatro) opera glasses pl

biografia [bjogra'fia] f biography

biologia [bjolo'ʒia] f biology

biombo ['bjõbu] m screen

bioterrorismo [bjotexo'riʒmu] m bioterrorism

bip [bip] n pager, paging device

biquíni [bi'kini] m bikini

birita [bi'rita] (col) f drink

biruta [bi'ruta] adj crazy ▷ f windsock

bis [biʃ] excl encore!

bisavô, -ó [biza'vo, ɔ] m/f great-grandfather/great-grandmother; **bisavós** [biza'vɔʃ] mpl great-grandparents

biscate [biʃ'katʃi] m odd job

biscoito [biʃ'kojtu] m biscuit (BRIT), cookie (US)

bispo ['biʃpu] m bishop

bissexto, -a [bi'seʃtu, a] adj: **ano ~** leap year

bit ['bitʃi] m (Comput) bit

bizarro, -a [bi'zaxu, a] adj bizarre

blasfemar [blaʃfe'maʳ] vt to curse ▷ vi to blaspheme; **blasfêmia** [blaʃ'femja] f blasphemy; (ultraje) curse

blazer ['blejzeʳ] (pl -s) m blazer

blecaute [ble'kawtʃi] m power cut

blindado, -a [blĩ'dadu, a] adj armoured (BRIT), armored (US)

blitz [blits] f police raid; (na estrada) police road block

bloco ['blɔku] m block; (Pol) bloc; (de escrever) writing pad; **~ de carnaval** carnival troupe

blog, blogue ['blɔgi] (pl -s) (col) m blog

blogueiro, -a [blo'gejru, a] (col) m/f blogger

bloqueador [blokja'doʳ] m: **~ solar** sunblock

bloquear [blo'kjaʳ] vt to blockade; (obstruir) to block; **bloqueio** [blo'keju] m blockade; blockage

blusa ['bluza] f (de mulher) blouse; (de homem) shirt; **~ de lã** jumper; **blusão** [blu'zãw] (pl -ões) m jacket

boa ['boa] adj f de **bom** ▷ f boa constrictor

boate ['bwatʃi] f nightclub

boato ['bwatu] m rumour (BRIT), rumor (US)

bobagem [bo'baʒẽ] (pl -ns) f silliness, nonsense; (dito, ato) silly thing

bobo, -a ['bobu, a] adj silly, daft ▷ m/f fool ▷ m (de corte) jester; **fazer-se de ~** to act the fool

bobó [bo'bɔ] m beans, palm oil and manioc

boca ['boka] f mouth; (entrada) entrance; (de fogão) ring; **de ~ aberta** amazed; **bater ~** to argue

bocadinho [boka'dʒiɲu] m: **um ~** (pouco tempo) a little while; (pouquinho) a little bit

bocado [bo'kadu] m mouthful, bite; (pedaço) piece, bit; **um ~ de tempo** quite some time

boçal [bo'saw] (pl -ais) adj ignorant; (grosseiro) uncouth

bocejar [bose'ʒaʳ] vi to yawn; **bocejo** [bo'seʒu] m yawn

bochecha [bo'ʃeʃa] f cheek; **bochecho** [bo'ʃeʃu] m mouthwash

boda ['boda] f wedding; **bodas** fpl (aniversário de casamento) wedding anniversary sg

bode ['bɔdʒi] *m* goat; **~ expiatório** scapegoat

bofetada [bofe'tada] *f* slap

bofetão [bofe'tãw] (*pl* **-ões**) *m* punch

boi [boj] *m* ox

bóia ['bɔja] *f* buoy; (*col*) grub; (*de braço*) armband, water wing

boiar [bo'ja*ʳ*] *vt*, *vi* to float

boi-bumbá [-bũ'ba] *n* *see boxed note*

boicotar [bojko'ta*ʳ*] *vt* to boycott; **boicote** [boj'kɔtʃi] *m* boycott

bola ['bɔla] *f* ball; **dar ~ para** (*flertar*) to flirt with; **ela não dá a menor ~ (para isso)** she couldn't care less (about it); **não ser certo da ~** (*col*) not to be right in the head

bolacha [bo'laʃa] *f* biscuit (*BRIT*), cookie (*US*); (*col: bofetada*) wallop; (*para chope*) beermat

boleia [bo'leja] *f* driver's seat; **dar uma ~ a alguém** (*PT*) to give sb a lift

boletim [bole'tʃĩ] (*pl* **-ns**) *m* report; (*publicação*) newsletter; **~ meteorológico** weather forecast

bolha ['boʎa] *f* (*na pele*) blister; (*de ar, sabão*) bubble

boliche [bo'liʃi] *m* bowling, skittles *sg*

bolinho [bo'liɲu] *m*: **~ de carne** meat ball; **~ de arroz/bacalhau** rice/dry cod cake

Bolívia [bo'livja] *f*: **a ~** Bolivia

bolo ['bolu] *m* cake; (*monte: de gente*) bunch; (: *de papéis*) bundle; **dar o ~ em alguém** to stand sb up; **vai dar ~** (*col*) there's going to be trouble

bolor [bo'lo*ʳ*] *m* mould (*BRIT*), mold (*US*); (*nas plantas*) mildew; (*bafio*) mustiness

bolota [bo'lɔta] *f* acorn

bolsa ['bowsa] *f* bag; (*Com: tb*: **~ de valores**) stock exchange; **~ (de**

estudos) scholarship

bolso ['bowsu] *m* pocket; **de ~** pocket *atr*

⬤ PALAVRA CHAVE

bom, boa [bõ, 'boa] (*pl* **bons/boas**) *adj*
1 (*ótimo*) good; **é um livro bom** *ou* **um bom livro** it's a good book; **a comida está boa** the food is delicious; **o tempo está bom** the weather's fine; **ele foi muito bom comigo** he was very nice *ou* kind to me
2 (*apropriado*): **ser bom para** to be good for; **acho bom você não ir** I think it's better if you don't go
3 (*irônico*): **um bom quarto de hora** a good quarter of an hour; **que bom motorista você é!** a fine *ou* some driver you are!; **seria bom que ...!** a fine thing it would be if ...!; **essa é boa!** what a cheek!
4 (*saudação*): **bom dia!** good morning!; **boa tarde!** good afternoon!; **boa noite!** good evening!; (*ao deitar-se*) good night!; **tudo bom?** how's it going?
5 (*outras frases*): **está bom?** OK?
▷ *excl*: **bom!** all right!; **bom, ...** right, ...

bomba ['bõba] *f* bomb; (*Tec*) pump; (*fig*) bombshell; **~ atômica/relógio/de fumaça** atomic/time/smoke bomb; **~ de gasolina** petrol (*BRIT*) *ou* gas (*US*) pump; **~ de incêndio** fire extinguisher

bombardear [bõbax'dʒja*ʳ*] *vt* to bomb; (*fig*) to bombard; **bombardeio** [bõbax'deju] *m* bombing, bombardment; **bombardeio suicida** suicide bombing

bombeiro [bõ'bejru] *m* fireman; (*BR: encanador*) plumber; **o corpo de ~s** fire brigade

bombom [bõ'bõ] (*pl* **-ns**) *m* chocolate

bondade [bõ'dadʒi] *f* goodness, kindness; **tenha a ~ de vir** would you please come

bonde ['bõdʒi] (*BR*) *m* tram

bondoso, -a [bõ'dozu, ɔza] *adj* kind, good

boné [bo'nɛ] *m* cap

boneca [bo'nɛka] *f* doll

boneco [bo'nɛku] *m* dummy

bonito, -a [bo'nitu, a] *adj* pretty; (*gesto, dia*) nice ▷ *m* (*peixe*) tuna (fish), tunny

bônus ['bonuʃ] *m inv* bonus

boquiaberto, -a [bokja'bextu, a] *adj* dumbfounded, astonished

borboleta [boxbo'leta] *f* butterfly; (*BR*:

roleta) turnstile

borbotão [boxbo'tãw] (*pl* **-ões**) *m* gush, spurt; **sair aos borbotões** to gush out

borbulhar [boxbu'ʎaʳ] *vi* to bubble

borda ['bɔxda] *f* edge; (*do rio*) bank; **à ~ de** on the edge of

bordado [box'dadu] *m* embroidery

bordar [box'daʳ] *vt* to embroider

bordo ['bɔxdu] *m* (*de navio*) side; **a ~ on** board

borra ['boxa] *f* dregs *pl*

borracha [bo'xaʃa] *f* rubber; **borracheiro** [boxa'ʃejru] *m* tyre (BRIT) ou tire (US) specialist

borrão [bo'xãw] (*pl* **-ões**) *m* (*rascunho*) rough draft; (*mancha*) blot

borrifar [boxi'faʳ] *vt* to sprinkle; **borrifo** [bo'xifu] *m* spray

borrões [bo'xõjʃ] *mpl de* **borrão**

bosque ['bɔʃki] *m* wood, forest

bossa ['bɔsa] *f* charm; (*inchaço*) swelling; **bossa nova** (*Mús*) *see boxed note*

⊛ **Bossa nova** is a type of music
⊛ invented by young, middle-class
⊛ inhabitants of Rio de Janeiro at the
⊛ end of the 1950s. It has an obvious jazz
⊛ influence, an unusual, rhythmic beat
⊛ and lyrics praising beauty and love.
⊛ **Bossa nova** became known around
⊛ the world through the work of the
⊛ conductor and composer Antônio
⊛ Carlos Jobim whose compositions,
⊛ working with the poet Vinícius de
⊛ Morais, include the famous song "The
⊛ Girl from Ipanema".

bota ['bɔta] *f* boot; **~s de borracha** wellingtons

botânica [bo'tanika] *f* botany

botão [bo'tãw] (*pl* **-ões**) *m* button; (*flor*) bud

botar [bo'taʳ] *vt* to put; (*roupa, sapatos*) to put on; (*mesa*) to set; (*defeito*) to find; (*ovos*) to lay

bote ['bɔtʃi] *m* boat; (*com arma*) thrust; (*salto*) spring

botequim [botʃi'kĩ] (*pl* **-ns**) *m* bar

botija [bo'tʃiʒa] *f* (*earthenware*) jug

botões [bo'tõjʃ] *mpl de* **botão**

boxe ['bɔksi] *m* boxing

brabo, -a ['brabu, a] *adj* fierce; (*zangado*) angry; (*ruim*) bad; (*calor*) unbearable

braçada [bra'sada] *f* armful; (*Natação*) stroke

bracelete [brase'letʃi] *m* bracelet

braço ['brasu] *m* arm; **de ~s cruzados** with arms folded; (*fig*) without lifting a finger; **de ~ dado** arm-in-arm

bradar [bra'daʳ] *vt*, *vi* to shout, yell; **brado** ['bradu] *m* shout, yell

braguilha [bra'giʎa] *f* flies *pl*

branco, -a ['brãku, a] *adj* white ▷ *m/f* white man/woman ▷ *m* (*espaço*) blank; **em ~** blank; **noite em ~** sleepless night; **brancura** [brã'kura] *f* whiteness

brando, -a ['brãdu, a] *adj* gentle; (*mole*) soft

brasão [bra'zãw] (*pl* **-ões**) *m* coat of arms

braseiro [bra'zejru] *m* brazier

Brasil [bra'ziw] *m*: **o ~** Brazil; **brasileiro, -a** [brazi'lejru, a] *adj*, *m/f* Brazilian

Brasília [bra'zilja] *n* Brasília

brasões [bra'zõjʃ] *mpl de* **brasão**

bravata [bra'vata] *f* bravado, boasting

bravio, -a [bra'viu, a] *adj* (*selvagem*) wild; (*feroz*) ferocious

bravo, -a ['bravu, a] *adj* brave; (*furioso*) angry; (*mar*) rough ▷ *m* brave man; **~!** bravo!; **bravura** [bra'vura] *f* courage, bravery

brecar [bre'kaʳ] *vt* (*carro*) to stop; (*reprimir*) to curb ▷ *vi* to brake

breu [brew] *m* tar, pitch

breve ['brevi] *adj* short; (*conciso, rápido*) brief ▷ *adv* soon; **em ~** soon, shortly; **até ~** see you soon

bridge ['bridʒi] *m* bridge

briga ['briga] *f* fight; (*verbal*) quarrel

brigada [bri'gada] *f* brigade

brigão, -ona [bri'gãw, ɔna] (*pl* **brigões/-s**) *adj* quarrelsome ▷ *m/f* troublemaker

brigar [bri'gaʳ] *vi* to fight; (*altercar*) to quarrel

brigões [bri'gõjʃ] *mpl de* **brigão**

brigona [bri'gɔna] *f de* **brigão**

brilhante [bri'ʎãtʃi] *adj* brilliant ▷ *m* diamond

brilhar [bri'ʎaʳ] *vi* to shine

brincadeira [brĩka'dejra] *f* fun; (*gracejo*) joke; (*de criança*) game; **deixe de ~s!** stop fooling!; **de ~** for fun

brincalhão, -ona [brĩka'ʎãw, ɔna] (*pl* **brincalhões/-s**) *adj* playful ▷ *m/f* joker, teaser

brincar [brĩ'kaʳ] *vi* to play; (*gracejar*) to joke; **estou brincando** I'm only kidding; **~ de soldados** to play (at) soldiers; **~ com alguém** to tease sb

brinco ['brĩku] *m* (*jóia*) earring

brindar [brī'da'] vt to drink to;
(presentear) to give a present to; **brinde**
['brīdʒi] m toast; free gift

brinquedo [brī'kedu] m toy

brio ['briu] m self-respect, dignity

brisa ['briza] f breeze

britânico, -a [bri'taniku, a] adj British
▷ m/f Briton

broche ['brɔʃi] m brooch

brochura [bro'ʃura] f (livro) paperback;
(folheto) brochure, pamphlet

brócolis ['brɔkoliʃ] mpl broccoli sg

bronca ['brōka] (col) f telling off; **dar
uma ~ em** to tell off; **levar uma ~** to get
told off

bronco, -a ['brōku, a] adj (rude) coarse;
(burro) thick

bronquite [brō'kitʃi] f bronchitis

bronze ['brōzi] m bronze; **bronzear**
[brō'zja'] vt to tan; **bronzear-se** vr to
get a tan

broto ['brotu] m bud; (fig) youngster

broxa ['brɔʃa] f (large) paint brush

bruços ['brusuʃ]: **de ~** adv face down

bruma ['bruma] f mist, haze

brusco, -a ['bruʃku, a] adj brusque;
(súbito) sudden

brutal [bru'taw] (pl -ais) adj brutal

bruto, -a ['brutu, a] adj brutish;
(grosseiro) coarse; (móvel) heavy; (petróleo)
crude; (peso, Com) gross ▷ m brute; **em ~**
raw, unworked

bruxa ['bruʃa] f witch; **bruxaria**
[bruʃa'ria] f witchcraft

Bruxelas [bru'ʃelaʃ] n Brussels

bruxo ['bruʃu] m wizard

budismo [bu'dʒiʒmu] m Buddhism

bufar [bu'fa'] vi to puff, pant; (com raiva)
to snort; (reclamar) to moan, grumble

bufê [bu'fe] m sideboard; (comida) buffet

buffer ['bafe'] (pl -s) m (Comput) buffer

bula ['bula] f (Med) directions pl for use

bule ['buli] m (de chá) teapot; (de café)
coffeepot

Bulgária [buw'garja] f: **a ~** Bulgaria;
búlgaro, -a ['buwgaru, a] adj, m/f
Bulgarian ▷ m (Ling) Bulgarian

bunda ['būda] (col) f bottom, backside

buquê [bu'ke] m bouquet

buraco [bu'raku] m hole; (de agulha) eye;
ser um ~ to be tough; **~ da fechadura**
keyhole

burguês, -guesa [bux'geʃ, 'geza] adj
middle-class, bourgeois; **burguesia**
[buxge'zia] f middle class, bourgeoisie

burocracia [burokra'sia] f bureaucracy

burro, -a ['buxu, a] adj stupid ▷ m/f
(Zool) donkey; (pessoa) fool, idiot; **pra ~**
(col) a lot; (com adj) really; **~ de carga** (fig)
hard worker

busca ['buʃka] f search; **em ~ de** in search
of; **dar ~ a** to search for

buscar [buʃ'ka'] vt to fetch; (procurar) to
look ou search for; **ir ~** to fetch, go for;
mandar ~ to send for

bússola ['busola] f compass

busto ['buʃtu] m bust

buzina [bu'zina] f horn; **buzinar**
[buzi'na'] vi to sound one's horn, toot
the horn ▷ vt to hoot

búzio ['buzju] m conch

C

c/ *abr* = **com**

Ca *abr* (= **companhia**) Co

cá [ka] *adv* here; **de cá** on this side; **para cá** here, over here; **para lá e para cá** back and forth; **de lá para cá** since then

caatinga [ka'tʃĩga] (BR) *f* scrub(-land)

cabana [ka'bana] *f* hut

cabeça [ka'besa] *f* head; (*inteligência*) brains *pl*; (*de uma lista*) top ▷ *m/f* leader; **de ~** off the top of one's head; (*calcular*) in one's head; **de ~ para baixo** upside down; **por ~** per person, per head; **cabeçada** [kabe'sada] *f* (*pancada com cabeça*) butt; (*Futebol*) header; (*asneira*) blunder; **cabeçalho** [kabe'saʎu] *m* (*de livro*) title page; (*de página, capítulo*) heading

cabeceira [kabe'sejra] *f* (*de cama*) head

cabeçudo, -a [kabe'sudu, a] *adj* big-headed; (*teimoso*) pigheaded

cabeleira [kabe'lejra] *f* head of hair; (*postiça*) wig; **cabeleireiro, -a** [kabelej'rejru, a] *m/f* hairdresser

cabelo [ka'belu] *m* hair; **cortar/fazer o ~** to have one's hair cut/done; **cabeludo, -a** [kabe'ludu, a] *adj* hairy

caber [ka'be^r] *vi*: **~ (em)** to fit; (*ser compatível*) to be appropriate (in); **~ a** (*em partilha*) to fall to; **cabe a alguém fazer** it is up to sb to do; **não cabe aqui fazer comentários** this is not the time or place to comment

cabide [ka'bidʒi] *m* (*coat*) hanger; (*móvel*) hat stand; (*fixo à parede*) coat rack

cabine [ka'bini] *f* cabin; (*em loja*) fitting room; **~ do piloto** (Aer) cockpit; **~ telefônica** telephone box (BRIT) *ou* booth

cabo ['kabu] *m* (*extremidade*) end; (*de faca, vassoura etc*) handle; (*corda*) rope; (*elétrico etc*) cable; (Geo) cape; (Mil) corporal; **ao ~ de** at the end of; **de ~ a rabo** from beginning to end; **levar a ~** to carry out; **dar ~ de** to do away with

caboclo, -a [ka'boklu, a] (BR) *m/f* mestizo

cabra ['kabra] *f* goat

cabreiro, -a [ka'brejru, a] (*col*) *adj* suspicious

cabrito [ka'britu] *m* kid

caça ['kasa] *f* hunting; (*busca*) hunt; (*animal*) quarry, game ▷ *m* (Aer) fighter (plane); **caçador, a** [kasa'do^r, a] *m/f* hunter

cação [ka'sãw] (*pl* **-ões**) *m* shark

caçar [ka'sa^r] *vt* to hunt; (*com espingarda*) to shoot; (*procurar*) to seek ▷ *vi* to hunt, go hunting

caçarola [kasa'rɔla] *f* (*sauce*)pan

cacau [ka'kaw] *m* cocoa; (Bot) cacao

cacetada [kase'tada] *f* blow (with a stick)

cachaça [ka'ʃasa] *f* (*white*) rum

cachaceiro, -a [kaʃa'sejru, a] *adj* drunk ▷ *m/f* drunkard

cachê [ka'ʃe] *m* fee

cachecol [kaʃe'kɔw] *m* (*pl* **-óis**) *m* scarf

cachimbo [ka'ʃĩbu] *m* pipe

cacho ['kaʃu] *m* bunch; (*de cabelo*) curl; (*: longo*) ringlet

cachoeira [kaʃ'wejra] *f* waterfall

cachorra [ka'ʃoxa] *f* bitch; (*cadela*) (female) puppy

cachorrinho, -a [kaʃo'xiɲu, a] *m/f* puppy

cachorro [ka'ʃoxu] *m* dog; (*cãozinho*) puppy; **cachorro-quente** (*pl* **cachorros-quentes**) *m* hot dog

cacique [ka'siki] *m* (Indian) chief; (*mandachuva*) local boss

caco ['kaku] *m* bit, fragment; (*pessoa velha*) old relic

caçoar [ka'swa^r] *vt, vi* to mock

cacoete [ka'kwetʃi] *m* twitch, tic

cacto ['kaktu] *m* cactus

cada ['kada] *adj inv* each; (*todo*) every; **~ um** each one; **~ semana** each week; **a ~ 3 horas** every 3 hours; **~ vez mais** more and more

cadastro [ka'daʃtru] *m* register; (*ato*) registration; (*de criminosos*) criminal record

cadáver [ka'daveʳ] *m* corpse, (dead) body

cadê [ka'de] (*col*) *adv*: **~ ...?** where's/ where are ...?, what's happened to ...?

cadeado [ka'dʒjadu] *m* padlock

cadeia [ka'deja] *f* chain; (*prisão*) prison; (*rede*) network

cadeira [ka'dejra] *f* chair; (*disciplina*) subject; (*Teatro*) stall; (*função*) post; **cadeiras** *fpl* (*Anat*) hips; **~ de balanço/rodas** rocking chair/wheelchair

cadela [ka'dela] *f* (*cão*) bitch

caderneta [kadex'neta] *f* notebook; **~ de poupança** savings account

caderno [ka'dexnu] *m* exercise book; (*de notas*) notebook; (*de jornal*) section

caducar [kadu'kaʳ] *vi* to lapse, expire; **caduco, -a** [ka'duku, a] *adj* invalid, expired; (*senil*) senile; (*Bot*) deciduous

cães [kãjʃ] *mpl de* **cão**

cafajeste [kafa'ʒeʃtʃi] (*col*) *adj* roguish; (*vulgar*) vulgar, coarse ▷ *m/f* rogue; rough customer

café [ka'fɛ] *m* coffee; (*estabelecimento*) café; **~ com leite** white coffee (BRIT), coffee with cream (US); **~ preto** black coffee; **~ da manhã** (BR) breakfast

cafeteira [kafe'tejra] *f* coffee pot; (*máquina*) percolator; **cafezal** [kafe'zaw] (*pl* **-ais**) *m* coffee plantation; **cafezinho** [kafe'ziɲu] *m* small black coffee

cágado ['kagadu] *m* turtle

cagüetar [kagwe'taʳ] *vt* to inform on; **cagüete** [ka'gwetʃi] *m* informer

caiba *etc* ['kajba] *vb ver* **caber**

cãibra ['kãjbra] *f* (*Med*) cramp

caída [ka'ida] *f* = **queda**

caído, -a [ka'idu, a] *adj* dejected; (*derrubado*) fallen; (*pendente*) droopy; **~ por** (*apaixonado*) in love with

cãimbra ['kãjbra] *f* = **cãibra**

caipirinha [kajpi'riɲa] *f* cocktail of cachaça, lemon and sugar

cair [ka'iʳ] *vi* to fall; **~ bem/mal** (*roupa*) to fit well/badly; (*col: pessoa*) to look good/bad; **~ em si** to come to one's

senses; **ao ~ da noite** at nightfall; **essa comida me caiu mal** that food did not agree with me

Cairo ['kajru] *m*: **o ~** Cairo

cais [kajʃ] *m* (*Náut*) quay; (*PT: Ferro*) platform

caixa ['kajʃa] *f* box; (*cofre*) safe; (*de uma loja*) cashdesk ▷ *m/f* (*pessoa*) cashier ▷ *m*: **~ automático** cash machine; **pequena ~** petty cash; **~ de correio** letter box; **~ econômica** savings bank; **~ de mudanças** (BR) *ou* **de velocidades** (PT) gearbox; **~ postal** P.O. box; **~ registradora** cash register; **caixa-forte** (*pl* **caixas-fortes**) *f* vault

caixão [kaj'ʃãw] (*pl* **-ões**) *m* (*ataúde*) coffin; (*caixa grande*) large box

caixeiro-viajante, caixeira-viajante (*pl* **caixeiros-viajantes** *or* **caixeiras-viajantes**) *m/f* commercial traveller (BRIT) *ou* traveler (US)

caixilho [kaj'ʃiʎu] *m* (*moldura*) frame

caixões [kaj'ʃõjʃ] *mpl de* **caixão**

caixote [kaj'ʃɔtʃi] *m* packing case; **~ do lixo** (PT) dustbin (BRIT), garbage can (US)

caju [ka'ʒu] *m* cashew fruit

cal [kaw] *f* lime; (*na água*) chalk; (*para caiar*) whitewash

calabouço [kala'bosu] *m* dungeon

calado, -a [ka'ladu, a] *adj* quiet

calafrio [kala'friu] *m* shiver; **ter ~s** to shiver

calamidade [kalami'dadʒi] *f* calamity, disaster

calão [ka'lãw] (PT) *m*: (**baixo**) **~** slang

calar [ka'laʳ] *vt* to keep quiet about; (*impor silêncio a*) to silence ▷ *vi* to go quiet; (*manter-se calado*) to keep quiet; **~-se** *vr* to go quiet; to keep quiet; **cala a boca!** shut up!

calça ['kawsa] *f* (*tb*: **~s**) trousers *pl* (BRIT), pants *pl* (US)

calçada [kaw'sada] *f* (BR: *passeio*) pavement (BRIT), sidewalk (US); (PT: *rua*) roadway

calçadão [kawsa'dãw] (*pl* **-ões**) *m* pedestrian precinct (BRIT)

calçado, -a [kaw'sadu, a] *adj* (*rua*) paved ▷ *m* shoe; **calçados** *mpl* (*para os pés*) footwear *sg*

calçadões [kawsa'dõjʃ] *mpl de* **calçadão**

calçamento [kawsa'mẽtu] *m* paving

calcanhar [kawka'ɲaʳ] *m* (*Anat*) heel

calção [kaw'sãw] (*pl* **-ões**) *m* shorts *pl*; **~ de banho** swimming trunks *pl*

calcar [kaw'ka^r] *vt* to tread on; (*espezinhar*) to trample (on)

calçar [kaw'sa^r] *vt* (*sapatos, luvas*) to put on; (*pavimentar*) to pave; **~-se** *vr* to put on one's shoes; **ela calça (número) 28** she takes size 28 (in shoes)

calcário [kaw'karju] *m* limestone

calcinha [kaw'siɲa] *f* panties *pl*

calço ['kawsu] *m* wedge

calções [kaw'sõjʃ] *mpl de* **calção**

calculador [kawkula'do^r] *m* = **calculadora**

calculadora [kawkula'dora] *f* calculator

calcular [kawku'la^r] *vt* to calculate; (*imaginar*) to imagine; **~ que** to reckon that

cálculo ['kawkulu] *m* calculation; (*Mat*) calculus; (*Med*) stone

calda ['kawda] *f* (*de doce*) syrup; **caldas** *fpl* (*águas termais*) hot springs

caldeirada [kawdej'rada] (*PT*) *f* (*guisado*) fish stew

caldo ['kawdu] *m* broth; (*de fruta*) juice; **~ de carne/galinha** beef/chicken stock; **~ verde** potato and cabbage broth

calendário [kalẽ'darju] *m* calendar

calhar [ka'ʎa^r] *vi*: **calhou viajarmos no mesmo avião** we happened to travel on the same plane; **calhou que** it so happened that; **~ a** (*cair bem*) to suit; **se ~** (*PT*) perhaps, maybe

calibre [ka'libri] *m* calibre (*BRIT*), caliber (*US*)

cálice ['kalisi] *m* wine glass; (*Rel*) chalice

calista [ka'liʃta] *m/f* chiropodist (*BRIT*), podiatrist (*US*)

calma ['kawma] *f* calm

calmante [kaw'mãtʃi] *adj* soothing ▷ *m* (*Med*) tranquillizer

calmo, -a ['kawmu, a] *adj* calm

calo ['kalu] *m* callus; (*no pé*) corn

calor [ka'lo^r] *m* heat; (*agradável, fig*) warmth; **está** *ou* **faz ~** it is hot; **estar com ~** to be hot

calorento, -a [kalo'rẽtu, a] *adj* (*pessoa*) sensitive to heat; (*lugar*) hot

caloria [calo'ria] *f* calorie

caloroso, -a [kalo'rozu, ɔza] *adj* warm; (*entusiástico*) enthusiastic

calouro, -a [ka'loru, a] *m/f* (*Educ*) fresher (*BRIT*), freshman (*US*)

calúnia [ka'lunja] *f* slander

calvo, -a ['kawvu, a] *adj* bald

cama ['kama] *f* bed; **~ de casal** double bed; **~ de solteiro** single bed; **de ~** (*doente*) ill (in bed)

camada [ka'mada] *f* layer; (*de tinta*) coat

câmara ['kamara] *f* chamber; (*Foto*) camera; **~ municipal** (*BR*) town council; (*PT*) town hall; **~ digital** digital camera; **em ~ lenta** in slow motion

câmara-de-ar (*pl* **câmaras-de-ar**) *f* inner tube

camarão [kama'rãw] (*pl* **-ões**) *m* shrimp; (*graúdo*) prawn

camarões [kama'rõjʃ] *mpl de* **camarão**

camarote [kama'rɔtʃi] *m* (*Náut*) cabin; (*Teatro*) box

cambaleante [kãba'ljãtʃi] *adj* unsteady (on one's feet)

cambalhota [kãba'ʎɔta] *f* somersault

câmbio ['kãbju] *m* (*dinheiro etc*) exchange; (*preço de câmbio*) rate of exchange; **~ livre** free trade; **~ paralelo** black market

cambista [kã'biʃta] *m* money changer

Camboja [kã'bɔja] *m*: **o ~** Cambodia

camelo [ka'melu] *m* camel

camião [ka'mjãw] (*pl* **-ões** (*PT*)) *m* lorry (*BRIT*), truck (*US*)

caminhada [kami'ɲada] *f* walk

caminhão [kami'ɲãw] (*pl* **-ões** (*BR*)) *m* lorry (*BRIT*), truck (*US*)

caminhar [kami'ɲa^r] *vi* to walk; (*processo*) to get under way; (*negócios*) to progress

caminho [ka'miɲu] *m* way; (*vereda*) road, path; **~ de ferro** (*PT*) railway (*BRIT*), railroad (*US*); **a ~** on the way, en route; **cortar ~** to take a short cut; **pôr-se a ~** to set off

caminhões [kami'ɲõjʃ] *mpl de* **caminhão**

caminhoneiro, -a [kamiɲo'nejru, a] *m/f* lorry driver (*BRIT*), truck driver (*US*)

camiões [ka'mjõjʃ] *mpl de* **camião**

camioneta [kamjo'neta] (*PT*) *f* (*para passageiros*) coach; (*comercial*) van

camionista [kamjo'niʃta] (*PT*) *m/f* lorry driver (*BRIT*), truck driver (*US*)

camisa [ka'miza] *f* shirt; **~ de dormir** nightshirt; **~ esporte/pólo/social** sports/polo/dress shirt; **mudar de ~** (*Esporte*) to change sides; **camisa-de-força** (*pl* **camisas-de-força**) *f* straitjacket

camiseta [kami'zeta] (*BR*) *f* T-shirt; (*interior*) vest

camisinha [kami'ziɲa] (*col*) *f* condom

camisola [kami'zɔla] f (BR) nightdress; (PT: *pulôver*) sweater; **~ interior** (PT) vest

campainha [kampa'iɲa] f bell

campanário [kãpa'narju] m church tower, steeple

campeão, -peã [kã'pjãw, 'pjã] (pl **campeões/-s**) m/f champion; **campeonato** [kãpjo'natu] m championship

campestre [kã'pɛʃtri] adj rural, rustic

camping ['kãpĩ] (BR): (pl **-s**) m camping; (*lugar*) campsite

campismo [kã'piʒmu] m camping; **parque de ~** campsite

campista [kã'piʃta] m/f camper

campo [kãpu] m field; (*fora da cidade*) countryside; (*Esporte*) ground; (*acampamento*) camp; (*Tênis*) court

camponês, -esa [kãpo'neʃ, eza] m/f countryman/woman; (*agricultor*) farmer

campus ['kãpuʃ] m inv campus

camuflagem [kamu'flaʒẽ] f camouflage

camundongo [kamũ'dõgu] (BR) m mouse

camurça [ka'muxsa] f suede

cana ['kana] f cane; (col: *cadeia*) nick; (*de açúcar*) sugar cane

Canadá [kana'da] m: **o ~** Canada; **canadense** [kana'dẽsi] adj, m/f Canadian

canal [ka'naw] (pl **-ais**) m channel; (*de navegação*) canal; (*Anat*) duct

canalização [kanaliza'sãw] f plumbing

canalizador, a [kanaliza'doʳ, a] (PT) m/f plumber

canário [ka'narju] m canary

canastra [ka'naʃtra] f (big) basket

canção [kã'sãw] (pl **-ões**) f song; **~ de ninar** lullaby

cancela [kã'sɛla] f gate

cancelamento [kãsela'mẽtu] m cancellation

cancelar [kãse'laʳ] vt to cancel; (*riscar*) to cross out

câncer ['kãseʳ] m cancer; **C~** (*Astrologia*) Cancer

canções [kã'sõjʃ] fpl de **canção**

cancro ['kãkru] (PT) m cancer

candelabro [kãde'labru] m candlestick; (*lustre*) chandelier

candidato, -a [kãdʒi'datu, a] m/f candidate; (*a cargo*) applicant

cândido, -a ['kãdʒidu, a] adj naive; (*inocente*) innocent

Candomblé [kãdõblɛ] m *see boxed note*

caneca [ka'nɛka] f mug

canela [ka'nɛla] f cinnamon; (*Anat*) shin

caneta [ka'neta] f pen; **~ esferográfica/ pilot** ballpoint/felt-tip pen; **~ seletora** (*Comput*) light pen

cangaceiro [kãga'sejru] (BR) m bandit

canguru [kãgu'ru] m kangaroo

canhão [ka'ɲãw] (pl **-ões**) m cannon; (*Geo*) canyon

canhoto, -a [ka'ɲotu, a] adj left-handed ▷ m/f left-handed person ▷ m (*de cheque*) stub

canibal [kani'baw] (pl **-ais**) m/f cannibal

canil [ka'niw] (pl **-is**) m kennel

canja ['kãʒa] f chicken broth; (*col*) cinch, pushover

canjica [kã'ʒika] f maize porridge

cano ['kanu] m pipe; (*tubo*) tube; (*de arma de fogo*) barrel; (*de bota*) top; **~ de esgoto** sewer

canoa [ka'noa] f canoe

cansaço [kã'sasu] m tiredness

cansado, -a [kã'sadu, a] adj tired

cansar [kã'saʳ] vt to tire; (*entediar*) to bore ▷ vi to get tired; **~-se** vr to get tired; **cansativo, -a** [kãsa'tʃivu, a] adj tiring; (*tedioso*) tedious

cantar [kã'taʳ] vt, vi to sing ▷ m song

canteiro [kã'tejru] m stonemason; (*de flores*) flower bed

cantiga [kã'tʃiga] f ballad; **~ de ninar** lullaby

cantil [kã'tʃiw] (pl **-is**) m canteen

cantina [kã'tʃina] f canteen

cantis [kã'tʃiʃ] mpl de **cantil**

canto ['kãtu] m corner; (*lugar*) place; (*canção*) song

cantor, a [kã'toʳ, a] m/f singer

cão [kãw] (pl **cães**) m dog

caolho, -a [ka'oʎu, a] adj cross-eyed

caos ['kaoʃ] *m* chaos

capa ['kapa] *f* cape; (*cobertura*) cover; **livro de ~ dura/mole** hardback/ paperback (book)

capacete [kapa'setʃi] *m* helmet

capacidade [kapasi'dadʒi] *f* capacity; (*aptidão*) ability, competence

capaz [ka'paʒ] *adj* able, capable; **ser ~ de** to be able to (*ou* capable of); **sou ~ de ...** (*talvez*) I might ...; **é ~ de chover hoje** it might rain today

capela [ka'pɛla] *f* chapel

capim [ka'pĩ] *m* grass

capitães [kapi'tãjʃ] *mpl de* **capitão**

capital [kapi'taw] (*pl* -**ais**) *adj, m* capital ▷ *f* (*cidade*) capital; **~ (em) ações** (*Com*) share capital

capitalismo [kapita'liʒmu] *m* capitalism; **capitalista** [kapita'liʃta] *m/f* capitalist

capitalizar [kapitali'zaʳ] *vt* to capitalize on; (*Com*) to capitalize

capitão [kapi'tãw] (*pl* -**ães**) *m* captain

capítulo [ka'pitulu] *m* chapter

capô [ka'po] *m* (*Auto*) bonnet (BRIT), hood (US)

capoeira [ca'pwejra] (PT) *f* hencoop; (*dança*) *see boxed note*

capota [ka'pɔta] *f* (*Auto*) hood, top

capotar [kapo'taʳ] *vi* to overturn

capricho [ka'priʃu] *m* whim, caprice; (*teimosia*) obstinacy; (*apuro*) care; **caprichoso, -a** [kapri'ʃozu, ɔza] *adj* capricious; (*com apuro*) meticulous

Capricórnio [kapri'kɔxnju] *m* Capricorn

cápsula ['kapsula] *f* capsule

captar [kap'taʳ] *vt* (*atrair*) to win; (*Rádio*) to pick up

captura [kap'tura] *f* capture; **capturar** [kaptu'raʳ] *vt* to capture

capuz [ka'puʒ] *m* hood

cáqui ['kaki] *adj* khaki

cara ['kara] *f* face; (*aspecto*) appearance ▷ *m* (*col*) guy; **~ ou coroa?** heads or tails?; **de ~** straightaway; **dar de ~ com** to bump into; **ser a ~ de** (*col*) to be the spitting image of; **ter ~ de** to look (like)

caracol [kara'kɔw] (*pl* -**óis**) *m* snail; (*de cabelo*) curl; **escada em ~** spiral staircase

caracteres [karak'tɛriʃ] *mpl de* **caráter**

característica [karakte'riʃtʃika] *f* characteristic, feature

característico, -a [karakte'riʃtʃiku, a] *adj* characteristic

cara-de-pau (*pl* **caras-de-pau**) *adj* brazen ▷ *m/f*: **ele é ~** he's very forward

caramelo [kara'mɛlu] *m* caramel; (*bala*) toffee

caranguejo [karã'geʒu] *m* crab

caras-pintadas *fpl see boxed note*

caratê [kara'te] *m* karate

caráter [ka'rateʳ] (*pl* **caracteres**) *m* character

caravana [kara'vana] *f* caravan

cardápio [kax'dapju] (BR) *m* menu

cardeal [kax'dʒjaw] (*pl* -**ais**) *adj, m* cardinal

cardigã [kaxdʒi'gã] *m* cardigan

careca [ka'rɛka] *adj* bald

carecer [kare'seʳ] *vi*: **~ de** to lack; (*precisar*) to need

carência [ka'rẽsja] *f* lack; (*necessidade*) need; (*privação*) deprivation; **carente** [ka'rẽtʃi] *adj* wanting; (*pessoa*) needy, deprived

carga ['kaxga] *f* load; (*de navio, avião*) cargo; (*ato de carregar*) loading; (*Elet*) charge; (*fig: peso*) burden; (*Mil*) attack, charge; **dar ~ em** (*Comput*) to boot (up)

cargo ['kaxgu] *m* responsibility; (*função*) post; **a ~ de** in charge of; **ter a ~** to be in charge of; **tomar a ~** to take charge of

Caribe [ka'ribi] *m*: **o ~** the Caribbean (Sea)

caridade [kari'dadʒi] *f* charity; **obra de**

~ charity
cárie [ˈkari] f tooth decay
carimbar [karĩˈbaʳ] vt to stamp; (no correio) to postmark
carimbo [kaˈrĩbu] m stamp; (postal) postmark
carinho [kaˈriɲu] m affection, fondness; (carícia) caress; **fazer ~** to caress; **com ~** affectionately; (com cuidado) with care; **carinhoso, -a** [kariˈɲozu, ɔza] adj affectionate
carioca [kaˈrjɔka] adj of Rio de Janeiro ▷ m/f native of Rio de Janeiro ▷ m (PT: café) type of weak coffee
carnal [kaxˈnaw] (pl **-ais**) adj carnal; **primo ~** first cousin
carnaval [kaxnaˈvaw] (pl **-ais**) m carnival; (fig) mess

※ **CARNAVAL**
※
※ In Brazil, **Carnaval** is the popular
※ festival held each year in the four days
※ before Lent. It is celebrated in very
※ different ways in different parts of the
※ country. In Rio de Janeiro, for example,
※ the big attraction is the parades of
※ the *escolas de samba*, in Salvador the
※ *trios elétricos*, in Recife the *frevo* and,
※ in Olinda, the giant figures, such as
※ the *Homem da meia-noite* and *Mulher
※ do meio-dia*. In Portugal, **Carnaval** is
※ celebrated on Shrove Tuesday, with
※ street parties and processions taking
※ place throughout the country.

carne [ˈkaxni] f flesh; (Culin) meat; **em ~ e osso** in the flesh
carnê [kaxˈne] m (para compras) payment book
carneiro [kaxˈnejru] m sheep; (macho) ram; **perna/costeleta de ~** leg of lamb/lamb chop
carnificina [kaxnifiˈsina] f slaughter
caro, -a [ˈkaru, a] adj dear; **cobrar/pagar ~** to charge a lot/pay dearly
carochinha [karoˈʃiɲa] f: **conto ou história da ~** fairy tale ou story
caroço [kaˈrosu] m (de frutos) stone; (endurecimento) lump
carona [kaˈrɔna] f lift; **viajar de ~** to hitchhike; **pegar uma ~** to get a lift
carpete [kaxˈpetʃi] m (fitted) carpet
carpinteiro [kaxpĩˈtejru] m carpenter
carrapato [kaxaˈpatu] m (inseto) tick
carrasco [kaˈxaʃku] m executioner; (fig)

tyrant
carregado, -a [kaxeˈgadu, a] adj loaded; (semblante) sullen; (céu) dark; (ambiente) tense
carregador [kaxegaˈdoʳ] m porter
carregamento [kaxegaˈmẽtu] m (ação) loading; (carga) load, cargo
carregar [kaxeˈgaʳ] vt to load; (levar) to carry; (bateria) to charge; (PT: apertar) to press; (levar para longe) to take away ▷ vi: **~ em** to overdo; (pôr enfase) to bring out
carreira [kaˈxejra] f run, running; (profissão) career; (Turfe) race; (Náut) slipway; (fileira) row; **às ~s** in a hurry
carretel [kaxeˈtɛw] (pl **-éis**) m spool, reel
carrinho [kaˈxiɲu] m trolley; (brinquedo) toy car; **~ (de criança)** pram; **~ de mão** wheelbarrow
carro [ˈkaxo] m car; (de bois) cart; (de mão) barrow; (de máquina de escrever) carriage; **~ de corrida/passeio/esporte** racing/saloon/sports car; **~ de praça** cab; **~ de bombeiro** fire engine
carroça [kaˈxɔsa] f cart, waggon
carroçeria [kaxoseˈria] f (Auto) bodywork
carro-chefe (pl **carros-chefes**) m (de desfile) main float; (fig) flagship, centrepiece (BRIT), centerpiece (US)
carrossel [kaxoˈsɛw] (pl **-éis**) m merry-go-round
carruagem [kaˈxwaʒẽ] (pl **-ns**) f carriage, coach
carta [ˈkaxta] f letter; (de jogar) card; (mapa) chart; **~ aérea/registrada** airmail/registered letter; **~ de condução** (PT) driving licence (BRIT), driver's license (US); **dar as ~s** to deal
cartão [kaxˈtãw] (pl **-ões**) m card; (PT: material) cardboard; **~ de crédito** credit card; **~ de recarga** (para celular) top-up card; **cartão-postal** (pl **cartões-postais**) m postcard
cartaz [kaxˈtaʒ] m poster, bill (US); (estar) **em ~** (Teatro, Cinema) (to be) showing
carteira [kaxˈtejra] f desk; (para dinheiro) wallet; (de ações) portfolio; **~ de identidade** identity card; **~ de motorista** driving licence (BRIT), driver's license (US)
carteiro [kaxˈtejru] m postman (BRIT), mailman (US)
cartões [kaxˈtõjʃ] mpl de **cartão**
cartola [kaxˈtola] f top hat
cartolina [kaxtoˈlina] f card

cartório [kax'tɔrju] *m* registry office
cartucho [kax'tuʃu] *m* cartridge; (*saco de papel*) packet
cartum [kax'tũ] (*pl* **-ns**) *m* cartoon
carvalho [kax'vaʎu] *m* oak
carvão [kax'vãw] (*pl* **-ões**) *m* coal; (*de madeira*) charcoal
casa ['kaza] *f* house; (*lar*) home; (*Com*) firm; (*Mat: decimal*) place; **em/para ~** (at) home/home; **~ de saúde** hospital; **~ da moeda** mint; **~ de banho** (PT) bathroom; **~ e comida** board and lodging; **~ de cômodos** tenement; **~ popular** ≈ council house
casacão [kaza'kãw] (*pl* **-ões**) *m* overcoat
casaco [ka'zaku] *m* coat; (*paletó*) jacket
casacões [kaza'kõjʃ] *mpl de* **casacão**
casal [ka'zaw] (*pl* **-ais**) *m* couple
casamento [kaza'mẽtu] *m* marriage; (*boda*) wedding
casar [ka'za'] *vt* to marry; (*combinar*) to match (up); **~-se** *vr* to get married; to combine well
casarão [kaza'rãw] (*pl* **-ões**) *m* mansion
casca ['kaʃka] *f* (*de árvore*) bark; (*de banana*) skin; (*de ferida*) scab; (*de laranja*) peel; (*de nozes, ovos*) shell; (*de milho etc*) husk; (*de pão*) crust
cascata [kaʃ'kata] *f* waterfall
casco ['kaʃku] *m* skull; (*de animal*) hoof; (*de navio*) hull; (*para bebidas*) empty bottle; (*de tartaruga*) shell
caseiro, -a [ka'zejru, a] *adj* home-made; (*pessoa, vida*) domestic ▷ *m/f* housekeeper
caso ['kazu] *m* case; (*tb*: **~ amoroso**) affair; (*estória*) story ▷ *conj* in case, if; **no ~ de** in case (of); **em todo ~** in any case; **neste ~** in that case; **~ necessário** if necessary; **criar ~** to cause trouble; **não fazer ~ de** to ignore; **~ de emergência** emergency
caspa ['kaʃpa] *f* dandruff
casquinha [kaʃ'kiɲa] *f* (*de sorvete*) cone; (*pele*) skin
cassar [ka'sa'] *vt* (*direitos, licença*) to cancel, withhold; (*políticos*) to ban
cassete [ka'sɛtʃi] *m* cassette
cassino [ka'sinu] *m* casino
castanha [kaʃ'taɲa] *f* chestnut; **~ de caju** cashew nut; **castanha-do-pará** [-pa'ra] (*pl* **castanhas-do-pará**) *f* Brazil nut
castanheiro [kaʃta'ɲejru] *m* chestnut tree
castanho, -a [kaʃ'taɲu, a] *adj* brown

castelo [kaʃ'tɛlu] *m* castle
castiçal [kaʃtʃi'saw] (*pl* **-ais**) *m* candlestick
castiço, -a [kaʃ'tʃisu, a] *adj* pure
castidade [kaʃtʃi'dadʒi] *f* chastity
castigar [kaʃtʃi'ga'] *vt* to punish; **castigo** [kaʃ'tʃigu] *m* punishment; (*fig*: *mortificação*) pain
casto, -a ['kaʃtu, a] *adj* chaste
casual [ka'zwaw] (*pl* **-ais**) *adj* chance *atr*, accidental; (*fortuito*) fortuitous; **casualidade** [kazwali'dadʒi] *f* chance; (*acidente*) accident
cata ['kata] *f*: **à ~ de** in search of
catalizador [kataliza'do'] *m* catalyst
catalogar [katalo'ga'] *vt* to catalogue (BRIT), catalog (US)
catálogo [ka'talogu] *m* catalogue (BRIT), catalog (US); **~ (telefônico)** telephone directory
catapora [kata'pɔra] (BR) *f* chickenpox
catar [ka'ta'] *vt* to pick (up); (*procurar*) to look for, search for; (*recolher*) to collect, gather
catarata [kata'rata] *f* waterfall; (*Med*) cataract
catarro [ka'taxu] *m* catarrh
catástrofe [ka'taʃtrofi] *f* catastrophe
cata-vento *m* weathercock
catedral [kate'draw] (*pl* **-ais**) *f* cathedral
categoria [katego'ria] *f* category; (*social*) rank; (*qualidade*) quality; **de alta ~** first-rate
cativar [katʃi'va'] *vt* to enslave; (*fascinar*) to captivate; (*atrair*) to charm
cativeiro [katʃi'vejru] *m* captivity; (*escravidão*) slavery; (*cadeia*) prison
católico, -a [ka'tɔliku, a] *adj, m/f* catholic
catorze [ka'toxzi] *num* fourteen
caução [kaw'sãw] (*pl* **-ões**) *f* security, guarantee; (*Jur*) bail; **sob ~** on bail
caule ['kauli] *m* stalk, stem
causa ['kawza] *f* cause; (*motivo*) motive, reason; (*Jur*) lawsuit, case; **por ~ de** because of; **causador, a** [kawza'do', a] *adj* which caused ▷ *m* cause; **causar** [kaw'za'] *vt* to cause, bring about
cautela [kaw'tɛla] *f* caution; (*senha*) ticket; **~ (de penhor)** pawn ticket; **cauteloso, -a** [kawte'lozu, ɔza] *adj* cautious, wary
cavado, -a [ka'vadu, a] *adj* (*olhos*) sunken; (*roupa*) low-cut
cavala [ka'vala] *f* mackerel
cavaleiro [kava'lejru] *m* rider,

horseman; (*medieval*) knight

cavalheiro, -a [kava'ʎejru, a] *adj* courteous, gallant ▷ *m* gentleman

cavalo [ka'valu] *m* horse; (*Xadrez*) knight; **a** ~ on horseback; **50 ~s(-vapor** ou **de força)** 50 horsepower; ~ **de corrida** racehorse

cavaquinho [kava'kiɲu] *m* small guitar

cavar [ka'va ͬ] *vt* to dig; (*esforçar-se para obter*) to try to get ▷ *vi* to dig; (*fig*) to delve; (*animal*) to burrow

cave ['kavi] (PT) *f* wine-cellar

caveira [ka'vejra] *f* skull

cavidade [kavi'dadʒi] *f* cavity

caxumba [ka'ʃũba] *f* mumps *sg*

CD *abr m* CD

cê [se] (*col*) *pron* = **você**

cear [sja ͬ] *vt* to have for supper ▷ *vi* to dine

cebola [se'bola] *f* onion; **cebolinha** [sebo'liɲa] *f* spring onion

ceder [se'de ͬ] *vt* to give up; (*dar*) to hand over; (*emprestar*) to lend ▷ *vi* to give in, yield

cedilha [se'dʒiʎa] *f* cedilla

cedo ['sedu] *adv* early; (*em breve*) soon

cedro ['sedru] *m* cedar

cédula ['sedula] *f* banknote; (*eleitoral*) ballot paper

CEE *abr f* (= *Comunidade Econômica Européia*) EEC

cegar [se'ga ͬ] *vt* to blind; (*ofuscar*) to dazzle ▷ *vi* to be dazzling

cego, -a ['sɛgu, a] *adj* blind; (*total*) complete, total; (*tesoura*) blunt ▷ *m/f* blind man/woman; **às cegas** blindly

ceia ['seja] *f* supper

cela ['sɛla] *f* cell

celebração [selebra'sãw] (*pl* **-ões**) *f* celebration

celebrar [sele'bra ͬ] *vt* to celebrate; (*exaltar*) to praise; (*acordo*) to seal

celeiro [se'lejru] *m* granary; (*depósito*) barn

celeste [se'lɛʃtʃi] *adj* celestial, heavenly

celibatário, -a [seliba'tarju, a] *adj* unmarried, single ▷ *m/f* bachelor/ spinster

celofane [selo'fani] *m* cellophane; **papel** ~ cling film

célula ['sɛlula] *f* (*Bio, Elet*) cell; **celular** [selu'la ͬ] *adj* cellular ▷ *n*: **(telefone) celular** mobile (phone) (BRIT), cellphone (US); **celular com câmera** camera phone

cem [sẽ] *num* hundred

cemitério [semi'tɛrju] *m* cemetery,

graveyard

cena ['sɛna] *f* scene; (*palco*) stage

cenário [se'narju] *m* scenery; (*Cinema*) scenario; (*de um acontecimento*) setting

cenoura [se'nora] *f* carrot

censo ['sẽsu] *m* census

censor, a [sẽ'so ͬ, a] *m/f* censor

censura [sẽ'sura] *f* censorship; (*reprovação*) censure, criticism; **censurar** [sẽsu'ra ͬ] *vt* to censure; (*filme, livro etc*) to censor

centavo [sẽ'tavu] *m* cent; **estar sem um** ~ to be penniless

centeio [sẽ'teju] *m* rye

centelha [sẽ'teʎa] *f* spark

centena [sẽ'tɛna] *f* hundred; **às ~s** in hundreds

centenário, -a [sẽte'narju, a] *m* centenary

centígrado [sẽ'tʃigradu] *m* centigrade

centímetro [sẽ'tʃimetru] *m* centimetre (BRIT), centimeter (US)

cento ['sẽtu] *m*: ~ **e um** one hundred and one; **por** ~ per cent

centopeia [sẽto'peja] *f* centipede

central [sẽ'traw] (*pl* **-ais**) *adj* central ▷ *f* (*de polícia etc*) head office; ~ **elétrica** (electric) power station; ~ **telefônica** telephone exchange; **centralizar** [sẽtrali'za ͬ] *vt* to centralize

centrar [sẽ'tra ͬ] *vt* to centre (BRIT), center (US)

centro ['sẽtru] *m* centre (BRIT), center (US); (*de uma cidade*) town centre; **centroavante** [sẽtroa'vãtʃi] *m* (*Futebol*) centre forward

CEP ['sɛpi] (BR) *abr m* (= *Código de Endereçamento Postal*) postcode (BRIT), zip code (US)

céptico, -a *etc* ['septiku, a] (PT) = **cético** *etc*

cera ['sera] *f* wax

cerâmica [se'ramika] *f* pottery

cerca ['sexka] *f* fence ▷ *prep*: ~ **de** (*aproximadamente*) around, about; ~ **viva** hedge

cercado [sex'kadu] *m* enclosure; (*para animais*) pen; (*para crianças*) playpen

cercanias [sexka'niaʃ] *fpl* outskirts; (*vizinhança*) neighbourhood *sg* (BRIT), neighborhood *sg* (US)

cerco ['sexku] *m* siege; **pôr ~ a** to besiege

cereal [se'rjaw] (*pl* **-ais**) *m* cereal

cérebro ['serebru] *m* brain; (*fig*) brains *pl*

cereja [se'reʒa] *f* cherry

cerimônia [seri'monja] *f* ceremony

cerração [sexa'sãw] f fog

cerrado, -a [se'xadu, a] adj shut, closed; (denso) thick ▷ m scrub(land)

certeza [sex'teza] f certainty; **com ~** certainly, surely; (provavelmente) probably; **ter ~ de/de que** to be certain ou sure of/to be sure that

certidão [sextʃi'dãw] (pl **-ões**) f certificate

certificado [sextʃifi'kadu] m certificate

certificar [sextʃifi'kaʳ] vt to certify; (assegurar) to assure; **~-se** vr: **~-se de** to make sure of

certo, -a ['sɛxtu, a] adj certain, sure; (exato, direito) right; (um, algum) a certain ▷ adv correctly; **na certa** certainly; **ao ~** for certain; **está ~** okay, all right

cerveja [sex'veʒa] f beer; **cervejaria** [sexveʒa'ria] f (fábrica) brewery; (bar) bar, public house

cervical [sexvi'kaw] (pl **-ais**) adj cervical

cessação [sesa'sãw] f halting, ceasing

cessão [se'sãw] (pl **-ões**) f surrender

cessar [se'saʳ] vi to cease, stop; **sem ~** continually; **cessar-fogo** m inv ceasefire

cessões [se'sõjʃ] fpl de **cessão**

cesta ['seʃta] f basket

cesto ['seʃtu] m basket; (com tampa) hamper

cético, -a ['sɛtʃiku, a] m/f sceptic (BRIT), skeptic (US)

cetim [se'tʃĩ] m satin

céu [sɛw] m sky; (Rel) heaven; (da boca) roof

cevada [se'vada] f barley

chá [ʃa] m tea

chácara ['ʃakara] f farm; (casa de campo) country house

chacina [ʃa'sina] f slaughter; **chacinar** [ʃasi'naʳ] vt (matar) to slaughter

chacota [ʃa'kɔta] f mockery

chafariz [ʃafa'riʒ] m fountain

chalé [ʃa'lɛ] m chalet

chaleira [ʃa'lejra] f kettle; (bajulador) crawler, toady

chama ['ʃama] f flame

chamada [ʃa'mada] f call; (Mil) roll call; (Educ) register; (no jornal) headline; **dar uma ~ em alguém** to tell sb off

chamar [ʃa'maʳ] vt to call; (convidar) to invite; (atenção) to attract ▷ vi to call; (telefone) to ring; **~-se** vr to be called; **chamo-me João** my name is John; **~ alguém de idiota/Dudu** to call sb an idiot/Dudu; **mandar ~** to summon, send for

chamariz [ʃama'riʒ] m decoy

chamativo, -a [ʃama'tʃivu, a] adj showy, flashy

chaminé [ʃami'nɛ] f chimney; (de navio) funnel

champanha [ʃã'paɲa] m ou f champagne

champanhe [ʃã'paɲi] m ou f = **champanha**

champu [ʃã'pu] (PT) m shampoo

chance ['ʃãsi] f chance

chantagear [ʃãta'ʒjaʳ] vt to blackmail

chantagem [ʃã'taʒẽ] f blackmail

chão [ʃãw] (pl **-s**) m ground; (terra) soil; (piso) floor

chapa ['ʃapa] f (placa) plate; (eleitoral) list; **~ de matrícula** (PT: Auto) number (BRIT) ou license (US) plate; **oi, meu ~!** hi, mate!

chapéu [ʃa'pɛw] m hat

charco ['ʃaxku] m marsh, bog

charme ['ʃaxmi] m charm; **fazer ~** to be nice, use one's charm; **charmoso, -a** [ʃax'mozu, ɔza] adj charming

charrete [ʃa'xɛtʃi] f cart

charuto [ʃa'rutu] m cigar

chassi [ʃa'si] m (Auto, Elet) chassis

chata ['ʃata] f barge; ver tb **chato**

chateação [ʃatʃja'sãw] (pl **-ões**) f bother, upset; (maçada) bore

chatear [ʃa'tʃjaʳ] vt to bother, upset; (importunar) to pester; (entediar) to bore; (irritar) to annoy ▷ vi to be upsetting; to be boring; to be annoying; **~-se** vr to get upset; to get bored; to get annoyed

chatice [ʃa'tʃisi] f nuisance

chato, -a ['ʃatu, a] adj flat; (tedioso) boring; (irritante) annoying; (que fica mal) rude ▷ m/f bore; (quem irrita) pain

chauvinista [ʃawvi'niʃta] adj chauvinistic ▷ m/f chauvinist

chavão [ʃa'vãw] (pl **-ões**) m cliché

chave ['ʃavi] f key; (Elet) switch; **~ de porcas** spanner; **~ inglesa** (monkey) wrench; **~ de fenda** screwdriver

chávena ['ʃavena] (PT) f cup

checar [ʃe'kaʳ] vt to check

check-up [tʃe'kapi] (pl **-s**) m check-up

chefe ['ʃɛfi] m/f head, chief; (patrão) boss; **~ de estação** stationmaster; **chefia** [ʃe'fia] f leadership; (direção) management; (repartição) headquarters sg; **chefiar** [ʃe'fjaʳ] vt to lead

chegada [ʃe'gada] f arrival

chegado, -a [ʃe'gadu, a] adj near; (íntimo) close

chegar [ʃe'gaʳ] *vt* to bring near ▷ *vi* to arrive; (*ser suficiente*) to be enough; **~-se** *vr:* **~-se a** to approach; **chega!** that's enough!; **~ a** (*atingir*) to reach; (*conseguir*) to manage to

cheio, -a ['ʃeju, a] *adj* full; (*repleto*) full up; (*col: farto*) fed up

cheirar [ʃej'raʳ] *vt, vi* to smell; **~ a** to smell of; **cheiro** ['ʃejru] *m* smell; **ter cheiro de** to smell of; **cheiroso, -a** [ʃej'rozu, ɔza] *adj:* **ser** *ou* **estar cheiroso/a** to smell nice

cheque ['ʃɛki] *m* cheque (*BRIT*), check (*US*); **~ de viagem** traveller's cheque (*BRIT*), traveler's check (*US*)

chiar [ʃjaʳ] *vi* to squeak; (*porta*) to creak; (*vapor*) to hiss; (*col: reclamar*) to grumble

chiclete [ʃi'klɛtʃi] *m* chewing gum

chicória [ʃi'kɔrja] *f* chicory

chicote [ʃi'kɔtʃi] *m* whip

chifre ['ʃifri] *m* horn

Chile ['ʃili] *m:* **o ~** Chile

chimarrão [ʃima'xãw] (*pl* **-ões**) *m* mate tea without sugar taken from a pipe-like cup

chimpanzé [ʃĩpã'zɛ] *m* chimpanzee

China ['ʃina] *f:* **a ~** China

chinelo [ʃi'nɛlu] *m* slipper

chinês, -esa [ʃi'neʃ, eza] *adj, m/f* Chinese ▷ *m* (*Ling*) Chinese

chip ['ʃipi] *m* (*Comput*) chip

Chipre ['ʃipri] *f* Cyprus

chique ['ʃiki] *adj* stylish, chic

chocalho [ʃo'kaʎu] *m* (*Mús, brinquedo*) rattle; (*para animais*) bell

chocante [ʃo'kãtʃi] *adj* shocking; (*col*) amazing

chocar [ʃo'kaʳ] *vt* to hatch, incubate; (*ofender*) to shock, offend ▷ *vi* to shock; **~-se** *vr* to crash, collide; to be shocked

chocho, -a ['ʃoʃu, a] *adj* hollow, empty; (*fraco*) weak; (*sem graça*) dull

chocolate [ʃoko'latʃi] *m* chocolate

chofer [ʃo'feʳ] *m* driver

chope ['ʃopi] *m* draught beer

choque¹ ['ʃɔki] *m* shock; (*colisão*) collision; (*impacto*) impact; (*conflito*) clash

choque² *etc vb ver* **chocar**

choramingar [ʃoramĩ'gaʳ] *vi* to whine, whimper

chorão, -rona [ʃo'rãw, rɔna] (*pl* **chorões/-s**) *adj* tearful ▷ *m/f* crybaby ▷ *m* (*Bot*) weeping willow

chorar [ʃo'raʳ] *vt, vi* to weep, cry

chorinho [ʃo'riɲu] *m* type of Brazilian music

choro ['ʃoru] *m* crying; (*Mús*) type of Brazilian music

choupana [ʃo'pana] *f* shack, hut

chouriço [ʃo'risu] *m* (*BR*) black pudding; (*PT*) spicy sausage

chover [ʃo'veʳ] *vi* to rain; **~ a cântaros** to rain cats and dogs

chulé [ʃu'lɛ] *m* foot odour (*BRIT*) *ou* odor (*US*)

chulo, -a ['ʃulu, a] *adj* vulgar

chumbo ['ʃũbu] *m* lead; (*de caça*) gunshot; (*PT: de dente*) filling; **sem ~** (*gasolina*) unleaded

chupar [ʃu'paʳ] *vt* to suck

chupeta [ʃu'peta] *f* dummy (*BRIT*), pacifier (*US*)

churrasco [ʃu'xaʃku] *m* , **churrasqueira** [ʃuxaʃ'kejra] ▷ *f* barbecue

churrasquinho [ʃuxaʃ'kiɲu] *m* kebab

chutar [ʃu'taʳ] *vt* to kick; (*col: adivinhar*) to guess at; (: *dar o fora em*) to dump ▷ *vi* to kick; to guess; (: *mentir*) to lie

chute ['ʃutʃi] *m* kick; (*col: mentira*) fib; **dar o ~ em alguém** (*col*) to give sb the boot

chuteira [ʃu'tejra] *f* football boot

chuva ['ʃuva] *f* rain; **chuveiro** [ʃu'vejru] *m* shower

chuviscar [ʃuviʃ'kaʳ] *vi* to drizzle; **chuvisco** [ʃu'viʃku] *m* drizzle

chuvoso, -a [ʃu'vozu, ɔza] *adj* rainy

Cia. *abr* (= *companhia*) Co.

cibercafé [sibexka'fɛ] *m* cybercafé

ciberespaço [sibexiʃ'pasu] *m* cyberspace

cicatriz [sika'triʒ] *f* scar; **cicatrizar** [sikatri'zaʳ] *vi* to heal; (*rosto*) to scar

cicerone [sise'roni] *m* tourist guide

ciclismo [si'kliʒmu] *m* cycling

ciclista [si'kliʃta] *m/f* cyclist

ciclo ['siklu] *m* cycle

ciclovia [siklo'via] *f* cycle lane or path

cidadã [sida'dã] *f de* **cidadão**

cidadania [sidada'nia] *f* citizenship

cidadão, -cidadã [sida'dãw, sida'dã] (*pl* **~s/-s**) *m/f* citizen

cidade [si'dadʒi] *f* town; (*grande*) city

ciência ['sjẽsja] *f* science

ciente ['sjẽtʃi] *adj* aware

científico, -a [sjẽ'tʃifiku, a] *adj* scientific

cientista [sjẽ'tʃiʃta] *m/f* scientist

cifra ['sifra] *f* cipher; (*algarismo*) number, figure; (*total*) sum

cigano, -a [si'ganu, a] *adj, m/f* gypsy

cigarra [si'gaxa] *f* cicada; (*Elet*) buzzer

cigarrilha [siga'xiʎa] *f* cheroot

cigarro [si'gaxu] *m* cigarette

cilada [si'lada] f ambush; (armadilha) trap; (embuste) trick

cilindro [si'lĩdru] m cylinder; (rolo) roller

cima ['sima] f: **de ~ para baixo** from top to bottom; **para ~** up; **em ~ de** on, on top of; **por ~ de** over; **de ~** from above; **lá em ~** up there; (em casa) upstairs; **ainda por ~** on top of that

cimento [si'mẽtu] m cement; (fig) foundation

cimo ['simu] m top, summit

cinco ['sĩku] num five

cineasta [sine'afta] m/f film maker

cinema [si'nɛma] f cinema

Cingapura [sĩga'pura] f Singapore

cinqüenta [sĩ'kwẽta] num fifty

cinta ['sĩta] f sash; (de mulher) girdle

cinto ['sĩtu] m belt; **~ de segurança** safety belt; (Auto) seatbelt

cintura [sĩ'tura] f waist; (linha) waistline

cinza ['sĩza] adj inv grey (BRIT), gray (US) ▷ f ash, ashes pl

cinzeiro [sĩ'zejru] m ashtray

cinzento, -a [sĩ'zẽtu, a] adj grey (BRIT), gray (US)

cio [siu] m: **no ~** on heat, in season

cipreste [si'preftfi] m cypress (tree)

cipriota [si'prjota] adj, m/f Cypriot

circo ['sixku] m circus

circuito [six'kwitu] m circuit

circulação [sixkula'sãw] f circulation

circular [sixku'la] adj circular ▷ f (carta) circular ▷ vi to circulate; (girar, andar) to go round ▷ vt to circulate; (estar em volta de) to surround; (percorrer em roda) to go round

círculo ['sixkulu] m circle

circundar [sixkũ'da] vt to surround

circunferência [sixkũfe'rẽsja] f circumference

circunflexo [sixkũ'flɛksu] m circumflex (accent)

circunstância [sixkũ'ftãsja] f circumstance; **~s atenuantes** mitigating circumstances

cirurgia [sirux'ʒia] f surgery; **~ plástica/estética** plastic/cosmetic surgery

cirurgião, -giã [sirux'ʒjãw, 'ʒjã] (pl cirurgiões/-s) m/f surgeon

cisco ['sifku] m speck

cismado, -a [siʒ'madu, a] adj with fixed ideas

cismar [siʒ'ma] vi (pensar): **~ em** to brood over; (antipatizar): **~ com** to take a dislike to ▷ vt: **~ que** to be convinced that; **~ de** ou **em fazer** (meter na cabeça)

to get into one's head to do; (insistir) to insist on doing

cisne ['siʒni] m swan

cisterna [sif'texna] f cistern, tank

citação [sita'sãw] (pl -ões) f quotation; (Jur) summons sg

citar [si'ta] vt to quote; (Jur) to summon

ciúme ['sjumi] m jealousy; **ter ~s de** to be jealous of; **ciumento, -a** [sju'mẽtu, a] adj jealous

cívico, -a ['siviku, a] adj civic

civil [si'viw] (pl -is) adj civil ▷ m/f civilian; **civilidade** [sivili'dadʒi] f politeness

civilização [siviliza'sãw] (pl -ões) f civilization

civis [si'vif] pl de **civil**

clamar [kla'ma] vt to clamour (BRIT) ou clamor (US) for ▷ vi to cry out, clamo(u)r

clamor [kla'mo] m outcry, uproar

clandestino, -a [klãdef'tfinu, a] adj clandestine; (ilegal) underground

clara ['klara] f egg white

clarão [kla'rãw] (pl -ões) m (cintilação) flash; (claridade) gleam

clarear [kla'rja] vi (dia) to dawn; (tempo) to clear up, brighten up ▷ vt to clarify

claridade [klari'dadʒi] f brightness

clarim [kla'rĩ] (pl -ns) m bugle

clarinete [klari'netfi] m clarinet

clarins [kla'rĩf] mpl de **clarim**

claro, -a ['klaru, a] adj clear; (luminoso) bright; (cor) light; (evidente) clear, evident ▷ m (na escrita) space; (clareira) clearing ▷ adv clearly; **~!** of course!; **~ que sim!/não!** of course!/of course not!; **às claras** openly

classe ['klasi] f class

clássico, -a ['klasiku, a] adj classical; (fig) classic; (habitual) usual ▷ m classic

classificação [klasifika'sãw] (pl -ões) f classification; (Esporte) place, placing

classificado, -a [klasifi'kadu, a] adj (em exame) successful; (anúncio) classified; (Esporte) placed ▷ m classified ad

classificar [klasifi'ka] vt to classify; **~-se** vr: **~-se de algo** to call o.s. sth, describe o.s. as sth

cláusula ['klawzula] f clause

clausura [klaw'zura] f enclosure

clavícula [kla'vikula] f collar bone

clemência [kle'mẽsja] f mercy

clero ['klɛru] m clergy

clicar [kli'ka] vi (Comput) to click

cliente ['kljẽtfi] m client, customer; (de médico) patient; **clientela** [kljẽ'tɛla] f clientele; (de loja) customers pl

clima ['klima] *m* climate

clímax ['klimaks] *m inv* climax

clipe ['klipi] *m* clip; (*para papéis*) paper clip

clique ['kliki] *m* (*Comput*) click; **dar um ~ duplo em** to double-click on

cloro ['klɔru] *m* chlorine

close ['klɔzi] *m* close-up

clube ['klubi] *m* club

coadjuvante [koadʒu'vãtʃi] *adj* supporting ▷ *m/f* (*num crime*) accomplice; (*Teatro, Cinema*) co-star

coador [koa'do^r] *m* strainer; (*de café*) filter bag; (*para legumes*) colander

coalhada [koa'ʎada] *f* curd

coalizão [koali'zãw] (*pl* **-ões**) *f* coalition

coar [ko'a^r] *vt* (*líquido*) to strain

coberta [ko'bɛxta] *f* cover, covering; (*Náut*) deck

cobertor [kobex'to^r] *m* blanket

cobertura [kobex'tura] *f* covering; (*telhado*) roof; (*apartamento*) penthouse; (*TV, Rádio, Jornalismo*) coverage; (*Seguros*) cover; (*Tel*) network coverage; **aqui não tem ~** there's no network coverage here

cobiça [ko'bisa] *f* greed

cobra ['kɔbra] *f* snake

cobrador, a [kobra'do^r, a] *m/f* collector; (*em transporte*) conductor

cobrança [ko'brãsa] *f* collection; (*ato de cobrar*) charging

cobrar [ko'bra^r] *vt* to collect; (*preço*) to charge

cobre ['kɔbri] *m* copper; **cobres** *mpl* (*dinheiro*) money *sg*

cobrir [ko'bri^r] *vt* to cover

cocada [ko'kada] *f* coconut sweet

cocaína [koka'ina] *f* cocaine

coçar [ko'sa^r] *vt* to scratch ▷ *vi* to itch; **~-se** *vr* to scratch o.s

cócegas ['kɔsegaʃ] *fpl*: **fazer ~ em** to tickle; **tenho ~ nos pés** my feet tickle; **sentir ~** to be ticklish

coceira [ko'sejra] *f* itch; (*qualidade*) itchiness

cochichar [koʃi'ʃa^r] *vi* to whisper; **cochicho** [ko'ʃiʃu] *m* whispering

cochilar [koʃi'la^r] *vi* to snooze, doze; **cochilo** [ko'ʃilu] *m* nap

coco ['koku] *m* coconut

cócoras ['kɔkoraʃ] *fpl*: **de ~** squatting; **ficar de ~** to squat (down)

código ['kɔdʒigu] *m* code; **~ de barras** bar code

coelho [ko'eʎu] *m* rabbit

coerente [koe'rẽtʃi] *adj* coherent; (*conseqüente*) consistent

cofre ['kɔfri] *m* safe; (*caixa*) strongbox; **os ~s públicos** public funds

cogitar [koʒi'ta^r] *vt, vi* to contemplate

cogumelo [kogu'mɛlu] *m* mushroom; **~ venenoso** toadstool

coice ['kojsi] *m* kick; (*de arma*) recoil; **dar ~s em** to kick

coincidência [koĩsi'dẽsja] *f* coincidence

coincidir [koĩsi'dʒi^r] *vi* to coincide; (*concordar*) to agree

coisa ['kojza] *f* thing; (*assunto*) matter; **~ de** about

coitado, -a [koj'tadu, a] *adj* poor, wretched

cola ['kɔla] *f* glue

colaborador, a [kolabora'do^r, a] *m/f* collaborator; (*em jornal*) contributor

colaborar [kolabo'ra^r] *vi* to collaborate; (*ajudar*) to help; (*escrever artigos etc*) to contribute

colante [ko'lãtʃi] *adj* (*roupa*) skin-tight

colapso [ko'lapsu] *m* collapse; **~ cardíaco** heart failure

colar [ko'la^r] *vt* to stick, glue; (*BR: copiar*) to crib ▷ *vi* to stick; to cheat ▷ *m* necklace

colarinho [kola'riɲu] *m* collar

colarinho-branco (*pl* **colarinhos-brancos**) *m* white-collar worker

colcha ['kowʃa] *f* bedspread

colchão [kow'ʃãw] (*pl* **-ões**) *m* mattress

colchete [kow'ʃetʃi] *m* clasp, fastening; (*parêntese*) square bracket; **~ de gancho** hook and eye; **~ de pressão** press stud, popper

colchões [kow'ʃõjʃ] *mpl de* **colchão**

coleção [kole'sãw] (*PT* **-cç-**) (*pl* **-ões**) *f* collection; **colecionador, a** [kolesjona'do^r, a] (*PT* **-cc-**) *m/f* collector; **colecionar** [kolesjo'na^r] (*PT* **-cc-**) *vt* to collect

colectar *etc* [kolek'ta^r] (*PT*) = **coletar** *etc*

colega [ko'lɛga] *m/f* colleague; (*de escola*) classmate

colegial [kole'ʒjaw] (*pl* **-ais**) *m/f* schoolboy/girl

colégio [ko'lɛʒu] *m* school

coleira [ko'lejra] *f* collar

cólera ['kɔlera] *f* anger ▷ *m ou f* (*Med*) cholera

colesterol [koleʃte'rɔw] *m* cholesterol

colete [ko'letʃi] *m* waistcoat (*BRIT*), vest (*US*); **~ salva-vidas** life jacket (*BRIT*), life preserver (*US*)

coletivo, -a [kole'tʃivu, a] *adj* collective;

(*transportes*) public ▷ *m* bus
colheita [ko'ʎejta] *f* harvest
colher [ko'ʎeʳ] *vt* to gather, pick; (*dados*) to gather ▷ *f* spoon; **~ de chá/sopa** teaspoon/tablespoon
colidir [koli'dʒiʳ] *vi*: **~ com** to collide with, crash into
coligação [koliga'sãw] (*pl* **-ões**) *f* coalition
colina [ko'lina] *f* hill
colisão [koli'zãw] (*pl* **-ões**) *f* collision
collant [ko'lã] (*pl* **-s**) *m* tights *pl* (BRIT), pantihose (US); (*blusa*) leotard
colmeia [kow'meja] *f* beehive
colo ['kɔlu] *m* neck; (*regaço*) lap
colocar [kolo'kaʳ] *vt* to put, place; (*empregar*) to find a job for, place; (*Com*) to market; (*pneus, tapetes*) to fit; (*questão, idéia*) to put forward; (*Comput: dados*) to key (in)
Colômbia [ko'lõbja] *f*: **a ~** Colombia
colônia [ko'lonja] *f* colony; (*perfume*) cologne; **colonial** [kolo'njaw] (*pl* **-ais**) *adj* colonial
colonizador, a [koloniza'doʳ, a] *m/f* colonist, settler
coloquial [kolo'kjaw] (*pl* **-ais**) *adj* colloquial
colóquio [ko'lɔkju] *m* conversation; (*congresso*) conference
colorido, -a [kolo'ridu, a] *adj* colourful (BRIT), colorful (US) ▷ *m* colouring (BRIT), coloring (US)
colorir [kolo'riʳ] *vt* to colour (BRIT), color (US)
coluna [ko'luna] *f* column; (*pilar*) pillar; **~ dorsal** *ou* **vertebral** spine; **colunável** [kolu'navew] (*pl* **-eis**) *adj* famous ▷ *m/f* celebrity; **colunista** [kolu'niʃta] *m/f* columnist
com [kõ] *prep* with; **~ cuidado** carefully; **estar ~ câncer** to have cancer; **estar ~ dinheiro** to have some money on one; **estar ~ fome** to be hungry
coma ['kɔma] *f* coma
comandante [komã'dãtʃi] *m* commander; (*Mil*) commandant; (*Náut*) captain
comandar [komã'daʳ] *vt* to command
comando [ko'mãdu] *m* command
combate [kõ'batʃi] *m* combat; **combater** [kõba'teʳ] *vt* to fight; (*opor-se a*) to oppose ▷ *vi* to fight; **combater-se** *vr* to fight
combinação [kõbina'sãw] (*pl* **-ões**) *f* combination; (*Quím*) compound; (*acordo*) arrangement; (*plano*) scheme; (*roupa*) slip
combinar [kõbi'naʳ] *vt* to combine; (*jantar etc*) to arrange; (*fuga etc*) to plan ▷ *vi* (*roupas etc*) to go together; **~-se** *vr* to combine; (*pessoas*) to get on well together; **~ com** (*harmonizar-se*) to go with; **~ de fazer** to arrange to do; **combinado!** agreed!
comboio [kõ'boju] *m* (PT) train; (*de navios, carros*) convoy
combustível [kõbuʃ'tʃivew] *m* fuel
começar [kome'saʳ] *vt, vi* to begin, start; **~ a fazer** to begin *ou* start to do
começo [ko'mesu] *m* beginning, start
comédia [ko'mɛdʒja] *f* comedy
comemorar [komemo'raʳ] *vt* to commemorate
comentar [komẽ'taʳ] *vt* to comment on; (*maliciosamente*) to make comments about
comentário [komẽ'tarju] *m* comment, remark; (*análise*) commentary
comer [ko'meʳ] *vt* to eat; (*Damas, Xadrez*) to take, capture ▷ *vi* to eat; **dar de ~ a** to feed
comercial [komex'sjaw] (*pl* **-ais**) *adj* commercial; (*relativo ao negócio*) business *atr* ▷ *m* commercial
comercializar [komexsjali'zaʳ] *vt* to market
comerciante [komex'sjãtʃi] *m/f* trader
comércio [ko'mɛxsju] *m* commerce; (*tráfico*) trade; (*negócio*) business; (*lojas*) shops *pl*; **~ eletrônico** e-commerce
comes ['kɔmiʃ] *mpl*: **~ e bebes** food and drink
comestíveis [komeʃ'tʃiveis] *mpl* foodstuffs, food *sg*
comestível [komeʃ'tʃivew] (*pl* **-eis**) *adj* edible
cometer [kome'teʳ] *vt* to commit
comício [ko'misju] *m* (Pol) rally, meeting; (*assembléia*) assembly
cômico, -a ['komiku, a] *adj* comic(al) ▷ *m* comedian; (*de teatro*) actor
comida [ko'mida] *f* (*alimento*) food; (*refeição*) meal
comigo [ko'migu] *pron* with me
comilão, -lona [komi'lãw, lona] (*pl* **comilões/-s**) *adj* greedy ▷ *m/f* glutton
comiserar-se [komize'raxsi] *vr*: **~-se (de)** to sympathize (with)
comissão [komi'sãw] (*pl* **-ões**) *f* commission; (*comitê*) committee
comissário [komi'sarju] *m* commissioner; (*Com*) agent; **~ de bordo**

(Aer) steward; (Náut) purser
comissões [komi'sõjʃ] fpl de **comissão**
comitê [komi'te] m committee

 PALAVRA CHAVE

como ['kɔmu] adv 1 (modo) as; **ela fez como eu pedi** she did as I asked; **como se** as if; **como quiser** as you wish; **seja como for** be that as it may
2 (assim como) like; **ela tem olhos azuis como o pai** she has blue eyes like her father's; **ela trabalha numa loja, como a mãe** she works in a shop, as does her mother
3 (de que maneira) how; **como?** pardon?; **como!** what!; **como assim?** what do you mean?; **como não!** of course!
▷ conj (porque) as, since; **como estava tarde ele dormiu aqui** since it was late he slept here

comoção [komo'sãw] (pl -**ões**) f distress; (revolta) commotion
cômoda ['kɔmoda] f chest of drawers (BRIT), bureau (US)
comodidade [komodʒi'dadʒi] f comfort; (conveniência) convenience
comodismo [komo'dʒiʒmu] m complacency
cômodo, -a ['kɔmodu, a] adj comfortable; (conveniente) convenient
▷ m room
comovente [komo'vẽtʃi] adj moving, touching
comover [komo've^r] vt to move ▷ vi to be moving; **~-se** vr to be moved
compacto, -a [kõ'paktu, a] adj compact; (espesso) thick; (sólido) solid
▷ m (disco) single
compadecer-se [kõpade'sexsi] vr: **~-se de** to be sorry for, pity
compadre [kõ'padri] m (col: companheiro) buddy, pal
compaixão [kõpaj'ʃãw] m compassion; (misericórdia) mercy
companheiro, -a [kõpa'ɲejru, a] m/f companion; (colega) friend; (col) buddy, mate
companhia [kõpa'ɲia] f company
comparação [kõpara'sãw] (pl -**ões**) f comparison
comparar [kõpa'ra^r] vt to compare; **~ a** to liken to; **~ com** to compare with
comparecer [kõpare'se^r] vi to appear, make an appearance; **~ a uma reunião** to attend a meeting

comparsa [kõ'paxsa] m/f (Teatro) extra; (cúmplice) accomplice
compartilhar [kõpaxtʃi'ʎa^r] vt to share
▷ vi: **~ de** to share in, participate in
compartimento [kõpaxtʃi'mẽtu] m compartment; (aposento) room
compasso [kõ'pasu] m (instrumento) pair of compasses; (Mús) time; (ritmo) beat
compatível [kõpa'tʃivew] (pl -**eis**) adj compatible
compensar [kõpẽ'sa^r] vt to make up for, compensate for; (equilibrar) to offset; (cheque) to clear
competência [kõpe'tẽsja] f competence, ability; (responsabilidade) responsibility; **competente** [kõpe'tẽtʃi] adj competent; (apropriado) appropriate; (responsável) responsible
competição [kõpetʃi'sãw] (pl -**ões**) f competition
competidor, a [kõpetʃi'do^r, a] m/f competitor
competir [kõpe'tʃi^r] vi to compete; **~ a alguém** to be sb's responsibility; (caber) to be up to sb
competitivo, -a [kõpetʃi'tʃivu, a] adj competitive
compito etc [kõ'pitu] vb ver **competir**
complementar [kõplemẽ'ta^r] adj complementary ▷ vt to supplement
complemento [kõple'mẽtu] m complement
completamente [kõpleta'mẽtʃi] adv completely, quite
completar [kõple'ta^r] vt to complete; (tanque, carro) to fill up; **~ dez anos** to be ten
completo, -a [kõ'pletu, a] adj complete; (cheio) full (up); **por ~** completely
complexo, -a [kõ'plɛksu, a] adj complex ▷ m complex
complicação [kõplika'sãw] (pl -**ões**) f complication
complicado, -a [kõpli'kadu, a] adj complicated
complicar [kõpli'ka^r] vt to complicate
complô [kõ'plo] m plot, conspiracy
componente [kõpo'nẽtʃi] adj, m component
compor [kõ'po^r] (irreg: como **pôr**) vt to compose; (discurso, livro) to write; (arranjar) to arrange ▷ vi to compose; **~-se** vr (controlar-se) to compose o.s.; **~-se de** to consist of
comportamento [kõpoxta'mẽtu] m

behaviour (BRIT), behavior (US)

comportar-se [kõpoxˈtaxsi] vt, vr to behave; **~ mal** to misbehave, behave badly

composição [kõpoziˈsãw] (pl -ões) f composition; (Tip) typesetting

compositor, a [kõpoziˈtoˑr, a] m/f composer; (Tip) typesetter

compota [kõˈpota] f fruit in syrup

compra [ˈkõpra] f purchase; **fazer ~s** to go shopping; **comprador, a** [kõpraˈdoˑr, a] m/f buyer, purchaser

comprar [kõˈpraˑr] vt to buy

compreender [kõprjeˈdeˑr] vt to understand; (constar de) to be comprised of, consist of; (abranger) to cover

compreensão [kõprjẽˈsãw] f understanding, comprehension; **compreensivo, -a** [kõprjẽˈsivu, a] adj understanding

compressa [kõˈprɛsa] f compress

comprido, -a [kõˈpridu, a] adj long; (alto) tall; **ao ~** lengthways

comprimento [kõpriˈmẽtu] m length

comprimido [kõpriˈmidu] m pill, tablet

comprimir [kõpriˈmiˑr] vt to compress

comprometer [kõpromeˈteˑr] vt to compromise; (envolver) to involve; (arriscar) to jeopardize; (empenhar) to pledge; **~-se** vr: **~-se a** to undertake to, promise to

compromisso [kõproˈmisu] m promise; (obrigação) commitment; (hora marcada) appointment; (acordo) agreement

comprovante [kõproˈvãtʃi] m receipt

comprovar [kõproˈvaˑr] vt to prove; (confirmar) to confirm; **compulsivo, -a** [kõpuwˈsivu, a] adj compulsive; **compulsório, -a** [kõpuwˈsɔrju, a] adj compulsory

computação [kõputaˈsãw] f computer science, computing

computador [kõputaˈdoˑr] m computer

computar [kõpuˈtaˑr] vt (calcular) to calculate; (contar) to count

comum [koˈmũ] (pl -ns) adj ordinary, common; (habitual) usual; **em ~** in common

comungar [komũˈgaˑr] vi to take communion

comunhão [komuˈɲãw] (pl -ões) f (ger, Rel) communion

comunicação [komunikaˈsãw] (pl -ões) f communication; (mensagem) message; (acesso) access

comunicado [komuniˈkadu] m notice

comunicar [komuniˈkaˑr] vt, vi to communicate; **~-se** vr to communicate; **~-se com** (entrar em contato) to get in touch with

comunidade [komuniˈdadʒi] f community; **C~ dos Estados Independentes** Commonwealth of Independent States

comunismo [komuˈniʒmu] m communism; **comunista** [komuˈniʃta] adj, m/f communist

comuns [koˈmũʃ] pl de **comum**

conceber [kõseˈbeˑr] vt, vi to conceive

conceder [kõseˈdeˑr] vt to allow; (outorgar) to grant; (dar) to give ▷ vi: **~ em** to agree to

conceito [kõˈsejtu] m concept, idea; (fama) reputation; (opinião) opinion; **conceituado, -a** [kõsejˈtwadu, a] adj well thought of, highly regarded

concentração [kõsẽtraˈsãw] (pl -ões) f concentration

concepção [kõsepˈsãw] (pl -ões) f (geração) conception; (noção) idea, concept; (opinião) opinion

concerto [kõˈsextu] m concert

concessão [kõseˈsãw] (pl -ões) f concession; (permissão) permission

concha [ˈkõʃa] f shell; (para líquidos) ladle

conchavo [kõˈʃavu] m conspiracy

conciliar [kõsiˈljaˑr] vt to reconcile

concluir [kõˈklwiˑr] vt, vi to conclude

conclusão [kõkluˈzãw] (pl -ões) f end; (dedução) conclusion

conclusões [kõkluˈzõjʃ] fpl de **conclusão**

concordância [kõkoxˈdãsja] f agreement

concordar [kõkoxˈdaˑr] vi, vt to agree

concorrência [kõkoˈxẽsja] f competition; (a um cargo) application

concorrente [kõkoˈxẽtʃi] m/f contestant; (candidato) candidate

concorrer [kõkoˈxeˑr] vi to compete; **~ a** to apply for

concretizar [kõkretʃiˈzaˑr] vt to make real; **~-se** vr (sonho) to come true; (ambições) to be realized

concreto, -a [kõˈkrɛtu, a] adj concrete ▷ m concrete

concurso [kõˈkuxsu] m contest; (exame) competition

conde [ˈkõdʒi] m count

condenar [kõdeˈnaˑr] vt to condemn; (Jur: sentenciar) to sentence; (: declarar culpado) to convict

condensar [kõdẽ'sa^r] vt to condense;
~-se vr to condense
condessa [kõ'desa] f countess
condimento [kõdʒi'mẽtu] m seasoning
condomínio [kõdo'minju] m
condominium
condução [kõdu'sãw] f driving;
(transporte) transport; (ônibus) bus
condutor, a [kõdu'to^r, a] m/f (de veículo)
driver ▷ m (Elet) conductor
conduzir [kõdu'zi^r] vt (levar) to lead;
(Fís) to conduct; **~-se** vr to behave; **~ a**
to lead to
cone ['kɔni] m cone
conectar [konek'ta^r] vt to connect
conexão [konek'sãw] (pl -**ões**) f
connection
confecção [kõfek'sãw] (pl -**ões**) f
making; (de um boletim) production;
(roupa) ready-to-wear clothes pl;
(negócio) business selling ready-to-wear
clothes
confeccionar [kõfeksjo'na^r] vt to make;
(fabricar) to manufacture
confecções [kõfek'sõjʃ] fpl de **confecção**
confeitaria [kõfejta'ria] f patisserie
conferência [kõfe'rẽsja] f conference;
(discurso) lecture
conferir [kõfe'ri^r] vt to check; (comparar)
to compare; (outorgar) to grant ▷ vi to
tally
confessar [kõfe'sa^r] vt, vi to confess;
~-se vr to confess
confiança [kõ'fjãsa] f confidence; (fé)
trust; **de ~** reliable; **ter ~ em alguém** to
trust sb
confiar [kõ'fja^r] vt to entrust; (segredo)
to confide ▷ vi: **~ em** to trust; (ter fé) to
have faith in
confiável [kõ'fjavew] (pl -**eis**) adj reliable
confidência [kõfi'dẽsja] f secret; **em ~** in
confidence; **confidencial** [kõfidẽ'sjaw]
(pl -**ais**) adj confidential
confirmação [kõfixma'sãw] (pl -**ões**) f
confirmation
confirmar [kõfix'ma^r] vt to confirm
confiro etc [kõ'firu] vb ver **conferir**
confissão [kõfi'sãw] (pl -**ões**) f
confession
conformar [kõfox'ma^r] vt to form ▷ vi: **~
com** to conform to; **~-se** vr: **~-se com** to
resign o.s. to; (acomodar-se) to conform to
conforme [kõ'foxmi] prep according to;
(dependendo de) depending on ▷ conj (logo
que) as soon as; (como) as, according to
what; (à medida que) as; **você vai? — ~** are

you going? — it depends
conformidade [kõfoxmi'dadʒi] f
agreement; **em ~ com** in accordance
with
confortar [kõfox'ta^r] vt to comfort,
console
confortável [kõfox'tavew] (pl -**eis**) adj
comfortable
conforto [kõ'foxtu] m comfort
confrontar [kõfrõ'ta^r] vt to confront;
(comparar) to compare
confronto [kõ'frõtu] m confrontation;
(comparação) comparison
confusão [kõfu'zãw] (pl -**ões**) f
confusion; (tumulto) uproar; (problemas)
trouble
confuso, -a [kõ'fuzu, a] adj confused;
(problema) confusing
confusões [kõfu'zõjʃ] fpl de **confusão**
congelador [kõʒela'do^r] m freezer, deep
freeze
congelamento [kõʒela'mẽtu] m
freezing; (Econ) freeze
congelar [kõʒe'la^r] vt to freeze; **~-se** vr
to freeze
congestão [kõʒeʃ'tãw] f congestion;
congestionado, -a [kõʒeʃtʃjo'nadu,
a] adj congested; (olhos) bloodshot;
(rosto) flushed; **congestionamento**
[kõʒeʃtʃjona'mẽtu] m congestion; **um
congestionamento (de tráfego)** a
traffic jam
congestionar [kõʒeʃtʃjo'na^r] vt to
congest; **~-se** vr (rosto) to go red
congressista [kõgre'siʃta] m/f
congressman/woman
congresso [kõ'gresu] m congress,
conference
conhaque [ko'ɲaki] m cognac, brandy
conhecedor, a [koɲese'do^r, a] adj
knowing ▷ m/f connoisseur, expert
conhecer [koɲe'se^r] vt to know; (travar
conhecimento com) to meet; (descobrir)
to discover; **~-se** vr to meet; (ter
conhecimento) to know each other
conhecido, -a [koɲe'sidu, a] adj known;
(célebre) well-known ▷ m/f acquaintance
conhecimento [koɲesi'mẽtu] m (tb:
~s) knowledge; (idéia) idea; (conhecido)
acquaintance; (Com) bill of lading; **levar
ao ~ de alguém** to bring to sb's notice
conjugado [kõʒu'gadu] m studio
cônjuge ['kõʒuʒi] m spouse
conjunção [kõʒũ'sãw] (pl -**ões**) f union;
(Ling) conjunction
conjuntivo [kõʒũ'tʃivu] (PT) m (Ling)

subjunctive

conosco [ko'noʃku] *pron* with us

conquista [kõ'kiʃta] *f* conquest;
conquistador, a [kõkiʃta'doʳ, a] *adj*
conquering ▷ *m* conqueror; **conquistar**
[kõkiʃ'taʳ] *vt* to conquer; (*alcançar*) to
achieve; (*ganhar*) to win

consciência [kõ'sjēsja] *f* conscience;
(*percepção*) awareness; (*senso de
responsabilidade*) conscientiousness

consciente [kõ'sjētʃi] *adj* conscious

conseguinte [kõse'gĩtʃi] *adj*: **por ~**
consequently

conseguir [kõse'giʳ] *vt* to get, obtain; **~
fazer** to manage to do, succeed in doing

conselho [kõ'seʎu] *m* piece of advice;
(*corporação*) council; **conselhos** *mpl*
(*advertência*) advice *sg*; **~ de guerra** court
martial; **C~ de ministros** (*Pol*) Cabinet

consentimento [kõsētʃi'mētu] *m*
consent

consentir [kõsē'tʃiʳ] *vt* to allow, permit;
(*aprovar*) to agree to ▷ *vi*: **~ em** to agree
to

conseqüência [kõse'kwēsja] *f*
consequence; **por ~** consequently

consertar [kõsex'taʳ] *vt* to mend,
repair; (*remediar*) to put right; **conserto**
[kõ'sextu] *m* repair

conserva [kõ'sexva] *f* pickle; **em ~**
pickled

conservação [kõsexva'sãw] *f*
conservation; (*de vida, alimentos*)
preservation

conservador, a [kõsexva'doʳ, a] *adj*
conservative ▷ *m/f* (*Pol*) conservative

conservante [kõsex'vãtʃi] *m*
preservative

conservar [kõsex'vaʳ] *vt* to preserve,
maintain; (*reter, manter*) to keep, retain;
~-se *vr* to keep

conservatório [kõsexva'tɔrju] *m*
conservatory

consideração [kõsidera'sãw] (*pl* **-ões**) *f*
consideration; (*estima*) respect, esteem;
levar em ~ to take into account

considerar [kõside'raʳ] *vt* to consider;
(*prezar*) to respect ▷ *vi* to consider

considerável [kõside'ravew] (*pl* **-eis**) *adj*
considerable

consigo¹ [kõ'sigu] *pron* (*m*) with him;
(*f*) with her; (*pl*) with them; (*com você*)
with you

consigo² *etc vb ver* **conseguir**

consinto *etc* [kõ'sĩtu] *vb ver* **consentir**

consistente [kõsiʃ'tētʃi] *adj* solid;

(*espesso*) thick

consistir [kõsiʃ'tʃiʳ] *vi*: **~ em** to be made
up of, consist of

consoante [kõso'ãtʃi] *f* consonant
▷ *prep* according to ▷ *conj*: **~ prometera**
as he had promised

consolação [kõsola'sãw] (*pl* **-ões**) *f*
consolation

consolar [kõso'laʳ] *vt* to console

consolidar [kõsoli'daʳ] *vt* to consolidate;
(*fratura*) to knit ▷ *vi* to become solid; to
knit together

consolo [kõ'solu] *m* consolation

consome *etc* [kõ'somi] *vb ver* **consumir**

consórcio [kõ'sɔxsju] *m* (*união*)
partnership; (*Com*) consortium

conspiração [kõʃpira'sãw] (*pl* **-ões**) *f*
plot, conspiracy

conspirar [kõʃpi'raʳ] *vt*, *vi* to plot

constante [kõʃ'tãtʃi] *adj* constant

constar [kõʃ'taʳ] *vi* to be in; **ao que me
consta** as far as I know

constatar [kõʃta'taʳ] *vt* to establish;
(*notar*) to notice; (*evidenciar*) to show up

consternado, -a [kõʃtex'nadu, a] *adj*
depressed; (*desolado*) distressed

constipação [kõʃtʃipa'sãw] (*pl* **-ões**) *f*
constipation; (*PT*) cold; **apanhar uma ~**
(*PT*) to catch a cold

constipado, -a [kõʃtʃi'padu, a] *adj*:
estar ~ to be constipated; (*PT*) to have
a cold

constituição [kõʃtʃitwi'sãw] (*pl* **-ões**) *f*
constitution

constituinte [kõʃtʃi'twĩtʃi] *m/f*
(*deputado*) member ▷ *f* (*BR*): **a C~** the
Constituent Assembly, ≈ Parliament

constituir [kõʃtʃi'twiʳ] *vt* to constitute;
(*formar*) to form; (*estabelecer*) to establish;
(*nomear*) to appoint

constrangimento [kõʃtrãʒi'mētu] *m*
constraint; embarrassment

construção [kõʃtru'sãw] (*pl* **-ões**) *f*
building, construction

construir [kõʃ'trwiʳ] *vt* to build,
construct

construtivo, -a [kõʃtru'tʃivu, a] *adj*
constructive

construtor, a [kõʃtru'toʳ, a] *m/f* builder

cônsul ['kõsuw] (*pl* **-es**) *m* consul;
consulado [kõsu'ladu] *m* consulate

consulta [kõ'suwta] *f* consultation;
livro de ~ reference book; **horário de
~** surgery hours *pl* (*BRIT*); office hours
pl (*US*); **consultar** [kõsuw'taʳ] *vt* to
consult; **consultor, a** [kõsuw'toʳ, a] *m/f*

consultant

consultório [kõsuw'tɔrju] *m* surgery

consumidor, a [kõsumi'doʳ, a] *adj*
consumer *atr* ▷ *m/f* consumer

consumir [kõsu'miʳ] *vt* to consume;
(*gastar*) to use up; **~-se** *vr* to waste away

consumo [kõ'sumu] *m* consumption;
artigos de ~ consumer goods

conta ['kõta] *f* count; (*em restaurante*) bill;
(*fatura*) invoice; (*bancária*) account; (*de
colar*) bead; **contas** *fpl* (Com) accounts;
levar *ou* **ter em ~** to take into account;
tomar ~ de to take care of; (*dominar*)
to take hold of; **afinal de ~s** after all;
dar-se ~ de to realize; (*notar*) to notice; **~
corrente** current account; **~ de e-mail**
ou **de correio eletrônico** e-mail account

contabilista [kõtabi'liʃta] (*PT*) *m/f*
accountant

contabilizar [kõtabili'zaʳ] *vt* to write
up, book

contacto *etc* [kõ'tatu] (*PT*) = **contato** *etc*

contador, a [kõta'doʳ, a] *m/f* (Com)
accountant ▷ *m* (Tec: *medidor*) meter

contagiante [kõta'ʒjãtʃi] *adj* (*alegria*)
contagious

contagiar [kõta'ʒjaʳ] *vt* to infect

contágio [kõ'taʒju] *m* infection

contagioso, -a [kõta'ʒjozu, ɔza] *adj*
(*doença*) contagious

contaminar [kõtami'naʳ] *vt* to
contaminate

contanto que [kõ'tãtu ki] *conj* provided
that

conta-quilómetros (*PT*) *m inv*
speedometer

contar [kõ'taʳ] *vt* to count; (*narrar*) to tell;
(*pretender*) to intend ▷ *vi* to count; **~ com**
to count on; (*esperar*) to expect; **~ em
fazer** to count on doing, expect to do

contatar [kõta'taʳ] *vt* to contact;
contato [kõ'tatu] *m* contact; **entrar
em contato com** to get in touch with,
contact

contemplar [kõtē'plaʳ] *vt* to
contemplate; (*olhar*) to gaze at

contemplativo, -a [kõtēpla'tʃivu, a] *adj*
(*pessoa*) thoughtful

contemporâneo, -a [kõtēpo'ranju, a]
adj, m/f contemporary

contentamento [kõtēta'mētu] *m*
(*felicidade*) happiness; (*satisfação*)
contentment

contente [kõ'tētʃi] *adj* happy; (*satisfeito*)
pleased, satisfied

contento [kõ'tētu] *m*: **a ~** satisfactorily

conter [kõ'teʳ] (*irreg: como* **ter**) *vt* to
contain, hold; (*refrear*) to restrain, hold
back; (*gastos*) to curb

contestação [kõteʃta'sãw] (*pl -ões*) *f*
challenge; (*negação*) denial

contestar [kõteʃ'taʳ] *vt* to dispute,
contest; (*impugnar*) to challenge

conteúdo [kõte'udu] *m* contents *pl*; (*de
um texto*) content

contexto [kõ'teʃtu] *m* context

contigo [kõ'tʃigu] *pron* with you

contíguo, -a [kõ'tʃigwu, a] *adj*: **~ a** next
to

continental [kõtʃinē'taw] (*pl -ais*) *adj*
continental

continente [kõtʃi'nētʃi] *m* continent

continuação [kõtʃinwa'sãw] *f*
continuation

continuar [kõtʃi'nwaʳ] *vt, vi* to continue;
~ falando *ou* **a falar** to go on talking; **ela
continua doente** she is still sick

continuidade [kõtʃinwi'dadʒi] *f*
continuity

conto ['kõtu] *m* story, tale; (*PT: dinheiro*)
1000 escudos

contorcer [kõtox'seʳ] *vt* to twist; **~-se** *vr*
to writhe

contornar [kõtox'naʳ] *vt* (*rodear*) to go
round; (*ladear*) to skirt; (*fig: problema*) to
get round

contorno [kõ'toxnu] *m* outline; (*da terra*)
contour; (*do rosto*) profile

contra ['kõtra] *prep* against ▷ *m*: **os prós
e os ~s** the pros and cons; **dar o ~ (a)** to
be opposed (to)

contra-ataque *m* counterattack

contrabandear [kõtrabã'dʒjaʳ]
vt to smuggle; **contrabandista**
[kõtrabã'dʒiʃta] *m/f* smuggler;
contrabando [kõtra'bãdu] *m*
smuggling; (*artigos*) contraband

contraceptivo, -a [kõtrasep'tʃivu, a]
adj contraceptive ▷ *m* contraceptive

contracheque [kõtra'ʃɛki] *m* pay slip
(BRIT), check stub (US)

contradição [kõtradʒi'sãw] (*pl -ões*) *f*
contradiction

contraditório, -a [kõtradʒi'tɔrju, a] *adj*
contradictory

contradizer [kõtradʒi'zeʳ] (*irreg: como*
dizer) *vt* to contradict

contragosto [kõtra'goʃtu] *m*: **a ~**
against one's will, unwillingly

contrair [kõtra'iʳ] *vt* to contract; (*hábito*)
to form

contramão [kõtra'mãw] *adj* one-way

▷ f: **na ~** the wrong way down a one-way street

contraproducente [kõtraprodu'sētʃi] adj counterproductive

contrário, -a [kõ'trarju, a] adj (oposto) opposite; (pessoa) opposed; (desfavorável) unfavourable (BRIT), unfavorable (US), adverse ▷ m opposite; **do ~** otherwise; **pelo** ou **ao ~** on the contrary; **ao ~** the other way round

contra-senso m nonsense

contrastar [kõtraʃ'taʳ] vt to contrast; **contraste** [kõ'traʃtʃi] m contrast

contratação [kõtrata'sãw] f (de pessoal) employment

contratar [kõtra'taʳ] vt (serviços) to contract; (pessoa) to employ, take on

contratempo [kõtra'tẽpu] m setback; (aborrecimento) upset; (dificuldade) difficulty

contrato [kõ'tratu] m contract; (acordo) agreement

contribuição [kõtribwi'sãw] (pl -ões) f contribution; (imposto) tax

contribuinte [kõtri'bwĩtʃi] m/f contributor; (que paga impostos) taxpayer

contribuir [kõtri'bwiʳ] vt to contribute ▷ vi to contribute; (pagar impostos) to pay taxes

controlar [kõtro'laʳ] vt to control

controle [kõ'trɔli] m control; **~ remoto** remote control; **~ de crédito** (Com) credit control; **~ de qualidade** (Com) quality control

controvérsia [kõtro'vɛxsja] f controversy; (discussão) debate; **controverso, -a** [kõtro'vɛxsu, a] adj controversial

contudo [kõ'tudu] conj nevertheless, however

contumaz [kõtu'majʒ] adj obstinate, stubborn

contusão [kõtu'zãw] (pl -ões) f bruise

convenção [kõvẽ'sãw] (pl -ões) f convention; (acordo) agreement

convencer [kõvẽ'seʳ] vt to convince; (persuadir) to persuade; **~-se** vr: **~-se de** to be convinced about; **convencido, -a** [kõvẽ'sidu, a] adj convinced; (col: imodesto) conceited, smug

convencional [kõvẽsjo'naw] (pl -ais) adj conventional

convenções [kõvẽ'sõjʃ] fpl de **convenção**

conveniência [kõve'njẽsja] f convenience

conveniente [kõve'njẽtʃi] adj convenient, suitable; (vantajoso) advantageous

convênio [kõ'venju] m (reunião) convention; (acordo) agreement

convento [kõ'vẽtu] m convent

conversa [kõ'vɛxsa] f conversation; **~- fiada** idle chat; (promessa falsa) hot air

conversão [kõvex'sãw] (pl -ões) f conversion

conversar [kõvex'saʳ] vi to talk

conversões [kõvex'sõjʃ] fpl de **conversão**

converter [kõvex'teʳ] vt to convert

convés [kõ'vɛʃ] (pl -eses) m (Náut) deck

convexo, -a [kõ'vɛksu, a] adj convex

convicção [kõvik'sãw] (pl -ões) f conviction

convidado, -a [kõvi'dadu, a] m/f guest

convidar [kõvi'daʳ] vt to invite

convincente [kõvĩ'sẽtʃi] adj convincing

convir [kõvi'ʳ] (irreg: como **vir**) vi to suit, be convenient; (ficar bem) to be appropriate; (concordar) to agree; **convém fazer isso o mais rápido possível** we must do this as soon as possible

convite [kõ'vitʃi] m invitation

convivência [kõvi'vẽsja] f living together; (familiaridade) familiarity, intimacy

conviver [kõvi'veʳ] vi: **~ com** (viver em comum) to live with; (ter familiaridade) to get on with; **convívio** [kõ'vivju] m living together; (familiaridade) familiarity

convocar [kõvo'kaʳ] vt to summon, call upon; (reunião, eleições) to call; (para o serviço militar) to call up

convosco [kõ'voʃku] adv with you

convulsão [kõvuw'sãw] (pl -ões) f convulsion

cooper ['kupeʳ] m jogging; **fazer ~** to go jogging

cooperação [koopera'sãw] f cooperation

cooperar [koope'raʳ] vi to cooperate

coordenada [kooxde'nada] f coordinate

copa ['kɔpa] f (de árvore) top; (torneio) cup; **copas** fpl (Cartas) hearts

cópia ['kɔpja] f copy; **tirar ~ de** to copy; **copiadora** [kopja'dora] f duplicating machine

copiar [ko'pjaʳ] vt to copy

copo ['kɔpu] m glass

coque ['kɔki] m (penteado) bun

coqueiro [ko'kejru] m (Bot) coconut

palm

coquetel [koke'tɛw] (*pl* **-éis**) *m* cocktail; (*festa*) cocktail party

cor¹ [kɔʳ] *m*: **de ~** by heart

cor² [koʳ] *f* colour (BRIT), color (US); **de ~** colo(u)red

coração [kora'sãw] (*pl* **-ões**) *m* heart; **de bom ~** kind-hearted; **de todo o ~** wholeheartedly

corado, -a [ko'radu, a] *adj* ruddy

coragem [ko'raʒẽ] *f* courage; (*atrevimento*) nerve

corais [ko'rajʃ] *mpl de* **coral**

corajoso, -a [kora'ʒozu, ɔza] *adj* courageous

coral [ko'raw] (*pl* **-ais**) *m* (*Mús*) choir; (*Zool*) coral

corar [ko'raʳ] *vt* (*roupa*) to bleach (in the sun) ▷ *vi* to blush; (*tornar-se branco*) to bleach

corda ['kɔxda] *f* rope, line; (*Mús*) string; (*varal*) clothes line; (*de relógio*) spring; **dar ~ em** to wind up; **~s vocais** vocal chords

cordão [kox'dãw] (*pl* **-ões**) *m* string, twine; (*jóia*) chain; (*no carnaval*) group; (*Elet*) lead; (*fileira*) row

cordeiro [kox'dejru] *m* lamb

cordel [kox'dɛw] (*pl* **-éis**) *m* (PT) string; **literatura de ~** pamphlet literature

cor-de-rosa *adj inv* pink

cordões [kox'dõjʃ] *mpl de* **cordão**

coreano, -a [ko'rjanu, a] *adj* Korean ▷ *m/f* Korean ▷ *m* (*Ling*) Korean

Coréia [ko'rɛja] *f*: **a ~** Korea

coreto [ko'retu] *m* bandstand

córner ['kɔxneʳ] *m* (*Futebol*) corner

coro ['koru] *m* chorus; (*conjunto de cantores*) choir

coroa [ko'roa] *f* crown; (*de flores*) garland ▷ *m/f* (BR: *col*) old timer

coroar [koro'aʳ] *vt* to crown; (*premiar*) to reward

coronel [koro'nɛw] (*pl* **-éis**) *m* colonel; (*político*) local political boss

corpo ['kɔxpu] *m* body; (*aparência física*) figure; (: *de homem*) build; (*de vestido*) bodice; (*Mil*) corps *sg*; **de ~ e alma** (*fig*) wholeheartedly; **~ diplomático** diplomatic corps *sg*

corpulento, -a [koxpu'lẽtu, a] *adj* stout

correção [koxe'sãw] (PT-**cç-**) (*pl* **-ões**) *f* correction; (*exatidão*) correctness; **casa de ~** reformatory

corre-corre [kɔxi'kɔxi] (*pl* **-s**) *m* rush

correcto, -a *etc* [ko'xektu, a] (PT) = **correto** *etc*

corredor, a [koxe'doʳ, a] *m/f* runner ▷ *m* corridor; (*em avião etc*) aisle; (*cavalo*) racehorse

correia [ko'xeja] *f* strap; (*de máquina*) belt; (*para cachorro*) leash

correio [ko'xeju] *m* mail, post; (*local*) post office; (*carteiro*) postman (BRIT), mailman (US); **~ aéreo** air mail; **pôr no ~** to post; **~ eletrônico** e-mail, electronic mail; **~ de voz** voice mail

corrente [ko'xẽtʃi] *adj* (*atual*) current; (*águas*) running; (*comum*) usual, common ▷ *f* current; (*cadeia, jóia*) chain; **~ de ar** draught (BRIT), draft (US); **correnteza** [koxẽ'teza] *f* (*de ar*) draught (BRIT), draft (US); (*de rio*) current

correr [ko'xeʳ] *vt* to run; (*viajar por*) to travel across ▷ *vi* to run; (*em carro*) to drive fast, speed; (*o tempo*) to elapse; (*boato*) to go round; (*atuar com rapidez*) to rush; **correria** [koxe'ria] *f* rush

correspondência [koxeʃpõ'dẽsja] *f* correspondence; **correspondente** [koxeʃpõ'dẽtʃi] *adj* corresponding ▷ *m* correspondent

corresponder [koxeʃpõ'deʳ] *vi*: **~ a** to correspond to; (*ser igual*) to match (up to); **~-se** *vr*: **~-se com** to correspond with

correto, -a [ko'xetu, a] *adj* correct; (*conduta*) right; (*pessoa*) straight, honest

corretor, a [koxe'toʳ, a] *m/f* broker; **~ de fundos** *ou* **de bolsa** stockbroker; **~ de imóveis** estate agent (BRIT), realtor (US)

corrida [ko'xida] *f* running; (*certame*) race; (*de taxi*) fare; **~ de cavalos** horse race

corrido, -a [ko'xidu, a] *adj* quick; (*expulso*) driven out ▷ *adv* quickly

corrigir [koxi'ʒiʳ] *vt* to correct

corriqueiro, -a [koxi'kejru, a] *adj* common; (*problema*) trivial

corromper [koxõ'peʳ] *vt* to corrupt; (*subornar*) to bribe; **~-se** *vr* to be corrupted

corrosão [koxo'zãw] *f* corrosion; (*fig*) erosion

corrosivo, -a [koxo'zivu, a] *adj* corrosive

corrupção [koxup'sãw] *f* corruption

corrupto, -a [ko'xuptu, a] *adj* corrupt

Córsega ['kɔxsega] *f*: **a ~** Corsica

cortada [kox'tada] *f*: **dar uma ~ em alguém** (*fig*) to cut sb short

cortante [kox'tãtʃi] *adj* cutting

cortar [kox'taʳ] *vt* to cut; (*eliminar*) to cut out; (*água, telefone etc*) to cut off; (*efeito*) to stop ▷ *vi* to cut; (*encurtar*

caminho) to take a short cut; **~ o cabelo**
(*no cabeleireiro*) to have one's hair cut; **~ a**
palavra de alguém to interrupt sb
corte¹ ['kɔxtʃi] *m* cut; (*de luz*) power cut;
sem ~ (*tesoura etc*) blunt; **~ de cabelo**
haircut
corte² ['kɔxtʃi] *f* court; **cortes** *fpl* (PT)
parliament *sg*
cortejo [kox'teʒu] *m* procession
cortesia [koxte'zia] *f* politeness; (*de*
empresa) free offer
cortiça [kox'tʃisa] *f* cork
cortiço [kox'tʃisu] *m* slum tenement
cortina [kox'tʃina] *f* curtain
coruja [ko'ruʒa] *f* owl
corvo ['koxvu] *m* crow
coser [ko'zeʳ] *vt, vi* to sew
cosmético, -a [koʒ'metʃiku, a] *adj*
cosmetic ▷ *m* cosmetic
cospe *etc* ['kɔʃpi] *vb ver* **cuspir**
costa ['kɔʃta] *f* coast; **costas** *fpl* (*dorso*)
back *sg*; **dar as ~s a** to turn one's back on
Costa Rica *f*: **a ~** Costa Rica
costela [koʃ'tɛla] *f* rib
costeleta [koʃte'leta] *f* chop, cutlet;
costeletas *fpl* (*suíças*) side-whiskers
costumar [koʃtu'maʳ] *vt* (*habituar*) to
accustom ▷ *vi*: **ele costuma chegar**
às 6.00 he usually arrives at 6.00;
costumava dizer ... he used to say ...
costume [koʃ'tumi] *m* custom,
habit; (*traje*) costume; **costumes** *mpl*
(*comportamento*) behaviour *sg* (BRIT),
behavior *sg* (US); (*conduta*) conduct *sg*; (*de*
um povo) customs; **de ~** usual; **como de**
~ as usual
costura [koʃ'tura] *f* sewing; (*sutura*)
seam; **costurar** [koʃtu'raʳ] *vt, vi* to sew;
costureira [koʃtu'rejra] *f* dressmaker
cota ['kɔta] *f* quota, share
cotação [kota'sãw] (*pl* -ões) *f* (*de*
preços) list, quotation; (*Bolsa*) price;
(*consideração*) esteem; **~ bancária** bank
rate
cotado, -a [ko'tadu, a] *adj* (Com: *ação*)
quoted; (*bem-conceituado*) well thought
of; (*num concurso*) fancied
cotar [ko'taʳ] *vt* (*ações*) to quote; **~ algo**
em to value sth at
cotejar [kote'ʒaʳ] *vt* to compare
cotidiano, -a [kotʃi'dʒianu, a] *adj* daily,
everyday ▷ *m* ~ daily life
cotonete [koto'nɛtʃi] *m* cotton bud
cotovelada [kotove'lada] *f* shove;
(*cutucada*) nudge
cotovelo [koto'velu] *m* (Anat) elbow;

(*curva*) bend; **falar pelos ~s** to talk
non-stop
coube *etc* ['kobi] *vb ver* **caber**
couro ['koru] *m* leather; (*de um animal*)
hide
couve ['kovi] *f* spring greens *pl*; **couve-**
flor (*pl* **couves-flores**) *f* cauliflower
couvert [ku'vɛx] *m* cover charge
cova ['kɔva] *f* pit; (*caverna*) cavern;
(*sepultura*) grave
covarde [ko'vaxdʒi] *adj* cowardly
▷ *m/f* coward; **covardia** [kovax'dʒia] *f*
cowardice
covil [ko'viw] (*pl* **-is**) *m* den, lair
covis [ko'viʃ] *mpl de* **covil**
coxa ['kɔʃa] *f* thigh
coxear [ko'ʃjaʳ] *vi* to limp
coxia [ko'ʃia] *f* aisle, gangway
coxo, -a ['koʃu, a] *adj* lame
cozer [ko'zeʳ] *vt, vi* to cook
cozido [ko'zidu] *m* stew
cozinha [ko'zina] *f* kitchen; (*arte*)
cookery
cozinhar [kozi'naʳ] *vt, vi* to cook
cozinheiro, -a [kozi'nejru, a] *m/f* cook
CP *abr* = **Caminhos de Ferro**
Portugueses
CPF (BR) *abr m* (= *Cadastro de Pessoa Física*)
identification number
CPLP *abr f* = **Comunidade de Países de**
Língua Portuguesa; *see boxed note*

crachá [kra'ʃa] *m* badge
crânio ['kranju] *m* skull
craque ['kraki] *m/f* ace, expert
crasso, -a ['krasu, a] *adj* crass
cratera [kra'tɛra] *f* crater
cravar [kra'vaʳ] *vt* (*prego etc*) to drive
(in); (*com os olhos*) to stare at; **~-se** *vr* to
penetrate
cravo ['kravu] *m* carnation; (*Mús*)
harpsichord; (*especiaria*) clove; (*na pele*)
blackhead; (*prego*) nail

creche [ˈkrɛʃi] f crèche
credenciais [kredẽˈsjajʃ] fpl credentials
creditar [kredʒiˈtaʳ] vt to guarantee; (Com) to credit; **~ algo a alguém** to credit sb with sth; (garantir) to assure sb of sth
crédito [ˈkrɛdʒitu] m credit; **digno de ~** reliable
creme [ˈkrɛmi] adj inv cream ▷ m cream; (Culin: doce) custard; **~ dental** toothpaste; **cremoso, -a** [kreˈmozu, ɔza] adj creamy
crença [ˈkrẽsa] f belief
crente [ˈkrẽtʃi] m/f believer
crepúsculo [kreˈpuʃkulu] m dusk, twilight
crer [kreʳ] vt, vi to believe; **~-se** vr to believe o.s. to be; **~ em** to believe in; **creio que sim** I think so
crescer [kreˈseʳ] vi to grow; **crescimento** [kresiˈmẽtu] m growth
crespo, -a [ˈkreʃpu, a] adj (cabelo) curly
cretinice [kretʃiˈnisi] f stupidity; (ato, dito) stupid thing
cretino [kreˈtʃinu] m cretin, imbecile
cria [ˈkria] f (animal: sg) baby animal; (: pl) young pl
criação [krjaˈsãw] (pl -ões) f creation; (de animais) raising, breeding; (educação) upbringing; (animais domésticos) livestock pl; **filho de ~** adopted child
criado, -a [ˈkrjadu, a] m/f servant
criador, a [krjaˈdoʳ, a] m/f creator; **~ de gado** cattle breeder
criança [ˈkrjãsa] adj childish ▷ f child; **criançada** [krjãˈsada] f: **a criançada** the kids
criar [krjaʳ] vt to create; (crianças) to bring up; (animais) to raise; (amamentar) to suckle, nurse; (planta) to grow; **~-se** vr: **~-se (com)** to grow up (with); **~ caso** to make trouble
criatura [kriaˈtura] f creature; (indivíduo) individual
crime [ˈkrimi] m crime; **criminal** [krimiˈnaw] (pl -ais) adj criminal; **criminalidade** [kriminaliˈdadʒi] f crime; **criminoso, -a** [krimiˈnozu, ɔza] adj, m/f criminal
crina [ˈkrina] f mane
crioulo, -a [ˈkrjolu, a] adj creole ▷ m/f creole; (BR: negro) Black (person)
crise [ˈkrizi] f crisis; (escassez) shortage; (Med) attack, fit
crista [ˈkriʃta] f (de serra, onda) crest; (de galo) cock's comb

cristal [kriʃˈtaw] (pl -ais) m crystal; (vidro) glass; **cristais** mpl (copos) glassware sg; **cristalino, -a** [kriʃtaˈlinu, a] adj crystal-clear
cristão, -tã [kriʃˈtãw, ˈtã] (pl ~s/-s) adj, m/f Christian
cristianismo [kriʃtʃjaˈniʒmu] m Christianity
Cristo [ˈkriʃtu] m Christ
critério [kriˈtɛrju] m criterion; (juízo) discretion, judgement; **criterioso, -a** [kriteˈrjozu, ɔza] adj thoughtful, careful
crítica [ˈkritʃika] f criticism; ver tb **crítico**
criticar [kritʃiˈkaʳ] vt to criticize; (um livro) to review
crítico, -a [ˈkritʃiku, a] adj critical ▷ m/f critic
crivar [kriˈvaʳ] vt (com balas etc) to riddle
crivo [ˈkrivu] m sieve
crocante [kroˈkãtʃi] adj crunchy
crônica [ˈkronika] f chronicle; (coluna de jornal) newspaper column; (texto jornalístico) feature; (conto) short story
crônico, -a [ˈkroniku, a] adj chronic
cronológico, -a [kronoˈlɔʒiku, a] adj chronological
croquete [kroˈkɛtʃi] m croquette
cru, a [kru, ˈkrua] adj raw; (não refinado) crude
crucial [kruˈsjaw] (pl -ais) adj crucial
crucificar [krusifiˈkaʳ] vt to crucify
crucifixo [krusiˈfiksu] m crucifix
cruel [kruˈew] (pl -éis) adj cruel; **crueldade** [kruewˈdadʒi] f cruelty
cruz [kruʒ] f cross; **C~ Vermelha** Red Cross
cruzado, -a [kruˈzadu, a] adj crossed ▷ m (moeda) cruzado
cruzamento [kruzaˈmẽtu] m crossroads
cruzar [kruˈzaʳ] vt to cross ▷ vi (Náut) to cruise; (pessoas) to pass each other by; **~ com** to meet
cruzeiro [kruˈzejru] m (cruz) (monumental) cross; (moeda) cruzeiro; (viagem de navio) cruise
Cuba [ˈkuba] f Cuba
cubro etc [ˈkubru] vb ver **cobrir**
cuca [ˈkuka] (col) f head; **fundir a ~** (quebrar a cabeça) to rack one's brain; (baratinar) to boggle the mind; (perturbar) to drive crazy
cuco [ˈkuku] m cuckoo
cueca [ˈkweka] f (BR: tb: ~s: para homens) underpants pl; **cuecas** fpl (PT) underpants pl; (para mulheres) panties pl
cuíca [ˈkwika] f kind of musical instrument

cuidado [kwi'dadu] *m* care; **aos ~s de** in the care of; **ter ~** to be careful; **~!** watch out!, be careful!; **tomar ~ (de)** to be careful (of); **cuidadoso, -a** [kwida'dozu, ɔza] *adj* careful

cuidar [kwi'da^r] *vi*: **~ de** to take care of, look after; **~-se** *vr* to look after o.s

cujo, -a ['kuʒu, a] *pron* (*de quem*) whose; (*de que*) of which

culinária [kuli'narja] *f* cookery

culpa ['kuwpa] *f* fault; (*Jur*) guilt; **ter ~ de** to be to blame for; **por ~ de** because of; **culpado, -a** [kuw'padu, a] *adj* guilty ▷ *m/f* culprit; **culpar** [kuw'pa^r] *vt* to blame; (*acusar*) to accuse; **culpar-se** *vr* to take the blame; **culpável** [kuw'pavew] (*pl* **-eis**) *adj* guilty

cultivar [kuwtʃi'va^r] *vt* to cultivate; (*plantas*) to grow; **cultivo** [kuw'tʃivu] *m* cultivation

culto, -a ['kuwtu, a] *adj* cultured ▷ *m* (*homenagem*) worship; (*religião*) cult

cultura [kuw'tura] *f* culture; (*da terra*) cultivation; **cultural** [kuwtu'raw] (*pl* **culturais**) *adj* cultural

cume ['kumi] *m* top, summit; (*fig*) climax

cúmplice ['kũplisi] *m/f* accomplice

cumprimentar [kũprimẽ'ta^r] *vt* to greet; (*dar parabéns*) to congratulate

cumprimento [kũpri'mẽtu] *m* fulfilment; (*saudação*) greeting; (*elogio*) compliment; **cumprimentos** *mpl* (*saudações*) best wishes; **~ de uma lei/ ordem** compliance with a law/an order

cumprir [kũ'pri^r] *vt* (*desempenhar*) to carry out; (*promessa*) to keep; (*lei*) to obey; (*pena*) to serve ▷ *vi* to be necessary; **~ a palavra** to keep one's word; **fazer ~** to enforce

cúmulo ['kumulu] *m* height; **é o ~!** that's the limit!

cunha ['kuɲa] *f* wedge

cunhado, -a [ku'ɲadu, a] *m/f* brother-in-law/sister-in-law

cunho ['kuɲu] *m* (*marca*) hallmark; (*caráter*) nature

cupim [ku'pĩ] (*pl* **-ns**) *m* termite

cupins [ku'pĩʃ] *mpl de* **cupim**

cúpula ['kupula] *f* dome; (*de abajur*) shade; (*de partido etc*) leadership; **(reunião de) ~** summit (meeting)

cura ['kura] *f* cure; (*tratamento*) treatment; (*de carnes etc*) curing, preservation ▷ *m* priest

curar [ku'ra^r] *vt* (*doença, carne*) to cure; (*ferida*) to treat; **~-se** *vr* to get well

curativo [kura'tʃivu] *m* dressing

curiosidade [kurjozi'dadʒi] *f* curiosity; (*objeto raro*) curio

curioso, -a [ku'rjozu, ɔza] *adj* curious ▷ *m/f* snooper, inquisitive person; **curiosos** *mpl* (*espectadores*) onlookers

curral [ku'xaw] (*pl* **-ais**) *m* pen, enclosure

currículo [ku'xikulu] *m* (*curriculum*) curriculum vitae

cursar [kux'sa^r] *vt* (*aulas, escola*) to attend; (*cursos*) to follow; **ele está cursando História** he's studying *ou* doing history

curso ['kuxsu] *m* course; (*direção*) direction; **em ~** (*ano etc*) current; (*processo*) in progress

cursor [kux'so^r] *m* (*Comput*) cursor

curtição [kuxtʃi'sãw] (*col*) *f* fun

curtir [kux'tʃi^r] *vt* (*couro*) to tan; (*tornar rijo*) to toughen up; (*padecer*) to suffer, endure; (*col*) to enjoy

curto, -a ['kuxtu, a] *adj* short ▷ *m* (*Elet*) short (circuit); **curto-circuito** (*pl* **curtos-circuitos**) *m* short circuit

curva ['kuxva] *f* curve; (*de estrada, rio*) bend; **~ fechada** hairpin bend

curvo, -a ['kuxvu, a] *adj* curved; (*estrada*) winding

cuscuz [kuʃ'kuʒ] *m* couscous

cuspe ['kuʃpi] *m* spit, spittle

cuspir [kuʃ'pi^r] *vt*, *vi* to spit

custa ['kuʃta] *f*: **à ~ de** at the expense of; **custas** *fpl* (*Jur*) costs

custar [kuʃ'ta^r] *vi* to cost; (*ser difícil*): **~ a fazer** to have trouble doing; (*demorar*): **~ a fazer** to take a long time to do; **~ caro** to be expensive

custo ['kuʃtu] *m* cost; **a ~** with difficulty; **a todo ~** at all costs

cutelo [ku'telu] *m* cleaver

cutícula [ku'tʃikula] *f* cuticle

cutucar [kutu'ka^r] *vt* (*com o dedo*) to prod, poke; (*com o cotovelo*) to nudge

d

D *abr* = **Dom; Dona**: (= *direito*) r; (= *deve*) d

d/ *abr* = **dia**

da [da] = **de + a**

dá [da] *vb ver* **dar**

dactilografar *etc* [datilogra'faʳ] (PT)
= **datilografar** *etc*

dado, -a ['dadu, a] *adj* given; (*sociável*)
sociable ▷ *m* (*em jogo*) die; (*fato*) fact;
dados *mpl* dice; (*fatos*, Comput) data
sg; **~ que** supposing that; (*uma vez que*)
given that

daí [da'ji] *adv* = **de + aí**; (*desse lugar*) from
there; (*desse momento*) from then; **~ a um
mês** a month later

dali [da'li] *adv* = **de + ali**; (*desse lugar*)
from there

daltônico, -a [daw'toniku, a] *adj* colour-
blind (BRIT), color-blind (US)

dama ['dama] *f* lady; (*Xadrez, Cartas*)
queen; **damas** *fpl* (*jogo*) draughts (BRIT),
checkers (US); **~ de honra** bridesmaid

damasco [da'maʃku] *m* apricot

danado, -a [da'nadu, a] *adj* damned;
(*zangado*) furious; (*menino*) mischievous

dança ['dãsa] *f* dance; **dançar** [dã'saʳ] *vi*
to dance

danificar [danifi'kaʳ] *vt* to damage

dano ['danu] *m* (*tb*: **~s**) damage, harm; (*a*

uma pessoa) injury

dantes ['dãtʃiʃ] *adv* before, formerly

daquele, -a [da'kɛli, a] = **de + aquele/a**

daqui [da'ki] *adv* = **de + aqui**; (*deste lugar*)
from here; **~ a pouco** soon, in a little
while; **~ a uma semana** a week from
now; **~ em diante** from now on

daquilo [da'kilu] = **de + aquilo**

 **PALAVRA CHAVE**

dar [daʳ] *vt* **1** (*ger*) to give; (*festa*) to hold;
(*problemas*) to cause; **dar algo a alguém**
to give sb sth, give sth to sb; **dar de
beber a alguém** to give sb a drink; **dar
aula de francês** to teach French

2 (*produzir: fruta etc*) to produce

3 (*notícias no jornal*) to publish

4 (*cartas*) to deal

5 (+ n: *perífrase de vb*): **me dá medo/pena**
it frightens/upsets me

▷ *vi* **1**: **dar com** (*coisa*) to find; (*pessoa*)
to meet

2: **dar em** (*bater*) to hit; (*resultar*) to lead
to; (*lugar*) to come to

3: **dá no mesmo** it's all the same

4: **dar de si** (*sapatos etc*) to stretch, give

5: **dar para** (*impess: ser possível*): **dá
para trocar dinheiro aqui?** can I
change money here?; **vai dar para eu ir
amanhã** I'll be able to go tomorrow; **dá
para você vir amanhã - não, amanhã
não vai dar** can you come tomorrow?
- no, I can't

6: **dar para** (*ser suficiente*): **dar para/
para fazer** to be enough for/to do; **dá
para todo mundo?** is there enough for
everyone?

dar-se *vr* **1** (*sair-se*): **dar-se bem/mal** to
do well/badly

2: **dar-se (com alguém)** to be
acquainted (with sb); **dar-se bem (com
alguém)** to get on well (with sb)

3: **dar-se por vencido** to give up

das [daʃ] = **de + as**

data ['data] *f* date; (*época*) time; **~ de
validade** best before date; **datar**
[da'taʳ] *vt* to date ▷ *vi*: **datar de** to date
from

datilografar [datʃilogra'faʳ] *vt* to type;
datilografia [datʃilogra'fia] *f* typing;
datilógrafo, -a [datʃi'lɔgrafu, a] *m/f*
typist (BRIT), stenographer (US)

d.C. *abr* (= *depois de Cristo*) A.D.

DDD *abr* (= *discagem direta à distância*)

STD (BRIT), direct dialling
DDI abr (= discagem direta internacional)
IDD, international direct call

🔘 **PALAVRA CHAVE**

de [dʒi] (de + o(s)/a(s) = do(s)/da(s); +
ele(s)/a(s) = dele(s)/a(s); + esse(s)/a(s) =
desse(s)/a(s); + isso = disso; + este(s)/a(s) =
deste(s)/a(s); + isto = disto; + aquele(s)/a(s)
= daquele(s)/a(s); + aquilo = daquilo) prep
1 (posse) of; **a casa de João/da irmã**
João's/my sister's house; **é dele** it's his;
um romance de a novel by
2 (origem, distância, com números) from;
sou de São Paulo I'm from São Paulo; **de
8 a 20** from 8 to 20; **sair do cinema** to
leave the cinema; **de dois em dois** two
by two, two at a time
3 (valor descritivo): **um copo de vinho**
a glass of wine; **um homem de cabelo
comprido** a man with long hair; **o
infeliz do homem** (col) the poor man;
um bilhete de avião an air ticket; **uma
criança de três anos** a three-year-old
(child); **uma máquina de costurar**
a sewing machine; **aulas de inglês**
English lessons; **feito de madeira** made
of wood; **vestido de branco** dressed in
white
4 (modo): **de trem/avião** by train/plane;
de lado sideways
5 (hora, tempo): **às 8 da manhã** at 8
o'clock in the morning; **de dia/noite** by
day/night; **de hoje a oito dias** a week
from now; **de dois em dois dias** every
other day
6 (comparações): **mais/menos de cem
pessoas** more/less than a hundred
people; **é o mais caro da loja** it's the
most expensive in the shop; **ela é mais
bonita do que sua irmã** she's prettier
than her sister; **gastei mais do que
pretendia** I spent more than I intended
7 (causa): **estou morto de calor** I'm
boiling hot; **ela morreu de câncer** she
died of cancer
8 (adj + de + infin): **fácil de entender** easy
to understand

dê etc [de] vb ver **dar**
debaixo [de'bajʃu] adv below,
underneath ▷ prep: ~ **de** under, beneath
debate [de'batʃi] m discussion, debate;
(disputa) argument; **debater** [deba'te**ʳ**]
vt to debate; (discutir) to discuss;

debater-se vr to struggle
débil ['dɛbiw] (pl **-eis**) adj weak, feeble
▷ m: ~ **mental** mentally handicapped
person; **debilidade** [debili'dadʒi] f
weakness; **debilidade mental** mental
handicap; **debilitar** [debili'ta**ʳ**] vt to
weaken; **debilitar-se** vr to become
weak, weaken; **debilóide** [debi'lɔjdʒi]
(col) adj idiotic ▷ m/f idiot
debitar [debi'ta**ʳ**] vt: ~ **$40 à** ou **na conta
de alguém** to debit $40 to sb's account;
débito ['dɛbitu] m debit
debochado, -a [debo'ʃadu, a] adj
(pessoa) sardonic; (jeito, tom) mocking
década ['dɛkada] f decade
decadência [deka'dẽsja] f decadence
decair [deka'i**ʳ**] vi to decline
decente [de'sẽtʃi] adj decent;
(apropriado) proper; (honrado) honourable
(BRIT), honorable (US); (trabalho) neat;
decentemente [desẽtʃi'mẽtʃi] adv
decently; properly; hono(u)rably
decepção [desep'sãw] (pl **-ões**) f
disappointment; **decepcionar**
[desepsjo'na**ʳ**] vt to disappoint;
(desiludir) to disillusion; **decepcionar-se**
vr to be disappointed; to be disillusioned
decidir [desi'dʒi**ʳ**] vt to decide;
(solucionar) to resolve; **~-se** vr: **~-se a**
to make up one's mind to; **~-se por** to
decide on, go for
decifrar [desi'fra**ʳ**] vt to decipher;
(futuro) to foretell; (compreender) to
understand
decimal [desi'maw] (pl **-ais**) adj, m
decimal
décimo, -a ['dɛsimu, a] adj tenth ▷ m
tenth
decisão [desi'zãw] (pl **-ões**) f decision;
decisivo, -a [desi'zivu, a] adj (fator)
decisive; (jogo) deciding
declaração [deklara'sãw] (pl **-ões**) f
declaration; (depoimento) statement
declarado, -a [dekla'radu, a] adj
(intenção) declared; (opinião) professed;
(inimigo) sworn; (alcoólatra) self-
confessed; (cristão etc) avowed
declarar [dekla'ra**ʳ**] vt to declare;
(confessar) to confess
declinar [dekli'na**ʳ**] vt (ger) to decline ▷ vi
(sol) to go down; (terreno) to slope down;
declínio [de'klinju] m decline
declive [de'klivi] m slope, incline
decolagem [deko'laʒẽ] (pl **-ns**) f (Aer)
take-off
decolar [deko'la**ʳ**] vi (Aer) to take off

decompor [dekõ'po'] (*irreg: como* **pôr**) *vt* to analyse; (*apodrecer*) to rot; **~-se** *vr* to rot, decompose

decomposição [dekõpozi'sãw] (*pl* **-ões**) *f* decomposition; (*análise*) dissection

decorar [deko'ra'] *vt* to decorate; (*aprender*) to learn by heart; **decorativo, -a** [dekora'tʃivu, a] *adj* decorative

decoro [de'koru] *m* decency; (*dignidade*) decorum

decorrente [deko'xẽtʃi] *adj*: **~ de** resulting from

decorrer [deko'xe'] *vi* (*tempo*) to pass; (*acontecer*) to take place, happen ▷ *m*: **no ~ de** in the course of; **~ de** to result from

decrescer [dekre'se'] *vi* to decrease, diminish

decretar [dekre'ta'] *vt* to decree, order; **decreto** [de'krɛtu] *m* decree, order; **decreto-lei** (*pl* **decretos-leis**) *m* act, law

dedetizar [dedetʃi'za'] *vt* to spray with insecticide

dedicação [dedʒika'sãw] *f* dedication; (*devotamento*) devotion

dedicar [dedʒi'ka'] *vt* to dedicate; (*tempo, atenção*) to devote; **~-se** *vr*: **~-se a** to devote o.s. to; **dedicatória** [dedʒika'tɔrja] *f* (*de obra*) dedication

dedo ['dedu] *m* finger; (*do pé*) toe; **~ anular/indicador/mínimo** *ou* **mindinho** ring/index/little finger; **~ polegar** thumb

dedução [dedu'sãw] (*pl* **-ões**) *f* deduction

deduzir [dedu'zi'] *vt* to deduct; (*concluir*) to deduce, infer

defasagem [defa'zaʒẽ] (*pl* **-ns**) *f* discrepancy

defeito [de'fejtu] *m* defect, flaw; **pôr ~s em** to find fault with; **com ~** broken, out of order; **para ninguém botar ~** (*col*) perfect; **defeituoso, -a** [defej'twozu, ɔza] *adj* defective, faulty

defender [defẽ'de'] *vt* to defend; **~-se** *vr* to stand up for o.s.; (*numa língua*) to get by

defensiva [defẽ'siva] *f*: **estar** *ou* **ficar na ~** to be on the defensive

defensor, a [defẽ'so', a] *m/f* defender; (*Jur*) defending counsel

defesa [de'feza] *f* defence (*BRIT*), defense (*US*); (*Jur*) counsel for the defence ▷ *m* (*Futebol*) back

deficiente [defi'sjẽtʃi] *adj* (*imperfeito*) defective; (*carente*): **~ (em)** deficient (in)

déficit ['dɛfisitʃi] (*pl* **-s**) *m* deficit

definição [defini'sãw] (*pl* **-ões**) *f* definition

definir [defi'ni'] *vt* to define; **~-se** *vr* to make a decision; (*explicar-se*) to make one's position clear; **~-se a favor de/contra algo** to come out in favo(u)r of/against sth

definitivamente [definitʃiva'mẽtʃi] *adv* definitively; (*permanentemente*) for good; (*sem dúvida*) definitely

definitivo, -a [defini'tʃivu, a] *adj* final, definitive; (*permanente*) permanent; (*resposta, data*) definite

defronte [de'frõtʃi] *adv* opposite ▷ *prep*: **~ de** opposite

defumar [defu'ma'] *vt* (*presunto*) to smoke; (*perfumar*) to perfume

defunto, -a [de'fũtu, a] *adj* dead ▷ *m/f* dead person

degelar [deʒe'la'] *vt* to thaw; (*geladeira*) to defrost ▷ *vi* to thaw out; to defrost

degradar [degra'da'] *vt* to degrade, debase; **~-se** *vr* to demean o.s

degrau [de'graw] *m* step; (*de escada de mão*) rung

degustação [deguʃta'sãw] (*pl* **-ões**) *f* tasting, sampling; (*saborear*) savouring (*BRIT*), savoring (*US*)

degustar [deguʃ'ta'] *vt* (*provar*) to taste; (*saborear*) to savour (*BRIT*), savor (*US*)

dei *etc* [dej] *vb ver* **dar**

deitada [dej'tada] (*col*) *f*: **dar uma ~** to have a lie-down

deitado, -a [dej'tadu, a] *adj* (*estendido*) lying down; (*na cama*) in bed

deitar [dej'ta'] *vt* to lay down; (*na cama*) to put to bed; (*colocar*) to put, place; (*lançar*) to cast; (*PT: líquido*) to pour; **~-se** *vr* to lie down; to go to bed; **~ sangue** (*PT*) to bleed; **~ abaixo** to knock down, flatten; **~ a fazer algo** to start doing sth; **~ uma carta** (*PT*) to post a letter; **~ fora** (*PT*) to throw away *ou* out; **~ e rolar** (*col*) to do as one likes

deixa ['dejʃa] *f* clue, hint; (*Teatro*) cue; (*chance*) chance

deixar [dej'ʃa'] *vt* to leave; (*abandonar*) to abandon; (*permitir*) to let, allow ▷ *vi*: **~ de** (*parar*) to stop; (*não fazer*) to fail to; **não posso ~ de ir** I must go; **~ cair** to drop; **~ alguém louco** to drive sb crazy *ou* mad; **~ alguém cansado/nervoso** *etc* to make sb tired/nervous *etc*; **deixa disso!** (*col*) come off it!; **deixa para lá!** (*col*) forget it!

dela ['dɛla] = **de** + **ela**

delatar [dela'ta'] *vt* (*pessoa*) to inform

on; (*abusos*) to reveal; (*à polícia*) to report;
delator, a [dela'to^r, a] *m/f* informer
dele ['deli] = **de + ele**
delegacia [delega'sia] *f* office; ~ **de polícia** police station
delegado, -a [dele'gadu, a] *m/f* delegate, representative; ~ **de polícia** police chief
delegar [dele'ga^r] *vt* to delegate
deleitar [delej'ta^r] *vt* to delight; ~**se** *vr*: ~**se com** to delight in
delgado, -a [dew'gadu, a] *adj* thin; (*esbelto*) slim; (*fino*) fine
deliberação [delibera'sãw] (*pl* -ões) *f* deliberation; (*decisão*) decision
deliberar [delibe'ra^r] *vt* to decide, resolve ▷ *vi* to deliberate
delicadeza [delika'deza] *f* delicacy; (*cortesia*) kindness
delicado, -a [deli'kadu, a] *adj* delicate; (*frágil*) fragile; (*cortês*) polite; (*sensível*) sensitive
delícia [de'lisja] *f* delight; (*prazer*) pleasure; **que ~!** how lovely!; **deliciar** [deli'sja^r] *vt* to delight; **deliciar-se** *vr*: **deliciar-se com algo** to take delight in sth
delicioso, -a [deli'sjozu, ɔza] *adj* lovely; (*comida, bebida*) delicious
delinear [deli'nja^r] *vt* to outline
delinqüente [delĩ'kwẽtʃi] *adj, m/f* delinquent, criminal
delirar [deli'ra^r] *vi* (*com febre*) to be delirious; (*de ódio, prazer*) to go mad, go wild
delírio [de'lirju] *m* (*Med*) delirium; (*êxtase*) ecstasy; (*excitação*) excitement
delito [de'litu] *m* (*crime*) crime; (*falta*) offence (*BRIT*), offense (*US*)
demais [dʒi'majʃ] *adv* (*em demasia*) too much; (*muitíssimo*) a lot, very much ▷ *pron*: **os/as ~** the rest (of them); **já é ~!** this is too much!; **é bom ~** it's really good; **foi ~** (*col: bacana*) it was great
demanda [de'mãda] *f* lawsuit; (*disputa*) claim; (*requisição*) request; (*Econ*) demand; **em ~ de** in search of; **demandar** [demã'da^r] *vt* (*Jur*) to sue; (*exigir, reclamar*) to demand
demasia [dema'zia] *f* excess, surplus; (*imoderação*) lack of moderation; **em ~** (*dinheiro, comida etc*) too much; (*cartas, problemas etc*) too many
demasiadamente [demazjada'mẽtʃi] *adv* too much; (*com adj*) too
demasiado, -a [dema'zjadu, a] *adj* too

much; (*pl*) too many ▷ *adv* too much; (*com adj*) too
demitir [demi'tʃi^r] *vt* to dismiss; (*col*) to sack, fire; ~**se** *vr* to resign
democracia [demokra'sia] *f* democracy
democrático, -a [demo'kratʃiku, a] *adj* democratic
demolir [demo'li^r] *vt* to demolish, knock down; (*fig*) to destroy
demonstração [demõʃtra'sãw] (*pl* -ões) *f* demonstration; (*de amizade*) show, display; (*prova*) proof
demonstrar [demõʃ'tra^r] *vt* to demonstrate; (*provar*) to prove; (*amizade etc*) to show
demora [de'mɔra] *f* delay; (*parada*) stop; **sem ~** at once, without delay; **qual é a ~ disso?** how long will this take?; **demorado, -a** [demo'radu, a] *adj* slow; **demorar** [demo'ra^r] *vt* to delay, slow down ▷ *vi* (*permanecer*) to stay; (*tardar a vir*) to be late; (*conserto*) to take (a long) time; **demorar-se** *vr* to stay for a long time, linger; **demorar a chegar** to be a long time coming; **vai demorar muito?** will it take long?; **não vou demorar** I won't be long
dendê [dẽ'de] *m* (*Culin: óleo*) palm oil; (*Bot*) oil palm
dengoso, -a [dẽ'gozu, ɔza] *adj* coy; (*criança: choraminguento*): **ser ~** to be a crybaby
dengue ['dẽgi] *m* (*Med*) dengue
denominar [denomi'na^r] *vt*: ~ **algo/ alguém ...** to call sth/sb ...; ~**se** *vr* to be called; (*a si mesmo*) to call o.s
denotar [deno'ta^r] *vt* (*indicar*) to show, indicate; (*significar*) to signify
densidade [dẽsi'dadʒi] *f* density; **disco de ~ simples/dupla** (*Comput*) single-/ double-density disk
denso, -a [dẽsu, a] *adj* dense; (*espesso*) thick; (*compacto*) compact
dentada [dẽ'tada] *f* bite
dentadura [dẽta'dura] *f* teeth *pl*, set of teeth; (*artificial*) dentures *pl*
dente ['dẽtʃi] *m* tooth; (*de animal*) fang; (*de elefante*) tusk; (*de alho*) clove; **falar entre os ~s** to mutter, mumble; ~ **de leite/do siso** milk/wisdom tooth; ~**s postiços** false teeth
dentista [dẽ'tʃiʃta] *m/f* dentist
dentre ['dẽtri] *prep* (from) among
dentro ['dẽtru] *adv* inside ▷ *prep*: ~ **de** inside; (*tempo*) (with)in; ~ **em pouco** *ou* **em breve** soon, before long; **de ~ para**

fora inside out; **dar uma ~** (col) to get it right; **aí ~** in there; **por ~** on the inside; **estar por ~** (col: fig) to be in the know

denúncia [de'nũsja] f denunciation; (acusação) accusation; (de roubo) report; **denunciar** [denũ'sja'] vt (acusar) to denounce; (delatar) to inform on; (revelar) to reveal

deparar [depa'ra'] vt to reveal; (fazer aparecer) to present ▷ vi: **~ com** to come across, meet; **~-se** vr: **~-se com** to come across, meet

departamento [depaxta'mẽtu] m department

dependência [depẽ'dẽsja] f dependence; (edificação) annexe (BRIT), annex (US); (colonial) dependency; (cômodo) room

dependente [depẽ'dẽtʃi] m/f dependant

depender [depẽ'de'] vi: **~ de** to depend on

depilar [depi'la'] vt (pernas) to wax; **depilatório** [depila'tɔrju] m hair-remover

deplorável [deplo'ravew] (pl -**eis**) adj deplorable; (lamentável) regrettable

depoimento [depoj'mẽtu] m testimony, evidence; (na polícia) statement

depois [de'pojʃ] adv afterwards ▷ prep: **~ de** after; **~ de comer** after eating; **~ que** after

depor [de'po'] (irreg: como **pôr**) vt (pôr) to place; (indicar) to indicate; (rei) to depose; (governo) to overthrow ▷ vi (Jur) to testify, give evidence; (na polícia) to give a statement

depositar [depozi'ta'] vt to deposit; (voto) to cast; (colocar) to place

depósito [de'pɔzitu] m deposit; (armazém) warehouse, depot; (de lixo) dump; (reservatório) tank; **~ de bagagens** left-luggage office (BRIT), checkroom (US)

depreciação [depresja'sãw] f depreciation

depredar [depre'da'] vt to wreck

depressa [dʒi'prɛsa] adv fast, quickly; **vamos ~** let's get a move on!

depressão [depre'sãw] (pl -**ões**) f depression

deprimente [depri'mẽtʃi] adj depressing

deprimido, -a [depri'midu, a] adj depressed

deprimir [depri'mi'] vt to depress; **~-se** vr to get depressed

deputado, -a [depu'tadu, a] m/f deputy; (agente) agent; (Pol) ≈ Member of Parliament (BRIT), ≈ Representative (US)

der etc [de'] vb ver **dar**

deriva [de'riva] f drift; **ir à ~** to drift; **ficar à ~** to be adrift

derivar [deri'va'] vt to divert; (Ling) to derive ▷ vi to drift; **~-se** vr to be derived; (ir à deriva) to drift; (provir): **~(-se) (de)** to derive ou be derived (from)

derradeiro, -a [dexa'dejru, a] adj last, final

derramamento [dexama'mẽtu] m spilling; (de sangue, lágrimas) shedding

derramar [dexa'ma'] vt to spill; (entornar) to pour; (sangue, lágrimas) to shed; **~-se** vr to pour out

derrame [de'xami] m haemorrhage (BRIT), hemorrhage (US)

derrapar [dexa'pa'] vi to skid

derreter [dexe'te'] vt to melt; **~-se** vr to melt; (coisa congelada) to thaw; (enternecer-se) to be touched

derrota [de'xɔta] f defeat, rout; (Náut) route; **derrotar** [dexo'ta'] vt (vencer) to defeat; (em jogo) to beat

derrubar [dexu'ba'] vt to knock down; (governo) to bring down; (suj: doença) to lay low; (col: prejudicar) to put down

desabafar [dʒizaba'fa'] vt (sentimentos) to give vent to ▷ vi: **~ (com)** to unburden o.s. (to); **~-se** vr: **~-se (com)** to unburden o.s. (to); **desabafo** [dʒiza'bafu] m confession

desabamento [dʒizaba'mẽtu] m collapse

desabar [dʒiza'ba'] vi (edifício, ponte) to collapse; (chuva) to pour down; (tempestade) to break

desabitado, -a [dʒizabi'tadu, a] adj uninhabited

desabotoar [dʒizabo'twa'] vt to unbutton

desabrigado, -a [dʒizabri'gadu, a] adj (sem casa) homeless; (exposto) exposed

desabrochar [dʒizabro'ʃa'] vi (flores, fig) to blossom

desacatar [dʒizaka'ta'] vt (desrespeitar) to have ou show no respect for; (afrontar) to defy; (desprezar) to scorn; **desacato** [dʒiza'katu] m disrespect; (desprezo) disregard

desaconselhar [dʒizakõse'ʎa'] vt: **~ algo (a alguém)** to advise (sb) against sth

desacordado, -a [dʒizakox'dadu, a] adj unconscious

desacordo [dʒiza'koxdu] m
disagreement; (*desarmonia*) discord

desacostumado, -a [dʒizakoʃtumadu,
a] *adj*: **~ (a)** unaccustomed (to)

desacreditar [dʒizakredʒi'ta'] *vt* to
discredit; **~-se** *vr* to lose one's reputation

desafiador, a [dʒizafja'do', a] *adj*
challenging; (*pessoa*) defiant ▷ *m/f*
challenger

desafiar [dʒiza'fja'] *vt* to challenge;
(*afrontar*) to defy

desafinado, -a [dʒizafi'nadu, a] *adj* out
of tune

desafio [dʒiza'fiu] m challenge; (PT:
Esporte) match, game

desaforado, -a [dʒizafo'radu, a] *adj*
rude, insolent

desaforo [dʒiza'foru] m insolence, abuse

desafortunado, -a [dʒizafoxtu'nadu,
a] *adj* unfortunate, unlucky

desagradar [dʒizagra'da'] *vt* to
displease ▷ *vi*: **~ a alguém** to displease
sb; **desagradável** [dʒizagra'davew]
(*pl* **-eis**) *adj* unpleasant; **desagrado**
[dʒiza'gradu] m displeasure

desaguar [dʒiza'gwa'] *vt* to drain ▷ *vi*: **~
(em)** to flow *ou* empty (into)

desajeitado, -a [dʒizaʒej'tadu, a] *adj*
clumsy, awkward

desalentado, -a [dʒizalẽ'tadu, a] *adj*
disheartened

desalentar [dʒizalẽ'ta'] *vt* to
discourage; (*deprimir*) to depress;
desalento [dʒiza'lẽtu] m
discouragement

desalmado, -a [dʒizaw'madu, a] *adj*
cruel, inhuman

desalojar [dʒizalo'ʒa'] *vt* (*expulsar*) to
oust; **~-se** *vr* to move out

desamarrar [dʒizama'xa'] *vt* to untie
▷ *vi* (*Náut*) to cast off

desamor [dʒiza'mo'] m dislike

desamparado, -a [dʒizãpa'radu, a] *adj*
abandoned; (*sem apoio*) helpless

desanimação [dʒizanima'sãw] f
dejection

desanimado, -a [dʒizani'madu, a] *adj*
(*pessoa*) fed up, dispirited; (*festa*) dull; **ser
~** (*pessoa*) to be apathetic

desanuviar [dʒizanu'vja'] *vt* (*céu*) to
clear; **~-se** *vr* to clear; (*fig*) to stop; **~
alguém** to put sb's mind at rest

desaparafusar [dʒizaparafu'za'] *vt* to
unscrew

desaparecer [dʒizapare'se'] *vi* to
disappear, vanish; **desaparecido,**

-a [dʒizapare'sidu, a] *adj* lost,
missing ▷ *m/f* missing person;
desaparecimento [dʒizaparesi'mẽtu]
m disappearance; (*falecimento*) death

desapego [dʒiza'pegu] m indifference,
detachment

desapercebido, -a [dʒizapexse'bidu, a]
adj unnoticed

desapertar [dʒizapex'ta'] *vt* to loosen;
(*livrar*) to free

desapontamento [dʒizapõta'mẽtu] m
disappointment

desapontar [dʒizapõ'ta'] *vt* to
disappoint

desapropriar [dʒizapro'prja'] *vt* (*bens*)
to expropriate; (*pessoa*) to dispossess

desaprovar [dʒizapro'va'] *vt* to
disapprove of; (*censurar*) to object to

desarmamento [dʒizaxma'mẽtu] m
disarmament

desarmar [dʒizax'ma'] *vt* to disarm;
(*desmontar*) to dismantle; (*bomba*) to
defuse

desarmonia [dʒizaxmo'nia] f discord

desarranjo [dʒiza'xãʒu] m disorder;
(*enguiço*) breakdown; (*diarréia*) diarrhoea
(BRIT), diarrhea (US)

desarrumado, -a [dʒizaxu'madu, a] *adj*
untidy, messy

desarrumar [dʒizaxu'ma'] *vt* to mess
up; (*mala*) to unpack

desassossego [dʒizaso'segu] m
(*inquietação*) disquiet; (*perturbação*)
restlessness

desastrado, -a [dʒizaʃ'tradu, a] *adj*
clumsy

desastre [dʒi'zaʃtri] m disaster;
(*acidente*) accident; (*de avião*) crash

desatar [dʒiza'ta'] *vt* (*nó*) to undo, untie
▷ *vi*: **~ a fazer** to begin to do; **~ a chorar**
to burst into tears; **~ a rir** to burst out
laughing

desatento, -a [dʒiza'tẽtu, a] *adj*
inattentive

desatinado, -a [dʒizatʃi'nadu, a] *adj*
crazy, wild ▷ *m/f* lunatic

desatino [dʒiza'tʃinu] m madness; (*ato*)
folly

desativar [dʒizatʃi'va'] *vt* (*firma, usina*)
to shut down; (*veículos*) to withdraw
from service; (*bomba*) to deactivate,
defuse

desatualizado, -a [dʒizatwali'zadu, a]
adj out of date; (*pessoa*) out of touch

desavença [dʒiza'vẽsa] f (*briga*) quarrel;
(*discórdia*) disagreement; **em ~ at**

loggerheads

desavergonhado, -a [dʒizavexɡoˈnadu, a] *adj* shameless

desavisado, -a [dʒizaviˈzadu, a] *adj* careless

desbastar [dʒiʒbaʃˈtaʳ] *vt* (*cabelo, plantas*) to thin (out); (*vegetação*) to trim

desbocado, -a [dʒiʒboˈkadu, a] *adj* foul-mouthed

desbotar [dʒiʒboˈtaʳ] *vt* to discolour (BRIT), discolor (US) ▷ *vi* to fade

desbragadamente [dʒiʒbragadaˈmetʃi] *adv* (*beber*) to excess; (*mentir*) blatantly

desbravar [dʒiʒbraˈvaʳ] *vt* (*terras desconhecidas*) to explore

descabelar [dʒiʃkabeˈlaʳ] *vt*: ~ **alguém** to mess up sb's hair; **~-se** *vr* to get one's hair messed up

descabido, -a [dʒiʃkaˈbidu, a] *adj* improper; (*inoportuno*) inappropriate

descafeinado [dʒiʃkafejˈnadu] *adj* decaffeinated ▷ *n* decaff

descalçar [dʒiʃkawˈsaʳ] *vt* (*sapatos*) to take off; **~-se** *vr* to take off one's shoes

descalço, -a [dʒiʃˈkawsu, a] *adj* barefoot

descansado, -a [dʒiʃkãˈsadu, a] *adj* calm, quiet; (*vagaroso*) slow; **fique ~** don't worry; **pode ficar ~ que ...** you can rest assured that ...

descansar [dʒiʃkãˈsaʳ] *vt* to rest; (*apoiar*) to lean ▷ *vi* to rest; to lean; **descanso** [dʒiʃˈkãsu] *m* rest; (*folga*) break; (*para prato*) mat

descarregamento [dʒiʃkaxegaˈmẽtu] *m* (*de carga*) unloading; (*Elet*) discharge

descarregar [dʒiʃkaxeˈgaʳ] *vt* (*carga*) to unload; (*Elet*) to discharge; (*aliviar*) to relieve; (*raiva*) to vent, give vent to; (*arma*) to fire ▷ *vi* to unload; (*bateria*) to run out; **~ a raiva em alguém** to take it out on sb

descartar [dʒiʃkaxˈtaʳ] *vt* to discard; **~-se** *vr*: **~-se de** to get rid of; **descartável** [dʒiʃkaxˈtavew] (*pl* **-eis**) *adj* disposable

descascar [dʒiʃkaʃˈkaʳ] *vt* (*fruta*) to peel; (*ervilhas*) to shell ▷ *vi* (*depois do sol*) to peel; (*cobra*) to shed its skin

descaso [dʒiʃˈkazu] *m* disregard

descendência [desẽˈdẽsja] *f* descendants *pl*, offspring *pl*

descendente [desẽˈdẽtʃi] *adj* descending, going down ▷ *m/f* descendant

descer [deˈseʳ] *vt* (*escada*) to go (*ou* come) down; (*bagagem*) to take down ▷ *vi* (*saltar*) to get off; (*baixar*) to go (*ou* come)

descida [deˈsida] *f* descent; (*declive*) slope; (*abaixamento*) fall, drop

desclassificar [dʒiʃklasifiˈkaʳ] *vt* to disqualify; (*desacreditar*) to discredit

descoberta [dʒiʃkoˈbexta] *f* discovery; (*invenção*) invention

descoberto, -a [dʒiʃkoˈbextu, a] *pp de* **descobrir** ▷ *adj* bare, naked; (*exposto*) exposed ▷ *m* overdraft; **a ~** openly; **conta a ~** overdrawn account; **pôr** *ou* **sacar a ~** (*conta*) to overdraw

descobridor, a [dʒiʃkobriˈdoʳ, a] *m/f* discoverer; (*explorador*) explorer

descobrimento [dʒiʃkobriˈmẽtu] *m* discovery; **Descobrimentos** *mpl*: **os Descobrimentos** the Discoveries; *see boxed note*

🔹 **DESCOBRIMENTOS**
🔹
🔹 Mainly due to the seafaring expertise
🔹 of Henry the Navigator, Portugal
🔹 enjoyed a period of unrivalled overseas
🔹 expansion during the 15th century.
🔹 He organized and financed several
🔹 voyages to Africa, which eventually led
🔹 to the rounding of the Cape of Good
🔹 Hope in 1488 by Bartolomeu Dias. In
🔹 1497, Vasco da Gama became the first
🔹 European to travel by sea to India,
🔹 where he established a lucrative spice
🔹 trade, and a few years later, in 1500,
🔹 Pedro Álvares Cabral reached Brazil,
🔹 which he claimed for Portugal. Brazil
🔹 remained under Portuguese rule until
🔹 1822.

descobrir [dʒiʃkoˈbriʳ] *vt* to discover; (*tirar a cobertura de*) to uncover; (*panela*) to take the lid off; (*averiguar*) to find out; (*enigma*) to solve

descolar [dʒiʃkoˈlaʳ] *vt* to unstick ▷ *vi*: **a criança não descola da mãe** the child won't leave his (*ou* her) mother's side

descolorante [dʒiʃkoloˈrãtʃi] *m* bleach

descolorir [dʒiʃkoloˈriʳ] *vt* to discolour (BRIT), discolor (US); (*cabelo*) to bleach ▷ *vi* to fade

descompostura [dʒiʃkõpoʃˈtura] *f* (*repreensão*) dressing-down; (*insulto*) abuse; **passar uma ~ em alguém** to give sb a dressing-down; to hurl abuse at sb

desconcentrar [dʒiʃkõsẽˈtraʳ] *vt* to distract; **~-se** *vr* to lose one's concentration

desconfiado, -a [dʒiʃkõˈfjadu, a] *adj*

suspicious, distrustful ▷ *m/f* suspicious person

desconfiança [dʒiʃkõˈfjãsa] *f* suspicion, distrust

desconfiar [dʒiʃkõˈfjaʳ] *vi* to be suspicious; **~ de alguém** (*não ter confiança em*) to distrust sb; (*suspeitar*) to suspect sb; **~ que ...** to have the feeling that ...

desconfortável [dʒiʃkõfoxˈtavew] (*pl* **-eis**) *adj* uncomfortable

desconforto [dʒiʃkõˈfoxtu] *m* discomfort

desconhecer [dʒiʃkoɲeˈseʳ] *vt* (*ignorar*) not to know; (*não reconhecer*) not to recognize; (*um benefício*) not to acknowledge; (*não admitir*) not to accept; **desconhecido, -a** [dʒiʃkoɲeˈsidu, a] *adj* unknown ▷ *m/f* stranger; **desconhecimento** [dʒiʃkoɲesiˈmẽtu] *m* ignorance

desconsolado, -a [dʒiʃkõsoˈladu, a] *adj* miserable, disconsolate

descontar [dʒiʃkõˈtaʳ] *vt* to deduct; (*não levar em conta*) to discount; (*não fazer caso de*) to make light of

descontentamento [dʒiʃkõtẽtaˈmẽtu] *m* discontent; (*desprazer*) displeasure

desconto [dʒiʃˈkõtu] *m* discount; **com ~** at a discount; **dar um ~ (para)** (*fig*) to make allowances (for)

descontraído, -a [dʒiʃkõtraˈidu, a] *adj* casual, relaxed

descontrair [dʒiʃkõtraˈiʳ] *vt* to relax; **~-se** *vr* to relax

descontrolar-se [dʒiʃkõtroˈlaxsi] *vr* (*situação*) to get out of control; (*pessoa*) to lose one's self-control

desconversar [dʒiʃkõvexˈsaʳ] *vi* to change the subject

descortesia [dʒiʃkoxteˈzia] *f* rudeness, impoliteness

descoser [dʒiʃkoˈzeʳ] *vt* (*descosturar*) to unstitch; (*rasgar*) to rip apart; **~-se** *vr* to come apart at the seams

descrença [dʒiʃˈkrẽsa] *f* disbelief, incredulity

descrente [dʒiʃˈkrẽtʃi] *adj* sceptical (BRIT), skeptical (US) ▷ *m/f* sceptic (BRIT), skeptic (US)

descrever [dʒiʃkreˈveʳ] *vt* to describe

descrição [dʒiʃkriˈsãw] (*pl* **-ões**) *f* description

descritivo, -a [dʒiʃkriˈtʃivu, a] *adj* descriptive

descrito, -a [dʒiʃˈkritu, a] *pp de* **descrever**

descubro *etc* [dʒiʃˈkubru] *vb ver* **descobrir**

descuidar [dʒiʃkwiˈdaʳ] *vt* to neglect ▷ *vi*: **~ de** to neglect, disregard; **descuido** [dʒiʃˈkwidu] *m* carelessness; (*negligência*) neglect; (*erro*) oversight, slip; **por descuido** inadvertently

desculpa [dʒiʃˈkuwpa] *f* excuse; (*perdão*) pardon; **pedir ~s a alguém por** *ou* **de algo** to apologise to sb for sth; **desculpar** [dʒiʃkuwˈpaʳ] *vt* to excuse; (*perdoar*) to pardon, forgive; **desculpar-se** *vr* to apologize; **desculpar algo a alguém** to forgive sb for sth; **desculpe!** (I'm) sorry, I beg your pardon; **desculpável** [dʒiʃkuwˈpavew] (*pl* **-eis**) *adj* forgivable

---

⊙ **PALAVRA CHAVE**

desde [ˈdeʒdʒi] *prep* **1** (*lugar*): **desde ... até ...** from ... to ...; **andamos desde a praia até o restaurante** we walked from the beach to the restaurant

2 (*tempo: + adv, n*): **desde então** from then on, ever since; **desde já** (*de agora*) from now on; (*imediatamente*) at once, right now; **desde o casamento** since the wedding

3 (*tempo: + vb*) since; for; **conhecemo-nos desde 1978/há 20 anos** we've known each other since 1978/for 20 years; **não o vejo desde 1983** I haven't seen him since 1983

4 (*variedade*): **desde os mais baratos até os mais luxuosos** from the cheapest to the most luxurious
▷ *conj*: **desde que** since; **desde que comecei a trabalhar não o vi mais** I haven't seen him since I started work; **não saiu de casa desde que chegou** he hasn't been out since he arrived

---

desdizer [dʒiʒdʒiˈzeʳ] (*irreg: como* **dizer**) *vt* to contradict; **~-se** *vr* to go back on one's word

desdobrar [dʒiʒdoˈbraʳ] *vt* (*abrir*) to unfold; (*esforços*) to increase, redouble; (*tropas*) to deploy; (*bandeira*) to unfurl; (*dividir em grupos*) to split up; **~-se** *vr* to unfold; (*empenhar-se*) to work hard, make a big effort

desejar [deseˈʒaʳ] *vt* to want, desire

desejo [deˈzeʒu] *m* wish, desire; **desejoso, -a** [dezeˈʒozu, ɔza] *adj*: **desejoso de algo** wishing for sth;

desejoso de fazer keen to do
desembaraçar [dʒizẽbara'sa^r] vt (livrar)
to free; (cabelo) to untangle; **~-se** vr
(desinibir-se) to lose one's inhibitions;
~-se de to get rid of
desembaraço [dʒizẽba'rasu] m
liveliness; (facilidade) ease; (confiança)
self-assurance
desembarcar [dʒizẽbax'ka^r] vt (carga)
to unload; (passageiros) to let off ▷ vi to
disembark; **desembarque** [dʒizẽ'baxki]
m landing, disembarkation;
"desembarque" (no aeroporto) "arrivals"
desembolsar [dʒizẽbow'sa^r] vt to spend
desembrulhar [dʒizẽbru'ʎa^r] vt to
unwrap
desempacotar [dʒizẽpako'ta^r] vt to
unpack
desempatar [dʒizẽpa'ta^r] vt to decide
▷ vi to decide the match (ou race etc);
desempate [dʒizẽ'patʃi] m: **partida de
desempate** (jogo) play-off, decider
desempenhar [dʒizẽpe'ɲa^r] vt (cumprir)
to carry out, fulfil (BRIT), fulfill (US); (papel)
to play; **desempenho** [dʒizẽ'peɲu]
m performance; (de obrigações etc)
fulfilment (BRIT), fulfillment (US)
desempregado, -a [dʒizẽpre'gadu,
a] adj unemployed ▷ m/f unemployed
person
desempregar-se [dʒizẽpre'gaxsi] vr to
lose one's job
desemprego [dʒizẽ'pregu] m
unemployment
desencadear [dʒizẽka'dʒia^r] vt to
unleash; (despertar) to provoke, trigger
off ▷ vi (chuva) to pour; **~-se** vr to break
loose; (tempestade) to break
desencaixar [dʒizẽkaj'ʃa^r] vt to put out
of joint; (deslocar) to dislodge; **~-se** vr to
become dislodged
desencaixotar [dʒizẽkajʃo'ta^r] vt to
unpack
desencarregar-se [dʒizẽkaxe'gaxsi] vr
(de obrigação) to discharge o.s
desencontrar-se [dʒizẽkõ'traxsi] vr
(não se encontrar) to miss each other;
(perder-se um do outro: perder-se) to
lose each other; **~ de** to miss; to get
separated from
desencorajar [dʒizẽkora'ʒa^r] vt to
discourage
desencostar [dʒizẽkoʃ'ta^r] vt to move
away; **~-se** vr: **~-se de** to move away
from
desenfreado, -a [dʒizẽ'frjadu, a] adj

wild
desenganado, -a [dʒizẽga'nadu, a] adj
incurable; (desiludido) disillusioned
desenganar [dʒizẽga'na^r] vt: **~ alguém**
to disillusion sb; (de falsas crenças)
to open sb's eyes; (doente) to give up
hope of curing; **~-se** vr to become
disillusioned; (sair de erro) to realize
the truth; **desengano** [dʒizẽ'ganu]
m disillusionment; (desapontamento)
disappointment
desengonçado, -a [dʒizẽgõ'sadu, a] adj
(mal-seguro) rickety; (pessoa) ungainly
desenhar [deze'ɲa^r] vt to draw; (Tec) to
design; **~-se** vr (destacar-se) to stand out;
(figurar-se) to take shape; **desenhista**
[deze'ɲiʃta] m/f (Tec) designer
desenho [de'zeɲu] m drawing; (modelo)
design; (esboço) sketch; (plano) plan; **~
animado** cartoon
desenlace [dʒizẽ'lasi] m outcome
desenrolar [dʒizẽxo'la^r] vt to unroll;
(narrativa) to develop; **~-se** vr to unfold
desentender [dʒizẽtẽ'de^r] vt to
misunderstand; **~-se** vr: **~-se com**
to have a disagreement with;
desentendido, -a [dʒizẽtẽ'dʒidu, a] adj:
fazer-se de desentendido to pretend
not to understand; **desentendimento**
[dʒizẽtẽdʒi'mẽtu] m misunderstanding
desenterrar [dʒizẽte'xa^r] vt (cadáver) to
exhume; (tesouro) to dig up; (descobrir) to
bring to light
desentupir [dʒizẽtu'pi^r] vt to unblock
desenvoltura [dʒizẽvow'tura] f self-
confidence
desenvolver [dʒizẽvow've^r] vt
to develop; **~-se** vr to develop;
desenvolvimento [dʒizẽvowvi'mẽtu]
m development; (crescimento) growth;
país em desenvolvimento developing
country
deserção [dezex'sãw] f desertion
desertar [desex'ta^r] vt to desert,
abandon ▷ vi to desert; **deserto, -a**
[de'zɛxtu, a] adj deserted ▷ m desert;
desertor, a [dezex'to^r, a] m/f deserter
desesperado, -a [dʒizeʃpe'radu, a] adj
desperate; (furioso) furious
desesperador, a [dʒizeʃpera'do^r, a] adj
desperate; (enfurecedor) maddening
desesperança [dʒizeʃpe'rãsa] f despair
desesperar [dʒizeʃpe'ra^r] vt to drive
to despair; (enfurecer) to infuriate; **~-se**
vr to despair; (enfurecer-se) to become
infuriated; **desespero** [dʒizeʃ'peru] m

despair, desperation; (*raiva*) fury

desestimular [dʒizeʃtʃimu'la^r] vt to discourage

desfalcar [dʒiʃfaw'ka^r] vt (*dinheiro*) to embezzle; (*reduzir*): **~ (de)** to reduce (by); **a jogo está desfalcado** the game is incomplete

desfalecer [dʒiʃfale'se^r] vt (*enfraquecer*) to weaken ▷ vi (*enfraquecer*) to weaken; (*desmaiar*) to faint

desfalque [dʒiʃ'fawki] m (*de dinheiro*) embezzlement; (*diminuição*) reduction

desfavorável [dʒiʃfavo'ravew] (*pl* **-eis**) adj unfavourable (*BRIT*), unfavorable (*US*)

desfazer [dʒifa'ze^r] (*irreg: como* **fazer**) vt (*costura*) to undo; (*dúvidas*) to dispel; (*agravo*) to redress; (*grupo*) to break up; (*contrato*) to dissolve; (*noivado*) to break off ▷ vi: **~ de alguém** to belittle sb; **~-se** vr to vanish; (*tecido*) to come to pieces; (*grupo*) to break up; (*vaso*) to break; **~-se de** (*livrar-se*) to get rid of; **~-se em lágrimas/gentilezas** to burst into tears/go out of one's way to please

desfecho [dʒiʃ'feʃu] m ending, outcome

desfeito, -a [dʒiʃ'fejtu, a] adj undone; (*cama*) unmade; (*contrato*) broken

desfilar [dʒiʃfi'la^r] vi to parade; **desfile** [dʒiʃ'fili] m parade, procession

desforra [dʒiʃ'fɔxa] f revenge; (*reparação*) redress; **tirar ~** to get even

desfrutar [dʒiʃfru'ta^r] vt to enjoy ▷ vi: **~ de** to enjoy

desgarrado, -a [dʒiʒga'xadu, a] adj stray; (*navio*) off course

desgastante [dʒiʒgaʃ'tãtʃi] adj (*fig*) stressful

desgrudar [dʒiʒgru'da^r] vt to unstick ▷ vi: **~ de** to tear o.s. away from; **~ algo de algo** to take sth off sth

desidratar [dʒizidra'ta^r] vt to dehydrate

design [dʒi'zãjn] m design

designar [dezig'na^r] vt to designate; (*nomear*) to name, appoint; (*dia, data*) to fix

desigual [dezi'gwaw] (*pl* **-ais**) adj unequal; (*terreno*) uneven; **desigualdade** [dʒizigwaw'dadʒi] f inequality

desiludir [dʒizilu'dʒi^r] vt to disillusion; (*causar decepção a*) to disappoint; **~-se** vr to lose one's illusions

desimpedido, -a [dʒizĩpe'dʒidu, a] adj free

desinfetante [dʒizĩfe'tãtʃi] (*PT* **-ct-**) adj, m disinfectant

desinfetar [dʒizĩfe'ta^r] (*PT* **-ct-**) vt to disinfect

desintegração [dʒizĩtegra'sãw] f disintegration, break-up

desintegrar [dʒizĩ'tegra^r] vt to separate; **~-se** vr to disintegrate, fall to pieces

desistir [deziʃ'tʃi^r] vi to give up; **~ de fumar** to stop smoking; **ele ia, mas no final desistiu** he was going, but in the end he gave up the idea *ou* he decided not to

desjejum [dʒiʒe'ʒũ] m breakfast

deslavado, -a [dʒiʒla'vadu, a] adj (*pessoa, atitude*) shameless; (*mentira*) blatant

desleal [dʒiʒle'aw] (*pl* **-ais**) adj disloyal

desleixo [dʒiʒ'lejʃu] m sloppiness

desligado, -a [dʒiʒli'gadu, a] adj (*eletricidade*) off; (*pessoa*) absent-minded; **estar ~** to be miles away

desligar [dʒiʒli'ga^r] vt (*Tec*) to disconnect; (*luz, TV, motor*) to switch off; (*telefone*) to hang up; **~-se de algo** (*afastar-se*) to leave sth; (*problemas etc*) to turn one's back on sth; **não desligue** (*Tel*) hold the line

deslizar [dʒiʒli'za^r] vi to slide; (*por acidente*) to slip; (*passar de leve*) to glide; **deslize** [dʒiʒ'lizi] m lapse; (*escorregadela*) slip

deslocado, -a [dʒiʒlo'kadu, a] adj (*membro*) dislocated; (*desambientado*) out of place

deslumbramento [dʒiʒlũbra'mẽtu] m dazzle; (*fascinação*) fascination

deslumbrante [dʒiʒlũ'brãtʃi] adj dazzling; (*casa, festa*) amazing

deslumbrar [dʒiʒlũ'bra^r] vt to dazzle; (*maravilhar*) to amaze; (*fascinar*) to fascinate ▷ vi to be dazzling; to be amazing; **~-se** vr: **~-se com** to be fascinated by

desmaiado, -a [dʒiʒma'jadu, a] adj unconscious; (*cor*) pale

desmaiar [dʒiʒma'ja^r] vi to faint; **desmaio** [dʒiʒ'maju] m faint

desmanchar [dʒiʒmaɲ'ʃa^r] vt (*costura*) to undo; (*contrato*) to break; (*noivado*) to break off; (*penteado*) to mess up; **~-se** vr (*costura*) to come undone

desmarcar [dʒiʒmax'ka^r] vt (*compromisso*) to cancel

desmascarar [dʒiʒmaʃka'ra^r] vt to unmask

desmazelado, -a [dʒiʒmaze'ladu, a] adj slovenly, untidy

desmedido, -a [dʒiʒme'dʒidu, a] adj
excessive
desmentido [dʒiʒmẽ'tʃidu] m (negação)
denial; (contradição) contradiction
desmentir [dʒiʒmẽ'tʃiʳ] vt (contradizer)
to contradict; (negar) to deny
desmiolado, -a [dʒiʒmjo'ladu, a] adj
brainless; (esquecido) forgetful
desmoronamento [dʒiʒmorona'mẽtu]
m collapse
desmoronar [dʒiʒmoro'naʳ] vt to knock
down ▷ vi to collapse
desnatado, -a [dʒiʒna'tadu, a] adj (leite)
skimmed
desnaturado, -a [dʒiʒnatu'radu, a] adj
inhumane ▷ m/f monster
desnecessário, -a [dʒiʒnese'sarju, a]
adj unnecessary
desnutrição [dʒiʒnutri'sãw] f
malnutrition
desobedecer [dʒizobede'seʳ]
vt to disobey; **desobediência**
[dʒizobe'dʒjẽsja] f disobedience;
desobediente [dʒizobe'dʒjẽtʃi] adj
disobedient
desobstruir [dʒizobiʃ'trwiʳ] vt to
unblock
desocupado, -a [dʒizoku'padu, a] adj
(casa) empty, vacant; (disponível) free;
(sem trabalho) unemployed
desocupar [dʒizoku'paʳ] vt (casa) to
vacate; (liberar) to free
desodorante [dʒizodo'rãtʃi] (PT
-dorante) m deodorant
desolação [dezola'sãw] f (consternação)
grief; (de um lugar) desolation; **desolado,
-a** [dezo'ladu, a] adj distressed; desolate
desonesto, -a [dezo'nɛʃtu, a] adj
dishonest
desordem [dʒi'zoxdẽ] f disorder,
confusion; **em ~** [ẽ ~] untidy
desorganizar [dʒizoxgani'zaʳ] vt to
disorganize; (dissolver) to break up; **~-se**
vr to become disorganized; to break up
desorientação [dʒizorjẽta'sãw] f
bewilderment, confusion
desorientar [dʒizorjẽ'taʳ] vt (desnortear)
to throw off course; (perturbar) to
confuse; (desvairar) to unhinge; **~-se** vr
to lose one's way; to get confused; to
go mad
desovar [dʒizo'vaʳ] vt to lay; (peixe) to
spawn
despachado, -a [dʒiʃpa'ʃadu, a] adj
(pessoa) efficient
despachar [dʒiʃpa'ʃaʳ] vt to dispatch,

send off; (atender, resolver) to deal with;
(despedir) to sack; **~-se** vr to hurry (up);
despacho [dʒiʃ'paʃu] m dispatch; (de
negócios) handling; (nota em requerimento)
ruling; (reunião) consultation; (macumba)
witchcraft
despeço etc [dʒiʃ'pɛsu] vb ver **despedir**
despedaçar [dʒiʃpeda'saʳ] vt (quebrar) to
smash; (rasgar) to tear apart; **~-se** vr to
smash; to tear
despedida [dʒiʃpe'dʒida] f farewell; (de
trabalhador) dismissal
despedir [dʒiʃpe'dʒiʳ] vt (de emprego) to
dismiss, sack; **~-se** vr: **~-se (de)** to say
goodbye (to)
despeitado, -a [dʒiʃpej'tadu, a] adj
spiteful; (ressentido) resentful
despeito [dʒiʃ'pejtu] m spite; **a ~ de** in
spite of, despite
despejar [dʒiʃpe'ʒaʳ] vt (água) to pour;
(esvaziar) to empty; (inquilino) to evict;
despejo [dʒiʃ'peʒu] m eviction; **quarto
de despejo** junk room
despencar [dʒiʃpẽ'kaʳ] vi to fall down,
tumble down
despentear [dʒiʃpẽ'tʃaʳ] vt (cabelo: sem
querer) to mess up; (: de propósito) to let
down; **~-se** vr to mess one's hair up; to
let one's hair down
despercebido, -a [dʒiʃpexse'bidu, a] adj
unnoticed
desperdiçar [dʒiʃpexdʒi'saʳ] vt to waste;
(dinheiro) to squander; **desperdício**
[dʒiʃpex'dʒisju] m waste
despertador [dʒiʃpexta'doʳ] m (tb:
relógio ~) alarm clock
despertar [dʒiʃpex'taʳ] vt to wake;
(suspeitas, interesse) to arouse;
(reminiscências) to revive; (apetite) to
whet ▷ vi to wake up ▷ m awakening;
desperto, -a [dʒiʃ'pextu, a] adj awake
despesa [dʒiʃ'peza] f expense; **despesas**
fpl (de uma empresa) expenses, costs; **~s
gerais** (Com) overheads
despido, -a [dʒiʃ'pidu, a] adj naked,
bare; (livre) free
despir [dʒiʃ'piʳ] vt (roupa) to take off;
(pessoa) to undress; (despojar) to strip;
~-se vr to undress
despojar [dʒiʃpo'ʒaʳ] vt (casas) to loot,
sack; (pessoas) to rob
despontar [dʒiʃpõ'taʳ] vi to emerge; (sol)
to come out; (: ao amanhecer) to come up;
ao ~ do dia at daybreak
desporto [dʒiʃ'poxtu] (esp PT) m sport
desprender [dʒiʃprẽ'deʳ] vt to loosen;

(*desatar*) to unfasten; (*emitir*) to emit; **~-se** *vr* (*botão*) to come off; (*cheiro*) to be given off

desprezar [dʒiʃpre'za'] *vt* to despise, disdain; (*não dar importância a*) to disregard, ignore; **desprezível** [dʒiʃpre'zivew] (*pl* **-eis**) *adj* despicable; **desprezo** [dʒiʃ'prezu] *m* scorn, contempt; **dar ao desprezo** to ignore

desproporcional [dʒiʃpropoxsjo'naw] *adj* disproportionate

despropósito [dʒiʃpro'pɔzitu] *m* nonsense

desprovido, -a [dʒiʃpro'vidu, a] *adj* deprived; **~ de** without

desqualificar [dʒiʃkwalifi'ka'] *vt* (*Esporte etc*) to disqualify; (*tornar indigno*) to disgrace, lower

desregrado, -a [dʒiʒxe'gradu, a] *adj* disorderly, unruly; (*devasso*) immoderate

desrespeito [dʒiʒxe'ʃpejtu] *m* disrespect

desse *etc* ['desi] *vb ver* **dar**

desse, -a ['desi, a] = **de + esse/a**

destacar [dʒiʃta'ka'] *vt* (*Mil*) to detail; (*separar*) to detach; (*enfatizar*) to emphasize ▷ *vi* to stand out; **~-se** *vr* to stand out; (*pessoa*) to be outstanding

destampar [dʒiʃtã'pa'] *vt* to take the lid off

destapar [dʒiʃta'pa'] *vt* to uncover

destaque [dʒiʃ'taki] *m* distinction; (*pessoa, coisa*) highlight

deste, -a ['deʃtʃi, a] = **de + este/a**

destemido, -a [deʃte'midu, a] *adj* fearless, intrepid

destilar [deʃtʃi'la'] *vt* to distil (BRIT), distill (US)

destinação [deʃtʃina'sãw] (*pl* **-ões**) *f* destination

destinar [deʃtʃina'] *vt* to destine; (*dinheiro*) **~ (para)** to set aside (for); **~-se** *vr*: **~-se a** to be intended for; (*carta*) to be addressed to

destinatário, -a [deʃtʃina'tarju, a] *m/f* addressee

destino [deʃ'tʃinu] *m* destiny, fate; (*lugar*) destination; **com ~ a** bound for

destituir [deʃtʃi'twi'] *vt* to dismiss; **~ de** (*privar de*) to deprive of

destrancar [dʒiʃtrã'ka'] *vt* to unlock

destratar [dʒiʃtra'ta'] *vt* to abuse, insult

destreza [deʃ'treza] *f* skill; (*agilidade*) dexterity

destro, -a ['dɛʃtru, a] *adj* skilful (BRIT), skillful (US); (*ágil*) agile; (*não canhoto*) right-handed

destrocar [dʒiʃtro'ka'] *vt* to give back, return

destroçar [dʒiʃtro'sa'] *vt* to destroy; (*quebrar*) to smash, break; **destroços** [dʒiʃ'trɔsuʃ] *mpl* wreckage *sg*

destruição [dʒiʃtrwi'sãw] *f* destruction

destruir [dʒiʃ'trwi'] *vt* to destroy

desvairado, -a [dʒiʒvaj'radu, a] *adj* (*louco*) crazy, demented; (*desorientado*) bewildered

desvalorizar [dʒiʒvalori'za'] *vt* to devalue

desvantagem [dʒiʒvã'taʒẽ] (*pl* **-ns**) *f* disadvantage

desvão [dʒiʒ'vãw] (*pl* **-s**) *m* loft

desventura [dʒiʒvẽ'tura] *f* misfortune; (*infelicidade*) unhappiness

desvio [dʒiʒ'viu] *m* diversion, detour; (*curva*) bend; (*fig*) deviation; (*de dinheiro*) embezzlement

detalhadamente [detaʎada'mẽtʃi] *adv* in detail

detalhado, -a [deta'ʎadu, a] *adj* detailed

detalhe [de'taʎi] *m* detail

detectar [detek'ta'] *vt* to detect

detective [detek'tivə] (PT) *m/f* = **detetive**

detector [detek'to'] *m* detector

detenção [detẽ'sãw] (*pl* **-ões**) *f* detention

deter [de'te'] (*irreg*: *como* **ter**) *vt* to stop; (*prender*) to arrest; (*manter preso*) to detain; (*reter*) to keep; (*conter: riso*) to contain; **~-se** *vr* to stop; (*ficar*) to stay; (*conter-se*) to restrain o.s

detergente [detex'ʒẽtʃi] *m* detergent

deteriorar [deterjo'ra'] *vt* to spoil, damage; **~-se** *vr* to deteriorate; (*relações*) to worsen

determinação [detexmina'sãw] *f* determination; (*decisão*) decision; (*ordem*) order

determinado, -a [detexmi'nadu, a] *adj* determined; (*certo*) certain, given

determinar [detexmi'na'] *vt* to determine; (*decretar*) to order; (*resolver*) to decide (on); (*causar*) to cause

detestar [deteʃ'ta'] *vt* to hate; **detestável** [deteʃ'tavew] (*pl* **-eis**) *adj* horrible, hateful

detetive [dete'tʃivi] *m/f* detective

detido, -a [de'tʃidu, a] *adj* (*preso*) under arrest; (*minucioso*) thorough ▷ *m/f* person under arrest, prisoner

detonação [detona'sãw] (*pl* **-ões**) *f*

explosion

detonar [deto'naʳ] *vt, vi* to detonate

detrás [de'trajʃ] *adv* behind ▷ *prep*: **~ de** behind

detrimento [detri'mẽtu] *m*: **em ~ de** to the detriment of

detrito [de'tritu] *m* debris *sg*; (*de comida*) remains *pl*; (*resíduo*) dregs *pl*

deturpação [detuxpa'sãw] *f* corruption; (*de palavras*) distortion

deturpar [detux'paʳ] *vt* to corrupt; (*desfigurar*) to disfigure; (*palavras*) to twist

deu [dew] *vb ver* **dar**

deus [dewʃ(sa)] *m/f* god/goddess; **D~ me livre!** God forbid!; **graças a D~** thank goodness; **meu D~!** good Lord!

devagar [dʒiva'gaʳ] *adv* slowly

devaneio [deva'neju] *m* daydream

devassa [de'vasa] *f* investigation, inquiry

devassidão [devasi'dãw] *f* debauchery

devasso, -a [de'vasu, a] *adj* dissolute

deve ['dɛvi] *m* debit

dever [de've ʳ] *m* duty ▷ *vt* to owe ▷ *vi* (*suposição*): **deve (de) estar doente** he must be ill; (*obrigação*): **devo partir às oito** I must go at eight; **você devia ir ao médico** you should go to the doctor; **que devo fazer?** what shall I do?

devido, -a [de'vidu, a] *adj* (*maneira*) proper; (*respeito*) due; **~ a** due to, owing to; **no ~ tempo** in due course

devoção [devo'sãw] *f* devotion

devolução [devolu'sãw] *f* devolution; (*restituição*) return; (*reembolso*) refund; **~ de impostos** tax rebate

devolver [devow've ʳ] *vt* to give back, return; (*Com*) to refund

devorar [devo'ra ʳ] *vt* to devour; (*destruir*) to destroy

devotar [devo'ta ʳ] *vt* to devote

dez [dɛʒ] *num* ten

dezanove [deza'nɔvɛ] (*PT*) *num* = **dezenove**

dezasseis [deza'sejʃ] (*PT*) *num* = **dezesseis**

dezassete [deza'setə] (*PT*) *num* = **dezessete**

dezembro [de'zẽbru] (*PT* **Dezembro**) *m* December

dezena [de'zena] *f*: **uma ~ de ...** ten ...

dezenove [deze'nɔvi] *num* nineteen

dezesseis [deze'sejʃ] *num* sixteen

dezessete [dezi'setʃi] *num* seventeen

dezoito [dʒi'zojtu] *num* eighteen

dia ['dʒia] *m* day; (*claridade*) daylight;

~ a ~ day by day; **~ santo** holy day; **~ útil** weekday; **estar** *ou* **andar em ~ (com)** to be up to date (with); **de ~** in the daytime, by day; **mais ~ menos ~** sooner or later; **~ sim, ~ não** every other day; **no ~ seguinte** the next day; **bom ~** good morning; **dia-a-dia** *m* daily life, everyday life

diabete(s) [dʒja'bɛtʃi(ʃ)] *f* diabetes *sg*; **diabético, -a** [dʒja'bɛtʃiku, a] *adj, m/f* diabetic

diabo ['dʒjabu] *m* devil; **que ~!** (*col*) damn it!

diabrura [dʒja'brura] *f* prank; **diabruras** *fpl* (*travessura*) mischief *sg*

diagnóstico [dʒjag'nɔʃtʃiku] *m* diagnosis

diagonal [dʒja'go'naw] (*pl* **-ais**) *adj, f* diagonal

diagrama [dʒja'grama] *m* diagram

dialeto [dʒja'letu] (*PT* **-ect-**) *m* dialect

dialogar [dʒjalo'ga ʳ] *vi*: **~ (com alguém)** to talk (to sb); (*Pol*) to have *ou* hold talks (with sb)

diálogo ['dʒjalogu] *m* dialogue; (*conversa*) talk, conversation

diamante [dʒja'mãtʃi] *m* diamond

diâmetro ['dʒjametru] *m* diameter

diante ['dʒjãtʃi] *prep*: **~ de** before; (*na frente de*) in front of; (*problemas etc*) in the face of; **e assim por ~** and so on; **para ~** forward

dianteira [dʒjã'tejra] *f* front, vanguard; **tomar a ~** to get ahead

dianteiro, -a [dʒjã'tejru, a] *adj* front

diapositivo [dʒjapozi'tʃivu] *m* (*Foto*) slide

diária ['dʒjarja] *f* (*de hotel*) daily rate

diário, -a ['dʒjarju, a] *adj* daily ▷ *m* diary; (*jornal*) (daily) newspaper; **~ de bordo** (*Aer*) logbook

diarréia [dʒja'xɛja] *f* diarrhoea (*BRIT*), diarrhea (*US*)

dica ['dʒika] (*col*) *f* hint

dicionário [dʒisjo'narju] *m* dictionary

dieta ['dʒjeta] *f* diet; **fazer ~** to be on a diet; (*começar*) to go on a diet

diferença [dʒife'rẽsa] *f* difference; **ela tem uma ~ comigo** she's got something against me

diferenciar [dʒiferẽ'sja ʳ] *vt* to differentiate

diferente [dʒife'rẽtʃi] *adj* different; **estar ~ com alguém** to be at odds with sb

difícil [dʒi'fisiw] (*pl* **-eis**) *adj* difficult; (*improvável*) unlikely; **o ~ é ...** the difficult thing is ...; **acho ~ ela aceitar nossa proposta** I think it's unlikely she will accept our proposal; **dificilmente** [dʒifisiw'mẽtʃi] adv with difficulty; (mal) hardly; (raramente) hardly ever

dificuldade [dʒifikuw'dadʒi] f difficulty; (aperto): **em ~s** in trouble

dificultar [dʒifikuw'taʳ] vt to make difficult; (complicar) to complicate

difundir [dʒifũ'dʒiʳ] vt to diffuse; (boato, rumor) to spread

digerir [dʒiʒe'riʳ] vt, vi to digest

digestão [dʒiʒeʃ'tãw] f digestion

digital [dʒiʒi'taw] (pl -**ais**) adj: **impressão ~** fingerprint

digitar [dʒiʒi'taʳ] vt (Comput: dados) to key (in)

dígito ['dʒiʒitu] m digit

dignidade [dʒigni'dadʒi] f dignity

digno, -a ['dʒignu, a] adj (merecedor) worthy; (nobre) dignified

digo etc ['dʒigu] vb ver **dizer**

dilatar [dʒila'taʳ] vt to dilate, expand; (prolongar) to prolong; (retardar) to delay

dilema [dʒi'lema] m dilemma

diluir [dʒi'lwiʳ] vt to dilute

dilúvio [dʒi'luvju] m flood

dimensão [dʒimẽ'sãw] (pl -**ões**) f dimension; **dimensões** fpl (medidas) measurements

diminuição [dʒiminwi'sãw] f reduction

diminuir [dʒimi'nwiʳ] vt to reduce; (som) to turn down; (interesse) to lessen ▷ vi to lessen, diminish; (preço) to go down; (dor) to wear off; (barulho) to die down

diminutivo, -a [dʒiminu'tʃivu, a] adj diminutive ▷ m (Ling) diminutive

Dinamarca [dʒina'maxka] f Denmark; **dinamarquês, -quesa** [dʒinamax'keʃ, 'keza] adj Danish ▷ m/f Dane ▷ m (Ling) Danish

dinâmico, -a [dʒi'namiku, a] adj dynamic

dínamo ['dʒinamu] m dynamo

dinheirão [dʒiɲej'rãw] m: **um ~** loads pl of money

dinheiro [dʒi'ɲejru] m money; **~ à vista** cash for paying in cash; **~ em caixa** money in the till; **~ em espécie** cash

dinossauro [dʒino'sawru] m dinosaur

diploma [dʒip'lɔma] m diploma

diplomacia [dʒiploma'sia] f diplomacy; (fig) tact

diplomata [dʒiplo'mata] m/f diplomat;

diplomático, -a [dʒiplo'matʃiku, a] adj diplomatic

dique ['dʒiki] m dam; (Geo) dyke

direção [dʒire'sãw] (PT -**cç**-) (pl -**ões**) f direction; (endereço) address; (Auto) steering; (administração) management; (comando) leadership; (diretoria) board of directors; **em ~ a** towards

directo, -a etc [di'rɛktu, a] (PT) = **direto** etc

direi etc [dʒi'rej] vb ver **dizer**

direita [dʒi'rejta] f (mão) right hand; (lado) right-hand side; (Pol) right wing; **à ~** on the right

direito, -a [dʒi'rejtu, a] adj (lado) right-hand; (mão) right; (honesto) honest; (devido) proper; (justo) right, just ▷ m right; (Jur) law ▷ adv straight; (bem) right; (de maneira certa) properly; **direitos** mpl (humanos) rights; (alfandegários) duty sg

direto, -a [dʒi'rɛtu, a] adj direct ▷ adv straight; **transmissão direta** (TV) live broadcast

diretor, a [dʒire'toʳ, a] adj directing, guiding ▷ m/f director; (de jornal) editor; (de escola) head teacher; **diretoria** [dʒireto'ria] f (Com) management

dirigente [dʒiri'ʒẽtʃi] m/f (de país, partido) leader; (diretor) director; (gerente) manager

dirigir [dʒiri'ʒiʳ] vt to direct; (Com) to manage; (veículo) to drive ▷ vi to drive; **~-se** vr: **~-se a** (falar com) to speak to; (ir, recorrer) to go to; (esforços) to be directed towards

discagem [dʒiʃ'kaʒẽ] f (Tel) dialling

discar [dʒiʃ'kaʳ] vt to dial

disciplina [dʒisi'plina] f discipline; **disciplinar** [dʒisipli'naʳ] vt to discipline

discípulo, -a [dʒi'sipulu, a] m/f disciple; (aluno) pupil

disc-jóquei [dʒiʃk-] m/f disc jockey, DJ

disco ['dʒiʃku] m disc; (Comput) disk; (Mús) record; (de telefone) dial; **~ laser** (máquina) compact disc player, CD player; (disco) compact disc, CD; **~ flexível/ rígido** (Comput) floppy/hard disk; **~ do sistema** system disk; **~ voador** flying saucer

discordar [dʒiʃkox'daʳ] vi: **~ de alguém em algo** to disagree with sb on sth

discórdia [dʒiʃ'kɔxdʒia] f discord, strife

discoteca [dʒiʃko'tɛka] f discotheque, disco

discrepância [dʒiʃkre'pãsja] f discrepancy; (desacordo) disagreement;

discrepante [dʒiʃkre'pãtʃi] *adj* conflicting

discreto, -a [dʒiʃ'krɛtu, a] *adj* discreet; (*modesto*) modest; (*prudente*) shrewd; (*roupa*) plain; **discrição** [dʒiʃkri'sãw] *f* discretion

discriminação [dʒiʃkrimina'sãw] *f* discrimination

discriminar [dʒiʃkrimi'naʳ] *vt* to distinguish ▷ *vi*: ~ **entre** to discriminate between

discurso [dʒiʃ'kuxsu] *m* speech

discussão [dʒiʃku'sãw] (*pl* **-ões**) *f* discussion; (*contenda*) argument

discutir [dʒiʃku'tʃiʳ] *vt* to discuss ▷ *vi*: ~ **(sobre algo)** to talk (about sth); (*contender*) to argue (about sth)

disenteria [dʒizẽte'ria] *f* dysentery

disfarçar [dʒiʃfax'saʳ] *vt* to disguise ▷ *vi* to pretend; **~-se** *vr*: **~-se em** *ou* **de algo** to disguise o.s. as sth; **disfarce** [dʒiʃ'faxsi] *m* disguise; (*máscara*) mask

dislexia [dʒiʒlek'sja] *f* dyslexia

disparar [dʒiʃpa'raʳ] *vt* to shoot, fire ▷ *vi* to fire; (*arma*) to go off; (*correr*) to shoot off, bolt

disparatado, -a [dʒiʃpara'tadu, a] *adj* silly, absurd

disparate [dʒiʃpa'ratʃi] *m* nonsense, rubbish

disparidade [dʒiʃpari'dadʒi] *f* disparity

dispensar [dʒiʃpẽ'saʳ] *vt* to excuse; (*prescindir de*) to do without; (*conferir*) to grant; **dispensável** [dʒiʃpẽ'savew] (*pl* **-eis**) *adj* expendable

dispersar [dʒiʃpex'saʳ] *vt*, *vi* to disperse; **disperso, -a** [dʒiʃ'pɛxsu, a] *adj* scattered

displicência [dʒiʃpli'sẽsja] (*BR*) *f* negligence, carelessness; **displicente** [dʒiʃpli'sẽtʃi] *adj* careless

dispo *etc* ['dʒiʃpu] *vb ver* **despir**

disponível [dʒiʃpo'nivew] (*pl* **-eis**) *adj* available

dispor [dʒiʃ'poʳ] (*irreg: como* **pôr**) *vt* to arrange ▷ *vi*: ~ **de** to have the use of; (*ter*) to have, own; (*pessoas*) to have at one's disposal; **~-se** *vr*: **~-se a** (*estar pronto a*) to be prepared to, be willing to; (*decidir*) to decide to; ~ **sobre** to talk about; **disponha!** feel free!

disposição [dʒiʃpozi'sãw] (*pl* **-ões**) *f* arrangement; (*humor*) disposition; (*inclinação*) inclination; **à sua ~** at your disposal

dispositivo [dʒiʃpozi'tʃivu] *m* gadget, device; (*determinação de lei*) provision

disputa [dʒiʃ'puta] *f* dispute, argument; (*competição*) contest; **disputar** [dʒiʃpu'taʳ] *vt* to dispute; (*concorrer a*) to compete for; (*lutar por*) to fight over ▷ *vi* to quarrel, argue; to compete; **disputar uma corrida** to run a race

disquete [dʒiʃ'ketʃi] *m* (*Comput*) floppy disk, diskette

disse *etc* ['dʒisi] *vb ver* **dizer**

disseminar [dʒisemi'naʳ] *vt* to disseminate; (*espalhar*) to spread

dissertar [dʒisex'taʳ] *vi* to speak

dissidência [dʒisi'dẽsja] *f* (*cisão*) difference of opinion

disso ['dʒisu] = **de** + **isso**

dissolução [dʒisolu'sãw] *f* (*libertinagem*) debauchery; (*de casamento*) dissolution

dissolver [dʒisow'veʳ] *vt* to dissolve; (*dispersar*) to disperse; (*motim*) to break up

dissuadir [dʒiswa'dʒiʳ] *vt* to dissuade; ~ **alguém de fazer algo** to talk sb out of doing sth, dissuade sb from doing sth

distância [dʒiʃ'tãsja] *f* distance; **a 3 quilômetros de ~** 3 kilometres (*BRIT*) *ou* kilometers (*US*) away

distanciar [dʒiʃtã'sjaʳ] *vt* to distance, set apart; (*colocar por intervalos*) to space out; **~-se** *vr* to move away; (*fig*) to distance o.s

distante [dʒiʃ'tãtʃi] *adj* distant

distender [dʒiʃtẽ'deʳ] *vt* to expand; (*estirar*) to stretch; (*dilatar*) to distend; (*músculo*) to pull; **~-se** *vr* to expand; to distend

distinção [dʒiʃtʃĩ'sãw] (*pl* **-ões**) *f* distinction; **fazer ~** to make a distinction

distinguir [dʒiʃtʃĩ'giʳ] *vt* to distinguish; (*avistar, ouvir*) to make out; **~-se** *vr* to stand out

distinto, -a [dʒiʃ'tʃĩtu, a] *adj* different; (*eminente*) distinguished; (*claro*) distinct; (*refinado*) refined

disto ['dʒiʃtu] = **de** + **isto**

distorcer [dʒiʃtox'seʳ] *vt* to distort

distração [dʒiʃtra'sãw] (*PT* **-cç-**) (*pl* **-ões**) *f* (*alheamento*) absent-mindedness; (*divertimento*) pastime; (*descuido*) oversight

distraído, -a [dʒiʃtra'idu, a] *adj* absent-minded; (*não atento*) inattentive

distrair [dʒiʃtra'iʳ] *vt* to distract; (*divertir*) to amuse

distribuição [dʒiʃtribwiˈsãw] f
distribution; (*de cartas*) delivery

distribuidor, a [dʒiʃtribwiˈdoʳ, a] m/f
distributor ▷ m (*Auto*) distributor ▷ f
(*Com*) distribution company, distributor

distribuir [dʒiʃtriˈbwiʳ] vt to distribute;
(*repartir*) to share out; (*cartas*) to deliver

distrito [dʒiʃˈtritu] m district; (*delegacia*)
police station; **~ eleitoral** constituency;
~ federal federal area

distúrbio [dʒiʃˈtuxbju] m disturbance

ditado [dʒiˈtadu] m dictation; (*provérbio*)
saying

ditador [dʒitaˈdoʳ] m dictator; **ditadura**
[dʒitaˈdura] f dictatorship

ditar [dʒiˈtaʳ] vt to dictate; (*impor*) to
impose

dito, -a [ˈdʒitu, a] pp de **dizer**; **~ e feito** no
sooner said than done

diurno, -a [ˈdʒiuxnu, a] adj daytime atr

divã [dʒiˈvã] m couch, divan

divergir [dʒivexˈʒiʳ] vi to diverge;
(*discordar*) **~ (de alguém)** to disagree
(with sb)

diversão [dʒivexˈsãw] (pl **-ões**) f
amusement; (*passatempo*) pastime

diverso, -a [dʒiˈvɛxsu, a] adj different; **~s**
various, several

diversões [dʒivexˈsõjʃ] fpl de **diversão**

diversos [dʒiˈvɛxsuʃ] mpl (*Com*) sundries

divertido, -a [dʒivexˈtʃidu, a] adj
amusing, funny

divertimento [dʒivextʃiˈmẽtu] m
amusement, entertainment

divertir [dʒivexˈtʃiʳ] vt to amuse,
entertain; **~-se** vr to enjoy o.s., have a
good time

dívida [ˈdʒivida] f debt; **contrair ~s** to
run into debt; **~ externa** foreign debt

dividir [dʒiviˈdʒiʳ] vt to divide; (*despesas,
lucro, comida etc*) to share; (*separar*) to
separate ▷ vi (*Mat*) to divide; **~-se** vr to
divide, split up

divino, -a [dʒiˈvinu, a] adj divine ▷ m
Holy Ghost

divirjo etc [dʒiˈvixʒu] vb ver **divergir**

divisa [dʒiˈviza] f emblem; (*frase*) slogan;
(*fronteira*) border; (*Mil*) stripe; **divisas** fpl
(*câmbio*) foreign exchange sg

divisão [dʒiviˈzãw] (pl **-ões**) f division;
(*discórdia*) split; (*partilha*) sharing

divisões [dʒiviˈzõjʃ] fpl de **divisão**

divisória [dʒiviˈzɔrja] f partition

divorciado, -a [dʒivoxˈsjadu, a] adj
divorced ▷ m/f divorcé(e)

divorciar [dʒivoxˈsjaʳ] vt to divorce; **~-se**

vr to get divorced; **divórcio** [dʒiˈvɔxsju]
m divorce

divulgar [dʒivuwˈgaʳ] vt (*notícias*) to
spread; (*segredo*) to divulge; (*produto*)
to market; (*livro*) to publish; **~-se** vr to
leak out

dizer [dʒiˈzeʳ] vt to say ▷ m saying;
dizer-se vr to claim to be; **diz-se** ou
dizem que ... it is said that ...; **dizer
algo a alguém** to tell sb sth; (*falar*) to
say sth to sb; **dizer a alguém que ...** to
tell sb that ...; **o que você diz da minha
sugestão?** what do you think of my
suggestion?; **querer dizer** to mean; **quer
dizer** that is to say; **digo** (*ou seja*) I mean;
não diga! you don't say!; **por assim
dizer** so to speak; **até dizer chega** as
much as possible

do [du] = **de +o**

doação [doaˈsãw] (pl **-ões**) f donation

doador, a [doaˈdoʳ, a] m/f donor

doar [doˈaʳ] vt to donate, give

dobra [ˈdɔbra] f fold; (*prega*) pleat; (*de
calças*) turn-up

dobradiça [dobraˈdʒisa] f hinge

dobradinha [dobraˈdʒiɲa] f (*Culin*) tripe
stew

dobrar [doˈbraʳ] vt to double; (*papel*) to
fold; (*joelho*) to bend; (*esquina*) to turn,
go round; (*fazer ceder*) **~ alguém** to talk
sb round ▷ vi to double; (*sino*) to toll;
(*vergar*) to bend; **~-se** vr to double (up)

dobro [ˈdobru] m double

doce [ˈdosi] adj sweet; (*terno*) gentle ▷ m
sweet

dóceis [ˈdɔsejʃ] adj pl de **dócil**

dócil [ˈdɔsiw] (pl **-eis**) adj docile

documentação [dokumẽtaˈsãw] f
documentation; (*documentos*) papers pl

documentário, -a [dokumẽˈtarju, a]
adj documentary ▷ m documentary

documento [dokuˈmẽtu] m document

doçura [doˈsura] f sweetness; (*brandura*)
gentleness

doença [doˈẽsa] f illness

doente [doˈẽtʃi] adj ill, sick ▷ m/f sick
person; (*cliente*) patient

doentio, -a [doẽˈtʃiu, a] adj (*pessoa*)
sickly; (*clima*) unhealthy; (*curiosidade*)
morbid

doer [doˈeʳ] vi to hurt, ache; **~ a alguém**
(*pesar*) to grieve sb

doido, -a [ˈdojdu, a] adj mad, crazy ▷ m/f
madman/woman

doído, -a [doˈidu, a] adj painful;
(*moralmente*) hurt; (*que causa dor*) painful

dois, duas [dojʃ, 'duaʃ] *num* two; **conversa a ~** tête-à-tête

dólar ['dɔlaʳ] *m* dollar; **~ oficial/paralelo** dollar at the official/black-market rate; **~-turismo** dollar at the special tourist rate; **doleiro, -a** [do'lejɾu, a] *m/f* (black market) dollar dealer

dolorido, -a [dolo'ɾidu, a] *adj* painful, sore

dom [dõ] *m* gift; *(aptidão)* knack

domar [do'maʳ] *vt* to tame

doméstica [do'mɛʃtʃika] *f* maid

domesticar [domeʃtʃi'kaʳ] *vt* to domesticate; *(povo)* to tame

doméstico, -a [do'mɛʃtʃiku, a] *adj* domestic; *(vida)* home *atr*

domicílio [domi'silju] *m* home, residence; **"entregamos a ~"** "we deliver"

dominador, a [domina'doʳ, a] *adj* *(pessoa)* domineering; *(olhar)* imposing ▷ *m/f* ruler

dominar [domi'naʳ] *vt* to dominate; *(reprimir)* to overcome ▷ *vi* to dominate; **~-se** *vr* to control o.s

domingo [do'mĩgu] *m* Sunday

domínio [do'minju] *m* power; *(dominação)* control; *(território)* domain; *(esfera)* sphere; **~ próprio** self-control

dona ['dɔna] *f* owner; *(col: mulher)* lady; **~ de casa** housewife; **D~ Lígia** Lígia; **D~ Luísa Souza** Mrs Luísa Souza

donde ['dõdə] *(PT) adv* from where; *(daí)* thus

dono ['donu] *m* owner

dopar [do'paʳ] *vt* to drug

dor [doʳ] *f* ache; *(aguda)* pain; *(fig)* grief, sorrow; **~ de cabeça/dentes/estômago** headache/toothache/stomachache

dormente [dox'mẽtʃi] *adj* numb ▷ *m* *(Ferro)* sleeper

dormir [dox'miʳ] *vi* to sleep; **~ fora** to spend the night away

dormitório [doxmi'tɔrju] *m* bedroom; *(coletivo)* dormitory

dorso ['dɔxsu] *m* back

dos [duʃ] = **de + os**

dosagem [do'zaʒẽ] *m* dosage

dose ['dɔzi] *f* dose

dossiê [do'sje] *m* dossier, file

dotado, -a [do'tadu, a] *adj* gifted; **~ de** endowed with

dotar [do'taʳ] *vt* to endow

dou [do] *vb ver* **dar**

dourado, -a [do'radu, a] *adj* golden; *(com camada de ouro)* gilt ▷ *m* gilt

doutor, a [do'toʳ, a] *m/f* doctor; **D~** *(forma de tratamento)* Sir; **D~ Eduardo Souza** Mr Eduardo Souza

doutrina [do'trina] *f* doctrine

doze ['dozi] *num* twelve

Dr(a). *abr* (= *Doutor(a)*) Dr.

dragão [dra'gãw] *(pl -ões) m* dragon

dragões [dra'gõjʃ] *mpl de* **dragão**

drama ['drama] *m* drama; **dramático, -a** [dra'matʃiku, a] *adj* dramatic; **dramatizar** [dramatʃi'zaʳ] *vt, vi* to dramatize

drástico, -a ['draʃtʃiku, a] *adj* drastic

dreno ['drɛnu] *m* drain

driblar [dri'blaʳ] *vt, vi* (*Futebol*) to dribble

drinque ['drĩki] *m* drink

droga ['drɔga] *f* drug; *(fig)* rubbish; **drogado, -a** [dro'gadu, a] *m/f* drug addict; **drogar** [dro'gaʳ] *vt* to drug; **drogar-se** *vr* to take drugs

drogaria [droga'ria] *f* chemist's shop (*BRIT*), drugstore (*US*)

DTP *abr m* (= *desktop publishing*) DTP

duas ['duaʃ] *f de* **dois**

ducha ['duʃa] *f* shower

dueto ['dwetu] *m* duet

duna ['duna] *f* dune

dupla ['dupla] *f* pair; (*Esporte*): **~ masculina/feminina/mista** men's/women's/mixed doubles

duplicar [dupli'kaʳ] *vt* to duplicate ▷ *vi* to double; **duplicata** [dupli'kata] *f* duplicate; *(título)* trade note, bill

duplo, -a ['duplu, a] *adj* double ▷ *m* double

duque ['duki] *m* duke

duração [dura'sãw] *f* duration; **de pouca ~** short-lived

durante [du'rãtʃi] *prep* during; **~ uma hora** for an hour

durar [du'raʳ] *vi* to last

durável [du'ravew] *(pl -eis) adj* lasting

durex® [du'reks] *adj:* **fita ~** adhesive tape, sellotape® (*BRIT*), scotchtape® (*US*)

durmo *etc* ['duxmu] *vb ver* **dormir**

duro, -a ['duru, a] *adj* hard; *(severo)* harsh; *(resistente, fig)* tough; **estar ~** *(col)* to be broke

dúvida ['duvida] *f* doubt; **sem ~** undoubtedly, without a doubt; **duvidar** [duvi'daʳ] *vt* to doubt ▷ *vi* to have one's doubts; **duvidar de alguém/algo** to doubt sb/sth; **duvidar que ...** to doubt that ...; **duvido!** I doubt it!; **duvidoso, -a**

[duvi'dozu, ɔza] *adj* doubtful; (*suspeito*) dubious

duzentos, -as [du'zētuʃ, aʃ] *num* two hundred

dúzia ['duzja] *f* dozen; **meia ~** half a dozen

DVD *abr m* (= *disco digital versátil*) DVD

dz. *abr* = **dúzia**

e [i] *conj* and; **e a bagagem?** what about the luggage?

é [ɛ] *vb ver* **ser**

eclipse [e'klipsi] *m* eclipse

eco ['ɛku] *m* echo; **ter ~** to catch on; **ecoar** [e'kwaʳ] *vt* to echo ▷ *vi* (*ressoar*) to echo

ecologia [ekolo'ʒia] *f* ecology

economia [ekono'mia] *f* economy; (*ciência*) economics *sg*; **economias** *fpl* (*poupanças*) savings; **fazer ~ (de)** to economize (with)

econômico, -a [eko'nomiku, a] *adj* economical; (*pessoa*) thrifty; (*Com*) economic

economizar [ekonomi'zaʳ] *vt* (*gastar com economia*) to economize on; (*poupar*) to save (up) ▷ *vi* to economize; to save up

écran ['ɛkrã] (PT) *m* screen

edição [edʒi'sãw] (*pl* **-ões**) *f* publication; (*conjunto de exemplares*) edition; (*TV, Cinema*) editing

edifício [edʒi'fisju] *m* building; **~ garagem** multistorey car park (BRIT), multistory parking lot (US)

Edimburgo [edʒĩ'buxgu] *n* Edinburgh

editar [edʒi'taʳ] *vt* to publish; (*Comput etc*) to edit

editor, a [edʒiˈtoʳ, a] *adj* publishing *atr* ▷ *m/f* publisher; *(redator)* editor ▷ *f* publishing company; **casa ~a** publishing house

editoração [edʒitoraˈsãw] *f*: **~ eletrônica** desktop publishing; **editorial** [edʒitorˈjaw] *(pl* -**ais)** *adj* publishing *atr* ▷ *m* editorial

edredão [adrəˈdãw] *(pl* -**ões** (PT)) *m* = **edredom**

edredom [edreˈdõ] *(pl* -**ns)** *m* eiderdown

educação [edukaˈsãw] *f* education; *(criação)* upbringing; *(de animais)* training; *(maneiras)* good manners *pl*; **educacional** [edukasjoˈnaw] *(pl* -**ais)** *adj* education *atr*

educar [eduˈkaʳ] *vt* to educate; *(criar)* to bring up; *(animal)* to train

efectivo, -a *etc* [efekˈtivu, a] (PT) *adj* = **efetivo** *etc*

efectuar [efekˈtwaʳ] (PT) *vt* = **efetuar**

efeito [eˈfejtu] *m* effect; **fazer ~** to work; **levar a ~** to put into effect; **com ~** indeed

efeminado [efemiˈnadu] *adj* effeminate

efervescente [efexveˈsẽtʃi] *adj* fizzy

efetivamente [efetʃivaˈmẽtʃi] *adv* effectively; *(realmente)* really, in fact

efetivo, -a [efeˈtʃivu, a] *adj* effective; *(real)* actual, real; *(cargo, funcionário)* permanent

efetuar [efeˈtwaʳ] *vt* to carry out; *(soma)* to do, perform

eficaz [efiˈkaʒ] *adj (pessoa)* efficient; *(tratamento)* effective

eficiência [efiˈsjẽsja] *f* efficiency; **eficiente** [efiˈsjẽtʃi] *adj* efficient

egípcio, -a [eˈʒipsju, a] *adj, m/f* Egyptian

Egito [eˈʒitu] (PT -**pt-**) *m*: **o ~** Egypt

egoísmo [egoˈiʒmu] *m* selfishness, egoism; **egoísta** [egoˈiʃta] *adj* selfish, egoistic ▷ *m/f* egoist

égua [ˈɛgwa] *f* mare

ei [ej] *excl* hey!

ei-lo *etc* = **eis + o**

eis [ejʃ] *adv (sg)* here is; *(pl)* here are; **~ aí** there is; there are

ejacular [eʒakuˈlaʳ] *vt (sêmen)* to ejaculate; *(líquido)* to spurt ▷ *vi* to ejaculate

ela [ˈɛla] *pron (pessoa)* she; *(coisa)* it; *(com prep)* her; **it; elas** *fpl* they; *(com prep)* them; **~s por ~s** *(col)* tit for tat

elaboração [elaboraˈsãw] *(pl* -**ões)** *f (de uma teoria)* working out; *(preparo)* preparation

elaborar [elaboˈraʳ] *vt* to prepare; *(fazer)* to make; *(teoria)* to work out

elástico, -a [eˈlaʃtʃiku, a] *adj* elastic; *(flexível)* flexible; *(colchão)* springy ▷ *m* elastic band

ele [ˈeli] *pron* he; *(coisa)* it; *(com prep)* him; it; **eles** *mpl* they; *(com prep)* them

electri... *etc* [eˈlektri] (PT) = **eletri...** *etc*

eléctrico, -a [eˈlɛktriku, a] (PT) *adj* = **elétrico** ▷ *m* tram (BRIT), streetcar (US)

electro... *etc* [eˈlektru] (PT) = **eletro...** *etc*

eléctrodo [eˈlektrodu] (PT) *m* = **eletrodo**

elefante, -ta [eleˈfãtʃi, ta] *m/f* elephant

elegante [eleˈgãtʃi] *adj* elegant; *(da moda)* fashionable

eleger [eleˈʒeʳ] *vt* to elect; *(escolher)* to choose

eleição [elejˈsãw] *(pl* -**ões)** *f* election; *(escolha)* choice

eleito, -a [eˈlejtu, a] *pp de* **eleger** ▷ *adj* elected; chosen

eleitor, a [elejˈtoʳ, a] *m/f* voter

elejo *etc* [eˈleʒu] *vb ver* **eleger**

elementar [elemẽˈtaʳ] *adj* elementary; *(fundamental)* basic, fundamental

elemento [eleˈmẽtu] *m* element; *(parte)* component; *(recurso)* means; *(informação)* grounds *pl*; **elementos** *mpl (rudimentos)* rudiments

elenco [eˈlẽku] *m* list; *(de atores)* cast

eletricidade [eletrisiˈdadʒi] *f* electricity

eletricista [eletriˈsiʃta] *m/f* electrician

elétrico, -a [eˈlɛtriku, a] *adj* electric; *(fig: agitado)* worked up

eletrificar [eletrifiˈkaʳ] *vt* to electrify

eletrizar [eletriˈzaʳ] *vt* to electrify; *(fig)* to thrill

eletro... [eletru] *prefixo* electro...;

eletrocutar [eletrokuˈtaʳ] *vt* to electrocute; **eletrodo** [eleˈtrodu] *m* electrode; **eletrodomésticos** [eletrodoˈmeʃtʃikuʃ] (BR) *mpl* (electrical) household appliances

eletrônica [eleˈtronika] *f* electronics *sg*

eletrônico, -a [eleˈtroniku, a] *adj* electronic

elevação [elevaˈsãw] *(pl* -**ões)** *f (Arq)* elevation; *(aumento)* rise; *(ato)* raising; *(altura)* height; *(promoção)* promotion; *(ponto elevado)* bump

elevador [elevaˈdoʳ] *m* lift (BRIT), elevator (US)

elevar [eleˈvaʳ] *vt* to lift up; *(voz, preço)* to raise; *(exaltar)* to exalt; *(promover)* to promote; **~-se** *vr* to rise

eliminar [elimiˈnaʳ] *vt* to remove; *(suprimir)* to delete; *(possibilidade)* to rule out; (*Med, banir*) to expel; (*Esporte*) to eliminate; **eliminatória** [elimina'tɔrja] *f* (*Esporte*) heat, preliminary round; (*exame*) test

elite [e'litʃi] *f* elite

elogiar [elo'ʒjaʳ] *vt* to praise; **elogio** [elo'ʒiu] *m* praise; (*cumprimento*) compliment

El Salvador [ew-] *n* El Salvador

⬤ **PALAVRA CHAVE**

em [ẽ] (*em* + *o*(*s*)/*a*(*s*) = *no*(*s*)/*na*(*s*); + *ele*(*s*)/*a*(*s*) = *nele*(*s*)/*a*(*s*); + *esse*(*s*)/*a*(*s*) = *nesse*(*s*)/*a*(*s*); + *isso* = *nisso*; + *este*(*s*)/*a*(*s*) = *neste*(*s*)/*a*(*s*); + *isto* = *nisto*; + *aquele*(*s*)/*a*(*s*) = *naquele*(*s*)/*a*(*s*); + *aquilo* = *naquilo*) *prep* **1** (*posição*) in; (: *sobre*) on; **está na gaveta/no bolso** it's in the drawer/pocket; **está na mesa/no chão** it's on the table/floor

2 (*lugar*) in; (: *casa, escritório etc*) at; (: *andar, meio de transporte*) on; **no Brasil/em São Paulo** in Brazil/São Paulo; **em casa/no dentista** at home/ the dentist; **no avião** on the plane; **no quinto andar** on the fifth floor

3 (*ação*) into; **ela entrou na sala de aula** she went into the classroom; **colocar algo na bolso** to put sth into one's bag

4 (*tempo*) in; on; **em 1962/3 semanas** in 1962/3 weeks; **no inverno** in the winter; **em janeiro, no mês de janeiro** in January; **nessa ocasião/altura** on that occasion/at that time; **em breve** soon

5 (*diferença*): **reduzir/aumentar em um 20%** to reduce/increase by 20%

6 (*modo*): **escrito em inglês** written in English

7 (*após vb que indica gastar etc*) on; **a metade do seu salário vai em comida** he spends half his salary on food

8 (*tema, ocupação*): **especialista no assunto** expert on the subject; **ele trabalha na construção civil** he works in the building industry

emagrecer [imagre'seʳ] *vt* to make thin ▷ *vi* to grow thin; (*mediante regime*) to slim; **emagrecimento** [imagresi'mẽtu] *m* (*mediante regime*) slimming

e-mail [i'mew] *m* e-mail; **mandar um ~ para** to e-mail; **mandar por ~** to e-mail

emaranhado, -a [imara'ɲadu, a] *adj* tangled ▷ *m* tangle

embaixada [ẽbaj'ʃada] *f* embassy

embaixador, a [ẽbajʃa'doʳ, a] *m/f* ambassador

embaixatriz [ẽbajʃa'triʒ] *f* ambassador; (*mulher de embaixador*) ambassador's wife

embaixo [ẽ'bajʃu] *adv* below, underneath ▷ *prep*: **~ de** under, underneath; **(lá) ~** (*em andar inferior*) downstairs

embalagem [ẽba'laʒẽ] *f* packing; (*de produto: caixa etc*) packaging

embalar [ẽba'laʳ] *vt* to pack; (*balançar*) to rock

embaraçar [ẽbara'saʳ] *vt* to hinder; (*complicar*) to complicate; (*encabular*) to embarrass; (*confundir*) to confuse; (*obstruir*) to block; **~-se** *vr* to become embarrassed

embaraço [ẽba'rasu] *m* hindrance; (*cábula*) embarrassment; **embaraçoso, -a** [ẽbara'sozu, ɔza] *adj* embarrassing

embarcação [ẽbaxka'sãw] (*pl* -**ões**) *f* vessel

embarcar [ẽbax'kaʳ] *vt* to embark, put on board; (*mercadorias*) to ship, stow ▷ *vi* to go on board, embark

embarque [ẽ'baxki] *m* (*de pessoas*) boarding, embarkation; (*de mercadorias*) shipment

embebedar [ẽbebe'daʳ] *vt* to make drunk ▷ *vi*: **o vinho embebeda** wine makes you drunk; **~-se** *vr* to get drunk

emblema [ẽ'blɛma] *m* emblem; (*na roupa*) badge

êmbolo [ẽ'bolu] *m* piston

embolsar [ẽbow'saʳ] *vt* to pocket; (*herança*) to come into; (*indenizar*) to refund

embora [ẽ'bɔra] *conj* though, although ▷ *excl* even so; **ir(-se) ~** to go away

emboscada [ẽboʃ'kada] *f* ambush

embriagar [ẽbrja'gaʳ] *vt* to make drunk, intoxicate; **~-se** *vr* to get drunk; **embriaguez** [ẽbrja'geʒ] *f* drunkenness; (*fig*) rapture

embrião [e'brjãw] (*pl* -**ões**) *m* embryo

embromar [ẽbro'maʳ] *vt* (*adiar*) to put off; (*enganar*) to cheat ▷ *vi* (*prometer e não cumprir*) to make empty promises, be all talk (and no action); (*protelar*) to stall; (*falar em rodeios*) to beat about the bush

embrulhar [ẽbru'ʎaʳ] *vt* (*pacote*) to wrap; (*enrolar*) to roll up; (*confundir*) to muddle up; (*enganar*) to cheat; (*estômago*) to upset; **~-se** *vr* to get into a muddle

embrulho [ẽ'bruʎu] *m* package, parcel;

(confusão) mix-up

emburrar [ēbu'xaʳ] vi to sulk

embutido, -a [ēbu'tʃidu, a] adj (armário) built-in, fitted

emenda [e'mẽda] f correction; (de lei) amendment; (de uma pessoa) improvement; (ligação) join; (sambladura) joint; (Costura) seam

emendar [emẽ'daʳ] vt to correct; (reparar) to mend; (injustiças) to make amends for; (lei) to amend; (ajuntar) to put together; **~-se** vr to mend one's ways

ementa [e'mẽta] (PT) f menu

emergência [imex'ʒẽsja] f emergence; (crise) emergency

emigrado, -a [emi'gradu, a] adj emigrant

emigrante [emi'grãtʃi] m/f emigrant

emigrar [emi'graʳ] vi to emigrate; (aves) to migrate

eminência [emi'nẽsja] f eminence; (altura) height; **eminente** [emi'nẽtʃi] adj eminent, distinguished; (Geo) high

emissão [emi'sãw] (pl -ões) f emission; (Rádio) broadcast; (de moeda, ações) issue

emissor, a [emi'soʳ, a] adj (de moeda-papel) issuing ▷ m (Rádio) transmitter ▷ f (estação) broadcasting station; (empresa) broadcasting company

emitir [emi'tʃiʳ] vt (som) to give out; (cheiro) to give off; (moeda, ações) to issue; (Rádio) to broadcast; (opinião) to express ▷ vi (emitir moeda) to print money

emoção [emo'sãw] (pl -ões) f emotion; (excitação) excitement; **emocional** [imosjo'naw] (pl -ais) adj emotional; **emocionante** [imosjo'nãtʃi] adj moving, exciting; **emocionar** [imosjo'naʳ] vt to move; (perturbar) to upset; (excitar) to excite, thrill ▷ vi to be exciting; (comover) to be moving; **emocionar-se** vr to get emotional

emotivo, -a [emo'tʃivu, a] adj emotional

empacotar [ēpako'taʳ] vt to pack, wrap up

empada [ē'pada] f pie

empadão [ēpa'dãw] (pl -ões) m pie

empalidecer [ēpalide'seʳ] vi to turn pale

empanturrar [ēpãtu'xaʳ] vt: **~ alguém de algo** to stuff sb full of sth

empatar [ēpa'taʳ] vt to hinder; (dinheiro) to tie up; (no jogo) to draw; (tempo) to take up ▷ vi (no jogo): **~ (com)** to draw (with); **empate** [ē'patʃi] m draw; tie; (Xadrez) stalemate; (em negociações) deadlock

empecilho [ēpe'siʎu] m obstacle; (col) snag

empenhar [ēpe'naʳ] vt (objeto) to pawn; (palavra) to pledge; (empregar) to exert; (compelir) to oblige; **~-se** vr: **~-se em fazer** to strive to do, do one's utmost to do; **empenho** [ē'peɲu] m pawning; pledge; (insistência): **empenho (em)** commitment (to)

empilhar [ēpi'ʎaʳ] vt to pile up

empinado, -a [ēpi'nadu, a] adj upright; (cavalo) rearing; (colina) steep

empinar [ēpi'naʳ] vt to raise, uplift

empobrecer [ēpobre'seʳ] vt to impoverish ▷ vi to become poor; **empobrecimento** [ēpobresi'mẽtu] m impoverishment

empolgação [ēpowga'sãw] f excitement; (entusiasmo) enthusiasm

empolgante [ēpow'gãtʃi] adj exciting

empolgar [ēpow'gaʳ] vt to stimulate, fill with enthusiasm; (prender a atenção de): **~ alguém** to keep sb riveted

empossar [ēpo'saʳ] vt to appoint

empreendedor, a [ēprjẽde'doʳ, a] adj enterprising ▷ m/f entrepreneur

empreender [ēprjẽ'deʳ] vt to undertake; **empreendimento** [ēprjẽdʒi'mẽtu] m undertaking

empregada [ēpre'gada] f (BR: doméstica) maid; (PT: de restaurante) waitress; ver tb **empregado**

empregado, -a [ēpre'gadu, a] m/f employee; (em escritório) clerk ▷ m (PT: de restaurante) waiter

empregador, a [ēprega'doʳ, a] m/f employer

empregar [ēpre'gaʳ] vt (pessoa) to employ; (coisa) to use; **~-se** vr to get a job

emprego [ē'pregu] m job; (uso) use

empreiteiro [ēprej'tejru] m contractor

empresa [ē'preza] f undertaking; (Com) enterprise, firm; **~ pontocom** dotcom; **empresário, -a** [ēpre'zarju, a] m/f businessman/woman; (de cantor, boxeador etc) manager

emprestado, -a [ēpres'tadu, a] adj on loan; **pedir ~** to borrow; **tomar algo ~** to borrow sth

emprestar [ēpres'taʳ] vt to lend; **empréstimo** [ē'prestʃimu] m loan

empunhar [ēpu'ɲaʳ] vt to grasp, seize

empurrão [ēpu'xãw] (pl -ões) m push, shove; **aos empurrões** jostling

empurrar [ēpu'xaʳ] vt to push

empurrões [ēpu'xõjʃ] mpl de **empurrão**

emudecer [emude'se'] *vt* to silence ▷ *vi* to fall silent, go quiet

enamorado, -a [enamo'radu, a] *adj* enchanted; (*apaixonado*) in love

encabulado, -a [ēkabu'ladu, a] *adj* shy

encadernação [ēkadexna'sãw] (*pl* **-ões**) *f* (*de livro*) binding

encadernado, -a [ēkadex'nadu, a] *adj* bound; (*de capa dura*) hardback

encadernar [ēkadex'na'] *vt* to bind

encaixar [ēkaj'ʃa'] *vt* (*colocar*) to fit in; (*inserir*) to insert ▷ *vi* to fit; **encaixe** [ē'kajʃi] *m* (*ato*) fitting; (*ranhura*) groove; (*buraco*) socket

encalço [ē'kawsu] *m* pursuit; **ir no ~ de** to pursue

encaminhar [ēkami'ɲa'] *vt* to direct; (*no bom caminho*) to put on the right path; (*processo*) to set in motion; **~-se para/a** to set out for/to

encanar [ēka'na'] *vt* to channel

encantado, -a [ēkã'tadu, a] *adj* delighted; (*castelo etc*) enchanted; (*fascinado*) **~ (por)** smitten (with)

encantamento [ēkãta'mētu] *m* (*magia*) spell; (*fascinação*) charm

encanto [ē'kãtu] *m* delight; charm

encarar [ēka'ra'] *vt* to face; (*olhar*) to look at; (*considerar*) to consider

encargo [ē'kaxgu] *m* responsibility; (*ocupação*) job, assignment; (*fardo*) burden

encarnação [ēkaxna'sãw] (*pl* **-ões**) *f* incarnation

encarnado, -a [ēkax'nadu, a] *adj* red, scarlet

encarnar [ēkax'na'] *vt* to embody, personify; (*Teatro*) to play

encarregado, -a [ēkaxe'gadu, a] *adj*: **~ de** in charge of ▷ *m/f* person in charge ▷ *m* (*de operários*) foreman

encarregar [ēkaxe'ga'] *vt*: **~ alguém de algo** to put sb in charge of sth; **~-se** *vr*: **~-se de fazer** to undertake to do

encenação [ēsena'sãw] (*pl* **-ões**) *f* (*de peça*) staging, putting on; (*produção*) production; (*fingimento*) playacting; (*atitude fingida*) put-on

encerar [ēse'ra'] *vt* to wax

encerramento [ēsexa'mētu] *m* close, end

encerrar [ēse'xa'] *vt* to shut in, lock up; (*conter*) to contain; (*concluir*) to close

encharcar [ēʃax'ka'] *vt* to flood; (*ensopar*) to soak, drench; **~-se** *vr* to get soaked *ou* drenched

enchente [ē'ʃētʃi] *f* flood

encher [ē'ʃe'] *vt* to fill (up); (*balão*) to blow up; (*tempo*) to fill, take up ▷ *vi* (*col*) to be annoying; **~-se** *vr* to fill up; **~-se (de)** (*col*) to get fed up (with); **enchimento** [ēʃi'mētu] *m* filling

enciclopédia [ēsiklo'pɛdʒja] *f* encyclopedia, encyclopaedia (BRIT)

encoberto, -a [ēko'bextu, a] *pp de* **encobrir** ▷ *adj* concealed; (*tempo*) overcast

encobrir [ēko'bri'] *vt* to conceal, hide

encolher [ēko'ʎe'] *vt* (*pernas*) to draw up; (*os ombros*) to shrug; (*roupa*) to shrink ▷ *vi* to shrink; **~-se** *vr* (*de frio*) to huddle

encomenda [ēko'mēda] *f* order; **feito de ~** made to order, custommade; **encomendar** [ēkomē'da'] *vt*: **encomendar algo a alguém** to order sth from sb

encontrar [ēkõ'tra'] *vt* to find; (*pessoa*) to meet; (*inesperadamente*) to come across; (*dar com*) to bump into ▷ *vi*: **~ com** to bump into; **~-se** *vr* (*achar-se*) to be; (*ter encontro*): **~-se (com alguém)** to meet (sb)

encontro [ē'kõtru] *m* (*de pessoas*) meeting; (*Mil*) encounter; **~ marcado** appointment; **ir/vir ao ~ de** to go/come and meet

encorajar [ēkora'ʒa'] *vt* to encourage

encosta [ē'kɔʃta] *f* slope

encostar [ēkoʃ'ta'] *vt* (*cabeça*) to put down; (*carro*) to park; (*pôr de lado*) to put to one side; (*pôr junto*) to put side by side; (*porta*) to leave ajar ▷ *vi* to pull in; **~-se** *vr*: **~-se em** to lean against; (*deitar-se*) to lie down on; **~ em** to lean against; **~ a mão em** (*bater*) to hit

encosto [ē'koʃtu] *m* (*arrimo*) support; (*de cadeira*) back

encrencar [ēkrē'ka'] (*col*) *vt* (*situação*) to complicate; (*pessoa*) to get into trouble ▷ *vi* to get complicated; (*carro*) to break down; **~-se** *vr* to get complicated; to get into trouble

encruzilhada [ēkruzi'ʎada] *f* crossroads *sg*

encurtar [ēkux'ta'] *vt* to shorten

endereçar [ēdere'sa'] *vt* (*carta*) to address; (*encaminhar*) to direct

endereço [ēde'resu] *m* address; **~ eletrônico** *ou* **de e-mail** e-mail address; **~ de site** web address

endiabrado, -a [ēdʒja'bradu, a] *adj* devilish; (*travesso*) mischievous

endinheirado, -a [ẽdʒiɲeˈradu, a] adj rich, wealthy

endireitar [ẽdʒirejˈtaʳ] vt (objeto) to straighten; (fig: retificar) to put right; **~-se** vr to straighten up

endividar-se [ẽdʒiviˈdaxsi] vr to run into debt

endossar [ẽdoˈsaʳ] vt to endorse

endurecer [ẽdureˈseʳ] vt, vi to harden

energia [enɛxˈʒia] f energy, drive; (Tec) power, energy; **enérgico, -a** [eˈnɛxʒiku, a] adj energetic, vigorous

enervante [enexˈvãtʃi] adj annoying

enevoado, -a [eneˈvwadu, a] adj misty, hazy

enfado [ẽˈfadu] m annoyance

ênfase [ˈẽfazi] f emphasis, stress

enfastiado, -a [ẽfaˈtʃjadu, a] adj bored

enfático, -a [ẽˈfatʃiku, a] adj emphatic

enfatizar [ẽfatʃiˈzaʳ] vt to emphasize

enfeitar [ẽfejˈtaʳ] vt to decorate; **~-se** vr to dress up; **enfeite** [ẽˈfejtʃi] m decoration

enfermeiro, -a [ẽfexˈmejru, a] m/f nurse

enfermidade [ẽfexmiˈdadʒi] f illness

enfermo, -a [ẽˈfexmu, a] adj ill, sick ▷ m/f sick person, patient

enferrujar [ẽfexuˈʒaʳ] vt to rust, corrode ▷ vi to go rusty

enfiar [ẽˈfjaʳ] vt (meter) to put; (agulha) to thread; (vestir) to slip on; **~-se** vr: **~-se em** to slip into

enfim [ẽˈfĩ] adv finally, at last; (em suma) in short; **até que ~!** at last!

enfoque [ẽˈfɔki] m approach

enforcar [ẽfoxˈkaʳ] vt to hang; (trabalho, aulas) to skip; **~-se** vr to hang o.s

enfraquecer [ẽfrakeˈseʳ] vt to weaken ▷ vi to grow weak

enfrentar [ẽfrẽˈtaʳ] vt to face; (confrontar) to confront; (problemas) to face up to

enfurecer [ẽfureˈseʳ] vt to infuriate; **~-se** vr to get furious

enganado, -a [ẽgaˈnadu, a] adj mistaken; (traído) deceived

enganar [ẽgaˈnaʳ] vt to deceive; (desonrar) to seduce; (cônjuge) to be unfaithful to; (fome) to stave off; **~-se** vr to be wrong, be mistaken; (iludir-se) to deceive o.s

engano [ẽˈgãnu] m mistake; (ilusão) deception; (logro) trick; **é ~** (Tel) I've (ou you've) got the wrong number

engarrafamento [ẽgaxafaˈmẽtu] m bottling; (de trânsito) traffic jam

engarrafar [ẽgaxaˈfaʳ] vt to bottle; (trânsito) to block

engasgar [ẽgazˈgaʳ] vt to choke ▷ vi to choke; (máquina) to splutter; **~-se** vr to choke

engatinhar [ẽgatʃiˈɲaʳ] vi to crawl

engenharia [ẽʒeɲaˈria] f engineering; **engenheiro, -a** [ẽʒeˈɲejru, a] m/f engineer

engenhoso, -a [ẽʒeˈɲozu, ɔza] adj clever, ingenious

engessar [ẽʒeˈsaʳ] vt (perna) to put in plaster; (parede) to plaster

englobar [ẽgloˈbaʳ] vt to include

engodo [ẽˈgodu] m bait

engolir [ẽgoˈliʳ] vt to swallow

engordar [ẽgoxˈdaʳ] vt to fatten ▷ vi to put on weight

engraçado, -a [ẽgraˈsadu, a] adj funny, amusing

engradado [ẽgraˈdadu] m crate

engraxador [ẽgraʃaˈdoʳ] (PT) m shoe shiner

engraxar [ẽgraˈʃaʳ] vt to polish

engrenagem [ẽgreˈnaʒẽ] (pl **-ns**) f (Auto) gear

engrenar [ẽgreˈnaʳ] vt to put into gear; (fig: conversa) to strike up ▷ vi: **~ com alguém** to get on with sb

engrossar [ẽgroˈsaʳ] vt (sopa) to thicken; (aumentar) to swell; (voz) to raise ▷ vi to thicken; to swell; to rise; (col: pessoa, conversa) to turn nasty

enguia [ẽˈgia] f eel

enguiçar [ẽgiˈsaʳ] vi (máquina) to break down ▷ vt to cause to break down; **enguiço** [ẽˈgisu] m snag; (desarranjo) breakdown

enigma [eˈnigima] m enigma; (mistério) mystery

enjeitado, -a [ẽʒejˈtadu, a] m/f foundling, waif

enjoado, -a [ẽˈʒwadu, a] adj sick; (enfastiado) bored; (enfadonho) boring; (mal-humorado) in a bad mood

enjoar [ẽˈʒwaʳ] vt to make sick; to bore ▷ vi (pessoa) to be sick; (remédio, comida) to cause nausea; **~-se** vr: **~-se de** to get sick of

enjôo [ẽˈʒou] m sickness; (em carro) travel sickness; (em navio) seasickness; boredom

enlatado, -a [ẽlaˈtadu, a] adj tinned (BRIT), canned ▷ m (pej: filme) foreign import; **enlatados** mpl (comida) tinned

(BRIT) ou canned foods

enlouquecer [ēloke'se^r] vt to drive mad
▷ vi to go mad

enlutado, -a [ēlu'tadu, a] adj in
mourning

enorme [e'nɔxmi] adj enormous,
huge; **enormidade** [enoxmi'dadʒi] f
enormity; **uma enormidade (de)** (col) a
hell of a lot (of)

enquanto [ē'kwãtu] conj while;
(considerado como) as; **~ isso** meanwhile;
por ~ for the time being; **~ ele não vem**
until he comes; **~ que** whereas

enquête [ē'ketʒi] f survey

enraivecer [ēxajve'se^r] vt to enrage

enredo [ē'xedu] m (de uma obra) plot;
(intriga) intrigue

enriquecer [ēxike'se^r] vt to make rich;
(fig) to enrich ▷ vi to get rich; **~-se** vr to
get rich

enrolar [ēxo'la^r] vt to roll up; (agasalhar)
to wrap up; (col: enganar) to con ▷ vi (col)
to waffle; **~-se** vr to roll up; to wrap up;
(col: confundir-se) to get mixed up

enroscar [ēxoʃ'ka^r] vt (torcer) to twist,
wind (round); **~-se** vr to coil up

enrugar [ēxu'ga^r] vt (pele) to wrinkle;
(testa) to furrow; (tecido) to crease ▷ vi
(pele, mãos) to go wrinkly; (pessoa) to get
wrinkles

ensaiar [ēsa'ja^r] vt to test, try out;
(treinar) to practise (BRIT), practice (US);
(Teatro) to rehearse

ensaio [ē'saju] m test; (tentativa)
attempt; (treino) practice; (Teatro)
rehearsal; (literário) essay

enseada [ē'sjada] f inlet, cove; (baía) bay

ensejo [ē'seʒu] m chance, opportunity

ensinamento [ēsina'mētu] m teaching;
(exemplo) lesson

ensinar [ēsi'na^r] vt, vi to teach

ensino [ē'sinu] m teaching, tuition;
(educação) education

ensopado, -a [ēso'padu, a] adj soaked
▷ m stew

ensurdecer [ēsuxde'se^r] vt to deafen
▷ vi to go deaf

entalar [ēta'la^r] vt to wedge, jam;
(encher): **ela me entalou de comida** she
stuffed me full of food

entalhar [ēta'ʎa^r] vt to carve; **entalhe**
[ē'taʎi] m groove, notch

entanto [ē'tãtu]: **no ~** adv yet, however

então [ē'tãw] adv then; **até ~** up to that
time; **desde ~** ever since; **e ~?** well then?;
para ~ so that; **pois ~** in that case; **~,**

você vai ou não? so, are you going or
not?

entardecer [ētaxde'se^r] vi to get late
▷ m sunset

ente [ˈētʃi] m being

enteado, -a [ē'tʃjadu, a] m/f stepson/
stepdaughter

entediar [ēte'dʒja^r] vt to bore; **~-se** vr to
get bored

entender [ētē'de^r] vt to understand;
(pensar) to think; (ouvir) to hear; **~-se**
vr to understand one another; **dar a ~**
to imply; **no meu ~** in my opinion; **~ de**
música to know about music; **~ de fazer**
to decide to do; **~-se por** to be meant by;
~-se com alguém to get along with sb;
(dialogar) to sort things out with sb

entendido, -a [ētē'dʒidu, a] adj (col) gay;
(conhecedor): **~ em** good at ▷ m/f expert;
(col) homosexual, gay; **bem ~** that is

entendimento [ētēdʒi'mētu] m
understanding; (opinião) opinion;
(combinação) agreement

enterrar [ēte'xa^r] vt to bury; (faca) to
plunge; (lever à ruina) to ruin; (assunto)
to close

enterro [ē'texu] m burial; (funeral)
funeral

entidade [ētʃi'dadʒi] f (ser) being;
(corporação) body; (coisa que existe) entity

entornar [ētox'na^r] vt to spill; (fig: copo)
to drink ▷ vi to drink a lot

entorpecente [ētoxpe'sētʃi] m narcotic

entorpecimento [ētoxpesi'mētu] m
numbness; (torpor) lethargy

entorse [ē'tɔxsi] f sprain

entortar [ētox'ta^r] vt (curvar) to bend;
(empenar) to warp; **~ os olhos** to squint

entrada [ē'trada] f (ato) entry; (lugar)
entrance; (Tec) inlet; (de casa) doorway;
(começo) beginning; (bilhete) ticket;
(Culin) starter, entrée; (Comput) input;
(pagamento inicial) down payment;
(corredor de casa) hall; **entradas** fpl (no
cabelo) receding hairline sg; **~ gratuita**
admission free; **"~ proibida"** "no entry",
"no admittance"; **meia ~** half-price ticket

entra-e-sai [ˈētrai'saj] m comings and
goings pl

entranhado, -a [ētra'ɲadu, a] adj deep-
rooted

entranhas [ē'traɲaʃ] fpl bowels,
entrails; (sentimentos) feelings; (centro)
heart sg

entrar [ē'tra^r] vi to go (ou come) in, enter;
~ com (Comput: dados etc) to enter; **eu**

entrei com £10 I contributed £10; **~ de férias/licença** to start one's holiday (BRIT) ou vacation (US)/leave; **~ em** to go (ou come) into, enter; (assunto) to get onto; (comida, bebida) to start in on

entrave [ĕ'travi] m (fig) impediment

entre ['ĕtri] prep (dois) between; (mais de dois) among(st); **~ si** amongst themselves

entreaberto, -a [ĕtrja'bɛxtu, a] adj half-open; (porta) ajar

entrega [ĕ'trɛga] f (de mercadorias) delivery; (a alguém) handing over; (rendição) surrender; **~ rápida** special delivery

entregar [ĕtre'gaʳ] vt to hand over; (mercadorias) to deliver; (confiar) to entrust; (devolver) to return; **~-se** vr (render-se) to give o.s. up; (dedicar-se) to devote o.s

entregue [ĕ'trɛgi] pp de **entregar**

entrelinha [ĕtre'liɲa] f line space; **ler nas ~s** to read between the lines

entreolhar-se [ĕtrio'ʎaxsi] vr to exchange glances

entretanto [ĕtri'tãtu] conj however

entretenimento [ĕtriteni'mĕtu] m entertainment; (distração) pastime

entreter [ĕtri'teʳ] (irreg: como **ter**) vt to entertain, amuse; (ocupar) to occupy; (manter) to keep up; (esperanças) to cherish; **~-se** vr to amuse o.s.; to occupy o.s

entrevista [ĕtre'viʃta] f interview; **~ coletiva (à imprensa)** press conference;

entrevistar [ĕtreviʃ'taʳ] vt to interview; **entrevistar-se** vr to have an interview

entristecer [ĕtriʃte'seʳ] vt to sadden, grieve ▷ vi to feel sad; **~-se** vr to feel sad

entroncamento [ĕtrõka'mĕtu] m junction

entrudo [ĕ'trudu] (PT) m carnival; (Rel) Shrovetide

entulhar [ĕtu'ʎaʳ] vt to cram full; (suj: multidão) to pack

entupido, -a [ĕtu'pidu, a] adj blocked; **estar ~** (col: congestionado) to have a blocked-up nose; (de comida) to be fit to burst, be full up

entupimento [ĕtupi'mĕtu] m blockage

entupir [ĕtu'piʳ] vt to block, clog; **~-se** vr to become blocked; (de comida) to stuff o.s

entusiasmar [ĕtuzjaʒ'maʳ] vt to fill with enthusiasm; (animar) to excite; **~-se** vr to get excited

entusiasmo [ĕtu'zjaʒmu] m enthusiasm; (júbilo) excitement

entusiasta [ĕtu'zjaʃta] adj enthusiastic ▷ m/f enthusiast

enumerar [enume'raʳ] vt to enumerate; (com números) to number

envelhecer [ĕveʎe'seʳ] vt to age ▷ vi to grow old, age

envelope [ĕve'lɔpi] m envelope

envenenamento [ĕvenena'mĕtu] m poisoning; **~ do sangue** blood poisoning

envenenar [ĕvene'naʳ] vt to poison; (fig) to corrupt; (: declaração, palavras) to distort, twist; (tornar amargo) to sour ▷ vi to be poisonous; **~-se** vr to poison o.s

envergonhado, -a [ĕvexgo'ɲadu, a] adj ashamed; (tímido) shy

envergonhar [ĕvexgo'ɲaʳ] vt to shame; (degradar) to disgrace; **~-se** vr to be ashamed

enviado, -a [ĕ'vjadu, a] m/f envoy, messenger

enviar [ĕ'vjaʳ] vt to send

envio [ĕ'viu] m sending; (expedição) dispatch; (remessa) remittance; (de mercadorias) consignment

enviuvar [ĕvju'vaʳ] vi to be widowed

envolver [ĕvow've'ʳ] vt to wrap (up); (cobrir) to cover; (comprometer, acarretar) to involve; (nos braços) to embrace; **~-se** vr (intrometer-se) to become involved; (cobrir-se) to wrap o.s. up; **envolvimento** [ĕvowvi'mĕtu] m involvement

enxada [ĕ'ʃada] f hoe

enxaguar [ĕʃa'gwaʳ] vt to rinse

enxame [ĕ'ʃami] m swarm

enxaqueca [ĕʃa'keka] f migraine

enxergar [ĕʃex'gaʳ] vt (avistar) to catch sight of; (divisar) to make out; (notar) to observe, see

enxofre [ĕ'ʃofri] m sulphur (BRIT), sulfur (US)

enxotar [ĕʃo'taʳ] vt to drive out

enxoval [ĕʃo'vaw] (pl **-ais**) m (de noiva) trousseau; (de recém-nascido) layette

enxugar [ĕʃu'gaʳ] vt to dry; (fig: texto) to tidy up

enxurrada [ĕʃu'xada] f (de água) torrent; (fig) spate

enxuto, -a [ĕ'ʃutu, a] adj dry; (corpo) shapely; (bonito) good-looking

épico, -a ['ɛpiku, a] adj epic ▷ m epic poet

epidemia [epide'mia] f epidemic

epilepsia [epile'psia] f epilepsy

episódio [epi'zɔdʒu] m episode

época ['ɛpoka] f time, period; (*da história*) age, epoch; **naquela ~** at that time; **fazer ~** to be epoch-making

equação [ekwa'sãw] (*pl* -**ões**) f equation

equador [ekwa'do^r] m equator; **o E~** Ecuador

equilibrar [ekili'bra^r] vt to balance; **~-se** vr to balance; **equilíbrio** [eki'librju] m balance

equipa [e'kipa] (PT) f team

equipamento [ekipa'mētu] m equipment, kit

equipar [eki'pa^r] vt: **~ (com)** (*navio*) to fit out (with); (*prover*) to equip (with)

equipe [e'kipi] (BR) f team

equitação [ekita'sãw] f (*ato*) riding; (*arte*) horsemanship

equivalente [ekiva'lēt∫i] adj, m equivalent

equivaler [ekiva'le^r] vi: **~ a** to be the same as, equal

equivocado, -a [ekivo'kadu, a] adj mistaken, wrong

equivocar-se [ekivo'kaxsi] vr to make a mistake, be wrong

era¹ ['ɛra] f era, age

era² etc vb ver **ser**

erário [e'rarju] m exchequer

erecto, -a [e'rɛktu, a] (PT) adj = **ereto**

ereto, -a [e'rɛtu, a] adj upright, erect

erguer [ex'ge^r] vt to raise, lift; (*edificar*) to build, erect; **~-se** vr to rise; (*pessoa*) to stand up

eriçar [eri'sa^r] vt: **~ o cabelo de alguém** to make sb's hair stand on end; **~-se** vr to bristle; (*cabelos*) to stand on end

erigir [eri'ʒi^r] vt to erect

erosão [ero'zãw] f erosion

erótico, -a [e'rɔt∫iku, a] adj erotic

errado, -a [e'xadu, a] adj wrong; **dar ~** to go wrong

errar [e'xa^r] vt (*alvo*) to miss; (*conta*) to get wrong ▷ vi to wander, roam; (*enganar-se*) to be wrong, make a mistake; **~ o caminho** to lose one's way

erro ['exu] m mistake; **salvo ~** unless I am mistaken; **~ de imprensa** misprint

errôneo, -a [e'xonju, a] adj wrong, mistaken; (*falso*) false, untrue

erva ['ɛxva] f herb; (*col: dinheiro*) dosh; (: *maconha*) dope; **~ daninha** weed

erva-mate (*pl* **ervas-mates**) f mate

ervilha [ex'viʎa] f pea

esbanjar [iʒbã'ʒa^r] vt to squander, waste

esbarrar [iʒba'xa^r] vi: **~ em** to bump into; (*obstáculo, problema*) to come up against

esbelto, -a [iʒ'bɛwtu, a] adj slim, slender

esboçar [iʒbo'sa^r] vt to sketch; (*delinear*) to outline; (*traçar*) to draw up; **esboço** [iʒ'bosu] m sketch; (*primeira versão*) draft; (*fig: resumo*) outline

esbofetear [iʒbofe't∫ja^r] vt to slap, hit

esburacar [iʒbura'ka^r] vt to make holes (*ou* a hole) in

esc (PT) abr = **escudo**

escabroso, -a [iʃka'brozu, ɔza] adj (*difícil*) tough; (*indecoroso*) indecent

escada [iʃ'kada] f (*dentro da casa*) staircase, stairs pl; (*fora da casa*) steps pl; (*de mão*) ladder; **~ de incêndio** fire escape; **~ rolante** escalator; **escadaria** [iʃkada'ria] f staircase

escala [iʃ'kala] f scale; (*Náut*) port of call; (*parada*) stop; **fazer ~ em** to call at; **sem ~** non-stop

escalada [iʃka'lada] f (*de guerra*) escalation

escalão [eʃka'lãw] (*pl* -**ões**) m step; (*Mil*) echelon

escalar [iʃka'la^r] vt (*montanha*) to climb; (*muro*) to scale; (*designar*) to select

escaldar [iʃkaw'da^r] vt to scald; **~-se** vr to scald o.s

escalões [eʃka'lõjʃ] mpl de **escalão**

escama [iʃ'kama] f (*de peixe*) scale; (*de pele*) flake

escancarado, -a [iʃkãka'radu, a] adj wide open

escandalizar [iʃkãdali'za^r] vt to shock; **~-se** vr to be shocked; (*ofender-se*) to be offended

escândalo [iʃ'kãdalu] m scandal; (*indignação*) outrage; **fazer** *ou* **dar um ~** to make a scene; **escandaloso, -a** [iʃkãda'lozu, ɔza] adj shocking, scandalous

Escandinávia [iʃkãdʒi'navja] f: **a ~** Scandinavia; **escandinavo, -a** [iʃkãdʒi'navu, a] adj, m/f Scandinavian

escangalhar [iʃkãga'ʎa^r] vt to break, smash (up); (*a própria saúde*) to ruin; **~-se** vr: **~-se de rir** to split one's sides laughing

escapar [iʃka'pa^r] vi: **~ a** *ou* **de** to escape from; (*fugir*) to run away from; **~-se** vr to run away, flee; **deixar ~** (*uma oportunidade*) to miss; (*palavras*) to blurt out; **~ de boa** (*col*) to have a close shave

escapatória [iʃkapa'tɔrja] f way out; (*desculpa*) excuse

escape [iʃ'kapi] m (*de gás*) leak; (*Auto*) exhaust

escapulir [iʃkapu'li^r] vi: **~ (de)** to get

away (from); (suj: coisa) to slip (from)

escarrar [iʃka'xaʳ] vt to spit, cough up
▷ vi to spit

escarro [iʃ'kaxu] m phlegm, spit

escassear [iʃka'sjaʳ] vt to skimp on ▷ vi
to become scarce

escassez [iʃka'seʒ] f (falta) shortage

escavar [iʃka'vaʳ] vt to excavate

esclarecer [iʃklare'seʳ] vt (situação)
to explain; (mistério) to clear up,
explain; ~-se vr: ~-se (sobre algo) to
find out (about sth); **esclarecimento**
[iʃklaresi'mẽtu] m explanation;
(informação) information

escoadouro [iʃkoa'doru] m drain; (cano)
drainpipe

escocês, -esa [iʃko'seʃ, seza] adj
Scottish, Scots ▷ m/f Scot, Scotsman/
woman

Escócia [iʃ'kɔsja] f Scotland

escola [iʃ'kɔla] f school; ~ **de línguas**
language school; ~ **naval** naval college;
~ **primária** primary (BRIT) ou elementary
(US) school; ~ **secundária** secondary
(BRIT) ou high (US) school; ~ **particular/
pública** private/state (BRIT) ou public
(US) school; ~ **de samba** see boxed note; ~
superior college

⬡ **ESCOLA DE SAMBA**
⬡
⬡ **Escolas de samba** are musical and
⬡ recreational associations made up,
⬡ among others, of samba dancers,
⬡ percussionists and carnival dancers.
⬡ Although they exist throughout
⬡ Brazil, the most famous schools
⬡ are in Rio de Janeiro. The schools
⬡ in Rio rehearse all year long for the
⬡ **carnaval**, where they appear for two
⬡ days in the **Sambódromo**, the samba
⬡ parade, and compete for the samba
⬡ school championship. Characterised
⬡ by their extravagance, the biggest
⬡ schools have up to 4,000 members
⬡ and are one of Brazil's major tourist
⬡ attractions.

escolar [iʃko'laʳ] adj school atr ▷ m/f
schoolboy/girl

escolha [iʃ'koʎa] f choice

escolher [iʃko'ʎeʳ] vt to choose, select

escolho [iʃ'koʎu] m (recife) reef; (rocha)
rock

escolta [iʃ'kɔwta] f escort; **escoltar**
[iʃkow'taʳ] vt to escort

escombros [iʃ'kõbruʃ] mpl ruins,
debris sg

esconde-esconde [iʃkõdʃiʃ'kõdʒi] m
hide-and-seek

esconder [iʃkõ'deʳ] vt to hide, conceal;
~-se vr to hide

escondidas [iʃkõ'dʒidaʃ] fpl: **às ~** secretly

escopo [iʃ'kopu] m aim, purpose

escorar [iʃko'raʳ] vt to prop (up);
(amparar) to support; (esperar de espreita)
to lie in wait for ▷ vi to lie in wait; ~-se
vr: ~-se em (fundamentar-se) to go by;
(amparar-se) to live off

escore [iʃ'kɔri] m score

escoriação [iʃkorja'sãw] (pl -ões) f
abrasion, scratch

escorpião [iʃkoxpi'ãw] (pl -ões) m
scorpion; **E~** (Astrologia) Scorpio

escorrega [iʃko'xɛga] f slide;
escorregadela [iʃkoxega'dɛla] f slip;
escorregadiço, -a [iʃkoxega'dʒi(s)u, a]
adj slippery; **escorregão** [iʃkoxe'gãw] (pl
-ões) m slip; (fig) slip(-up); **escorregar**
[iʃkoxe'gaʳ] vi to slip; (errar) to slip up

escorrer [iʃko'xeʳ] vt to drain (off);
(verter) to pour out ▷ vi (pingar) to drip;
(correr em fio) to trickle

escoteiro [iʃko'tejru] m scout

escova [iʃ'kova] f brush; (penteado) blow-
dry; ~ **de dentes** toothbrush; **escovar**
[iʃko'vaʳ] vt to brush

escravatura [iʃkrava'tura] f (tráfico)
slave trade; (escravidão) slavery

escravidão [iʃkravi'dãw] f slavery

escravizar [iʃkravi'zaʳ] vt to enslave;
(cativar) to captivate

escravo, -a [iʃ'kravu, a] adj captive
▷ m/f slave

escrever [iʃkre'veʳ] vt, vi to write; ~-se
vr to write to each other; ~ **à máquina**
to type

escrita [eʃ'krita] f writing; (letra)
handwriting

escrito, -a [eʃ'kritu, a] pp de **escrever**
▷ adj written ▷ m piece of writing; ~ **à
mão** handwritten; **dar por ~** to put in
writing

escritor, a [iʃkri'toʳ, a] m/f writer; (autor)
author

escritório [iʃkri'tɔrju] m office; (em casa)
study

escritura [iʃkri'tura] f (Jur) deed;
(na compra de imóveis) ≈ exchange
of contracts; **as Sagradas E~s** the
Scriptures

escrivã [iʃkri'vã] f de **escrivão**

escrivaninha [iʃkriva'niɲa] f writing desk

escrivão, -vã [iʃkri'vãw, vã] (pl **escrivões/-s**) m/f registrar, recorder

escrupuloso, -a [iʃkrupu'lozu, ɔza] adj scrupulous; careful

escudo [iʃ'kudu] m shield; (moeda) escudo

esculhambado, -a [iʃkuʎã'badu, a] (col!) adj shabby, slovenly; (estragado) knackered

esculhambar [iʃkuʎã'baʳ] (col!) vt to mess up; **~ alguém** (criticar) to give sb stick; (descompor) to give sb a bollocking (!)

esculpir [iʃkuw'piʳ] vt to carve, sculpt; (gravar) to engrave

escultor, a [iʃkuw'toʳ, a] m/f sculptor

escultura [iʃkuw'tura] f sculpture

escuras [iʃ'kuraʃ] fpl: **às ~** in the dark

escurecer [iʃkure'seʳ] vt to darken ▷ vi to get dark; **ao ~** at dusk

escuridão [iʃkuri'dãw] f (trevas) dark

escuro, -a [iʃ'kuru, a] adj dark; (dia) overcast; (pessoa) swarthy; (negócios) shady ▷ m darkness

escusar [iʃku'zaʳ] vt to excuse, forgive; (justificar) to justify; (dispensar) to exempt; (não precisar de) not to need; **~-se** vr to apologize; **~-se de fazer** to refuse to do

escuta [iʃ'kuta] f listening; **à ~** listening out; **ficar na ~** to stand by

escutar [iʃku'taʳ] vt to listen to; (sem prestar atenção) to hear ▷ vi to listen; to hear

esfacelar [iʃfase'laʳ] vt to destroy

esfaquear [iʃfaki'aʳ] vt to stab

esfarrapado, -a [iʃfaxa'padu, a] adj ragged, tattered

esfera [iʃ'fɛra] f sphere; (globo) globe; (Tip, Comput) golfball

esfolar [iʃfo'laʳ] vt to skin; (arranhar) to graze; (cobrar demais a) to overcharge, fleece

esfomeado, -a [iʃfo'mjadu, a] adj famished, starving

esforçado, -a [iʃfox'sadu, a] adj committed, dedicated

esforçar-se [iʃfox'saxsi] vr: **~ para** to try hard to, strive to

esforço [iʃ'foxsu] m effort

esfregar [iʃfre'gaʳ] vt to rub; (com água) to scrub

esfriar [iʃ'frja] vt to cool, chill ▷ vi to get cold; (fig) to cool off

esganar [iʃga'naʳ] vt to strangle, choke

esgotado, -a [iʃgo'tadu, a] adj exhausted; (consumido) used up; (livros) out of print; (ingressos) sold out

esgotamento [iʒgota'mẽtu] m exhaustion

esgotar [iʒgo'taʳ] vt to drain, empty; (recursos) to use up; (pessoa, assunto) to exhaust; **~-se** vr to become exhausted; (mercadorias, edição) to be sold out; (recursos) to run out

esgoto [iʒ'gotu] m drain; (público) sewer

esgrima [iʒ'grima] f (esporte) fencing

esgueirar-se [iʒgej'raxsi] vr to slip away, sneak off

esguelha [iʒ'geʎa] f slant; **olhar alguém de ~** to look at sb out of the corner of one's eye

esguio, -a [eʒ'giu, a] adj slender

esmaecer [iʒmaje'seʳ] vi to fade

esmagador, a [iʒmagado̖ʳ, a] adj crushing; (provas) irrefutable; (maioria) overwhelming

esmalte [iʒ'mawtʃi] m enamel; (de unhas) nail polish

esmeralda [iʒme'rawda] f emerald

esmerar-se [iʒme'raxsi] vr: **~ em fazer algo** to take great care in doing sth

esmigalhar [iʒmiga'ʎaʳ] vt to crumble; (despedaçar) to shatter; (esmagar) to crush; **~-se** vr to crumble; to smash, shatter

esmo ['eʒmu] m: **a ~** at random; **falar a ~** to prattle

esmola [iʒ'mɔla] f alms pl; **pedir ~s** to beg

esmurrar [iʒmu'xaʳ] vt to punch

espacial [iʃpa'sjaw] (pl -**ais**) adj space atr; **nave ~** spaceship

espaço [iʃ'pasu] m space; (tempo) period; **~ para 3 pessoas** room for 3 people; **a ~s** from time to time; **espaçoso, -a** [iʃpa'sozu, ɔza] adj spacious, roomy

espada [iʃ'pada] f sword; **espadas** fpl (Cartas) spades

espadarte [iʃpa'daxtʃi] m swordfish

espairecer [iʃpajre'seʳ] vt to amuse, entertain ▷ vi to relax; **~-se** vr to relax

espaldar [iʃpaw'daʳ] m (chair) back

espalhafato [iʃpaʎa'fatu] m din, commotion

espalhar [iʃpa'ʎaʳ] vt to scatter; (boato, medo) to spread; (luz) to shed; **~-se** vr to spread; (refestelar-se) to lounge

espanador [iʃpana'do̖ʳ] m duster

espancar [iʃpã'kaʳ] vt to beat up

Espanha [iʃ'paɲa] f: a ~ Spain; **espanhol, a** [iʃpa'ɲow, ola] (pl **espanhóis/ espanhas**) adj Spanish ▷ m/f Spaniard ▷ m (Ling) Spanish; **os espanhóis** mpl the Spanish

espantado, -a [iʃpã'tadu, a] adj astonished, amazed; (assustado) frightened

espantalho [iʃpã'taʎu] m scarecrow

espantar [iʃpã'taʳ] vt to frighten; (admirar) to amaze, astonish; (afugentar) to frighten away ▷ vi to be amazing; **~-se** vr to be astonished ou amazed; to be frightened

espanto [iʃ'pãtu] m fright, fear; (admiração) astonishment, amazement; **espantoso, -a** [iʃpã'tozu, ɔza] adj amazing

esparadrapo [iʃpara'drapu] m (sticking) plaster (BRIT), bandaid® (US)

esparramar [iʃpaxa'maʳ] vt to splash; (espalhar) to scatter

esparso, -a [iʃ'paxsu, a] adj scattered; (solto) loose

espasmo [iʃ'paʒmu] m spasm, convulsion

espatifar [iʃpatʃi'faʳ] vt to smash; **~-se** vr to smash; (avião) to crash

especial [iʃpe'sjaw] (pl **-ais**) adj special; **em ~** especially; **especialidade** [iʃpesjali'dadʒi] f speciality (BRIT), specialty (US); (ramo de atividades) specialization; **especialista** [iʃpesja'liʃta] m/f specialist; (perito) expert; **especializar-se** [iʃpesjali'zaxsi] vr: **especializar-se (em)** to specialize (in)

espécie [iʃ'pɛsi] f (Bio) species; (tipo) sort, kind; **causar ~** to be surprising; **pagar em ~** to pay in cash

especificar [iʃpesifi'kaʳ] vt to specify; **específico, -a** [iʃpe'sifiku, a] adj specific

espécime [iʃ'pɛsimi] m specimen

espécimen [iʃ'pɛsimẽ] (pl **-s**) m = **espécime**

espectáculo etc [iʃpek'takulu] (PT) m = **espetáculo** etc

espectador, a [iʃpekta'doʳ, a] m/f onlooker; (TV) viewer; (Esporte) spectator; (Teatro) member of the audience; **espectadores** mpl (TV, Teatro) audience sg

especular [iʃpeku'laʳ] vi: **~ (sobre)** to speculate (on)

espelho [iʃ'peʎu] m mirror; (fig) model; **~ retrovisor** (Auto) rearview mirror

espera [iʃ'pɛra] f (demora) wait; (expectativa) expectation; **à ~ de** waiting for; **à minha ~** waiting for me

esperança [iʃpe'rãsa] f hope; (expectativa) expectation; **dar ~s a alguém** to raise sb's hopes; **esperançoso, -a** [iʃperã'sozu, ɔza] adj hopeful

esperar [iʃpe'raʳ] vt to wait for; (contar com: bebê) to expect; (desejar) to hope for ▷ vi to wait; to hope; to expect

esperma [iʃ'pexma] f sperm

espertalhão, -lhona [iʃpexta'ʎãw, ʎɔna] (pl **espertalhões/-s**) adj crafty, shrewd

esperteza [iʃpex'teza] f cleverness; (astúcia) cunning

esperto, -a [iʃ'pextu, a] adj clever; (espertalhão) crafty

espetacular [iʃpetaku'laʳ] adj spectacular

espetáculo [iʃpe'takulu] m (Teatro) show; (vista) sight; (cena ridícula) spectacle; **dar ~** to make a spectacle of o.s.

espetar [iʃpe'taʳ] vt (carne) to put on a spit; (cravar) to stick; **~-se** vr to prick o.s.; **~ algo em algo** to pin sth to sth

espeto [iʃ'petu] m spit; (pau) pointed stick; **ser um ~** (ser difícil) to be awkward

espevitado, -a [iʃpevi'tadu, a] adj (fig: vivo) lively

espiã [iʃ'pjã] f de **espião**

espiada [iʃ'pjada] f: **dar uma ~** to have a look

espião, -piã [iʃ'pjãw, 'pjã] (pl **espiões/-s**) m/f spy

espiar [iʃ'pjaʳ] vt to spy on; (uma ocasião) to watch out for; (olhar) to watch ▷ vi to spy; (olhar) to peer

espiga [iʃ'piga] f (de milho) ear

espinafre [iʃpi'nafri] m spinach

espingarda [iʃpĩ'gaxda] f shotgun, rifle

espinha [iʃ'piɲa] f (de peixe) bone; (na pele) spot, pimple; (coluna vertebral) spine

espinho [iʃ'piɲu] m thorn; (de animal) spine; (fig: dificuldade) snag; **espinhoso, -a** [iʃpi'ɲozu, ɔza] adj (planta) prickly, thorny; (fig: difícil) difficult; (: problema) thorny

espiões [iʃ'pjõjʃ] mpl de **espião**

espionar [iʃpjo'naʳ] vt to spy on ▷ vi to spy, snoop

espírito [iʃ'piritu] m spirit; (pensamento) mind; **~ esportivo** sense of humo(u)r; **E~ Santo** Holy Spirit

espiritual [iʃpiri'twaw] (pl **-ais**) adj

spiritual

espirituoso, -a [iʃpiri'twozu, ɔza] adj witty

espirrar [iʃpi'xaʳ] vi to sneeze; (jorrar) to spurt out ▷ vt (água) to spurt; **espirro** [iʃ'pixu] m sneeze

esplêndido, -a [iʃ'plẽdʒidu, a] adj splendid

esplendor [iʃple'doʳ] m splendour (BRIT), splendor (US)

esponja [iʃ'põʒa] f sponge

espontâneo, -a [iʃpõ'tanju, a] adj spontaneous; (pessoa) straightforward

esporádico, -a [iʃpo'radʒiku, a] adj sporadic

esporte [iʃ'pɔxtʃi] (BR) m sport; **esportista** [iʃpox'tʃiʃta] adj sporting ▷ m/f sportsman/woman; **esportivo, -a** [iʃpox'tʃivu, a] adj sporting

esposa [iʃ'poza] f wife

esposo [iʃ'pozu] m husband

espreguiçadeira [iʃpregiza'dejra] f deck chair; (com lugar para as pernas) lounger

espreguiçar-se [iʃpregi'saxsi] vr to stretch

espreita [iʃ'prejta] f: **ficar à ~** to keep watch

espreitar [iʃprej'taʳ] vt to spy on; (observar) to observe, watch

espremer [iʃpre'meʳ] vt (fruta) to squeeze; (roupa molhada) to wring out; (pessoas) to squash; **~-se** vr (multidão) to be squashed together; (uma pessoa) to squash up

espuma [iʃ'puma] f foam; (de cerveja) froth, head; (de sabão) lather; (de ondas) surf; **~ de borracha** foam rubber; **espumante** [iʃpu'mãtʃi] adj frothy, foamy; (vinho) sparkling

esq. abr (= esquerdo/a) l

esquadra [iʃ'kwadra] f (Náut) fleet; (PT: da polícia) police station

esquadrão [iʃkwa'drãw] (pl -ões) m squadron

esquadrilha [iʃkwa'driʎa] f squadron

esquadrões [iʃkwa'drõjʃ] mpl de **esquadrão**

esquartejar [iʃkwaxte'ʒaʳ] vt to quarter

esquecer [iʃke'seʳ] vt, vi to forget; **~-se** vr: **~-se de** to forget; **esquecido, -a** [iʃke'sidu, a] adj forgotten; (pessoa) forgetful

esqueleto [iʃke'letu] m skeleton; (arcabouço) framework

esquema [iʃ'kɛma] m outline; (plano) scheme; (diagrama) diagram, plan

esquentar [iʃkẽ'taʳ] vt to heat (up), warm (up); (fig: irritar) to annoy ▷ vi to warm up; (casaco) to be warm; **~-se** vr to get annoyed

esquerda [iʃ'kexda] f (tb Pol) left; **à ~** on the left

esquerdista [iʃkex'dʒiʃta] adj left-wing ▷ m/f left-winger

esquerdo, -a [iʃ'kexdu, a] adj left

esqui [iʃ'ki] m (patim) ski; (esporte) skiing; **~ aquático** water skiing; **fazer ~** to go skiing; **esquiar** [iʃ'kjaʳ] vi to ski

esquilo [iʃ'kilu] m squirrel

esquina [iʃ'kina] f corner

esquisito, -a [iʃki'zitu, a] adj strange, odd

esquivar-se [iʃki'vaxsi] vr: **~ de** to escape from, get away from; (deveres) to get out of

esquivo, -a [iʃ'kivu, a] adj aloof, standoffish

essa ['ɛsa] pron: **~ é/foi boa** that is/was a good one; **~ não, sem ~** come off it!; **vamos nessa** let's go!; **ainda mais ~!** that's all I need!; **corta ~!** cut it out!; **por ~s e outras** for these and other reasons; **~ de fazer ...** this business of doing ...

esse ['esi] adj (sg) that; (pl) those; (BR: este: sg) this; (: pl) these ▷ pron (sg) that one; (pl) those; (BR: este: sg) this one; (: pl) these

essência [e'sẽsja] f essence; **essencial** [esẽ'sjaw] (pl -ais) adj essential; (principal) main ▷ m: **o essencial** the main thing

esta ['ɛʃta] f de **este**

estabelecer [iʃtabele'seʳ] vt to establish; (fundar) to set up

estabelecimento [iʃtabelesi'mẽtu] m establishment; (casa comercial) business

estábulo [iʃ'tabulu] m cow-shed

estaca [iʃ'taka] f post, stake; (de barraca) peg

estação [iʃta'sãw] (pl -ões) f station; (do ano) season; **~ de águas** spa; **~ balneária** seaside resort; **~ emissora** broadcasting station

estacionamento [iʃtasjona'mẽtu] m (ato) parking; (lugar) car park (BRIT), parking lot (US)

estacionar [iʃtasjo'naʳ] vt to park ▷ vi to park; (não mover) to remain stationary

estacionário, -a [iʃtasjo'narju, a] adj (veículo) stationary; (Com) slack

estações [iʃta'sõjʃ] fpl de **estação**

estada [iʃˈtada] f stay
estadia [iʃtaˈdʒia] f = **estada**
estádio [iʃˈtadʒu] m stadium
estadista [iʃtaˈdʒiʃta] m/f statesman/ woman
estado [iˈʃtadu] m state; **E~s Unidos (da América)** United States (of America); **~ civil** marital status; **~ de espírito** state of mind; **~ maior** staff; **estadual** [iʃtaˈdwaw] (pl **-ais**) adj state atr
estafa [iʃˈtafa] f fatigue; (esgotamento) nervous exhaustion
estagiário, -a [iʃtaˈʒjarju, a] m/f probationer, trainee; (professor) student teacher; (médico) junior doctor
estágio [iʃˈtaʒu] m (aprendizado) traineeship; (fase) stage
estagnado, -a [iʃtagˈnadu, a] adj stagnant
estalar [iʃtaˈlaʳ] vt to break; (os dedos) to snap ▷ vi to split, crack; (crepitar) to crackle
estalido [iʃtaˈlidu] m pop
estalo [iʃˈtalu] m (do chicote) crack; (dos dedos) snap; (dos lábios) smack; (de foguete) bang; **~ de trovão** thunderclap; **de ~** suddenly
estampa [iʃˈtãpa] f (figura impressa) print; (ilustração) picture
estampado, -a [iʃtãˈpadu, a] adj printed ▷ m (tecido) print; (num tecido) pattern
estampar [iʃtãˈpaʳ] vt to print; (marcar) to stamp
estancar [iʃtãˈkaʳ] vt to staunch; (fazer cessar) to stop; **~-se** vr to stop
estância [iʃˈtãsja] f ranch, farm
estandarte [iʃtãˈdaxtʃi] m standard, banner
estanho [iʃˈtaɲu] m (metal) tin
estante [iʃˈtãtʃi] f bookcase; (suporte) stand

🔵 **PALAVRA CHAVE**

estar [iʃˈtaʳ] vi **1** (lugar) to be; (em casa) to be in; (no telefone): **a Lúcia está? - não, ela não está** is Lúcia there? - no, she's not here
2 (estado) to be; **estar doente** to be ill; **estar bem** (de saúde) to be well; (financeiramente) to be well off; **estar calor/frio** to be hot/cold; **estar com fome/sede/medo** to be hungry/thirsty/afraid
3 (ação contínua): **estar fazendo** (BR) ou **a fazer** (PT) to be doing

4 (+ pp: = adj): **estar sentado/cansado** to be sitting down/tired
5 (+ pp: uso passivo): **está condenado à morte** he's been condemned to death; **o livro está emprestado** the book's been borrowed
6: **estar de**: **estar de férias/licença** to be on holiday (BRIT) ou vacation (US)/ leave; **ela estava de chapéu** she had a hat on, she was wearing a hat
7: **estar para**: **estar para fazer** to be about to do; **ele está para chegar a qualquer momento** he'll be here any minute; **não estar para conversas** not to be in the mood for talking
8: **estar por fazer** to be still to be done
9: **estar sem**: **estar sem dinheiro** to have no money; **estar sem dormir** not to have slept; **estou sem dormir há três dias** I haven't slept for three days; **está sem terminar** it isn't finished yet
10 (frases): **está bem, tá (bem)** (col) OK; **estar bem com** to be on good terms with

estardalhaço [iʃtaxdaˈʎasu] m fuss; (ostentação) ostentation
estas [ˈɛʃtaʃ] fpl de **este**
estatal [iʃtaˈtaw] (pl **-ais**) adj nationalized, state-owned ▷ f state-owned company
estático, -a [iʃˈtatʃiku, a] adj static
estatística [iʃtaˈtʃiʃtʃika] f statistic; (ciência) statistics sg
estatizar [iʃtatʃiˈzaʳ] vt to nationalize
estátua [iʃˈtatwa] f statue
estatura [iʃtaˈtura] f stature
estável [iʃˈtavew] (pl **-eis**) adj stable
este¹ [ˈɛʃtʃi] m east ▷ adj inv (região) eastern; (vento, direção) easterly
este², -ta [ˈeʃtʃi, ˈɛʃta] adj (sg) this; (pl) these ▷ pron this one; (pl) these; (a quem/ que se referiu por último) the latter; **esta noite** (noite passada) last night; (noite de hoje) tonight
esteira [iʃˈtejra] f mat; (de navio) wake; (rumo) path
esteja etc [iʃˈteʒa] vb ver **estar**
estelionato [iʃteljoˈnatu] m fraud
estender [iʃtẽˈdeʳ] vt to extend; (mapa) to spread out; (pernas) to stretch; (massa) to roll out; (conversa) to draw out; (corda) to pull tight; (roupa molhada) to hang out; **~-se** vr to lie down; (fila, terreno) to stretch, extend; **~ a mão** to hold out one's hand; **~-se sobre algo** to

dwell on sth, expand on sth
estéreis [iʃˈtɛrejʃ] adj pl de **estéril**
estereo... [iʃˈterju] prefixo stereo...;
estereofônico, -a [iʃterjoˈfoniku,
a] adj stereo(phonic); **estereótipo**
[iʃteˈrjɔtʃipu] m stereotype
estéril [iʃˈteriw] (pl **-eis**) adj sterile;
(terra) infertile; (fig) futile; **esterilizar**
[iʃteriliˈzaʳ] vt to sterilize
esteve [iʃˈtevi] vb ver **estar**
esticar [iʃtʃiˈkaʳ] vt to stretch; **~-se** vr to
stretch out
estigma [iʃˈtʃigima] m mark, scar; (fig)
stigma
estilhaçar [iʃtʃiʎaˈsaʳ] vt to splinter;
(despedaçar) to shatter; **~-se** vr to
shatter; **estilhaço** [iʃtʃiˈʎasu] m
fragment; (de pedra) chip; (de madeira,
metal) splinter
estilo [iʃˈtʃilu] m style; (Tec) stylus; **~ de
vida** way of life
estima [iʃˈtʃima] f esteem; (afeto)
affection; **ter ~ a** to have a high regard
for
estimação [iʃtʃimaˈsãw] f: ... **de ~**
favourite (BRIT) ..., favorite (US) ...
estimado, -a [iʃtʃiˈmadu, a] adj
respected; (em cartas): **E~ Senhor** Dear
Sir
estimar [iʃtʃiˈmaʳ] vt to appreciate;
(avaliar) to value; (ter estima a) to
have a high regard for; (calcular
aproximadamente) to estimate
estimativa [iʃtʃimaˈtʃiva] f estimate
estimulante [iʃtʃimuˈlãtʃi] adj
stimulating ▷ m stimulant
estimular [iʃtʃimuˈlaʳ] vt to stimulate;
(incentivar) to encourage; **estímulo**
[iʃˈtʃimulu] m stimulus; (ânimo)
encouragement
estipular [iʃtʃipuˈlaʳ] vt to stipulate
estirar [iʃtʃiˈraʳ] vt to stretch (out); **~-se**
vr to stretch
estive etc [iʃˈtʃivi] vb ver **estar**
estocada [iʃtoˈkada] f stab, thrust
estocar [iʃtoˈkaʳ] vt to stock
estofo [iʃˈtofu] m (tecido) material; (para
acolchoar) padding, stuffing
estojo [iʃˈtoʒu] m case; **~ de
ferramentas** tool kit; **~ de unhas**
manicure set
estômago [iʃˈtomagu] m stomach; **ter ~
para (fazer) algo** to be up to (doing) sth
estontear [iʃtõˈtʃjaʳ] vt to stun, daze
estoque [iʃˈtɔki] m (Com) stock
estourado, -a [iʃtoˈradu, a] adj

(temperamental) explosive; (col: cansado)
shattered, worn out
estourar [iʃtoˈraʳ] vi to explode; (pneu) to
burst; (escândalo) to blow up; (guerra) to
break out; (BR: chegar) to turn up, arrive;
~ (com alguém) (zangar-se) to blow up
(at sb)
estouro [iʃˈtoru] m explosion; **dar o ~**
(fig: zangar-se) to blow up, blow one's top
estrábico, -a [iʃˈtrabiku, a] adj cross-
eyed
estraçalhar [iʃtrasaˈʎaʳ] vt (livro, objeto)
to pull to pieces; (pessoa) to tear to pieces
estrada [iʃˈtrada] f road; **~ de ferro** (BR)
railway (BRIT), railroad (US); **~ principal**
main road (BRIT), state highway (US)
estrado [iʃˈtradu] m (tablado) platform;
(de cama) base
estragado, -a [iʃtraˈgadu, a] adj ruined;
(fruta) rotten; (muito mimado) spoiled,
spoilt (BRIT)
estraga-prazeres [iʃtraga-] m/f inv
spoilsport
estragar [iʃtraˈgaʳ] vt to spoil; (arruinar)
to ruin, wreck; (desperdiçar) to waste;
(saúde) to damage; (mimar) to spoil;
estrago [iʃˈtragu] m destruction; waste;
damage; **os estragos da guerra** the
ravages of war
estrangeiro, -a [iʃtrãˈʒejru, a] adj
foreign ▷ m/f foreigner; **no ~** abroad
estrangular [iʃtrãguˈlaʳ] vt to strangle
estranhar [iʃtraˈɲaʳ] vt to be surprised
at; (achar estranho): **~ algo** to find sth
strange; **estranhei o clima** the climate
did not agree with me; **não é de se ~** it's
not surprising
estranho, -a [iʃˈtraɲu, a] adj strange,
odd; (influências) outside ▷ m/f
(desconhecido) stranger; (de fora) outsider
estratégia [iʃtraˈtɛʒa] f strategy
estrear [iʃˈtrjaʳ] vt (vestido) to wear for
the first time; (peça de teatro) to perform
for the first time; (veículo) to use for the
first time; (filme) to show for the first
time, première; (iniciar): **~ uma carreira**
to embark on ou begin a career ▷ vi (ator,
jogador) to make one's first appearance;
(filme, peça) to open
estrebaria [iʃtrebaˈria] f stable
estréia [iʃˈtreja] f (de artista) debut;
(de uma peça) first night; (de um filme)
première, opening
estreitar [iʃtrejˈtaʳ] vt to narrow;
(roupa) to take in; (abraçar) to hug; (laços
de amizade) to strengthen ▷ vi (estrada)

to narrow

estreito, -a [iʃ'trejtu, a] *adj* narrow; (*saia*) straight; (*vínculo, relação*) close; (*medida*) strict ▷ *m* strait

estrela [iʃ'trela] *f* star; ~ **cadente** falling star; **estrelado, -a** [iʃtre'ladu, a] *adj* (*céu*) starry; (*ovo*) fried

estremecer [iʃtreme'seʳ] *vt* to shake; (*amizade*) to strain; (*fazer tremer*): ~ **alguém** to make sb shudder ▷ *vi* to shake; (*tremer*) to tremble; (*horrorizar-se*) to shudder; (*amizade*) to be strained

estremecimento [iʃtremesi'mẽtu] *m* shaking, trembling; (*tremor*) tremor; (*numa amizade*) tension

estresse [iʃ'trɛsi] *m* stress

estribeira [iʃtri'bejra] *f*: **perder as ~s** (*col*) to fly off the handle, lose one's temper

estridente [iʃtri'dẽtʃi] *adj* shrill, piercing

estrofe [iʃ'trɔfi] *f* stanza

estrondo [iʃ'trõdu] *m* (*de trovão*) rumble; (*de armas*) din

estrutura [iʃtru'tura] *f* structure; (*armação*) framework; (*de edifício*) fabric

estudante [iʃtu'dãtʃi] *m/f* student; **estudantil** [iʃtuda'tʃiw] (*pl* -**is**) *adj* student *atr*

estudar [iʃtu'daʳ] *vt, vi* to study

estúdio [iʃ'tudʒu] *m* studio

estudo [iʃ'tudu] *m* study

estufa [iʃ'tufa] *f* (*fogão*) stove; (*de plantas*) greenhouse; (*de fogão*) plate warmer; **efeito ~** greenhouse effect

estufado [iʃtu'fadu] (*PT*) *m* stew

estupefato, -a [iʃtupe'fatu, a] (*PT* -**ct**-) *adj* dumbfounded

estupendo, -a [iʃtu'pẽdu, a] *adj* wonderful, terrific

estupidez [iʃtupi'deʒ] *f* stupidity; (*ato, dito*) stupid thing; (*grosseria*) rudeness

estúpido, -a [iʃ'tupidu, a] *adj* stupid; (*grosseiro*) rude, churlish ▷ *m/f* idiot; oaf

estuprar [iʃtu'praʳ] *vt* to rape; **estupro** [iʃ'tupru] *m* rape

esvaziar [iʒva'zjaʳ] *vt* to empty; ~**se** *vr* to empty

etapa [e'tapa] *f* stage

etc. *abr* (= *et cetera*) etc.

eternidade [etexni'dadʒi] *f* eternity

ética ['ɛtʃika] *f* ethics *pl*

ético, -a ['ɛtʃiku, a] *adj* ethical

Etiópia [e'tʃjɔpja] *f*: **a ~** Ethiopia

etiqueta [etʃi'keta] *f* etiquette; (*rótulo, em roupa*) label; (*que se amarra*) tag

étnico, -a ['ɛtʃniku, a] *adj* ethnic

etos ['ɛtuʃ] *m inv* ethos

eu [ew] *pron* I ▷ *m* self; **sou eu** it's me

EUA *abr mpl* (= *Estados Unidos da América*) USA

eucaristia [ewkariʃ'tʃia] *f* Holy Communion

euro ['ewru] *m* (*moeda*) euro

Europa [ew'rɔpa] *f*: **a ~** Europe; **europeu, -péia** [ewro'peu, 'peja] *adj, m/f* European

evacuar [eva'kwaʳ] *vt* to evacuate; (*sair de*) to leave; (*Med*) to discharge ▷ *vi* to defecate

evadir [eva'dʒiʳ] *vt* to evade; ~**se** *vr* to escape

evangelho [evã'ʒeʎu] *m* gospel

evaporar [evapo'raʳ] *vt, vi* to evaporate; ~**se** *vr* to evaporate; (*desaparecer*) to vanish

evasão [eva'zãw] (*pl* -**ões**) *f* escape, flight; (*fig*) evasion

evasiva [eva'ziva] *f* excuse

evasivo, -a [eva'zivu, a] *adj* evasive

evasões [eva'zõjʃ] *fpl de* **evasão**

evento [e'vẽtu] *m* event; (*eventualidade*) eventuality

eventual [evẽ'tuaw] (*pl* -**ais**) *adj* fortuitous, accidental; **eventualidade** [evẽtwali'dadʒi] *f* eventuality

evidência [evi'dẽsja] *f* evidence, proof; **evidenciar** [evidẽ'sjaʳ] *vt* to prove; (*mostrar*) to show; **evidenciar-se** *vr* to be evident, be obvious

evidente [evi'dẽtʃi] *adj* obvious, evident

evitar [evi'taʳ] *vt* to avoid; ~ **de fazer algo** to avoid doing sth

evocar [evo'kaʳ] *vt* to evoke; (*espíritos*) to invoke

evolução [evolu'sãw] (*pl* -**ões**) *f* development; (*Mil*) manoeuvre (*BRIT*), maneuver (*US*); (*movimento*) movement; (*Bio*) evolution

evoluir [evo'lwiʳ] *vi* to evolve; ~ **para** to evolve into

Ex.ª *abr* = **Excelência**

exacto, -a *etc* [e'zatu, a] (*PT*) = **exato** *etc*

exagerar [ezaʒe'raʳ] *vt* to exaggerate ▷ *vi* to exaggerate; (*agir com exagero*) to overdo it; **exagero** [eza'ʒeru] *m* exaggeration

exalar [eza'laʳ] *vt* (*odor*) to give off

exaltado, -a [ezaw'tadu, a] *adj* fanatical; (*apaixonado*) overexcited

exaltar [ezaw'taʳ] *vt* (*elevar: pessoa, virtude*) to exalt; (*louvar*) to praise; (*excitar*) to excite; (*irritar*) to annoy; ~**se**

vr (*irritar-se*) to get worked up; (*arrebatar-se*) to get carried away

exame [e'zami] *m* (*Educ*) examination, exam; (*Med etc*) examination; **fazer um ~** (*Educ*) to take an exam; (*Med*) to have an examination

examinar [ezami'na^r] *vt* to examine

exatidão [ezatʃi'dãw] *f* accuracy; (*perfeição*) correctness

exato, -a [e'zatu, a] *adj* right, correct; (*preciso*) exact; **~!** exactly!

exaustão [ezaw'ʃtãw] *f* exhaustion; **exausto, -a** [e'zawʃtu, a] *adj* exhausted

exaustor [ezaw'ʃto^r] *m* extractor fan

exceção [ese'sãw] (*pl* -**ões**) *f* exception; **com ~ de** with the exception of; **abrir ~** to make an exception

excedente [ese'dẽtʃi] *adj* excess; (*Com*) surplus ▷ *m* (*Com*) surplus

exceder [ese'de^r] *vt* to exceed; (*superar*) to surpass; **~-se** *vr* (*cometer excessos*) to go too far; (*cansar-se*) to overdo things

excelência [ese'lẽsja] *f* excellence; **por ~** par excellence; **Vossa E~** Your Excellency; **excelente** [ese'lẽtʃi] *adj* excellent

excêntrico, -a [e'sẽtriku, a] *adj, m/f* eccentric

excepção [ese'sãw] (*PT*) *f* = **exceção**

excepcional [esepsjo'naw] (*pl* -**ais**) *adj* exceptional; (*especial*) special; (*Med*) handicapped

excepto *etc* [e'sɛtu] (*PT*) = **exceto** *etc*

excesso [e'sɛsu] *m* excess; (*Com*) surplus

exceto [e'sɛtu] *prep* except (for), apart from

excitação [esita'sãw] *f* excitement

excitado, -a [esi'tadu, a] *adj* excited; (*estimulado*) aroused

excitante [esi'tãtʃi] *adj* exciting

exclamação [iʃklama'sãw] (*pl* -**ões**) *f* exclamation

exclamar [iʃkla'ma^r] *vi* to exclaim

excluir [iʃ'klwi^r] *vt* to exclude, leave out; (*eliminar*) to rule out; (*ser incompatível com*) to preclude; **exclusão** [iʃklu'zãw] *f* exclusion; **exclusivo, -a** [iʃklu'zivu, a] *adj* exclusive

excursão [iʃkux'sãw] (*pl* -**ões**) *f* outing, excursion; **~ a pé** hike; **excursionista** [iʃkuxsjo'niʃta] *m/f* tourist; (*para o dia*) day-tripper; (*a pé*) hiker

execução [ezeku'sãw] (*pl* -**ões**) *f* execution; (*de música*) performance

executar [ezeku'ta^r] *vt* to execute; (*Mús*) to perform; (*plano*) to carry out; (*papel teatral*) to play

executivo, -a [ezeku'tʃivu, a] *adj, m/f* executive

exemplar [ezẽ'pla^r] *adj* exemplary ▷ *m* model, example; (*Bio*) specimen; (*livro*) copy; (*peça*) piece

exemplo [e'zẽplu] *m* example; **por ~** for example

exercer [ezex'se^r] *vt* to exercise; (*influência, pressão*) to exert; (*função*) to perform; (*profissão*) to practise (*BRIT*), practice (*US*); (*obrigações*) to carry out

exercício [ezex'sisju] *m* exercise; (*de medicina*) practice; (*Mil*) drill; (*Com*) financial year

exercitar [ezexsi'ta^r] *vt* (*profissão*) to practise (*BRIT*), practice (*US*); (*direitos, músculos*) to exercise; (*adestrar*) to train

exército [e'zɛxsito] *m* army

exibição [ezibi'sãw] (*pl* -**ões**) *f* show, display; (*de filme*) showing

exibir [ezi'bi^r] *vt* to show, display; (*alardear*) to show off; (*filme*) to show, screen; **~-se** *vr* to show off; (*indecentemente*) to expose o.s

exigência [ezi'ʒẽsja] *f* demand; (*o necessário*) requirement; **exigente** [ezi'ʒẽtʃi] *adj* demanding

exigir [ezi'ʒi^r] *vt* to demand

exíguo, -a [e'zigwu, a] *adj* (*diminuto*) small; (*escasso*) scanty

exilado, -a [ezi'ladu, a] *adj, m/f* exile

exilar [ezi'la^r] *vt* to exile; **~-se** *vr* to go into exile; **exílio** [e'zilju] *m* exile; (*forçado*) deportation

existência [eziʃ'tẽsja] *f* existence; (*vida*) life

existir [eziʃ'tʃi^r] *vi* to exist; **existe/existem** ... (*há*) there is/are ...

êxito ['ezitu] *m* result; (*sucesso*) success; (*música, filme etc*) hit; **ter ~ (em)** to succeed (in), be successful (in)

Exmo(s)/a(s) *abr* (= *Excelentíssimo(s)/a(s)*) Dear

êxodo ['ezodu] *m* exodus

exorcista [ezox'siʃta] *m/f* exorcist

exótico, -a [e'zɔtʃiku, a] *adj* exotic

expandir [iʃpã'dʒi^r] *vt* to expand; (*espalhar*) to spread; **~-se** *vr* to expand; **~-se com alguém** to be frank with sb

expansão [iʃpã'sãw] *f* expansion, spread; (*de alegria*) effusiveness

expansivo, -a [iʃpã'sivu, a] *adj* (*pessoa*) outgoing

expeça *etc* [iʃ'pɛsa] *vb ver* **expedir**

expectativa [iʃpekta'tʃiva] *f* expectation

expedição [iʃpedʒi'sãw] (pl **-ões**) f (viagem) expedition; (de mercadorias) despatch; (por navio) shipment; (de passaporte etc) issue

expediente [iʃpe'dʒjẽtʃi] m means; (serviço) working day; (correspondência) correspondence ▷ adj expedient; ~ **bancário** banking hours pl; ~ **do escritório** office hours pl

expedir [iʃpe'dʒiʳ] vt to send, despatch; (bilhete, passaporte, decreto) to issue

expelir [iʃpe'liʳ] vt to expel; (sangue) to spit

experiência [iʃpe'rjẽsja] f experience; (prova) experiment, test; **em ~** on trial

experimentar [iʃperimẽ'taʳ] vt (comida) to taste; (vestido) to try on; (pôr à prova) to try out, test; (conhecer pela experiência) to experience; (sofrer) to suffer, undergo; **experimento** [iʃperi'mẽtu] m experiment

expilo etc [iʃ'pilu] vb ver **expelir**

expirar [iʃpi'raʳ] vt to exhale, breathe out ▷ vi to die; (terminar) to end

explicação [iʃplika'sãw] (pl **-ões**) f explanation

explicar [iʃpli'kaʳ] vt, vi to explain; **~-se** vr to explain o.s

explícito, -a [iʃ'plisitu, a] adj explicit, clear

explodir [iʃplo'dʒiʳ] vt, vi to explode

exploração [iʃplora'sãw] f exploration; (abuso) exploitation; (de uma mina) working

explorador, a [iʃplora'doʳ, a] m/f explorer; (de outros) exploiter

explorar [iʃplo'raʳ] vt (região) to explore; (mina) to work, run; (ferida) to probe; (trabalhadores etc) to exploit

explosão [iʃplo'zãw] (pl **-ões**) f explosion; (fig) outburst; **explosivo, -a** [iʃplo'zivu, a] adj explosive; (pessoa) hot-headed ▷ m explosive

expor [iʃ'poʳ] (irreg: como **pôr**) vt to expose; (a vida) to risk; (teoria) to explain; (revelar) to reveal; (mercadorias) to display; (quadros) to exhibit; **~-se** vr to expose o.s

exportação [iʃpoxta'sãw] f (ato) export(ing); (mercadorias) exports pl

exportador, a [iʃpoxta'doʳ, a] adj exporting ▷ m/f exporter

exportar [iʃpox'taʳ] vt to export

exposição [iʃposi'sãw] (pl **-ões**) f exhibition; (explicação) explanation; (declaração) statement; (narração) account; (Foto) exposure

exposto, -a [iʃ'poʃtu, 'poʃta] adj (lugar) exposed; (quadro, mercadoria) on show ou display ▷ m: **o acima ~** the above

expressão [iʃpre'sãw] (pl **-ões**) f expression

expressar [iʃpre'saʳ] vt to express; **expressivo, -a** [iʃpre'sivu, a] adj expressive; (pessoa) demonstrative

expresso, -a [iʃ'prɛsu, a] pp de **exprimir** ▷ adj definite, clear; (trem, ordem, carta) express ▷ m express

expressões [iʃpre'sõjʃ] fpl de **expressão**

exprimir [iʃpri'miʳ] vt to express

expulsão [iʃpul'sãw] (pl **-ões**) f expulsion; (Esporte) sending off

expulsar [iʃpuw'saʳ] vt to expel; (de uma festa, clube etc) to throw out; (inimigo) to drive out; (estrangeiro) to expel, deport; (jogador) to send off

expulso, -a [iʃ'puwsu, a] pp de **expulsar**

expulsões [iʃpul'sõjʃ] fpl de **expulsão**

êxtase ['eʃtazi] m ecstasy

extenso, -a [iʃ'tẽsu, a] adj extensive; (comprido) long; (artigo) full, comprehensive; **por ~** in full

extenuante [iʃte'nwãtʃi] adj exhausting; (debilitante) debilitating

exterior [iʃte'rjoʳ] adj (de fora) outside, exterior; (aparência) outward; (comércio) foreign ▷ m (da casa) outside; (aspecto) outward appearance; **do ~** (do estrangeiro) from abroad; **no ~** abroad

exterminar [iʃtexmi'naʳ] vt (inimigo) to wipe out, exterminate; (acabar com) to do away with

externo, -a [iʃ'texnu, a] adj external; (aparente) outward; **aluno ~** day pupil

extinguir [iʃtʃi'giʳ] vt (fogo) to put out, extinguish; (um povo) to wipe out; **~-se** vr (fogo, luz) to go out; (Bio) to become extinct

extinto, -a [iʃ'tʃĩtu, a] adj (fogo) extinguished; (língua, pessoa) dead; (animal, vulcão) extinct; (associação etc) defunct; **extintor** [iʃtʃĩ'toʳ] m (fire) extinguisher

extorsão [iʃtox'sãw] f extortion

extra ['ɛʃtra] adj extra ▷ m/f extra person; (Teatro) extra

extração [iʃtra'sãw] (PT **-cç-**) (pl **-ões**) f extraction; (de loteria) draw

extracto [iʃ'tratu] (PT) m = **extrato**

extrair [iʃtra'jiʳ] vt to extract, take out

extraordinário, -a [iʃtraoxdʒi'narju, a] adj extraordinary; (despesa) extra;

(reunião) special
extrato [iʃ'tratu] *m* extract; (*resumo*)
summary; **~ (bancário)** (bank)
statement
extravagância [iʃtrava'gãsja]
f extravagance; **extravagante**
[iʃtrava'gãtʃi] *adj* extravagant; (*roupa*)
outlandish; (*conduta*) wild
extravasar [iʃtrava'za^r] *vi* to overflow
extraviado, -a [iʃtra'vjadu, a] *adj* lost,
missing
extraviar [iʃtra'vja^r] *vt* to mislay;
(*pessoa*) to lead astray; (*dinheiro*) to
embezzle; **~-se** *vr* to get lost; **extravio**
[iʃtra'viu] *m* loss; embezzlement; (*fig*)
deviation
extremado, -a [iʃtre'madu, a] *adj*
extreme
extremidade [iʃtremi'dadʒi] *f*
extremity; (*do dedo*) tip; (*ponta*) end;
(*beira*) edge
extremo, -a [iʃ'tremu, a] *adj* extreme
▷ *m* extreme; **ao ~** extremely
extrovertido, -a [eʃtrovex'tʃidu, a] *adj*
extrovert, outgoing ▷ *m/f* extrovert
exultante [ezuw'tãtʃi] *adj* jubilant,
exultant

fã [fã] (*col*) *m/f* fan
fábrica ['fabrika] *f* factory; **~ de cerveja**
brewery; **a preço de ~** wholesale
fabricação [fabrika'sãw] *f*
manufacture; **~ em série** mass
production
fabuloso, -a [fabu'lozu, ɔza] *adj*
fabulous
faca ['faka] *f* knife; **facada** [fa'kada] *f*
stab, cut
façanha [fa'saɲa] *f* exploit, deed
facção [fak'sãw] (*pl* **-ões**) *f* faction
face ['fasi] *f* face; (*bochecha*) cheek; **em**
~ de in view of; **fazer ~ a** to face up to;
disquete de ~ simples/dupla (*Comput*)
single-/double-sided disk
fáceis ['fasejʃ] *adj pl de* **fácil**
faceta [fa'seta] *f* facet
fachada [fa'ʃada] *f* façade, front
fácil ['fasiw] (*pl* **-eis**) *adj* easy;
(*temperamento, pessoa*) easy-going
▷ *adv* easily; **facilidade** [fasili'dadʒi] *f*
ease; (*jeito*) facility; **fácils** *fpl* (*recursos*)
facilities; **ter facilidade para algo** to
have a talent for sth
facilitar [fasili'ta^r] *vt* to facilitate, make
easy; (*fornecer*): **~ algo a alguém** to
provide sb with sth

faço etc ['fasu] vb ver **fazer**
facto ['faktu] (PT) m = **fato**
factor [fak'to'] (PT) m = **fator**
factual [fak'twaw] (pl **-ais**) adj factual
factura etc [fak'tura] (PT) = **fatura** etc
faculdade [fakuw'dadʒi] f (ger, Educ) faculty; (poder) power
facultativo, -a [fakuwta'tʃivu, a] adj optional ▷ m/f doctor
fadado, -a [fa'dadu, a] adj destined
fadiga [fa'dʒiga] f fatigue
fadista [fa'dʒiʃta] m/f fado singer ▷ m (PT) ruffian
fado ['fadu] m fate; (canção) fado

⚜ **FADO**
⚜
⚜ The best-known musical form in
⚜ Portugal is the melancholic **fado**,
⚜ which is traditionally sung by a soloist
⚜ (known as a *fadista*) accompanied by
⚜ the Portuguese *guitarra*. There are two
⚜ main types of Fado: Coimbra **fado**
⚜ is traditionally sung by men, and is
⚜ considered to be more cerebral than
⚜ the fado from Lisbon, which is sung
⚜ by both men and women. The theme
⚜ is nearly always one of deep nostalgia
⚜ known as *saudade*, and the harsh
⚜ reality of life.

faia ['faja] f beech (tree)
faisão [faj'zãw] (pl **-ães** or **-ões**) m pheasant
faísca [fa'iʃka] f spark; (brilho) flash
faisões [faj'zõjʃ] mpl de **faisão**
faixa ['fajʃa] f (cinto, Judô) belt; (tira) strip; (área) zone; (Auto: pista) lane; (BR: para pedestres) zebra crossing (BRIT), crosswalk (US); (Med) bandage; (num disco) track
fala ['fala] f speech; **chamar às ~s** to call to account; **sem ~** speechless
falante [fa'lãtʃi] adj talkative
falar [fa'la'] vt (língua) to speak; (besteira etc) to talk; (dizer) to say; (verdade, mentira) to tell ▷ vi to speak; **~ algo a alguém** to tell sb sth; **~ de ou em algo** to talk about sth; **~ com alguém** to talk to sb; **por ~ em** speaking of; **sem ~ em** not to mention; **falou!, 'tá falado!** (col) OK!
falcão [faw'kãw] (pl **-ões**) m falcon
falecer [fale'se'] vi to die; **falecimento** [falesi'mẽtu] m death
falência [fa'lẽsja] f bankruptcy; **abrir ~** to declare o.s. bankrupt; **ir à ~** to go

bankrupt; **levar à ~** to bankrupt
falésia [fa'lɛzja] f cliff
falha ['faʎa] f fault; (lacuna) omission; (de caráter) flaw
falhar [fa'ʎa'] vi to fail; (não acertar) to miss; (errar) to be wrong; **sua voz está falhando** (Tel) you're breaking up
falho, -a ['faʎu, a] adj faulty; (deficiente) wanting
falido, -a [fa'lidu, a] adj, m/f bankrupt
falir [fa'li'] vi to fail; (Com) to go bankrupt
falsário, -a [faw'sarju, a] m/f forger
falsidade [fawsi'dadʒi] f falsehood; (fingimento) pretence (BRIT), pretense (US)
falsificar [fawsifi'ka'] vt (forjar) to forge; (falsear) to falsify; (adulterar) to adulterate; (desvirtuar) to misrepresent
falso, -a ['fawsu, a] adj false; (fraudulento) dishonest; (errôneo) wrong; (jóia, moeda, quadro) fake; **pisar em ~** to blunder
falta ['fawta] f (carência) lack; (ausência) absence; (defeito, culpa) fault; (Futebol) foul; **por ou na ~ de** for lack of; **sem ~** without fail; **fazer ~** to be lacking, be needed; **sentir ~ de alguém/algo** to miss sb/sth; **ter ~ de** to lack, be in need of
faltar [faw'ta'] vi to be lacking, be wanting; (pessoa) to be absent; (falhar) to fail; **~ ao trabalho** to be absent from work; **~ à palavra** to break one's word; **falta pouco para ...** it won't be long until ...
fama ['fama] f (renome) fame; (reputação) reputation
família [fa'milja] f family
familiar [fami'lja'] adj (da família) family atr; (conhecido) familiar ▷ m/f relation, relative; **familiaridade** [familjari'dadʒi] f familiarity; (sem-cerimônia) informality
famoso, -a [fa'mozu, ɔza] adj famous
fanático, -a [fa'natʃiku, a] adj fanatical ▷ m/f fanatic
fantasia [fãta'zia] f fantasy; (imaginação) imagination; (capricho) fancy; (traje) fancy dress
fantasiar [fãta'zja'] vt to imagine ▷ vi to daydream; **~-se** vr to dress up (in fancy dress)
fantasma [fã'taʒma] m ghost; (alucinação) illusion
fantástico, -a [fã'taʃtʃiku, a] adj fantastic; (ilusório) imaginary; (incrível) unbelievable
fantoche [fã'tɔʃi] m puppet
farda ['faxda] f uniform
farei etc [fa'rej] vb ver **fazer**

farinha [faˈriɲa] f: ~ **(de mesa)** (manioc) flour; ~ **de rosca** breadcrumbs pl; ~ **de trigo** plain flour

farmacêutico, -a [faxmaˈsewtʃiku, a] adj pharmaceutical ▷ m/f pharmacist, chemist (BRIT)

farmácia [faxˈmasja] f pharmacy, chemist's (shop) (BRIT)

faro [ˈfaru] m sense of smell; (fig) flair

farofa [faˈrɔfa] f (Culin) side dish based on manioc flour

farol [faˈrɔw] (pl -óis) m lighthouse; (Auto) headlight; **com ~ alto** (Auto) on full (BRIT) ou high (US) beam; **com ~ baixo** dipped headlights pl (BRIT), dimmed beam (US)

farra [ˈfaxa] f binge, spree

farrapo [faˈxapu] m rag

farsa [ˈfaxsa] f farce; **farsante** [fax'sãtʃi] m/f joker

fartar [faxˈtar] vt to satiate; (encher) to fill up; ~-**se** vr to gorge o.s

farto, -a [ˈfaxtu, a] adj full, satiated; (abundante) plentiful; (aborrecido) fed up

fartura [faxˈtura] f abundance

fascinante [fasiˈnãtʃi] adj fascinating

fascinar [fasiˈnar] vt to fascinate; (encantar) to charm; **fascínio** [faˈsinju] m fascination

fase [ˈfazi] f phase

fashion [ˈfɛʃjõ] (col) adj trendy

fatal [faˈtaw] (pl -ais) adj (mortal) fatal; (inevitável) inevitable; **fatalidade** [fatali'dadʒi] f fate; (desgraça) disaster

fatia [faˈtʃia] f slice

fatigante [fatʃiˈgãtʃi] adj tiring; (aborrecido) tiresome

fatigar [fatʃiˈgar] vt to tire; (aborrecer) to bore; ~-**se** vr to get tired

Fátima [ˈfatima] f Fatima; see boxed note

❋ **FÁTIMA**
❋
❋ Fátima, situated in central Portugal,
❋ is know worldwide as a site of
❋ pilgrimage for Catholics. It is said that,
❋ in 1917, the Virgin Mary appeared six
❋ times to three shepherd children (os
❋ três pastorinhos). Millions of pilgrims
❋ visit Fátima every year.

fato [ˈfatu] m fact; (acontecimento) event; (PT: traje) suit; ~ **de banho** (PT) swimming costume (BRIT), bathing suit (US); **de ~** in fact, really

fator [faˈtor] m factor

fatura [faˈtura] f bill, invoice; **faturar** [fatuˈrar] vt to invoice; (dinheiro) to make ▷ vi (col: ganhar dinheiro): **faturar (alto)** to rake it in

fava [ˈfava] f broad bean; **mandar alguém às ~s** to send sb packing

favela [faˈvɛla] f slum

favor [faˈvor] m favour (BRIT), favor (US); **a ~ de** in favo(u)r of; **por ~** please; **faça** ou **faz o ~ de ...** would you be so good as to ..., kindly ...; **favorável** [favoˈravew] (pl -eis) adj: **favorável (a)** favo(u)rable (to); **favorecer** [favoreˈser] vt to favo(u)r; (beneficiar) to benefit; (suj: vestido) to suit; (: retrato) to flatter; **favorito** [favoˈritu, a] adj, m/f favo(u)rite

fax [faks] m (carta) fax; (máquina) fax (machine); **enviar por ~** to fax

faxina [faˈʃina] f: **fazer ~** to clean up; **faxineiro, -a** [faʃiˈnejru, a] m/f cleaner

fazenda [faˈzẽda] f farm; (de café) plantation; (de gado) ranch; (pano) cloth, fabric; (Econ) treasury; **fazendeiro** [fazẽˈdejru] m farmer; (de café) plantation-owner; (de gado) rancher, ranch-owner

⊙ **PALAVRA CHAVE**

fazer [faˈzer] vt **1** (fabricar, produzir) to make; (construir) to build; (pergunta) to ask; (poema, música) to write; **fazer um filme/ruído** to make a film/noise

2 (executar) to do; **o que você está fazendo?** what are you doing?; **fazer a comida** to do the cooking; **fazer o papel de** (Teatro) to play

3 (estudos, alguns esportes) to do; **fazer medicina/direito** to do ou study medicine/law; **fazer ioga/ginástica** to do yoga/keep-fit

4 (transformar, tornar): **sair o fará sentir melhor** going out will make him feel better; **sua partida fará o trabalho mais difícil** his departure will make work more difficult

5 (como sustituto de vb): **ele bebeu e eu fiz o mesmo** he drank and I did likewise

6: **fazer anos**: **ele faz anos hoje** it's his birthday today; **fiz 30 anos ontem** I was 30 yesterday

▷ vi **1** (portar-se) to act, behave; **fazer bem/mal** to do the right/wrong thing; **não fiz por mal** I didn't mean it; **faz como quem não sabe** act as if you don't

know anything
2: fazer com que alguém faça algo to make sb do sth
▷ *vb impess* **1: faz calor/frio** it's hot/cold **2** (*tempo*): **faz um ano** a year ago; **faz dois anos que ele se formou** it's two years since he graduated; **faz três meses que ele está aqui** he's been here for three months
3: não faz mal never mind; **tanto faz** it's all the same
fazer-se *vr* **1: fazer-se de desentendido** to pretend not to understand
2: faz-se com ovos e leite it's made with eggs and milk; **isso não se faz** that's not done

fé [fɛ] *f* faith; (*crença*) belief; (*confiança*) trust; **de boa/má fé** in good/bad faith
febre ['fɛbri] *f* fever; (*fig*) excitement; **~ do feno** hay fever; **febril** [fe'briw] (*pl* **-is**) *adj* feverish
fechado, -a [fe'ʃadu, a] *adj* shut, closed; (*pessoa*) reserved; (*sinal*) red; (*luz, torneira*) off; (*tempo*) overcast; (*cara*) stern
fechadura [feʃa'dura] *f* (*de porta*) lock
fechar [fe'ʃaʳ] *vt* to close, shut; (*concluir*) to finish, conclude; (*luz, torneira*) to turn off; (*rua*) to close off; (*ferida*) to close up; (*bar, loja*) to close down ▷ *vi* to close (up), shut; to close down; (*tempo*) to cloud over; **~-se** *vr* to close, shut; (*pessoa*) to withdraw; **~ à chave** to lock
fecho ['feʃu] *m* fastening; (*trinco*) latch; (*término*) close; **~ ecler** zip fastener (*BRIT*), zipper (*US*)
fécula ['fɛkula] *f* starch
feder [fe'deʳ] *vi* to stink
federação [federa'sãw] (*pl* **-ões**) *f* federation
federal [fede'raw] (*pl* **-ais**) *adj* federal; (*col: grande*) huge
fedor [fe'doʳ] *m* stench
feijão [fej'ʒãw] (*pl* **-ões**) *m* bean(s) (*pl*); (*preto*) black bean(s) (*pl*); **feijoada** [fej'ʒwada] *f* (*Culin*) meat, rice and black beans
feio, -a ['feju, a] *adj* ugly; (*situação*) grim; (*atitude*) bad; (*tempo*) horrible ▷ *adv* (*perder*) badly
feira ['fejra] *f* fair; (*mercado*) market
feiticeira [fejtʃi'sejra] *f* witch
feiticeiro, -a [fejtʃi'sejru, a] *adj* bewitching, enchanting ▷ *m* wizard
feitiço [fej'tʃisu] *m* charm, spell

feitio [fej'tʃiu] *m* shape, pattern; (*caráter*) nature, manner; (*Tec*) workmanship
feito, -a ['fejtu, a] *pp de* **fazer** ▷ *adj* finished, ready ▷ *m* act, deed; (*façanha*) feat ▷ *conj* like; **~ a mão** hand-made; **homem ~** grown man
feiúra [fe'jura] *f* ugliness
felicidade [felisi'dadʒi] *f* happiness; (*sorte*) good luck; (*êxito*) success; **felicidades** *fpl* (*congratulações*) congratulations
felicitações [felisita'sõjʃ] *fpl* congratulations, best wishes
feliz [fe'liʒ] *adj* happy; (*afortunado*) lucky; **felizmente** [feliʒ'mẽtʃi] *adv* fortunately
feltro ['fewtru] *m* felt
fêmea ['femja] *f* female
feminino, -a [femi'ninu, a] *adj* feminine; (*sexo*) female; (*equipe, roupa*) women's ▷ *m* (*Ling*) feminine
feminista [femi'niʃta] *adj, m/f* feminist
feno ['fenu] *m* hay
fenomenal [fenome'naw] (*pl* **-ais**) *adj* phenomenal; (*espantoso*) amazing; (*pessoa*) brilliant
fenômeno [fe'nomenu] *m* phenomenon
fera ['fɛra] *f* wild animal
feriado [fe'rjadu] *m* holiday (*BRIT*), vacation (*US*)
férias ['fɛrjaʃ] *fpl* holidays, vacation *sg*; **de ~** on holiday; **tirar ~** to have *ou* take a holiday
ferida [fe'rida] *f* wound, injury; *ver tb* **ferido**
ferido, -a [fe'ridu, a] *adj* injured; (*em batalha*) wounded; (*magoado*) hurt ▷ *m/f* casualty
ferimento [feri'mẽtu] *m* injury; (*em batalha*) wound
ferir [fe'riʳ] *vt* to injure; (*tb fig*) to hurt; (*em batalha*) to wound; (*ofender*) to offend
fermentar [fexmẽ'taʳ] *vi* to ferment
fermento [fex'mẽtu] *m* yeast; **~ em pó** baking powder
feroz [fe'rɔʒ] *adj* fierce, ferocious; (*cruel*) cruel
ferragem [fe'xaʒẽ] (*pl* **-ns**) *f* (*peças*) hardware; (*guarnição*) metalwork; **loja de ferragens** ironmonger's (*BRIT*), hardware store
ferramenta [fexa'mẽta] *f* tool; (*caixa de ferramentas*) tool kit; **~ de busca** (*Comput*) search engine

ferrão [fe'xãw] (pl **-ões**) m goad; (de inseto) sting

ferrenho, -a [fe'xeɲu, a] adj (vontade) iron

ferro ['fɛxu] m iron; **ferros** mpl (algemas) shackles, chains; **~ batido** wrought iron; **~ de passar** iron; **~ fundido** cast iron; **~ ondulado** corrugated iron

ferrões [fe'xõjʃ] mpl de **ferrão**

ferrolho [fe'xoʎu] m (trinco) bolt

ferrovia [fexo'via] f railway (BRIT), railroad (US); **ferroviário, -a** [fexo'vjarju, a] adj railway atr (BRIT), railroad atr (US) ▷ m/f railway ou railroad worker

ferrugem [fe'xuʒẽ] f rust

fértil ['fɛxtʃiw] (pl **-eis**) adj fertile; **fertilizante** [fextʃili'zãtʃi] m fertilizer; **fertilizar** [fextʃili'za^r] vt to fertilize

ferver [fex've^r] vt, vi to boil; **~ de raiva/indignação** to seethe with rage/ indignation; **~ em fogo baixo** (Culin) to simmer

fervilhar [fexvi'ʎa^r] vi to simmer; (com atividade) to hum; (pulular): **~ de** to swarm with

fervor [fex'vo^r] m fervour (BRIT), fervor (US)

festa ['fɛʃta] f (reunião) party; (conjunto de ceremônias) festival; **festas** fpl (carícia) embrace sg; **boas ~s** Merry Christmas and a Happy New Year; **dia de ~** public holiday

festejar [feʃte'ʒa^r] vt to celebrate; (acolher) to welcome, greet; **festejo** [feʃ'teʒu] m festivity; (ato) celebration

festival [feʃtʃi'vaw] (pl **-ais**) m festival

festividade [feʃtʃivi'dadʒi] f festivity

festivo, -a [feʃ'tʃivu, a] adj festive

fetiche [fe'tʃiʃi] m fetish

feto ['fɛtu] m (Med) foetus (BRIT), fetus (US)

fevereiro [feve'rejru] (PT **F-**) m February

fez [feʒ] vb ver **fazer**

fezes ['feziʃ] fpl faeces (BRIT), feces (US)

fiado, -a ['fjadu, a] adv: **comprar/ vender ~** to buy/sell on credit

fiador, a [fja'do^r, a] m/f (Jur) guarantor; (Com) backer

fiambre ['fjãbri] m cold meat; (presunto) ham

fiança ['fjãsa] f guarantee; (Jur) bail; **prestar ~ por** to stand bail for; **sob ~** on bail

fiar ['fja^r] vt (algodão etc) to spin; (confiar) to entrust; (vender a crédito) to sell on

credit; **~-se** vr: **~-se em** to trust

fibra ['fibra] f fibre (BRIT), fiber (US)

⊙ **PALAVRA CHAVE**

ficar [fi'ka^r] vi **1** (permanecer) to stay; (sobrar) to be left; **ficar perguntando/ olhando** etc to keep asking/looking etc; **ficar por fazer** to have still to be done; **ficar para trás** to be left behind

2 (tornar-se) to become; **ficar cego/ surdo/louco** to go blind/deaf/mad; **fiquei contente ao saber da notícia** I was happy when I heard the news; **ficar com raiva/medo** to get angry/ frightened; **ficar de bem/mal com alguém** (col) to make up/fall out with sb

3 (posição) to be; **a casa fica ao lado da igreja** the house is next to the church; **ficar sentado/deitado** to be sitting down/lying down

4 (tempo: durar): **ele ficou duas horas para resolver** he took two hours to decide; (: ser adiado): **a reunião ficou para amanhã** the meeting was postponed until the following day

5: ficar bem (comportamento): **sua atitude não ficou bem** his (ou her etc) behaviour was inappropriate; (cor): **você fica bem em azul** blue suits you, you look good in blue; (roupa): **ficar bem para** to suit

6: ficar bom (de saúde) to be cured; (trabalho, foto etc) to turn out well

7: ficar de fazer algo (combinar) to arrange to do sth; (prometer) to promise to do sth

8: ficar de pé to stand up

ficção [fik'sãw] f fiction

ficha ['fiʃa] f (tb: **~ de telefone**) token; (tb: **~ de jogo**) chip; (de fichário) (index) card; (Polícia) record; (PT: Elet) plug; (em loja, lanchonete) ticket

fichário [fi'ʃarju] m filing cabinet; (caixa) card index; (caderno) file

ficheiro [fi'ʃejru] (PT) m = **fichário**

fidelidade [fideli'dadʒi] f fidelity, loyalty; (exatidão) accuracy

fiel [fjɛw] (pl **-éis**) adj (leal) faithful, loyal; (acurado) accurate; (que não falha) reliable

figa ['figa] f talisman; **fazer uma ~** to make a figa, ≈ cross one's fingers; **de uma ~** (col) damned

fígado ['figadu] m liver

figo ['figu] m fig; **figueira** [fi'gejra] f fig

figura | 308

tree
figura [fi'gura] *f* figure; (*forma*) form, shape; (*Ling*) figure of speech; (*aspecto*) appearance
figurino [figu'rinu] *m* model; (*revista*) fashion magazine
fila ['fila] *f* row, line; (BR: *fileira de pessoas*) queue (US); (*num teatro*, *cinema*) row; **em ~** in a row; **fazer ~ to** form a line, queue; **~ indiana** single file
filé [fi'lε] *m* (*bife*) steak; (*peixe*) fillet
fileira [fi'lejru] *f* row, line; **fileiras** *fpl* (*serviço militar*) military service *sg*
filho, -a ['fiʎu, a] *m/f* son/daughter; **filhos** *mpl* children; (*de animais*) young
filhote [fi'ʎɔtʃi] *m* (*de leão*, *urso etc*) cub; (*cachorro*) pup(py)
filial [fi'ljaw] (*pl* **-ais**) *f* (*sucursal*) branch
Filipinas [fili'pinaʃ] *fpl*: **as ~** the Philippines
filmadora [fiwma'dora] *f* camcorder
filmar [fiw'maʳ] *vt*, *vi* to film
filme ['fiwmi] *m* film (BRIT), movie (US)
filosofia [filozo'fia] *f* philosophy; **filósofo, -a** [fi'lɔzofu, a] *m/f* philosopher
filtrar [fiw'traʳ] *vt* to filter; **~-se** *vr* to filter; (*infiltrar-se*) to infiltrate
filtro ['fiwtru] *m* (*Tec*) filter
fim [fĩ] (*pl* **-ns**) *m* end; (*motivo*) aim, purpose; (*de história*, *filme*) ending; **a ~ de** in order to; **no ~ das contas** after all; **por ~** finally; **sem ~** endless; **levar ao ~** to carry through; **pôr** *ou* **dar ~ a** to put an end to; **ter ~** to come to an end; **~ de semana** weekend
finado, -a [fi'nadu, a] *adj*, *m/f* deceased; **dia dos F~s** day of the dead; *see boxed note*

final [fi'naw] (*pl* **-ais**) *adj* final, last ▷ *m* end; (*Mús*) finale ▷ *f* (*Esporte*) final;

finalista [fina'liʃta] *m/f* finalist;
finalizar [finali'zaʳ] *vt* to finish, conclude
finanças [fi'nãsaʃ] *fpl* finance *sg*; **financeiro, -a** [finã'sejru, a] *adj* financial ▷ *m/f* financier; **financiar** [finã'sjaʳ] *vt* to finance
fingimento [fiʒi'mẽtu] *m* pretence (BRIT), pretense (US)
fingir [fĩ'ʒiʳ] *vt* to feign ▷ *vi* to pretend; **~-se** *vr*: **~-se de** to pretend to be
finito, -a [fi'nitu, a] *adj* finite
finlandês, -esa [fĩlã'deʃ, eza] *adj* Finnish ▷ *m/f* Finn ▷ *m* (*Ling*) Finnish
Finlândia [fĩ'lãdʒia] *f*: **a ~** Finland
fino, -a ['finu, a] *adj* fine; (*delgado*) slender; (*educado*) polite; (*som*, *voz*) shrill; (*elegante*) refined ▷ *adv*: **falar ~** to talk in a high voice
fins [fĩʃ] *mpl de* **fim**
fio ['fiu] *m* thread; (*Bot*) fibre (BRIT), fiber (US); (*Elet*) wire; (*Tel*) line; (*de líquido*) trickle; (*gume*) edge; (*encadeamento*) series; **horas/dias a ~** hours/days on end
firewall [fajau'aw] *m* firewall
firma ['fixma] *f* signature; (*Com*) firm, company
firmar [fix'maʳ] *vt* to secure, make firm; (*assinar*) to sign; (*estabelecer*) to establish; (*basear*) to base ▷ *vi* (*tempo*) to settle; **~-se** *vr*: **~-se em** (*basear-se*) to rest on, be based on
firme ['fixmi] *adj* firm; (*estável*) stable; (*sólido*) solid; (*tempo*) settled ▷ *adv* firmly; **firmeza** [fix'meza] *f* firmness; stability; solidity
fiscal [fiʃ'kaw] (*pl* **-ais**) *m/f* supervisor; (*aduaneiro*) customs officer; (*de impostos*) tax inspector; **fiscalizar** [fiʃkali'zaʳ] *vt* to supervise; (*examinar*) to inspect, check
fisco ['fiʃku] *m*: **o ~** ≈ the Inland Revenue (BRIT), ≈ the Internal Revenue Service (US)
física ['fizika] *f* physics *sg*; *ver tb* **físico**
físico, -a ['fiziku, a] *adj* physical ▷ *m/f* (*cientista*) physicist ▷ *m* (*corpo*) physique
fisionomia [fizjono'mia] *f* (*rosto*) face; (*ar*) expression, look; (*aspecto de algo*) appearance
fissura [fi'sura] *f* crack
fita ['fita] *f* tape; (*tira*) strip, band; (*filme*) film; (*para máquina de escrever*) ribbon; **~ durex®** adhesive tape, sellotape® (BRIT), scotchtape® (US); **~ métrica** tape

measure

fitar [fi'ta^r] vt to stare at, gaze at

fivela [fi'vɛla] f buckle

fixar [fik'sa^r] vt to fix; (colar, prender) to stick; (data, prazo, regras) to set; (atenção) to concentrate; **~-se** vr: **~-se em** (assunto) to concentrate on; (detalhe) to fix on; (apegar-se a) to be attached to; **~ os olhos em** to stare at; **~ residência** to set up house

fixo, -a ['fiksu, a] adj fixed; (firme) firm; (permanente) permanent; (cor) fast

fiz etc [fiʒ] vb ver**fazer**

flagelado, -a [flaʒe'ladu, a] m/f: **os ~s** the afflicted, the victims

flagrante [fla'grãtʃi] adj flagrant; **apanhar em ~ (delito)** to catch red-handed ou in the act

flagrar [fla'gra^r] vt to catch

flanela [fla'nɛla] f flannel

flash [flaʃ] m (Foto) flash

flauta ['flawta] f flute

flecha ['flɛʃa] f arrow

fleu(g)ma ['flewma] f phlegm

floco ['flɔku] m flake; **~ de milho** cornflake; **~ de neve** snowflake

flor [flo^r] f flower; (o melhor): **a ~ de** the cream of, the pick of; **em ~** in bloom; **à ~ de** on the surface of

florescente [flore'sẽtʃi] adj (Bot) in flower; (próspero) flourishing

florescer [flore'se^r] vi (Bot) to flower; (prosperar) to flourish

floresta [flo'rɛʃta] f forest; **~ tropical** rainforest; **florestal** [floreʃ'taw] (pl **florestais**) adj forest atr

florido, -a [flo'ridu, a] adj (jardim) in flower

fluente [flu'ẽtʃi] adj fluent

fluido, -a ['flwidu, a] adj fluid ▷ m fluid

fluir [flwi^r] vi to flow

fluminense [flumi'nẽsi] adj from the state of Rio de Janeiro ▷ m/f native ou inhabitant of the state of Rio de Janeiro

flutuar [flu'twa^r] vi to float; (bandeira) to flutter; (fig: vacilar) to waver

fluvial [flu'vjaw] (pl **-ais**) adj river atr

fluxo ['fluksu] m (corrente) flow; (Elet) flux; **~ de caixa** (Com) cash flow

fobia [fo'bia] f phobia

foca ['fɔka] f seal

foco ['fɔku] m focus; (Med, fig) seat, centre (BRIT), center (US); **fora de ~, em/ fora de ~** out of focus, in/out of focus

fofo, -a ['fofu, a] adj soft; (col: pessoa) cute

fofoca [fo'fɔka] f piece of gossip; **fofocas** fpl (mexericos) gossip sg; **fofocar** [fofo'ka^r] vi to gossip

fogão [fo'gãw] (pl **-ões**) m stove, cooker

fogareiro [foga'rejru] m stove

foge etc ['fɔʒi] vb ver**fugir**

fogo ['fogu] m fire; (fig) ardour (BRIT), ardor (US); **você tem ~?** have you got a light?; **~s de artifício** fireworks; **pôr ~ a** to set fire to

fogões [fo'gõjʃ] mpl de**fogão**

fogueira [fo'gejra] f bonfire

foguete [fo'getʃi] m rocket

foi [foj] vb ver**ir; ser**

folclore [fowk'lɔri] m folklore

folclórico, -a [fowk'lɔriku, a] adj (música etc) folk; (comida, roupa) ethnic

fôlego ['folegu] m breath; (folga) breathing space; **perder o ~** to get out of breath

folga ['fɔwga] f rest, break; (espaço livre) clearance; (ócio) inactivity; (col: atrevimento) cheek; **dia de ~** day off; **folgado, -a** [fow'gadu, a] adj (roupa) loose; (vida) leisurely; (col: atrevido) cheeky; **folgar** [fow'ga^r] vt to loosen ▷ vi (descansar) to rest; (divertir-se) to have fun

folha ['foʎa] f leaf; (de papel, de metal) sheet; (página) page; (de faca) blade; (jornal) paper; **novo em ~** brand new; **~ de estanho** tinfoil (BRIT), aluminum foil (US); **~ de exercícios** worksheet

folhagem [fo'ʎaʒẽ] f foliage

folheto [fo'ʎetu] m booklet, pamphlet

fome ['fɔmi] f hunger; (escassez) famine; (fig: avidez) longing; **passar ~** to go hungry; **estar com** ou **ter ~** to be hungry

fone ['fɔni] m telephone, phone; (peça do telefone) receiver

fonte ['fõtʃi] f (nascente) spring; (chafariz) fountain; (origem) source; (Anat) temple

for etc [fo^r] vb ver**ir; ser**

fora[^1] ['fɔra] adv out, outside ▷ prep (além de) apart from ▷ m: **dar o ~** (bateria, radio) to give out; (pessoa) to leave, be off; **dar um ~** to slip up; **dar um ~ em/levar um ~** (namorado) to chuck ou dump/be given the boot; (esnobar) to snub sb/get the brush-off; **~ de** outside; **~ de si** beside o.s.; **estar ~** (viajando) to be away; **estar ~ (de casa)** (de casa) to be out; **lá ~** outside; (no exterior) abroad; **jantar ~** to eat out; **com os braços de ~** with bare arms; **ser de ~** to be from out of town; **ficar de ~** not to join in; **lá para ~** outside; **ir para ~** (viajar) to go out of town; **com a cabeça para ~ da janela** with one's head sticking out of the window; **costurar/cozinhar para ~** to do sewing/cooking for other people; **por ~** on the outside; **cobrar por ~** (*cobrar*) to charge extra, extra; **~ de dúvida** beyond doubt; **~ de propósito** irrelevant

fora² *etc vb ver* **ir; ser**

foragido, -a [fora'ʒidu, a] *adj, m/f* (*fugitivo*) fugitive

forasteiro, -a [foraʃ'tejru, a] *m/f* outsider, stranger; (*de outro país*) foreigner

força ['foxsa] *f* strength; (*Tec, Elet*) power; (*esforço*) effort; (*coerção*) force; **à ~** by force; **à ~ de** by dint of; **com ~** hard; **por ~ de** of necessity; **fazer ~** to try (hard); **~ de trabalho** workforce

forçado, -a [fox'sadu, a] *adj* forced; (*afetado*) false

forçar [fox'sa'] *vt* to force; (*olhos, voz*) to strain

forma ['fɔxma] *f* form; (*de um objeto*) shape; (*físico*) figure; (*maneira*) way; (*Med*) fitness; **desta ~** in this way; **de qualquer ~** anyway; **manter a ~** to keep fit

fôrma ['fɔxma] *f* (*Culin*) cake tin; (*molde*) mould (*BRIT*), mold (*US*)

formação [foxma'sãw] (*pl* -**ões**) *f* formation; (*antecedentes*) background; (*caráter*) make-up; (*profissional*) training

formado, -a [fox'madu, a] *adj* (*modelado*): **ser ~ de** to consist of ▷ *m/f* graduate

formal [fox'maw] (*pl* -**ais**) *adj* formal; **formalidade** [foxmali'dadʒi] *f* formality

formar [fox'ma'] *vt* to form; (*constituir*) to constitute, make up; (*educar*) to train; **~-se** *vr* to form; (*Educ*) to graduate

formatar [foxma'ta'] *vt* (*Comput*) to format

formidável [foxmi'davew] (*pl* -**eis**) *adj* tremendous, great

formiga [fox'miga] *f* ant

formigar [foxmi'ga'] *vi* to abound; (*sentir comichão*) to itch

formoso, -a [fox'mozu, ɔza] *adj* beautiful; (*esplêndido*) superb

fórmula ['fɔxmula] *f* formula

formular [foxmu'la'] *vt* to formulate; (*queixas*) to voice

formulário [foxmu'larju] *m* form; **formulários** *mpl*: **~s contínuos** (*Comput*) continuous stationery *sg*

fornecedor, a [foxnese'do', a] *m/f*

supplier ▷ *f* (*empresa*) supplier

fornecer [foxne'se'] *vt* to supply, provide; **fornecimento** [foxnesi'mẽtu] *m* supply

forno ['foxnu] *m* (*Culin*) oven; (*Tec*) furnace; (*para cerâmica*) kiln; **alto ~** blast furnace

foro ['foru] *m* forum; (*Jur*) Court of Justice; **foros** *mpl* (*privilégios*) privileges

forro ['foxu] *m* covering; lining

fortalecer [foxtale'se'] *vt* to strengthen

fortaleza [foxta'leza] *f* fortress; (*força*) strength; (*moral*) fortitude

forte ['fɔxtʃi] *adj* strong; (*pancada*) hard; (*chuva*) heavy; (*tocar*) loud; (*dor*) sharp ▷ *adv* strongly; (*tocar*) loud(ly) ▷ *m* fort; (*talento*) strength; **ser ~ em algo** (*versado*) to be good at sth *ou* strong in sth

fortuito, -a [fox'twitu, a] *adj* accidental

fortuna [fox'tuna] *f* fortune, (good) luck; (*riqueza*) fortune, wealth

fosco, -a ['foʃku, a] *adj* dull; (*opaco*) opaque

fósforo ['fɔʃforu] *m* match

fossa ['fɔsa] *f* pit

fosse *etc* ['fosi] *vb ver* **ir; ser**

fóssil ['fɔsiw] (*pl* -**eis**) *m* fossil

fosso ['fosu] *m* trench, ditch

foto ['fɔtu] *f* photo

fotocópia [foto'kɔpja] *f* photocopy; **fotocopiadora** [fotokopja'dora] *f* photocopier; **fotocopiar** [fotoko'pja'] *vt* to photocopy

fotografar [fotogra'fa'] *vt* to photograph

fotografia [fotogra'fia] *f* photography; (*uma fotografia*) photograph

fotógrafo, -a [fo'tɔgrafu, a] *m/f* photographer

foz [fɔʒ] *f* mouth of river

fração [fra'sãw] (*pl* -**ões**) *f* fraction

fracassar [fraka'sa'] *vi* to fail; **fracasso** [fra'kasu] *m* failure

fracção [fra'sãw] (*PT*) *f* = **fração**

fraco, -a ['fraku, a] *adj* weak; (*sol, som*) faint

fractura *etc* [fra'tura] (*PT*) *f* = **fratura** *etc*

frágil ['fraʒiw] (*pl* -**eis**) *adj* (*débil*) fragile; (*Com*) breakable; (*pessoa*) frail; (*saúde*) delicate, poor

fragmento [frag'mẽtu] *m* fragment

fragrância [fra'grãsja] *f* fragrance, perfume

fralda ['frawda] *f* (*da camisa*) shirt tail; (*para bebê*) nappy (*BRIT*), diaper (*US*); (*de montanha*) foot

framboesa [frã'beza] f raspberry

França ['frãsa] f France

francamente [frãka'mẽtʃi] adv (abertamente) frankly; (realmente) really

francês, -esa [frã'seʃ, eza] adj French ▷ m/f Frenchman/woman ▷ m (Ling) French

franco, -a ['frãku, a] adj frank; (isento de pagamento) free; (óbvio) clear ▷ m franc; **entrada franca** free admission

frango ['frãgu] m chicken

franja ['frãʒa] f fringe (BRIT), bangs pl (US)

franquia [frã'kia] f (Com) franchise; (isenção) exemption

franzino, -a [frã'zinu, a] adj skinny

fraqueza [fra'keza] f weakness

frasco ['fraʃku] m bottle

frase ['frazi] f sentence; **~ feita** set phrase

fratura [fra'tura] f fracture, break; **fraturar** [fratu'ra'] vt to fracture

freada [fre'ada] (BR) f: **dar uma ~** to slam on the brakes

frear [fre'a'] (BR) vt to curb, restrain; (veículo) to stop ▷ vi (veículo) to brake

freezer ['frize'] m freezer

freguês, -guesa [fre'geʃ, 'geza] m/f customer; (PT) parishioner; **freguesia** [frege'zia] f customers pl; parish

freio ['freju] m (BR: de veículo) brake; (de cavalo) bridle; (bocado do freio) bit; **~ de mão** handbrake

freira ['frejra] f nun

frenesi [frene'zi] m frenzy; **frenético, -a** [fre'nɛtʃiku, a] adj frantic, frenzied

frente ['frẽtʃi] f front; (rosto) face; (fachada) façade; **~ a ~** face to face; **de ~ para** facing; **em ~ de** in front of; (de frente a) opposite; **para a ~** ahead, forward; **porta da ~** front door; **seguir em ~** to go straight on; **na minha** (ou **sua** etc) **~** in front of me (ou you etc); **sair da ~** to get out of the way; **pra ~** (col) fashionable, trendy

freqüência [fre'kwẽsja] f frequency; **com ~** often, frequently

freqüentar [frekwẽ'ta'] vt to frequent

freqüente [fre'kwẽtʃi] adj frequent

fresco, -a ['freʃku, a] adj fresh; (vento, tempo) cool; (col: efeminado) camp; (: afetado) pretentious; (: cheio de luxo) fussy ▷ m (ar) fresh air

frescobol [freʃko'bɔw] m (kind of) racketball (played mainly on the beach)

frescura [freʃ'kura] f freshness; (frialdade) coolness; (col: luxo) fussiness;

(: afetaçao) pretentiousness

frete ['frɛtʃi] m (carregamento) freight, cargo; (tarifa) freightage

frevo ['frevu] m improvised Carnival dance

fria ['fria] f: **dar uma ~ em alguém** to give sb the cold shoulder; **estar/entrar numa ~** (col) to be in/get into a mess

fricção [frik'sãw] f friction; (ato) rubbing; (Med) massage; **friccionar** [friksjo'na'] vt to rub

frieza ['frjeza] f coldness; (indiferença) coolness

frigideira [friʒi'dejra] f frying pan

frigorífico [frigo'rifiku] m refrigerator; (congelador) freezer

frio, -a ['friu, a] adj cold ▷ m cold; **frios** mpl (Culin) cold meats; **estou com ~** I'm cold; **faz** ou **está ~** it's cold

frisar [fri'za'] vt (encrespar) to curl; (salientar) to emphasize

fritar [fri'ta'] vt to fry

fritas ['fritas] fpl chips (BRIT), French fries (US)

frito, -a ['fritu, a] adj fried; (col): **estar ~** to be done for

frívolo, -a ['frivolu, a] adj frivolous

fronha ['froɲa] f pillowcase

fronteira [frõ'tejra] f frontier, border

frota ['frota] f fleet

frouxo, -a ['froʃu, a] adj loose; (corda, fig: pessoa) slack; (fraco) weak; (col: condescendente) soft

frustrar [fruʃ'tra'] vt to frustrate

fruta ['fruta] f fruit; **frutífero, -a** [fru'tʃiferu, a] adj (proveitoso) fruitful; (árvore) fruit-bearing

fruto ['frutu] m (Bot) fruit; (resultado) result, product; **dar ~** (fig) to bear fruit

fubá [fu'ba] m corn meal

fugir [fu'ʒi'] vi to flee, escape; (prisioneiro) to escape

fui [fuj] vb ver **ir; ser**

fulano, -a [fu'lanu, a] m/f so-and-so

fulminante [fuwmi'nãtʃi] adj devastating; (palavras) scathing

fulo, -a ['fulu, a] adj: **estar** ou **ficar ~ de raiva** to be furious

fumaça [fu'masa] (BR) f (de fogo) smoke; (de gás) fumes pl

fumador, a [fuma'do', a] (PT) m/f smoker

fumante [fu'mãtʃi] m/f smoker

fumar [fu'ma'] vt, vi to smoke

fumo ['fumu] m (PT: de fogo) smoke; (: de gás) fumes pl; (BR: tabaco) tobacco; (fumar) smoking

função [fũ'sãw] (pl **-ões**) f function; (ofício) duty; (papel) role; (espetáculo) performance

funcionalismo [fũsjona'liʒmu] m: **~ público** civil service

funcionamento [fũsjona'mẽtu] m functioning, working; **pôr em ~** to set going, start

funcionar [fũsjo'na^r] vi to function; (máquina) to work, run; (dar bom resultado) to work

funcionário, -a [fũsjo'narju, a] m/f official; **~ (público)** civil servant

funções [fũ'sõjʃ] fpl de **função**

fundação [fũda'sãw] (pl **-ões**) f foundation

fundamental [fũdamẽ'taw] (pl **-ais**) adj fundamental, basic

fundamento [fũda'mẽtu] m (fig) foundation, basis; (motivo) motive

fundar [fũ'da^r] vt to establish, found; (basear) to base; **~-se** vr: **~-se em** to be based on

fundir [fũ'dʒi^r] vt to fuse; (metal) to smelt, melt down; (Com: empresas) to merge; (em molde) to cast; **~-se** vr to melt; (juntar-se) to merge

fundo, -a ['fũdu, a] adj deep; (fig) profound ▷ m (do mar, jardim) bottom; (profundidade) depth; (base) basis; (da loja, casa, do papel) back; (de quadro) background; (de dinheiro) fund ▷ adv deeply; **fundos** mpl (Com) funds; (da casa etc) back sg; **a ~** thoroughly; **no ~** at the bottom; (da casa etc) at the back; (fig) basically

fúnebre ['funebri] adj funeral atr, funereal; (fig) gloomy

funeral [fune'raw] (pl **-ais**) m funeral

funil [fu'niw] (pl **-is**) m funnel

furacão [fura'kãw] (pl **-ões**) m hurricane

furado, -a [fu'radu, a] adj perforated; (pneu) flat; (orelha) pierced

furão, -rona [fu'rãw, 'rɔna] (pl **furões/ -s**) m ferret ▷ m/f (col) go-getter ▷ adj (col) hard-working, dynamic

furar [fu'ra^r] vt to perforate; (orelha) to pierce; (penetrar) to penetrate; (frustrar) to foil; (fila) to jump ▷ vi (col: programa) to fall through

fúria ['furja] f fury, rage; **furioso, -a** [fu'rjozu, ɔza] adj furious

furo ['furu] m hole; (num pneu) puncture

furões [fu'rõjʃ] mpl de **furão**

furona [fu'rɔna] f de **furão**

furor [fu'ro^r] m fury, rage; **fazer ~** to be

all the rage

furtar [fux'ta^r] vt, vi to steal; **~-se** vr: **~-se a** to avoid

furtivo, -a [fux'tʃivu, a] adj furtive, stealthy

furto ['fuxtu] m theft

fusível [fu'zivew] (pl **-eis**) m (Elet) fuse

fuso ['fuzu] m (Tec) spindle; **~ horário** time zone

fusões [fu'zõjʃ] fpl de **fusão**

futebol [futʃi'bɔw] m football; **~ de salão** five-a-side football

futevôlei [futʃi'volej] m see boxed note

fútil ['futʃiw] (pl **-eis**) adj (pessoa) shallow; (insignificante) trivial

futilidade [futʃili'dadʒi] f (de pessoa) shallowness; (insignificância) triviality; (coisa) trivial thing

futuro, -a [fu'turu, a] adj future ▷ m future; **no ~** in the future

fuzil [fu'ziw] (pl **-is**) m rifle; **fuzilar** [fuzi'la^r] vt to shoot

fuzis [fu'ziʃ] mpl de **fuzil**

g

g. abr (= grama) gr.

gabar [ga'ba^r] vt to praise; **~-se** vr: **~-se de** to boast about

gabinete [gabi'netʃi] m (Com) office; (escritório) study; (Pol) cabinet

gado ['gadu] m livestock; (bovino) cattle; **~ leiteiro** dairy cattle; **~ suíno** pigs pl

gafanhoto [gafa'ɲotu] m grasshopper

gafe ['gafi] f gaffe, faux pas

gagueira [ga'gejra] f stutter

gaguejar [gage'ʒa^r] vi to stammer, stutter

gaiato, -a [ga'jatu, a] adj funny

gaiola [ga'jɔla] f cage; (cadeia) jail ▷ m (barco) riverboat

gaita ['gajta] f harmonica; **~ de foles** bagpipes pl

gaivota [gaj'vɔta] f seagull

gajo ['gaʒu] (PT: col) m guy, fellow

gala ['gala] f: **traje de ~** evening dress; **festa de ~** gala

galão [ga'lãw] (pl -ões) m (Mil) stripe; (medida) gallon; (PT: café) white coffee; (passamanaria) braid

Galápagos [ga'lapaguʃ]: **(as) Ilhas ~** fpl (the) Galapagos Islands

galáxia [ga'laksja] m galaxy

galera [ga'lɛra] f (Náut) galley; (col:

pessoas, público) crowd

galeria [gale'ria] f gallery; (Teatro) circle

Gales ['galiʃ] m: **País de ~** Wales

galho ['gaʎu] m (de árvore) branch

galinha [ga'liɲa] f hen; (Culin) chicken; **galinheiro** [gali'ɲejru] m hen-house

galo ['galu] m cock, rooster; (inchação) bump; **missa do ~** midnight mass

galões [ga'lõjʃ] mpl de **galão**

galopar [galo'pa^r] vi to gallop; **galope** [ga'lɔpi] m gallop

gama ['gama] f (Mús) scale; (fig) range; (Zool) doe

gambá [gã'ba] m (Zool) opossum

Gana ['gana] m Ghana

gana ['gana] f craving, desire; (ódio) hate; **ter ~s de (fazer) algo** to feel like (doing) sth; **ter ~ de alguém** to hate sb

ganância [ga'nãsja] f greed; **ganancioso, -a** [ganã'sjozu, ɔza] adj greedy

gancho ['gãʃu] m hook; (de calça) crotch

gangue ['gãgi] (col) f gang

ganhador, a [gaɲa'do^r, a] adj winning ▷ m/f winner

ganha-pão ['gaɲa-] (pl -ães) m living, livelihood

ganhar [ga'ɲa^r] vt to win; (salário) to earn; (adquirir) to get; (lugar) to reach; (lucrar) to gain ▷ vi to win; **~ de alguém** (num jogo) to beat sb; **ganho, -a** ['gaɲu, a] pp de **ganhar** ▷ m profit, gain; **ganhos** mpl (ao jogo) winnings

ganso, -a ['gãsu, a] m/f gander/goose

garagem [ga'raʒẽ] (pl -ns) f garage

garantia [garã'tʃia] f guarantee; (de dívida) surety

garçom [gax'sõ] (BR): (pl -ns) m waiter

garçonete [gaxso'netʃi] (BR) f waitress

garçons [gax'sõʃ] mpl de **garçom**

garfo ['gaxfu] m fork

gargalhada [gaxga'ʎada] f burst of laughter; **rir às ~s** to roar with laughter; **dar ou soltar uma ~** to burst out laughing

gargalo [gax'galu] m (tb fig) bottleneck

garganta [gax'gãta] f throat; (Geo) gorge, ravine

gargarejo [gaxga'reʒu] m (ato) gargling; (líquido) gargle

gari ['gari] m/f (na rua) roadsweeper (BRIT), streetsweeper (US); (lixeiro) dustman (BRIT), garbage man (US)

garoa [ga'roa] f drizzle; **garoar** [ga'rwa^r] vi to drizzle

garotada [garo'tada] f: **a ~** the kids pl

garoto, -a [ga'rotu, a] *m/f* boy/girl;
(*namorado*) boyfriend/girlfriend ▷ *m* (PT:
café) coffee with milk
garoupa [ga'ropa] *f* (*peixe*) grouper
garrafa [ga'xafa] *f* bottle
garupa [ga'rupa] *f* (*de cavalo*)
hindquarters *pl*; (*de moto*) back seat;
andar na ~ (*de moto*) to ride pillion
gás [gajʃ] *m* gas; **gases** *mpl* (*do intestino*)
wind *sg*; **~ natural** natural gas
gasóleo [ga'zɔlju] *m* diesel oil
gasolina [gazo'lina] *f* petrol (BRIT),
gas(oline) (US)
gasosa [ga'zɔza] *f* fizzy drink
gasoso, -a [ga'zozu, ɔza] *adj* (*água*)
sparkling; (*bebida*) fizzy
gastador, -deira [gaʃta'doʳ, 'dejra] *adj*,
m/f spendthrift
gastar [gaʃ'taʳ] *vt* to spend; (*gasolina*,
eletricidade) to use; (*roupa, sapato*) to wear
out; (*salto, piso etc*) to wear down; (*saúde*)
to damage; (*desperdiçar*) to waste ▷ *vi* to
spend; to wear out; to wear down; **~-se**
vr to wear out; to wear down
gata ['gata] *f* (she-)cat
gatilho [ga'tʃiʎu] *m* trigger
gato ['gatu] *m* cat; **~ montês** wild cat
gatuno, -a [ga'tunu, a] *adj* thieving
▷ *m/f* thief
gaveta [ga'veta] *f* drawer
geada ['ʒjada] *f* frost
geladeira [ʒela'dejra] *f* (BR) refrigerator,
icebox (US)
gelado, -a [ʒe'ladu, a] *adj* frozen ▷ *m* (PT:
sorvete) ice cream
gelar [ʒe'laʳ] *vt* to freeze; (*vinho etc*) to
chill ▷ *vi* to freeze
gelatina [ʒela'tʃina] *f* gelatine;
(*sobremesa*) jelly (BRIT), jello (US)
geléia [ʒe'lɛja] *f* jam
gélido, -a ['ʒɛlidu, a] *adj* chill, icy
gelo ['ʒelu] *adj inv* light grey (BRIT) *ou*
gray (US) ▷ *m* ice; (*cor*) light grey (BRIT)
ou gray (US)
gema ['ʒɛma] *f* yolk; (*pedra preciosa*) gem
gêmeo, -a ['ʒemju, a] *adj, m/f* twin;
Gêmeos *mpl* (*Astrologia*) Gemini *sg*
gemer [ʒe'meʳ] *vi* (*de dor*) to groan, moan;
(*lamentar-se*) to wail; (*animal*) to whine;
(*vento*) to howl; **gemido** [ʒe'midu] *m*
groan, moan; wail; whine
gene ['ʒeni] *m* gene
Genebra [ʒe'nɛbra] *n* Geneva
general [ʒene'raw] (*pl* **-ais**) *m* general
generalizar [ʒenerali'zaʳ] *vt* to
propagate ▷ *vi* to generalize; **~-se** *vr* to

become general, spread
gênero ['ʒeneru] *m* type, kind; (*Bio*)
genus; (*Ling*) gender; **gêneros** *mpl*
(*produtos*) goods; **~s alimentícios**
foodstuffs; **~ humano** humankind,
human race
generosidade [ʒenerozi'dadʒi] *f*
generosity
generoso, -a [ʒene'rozu, ɔza] *adj*
generous
genética [ʒe'nɛtʃika] *f* genetics *sg*
gengibre [ʒẽ'ʒibri] *m* ginger
gengiva [ʒẽ'ʒiva] *f* (*Anat*) gum
genial [ʒe'njaw] (*pl* **-ais**) *adj* inspired,
brilliant; (*col*) terrific, fantastic
gênio ['ʒenju] *m* (*temperamento*) nature;
(*irascibilidade*) temper; (*talento, pessoa*)
genius; **de bom/mau ~** good-natured/
bad-tempered
genital [ʒeni'taw] (*pl* **-ais**) *adj*: **órgãos
genitais** genitals *pl*
genro ['ʒẽxu] *m* son-in-law
gente ['ʒẽtʃi] *f* people *pl*; (*col*) folks *pl*,
family; (: *alguém*): **tem ~ batendo à
porta** there's somebody knocking at the
door; **a ~** (*nós: suj*) we; (: *objeto*) us; **a casa
da ~** our house; **toda a ~** everybody; **~
grande** grown-ups *pl*
gentil [ʒẽ'tʃiw] (*pl* **-is**) *adj* kind; **gentileza**
[ʒẽtʃi'leza] *f* kindness; **por gentileza**
if you please; **tenha a gentileza de
fazer ...?** would you be so kind as to do ...?
genuíno, -a [ʒe'nwinu, a] *adj* genuine
geografia [ʒeogra'fia] *f* geography
geometria [ʒeome'tria] *f* geometry
geração [ʒera'sãw] (*pl* **-ões**) *f* generation
gerador, a [ʒera'doʳ, a] *m/f* (*produtor*)
creator ▷ *m* (*Tec*) generator
geral [ʒe'raw] (*pl* **-ais**) *adj* general
▷ *f* (*Teatro*) gallery; **em ~** in general,
generally; **de um modo ~** on the
whole; **geralmente** [ʒeraw'mẽtʃi] *adv*
generally, usually
gerânio [ʒe'ranju] *m* geranium
gerar [ʒe'raʳ] *vt* to produce; (*eletricidade*)
to generate
gerência [ʒe'rẽsja] *f* management;
gerenciar [ʒerẽ'sjaʳ] *vt, vi* to manage
gerente [ʒe'rẽtʃi] *adj* managing ▷ *m/f*
manager
gerir [ʒe'riʳ] *vt* to manage, run
germe ['ʒɛxmi] *m* (*embrião*) embryo;
(*micróbio*) germ
gesso ['ʒesu] *m* plaster (of Paris)
gesticular [ʒeʃtʃiku'laʳ] *vi* to make
gestures, gesture

gesto ['ʒɛʃtu] m gesture
Gibraltar [ʒibraw'taʳ] f Gibraltar
gigante, -ta [ʒi'gãtʃi, ta] adj gigantic, huge ▷ m giant; **gigantesco, -a** [ʒigã'teʃku, a] adj gigantic
gim [ʒĩ] (pl **-ns**) m gin
ginásio [ʒi'nazju] m gymnasium; (escola) secondary (BRIT) ou high (US) school
ginástica [ʒi'naʃtʃika] f gymnastics sg; (para fortalecer o corpo) keep-fit
ginecologia [ʒinekolo'ʒia] f gynaecology (BRIT), gynecology (US)
ginecologista [ʒinekolo'ʒiʃta] m/f gynaecologist (BRIT), gynecologist (US)
ginjinha [ʒĩ'ʒiɲa] (PT) f cherry brandy
gira-discos ['ʒira-] (PT) m inv record-player
girafa [ʒi'rafa] f giraffe
girar [ʒi'raʳ] vt to turn, rotate; (como pião) to spin ▷ vi to go round; to spin; (vaguear) to wander
girassol [ʒira'sɔw] (pl **-óis**) m sunflower
gíria ['ʒirja] f (calão) slang; (jargão) jargon
giro¹ ['ʒiru] m turn; **dar um ~** to go for a wander; (em veículo) to go for a spin; **que ~!** (PT) terrific!
giro² etc vb ver **gerir**
giz [ʒiʃ] m chalk
glacê [gla'se] m icing
glacial [gla'sjaw] (pl **-ais**) adj icy
glamouroso, -a [glamu'rozu, ɔza] adj glamorous
glândula ['glãdula] f gland
global [glo'baw] (pl **-ais**) adj global; (total) overall; **quantia ~** lump sum; **globalização** [globaliza'sãw] (pl **globalizações**) f globalization
globo ['globu] m globe; **~ ocular** eyeball
glória ['glɔrja] f glory; **glorificar** [glorifi'kaʳ] vt to glorify; **glorioso, -a** [glo'rjozu, ɔza] adj glorious
glossário [glo'sarju] m glossary
gnomo ['gnomu] m gnome
goiaba [go'jaba] f guava; **goiabada** [goja'bada] f guava jelly
gol [gow] (pl **-s**) m goal
gola ['gɔla] f collar
gole ['gɔli] m gulp, swallow; (pequeno) sip; **tomar um ~ de** to sip
goleiro [go'lejru] (BR) m goalkeeper
golfe ['gowfi] m golf; **campo de ~** golf course
golfinho [gow'fiɲu] m (Zool) dolphin
golfo ['gowfu] m gulf
golinho [go'liɲu] m sip; **beber algo aos ~s** to sip sth

golo ['golu] (PT) m = **gol**
golpe ['gɔwpi] m (tb fig) blow; (de mão) smack; (de punho) punch; (manobra) ploy; (de vento) gust; **de um só ~** at a stroke; **dar um ~ em alguém** to hit sb; (fig: trapacear) to trick sb; **~ (de estado)** coup (d'état); **~ de mestre** masterstroke; **golpear** [gow'pjaʳ] vt to hit; (com navalha) to stab; (com o punho) to punch
goma ['goma] f gum, glue; (de roupa) starch; **~ de mascar** chewing gum
gomo ['gomu] m (de laranja) slice
gordo, -a ['goxdu, a] adj fat; (gordurento) greasy; (carne) fatty; (fig: quantia) considerable, ample ▷ m/f fat man/woman
gordura [gox'dura] f fat; (derretida) grease; (obesidade) fatness; **gorduroso, -a** [goxdu'rozu, ɔza] adj (pele) greasy; (comida) fatty
gorila [go'rila] m gorilla
gorjeta [gox'ʒeta] f tip, gratuity
gorro ['goxu] m cap; (de lã) hat
gosma ['gɔʒma] f spittle; (fig: quantia) slime
gostar [goʃ'taʳ] vi: **~ de** to like; (férias, viagem etc) to enjoy; **~-se** vr to like each other; **~ mais de ...** to prefer ..., like ... better
gosto ['goʃtu] m taste; (prazer) pleasure; **a seu ~** to your liking; **com ~** willingly; (vestir-se) tastefully; (comer) heartily; **de bom/mau ~** in good/bad taste; **ter ~ de** to taste of; **gostoso, -a** [goʃ'tozu, ɔza] adj tasty; (agradável) pleasant; (cheiro) lovely; (risada) good; (col: pessoa) gorgeous
gota ['gota] f drop; (de suor) bead; (Med) gout; **~ a ~** drop by drop
goteira [go'tejra] f (cano) gutter; (buraco) leak
gourmet [gux'me] (pl **-s**) m/f gourmet
governador, a [govexnadoʳ, a] m/f governor
governamental [govexname'taw] (pl **-ais**) adj government atr
governante [govex'nãtʃi] adj ruling ▷ m/f ruler ▷ f governess
governar [govex'naʳ] vt to govern, rule; (barco) to steer
governo [go'vexnu] m government; (controle) control
gozação [goza'sãw] (pl **-ões**) f enjoyment; (zombaria) teasing; (uma gozação) joke
gozado, -a [go'zadu, a] adj funny; (estranho) strange, odd

gozar [go'za^r] vt to enjoy; (col: rir de) to make fun of ▷ vi to enjoy o.s.; **~ de** to enjoy; to make fun of; **gozo** ['gozu] m (prazer) pleasure; (uso) enjoyment, use; (orgasmo) orgasm

Grã-Bretanha [grã-bre'taɲa] f Great Britain

graça ['grasa] f (Rel) grace; (charme) charm; (gracejo) joke; (Jur) pardon; **de ~** (grátis) for nothing; (sem motivo) for no reason; **sem ~** dull, boring; **fazer ou ter ~** to be funny; **ficar sem ~** to be embarrassed; **~s a** thanks to

gracejar [grase'ʒa^r] vi to joke; **gracejo** [gra'seʒu] m joke

gracioso, -a [gra'sjozu, ɔza] adj (pessoa) charming; (gestos) gracious

grade ['gradʒi] f (no chão) grating; (grelha) grill; (na janela) bars pl; (col: cadeia) nick, clink

gradear [gra'dʒja^r] vt (janela) to put bars up at; (jardim) to fence off

graduação [gradwa'sãw] (pl -ões) f (classificação) grading; (Educ) graduation; (Mil) rank

gradual [gra'dwaw] (pl -ais) adj gradual

graduar [gra'dwa^r] vt (classificar) to grade; (luz, fogo) to regulate; **~-se** vr to graduate

gráfica ['grafika] f graphics sg; ver tb **gráfico**

gráfico, -a ['grafiku, a] adj graphic ▷ m/f printer ▷ m (Mat) graph; (diagrama) diagram, chart; **gráficos** mpl (Comput) graphics; **~ de barras** bar chart

grã-fino, -a [grã'finu, a] (col) adj posh ▷ m/f nob, toff

grama ['grama] m gramme ▷ f (BR: capim) grass

gramado [gra'madu] (BR) m lawn; (Futebol) pitch

gramática [gra'matʃika] f grammar

grampear [grã'pja^r] vt to staple

grampo ['grãpu] m staple; (no cabelo) hairgrip; (de carpinteiro) clamp; (de chapéu) hatpin

grande ['grãdʒi] adj big, large; (alto) tall; (notável, intenso) great; (longo) long; (adulto) grown-up; **mulher ~** big woman; **~ mulher** great woman; **grandeza** [grã'deza] f size; (fig) greatness; (ostentação) grandeur

grandioso, -a [grã'dʒjozu, ɔza] adj magnificent, grand

granito [gra'nitu] m granite

granizo [gra'nizu] m hailstone; **chover**

~ to hail; **chuva de ~** hailstorm

granulado, -a [granu'ladu, a] adj grainy; (açúcar) granulated

grão ['grãw] (pl ~s) m grain; (semente) seed; (de café) bean; **grão-de-bico** (pl **grãos-de-bico**) m chickpea

gratidão [gratʃi'dãw] f gratitude

gratificar [gratʃifi'ka^r] vt to tip; (dar bônus a) to give a bonus to; (recompensar) to reward

grátis ['gratʃiʃ] adj free

grato, -a ['gratu, a] adj grateful; (agradável) pleasant

gratuito, -a [gra'twitu, a] adj (grátis) free; (infundado) gratuitous

grau [graw] m degree; (nível) level; (Educ) class; **em alto ~** to a high degree; **ensino de primeiro/segundo ~** primary (BRIT) ou elementary (US) /secondary education

gravação [grava'sãw] f (em madeira) carving; (em disco, fita) recording

gravador [grava'do^r] m tape recorder; **~ de CD/DVD** CD/DVD burner, CD/DVD writer

gravar [gra'va^r] vt to carve; (metal, pedra) to engrave; (na memória) to fix; (disco, fita) to record

gravata [gra'vata] f tie; **~ borboleta** bow tie

grave ['gravi] adj serious; (tom) deep; **gravemente** [grave'mẽtʃi] adv (doente, ferido) seriously

grávida ['gravida] adj pregnant

gravidade [gravi'dadʒi] f gravity

gravidez [gravi'deʒ] f pregnancy

gravura [gra'vura] f (em madeira) engraving; (estampa) print

graxa ['graʃa] f (para sapatos) polish; (lubrificante) grease

Grécia ['grɛsja] f: **a ~** Greece; **grego, -a** ['gregu, a] adj, m/f Greek ▷ m (Ling) Greek

grelha ['greʎa] f grill; (de fornalha) grate; **bife na ~** grilled steak; **grelhado** [gre'ʎadu] m (prato) grill

grêmio ['gremju] m (associação) guild; (clube) club

grená [gre'na] adj, m dark red

greve ['grevi] f strike; **fazer ~** to go on strike; **~ branca** go-slow; **grevista** [gre'viʃta] m/f striker

grilo ['grilu] m cricket; (Auto) squeak; (col: de pessoa) hang-up; **qual é o ~?** what's the matter?; **não tem ~!** (col) (there's) no problem!

gringo, -a ['grĩgu, a] (col: pej) m/f
foreigner

gripado, -a [gri'padu, a] adj: **estar/ficar
~** to have/get a cold

gripe ['gripi] f flu, influenza

grisalho, -a [gri'zaʎu, a] adj (cabelo) grey
(BRIT), gray (US)

gritante [gri'tãtʃi] adj (hipocrisia) glaring;
(desigualdade) gross; (mentira) blatant;
(cor) loud, garish

gritar [gri'taʳ] vt to shout, yell ▷ vi
to shout; (de dor, medo) to scream; **~
com alguém** to shout at sb; **gritaria**
[grita'ria] f shouting, din; **grito** ['gritu]
m shout; (de medo) scream; (de dor) cry;
(de animal) call; **dar um grito** to cry out;
falar/protestar aos gritos to shout/
shout protests

Groenlândia [grwẽ'lãdʒja] f: **a ~**
Greenland

grosseiro, -a [gro'sejru, a] adj rude;
(piada) crude; (modos, tecido) coarse;
grosseria [grose'ria] f rudeness; (ato):
fazer uma grosseria to be rude; (dito):
dizer uma grosseria to be rude, say
something rude

grosso, -a ['grosu, 'grɔsa] adj thick;
(áspero) rough; (voz) deep; (col: pessoa,
piada) rude ▷ m: **o ~ de** the bulk of;
grossura [gro'sura] f thickness

grotesco, -a [gro'teʃku, a] adj grotesque

grudar [gru'daʳ] vt to glue, stick ▷ vi to
stick

grude ['grudʒi] f glue; **grudento, -a**
[gru'dẽtu, a] adj sticky

grunhir [gru'niʳ] vi (porco) to grunt;
(tigre) to growl; (resmungar) to grumble

grupo ['grupu] m group

guarda ['gwaxda] m/f policeman/
woman ▷ f (vigilância) guarding; (de
objeto) safekeeping ▷ m (Mil) guard;
estar de ~ to be on guard; **pôr-se em ~**
to be on one's guard; **a G~ Civil** the Civil
Guard; **guarda-chuva** (pl **guarda-
chuvas**) m umbrella; **guarda-costas**
m inv (Náut) coastguard boat; (capanga)
bodyguard; **guardados** [gwax'daduʃ]
mpl keepsakes, valuables; **guarda-fogo**
(pl **guarda-fogos**) m fireguard; **guarda-
louça** [gwaxda'losa] (pl **guarda-
louças**) m sideboard; **guardanapo**
[gwaxda'napu] m napkin; **guarda-
noturno** (pl **guardas-noturnos**) m
night watchman; **guardar** [gwax'daʳ]
vt to put away; (zelar por) to guard;
(lembrança, segredo) to keep; **guardar-se**

vr (defender-se) to protect o.s.; **guardar-
se de** (acautelar-se) to guard against;
guarda-redes (PT) m inv goalkeeper;
guarda-roupa (pl **guarda-roupas**) m
wardrobe; **guarda-sol** (pl **guarda-sóis**)
m sunshade, parasol

guardião, -diã [gwax'dʒjãw, 'dʒjã]
(pl **guardiães** or **guardiões/-s**) m/f
guardian

guarnição [gwaxni'sãw] (pl **-ões**) f (Mil)
garrison; (Náut) crew; (Culin) garnish

Guatemala [gwate'mala] f: **a ~**
Guatemala

gude ['gudʒi] m: **bola de ~** marble; (jogo)
marbles pl

guerra ['gexa] f war; **em ~** at war; **fazer ~**
to wage war; **~ civil** civil war; **~ mundial**
world war; **~ civil/mundial** civil/world
war; **guerreiro, -a** [ge'xejru, a] adj
(espírito) fighting; (belicoso) warlike ▷ m
warrior

guerrilha [ge'xiʎa] f (luta) guerrilla
warfare; (tropa) guerrilla band;
guerrilheiro, -a [gexi'ʎejru, a] m/f
guerrilla

guia ['gia] f guidance; (Com) permit, bill of
lading; (formulário) advice slip ▷ m (livro)
guide(book) ▷ m/f (pessoa) guide

Guiana ['gjana] f: **a ~** Guyana

guiar [gjaʳ] vt to guide; (Auto) to drive ▷ vi
to drive; **~-se** vr: **~-se por** to go by

guichê [gi'ʃe] m ticket window; (em
banco, repartição) window, counter

guinada [gi'nada] f: **dar uma ~** (com o
carro) to swerve

guindaste [gi'daʃtʃi] m hoist, crane

guisado [gi'zadu] m stew

guitarra [gi'taxa] f (electric) guitar

guloso, -a [gu'lozu, ɔza] adj greedy

h

há [a] *vb ver* **haver**
hábil ['abiw] (*pl* **-eis**) *adj* competent, capable; (*astucioso, esperto*) clever; (*sutil*) diplomatic; **em tempo ~** in reasonable time; **habilidade** [abili'dadʒi] *f* skill, ability; (*astúcia, esperteza*) shrewdness; (*tato*) discretion; **habilidoso, -a** [abili'dozu, ɔza] *adj* skilled, clever
habilitação [abilita'sãw] (*pl* **-ões**) *f* competence; (*ato*) qualification; **habilitações** *fpl* (*conhecimentos*) qualifications
habilitar [abili'ta'] *vt* to enable; (*dar direito a*) to qualify, entitle; (*preparar*) to prepare
habitação [abita'sãw] (*pl* **-ões**) *f* dwelling, residence; (*alojamento*) housing
habitante [abi'tãtʃi] *m/f* inhabitant
habitar [abi'ta'] *vt* to live in; (*povoar*) to inhabit ▷ *vi* to live
hábito ['abitu] *m* habit; (*social*) custom; (*Rel: traje*) habit
habituado, -a [abi'twadu, a] *adj*: **~ a (fazer) algo** used to (doing) sth
habituar [abi'twa'] *vt*: **~ alguém a** to get sb used to, accustom sb to; **~-se** *vr*: **~-se a** to get used to
hacker ['ake'] (*pl* **-s**) *m* (*Comput*) hacker

Haia ['aja] *n* the Hague
haja *etc* ['aʒa] *vb ver* **haver**
hálito ['alitu] *m* breath
hall [xɔw] (*pl* **-s**) *m* hall; (*de teatro, hotel*) foyer; **~ de entrada** entrance hall
hambúrguer [ã'buxge'] *m* hamburger
hão [ãw] *vb ver* **haver**
hardware ['xadwe'] *m* (*Comput*) hardware
harmonia [axmo'nia] *f* harmony
harmonioso, -a [axmo'njozu, ɔza] *adj* harmonious
harmonizar [axmoni'za'] *vt* (*Mús*) to harmonize; (*conciliar*): **~ algo (com algo)** to reconcile sth (with sth); **~-se** *vr*: **~(-se)** (*idéias etc*) to coincide; (*pessoas*) to be in agreement
harpa ['axpa] *f* harp
Havaí [ava'i] *m*: **o ~** Hawaii

 PALAVRA CHAVE

haver [a've'] *vb aux* **1** (*ter*) to have; **ele havia saído/comido** he had left/eaten
2: **haver de: quem haveria de dizer que ...** who would have thought that ...
▷ *vb impess* **1** (*existência*): **há** (*sg*) there is; (*pl*) there are; **o que é que há?** what's the matter?; **o que é que houve?** what happened?, what was that?; **não há de quê** don't mention it, you're welcome; **haja o que houver** come what may
2 (*tempo*): **há séculos/cinco dias que não o vejo** I haven't seen him for ages/five days; **há um ano que ela chegou** it's a year since she arrived; **há cinco dias (atrás)** five days ago
haver-se *vr*: **haver-se com alguém** to sort things out with sb
▷ *m* (*Com*) credit; **haveres** *mpl* (*pertences*) property *sg*, possessions; (*riqueza*) wealth *sg*

haxixe [a'ʃiʃi] *m* hashish
hebraico, -a [e'brajku, a] *adj* Hebrew ▷ *m* (*Ling*) Hebrew
Hébridas ['ɛbridaʃ] *fpl*: **as (ilhas) ~** the Hebrides
hediondo, -a [e'dʒjõdu, a] *adj* vile, revolting; (*crime*) heinous
hei [ej] *vb ver* **haver**
hélice ['ɛlisi] *f* propeller
helicóptero [eli'kɔpteru] *m* helicopter
hematoma [ema'tɔma] *m* bruise
hemorragia [emoxa'ʒia] *f* haemorrhage (*BRIT*), hemorrhage (*US*);

~ nasal nosebleed
hemorróidas [emo'xɔjdaʃ] *fpl*
haemorrhoids (BRIT), hemorrhoids (US),
piles
hepatite [epa'tʃitʃi] *f* hepatitis
hera ['ɛra] *f* ivy
herança [e'rãsa] *f* inheritance; (*fig*)
heritage
herdar [ex'da^r] *vt*: **~ algo (de)** to inherit
sth (from); **~ a** to bequeath to
herdeiro, -a [ex'dejru, a] *m/f* heir(ess)
herói [e'rɔj] *m* hero
heroína [ero'ina] *f* heroine; (*droga*)
heroin
hesitação [ezita'sãw] *f* (*pl* -**ões**)
hesitation
hesitante [ezi'tãtʃi] *adj* hesitant
hesitar [ezi'ta^r] *vi* to hesitate
heterossexual [eterosek'swaw] (*pl* -**ais**)
adj, m/f heterosexual
híbrido, -a ['ibridu, a] *adj* hybrid
hidratante [idra'tãtʃi] *m* moisturizer
hidráulico, -a [i'drawliku, a] *adj*
hydraulic
hidrelétrico, -a [idre'lɛtriku, a] (*PT* -**ct-**)
adj hydroelectric
hidro... [idru] *prefixo* hydro..., water... *atr*
hidrogênio [idro'ʒenju] *m* hydrogen
hífen ['ifẽ] (*pl* -**s**) *m* hyphen
higiene [i'ʒjeni] *f* hygiene; **higiênico, -a**
[i'ʒjeniku, a] *adj* hygienic; (*pessoa*) clean;
papel higiênico toilet paper
hindu [ĩ'du] *adj, m/f* Hindu
hino ['inu] *m* hymn; **~ nacional** national
anthem
hipermercado [ipexmex'kadu] *m*
hypermarket
hipertensão [ipextẽ'sãw] *f* high blood
pressure
hipismo [i'piʒmu] *m* (*turfe*) horse racing;
(*equitação*) (horse) riding
hipocrisia [ipokri'sia] *f* hypocrisy;
hipócrita [i'pɔkrita] *adj* hypocritical
▷ *m/f* hypocrite
hipódromo [i'pɔdromu] *m* racecourse
hipopótamo [ipo'pɔtamu] *m*
hippopotamus
hipoteca [ipo'tɛka] *f* mortgage;
hipotecar [ipote'ka^r] *vt* to mortgage
hipótese [i'pɔtezi] *f* hypothesis; **na ~ de**
in the event of; **em ~ alguma** under no
circumstances; **na melhor/pior das ~s**
at best/worst
hispânico, -a [iʃ'paniku, a] *adj* Hispanic
histeria [iʃte'ria] *f* hysteria; **histérico, -a**
[iʃ'tɛriku, a] *adj* hysterical

história [iʃ'tɔrja] *f* history; (*conto*) story;
histórias *fpl* (*chateação*) bother *sg*,
fuss *sg*; **isso é outra ~** that's a different
matter; **que ~ é essa?** what's going
on?; **historiador, a** [iʃtorja'do^r, a] *m/f*
historian; **histórico, -a** [iʃ'tɔriku, a]
adj historical; (*fig: notável*) historic ▷ *m*
history
hobby ['xɔbi] (*pl* -**bies**) *m* hobby
hoje ['oʒi] *adv* today; (*tb*: **~ em dia**)
now(adays); **~ à noite** tonight
Holanda [o'lãda] *f*: **a ~** Holland;
holandês, -esa [olã'deʃ, eza] *adj* Dutch
▷ *m/f* Dutchman/woman ▷ *m* (*Ling*)
Dutch
holocausto [olo'kawʃtu] *m* holocaust
homem ['omẽ] (*pl* -**ns**) *m* man; (*a
humanidade*) mankind; **~ de empresa**
ou **negócios** businessman; **~ de
estado** statesman; **homem-bomba** (*pl*
homens-bomba) *m* suicide bomber
homenagear [omena'ʒja^r] *vt* (*pessoa*) to
pay tribute to, honour (BRIT), honor (US)
homenagem [ome'naʒẽ] *f* tribute; (*Rel*)
homage; **prestar ~ a alguém** to pay
tribute to sb
homens ['omẽʃ] *mpl de* **homem**
homeopático, -a [omjo'patʃiku] *adj*
homoeopathic
homicida [omi'sida] *adj* homicidal
▷ *m/f* murderer; **homicídio** [omi'sidʒju]
m murder; **homicídio involuntário**
manslaughter
homologar [omolo'ga^r] *vt* to ratify
homólogo, -a [o'mɔlogu, a] *adj*
homologous; (*fig*) equivalent ▷ *m/f*
opposite number
homossexual [omosek'swal] (*pl* -**ais**)
adj, m/f homosexual
Honduras [õ'duraʃ] *f* Honduras
honestidade [oneʃtʃi'dadʒi] *f* honesty;
(*decência*) decency; (*justeza*) fairness
honesto, -a [o'nɛʃtu, a] *adj* honest;
(*decente*) decent; (*justo*) fair, just
honorário, -a [ono'rarju, a] *adj*
honorary; **honorários** [ono'rarjuʃ] *mpl*
fees
honra ['õxa] *f* honour (BRIT), honor (US);
em ~ de in hono(u)r of
honrado, -a [õ'xadu, a] *adj* honest;
(*respeitado*) honourable (BRIT),
honorable (US)
honrar [õ'xa^r] *vt* to honour (BRIT), honor
(US)
honroso, -a [õ'xozu, ɔza] *adj*
hono(u)rable

hóquei ['ɔkej] *m* hockey; **~ sobre gelo** ice hockey

hora ['ɔra] *f* (*60 minutos*) hour; (*momento*) time; **a que ~s?** (at) what time?; **que ~s são?** what time is it?; **são duas ~s** it's two o'clock; **você tem as ~s?** have you got the time?; **fazer ~** to kill time; **de ~ em ~** every hour; **na ~** on the spot; **chegar na ~** to be on time; **de última ~** *adj* last-minute ▷ *adv* at the last minute; **meia ~** half an hour; **~s extras** overtime *sg*; **horário, -a** [o'rarju, a] *adj*: **100 km horários** 100 km an hour ▷ *m* timetable; (*hora*) time; **horário de expediente** working hours *pl*; (*de um escritório*) office hours *pl*

horizontal [orizõ'taw] (*pl* **-ais**) *adj* horizontal

horizonte [ori'zõtʃi] *m* horizon

horóscopo [o'rɔʃkopu] *m* horoscope

horrível [o'xivew] (*pl* **-eis**) *adj* awful, horrible

horror [o'xoʳ] *m* horror; **que ~!** how awful!; **ter ~ a algo** to hate sth; **horrorizar** [oxori'zaʳ] *vt* to horrify, frighten; **horroroso, -a** [oxo'rozu, ɔza] *adj* horrible, ghastly

hortaliças [oxta'lisaʃ] *fpl* vegetables

hortelã [oxte'lã] *f* mint; **~ pimenta** peppermint

horticultor, a [oxtʃikuw'toʳ, a] *m/f* market gardener (*BRIT*), truck farmer (*US*)

hortifrutigranjeiros [oxtʃifrutʃigrã-'ʒejruʃ] *mpl* fruit and vegetables

horto ['oxtu] *m* market garden (*BRIT*), truck farm (*US*)

hospedagem [oʃpe'daʒẽ] *f* guest house

hospedar [oʃpe'daʳ] *vt* to put up; **~-se** *vr* to stay, lodge; **hospedaria** [oʃpeda'ria] *f* guest house

hóspede ['oʃpedʒi] *m* (*amigo*) guest; (*estranho*) lodger

hospedeira [oʃpe'dejra] *f* landlady; (*PT*: *de bordo*) stewardess, air hostess (*BRIT*)

hospício [oʃ'pisju] *m* mental hospital

hospital [oʃpi'taw] (*pl* **-ais**) *m* hospital

hospitalidade [oʃpitali'dadʒi] *f* hospitality

hostil [oʃ'tʃiw] (*pl* **-is**) *adj* hostile; **hostilizar** [oʃtʃili'zaʳ] *vt* to antagonize; (*Mil*) to wage war on

hotel [o'tew] (*pl* **-éis**) *m* hotel; **hoteleiro, -a** [ote'lejru, a] *m/f* hotelier

houve *etc* ['ovi] *vb ver* **haver**

humanidade [umani'dadʒi] *f* (*os homens*) man(kind); (*compaixão*) humanity

humanitário, -a [umani'tarju, a] *adj* humane

humano, -a [u'manu, a] *adj* human; (*bondoso*) humane

húmido, -a (*PT*) *adj* = **úmido**

humildade [umiw'dadʒi] *f* humility; (*pobreza*) poverty

humilde [u'miwdʒi] *adj* humble; (*pobre*) poor

humilhar [umi'ʎaʳ] *vt* to humiliate

humor [u'moʳ] *m* mood, temper; (*graça*) humour (*BRIT*), humor (*US*); **de bom/mau ~** in a good/bad mood; **humorista** [umo'riʃta] *m/f* comedian; **humorístico, -a** [umo'riʃtʃiku, a] *adj* humorous

húngaro, -a ['ũgaru, a] *adj, m/f* Hungarian

Hungria [ũ'gria] *f*: **a ~** Hungary

hurra ['uxa] *m* cheer ▷ *excl* hurrah!

I

ia etc ['ia] vb ver **ir**
iate ['jatʃi] m yacht; **~ clube** yacht club
ibérico, -a [i'bɛriku, a] adj, m/f Iberian
ibero-americano, -a [iberu-] adj, m/f
Ibero-American
ICM (BR) abr m (= Imposto sobre Circulação
de Mercadorias) ≈ VAT
ícone [i'kɔni] m (gen, Comput) icon
ida ['ida] f going, departure; **~ e volta**
round trip, return; **a (viagem de) ~** the
outward journey; **na ~** on the way there
idade [i'dadʒi] f age; **ter cinco anos de ~**
to be five (years old); **de meia ~** middle-
aged; **qual é a ~ dele?** how old is he?; **na
minha ~** at my age; **ser menor/maior
de ~** to be under/of age; **pessoa de ~**
elderly person; **I~ Média** Middle Ages pl
ideal [ide'jaw] (pl **-ais**) adj, m ideal;
idealista [idea'liʃta] adj idealistic ▷ m/f
idealist
idéia [i'dɛja] f idea; (mente) mind; **mudar
de ~** to change one's mind; **não ter a
mínima ~** to have no idea; **não faço ~** I
can't imagine; **estar com ~ de fazer** to
plan to do
idem ['idẽ] pron ditto
idêntico, -a [i'dẽtʃiku, a] adj identical
identidade [idẽtʃi'dadʒi] f identity

identificação [idẽtʃifika'sãw] f
identification
identificar [idẽtʃifi'kaʳ] vt to identify;
~-se vr: **~-se com** to identify with
idioma [i'dʒɔma] m language
idiota [i'dʒɔta] adj idiotic ▷ m/f idiot
ido, -a ['idu, a] adj past
ídolo ['idolu] m idol
idoso, -a [i'dozu, ɔza] adj elderly, old
ignorado, -a [igno'radu, a] adj unknown
ignorância [igno'rãsja] f ignorance;
ignorante [igno'rãtʃi] adj ignorant,
uneducated ▷ m/f ignoramus
ignorar [igno'raʳ] vt not to know; (não
dar atenção a) to ignore
igreja [i'greʒa] f church
igual [i'gwaw] (pl **-ais**) adj equal;
(superfície) even ▷ m/f equal
igualar [igwa'laʳ] vt to equal; (fazer igual)
to make equal; (nivelar) to level ▷ vi: **~ a
ou com** to be equal to, be the same as;
(ficar no mesmo nível) to be level with; **~-se**
vr: **~-se a alguém** to be sb's equal
igualdade [igwaw'dadʒi] f equality;
(uniformidade) uniformity
igualmente [igwaw'mẽtʃi] adv equally;
(também) likewise, also; **~!** (saudação) the
same to you!
ilegal [ile'gaw] (pl **-ais**) adj illegal
ilegítimo, -a [ile'ʒitʃimu, a] adj
illegitimate; (ilegal) unlawful
ilegível [ile'ʒivew] (pl **-eis**) adj illegible
iletrado, -a [ile'tradu, a] adj illiterate
ilha ['iʎa] f island; **ilhéu, ilhoa** [i'ʎɛw,
i'ʎoa] m/f islander
ilícito, -a [i'lisitu, a] adj illicit
ilimitado, -a [ilimi'tadu, a] adj
unlimited
iluminar [ilumi'naʳ] vt to light up;
(estádio etc) to floodlight; (fig) to
enlighten
ilusão [ilu'zãw] (pl **-ões**) f illusion;
(quimera) delusion; **ilusório, -a**
[ilu'zɔrju, a] adj deceptive
ilustração [iluʃtra'sãw] (pl **-ões**) f
illustration
ilustrado, -a [iluʃ'tradu, a] adj
illustrated; (erudito) learned
ilustrar [iluʃ'traʳ] vt to illustrate;
(instruir) to instruct
ilustre [i'luʃtri] adj illustrious; **um ~
desconhecido** a complete stranger
ímã ['imã] m magnet
imagem [i'maʒẽ] (pl **-ns**) f image;
(semelhança) likeness; (TV) picture;
imagens fpl (Literatura) imagery sg

imaginação [imaʒina'sãw] (pl -ões) f
imagination

imaginar [imaʒi'naʳ] vt to imagine;
(supor) to suppose; **~-se** vr to imagine
o.s.; **imagine só!** just imagine!;
imaginário, -a [imaʒi'narju, a] adj
imaginary

imaturo, -a [ima'turu, a] adj immature

imbatível [ĩba'tʃivew] (pl -eis) adj
invincible

imbecil [ĩbe'siw] (pl -is) adj stupid ▷ m/f
imbecile; **imbecilidade** [ĩbesili'dadʒi]
f stupidity

imediações [imedʒa'sõjʃ] fpl vicinity sg,
neighbourhood sg (BRIT), neighborhood
sg (US)

imediatamente [imedʒata'mẽtʃi] adv
immediately, right away

imediato, -a [ime'dʒatu, a] adj
immediate; (seguinte) next; **~ a** next to;
de ~ straight away

imenso, -a [i'mẽsu, a] adj immense,
huge; (ódio, amor) great

imigração [imigra'sãw] (pl -ões) f
immigration

imigrante [imi'grãtʃi] adj, m/f
immigrant

iminente [imi'nẽtʃi] adj imminent

imitação [imita'sãw] (pl -ões) f
imitation

imitar [imi'taʳ] vt to imitate; (assinatura)
to copy

imobiliária [imobi'ljarja] f estate
agent's (BRIT), real estate broker's (US)

imobiliário, -a [imobi'ljarju, a] adj
property atr

imobilizar [imobili'zaʳ] vt to
immobilize; (fig) to bring to a standstill

imoral [imo'raw] (pl -ais) adj immoral

imortal [imox'taw] (pl -ais) adj immortal

imóvel [i'mɔvew] (pl -eis) adj
motionless, still; (não movediço)
immovable ▷ m property; (edifício)
building; **imóveis** mpl (propriedade) real
estate sg, property sg

impaciência [ĩpa'sjẽsja] f impatience;
impacientar-se [ĩpasjẽ'taxsi] vr to lose
one's patience; **impaciente** [ĩpa'sjẽtʃi]
adj impatient

impacto [ĩ'paktu] (PT -cte) m impact

ímpar [ĩ'paʳ] adj (número) odd; (sem igual)
unique, unequalled

imparcial [ĩpax'sjaw] (pl -ais) adj fair,
impartial

impecável [ĩpe'kavew] (pl -eis) adj
perfect, impeccable

impeço etc [ĩ'pɛsu] vb ver **impedir**

impedido, -a [ĩpe'dʒidu, a] adj (Futebol)
offside; (PT: Tel) engaged (BRIT), busy (US)

impedimento [ĩpedʒi'mẽtu] m
impediment

impedir [ĩpe'dʒiʳ] vt to obstruct; (estrada,
tráfego) to block; (movimento, progresso)
to impede; **~ alguém de fazer algo** to
prevent sb from doing sth; (proibir) to
forbid sb to do sth; **~ (que aconteça)
algo** to prevent sth (happening)

impenetrável [ĩpene'travew] (pl -eis)
adj impenetrable

impensado, -a [ĩpẽ'sadu, a]
adj thoughtless; (não calculado)
unpremeditated; (imprevisto) unforeseen

imperador [ĩpera'doʳ] m emperor

imperativo, -a [ĩpera'tʃivu, a] adj
imperative ▷ m imperative

imperatriz [ĩpera'triʒ] f empress

imperdoável [ĩpex'dwavew] (pl -eis) adj
unforgivable, inexcusable

imperfeito, -a [ĩpex'fejtu, a] adj
imperfect ▷ m (Ling) imperfect (tense)

imperial [ĩpe'rjaw] (pl -ais) adj imperial

imperícia [ĩpe'risja] f inability;
(inexperiência) inexperience

império [ĩ'perju] m empire

impermeável [ĩpex'mjavew] (pl -eis)
adj: **~ a** (tb fig) impervious to; (à água)
waterproof ▷ m raincoat

impessoal [ĩpe'swaw] (pl -ais) adj
impersonal

ímpeto [ĩ'petu] m (Tec) impetus;
(movimento súbito) start; (de cólera) fit; (de
emoção) surge; (de chamas) fury; **agir com
~** to act on impulse; **levantar-se num ~**
to get up with a start

impiedoso, -a [ĩpje'dozu, ɔza] adj
merciless, cruel

implacável [ĩpla'kavew] (pl -eis) adj
relentless; (pessoa) unforgiving

implantação [ĩplãta'sãw] (pl -ões) f
introduction; (Med) implant

implementar [ĩplemẽ'taʳ] vt to
implement

implicar [ĩpli'kaʳ] vt (envolver) to
implicate; (pressupor) to imply ▷ vi: **~ com
alguém** (chatear) to tease sb, pick on sb;
~-se vr to get involved; **~ (em) algo** to
involve sth

implícito, -a [ĩ'plisitu, a] adj implicit

implorar [ĩplo'raʳ] vt: **~ (algo a alguém)**
to beg ou implore (sb for sth)

impopular [ĩpopu'laʳ] adj unpopular;
impopularidade [ĩpopulari'dadʒi] f

unpopularity
impor [ĩ'poʳ] (*irreg: como* **pôr**) *vt* to impose; (*respeito*) to command; **~-se** *vr* to assert o.s.; **~ algo a alguém** to impose sth on sb
importação [impoxta'sãw] (*pl* **-ões**) *f* (*ato*) importing; (*mercadoria*) import
importador, a [ĩpoxta'doʳ, a] *adj* import *atr* ▷ *m/f* importer
importância [ĩpox'tãsja] *f* importance; (*de dinheiro*) sum, amount; **não tem ~** it doesn't matter, never mind; **ter ~** to be important; **sem ~** unimportant; **importante** [ĩpox'tãtʃi] *adj* important ▷ *m*: **o (mais) importante** the (most) important thing
importar [ĩpox'taʳ] *vt* (*Com*) to import; (*trazer*) to bring in; (*causar: prejuízos etc*) to cause; (*implicar*) to imply, involve ▷ *vi* to matter, be important; **~-se** *vr*: **~-se com algo** to mind sth; **não me importo** I don't care
importunar [ĩpoxtu'naʳ] *vt* to bother, annoy
importuno, -a [ĩpox'tunu, a] *adj* annoying; (*inoportuno*) inopportune ▷ *m/f* nuisance
impossibilitado, -a [ĩposibili'tadu, a] *adj*: **~ de fazer** unable to do
impossibilitar [ĩposibili'taʳ] *vt*: **~ algo** to make sth impossible; **~ alguém de fazer, ~ a alguém fazer** to prevent sb doing; **~ algo a alguém, ~ alguém para algo** to make sth impossible for sb
impossível [ĩpo'sivew] (*pl* **-eis**) *adj* impossible; (*insuportável: pessoa*) insufferable; (*incrível*) incredible
imposto [ĩ'poʃtu] *m* tax; **antes/depois de ~s** before/after tax; **~ de renda** (BR) income tax; **~ predial** rates *pl*; **I~ sobre Circulação de Mercadorias (e Serviços)** (BR), **~ sobre valor acrescentado** (PT) value added tax (BRIT), sales tax (US)
impotente [ĩpo'tẽtʃi] *adj* powerless; (*Med*) impotent
impraticável [ĩpratʃi'kavew] (*pl* **-eis**) *adj* impracticable; (*rua, rio etc*) impassable
impreciso, -a [ĩpre'sizu, a] *adj* vague; (*falto de rigor*) inaccurate
imprensa [ĩ'prẽsa] *f* printing; (*máquina, jornais*) press
imprescindível [ĩpresĩ'dʒivew] (*pl* **-eis**) *adj* essential, indispensable
impressão [impre'sãw] (*pl* **-ões**) *f* impression; (*de livros*) printing; (*marca*) imprint; **causar boa ~** to make a good impression; **ficar com/ter a ~ (de) que** to get/have the impression that
impressionante [ĩpresjo'nãtʃi] *adj* impressive
impressionar [ĩpresjo'naʳ] *vt* to affect ▷ *vi* to be impressive; (*pessoa*) to make an impression; **~-se** *vr*: **~-se (com algo)** to be moved (by sth)
impresso, -a [ĩ'prɛsu, a] *pp de* **imprimir** ▷ *adj* printed ▷ *m* (*para preencher*) form; (*folheto*) leaflet; **impressos** *mpl* (*formulário*) printed matter *sg*
impressões [impre'sõjʃ] *fpl de* **impressão**
impressora [ĩpre'sora] *f* printing machine; (*Comput*) printer; **~ matricial/a laser** dot-matrix/laser printer
imprestável [ĩpreʃ'tavew] (*pl* **-eis**) *adj* (*inútil*) useless; (*pessoa*) unhelpful
imprevisível [ĩprevi'zivew] (*pl* **-eis**) *adj* unforeseeable
imprevisto, -a [ĩpre'viʃtu, a] *adj* unexpected, unforeseen ▷ *m*: **um ~** something unexpected
imprimir [ĩpri'miʳ] *vt* to print; (*marca*) to stamp; (*infundir*) to instil (BRIT), instill (US); (*Comput*) to print out
impróprio, -a [ĩ'prɔprju, a] *adj* inappropriate; (*indecente*) improper
improvável [ĩpro'vavew] (*pl* **-eis**) *adj* unlikely
improviso [ĩpro'vizu]: **de ~** *adv* (*de repente*) suddenly; (*sem preparação*) without preparation
imprudente [ĩpru'dẽtʃi] *adj* (*irrefletido*) rash; (*motorista*) careless
impulsivo, -a [ĩpuw'sivu, a] *adj* impulsive
impulso [ĩ'puwsu] *m* impulse; (*fig: estímulo*) urge
impune [ĩ'puni] *adj* unpunished; **impunidade** [ĩpuni'dadʒi] *f* impunity
imundície [imũ'dʒisji] *f* filth; **imundo, -a** [i'mũdu, a] *adj* filthy; (*obsceno*) dirty
imune [i'muni] *adj*: **~ a** immune to; **imunidade** [imuni'dadʒi] *f* immunity
inábil [i'nabiw] (*pl* **-eis**) *adj* incapable; (*desajeitado*) clumsy
inabitado, -a [inabi'tadu, a] *adj* uninhabited
inacabado, -a [inaka'badu, a] *adj* unfinished
inacreditável [inakredʒi'tavew] (*pl* **-eis**) *adj* unbelievable, incredible
inactivo, -a [ina'tivu, a] (PT)

= **inativo/a**

inadequado, -a [inade'kwadu, a] *adj*
inadequate; (*impróprio*) unsuitable

inadiável [ina'dʒjavew] (*pl* -eis) *adj*
pressing

inadimplência [inadʒĩ'plẽsja] *f* (*Jur*)
breach of contract, default

inaptidão [inapt'ʃi'dãw] (*pl* -ões) *f*
inability

inatingível [inat'ʃĩ'ʒivew] (*pl* -eis) *adj*
unattainable

inativo, -a [ina't'ʃivu, a] *adj* inactive;
(*aposentado, reformado*) retired

inauguração [inawgura'sãw] (*pl* -ões)
f inauguration; (*de exposição*) opening;
inaugural [inawgu'raw] (*pl* -ais) *adj*
inaugural; **inaugurar** [inawgu'ra'] *vt* to
inaugurate; (*exposição*) to open

incapacidade [ĩkapasi'dadʒi]
f incapacity; (*incompetência*)
incompetence

incapacitado, -a [ĩkapasi'tadu, a] *adj*
(*inválido*) disabled, handicapped ▷ *m/f*
handicapped person; **estar ~ de fazer** to
be unable to do

incapaz [ĩka'pajʒ] *adj*, *m/f* incompetent;
~ de fazer incapable of doing; **~ para**
unfit for

incendiar [ĩse'dʒja'] *vt* to set fire to; (*fig*)
to inflame; **~-se** *vr* to catch fire

incêndio [ĩ'sẽdʒju] *m* fire; **~ criminoso**
ou **premeditado** arson

incenso [ĩ'sẽsu] *m* incense

incentivar [ĩsẽt'ʃi'va'] *vt* to stimulate,
encourage

incentivo [ĩsẽ't'ʃivu] *m* incentive; **~
fiscal** tax incentive

incerteza [ĩsex'teza] *f* uncertainty

incerto, -a [ĩ'sɛxtu, a] *adj* uncertain

incesto [ĩ'sɛstu] *m* incest

inchado, -a [ĩ'ʃadu, a] *adj* swollen; (*fig*)
conceited

inchar [ĩ'ʃa'] *vt*, *vi* to swell

incidência [ĩsi'dẽsja] *f* incidence,
ocurrence

incidente [ĩsi'dẽt'ʃi] *m* incident

incisivo, -a [ĩsi'zivu, a] *adj* cutting,
sharp; (*fig*) incisive

incitar [ĩsi'ta'] *vt* to incite; (*pessoa,
animal*) to drive on

inclinação [ĩklina'sãw] (*pl* -ões) *f*
inclination; **~ da cabeça** nod

inclinar [ĩkli'na'] *vt* to tilt; (*cabeça*) to
nod ▷ *vi* to slope; (*objeto*) to tilt; **~-se** *vr*
to tilt; (*dobrar o corpo*) to bow, stoop; **~-se
sobre algo** to lean over sth

incluir [ĩ'klwi'] *vt* to include; (*em carta*) to
enclose; **~-se** *vr* to be included

inclusão [ĩklu'zãw] *f* inclusion;
inclusive [ĩklu'zivi] *prep* including ▷ *adv*
inclusive; (*até mesmo*) even

incoerente [ĩkoe'rẽt'ʃi] *adj* incoherent;
(*contraditório*) inconsistent

incógnita [ĩ'kɔgnita] *f* (*Mat*) unknown;
(*fato incógnito*) mystery; **incógnito,
-a** [ĩ'kɔgnitu, a] *adj* unknown ▷ *adv*
incognito

incolor [ĩko'lo'] *adj* colourless (*BRIT*),
colorless (*US*)

incomodar [ĩkomo'da'] *vt* to bother,
trouble; (*aborrecer*) to annoy ▷ *vi* to be
bothersome; **~-se** *vr* to bother, put o.s.
out; **~-se com algo** to be bothered by
sth, mind sth; **não se incomode!** don't
worry!

incômodo, -a [ĩ'komodu, a] *adj*
uncomfortable; (*incomodativo*)
troublesome; (*inoportuno*) inconvenient

incompetente [ĩkõpe'tẽt'ʃi] *adj*, *m/f*
incompetent

incompreendido, -a [ĩkõprjẽ'dʒidu, a]
adj misunderstood

incomum [ĩko'mũ] *adj* uncommon

incomunicável [ĩkomuni'kavew] (*pl*
-eis) *adj* cut off; (*privado de comunicação,
fig*) incommunicado; (*preso*) in solitary
confinement

inconformado, -a [ĩkõfox'madu, a] *adj*
bitter; **~ com** unreconciled to

inconfundível [ĩkõfũ'dʒivew] (*pl* -eis)
adj unmistakeable

inconsciência [ĩkõ'sjẽsja] *f* (*Med*)
unconsciousness; (*irreflexão*)
thoughtlessness

inconsciente [ĩkõ'sjẽt'ʃi] *adj*
unconscious ▷ *m* unconscious

inconseqüente [ĩkõse'kwẽt'ʃi] *adj*
inconsistent; (*contraditório*) illogical;
(*irresponsável*) irresponsible

inconsistente [ĩkõsiʃ'tẽt'ʃi] *adj*
inconsistent; (*sem solidez*) runny

inconstante [ĩkõʃ'tãt'ʃi] *adj* fickle;
(*tempo*) changeable

incontrolável [ĩkõtro'lavew] (*pl* -eis) *adj*
uncontrollable

inconveniência [ĩkõve'njẽsja]
f inconvenience; (*impropriedade*)
inappropriateness

inconveniente [ĩkõve'njẽt'ʃi] *adj*
inconvenient; (*inoportuno*) awkward;
(*grosseiro*) rude; (*importuno*) annoying
▷ *m* disadvantage; (*obstáculo*) difficulty,

problem

incorreto, -a [ĩko'xɛtu, a] (PT **-ect-**) *adj* incorrect; (*desonesto*) dishonest

incrédulo, -a [ĩ'krɛdulu, a] *adj* incredulous; (*cético*) sceptical (BRIT), skeptical (US) ▷ *m/f* sceptic (BRIT), skeptic (US)

incrível [ĩ'krivew] (*pl* **-eis**) *adj* incredible

incumbência [ĩkũ'bẽsja] *f* task, duty

incumbir [ĩkũ'bi'] *vt*: ~ **alguém de algo** *ou* **algo a alguém** to put sb in charge of sth ▷ *vi*: ~ **a alguém** to be sb's duty; ~**-se** *vr*: ~**-se de** to undertake, take charge of

indagação [ĩdaga'sãw] (*pl* **-ões**) *f* investigation; (*pergunta*) inquiry, question

indagar [ĩda'ga'] *vt* to investigate ▷ *vi* to inquire; ~**-se** *vr*: ~**-se a si mesmo** to ask o.s.; ~ **algo de alguém** to ask sb about sth

indecente [ĩde'sẽtʃi] *adj* indecent, improper; (*obsceno*) rude, vulgar

indecoroso, -a [ĩdeko'rozu, ɔza] *adj* indecent, improper

indefinido, -a [ĩdefi'nidu, a] *adj* indefinite; (*vago*) vague, undefined; **por tempo ~** indefinitely

indelicado, -a [ĩdeli'kadu, a] *adj* impolite, rude

indenização [indeniza'sãw] (PT **-mn-**) (*pl* **-ões**) *f* compensation; (*Com*) indemnity

indenizar [ĩdeni'za'] (PT **-mn-**) *vt*: ~ **alguém por** *ou* **de algo** (*compensar*) to compensate sb for sth; (*por gastos*) to reimburse sb for sth

independência [ĩdepẽ'dẽsja] *f* independence; **independente** [ĩdepẽ'dẽtʃi] *adj* independent

indesejável [ĩdeze'ʒavew] (*pl* **-eis**) *adj* undesirable

indevido, -a [ĩde'vidu, a] *adj* (*imerecido*) unjust; (*impróprio*) inappropriate

Índia [ˈĩdʒa] *f*: **a ~** India; **as ~s Ocidentais** the West Indies; **indiano, -a** [ĩ'dʒjanu, a] *adj, m/f* Indian

indicação [ĩdʒika'sãw] (*pl* **-ões**) *f* indication; (*de termômetro*) reading; (*para um cargo, prêmio*) nomination; (*recomendação*) recommendation; (*de um caminho*) directions *pl*

indicado, -a [ĩdʒi'kadu, a] *adj* appropriate

indicador, a [ĩdʒika'do', a] *adj*: ~ **de** indicative of ▷ *m* indicator; (*Tec*) gauge; (*dedo*) index finger; (*ponteiro*) pointer

indicar [ĩdʒi'ka'] *vt* to indicate; (*apontar*) to point to; (*temperatura*) to register; (*recomendar*) to recommend; (*para um cargo*) to nominate; (*determinar*) to determine; ~ **o caminho a alguém** to give sb directions

índice [ˈĩdʒisi] *m* (*de livro*) index; (*taxa*) rate

indício [in'dʒisju] *m* (*sinal*) sign; (*vestígio*) trace; (*Jur*) clue

indiferença [ĩdʒife'rẽsa] *f* indifference; **indiferente** [ĩdʒife'rẽtʃi] *adj* indifferent; **isso me é indiferente** it's all the same to me

indígena [ĩ'dʒiʒena] *adj, m/f* native; (*índio: da América*) Indian

indigência [ĩdʒi'ʒẽsja] *f* poverty; (*fig*) lack, need

indigestão [ĩdʒiʒeʃ'tãw] *f* indigestion

indigesto, -a [ĩdʒi'ʒɛʃtu, a] *adj* indigestible

indignação [ĩdʒigna'sãw] *f* indignation; **indignado, -a** [ĩdʒig'nadu, a] *adj* indignant

indignar [ĩdʒig'na'] *vt* to anger, incense; ~**-se** *vr* to get angry

índio, -a [ˈĩdʒju, a] *adj, m/f* (*da América*) Indian; **o Oceano Í~** the Indian Ocean

indireto, -a [ĩdʒi'rɛtu, a] (PT **-ct-**) *adj* indirect

indiscreto, -a [ĩdʒiʃ'krɛtu, a] *adj* indiscreet

indiscutível [ĩdʒiʃku'tʃivew] (*pl* **-eis**) *adj* indisputable

indispensável [ĩdʒiʃpẽ'savew] (*pl* **-eis**) *adj* essential, vital ▷ *m*: **o ~** the essentials *pl*

indispor [ĩdʒiʃ'po'] (*irreg: como* **pôr**) *vt* (*de saúde*) to make ill; (*aborrecer*) to upset; **indisposto, -a** [ĩdʒiʃ'poʃtu, 'pɔʃta] *adj* unwell, poorly; upset

indistinto, -a [ĩdʒiʃ'tʃĩtu, a] *adj* indistinct

individual [ĩdʒivi'dwaw] (*pl* **-ais**) *adj* individual

indivíduo [ĩdʒi'vidwu] *m* individual; (*col: sujeito*) guy

indócil [ĩ'dɔsiw] (*pl* **-eis**) *adj* unruly, wayward; (*impaciente*) restless

índole [ˈĩdoli] *f* (*temperamento*) nature; (*tipo*) sort, type

indolor [ĩdo'lo'] *adj* painless

Indonésia [ĩdo'nɛzja] *f*: **a ~** Indonesia

indústria [ĩ'duʃtrja] *f* industry; **industrial** [ĩduʃ'trjaw] (*pl* **-ais**) *adj* industrial ▷ *m/f* industrialist;

industrializar [ĩduʃtrjali'za^r] vt (país) to industrialize; (aproveitar) to process

induzir [ĩdu'zi^r] vt to induce; (persuadir) to persuade

inédito, -a [i'nɛdʒitu, a] adj (livro) unpublished; (incomum) unheard-of, rare

inegável [ine'gavew] (pl -eis) adj undeniable

inelutável [inelu'tavew] (pl -eis) adj inescapable

inepto, -a [i'nɛptu, a] adj inept, incompetent

inequívoco, -a [ine'kivoku, a] adj (evidente) clear; (inconfundível) unmistakeable

inércia [i'nɛxsja] f lethargy; (Fís) inertia

inerente [ine'rẽtʃi] adj: ~ **a** inherent in ou to

inerte [i'nɛxtʃi] adj lethargic; (Fís) inert

inesgotável [inezgo'tavew] (pl -eis) adj inexhaustible; (superabundante) boundless

inesperado, -a [ineʃpe'radu, a] adj unexpected, unforeseen ▷ m: **o ~** the unexpected

inesquecível [ineʃke'sivew] (pl -eis) adj unforgettable

inestimável [ineʃtʃi'mavew] (pl -eis) adj invaluable

inexato, -a [ine'zatu, a] (PT -ct-) adj inaccurate

inexistência [inezíʃ'tẽsja] f lack

inexperiência [ineʃpe'rjẽsja] f inexperience; **inexperiente** [ineʃpe'rjẽtʃi] adj inexperienced; (ingênuo) naive

inexpressivo, -a [ineʃpre'sivu, a] adj expressionless

infância [ĩ'fãsja] f childhood

infantil [ĩfã'tʃiw] (pl -is) adj (ingênuo) childlike; (pueril) childish; (para crianças) children's

infarto [ĩ'faxtu] m heart attack

infecção [ĩfek'sãw] (pl -ões) f infection; **infeccionar** [ĩfeksjo'na^r] vt (ferida) to infect; **infeccioso, -a** [ĩfek'sjozu, ɔza] adj infectious

infectar [ĩfek'ta^r] (PT) vt = **infetar**

infelicidade [ĩfelisi'dadʒi] f unhappiness; (desgraça) misfortune

infeliz [ĩfe'liʒ] adj unhappy; (infausto) unlucky; (ação, medida) unfortunate; (sugestão, idéia) inappropriate ▷ m/f unhappy person; **infelizmente** [ĩfeliʒ'mẽtʃi] adv unfortunately

inferior [ĩfe'rjo^r] adj: ~ **(a)** (em valor, qualidade) inferior (to); (mais baixo) lower (than) ▷ m/f inferior, subordinate; **inferioridade** [ĩferjori'dadʒi] f inferiority

infernal [ĩfex'naw] (pl -ais) adj infernal

inferno [ĩ'fɛxnu] m hell; **vá pro ~!** (col) piss off!

infetar [ĩfe'ta^r] vt to infect

infiel [ĩ'fjɛw] (pl -éis) adj disloyal; (marido, mulher) unfaithful; (texto) inaccurate ▷ m/f (Rel) non-believer

ínfimo, -a ['ĩfimu, a] adj lowest; (qualidade) poorest

infindável [ĩfĩ'davew] (pl -eis) adj unending, constant

infinidade [ĩfini'dadʒi] f infinity; **uma ~ de** countless

infinitivo [ĩfini'tʃivu] m (Ling) infinitive

inflação [ĩfla'sãw] f inflation; **inflacionário, -a** [ĩflasjo'narju, a] adj inflationary

inflamação [ĩflama'sãw] (pl -ões) f inflammation; **inflamado, -a** [ĩfla'madu, a] adj (Med) inflamed; (discurso) heated

inflamar [ĩfla'ma^r] vt (madeira, pólvora) to set fire to; (Med, fig) to inflame; **~-se** vr to catch fire; (fig) to get worked up; **~-se de algo** to be consumed with sth

inflamável [ĩfla'mavew] (pl -eis) adj inflammable

inflar [ĩ'fla^r] vt to inflate, blow up; **~-se** vr to swell (up)

inflexível [ĩflek'sivew] (pl -eis) adj stiff, rigid; (fig) unyielding

influência [ĩ'flwẽsja] f influence; **sob a ~ de** under the influence of; **influenciar** [ĩflwẽ'sja^r] vt to influence ▷ vi: **influenciar em algo** to influence sth, have an influence on sth; **influenciar-se** vr: **influenciar-se por** to be influenced by; **influente** [ĩ'flwẽtʃi] adj influential; **influir** [ĩ'flwi^r] vi to matter, be important; **influir em** ou **sobre** to influence, have an influence on

informação [ĩfoxma'sãw] (pl -ões) f (piece of) information; (notícia) news sg; **informações** fpl (detalhes) information sg; **Informações** (Tel) directory enquiries (BRIT), information (US); **pedir informações sobre** to ask about, inquire about

informal [ĩfox'maw] (pl -ais) adj informal

informar [ĩfox'ma^r] vt: ~ **alguém (de/ sobre algo)** to inform sb (of/about sth)

▷ *vi* to inform, be informative; **~-se** *vr*: **~-se de** to find out about, inquire about; **~ de** to report on

informática [ĩfox'matʃika] *f* computer science; (*ramo*) computing, computers *pl*

informativo, -a [ĩfoxma'tʃivu, a] *adj* informative

informatizar [ĩfoxmatʃi'za^r] *vt* to computerize

infortúnio [ĩfox'tunju] *m* misfortune

infração [ĩfra'sãw] (*PT* **-cç-**) (*pl* **-ões**) *f* breach, infringement; (*Esporte*) foul

infractor, a [ĩfra'to^r, a] (*PT*) *m/f* = **infrator, a**

infrator, a [ĩfra'to^r, a] *m/f* offender

infrutífero, -a [ĩfru'tʃiferu, a] *adj* fruitless

ingênuo, -a [ĩ'ʒenwu, a] *adj* ingenuous, naïve; (*comentário*) harmless ▷ *m/f* naïve person

ingerir [ĩʒe'ri^r] *vt* to ingest; (*engolir*) to swallow

Inglaterra [ĩgla'tɛxa] *f*: **a ~** England; **inglês, -esa** [ĩ'gleʃ, eza] *adj* English ▷ *m/f* Englishman/woman ▷ *m* (*Ling*) English; **os ingleses** *mpl* the English

ingrediente [ĩgre'dʒjẽtʃi] *m* ingredient

íngreme ['ĩgremi] *adj* steep

ingressar [ĩgre'sa^r] *vi*: **~ em** to enter, go into; (*um clube*) to join

ingresso [ĩ'grɛsu] *m* (*entrada*) entry; (*admissão*) admission; (*bilhete*) ticket

inibição [inibi'sãw] (*pl* **-ões**) *f* inhibition

inibido, -a [ini'bidu, a] *adj* inhibited

inibir [ini'bi^r] *vt* to inhibit

inicial [ini'sjaw] (*pl* **-ais**) *adj*, *f* initial

iniciar [ini'sja^r] *vt*, *vi* (*começar*) to begin, start; **~ alguém em algo** (*arte, seita*) to initiate sb into sth

iniciativa [inisja'tʃiva] *f* initiative; **a ~ privada** (*Econ*) private enterprise

início [i'nisju] *m* beginning, start; **no ~** at the start

inimigo, -a [ini'migu, a] *adj*, *m/f* enemy

injeção [ĩʒe'sãw] (*PT* **-cç-**) (*pl* **-ões**) *f* injection

injetar [ĩʒe'ta^r] (*PT* **-ct-**) *vt* to inject

injúria [ĩ'ʒurja] *f* insult

injustiça [ĩʒuʃ'tʃisa] *f* injustice

inocência [ino'sẽsja] *f* innocence

inocentar [inosẽ'ta^r] *vt*: **~ alguém (de algo)** to clear sb (of sth)

inocente [ino'sẽtʃi] *adj* innocent ▷ *m/f* innocent man/woman

inofensivo, -a [inofẽ'sivu, a] *adj* harmless, inoffensive

inovação [inova'sãw] (*pl* **-ões**) *f* innovation

INPS (*BR*) *abr m* (= *Instituto Nacional de Previdência Social*) ≈ DSS (*BRIT*), ≈ Welfare Dept (*US*)

inquérito [ĩ'kɛritu] *m* inquiry; (*Jur*) inquest

inquietação [ĩkjeta'sãw] *f* anxiety, uneasiness; (*agitação*) restlessness

inquietante [ĩkje'tãtʃi] *adj* worrying, disturbing

inquietar [ĩkje'ta^r] *vt* to worry, disturb; **~-se** *vr* to worry, bother; **inquieto, -a** [ĩ'kjɛtu, a] *adj* anxious, worried; (*agitado*) restless

inquilino, -a [ĩki'linu, a] *m/f* tenant

insalubre [ĩsa'lubri] *adj* unhealthy

insanidade [ĩsani'dadʒi] *f* madness, insanity; **insano, -a** [ĩ'sanu, a] *adj* insane

insatisfatório, -a [ĩsatʃiʃfa'tɔrju, a] *adj* unsatisfactory

insatisfeito, -a [ĩsatʃiʃ'fejtu, a] *adj* dissatisfied, unhappy

inscrever [ĩʃkre've^r] *vt* to inscribe; (*aluno*) to enrol (*BRIT*), enroll (*US*); (*em registro*) to register

inscrito, -a [ĩ'ʃkritu, a] *pp de* **inscrever**

insecto *etc* [ĩ'sɛktu] (*PT*) = **inseto** *etc*

insegurança [ĩsegu'rãsa] *f* insecurity; **inseguro, -a** [ĩse'guru, a] *adj* insecure; **insensato, -a** [ĩsẽ'satu, a] *adj* unreasonable, foolish

inserir [ĩse'ri^r] *vt* to insert, put in; (*Comput: dados*) to enter

inseticida [ĩsetʃi'sida] *m* insecticide

inseto [ĩ'sɛtu] *m* insect

insípido, -a [ĩ'sipidu, a] *adj* insipid

insiro *etc* [ĩ'siru] *vb ver* **inserir**

insistência [ĩsiʃ'tẽsja] *f*: **~ (em)** insistence (on); (*obstinação*) persistence (in); **insistente** [ĩsiʃ'tẽtʃi] *adj* (*pessoa*) insistent; (*apelo*) urgent

insistir [ĩsiʃ'tʃi^r] *vi*: **~ (em)** to insist (on); (*perseverar*) to persist (in); **~ (em) que** to insist that

insolação [ĩsola'sãw] *f* sunstroke; **pegar uma ~** to get sunstroke

insólito, -a [ĩ'sɔlitu, a] *adj* unusual

insônia [ĩ'sonja] *f* insomnia

insosso, -a [ĩ'sosu, a] *adj* unsalted; (*sem sabor*) tasteless; (*pessoa*) uninteresting, dull

inspeção [ĩʃpe'sãw] (*PT* **-cç-**) (*pl* **-ões**) *f* inspection, check; **inspecionar** [ĩʃpesjo'na^r] (*PT* **-cc-**) *vt* to inspect

inspetor, a [ĩʃpe'toʳ, a] (PT **-ct-**) m/f
inspector

inspirar [ĩʃpi'raʳ] vt to inspire; (Med) to
inhale; **~-se** vr to be inspired

instalação [ĩʃtala'sãw] (pl **-ões**) f
installation; **~ elétrica** (de casa) wiring

instalar [ĩʃta'laʳ] vt to install; (estabelecer)
to set up; **~-se** vr (numa cadeira) to settle
down

instantâneo, -a [ĩʃtã'tanju, a] adj
instant, instantaneous ▷ m (Foto) snap

instante [ĩʃ'tãtʃi] adj urgent ▷ m
moment; **num ~** in an instant, quickly;
só um ~! just a moment!

instável [ĩʃ'tavew] (pl **-eis**) adj unstable;
(tempo) unsettled

instintivo, -a [ĩʃtʃĩ'tʃivu, a] adj
instinctive

instinto [ĩʃ'tʃĩtu] m instinct; **por ~**
instinctively

instituição [ĩʃtʃĩtwi'sãw] (pl **-ões**) f
institution

instituto [ĩʃtʃĩ'tutu] m (escola) institute;
(instituição) institution; **~ de beleza**
beauty salon

instrução [ĩʃtru'sãw] (PT **-cç-**) (pl **-ões**) f
education; (erudição) learning; (diretriz)
instruction; (Mil) training; **instruções** fpl
(para o uso) instructions (for use)

instructor, a [ĩʃtru'toʳ, a] (PT) m/f
= **instrutor, a**

instruído, -a [ĩʃ'trwidu, a] adj educated

instruir [ĩʃ'trwiʳ] vt to instruct; (Mil) to
train; **~-se** vr: **~-se em algo** to learn sth;
~ alguém de ou **sobre algo** to inform sb
about sth

instrumento [ĩʃtru'mẽtu] m
instrument; (ferramenta) implement;
(Jur) deed, document; **~ de cordas/
percussão/sopro** stringed/percussion/
wind instrument; **~ de trabalho** tool

instrutivo, -a [ĩʃtru'tʃivu, a] adj
instructive

instrutor, a [ĩʃtru'toʳ, a] m/f instructor;
(Esporte) coach

insubordinação [ĩsuboxdʒina'sãw] f
rebellion; (Mil) insubordination

insubstituível [ĩsubiʃtʃi'twivew] (pl
-eis) adj irreplaceable

insuficiência [ĩsufi'sjẽsja] f
inadequacy; (carência) shortage;
(Med) deficiency; **~ cardíaca** heart
failure; **insuficiente** [ĩsufi'sjẽtʃi] adj
insufficient; (Educ: nota) ≈ fail; (pessoa)
incompetent

insulina [ĩsu'lina] f insulin

insultar [ĩsuw'taʳ] vt to insult; **insulto**
[ĩ'suwtu] m insult

insuportável [ĩsupox'tavew] (pl **-eis**)
adj unbearable

insurgir-se [ĩsux'ʒixsi] vr to rebel,
revolt

insurreição [ĩsuxej'sãw] (pl **-ões**) f
rebellion, insurrection

intato, -a [ĩ'tatu, a] (PT **-act-**) adj intact

íntegra [ĩtegra] f: **na ~** in full

integral [ĩte'graw] (pl **-ais**) adj whole
▷ f (Mat) integral; **pão ~** wholemeal
(BRIT) ou wholewheat (US) bread;
integralmente [ĩtegraw'mẽtʃi] adv in
full, fully

integrar [ĩte'graʳ] vt to unite, combine;
(completar) to form, make up; (Mat,
raças) to integrate; **~-se** vr to become
complete; **~-se em** ou **a algo** to join sth;
(adaptar-se) to integrate into sth

integridade [ĩtegri'dadʒi] f entirety;
(fig: de pessoa) integrity

íntegro, -a [ĩtegru, a] adj entire;
(honesto) upright, honest

inteiramente [ĩtejra'mẽtʃi] adv
completely

inteirar [ĩtej'raʳ] vt (completar) to
complete; **~-se** vr: **~-se de** to find out
about; **~ alguém de** to inform sb of

inteiro, -a [ĩ'tejru, a] adj whole,
entire; (ileso) unharmed; (não quebrado)
undamaged

intelecto [ĩte'lɛktu] m intellect;
intelectual [ĩtelek'twaw] (pl **-ais**) adj,
m/f intellectual

inteligência [ĩteli'ʒẽsja] f intelligence;
inteligente [ĩteli'ʒẽtʃi] adj intelligent,
clever

inteligível [ĩteli'ʒivew] (pl **-eis**) adj
intelligible

intenção [ĩtẽ'sãw] (pl **-ões**) f intention;
segundas intenções ulterior
motives; **ter a ~ de** to intend to;
intencionado, -a [ĩtẽsjo'nadu, a] adj:
bem intencionado well-meaning; **mal
intencionado** spiteful; **intencional**
[ĩtẽsjo'naw] (pl **-ais**) adj intentional,
deliberate; **intencionar** [ĩtẽsjo'naʳ] vt
to intend

intensificar [ĩtẽsifi'kaʳ] vt to intensify;
~-se vr to intensify

intensivo, -a [ĩtẽ'sivu, a] adj intensive

intenso, -a [ĩ'tẽsu, a] adj intense;
(emoção) deep; (impressão) vivid; (vida
social) full

interação [ĩtera'sãw] (PT **-cç-**) f

interaction

interativo, -a [ītera'tʃivu, a] (PT **-ct-**) adj (Comput) interactive

intercâmbio [ītex'kãbju] m exchange

interdição [ītexdʒi'sãw] (pl **-ões**) f (de estrada, porta) closure; (Jur) injunction

interditar [ītexdʒi'ta'] vt (importação etc) to ban; (estrada, praia) to close off; (cinema etc) to close down

interessado, -a [ītere'sadu, a] adj interested; (amizade) self-seeking

interessante [ītere'sātʃi] adj interesting

interessar [ītere'sa'] vt to interest ▷ vi to be interesting; **~-se** vr: **~-se em** ou **por** to take an interest in, be interested in; **a quem possa ~** to whom it may concern

interesse [īte'resi] m interest; (próprio) self-interest; (proveito) advantage; **no ~ de** for the sake of; **por ~ (próprio)** for one's own ends; **interesseiro, -a** [ītere'sejru, a] adj self-seeking

interface [ītex'fasi] f (Comput) interface

interferência [ītexfe'rẽsja] f interference

interferir [ītexfe'ri'] vi: **~ em** to interfere in; (rádio) to jam

interfone [ītex'fɔni] m intercom

interior [īte'rjo'] adj inner, inside; (Com) domestic, internal ▷ m inside, interior; (do país): **no ~** inland; **Ministério do I~** ≈ Home Office (BRIT), ≈ Department of the Interior (US)

interjeição [ītexʒej'sãw] (pl **-ões**) f interjection

interlocutor, a [ītexloku'to', a] m/f speaker; **meu ~** the person I was speaking to

intermediário, -a [ītexme'dʒjarju, a] adj intermediary ▷ m/f (Com) middleman; (mediador) intermediary, mediator

intermédio [ītex'mɛdʒu] m: **por ~ de** through

internação [ītexna'sãw] (pl **-ões**) f (de doente) admission

internacional [ītexnasjo'naw] (pl **-ais**) adj international

internações [ītexna'sõjʃ] fpl de **internação**

internar [ītex'na'] vt (aluno) to put into boarding school; (doente) to take into hospital; (Mil, Pol) to intern

internauta [ītex'nawta] m/f Internet user, web ou net surfer (col)

Internet [ītex'nɛtʃi] f: **a ~** the Internet

interno, -a [ī'texnu, a] adj internal; (Pol) domestic ▷ m/f (tb: **aluno ~**) boarder; (Med: estudante) houseman (BRIT), intern (US); **de uso ~** (Med) for internal use

interpretação [ītexpreta'sãw] (pl **-ões**) f interpretation; (Teatro) performance

interpretar [ītexpre'ta'] vt to interpret; (um papel) to play; **intérprete** [ī'tɛxpretʃi] m/f interpreter; (Teatro) performer, artist

interrogação [ītexoga'sãw] (pl **-ões**) f interrogation; **ponto de ~** question mark

interrogar [ītexo'ga'] vt to question, interrogate; (Jur) to cross-examine

interromper [ītexõ'pe'] vt to interrupt; (parar) to stop; (Elet) to cut off

interruptor [ītexup'to'] m (Elet) switch

interseção [ītexse'sãw] (PT **-cç-**) (pl **-ões**) f intersection

interurbano, -a [īterux'banu, a] adj (Tel) long-distance ▷ m long-distance ou trunk call

intervalo [ītex'valu] m interval; (descanso) break; **a ~s** every now and then

intervir [ītex'vi'] (irreg: como **vir**) vi to intervene; (sobrevir) to come up

intimação [ītʃima'sãw] (pl **-ões**) f (ordem) order; (Jur) summons

intimar [ītʃi'ma'] vt (Jur) to summon; **~ alguém a fazer** ou **a alguém que faça** to order sb to do

íntimo, -a [ī'tʃimu, a] adj intimate; (sentimentos) innermost; (amigo) close; (vida) private ▷ m/f close friend; **no ~** at heart

intolerante [ītole'rãtʃi] adj intolerant

intolerável [ītole'ravew] (pl **-eis**) adj intolerable, unbearable

intoxicação [ītoksika'sãw] f poisoning; **~ alimentar** food poisoning

intoxicar [ītoksi'ka'] vt to poison

intranet [ītra'nɛtʃi] f intranet

intransitável [ītrãsi'tavew] (pl **-eis**) adj impassable

intratável [ītra'tavew] (pl **-eis**) adj (pessoa) contrary, awkward; (doença) untreatable; (problema) insurmountable

intriga [ī'triga] f intrigue; (enredo) plot; (fofoca) piece of gossip; **intrigas** (fofocas) gossip sg; **~ amorosa** (PT) love affair; **intrigante** [ītri'gãtʃi] m/f troublemaker ▷ adj intriguing; **intrigar** [ītri'ga'] vt to intrigue ▷ vi to be intriguing

introdução [ĩtrodu'sãw] (*pl* **-ões**) *f* introduction

introduzir [ĩtrodu'zi^r] *vt* to introduce

intrometer-se [ĩtrome'texsi] *vr* to interfere, meddle; **intrometido, -a** [ĩtrome'tʃidu, a] *adj* interfering; (*col*) nosey ▷ *m/f* busybody

introvertido, -a [ĩtrovex'tʃidu, a] *adj* introverted ▷ *m/f* introvert

intruso, -a [ĩ'truzu, a] *m/f* intruder

intuição [ĩtwi'sãw] (*pl* **-ões**) *f* intuition

intuito [ĩ'tuito] *m* intention, aim

inúmero, -a [i'numeru, a] *adj* countless, innumerable

inundação [inũda'sãw] (*pl* **-ões**) *f* (*enchente*) flood; (*ato*) flooding

inundar [inũ'da^r] *vt* to flood; (*fig*) to inundate ▷ *vi* to flood

inusitado, -a [inuzi'tadu, a] *adj* unusual

inútil [i'nutʃiw] (*pl* **-eis**) *adj* useless; (*esforço*) futile; (*desnecessário*) pointless;

inutilizar [inutʃili'za^r] *vt* to make useless, render useless; (*incapacitar*) to put out of action; (*danificar*) to ruin; (*esforços*) to thwart; **inutilmente** [inutʃiw'mẽtʃi] *adv* in vain

invadir [ĩva'dʒi^r] *vt* to invade; (*suj: água*) to overrun; (: *sentimento*) to overcome

inválido, -a [ĩ'validu, a] *adj*, *m/f* invalid

invasão [ĩva'zãw] (*pl* **-ões**) *f* invasion

inveja [ĩ'vɛʒa] *f* envy; **invejar** [ĩve'ʒa^r] *vt* to envy; (*cobiçar*) to covet ▷ *vi* to be envious; **invejoso, -a** [ĩve'ʒozu, ɔza] *adj* envious

invenção [ĩvẽ'sãw] (*pl* **-ões**) *f* invention

inventar [ĩvẽ'ta^r] *vt* to invent

inventivo, -a [ĩvẽ'tʃivu, a] *adj* inventive

inventor, a [ĩvẽ'to^r, a] *m/f* inventor

inverno [ĩ'vɛxnu] *m* winter

inverossímil [ĩvero'simiw] (*PT* **-osí-**) (*pl* **-eis**) *adj* unlikely, improbable; (*inacreditável*) implausible

invés [ĩ'vɛʃ] *m*: **ao ~ de** instead of

investigação [ĩveʃtʃiga'sãw] (*pl* **-ões**) *f* investigation; (*pesquisa*) research

investigar [ĩveʃtʃi'ga^r] *vt* to investigate; (*examinar*) to examine

investimento [ĩveʃtʃi'mẽtu] *m* investment

investir [ĩveʃ'tʃi^r] *vt* (*dinheiro*) to invest

inviável [ĩ'vjavew] (*pl* **-eis**) *adj* impracticable

invisível [ĩvi'zivew] (*pl* **-eis**) *adj* invisible

invisto *etc* [ĩ'viʃtu] *vb ver* **investir**

invocar [ĩvo'ka^r] *vt* to invoke

ioga ['jɔga] *f* yoga

iogurte [jo'guxtʃi] *m* yogurt

IR (BR) *abr m* = **Imposto de Renda**

○ **PALAVRA CHAVE**

ir [i^r] *vi* **1** to go; (*a pé*) to walk; (*a cavalo*) to ride; (*viajar*) to travel; **ir caminhando** to walk; **fui de trem** I went *ou* travelled by train; **vamos!, vamos embora!, vamos nessa!** (*col*) let's go!; **já vou!** I'm coming!; **ir atrás de alguém** (*seguir*) to follow sb; (*confiar*) to take sb's word for it

2 (*progredir: pessoa, coisa*) to go; **o trabalho vai muito bem** work is going very well; **como vão as coisas?** how are things going?; **vou muito bem** I'm very well; (*na escola etc*) I'm getting on very well

▷ *vb aux* **1** (+ *infin*): **vou fazer** I will do, I am going to do

2 (+ *gerúndio*): **ir fazendo** to keep on doing

ir-se *vr* to go away, leave

ira ['ira] *f* anger, rage

Irã [i'rã] *m*: **o ~** Iran

iraniano, -a [ira'njanu, a] *adj*, *m/f* Iranian

Irão [i'rãw] (PT) *m* = **Irã**

Iraque [i'raki] *m*: **o ~** Iraq; **iraquiano, -a** [ira'kjanu, a] *adj*, *m/f* Iraqi

ir-e-vir (*pl* **ires-e-vires**) *m* comings and goings *pl*

Irlanda [ix'lãda] *f*: **a ~** Ireland; **a ~ do Norte** Northern Ireland; **irlandês, -esa** [ixlã'deʃ, eza] *adj* Irish ▷ *m/f* Irishman/woman ▷ *m* (*Ling*) Irish

irmã [ix'mã] *f* sister; **~ de criação** adoptive sister; **~ gêmea** twin sister

irmão [ix'mãw] (*pl* **-s**) *m* brother; (*fig: similar*) twin; (*col: companheiro*) mate; **~ de criação** adoptive brother; **~ gêmeo** twin brother

ironia [iro'nia] *f* irony

irra! ['ixa] (PT) *excl* damn!

irracional [ixasjo'naw] (*pl* **-ais**) *adj* irrational

irreal [ixe'aw] (*pl* **-ais**) *adj* unreal

irregular [ixegu'la^r] *adj* irregular; (*vida*) unconventional; (*feições*) unusual; (*aluno, gênio*) erratic

irremediável [ixeme'dʒjavew] (*pl* **-eis**) *adj* irremediable; (*sem remédio*) incurable

irrequieto, -a [ixe'kjetu, a] *adj* restless

irresistível [ixeziʃ'tʃívew] (pl -eis) adj
irresistible

irresponsável [ixeʃpõ'savew] (pl -eis)
adj irresponsible

irrigar [ixi'gaʳ] vt to irrigate

irritação [ixita'sãw] (pl -ões) f irritation

irritadiço, -a [ixita'dʒisu, a] adj irritable

irritante [ixi'tãtʃi] adj irritating,
annoying

irritar [ixi'taʳ] vt to irritate; ~**-se** vr to get
angry, get annoyed

irromper [ixõ'peʳ] vi (entrar subitamente):
~ **(em)** to burst in(to)

isca ['iʃka] f (Pesca) bait; (fig) lure, bait

isenção [izẽ'sãw] (pl -ões) f exemption

isentar [izẽ'taʳ] vt to exempt; (livrar) to
free

Islã [iʒ'lã] m Islam

Islândia [iʒ'lãdʒa] f: **a** ~ Iceland

isolado, -a [izo'ladu, a] adj isolated;
(solitário) lonely

isolamento [izola'mẽtu] m isolation;
(Elet) insulation

isqueiro [iʃ'kejru] m (cigarette) lighter

Israel [iʒxa'ɛw] m Israel; **israelense**
[iʒxae'lẽsi] adj, m/f Israeli

isso ['isu] pron that; (col: isto) this; ~
mesmo exactly; **por** ~ therefore, so; **por**
~ **mesmo** for that very reason; **só ~?** is
that all?

isto ['iʃtu] pron this; ~ **é** that is, namely

Itália [i'talja] f: **a** ~ Italy; **italiano, -a**
[ita'ljanu, a] adj, m/f Italian ▷ m (Ling)
Italian

Itamarati [itamara'tʃi] m: **o Itamarati**
the Brazilian Foreign Ministry; see boxed
note

◈ **ITAMARATI**
◈
◈ The Palace of Itamarati was built
◈ in 1855 in Rio de Janeiro. It became
◈ the seat of government when Brazil
◈ became a republic in 1889, and was
◈ later the Foreign Ministry. It ceased to
◈ be this when the Brazilian capital was
◈ transferred to Brasília, but **Itamarati**
◈ is still used to refer to the Foreign
◈ Ministry.

item ['itẽ] (pl -ns) m item

itinerário [itʃine'rarju] m itinerary;
(caminho) route

já [ʒa] adv already; (em perguntas) yet;
(agora) now; (imediatamente) right away;
(agora mesmo) right now ▷ conj on the
other hand; **até já** bye; **desde já** from
now on; **já não** no longer; **já que** as,
since; **já se vê** of course; **já vou** I'm
coming; **já até** even; **já, já** right away

jabuti [ʒabu'tʃi] m giant tortoise

jabuticaba [ʒabutʃi'kaba] f jaboticaba
(type of berry)

jaca ['ʒaka] f jackfruit

jacaré [ʒaka'rɛ] (BR) m alligator

jacto ['ʒaktu] (PT) m = **jato**

jaguar [ʒa'gwaʳ] m jaguar

jaguatirica [ʒagwatʃi'rika] f leopard cat

Jamaica [ʒa'majka] f: **a** ~ Jamaica

jamais [ʒa'majʃ] adv never; (com palavra
negativa) ever

janeiro [ʒa'nejru] (PT J-) m January

janela [ʒa'nɛla] f window

jangada [ʒã'gada] f raft

jantar [ʒã'taʳ] m dinner ▷ vt to have for
dinner ▷ vi to have dinner

Japão [ʒa'pãw] m: **o** ~ Japan; **japonês,
-esa** [ʒapo'neʃ, eza] adj, m/f Japanese
▷ m (Ling) Japanese

jararaca [ʒara'raka] f jararaca (snake)

jardim [ʒax'dʒĩ] (pl -ns) m garden; ~

zoológico zoo; **jardim-de-infância** (*pl* **jardins-de-infância**) *m* kindergarten; **jardinagem** [ʒaxdʒi'naʒẽ] *f* gardening

jardineira [ʒaxdʒi'nejra] *f* (*caixa*) trough; (*calça*) dungarees *pl*; *ver tb* **jardineiro**

jardineiro, -a [ʒaxdʒi'nejru, a] *m/f* gardener

jardins [ʒax'dʒĩʃ] *mpl de* **jardim**

jargão [ʒax'gãw] *m* jargon

jarra ['ʒaxa] *f* pot

jarro ['ʒaxu] *m* jug

jasmim [ʒaʒ'mĩ] *m* jasmine

jato ['ʒatu] *m* jet; (*de luz*) flash; (*de ar*) blast; **a ~** at top speed

jaula ['ʒawla] *f* cage

jazigo [ʒa'zigu] *m* grave; (*monumento*) tomb

jazz [dʒɛz] *m* jazz

jeito ['ʒejtu] *m* (*maneira*) way; (*aspecto*) appearance; (*habilidade*) skill, knack; (*modos pessoais*) manner; **ter ~ de** to look like; **não ter ~** (*pessoa*) to be awkward; (*situação*) to be hopeless; **dar um ~ em** (*pé*) to twist; (*quarto, casa, papéis*) to tidy up; (*consertar*) to fix; **dar um ~** to find a way; **o ~ é ...** the thing to do is ...; **é o ~** it's the best way; **ao ~ de** in the style of; **com ~** tactfully; **daquele ~** (in) that way; (*col: em desordem, mal*) anyhow; **de qualquer ~** anyway; **de ~ nenhum!** no way!

jejuar [ʒe'ʒwaʳ] *vi* to fast

jejum [ʒe'ʒũ] (*pl* **-ns**) *m* fast; **em ~** fasting

Jesus [ʒe'zuʃ] *m* Jesus ▷ *excl* heavens!

jibóia [ʒi'bɔja] *f* boa (constrictor)

jiló [ʒi'lɔ] *m* kind of vegetable

jingle ['dʒĩgew] *m* jingle

joalheria [ʒoaʎe'ria] *f* jeweller's (shop) (BRIT), jewelry store (US)

joaninha [ʒwa'niɲa] *f* ladybird (BRIT), ladybug (US)

joelho [ʒo'eʎu] *m* knee; **de ~s** kneeling; **ficar de ~s** to kneel down

jogada [ʒo'gada] *f* move; (*lanço*) throw; (*negócio*) move

jogador, a [ʒoga'doʳ, a] *m/f* player; (*de jogo de azar*) gambler

jogar [ʒo'gaʳ] *vt* to play; (*em jogo de azar*) to gamble; (*atirar*) to throw; (*indiretas*) to drop ▷ *vi* to play; to gamble; (*barco*) to pitch; **~ fora** to throw away

jogging ['ʒɔgĩ] *m* jogging; (*roupa*) track suit; **fazer ~** to go jogging, jog

jogo ['ʒogu] *m* game; (*jogar*) play; (*de azar*) gambling; (*conjunto*) set; (*artimanha*) trick; **J~s Olímpicos** Olympic Games

jóia ['ʒɔja] *f* jewel

Jordânia [ʒox'danja] *f*: **a ~** Jordan; **Jordão** [ʒox'dãw] *m*: **o (rio) Jordão** the Jordan (River)

jornada [ʒox'nada] *f* journey; **~ de trabalho** working day

jornal [ʒox'naw] (*pl* **-ais**) *m* newspaper; (*TV, Rádio*) news *sg*; **jornaleiro, -a** [ʒoxna'lejru, a] *m/f* newsagent (BRIT), newsdealer (US)

jornalismo [ʒoxna'liʒmu] *m* journalism; **jornalista** [ʃoxna'liʃta] *m/f* journalist

jovem ['ʒɔvẽ] (*pl* **-ns**) *adj* young ▷ *m/f* young person

jovial [ʒo'vjaw] (*pl* **-ais**) *adj* jovial, cheerful

Jr *abr* = **Júnior**

judaico, -a [ʒu'dajku, a] *adj* Jewish

judeu, judia [ʒu'dew, ʒu'dʒia] *adj* Jewish ▷ *m/f* Jew

judiar [ʒu'dʒjaʳ] *vi*: **~ de** to ill-treat

judicial [ʒudʒi'sjaw] (*pl* **-ais**) *adj* judicial; **judiciário, -a** [ʒudʒi'sjarju, a] *adj* judicial; **o (poder) ~** the judiciary

judô [ʒu'do] *m* judo

juiz, -íza [ʒwiʒ, 'iza] *m/f* judge; (*em jogos*) referee; **~ de paz** justice of the peace; **juizado** [ʒwi'zado] *m* court

juízo ['ʒwizu] *m* judgement; (*parecer*) opinion; (*siso*) common sense; (*foro*) court; **perder o ~** to lose one's mind; **não ter ~** to be foolish; **tomar** *ou* **criar ~** to come to one's senses; **chamar/levar a ~** to summon/take to court; **~!** behave yourself!

julgamento [ʒuwga'mẽtu] *m* judgement; (*audiência*) trial; (*sentença*) sentence

julgar [ʒuw'gaʳ] *vt* to judge; (*achar*) to think; (*Jur: sentenciar*) to sentence; **~-se** *vr*: **~-se algo** to consider o.s. sth, think of o.s. as sth

julho ['ʒuʎu] (*PT* **J-**) *m* July

jumento, -a [ʒu'mẽtu, a] *m/f* donkey

junção [ʒũ'sãw] (*pl* **-ões**) *f* (*ato*) joining; (*junta*) join

junco ['ʒũku] *m* reed, rush

junções [ʒũ'sõjʃ] *fpl de* **junção**

junho ['ʒuɲu] (*PT* **J-**) *m* June

júnior ['ʒunjoʳ] (*pl* **juniores**) *adj* younger, junior ▷ *m/f* (*Esporte*) junior; **Eduardo Autran J~** Eduardo Autran Junior

juntar [ʒũ'taʳ] *vt* to join; (*reunir*) to bring together; (*aglomerar*) to gather together; (*recolher*) to collect up; (*acrescentar*) to add; (*dinheiro*) to save up ▷ *vi* to gather; **~-se** *vr* to gather; (*associar-se*) to join up;

~-se a alguém to join sb

junto, -a [ˈʒũtu, a] *adj* joined; *(chegado)* near; **ir ~s** to go together; **~ a/de** near/next to; **segue ~** *(Com)* please find enclosed

jura [ˈʒura] *f* vow

jurado, -a [ʒuˈradu, a] *adj* sworn ▷ *m/f* juror

juramento [ʒuraˈmẽtu] *m* oath

jurar [ʒuˈraʳ] *vt, vi* to swear; **jura?** really?

júri [ˈʒuri] *m* jury

jurídico, -a [ʒuˈridʒiku, a] *adj* legal

juros [ˈʒuruʃ] *mpl* *(Econ)* interest *sg*; **~ simples/compostos** simple/compound interest

justamente [ʒuʃtaˈmẽtʃi] *adv* fairly, justly; *(precisamente)* exactly

justiça [ʒuʃˈtʃisa] *f* justice; *(poder judiciário)* judiciary; *(eqüidade)* fairness; *(tribunal)* court; **com ~** justly, fairly; **ir à ~** to go to court

justificar [ʒuʃtʃifiˈkaʳ] *vt* to justify

justo, -a [ˈʒuʃtu, a] *adj* just, fair; *(legítimo: queixa)* legitimate, justified; *(exato)* exact; *(apertado)* tight ▷ *adv* just

juvenil [ʒuveˈniw] *(pl* **-is***)* *adj* youthful; *(roupa)* young; *(livro)* for young people; *(Esporte: equipe, campeonato)* youth *atr*, junior

juventude [ʒuvẽˈtudʒi] *f* youth; *(jovialidade)* youthfulness; *(jovens)* young people *pl*, youth

k

kg *abr* (= *quilograma*) kg

kit [ˈkitʃi] *(pl* **~s***)* *m* kit

kitchenette [kitʃeˈnetʃi] *f* studio flat

km *abr* (= *quilômetro*) km

km/h *abr* (= *quilômetros por hora*) km/h

l

-**la** [la] *pron* her; (*você*) you; (*coisa*) it

lá [la] *adv* there ▷ *m* (*Mús*) A; **lá fora** outside; **lá em baixo** down there; **por lá** (*direção*) that way; (*situação*) over there; **até lá** (*no espaço*) there; (*no tempo*) until then

lã [lã] *f* wool

labia ['labja] *f* (*astúcia*) cunning; **ter ~** to have the gift of the gab

lábio ['labju] *m* lip

labirinto [labi'rĩtu] *m* labyrinth, maze

laboratório [labora'tɔrju] *m* laboratory

laca ['laka] *f* lacquer

laçar [la'saʳ] *vt* to bind, tie

laço ['lasu] *m* bow; (*de gravata*) knot; (*armadilha*) snare; (*fig*) bond, tie; **dar um ~** to tie a bow

lacrar [la'kraʳ] *vt* to seal (with wax); **lacre** ['lakri] *m* sealing wax

lacuna [la'kuna] *f* gap; (*omissão*) omission; (*espaço em branco*) blank

ladeira [la'dejra] *f* slope

lado ['ladu] *m* side; (*Mil*) flank; (*rumo*) direction; **ao ~** (*perto*) close by; **a casa ao ~** the house next door; **ao ~ de** beside; **deixar de ~** to set aside; (*fig*) to leave out; **de um ~ para outro** back and forth

ladra ['ladra] *f* thief, robber; (*picareta*) crook

ladrão, -ona [la'drãw, ɔna] (*pl* **ladrões/-s**) *adj* thieving ▷ *m/f* thief, robber; (*picareta*) crook

ladrilho [la'driʎu] *m* tile; (*chão*) tiled floor, tiles *pl*

ladrões [la'drõjʃ] *mpl de* **ladrão**

lagarta [la'gaxta] *f* caterpillar

lagartixa [lagax'tʃiʃa] *f* gecko

lagarto [la'gaxtu] *m* lizard

lago ['lagu] *m* lake; (*de jardim*) pond

lagoa [la'goa] *f* pool, pond; (*lago*) lake

lagosta [la'goʃta] *f* lobster

lagostim [lagoʃ'tʃĩ] (*pl* -**ns**) *m* crayfish

lágrima ['lagrima] *f* tear

lama ['lama] *f* mud

lamaçal [lama'saw] (*pl* -**ais**) *m* quagmire; (*pântano*) bog, marsh

lamber [lã'beʳ] *vt* to lick; **lambida** [lã'bida] *f*: **dar uma lambida em algo** to lick sth

lambuzar [lãbu'zaʳ] *vt* to smear

lamentar [lamẽ'taʳ] *vt* to lament; (*sentir*) to regret; **~-se** *vr*: **~-se (de algo)** to lament (sth); **~ (que)** to be sorry (that); **lamentável** [lamẽ'tavew] (*pl* -**eis**) *adj* regrettable; (*deplorável*) deplorable; **lamento** [la'mẽtu] *m* lament; (*gemido*) moan

lâmina ['lamina] *f* (*chapa*) sheet; (*placa*) plate; (*de faca*) blade; (*de persiana*) slat

lâmpada ['lãpada] *f* lamp; (*tb*: **~ elétrica**) light bulb; **~ de mesa** table lamp

lançar [lã'saʳ] *vt* to throw; (*navio, produto, campanha*) to launch; (*disco, filme*) to release; (*Com: em livro*) to enter; (*em leilão*) to bid

lancha ['lãʃa] *f* launch; **~ torpedeira** torpedo boat

lanchar [lã'ʃaʳ] *vi* to have a snack ▷ *vt* to have as a snack; **lanche** ['lãʃi] *m* snack

lanchonete [lãʃo'netʃi] (*BR*) *f* snack bar

lanterna [lã'texna] *f* lantern; (*portátil*) torch (*BRIT*), flashlight (*US*)

lápide ['lapidʒi] *f* (*tumular*) tombstone; (*comemorativa*) memorial stone

lápis ['lapiʃ] *m inv* pencil; **~ de cor** coloured (*BRIT*) *ou* colored (*US*) pencil, crayon; **~ de olho** eyebrow pencil; **lapiseira** [lapi'zejra] *f* propelling (*BRIT*) *ou* mechanical (*US*) pencil; (*caixa*) pencil case

lapso ['lapsu] *m* lapse; (*de tempo*) interval; (*erro*) slip

lar [laʳ] *m* home

laranja [la'rãʒa] *adj inv* orange ▷ *f*
orange ▷ *m* (*cor*) orange; **laranjada**
[larã'ʒada] *f* orangeade; **laranjeira**
[larã'ʒejra] *f* orange tree

lareira [la'rejra] *f* hearth, fireside

larga ['laxga] *f*: **à** ~ lavishly; **dar ~s a**
to give free rein to; **viver à** ~ to lead a
lavish life

largada [lax'gada] *f* start; **dar a** ~ to
start; (*fig*) to make a start

largar [lax'ga^r] *vt* to let go of, release;
(*deixar*) to leave; (*deixar cair*) to drop;
(*risada*) to let out; (*velas*) to unfurl; (*piada*)
to tell; (*pôr em liberdade*) to let go ▷ *vi*
(*Náut*) to set sail; **~-se** *vr* (*desprender-se*)
to free o.s.; (*ir-se*) to go off; (*pôr-se*) to
proceed

largo, -a ['laxgu, a] *adj* wide, broad;
(*amplo*) extensive; (*roupa*) loose, baggy;
(*conversa*) long ▷ *m* (*praça*) square; (*alto-
mar*) open sea; **ao** ~ at a distance, far
off; **passar de ~ sobre um assunto** to
gloss over a subject; **passar ao ~ de algo**
(*fig*) to sidestep sth; **largura** [lax'gura] *f*
width, breadth

laringite [larĩ'ʒitʃi] *f* laryngitis

lasanha [la'zaɲa] *f* lasagna

laser ['lejze^r] *m* laser; **raio ~** laser beam

lástima ['laʃtʃima] *f* pity, compassion;
(*infortúnio*) misfortune; **é uma ~ (que)**
it's a shame (that); **lastimar** [laʃtʃi'ma^r]
vt to lament; **lastimar-se** *vr* to
complain, be sorry for o.s

lata ['lata] *f* tin (*BRIT*), can; (*material*)
tin-plate; ~ **de lixo** rubbish bin (*BRIT*),
garbage can (*US*); ~ **velha** (*col: carro*) old
banger (*BRIT*) *ou* clunker (*US*)

latão [la'tãw] *m* brass

lataria [lata'ria] *f* (*Auto*) bodywork;
(*enlatados*) canned food

latejar [late'ʒa^r] *vi* to throb

latente [la'tẽtʃi] *adj* latent

lateral [late'raw] (*pl* **-ais**) *adj* side,
lateral ▷ *f* (*Futebol*) sideline ▷ *m* (*Futebol*)
throw-in

latido [la'tʃidu] *m* bark(ing), yelp(ing)

latifundiário, -a [latʃifũ'dʒjarju, a] *m/f*
landowner

latifúndio [latʃi'fũdʒju] *m* large estate

latim [la'tʃĩ] *m* (*Ling*) Latin; **gastar o seu**
~ to waste one's breath

latino, -a [la'tʃinu, a] *adj* Latin; **latino-
americano, -a** *adj*, *m/f* Latin-American

latir [la'tʃi^r] *vi* to bark, yelp

latitude [latʃi'tudʒi] *f* latitude; (*largura*)
breadth; (*fig*) scope

latrocínio [latro'sinju] *m* armed robbery

laudo ['lawdu] *m* (*Jur*) decision;
(*resultados*) findings *pl*; (*peça escrita*)
report

lava ['lava] *f* lava

lavabo [la'vabu] *m* toilet

lavadeira [lava'dejra] *f* washerwoman

lavagem [la'vaʒẽ] *f* washing; ~ **a seco**
dry cleaning; ~ **cerebral** brainwashing

lavanda [la'vãda] *f* (*Bot*) lavender;
(*colônia*) lavender water; (*para lavar os
dedos*) fingerbowl

lavar [la'va^r] *vt* to wash; (*culpa*) to wash
away; ~ **a seco** to dry clean

lavatório [lava'tɔrju] *m* washbasin;
(*aposento*) toilet

lavoura [la'vora] *f* tilling; (*agricultura*)
farming; (*terreno*) plantation

laxativo, -a [laʃa'tʃivu, a] *adj* laxative
▷ *m* laxative

lazer [la'ze^r] *m* leisure

leal [le'aw] (*pl* **-ais**) *adj* loyal; **lealdade**
[leaw'dadʒi] *f* loyalty

leão [le'ãw] (*pl* **-ões**) *m* lion; **L~**
(*Astrologia*) Leo

lebre ['lɛbri] *f* hare

lecionar [lesjo'na^r] (*PT* **-cc-**) *vt*, *vi* to
teach

lectivo, -a [lek'tivu, a] (*PT*) *adj* = **letivo**

legal [le'gaw] (*pl* **-ais**) *adj* legal, lawful;
(*col*) fine; (: *pessoa*) nice ▷ *adv* (*col*) well;
(**tá**) ~! OK!; **legalidade** [legali'dadʒi]
f legality, lawfulness; **legalizar**
[legali'za^r] *vt* to legalize; (*documento*) to
authenticate

legendário, -a [leʒẽ'darju, a] *adj*
legendary

legislação [leʒiʒla'sãw] *f* legislation

legislar [leʒiʒ'la^r] *vi* to legislate ▷ *vt* to
pass

legislativo, -a [leʒiʒla'tʃivu, a] *adj*
legislative ▷ *m* legislature

legitimar [leʒitʃi'ma^r] *vt* to legitimize;
(*justificar*) to legitimate

legume [le'gumi] *m* vegetable

lei [lej] *f* law; (*regra*) rule; (*metal*) standard

leigo, -a ['lejgu, a] *adj* (*Rel*) lay, secular
▷ *m* layman; **ser ~ em algo** (*fig*) to be no
expert at sth, be unversed in sth

leilão [lej'lãw] (*pl* **-ões**) *m* auction;
vender em ~ to sell by auction, auction
off; **leiloar** [lej'lwa^r] *vt* to auction

leio *etc* ['leju] *vb ver* **ler**

leitão, -toa [lej'tãw, 'toa] (*pl* **leitões/-s**)
m/f sucking (*BRIT*) *ou* suckling (*US*) pig

leite ['lejtʃi] *m* milk; ~ **em pó** powdered

milk; ~ **desnatado** ou **magro** skimmed milk; ~ **de magnésia** milk of magnesia; ~ **semidesnatado** semi-skimmed milk;

leiteira [lej'tejra] f (para ferver) milk pan; (para servir) milk jug; **leiteiro, -a** [lej'tejru, a] adj (vaca, gado) dairy ▷ m/f milkman/woman

leitões [lej'tõjʃ] mpl de **leitão**

leitor, a [lej'tor, a] m/f reader; (professor) lector

leitura [lej'tura] f reading; (livro etc) reading matter

lema ['lɛma] m motto; (Pol) slogan

lembrança [lẽ'brãsa] f recollection, memory; (presente) souvenir; **lembranças** fpl (recomendações): **~s a sua mãe!** regards to your mother!

lembrar [lẽ'bra^r] vt, vi to remember; **~-se** vr: **~(-se) de** to remember; **~(-se) (de) que** to remember that; **~ algo a alguém, ~ alguém de algo** to remind sb of sth; **~ alguém de que, ~ a alguém que** to remind sb that; **ele lembra meu irmão** he reminds me of my brother, he is like my brother; **lembrete** [lẽ'bretʃi] m reminder

leme ['lɛmi] m rudder; (Náut) helm; (fig) control

lenço ['lẽsu] m handkerchief; (de pescoço) scarf; (de cabeça) headscarf; **~ de papel** tissue

lençol [lẽ'sɔw] (pl **-óis**) m sheet; **estar em maus lençóis** to be in a fix

lenda ['lẽda] f legend; (fig: mentira) lie; **lendário, -a** [lẽ'darju, a] adj legendary

lenha ['lɛɲa] f firewood

lente ['lẽtʃi] f lens sg; **~ de aumento** magnifying glass; **~s de contato** contact lenses

lentidão [lẽtʃi'dãw] f slowness

lento, -a ['lẽtu, a] adj slow

leoa [le'oa] f lioness

leões [le'õjʃ] mpl de **leão**

leopardo [ljo'paxdu] m leopard

lepra ['lɛpra] f leprosy

leque ['lɛki] m fan; (fig) array

ler [le^r] vt, vi to read

lesão [le'zãw] (pl **-ões**) f harm, injury; (Jur) violation; (Med) lesion; **~ corporal** (Jur) bodily harm

lesar [le'za^r] vt to harm, damage; (direitos) to violate

lésbica ['lɛʒbika] f lesbian

lesma ['lɛʒma] f slug; (fig: pessoa) slowcoach

lesões [le'zõjʃ] fpl de **lesão**

lesse etc ['lesi] vb ver **ler**

leste ['lɛʃtʃi] m east

letal [le'taw] (pl **-ais**) adj lethal

letargia [letax'ʒia] f lethargy

letivo, -a [le'tʃivu, a] adj school atr; **ano ~** academic year

letra ['letra] f letter; (caligrafia) handwriting; (de canção) lyrics pl; **Letras** fpl (curso) language and literature; **à ~** literally; **ao pé da ~** literally, word for word; **~ de câmbio** (Com) bill of exchange; **~ de imprensa** print; **letrado, -a** [le'tradu, a] adj learned, erudite ▷ m/f scholar; **letreiro** [le'trejru] m sign, notice; (inscrição) inscription; (Cinema) subtitle

leu etc [lew] vb ver **ler**

léu [lɛw] m: **ao ~** (à toa) aimlessly; (à mostra) uncovered

leucemia [lewse'mia] f leukaemia (BRIT), leukemia (US)

levado, -a [le'vadu, a] adj mischievous; (criança) naughty

levantador, a [levãta'do^r, a] adj lifting ▷ m/f: **~ de pesos** weightlifter

levantamento [levãta'mẽtu] m lifting, raising; (revolta) uprising, rebellion; (arrolamento) survey

levantar [levã'ta^r] vt to lift, raise; (voz, capital) to raise; (apanhar) to pick up; (suscitar) to arouse; (ambiente) to brighten up ▷ vi to stand up; (da cama) to get up; (dar vida) to brighten; **~-se** vr to stand up; (da cama) to get up; (rebelar-se) to rebel

levar [le'va^r] vt to take; (portar) to carry; (tempo) to pass, spend; (roupa) to wear; (lidar com) to handle; (induzir) to lead; (filme) to show; (peça teatral) to do, put on; (vida) to lead ▷ vi to get a beating; **~ a** to lead to; **~ a mal** to take amiss

leve ['lɛvi] adj light; (insignificante) slight; **de ~** lightly, softly

leviandade [levjã'dadʒi] f frivolity

leviano, -a [le'vjanu, a] adj frivolous

lha(s) [ʎa(ʃ)] = **lhe + a(s)**

lhe [ʎi] pron (a ele) to him; (a ela) to her; (a você) to you

lhes [ʎiʃ] pron pl (a eles/elas) to them; (a vocês) to you

lho(s) [ʎu(ʃ)] = **lhe + o(s)**

li etc [li] vb ver **ler**

Líbano ['libanu] m: **o ~** (the) Lebanon

libélula [li'bɛlula] f dragonfly

liberação [libera'sãw] f liberation

liberal [libe'raw] (pl **-ais**) adj, m/f liberal

liberar [libe'ra[^r]] vt to release; (*libertar*) to free

liberdade [libex'dadʒi] f freedom; **liberdades** fpl (*direitos*) liberties; **pôr alguém em ~** to set sb free; **~ condicional** probation; **~ de palavra** freedom of speech; **~ sob palavra** parole

libertação [libexta'sãw] f release

libertino, -a [libex'tʃinu, a] adj loose-living ▷ m/f libertine

Líbia ['libja] f: **a ~** Libya

libidinoso, -a [libidʒi'nozu, ɔza] adj lecherous, lustful

líbio, -a ['libju, a] adj, m/f Libyan

libra ['libra] f pound; **L~** (*Astrologia*) Libra

lição [li'sãw] (pl **-ões**) m lesson

licença [li'sẽsa] f licence (BRIT), license (US); (*permissão*) permission; (*do trabalho, Mil*) leave; **com ~** excuse me; **estar de ~** to be on leave; **dá ~?** may I?

licenciado, -a [lisẽ'sjadu, a] m/f graduate

licenciar [lisẽ'sja[^r]] vt to license; **~-se** vr (*Educ*) to graduate; (*ficar de licença*) to take leave; **licenciatura** [lisẽsja'tura] f (*título*) degree; (*curso*) degree course

liceu [li'sew] (PT) m secondary (BRIT) ou high (US) school

lições [li'sõjʃ] fpl de **lição**

licor [li'ko[^r]] m liqueur

lidar [li'da[^r]] vi: **~ com** (*ocupar-se*) to deal with; (*combater*) to struggle against; **~ em algo** to work in sth

líder ['lide[^r]] m/f leader; **liderança** [lide'rãsa] f leadership; (*Esporte*) lead; **liderar** [lide'ra[^r]] vt to lead

ligado, -a [li'gadu, a] adj (*Tec*) connected; (*luz, rádio etc*) on; (*metal*) alloy

ligadura [liga'dura] f bandage

ligamento [liga'mẽtu] m ligament

ligar [li'ga[^r]] vt to tie, bind; (*unir*) to join, connect; (*luz, TV*) to switch on; (*afetivamente*) to bind together; (*carro*) to start (up) ▷ vi (*telefonar*) to ring; **~-se** vr to join; **~-se com alguém** to join with sb; **~-se a algo** to be connected with sth; **~ para alguém** to ring sb up; **~ para ou a algo** (*dar atenção*) to take notice of sth; (*dar importância*) to care about sth; **eu nem ligo** it doesn't bother me; **não ligo a mínima (para)** I couldn't care less (about)

ligeiro, -a [li'ʒejru, a] adj light; (*ferimento*) slight; (*referência*) passing; (*conhecimentos*) scant; (*rápido*) quick, swift; (*ágil*) nimble ▷ adv swiftly, nimbly

lilás [li'laʃ] adj, m lilac

lima ['lima] f (*laranja*) type of (very sweet) orange; (*ferramenta*) file; **~ de unhas** nailfile

limão [li'mãw] (pl **-ões**) m lime; **limão (-galego)** (pl **limões(-galegos)**) m lemon

limiar [li'mja[^r]] m threshold

limitação [limita'sãw] (pl **-ões**) f limitation, restriction

limitar [limi'ta[^r]] vt to limit, restrict; **~-se** vr: **~-se a** to limit o.s. to; **~-se com** to border on; **limite** [li'mitʃi] m limit, boundary; (*fig*) limit; **passar dos limites** to go too far

limo ['limu] m (*Bot*) water weed; (*lodo*) slime

limoeiro [li'mwejru] m lemon tree

limões [li'mõjʃ] mpl de **limão**

limonada [limo'nada] f lemonade (BRIT), lemon soda (US)

limpar [lĩ'pa[^r]] vt to clean; (*lágrimas, suor*) to wipe away; (*polir*) to shine, polish; (*fig*) to clean up; (*roubar*) to rob

limpo, -a ['lĩpu, a] pp de **limpar** ▷ adj clean; (*céu, consciência*) clear; (*Com*) net; (*fig*) pure; (*col: pronto*) ready; **passar a ~** to make a fair copy; **tirar a ~** to find out the truth about, clear up; **estar ~ com alguém** (*col*) to be in with sb

linchar [lĩ'ʃa[^r]] vt to lynch

lindo, -a ['lĩdu, a] adj lovely

lingerie [lĩʒe'ri] m lingerie

língua ['lĩgwa] f tongue; (*linguagem*) language; **botar a ~ para fora** to stick out one's tongue; **dar com a ~ nos dentes** to let the cat out of the bag; **estar na ponta da ~** to be on the tip of one's tongue

linguado [lĩ'gwadu] m (*peixe*) sole

linguagem [lĩ'gwaʒẽ] (pl **-ns**) f (tb Comput) language; (*falada*) speech; **~ de máquina** (Comput) machine language

linguarudo, -a [lĩgwa'rudu, a] adj gossiping ▷ m/f gossip

lingüiça [lĩ'gwisa] f sausage

linha ['liɲa] f line; (*para costura*) thread; (*barbante*) string, cord; **linhas** fpl (*carta*) letter sg; **em ~** in line, in a row; (Comput) on line; **fora de ~** (Comput) off line; **manter/perder a ~** to keep/lose one's cool; **o telefone não deu ~** the line was dead; **~ aérea** airline; **~ de mira** sights pl; **~ de montagem** assembly line; **~ férrea** railway (BRIT), railroad (US)

linho ['liɲu] m linen; (*planta*) flax

liquidação [likida'sãw] (pl **-ões**) f

liquidation; (*em loja*) (clearance) sale; (*de conta*) settlement; **em ~ on** sale

liquidar [liki'da^r] *vt* to liquidate; (*conta*) to settle; (*mercadoria*) to sell off; (*assunto*) to lay to rest ▷ *vi* (*loja*) to have a sale; **~-se** *vr* (*destruir-se*) to be destroyed; **~ (com) alguém** (*fig: arrasar*) to destroy sb; (: *matar*) to do away with sb

liqüidificador [likwidʒifika'do^r] *m* liquidizer

líquido, -a ['likidu, a] *adj* liquid, fluid; (*Com*) net ▷ *m* liquid

lira ['lira] *f* lyre; (*moeda*) lira

lírio ['lirju] *m* lily

Lisboa [liʒ'boa] *n* Lisbon; **lisboeta** [liʒ'bweta] *adj* Lisbon *atr* ▷ *m/f* inhabitant *ou* native of Lisbon

liso, -a ['lizu, a] *adj* smooth; (*tecido*) plain; (*cabelo*) straight; (*col: sem dinheiro*) broke

lisonjear [lizõ'ʒja^r] *vt* to flatter

lista ['liʃta] *f* list; (*listra*) stripe; (*PT: menu*) menu; **~ negra** blacklist; **~ telefônica** telephone directory; **listar** [liʃ'ta^r] *vt* (*Comput*) to list

listra ['liʃtra] *f* stripe; **listrado, -a** [liʃ'tradu, a] *adj* striped

literal [lite'raw] (*pl* **-ais**) *adj* literal

literário, -a [lite'rarju, a] *adj* literary

literatura [litera'tura] *f* literature; **literatura de cordel** *see boxed note*

※ **LITERATURA DE CORDEL**
※
※ **Literatura de cordel** is a type of
※ literature typical of the north-east
※ of Brazil, and published in the form
※ of cheaply printed booklets. Their
※ authors hang these booklets from
※ wires attached to walls in the street
※ so that people can look at them.
※ While they do this, the authors sing
※ their stories aloud. **Literatura de**
※ **cordel** deals both with local events
※ and people, and with everyday public
※ life, almost always in an irreverent
※ manner.

---

litoral [lito'raw] (*pl* **-ais**) *adj* coastal ▷ *m* coast, seaboard

litro ['litru] *m* litre (*BRIT*), liter (*US*)

livrar [li'vra^r] *vt* to release, liberate; (*salvar*) to save; **~-se** *vr* to escape; **~-se de** to get rid of; (*compromisso*) to get out of; **Deus me livre!** Heaven forbid!

livraria [livra'ria] *f* bookshop (*BRIT*), bookstore (*US*)

livre ['livri] *adj* free; (*lugar*) unoccupied; (*desimpedido*) clear, open; **~ de impostos** tax-free; **livre-arbítrio** *m* free will

livro ['livru] *m* book; **~ brochado** paperback; **~ de bolso** pocket-sized book; **~ de cheques** cheque book (*BRIT*), check book (*US*); **~ de consulta** reference book; **~ encadernado** *ou* **de capa dura** hardback

lixa ['liʃa] *f* sandpaper; (*de unhas*) nailfile; (*peixe*) dogfish; **lixar** [li'ʃa^r] *vt* to sand

lixeira [li'ʃejra] *f* dustbin (*BRIT*), garbage can (*US*)

lixeiro [li'ʃejru] *m* dustman (*BRIT*), garbage man (*US*)

lixo ['liʃu] *m* rubbish, garbage (*US*); **ser um ~** (*col*) to be rubbish; **~ atômico** nuclear waste

-lo [lu] *pron* him; (*você*) you; (*coisa*) it

lobo ['lobu] *m* wolf

locação [loka'sãw] (*pl* **-ões**) *f* lease; (*de vídeo etc*) rental

locador, a [loka'do^r, a] *m/f* (*de casa*) landlord; (*de carro, filme*) rental agent ▷ *f* rental company; **~a de vídeo** video rental shop

local [lo'kaw] (*pl* **-ais**) *adj* local ▷ *m* site, place ▷ *f* (*notícia*) story; **localidade** [lokali'dadʒi] *f* (*lugar*) locality; (*povoação*) town; **localização** [lokaliza'sãw] (*pl* **-ões**) *f* location; **localizar** [lokali'za^r] *vt* to locate; (*situar*) to place; **localizar-se** *vr* to be located; (*orientar-se*) to get one's bearings

loção [lo'sãw] (*pl* **-ões**) *f* lotion; **~ após-barba** aftershave (lotion)

locatário, -a [loka'tarju, a] *m/f* (*de casa*) tenant; (*de carro, filme*) hirer

loções [lo'sõjʃ] *fpl* de **loção**

locomotiva [lokomo'tʃiva] *f* railway (*BRIT*) *ou* railroad (*US*) engine, locomotive

locomover-se [lokomo'vexsi] *vr* to move around

locutor, a [loku'to^r, a] *m/f* (*TV, Rádio*) announcer

lógica ['lɔʒika] *f* logic; **lógico, -a** ['lɔʒiku, a] *adj* logical; **(é) lógico!** of course!

logo ['lɔgu] *adv* (*imediatamente*) right away, at once; (*em breve*) soon; (*justamente*) just, right; (*mais tarde*) later; **~, ~** straightaway, without delay; **~ mais** later; **~ no começo** right at the start; **~ que, tão** as soon as; **até ~!** bye!; **~ antes/depois** just before/shortly afterwards; **~ de saída** *ou* **de cara** straightaway, right away

logotipo [logo'tʃipu] *m* logo
lograr [lo'graʳ] *vt* (*alcançar*) to achieve; (*obter*) to get, obtain; (*enganar*) to cheat; **~ fazer** to manage to do
loiro, -a ['lojru, a] *adj* = **louro/a**
loja ['lɔʒa] *f* shop; **lojista** [lo'ʒiʃta] *m/f* shopkeeper
lombo ['lõbu] *m* back; (*carne*) loin
lona ['lona] *f* canvas
Londres ['lõdriʃ] *n* London; **londrino, -a** [lõ'drinu, a] *adj* London *atr* ▷ *m/f* Londoner
longa-metragem (*pl* **longas-metragens**) *m*: **(filme de) ~** feature (film)
longe ['lõʒi] *adv* far, far away ▷ *adj* distant; **ao ~** in the distance; **de ~** from far away; (*sem dúvida*) by a long way; **~ de** a long way *ou* far from; **~ disso** far from it; **ir ~ demais** (*fig*) to go too far
longínquo, -a [lõ'ʒĩkwu, a] *adj* distant, remote
longitude [lõʒi'tudʒi] *f* (*Geo*) longitude
longo, -a ['lõgu, a] *adj* long ▷ *m* (*vestido*) long dress, evening dress; **ao ~ de** along, alongside
lotação [lota'sãw] *f* capacity; (*de funcionários*) complement; (BR: *ônibus*) bus; **~ completa** *ou* **esgotada** (*Teatro*) sold out
lotado, -a [lo'tadu, a] *adj* (*Teatro*) full; (*ônibus*) full up; (*bar, praia*) packed, crowded
lotar [lo'taʳ] *vt* to fill, pack; (*funcionário*) to place ▷ *vi* to fill up
lote ['lɔtʃi] *m* portion, share; (*em leilão*) lot; (*terreno*) plot; (*de ações*) parcel, batch
loteria [lote'ria] *f* lottery; **~ esportiva** football pools *pl* (BRIT), lottery (US)
louça ['losa] *f* china; (*conjunto*) crockery; (*tb*: **~ sanitária**) bathroom suite; **de ~** china *atr*; **~ de barro** earthenware; **~ de jantar** dinner service; **lavar a ~** to do the washing up *ou* the dishes
louco, -a ['loku, a] *adj* crazy, mad; (*sucesso*) runaway; (*frio*) freezing ▷ *m/f* lunatic; **~ varrido** raving mad; **~ de fome/raiva** ravenous/hopping mad; **~ por** crazy about; **deixar alguém ~** to drive sb crazy; **loucura** [lo'kura] *f* madness; (*ato*) crazy thing; **ser loucura (fazer)** to be crazy (to do); **ser uma loucura** to be crazy; (*col*: *ser muito bom*) to be fantastic
louro, -a ['loru, a] *adj* blond, fair ▷ *m* laurel; (*Culin*) bay leaf; (*papagaio*) parrot;

louros *mpl* (*fig*) laurels
louva-a-deus ['lova-] *m inv* praying mantis
louvar [lo'vaʳ] *vt* to praise ▷ *vi*: **~ a** to praise; **louvável** [lo'vavew] (*pl* **-eis**) *adj* praiseworthy
louvor [lo'voʳ] *m* praise
LP *abr m* LP
Ltda. *abr* (= *Limitada*) Ltd (BRIT), Inc. (US)
lua ['lua] *f* moon; **estar** *ou* **viver no mundo da ~** to have one's head in the clouds; **estar de ~** (*col*) to be in a mood; **ser de ~** (*col*) to be moody; **~ cheia/nova** full/new moon; **lua-de-mel** *f* honeymoon
luar ['lwaʳ] *m* moonlight
lubrificante [lubrifi'kãtʃi] *m* lubricant
lúcido, -a ['lusidu, a] *adj* lucid
lúcio ['lusju] *m* (*peixe*) pike
lucrar [lu'kraʳ] *vt* (*tirar proveito*) to profit from *ou* by; (*dinheiro*) to make; (*gozar*) to enjoy ▷ *vi* to make a profit; **~ com** *ou* **em** to profit by
lucrativo, -a [lukra'tʃivu, a] *adj* lucrative, profitable
lucro ['lukru] *m* gain; (*Com*) profit; **~s e perdas** (*Com*) profit and loss
lugar [lu'gaʳ] *m* place; (*espaço*) space, room; (*para sentar*) seat; (*emprego*) job; (*ocasião*) opportunity; **em ~ de** instead of; **dar ~ a** (*causar*) to give rise to; **~ comum** commonplace; **em primeiro ~** in the first place; **em algum/nenhum/todo ~** somewhere/nowhere/everywhere; **em outro ~** somewhere else, elsewhere; **ter ~** (*acontecer*) to take place; **~ de nascimento** place of birth; **lugarejo** [luga'reʒu] *m* village
lula ['lula] *f* squid
lume ['lumi] *m* fire; (*luz*) light
luminária [lumi'narja] *f* lamp; **luminárias** *fpl* (*iluminações*) illuminations
luminosidade [luminozi'dadʒi] *f* brightness
luminoso, -a [lumi'nozu, ɔza] *adj* luminous; (*fig*: *raciocínio*) clear; (: *idéia, talento*) brilliant; (*letreiro*) illuminated
lunar [lu'naʳ] *adj* lunar ▷ *m* (*na pele*) mole
lunático, -a [lu'natʃiku, a] *adj* mad
lusitano, -a [luzi'tanu, a] *adj* Portuguese, Lusitanian
luso, -a ['luzu, a] *adj* Portuguese; **luso-brasileiro, -a** (*pl* **lusos-brasileiros/as**) *adj* Luso-Brazilian
lustre ['luʃtri] *m* gloss, sheen; (*fig*) lustre

(BRIT), luster (US); (luminária) chandelier

luta ['luta] f fight, struggle; **~ de boxe**
boxing; **~ livre** wrestling; **lutador, a**
[luta'do^r, a] m/f fighter; (atleta) wrestler;
lutar [lu'ta^r] vi to fight, struggle; (luta
livre) to wrestle ▷ vt (caratê, judô) to
do; **lutar contra/por algo** to fight
against/for sth; **lutar para fazer algo**
to fight ou struggle to do sth; **lutar**
com (dificuldades) to struggle against;
(competir) to fight with

luto ['lutu] m mourning; (tristeza) grief;
de ~ in mourning; **pôr ~** to go into
mourning

luva ['luva] f glove; **luvas** fpl (pagamento)
payment sg; (ao locador) fee sg

Luxemburgo [luʃē'buxgu] m: **o ~**
Luxembourg

luxo ['luʃu] m luxury; **de ~** luxury atr; **dar-**
se ao ~ de to allow o.s. to; **luxuoso, -a**
[lu'ʃwozu, ɔza] adj luxurious

luxúria [lu'ʃurja] f lust

luz [luʒ] f light; (eletricidade) electricity;
à ~ de by the light of; (fig) in the light of;
a meia ~ with subdued lighting; **dar à ~**
(um filho) to give birth (to a son); **deu-**
me uma ~ I had an idea

m

ma [ma] pron = me + a

má [ma] f de mau

maca ['maka] f stretcher

maçã [ma'sã] f apple; **~ do rosto**
cheekbone

macabro, -a [ma'kabru, a] adj macabre

macacão [maka'kãw] (pl **-ões**) m (de
trabalhador) overalls pl (BRIT), coveralls pl
(US); (da moda) jump-suit

macaco, -a [ma'kaku, a] m/f monkey
▷ m (Mecânica) jack; (fato) **~** (PT) overalls
pl (BRIT), coveralls pl (US); **~ velho** (fig)
old hand

macacões [maka'kõjʃ] mpl de **macacão**

maçador, a [masa'do^r, a] (PT) adj boring

maçaneta [masa'neta] f knob

maçante [ma'sãtʃi] (BR) adj boring

macarrão [maka'xãw] m pasta;
(em forma de canudo) spaghetti;
macarronada [makaxo'nada] f pasta
with cheese and tomato sauce

macete [ma'setʃi] m mallet

machado [ma'ʃadu] m axe (BRIT), ax (US)

machista [ma'ʃiʃta] adj chauvinistic,
macho ▷ m male chauvinist

macho ['maʃu] adj male; (fig) virile,
manly; (valentão) tough ▷ m male; (Tec)
tap

machucado, -a [maʃuˈkadu, a] adj
hurt; (pé, braço) bad ▷ m injury; (área
machucada) sore patch
machucar [maʃuˈkaʳ] vt to hurt;
(produzir contusão) to bruise ▷ vi to hurt;
~-se vr to hurt o.s
maciço, -a [maˈsisu, a] adj solid;
(espesso) thick; (quantidade) massive
macio, -a [maˈsiu, a] adj soft; (liso)
smooth
maço [ˈmasu] m (de folhas, notas) bundle;
(de cigarros) packet
maçom [maˈsõ] (pl -ns) m (free)mason
maconha [maˈkɔɲa] f dope; **cigarro de
~** joint
maçons [maˈsõʃ] mpl de **maçom**
má-criação (pl -ões) f rudeness; (ato,
dito) rude thing
mácula [ˈmakula] f stain, blemish
macumba [maˈkũba] f ≈ voodoo;
(despacho) macumba offering;
macumbeiro, -a [makũˈbejru, a] adj
≈ voodoo atr ▷ m/f follower of macumba
madama [maˈdama] f = **madame**
madame [maˈdami] f (senhora) lady; (col:
dona-de-casa) lady of the house
madeira [maˈdejra] f wood ▷ m Madeira
(wine); **de ~** wooden; **bater na ~** (fig) to
touch (BRIT) ou knock on (US) wood; **~
compensada** plywood
madeirense [madejˈrẽsi] adj, m/f
Madeiran
madeixa [maˈdejʃa] f (de cabelo) lock
madrasta [maˈdraʃta] f stepmother
madrepérola [madreˈpɛrola] f mother
of pearl
Madri [maˈdri] n Madrid
Madrid [maˈdrid] (PT) n Madrid
madrinha [maˈdriɲa] f godmother
madrugada [madruˈgada] f (early)
morning; (alvorada) dawn, daybreak
madrugar [madruˈgaʳ] vi to get up early;
(aparecer cedo) to be early
maduro, -a [maˈduru, a] adj ripe; (fig)
mature; (: prudente) prudent
mãe [mãj] f mother; **~ adotiva** ou **de
criação** adoptive mother
maestro, -trina [maˈɛʃtru, ˈtrina] m/f
conductor
má-fé f malicious intent
magia [maˈʒia] f magic
mágica [ˈmaʒika] f magic; (truque) magic
trick; ver tb **mágico**
mágico, -a [ˈmaʒiku, a] adj magic ▷ m/f
magician
magistério [maʒiʃˈtɛrju] m (ensino)

teaching; (profissão) teaching profession;
(professorado) teachers pl
magnético, -a [magˈnɛtʃiku, a] adj
magnetic
magnífico, -a [magˈnifiku, a] adj
splendid, magnificent
mago [ˈmagu] m magician; **os reis ~s** the
Three Wise Men, the Three Kings
mágoa [ˈmagwa] f (tristeza) sorrow,
grief; (fig: desagrado) hurt
magoado, -a [maˈgwadu, a] adj hurt
magoar [maˈgwaʳ] vt, vi to hurt; **~-se** vr:
~-se com algo to be hurt by sth
magro, -a [ˈmagru, a] adj (pessoa) slim;
(carne) lean; (fig: parco) meagre (BRIT),
meager (US); (leite) skimmed
maio [ˈmaju] (PT M-) m May
maiô [maˈjo] (BR) m swimsuit
maionese [majoˈnezi] f mayonnaise
maior [maˈjɔʳ] adj (compar: de tamanho)
bigger; (: de importância) greater; (superl:
de tamanho) biggest; (: de importância)
greatest ▷ m/f adult; **~ de idade** of age,
adult; **~ de 21 anos** over 21; **maioria**
[majoˈria] f majority; **a maioria de**
most of; **maioridade** [majoriˈdadʒi] f
adulthood

⊙ **PALAVRA CHAVE**

mais [majʃ] adv **1** (compar): **mais magro/
inteligente (do que)** thinner/more
intelligent (than); **ele trabalha mais (do
que eu)** he works more (than me)
2 (superl): **o mais ... the** most ...; **o mais
magro/inteligente** the thinnest/most
intelligent
3 (negativo): **ele não trabalha mais aqui**
he doesn't work here any more; **nunca
mais** never again
4 (+ adj: valor intensivo): **que livro mais
chato!** what a boring book!
5: por mais que however much; **por
mais que se esforce ...** no matter
how hard you try ...; **por mais que eu
quisesse ...** much as I should like to ...
6: a mais: temos um a mais we've got
one extra
7 (tempo): **mais cedo ou mais tarde**
sooner or later; **a mais tempo** sooner;
logo mais later on; **no mais tardar** at
the latest
8 (frases): **mais ou menos** more or less;
mais uma vez once more; **cada vez
mais** more and more; **sem mais nem
menos** out of the blue

▷ *adj* **1** (*compar*): **mais (do que)** more (than); **ele tem mais dinheiro (do que o irmão)** he's got more money (than his brother)

2 (*superl*): **ele é quem tem mais dinheiro** he's got most money

3 (+*números*): **ela tem mais de dez bolsas** she's got more than ten bags

4 (*negativo*): **não tenho mais dinheiro** I haven't got any more money

5 (*adicional*) else; **mais alguma coisa?** anything else?; **nada/ninguém mais** nothing/no-one else

▷ *prep*: **2 mais 2 são 4** 2 and 2 ou plus 2 are 4

▷ *m*: **o mais** the rest

maisena [maj'zena] *f* cornflower
maiúscula [ma'juʃkula] *f* capital letter
majestade [maʒeʃ'tadʒi] *f* majesty; **majestoso, -a** [maʒeʃ'tozu, ɔza] *adj* majestic
major [ma'ʒɔr] *m* (*Mil*) major
majoritário, -a [maʒori'tarju, a] *adj* majority *atr*
mal [maw] (*pl* **-es**) *m* harm; (*Med*) illness ▷ *adv* badly; (*quase não*) hardly ▷ *conj* hardly; **~ desliguei o fone, a campainha tocou** I had hardly put the phone down when the doorbell rang; **falar ~ de alguém** to speak ill of sb, run sb down; **não faz ~** never mind; **estar ~** (*doente*) to be ill; **passar ~** to be sick; **estar de ~ com alguém** not to be speaking to sb
mal- [mal-] *prefixo* badly
mala ['mala] *f* suitcase; (*BR: Auto*) boot, trunk (*US*); **malas** *fpl* (*bagagem*) luggage *sg*; **fazer as ~s** to pack
malabarismo [malaba'riʒmu] *m* juggling; **malabarista** [malaba'riʃta] *m/f* juggler
mal-acabado, -a *adj* badly finished; (*pessoa*) deformed
malagueta [mala'geta] *f* chilli (*BRIT*) ou chili (*US*) pepper
Malaísia [mala'izja] *f*: **a ~** Malaysia
malandragem [malã'draʒẽ] *f* (*patifaria*) double-dealing; (*preguiça*) idleness; (*esperteza*) cunning
malária [ma'larja] *f* malaria
mal-arrumado, -a [-axu'madu, a] *adj* untidy
malcomportado, -a [mawkõpox'tadu, a] *adj* badly behaved
malcriado, -a [maw'krjadu, a] *adj* rude

▷ *m/f* slob
maldade [maw'dadʒi] *f* cruelty; (*malícia*) malice
maldição [mawdʒi'sãw] (*pl* **-ões**) *f* curse
maldizer [mawdʒi'zer] (*irreg*: *como* **dizer**) *vt* to curse
maldoso, -a [maw'dozu, ɔza] *adj* wicked; (*malicioso*) malicious
maledicência [maledʒi'sẽsja] *f* slander
mal-educado, -a *adj* rude ▷ *m/f* slob
malefício [male'fisju] *m* harm; **maléfico, -a** [ma'lɛfiku, a] *adj* (*pessoa*) malicious; (*prejudicial*: *efeito*) harmful, injurious
mal-entendido, -a *adj* misunderstood ▷ *m* misunderstanding
mal-estar *m* indisposition; (*embaraço*) uneasiness
malfeito, -a [mal'fejtu, a] *adj* (*roupa*) poorly made; (*corpo*) misshapen
malfeitor, a [mawfej'tor, a] *m/f* wrong-doer
malha ['maʎa] *f* (*de rede*) mesh; (*tecido*) jersey; (*suéter*) sweater; (*de ginástica*) leotard; **fazer ~** (*PT*) to knit; **artigos de ~** knitwear
malhar [ma'ʎar] *vt* (*bater*) to beat; (*cereais*) to thresh; (*col*: *criticar*) to knock, run down
mal-humorado, -a [-umo'radu, a] *adj* grumpy, sullen
maligno, -a [ma'lignu, a] *adj* evil, malicious; (*danoso*) harmful; (*Med*) malignant
malograr [malo'grar] *vt* (*planos*) to upset; (*frustrar*) to thwart, frustrate ▷ *vi* (*planos*) to fall through; (*fracassar*) to fail; **~-se** *vr* to fall through; to fail
mal-passado, -a *adj* underdone; (*bife*) rare
malsucedido, -a [mawsuse'dʒidu, a] *adj* unsuccessful
Malta ['mawta] *f* Malta
malta ['mawta] (*PT*) *f* gang, mob
maltrapilho, -a [mawtra'piʎu, a] *adj* in rags, ragged ▷ *m/f* ragamuffin
maluco, -a [ma'luku, a] *adj* crazy, daft ▷ *m/f* madman/woman
malvadeza [mawva'deza] *f* wickedness; (*ato*) wicked thing
malvado, -a [maw'vadu, a] *adj* wicked
Malvinas [maw'vinaʃ] *fpl*: **as (ilhas) ~** the Falklands, the Falkland Islands
mama ['mama] *f* breast
mamadeira [mama'dejra] (*BR*) *f* feeding bottle

mamãe [maˈmãj] f mum, mummy

mamão [maˈmãw] (pl -ões) m papaya

mamar [maˈmaˈ] vt to suck; (dinheiro) to extort ▷ vi to be breastfed; **dar de ~ a um bebê** to (breast)feed a baby

mamífero [maˈmiferu] m mammal

mamilo [maˈmilu] m nipple

mamões [maˈmõjʃ] mpl de **mamão**

manada [maˈnada] f herd, drove

mancada [mãˈkada] f (erro) mistake; (gafe) blunder; **dar uma ~** to blunder

mancar [mãˈkaˈ] vt to cripple ▷ vi to limp; **~-se** vr (col) to get the message, take the hint

Mancha [ˈmãʃa] f: **o canal da ~** the English Channel

mancha [ˈmãʃa] f stain; (na pele) mark, spot; **sem ~s** (reputação) spotless; **manchado, -a** [mãˈʃadu, a] adj soiled; (malhado) mottled, spotted; **manchar** [mãˈʃaˈ] vt to stain, mark; (reputação) to soil

manchete [mãˈʃɛtʃi] f headline

manco, -a [ˈmãku, a] adj crippled, lame ▷ m/f cripple

mandado [mãˈdadu] m order; (Jur) writ; (: tb: **~ de segurança**) injunction; **~ de prisão/busca** warrant for sb's arrest/search warrant; **~ de segurança** injunction

mandão, -dona [mãˈdãw, ˈdɔna] (pl mandões/-s) adj bossy, domineering

mandar [mãˈdaˈ] vt (ordenar) to order; (enviar) to send ▷ vi to be in charge; **~-se** vr (col: partir) to make tracks, get going; (fugir) to take off; **~ buscar** ou **chamar** to send for; **~ fazer um vestido** to have a dress made; **~ que alguém faça**, **~ alguém fazer** to tell sb to do; **o que é que você manda?** (col) what can I do for you?; **~ em alguém** to boss sb around

mandato [mãˈdatu] m mandate; (ordem) order; (Pol) term of office

mandioca [mãˈdʒjɔka] f cassava, manioc

mandões [mãˈdõjʃ] mpl de **mandão**

mandona [mãˈdɔna] f de **mandão**

maneira [maˈnejra] f (modo) way; (estilo) style, manner; **maneiras** fpl (modas) manners; **à ~ de** like; **de ~ que** so that; **de ~ alguma** ou **nenhuma** not at all; **desta ~** in this way; **de qualquer ~** anyway; **não houve ~ de convencê-lo** it was impossible to convince him

maneiro, -a [maˈnejru, a] adj (ferramenta) easy to use; (roupa)

attractive; (trabalho) easy; (pessoa) capable; (col: bacana) great, brilliant

manejar [maneˈʒaˈ] vt (instrumento) to handle; (máquina) to work; **manejo** [maˈneʒu] m handling

manequim [maneˈkĩ] (pl -ns) m (boneco) dummy ▷ m/f model

manga [ˈmãga] f sleeve; (fruta) mango; **em ~s de camisa** in (one's) shirt sleeves

mangueira [mãˈgejra] f hose(pipe); (árvore) mango tree

manha [ˈmaɲa] f guile, craftiness; (destreza) skill; (ardil) trick; (birra) tantrum; **fazer ~** to have a tantrum

manhã [maˈɲã] f morning; **de** ou **pela ~** in the morning; **amanhã/hoje de ~** tomorrow/this morning

manhoso, -a [maˈɲozu, ɔza] adj crafty, sly; (criança) whining

mania [maˈnia] f (Med) mania; (obsessão) craze; **estar com ~ de ...** to have a thing about ...; **maníaco, -a** [maˈniaku, a] adj manic ▷ m/f maniac

manicômio [maniˈkomju] m asylum, mental hospital

manifestação [manifeʃtaˈsãw] (pl -ões) f show, display; (expressão) expression, declaration; (política) demonstration

manifestante [mãnifeʃˈtãtʃi] m/f demonstrator

manifestar [manifeʃˈtaˈ] vt to show, display; (declarar) to express, declare

manifesto, -a [mãniˈfeʃtu, a] adj obvious, clear ▷ m manifesto

manipulação [manipulaˈsãw] f handling; (fig) manipulation

manipular [manipuˈlaˈ] vt to manipulate; (manejar) to handle

manjericão [mãʒeriˈkãw] m basil

manobra [maˈnɔbra] f manoeuvre (BRIT), maneuver (US); (de mecanismo) operation; (de trens) shunting; **manobrar** [manoˈbraˈ] vt to manoeuvre ou maneuver; (mecanismo) to operate, work; (governar) to take charge of; (manipular) to manipulate ▷ vi to manoeuvre ou maneuver

manso, -a [ˈmãsu, a] adj gentle; (mar) calm; (animal) tame

manta [ˈmãta] f blanket; (xale) shawl; (agasalho) cloak

manteiga [mãˈtejga] f butter; **~ de cacau** cocoa butter

manter [mãˈteˈ] (irreg: como **ter**) vt to maintain; (num lugar) to keep; (uma família) to support; (a palavra)

to keep; (*princípios*) to abide by; **~-se**
vr to support o.s.; (*permanecer*) to
remain; **mantimento** [mãtʃi'mẽtu]
m maintenance; **mantimentos** *mpl*
(*alimentos*) provisions
manual [ma'nwaw] (*pl* -**ais**) *adj* manual
▷ *m* handbook, manual
manufatura [manufa'tura] (*PT*
-**ct-**) *f* manufacture; **manufaturar**
[manufatu'ra^r] (*PT* -**ct-**) *vt* to
manufacture
manusear [manu'zja^r] *vt* to handle;
(*livro*) to leaf through
mão [mãw] (*pl* ~**s**) *f* hand; (*de animal*)
paw; (*de pintura*) coat; (*de direção*) flow
of traffic; **à ~** by hand; (*perto*) at hand;
de segunda ~ second-hand; **em ~** by
hand; **dar a ~ a alguém** to hold sb's
hand; (*cumprimentar*) to shake hands
with sb; **dar uma ~ a alguém** to give
sb a hand, help sb out; **~ única/dupla**
one-way/two-way traffic; **rua de duas
~s** two-way street; **mão-de-obra** *f*
(*trabalhadores*) labour (*BRIT*), labor (*US*);
(*coisa difícil*) tricky thing
mapa ['mapa] *m* map; (*gráfico*) chart
maquiagem [ma'kjaʒẽ] *f*
= **maquilagem**
maquiar [ma'kja^r] *vt* to make up; **~-se** *vr*
to make o.s. up, put on one's make-up
maquilagem [maki'laʒẽ] (*PT* -**lha-**) *f*
make-up; (*ato*) making up
máquina ['makina] *f* machine; (*de trem*)
engine; (*fig*) machinery; **~ de calcular/
costura/escrever** calculator/sewing
machine/typewriter; **~ fotográfica**
camera; (*de filmar*) camera; (*de vídeo*)
camcorder; **~ de lavar (roupa)/pratos**
washing machine/dishwasher; **escrito
à ~** typewritten
maquinar [maki'na^r] *vt* to plot ▷ *vi* to
conspire
maquinista [maki'niʃta] *m* (*Ferro*)
engine driver; (*Náut*) engineer
mar [ma^r] *m* sea; **por ~** by sea; **fazer-se
ao ~** to set sail; **pleno ~, ~ alto** high
sea; **o ~ Morto/Negro/Vermelho** the
Dead/Black/Red Sea
maracujá [maraku'ʒa] *m* passion fruit;
pé de ~ passion flower
maratona [mara'tona] *f* marathon
maravilha [mara'viʎa] *f* marvel,
wonder; **maravilhoso, -a** [maravi'ʎozu,
ɔza] *adj* marvellous (*BRIT*), marvelous
(*US*)
marca ['maxka] *f* mark; (*Com*) make,

brand; (*carimbo*) stamp; **~ de fábrica**
trademark; **~ registrada** registered
trademark
marcação [maxka'sãw] (*pl* -**ões**)
f marking; (*em jogo*) scoring; (*de
instrumento*) reading; (*Teatro*) action; (*PT:
Tel*) dialling
marcador [maxka'do^r] *m* marker;
(*de livro*) bookmark; (*Esporte: quadro*)
scoreboard; (: *jogador*) scorer
marcapasso [maxka'pasu] *m* (*Med*)
pacemaker
marcar [max'ka^r] *vt* to mark; (*hora,
data*) to fix, set; (*PT: Tel*) to dial; (*gol,
ponto*) to score ▷ *vi* to make one's mark;
~ uma consulta, ~ hora to make an
appointment; **~ um encontro com
alguém** to arrange to meet sb
marcha ['maxʃa] *f* march; (*de
acontecimentos*) course; (*passo*) pace;
(*Auto*) gear; (*progresso*) progress; **~ à ré**
(*BR*), **~ atrás** (*PT*) reverse (gear); **pôr-se
em ~** to set off
marchar [max'ʃa^r] *vi* to go; (*andar a pé*) to
walk; (*Mil*) to march
marco ['maxku] *m* landmark; (*de janela*)
frame; (*fig*) frontier; (*moeda*) mark
março ['maxsu] (*PT* **M-**) *m* March
maré [ma're] *f* tide
marechal [mare'ʃaw] (*pl* -**ais**) *m* marshal
maremoto [mare'mɔtu] *m* tidal wave
marfim [max'fĩ] *m* ivory
margarida [maxga'rida] *f* daisy;
(*Comput*) daisy wheel
margarina [maxga'rina] *f* margarine
margem ['maxʒẽ] (*pl* -**ns**) *f* (*borda*) edge;
(*de rio*) bank; (*litoral*) shore; (*de impresso*)
margin; (*fig: tempo*) time; (: *lugar*) space; **à
~ de** alongside
marginal [maxʒi'naw] (*pl* -**ais**) *adj*
marginal ▷ *m/f* delinquent
marido [ma'ridu] *m* husband
marimbondo [marĩ'bõdu] *m* hornet
marinha [ma'riɲa] *f* (*tb:* **~ de guerra**)
navy; **~ mercante** merchant navy;
marinheiro [mari'ɲejru] *m* seaman,
sailor
marinho, -a [ma'riɲu, a] *adj* sea *atr*,
marine
mariposa [mari'poza] *f* moth
marítimo, -a [ma'ritʃimu, a] *adj* sea *atr*
marketing ['maxketʃĩŋ] *m* marketing
marmelada [maxme'lada] *f* quince jam
marmelo [max'mɛlu] *m* quince
marmita [max'mita] *f* (*vasilha*) pot
mármore ['maxmori] *m* marble

marquês, -quesa [max'keʃ, 'keza] *m/f* marquis/marchioness

marquise [max'kizi] *f* awning, canopy

Marrocos [ma'xɔkuʃ] *m*: **o ~** Morocco

marrom [ma'xõ] (*pl* **-ns**) *adj, m* brown

martelar [maxte'la'] *vt* to hammer; (*amolar*) to bother ▷ *vi* to hammer; (*insistir*): **~ (em algo)** to keep *ou* harp on (about sth); **martelo** [max'tɛlu] *m* hammer

mártir ['maxtʃi'] *m/f* martyr; **martírio** [max'tʃirju] *m* martyrdom; (*fig*) torment

marxista [max'ksiʃta] *adj, m/f* Marxist

mas [ma(j)ʃ] *conj* but ▷ *pron* = **me** + **as**

mascar [maʃ'ka'] *vt* to chew

máscara ['maʃkara] *f* mask; (*para limpeza de pele*) face pack; **sob a ~ de** under the guise of; **mascarar** [maʃka'ra'] *vt* to mask; (*disfarçar*) to disguise; (*encobrir*) to cover up

mascote [maʃ'kɔtʃi] *f* mascot

masculino, -a [maʃku'linu, a] *adj* masculine; (*Bio*) male

massa ['masa] *f* (*Fís, fig*) mass; (*de tomate*) paste; (*Culin: de pão*) dough; (: *macarrão etc*) pasta

massacrar [masa'kra'] *vt* to massacre; **massacre** [ma'sakri] *f* massacre

massagear [masa'ʒja'] *vt* to massage; **massagem** [ma'saʒē] (*pl* **-ns**) *f* massage

mastigar [maʃtʃi'ga'] *vt* to chew

mastro ['maʃtru] *m* (*Náut*) mast; (*para bandeira*) flagpole

masturbar-se [maʃtux'baxsi] *vr* to masturbate

mata ['mata] *f* forest, wood

matadouro [mata'doru] *m* slaughterhouse

matança [ma'tãsa] *f* massacre; (*de reses*) slaughter(ing)

matar [ma'ta'] *vt* to kill; (*sede*) to quench; (*fome*) to satisfy; (*aula*) to skip; (*trabalho: não aparecer*) to skive off; (: *fazer rápido*) to dash off; (*adivinhar*) to guess ▷ *vi* to kill; **~-se** *vr* to kill o.s.; (*esfalfar-se*) to wear o.s. out; **um calor/uma dor de ~** stifling heat/excruciating pain

mate ['matʃi] *adj* matt ▷ *m* (*chá*) maté tea; (*xeque-mate*) checkmate

matemática [mate'matʃika] *f* mathematics *sg*, maths *sg* (*BRIT*), math (*US*); **matemático, -a** [mate'matʃiku, a] *adj* mathematical ▷ *m/f* mathematician

matéria [ma'tɛrja] *f* matter; (*Tec*) material; (*Educ: assunto*) subject; (*tema*) topic; (*jornalística*) story, article; **em ~ de** on the subject of

material [mate'rjaw] (*pl* **-ais**) *adj* material; (*físico*) physical ▷ *m* material; (*Tec*) equipment; **materialista** [materja'liʃta] *adj* materialistic; **materializar** [materjali'za'] *vt* to materialize; **materializar-se** *vr* to materialize

maternal [matex'naw] (*pl* **-ais**) *adj* motherly, maternal; **escola ~** nursery (school); **maternidade** [matexni'dadʒi] *f* motherhood, maternity; (*hospital*) maternity hospital

materno, -a [ma'tɛxnu, a] *adj* motherly, maternal; (*língua*) native

matinê [matʃi'ne] *f* matinée

matiz [ma'tʃiʒ] *m* (*de cor*) shade

mato ['matu] *m* scrubland, bush; (*plantas agrestes*) scrub; (*o campo*) country

matraca [ma'traka] *f* rattle

matrícula [ma'trikula] *f* (*lista*) register; (*inscrição*) registration; (*pagamento*) enrolment (*BRIT*) *ou* enrollment (*US*) fee; (*PT: Auto*) registration number (*BRIT*), license number (*US*); **fazer a ~** to enrol (*BRIT*), enroll (*US*)

matrimonial [matrimo'njaw] (*pl* **-ais**) *adj* marriage *atr*, matrimonial

matrimônio [matri'monju] *m* marriage

matriz [ma'triʒ] *f* (*Med*) womb; (*fonte*) source; (*molde*) mould (*BRIT*), mold (*US*); (*Com*) head office

maturidade [maturi'dadʒi] *f* maturity

mau, má [maw, ma] *adj* bad; (*malvado*) evil, wicked ▷ *m* bad; (*Rel*) evil; **os maus** *mpl* (*pessoas*) bad people; (*num filme*) the baddies

maus-tratos *mpl* ill-treatment *sg*

maxila [mak'sila] *f* jawbone

maxilar [maksi'la'] *m* jawbone

máxima ['masima] *f* maxim

máximo, -a ['masimu, a] *adj* (*maior que todos*) greatest; (*o maior possível*) maximum ▷ *m* maximum; (*o cúmulo*) peak; (*temperature*) high; **no ~** at most; **ao ~** to the utmost

MCE *abr m* = **Mercado Comum Europeu**

me [mi] *pron* (*direto*) me; (*indireto*) (to) me; (*reflexivo*) (to) myself

meado ['mjadu] *m* middle; **em ~s** *ou* **no(s) ~(s) de julho** in mid-July

Meca ['mɛka] *n* Mecca

mecânica [me'kanika] *f* (*ciência*) mechanics *sg*; (*mecanismo*) mechanism; *ver tb* **mecânico**

mecânico, -a [me'kaniku, a] *adj*

mechanical ▷ *m/f* mechanic
mecanismo [meka'nizmu] *m*
mechanism; **~ de busca** (BR: *Comput*)
search engine
meço *etc* ['mɛsu] *vb ver* **medir**
medalha [me'daʎa] *f* medal; **medalhão**
[meda'ʎãw] (*pl* **-ões**) *m* medallion
média ['mɛdʒja] *f* average; (*café*) coffee
with milk; **em ~** on average
mediano, -a [me'dʒjanu, a] *adj*
medium; (*médio*) average; (*medíocre*)
mediocre
mediante [me'dʒjãtʃi] *prep* by (means
of), through; (*a troca de*) in return for
medicamento [medʒika'mẽtu] *m*
medicine
medicina [medʒi'sina] *f* medicine
médico, -a ['mɛdʒiku, a] *adj* medical
▷ *m/f* doctor; **receita médica**
prescription
medida [me'dʒida] *f* measure;
(*providência*) step; (*medição*)
measurement; (*moderação*) prudence; **à
~ que** while, as; **na ~ em que** in so far as;
feito sob ~ made to measure; **ir além
da ~** to go too far; **tirar as ~s de alguém**
to take sb's measurements; **~s to**
take steps; **tomar as ~s de** to measure
medieval [medʒje'vaw] (*pl* **-ais**) *adj*
medieval
médio, -a ['mɛdʒju, a] *adj* (*dedo, classe*)
middle; (*tamanho, estatura*) medium;
(*mediano*) average; **ensino ~** secondary
education
medir [me'dʒiʳ] *vt* to measure; (*atos,
palavras*) to weigh; (*avaliar: conseqüências,
distâncias*) to weigh up ▷ *vi* to measure;
quanto você mede? — meço 1.60 m
how tall are you? — I'm 1.60 m (tall)
meditar [medʒi'taʳ] *vi* to meditate; **~
sobre algo** to ponder (on) sth
mediterrâneo, -a [medʒite'xanju,
a] *adj* Mediterranean ▷ *m*: **o M~** the
Mediterranean
medo ['medu] *m* fear; **com ~** afraid;
meter ~ em alguém to frighten sb; **ter ~
de** to be afraid of
medonho, -a [me'doɲu, a] *adj* terrible,
awful
medroso, -a [me'drozu, ɔza] *adj* (*com
medo*) frightened; (*tímido*) timid
megabyte [mega'bajtʃi] *m* megabyte
meia ['meja] *f* stocking; (*curta*) sock;
(*meia-entrada*) half-price ticket ▷ *num* six;
meia-idade *f* middle age; **pessoa de
meia-idade** middle-aged person; **meia-**

noite *f* midnight
meigo, -a ['mejgu, a] *adj* sweet
meio, -a ['meju, a] *adj* half ▷ *adv* a bit,
rather ▷ *m* middle; (*social, profissional*)
milieu; (*tb:* **~ ambiente**) environment;
(*maneira*) way; (*recursos: tb:* **~s**) means
pl; **~ quilo** half a kilo; **um mês e ~** one
and a half months; **cortar ao ~** to cut in
half; **dividir algo ~ a ~** to divide sth in
half *ou* fifty-fifty; **em ~ a** amid; **no ~ (de)**
in the middle (of); **~s de comunicação
(de massa)** (mass) media *pl;* **por ~ de**
through; **meio-dia** *m* midday, noon;
meio-fio *m* kerb (BRIT), curb (US);
meio-termo (*pl* **meios-termos**) *m* (*fig*)
compromise
mel [mɛw] *m* honey
melaço [me'lasu] *m* treacle (BRIT),
molasses *pl* (US)
melancia [melã'sia] *f* watermelon
melancolia [melãko'lia] *f* melancholy,
sadness; **melancólico, -a** [melã'kɔliku,
a] *adj* melancholy, sad
melão [me'lãw] (*pl* **-ões**) *m* melon
melhor [me'ʎɔʳ] *adj, adv* (*compar*) better;
(*superl*) best; **~ que nunca** better than
ever; **quanto mais ~** the more the
better; **seria ~ começarmos** we had
better begin; **tanto ~** so much the better;
ou ~ ... (*ou antes*) or rather ...; **melhora**
[me'ʎɔra] *f* improvement; **melhoras!**
get well soon!; **melhorar** [meʎo'raʳ] *vt*
to improve, make better; (*doente*) to cure
▷ *vi* to improve, get better
melodia [melo'dʒia] *f* melody;
(*composição*) tune
melões [me'lõjʃ] *mpl de* **melão**
melro ['mɛwxu] *m* blackbird
membro ['mẽbru] *m* member; (*Anat:
braço, perna*) limb
memória [me'mɔrja] *f* memory;
memórias *fpl* (*de autor*) memoirs; **de ~**
by heart
memorizar [memori'zaʳ] *vt* to
memorize
mencionar [mẽsjo'naʳ] *vt* to mention
mendigar [mẽdʒi'gaʳ] *vt* to beg for ▷ *vi*
to beg; **mendigo, -a** [mẽ'dʒigu, a] *m/f*
beggar
menina [me'nina] *f*: **~ do olho** pupil; **ser
a ~ dos olhos de alguém** (*fig*) to be the
apple of sb's eye; *ver tb* **menino**
meninada [meni'nada] *f* kids *pl*
menino, -a [me'ninu, a] *m/f* boy/girl
menopausa [meno'pawza] *f*
menopause

menor [me'nɔʳ] *adj* (*mais pequeno:*
compar) smaller; (: *superl*) smallest;
(*mais jovem: compar*) younger; (: *superl*)
youngest; (*o mínimo*) least, slightest; (*tb:*
~ de idade) under age ▷ *m/f* juvenile,
young person; (*Jur*) minor; **não tenho a ~
idéia** I haven't the slightest idea

O **PALAVRA CHAVE**

menos ['menuʃ] *adj* **1** (*compar*): **menos
(do que)** (*quantidade*) less (than);
(*número*) fewer (than); **com menos
entusiasmo** with less enthusiasm;
menos gente fewer people
2 (*superl*) least; **é o que tem menos
culpa** he is the least to blame
▷ *adv* **1** (*compar*): **menos (do que)** less
(than); **gostei menos do que do outro** I
liked it less than the other one
2 (*superl*): **é o menos inteligente da
classe** he is the least bright in his class;
**de todas elas é a que menos me
agrada** out of all of them she's the one I
like least; **pelo menos** at (the very) least
3 (*frases*): **temos sete a menos** we are
seven short; **não é para menos** it's
no wonder; **isso é o de menos** that's
nothing
▷ *prep* (*exceção*) except; (*números*) minus;
todos menos eu everyone except (for)
me; **5 menos 2** 5 minus 2
▷ *conj*: **a menos que** unless; **a menos
que ele venha amanhã** unless he
comes tomorrow
▷ *m*: **o menos** the least

menosprezar [menuʃpre'zaʳ] *vt*
(*subestimar*) to underrate; (*desprezar*) to
despise, scorn
mensageiro, -a [mēsa'ʒejru, a] *m/f*
messenger
mensagem [mē'saʒē] (*pl* **-ns**) *f*
message; **~ de texto** text (message);
mandar uma ~ de texto para to text;
**eu te mando uma ~ de texto quando
voltar** I'll text you when I get back;
(**sistema de) ~s instantâneas** instant
messaging
mensal [mē'saw] (*pl* **-ais**) *adj* monthly;
ele ganha £1000 mensais he earns
£1000 a month; **mensalidade**
[mēsali'dadʒi] *f* monthly payment;
mensalmente [mēsaw'mētʃi] *adv*
monthly
menstruação [mēʃtrwa'sãw] *f* period;

(*Med*) menstruation
menta ['mēta] *f* mint
mental [mē'taw] (*pl* **-ais**) *adj* mental;
mentalidade [mētali'dadʒi] *f*
mentality
mente ['mētʃi] *f* mind; **de boa ~** willingly;
ter em ~ to bear in mind
mentir [mē'tʃiʳ] *vi* to lie
mentira [mē'tʃira] *f* lie; (*ato*) lying;
parece ~ que it seems incredible that;
de ~ not for real; **~!** (*acusação*) that's a lie!,
you're lying; (*de surpresa*) you don't say!,
no!; **mentiroso, -a** [mētʃi'rozu, ɔza] *adj*
lying ▷ *m/f* liar
menu [me'nu] *m* (*tb: Comput*) menu
mercado [mex'kadu] *m* market; **M~
Comum** Common Market; **~ negro** ou
paralelo black market
mercadoria [mexkado'ria] *f*
commodity; **mercadorias** *fpl* (*produtos*)
goods
mercearia [mexsja'ria] *f* grocer's (shop)
(*BRIT*), grocery store
mercúrio [mex'kurju] *m* mercury
merecer [mere'seʳ] *vt* to deserve;
(*consideração*) to merit; (*valer*) to be
worth ▷ *vi* to be worthy; **merecido, -a**
[mere'sidu, a] *adj* deserved; (*castigo,
prêmio*) just
merenda [me'rēda] *f* packed lunch
merengue [me'rēgi] *m* meringue
mergulhador, a [mexguʎa'doʳ, a] *m/f*
diver
mergulhar [mexgu'ʎaʳ] *vi* to dive;
(*penetrar*) to plunge ▷ *vt*: **~ algo em algo**
(*num líquido*) to dip sth into sth; (*na terra
etc*) to plunge sth into sth; **mergulho**
[mex'guʎu] *m* dip(ping), immersion;
(*em natação*) dive; **dar um mergulho** (*na
praia*) to go for a dip
mérito ['meritu] *m* merit
mero, -a ['mɛru, a] *adj* mere
mês [meʃ] *m* month
mesa ['meza] *f* table; (*de trabalho*) desk;
(*comitê*) board; (*numa reunião*) panel;
pôr/tirar a ~ to lay/clear the table; **à ~** at
the table; **~ de toalete** dressing table; **~
telefônica** switchboard
mesada [me'zada] *f* monthly allowance;
(*de criança*) pocket money
mesa-de-cabeceira (*pl* **mesas-de-
cabeceira**) *f* bedside table
mesmo, -a ['meʒmu, a] *adj* same;
(*enfático*) very ▷ *adv* (*exatamente*) right;
(*até*) even; (*realmente*) really ▷ *m/f*: **o ~/a
mesma** the same (one); **o ~** (*a mesma*

coisa) the same (thing); **este ~ homem** this very man; **ele ~ o fez** he did it himself; **dá no ~ ou na mesma** it's all the same; **aqui/agora/hoje ~** right here/right now/this very day; **~ que** even if; **é ~** it's true; **é ~?** really?; **(é) isso ~!** exactly!; **por isso ~** that's why; **nem ~** not even; **só ~** only; **por si ~** by oneself

mesquinho, -a [meʃˈkiɲu, a] *adj* mean

mesquita [meʃˈkita] *f* mosque

mestre, -a [ˈmɛʃtri, a] *adj* (*chave, viga*) master; (*linha, estrada*) main ▷ *m/f* master/mistress; (*professor*) teacher; **obra mestra** masterpiece

meta [ˈmɛta] *f* (*em corrida*) finishing post; (*gol*) goal; (*objetivo*) aim

metade [meˈtadʒi] *f* half; (*meio*) middle

metáfora [meˈtafora] *f* metaphor

metal [meˈtaw] (*pl* **-ais**) *m* metal; **metais** *mpl* (*Mús*) brass *sg*; **metálico, -a** [meˈtaliku, a] *adj* metallic; (*de metal*) metal *atr*

meteorologia [meteoroloˈʒia] *f* meteorology; **meteorologista** [meteoroloˈʒiʃta] *m/f* meteorologist; (*TV, Rádio*) weather forecaster

meter [meˈteʳ] *vt* (*colocar*) to put; (*envolver*) to involve; (*introduzir*) to introduce; **~-se** *vr* (*esconder-se*) to hide; **~-se a fazer algo** to decide to have a go at sth; **~-se com** (*provocar*) to pick a quarrel with; (*associar-se*) to get involved with; **~-se em** to get involved in; (*intrometer-se*) to interfere in

meticuloso, -a [metʃikuˈlozu, ɔza] *adj* meticulous

metido, -a [meˈtʃidu, a] *adj* (*envolvido*) involved; (*intrometido*) meddling; **~ (a besta)** snobbish

metódico, -a [meˈtɔdʒiku, a] *adj* methodical

método [ˈmɛtodu] *m* method

metralhadora [metraʎaˈdora] *f* sub-machine gun

métrico, -a [ˈmɛtriku, a] *adj* metric

metro [ˈmɛtru] *m* metre (*BRIT*), meter (*US*); (*PT*) = **metrô**

metrô [meˈtro] (*BR*) *m* underground (*BRIT*), subway (*US*)

metrópole [meˈtrɔpoli] *f* metropolis; (*capital*) capital

meu, minha [mew, ˈmiɲa] *adj* my ▷ *pron* mine; **os meus** *mpl* (*minha família*) my family *ou* folks (*col*); **um amigo ~** a friend of mine

mexer [meˈʃeʳ] *vt* to move; (*cabeça:*

dizendo sim) to nod; (*: dizendo não*) to shake; (*misturar*) to stir; (*ovos*) to scramble ▷ *vi* to move; **~-se** *vr* to move; (*apressar-se*) to get a move on; **~ em algo** to touch sth; **mexa-se!** get going!, move yourself!

mexerico [meʃeˈriku] *m* piece of gossip; **mexericos** *mpl* (*fofocas*) gossip *sg*

México [ˈmɛʃiku] *m*: **o ~** Mexico

mexido, -a [meˈʃidu, a] *adj* (*papéis*) mixed up; (*ovos*) scrambled

mexilhão [meʃiˈʎãw] (*pl* **-ões**) *m* mussel

mi [mi] *m* (*Mús*) E

miau [mjaw] *m* miaow

micro... [mikru] *prefixo* micro...; **micro(computador)** [mikro(kõputaˈdoʳ)] *m* micro(computer); **microfone** [mikroˈfoni] *m* microphone; **microondas** [mikroˈõdaʃ] *m inv* (*tb:* **forno de microondas**) microwave (oven); **microprocessador** [mikroprosesaˈdoʳ] *m* microprocessor; **microscópio** [mikroˈʃkɔpju] *m* microscope

mídia [ˈmidʒja] *f* media *pl*

migalha [miˈgaʎa] *f* crumb; **migalhas** *fpl* (*restos, sobras*) scraps

migrar [miˈgraʳ] *vi* to migrate

mijar [miˈʒaʳ] (*col*) *vi* to pee; **~-se** *vr* to wet o.s

mil [miw] *num* thousand; **dois ~** two thousand

milagre [miˈlagri] *m* miracle; **por ~** miraculously; **milagroso, -a** [milaˈgrozu, ɔza] *adj* miraculous

milhão [miˈʎãw] (*pl* **-ões**) *m* million; **um ~ de vezes** hundreds of times

milhar [miˈʎaʳ] *m* thousand; **turistas aos ~es** tourists in their thousands

milho [ˈmiʎu] *m* maize (*BRIT*), corn (*US*)

milhões [miˈʎõjʃ] *mpl de* **milhão**

miligrama [miliˈgrama] *m* milligram(me)

milionário, -a [miljoˈnarju, a] *m/f* millionaire

militar [miliˈtaʳ] *adj* military ▷ *m* soldier ▷ *vi* to fight; **~ em** (*Mil: regimento*) to serve in; (*Pol: partido*) to belong to, be active in; (*profissão*) to work in

mim [mĩ] *pron* me; (*reflexivo*) myself; **de ~ para ~** to myself

mímica [ˈmimika] *f* mime

mimo [ˈmimu] *m* gift; (*pessoa, coisa encantadora*) delight; (*carinho*) tenderness; (*gentileza*) kindness;

cheio de ~s (*criança*) spoiled, spoilt
(BRIT); **mimoso, -a** [mi'mozu, ɔza] *adj*
(*delicado*) delicate; (*carinhoso*) tender,
loving; (*encantador*) delightful
mina ['mina] *f* mine
mindinho [mĩ'dʒiɲu] *m* (*tb:* **dedo ~**)
little finger
mineiro, -a [mi'nejru, a] *adj* mining *atr*
▷ *m/f* miner
mineral [mine'raw] (*pl* -**ais**) *adj, m*
mineral
minério [mi'nɛrju] *m* ore
míngua ['mĩgwa] *f* lack; **à ~ de** for
want of; **viver à ~** to live in poverty;
minguado, -a [mĩ'gwadu, a] *adj* scant;
(*criança*) stunted; **minguado de algo**
short of sth
minguar [mĩ'gwaʳ] *vi* (*diminuir*) to
decrease, dwindle; (*faltar*) to run short
minha ['miɲa] *f de* **meu**
minhoca [mi'ɲɔka] *f* (earth)worm
mini... [mini] *prefixo* mini...
miniatura [minja'tura] *adj, f* miniature
MiniDisc® [mini'dʒiʃki] *m* MiniDisc®
mínima ['minima] *f* (*temperatura*) low;
(*Mús*) minim
mínimo, -a ['minimu, a] *adj* minimum
▷ *m* minimum; (*tb:* **dedo ~**) little finger;
não dou *ou* **ligo a mínima para isso**
I couldn't care less about it; **a mínima
importância/idéia** the slightest
importance/idea; **no ~** at least
minissaia [mini'saja] *f* miniskirt
ministério [mini'tɛrju] *m* ministry; ~
da Fazenda ≈ Treasury (BRIT), ≈ Treasury
Department (US); **M~ das Relações
Exteriores** ≈ Foreign Office (BRIT),
≈ State Department (US)
ministro, -a [mi'niʃtru, a] *m/f* minister
minoria [mino'ria] *f* minority
minto *etc* ['mĩtu] *vb ver* **mentir**
minucioso, -a [minu'sjozu, ɔza] *adj*
(*indivíduo, busca*) thorough; (*explicação*)
detailed
minúsculo, -a [mi'nuʃkulu, a] *adj*
minute, tiny; **letra minúscula** lower
case
minuta [mi'nuta] *f* rough draft
minuto [mi'nutu] *m* minute
miolo ['mjolu] *m* inside; (*polpa*) pulp;
(*de maçã*) core; **miolos** *mpl* (*cérebro,
inteligência*) brains
míope ['miopi] *adj* short-sighted
mira ['mira] *f* (*de fuzil*) sight; (*pontaria*)
aim; (*fig*) aim, purpose; **à ~ de** on the
lookout for; **ter em ~** to have one's eye on

miragem [mi'raʒẽ] (*pl* -**ns**) *f* mirage
miserável [mize'ravew] (*pl* -**eis**) *adj*
(*digno de compaixão*) wretched; (*pobre*)
impoverished; (*avaro*) stingy, mean;
(*insignificante*) paltry; (*lugar*) squalid;
(*infame*) despicable ▷ *m* wretch;
(*coitado*) poor thing; (*pessoa infame*)
rotter
miséria [mi'zɛrja] *f* misery; (*pobreza*)
poverty; (*avareza*) stinginess
misericórdia [mizeri'kɔxdʒja] *f*
(*compaixão*) pity, compassion; (*graça*)
mercy
missa ['misa] *f* (*Rel*) mass
missão [mi'sãw] (*pl* -**ões**) *f* mission;
(*dever*) duty
míssil ['misiw] (*pl* -**eis**) *m* missile
missionário, -a [misjo'narju, a] *m/f*
missionary
missões [mi'sõjʃ] *fpl de* **missão**
mistério [miʃ'tɛrju] *m* mystery;
misterioso, -a [miʃte'rjozu, ɔza] *adj*
mysterious
mistificar [miʃtʃifi'kaʳ] *vt, vi* to fool
misto, -a ['miʃtu, a] *adj* mixed; (*confuso*)
mixed up ▷ *m* mixture; **misto-quente**
(*pl* **mistos-quentes**) *m* toasted cheese
and ham sandwich
mistura [miʃ'tura] *f* mixture; (*ato*)
mixing; **misturar** [miʃtu'raʳ] *vt* to mix;
(*confundir*) to mix up; **misturar-se** *vr*:
misturar-se com to mingle with
mito ['mitu] *m* myth
miudezas [mju'dezaʃ] *fpl* minutiae;
(*bugigangas*) odds and ends; (*objetos
pequenos*) trinkets
miúdo, -a ['mjudu, a] *adj* tiny, minute
▷ *m/f* (PT: *criança*) youngster, kid;
miúdos *mpl* (*dinheiro*) change *sg*; (*de
aves*) giblets; **dinheiro ~** small change
mm *abr* (= *milímetro*) mm
mo [mu] *pron* = **me + o**
moa *etc* ['moa] *vb ver* **moer**
móbil ['mɔbiw] (*pl* -**eis**) *adj* = **móvel**
móbile ['mɔbili] *m* mobile
mobília [mo'bilja] *f* furniture; **mobiliar**
[mobi'ljaʳ] (BR) *vt* to furnish; **mobiliário**
[mobi'ljarju] *m* furnishings *pl*
moça ['mosa] *f* girl, young woman
Moçambique [mosã'biki] *m*
Mozambique
moção [mo'sãw] (*pl* -**ões**) *f* motion
mochila [mo'ʃila] *f* rucksack
mocidade [mosi'dadʒi] *f* youth; (*os
moços*) young people *pl*
moço, -a ['mosu, a] *adj* young ▷ *m*

young man, lad

moções [mo'sõjʃ] *fpl de* **moção**

moda ['mɔda] *f* fashion; **estar na ~** to be in fashion, be all the rage; **fora da ~** old-fashioned; **sair da** *ou* **cair de ~** to go out of fashion

modalidade [modali'dadʒi] *f* kind; (*Esporte*) event

modelo [mo'dɛlu] *m* model; (*criação de estilista*) design

moderar [mode'raʰ] *vt* to moderate; (*violência*) to control, restrain; (*velocidade*) to reduce; (*voz*) to lower; (*gastos*) to cut down

modernizar [modexni'zaʰ] *vt* to modernize; **~-se** *vr* to modernize

moderno, -a [mo'dɛxnu, a] *adj* modern; (*atual*) present-day

modéstia [mo'dɛʃtʃja] *f* modesty

módico, -a ['mɔdʒiku, a] *adj* moderate; (*preço*) reasonable; (*bens*) scant

modificar [modʒifi'kaʰ] *vt* to modify, alter

modista [mo'dʒiʃta] *f* dressmaker

modo ['mɔdu] *m* (*maneira*) way, manner; (*método*) way; (*Mús*) mode; **modos** *mpl* (*comportamento*) manners; **de (tal) ~ que** so (that); **de ~ nenhum** in no way; **de qualquer ~** anyway, anyhow; **~ de emprego** instructions *pl* for use

módulo ['mɔdulu] *m* module

moeda ['mwɛda] *f* (*uma moeda*) coin; (*dinheiro*) currency; **uma ~ de 10p** a 10p piece; **~ corrente** currency; **Casa da M~** ≈ the Mint (*BRIT*), ≈ the (US) Mint

moedor [moe'doʰ] *m* (*de café*) grinder; (*de carne*) mincer

moer [mwɛʰ] *vt* (*café*) to grind; (*cana*) to crush

mofado, -a [mo'fadu, a] *adj* mouldy (*BRIT*), moldy (*US*)

mofo ['mofu] *m* (*Bot*) mo(u)ld; **cheiro de ~** musty smell

mogno ['mɔgnu] *m* mahogany

mói *etc* [mɔj] *vb ver* **moer**

moía *etc* [mo'ia] *vb ver* **moer**

moído, -a [mo'idu, a] *adj* (*café*) ground; (*carne*) minced; (*cansado*) tired out; (*corpo*) aching

moinho ['mwiɲu] *m* mill; (*de café*) grinder; **~ de vento** windmill

mola ['mɔla] *f* (*Tec*) spring; (*fig*) motive, motivation

moldar [mow'daʰ] *vt* to mould (*BRIT*), mold (*US*); (*metal*) to cast; **molde** ['mɔwdʒi] *m* mo(u)ld; (*de papel*) pattern;

(*fig*) model; **molde de vestido** dress pattern

moldura [mow'dura] *f* (*de pintura*) frame

mole ['mɔli] *adj* soft; (*sem energia*) listless; (*carnes*) flabby; (*col: fácil*) easy; (*lento*) slow; (*preguiçoso*) sluggish ▷ *adv* (*lentamente*) slowly

moleque [mo'lɛki] *m* (*de rua*) urchin; (*menino*) youngster; (*pessoa sem palavra*) unreliable person; (*canalha*) scoundrel ▷ *adj* (*levado*) mischievous; (*brincalhão*) funny

molestar [moleʃ'taʰ] *vt* to upset; (*enfadar*) to annoy; (*importunar*) to bother

moléstia [mo'lɛʃtʃja] *f* illness

moleza [mo'leza] *f* softness; (*falta de energia*) listlessness; (*falta de força*) weakness; **ser (uma) ~** (*col*) to be easy; **na ~** without exerting oneself

molhado, -a [mo'ʎadu, a] *adj* wet, damp

molhar [mo'ʎaʰ] *vt* to wet; (*de leve*) to moisten, dampen; (*mergulhar*) to dip; **~-se** *vr* to get wet

molho¹ ['mɔʎu] *m* (*de chaves*) bunch; (*de trigo*) sheaf

molho² ['moʎu] *m* (*Culin*) sauce; (: *de salada*) dressing; (: *de carne*) gravy; **pôr de ~** to soak; **estar/deixar de ~** (*roupa etc*) to be/leave to soak

momentâneo, -a [momẽ'tanju, a] *adj* momentary

momento [mo'mẽtu] *m* moment; (*Tec*) momentum; **a todo ~** constantly; **de um ~ para outro** suddenly; **no ~ em que** just as

Mônaco ['monaku] *m* Monaco

monarquia [monax'kia] *f* monarchy

monitor [moni'toʰ] *m* monitor

monopólio [mono'pɔlju] *m* monopoly; **monopolizar** [monopoli'zaʰ] *vt* to monopolize

monotonia [monoto'nia] *f* monotony; **monótono, -a** [mo'nɔtonu, a] *adj* monotonous

monstro, -a ['mõʃtru, a] *adj inv* giant ▷ *m* (*tb fig*) monster; **monstruoso, -a** [mõʃtrwozu, ɔza] *adj* monstrous; (*enorme*) gigantic, huge

montagem [mõ'taʒẽ] (*pl* **-ns**) *f* assembly; (*Arq*) erection; (*Cinema*) editing; (*Teatro*) production

montanha [mõ'taɲa] *f* mountain; **montanha-russa** *f* roller coaster

montante [mõ'tãtʃi] *m* amount, sum; **a ~** (*nadar*) upstream

montar [mõ'ta^r] vt (cavalo) to mount, get on; (colocar em) to put on; (cavalgar) to ride; (peças) to assemble, put together; (loja, máquina) to set up; (casa) to put up; (peça teatral) to put on ▷ vi to ride; **~ a** ou **em** (animal) to get on; (cavalgar) to ride; (despesa) to come to

monte ['mõtʃi] m hill; (pilha) heap, pile; **um ~ de** (muitos) a lot of, lots of; **gente aos ~s** loads of people

montra ['mõtra] (PT) f shop window

monumento [monu'mẽtu] m monument

moqueca [mo'kɛka] f fish or seafood simmered in coconut cream and palm oil; **~ de camarão** prawn moqueca

morada [mo'rada] f home, residence; (PT: endereço) address; **moradia** [mora'dʒia] f home, dwelling; **morador, a** [mora'do^r, a] m/f resident; (de casa alugada) tenant

moral [mo'raw] (pl **-ais**) adj moral ▷ f (ética) ethics pl; (conclusão) moral ▷ m (de pessoa) sense of morality; (ânimo) morale; **moralidade** [morali'dadʒi] f morality

morango [mo'rãgu] m strawberry

morar [mo'ra^r] vi to live, reside

mórbido, -a [ˈmɔxbidu, a] adj morbid

morcego [mox'segu] m (Bio) bat

mordaça [mox'dasa] f (de animal) muzzle; (fig) gag

morder [mox'de^r] vt to bite; (corroer) to corrode; **mordida** [mox'dʒida] f bite

mordomia [moxdo'mia] f (de executivos) perk; (col: regalia) luxury, comfort

mordomo [mox'dɔmu] m butler

moreno, -a [mo'renu, a] adj dark(-skinned); (de cabelos) dark(-haired); (de tomar sol) brown ▷ m/f dark person

mormaço [mox'masu] m sultry weather

morno, -a ['moxnu, 'mɔxna] adj lukewarm, tepid

morrer [mo'xe^r] vi to die; (luz, cor) to fade; (fogo) to die down; (Auto) to stall

morro ['moxu] m hill; (favela) slum

mortadela [moxta'dɛla] f salami

mortal [mox'taw] (pl **-ais**) adj mortal; (letal, insuportável) deadly ▷ m mortal

mortalidade [moxtali'dadʒi] f mortality

morte ['mɔxtʃi] f death

mortífero, -a [mox'tʃiferu, a] adj deadly, lethal

morto, -a ['moxtu, 'mɔxta] pp de **matar** ▷ pp de **morrer** ▷ adj dead; (cor) dull; (exausto) exhausted; (inexpressivo) lifeless

▷ m/f dead man/woman; **estar/ser ~** to be dead/killed; **estar ~ de inveja** to be green with envy; **estar ~ de vontade de** to be dying to

mos [muʃ] pron = **me + os**

mosca ['moʃka] f fly; **estar às ~s** (bar etc) to be deserted

Moscou [moʃ'ku] (BR) n Moscow

Moscovo [moʃ'kovu] (PT) n Moscow

mosquito [moʃ'kitu] m mosquito

mostarda [moʃ'taxda] f mustard

mosteiro [moʃ'tejru] m monastery; (de monjas) convent

mostrador [moʃtra'do^r] m (de relógio) face, dial

mostrar [moʃ'tra^r] vt to show; (mercadorias) to display; (provar) to demonstrate, prove; **~-se** vr to show o.s. to be; (exibir-se) to show off

motel [mo'tɛw] (pl **-éis**) m motel

motivar [motʃi'va^r] vt (causar) to cause, bring about; (estimular) to motivate; **motivo** [mo'tʃivu] m (causa): **motivo (de** ou **para)** cause (of), reason (for); (fim) motive; (Arte, Mús) motif; **por motivo de** because of, owing to

moto ['mɔtu] f motorbike ▷ m (lema) motto

motocicleta [motosi'kleta] f motorcycle, motorbike

motociclista [motosi'kliʃta] m/f motorcyclist

motociclo [moto'siklu] (PT) m = **motocicleta**

motor, motriz [mo'to^r, mo'triʒ] adj: **força motriz** driving force ▷ m motor; (de carro, avião) engine; **~ diesel/de explosão** diesel/internal combustion engine; **~ de pesquisa** (PT: Comput) search engine

motorista [moto'riʃta] m/f driver

móvel ['mɔvew] (pl **-eis**) adj movable ▷ m piece of furniture; **móveis** mpl (mobília) furniture sg

mover [mo've^r] vt to move; (cabeça) to shake; (mecanismo) to drive; (campanha) to start (up); **~-se** vr to move

movimentado, -a [movimẽ'tadu, a] adj (rua, lugar) busy; (pessoa) active; (show, música) up-tempo

movimentar [movimẽ'ta^r] vt to move; (animar) to liven up

movimento [movi'mẽtu] m movement; (Tec) motion; (na rua) activity, bustle; **de muito ~** busy

muamba ['mwãba] (col) f (contrabando)

contraband; (*objetos roubados*) loot

muçulmano, -a [musuw'manu, a] *adj*, *m/f* Moslem

muda ['muda] *f* (*planta*) seedling; (*vestuário*) outfit; **~ de roupa** change of clothes

mudança [mu'dãsa] *f* change; (*de casa*) move; (*Auto*) gear

mudar [mu'da^r] *vt* to change; (*deslocar*) to move ▷ *vi* to change; (*ave*) to moult (*BRIT*), molt (*US*); **~-se** *vr* (*de casa*) to move (away); **~ de roupa/de assunto** to change clothes/the subject; **~ de casa** to move (house); **~ de idéia** to change one's mind

mudo, -a ['mudu, a] *adj* dumb; (*calado*, *Cinema*) silent; (*telefone*) dead ▷ *m/f* mute

⬤ **PALAVRA CHAVE**

muito, -a ['mwĩtu, a] *adj* (*quantidade*) a lot of; (: *em frase negativa ou interrogativa*) much; (*número*) lots of, a lot of; many; **muito esforço** a lot of effort; **faz muito calor** it's very hot; **muito tempo** a long time; **muitas amigas** lots *ou* a lot of friends; **muitas vezes** often ▷ *pron* a lot; (*em frase negativa ou interrogativa*: *sg*) much; (: *pl*) many; **tenho muito que fazer** I've got a lot to do; **muitos dizem que ...** a lot of people say that ...
▷ *adv* **1** a lot; (+ *adj*) very; (+ *compar*): **muito melhor** much *ou* far *ou* a lot better; **gosto muito disto** I like it a lot; **sinto muito** I'm very sorry; **muito interessante** very interesting
2 (*resposta*) very; **está cansado? - muito** are you tired? - very
3 (*tempo*): **muito depois** long after; **há muito** a long time ago; **não demorou muito** it didn't take long

mula ['mula] *f* mule

mulato, -a [mu'latu, a] *adj*, *m/f* mulatto

muleta [mu'leta] *f* crutch; (*fig*) support

mulher [mu'ʎe^r] *f* woman; (*esposa*) wife; **mulher-bomba** (*pl* **mulheres-bomba**) *f* suicide bomber

multa ['muwta] *f* fine; **levar uma ~** to be fined; **multar** [muw'ta^r] *vt* to fine; **multar alguém em $1000** to fine sb $1000

multi... [muwtʃi] *prefixo* multi...

multidão [muwtʃi'dãw] (*pl* **-ões**) *f* crowd; **uma ~ de** (*muitos*) lots of

multimídia [muwtʃi'midʒja] *adj* multimedia

multinacional [muwtʃinasjo'naw] (*pl* **-ais**) *adj*, *f* multinational

multiplicar [muwtʃipli'ka^r] *vt* to multiply; (*aumentar*) to increase

múltiplo, -a ['muwtʃiplu, a] *adj* multiple ▷ *m* multiple

múmia ['mumja] *f* mummy

mundial [mũ'dʒjaw] (*pl* **-ais**) *adj* worldwide; (*guerra, recorde*) world *atr* ▷ *m* world championship

mundo ['mũdu] *m* world; **todo o ~** everybody; **um ~ de** lots of, a great many

munição [muni'sãw] (*pl* **-ões**) *f* (*de armas*) ammunition; (*chumbo*) shot; (*Mil*) munitions *pl*, supplies *pl*

municipal [munisi'paw] (*pl* **-ais**) *adj* municipal

município [muni'sipju] *m* local authority; (*cidade*) town; (*condado*) county

munições [muni'sõjʃ] *fpl de* **munição**

munir [mu'ni^r] *vt*: **~ de** to provide with, supply with; **~-se** *vr*: **~-se de** (*provisões*) to equip o.s. with

muralha [mu'raʎa] *f* (*de fortaleza*) rampart; (*muro*) wall

murchar [mux'ʃa^r] *vt* (*Bot*) to wither; (*sentimentos*) to dull; (*pessoa*) to sadden ▷ *vi* to wither, wilt; (*fig*) to fade

murmurar [muxmu'ra^r] *vi* to murmur, whisper; (*queixar-se*) to mutter, grumble; (*água*) to ripple; (*folhagem*) to rustle ▷ *vt* to murmur; **murmúrio** [mux'murju] *m* murmuring, whispering; grumbling; rippling; rustling

muro ['muru] *m* wall

murro ['muxu] *m* punch; **dar um ~ em alguém** to punch sb

musa ['muza] *f* muse

musculação [muʃkula'sãw] *f* body-building

músculo ['muʃkulu] *m* muscle; **musculoso, -a** [muʃku'lozu, ɔza] *adj* muscular

museu [mu'zew] *m* museum; (*de pintura*) gallery

musgo ['muʒgu] *m* moss

música ['muzika] *f* music; (*canção*) song; **músico, -a** ['muziku, a] *adj* musical ▷ *m/f* musician

mútuo, -a ['mutwu, a] *adj* mutual

boyfriend/girlfriend
namorar [namo'ra^r] *vt* (*ser namorado de*)
to be going out with
namoro [na'moru] *m* relationship
não [nãw] *adv* not; (*resposta*) no ▷ *m* no;
~ sei I don't know; **~ muito** not much; **~
só ... mas também** not only ... but also; **~
agora** ~ not now; **~ tem de quê** don't
mention it; **~ é?** isn't it?, won't you? (*etc*,
segundo o verbo precedente); **eles são
brasileiros, ~ é?** they're Brazilian, aren't
they?
não- [nãw-] *prefixo* non-
naquele(s), -a(s) [na'keli(ʃ), na'kɛla(ʃ)]
= **em + aquele(s)/a(s)**
naquilo [na'kilu] = **em + aquilo**
narina [na'rina] *f* nostril
nariz [na'riʒ] *m* nose
narração [naxa'sãw] (*pl* **-ões**) *f*
narration; (*relato*) account
narrar [na'xa^r] *vt* to narrate
narrativa [naxa'tʃiva] *f* narrative;
(*história*) story
nas [naʃ] = **em + as**
-nas [naʃ] *pron* them
nascença [na'sẽsa] *f* birth; **de ~** by birth;
ele é surdo de ~ he was born deaf
nascente [na'sẽtʃi] *m*: **o ~** the East, the
Orient ▷ *f* (*fonte*) spring
nascer [na'se^r] *vi* to be born; (*plantas*) to
sprout; (*o sol*) to rise; (*ave*) to hatch; (*fig*:
ter origem) to come into being ▷ *m*: **~ do
sol** sunrise; **ele nasceu para médico**
etc he's a born doctor *etc*; **nascimento**
[nasi'mẽtu] *m* birth; (*fig*) origin; (*estirpe*)
descent
nata ['nata] *f* cream
natação [nata'sãw] *f* swimming
natais [na'tajʃ] *adj pl* de **natal**
Natal [na'taw] *m* Christmas; **Feliz ~!**
Merry Christmas!
natal [na'taw] (*pl* **-ais**) *adj* (*relativo ao
nascimento*) natal; (*país*) native; **cidade ~**
home town
natalino, -a [nata'linu, a] *adj*
Christmas *atr*
nativo, -a [na'tʃivu, a] *adj, m/f* native
natural [natu'raw] (*pl* **-ais**) *adj* natural;
(*nativo*) native ▷ *m/f* native; **ao ~**
(*Culin*) fresh, uncooked; **naturalidade**
[naturali'dadʒi] *f* naturalness; **de
naturalidade paulista** *etc* born in São
Paulo *etc*; **naturalizar** [naturali'za^r]
vt to naturalize; **naturalizar-se** *vr* to
become naturalized; **naturalmente**
[naturaw'mẽtʃi] *adv* naturally;

N *abr* (= *norte*) N
na [na] = **em + a**
-na [na] *pron* her; (*coisa*) it
nabo ['nabu] *m* turnip
nação [na'sãw] (*pl* **-ões**) *f* nation
nacional [nasjo'naw] (*pl* **-ais**) *adj*
national; (*carro, vinho etc*) domestic,
home-produced; **nacionalidade**
[nasjonali'dadʒi] *f* nationality;
nacionalismo [nasjona'liʒmu]
m nationalism; **nacionalista**
[nasjona'liʃta] *adj, m/f* nationalist
nações [na'sõjʃ] *fpl* de **nação**
nada ['nada] *pron* nothing ▷ *adv* at all;
antes de mais ~ first of all; **não é ~
difícil** it's not at all hard, it's not hard
at all; **~ mais** nothing else; **~ de novo**
nothing new; **obrigado — de ~** thank
you — not at all *ou* don't mention it
nadador, a [nada'do^r, a] *m/f* swimmer
nadar [na'da^r] *vi* to swim
nádegas ['nadegaʃ] *fpl* buttocks
nado ['nadu] *m*: **atravessar a ~** to swim
across; **~ borboleta/de costas/de
peito** butterfly (stroke)/backstroke/
breaststroke
naipe ['najpi] *m* (*cartas*) suit
namorado, -a [namo'radu, a] *m/f*

naturalmente! of course!
natureza [natu'reza] f nature; (*espécie*) kind, type
nau [naw] f (*literário*) ship
náusea ['nawzea] f nausea; **dar ~s a alguém** to make sb feel sick; **sentir ~s** to feel sick
náutico, -a ['nawtʃiku, a] adj nautical
naval [na'vaw] (*pl* -**ais**) adj naval; **construção ~** shipbuilding
navalha [na'vaʎa] f (*de barba*) razor; (*faca*) knife
nave ['navi] f (*de igreja*) nave
navegação [navega'sãw] f navigation, sailing; **~ aérea** air traffic; **companhia de ~** shipping line
navegar [nave'gaʳ] vt to navigate; (*mares*) to sail ▷ vi to sail; (*dirigir o rumo*) to navigate
navio [na'viu] m ship; **~ aeródromo/ cargueiro/petroleiro** aircraft carrier/ cargo ship/oil tanker; **~ de guerra** (BR) battleship
nazi [na'zi] (PT) adj, m/f = **nazista**
nazista [na'ziʃta] adj, m/f Nazi
NB abr (= *note bem*) NB
neblina [ne'blina] f fog, mist
nebuloso, -a [nebu'lozu, ɔza] adj foggy, misty; (*céu*) cloudy; (*fig*) vague
necessário, -a [nese'sarju, a] adj necessary ▷ m: **o ~** the necessities pl
necessidade [nesesi'dadʒi] f need, necessity; (*o que se necessita*) need; (*pobreza*) poverty, need; **ter ~ de** to need; **em caso de ~** if need be
necessitado, -a [nesesi'tadu, a] adj needy, poor; **~ de** in need of
necessitar [nesesi'taʳ] vt to need, require ▷ vi: **~ de** to need
neerlandês, -esa [neexlã'deʃ, eza] adj Dutch ▷ m/f Dutchman/woman
Neerlândia [neex'lãdʒa] f the Netherlands pl
negar [ne'gaʳ] vt to deny; (*recusar*) to refuse; **~-se** vr: **~-se a** to refuse to
negativa [nega'tiiva] f negative; (*recusa*) denial
negativo, -a [nega'tʃivu, a] adj negative ▷ m (Tec, Foto) negative ▷ excl (col) nope!
negligência [negli'ʒẽsja] f negligence, carelessness; **negligente** [negli'ʒẽtʃi] adj negligent, careless
negociação [negosja'sãw] (*pl* -**ões**) f negotiation
negociante [nego'sjãtʃi] m/f businessman/woman

negociar [nego'sjaʳ] vt to negotiate; (Com) to trade ▷ vi: **~ (com)** to trade ou deal (in); to negotiate (with)
negócio [ne'gɔsju] m (Com) business; (*transação*) deal; (*questão*) matter; (*col: troço*) thing; (*assunto*) affair, business; **homem de ~s** businessman; **a ~s** on business; **fechar um ~** to make a deal
negro, -a ['negru, a] adj black; (*raça*) Black; (*fig: lúgubre*) black, gloomy ▷ m/f Black man/woman
nele(s), -a(s) ['neli(ʃ), 'nɛla(ʃ)] = **em + ele(s)/a(s)**
nem [nẽj] conj nor, neither; **~ (sequer)** not even; **~ que** even if; **~ bem** hardly; **~ um só** not a single one; **~ estuda ~ trabalha** he neither studies nor works; **~ eu** nor me; **~ sem ~** without even; **~ todos** not all; **~ tanto** not so much; **~ sempre** not always
nenê [ne'ne] m/f baby
neném [ne'nẽj] (*pl* -**ns**) m/f = **nenê**
nenhum, a [ne'nũ, 'numa] adj no, not any ▷ pron (*nem um só*) none, not one; (*de dois*) neither; **~ lugar** nowhere
nervo ['nexvu] m (Anat) nerve; (*fig*) energy, strength; (*em carne*) sinew; **nervosismo** [nexvo'ziʒmu] m (*nervosidade*) nervousness; (*irritabilidade*) irritability; **nervoso** [nex'vozu, ɔza] adj nervous; (*irritável*) touchy, on edge; (*exaltado*) worked up; **isso/ele me deixa nervoso** he gets on my nerves
nesse(s), -a(s) ['nesi(ʃ), 'nɛsa(ʃ)] = **em + esse(s)/a(s)**
neste(s), -a(s) ['neʃtʃi(ʃ), 'nɛʃta(ʃ)] = **em + este(s)/a(s)**
neto, -a ['nɛtu, a] m/f grandson/ daughter; **netos** mpl grandchildren
neurose [new'rozi] f neurosis; **neurótico, -a** [new'rɔtʃiku, a] adj, m/f neurotic
neutro, -a ['newtru, a] adj (Ling) neuter; (*imparcial*) neutral
nevar [ne'vaʳ] vi to snow; **nevasca** [ne'vaʃka] f snowstorm; **neve** ['nɛvi] f snow
névoa ['nɛvoa] f fog; **nevoeiro** [nevo'ejru] m thick fog
nexo ['nɛksu] m connection, link; **sem ~** disconnected, incoherent
Nicarágua [nika'ragwa] f: **a ~** Nicaragua
nicotina [niko'tʃina] f nicotine
Nigéria [ni'ʒɛrja] f: **a ~** Nigeria
Nilo ['nilu] m: **o ~** the Nile
ninguém [nĩ'gẽj] pron nobody, no-one

ninho ['niɲu] m nest; (toca) lair; (lar) home

nisso ['nisu] = **em + isso**

nisto ['niʃtu] = **em + isto**

nitidez [nitʃi'deʒ] f (clareza) clarity; (brilho) brightness; (imagem) sharpness

nítido, -a ['nitʃidu, a] adj clear, distinct; (brilhante) bright; (imagem) sharp, clear

nível ['nivew] (pl -eis) m level; (fig: padrão) standard; (: ponto) point, pitch; **~ de vida** standard of living

no [nu] = **em + o**

-no [nu] pron him; (coisa) it

nº abr (= número) no

nó [nɔ] m knot; (de uma questão) crux; **nós dos dedos** knuckles; **dar um nó** to tie a knot

nobre ['nɔbri] adj, m/f noble; **horário ~** prime time; **nobreza** [no'breza] f nobility

noção [no'sãw] (pl -ões) f notion; **noções** fpl (rudimentos) rudiments, basics; **~ vaga** inkling; **não ter a menor ~ de algo** not to have the slightest idea about sth

nocaute [no'kawtʃi] m knockout ▷ adv: **pôr alguém ~** to knock sb out

nocivo, -a [no'sivu, a] adj harmful

noções [no'sõjʃ] fpl de **noção**

nocturno, -a [no'tuxnu, a] (PT) adj = **noturno**

nódoa ['nɔdwa] f spot; (mancha) stain

nogueira [no'gejra] f (árvore) walnut tree; (madeira) walnut

noite ['nojtʃi] f night; **à** ou **de ~** at night, in the evening; **boa ~** good evening; (despedida) good night; **da ~ para o dia** overnight; **tarde da ~** late at night

noivado [noj'vadu] m engagement

noivo, -a ['nojvu, a] m/f (prometido) fiancé(e); (no casamento) bridegroom/bride; **os noivos** mpl (prometidos) the engaged couple; (no casamento) the bride and groom; (recém-casados) the newly-weds

nojento, -a [no'ʒẽtu, a] adj disgusting

nojo ['noʒu] m nausea; (repulsão) disgust, loathing; **ela é um ~** she's horrible; **este trabalho está um ~** this work is messy

no-la(s) = **nos + a(s)**

no-lo(s) = **nos + o(s)**

nome ['nɔmi] m name; (fama) fame; **de ~** by name; **escritor de ~** famous writer; **um restaurante de ~** a restaurant with a good reputation; **em ~ de** in the name of; **~ de batismo** Christian name

nomear [no'mjaʳ] vt to nominate; (conferir um cargo a) to appoint; (dar nome a) to name

nono, -a ['nɔnu, a] num ninth

nora ['nɔra] f daughter-in-law

nordeste [nox'dɛʃtʃi] m, adj northeast

norma ['nɔxma] f standard, norm; (regra) rule; **como ~** as a rule

normal [nox'maw] (pl -ais) adj normal; (habitual) usual; **normalizar** [noxmali'zaʳ] vt to bring back to normal; **normalizar-se** vr to return to normal

noroeste [nor'wɛʃtʃi] adj northwest, northwestern ▷ m northwest

norte ['nɔxtʃi] adj northern, north; (vento, direção) northerly ▷ m north; **norte-americano, -a** adj, m/f (North) American

Noruega [nor'wega] f Norway; **norueguês, -esa** [norwe'geʃ, geza] adj, m/f Norwegian ▷ m (Ling) Norwegian

nos [nuʃ] = **em + os** pron (direto) us; (indireto) us, to us, for us; (reflexivo) ourselves; (recíproco) (to) each other

-nos [nuʃ] pron them

nós [nɔʃ] pron we; (depois de prep) us; **~ mesmos** we ourselves

nosso, -a ['nɔsu, a] adj our ▷ pron ours; **um amigo ~** a friend of ours; **Nossa Senhora** (Rel) Our Lady

nostalgia [noʃtaw'ʒia] f nostalgia; (saudades da pátria etc) homesickness; **nostálgico, -a** [noʃ'tawʒiku, a] adj nostalgic; homesick

nota ['nɔta] f note; (Educ) mark; (conta) bill; (cédula) banknote; **~ de venda** sales receipt; **~ fiscal** receipt

notar [no'taʳ] vt to notice, note; **~-se** vr to be obvious; **fazer ~** to call attention to; **notável** [no'tavew] (pl -eis) adj notable, remarkable

notícia [no'tʃisja] f (uma notícia) piece of news; (TV etc) news item; **notícias** fpl (informações) news sg; **pedir ~s de** to inquire about; **ter ~s de** to hear from; **noticiário** [notʃi'sjarju] m (de jornal) news section; (Cinema) newsreel; (TV, Rádio) news bulletin

notório, -a [no'tɔrju, a] adj well-known

noturno, -a [no'tuxnu, a] adj nocturnal, nightly; (trabalho) night atr ▷ m (trem) night train

nova ['nɔva] f piece of news; **novas** fpl (novidades) news sg

novamente [nova'mẽtʃi] adv again

novato, -a [no'vatu, a] *adj* inexperienced, raw ▷ *m/f* beginner, novice; (*Educ*) fresher

nove ['nɔvi] *num* nine

novela [no'vɛla] *f* short novel, novella; (*Rádio, TV*) soap opera

novelo [no'velu] *m* ball of thread

novembro [no'vẽbru] (*PT* **N-**) *m* November

noventa [no'vẽta] *num* ninety

novidade [novi'dadʒi] *f* novelty; (*notícia*) piece of news; **novidades** *fpl* (*notícias*) news *sg*

novilho, -a [no'viʎu, a] *m/f* young bull/heifer

novo, -a ['novu, 'nɔva] *adj* new; (*jovem*) young; (*adicional*) further; **de ~** again

noz [nɔʒ] *f* nut; (*da nogueira*) walnut; **~ moscada** nutmeg

nu, a [nu, 'nua] *adj* naked; (*arvore, sala, parede*) bare ▷ *m* nude

nublado, -a [nu'bladu, a] *adj* cloudy, overcast

nuclear [nu'kljaʳ] *adj* nuclear

núcleo ['nuklju] *m* nucleus *sg*; (*centro*) centre (*BRIT*), center (*US*)

nudez [nu'deʒ] *f* nakedness, nudity; (*de paredes etc*) bareness

nudista [nu'dʒiʃta] *adj, m/f* nudist

nulo, -a ['nulu, a] *adj* (*Jur*) null, void; (*nenhum*) non-existent; (*sem valor*) worthless; (*esforço*) vain, useless

num [nũ] = **em** + **um**

numa(s) ['numa(ʃ)] = **em** + **uma(s)**

numeral [nume'raw] (*pl* **-ais**) *m* numeral

numerar [nume'raʳ] *vt* to number

numérico, -a [nu'mɛriku, a] *adj* numerical

número ['numeru] *m* number; (*de jornal*) issue; (*Teatro etc*) act; (*de sapatos, roupa*) size; **sem ~** countless; **~ de matrícula** registration (*BRIT*) *ou* license plate (*US*) number; **numeroso, -a** [nume'rozu, ɔza] *adj* numerous

nunca ['nũka] *adv* never; **~ mais** never again; **quase ~** hardly ever; **mais que ~** more than ever

nuns [nũʃ] = **em** + **uns**

núpcias ['nupsjaʃ] *fpl* nuptials, wedding *sg*

nutrição [nutri'sãw] *f* nutrition

nuvem ['nuvẽj] (*pl* **-ns**) *f* cloud; (*de insetos*) swarm

O

o, a [u, a] *art def* **1** the; **o livro/a mesa/os estudantes** the book/table/students

2 (*com n abstrato: não se traduz*): **o amor/a juventude** love/youth

3 (*posse: traduz-se muitas vezes por adj possessivo*): **quebrar o braço** to break one's arm; **ele levantou a mão** he put his hand up; **ela colocou o chapéu** she put her hat on

4 (*valor descritivo*): **ter a boca grande/os olhos azuis** to have a big mouth/blue eyes

▷ *pron demostrativo*: **meu livro e o seu** my book and yours; **as de Pedro são melhores** Pedro's are better; **não a(s) branca(s) mas a(s) cinza(s)** not the white one(s) but the grey one(s)

▷ *pron relativo*: **o(s) que quiser(em) pode(m) sair** anyone who wants to can leave; **leve o que mais gustar** take the one you like best

2 (*def*): **o que comprei ontem** the one I bought yesterday; **os que sairam** those who left

3: **o que** what; **o que eu acho/mais gosto** what I think/like most

▷ *pron pessoal* **1** (*pessoa: m*) him; (*: f*) her; (*: pl*) them; **não posso vê-lo(s)** I can't see him/them; **vemo-la todas as semanas** we see her every week **2** (*animal, coisa: sg*) it; (*: pl*) them; **não posso vê-lo(s)** I can't see it/them; **acharam-nos na praia** they found us on the beach

obedecer [obede'seʳ] *vi*: ~ **a** to obey; **obediência** [obe'dʒẽsja] *f* obedience; **obediente** [obe'dʒẽtʃi] *adj* obedient

óbito ['ɔbitu] *m* death; **atestado de ~** death certificate

objeção [obʒe'sãw] (*PT* -**cç**-) (*pl* -**ões**) *f* objection; **fazer** *ou* **pôr objeções a** to object to

objetivo, -a [obʒe'tʃivu, a] (*PT* -**ct**-) *adj* objective ▷ *m* objective

objeto [ob'ʒɛtu] (*PT* -**ct**-) *m* object

obra ['ɔbra] *f* work; (*Arq*) building, construction; (*Teatro*) play; **em ~s** under repair; **ser ~ de alguém/algo** to be the work of sb/the result of sth; **~ de arte** work of art; **~s públicas** public works; **obra-prima** (*pl* **obras-primas**) *f* masterpiece

obrigação [obriga'sãw] (*pl* -**ões**) *f* obligation; (*Com*) bond

obrigado, -a [obri'gadu, a] *adj* obliged, compelled ▷ *excl* thank you; (*recusa*) no, thank you

obrigar [obri'gaʳ] *vt* to oblige, compel; **~-se** *vr*: **~-se a fazer algo** to undertake to do sth; **obrigatório, -a** [obriga'tɔrju, a] *adj* compulsory, obligatory

obsceno, -a [obi'sɛnu, a] *adj* obscene

obscurecer [obiʃkure'seʳ] *vt* to darken; (*entendimento, verdade etc*) to obscure ▷ *vi* to get dark

obscuro, -a [obi'ʃkuru, a] *adj* dark; (*fig*) obscure

observação [obisexva'sãw] (*pl* -**ões**) *f* observation; (*comentário*) remark, comment; (*de leis, regras*) observance

observador, a [obisexva'doʳ, a] *m/f* observer

observar [obisex'vaʳ] *vt* to observe; (*notar*) to notice; **~ algo a alguém** to point sth out to sb

observatório [obisexva'tɔrju] *m* observatory

obsessão [obise'sãw] (*pl* -**ões**) *f* obsession; **obsessivo, -a** [obise'sivu, a] *adj* obsessive

obsoleto, -a [obiso'lɛtu, a] *adj* obsolete

obstinado, -a [obiʃtʃi'nadu, a] *adj* obstinate, stubborn

obstrução [obiʃtru'sãw] (*pl* -**ões**) *f* obstruction; **obstruir** [obiʃtrwiʳ] *vt* to obstruct; (*impedir*) to impede

obter [obi'teʳ] (*irreg: como* **ter**) *vt* to obtain, get; (*alcançar*) to gain

obturação [obitura'sãw] (*pl* -**ões**) *f* (*de dente*) filling

obtuso, -a [obi'tuzu, a] *adj* (*ger*) obtuse; (*fig: pessoa*) thick

óbvio, -a ['ɔbvju, a] *adj* obvious; **(é) ~!** of course!

ocasião [oka'zjãw] (*pl* -**ões**) *f* opportunity, chance; (*momento, tempo*) occasion; **ocasionar** [okazjo'naʳ] *vt* to cause, bring about

oceano [o'sjanu] *m* ocean

ocidental [osidẽ'taw] (*pl* -**ais**) *adj* western ▷ *m/f* westerner

ocidente [osi'dẽtʃi] *m* west

ócio ['ɔsju] *m* (*lazer*) leisure; (*inação*) idleness; **ocioso, -a** [o'sjozu, ɔza] *adj* idle; (*vaga*) unfilled

oco, -a ['oku, a] *adj* hollow, empty

ocorrência [oko'xẽsja] *f* incident, event; (*circunstância*) circumstance

ocorrer [oko'xeʳ] *vi* to happen, occur; (*vir ao pensamento*) to come to mind; **~ a alguém** to happen to sb; to occur to sb

oculista [oku'liʃta] *m/f* optician

óculo ['ɔkulu] *m* spyglass; **óculos** *mpl* (*para ver melhor*) glasses, spectacles; **~s de proteção** goggles

ocultar [okuw'taʳ] *vt* to hide, conceal; **oculto, -a** [o'kuwtu, a] *adj* hidden; (*desconhecido*) unknown; (*secreto*) secret; (*sobrenatural*) occult

ocupação [okupa'sãw] (*pl* -**ões**) *f* occupation

ocupado, -a [oku'padu, a] *adj* (*pessoa*) busy; (*lugar*) taken, occupied; (*BR: telefone*) engaged (*BRIT*), busy (*US*); **sinal de ~** (*BR: Tel*) engaged tone (*BRIT*), busy signal (*US*)

ocupar [oku'paʳ] *vt* to occupy; (*tempo*) to take up; (*pessoa*) to keep busy; **~-se** *vr*: **~-se com** *ou* **de** *ou* **em algo** (*dedicar-se a*) to deal with sth; (*cuidar de*) to look after sth; (*passar seu tempo com*) to occupy o.s. with sth

odiar [o'dʒjaʳ] *vt* to hate; **ódio** ['ɔdʒju] *m* hate, hatred; **odioso, -a** [o'dʒjozu, ɔza] *adj* hateful

odor [o'doʳ] *m* smell

oeste ['wɛʃtʃi] *m* west ▷ *adj inv* (*região*)

western; (direção, vento) westerly

ofegante [ofe'gãtʃi] adj breathless, panting

ofender [ofē'deʳ] vt to offend; **~-se** vr: **~-se (com)** to take offence (BRIT) ou offense (US) (at)

ofensa [o'fẽsa] f insult; (à lei, moral) offence (BRIT), offense (US); **ofensiva** [ofẽ'siva] f offensive; **ofensivo, -a** [ofẽ'sivu, a] adj offensive

oferecer [ofere'seʳ] vt to offer; (dar) to give; (jantar) to give; (propor) to propose; (dedicar) to dedicate; **~-se** vr (pessoa) to offer o.s., volunteer; (oportunidade) to present itself, arise; **~-se para fazer** to offer to do; **oferecimento** [oferesi'mẽtu] m offer; **oferta** [o'fɛxta] f offer; (dádiva) gift; (Com) bid; (em loja) special offer

oficial [ofi'sjaw] (pl **-ais**) adj official ▷ m/f official; (Mil) officer; **~ de justiça** bailiff

oficina [ofi'sina] f workshop; **~ mecânica** garage

ofício [o'fisju] m profession, trade; (Rel) service; (carta) official letter; (função) function; (encargo) job, task

oitavo, -a [oj'tavu, a] num eighth

oitenta [oj'tẽta] num eighty

oito [ojtu] num eight

olá [o'la] excl hello!

olaria [ola'ria] f (fábrica: de louças de barro) pottery; (: de tijolos) brickworks sg

óleo ['ɔlju] m (lubricante) oil; **~ diesel/de bronzear** diesel/suntan oil; **oleoso, -a** [o'ljozu, ɔza] adj oily; (gorduroso) greasy

olfato [ow'fatu] m sense of smell

olhada [o'ʎada] f glance, look; **dar uma ~** to have a look

olhadela [oʎa'dɛla] f peep

olhar [o'ʎaʳ] vt to look at; (observar) to watch; (ponderar) to consider; (cuidar de) to look after ▷ vi to look ▷ m look; **~-se** vr to look at o.s.; (duas pessoas) to look at each other; **~ fixamente** to stare at; **~ para** to look at; **~ por** to look after; **~ fixo** stare

olho ['oʎu] m (Anat, de agulha) eye; (vista) eyesight; **~ nele!** watch him!; **~ vivo!** keep your eyes open!; **a ~** (medir, calcular etc) by eye; **~ mágico** (na porta) peephole; **~ roxo** black eye; **num abrir e fechar de ~s** in a flash

olimpíada [olĩ'piada] f: **as O~s** the Olympics

oliveira [oli'vejra] f olive tree

ombro ['õbru] m shoulder; **encolher os**

~s , dar de ~s to shrug one's shoulders

omeleta [ome'leta] (PT) f = **omelete**

omelete [ome'letʃi] (BR) f omelette (BRIT), omelet (US)

omissão [omi'sãw] (pl **-ões**) f omission; (negligência) negligence

omitir [omi'tʃiʳ] vt to omit

omoplata [omo'plata] f shoulder blade

onça ['õsa] f ounce; (animal) jaguar

onda ['õda] f wave; (moda) fashion; **~ curta/média/longa** short/medium/long wave; **~ de calor** heat wave

onde ['õdʒi] adv where ▷ conj where, in which; **de ~ você é?** where are you from?; **por ~** through which; **por ~?** which way?; **~ quer que** wherever

ondulado, -a [õdu'ladu, a] adj wavy

ônibus ['onibuʃ] (BR) m inv bus; **ponto de ~** bus-stop

ontem ['õtẽ] adv yesterday; **~ à noite** last night

ONU ['onu] abr f (= Organização das Nações Unidas) UNO

ônus ['onuʃ] m inv onus; (obrigação) obligation; (Com) charge; (encargo desagradável) burden

onze ['õzi] num eleven

opaco, -a [o'paku, a] adj opaque; (obscuro) dark

opção [op'sãw] (pl **-ões**) f option, choice; (preferência) first claim, right

ópera ['ɔpera] f opera

operação [opera'sãw] (pl **-ões**) f operation; (Com) transaction

operador, a [opera'doʳ, a] m/f operator; (cirurgião) surgeon; (num cinema) projectionist

operar [ope'raʳ] vt to operate; (produzir) to effect, bring about; (Med) to operate on ▷ vi to operate; (agir) to act, function; **~-se** vr (suceder) to take place; (Med) to have an operation

operário, -a [ope'rarju, a] adj working ▷ m/f worker; **classe operária** working class

opinar [opi'naʳ] vt to think ▷ vi to give one's opinion

opinião [opi'njãw] (pl **-ões**) f opinion; **mudar de ~** to change one's mind

oponente [opo'nẽtʃi] adj opposing ▷ m/f opponent

opor [o'poʳ] (irreg: como **pôr**) vt to oppose; (resistência) to put up, offer; (objeção, dificuldade) to raise; **~-se** vr: **~-se a** to object to; (resistir) to oppose

oportunidade [opoxtuni'dadʒi] f

opportunity

oportunista [opoxtu'niʃta] *adj, m/f* opportunist

oportuno, -a [opox'tunu, a] *adj* (*momento*) opportune, right; (*oferta de ajuda*) well-timed; (*conveniente*) convenient, suitable

oposição [opozi'sãw] *f* opposition; **em ~ a** against; **fazer ~ a** to oppose

opressão [opre'sãw] (*pl* **-ões**) *f* oppression; **opressivo, -a** [opre'sivu, a] *adj* oppressive

oprimir [opri'miʳ] *vt* to oppress; (*comprimir*) to press

optar [op'taʳ] *vi* to choose; **~ por** to opt for; **~ por fazer** to opt to do

óptico, -a *etc* ['ɔtiku, a] (*PT*) = **ótico** *etc*

óptimo, -a *etc* ['ɔtimu, a] (*PT*) *adj* = **ótimo** *etc*

ora ['ɔra] *adv* now ▷ *conj* well; **por ~** for the time being; **~ ..., ~ ...** one moment ..., the next ...; **~ bem** now then

oração [ora'sãw] (*pl* **-ões**) *f* prayer; (*discurso*) speech; (*Ling*) clause

oral [o'raw] (*pl* **-ais**) *adj* oral ▷ *f* oral (*exam*)

orar [o'raʳ] *vi* (*Rel*) to pray

órbita ['ɔxbita] *f* orbit; (*do olho*) socket

Órcades ['ɔxkadʒiʃ] *fpl*: **as ~** the Orkneys

orçamento [oxsa'mẽtu] *m* (*do estado etc*) budget; (*avaliação*) estimate

orçar [ox'saʳ] *vt* to value, estimate ▷ *vi*: **~ em** (*gastos etc*) to be valued at, be put at

ordem ['oxdẽ] (*pl* **-ns**) *f* order; **até nova ~** until further notice; **de primeira ~** first-rate; **estar em ~** to be tidy; **por ~** in order, in turn; **~ do dia** agenda; **~ pública** public order, law and order

ordenado, -a [oxde'nadu, a] *adj* (*posto em ordem*) in order; (*metódico*) orderly ▷ *m* salary, wages *pl*

ordens ['oxdẽʃ] *fpl de* **ordem**

ordinário, -a [oxdʒi'narju, a] *adj* ordinary; (*comum*) usual; (*medíocre*) mediocre; (*grosseiro*) coarse, vulgar; (*de má qualidade*) inferior; **de ~** usually

orelha [o'reʎa] *f* ear; (*aba*) flap

orelhão [ore'ʎjãw] (*col*) *m* payphone

órfão, -fã ['ɔxfãw, fã] (*pl* **~s**) *adj, m/f* orphan

orgânico, -a [ox'ganiku, a] *adj* organic

organismo [oxga'niʒmu] *m* organism; (*entidade*) organization

organização [oxganiza'sãw] (*pl* **-ões**) *f* organization; **organizar** [oxgani'zaʳ] *vt* to organize

órgão ['ɔxgãw] (*pl* **~s**) *m* organ; (*governamental etc*) institution, body

orgasmo [ox'gaʒmu] *m* orgasm

orgia [ox'ʒia] *f* orgy

orgulho [ox'guʎu] *m* pride; (*arrogância*) arrogance; **orgulhoso, -a** [oxgu'ʎozu, ɔza] *adj* proud; haughty

orientação [orjẽta'sãw] *f* direction; (*posição*) position; **~ educacional** training, guidance

oriental [orjẽ'taw] (*pl* **-ais**) *adj* eastern; (*do Extremo Oriente*) oriental

orientar [orjẽ'taʳ] *vt* to orientate; (*indicar o rumo*) to direct; (*aconselhar*) to guide; **~-se** *vr* to get one's bearings; **~-se por algo** to follow sth

oriente [o'rjẽtʃi] *m*: **o O~** the East; **Extremo O~** Far East; **O~ Médio** Middle East

origem [o'riʒẽ] (*pl* **-ns**) *f* origin; (*ascendência*) lineage, descent; **lugar de ~** birthplace

original [oriʒi'naw] (*pl* **-ais**) *adj* original; (*estranho*) strange, odd ▷ *m* original; **originalidade** [oriʒinali'dadʒi] *f* originality; (*excentricidade*) eccentricity

originar [oriʒi'naʳ] *vt* to give rise to, start; **~-se** *vr* to arise; **~-se de** to originate from

oriundo, -a [o'rjũdu, a] *adj*: **~ de** arising from; (*natural*) native of

orla ['ɔxla] *f*: **~ marítima** seafront

ornamento [oxna'mẽtu] *m* adornment, decoration

orquestra [ox'kɛʃtra] (*PT* **-esta**) *f* orchestra

orquídea [ox'kidʒja] *f* orchid

ortodoxo, -a [oxto'dɔksu, a] *adj* orthodox

ortografia [oxtogra'fia] *f* spelling

orvalho [ox'vaʎu] *m* dew

os [uʃ] *art def ver* **o**

osso ['osu] *m* bone

ostensivo, -a [oʃtẽ'sivu, a] *adj* ostensible

ostentar [oʃtẽ'taʳ] *vt* to show; (*alardear*) to show off, flaunt

ostra ['oʃtra] *f* oyster

OTAN ['otã] *abr f* (= *Organização do Tratado do Atlântico Norte*) NATO

ótica ['ɔtʃika] *f* optics *sg*; (*loja*) optician's; (*fig*: *ponto de vista*) viewpoint; *ver tb* **ótico**

ótico, -a ['ɔtʃiku, a] *adj* optical ▷ *m/f* optician

otimista [otʃi'miʃta] *adj* optimistic ▷ *m/f* optimist

ótimo, -a ['ɔtʃimu, a] *adj* excellent,
splendid ▷ *excl* great!, super!
ou [o] *conj* or; **ou este ou aquele** either
this one or that one; **ou seja** in other
words
ouço *etc* ['osu] *vb ver* **ouvir**
ouriço [o'risu] *m* (*europeu*) hedgehog;
(*casca*) shell
ouro ['oru] *m* gold; **ouros** *mpl* (*Cartas*)
diamonds
ousadia [oza'dʒia] *f* daring; **ousado, -a**
[o'zadu, a] *adj* daring, bold
ousar [o'za*] *vt, vi* to dare
outono [o'tɔnu] *m* autumn

 PALAVRA CHAVE

outro, -a ['otru, a] *adj* **1** (*distinto: sg*)
another; (: *pl*) other; **outra coisa**
something else; **de outro modo, de
outra maneira** otherwise; **no outro dia**
the next day; **ela está outra** (*mudada*)
she's changed
2 (*adicional*): **traga-me outro café, por
favor** can I have another coffee please?;
outra vez again
▷ *pron* **1**: **o outro** the other one; **(os)
outros** (the) others; **de outro** somebody
else's
2 (*recíproco*): **odeiam-se uns aos outros**
they hate one another *ou* each other
3: **outro tanto** the same again; **comer
outro tanto** to eat the same *ou* as
much again; **ele recebeu uma dezena
de telegramas e outras tantas
chamadas** he got about ten telegrams
and as many calls

outubro [o'tubru] (*PT* **O-**) *m* October
ouvido [o'vidu] *m* (*Anat*) ear; (*sentido*)
hearing; **de ~** by ear; **dar ~s a** to listen to
ouvinte [o'vĩtʃi] *m/f* listener; (*estudante*)
auditor
ouvir [o'vi*] *vt* to hear; (*com atenção*) to
listen to; (*missa*) to attend ▷ *vi* to hear;
to listen; **~ dizer que ...** to hear that ...; **~
falar de** to hear of
ova ['ɔva] *f* roe
oval [o'vaw] (*pl* **-ais**) *adj, f* oval
ovário [o'varju] *m* ovary
ovelha [o'veʎa] *f* sheep
óvni ['ɔvni] *m* UFO
ovo ['ovu] *m* egg; **~s de granja** free-
range eggs; **~ pochê** (*BR*) *ou* **escalfado**
(*PT*) poached egg; **~ estrelado** *ou* **frito**
fried egg; **~s mexidos** scrambled eggs; **~**

quente/cozido duro hard-boiled/soft-
boiled egg
oxidar [oksi'da*] *vt* to rust; **~-se** *vr* to
rust, go rusty
oxigenado, -a [oksiʒe'nadu, a] *adj*
(*cabelo*) bleached; **água oxigenada**
peroxide
oxigênio [oksi'ʒenju] *m* oxygen
ozônio [o'zonju] *m* ozone; **camada de ~**
ozone layer

P

P. abr (= Praça) Sq.

pá [pa] f shovel; (de remo, hélice) blade ▷ m (PT) pal, mate; **pá de lixo** dustpan

paca ['paka] f (Zool) paca

pacato, -a [pa'katu, a] adj (pessoa) quiet; (lugar) peaceful

paciência [pa'sjēsja] f patience; **paciente** [pa'sjētʃi] adj, m/f patient

pacífico, -a [pa'sifiku, a] adj (pessoa) peace-loving; (aceito sem discussão) undisputed; (sossegado) peaceful; **o (Oceano) P~** the Pacific (Ocean)

pacote [pa'kotʃi] m packet; (embrulho) parcel; (Econ, Comput, Turismo) package

pacto ['paktu] m pact; (ajuste) agreement

padaria [pada'ria] f bakery, baker's (shop)

padeiro [pa'dejru] m baker

padiola [pa'dʒjɔla] f stretcher

padrão [pa'drãw] (pl -ões) m standard; (medida) gauge; (desenho) pattern; (fig: modelo) model; **~ de vida** standard of living

padrasto [pa'draʃtu] m stepfather

padre ['padri] m priest

padrinho [pa'driɲu] m godfather; (de noivo) best man; (patrono) sponsor

padroeiro, -a [pa'drwejru, a] m/f patron; (santo) patron saint

padrões [pa'drõjʃ] mpl de **padrão**

pães [pãjʃ] mpl de **pão**

pagador, a [paga'doʳ, a] adj paying ▷ m/f payer; (de salário) pay clerk; (de banco) teller

pagamento [paga'mētu] m payment; **~ a prazo** ou **em prestações** payment in instal(l)ments; **~ à vista** cash payment; **~ contra entrega** (Com) COD, cash on delivery

pagar [pa'gaʳ] vt to pay; (compras, pecados) to pay for; (o que devia) to pay back; (retribuir) to repay ▷ vi to pay; **~ por algo** (tb fig) to pay for sth; **~ a prestações** to pay in instal(l)ments; **~ de contado** (PT) to pay cash

página ['paʒina] f page; **~ (da) web** web page

pago, -a ['pagu, a] pp de **pagar** ▷ adj paid; (fig) even ▷ m pay

pai [paj] m father; **pais** mpl parents

painel [paj'nɛw] (pl -éis) m panel; (quadro) picture; (Auto) dashboard; (de avião) instrument panel

país [pa'jiʃ] m country; (região) land; **~ natal** native land

paisagem [paj'zaʒē] (pl -ns) f scenery, landscape

paisano, -a [paj'zanu, a] adj civilian ▷ m/f (não militar) civilian; (compatriota) fellow countryman

Países Baixos mpl: **os ~** the Netherlands

paixão [paj'ʃãw] (pl -ões) f passion

palácio [pa'lasju] m palace; **~ da justiça** courthouse; **palácio do Planalto** see boxed note

⬤ **PALÁCIO DO PLANALTO**
⬤
⬤ **Palácio de Planalto** is the seat of
⬤ the Brazilian government, in Brasília.
⬤ The name comes from the fact that
⬤ the Brazilian capital is situated on a
⬤ plateau. It has come to be a byword for
⬤ central government.

paladar [pala'daʳ] m taste; (Anat) palate

palafita [pala'fita] f (estacaria) stilts pl; (habitação) stilt house

palavra [pa'lavra] f word; (fala) speech; (promessa) promise; (direito de falar) right to speak; **dar a ~ a alguém** to give sb the chance to speak; **ter ~** (pessoa) to

be reliable; **~s cruzadas** crossword
(puzzle) *sg*; **palavrão** [pala'vrãw] (*pl*
-ões) *m* swearword
palco ['palku] *m* (*Teatro*) stage; (*fig: local*)
scene
Palestina [paleʃ'tʃina] *f*: **a ~** Palestine;
palestino, -a [paleʃ'tʃinu, a] *adj, m/f*
Palestinian
palestra [pa'lɛʃtra] *f* chat, talk;
(*conferência*) lecture
paletó [pale'tɔ] *m* jacket
palha ['paʎa] *f* straw
palhaço [pa'ʎasu] *m* clown
pálido, -a ['palidu, a] *adj* pale
palito [pa'litu] *m* stick; (*para os dentes*)
toothpick
palma ['pawma] *f* (*folha*) palm leaf; (*da
mão*) palm; **bater ~s** to clap; **palmada**
[paw'mada] *f* slap
palmeira [paw'mejra] *f* palm tree
palmo ['pawmu] *m* span; **~ a ~** inch by
inch
palpável [paw'pavew] (*pl* **-eis**) *adj*
tangible; (*fig*) obvious
pálpebra ['pawpebra] *f* eyelid
palpitação [pawpita'sãw] (*pl* **-ões**) *f*
beating, throbbing; **palpitações** *fpl*
(*batimentos cardíacos*) palpitations
palpitante [pawpi'tãtʃi] *adj* beating,
throbbing; (*fig: emocionante*) thrilling;
(: *de interesse atual*) sensational
palpitar [pawpi'ta'] *vi* (*coração*) to beat
palpite [paw'pitʃi] *m* (*intuição*) hunch;
(*Jogo, Turfe*) tip; (*opinião*) opinion
pampa ['pãpa] *f* pampas
Panamá [pana'ma] *m*: **o ~** Panama, the
Panama Canal
pancada [pã'kada] *f* (*no corpo*) blow,
hit; (*choque*) knock; (*de relógio*) stroke;
dar ~ em alguém to hit sb; **pancadaria**
[pãkada'ria] *f* (*surra*) beating; (*tumulto*)
fight
pandeiro [pã'dejru] *m* tambourine
pane ['pani] *f* breakdown
panela [pa'nɛla] *f* (*de barro*) pot; (*de
metal*) pan; (*de cozinhar*) saucepan; (*no
dente*) hole; **~ de pressão** pressure
cooker
panfleto [pã'fletu] *m* pamphlet
pânico ['paniku] *m* panic; **entrar em ~**
to panic
pano ['panu] *m* cloth; (*Teatro*) curtain;
(*vela*) sheet, sail; **~ de pratos** tea-towel;
~ de pó duster; **~ de fundo** (*tb fig*)
backdrop
panorama [pano'rama] *m* view

panqueca [pã'kɛka] *f* pancake
pantanal [pãta'naw] (*pl* **-ais**) *m*
swampland
pântano ['pãtanu] *m* marsh, swamp
pantera [pã'tɛra] *f* panther
pão [pãw] (*pl* **pães**) *m* bread; **o P~ de
Açúcar** (*no Rio*) Sugarloaf Mountain; **~
torrado** toast; **pão-duro** (*pl* **pães-
duros**) (*col*) *adj* mean, stingy ▷ *m/f*
miser; **pãozinho** [pãw'zinu] *m* roll
papa ['papa] *m* Pope; (*mingau*) porridge
papagaio [papa'gaju] *m* parrot; (*pipa*)
kite
papai [pa'paj] *m* dad, daddy; **P~ Noel**
Santa Claus, Father Christmas
papel [pa'pɛw] (*pl* **-éis**) *m* paper;
(*Teatro, função*) role; **~ de embrulho/
de escrever/de alumínio** wrapping
paper/writing paper/tinfoil; **~
higiênico/usado** toilet/waste paper;
~ de parede/de seda/transparente
wallpaper/tissue paper/tracing paper;
papelada [pape'lada] *f* pile of papers;
(*burocracia*) paperwork, red tape;
papelão [pape'lãw] *m* cardboard;
(*fig*) fiasco; **papelaria** [papela'ria] *f*
stationer's (shop); **papel-carbono** *m*
carbon paper
papo ['papu] (*col*) *m* (*queixo duplo*) double
chin; (*conversa*) chat; **bater (um) ~** to
have a chat, chat (*tb internet*); **ficar de ~
para o ar** (*fig*) to laze around
paquerar [pake'ra'] (*col*) *vi* to flirt ▷ *vt*
to chat up
paquistanês, -esa [pakiʃta'neʃ, eza] *adj,
m/f* Pakistani
Paquistão [pakiʃ'tãw] *m*: **o ~** Pakistan
par [pa'] *adj* (*igual*) equal; (*número*) even
▷ *m* pair; (*casal*) couple; (*pessoa na dança*)
partner; **~ a ~** side by side, level; **sem ~**
incomparable
para ['para] *prep* for; (*direção*) to,
towards; **~ que** so that, in order that;
~ quê? what for?, why?; **ir ~ casa** to go
home; **~ com** (*atitude*) towards; **de lá ~
cá** since then; **~ a semana** next week;
estar ~ to be about to; **é ~ nós ficarmos
aqui?** should we stay here?
parabéns [para'bẽjʃ] *mpl*
congratulations; (*no aniversário*) happy
birthday; **dar ~ a** to congratulate
pára-brisa ['para-] (*pl* **~s**) *m* windscreen
(*BRIT*), windshield (*US*)
pára-choque ['para-] (*pl* **~s**) *m* (*Auto*)
bumper
parada [pa'rada] *f* stop; (*Com*) stoppage;

(*militar, colegial*) parade
parado, -a [pa'radu, a] *adj* (*imóvel*)
standing still; (*sem vida*) lifeless; (*carro*)
stationary; (*máquina*) out of action;
(*olhar*) fixed; (*trabalhador, fábrica*) idle
paradoxo [para'dɔksu] *m* paradox
parafuso [para'fuzu] *m* screw
paragem [pa'raʒẽ] (*pl* **-ns**) *f* stop;
paragens *fpl* (*lugares*) places, parts; **~
de eléctrico** (PT) tram (BRIT) *ou* streetcar
(US) stop
parágrafo [pa'ragrafu] *m* paragraph
Paraguai [para'gwaj] *m*: **o ~** Paraguay;
paraguaio, -a [para'gwaju, a] *adj, m/f*
Paraguayan
paraíso [para'izu] *m* paradise
pára-lama ['para-] (*pl* **-s**) *m* wing (BRIT),
fender (US); (*de bicicleta*) mudguard
paralelepípedo [paralele'pipedu] *m*
paving stone
paralelo, -a [para'lɛlu, a] *adj* parallel
parapeito [para'pejtu] *m* wall, parapet;
(*da janela*) windowsill
parapente [para'pẽtʃi] *m* (*Esporte*)
paragliding; (*equipamento*) paraglider
pára-quedas ['para-] *m inv* parachute
parar [pa'raʳ] *vi* to stop; (*ficar*) to stay
▷ *vt* to stop; **fazer ~** (*deter*) to stop; **~ na
cadeia** to end up in jail; **~ de fazer** to
stop doing
pára-raios ['para-] *m inv* lightning
conductor
parasita [para'zita] *m* parasite
parceiro, -a [pax'sejru, a] *adj* matching
▷ *m/f* partner
parcela [pax'sɛla] *f* piece, bit;
(*de pagamento*) instalment (BRIT),
installment (US); (*de terra*) plot; (*do
eleitorado etc*) section; (*Mat*) item
parceria [paxse'ria] *f* partnership
parcial [pax'sjaw] *adj* partial;
(*feito por partes*) in parts; (*pessoa*)
bias(s)ed; (*Pol*) partisan; **parcialidade**
[paxsjali'dadʒi] *f* bias, partiality
pardal [pax'daw] (*pl* **-ais**) *m* sparrow
pardieiro [pax'dʒjejru] *m* ruin, heap
pardo, -a ['paxdu, a] *adj* (*cinzento*) grey
(BRIT), gray (US); (*castanho*) brown;
(*mulato*) mulatto
parecer [pare'seʳ] *m, vi* (*ter a aparência
de*) to look, seem; **~-se** *vr*: **~-se com
alguém** to look like sb; **~ (com)** (*ter
semelhança com*) to look (like); **ao que
parece** apparently; **parece-me que** I
think that, it seems to me that; **que lhe
parece?** what do you think?; **parece que**

it looks as if
parecido, -a [pare'sidu, a] *adj* alike,
similar; **~ com** like
parede [pa'redʒi] *f* wall
parente, -a [pa'rẽtʃi] *m/f* relative,
relation; **parentesco** [parẽ'teʃku] *m*
relationship; (*fig*) connection
parêntese [pa'rẽtezi] *m* parenthesis;
(*na escrita*) bracket; (*fig: digressão*)
digression
páreo ['parju] *m* race; (*fig*) competition
parir [pa'riʳ] *vt* to give birth to ▷ *vi* to give
birth; (*mulher*) to have a baby
Paris [pa'riʃ] *n* Paris; **parisiense**
[pari'zjẽsi] *adj, m/f* Parisian
parlamentar [paxlamẽ'taʳ] *adj*
parliamentary ▷ *m/f* member of
parliament
parlamento [paxla'mẽtu] *m*
parliament
paróquia [pa'rɔkja] *f* (*Rel*) parish
parque ['paxki] *m* park; **~ industrial/
infantil** industrial estate/children's
playground; **~ nacional** national park
parte ['paxtʃi] *f* part; (*quinhão*) share;
(*lado*) side; (*ponto*) point; (*Jur*) party;
(*papel*) role; **a maior ~ de** most
of; **à ~** aside; (*separado*) separate;
(*separadamente*) separately; (*além de*)
apart from; **da ~ de alguém** on sb's part;
em alguma/qualquer ~ somewhere;
anywhere; **em ~ alguma** nowhere; **por
toda (a) ~** everywhere; **pôr de ~** to set
aside; **tomar ~ em** to take part in; **dar
~ de alguém à polícia** to report sb to
the police
participar [paxtʃisi'paʳ] *vt* to
announce, notify of ▷ *vi*: **~ de** *ou*
em to participate in, take part in;
(*compartilhar*) to share in
particípio [paxtʃi'sipju] *m* participle
particular [paxtʃiku'laʳ] *adj* particular,
special; (*privativo, pessoal*) private
▷ *m* particular; (*indivíduo*) individual;
particulares *mpl* (*pormenores*) details;
em ~ in private; **particularmente**
[paxtʃikulax'mẽtʃi] *adv* privately;
(*especialmente*) particularly
partida [pax'tʃida] *f* (*saída*) departure;
(*Esporte*) game, match
partidário, -a [paxtʃi'darju, a] *adj*
supporting ▷ *m/f* supporter, follower
partido [pax'tʃidu] *m* (*Pol*) party; **tirar
~ de** to profit from; **tomar o ~ de** to side
with
partilhar [paxtʃi'ʎaʳ] *vt* to share;

(*distribuir*) to share out
partir [pax'tʃiʳ] vt to break; (*dividir*)
to divide, split ▷ vi (*pôr-se a caminho*)
to set off, set out; (*ir-se embora*) to
leave, depart; **~-se** vr to break; **a ~ de**
(starting) from
parto ['paxtu] m (child)birth; **estar em
trabalho de ~** to be in labour (BRIT) *ou*
labor (US)
Páscoa ['paʃkwa] f Easter; (*dos judeus*)
Passover
pasmo, -a ['paʒmu, a] adj astonished
▷ m amazement
passa ['pasa] f raisin
passadeira [pasa'dejra] f (*tapete*) stair
carpet; (*mulher*) ironing lady; (PT: *para
peões*) zebra crossing (BRIT), crosswalk
(US)
passado, -a [pa'sadu, a] adj past;
(*antiquado*) old-fashioned; (*fruta*) bad;
(*peixe*) off ▷ m past; **o ano ~** last year;
bem/mal ~ (*carne*) well done/rare
passageiro, -a [pasa'ʒejru, a] adj
passing ▷ m/f passenger
passagem [pa'saʒẽ] (*pl* **-ns**) f passage;
(*preço de condução*) fare; (*bilhete*) ticket;
~ de ida e volta return ticket, round
trip ticket (US); **~ de nível** level (BRIT)
ou grade (US) crossing; **~ de pedestres**
pedestrian crossing (BRIT), crosswalk
(US); **~ subterrânea** underpass, subway
(BRIT)
passaporte [pasa'pɔxtʃi] m passport
passar [pa'saʳ] vt to pass; (*exceder*) to
go beyond, exceed; (*a ferro*) to iron; (*o
tempo*) to spend; (*a outra pessoa*) to pass
on; (*pomada*) to put on ▷ vi to pass; (*na
rua*) to go past; (*tempo*) to go by; (*dor*)
to wear off; (*terminar*) to be over; **~-se**
vr (*acontecer*) to go on, happen; **~ bem**
(*de saúde*) to be well; **passava das dez
horas** it was past ten o' clock; **~ alguém
para trás** to con sb; (*cônjuge*) to cheat on
sb; **~ por algo** (*sofrer*) to go through sth;
(*transitar: estrada*) to go along sth; (*ser
considerado como*) to be thought of as sth;
~ sem to do without
passarela [pasa'rɛla] f footbridge
pássaro ['pasaru] m bird
passatempo [pasa'tẽpu] m pastime
passe ['pasi] m pass
passear [pa'sjaʳ] vt to take for a walk
▷ vi (*a pé*) to go for a walk; (*sair*) to go
out; **~ a cavalo** (*ou de carro*) to go for
a ride; **passeata** [pa'sjata] f (*marcha
coletiva*) protest march; **passeio**

[pa'seju] m walk; (*de carro*) drive, ride;
(*excursão*) outing; (*calçada*) pavement
(BRIT), sidewalk (US); **dar um passeio** to
go for a walk; (*de carro*) to go for a drive
ou ride
passível [pa'sivew] (*pl* **-eis**) adj: **~ de** (*dor
etc*) susceptible to; (*pena, multa*) subject
to
passivo, -a [pa'sivu, a] adj passive ▷ m
(Com) liabilities pl
passo ['pasu] m step; (*medida*) pace;
(*modo de andar*) walk; (*ruído dos passos*)
footstep; (*sinal de pé*) footprint; **ao ~ que**
while; **ceder o ~ a** to give way to
pasta ['paʃta] f paste; (*de couro*) briefcase;
(*de cartolina*) folder; (*de ministro*)
portfolio; **~ dentifrícia** *ou* **de dentes**
toothpaste
pastar [paʃ'taʳ] vt to graze on ▷ vi to
graze
pastel [paʃ'tɛw] (*pl* **-éis**) adj inv (*cor*)
pastel ▷ m samosa
pastelão [paʃte'lãw] m slapstick
pastelaria [paʃtela'ria] f cake shop;
(*comida*) pastry
pasteurizado, -a [paʃtewri'zadu, a] adj
pasteurized
pastilha [paʃ'tʃiʎa] f (Med) tablet; (*doce*)
pastille; (Comput) chip
pastor, a [paʃ'toʳ, a] m/f shepherd(ess)
▷ m (Rel) clergyman, pastor
pata ['pata] f (*pé de animal*) foot, paw;
(*ave*) duck; (*col: pé*) foot
patamar [pata'maʳ] m (*de escada*)
landing; (*fig*) level
pateta [pa'tɛta] adj stupid, daft ▷ m/f
idiot
patético, -a [pa'tɛtʃiku, a] adj pathetic,
moving
patife [pa'tʃifi] m scoundrel, rogue
patim [pa'tʃĩ] (*pl* **-ns**) m skate; **~ de rodas**
roller skate; **~s em linha** Rollerblades®;
patinar [patʃi'naʳ] vi to skate; (*Auto:
derrapar*) to skid
patins [pa'tʃĩʃ] mpl de **patim**
pátio ['patʃju] m (*de uma casa*) patio,
backyard; (*espaço cercado de edifícios*)
courtyard; (*tb*: **~ de recreio**) playground;
(*Mil*) parade ground
pato ['patu] m duck; (*macho*) drake
patologia [patolo'ʒia] f pathology;
patológico, -a [pato'lɔʒiku, a] adj
pathological
patrão [pa'trãw] (*pl* **-ões**) m (Com) boss;
(*dono de casa*) master; (*proprietário*)
landlord; (*Náut*) skipper

pátria ['patrja] f homeland
patrimônio [patri'monju] m (*herança*) inheritance; (*fig*) heritage; (*bens*) property
patriota [pa'trjɔta] m/f patriot
patrocinar [patrosi'na^r] vt to sponsor; (*proteger*) to support; **patrocínio** [patro'sinju] m sponsorship, backing, support
patrões [pa'trõjʃ] mpl de **patrão**
patrulha [pa'truʎa] f patrol; **patrulhar** [patru'ʎa^r] vt, vi to patrol
pau [paw] m (*madeira*) wood; (*vara*) stick; **paus** mpl (*Cartas*) clubs; **~ a ~** neck and neck; **~ de bandeira** flagpole
pausa ['pawza] f pause; (*intervalo*) break; (*descanso*) rest
pauta ['pawta] f (*linha*) (guide)line; (*ordem do dia*) agenda; (*indicações*) guidelines pl; **sem ~** (*papel*) plain; **em ~** on the agenda
pavão, -voa [pa'vãw, 'voa] (pl **pavões/-s**) m/f peacock/peahen
pavilhão [pavi'ʎãw] (pl **-ões**) m tent; (*de madeira*) hut; (*no jardim*) summerhouse; (*em exposição*) pavilion; (*bandeira*) flag
pavimento [pavi'mẽtu] m (*chão, andar*) floor; (*da rua*) road surface
pavões [pa'võjʃ] mpl de **pavão**
pavor [pa'vo^r] m dread, terror; **ter ~ de** to be terrified of; **pavoroso, -a** [pavo'rozu, ɔza] adj dreadful, terrible
paz [pajʒ] f peace; **fazer as ~es** to make up, be friends again
PC abr m = **personal computer**
Pça. abr (= *Praça*) Sq.
pé [pɛ] m foot; (*da mesa*) leg; (*fig: base*) footing; (*de milho, café*) plant; **ir a pé** to walk, go on foot; **ao pé de** near, by; **ao pé da letra** literally; **estar de pé** (*festa etc*) to be on; **em ou de pé** standing (up); **dar no pé** (*col*) to run away, take off; **não ter pé nem cabeça** (*fig*) to make no sense
peão [pjãw] (PT): (pl **-ões**) m pedestrian
peça ['pɛsa] f piece; (*Auto*) part; (*aposento*) room; (*Teatro*) play; **~ de reposição** spare part; **~ de roupa** garment
pecado [pe'kadu] m sin
pecar [pe'ka^r] vi to sin; **~ por excesso de zelo** to be over-zealous
pechincha [pe'ʃĩʃa] f (*vantagem*) godsend; (*coisa barata*) bargain; **pechinchar** [peʃĩ'ʃa^r] vi to bargain, haggle

peço etc ['pɛsu] vb ver **pedir**
peculiar [peku'lja^r] adj special, peculiar; (*particular*) particular; **peculiaridade** [pekuljari'dadʒi] f peculiarity
pedaço [pe'dasu] m piece; (*fig: trecho*) bit; **aos ~s** in pieces
pedágio [pe'daʒju] (BR) m (*pagamento*) toll
pedal [pe'daw] (pl **-ais**) m pedal; **pedalar** [peda'la^r] vt, vi to pedal
pedante [pe'dãtʃi] adj pretentious ▷ m/f pseud
pedestre [pe'dɛʃtri] (BR) m pedestrian
pedicuro, -a [pedʒi'kuru, a] m/f chiropodist (BRIT), podiatrist (US)
pedido [pe'dʒidu] m request; (*Com*) order; **~ de demissão** resignation; **~ de desculpa** apology
pedinte [pe'dʒĩtʃi] m/f beggar
pedir [pe'dʒi^r] vt to ask for; (*Com, comida*) to order; (*exigir*) to demand ▷ vi to ask; (*num restaurante*) to order; **~ algo a alguém** to ask sb for sth; **~ a alguém que faça, ~ para alguém fazer** to ask sb to do
pedra ['pɛdra] f stone; (*rochedo*) rock; (*de granizo*) hailstone; (*de açúcar*) lump; (*quadro-negro*) slate; **~ de gelo** ice cube; **pedreiro** [pe'drejru] m stonemason
pegada [pe'gada] f (*de pé*) footprint; (*Futebol*) save
pegado, -a [pe'gadu, a] adj stuck; (*unido*) together
pegajoso, -a [pega'ʒozu, ɔza] adj sticky
pegar [pe'ga^r] vt to catch; (*selos*) to stick (on); (*segurar*) to take hold of; (*hábito, mania*) to get into; (*compreender*) to take in; (*trabalho*) to take on; (*estação de rádio*) to pick up, get ▷ vi to stick; (*planta*) to take; (*moda*) to catch on; (*doença*) to be catching; (*motor*) to start; **~ em** (*segurar*) to grab, pick up; **ir ~** (*buscar*) to go and get; **~ um emprego** to get a job; **~ fogo a algo** to set fire to sth; **~ no sono** to fall asleep
pego, -a ['pɛgu, a] pp de **pegar**
peito ['pejtu] m (*Anat*) chest; (*de ave, mulher*) breast; (*fig*) courage
peitoril [pejto'riw] (pl **-is**) m windowsill
peixada [pej'ʃada] f fish cooked in a seafood sauce
peixaria [pejʃa'ria] f fish shop, fishmonger's (BRIT)
peixe ['pejʃi] m fish; **Peixes** mpl (*Astrologia*) Pisces sg
pela ['pɛla] = **por + a**

pelada [pe'lada] f football game

❀ **PELADA**

❀ **Pelada** is an improvised, generally
❀ short, game of football, which in the
❀ past was played with a ball made out
❀ of socks, or an inflatable rubber ball.
❀ It is still played today on any piece of
❀ open land, or even in the street.

pelado, -a [pe'ladu, a] adj (sem pele)
skinned; (sem pêlo, cabelo) shorn; (nu)
naked, in the nude; (sem dinheiro) broke
pelar [pe'la^r] vt (tirar a pele) to skin; (tirar o
pêlo) to shear
pelas ['pelaʃ] = por + as
pele ['pɛli] f skin; (couro) leather; (como
agasalho) fur; (de animal) hide
película [pe'likula] f film
pelo ['pɛlu] = por + o
pêlo ['pelu] m hair; (de animal) fur, coat;
nu em ~ stark naked
pelos ['pɛluʃ] = por + os
peludo, -a [pe'ludu, a] adj hairy; (animal)
furry
pena ['pena] f feather; (de caneta)
nib; (escrita) writing; (Jur) penalty,
punishment; (sofrimento) suffering;
(piedade) pity; **que ~!** what a shame!; **dar
~** to be upsetting; **ter ~ de** to feel sorry
for; **~ capital** capital punishment
pênalti ['penawtʃi] m (Futebol) penalty
(kick)
penar [pe'na^r] vt to grieve ▷ vi to suffer
pendência [pẽ'dẽsja] f dispute, quarrel
pendente [pẽ'dẽtʃi] adj hanging; (por
decidir) pending; (inclinado) sloping;
(dependente): **~ (de)** dependent (on) ▷ m
pendant
pêndulo ['pẽdulu] m pendulum
pendurar [pẽdu'ra^r] vt to hang
penedo [pe'nedu] m rock, boulder
peneira [pe'nejra] f sieve; **peneirar**
[penej'ra^r] vt to sift, sieve ▷ vi (chover)
to drizzle
penetrar [pene'tra^r] vt to get into,
penetrate; (compreender) to understand
▷ vi: **~ em** ou **por** ou **entre** to penetrate; **~
em** (segredo) to find out
penhasco [pe'ɲaʃku] m cliff, crag
penhorar [peɲo'ra^r] vt (dar em penhor) to
pledge, pawn
penicilina [penisi'lina] f penicillin
península [pe'nĩsula] f peninsula
pênis ['peniʃ] m inv penis

penitência [peni'tẽsja] f penitence;
(expiação) penance; **penitenciária**
[penitẽ'sjarja] f prison
penoso, -a [pe'nozu, ɔza] adj (assunto,
tratamento) painful; (trabalho) hard
pensamento [pẽsa'mẽtu] m thought;
(mente) mind; (opinião) way of thinking;
(idéia) idea
pensão [pẽ'sãw] (pl -ões) f (tb: **casa
de ~**) boarding house; (comida)
board; **~ completa** full board; **~ de
aposentadoria** (retirement) pension
pensar [pẽ'sa^r] vi to think; (imaginar)
to imagine; **~ em** to think of ou about;
~ fazer to intend to do; **pensativo, -a**
[pẽsa'tʃivu, a] adj thoughtful, pensive
pensionista [pẽsjo'niʃta] m/f pensioner
pensões [pẽ'sõjʃ] fpl de **pensão**
pente ['pẽtʃi] m comb; **penteado,
-a** [pẽ'tʃjadu, a] adj (cabelo) in place;
(pessoa) smart ▷ m hairdo, hairstyle;
pentear [pẽ'tʃja^r] vt to comb; (arranjar
o cabelo) to do, style; **pentear-se** vr to
comb one's hair; to do one's hair
penúltimo, -a [pe'nuwtʃimu, a] adj last
but one, penultimate
penumbra [pe'nũbra] f twilight, dusk;
(sombra) shadow; (meia-luz) half-light
penúria [pe'nurja] f poverty
peões [pjõjʃ] mpl de **peão**
pepino [pe'pinu] m cucumber
pequeno, -a [pe'kenu, a] adj small;
(mesquinho) petty ▷ m boy
pequerrucho [peke'xuʃu] m thimble
Pequim [pe'kĩ] n Peking, Beijing
pêra ['pera] f pear
perambular [perãbu'la^r] vi to wander
perante [pe'rãtʃi] prep before, in the
presence of
per capita [pex'kapita] adv, adj per
capita
perceber [pexse'be^r] vt to realize;
(por meio dos sentidos) to perceive;
(compreender) to understand; (ver) to see;
(ouvir) to hear; (ver ao longe) to make out;
(dinheiro: receber) to receive
percentagem [pexsẽ'taʒẽ] f percentage
percepção [pexsep'sãw] f perception;
perceptível [pexsep'tʃivew] (pl -eis) adj
perceptible, noticeable; (som) audible
percevejo [pexse'veʒu] m (inseto) bug;
(prego) drawing pin (BRIT), thumbtack
(US)
perco etc ['pexku] vb ver **perder**
percorrer [pexko'xe^r] vt (viajar por) to
travel (across ou over); (passar por) to go

through, traverse; (*investigar*) to search
through

percurso [pex'kuxsu] *m* (*espaço
percorrido*) distance (covered); (*trajeto*)
route; (*viagem*) journey

percussão [pexku'sãw] *f* (*Mús*)
percussion

perda ['pexda] *f* loss; (*desperdício*) waste;
~s e danos damages, losses

perdão [pex'dãw] *m* pardon, forgiveness;
~! sorry!, I beg your pardon!

perder [pex'deᴿ] *vt* to lose; (*tempo*) to
waste; (*trem, show, oportunidade*) to
miss ▷ *vi* to lose; **~-se** *vr* to get lost;
(*arruinar-se*) to be ruined; (*desaparecer*) to
disappear; **~-se de alguém** to lose sb

perdido, -a [pex'dʒidu, a] *adj* lost; **~s e
achados** lost and found, lost property

perdiz [pex'dʒiʒ] *f* partridge

perdoar [pex'dwaᴿ] *vt* to forgive

perdurar [pexdu'raᴿ] *vi* to last a long
time; (*continuar a existir*) to still exist

perecível [pere'sivew] (*pl* **-eis**) *adj*
perishable

peregrinação [peregrina'sãw] (*pl* **-ões**) *f*
(*viagem*) travels *pl*; (*Rel*) pilgrimage

peregrino, -a [pere'grinu, a] *m/f* pilgrim

peremptório, -a [perẽp'tɔrju, a] *adj*
final; (*decisivo*) decisive

perene [pe'reni] *adj* everlasting; (*Bot*)
perennial

perfeição [pexfej'sãw] *f* perfection

perfeitamente [pexfejta'mẽtʃi] *adv*
perfectly ▷ *excl* exactly!

perfeito, -a [pex'fejtu, a] *adj* perfect ▷ *m*
(*Ling*) perfect

perfil [pex'fiw] (*pl* **-is**) *m* profile; (*silhueta*)
silhouette, outline; (*Arq*) (cross) section

perfume [pex'fumi] *m* perfume, scent

perfurar [pexfu'raᴿ] *vt* (*o chão*) to drill a
hole in; (*papel*) to punch (a hole in)

pergunta [pex'gũta] *f* question; **fazer
uma ~ a alguém** to ask sb a question;
perguntar [pexgũ'taᴿ] *vt* to ask;
(*interrogar*) to question ▷ *vi*: **perguntar
por alguém** to ask after sb; **perguntar-
se** *vr* to wonder; **perguntar algo a
alguém** to ask sb sth

perícia [pe'risja] *f* expertise; (*destreza*)
skill; (*exame*) investigation

periferia [perife'ria] *f* periphery; (*da
cidade*) outskirts *pl*

perigo [pe'rigu] *m* danger; **perigoso,
-a** [peri'gozu, ɔza] *adj* dangerous;
(*arriscado*) risky

período [pe'riodu] *m* period; (*estação*)

season

periquito [peri'kitu] *m* parakeet

perito, -a [pe'ritu, a] *adj* expert ▷ *m/f*
expert; (*quem faz perícia*) investigator

permanecer [pexmane'seᴿ] *vi* to
remain; (*num lugar*) to stay; (*continuar a
ser*) to remain, keep; **~ parado** to keep
still

permanência [pexma'nẽsja] *f*
permanence; (*estada*) stay; **permanente**
[pexma'nẽtʃi] *adj* (*dor*) constant; (*cor*)
fast; (*residência, pregas*) permanent ▷ *m*
(*cartão*) pass ▷ *f* perm

permissão [pexmi'sãw] *f* permission,
consent; **permissivo, -a** [pexmi'sivu, a]
adj permissive

permitir [pexmi'tʃiᴿ] *vt* to allow, permit

perna ['pexna] *f* leg; **~s tortas** bow legs

pernil [pex'niw] (*pl* **-is**) *m* (*de animal*)
haunch; (*Culin*) leg

pernilongo [pexni'lõgu] *m* mosquito

pernis [pex'niʃ] *mpl de* **pernil**

pernoitar [pexnoj'taᴿ] *vi* to spend the
night

pérola ['pɛrola] *f* pearl

perpendicular [pexpẽdʒiku'laᴿ] *adj, f*
perpendicular

perpetuar [pexpe'twaᴿ] *vt* to
perpetuate; **perpétuo, -a** [pex'pɛtwu, a]
adj perpetual

persa ['pɛxsa] *adj, m/f* Persian

perseguição [pexsegi'sãw] *f* pursuit;
(*Rel, Pol*) persecution

perseguir [pexse'giᴿ] *vt* to pursue;
(*correr atrás*) to chase (after); (*Rel, Pol*) to
persecute; (*importunar*) to harass, pester

perseverante [pexseve'rãtʃi] *adj*
persistent

perseverar [pexseve'raᴿ] *vi*: **~ (em)** to
persevere (in), persist (in)

Pérsia ['pɛxsja] *f*: **a ~** Persia

persiana [pex'sjana] *f* blind

Pérsico, -a ['pɛxsiku, a] *adj*: **o golfo ~** the
Persian Gulf

persigo *etc* [pex'sigu] *vb ver* **perseguir**

persistir [pexsiʃ'tʃiᴿ] *vi*: **~ (em)** to persist
(in)

personagem [pexso'naʒẽ] (*pl* **-ns**) *m/f*
famous person, celebrity; (*num livro,
filme*) character

personalidade [pexsonali'dadʒi] *f*
personality

perspectiva [pexʃpek'tʃiva] *f*
perspective; (*panorama*) view;
(*probabilidade*) prospect

perspicácia [pexʃpi'kasja] *f* insight,

perceptiveness; **perspicaz** [pexʃpi'kaj3]
adj observant; (*sagaz*) shrewd
persuadir [pexswa'dʒiʳ] *vt* to
persuade; **~-se** *vr* to convince o.s.;
persuasão [pexswa'zãw] *f* persuasion;
persuasivo, -a [pexswa'zivu, a] *adj*
persuasive
pertencente [pextẽ'sẽtʃi] *adj*: **~ a**
pertaining to
pertencer [pextẽ'seʳ] *vi*: **~ a** to belong to;
(*referir-se*) to concern
pertences [pex'tẽsiʃ] *mpl* (*de uma pessoa*)
belongings
pertinência [pextʃi'nẽsja] *f* relevance;
pertinente [pextʃi'nẽtʃi] *adj* relevant;
(*apropriado*) appropriate
perto, -a [ˈpɛxtu, a] *adj* nearby ▷ *adv*
near; **~ de** near to; (*em comparação com*)
next to; **de ~** closely; (*ver*) close up;
(*conhecer*) very well
perturbar [pextux'baʳ] *vt* to disturb;
(*abalar*) to upset, trouble; (*atrapalhar*) to
put off; (*andamento, trânsito*) to disrupt;
(*envergonhar*) to embarrass; (*alterar*) to
affect
Peru [pe'ru] *m*: **o ~** Peru
peru, a [pe'ru, a] *m/f* turkey
peruca [pe'ruka] *f* wig
perverso, -a [pex'vɛxsu, a] *adj* perverse;
(*malvado*) wicked
perverter [pexvex'teʳ] *vt* to corrupt,
pervert; **pervertido, -a** [pexvex'tʃidu, a]
adj perverted ▷ *m/f* pervert
pesadelo [peza'delu] *m* nightmare
pesado, -a [pe'zadu, a] *adj* heavy;
(*ambiente*) tense; (*trabalho*) hard; (*estilo*)
dull, boring; (*andar*) slow; (*piada*) coarse;
(*comida*) stodgy; (*tempo*) sultry ▷ *adv*
heavily
pêsames [ˈpesamiʃ] *mpl* condolences,
sympathy *sg*
pesar [pe'zaʳ] *vt* to weigh; (*fig*) to weigh
up ▷ *vi* to weigh; (*ser pesado*) to be heavy;
(*influir*) to carry weight; (*causar mágoa*):
~ a to hurt, grieve ▷ *m* grief; **~ sobre**
(*recair*) to fall upon
pesaroso, -a [peza'rozu, ɔza] *adj*
sorrowful, sad; (*arrependido*) regretful,
sorry
pesca [ˈpɛʃka] *f* fishing; (*os peixes*) catch;
ir à ~ to go fishing
pescada [peʃ'kada] *f* whiting
pescado [peʃ'kadu] *m* fish
pescador, a [peʃka'doʳ, a] *m/f*
fisherman/woman; **~ à linha** angler
pescar [peʃ'kaʳ] *vt* (*peixe*) to catch; (*tentar*

apanhar) to fish for; (*retirar da água*) to fish
out ▷ *vi* to fish
pescoço [peʃ'kosu] *m* neck
peso [ˈpezu] *m* weight; (*fig*: *ônus*) burden;
(*importância*) importance; **~ bruto/
líquido** gross/net weight
pesquisa [peʃ'kiza] *f* inquiry,
investigation; (*científica, de mercado*)
research; **pesquisar** [peʃki'zaʳ] *vt*, *vi* to
investigate; to research
pêssego [ˈpesegu] *m* peach
pessimista [pesi'miʃta] *adj* pessimistic
▷ *m/f* pessimist
péssimo, -a [ˈpɛsimu, a] *adj* very bad,
awful
pessoa [pe'soa] *f* person; **pessoas** *fpl*
(*gente*) people; **pessoal** [pe'swaw] (*pl*
pessoais) *adj* personal ▷ *m* personnel *pl*,
staff *pl*; (*col*) people *pl*, folks *pl*
pestana [peʃ'tana] *f* eyelash
peste [ˈpɛʃtʃi] *f* epidemic; (*bubônica*)
plague; (*fig*) pest, nuisance
pétala [ˈpɛtala] *f* petal
petição [petʃi'sãw] (*pl* **-ões**) *f* request;
(*documento*) petition
petisco [pe'tʃiʃku] *m* savoury (BRIT),
savory (US), titbit (BRIT), tidbit (US)
petróleo [pe'trɔlju] *m* oil, petroleum; **~
bruto** crude oil
peúga [ˈpjuga] (PT) *f* sock
pevide [pe'vidʒi] (PT) *f* (*de melão*) seed;
(*de maçã*) pip
p. ex. *abr* (= *por exemplo*) e.g.
pia [ˈpia] *f* wash basin; (*da cozinha*) sink; **~
batismal** font
piada [ˈpjada] *f* joke
pianista [pja'niʃta] *m/f* pianist
piano [ˈpjanu] *m* piano
piar [pjaʳ] *vi* (*pinto*) to cheep; (*coruja*) to
hoot
picada [pi'kada] *f* (*de agulha etc*) prick;
(*de abelha*) sting; (*de mosquito, cobra*) bite;
(*de avião*) dive; (*de navalha*) stab; (*atalho*)
path, trail
picante [pi'kãtʃi] *adj* (*tempero*) hot
picar [pi'kaʳ] *vt* to prick; (*suj*: *abelha*)
to sting; (: *mosquito*) to bite; (: *pássaro*)
to peck; (*um animal*) to goad; (*carne*) to
mince; (*papel*) to shred; (*fruta*) to chop up
▷ *vi* (*comichar*) to prickle
picareta [pika'reta] *f* pickaxe (BRIT),
pickax (US) ▷ *m/f* crook
pico [ˈpiku] *m* (*cume*) peak; (*ponta aguda*)
sharp point; (PT: *um pouco*) a bit; **mil e ~**
just over a thousand
picolé [piko'lɛ] *m* lolly

picotar [piko'ta^r] vt to perforate; (bilhete) to punch

piedade [pje'dadʒi] f piety; (compaixão) pity; **ter ~ de** to have pity on; **piedoso, -a** [pje'dozu, ɔza] adj pious; (compassivo) merciful

piercing ['pixsī] (pl **~s**) m piercing

pifar [pi'fa^r] (col) vi (carro) to break down; (rádio etc) to go wrong; (plano, programa) to fall through

pijama [pi'ʒama] m ou f pyjamas pl (BRIT), pajamas pl (US)

pilantra [pi'lãtra] (col) m/f crook

pilar [pi'la^r] vt to pound, crush ▷ m pillar

pilha ['piʎa] f (Elet) battery; (monte) pile, heap

pilhar [pi'ʎa^r] vt to plunder, pillage; (roubar) to rob; (surpreender) to catch

pilotar [pilo'ta^r] vt (avião) to fly

piloto [pi'lotu] m pilot; (motorista) (racing) driver; (bico de gás) pilot light ▷ adj inv (usina, plano) pilot; (peça) sample atr

pílula ['pilula] f pill; **a ~ (anticoncepcional)** the pill

pimenta [pi'mēta] f (Culin) pepper; **~ de Caiena** cayenne pepper; **pimenta-do-reino** f black pepper; **pimenta-malagueta** (pl **pimentas-malagueta**) f chilli (BRIT) ou chili (US) pepper; **pimentão** [pimē'tãw] (pl **-ões**) m (Bot) pepper

pinça ['pĩsa] f (de sobrancelhas) tweezers pl; (de casa) tongs pl; (Med) callipers pl (BRIT), calipers pl (US)

pincel [pĩ'sew] (pl **-éis**) m brush; (para pintar) paintbrush; **pincelar** [pĩse'la^r] vt to paint

pinga ['pĩga] f (cachaça) rum; (PT: trago) drink

pingar [pĩ'ga^r] vi to drip

pingo ['pĩgu] m (gota) drop

pingue-pongue® [pĩgi-'põgi] m ping-pong®

pingüim [pĩ'gwĩ] (pl **-ns**) m penguin

pinheiro [pi'nejru] m pine (tree)

pinho ['piɲu] m pine

pino ['pinu] m (peça) pin; (Auto: na porta) lock; **a ~** upright

pinta ['pĩta] f (mancha) spot

pintar [pĩ'ta^r] vt to paint; (cabelo) to dye; (rosto) to make up; (descrever) to describe; (imaginar) to picture ▷ vi to paint; **~-se** vr to make o.s. up

pintarroxo [pĩta'xoʃu] m (BR) linnet; (PT) robin

pinto ['pĩtu] m chick

pintor, a [pĩ'to^r, a] m/f painter

pintura [pĩ'tura] f painting; (maquiagem) make-up

piolho ['pjoʎu] m louse

pioneiro, -a [pjo'nejru, a] m/f pioneer

pior ['pjo^r] adj, adv (compar) worse; (superl) worst ▷ m: **o ~** worst of all; **piorar** [pjo'ra^r] vt to make worse, worsen ▷ vi to get worse

pipa ['pipa] f barrel, cask; (de papel) kite

pipi [pi'pi] (col) m pee; **fazer ~** to have a pee

pipoca [pi'pɔka] f popcorn

pipocar [pipo'ka^r] vi to go pop, pop

pique etc vb ver **picar**

piquenique [piki'niki] m picnic

pirâmide [pi'ramidʒi] f pyramid

piranha [pi'raɲa] f piranha (fish)

pirata [pi'rata] m pirate

pires ['piriʃ] m inv saucer

Pirineus [piri'newʃ] mpl: **os ~** the Pyrenees

pirulito [piru'litu] (BR) m lollipop

pisar [pi'za^r] vt to tread on; (esmagar, subjugar) to crush ▷ vi to step, tread

pisca-pisca [piʃka-'piʃka] (pl **~s**) m (Auto) indicator

piscar [piʃ'ka^r] vt to blink; (dar sinal) to wink; (estrelas) to twinkle ▷ m: **num ~ de olhos** in a flash

piscina [pi'sina] f swimming pool

piso ['pizu] m floor

pisotear [pizo'tʃja^r] vt to trample (on)

pista ['piʃta] f (vestígio) trace; (indicação) clue; (de corridas) track; (Aviat) runway; (de estrada) lane; (de dança) (dance) floor

pistola [piʃ'tɔla] f pistol

pitada [pi'tada] f (porção) pinch

pivete [pi'vetʃi] m child thief

pivô [pi'vo] m pivot; (fig) central figure, prime mover

pizza ['pitsa] f pizza

placa ['plaka] f plate; (Auto) number plate (BRIT), license plate (US); (comemorativa) plaque; (na pele) blotch; **~ de memória** (Phot) memory card; **~ de sinalização** roadsign

placar [pla'ka^r] m scoreboard

plácido, -a ['plasidu, a] adj calm; (manso) placid

plágio ['plaʒu] m plagiarism

planalto [pla'nawtu] m tableland, plateau

planar [pla'na^r] vi to glide

planear [pla'nja^r] (PT) vt = **planejar**

planejamento [planeʒaˈmẽtu] *m*
planning; **~ familiar** family planning
planejar [planeˈʒaʳ] (BR) *vt* to plan;
(*edifício*) to design
planeta [plaˈneta] *m* planet
planície [plaˈnisi] *f* plain
planilha [plˈniʎa] *f* speadsheet
plano, -a [ˈplanu, a] *adj* flat, level; (*liso*)
smooth ▷ *m* plan; **em primeiro/em**
último ~ in the foreground/background;
Plano Real *see boxed note*

planta [ˈplãta] *f* plant; (*de pé*) sole; (*Arq*)
plan
plantação [plãtaˈsãw] *f* (*ato*) planting;
(*terreno*) planted land; (*plantio*) crops *pl*
plantão [plãˈtãw] (*pl* **-ões**) *m* duty;
(*noturno*) night duty; (*plantonista*) person
on duty; (*Mil: serviço*) sentry duty;
(: *pessoa*) sentry; **estar de ~** to be on duty
plantar [plãˈtaʳ] *vt* to plant; (*estaca*) to
drive in; (*estabelecer*) to set up
plantões [plãˈtõjʃ] *mpl de* **plantão**
plástico, -a [ˈplaʃtʃiku, a] *adj* plastic ▷ *m*
plastic
plataforma [plataˈfɔxma] *f* platform; **~**
de exploração de petróleo oil rig; **~ de**
lançamento launch pad
platéia [plaˈtɛja] *f* (*Teatro etc*) stalls *pl*
(BRIT), orchestra (US); (*espectadores*)
audience
platina [plaˈtʃina] *f* platinum
platinados [platʃiˈnaduʃ] *mpl* (*Auto*)
points
plausível [plawˈzivew] (*pl* **-eis**) *adj*
credible, plausible
playground [plejˈgrãwdʒi] (*pl* **-s**) *m*
(children's) playground
plenamente [plenaˈmẽtʃi] *adv* fully,
completely
pleno, -a [ˈplenu, a] *adj* full; (*completo*)

complete; **em ~ dia** in broad daylight;
em ~ inverno in the middle *ou* depths
of winter
plural [pluˈraw] (*pl* **-ais**) *adj, m* plural
pneu [ˈpnew] *m* tyre (BRIT), tire (US)
pneumonia [pnewmoˈnia] *f* pneumonia
pó [pɔ] *m* powder; (*sujeira*) dust; **sabão**
em pó soap powder; **tirar o pó (de algo)**
to dust (sth)
pobre [ˈpɔbri] *adj* poor ▷ *m/f* poor
person; **pobreza** [poˈbreza] *f* poverty
poça [ˈpɔsa] *f* puddle, pool
poção [poˈsãw] (*pl* **-ões**) *f* potion
poço [ˈposu] *m* well; (*de mina, elevador*)
shaft
poções [poˈsõjʃ] *fpl de* **poção**
pôde *etc* [ˈpodʒi] *vb ver* **poder**
pó-de-arroz *m* face powder

🅞 **PALAVRA CHAVE**

poder [poˈdeʳ] *vi* **1** (*capacidade*) can, be
able to; **não posso fazê-lo** I can't do it,
I'm unable to do it
2 (*ter o direito de*) can, may, be allowed to;
posso fumar aqui? can I smoke here?;
pode entrar? (*posso?*) can I come in?
3 (*possibilidade*) may, might, could; **pode**
ser maybe; **pode ser que** it may be that;
ele poderá vir amanhã he might come
tomorrow
4: **não poder com, não posso com ele** I
cannot cope with him
5 (*col: indignação*): **pudera!** no wonder!;
como é que pode? you're joking!
▷ *m* power; (*autoridade*) authority; **poder**
aquisitivo purchasing power; **estar**
no poder to be in power; **em poder de**
alguém in sb's hands

poderoso, -a [podeˈrozu, ɔza] *adj*
mighty, powerful
podre [ˈpodri] *adj* rotten; **podridão**
[podriˈdãw] *f* decay, rottenness; (*fig*)
corruption
põe *etc* [põj] *vb ver* **pôr**
poeira [ˈpwejra] *f* dust; **~ radioativa**
fall-out; **poeirento, -a** [pwejˈrẽtu, a]
adj dusty
poema [ˈpwɛma] *m* poem
poesia [poeˈzia] *f* poetry; (*poema*) poem
poeta [ˈpwɛta] *m* poet; **poético, -a**
[ˈpwɛtʃiku, a] *adj* poetic; **poetisa**
[pweˈtʃiza] *f* (woman) poet
pois [pojʃ] *adv* (*portanto*) so; (PT:
assentimento) yes ▷ *conj* as, since; (*mas*)

but; **~ bem** well then; **~ é** that's right; **~ não!** (BR) of course!; **~ não?** (BR: *numa loja*) what can I do for you?; (PT) isn't it?, aren't you?, didn't they? *etc*; **~ sim!** certainly not!; **~ (então)** then

polaco, -a [po'laku, a] *adj* Polish ▷ *m/f* Pole ▷ *m* (Ling) Polish

polar [po'la^r] *adj* polar

polegada [pole'gada] *f* inch

polegar [pole'ga^r] *m* (*tb*: **dedo ~**) thumb

polêmica [po'lemika] *f* controversy; **polêmico, -a** [po'lemiku, a] *adj* controversial

pólen ['pɔlẽ] *m* pollen

polícia [po'lisja] *f* police, police force ▷ *m/f* policeman/woman; **policial** [poli'sjaw] (*pl* **-ais**) *adj* police *atr* ▷ *m/f* (BR) policeman/woman; **novela** *ou* **romance policial** detective novel; **policiar** [poli'sja^r] *vt* to police; (*instintos, modos*) to control, keep in check

polidez [poli'deʒ] *f* good manners *pl*, politeness

polido, -a [po'lidu, a] *adj* polished, shiny; (*cortês*) well-mannered, polite

pólio ['pɔlju] *f* polio

polir [po'li^r] *vt* to polish

política [po'litʃika] *f* politics *sg*; (*programa*) policy; **político, -a** [po'litʃiku, a] *adj* political ▷ *m/f* politician

pólo ['pɔlu] *m* pole; (*Esporte*) polo; **P~ Norte/Sul** North/South Pole

polonês, -esa [polo'neʃ, eza] *adj* Polish ▷ *m/f* Pole ▷ *m* (Ling) Polish

Polônia [po'lonja] *f*: **a ~** Poland

polpa ['powpa] *f* pulp

poltrona [pow'trɔna] *f* armchair

poluição [polwi'sãw] *f* pollution; **poluir** [po'lwi^r] *vt* to pollute

polvo ['powvu] *m* octopus

pólvora ['pɔwvora] *f* gunpowder

pomada [po'mada] *f* ointment

pomar [po'ma^r] *m* orchard

pomba ['põba] *f* dove

pombo ['põbu] *m* pigeon

ponderação [põdera'sãw] *f* consideration, meditation; (*prudência*) prudence

ponderado, -a [põde'radu, a] *adj* prudent

ponderar [põde'ra^r] *vt* to consider, weigh up ▷ *vi* to meditate, muse

ponho *etc* ['poɲu] *vb ver* **pôr**

ponta ['põta] *f* tip; (*de faca*) point; (*de sapato*) toe; (*extremidade*) end; (*Futebol: posição*) wing; (: *jogador*) winger; **uma**

~ de (*um pouco*) a touch of; **~ do dedo** fingertip

pontapé [põta'pɛ] *m* kick; **dar ~s em alguém** to kick sb

pontaria [põta'ria] *f* aim; **fazer ~** to take aim

ponte ['põtʃi] *f* bridge; **~ aérea** air shuttle, airlift; **~ de safena** (heart) bypass operation

ponteiro [põ'tejru] *m* (*indicador*) pointer; (*de relógio*) hand

pontiagudo, -a [põtʃja'gudu, a] *adj* sharp, pointed

ponto ['põtu] *m* point; (*Med, Costura, Tricô*) stitch; (*pequeno sinal, do i*) dot; (*na pontuação*) full stop (BRIT), period (US); (*na pele*) spot; (*de ônibus*) stop; (*de táxi*) rank (BRIT), stand (US); (*matéria escolar*) subject; **estar a ~ de fazer** to be on the point of doing; **às cinco em ~** at five o'clock on the dot; **dois ~s** colon *sg*; **~ de admiração** (PT) exclamation mark; **~ de exclamação/interrogação** exclamation/question mark; **~ de vista** point of view, viewpoint; **ponto-e-vírgula** (*pl* **ponto-e-vírgulas**) *m* semicolon

pontuação [põtwa'sãw] *f* punctuation

pontual [põ'twaw] (*pl* **-ais**) *adj* punctual

pontudo, -a [põ'tudu, a] *adj* pointed

popa ['popa] *f* stern

população [popula'sãw] (*pl* **-ões**) *f* population

popular [popu'la^r] *adj* popular; **popularidade** [populari'dadʒi] *f* popularity

pôquer ['poke^r] *m* poker

◯ **PALAVRA CHAVE**

por [po^r] (*por + o(s)/a(s) = pelo(s)/a(s)*) *prep*
1 (*objetivo*) for; **lutar pela pátria** to fight for one's country

2 (*+ infin*): **está por acontecer** it is about to happen, it is yet to happen; **está por fazer** it is still to be done

3 (*causa*) out of, because of; **por falta de fundos** through lack of funds; **por hábito/natureza** out of habit/by nature; **faço isso por ela** I do it for her; **por isso** therefore; **a razão pela qual ...** the reason why ...; **pelo amor de Deus!** for Heaven's sake!

4 (*tempo*): **pela manhã** in the morning; **por volta das duas horas** at about two o'clock; **ele vai ficar por uma semana**

he's staying for a week

5 (*lugar*): **por aqui** this way; **viemos pelo parque** we came through the park; **passar por São Paulo** to pass through São Paulo; **por fora/dentro** outside/ inside

6 (*troca, preço*) for; **trocar o velho pelo novo** to change old for new; **comprei o livro por dez libras** I bought the book for ten pounds

7 (*valor proporcional*): **por cento** per cent; **por hora/dia/semana/mês/ano** hourly/daily/weekly/monthly/yearly; **por cabeça** a *ou* per head; **por mais difícil** *etc* **que seja** however difficult *etc* it is

8 (*modo, meio*) by; **por correio/avião** by post/air; **por si** by o.s.; **por escrito** in writing; **entrar pela entrada principal** to go in through the main entrance

9: **por que** (*por causa*) because (*PT*), why (*BR*); **por quê?** why?

10: **por mim tudo bem** as far as I'm concerned that's OK

O PALAVRA CHAVE

pôr [po^r] *vt* **1** (*colocar*) to put; (*roupas*) to put on; (*objeções, dúvidas*) to raise; (*ovos, mesa*) to lay; (*defeito*) to find; **põe mais forte** turn it up; **você põe açúcar?** do you take sugar?; **pôr de lado** to set aside **2** (+ *adj*) to make; **você está me pondo nervoso** you're making me nervous **pôr-se** *vr* **1** (*sol*) to set **2** (*colocar-se*) **pôr-se de pé** to stand up; **ponha-se no meu lugar** put yourself in my position **3**: **pôr-se a** to start to; **ela pôs-se a chorar** she started crying ▷ *m*: **o pôr do sol** sunset

porão [po'rãw] (*pl* **-ões**) *m* (*de casa*) basement; (: *armazém*) cellar
porca ['pɔxka] *f* (*animal*) sow
porção [pox'sãw] (*pl* **-ões**) *f* portion, piece; **uma ~ de** a lot of
porcaria [poxka'ria] *f* filth; (*dito sujo*) obscenity; (*coisa ruim*) piece of junk
porcelana [poxse'lana] *f* porcelain
porcentagem [poxsẽ'taʒẽ] (*pl* **-ns**) *f* percentage
porco, -a ['poxku, 'pɔxka] *adj* filthy ▷ *m* (*animal*) pig; (*carne*) pork
porções [pox'sõjʃ] *fpl de* **porção**
porém [po'rẽ] *conj* however

pormenor [poxme'no^r] *m* detail
pornografia [poxnogra'fia] *f* pornography
poro ['pɔru] *m* pore
porões [po'rõjs] *mpl de* **porão**
porque ['poxke] *conj* because; (*interrogativo*: *PT*) why
porquê [pox'ke] *adv* why ▷ *m* reason, motive; **~?** (*PT*) why?
porrete [po'xetʃi] *m* club
porta ['pɔxta] *f* door; (*vão da porta*) doorway; (*de um jardim*) gate
portador, a [poxta'do^r, a] *m/f* bearer
portagem [pox'taʒẽ] (*PT*): (*pl* **-ns**) *f* toll
portal [pox'taw] (*pl* **-ais**) *m* doorway
porta-luvas *m inv* (*Auto*) glove compartment
porta-malas *m inv* (*Auto*) boot (*BRIT*), trunk (*US*)
porta-níqueis *m inv* purse
portanto [pox'tãtu] *conj* so, therefore
portão [pox'tãw] (*pl* **-ões**) *m* gate
portar [pox'ta^r] *vt* to carry; **~-se** *vr* to behave
portaria [poxta'ria] *f* (*de um edifício*) entrance hall; (*recepção*) reception desk; (*do governo*) edict, decree
portátil [pox'tatʃiw] (*pl* **-eis**) *adj* portable
porta-voz (*pl* **-es**) *m/f* (*pessoa*) spokesman/woman
porte ['pɔxtʃi] *m* transport; (*custo*) freight charge, carriage; **~ pago** post paid; **de grande ~** far-reaching, important
porteiro, -a [pox'tejru, a] *m/f* caretaker; **~ eletrônico** entryphone
pórtico ['pɔxtʃiku] *m* porch, portico
porto ['poxtu] *m* (*do mar*) port, harbour (*BRIT*), harbor (*US*); (*vinho*) port; **o P~** Oporto
portões [pox'tõjʃ] *mpl de* **portão**
Portugal [poxtu'gaw] *m* Portugal; **português, -guesa** [portu'geʃ, 'geza] *adj* Portuguese ▷ *m/f* Portuguese *inv* ▷ *m* (*Ling*) Portuguese
porventura [poxvẽ'tura] *adj* by chance; **se ~ você …** if you happen to …
pôs [poʃ] *vb ver* **pôr**
posar [po'za^r] *vi* (*Foto*): **~ (para)** to pose (for)
posição [pozi'sãw] (*pl* **-ões**) *f* position; (*social*) standing, status; **posicionar** [pozisjo'na^r] *vt* to position
positivo, -a [pozi'tʃivu, a] *adj* positive
possante [po'sãtʃi] *adj* powerful, strong; (*carro*) flashy

possessão [pose'sãw] f possession;
  possessivo, -a [pose'sivu, a] adj
  possessive
possibilidade [posibili'dadʒi] f
  possibility; **possibilidades** fpl (recursos)
  means
possibilitar [posibili'ta^r] vt to make
  possible, permit
possível [po'sivew] (pl -eis) adj possible;
  fazer todo o ~ to do one's best
posso etc ['posu] vb ver **poder**
possuidor, a [poswi'do^r, a] m/f owner
possuir [po'swi^r] vt (casa, livro etc) to
  own; (dinheiro, talento) to possess
postal [poʃ'taw] (pl -ais) adj postal ⊳ m
  postcard
poste ['pɔʃtʃi] m pole, post
posterior [poʃte'rjo^r] adj (mais tarde)
  subsequent, later; (traseiro) rear, back;
  posteriormente [poʃterjox'mẽtʃi] adv
  later, subsequently
postiço, -a [poʃ'tʃisu, a] adj false,
  artificial
posto, -a ['poʃtu, 'pɔʃta] pp de **pôr**
  ⊳ m post, position; (emprego) job; **~ de
  gasolina** service ou petrol station; **~ que**
  although; **~ de saúde** health centre ou
  center
póstumo, -a ['pɔʃtumu, a] adj
  posthumous
postura [poʃ'tura] f posture; (aspecto
  físico) appearance
potável [po'tavew] (pl -eis) adj drinkable;
  água ~ drinking water
pote ['pɔtʃi] m jug, pitcher; (de geléia) jar;
  (de creme) pot; **chover a ~s** (PT) to rain
  cats and dogs
potência [po'tẽsja] f power
potencial [potẽ'sjaw] (pl -ais) adj, m
  potential
potente [po'tẽtʃi] adj powerful, potent

○ **PALAVRA CHAVE**

pouco, -a ['poku, a] adj **1** (sg) little,
  not much; **pouco tempo** little ou not
  much time; **de pouco interesse** of little
  interest, not very interesting; **pouca
  coisa** not much
  2 (pl) few, not many; **uns poucos** a few,
  some; **poucas vezes** rarely; **poucas
  crianças comem o que devem** few
  children eat what they should
  ⊳ adv **1** little, not much; **custa pouco** it
  doesn't cost much; **dentro em pouco,
  daqui a pouco** shortly; **pouco antes**

shortly before
  2 (+ adj: = negativo): **ela é pouco
  inteligente/simpática** she's not very
  bright/friendly
  3: **por pouco eu não morri** I almost died
  4: **pouco a pouco** little by little
  5: **aos poucos** gradually
  ⊳ m: **um pouco** a little, a bit; **nem um
  pouco** not at all

poupador, a [popa'do^r, a] adj thrifty
poupança [po'pãsa] f thrift; (economias)
  savings pl; (tb: **caderneta de ~**) savings
  bank
poupar [po'pa^r] vt to save; (vida) to spare
pousada [po'zada] f (hospedagem)
  lodging; (hospedaria) inn
pousar [po'za^r] vt to place; (mão) to rest
  ⊳ vi (avião, pássaro) to land; (pernoitar) to
  spend the night
povo ['povu] m people; (raça) people
  pl, race; (plebe) common people pl;
  (multidão) crowd
povoação [povwa'sãw] (pl -ões) f
  (aldeia) village, settlement; (habitantes)
  population
povoado [po'vwadu] m village
povoar [po'vwa^r] vt (de habitantes) to
  people, populate; (de animais etc) to stock
pra [pra] (col) prep = **para a**
praça ['prasa] f (largo) square; (mercado)
  marketplace; (soldado) soldier; **~ de
  touros** bullring
praga ['praga] f nuisance; (maldição)
  curse; (desgraça) misfortune; (erva
  daninha) weed
pragmático, -a [prag'matʃiku, a] adj
  pragmatic
praia ['praja] f beach
prancha ['prãʃa] f plank; (de surfe) board
prata ['prata] f silver; (col: cruzeiro) ≈ quid
  (BRIT), ≈ buck (US)
prateleira [prate'lejra] f shelf
prática ['pratʃika] f practice; (experiência)
  experience, know-how; (costume) habit,
  custom; ver tb **prático**
praticante [pratʃi'kãtʃi] adj practising
  (BRIT), practicing (US) ⊳ m/f apprentice;
  (de esporte) practitioner
praticar [pratʃi'ka^r] vt to practise
  (BRIT), practice (US); (roubo, operação) to
  carry out; **prático, -a** ['pratʃiku, a] adj
  practical ⊳ m/f expert
prato ['pratu] m plate; (comida) dish;
  (de uma refeição) course; (de toca-discos)
  turntable; **pratos** mpl (Mús) cymbals

praxe ['praksi] f custom, usage; **de ~** usually; **ser de ~** to be the norm

prazer [pra'ze'] m pleasure; **muito ~ em conhecê-lo** pleased to meet you

prazo ['prazu] m term, period; *(vencimento)* expiry date, time limit; **a curto/médio/longo ~** in the short/ medium/long term; **comprar a ~** to buy on hire purchase *(BRIT) ou* on the installment plan *(US)*

precário, -a [pre'karju, a] adj precarious; *(escasso)* failing

precaução [prekaw'sãw] *(pl -ões)* f precaution

precaver-se [preka'vexsi] vr: **~ (contra ou de)** to be on one's guard (against); **precavido, -a** [preka'vidu, a] adj cautious

prece ['prɛsi] f prayer; *(súplica)* entreaty

precedente [prese'dẽtʃi] adj preceding ▷ m precedent

preceder [prese'de'] vt, vi to precede; **~ a algo** to precede sth; *(ter primazia)* to take precedence over sth

precioso, -a [pre'sjozu, ɔza] adj precious

precipício [presi'pisju] m precipice; *(fig)* abyss

precipitação [presipita'sãw] f haste; *(imprudência)* rashness

precipitado, -a [presipi'tadu, a] adj hasty; *(imprudente)* rash

precisamente [presiza'mẽtʃi] adv precisely

precisar [presi'za'] vt to need; *(especificar)* to specify; **~-se** vr: **"precisa-se"** "needed"; **~ de** to need; *(uso impess)*: **não precisa você se preocupar** you needn't worry

preciso, -a [pre'sizu, a] adj precise, accurate; *(necessário)* necessary; *(claro)* concise; **é ~ você ir** you must go

preço ['presu] m price; *(custo)* cost; *(valor)* value; **a ~ de banana** *(BR) ou* **de chuva** *(PT)* dirt cheap

preconceito [prekõ'sejtu] m prejudice

predador [preda'do'] m predator

predileto, -a [predʒi'letu, a] *(PT -ct-)* adj favourite *(BRIT)*, favorite *(US)*

prédio ['predʒju] m building; **~ de apartamentos** block of flats *(BRIT)*, apartment house *(US)*

predispor [predʒis'po'] *(irreg: como* **pôr***)* vt: **~ alguém contra** to prejudice sb against; **~-se** vr: **~-se a/para** to get o.s. in the mood to/for

predominar [predomi'na'] vi to predominate, prevail

preencher [preẽ'ʃe'] vt *(formulário)* to fill in *(BRIT) ou* out, complete; *(requisitos)* to fulfil *(BRIT)*, fulfill *(US)*, meet, to fill

prefácio [pre'fasju] m preface

prefeito, -a [pre'fejtu, a] m/f mayor; **prefeitura** [prefej'tura] f town hall; **preferencial** [preferẽ'sjaw] *(pl -ais)* adj *(rua)* main ▷ f main road *(with priority)*

preferido, -a [prefe'ridu, a] adj favourite *(BRIT)*, favorite *(US)*

preferir [prefe'ri'] vt to prefer

prefiro *etc* [pre'firu] vb **ver preferir**

prefixo [pre'fiksu] m *(Ling)* prefix; *(Tel)* code

prega ['prɛga] f pleat, fold

pregar¹ [pre'ga'] vt, vi to preach

pregar² [pre'ga'] vt *(com prego)* to nail; *(fixar)* to pin, fasten; *(cosendo)* to sew on; **~ uma peça** to play a trick; **~ um susto em alguém** to give sb a fright

prego ['prɛgu] m nail; *(col: casa de penhor)* pawn shop

preguiça [pre'gisa] f laziness; *(animal)* sloth; **estar com ~** to feel lazy; **preguiçoso, -a** [pregi'sozu, ɔza] adj lazy

pré-histórico, -a [pre-] adj prehistoric

preia-mar *(PT)* f high tide

prejuízo [pre'ʒwizu] m damage, harm; *(em dinheiro)* loss; **em ~ de** to the detriment of

prematuro, -a [prema'turu, a] adj premature

premiado, -a [pre'mjadu, a] adj prize-winning; *(bilhete)* winning ▷ m/f prize-winner

premiar [pre'mja'] vt to award a prize to; *(recompensar)* to reward

prêmio ['premju] m prize; *(recompensa)* reward; *(Seguros)* premium

prenda ['prẽda] f gift, present; *(em jogo)* forfeit; **~s domésticas** housework *sg*

prendedor [prēde'do'] m fastener; (de cabelo, gravata) clip; **~ de roupa** clothes peg; **~ de papéis** paper clip

prender [prē'de'] vt to fasten, fix; (roupa) to pin; (cabelo) to put back; (capturar) to arrest; (atar, ligar) to tie; (atenção) to catch; (afetivamente) to tie, bind; (reter: doença, compromisso) to keep; (movimentos) to restrict; **~-se** vr to get caught, stick; **~-se a alguém** (por amizade) to be attached to sb

preocupação [preokupa'sãw] (pl -ões) f preoccupation; (inquietação) worry, concern

preocupar [preoku'pa'] vt to preoccupy; (inquietar) to worry; **~-se** vr: **~-se com** to worry about, be worried about

preparação [prepara'sãw] (pl -ões) f preparation

preparar [prepa'ra'] vt to prepare; **~-se** vr to get ready; **preparativos** [prepara'tʃivuʃ] mpl preparations, arrangements

preponderante [prepõde'rãtʃi] adj predominant

preposição [prepozi'sãw] (pl -ões) f preposition

prepotente [prepo'tētʃi] adj predominant; (despótico) despotic; (atitude) overbearing

prescrever [preʃkre've'] vt to prescribe; (prazo) to set

presença [pre'zēsa] f presence; (freqüência) attendance; **ter boa ~** to be presentable; **presenciar** [prezē'sja'] vt to be present at; (testemunhar) to witness

presente [pre'zētʃi] adj present; (fig: interessado) attentive; (: evidente) clear, obvious ▷ m present ▷ f (Com: carta): **a ~** this letter; **os presentes** mpl (pessoas) those present; **presentear** [prezē'tʃja'] vt: **presentear alguém (com algo)** to give sb (sth as) a present

preservação [prezexva'sãw] f preservation

presidente, -a [prezi'dētʃi, ta] m/f president

presidiário, -a [prezi'dʒjarju, a] m/f convict

presídio [pre'zidʒju] m prison

presidir [prezi'dʒi'] vt, vi: **~ (a)** to preside over; (reunião) to chair; (suj: leis, critérios) to govern

preso, -a [pre'zu, a] adj imprisoned; (capturado) under arrest; (atado) tied ▷ m/f prisoner; **estar ~ a alguém** to be

attached to sb

pressa ['prɛsa] f haste, hurry; (rapidez) speed; (urgência) urgency; **às ~s** hurriedly; **estar com ~** to be in a hurry; **ter ~ de** ou **em fazer** to be in a hurry to do

presságio [pre'saʒu] m omen, sign; (pressentimento) premonition

pressão [pre'sãw] (pl -ões) f pressure; (colchete de) **~** press stud, popper

pressentimento [presētʃi'mētu] m premonition

pressentir [presē'tʃi'] vt to foresee; (suspeitar) to sense

pressionar [presjo'na'] vt (botão) to press; (coagir) to pressure ▷ vi to press, put on pressure

pressões [pre'sõjʃ] fpl de **pressão**

pressupor [presu'po'] (irreg: como **pôr**) vt to presuppose

prestação [preʃta'sãw] (pl -ões) f instalment (BRIT), installment (US); (por uma casa) repayment

prestar [preʃ'ta'] vt (cuidados) to give; (favores, serviços) to do; (contas) to render; (informações) to supply; (uma qualidade a algo) to lend ▷ vi: **~ a alguém para algo** to be of use to sb for sth; **~-se** vr: **~-se a** to be suitable for; (admitir) to lend o.s. to; (dispor-se) to be willing to; **~ atenção** to pay attention

prestes ['prɛʃtʃiʃ] adj inv ready; (a ponto de): **~ a partir** about to leave

prestígio [preʃ'tʃiʒu] m prestige

presunção [prezũ'sãw] (pl -ões) f presumption; (vaidade) conceit, self-importance; **presunçoso, -a** [prezũ'sozu, ɔza] adj vain, self-important

presunto [pre'zũtu] m ham

pretender [pretē'de'] vt to claim; (cargo, emprego) to go for; **~ fazer** to intend to do

pretensão [pretē'sãw] (pl -ões) f claim; (vaidade) pretension; (propósito) aim; (aspiração) aspiration; **pretensioso, -a** [pretē'sjozu, ɔza] adj pretentious

pretérito [pre'tɛritu] m (Ling) preterite

pretexto [pre'teʃtu] m pretext

preto, -a ['pretu, a] adj black ▷ m/f Black (man/woman)

prevalecer [prevale'se'] vi to prevail; **~-se** vr: **~-se de** (aproveitar-se) to take advantage of

prevenção [prevē'sãw] (pl -ões) f prevention; (preconceito) prejudice; (cautela) caution; **estar de ~ com** ou

contra alguém to be bias(s)ed against sb

prevenido, -a [preve'nidu, a] *adj* cautious, wary

prevenir [preve'ni^r] *vt* to prevent; (*avisar*) to warn; (*preparar*) to prepare

prever [pre've^r] (*irreg: como* **ver**) *vt* to predict, foresee; (*pressupor*) to presuppose

prévio, -a ['prɛvju, a] *adj* prior; (*preliminar*) preliminary

previsão [previ'zãw] (*pl* -**ões**) *f* foresight; (*prognóstico*) prediction, forecast; ~ **do tempo** weather forecast

previsível [previ'zivew] (*pl* -**eis**) *adj* predictable

previsões [previ'zõjʃ] *fpl de* **previsão**

prezado, -a [pre'zadu, a] *adj* esteemed; (*numa carta*) dear

prezar [pre'za^r] *vt* (*amigos*) to value highly; (*autoridade*) to respect; (*gostar de*) to appreciate

primário, -a [pri'marju, a] *adj* primary; (*elementar*) basic, rudimentary; (*primitivo*) primitive ▷ *m* (*curso*) elementary education

primavera [prima'vɛra] *f* spring; (*planta*) primrose

primeira [pri'mejra] *f* (*Auto*) first (gear)

primeiro, -a [pri'mejru, a] *adj, adv* first; **de primeira** first-class

primo, -a ['primu, a] *m/f* cousin; ~ **irmão** first cousin

princesa [prĩ'seza] *f* princess

principal [prĩsi'paw] (*pl* -**ais**) *adj* principal; (*entrada, razão, rua*) main ▷ *m* head, principal; (*essencial, de dívida*) principal

príncipe ['prĩsipi] *m* prince

principiante [prĩsi'pjãtʃi] *m/f* beginner

principiar [prĩsi'pja^r] *vt, vi* to begin

princípio [prĩ'sipju] *m* beginning, start; (*origem*) origin; (*legal, moral*) principle; **princípios** *mpl* (*de matéria*) rudiments

prioridade [prjori'dadʒi] *f* priority

prisão [pri'zãw] (*pl* -**ões**) *f* imprisonment; (*cadeia*) prison, jail; (*detenção*) arrest; ~ **de ventre** constipation; **prisioneiro, -a** [prizjo'nejru, a] *m/f* prisoner

privacidade [privasi'dadʒi] *f* privacy

privada [pri'vada] *f* toilet

privado, -a [pri'vadu, a] *adj* private; (*carente*) deprived

privar [pri'va^r] *vt* to deprive

privativo, -a [priva'tʃivu, a] *adj*

(*particular*) private; ~ **de** peculiar to

privilegiado, -a [privile'ʒjadu, a] *adj* privileged; (*excepcional*) unique, exceptional

privilegiar [privile'ʒja^r] *vt* to privilege; (*favorecer*) to favour (BRIT), favor (US)

privilégio [privi'lɛʒu] *m* privilege

pró [prɔ] *adv* for, in favour (BRIT) *ou* favor (US) ▷ *m* advantage; **os ~s e os contras** the pros and cons; **em ~ de** in favo(u)r of

pró- [prɔ] *prefixo* pro-

proa ['proa] *f* prow, bow

probabilidade [probabili'dadʒi] *f* probability; **probabilidades** *fpl* (*chances*) odds

problema [prob'lɛma] *m* problem

procedência [prose'dẽsja] *f* origin, source; (*lugar de saída*) point of departure

proceder [prose'de^r] *vi* to proceed; (*comportar-se*) to behave; (*agir*) to act ▷ *m* conduct; **procedimento** [prosedʒi'mẽtu] *m* conduct, behaviour (BRIT), behavior (US); (*processo*) procedure; (*Jur*) proceedings *pl*

processamento [prosesa'mẽtu] *m* processing; (*Jur*) prosecution; (*verificação*) verification; ~ **de texto** word processing

processar [prose'sa^r] *vt* (*Jur*) to take proceedings against, prosecute; (*requerimentos, Comput*) to process

processo [pro'sɛsu] *m* process; (*procedimento*) procedure; (*Jur*) lawsuit, legal proceedings *pl*; (: *autos*) record; (*conjunto de documentos*) documents *pl*

procissão [prosi'sãw] (*pl* -**ões**) *f* procession

Proclamação da República (PT) *see boxed note*

※ **PROCLAMAÇÃO DA REPÚBLICA**
※
※ Commemorated on 15 November,
※ which is a public holiday, the
※ proclamation of the republic in 1889
※ was a military coup, led by Marshal
※ Deodoro da Fonseca. It brought
※ down the empire which had been
※ established after independence and
※ installed a federal republic in Brazil.

proclamar [prokla'ma^r] *vt* to proclaim

procura [pro'kura] *f* search; (*Com*) demand

procuração [prokura'sãw] *f*: **por ~** by

proxy

procurador, a [prokura'doʳ, a]
m/f attorney; **P~ Geral da República**
Attorney General

procurar [proku'raʳ] vt to look for, seek;
(emprego) to apply for; (ir visitar) to call
on; (contatar) to get in touch with; ~
fazer to try to do

produção [produ'sãw] (pl -ões) f
production; (volume de produção) output;
(produto) product; ~ **em massa, ~ em
série** mass production

produtivo, -a [produ'tʃivu, a] adj
productive; (rendoso) profitable

produto [pro'dutu] m product; (renda)
proceeds pl, profit

produtor, a [produ'toʳ, a] adj producing
▷ m/f producer

produzir [produ'ziʳ] vt to produce;
(ocasionar) to cause, bring about; (render)
to bring in

proeminente [proemi'nētʃi] adj
prominent

proeza [pro'eza] f achievement, feat

profanar [profa'naʳ] vt to desecrate,
profane; **profano, -a** [pro'fanu, a] adj
profane ▷ m/f layman/woman

profecia [profe'sia] f prophecy

professor, a [profe'soʳ, a] m/f teacher;
(universitário) lecturer

profeta, -isa [pro'feta, profe'tʃiza] m/f
prophet; **profetizar** [profetʃi'zaʳ] vt, vi
to prophesy, predict

profissão [profi'sãw] (pl -ões) f
profession; **profissional** [profisjo'naw]
(pl -ais) adj, m/f professional;
profissionalizante [profisjonali'zãtʃi]
adj (ensino) vocational

profundidade [profũdʒi'dadʒi] f depth

profundo, -a [pro'fũdu, a] adj deep; (fig)
profound

profusão [profu'zãw] f profusion,
abundance

prognóstico [prog'nɔʃtʃiku] m
prediction, forecast

programa [pro'grama] m programme
(BRIT), program (US); (Comput) program;
(plano) plan; (diversão) thing to do;
(de um curso) syllabus; **programação**
[programa'sãw] f planning; (TV, Rádio,
Comput) programming; **programador,
a** [programa'doʳ, a] m/f programmer;
programar [progra'maʳ] vt to plan;
(Comput) to program

progredir [progre'dʒiʳ] vi to progress;
(avançar) to move forward; (infecção) to

progress

progressista [progre'siʃta] adj, m/f
progressive

progressivo, -a [progre'sivu, a] adj
progressive; (gradual) gradual

progresso [pro'grɛsu] m progress

progrido etc [pro'gridu] vb ver
progredir

proibição [proibi'sãw] (pl -ões) f
prohibition, ban

proibir [proi'biʳ] vt to prohibit; (livro,
espetáculo) to ban; **"é proibido fumar"**
"no smoking"; ~ **alguém de fazer, ~ que
alguém faça** to forbid sb to do

projeção [proʒe'sãw] (PT -cç-) (pl -ões) f
projection

projetar [proʒe'taʳ] (PT -ct-) vt to project

projétil [pro'ʒetʃiw] (PT -ct-) (pl -eis) m
projectile, missile

projeto [pro'ʒetu] (PT -ct-) m project;
(plano, Arq) plan; (Tec) design; ~ **de lei** bill

projetor [proʒe'toʳ] (PT -ct-) m (Cinema)
projector

proliferar [prolife'raʳ] vi to proliferate

prolongação [prolõga'sãw] f extension

prolongado, -a [prolõ'gadu, a] adj
prolonged; (alongado) extended

prolongar [prolõ'gaʳ] vt to extend,
lengthen; (decisão etc) to postpone; (vida)
to prolong; **~-se** vr to extend; (durar)
to last

promessa [pro'mɛsa] f promise

prometer [prome'teʳ] vt, vi to promise

promíscuo, -a [pro'miʃkwu, a] adj
disorderly, mixed up; (comportamento
sexual) promiscuous

promissor, a [promi'soʳ, a] adj
promising

promoção [promo'sãw] (pl -ões) f
promotion; **fazer ~ de alguém/algo** to
promote sb/sth

promotor, a [promo'toʳ, a] m/f
promoter; (Jur) prosecutor

promover [promo'veʳ] vt to promote;
(causar) to cause, bring about

pronome [pro'nɔmi] m pronoun

pronto, -a [prõtu, a] adj ready; (rápido)
quick, speedy; (imediato) prompt ▷ adv
promptly; **de ~** promptly; **estar ~ a ...** to
be prepared ou willing to ...; **pronto-
socorro** (pl **prontos-socorros** (PT)) m
towtruck

pronúncia [pro'nũsja] f pronunciation;
(Jur) indictment

pronunciar [pronũ'sjaʳ] vt to
pronounce; (discurso) to make, deliver;

(Jur: réu) to indict; *(: sentença)* to pass
propaganda [propa'gãda] *f (Pol)*
propaganda; *(Com)* advertising; *(: uma
propaganda)* advert, advertisement;
fazer ~ de to advertise
propagar [propa'gaʳ] *vt* to propagate;
(fig: difundir) to disseminate
propensão [propẽ'sãw] *(pl -ões) f*
inclination, tendency; **propenso, -a**
[pro'pẽsu, a] *adj*: **propenso a** inclined to;
ser propenso a to be inclined to, have a
tendency to
propina [pro'pina] *f (gorjeta)* tip; *(PT:
cota)* fee
propor [pro'poʳ] *(irreg: como pôr) vt* to
propose; *(oferecer)* to offer; *(um problema)*
to pose; **~-se** *vr*: **~-se (a) fazer** *(pretender)*
to intend to do; *(visar)* to aim to do;
(dispor-se) to decide to do; *(oferecer-se)* to
offer to do
proporção [propox'sãw] *(pl -ões)
f* proportion; **proporções**
fpl (dimensões) dimensions;
proporcional [propoxsjo'naw] *(pl
-ais) adj* proportional; **proporcionar**
[propoxsjo'naʳ] *vt* to provide, give;
(adaptar) to adapt, adapt
proposição [propozi'sãw] *(pl -ões) f*
proposition, proposal
proposital [propozi'taw] *(pl -ais) adj*
intentional
propósito [pro'pɔzitu] *m (intenção)*
purpose; *(objetivo)* aim; **a ~** by the way; **a
~ de** with regard to; **de ~** on purpose
proposta [pro'pɔʃta] *f* proposal;
(oferecimento) offer
propriamente [proprja'mẽtʃi] *adv*
properly, exactly; **~ falando** *ou* **dito**
strictly speaking
propriedade [proprje'dadʒi] *f* property;
(direito de proprietário) ownership; *(o que é
apropriado)* propriety
proprietário, -a [proprje'tarju, a] *m/f*
owner, proprietor
próprio, -a ['prɔprju, a] *adj* own, of
one's own; *(mesmo)* very, selfsame; *(hora,
momento)* opportune, right; *(nome)*
proper; *(característico)* characteristic;
(sentido) proper, true; *(depois de pronome)*
-self; **~ (para)** suitable (for); **eu ~** I myself;
por si ~ of one's own accord; **ele é o ~
inglês** he's a typical Englishman; **é o ~** it's
him himself
prorrogação [proxoga'sãw] *(pl -ões) f*
extension
prosa ['prɔza] *f* prose; *(conversa)* chatter;

(fanfarrice) boasting, bragging ▷ *adj* full
of oneself
prospecto [proʃ'pɛktu] *m* leaflet; *(em
forma de livro)* brochure
prosperar [proʃpe'raʳ] *vi* to prosper,
thrive; **prosperidade** [proʃperi'dadʒi]
f prosperity; *(bom êxito)* success;
próspero, -a ['prɔʃperu, a] *adj*
prosperous; *(bem sucedido)* successful;
(favorável) favourable (BRIT), favorable
(US)
prosseguir [prose'giʳ] *vt, vi* to continue;
~ em to continue (with)
prostíbulo [proʃ'tʃibulu] *m* brothel
prostituta [proʃtʃi'tuta] *f* prostitute
prostrado, -a [proʃ'tradu, a] *adj*
prostrate
protagonista [protago'niʃta] *m/f*
protagonist
proteção [prote'sãw] *(PT -çç-) f*
protection
protector, a [protek'toʳ, a] *(PT)*
= **protetor, a**
proteger [prote'ʒeʳ] *vt* to protect;
protegido, -a [prote'ʒidu, a] *m/f*
protégé(e)
proteína [prote'ina] *f* protein
protejo *etc* [pro'teʒu] *vb ver* **proteger**
protestante [proteʃ'tãtʃi] *adj, m/f*
Protestant
protestar [proteʃ'taʳ] *vt, vi* to protest;
protesto [pro'teʃtu] *m* protest
protetor, a [prote'toʳ, a] *adj* protective
▷ *m/f* protector; **~ solar** sunscreen; **~ de
tela** *(Comput)* screensaver
protuberância [protube'rãsja] *f* bump;
protuberante [protube'rãtʃi] *adj*
sticking out
prova ['prɔva] *f* proof; *(Tec: teste)* test,
trial; *(Educ: exame)* examination; *(sinal)*
sign; *(de comida, bebida)* taste; *(de roupa)*
fitting; *(Esporte)* competition; *(Tip)*
proof; **prova(s)** *f(pl)* *(Jur)* evidence *sg*;
à ~ de bala/fogo/água bulletproof/
fireproof/waterproof; **pôr à ~** to put to
the test
provar [pro'vaʳ] *vt* to prove; *(comida)* to
taste, try; *(roupa)* to try on ▷ *vi* to try
provável [pro'vavew] *(pl -eis) adj*
probable, likely
provedor, a [prove'doʳ, a] *m/f* supplier;
~ de acesso à Internet Internet service
provider
proveito [pro'vejtu] *m* advantage;
(ganho) profit; **em ~ de** for the benefit of;
fazer ~ de to make use of; **proveitoso,**

-a [prove'tozu, ɔza] adj profitable, advantageous; (útil) useful

proveniente [prove'njẽtʃi] adj: **~ de** originating from; (que resulta de) arising from

prover [pro've^r] (irreg: como **ver**) vt to provide, supply; (vaga) to fill ▷ vi: **~ a** to take care of, see to

provérbio [pro'vɛxbju] m proverb

providência [provi'dẽsja] f providence; **providências** fpl (medidas) measures, steps; **providencial** [providẽ'sjaw] (pl **-ais**) adj opportune; **providenciar** [providẽ'sja^r] vt to provide; (tomar providências) to arrange ▷ vi to make arrangements, take steps; **providenciar para que** to see to it that

província [pro'vĩsja] f province; **provinciano, -a** [provĩ'sjanu, a] adj provincial

provisório, -a [provi'zɔrju, a] adj provisional, temporary

provocador, a [provoka'do^r, a] adj provocative

provocante [provo'kãtʃi] adj provocative

provocar [provo'ka^r] vt to provoke; (ocasionar) to cause; (atrair) to tempt, attract; (estimular) to rouse, stimulate

próximo, -a [ˈprɔsimu, a] adj (no espaço) near, close; (no tempo) close; (seguinte) next; (amigo, parente) close; (vizinho) neighbouring (BRIT), neighboring (US) ▷ adv near ▷ m fellow man; **~ a ou de** near, close to; **até a próxima!** see you again soon!

prudência [pru'dẽsja] f care, prudence; **prudente** [pru'dẽtʃi] adj prudent

prurido [pru'ridu] m itch

psicanálise [psika'nalizi] f psychoanalysis

psicologia [psikolo'ʒia] f psychology; **psicológico, -a** [psiko'lɔʒiku, a] adj psychological; **psicólogo, -a** [psi'kɔlogu, a] m/f psychologist

psique ['psiki] f psyche

psiquiatra [psi'kjatra] m/f psychiatrist

psiquiatria [psikja'tria] f psychiatry

psíquico, -a ['psikiku, a] adj psychological

puberdade [pubex'dadʒi] f puberty

publicação [publika'sãw] f publication

publicar [publi'ka^r] vt to publish; (divulgar) to divulge; (proclamar) to announce

publicidade [publisi'dadʒi] f publicity;

(Com) advertising; **publicitário, -a** [publisi'tarju, a] adj publicity atr; advertising atr

público, -a ['publiku, a] adj public ▷ m public; (Cinema, Teatro etc) audience

pude etc ['pudʒi] vb ver **poder**

pudera etc [pu'dɛra] vb ver **poder**

pudim [pu'dʒĩ] (pl **-ns**) m pudding

pudor [pu'do^r] m bashfulness, modesty; (moral) decency

pular [pu'la^r] vi to jump; (no Carnaval) to celebrate ▷ vt to jump (over); (páginas, trechos) to skip; **~ Carnaval** to celebrate Carnival; **~ corda** to skip

pulga ['puwga] f flea

pulmão [puw'mãw] (pl **-ões**) m lung

pulo¹ ['pulu] m jump; **dar um ~ em** to stop off at

pulo² etc vb ver **polir**

pulôver [pu'love^r] (BR) m pullover

pulsação [puwsa'sãw] f pulsation, beating; (Med) pulse

pulseira [puw'sejra] f bracelet; (de sapato) strap

pulso ['puwsu] m (Anat) wrist; (Med) pulse; (fig) vigour (BRIT), vigor (US), energy

punha etc ['puɲa] vb ver **pôr**

punhado [pu'ɲadu] m handful

punhal [pu'ɲaw] (pl **-ais**) m dagger

punho ['puɲu] m fist; (de manga) cuff; (de espada) hilt

punição [puni'sãw] (pl **-ões**) f punishment

punir [pu'ni^r] vt to punish

pupila [pu'pila] f (Anat) pupil

purê [pu're] m purée; **~ de batatas** mashed potatoes

pureza [pu'reza] f purity

purificar [purifi'ka^r] vt to purify

puritano, -a [puri'tanu, a] adj puritanical; (seita) puritan ▷ m/f puritan

puro, -a ['puru, a] adj pure; (uísque etc) neat; (verdade) plain; (intenções) honourable (BRIT), honorable (US); (estilo) clear

pus¹ [puʃ] m pus

pus² etc [puʃ] vb ver **pôr**

puser etc [pu'ze^r] vb ver **pôr**

puto, -a ['putu, a] (col!) adj (zangado) furious; (incrível): **um ~ ...** a hell of a ...; **o ~ de ...** the bloody ...

pútrido, -a ['putridu, a] adj putrid, rotten

puxador [puʃa'do^r] m handle, knob

puxão [pu'ʃãw] (*pl* **-ões**) *m* tug, jerk
puxar [pu'ʃaʳ] *vt* to pull; (*sacar*) to pull
out; (*assunto*) to bring up; (*conversa*) to
strike up; (*briga*) to pick ▷ *vi*: **~ de uma
perna** to limp; **~ a** to take after
puxões [pu'ʃõjʃ] *mpl de* **puxão**

QG *abr m* (= *Quartel-General*) HQ
QI *abr m* (= *Quociente de Inteligência*) IQ
quadra ['kwadra] *f* (*quarteirão*) block; (*de
tênis etc*) court; (*período*) time, period
quadrado, -a [kwa'dradu, a] *adj* square
▷ *m* square ▷ *m/f* (*col*) square
quadril [kwa'driw] (*pl* **-is**) *m* hip
quadrinho [kwa'driɲu] *m*: **história em
~s** (BR) cartoon, comic strip
quadris [kwa'driʃ] *mpl de* **quadril**
quadro ['kwadru] *m* painting; (*gravura,
foto*) picture; (*lista*) list; (*tabela*) chart,
table; (*Tec: painel*) panel; (*pessoal*)
staff; (*time*) team; (*Teatro, fig*) scene;
quadro-negro (*pl* **quadros-negros**) *m*
blackboard
quadruplicar [kwadrupli'kaʳ] *vt, vi* to
quadruple
qual [kwaw] (*pl* **-ais**) *pron* which ▷ *conj*
as, like ▷ *excl* what!; **o ~** which; (*pessoa:
suj*) who; (: *objeto*) whom; **seja ~ for**
whatever *ou* whichever it may be; **cada
~** each one
qualidade [kwali'dadʒi] *f* quality
qualificação [kwalifika'sãw] (*pl* **-ões**) *f*
qualification
qualificado, -a [kwalifi'kadu, a] *adj*
qualified

qualificar [kwalifiˈkaʳ] vt to qualify; (avaliar) to evaluate; **~-se** vr to qualify; **~ de** ou **como** to classify as

qualquer [kwawˈkeʳ] (pl **quaisquer**) adj, pron any; **~ pessoa** anyone, anybody; **~ um dos dois** either; **~ que seja** whichever it may be; **a ~ momento** at any moment

quando [ˈkwãdu] adv when ▷ conj when; (interrogativo) when?; (ao passo que) whilst; **~ muito** at most

quantia [kwãˈtʃia] f sum, amount

quantidade [kwãtʃiˈdadʒi] f quantity, amount

🅞 **PALAVRA CHAVE**

quanto, -a [ˈkwãtu, a] adj
1 (interrogativo: sg) how much?; (: pl) how many?; **quanto tempo?** how long?
2 (o (que for) necessário) all that, as much as; **daremos quantos exemplares ele precisar** we'll give him as many copies as ou all the copies he needs
3: **tanto/tantos ... quanto** as much/ many ... as
▷ pron **1** how much?; how many?; **quanto custa?** how much?; **a quanto está o jogo?** what's the score?
2: **tudo quanto** everything that, as much as
3: **tanto/tantos quanto ...** as much/as many as ...
4: **um tanto quanto** somewhat, rather
▷ adv **1**: **quanto a** as regards; **quanto a mim** as for me
2: **quanto antes** as soon as possible
3: **quanto mais** (principalmente) especially; (muito menos) let alone; **quanto mais cedo melhor** the sooner the better
4: **tanto quanto possível** as much as possible; **tão ... quanto ...** as ... as ...
▷ conj: **quanto mais trabalha, mais ele ganha** the more he works, the more he earns; **quanto mais, (tanto) melhor** the more, the better

---

quarenta [kwaˈrẽta] num forty

quarentena [kwarẽˈtɛna] f quarantine

quaresma [kwaˈreʒma] f Lent

quarta [ˈkwaxta] f (tb: **~-feira**) Wednesday; (parte) quarter; (Auto) fourth (gear); **quarta-feira** (pl **quartas-feiras**) f Wednesday; **quarta-feira de cinzas** Ash Wednesday

quarteirão [kwaxtejˈrãw] (pl -**ões**) m (de casas) block

quartel [kwaxˈtɛw] (pl -**éis**) m barracks sg; **quartel-general** m headquarters pl

quarteto [kwaxˈtetu] m quartet(te)

quarto, -a [ˈkwaxtu, a] num fourth ▷ m quarter; (aposento) room; **~ de banho/ dormir** bathroom/bedroom; **três ~s de hora** three quarters of an hour

quase [ˈkwazi] adv almost, nearly; **~ nunca** hardly ever

quatorze [kwaˈtoxzi] num fourteen

quatro [ˈkwatru] num four

🅞 **PALAVRA CHAVE**

que [ki] conj **1** (com oração subordinada: muitas vezes não se traduz) that; **ele disse que viria** he said (that) he would come; **não há nada que fazer** there's nothing to be done; **espero que sim/não** I hope so/not; **dizer que sim/não** to say yes/no
2 (consecutivo: muitas vezes não se traduz) that; **é tão pesado que não consigo levantá-lo** it's so heavy (that) I can't lift it
3 (comparações): **(do) que** than; ver tb **mais; menos; mesmo**
▷ pron **1** (coisa) which, that; (+ prep) which; **o chapéu que você comprou** the hat (that ou which) you bought
2 (pessoa: suj) who, that; (: complemento) whom, that; **o amigo que me levou ao museu** the friend who took me to the museum; **a moça que eu convidei** the girl (that ou whom) I invited
3 (interrogativo) what?; **o que você disse?** what did you say?
4 (exclamação) what!; **que pena!** what a pity!; **que lindo!** how lovely!

---

quê [ke] m (col) something ▷ pron what; **~!** what!; **não tem de ~** don't mention it; **para ~?** what for?; **por ~?** why?

quebra [ˈkɛbra] f break, rupture; (falência) bankruptcy; (de energia elétrica) cut; **de ~** in addition; **quebra-cabeça** (pl **quebra-cabeças**) m puzzle, problem; (jogo) jigsaw puzzle

quebrado, -a [keˈbradu, a] adj broken; (cansado) exhausted; (falido) bankrupt; (carro, máquina) broken down; (telefone) out of order

quebrar [keˈbraʳ] vt to break ▷ vi to break; (carro) to break down; (Com) to go bankrupt; (ficar sem dinheiro) to go broke

queda ['kɛda] f fall; (fig) downfall; **ter ~ para algo** to have a bent for sth; **~ de barreira** landslide; **queda-d'água** (pl **quedas-d'água**) f waterfall

queijo ['kejʒu] m cheese

queimado, -a [kej'madu, a] adj burnt; (de sol: machucado) sunburnt; (: bronzeado) brown, tanned; (plantas, folhas) dried up

queimadura [kejma'dura] f burn; (de sol) sunburn

queimar [kej'maʳ] vt to burn; (roupa) to scorch; (com líquido) to scald; (bronzear a pele) to tan; (planta, folha) to wither ▷ vi to burn; **~-se** vr (pessoa) to burn o.s.; (de sol) to tan

queima-roupa f: **à ~** point-blank, at point-blank range

queira etc ['kejra] vb ver **querer**

queixa ['kejʃa] f complaint; (lamentação) lament; **fazer ~ de alguém** to complain about sb

queixar-se [kej'ʃaxsi] vr to complain; **~ de** to complain about; (dores etc) to complain of

queixo ['kejʃu] m chin; (maxilar) jaw; **bater o ~** to shiver

quem [kẽj] pron who; (como objeto) who(m); **de ~ é isto?** whose is this?; **~ diria!** who would have thought (it)!; **~ sabe** (talvez) perhaps

Quênia ['kenja] m: **o ~** Kenya

quente ['kẽtʃi] adj hot; (roupa) warm

quer [kɛʳ] vb ver **querer** ▷ conj: **~ ... ~ ...** whether ... or ...; **~ chova ~ não** whether it rains or not; **onde/quando/quem ~ que** wherever/whenever/whoever; **o que ~ que seja** whatever it is

PALAVRA CHAVE

querer [ke're̊ʳ] vt **1** (desejar) to want; **quero mais dinheiro** I want more money; **queria um chá** I'd like a cup of tea; **quero ajudar/que vá** I want to help/you to go; **você vai querer sair amanhã?** do you want to go out tomorrow?; **eu vou querer uma cerveja** (num bar etc) I'd like a beer; **por/sem querer** intentionally/unintentionally; **como queira** as you wish

2 (perguntas para pedir algo): **você quer fechar a janela?** will you shut the window?; **quer me dar uma mão?** can you give me a hand?

3 (amar) to love

4 (convite): **quer entrar/sentar** do come in/sit down

5: **querer dizer** (significar) to mean; (pretender dizer) to mean to say; **quero dizer** I mean; **quer dizer** (com outras palavras) in other words

▷ vi: **querer bem a** to be fond of

querer-se vr to love one another

▷ m (vontade) wish; (afeto) affection

querido, -a [ke'ridu, a] adj dear ▷ m/f darling; **Q~ João** Dear John

querosene [kero'zeni] m kerosene

questão [keʃ'tãw] (pl -ões) f question, inquiry; (problema) matter, question; (Jur) case; (contenda) dispute, quarrel; **fazer ~ (de)** to insist (on); **em ~** in question; **há ~ de um ano** a year ago; **questionar** [keʃtʃjo'naʳ] vi to question ▷ vt to question, call into question; **questionário** [keʃtʃjo'narju] m questionnaire; **questionável** [keʃtʃjo'navew] (pl -eis) adj questionable

quicar [ki'kaʳ] vt, vi to bounce

quieto, -a ['kjetu, a] adj quiet; (imóvel) still; **quietude** [kje'tudʒi] f calm, tranquillity

quilate [ki'latʃi] m carat

quilo ['kilu] m kilo; **quilobyte** [kilo'bajtʃi] m kilobyte; **quilograma** [kilo'grama] m kilogram; **quilometragem** [kilome'traʒẽ] f number of kilometres ou kilometers travelled, ≈ mileage; **quilômetro** [ki'lometru] m kilometre (BRIT), kilometer (US); **quilowatt** [kilo'watʃi] m kilowatt

química ['kimika] f chemistry

químico, -a ['kimiku, a] adj chemical ▷ m/f chemist

quina ['kina] f corner; (de mesa etc) edge; **de ~** edgeways (BRIT), edgewise (US)

quindim [kĩ'dʒĩ] m sweet made of egg yolks, coconut and sugar

quinhão [ki'nãw] (pl -ões) m share, portion

quinhentos, -as [ki'ɲẽtuʃ, aʃ] num five hundred

quinhões [ki'ɲõjʃ] mpl de **quinhão**

quinquilharias [kĩkiʎa'riaʃ] fpl odds and ends; (miudezas) knicknacks, trinkets

quinta ['kĩta] f (tb: **~-feira**) Thursday; (propriedade) estate; (PT) farm; **quinta-feira** ['kĩta-'fejra] (pl **quintas-feiras**) f Thursday

quintal [kĩ'taw] (pl -ais) m back yard

quinteto [kĩ'tetu] *m* quintet(te)

quinto, -a ['kĩtu, a] *num* fifth

quinze ['kĩzɪ] *num* fifteen; **duas e ~** a quarter past (BRIT) *ou* after (US) two; **~ para as sete** a quarter to (BRIT) *ou* of (US) seven

quinzena [kĩ'zɛna] *f* two weeks, fortnight (BRIT); **quinzenal** [kĩze'naw] (*pl* **quinzenais**) *adj* fortnightly; **quinzenalmente** [kĩzenaw'mẽtʃi] *adv* fortnightly

quiosque ['kjɔʃki] *m* kiosk

quis *etc* [kiʃ] *vb ver* **querer**

quiser *etc* [ki'zeʳ] *vb ver* **querer**

quisto ['kiʃtu] *m* cyst

quitanda [ki'tãda] *f* grocer's (shop) (BRIT), grocery store (US)

quitar [ki'taʳ] *vt* (*dívida: pagar*) to pay off; (: *perdoar*) to cancel; (*devedor*) to release

quite ['kitʃi] *adj* (*livre*) free; (*com um credor*) squared up; (*igualado*) even; **estar ~ (com alguém)** to be quits (with sb)

quitute [ki'tutʃi] *m* titbit (BRIT), tidbit (US)

quota ['kwɔta] *f* quota; (*porção*) share, portion

quotidiano, -a [kwotʃi'dʒjanu, a] *adj* everyday

r

R *abr* (= *rua*) St

R$ *abr* = **real**

rã [xã] *f* frog

rabanete [xaba'netʃi] *m* radish

rabiscar [xabiʃ'kaʳ] *vt* to scribble; (*papel*) to scribble on ▷ *vi* to scribble; (*desenhar*) to doodle; **rabisco** [xa'biʃku] *m* scribble

rabo ['xabu] *m* tail

rabugento, -a [xabu'ʒẽtu, a] *adj* grumpy

raça ['xasa] *f* breed; (*grupo étnico*) race; **cão/cavalo de ~** pedigree dog/ thoroughbred horse

racha ['xaʃa] *f* (*fenda*) split; (*greta*) crack; **rachadura** [xaʃa'dura] *f* crack; **rachar** [xa'ʃaʳ] *vt* to crack; (*objeto, despesas*) to split; (*lenha*) to chop ▷ *vi* to split; (*cristal*) to crack; **rachar-se** *vr* to split; to crack

racial [xa'sjaw] (*pl* **-ais**) *adj* racial

raciocínio [xasjo'sinju] *m* reasoning

racional [xasjo'naw] (*pl* **-ais**) *adj* rational; **racionalizar** [xasjonali'zaʳ] *vt* to rationalize

racionamento [xasjona'mẽtu] *m* rationing

racismo [xa'siʒmu] *m* racism; **racista** [xa'siʃta] *adj, m/f* racist

radar [xa'daʳ] *m* radar

radiação [xadʒja'sãw] f radiation
radiador [xadʒja'doʳ] m radiator
radical [xadʒi'kaw] (pl **-ais**) adj radical
radicar-se [xadʒi'kaxsi] vr to take root;
(fixar residência) to settle
rádio ['xadʒu] m radio; (Quím) radium;
radioativo, -a [xadʒjua'tʃivu, a] (PT
-act-) adj radioactive; **radiodifusão**
[xadʒjodʒifu'zãw] f broadcasting;
radiografar [xadʒjogra'faʳ] vt to X-ray;
radiografia [xadʒjogra'fia] f X-ray
raia ['xaja] f (risca) line; (fronteira)
boundary; (limite) limit; (de corrida) lane;
(peixe) ray
raiar [xa'jaʳ] vi to shine
rainha [xa'iɲa] f queen
raio ['xaju] m (de sol) ray; (de luz) beam;
(de roda) spoke; (relâmpago) flash of
lightning; (alcance) range; (Mat) radius;
~s X X-rays
raiva ['xajva] f rage, fury; (Med) rabies sg;
estar/ficar com ~ (de) to be/get angry
(with); **ter ~ de** to hate; **raivoso, -a**
[xaj'vozu, ɔza] adj furious
raiz [xa'iʒ] f root; (origem) origin, source;
~ quadrada square root
rajada [xa'ʒada] f (vento) gust
ralado, -a [xa'ladu, a] adj grated;
ralador [xala'doʳ] m grater
ralar [xa'laʳ] vt to grate
ralhar [xa'ʎaʳ] vi to scold; **~ com alguém**
to tell sb off
rali [xa'li] m rally
ralo, -a ['xalu, a] adj (cabelo) thinning;
(tecido) flimsy; (vegetação) sparse; (sopa)
thin, watery; (café) weak ▷ m (de regador)
rose, nozzle; (de pia, banheiro) drain
rama ['xama] f branches pl, foliage; **pela**
~ superficially; **ramagem** [xa'maʒẽ] f
branches pl, foliage; **ramal** [xa'maw]
(pl **ramais**) m (Ferro) branch line; (Tel)
extension; (Auto) side road
ramificar-se [xamifi'kaxsi] vr to branch
out
ramo ['xamu] m branch; (profissão,
negócios) line; (de flores) bunch; **Domingo**
de R~s Palm Sunday
rampa ['xãpa] f ramp; (ladeira) slope
ranger [xã'ʒeʳ] vi to creak ▷ vt: **~ os**
dentes to grind one's teeth
ranhura [xa'ɲura] f groove; (para moeda)
slot
rapar [xa'paʳ] vt to scrape; (a barba) to
shave; (o cabelo) to crop
rapariga [xapa'riga] f girl
rapaz [xa'pajʒ] m boy; (col) lad

rapidez [xapi'deʒ] f speed
rápido, -a ['xapidu, a] adj fast, quick
▷ adv fast, quickly ▷ m (trem) express
rapina [xa'pina] f robbery; **ave de ~** bird
of prey
raptar [xap'taʳ] vt to kidnap; **rapto**
['xaptu] m kidnapping; **raptor** [xap'toʳ]
m kidnapper
raquete [xa'ketʃi] f racquet
raquítico, -a [xa'kitʃiku, a] adj (franzino)
puny; (vegetação) poor
raramente [xara'mẽtʃi] adv rarely,
seldom
raro, -a ['xaru, a] adj rare ▷ adv rarely,
seldom
rasgado, -a [xaʒ'gadu, a] adj (roupa)
torn, ripped
rasgão [xaʒ'gãw] (pl **-ões**) m tear, rip
rasgar [xaʒ'gaʳ] vt to tear, rip; (destruir)
to tear up, rip up; **~-se** vr to split; **rasgo**
['xaʒgu] m tear, rip
rasgões [xaʒ'gõjʃ] mpl de **rasgão**
raso, -a ['xazu, a] adj (liso) flat, level; (não
fundo) shallow; (baixo) low; **soldado ~**
private
raspa ['xaʃpa] f (de madeira) shaving; (de
metal) filing
raspão [xaʃ'pãw] (pl **-ões**) m scratch,
graze
raspar [xaʃ'paʳ] vt to scrape; (alisar) to
file; (tocar de raspão) to graze; (arranhar) to
scratch; (pêlos, cabeça) to shave; (apagar)
to rub out ▷ vi: **~ em** to scrape
raspões [xaʃ'põjʃ] mpl de **raspão**
rasteira [xaʃ'tejra] f: **dar uma ~ em**
alguém to trip sb up
rasteiro, -a [xaʃ'tejru, a] adj crawling;
(planta) creeping
rastejar [xaʃte'ʒaʳ] vi to crawl;
(furtivamente) to creep; (fig: rebaixar-se) to
grovel ▷ vt (fugitivo etc) to track
rasto ['xaʃtu] m (pegada) track; (de veículo)
trail; (fig) sign, trace; **andar de ~s** to
crawl
rastro ['xaʃtru] m = **rasto**
rata ['xata] f rat; (pequena) mouse
ratificar [xatʃifi'kaʳ] vt to ratify
rato ['xatu] m rat; (pequeno) mouse; **~ de**
hotel/praia hotel/beach thief; **ratoeira**
[xa'twejra] f rat trap; mousetrap
ravina [xa'vina] f ravine
razão [xa'zãw] (pl **-ões**) f reason;
(argumento) reasoning; (Mat) ratio ▷ m
(Com) ledger; **à ~ de** at the rate of; **em**
~ de on account of; **dar ~ a alguém** to
support sb; **ter/não ter ~** to be right/

wrong; **razoável** [xa'zwavew] (*pl* -**eis**) *adj* reasonable

r/c (*PT*) *abr* = **rés-do-chão**

ré [xɛ] *f* (*Auto*) reverse (gear); **dar (marcha à) ré** to reverse, back up; *ver tb* **réu**

reabastecer [xeabaʃte'seʳ] *vt* (*avião*) to refuel; (*carro*) to fill up; **~-se** *vr*: **~-se de** to replenish one's supply of

reação [xea'sãw] (*PT* -**çç**-; *pl* -**ões**) *f* reaction

reagir [xea'ʒiʳ] *vi* to react; (*doente, time perdedor*) to fight back; **~ a** (*resistir*) to resist; (*protestar*) to rebel against

reais [xe'ajʃ] *adj pl de* **real**

reaja *etc* [xe'aʒa] *vb ver* **reagir; reaver**

reajuste [xea'ʒuʃtʃi] *m* adjustment

real [xe'aw] (*pl* -**ais**) *adj* real; (*relativo à realeza*) royal ▷ *m* (*moeda*) real

realçar [xeaw'saʳ] *vt* to highlight; **realce** [xe'awsi] *m* emphasis; (*mais brilho*) highlight; **dar realce a** to enhance

realeza [xea'leza] *f* royalty

realidade [xeali'dadʒi] *f* reality; **na ~** actually, in fact

realista [xea'liʃta] *adj* realistic ▷ *m/f* realist

realização [xealiza'sãw] *f* fulfilment (*BRIT*), fulfillment (*US*), realization; (*de projeto*) execution, carrying out

realizador, a [xealiza'doʳ, a] *adj* enterprising

realizar [xeali'zaʳ] *vt* to achieve; (*projeto*) to carry out; (*ambições, sonho*) to fulfil (*BRIT*), fulfill (*US*), realize; (*negócios*) to transact; (*perceber*) to realize; **~-se** *vr* to take place; (*ambições*) to be realized; (*sonhos*) to come true

realmente [xeaw'mẽtʃi] *adv* really; (*de fato*) actually

reanimar [xeani'maʳ] *vt* to revive; (*encorajar*) to encourage; **~-se** *vr* to cheer up

reatar [xea'taʳ] *vt* to resume, take up again

reaver [xea'veʳ] *vt* to recover, get back

rebaixar [xebaj'ʃaʳ] *vt* to lower; (*mercadorias*) to lower the price of; (*humilhar*) to put down, humiliate ▷ *vi* to drop; **~-se** *vr* to demean o.s.

rebanho [xe'baɲu] *m* (*de carneiros, fig*) flock; (*de gado, elefantes*) herd

rebelar-se [xebe'laxsi] *vr* to rebel;

rebelde [xe'bɛwdʒi] *adj* rebellious; (*indisciplinado*) unruly, wild ▷ *m/f* rebel

rebeldia [xebew'dʒia] *f* rebelliousness;

(*fig: obstinação*) stubbornness; (: *oposição*) defiance

rebelião [xebe'ljãw] (*pl* -**ões**) *f* rebellion

rebentar [xebẽ'taʳ] *vi* (*guerra*) to break out; (*louça*) to smash; (*corda*) to snap; (*represa*) to burst; (*ondas*) to break ▷ *vt* to smash; to snap; (*porta*) to break down

rebocador [xeboka'doʳ] *m* tug (boat)

rebocar [xebo'kaʳ] *vt* (*paredes*) to plaster; (*veículo*) to tow

rebolar [xebo'laʳ] *vt* to swing ▷ *vi* to sway

reboque[1] [xe'bɔki] *m* tow; (*veículo: tb*: **carro ~**) trailer; (*cabo*) towrope; (*BR*: **de socorro**) towtruck; **a ~** on *ou* in (*US*) tow

reboque[2] *etc vb ver* **rebocar**

rebuçado [xebu'sadu] (*PT*) *m* sweet, candy (*US*)

recado [xe'kadu] *m* message; **deixar ~** to leave a message

recair [xeka'iʳ] *vi* (*doente*) to relapse

recalcar [xekaw'kaʳ] *vt* to repress

recalque *etc* [xe'kawki] *vb ver* **recalcar**

recanto [xe'kãtu] *m* corner, nook

recapitular [xekapitu'laʳ] *vt* to sum up, recapitulate; (*fatos*) to review; (*matéria escolar*) to revise

recarga [xe'kaxga] *f* (*de celular*) top-up; **preciso fazer a ~ do meu celular** I need to top up my mobile

recarregar [xekaxe'gaʳ] *vt* (*celular*) to top up; (*bateria*) recharge; (*cartucho*) refill

recatado, -a [xeka'tadu, a] *adj* (*modesto*) modest; (*reservado*) reserved

recauchutado, -a [xekawʃu'tadu, a] *adj*: **pneu ~** (*Auto*) retread, remould (*BRIT*)

recear [xe'sjaʳ] *vt* to fear ▷ *vi*: **~ por** to fear for; **~ fazer/que** to be afraid to do/that

receber [xese'beʳ] *vt* to receive; (*ganhar*) to earn, get; (*hóspedes*) to take in; (*convidados*) to entertain; (*acolher bem*) to welcome ▷ *vi* (*receber convidados*) to entertain; **recebimento**; (*receb*) (*BR*) *m* reception; (*de uma carta*) receipt; **acusar o recebimento de** to acknowledge receipt of

receio [xe'seju] *m* fear; **ter ~ de que** to fear that

receita [xe'sejta] *f* income; (*do Estado*) revenue; (*Med*) prescription; (*Culin*) recipe; **R~ Federal** ≈ Inland Revenue (*BRIT*), ≈ IRS (*US*); **receitar** [xesej'taʳ] *vt* to prescribe

recém [xe'sẽ] *adv* recently, newly; **recém-casado, -a** *adj*: **os recém-**

casados the newlyweds; **recém-chegado, -a** *m/f* newcomer; **recém-nascido, -a** *m/f* newborn child

recente [xe'sẽtʃi] *adj* recent; *(novo)* new ▷ *adv* recently; **recentemente** [xesẽtʃi'mẽtʃi] *adv* recently

receoso, -a [xe'sjozu, ɔza] *adj* frightened, fearful; **estar ~ de (fazer)** to be afraid of (doing)

recepção [xesep'sãw] *(pl* **-ões)** *f* reception; *(PT: de uma carta)* receipt; **acusar a ~ de** *(PT)* to acknowledge receipt of; **recepcionista** [xesepsjo'niʃta] *m/f* receptionist

receptivo, -a [xesep'tʃivu, a] *adj* receptive; *(acolhedor)* welcoming

receptor [xesep'to'] *m* receiver

recessão [xese'sãw] *(pl* **-ões)** *f* recession; **recessões** [xese'sõjʃ] *fpl de* **recessão**

recheado, -a [xe'ʃjadu, a] *adj (ave, carne)* stuffed; *(empada, bolo)* filled; *(cheio)* full, crammed

rechear [xe'ʃja'] *vt* to fill; *(ave, carne)* to stuff; **recheio** [xe'ʃeju] *m* stuffing; *(de empada, de bolo)* filling; *(o conteúdo)* contents *pl*

rechonchudo, -a [xeʃõ'ʃudu, a] *adj* chubby, plump

recibo [xe'sibu] *m* receipt

reciclar [xesi'kla'] *vt* to recycle

reciclável [xesi'klavew] *(pl* **-eis)** *adj* recyclable

recinto [xe'sĩtu] *m* enclosure; *(lugar)* area

recipiente [xesi'pjẽtʃi] *m* container, receptacle

recíproco, -a [xe'siproku, a] *adj* reciprocal

recitar [xesi'ta'] *vt* to recite

reclamação [xeklama'sãw] *(pl* **-ões)** *f* complaint

reclamar [xekla'ma'] *vt* to demand; *(herança)* to claim ▷ *vi* to complain

reclinar [xekli'na'] *vt* to rest, lean; **~-se** *vr* to lie back; *(deitar-se)* to lie down

recobrar [xeko'bra'] *vt* to recover, get back; **~-se** *vr* to recover

recolher [xeko'ʎe'] *vt* to collect; *(coisas dispersas)* to pick up; *(gado, roupa do varal)* to bring in; *(juntar)* to gather together; **recolhido, -a** [xeko'ʎidu, a] *adj (lugar)* secluded; *(pessoa)* withdrawn; **recolhimento** [xekoʎi'mẽtu] *m* retirement; *(arrecadação)* collection; *(ato de levar)* taking

recomeçar [xekome'sa'] *vt, vi* to restart

recomendação [xekomẽda'sãw] *(pl* **-ões)** *f* recommendation; **recomendações** *fpl (cumprimentos)* regards

recomendar [xekomẽ'da'] *vt* to recommend; **recomendável** [xekomẽ'davew] *(pl* **-eis)** *adj* advisable

recompensa [xekõ'pẽsa] *f* reward; **recompensar** [xekõpẽ'sa'] *vt* to reward

recompor [xekõ'po'] *(irreg: como* **pôr**) *vt* to reorganize; *(restabelecer)* to restore

reconciliar [xekõsi'lja'] *vt* to reconcile

reconhecer [xekoɲe'se'] *vt* to recognize; *(Mil)* to reconnoitre *(BRIT)*, reconnoiter *(US)*; **reconhecido, -a** [xekoɲe'sidu, a] *adj* recognized; *(agradecido)* grateful, thankful; **reconhecimento** [xekoɲesi'mẽtu] *m* recognition; *(admissão)* admission; *(gratidão)* gratitude; *(Mil)* reconnaissance; **reconhecível** [xekoɲe'sivew] *(pl* **-eis)** *adj* recognizable

reconstruir [xekõʃ'trwi'] *vt* to rebuild

recordação [xekoxda'sãw] *(pl* **-ões)** *f (reminiscência)* memory; *(objeto)* memento

recordar [xekox'da'] *vt* to remember; *(parecer)* to look like; *(recapitular)* to revise; **~-se** *vr*: **~-se de** to remember; **~ algo a alguém** to remind sb of sth

recorde [xe'kɔxdʒi] *adj inv* record *atr* ▷ *m* record

recorrer [xeko'xe'] *vi*: **~ a** to turn to; *(valer-se de)* to resort to

recortar [xekox'ta'] *vt* to cut out; **recorte** [xe'kɔxtʃi] *m (ato)* cutting out; *(de jornal)* cutting, clipping

recreação [xekrja'sãw] *f* recreation

recreio [xe'kreju] *m* recreation

recriminar [xekrimi'na'] *vt* to reproach, reprove

recrutamento [xekruta'mẽtu] *m* recruitment

recrutar [xekru'ta'] *vt* to recruit

rectângulo [xek'tãgulu] *(PT)* = **retângulo**

recto, -a *etc* ['xɛkto, a] *(PT)* = **reto** *etc*

recuar [xe'kwa'] *vt* to move back ▷ *vi* to move back; *(exército)* to retreat

recuperar [xekupe'ra'] *vt* to recover; *(tempo perdido)* to make up for; *(reabilitar)* to rehabilitate; **~-se** *vr* to recover

recurso [xe'kuxsu] *m* resource; *(Jur)* appeal; **recursos** *mpl (financeiros)* resources

recusa [xe'kuza] *f* refusal; *(negação)*

denial; **recusar** [xeku'za^r] vt to refuse; to deny; **recusar-se** vr: **recusar-se a** to refuse to

redação [xeda'sãw] (PT -cç-) (pl -ões) f (ato) writing; (Educ) composition, essay; (redatores) editorial staff

redator, a [xeda'to^r, a] (PT -act-) m/f journalist; (editor) editor; (quem redige) writer

rede ['xedʒi] f net; (de dormir) hammock; (cilada) trap; (Ferro, Tec, fig) network; **a R~** (a Internet) the Net

rédea ['xɛdʒja] f rein

redentor, a [xede'to^r, a] adj redeeming

redigir [xedʒi'ʒi^r] vt, vi to write

redobrar [xedo'bra^r] vt (aumentar) to increase; (esforços) to redouble

redondamente [xedõda'mẽtʃi] adv (completamente) completely

redondezas [xedõ'dezaʃ] fpl surroundings

redondo, -a [xe'dõdu, a] adj round

redor [xe'do^r] m: **ao** ou **em ~ (de)** around, round about

redução [xedu'sãw] (pl -ões) f reduction

redundância [xedũ'dãsja] f redundancy; **redundante** [xedũ'dãtʃi] adj redundant

reduzido, -a [xedu'zidu, a] adj reduced; (limitado) limited; (pequeno) small

reduzir [xedu'zi^r] vt to reduce; **~-se** vr: **~-se a** to be reduced to; (fig: resumir-se em) to come down to

reembolsar [xeẽbow'sa^r] vt to recover; (restituir) to reimburse; (depósito) to refund; **reembolso** [xeẽ'bowsu] m (de depósito) refund; (de despesa) reimbursement

reencontro [xeẽ'kõtru] m reunion

refeição [xefej'sãw] (pl -ões) f meal; **refeitório** [xefej'tɔrju] m refectory

refém [xe'fẽ] (pl -ns) m hostage

referência [xefe'rẽsja] f reference; **referências** fpl (informaçoes para emprego) references; **fazer ~ a** to make reference to, refer to

referente [xefe'rẽtʃi] adj: **~ a** concerning, regarding

referir [xefe'ri^r] vt to relate, tell; **~-se** vr: **~-se a** to refer to

REFESA f (= Rede Ferroviária SA) ≈ BR

refinamento [xefina'mẽtu] m refinement

refinaria [xefina'ria] f refinery

refiro etc [xe'firu] vb ver **referir**

refletir [xefle'tʃi^r] (PT -ct-) vt to reflect ▷ vi: **~ em** ou **sobre** to consider, think about

reflexão [xeflek'sãw] (pl -ões) f reflection

reflexo, -a [xe'flɛksu, a] adj (luz) reflected; (ação) reflex ▷ m reflection; (Anat) reflex; (no cabelo) highlight

reflexões [xeflek'sõjʃ] fpl de **reflexão**

reflito etc [xe'flitu] vb ver **refletir**

reforçado, -a [xefox'sadu, a] adj reinforced; (pessoa) strong; (café da manhã, jantar) hearty

reforçar [xefox'sa^r] vt to reinforce; (revigorar) to invigorate; **reforço** [xe'foxsu] m reinforcement

reforma [xe'fɔxma] f reform; (Arq) renovation; **reformado, -a** [xefox'madu, a] adj reformed; renovated; (Mil) retired; **reformar** [xefox'ma^r] vt to reform; to renovate; **reformar-se** vr to reform

refractário, -a [xefra'tarju, a] (PT) adj = **refratário/a**

refrão [xe'frãw] (pl -ãos or -ães) m chorus, refrain; (provérbio) saying

refratário, -a [xefra'tarju, a] adj (Tec) heat-resistant; (Culin) ovenproof

refrear [xefre'a^r] vt (cavalo) to rein in; (inimigo) to contain, check; (paixões, raiva) to control; **~-se** vr to restrain o.s.

refrescante [xefreʃ'kãtʃi] adj refreshing

refrescar [xefreʃ'ka^r] vt (ar, ambiente) to cool; (pessoa) to refresh ▷ vi to cool down

refresco [xe'freʃku] m cool fruit drink, squash; **refrescos** mpl (refrigerantes) refreshments

refrigerador [xefriʒera'do^r] m refrigerator, fridge (BRIT)

refrigerante [xefriʒe'rãtʃi] m soft drink

refugiado, -a [xefu'ʒjadu, a] adj, m/f refugee

refugiar-se [xefu'ʒjaxsi] vr to take refuge; **refúgio** [xe'fuʒju] m refuge

refugo [xe'fugu] m rubbish, garbage (US); (mercadoria) reject

rega ['xɛga] (PT) f irrigation

regador [xega'do^r] m watering can

regalia [xega'lia] f privilege

regar [xe'ga^r] vt (plantas, jardim) to water; (umedecer) to sprinkle

regatear [xega'tʃja^r] vt (o preço) to haggle over, bargain for ▷ vi to haggle

regenerar [xeʒene'ra^r] vt to regenerate

reger [xe'ʒe^r] vt to govern; (orquestra) to conduct; (empresa) to run ▷ vi to rule; (maestro) to conduct

região [xe'ʒjãw] (pl -ões) f region, area

regime [xe'ʒimi] m (Pol) regime; (dieta) diet; (maneira) way; **estar de ~** to be on a diet

regimento [xeʒi'mẽtu] m regiment

regiões [xe'ʒjõjʃ] fpl de **região**

regional [xeʒjo'naw] (pl **-ais**) adj regional

registrar [xeʒiʃ'tra'] (PT **-ista-**) vt to register; (anotar) to record

registro [xe'ʒiʃtru] (PT **-to**) m registration; (anotação) recording; (livro, Ling) register; (histórico) record; **~ civil** registry office

regra ['xɛgra] f rule; **regras** fpl (Med) periods

regravável [xegra'vavew] (pl **-eis**) adj rewritable

regressar [xegre'sa'] vi to come (ou go) back, return; **regresso** [xe'grɛsu] m return

régua ['xɛgwa] f ruler; **~ de calcular** slide rule

regulador [xegula'do'] m regulator

regulamento [xegula'mẽtu] m rules pl, regulations pl

regular [xegu'la'] adj regular; (estatura) average, medium; (tamanho) normal; (razoável) not bad ▷ vt to regulate; (reger) to govern; (máquina) to adjust; (carro, motor) to tune ▷ vi to work, function; **regularidade** [xegulari'dadʒi] f regularity

rei [xej] m king; **Dia de R~s** Epiphany; **R~ Momo** carnival king

reinado [xej'nadu] m reign

reinar [xej'na'] vi to reign

reino ['xejnu] m kingdom; (fig) realm; **o R~ Unido** the United Kingdom

reivindicação [xejvĩdʒika'sãw] (pl **-ões**) f claim, demand

reivindicar [xejvĩdʒi'ka'] vt to claim; (aumento salarial, direitos) to demand

rejeição [xeʒej'sãw] (pl **-ões**) f rejection

rejeitar [xeʒej'ta'] vt to reject; (recusar) to refuse

rejo etc ['xeʒu] vb ver **reger**

rejuvenescer [xeʒuvene'se'] vt to rejuvenate

relação [xela'sãw] (pl **-ões**) f relation; (conexão) connection; (relacionamento) relationship; (Mat) ratio; (lista) list; **com ou em ~ a** regarding, with reference to; **relações públicas** public relations; **relacionamento** [xelasjona'mẽtu] m relationship; **relacionar** [xelasjo'na'] vt to make a list of; (ligar): **relação**

algo com algo to connect sth with sth, relate sth to sth; **relacionar-se** vr to be connected ou related

relâmpago [xe'lãpagu] m flash of lightning; **relâmpagos** mpl (clarões) lightning sg

relance [xe'lãsi] m glance; **olhar de ~** to glance at

relapso, -a [xe'lapsu, a] adj (negligente) negligent

relatar [xela'ta'] vt to give an account of

relativo, -a [xela'tʃivu, a] adj relative

relato [xe'latu] m account

relatório [xela'tɔrju] m report

relaxado, -a [xela'ʃadu, a] adj relaxed; (desleixado) slovenly, sloppy; (relapso) negligent

relaxante [xela'ʃãtʃi] adj relaxing

relaxar [xela'ʃa'] vt, vi to relax

relegar [xele'ga'] vt to relegate

relembrar [xelẽ'bra'] vt to recall

relevante [xele'vãtʃi] adj relevant

relevo [xe'levu] m relief

religião [xeli'ʒãw] (pl **-ões**) f religion; **religioso, -a** [xeli'ʒozu, ɔza] adj religious ▷ m/f religious person; (frade/freira) monk/nun

relíquia [xe'likja] f relic; **~ de família** family heirloom

relógio [xe'lɔʒu] m clock; (de gás) meter; **~ (de pulso)** (wrist)watch; **~ de sol** sundial

relutante [xelu'tãtʃi] adj reluctant

relva ['xɛwva] f grass; (terreno gramado) lawn

relvado [xew'vadu] (PT) m lawn

remar [xe'ma'] vt, vi to row

rematar [xema'ta'] vt to finish off; **remate** [xe'matʃi] m (fim) end; (acabamento) finishing touch

remediar [xeme'dʒja'] vt to put right, remedy

remédio [xe'mɛdʒu] m (medicamento) medicine; (recurso, solução) remedy; (Jur) recourse; **não tem ~** there's no way

remendar [xemẽ'da'] vt to mend; (com pano) to patch; **remendo** [xe'mẽdu] m repair; patch

remessa [xe'mɛsa] f shipment; (de dinheiro) remittance

remetente [xeme'tẽtʃi] m/f sender

remexer [xeme'ʃe'] vt (papéis) to shuffle; (sacudir: braços) to wave; (folhas) to shake; (revolver: areia, lama) to stir up ▷ vi: **~ em** to rummage through

reminiscência [xemini'sẽsja] f

reminiscence

remo ['xɛmu] *m* oar; (*Esporte*) rowing

remoção [xemo'sãw] *f* removal

remorso [xe'mɔxsu] *m* remorse

remover [xemo've'] *vt* to move; (*transferir*) to transfer; (*demitir*) to dismiss; (*retirar, afastar*) to remove; (*terra*) to churn up

renal [xe'naw] (*pl* -**ais**) *adj* renal, kidney *atr*

Renascença [xena'sẽsa] *f*: **a ~** the Renaissance

renascer [xena'se'] *vi* to be reborn; (*fig*) to revive

renascimento [xenasi'mẽtu] *m* rebirth; (*fig*) revival; **o R~** the Renaissance

renda ['xẽda] *f* income; (*nacional*) revenue; (*de aplicação, locação*) yield; (*tecido*) lace

render [xẽ'de'] *vt* (*lucro, dinheiro*) to bring in, yield; (*preço*) to fetch; (*homenagem*) to pay; (*graças*) to give; (*serviços*) to render; (*armas*) to surrender; (*guarda*) to relieve; (*causar*) to bring ▷ *vi* (*dar lucro*) to pay; **~-se** *vr* to surrender; **rendição** [xẽdʒi'sãw] *f* surrender

rendimento [xẽdʒi'mẽtu] *m* income; (*lucro*) profit; (*juro*) yield, interest

renegar [xene'ga'] *vt* (*crença*) to renounce; (*detestar*) to hate; (*trair*) to betray; (*negar*) to deny; (*desprezar*) to reject

renomado, -a [xeno'madu, a] *adj* renowned

renovar [xeno'va'] *vt* to renew; (*Arq*) to renovate

rentabilidade [xẽtabili'dadʒi] *f* profitability

rentável [xẽ'tavew] (*pl* -**eis**) *adj* profitable

renúncia [xe'nũsja] *f* resignation

renunciar [xenũ'sja'] *vt* to give up, renounce ▷ *vi* to resign; (*abandonar*): **~ a algo** to give sth up

reouve *etc* [xe'ovi] *vb ver* **reaver**

reouver *etc* [xeo've'] *vb ver* **reaver**

reparação [xepara'sãw] (*pl* -**ões**) *f* mending, repairing; (*de mal, erros*) remedying; (*fig*) amends *pl*, reparation

reparar [xepa'ra'] *vt* to repair; (*forças*) to restore; (*mal, erros*) to remedy; (*prejuízo, danos, ofensa*) to make amends for; (*notar*) to notice ▷ *vi*: **~ em** to notice; **reparo** [xe'paru] *m* repair; (*crítica*) criticism; (*observação*) observation

repartição [xepaxtʃi'sãw] (*pl* -**ões**) *f* distribution

repartir [xepax'tʃi'] *vt* (*distribuir*) to distribute; (*dividir entre vários*) to share out; (*dividir em várias porções*) to divide up

repelente [xepe'lẽtʃi] *adj, m* repellent

repente [xe'pẽtʃi] *m* outburst; **de ~** suddenly; (*col: talvez*) maybe

repentino, -a [xepẽ'tʃinu, a] *adj* sudden

repercussão [xepexku'sãw] (*pl* -**ões**) *f* repercussion

repercutir [xepexku'tʃi'] *vt* to echo ▷ *vi* to reverberate, echo; (*fig*): **~ (em)** to have repercussions (on)

repertório [xepex'tɔrju] *m* list; (*coleção*) collection; (*Mús*) repertoire

repetidamente [xepetʃida'mẽtʃi] *adv* repeatedly

repetir [xepe'tʃi'] *vt* to repeat ▷ *vi* (*ao comer*) to have seconds; **~-se** *vr* to happen again; (*pessoa*) to repeat o.s.; **repetitivo, -a** [xepetʃi'tʃivu, a] *adj* repetitive

repito *etc* [xe'pitu] *vb ver* **repetir**

repleto, -a [xe'plɛtu, a] *adj* replete, full up

réplica ['xɛplika] *f* replica; (*contestação*) reply, retort

replicar [xepli'ka'] *vt* to answer, reply to ▷ *vi* to reply, answer back

repolho [xe'poʎu] *m* cabbage

repor [xe'po'] (*irreg: como* **pôr**) *vt* to put back, replace; (*restituir*) to return; **~-se** *vr* to recover

reportagem [xepox'taʒẽ] (*pl* -**ns**) *f* reporting; (*notícia*) report

repórter [xe'pɔxte'] *m/f* reporter

repousar [xepo'za'] *vi* to rest; **repouso** [xe'pozu] *m* rest

representação [xeprezẽta'sãw] (*pl* -**ões**) *f* representation; (*Teatro*) performance; **representante** [xeprezẽ'tãtʃi] *m/f* representative

representar [xeprezẽ'ta'] *vt* to represent; (*Teatro: papel*) to play; (*: peça*) to put on ▷ *vi* to act; **representativo, -a** [xeprezẽta'tʃivu, a] *adj* representative

repressão [xepre'sãw] (*pl* -**ões**) *f* repression

reprimir [xepri'mi'] *vt* to repress

reprodução [xeprodu'sãw] (*pl* -**ões**) *f* reproduction

reproduzir [xeprodu'zi'] *vt* to reproduce; (*repetir*) to repeat; **~-se** *vr* to breed

reprovar [xepro'va'] *vt* to disapprove of; (*aluno*) to fail

réptil ['xɛptʃiw] (pl **-eis**) m reptile
república [xe'publika] f republic;
republicano, -a [xepubli'kanu, a] adj,
m/f republican
repudiar [xepu'dʒjaʳ] vt to repudiate;
repúdio [xe'pudʒju] m repudiation;
repulsivo, -a [xepuw'sivu, a] adj
repulsive
reputação [reputa'sãw] (pl **-ões**) f
reputation
requeijão [xekej'ʒãw] m cheese spread
requerer [xeke'reʳ] vt (emprego) to
apply for; (pedir) to request; (exigir) to
require; **requerimento** [xekeri'mẽtu] m
application; request; (petição) petition
requintado, -a [xekĩ'tadu, a] adj
refined, elegant
requinte [xe'kĩtʃi] m refinement,
elegance; (cúmulo) height
requisito [xeki'zitu] m requirement
rês-do-chão [xɛʒ-] (PT) m inv ground
floor (BRIT), first floor (US)
reserva [xe'zɛxva] f reserve; (para hotel,
fig) reservation ▷ m/f (Esporte) reserve
reservado, -a [xezex'vadu, a] adj
reserved
reservar [xezex'vaʳ] vt to reserve;
(guardar de reserva) to keep; (forças) to
conserve; **~-se** vr to save o.s.
reservatório [xezexva'tɔrju] m
reservoir
resfriado, -a [xeʃ'frjadu, a] (BR) adj:
estar/ficar ~ to have a cold/catch (a)
cold ▷ m cold, chill
resgatar [xeʒga'taʳ] vt (salvar) to rescue;
(prisioneiro) to ransom; (retomar) to get
back, recover; **resgate** [xeʒ'gatʃi] m
rescue; ransom; recovery
residência [xezi'dẽsja] f residence;
residencial [xezidẽ'sjaw] (pl **-ais**) adj
residential; (computador, telefone etc)
home atr; **residente** [xezi'dẽtʃi] adj, m/f
resident
residir [xezi'dʒiʳ] vi to live, reside
resíduo [xe'zidwu] m residue
resignação [xezigna'sãw] (pl **-ões**) f
resignation
resignar-se [xezig'naxsi] vr: **~ com** to
resign o.s. to
resina [xe'zina] f resin
resistente [xeziʃ'tẽtʃi] adj resistant;
(material, objeto) hard-wearing, strong
resistir [xeziʃ'tʃiʳ] vi to hold; (pessoa)
to hold out; **~ a** to resist; (sobreviver) to
survive
resmungar [xeʒmũ'gaʳ] vt, vi to mutter,
mumble

resolução [xezolu'sãw] (pl **-ões**) f
resolution; (de um problema) solution;
resoluto, -a [xezo'lutu, a] adj decisive
resolver [xezow've'] vt to sort out;
(problema) to solve; (questão) to resolve;
(decidir) to decide; **~-se** vr: **~-se (a fazer)**
to make up one's mind (to do), decide
(to do)
respectivo, -a [xeʃpek'tʃivu, a] adj
respective
respeitar [xeʃpej'taʳ] vt to respect;
respeitável [xeʃpej'tavew] (pl **-eis**) adj
respectable; (considerável) considerable
respeito [xeʃ'pejtu] m: **~ (a** ou
por) respect (for); **respeitos** mpl
(cumprimentos) regards; **a ~ de, com ~ a**
as to, as regards; (sobre) about; **dizer ~ a**
to concern; **em ~ a** with respect to
respiração [xeʃpira'sãw] f breathing
respirar [xeʃpi'raʳ] vt, vi to breathe
respiro [xeʃ'piru] m breath
resplandecente [xeʃplãde'sẽtʃi] adj
resplendent
responder [xeʃpõ'deʳ] vt to answer ▷ vi
to answer; (ser respondão) to answer
back; **~ por** to be responsible for, answer
for
responsabilidade [xeʃpõsabili'dadʒi] f
responsibility
responsabilizar [xeʃpõsabili'zaʳ]
vt: **~ alguém (por algo)** to hold sb
responsible (for sth); **~-se** vr: **~-se por** to
take responsibility for
responsável [xeʃpõ'savew] (pl **-eis**) adj:
~ (por) responsible (for); **~ a** answerable
to, accountable to
resposta [xeʃ'pɔʃta] f answer, reply
resquício [xeʃ'kisju] m (vestígio) trace
ressabiado, -a [xesa'bjadu, a] adj wary;
(ressentido) resentful
ressaca [xe'saka] f undertow; (mar bravo)
rough sea; (fig: de quem bebeu) hangover
ressalva [xe'sawva] f safeguard
ressentido, -a [xesẽ'tʃidu, a] adj
resentful
ressentimento [xesẽtʃi'mẽtu] m
resentment
ressentir-se [xesẽ'tʃixsi] vr: **~ de**
(ofender-se) to resent; (magoar-se) to be
hurt by; (sofrer) to suffer from, feel the
effects of
ressurgimento [xesuxʒi'mẽtu] m
resurgence, revival
ressuscitar [xesusi'taʳ] vt, vi to revive
restabelecer [xeʃtabele'seʳ] vt to re-

establish, restore; **~-se** vr to recover,
recuperate; **restabelecimento**
[xeʃtabelesi'mẽtu] m re-establishment;
restoration; recovery

restante [xeʃ'tãtʃi] adj remaining ▷ m
rest

restar [xeʃ'ta'] vi to remain, be left

restauração [xeʃtawra'sãw] (pl -ões) f
restoration; (de costumes, usos) revival

restaurante [xeʃtaw'rãtʃi] m restaurant

restaurar [xeʃtaw'ra'] vt to restore

restituição [xeʃtʃitwi'sãw] (pl -ões)
f restitution, return; (de dinheiro)
repayment

restituir [xeʃtʃi'twi'] vt to return;
(dinheiro) to repay; (forças, saúde) to
restore; (usos) to revive; (reempossar) to
reinstate

resto ['xeʃtu] m rest; (Mat) remainder;
restos mpl (sobras) remains; (de comida)
scraps

restrição [xeʃtri'sãw] (pl -ões) f
restriction

resultado [xezuw'tadu] m result

resultante [xezuw'tãtʃi] adj resultant; **~
de** resulting from

resultar [xezuw'ta'] vi: **~ (de/em)** to
result (from/in) ▷ vi (vir a ser) to turn
out to be

resumir [xezu'mi'] vt to summarize;
(livro) to abridge; (reduzir) to reduce;
(conter em resumo) to sum up; **resumo**
[xe'zumu] m summary, résumé; **em
resumo** in short, briefly

retaguarda [xeta'gwaxda] f rearguard;
(posição) rear

retaliação [xetalja'sãw] (pl -ões) f
retaliation

retângulo [xe'tãgulu] m rectangle

retardar [xetax'da'] vt to hold up, delay;
(adiar) to postpone

reter [xe'te'] (irreg: como **ter**) vt (guardar,
manter) to keep; (deter) to stop; (segurar)
to hold; (ladrão, suspeito) to detain; (na
memória) to retain; (lágrimas, impulsos) to
hold back; (impedir de sair) to keep back

reticente [xetʃi'sẽtʃi] adj reticent

retificar [xetʃifi'ka'] vt to rectify

retirada [xetʃi'rada] f (Mil) retreat;
(salário, saque) withdrawal

reto, -a ['xetu, a] adj straight; (fig: justo)
fair; (: honesto) honest, upright ▷ m
(Anat) rectum

retorcer [xetox'se'] vt to twist; **~-se** vr to
wriggle, writhe

retornar [xetox'na'] vi to return, go

back; **retorno** [xe'toxnu] m return; **dar
retorno** to do a U-turn; **retorno (do
carro)** (Comput) (carriage) return

retraído, -a [xetra'idu, a] adj (tímido)
reserved, timid

retrair [xetra'i'] vt to withdraw; (contrair)
to contract; (pessoa) to make reserved

retrato [xe'tratu] m portrait;
(Foto) photo; (fig: efígie) likeness;
(: representação) portrayal; **~ falado**
identikit® picture

retribuir [xetri'bwi'] vt to reward,
recompense; (pagar) to remunerate;
(hospitalidade, favor, sentimento, visita) to
return

retroceder [xetrose'de'] vi to retreat, fall
back; **retrocesso** [xetro'sɛsu] m retreat;
(ao passado) return

retrógrado, -a [xe'trɔgradu, a] adj
retrograde; (reacionário) reactionary

retrospecto [xetro'ʃpektu] m: **em ~** in
retrospect

retrovisor [xetrovi'zo'] adj, m: **(espelho)
~** (rear-view) mirror

réu, -ré [xɛw, xɛ] m/f defendant;
(culpado) culprit, criminal

reumatismo [xewma'tʃiʒmu] m
rheumatism

reunião [xeu'njãw] (pl -ões) f meeting;
(ato, reencontro) reunion; (festa) get-
together, party; **~ de cúpula** summit
(meeting)

revanche [xe'vãʃi] f revenge

reveillon [xeve'jõ] m New Year's Eve

revelação [xevela'sãw] (pl -ões) f
revelation

revelar [xeve'la'] vt to reveal; (Foto) to
develop; **~-se** vr to turn out to be

revelia [xeve'lia] f default; **à ~** by default;
à ~ de without the knowledge ou
consent of

revendedor, a [xevẽde'do', a] m/f dealer

rever [xe've'] (irreg: como **ver**) vt to see
again; (examinar) to check; (revisar) to
revise

reverência [xeve'rẽsja] f reverence,
respect; (ato) bow; (: de mulher) curtsey;
fazer uma ~ to bow; to curtsey

reverso [xe'vɛxsu] m reverse

reverter [xevex'te'] vt to revert

revestir [xeveʃ'tʃi'] vt (paredes etc) to
cover; (interior de uma caixa etc) to line

revezar [xeve'za'] vt, vi to alternate; **~-se**
vr to take turns, alternate

revidar [xevi'da'] vt (soco, insulto) to
return; (retrucar) to answer; (crítica)

to rise to, respond to ▷ *vi* to hit back;
(*retrucar*) to respond
revirar [xevi'ra^r] *vt* to turn round;
(*gaveta*) to turn out, go through
revisão [xevi'zãw] (*pl* -ões) *f* revision;
(*de máquina*) overhaul; (*de carro*) service;
(*Jur*) appeal
revisar [xevi'za^r] *vt* to revise
revisões [xevi'zõjʃ] *fpl de* **revisão**
revista [xe'viʃta] *f* (*busca*) search; (*Mil,
exame*) inspection; (*profissional,
erudita*) journal; (*Teatro*)
revue
revisto *etc* [xe'viʃtu] *vb ver* **revestir**
revogar [xevo'ga^r] *vt* to revoke
revolta [xe'vɔwta] *f* revolt; (*fig:
indignação*) disgust; **R~ da Vacina** *see
boxed note*; **revoltado, -a** [xevow'tadu,
a] *adj* in revolt; (*indignado*) disgusted;
(*amargo*) bitter; **revoltante** [xevow'tãtʃi]
adj disgusting, revolting

⬢ **REVOLTA DA VACINA**
⬢
⬢ This was a popular movement of
⬢ opposition to the government which
⬢ took place in Rio de Janeiro in 1904,
⬢ following the passing of a law which
⬢ made vaccination against smallpox
⬢ compulsory. It was the culmination
⬢ of general dissatisfaction with health
⬢ reforms undertaken at that time by
⬢ the scientist Osvaldo Cruz, and the
⬢ relocation programme of the prefect
⬢ Pereira Passos, as a result of which
⬢ part of the population of Rio had been
⬢ moved from the slums and shanty
⬢ towns of the central region to suburbs
⬢ much further out.

revoltar [xevow'ta^r] *vt* to disgust; **~-se**
vr to rebel, revolt; (*indignar-se*) to be
disgusted
revolto, -a [xe'vowtu, a] *pp de* **revolver**
▷ *adj* (*década*) turbulent; (*mundo*)
troubled; (*cabelo*) untidy, unkempt; (*mar*)
rough; (*desarrumado*) untidy
revolução [xevolu'sãw] (*pl* -ões)
f revolution; **revolucionar**
[xevolusjo'na^r] *vt* to revolutionize;
revolucionário, -a [xevolusjo'narju, a]
adj, m/f revolutionary
revolver [xevow've^r] *vi* to revolve, rotate
revólver [xe'vɔwve^r] *m* revolver
reza [ˈxɛza] *f* prayer; **rezar** [xe'za^r] *vi* to
pray

riacho [ˈxjaʃu] *m* brook, stream
ribeiro [xi'bejru] *m* brook, stream
rico, -a [ˈxiku, a] *adj* rich; (PT: *lindo*)
beautiful; (: *excelente*) splendid ▷ *m/f* rich
man/woman
ridicularizar [xidʒikulari'za^r] *vt* to
ridicule
ridículo, -a [xi'dʒikulu, a] *adj* ridiculous
rifa [ˈxifa] *f* raffle
rifle [ˈxifli] *m* rifle
rigidez [xiʒi'deʒ] *f* rigidity, stiffness;
(*austeridade*) severity, strictness
rígido, -a [ˈxiʒidu, a] *adj* rigid, stiff; (*fig*)
strict
rigor [xi'go^r] *m* rigidity; (*meticulosidade*)
rigour (BRIT), rigor (US); (*severidade*)
harshness, severity; (*exatidão*) precision;
ser de ~ to be essential *ou* obligatory;
rigoroso, -a [xigo'rozu, ɔza] *adj*
rigorous; (*severo*) strict; (*exigente*)
demanding; (*minucioso*) precise,
accurate; (*inverno*) hard, harsh
rijo, -a [ˈxiʒu, a] *adj* tough, hard; (*severo*)
harsh, severe
rim [xĩ] (*pl* -ns) *m* kidney; **rins** *mpl* (*parte
inferior das costas*) small *sg* of the back
rima [ˈxima] *f* rhyme; (*poema*) verse,
poem; **rimar** [xi'ma^r] *vt, vi* to rhyme
rímel [ˈximew] (TM): (*pl* -eis) *m* mascara
ringue [ˈxĩgi] *m* ring
rins [xĩʃ] *mpl de* **rim**
Rio [ˈxiu] *m*: **o ~ (de Janeiro)** Rio (de
Janeiro)
rio [ˈxiu] *m* river
riqueza [xi'keza] *f* wealth, riches *pl*;
(*qualidade*) richness
rir [xi^r] *vi* to laugh; **~ de** to laugh at
risada [xi'zada] *f* laughter
risca [ˈxiʃka] *f* stroke; (*listra*) stripe; (*no
cabelo*) parting
riscar [xiʃ'ka^r] *vt* (*marcar*) to mark;
(*apagar*) to cross out; (*desenhar*) to outline
risco [ˈxiʃku] *m* (*marca*) mark, scratch;
(*traço*) stroke; (*desenho*) drawing, sketch;
(*perigo*) risk; **correr o ~ de** to run the
risk of
riso [ˈxizu] *m* laughter; **risonho, -a**
[xi'zoɲu, a] *adj* smiling; (*contente*)
cheerful
ríspido, -a [ˈxiʃpidu, a] *adj* brusque;
(*áspero*) harsh
ritmo [ˈxitʃmu] *m* rhythm
rito [ˈxitu] *m* rite
ritual [xi'twaw] (*pl* -ais) *adj, m* ritual
rival [xi'vaw] (*pl* -ais) *adj, m/f* rival;
rivalidade [xivali'dadʒi] *f* rivalry;

rivalizar [xivali'za'] vt to rival ▷ vi:
  rivalizar com to compete with, vie with
roa etc ['xɔa] vb ver **roer**
robô [xo'bo] m robot
roça ['xɔsa] f plantation; (no mato)
  clearing; (campo) country
rocha ['xɔʃa] f rock; (penedo) crag
rochedo [xo'ʃedu] m crag, cliff
rock-and-roll [-ã'xɔw] m rock and roll
roda ['xɔda] f wheel; (círculo) circle; **~
  dentada** cog(wheel); **em** ou **à ~ de**
  round, around
rodada [xo'dada] f (de bebidas, Esporte)
  round
rodar [xo'da'] vt to turn, spin; (viajar por)
  to tour, travel round; (quilômetros) to
  do; (filme) to make; (imprimir) to print;
  (Comput: programa) to run ▷ vi to turn
  round; (Auto) to drive around; **~ por** (a
  pé) to wander around; (de carro) to drive
  around
rodela [xo'dɛla] f (pedaço) slice
rodízio [xo'dʒizju] m rota; **em ~** on a
  rota basis
rodopiar [xodo'pja'] vi to whirl around,
  swirl
rodovia [xodo'via] f highway,
  ≈ motorway (BRIT), ≈ interstate (US)
rodoviária [xodo'vjarja] f (tb: **estação
  ~**) bus station; ver tb **rodoviário**
rodoviário, -a [xodo'vjarju, a] adj road
  atr; (polícia) traffic atr
roer [xwe'] vt to gnaw, nibble; (enferrujar)
  to corrode; (afligir) to eat away
rogar [xo'ga'] vt to ask, request; **~ a
  alguém que faça (algo)** to beg sb to
  do (sth)
rói [xɔj] vb ver **roer**
roía etc [xo'ia] vb ver **roer**
rolar [xo'la'] vt, vi to roll
roleta [xo'leta] f roulette; (borboleta)
  turnstile
rolha ['xoʎa] f cork
roliço, -a [xo'lisu, a] adj (pessoa) plump,
  chubby; (objeto) round, cylindrical
rolo ['xolu] m (de papel etc) roll; (para
  nivelar o solo, para pintura) roller; (para
  cabelo) curler; (col: briga) brawl, fight;
  cortina de ~ roller blind; **~ compressor**
  steamroller
Roma ['xoma] n Rome
romã [xo'mã] f pomegranate
romance [xo'mãsi] m novel; (caso
  amoroso) romance; **~ policial** detective
  story
romano, -a [xo'manu, a] adj, m/f
Roman
romântico, -a [xo'mãtʃiku, a] adj
romantic
rombo ['xõbu] m (buraco) hole; (fig:
  desfalque) embezzlement; (: prejuízo) loss,
  shortfall
Romênia [xo'menja] f: **a ~** Romania;
  romeno, -a [xo'mɛnu, a] adj, m/f
  Rumanian ▷ m (Ling) Rumanian
romper [xõ'pe'] vt to break; (rasgar)
  to tear; (relações) to break off ▷ vi (sol)
  to appear, emerge; (: surgir) to break
  through; (ano, dia) to start, begin; **~ em
  pranto** ou **lágrimas** to burst into tears;
  rompimento [xõpi'mẽtu] m breakage;
  (fenda) break; (de relações) breaking off
roncar [xõ'ka'] vi to snore; **ronco** ['xõku]
  m snore
ronda ['xõda] f patrol, beat; **fazer a ~
  de** to go the rounds of, patrol; **rondar**
  [xõ'da'] vt to patrol; (espreitar) to prowl
  ▷ vi to prowl, lurk; (fazer a ronda) to
  patrol; **a inflação ronda os 30% ao mês**
  inflation is in the region of 30% a month
rosa ['xɔza] adj inv pink ▷ f rose; **rosado,
  -a** [xo'zadu, a] adj rosy, pink
rosário [xo'zarju] m rosary
rosbife [xoʒ'bifi] m roast beef
roseira [xo'zejra] f rosebush
rosnar [xoʒ'na'] vi (cão) to growl, snarl;
  (murmurar) to mutter, mumble
rosto ['xoʃtu] m face
rota ['xɔta] f route, course
roteiro [xo'tejru] m itinerary; (ordem)
  schedule; (guia) guidebook; (de filme)
  script
rotina [xo'tʃina] f routine; **rotineiro, -a**
  [xotʃi'nejru, a] adj routine
roto, -a ['xotu, a] adj broken; (rasgado)
  torn
rotular [xotu'la'] vt to label; **rótulo**
  ['xɔtulu] m label
roubar [xo'ba'] vt to steal; (loja, casa,
  pessoa) to rob ▷ vi to steal; (em jogo, no
  preço) to cheat; **~ algo a alguém** to steal
  sth from sb; **roubo** ['xobu] m theft,
  robbery
rouco, -a ['xoku, a] adj hoarse
round ['xãwdʒi] (pl **~s**) m (Boxe) round
roupa ['xopa] f clothes pl, clothing; **~ de
  baixo** underwear; **~ de cama** bedclothes
  pl, bed linen
roupão [xo'pãw] (pl **-ões**) m dressing
  gown
rouxinol [xoʃi'nɔw] (pl **-óis**) m
  nightingale

roxo, -a ['xoʃu, a] *adj* purple, violet
royalty ['xɔjawtʃi] (*pl* -**ies**) *m* royalty
rua ['xua] *f* street; ~ **principal** main
  street; ~ **sem saída** no through road,
  cul-de-sac
rubéola [xu'bɛola] *f* (*Med*) German
  measles *sg*
rubi [xu'bi] *m* ruby
rubor [xu'boʳ] *m* blush; (*fig*) shyness,
  bashfulness; **ruborizar-se** [xubori'axsi]
  vr to blush
rubrica [xu'brika] *f* (signed) initials *pl*
rubro, -a ['xubru, a] *adj* (*faces*) rosy,
  ruddy
ruço, -a ['xusu, a] *adj* grey (*BRIT*), gray
  (*US*), dun; (*desbotado*) faded
ruela ['xwɛla] *f* lane, alley
ruga ['xuga] *f* (*na pele*) wrinkle; (*na roupa*)
  crease
ruge ['xuʒi] *m* rouge
rugido [xu'ʒidu] *m* roar
rugir [xu'ʒiʳ] *vi* to roar
ruído ['xwidu] *m* noise; **ruidoso, -a**
  [xwi'dozu, ɔza] *adj* noisy
ruim [xu'ĩ] (*pl* -**ns**) *adj* bad; (*defeituoso*)
  defective
ruína ['xwina] *f* ruin; (*decadência*)
  downfall
ruins [xu'ĩʃ] *pl de* **ruim**
ruir ['xwiʳ] *vi* to collapse, go to ruin
ruivo, -a ['xwivu, a] *adj* red-haired ▷ *m/f*
  redhead
rum [xũ] *m* rum
rumo ['xumu] *m* course, bearing; (*fig*)
  course; ~ **a** bound for; **sem** ~ adrift
rumor [xu'moʳ] *m* noise; (*notícia*) rumour
  (*BRIT*), rumor (*US*), report
ruptura [xup'tura] *f* break, rupture
rural [xu'raw] (*pl* -**ais**) *adj* rural
rush [xaʃ] *m* rush; (**a hora do**) ~ rush hour
Rússia ['xusja] *f*: **a** ~ Russia; **russo, -a**
  ['xusu, a] *adj, m/f* Russian ▷ *m* (*Ling*)
  Russian

S. *abr* (= *Santo/a ou São*) St
SA *abr* (= *Sociedade Anônima*) Ltd (*BRIT*),
  Inc. (*US*)
sã [sã] *f de* **são**
Saara [sa'ara] *m*: **o** ~ the Sahara
sábado ['sabadu] *m* Saturday
sabão [sa'bãw] (*pl* -**ões**) *m* soap
sabedoria [sabedo'ria] *f* wisdom;
  (*erudição*) learning
saber [sa'beʳ] *vt, vi* to know; (*descobrir*) to
  find out ▷ *m* knowledge; **a** ~ namely; ~
  fazer to know how to do, be able to do;
  que eu saiba as far as I know
sabiá [sa'bja] *m/f* thrush
sabido, -a [sa'bidu, a] *adj*
  knowledgeable; (*esperto*) shrewd
sabões [sa'bõjʃ] *mpl de* **sabão**
sabonete [sabo'netʃi] *m* toilet soap
sabor [sa'boʳ] *m* taste, flavour (*BRIT*),
  flavor (*US*); **saborear** [sabo'rjaʳ] *vt*
  to taste, savour (*BRIT*), savor (*US*);
  saboroso, -a [sabo'rozu, ɔza] *adj* tasty,
  delicious
sabotagem [sabo'taʒẽ] *f* sabotage
sabotar [sabo'taʳ] *vt* to sabotage
saca ['saka] *f* sack
sacar [sa'kaʳ] *vt* to take out; (*dinheiro*)
  to withdraw; (*arma, cheque*) to draw;

(*Esporte*) to serve; (*col: entender*) to understand ▷ *vi* (*col: entender*) to understand; **~ sobre um devedor** to borrow money from sb

saca-rolhas *m inv* corkscrew

sacerdote [sasex'dɔtʃi] *m* priest

saciar [sa'sjaʳ] *vt* (*fome, curiosidade*) to satisfy; (*sede*) to quench

saco ['saku] *m* bag; (*enseada*) inlet; **~ de café** coffee filter; **~ de dormir** sleeping bag

sacode *etc* [sa'kɔdʒi] *vb ver* **sacudir**

sacola [sa'kɔla] *f* bag

sacramento [sakra'mẽtu] *m* sacrament

sacrificar [sakrifi'kaʳ] *vt* to sacrifice; **sacrifício** [sakri'fisju] *m* sacrifice

sacrilégio [sakri'lɛʒju] *m* sacrilege

sacro, -a ['sakru, a] *adj* sacred

sacudida [saku'dʒida] *f* shake

sacudir [saku'dʒiʳ] *vt* to shake; **~-se** *vr* to shake

sádico, -a ['sadʒiku, a] *adj* sadistic

sadio, -a [sa'dʒiu, a] *adj* healthy

safado, -a [sa'fadu, a] *adj* shameless; (*imoral*) dirty; (*travesso*) mischievous ▷ *m* rogue

safira [sa'fira] *f* sapphire

safra ['safra] *f* harvest

Sagitário [saʒi'tarju] *m* Sagittarius

sagrado, -a [sa'gradu, a] *adj* sacred, holy

saia ['saja] *f* skirt

saiba *etc* ['sajba] *vb ver* **saber**

saída [sa'ida] *f* exit, way out; (*partida*) departure; (*ato: de pessoa*) going out; (*fig: solução*) way out; (*Comput: de programa*) exit; (: *de dados*) output; **~ de emergência** emergency exit

sair [sa'iʳ] *vi* to go (*ou* come) out; (*partir*) to leave; (*realizar-se*) to turn out; (*Comput*) to exit; **~-se** *vr*: **~-se bem/mal de** to be successful/unsuccessful in

sal [saw] (*pl* **sais**) *m* salt; **sem ~** (*comida*) salt-free; (*pessoa*) lacklustre (*BRIT*), lackluster (*US*)

sala ['sala] *f* room; (*num edifício público*) hall; (*classe, turma*) class; **~ (de aula)** classroom; (*Internet*) chatroom; **~ de bate-papo** (*Internet*) chatroom; **~ de espera/(de estar)/de jantar** waiting/living/dining room; **~ de operação** (*Med*) operating theatre (*BRIT*) *ou* theater (*US*)

salada [sa'lada] *f* salad; (*fig*) confusion, jumble

sala-e-quarto (*pl* **~s** *or* **salas-e-quarto**) *m* two-room flat (*BRIT*) *ou* apartment (*US*)

salão [sa'lãw] (*pl* **-ões**) *m* large room,

hall; (*exposição*) show; **~ de beleza** beauty salon

salário [sa'larju] *m* wages *pl*, salary

saldo ['sawdu] *m* balance; (*sobra*) surplus

saleiro [sa'lejru] *m* salt cellar

salgadinho [sawga'dʒiɲu] *m* savoury (*BRIT*), savory (*US*), snack

salgado, -a [saw'gadu, a] *adj* salty, salted

salgueiro [saw'gejru] *m* willow; **~ chorão** weeping willow

salientar [saljẽ'taʳ] *vt* to point out; (*acentuar*) to stress, emphasize; **saliente** [sa'ljẽtʃi] *adj* prominent; (*evidente*) clear, conspicuous; (*importante*) outstanding; (*assanhado*) forward

saliva [sa'liva] *f* saliva

salmão [saw'mãw] (*pl* **-ões**) *m* salmon

salmoura [saw'mora] *f* brine

salões [sa'lõjʃ] *mpl de* **salão**

salsa ['sawsa] *f* parsley

salsicha [saw'sifa] *f* sausage; **salsichão** [sawsi'fãw] (*pl* **-ões**) *m* sausage

saltar [saw'taʳ] *vt* to jump (over), leap (over); (*omitir*) to skip ▷ *vi* to jump, leap; (*sangue*) to spurt out; (*de ônibus, cavalo*): **~ de** to get off

salto ['sawtu] *m* jump, leap; (*de calçado*) heel; **~ de vara/em altura/em distância** pole vault/high jump/long jump

salubre [sa'lubri] *adj* healthy, salubrious

salvamento [sawva'mẽtu] *m* rescue; (*de naufrágio*) salvage

salvar [saw'vaʳ] *vt* to save; (*resgatar*) to rescue; (*objetos, de ruína*) to salvage; (*honra*) to defend; **~-se** *vr* to escape

salva-vidas *m inv* (*bóia*) lifebuoy ▷ *m/f inv* (*pessoa*) lifeguard; **barco ~** lifeboat

salvo, -a ['sawvu, a] *adj* safe ▷ *prep* except, save; **a ~** in safety

samba ['sãba] *m* samba; *see boxed note*

🔵 SAMBA

- The greatest form of musical expression of the Brazilian people, the **samba** is a type of music and dance of African origin. It embraces a number of rhythmic styles, such as *samba de breque*, *samba-enredo*, *samba-canção* and *pagode*, among others. Officially, the first samba, entitled *Pelo telefone*, was written in Rio in 1917.

---

sanar [sa'naʳ] *vt* to cure; (*remediar*) to

remedy

sanção [sã'sãw] (pl **-ões**) f sanction; **sancionar** [sãsjo'na^r] vt to sanction

sandália [sã'dalja] f sandal

sandes ['sãdəʃ] (PT) f inv sandwich

sanduíche [sand'wiʃi] (BR) m sandwich

saneamento [sanja'mẽtu] m sanitation

sanear [sa'nja^r] vt to clean up

sangrar [sã'gra^r] vt, vi to bleed; **sangrento, -a** [sã'grẽtu, a] adj bloody; (Culin: carne) rare

sangue ['sãgi] m blood

sanguinário, -a [sãgi'narju, a] adj bloodthirsty

sanguíneo, -a [sã'ginju, a] adj: **grupo ~** blood group; **pressão sanguínea** blood pressure; **vaso ~** blood vessel

sanidade [sani'dadʒi] f (saúde) health; (mental) sanity

sanita [sa'nita] (PT) f toilet, lavatory

sanitário, -a [sani'tarju, a] adj sanitary; **vaso ~** toilet, lavatory (bowl); **sanitários** [sani'tarjuʃ] mpl toilets

santo, -a ['sãtu, a] adj holy ▷ m/f saint

santuário [sã'twarju] m shrine, sanctuary

São [sãw] m Saint

são, sã [sãw, sã] (pl **~s/-s**) adj healthy; (conselho) sound; (mentalmente) sane; **~ e salvo** safe and sound

São Paulo [-'pawlu] n São Paulo

sapataria [sapata'ria] f shoe shop

sapateiro [sapa'tejru] m shoemaker; (vendedor) shoe salesman; (que conserta) shoe repairer; (loja) shoe repairer's

sapatilha [sapa'tʃiʎa] f (de balé) shoe; (sapato) pump; (de atleta) running shoe

sapato [sa'patu] m shoe

sapo [sa'pu] m toad

saque¹ [saki] m (de dinheiro) withdrawal; (Com) draft, bill; (Esporte) serve; (pilhagem) plunder, pillage; **~ a descoberto** (Com) overdraft

saque² etc vb ver **sacar**

saquear [sa'kja^r] vt to pillage, plunder

sarampo [sa'rãpu] m measles sg

sarar [sa'ra^r] vt to cure; (ferida) to heal ▷ vi to recover

sarcasmo [sax'kaʒmu] m sarcasm

sarda ['saxda] f freckle

Sardenha [sax'dɛɲa] f: **a ~** Sardinia

sardinha [sax'dʒiɲa] f sardine

sargento [sax'ʒẽtu] m sergeant

sarjeta [sax'ʒeta] f gutter

Satã [sa'tã] m Satan

Satanás [sata'naʃ] m Satan

satélite [sa'tɛlitʃi] m satellite

sátira ['satʃira] f satire

satisfazer [satʃiʃfa'ze^r] (irreg: como **fazer**) vt to satisfy ▷ vi to be satisfactory; **~-se** vr to be satisfied; (saciar-se) to fill o.s. up; **~ a** to satisfy; **satisfeito, -a** [satʃiʃ'fejtu, a] adj satisfied; (saciado) full; **dar-se por satisfeito com algo** to be content with sth

saudação [sawda'sãw] (pl **-ões**) f greeting

saudade [saw'dadʒi] f longing, yearning; (lembrança nostálgica) nostalgia; **deixar ~s** to be greatly missed; **ter ~(s) de** (desejar) to long for; (sentir falta de) to miss; **~(s) de casa, ~(s) da pátria** homesickness sg

saudar [saw'da^r] vt to greet; (dar as boas vindas) to welcome; (aclamar) to acclaim

saudável [saw'davew] (pl **-eis**) adj healthy; (moralmente) wholesome

saúde [sa'udʒi] f health; (brinde) toast; **~!** (brindando) cheers!; (quando se espirra) bless you!; **beber à ~ de** to drink to, toast; **estar bem/mal de ~** to be well/ill

saudosismo [sawdo'ziʒmu] m nostalgia

saudoso, -a [saw'dozu, ɔza] adj (nostálgico) nostalgic; (da família ou terra natal) homesick; (de uma pessoa) longing; (que causa saudades) much-missed

sauna ['sawna] f sauna

saxofone [sakso'fɔni] m saxophone

sazonal [sazo'naw] (pl **-ais**) adj seasonal

scanner ['skane^r] m scanner

🔵 **PALAVRA CHAVE**

se [si] pron **1** (reflexivo: impess) oneself; (: m) himself; (: f) herself; (: coisa) itself; (: você) yourself; (: pl) themselves; (: vocês) yourselves; **ela está se vestindo** she's getting dressed; (usos léxicos del pron) o vb em questão p. ex. **arrepender-se**
2 (uso recíproco) each other, one another; **olharam-se** they looked at each other
3 (impess): **come-se bem aqui** you can eat well here; **sabe-se que ...** it is known that ...; **vende(m)-se jornais naquela loja** they sell newspapers in that shop ▷ conj if; (em pergunta indireta) whether; **se bem que** even though

sê [se] vb ver **ser**

sebe ['sɛbi] (PT) f fence; **~ viva** hedge

sebo ['sebu] *m* tallow; **seboso, -a** [se'bozu, ɔza] *adj* greasy; (*sujo*) dirty

seca ['seka] *f* drought

secador [seka'do^r] *m*: **~ de cabelo/roupa** hairdryer/clothes horse

seção [se'sãw] (*pl* **-ões**) *f* section; (*em loja, repartição*) department

secar [se'ka^r] *vt* to dry; (*planta*) to parch ▷ *vi* to dry; to wither; (*fonte*) to dry up

secção [sek'sãw] (*PT*) = **seção**

seco, -a ['seku, a] *adj* dry; (*ríspido*) curt, brusque; (*magro*) thin; (*pessoa: frio*) cold; (: *sério*) serious

seções [se'sõjʃ] *fpl de* **seção**

secretaria [sekreta'ria] *f* general office; (*de secretário*) secretary's office; (*ministério*) ministry

secretária [sekre'tarja] *f* writing desk; **~ eletrônica** (*telephone*) answering machine; *ver tb* **secretário**

secretário, -a [sekre'tarju, a] *m/f* secretary; **S~ de Estado de ...** Secretary of State for ...

sector [sek'to^r] (*PT*) *m* = **setor**

século ['sɛkulu] *m* century; (*época*) age

secundário, -a [seku'darju, a] *adj* secondary

seda ['seda] *f* silk

sedativo [seda'tʃivu] *m* sedative

sede¹ ['sɛdʒi] *f* (*de empresa, instituição*) headquarters *sg*; (*de governo*) seat; (*Rel*) see, diocese

sede² ['sedʒi] *f* thirst; **estar com** *ou* **ter ~** to be thirsty; **sedento, -a** [se'dẽtu, a] *adj* thirsty

sediar [se'dʒja^r] *vt* to base

sedução [sedu'sãw] (*pl* **-ões**) *f* seduction

sedutor, a [sedu'to^r, a] *adj* seductive; (*oferta etc*) tempting

seduzir [sedu'zi^r] *vt* to seduce; (*fascinar*) to fascinate

segmento [seg'mẽtu] *m* segment

segredo [se'gredu] *m* secret; (*sigilo*) secrecy; (*de fechadura*) combination

segregar [segre'ga^r] *vt* to segregate

seguidamente [segida'mẽtʃi] *adv* (*sem parar*) continuously; (*logo depois*) soon afterwards

seguido, -a [se'gidu, a] *adj* following; (*contínuo*) continuous, consecutive; **~ de** *ou* **por** followed by; **três dias ~s** three days running; **horas seguidas** for hours on end; **em seguida** next; (*logo depois*) soon afterwards; (*imediatamente*) immediately, right away

seguimento [segi'mẽtu] *m* continuation; **dar ~ a** to proceed with; **em ~ de** after

seguinte [se'gĩtʃi] *adj* following, next; **eu lhe disse o ~** this is what I said to him

seguir [se'gi^r] *vt* to follow; (*continuar*) to continue ▷ *vi* to follow; to continue, carry on; (*ir*) to go; **~-se** *vr*: **~-se (a)** to follow; **logo a ~** next; **~-se (de)** to result (from)

segunda [se'gũda] *f* (*tb*: **~-feira**) Monday; (*Auto*) second (gear); **de ~** second-rate; **segunda-feira** (*pl* **segundas-feiras**) *f* Monday

segundo, -a [se'gũdu, a] *adj* second ▷ *prep* according to ▷ *conj* as, from what ▷ *adv* secondly ▷ *m* second; **de segunda mão** second-hand; **de segunda (classe)** second-class; **~ ele disse** according to what he said; **~ dizem** apparently; **~ me consta** as far as I know; **segundas intenções** ulterior motives

seguramente [segura'mẽtʃi] *adv* certainly; (*muito provavelmente*) surely

segurança [segu'rãsa] *f* security; (*ausência de perigo*) safety; (*confiança*) confidence ▷ *m/f* security guard; **com ~** assuredly

segurar [segu'ra^r] *vt* to hold; (*amparar*) to hold up; (*Com: bens*) to insure ▷ *vi*: **~ em** to hold; **~-se** *vr*: **~-se em** to hold on to

seguro, -a [se'guru, a] *adj* safe; (*livre de risco, firme*) secure; (*certo*) certain, assured; (*confiável*) reliable; (*de si mesmo*) confident; (*tempo*) settled ▷ *adv* confidently ▷ *m* (*Com*) insurance; **estar ~ de/de que** to be sure of/that; **fazer ~** to take out an insurance policy; **~ contra acidentes/incêndio** accident/fire insurance; **seguro-saúde** (*pl* **seguros-saúde**) *m* health insurance

sei [sej] *vb ver* **saber**

seio ['seju] *m* breast, bosom; (*âmago*) heart; **~ paranasal** sinus

seis [sejʃ] *num* six

seita ['sejta] *f* sect

seixo ['sejʃu] *m* pebble

seja *etc* ['seʒa] *vb ver* **ser**

sela ['sɛla] *f* saddle

selar [se'la^r] *vt* (*carta*) to stamp; (*documento oficial, pacto*) to seal; (*cavalo*) to saddle

seleção [sele'sãw] (*PT* **-cç-**) (*pl* **-ões**) *f* selection; (*Esporte*) team

selecionar [selesjo'na^r] (PT **-cc-**) vt to select

seleções [sele'sõjʃ] fpl de **seleção**

seleto, -a [se'lɛtu, a] (PT **-ct-**) adj select

selim [se'lĩ] (pl **-ns**) m saddle

selo ['selu] m stamp; (carimbo, sinete) seal

selva ['sɛwva] f jungle

selvagem [sew'vaʒē] (pl **-ns**) adj wild; (feroz) fierce; (povo) savage; **selvageria** [sewvaʒe'ria] f savagery

sem [sē] prep without ▷ conj: ~ que eu peça without my asking; **estar/ficar ~ dinheiro/gasolina** to have no/have run out of money/petrol

semáforo [se'maforu] m (Auto) traffic lights pl; (Ferro) signal

semana [se'mana] f week; **semanal** [sema'naw] (pl **semanais**) adj weekly; **semanário** [sema'narju] m weekly (publication)

semear [se'mja^r] vt to sow; **semelhante** [seme'ʎãtʃi] adj similar; (tal) such ▷ m fellow creature

sêmen ['semē] m semen

semente [se'mētʃi] f seed

semestral [semeʃ'traw] (pl **-ais**) adj half-yearly, bi-annual

semestre [se'mɛʃtri] m six months; (Educ) semester

semi... [semi] prefixo semi..., half...; **semicírculo** [semi'sixkulu] m semicircle; **semifinal** [semi'finaw] (pl **semifinais**) f semi-final

seminário [semi'narju] m seminar; (Rel) seminary

sem-número m: **um ~ de coisas** loads of things

sempre ['sēpri] adv always; **você ~ vai?** (PT) are you still going?; **~ que** whenever; **como ~** as usual; **a comida/hora etc de ~** the usual food/time etc

sem-terra m/f inv landless labourer (BRIT) ou laborer (US)

sem-teto m/f inv: **os ~** the homeless

sem-vergonha adj inv shameless ▷ m/f inv (pessoa) rogue

senado [se'nadu] m senate; **senador, a** [sena'do^r, a] m/f senator

senão [se'nãw] (pl **-ões**) conj otherwise; (mas sim) but, but rather ▷ prep except ▷ m flaw, defect

senha ['sɛɲa] f sign; (palavra de passe) password; (de caixa automático) PIN number; (recibo) receipt; (passe) pass

senhor, a [se'ɲo^r, a] m (homem) man; (formal) gentleman; (homem idoso) elderly man; (Rel) lord; (dono) owner; (tratamento) Mr(.); (tratamento respeitoso) sir ▷ f (mulher) lady; (esposa) wife; (mulher idosa) elderly lady; (dona) owner; (tratamento) Mrs(.), Ms(.); (tratamento respeitoso) madam; **o ~/a ~a** (você) you; **nossa ~a!** (col) gosh; **sim, ~(a)!** yes indeed

senhorita [seɲo'rita] f young lady; (tratamento) Miss, Ms(.); **a ~** (você) you

senil [se'niw] (pl **-is**) adj senile

senões [se'nõjʃ] mpl de **senão**

sensação [sēsa'sãw] (pl **-ões**) f sensation; **sensacional** [sēsasjo'naw] (pl **-ais**) adj sensational

sensível [sē'sivew] (pl **-eis**) adj sensitive; (visível) noticeable; (considerável) considerable; (dolorido) tender

senso ['sēsu] m sense; (juízo) judgement

sensual [sē'swaw] (pl **-ais**) adj sensual

sentado, -a [sē'tadu, a] adj sitting

sentar [sē'ta^r] vt to seat ▷ vi to sit; **~-se** vr to sit down

sentença [sē'tēsa] f (Jur) sentence; **sentenciar** [sētē'sja^r] vt (julgar) to pass judgement on; (condenar por sentença) to sentence

sentido, -a [sē'tʃidu, a] adj (magoado) hurt; (choro, queixa) heartfelt ▷ m sense; (direção) direction; (atenção) attention; (aspecto) respect; **~!** (Mil) attention!; **em certo ~** in a sense; **(não) ter ~** (not) to be acceptable; **"~ único"** (PT: sinal) "one-way"

sentimental [sētʃimē'taw] (pl **-ais**) adj sentimental; **vida ~** love life

sentimento [sētʃi'mētu] m feeling; (senso) sense; **sentimentos** mpl (pêsames) condolences

sentinela [sētʃi'nɛla] f sentry, guard

sentir [sē'tʃi^r] vt to feel; (perceber, pressentir) to sense; (ser afetado por) to be affected by; (magoar-se) to be upset by ▷ vi to feel; (sofrer) to suffer; **~-se** vr to feel; (julgar-se) to consider o.s. (to be); **~ (a) falta de** to miss; **~ cheiro/gosto (de)** to smell/taste; **~ vontade de** to feel like; **sinto muito** I am very sorry

separação [separa'sãw] (pl **-ões**) f separation

separado, -a [sepa'radu, a] adj separate; **em ~** separately, apart

separar [sepa'ra^r] vt to separate; (dividir)

to divide; (*pôr de lado*) to put aside; **~-se** *vr* to separate; to be divided

sepultamento [sepuwta'mẽtu] *m* burial

sepultar [sepuw'ta^r] *vt* to bury; **sepultura** [sepuw'tura] *f* grave, tomb

seqüência [se'kwẽsja] *f* sequence

sequer [se'kɛ^r] *adv* at least; **(nem) ~** not even

seqüestrar [sekweʃ'tra^r] *vt* (*bens*) to seize, confiscate; (*raptar*) to kidnap; (*avião etc*) to hijack; **seqüestro** [se'kwɛʃtru] *m* seizure; abduction, kidnapping; hijack

PALAVRA CHAVE

ser [se^r] *vi* **1** (*descrição*) to be; **ela é médica/muito alta** she's a doctor/very tall; **é Ana** (*Tel*) Ana speaking *ou* here; **ela é de uma bondade incrível** she's incredibly kind; **ele está é danado** he's really angry; **ser de mentir/briga** to be the sort to lie/fight
2 (*horas, datas, números*): **é uma hora** it's one o'clock; **são seis e meia** it's half past six; **é dia 1º de junho** it's the first of June; **somos/são seis** there are six of us/them
3 (*origem, material*): **ser de** to be *ou* come from; (*feito de*) to be made of; (*pertencer*) to belong to; **sua família é da Bahia** his (*ou* her *etc*) family is from Bahia; **a mesa é de mármore** the table is made of marble; **é de Pedro** it's Pedro's, it belongs to Pedro
4 (*em orações passivas*): **já foi descoberto** it had already been discovered
5 (*locuções com subjun*): **ou seja** that is to say; **seja quem for** whoever it may be; **se eu fosse você** if I were you; **se não fosse você, ...** if it hadn't been for you ...
6 (*locuções*): **a não ser** except; **a não ser que** unless; **é** (*resposta afirmativa*) yes; **..., não é?** isn't it?, don't you? *etc*; **ah, é?** really?; **que foi?** (*o que aconteceu?*) what happened?; (*qual é o problema?*) what's the problem?; **será que ...?** I wonder if ...?
▷ *m* being; **seres** *mpl* (*criaturas*) creatures

sereia [se'reja] *f* mermaid

série ['sɛri] *f* series; (*seqüência*) sequence, succession; (*Educ*) grade; (*categoria*)

category; **fora de ~** out of order; (*fig*) extraordinary

seriedade [serje'dadʒi] *f* seriousness; (*honestidade*) honesty

seringa [se'rĩga] *f* syringe

sério, -a ['sɛrju, a] *adj* serious; (*honesto*) honest, decent; (*responsável*) responsible; (*confiável*) reliable; (*roupa*) sober ▷ *adv* seriously; **a ~** seriously; **~?** really?

sermão [sex'mãw] (*pl* **-ões**) *m* sermon; (*fig*) telling-off

serpente [sex'pẽtʃi] *f* snake

serra ['sɛxa] *f* (*montanhas*) mountain range; (*Tec*) saw

serralheiro, -a [sexa'ʎejru, a] *m/f* locksmith

serrano, -a [se'xanu, a] *adj* highland *atr* ▷ *m/f* highlander

serrar [se'xa^r] *vt* to saw

sertanejo, -a [sexta'neʒu, a] *adj* rustic, country ▷ *m/f* inhabitant of the sertão

sertão [sex'tãw] (*pl* **-ões**) *m* backwoods *pl*, bush (country)

servente [sex'vẽtʃi] *m/f* servant; (*operário*) labourer (BRIT), laborer (US)

serviçal [sexvi'saw] (*pl* **-ais**) *adj* obliging, helpful ▷ *m/f* servant; (*trabalhador*) wage earner

serviço [sex'visu] *m* service; (*de chá etc*) set; **estar de ~** to be on duty; **prestar ~** to help

servidor, a [sexvi'do^r, a] *m/f* servant; (*funcionário*) employee; **~ público** civil servant

servil [sex'viw] (*pl* **-is**) *adj* servile

servir [sex'vi^r] *vt* to serve ▷ *vi* to serve; (*ser útil*) to be useful; (*ajudar*) to help; (*roupa: caber*) to fit; **~-se** *vr*: **~-se (de)** (*comida, café*) to help o.s. (to); (*meios*): **~-se de** to use, make use of; **~ de** (*prover*) to supply with, provide with; **você está servido?** (*num bar*) are you all right for a drink?; **~ de algo** to serve as sth; **qualquer ônibus serve** any bus will do

servis [sex'viʃ] *adj pl de* **servil**

sessão [se'sãw] (*pl* **-ões**) *f* (*do parlamento etc*) session; (*reunião*) meeting; (*de cinema*) showing

sessenta [se'sẽta] *num* sixty

sessões [se'sõjʃ] *fpl de* **sessão**

sesta ['sɛʃta] *f* siesta, nap

seta ['sɛta] *f* arrow

sete ['sɛtʃi] *num* seven

setembro [se'tẽbru] (*PT* **S-**) *m*

September; **7 de setembro** see boxed note

setenta [se'tẽta] num seventy
sétimo, -a ['sɛtʃimu, a] num seventh
setor [se'toʳ] m sector
seu, sua [sew, 'sua] adj (dele) his; (dela)
her; (de coisa) its; (deles, delas) their; (de
você, vocês) your ▷ pron: **(o) ~/(a) sua** his;
hers; its; theirs; yours ▷ m (senhor) Mr(.)
severidade [severi'dadʒi] f severity
severo, -a [se'vɛru, a] adj severe
sexo ['sɛksu] m sex
sexta ['sɛʃta] f (tb: **~-feira**) Friday; **sexta-
feira** (pl **sextas-feiras**) f Friday; **Sexta-
feira Santa** Good Friday
sexto, -a ['sɛʃtu, a] num sixth
sexual [se'kswaw] (pl **-ais**) adj sexual;
(vida, ato) sex atr
sexy ['sɛksi] (pl **~s**) adj sexy
s.f.f. (PT) abr = **se faz favor**
short ['ʃɔxtʃi] m (pair of) shorts pl
si [si] pron oneself; (ele) himself; (ela)
herself; (coisa) itself; (PT: você) yourself,
you; (: vocês) yourselves; (eles, elas)
themselves
SIDA ['sida] (PT) abr f = **síndrome de
deficiência imunológica adquirida**;
a ~AIDS
siderúrgica [side'ruxʒika] f steel
industry
sigilo [si'ʒilu] m secrecy
sigla ['sigla] f acronym; (abreviação)
abbreviation
significado [signifi'kadu] m meaning
significar [signifi'kaʳ] vt to
mean, signify; **significativo, -a**
[signifika'tʃivu, a] adj significant
signo ['signu] m sign
sigo etc ['sigu] vb ver **seguir**
sílaba ['silaba] f syllable
silenciar [silẽ'sjaʳ] vt to silence

silêncio [si'lẽsju] m silence, quiet;
silencioso, -a [silẽ'sjozu, ɔza] adj silent,
quiet ▷ m (Auto) silencer (BRIT), muffler
(US)
silhueta [si'ʎweta] f silhouette
silvestre [siw'vɛʃtri] adj wild
sim [sĩ] adv yes; **creio que ~** I think so
símbolo ['sĩbolu] m symbol
simetria [sime'tria] f symmetry
similar [simi'laʳ] adj similar
simpatia [sĩpa'tʃia] f liking; (afeto)
affection; (afinidade, solidariedade)
sympathy; **simpatias** fpl (inclinações)
sympathies; **simpático, -a** [sĩ'patʃiku,
a] adj (pessoa, decoração etc) nice;
(lugar) pleasant, nice; (amável) kind;
simpatizante [sĩpatʃi'zãtʃi] adj
sympathetic ▷ m/f sympathizer;
simpatizar [sĩpatʃi'zaʳ] vi: **simpatizar
com** (pessoa) to like; (causa) to
sympathize with
simples ['sĩpliʃ] adj inv simple; (único)
single; (fácil) easy; (mero) mere; (ingênuo)
naïve ▷ adv simply; **simplicidade**
[sĩplisi'dadʒi] f simplicity; **simplificar**
[sĩplifi'kaʳ] vt to simplify
simular [simu'laʳ] vt to simulate
simultaneamente [simuwtanja'mẽtʃi]
adv simultaneously
simultâneo, -a [simuw'tanju, a] adj
simultaneous
sinagoga [sina'goga] f synagogue
sinal [si'naw] (pl **-ais**) m sign; (gesto,
Tel) signal; (na pele) mole; (: de nascença)
birthmark; (depósito) deposit; (tb: **~
de tráfego, ~ luminoso**) traffic light; **~
por ~** (por falar nisso) by the way; (aliás)
as a matter of fact; **~ de chamada**
(Tel) ringing tone; **~ de discar** (BR) ou
de marcar (PT) dialling tone (BRIT),
dial tone (US); **~ de ocupado** (BR)
ou **de impedido** (PT) engaged tone
(BRIT), busy signal (US); **sinalização**
[sinaliza'sãw] f (ato) signalling; (para
motoristas) traffic signs pl
sincero, -a [sĩ'sɛru, a] adj sincere
sindicalista [sĩdʒika'liʃta] m/f trade
unionist
sindicato [sĩdʒi'katu] m trade union;
(financeiro) syndicate
síndrome ['sĩdromi] f syndrome; **~ de
Down** Down's syndrome
sinfonia [sĩfo'nia] f symphony
singular [sĩgu'laʳ] adj singular;
(extraordinário) exceptional; (bizarro) odd,
peculiar

sino ['sinu] m bell
sintaxe [sĩ'tasi] f syntax
síntese ['sĩtezi] f synthesis; **sintético, -a** [sĩ'tɛtʃiku, a] adj synthetic; **sintetizar** [sĩtetʃi'zaʳ] vt to synthesize
sinto etc ['sĩtu] vb ver **sentir**
sintoma [sĩ'tɔma] m symptom
sinuca [si'nuka] f snooker
sinuoso, -a [si'nwozu, ɔza] adj (caminho) winding; (linha) wavy
siri [si'ri] m crab
sirvo etc ['sixvu] vb ver **servir**
sistema [siʃ'tema] m system; (método) method
site ['sajtʃi] m (na Internet) website
sítio ['sitʃju] m (Mil) siege; (propriedade rural) small farm; (PT: lugar) place
situação [sitwa'sãw] (pl -ões) f situation; (posição) position
situado, -a [si'twadu, a] adj situated
situar [si'twaʳ] vt to place, put; (edifício) to situate, locate; **--se** vr to position o.s.; (estar situado) to be situated
slogan [iʃ'lɔgã] (pl -s) m slogan
SME abr m (= Sistema Monetário Europeu) ERM
smoking [iʒ'mokĩʃ] (pl -s) m dinner jacket (BRIT), tuxedo (US)
só [sɔ] adj alone; (único) single; (solitário) solitary ▷ adv only; **a sós** alone
soar [swaʳ] vi to sound ▷ vt (horas) to strike; (instrumento) to play; **~ a** to sound like; **~ bem/mal** (fig) to go down well/badly
sob [sob] prep under; **~ juramento** on oath; **~ medida** (roupa) made to measure
sobe etc ['sɔbi] vb ver **subir**
soberano, -a [sobe'ranu, a] adj sovereign; (fig: supremo) supreme ▷ m/f sovereign
sobra ['sɔbra] f surplus, remnant; **sobras** fpl (restos) remains; (de tecido) remnants; (de comida) leftovers; **ter algo de ~** to have sth extra; (tempo, comida, motivos) to have plenty of sth; **ficar de ~** to be left over
sobrado [so'bradu] m (andar) floor; (casa) house (of two or more storeys)
sobrancelha [sobrã'seʎa] f eyebrow
sobrar [so'braʳ] vi to be left; (dúvidas) to remain
sobre ['sobri] prep on; (por cima de) over; (acima de) above; (a respeito de) about
sobrecarregar [sobrikaxe'gaʳ] vt to overload
sobremesa [sobri'meza] f dessert

sobrenatural [sobrinatu'raw] (pl -ais) adj supernatural
sobrenome [sobri'nɔmi] (BR) m surname, family name
sobrepor [sobri'poʳ] (irreg: como **pôr**) vt: **~ algo a algo** to put sth on top of sth
sobressair [sobrisa'iʳ] vi to stand out; **--se** vr to stand out
sobressalente [sobrisa'lẽtʃi] adj, m spare
sobressalto [sobri'sawtu] m start; (temor) trepidation; **de ~** suddenly
sobretaxa [sobri'taʃa] f surcharge
sobretudo [sobri'tudu] m overcoat ▷ adv above all, especially
sobrevivência [sobrivi'vẽsja] f survival; **sobrevivente** [sobrivi'vẽtʃi] adj surviving ▷ m/f survivor
sobreviver [sobrivi'veʳ] vi: **~ (a)** to survive
sobrinho, -a [so'briɲu, a] m/f nephew/niece
sóbrio, -a ['sɔbrju, a] adj sober; (moderado) moderate, restrained
socar [so'kaʳ] vt to hit, strike; (calcar) to crush, pound; (massa de pão) to knead
social [so'sjaw] (pl -ais) adj social; **socialista** [sosja'liʃta] adj, m/f socialist
sociedade [sosje'dadʒi] f society; (Com: empresa) company; (associação) association; **~ anônima** limited company (BRIT), incorporated company (US)
sócio, -a ['sɔsju, a] m/f (Com) partner; (de clube) member
soco ['soku] m punch; **dar um ~ em** to punch
socorrer [soko'xeʳ] vt to help, assist; (salvar) to rescue; **--se** vr: **--se de** to resort to, have recourse to; **socorro** [so'koxu] m help, assistance; (reboque) breakdown (BRIT) ou tow (US) truck; **socorro!** help!; **primeiros socorros** first aid sg
soda ['sɔda] f soda (water)
sofá [so'fa] m sofa, settee; **sofá-cama** (pl **sofás-camas**) m sofa-bed
sofisticado, -a [sofiʃtʃi'kadu, a] adj sophisticated; (afetado) pretentious
sofrer [so'freʳ] vt to suffer; (acidente) to have; (agüentar) to bear, put up with; (experimentar) to undergo ▷ vi to suffer; **sofrido, -a** [so'fridu, a] adj long-suffering; **sofrimento** [sofri'mẽtu] m suffering
software [sof'tweʳ] m (Comput) software

sogro, -a ['sogru, 'sɔgra] *m/f* father-in-law/mother-in-law

sóis [sɔjʃ] *mpl de* **sol**

soja ['sɔʒa] *f* soya (BRIT), soy (US)

sol [sɔw] (*pl* **sóis**) *m* sun; (*luz*) sunshine, sunlight; **fazer ~** to be sunny; **tomar ~** to sunbathe

sola ['sɔla] *f* sole

solar [sola^r] *adj* solar; **energia/painel ~** solar energy/panel

soldado [sow'dadu] *m* soldier

soleira [so'lejra] *f* doorstep

solene [so'lɛni] *adj* solemn; **solenidade** [soleni'dadʒi] *f* solemnity; (*cerimônia*) ceremony

soletrar [sole'tra^r] *vt* to spell

solicitar [solisi'ta^r] *vt* to ask for; (*emprego etc*) to apply for; (*amizade, atenção*) to seek; **~ algo a alguém** to ask sb for sth

solícito, -a [so'lisitu, a] *adj* helpful

solidão [soli'dãw] *f* solitude; (*sensação*) loneliness

solidariedade [solidarje'dadʒi] *f* solidarity

solidário, -a [soli'darju, a] *adj*: **ser ~ a** *ou* **com** (*pessoa*) to stand by; (*causa*) to be sympathetic to, sympathize with

sólido, -a ['sɔlidu, a] *adj* solid

solitário, -a [soli'tarju, a] *adj* lonely; (*isolado*) solitary ▷ *m* hermit

solo ['sɔlu] *m* ground, earth; (*Mús*) solo

soltar [sow'ta^r] *vt* to set free; (*desatar*) to loosen; (*largar*) to let go of; (*emitir*) to emit; (*grito*) to let out; (*cabelo*) to let down; (*freio*) to release; **~-se** *vr* to come loose; (*desinibir-se*) to let o.s. go

solteirão, -ona [sowtej'rãw, rɔna] (*pl* **solteirões/-s**) *adj* unmarried, single ▷ *m/f* confirmed bachelor/spinster

solteiro, -a [sow'tejru, a] *adj* unmarried, single ▷ *m/f* bachelor/single woman

solteirões [sowtej'rõjʃ] *mpl de* **solteirão**

solteirona [sowtej'rɔna] *f de* **solteirão**

solto, -a ['sowtu, a] *pp de* **soltar** ▷ *adj* loose; (*livre*) free; (*sozinho*) alone

solução [solu'sãw] (*pl* **-ões**) *f* solution

soluçar [solu'sa^r] *vi* (*chorar*) to sob; (*Med*) to hiccup

solucionar [solusjo'na^r] *vt* to solve; (*decidir*) to resolve

soluço [so'lusu] *m* sob; (*Med*) hiccup

soluções [solu'sõjʃ] *fpl de* **solução**

som [sõ] (*pl* **-ns**) *m* sound; **~ cd** compact disc player

soma ['sɔma] *f* sum; **somar** [so'ma^r] *vt* (*adicionar*) to add (up); (*chegar a*) to add

up to, amount to ▷ *vi* to add up

sombra ['sõbra] *f* shadow; (*proteção*) shade; (*indício*) trace, sign

sombrinha [sõ'brina] *f* parasol, sunshade

some *etc* ['sɔmi] *vb ver* **sumir**

somente [sɔ'mẽtʃi] *adv* only

somos ['sõmuʃ] *vb ver* **ser**

sonâmbulo, -a [so'nãbulu, a] *m/f* sleepwalker

sondar [sõ'da^r] *vt* to probe; (*opinião etc*) to sound out

soneca [so'nɛka] *f* nap, snooze

sonegar [sone'ga^r] *vt* (*dinheiro, valores*) to conceal, withhold; (*furtar*) to steal, pilfer; (*impostos*) to dodge, evade; (*informações, dados*) to withhold

soneto [so'netu] *m* sonnet

sonhar [so'na^r] *vt, vi* to dream; **~ com** to dream about; **sonho** ['sɔnu] *m* dream; (*Culin*) doughnut

sono ['sɔnu] *m* sleep; **estar com** *ou* **ter ~** to be sleepy

sonolento, -a [sono'lẽtu, a] *adj* sleepy, drowsy

sonoro, -a [so'nɔru, a] *adj* resonant

sons [sõʃ] *mpl de* **som**

sonso, -a ['sõsu, a] *adj* sly, artful

sopa ['sɔpa] *f* soup

soporífero [sopo'riferu], **soporífico** [sopo'rifiku] *m* sleeping drug

soprar [so'pra^r] *vt* to blow; (*balão*) to blow up; (*vela*) to blow out; (*dizer em voz baixa*) to whisper ▷ *vi* to blow; **sopro** ['sopru] *m* blow, puff; (*de vento*) gust

sórdido, -a ['sɔxdʒidu, a] *adj* sordid; (*imundo*) squalid

soro ['soru] *m* (*Med*) serum

sorridente [soxi'dẽtʃi] *adj* smiling

sorrir [so'xi^r] *vi* to smile; **sorriso** [so'xizu] *m* smile

sorte ['sɔxtʃi] *f* luck; (*casualidade*) chance; (*destino*) fate, destiny; (*condição*) lot; (*espécie*) sort, kind; **de ~ que** so that; **dar ~** (*trazer sorte*) to bring good luck; (*ter sorte*) to be lucky; **estar com** *ou* **ter ~** to be lucky

sortear [sox'tʃia^r] *vt* to draw lots for; (*rifar*) to raffle; (*Mil*) to draft; **sorteio** [sox'teju] *m* draw; raffle; draft

sortido, -a [sox'tʃidu, a] *adj* (*abastecido*) supplied, stocked; (*variado*) assorted; (*loja*) well-stocked

sortudo, -a [sox'tudu, a] (*col*) *adj* lucky

sorvete [sox'vetʃi] (BR) *m* ice cream

SOS *abr* SOS

sossegado, -a [sose'gadu, a] *adj* peaceful, calm

sossegar [sose'gaʳ] *vt* to calm, quieten ▷ *vi* to quieten down

sossego [so'segu] *m* peace (and quiet)

sótão ['sɔtãw] (*pl* **-s**) *m* attic, loft

sotaque [so'taki] *m* accent

soterrar [sote'xaʳ] *vt* to bury

sou [so] *vb ver* **ser**

soube *etc* ['sobi] *vb ver* **saber**

soutien [su'tʃjã] (*PT*) *m* = **sutiã**

sova ['sɔva] *f* beating, thrashing

sovaco [so'vaku] *m* armpit

sovina [so'vina] *adj* mean, stingy ▷ *m/f* miser

sozinho, -a [sɔ'ziɲu, a] *adj* (all) alone, by oneself; (*por si mesmo*) by oneself

spam [iʃpã] (*pl* **-s**) *m* (*Comput*) spam

squash [iʃ'kweʃ] *m* squash

Sr. *abr* (= *senhor*) Mr(.)

Sr.ª *abr* (= *senhora*) Mrs(.)

Sr.ta *abr* (= *senhorita*) Miss

sua ['sua] *f de* **seu**

suar [swaʳ] *vt, vi* to sweat

suave ['swavi] *adj* gentle; (*música, voz*) soft; (*sabor, vinho*) smooth; (*cheiro*) delicate; (*dor*) mild; (*trabalho*) light; **suavidade** [suavi'dadʒi] *f* gentleness; softness

subalterno, -a [subaw'tɛxnu, a] *adj, m/f* subordinate

subconsciente [subkõ'sjẽtʃi] *adj, m* subconscious

subdesenvolvido, -a [subdʒizẽvow'vidu, a] *adj* underdeveloped

subentender [subẽtẽ'deʳ] *vt* to understand, assume; **subentendido, -a** [subẽtẽ'dʒidu, a] *adj* implied ▷ *m* implication

subestimar [subeʃtʃi'maʳ] *vt* to underestimate

subida [su'bida] *f* ascent, climb; (*ladeira*) slope; (*de preços*) rise

subir [su'biʳ] *vi* to go up; (*preço, de posto etc*) to rise ▷ *vt* to raise; (*ladeira, escada, rio*) to climb, go up; **~ em** to climb, go up; (*cadeira, palanque*) to climb onto, get up onto; (*ônibus*) to get on

súbito, -a ['subitu, a] *adj* sudden ▷ *adv* (*tb*: **de ~**) suddenly

subjetivo, -a [subʒe'tʃivu, a] (*PT* **-ct-**) *adj* subjective

subjuntivo, -a [subʒũ'tʃivu, a] *adj* subjunctive ▷ *m* subjunctive

sublime [su'blimi] *adj* sublime

sublinhar [subli'ɲaʳ] *vt* to underline; (*destacar*) to emphasize, stress

submarino, -a [subma'rinu, a] *adj* underwater ▷ *m* submarine

submeter [subme'teʳ] *vt* to subdue; (*plano*) to submit; (*sujeitar*): **~ a** to subject to; **~-se** *vr*: **~-se a** to submit to; (*operação*) to undergo

submisso, -a [sub'misu, a] *adj* submissive

subnutrição [subnutri'sãw] *f* malnutrition

subornar [subox'naʳ] *vt* to bribe; **suborno** [su'boxnu] *m* bribery

subseqüente [subse'kwẽtʃi] *adj* subsequent

subserviente [subsex'vjẽtʃi] *adj* obsequious, servile

subsidiária [subsi'dʒjarja] *f* (*Com*) subsidiary (company)

subsidiário, -a [subsi'dʒjarju, a] *adj* subsidiary

subsídio [sub'sidʒu] *m* subsidy; (*ajuda*) aid

subsistência [subsiʃ'tẽsja] *f* subsistence

subsistir [subsiʃ'tʃiʳ] *vi* to exist; (*viver*) to subsist

subsolo [sub'sɔlu] *m* (*de prédio*) basement

substância [subʃ'tãsja] *f* substance; **substancial** [subʃtã'sjaw] (*pl* **-ais**) *adj* substantial

substantivo [subʃtã'tʃivu] *m* noun

substituir [subʃtʃi'twiʳ] *vt* to substitute

subtil *etc* [sub'tiw] (*PT*) = **sutil** *etc*

subtrair [subtra'iʳ] *vt* to steal; (*deduzir*) to subtract ▷ *vi* to subtract

subumano, -a [subu'manu, a] *adj* subhuman; (*desumano*) inhuman

suburbano, -a [subux'banu, a] *adj* suburban

subúrbio [su'buxbju] *m* suburb

subvenção [subvẽ'sãw] (*pl* **-ões**) *f* subsidy, grant

subversivo, -a [subvex'sivu, a] *adj, m/f* subversive

sucata [su'kata] *f* scrap metal

sucção [suk'sãw] *f* suction

suceder [suse'deʳ] *vi* to happen ▷ *vt* to succeed; **~ a** (*num cargo*) to succeed; (*seguir*) to follow

sucessão [suse'sãw] (*pl* **-ões**) *f* succession; **sucessivo, -a** [suse'sivu, a] *adj* successive

sucesso [su'sɛsu] *m* success; (*música, filme*) hit; **fazer** *ou* **ter ~** to be successful

sucinto, -a [su'sĩtu, a] *adj* succinct
suco ['suku] (BR) *m* juice
suculento, -a [suku'lẽtu, a] *adj* succulent
sucumbir [sukũ'bi\`] *vi* to succumb; (*morrer*) to die, perish
sucursal [sukux'saw] (*pl* **-ais**) *f* (Com) branch
Sudão [su'dãw] *m*: **o ~** (the) Sudan
sudeste [su'dɛʃtʃi] *m* south-east
súdito ['sudʒitu] *m* (*de rei etc*) subject
sudoeste [sud'wɛʃtʃi] *m* south-west
Suécia ['swɛsja] *f*: **a ~** Sweden; **sueco, -a** ['sweku, a] *adj* Swedish ▷ *m/f* Swede ▷ *m* (Ling) Swedish
suéter ['swete\`] (BR) *m ou f* sweater
suficiente [sufi'sjẽtʃi] *adj* sufficient, enough
sufixo [su'fiksu] *m* suffix
sufocar [sufo'ka\`] *vt, vi* to suffocate
sugar [su'ga\`] *vt* to suck
sugerir [suʒe'ri\`] *vt* to suggest
sugestão [suʒeʃ'tãw] (*pl* **-ões**) *f* suggestion; **dar uma ~** to make a suggestion; **sugestivo, -a** [suʒeʃ'tʃivu, a] *adj* suggestive
sugiro *etc* [su'ʒiru] *vb ver* **sugerir**
Suíça ['swisa] *f*: **a ~** Switzerland
suíças ['swisaʃ] *fpl* sideburns; *ver tb* **suíço**
suicida [swi'sida] *adj* suicidal ▷ *m/f* suicidal person; (*morto*) suicide; **suicidar-se** [swisi'daxsi] *vr* to commit suicide; **suicídio** [swi'sidʒju] *m* suicide
suíço, -a ['swisu, a] *adj, m/f* Swiss
suíte ['switʃi] *f* (Mús, *em hotel*) suite
sujar [su'ʒa\`] *vt* to dirty ▷ *vi* to make a mess; **~-se** *vr* to get dirty
sujeira [su'ʒejra] *f* dirt; (*estado*) dirtiness; (*col*) dirty trick
sujeito, -a [su'ʒejtu, a] *adj*: **~ a** subject to ▷ *m* (Ling) subject ▷ *m/f* man/woman
sujo, -a ['suʒu, a] *adj* dirty; (*fig*: *desonesto*) dishonest ▷ *m* dirt
sul [suw] *adj inv* south, southern ▷ *m*: **o ~** the south; **sul-africano, -a** *adj, m/f* South African; **sul-americano, -a** *adj, m/f* South American; **sulco** [suw'ku] *m* furrow
suma ['suma] *f*: **em ~** in short
sumário, -a [su'marju, a] *adj* (*breve*) brief, concise; (*Jur*) summary; (*biquíni*) skimpy ▷ *m* summary
sumiço [su'misu] *m* disappearance
sumir [su'mi\`] *vi* to disappear, vanish
sumo, -a ['sumu, a] *adj* (*importância*) extreme; (*qualidade*) supreme ▷ *m* (PT)

juice
sunga ['sũga] *f* swimming trunks *pl*
suor [swɔ\`] *m* sweat
super- [supe\`-] *prefixo* super-
superado, -a [supe'radu, a] *adj* (*idéias*) outmoded
superar [supe'ra\`] *vt* (*rival*) to surpass; (*inimigo, dificuldade*) to overcome; (*expectativa*) to exceed
superfície [supex'fisi] *f* surface; (*extensão*) area; (*fig*: *aparência*) appearance
supérfluo, -a [su'pexflwu, a] *adj* superfluous
superior [supe'rjo\`] *adj* superior; (*mais elevado*) higher; (*quantidade*) greater; (*mais acima*) upper ▷ *m* superior; **superioridade** [superjori'dadʒi] *f* superiority
superlotado, -a [supexlo'tadu, a] *adj* crowded; (*excessivamente cheio*) overcrowded
supermercado [supexmex'kadu] *m* supermarket
superpotência [supexpo'tẽsja] *f* superpower
superstição [supexʃtʃi'sãw] (*pl* **-ões**) *f* superstition; **supersticioso, -a** [supexʃtʃi'sjozu, ɔza] *adj* superstitious
supervisão [supexvi'zãw] *f* supervision; **supervisionar** [supexvizjo'na\`] *vt* to supervise; **supervisor, a** [supexvi'zo\`, a] *m/f* supervisor
suplemento [suple'mẽtu] *m* supplement
súplica ['suplika] *f* supplication, plea; **suplicar** [supli'ka\`] *vt, vi* to plead, beg
suplício [su'plisju] *m* torture
supor [su'po\`] (*irreg*: *como* **pôr**) *vt* to suppose; (*julgar*) to think
suportar [supox'ta\`] *vt* to hold up, support; (*tolerar*) to bear, tolerate; **suportável** [supox'tavew] (*pl* **-eis**) *adj* bearable; **suporte** [su'pɔxtʃi] *m* support
suposto, -a [su'poʃtu, 'pɔʃta] *adj* supposed ▷ *m* assumption, supposition
supremo, -a [su'premu, a] *adj* supreme
suprimir [supri'mi\`] *vt* to suppress
surdo, -a ['suxdu, a] *adj* deaf; (*som*) muffled, dull ▷ *m/f* deaf person; **surdo-mudo, surda-muda** *adj* deaf and dumb ▷ *m/f* deaf-mute
surfe ['suxfi] *m* surfing
surfista [sux'fiʃta] *m/f* surfer
surgir [sux'ʒi\`] *vi* to appear; (*problema, oportunidade*) to arise

surjo etc ['suxju] vb ver **surgir**

surpreendente [suxprjẽ'dẽtʃi] adj surprising

surpreender [suxprjẽ'de'] vt to surprise; **~-se** vr: **~-se (de)** to be surprised (at); **surpresa** [sux'preza] f surprise; **surpreso, -a** [sux'prezu, a] pp de **surpreender** ▷ adj surprised

surra ['suxa] f (ger, Esporte): **dar uma ~ em** to thrash; **levar uma ~ (de)** to get thrashed (by); **surrar** [su'xa'] vt to beat, thrash

surtir [sux'tʃi'] vt to produce, bring about

surto ['suxtu] m outbreak

suspeita [suʃ'pejta] f suspicion; **suspeitar** [suʃpej'ta'] vt to suspect ▷ vi: **suspeitar de algo** to suspect sth; **suspeito, -a** [suʃ'pejtu, a] adj, m/f suspect

suspender [suʃpẽ'de'] vt (levantar) to lift; (pendurar) to hang; (trabalho, funcionário etc) to suspend; (encomenda) to cancel; (sessão) to adjourn, defer; (viagem) to put off; **suspensão** [suʃpẽ'sãw] (pl **-ões**) f (ger, Auto) suspension; (de trabalho, pagamento) stoppage; (de viagem, sessão) deferment; (de encomenda) cancellation; **suspense** [suʃ'pẽsi] m suspense; **filme de suspense** thriller; **suspenso, -a** [suʃ'pẽsu, a] pp de **suspender**

suspensórios [suʃpẽ'sɔrjuʃ] mpl braces (BRIT), suspenders (US)

suspirar [suʃpi'ra'] vi to sigh; **suspiro** [suʃ'piru] m sigh; (doce) meringue

sussurrar [susu'xa'] vt, vi to whisper; **sussurro** [su'suxu] m whisper

sustentar [suʃtẽ'ta'] vt to sustain; (prédio) to hold up; (padrão) to maintain; (financeiramente, acusação) to support; **sustentável** [suʃtẽ'tavew] (pl **-eis**) adj sustainable; **sustento** [suʃ'tẽtu] m sustenance; (subsistência) livelihood; (amparo) support

susto ['suʃtu] m fright, scare

sutiã [su'tʃjã] m bra(ssiere)

sutil [su'tʃiw] (pl **-is**) adj subtle; **sutileza** [sutʃi'leza] f subtlety

ta [ta] = **te + a**

tabacaria [tabaka'ria] f tobacconist's (shop)

tabaco [ta'baku] m tobacco

tabela [ta'bɛla] f table, chart; (lista) list; **por ~** indirectly

taberna [ta'bɛxna] f tavern, bar

tablete [ta'blɛtʃi] m (de chocolate) bar

tabu [ta'bu] adj, m taboo

tábua ['tabwa] f plank, board; (Mat) table; **~ de passar roupa** ironing board

tabuleiro [tabu'lejru] m tray; (Xadrez) board

tabuleta [tabu'leta] f (letreiro) sign, signboard

taça ['tasa] f cup

tacha ['taʃa] f tack

tachinha [ta'ʃina] f drawing pin (BRIT), thumb tack (US)

taco ['taku] m (Bilhar) cue; (Golfe) club

táctico, -a etc ['tatiku, a] (PT) = **tático** etc

tacto ['tatu] (PT) m = **tato**

tagarela [taga'rɛla] adj talkative ▷ m/f chatterbox; **tagarelar** [tagare'la'] vi to chatter

Tailândia [taj'lãdʒja] f: **a ~** Thailand

tal [taw] (pl **tais**) adj such; **~ e coisa** this

and that; **um ~ de Sr. X** a certain Mr. X; **que ~?** what do you think?; (PT) how are things?; **que ~ um cafezinho?** what about a coffee?; **que ~ nós irmos ao cinema?** what about (us) going to the cinema?; **~ pai, ~ filho** like father, like son; **~ como** such as; (da maneira que) just as; **~ qual** just like; **o ~ professor** that teacher; **a ~ ponto** to such an extent; **de ~ maneira** in such a way; **e ~** and so on; **o/a ~** (col) the greatest; **o Pedro de ~** Peter what's-his-name; **na rua ~** in such and such a street; **foi um ~ de gente ligar lá para casa** there were people ringing home non-stop

talão [ta'lãw] (pl -ões) m (de recibo) stub; **~ de cheques** cheque book (BRIT), check book (US)

talco ['tawku] m talcum powder; **pó de ~** (PT) talcum powder

talento [ta'lẽtu] m talent; (aptidão) ability

talha ['taʎa] f carving; (vaso) pitcher; (Náut) tackle

talher [ta'ʎeʳ] m set of cutlery; **talheres** mpl cutlery sg

talo ['talu] m stalk, stem

talões [ta'lõjʃ] mpl de **talão**

talvez [taw'veʒ] adv perhaps, maybe

tamanco [ta'mãku] m clog, wooden shoe

tamanduá [tamã'dwa] m anteater

tamanho, -a [ta'maɲu, a] adj such (a) great ▷ m size

tâmara ['tamara] f date

também [tã'bẽj] adv also, too, as well; (além disso) besides; **~ não** not ... either, nor

tambor [tã'boʳ] m drum

tamborim [tãbo'rĩ] (pl -ns) m tambourine

Tâmisa ['tamiza] m: **o ~** the Thames

tampa ['tãpa] f lid; (de garrafa) cap

tampão [tã'pãw] (pl -ões) m tampon; (de olho) (eye) patch

tampar [tã'paʳ] vt (lata, garrafa) to put the lid on; (cobrir) to cover

tampinha [tã'piɲa] f lid, top

tampo ['tãpu] m lid

tampões [tã'põjʃ] mpl de **tampão**

tampouco [tã'poku] adv nor, neither

tangerina [tãʒe'rina] f tangerine

tanque ['tãki] m tank; (de lavar roupa) sink

tanto, -a ['tãtu, a] adj, pron (sg) so much; (: + interrogativa/negativa) as much; (pl) so many; (: + interrogativa/negativa) as many ▷ adv so much; **~ ... como ...** both ... and ...; **~ ... quanto ...** as much ... as ...; **~ tempo** so long; **quarenta e ~s anos** forty-odd years; **~ faz** it's all the same to me, I don't mind; **um ~ (quanto)** (como adv) rather, somewhat; **~ (assim) que** so much so that

tão [tãw] adv so; **~ rico quanto** as rich as; **tão-só** adv only

tapa ['tapa] m ou f slap

tapar [ta'paʳ] vt to cover; (garrafa) to cork; (caixa) to put the lid on; (orifício) to block up; (encobrir) to block out

tapear [ta'pjaʳ] vt, vi to cheat

tapeçaria [tapesa'ria] f tapestry

tapete [ta'petʃi] m carpet, rug

tardar [tax'daʳ] vi to delay; (chegar tarde) to be late ▷ vt to delay; **sem mais ~** without delay; **~ a ou em fazer** to take a long time to do; **o mais ~** at the latest

tarde ['taxdʒi] f afternoon ▷ adv late; **mais cedo ou mais ~** sooner or later; **antes ~ do que nunca** better late than never; **boa ~!** good afternoon!; **à ou de ~** in the afternoon

tardio, -a [tax'dʒiu, a] adj late

tarefa [ta'rɛfa] f task, job; (faina) chore

tarifa [ta'rifa] f tariff; (para transportes) fare; (lista de preços) price list; **~ alfandegária** customs duty

tartaruga [taxta'ruga] f turtle

tasca ['taʃka] (PT) f cheap eating place

tática ['tatʃika] f tactics pl

tático, -a ['tatʃiku, a] adj tactical

tato ['tatu] m touch; (fig: diplomacia) tact

tatu [ta'tu] m armadillo

tatuagem [ta'twaʒẽ] (pl -ns) f tattoo

taxa ['taʃa] f (imposto) tax; (preço) fee; (índice) rate; **~ de câmbio/juros** exchange/interest rate; **~ de taxação** [taʃa'sãw] f taxation; **taxar** [ta'ʃaʳ] vt (fixar o preço de) to fix the price of; (lançar impostos sobre) to tax

táxi ['taksi] m taxi

tchau [tʃaw] excl bye!

tcheco, -a ['tʃɛku, a] adj, m/f Czech

Tcheco-Eslováquia [tʃekuiʒlo'vakja] f = **Tchecoslováquia**

Tchecoslováquia [tʃekoʒlo'vakja] f: **a ~** Czechoslovakia

te [tʃi] pron you; (para você) (to) you

teatro ['tʃjatru] m theatre (BRIT), theater (US); (obras) plays pl, dramatic works pl; (gênero, curso) drama; **peça de ~** play

tecer [te'se^r] *vt, vi* to weave; **tecido** [te'sidu] *m* cloth, material; (*Anat*) tissue

tecla ['tɛkla] *f* key; **teclado** [tek'ladu] *m* keyboard

técnica ['tɛtknika] *f* technique; *vertb* **técnico**

técnico, -a ['tɛkniku, a] *adj* technical ▷ *m/f* technician; (*especialista*) expert

tecnologia [teknolo'ʒia] *f* technology; **tecnológico, -a** [tekno'lɔʒiku, a] *adj* technological

tecto ['tɛktu] (*PT*) *m* = **teto**

tédio ['tɛdʒju] *m* tedium, boredom; **tedioso, -a** [te'dʒjozu, ɔza] *adj* tedious, boring

teia ['teja] *f* web; **~ de aranha** cobweb

teimar [tej'ma^r] *vi* to insist, keep on; **~ em** to insist on

teimosia [tejmo'zia] *f* stubbornness; **~ em fazer** insistence on doing

teimoso, -a [tej'mozu, ɔza] *adj* obstinate; (*criança*) wilful (*BRIT*), willful (*US*)

Tejo ['teʒu] *m*: **o (rio) ~** the (river) Tagus

tela ['tɛla] *f* fabric, material; (*de pintar*) canvas; (*Cinema, TV*) screen

tele... ['tele] *prefixo* tele...; **telecomunicações** [telekomunika'sõjʃ] *fpl* telecommunications; **teleconferência** [telekõfe'rẽsja] *f* teleconference

teleférico [tele'feriku] *m* cable car

telefonar [telefo'na^r] *vi*: **~ para alguém** to (tele)phone sb

telefone [tele'foni] *m* phone, telephone; (*número*) (tele)phone number; (*telefonema*) phone call; **~ celular** cellphone, mobile phone; **~ de carro** carphone; **telefonema** [telefo'nɛma] *m* phone call; **dar um telefonema** to make a phone call; **telefônico, -a** [tele'foniku, a] *adj* telephone *atr*; **telefonista** [telefo'niʃta] *m/f* telephonist; (*na companhia telefônica*) operator

telegrama [tele'grama] *m* telegram, cable; **passar um ~** to send a telegram

telejornal [teleʒox'naw] (*pl* **telejornais**) *m* television news *sg*

telemóvel [tɛle'mɔvel] (*pl* **-eis**) *m* (*PT*) mobile (phone) (*BRIT*), cellphone (*US*); **telenovela** [teleno'vɛla] *f* (TV) soap opera; **telescópio** [tele'skɔpju] *m* telescope; **telespectador, a** [teleʃpekta'do^r, a] *m/f* viewer

televendas [tele'vẽdaʃ] *fpl* telesales

televisão [televi'zãw] *f* television;

~ por assinatura pay television; **~ a cabo** cable television; **~ a cores** colo(u)r television; **~ digital** digital television; **~ via satélite** satellite television; **aparelho de ~** television set; **televisionar** [televizjo'na^r] *vt* to televise; **televisivo, -a** [televi'zivu, a] *adj* television *atr*

televisor [televi'zo^r] *m* (*aparelho*) television (set), TV (set)

telha ['teʎa] *f* tile; (*col*: *cabeça*) head; **ter uma ~ de menos** to have a screw loose

telhado [te'ʎadu] *m* roof

tema ['tɛma] *m* theme; (*assunto*) subject; **temática** [te'matʃika] *f* theme

temer [te'me^r] *vt* to fear, be afraid of ▷ *vi* to be afraid

temeroso, -a [teme'rozu, ɔza] *adj* fearful, afraid; (*pavoroso*) dreadful

temido, -a [te'midu, a] *adj* fearsome, frightening

temível [te'mivew] (*pl* **-eis**) *adj* = **temido**

temor [te'mo^r] *m* fear

temperado, -a [tẽpe'radu, a] *adj* (*clima*) temperate; (*comida*) seasoned

temperamento [tẽpera'mẽtu] *m* temperament, nature

temperar [tẽpe'ra^r] *vt* to season

temperatura [tẽpera'tura] *f* temperature

tempero [tẽ'peru] *m* seasoning, flavouring (*BRIT*), flavoring (*US*)

tempestade [tẽpeʃ'tadʒi] *f* storm; **tempestuoso, -a** [tẽpeʃ'twozu, ɔza] *adj* stormy

templo ['tẽplu] *m* temple; (*igreja*) church

tempo ['tẽpu] *m* time; (*meteorológico*) weather; (*Ling*) tense; **o ~ todo** the whole time; **a ~** on time; **ao mesmo ~** at the same time; **a um ~** at once; **com ~** in good time; **de ~ em ~** from time to time; **nesse meio ~** in the meantime; **quanto ~?** how long?; **mais ~** longer; **há ~s** for ages; (*atrás*) ages ago; **~ livre** spare time; **primeiro/segundo ~** (*Esporte*) first/second half

temporada [tẽpo'rada] *f* season; (*tempo*) spell

temporal [tẽpo'raw] (*pl* **-ais**) *m* storm, gale

temporário, -a [tẽpo'rarju, a] *adj* temporary, provisional

tenacidade [tenasi'dadʒi] *f* tenacity

tencionar [tẽsjoˈnaʳ] vt to intend, plan
tenda [ˈtẽda] f tent
tendão [tẽˈdãw] (pl -ões) m tendon
tendões [tẽˈdõjʃ] mpl de **tendão**
tenebroso, -a [teneˈbrozu, ɔza] adj
dark, gloomy; (fig) horrible
tenho etc [ˈteɲu] vb ver **ter**
tênis [ˈteniʃ] m inv tennis; (sapatos)
training shoes pl; (um sapato) training
shoe; ~ **de mesa** table tennis; **tenista**
[teˈniʃta] m/f tennis player
tenor [teˈnoʳ] m (Mús) tenor
tenro, -a [ˈtẽxu, a] adj tender; (macio)
soft; (delicado) delicate; (novo) young
tensão [tẽˈsãw] f tension; (pressão)
pressure, strain; (rigidez) tightness; (Elet:
voltagem) voltage
tenso, -a [ˈtẽsu, a] adj tense; (sob pressão)
under stress, strained
tentação [tẽtaˈsãw] f temptation
tentáculo [tẽˈtakulu] m tentacle
tentar [tẽˈtaʳ] vt to try; (seduzir) to
tempt ▷ vi to try; **tentativa** [tẽtaˈtʃiva]
f attempt; **tentiva de homicídio/
suicídio/roubo** attempted murder/
suicide/robbery; **por tentativas** by trial
and error
tênue [ˈtenwi] adj tenuous; (fino)
thin; (delicado) delicate; (luz, voz) faint;
(pequeníssimo) minute
teor [teˈoʳ] m (conteúdo) tenor; (sentido)
meaning, drift
teoria [teoˈria] f theory; **teoricamente**
[teorikaˈmẽtʃi] adv theoretically, in
theory; **teórico, -a** [teˈɔriku, a] adj
theoretical ▷ m/f theoretician
tépido, -a [ˈtɛpidu, a] adj tepid

⬤ **PALAVRA CHAVE**

ter [teʳ] vt 1 (possuir, ger) to have; (na mão)
to hold; **você tem uma caneta?** have
you got a pen?; **ela vai ter neném** she is
going to have a baby
2 (idade, medidas, estado) to be; **ela tem
7 anos** she's 7 (years old); **a mesa tem
1 metro de comprimento** the table
is 1 metre long; **ter fome/sorte** to be
hungry/lucky; **ter frio/calor** to be
cold/hot
3 (conter) to hold, contain; **a caixa tem
um quilo de chocolates** the box holds
one kilo of chocolates
4: **ter que** ou **de fazer** to have to do
5: **ter a ver com** to have to do with
6: **ir ter com** to (go and) meet

▷ vb impess 1: **tem** (sg) there is; (pl) there
are; **tem 3 dias que não saio de casa** I
haven't been out for 3 days
2: **não tem de quê** don't mention it

terapeuta [teraˈpewta] m/f therapist
terapia [teraˈpia] f therapy
terça [ˈtexsa] f (tb: ~-feira) Tuesday;
terça-feira (pl **terças-feiras**) f Tuesday;
terça-feira gorda Shrove Tuesday
terceiro, -a [texˈsejru, a] num third;
terceiros mpl (os outros) outsiders
terço [ˈtexsu] m third (part)
termas [ˈtexmaʃ] fpl bathhouse sg
térmico, -a [ˈtexmiku, a] adj thermal;
garrafa térmica (Thermos®) flask
terminal [texmiˈnaw] (pl -**ais**) adj
terminal ▷ m (de rede, Elet, Comput)
terminal ▷ f terminal; ~ (**de vídeo**)
monitor, visual display unit
terminar [texmiˈnaʳ] vt to finish ▷ vi
(pessoa) to finish; (coisa) to end; ~ **de
fazer** to finish doing; (ter feito há pouco) to
have just done; ~ **por fazer algo** to end
up doing sth
término [ˈtexminu] m end, termination
termo [ˈtexmu] m term; (fim) end,
termination; (limite) limit, boundary;
(prazo) period; (PT: garrafa) (Thermos®)
flask; **meio** ~ compromise; **em ~s (de)** in
terms (of)
termômetro [texˈmometru] m
thermometer
terno, -a [ˈtexnu, a] adj gentle, tender
▷ m (BR: roupa) suit; **ternura** [texˈnura] f
gentleness, tenderness
terra [ˈtexa] f earth, world; (Agr,
propriedade) land; (pátria) country; (chão)
ground; (Geo) soil; (pó) dirt
terraço [teˈxasu] m terrace
terramoto [texaˈmɔtu] (PT) m
= **terremoto**
terreiro [teˈxejru] m yard, square
terremoto [texeˈmɔtu] m earthquake
terreno, -a [teˈxenu, a] m ground, land;
(porção de terra) plot of land ▷ adj earthly
térreo, -a [ˈtexju, a] adj: **andar** ~ (BR)
ground floor (BRIT), first floor (US)
terrestre [teˈxeʃtri] adj land atr
território [texiˈtɔrju] m territory
terrível [teˈxivew] (pl -**eis**) adj terrible,
dreadful
terror [teˈxoʳ] m terror, dread; **terrorista**
[texoˈriʃta] adj, m/f terrorist; **terrorista
suicida** suicide bomber
tese [ˈtɛzi] f proposition, theory; (Educ)

thesis; **em ~** in theory

teso, -a ['tezu, a] adj (cabo) taut; (rígido) stiff

tesouraria [tezora'ria] f treasury

tesouro [te'zoru] m treasure; (erário) treasury, exchequer; (livro) thesaurus

testa ['tɛʃta] f brow, forehead

testar [teʃ'taʳ] vt to test; (deixar em testamento) to bequeath

teste ['tɛʃtʃi] m test

testemunha [teʃte'muɲa] f witness; **testemunhar** [teʃtemu'ɲaʳ] vi to testify ▷ vt to give evidence about; (presenciar) to witness; (confirmar) to demonstrate; **testemunho** [teʃte'muɲu] m evidence

testículo [teʃ'tʃikulu] m testicle

teta ['teta] f teat, nipple

tétano ['tetanu] m tetanus

teto ['tɛtu] m ceiling; (telhado) roof; (habitação) home

teu, tua [tew, 'tua] adj your ▷ pron yours

teve ['tevi] vb ver **ter**

têxtil ['teʃtʃiw] (pl **-eis**) m textile

texto ['teʃtu] m text

textura [teʃ'tura] f texture

thriller ['srila'] (BR) (pl **-s**) m thriller

ti [tʃi] pron you

tia ['tʃia] f aunt

Tibete [tʃi'bɛtʃi] m: **o ~** Tibet

tido, -a [t'tʃidu, a] pp de **ter** ▷ adj: **~ como ou por** considered to be

tigela [tʃi'ʒela] f bowl

tigre ['tʃigri] m tiger

tijolo [tʃi'ʒolu] m brick

til [tʃiw] (pl **tis**) m tilde

timbre ['tʃibri] m insignia, emblem; (selo) stamp; (Mús) tone, timbre; (de voz) tone; (em papel de carta) heading

time ['tʃimi] (BR) m team; **de segundo ~** (fig) second-rate

tímido, -a ['tʃimidu, a] adj shy, timid

tímpano ['tʃipanu] m eardrum; (Mús) kettledrum

tingir [tʃi'ʒiʳ] vt to dye; (fig) to tinge

tinha etc ['tʃiɲa] vb ver **ter**

tinjo etc ['tʃiʒu] vb ver **tingir**

tinta ['tʃita] f (de pintar) paint; (de escrever) ink; (para tingir) dye; (fig: vestígio) shade, tinge

tinto, -a ['tʃitu, a] adj dyed; (fig) stained; **vinho ~** red wine

tintura [tʃi'tura] f dye; (ato) dyeing; (fig) tinge, hint

tinturaria [tʃitura'ria] f dry-cleaner's

tio ['tʃiu] m uncle

típico, -a ['tʃipiku, a] adj typical

tipo ['tʃipu] m type; (de imprensa) print; (de impressora) typeface; (col: sujeito) guy, chap; (pessoa) person

tipografia [tʃipogra'fia] f printing; (estabelecimento) printer's

tíquete ['tʃiketʃi] m ticket

tira ['tʃira] f strip ▷ m (BR: col) cop

tira-gosto (pl **-s**) m snack, savoury (BRIT); **tirano, -a** [tʃi'ranu, a] adj tyrannical ▷ m/f tyrant

tirar [tʃi'raʳ] vt to take away; (de dentro) to take out; (de cima) to take off; (roupa, sapatos) to take off; (arrancar) to pull out; (férias) to take, have; (boas notas) to get; (salário) to earn; (curso) to do, take; (mancha) to remove; (foto, cópia) to take; (mesa) to clear; **~ algo a alguém** to take sth from sb

tiritar [tʃiri'taʳ] vi to shiver

tiro ['tʃiru] m shot; (ato de disparar) shooting; **~ ao alvo** target practice; **trocar ~s** to fire at one another

tiroteio [tʃiro'teju] m shooting, exchange of shots

tis [tʃiʃ] mpl de **til**

titular [tʃitu'laʳ] adj titular ▷ m/f holder

título ['tʃitulu] m title; (Com) bond; (universitário) degree; **~ de propriedade** title deed

tive etc ['tʃivi] vb ver **ter**

to [tu] = **te + o**

toa ['toa] f towrope; **à ~** at random; (sem motivo) for no reason; (inutilmente) in vain, for nothing

toalete [twa'letʃi] m (banheiro) toilet; (traje) outfit ▷ f: **fazer a ~** to have a wash

toalha [to'aʎa] f towel

toca ['tɔka] f burrow, hole

toca-discos (BR) m inv record-player

tocador [toka'doʳ] m player; **~ MP3** MP3 player

toca-fitas m inv cassette player

tocaia [to'kaja] f ambush

tocante [to'kãtʃi] adj moving, touching; **no ~ a** regarding, concerning

tocar [to'kaʳ] vt to touch; (Mús) to play ▷ vi to touch; to play; (campainha, sino, telefone) to ring; **~-se** vr to touch (each other); **~ a** (dizer respeito a) to concern, affect; **~ em** to touch; (assunto) to touch upon; **~ para alguém** (telefonar) to ring sb (up), call sb (up); **pelo que me toca** as far as I am concerned

tocha ['tɔʃa] f torch

todavia [toda'via] *adv* yet, still, however

PALAVRA CHAVE

todo, a ['todu, 'tɔda] *adj* **1** (*com artigo sg*) all; **toda a carne** all the meat; **toda a noite** all night, the whole night; **todo o Brasil** the whole of Brazil; **a toda (velocidade)** at full speed; **todo o mundo** (BR), **toda a gente** (PT) everybody, everyone; **em toda (a) parte** everywhere

2 (*com artigo pl*) all; (: *cada*) every; **todos os livros** all the books; **todos os dias/todas as noites** every day/night; **todos os que querem sair** all those who want to leave; **todos nós** all of us ▷ *adv*: **ao todo** altogether; (*no total*) in all; **de todo** completely ▷ *pron*: **todos** *mpl* everybody *sg*, everyone *sg*

todo-poderoso, -a *adj* all-powerful ▷ *m*: **o T~** the Almighty
toicinho [toj'siɲu] *m* bacon fat
tolerância [tole'rãsja] *f* tolerance; **tolerante** [tole'rãtʃi] *adj* tolerant
tolerar [tole'ra'] *vt* to tolerate; **tolerável** [tole'ravew] (*pl -eis*) *adj* tolerable, bearable; (*satisfatório*) passable; (*falta*) excusable
tolice [to'lisi] *f* stupidity, foolishness; (*ato, dito*) stupid thing
tom [tõ] (*pl -ns*) *m* tone; (*Mús: altura*) pitch; (: *escala*) key; (*cor*) shade
tomada [to'mada] *f* capture; (*Elet*) socket
tomar [to'ma'] *vt* to take; (*capturar*) to capture, seize; (*decisão*) to make; (*bebida*) to drink; **~ café** (*de manhã*) to have breakfast
tomara [to'mara] *excl*: **~!** if only!; **~ que venha hoje** I hope he comes today
tomate [to'matʃi] *m* tomato
tombadilho [tõba'dʒiʎu] *m* deck
tombar [tõ'ba'] *vi* to fall down, tumble down ▷ *vt* to knock down, knock over; **tombo** ['tõbu] *m* tumble, fall
tomilho [to'miʎu] *m* thyme
tona ['tɔna] *f* surface; **vir à ~** to come to the surface; (*fig*) to emerge; **trazer à ~** to bring up; (*recordações*) to bring back
tonalidade [tonali'dadʒi] *f* (*de cor*) shade; (*Mús: tom*) key
tonelada [tone'lada] *f* ton
tônica ['tonika] *f* (*água*) tonic (water); (*fig*) keynote

tônico ['toniku] *m* tonic; **acento ~** stress
tons [tõʃ] *mpl de* **tom**
tonteira [tõ'tejra] *f* dizziness
tonto, -a ['tõtu, a] *adj* stupid, silly; (*zonzo*) dizzy, lightheaded; (*atarantado*) flustered
topar [to'pa'] *vt* to agree to ▷ *vi*: **~ com** to come across; **~-se** *vr* (*duas pessoas*) to run into one another; **~ em** (*tropeçar*) to stub one's toe on; (*esbarrar*) to run into; (*tocar*) to touch
tópico, -a ['tɔpiku, a] *adj* topical ▷ *m* topic
topless [tɔp'lɛs] *adj inv* topless
topo ['topu] *m* top; (*extremidade*) end, extremity
toque *etc vb ver* **tocar**
Tóquio ['tɔkju] *n* Tokyo
tora ['tɔra] *f* (*pedaço*) piece; (*de madeira*) log; (*sesta*) nap
toranja [to'rãʒa] *f* grapefruit
torção [tox'sãw] (*pl -ões*) *m* twist; (*Med*) sprain
torcedor, a [toxse'do', a] *m/f* supporter, fan
torcer [tox'se'] *vt* to twist; (*Med*) to sprain; (*desvirtuar*) to distort, misconstrue; (*roupa: espremer*) to wring; (: *na máquina*) to spin; (*vergar*) to bend ▷ *vi*: **~ por** (*time*) to support; **~-se** *vr* to squirm, writhe
torcicolo [toxsi'kɔlu] *m* stiff neck
torcida [tox'sida] *f* (*pavio*) wick; (*Esporte: ato de torcer*) cheering; (: *torcedores*) supporters *pl*
torções [tox'sõjʃ] *mpl de* **torção**
tormenta [tox'mẽta] *f* storm
tormento [tox'mẽtu] *m* torment; (*angústia*) anguish
tornar [tox'na'] *vi* to return, go back ▷ *vt*: **~ algo em algo** to turn ou make sth into sth; **~-se** *vr* to become; **~ a fazer algo** to do sth again
torneio [tox'neju] *m* tournament
torneira [tox'nejra] *f* tap (BRIT), faucet (US)
tornozelo [toxno'zelu] *m* ankle
torpedo [tox'pedu] *m* (*bomba*) torpedo; (*col: mensagem*) text (message)
torrada [to'xada] *f* toast; **uma ~a** piece of toast; **torradeira** [toxa'dejra] *f* toaster
torrão [to'xãw] (*pl -ões*) *m* turf, sod; (*terra*) soil, land; (*de açúcar*) lump
torrar [to'xa'] *vt* to toast; (*café*) to roast
torre ['toxi] *f* tower; (*Xadrez*) castle, rook;

(*Elet*) pylon; **~ de controle** (*Aer*) control tower

tórrido, -a ['tɔxidu, a] *adj* torrid

torrões [to'xõjʃ] *mpl de* **torrão**

torso ['toxsu] *m* torso

torta ['tɔxta] *f* pie, tart

torto, -a ['toxtu, 'tɔxta] *adj* twisted, crooked; **a ~ e a direito** indiscriminately

tortuoso, -a [tox'twozu, ɔza] *adj* winding

tortura [tox'tura] *f* torture; (*fig*) anguish; **torturar** [toxtu'ra^r] *vt* to torture; to torment

tos [tuʃ] = **te + os**

tosco, -a ['toʃku, a] *adj* rough, unpolished; (*grosseiro*) coarse, crude

tosse ['tɔsi] *f* cough; **~ de cachorro** whooping cough; **tossir** [to'si^r] *vi* to cough

tosta ['tɔʃta] (*PT*) *f* toast; **~ mista** toasted cheese and ham sandwich

tostão [toʃ'tãw] *m* cash

tostar [toʃ'ta^r] *vt* to toast; (*pele, pessoa*) to tan; **~-se** *vr* to get tanned

total [to'taw] (*pl* **-ais**) *adj, m* total

touca ['toka] *f* bonnet; **~ de banho** bathing cap

tourada [to'rada] *f* bullfight; **toureiro** [to'rejru] *m* bullfighter

touro ['toru] *m* bull; **T~** (*Astrologia*) Taurus

tóxico, -a ['tɔksiku, a] *adj* toxic ▷ *m* poison; (*droga*) drug; **toxicômano, -a** [toksi'komanu, a] *m/f* drug addict

TPM *abr f* (= *tensão pré-menstrual*) PMT

trabalhador, a [trabaʎa'do^r, a] *adj* hard-working, industrious; (*Pol: classe*) working ▷ *m/f* worker

trabalhar [traba'ʎa^r] *vi* to work ▷ *vt* (*terra*) to till; (*madeira, metal*) to work; (*texto*) to work on; **~ com** (*comerciar*) to deal in; **~ de** *ou* **como** to work as; **trabalhista** [traba'ʎiʃta] *adj* labour *atr* (*BRIT*), labor *atr* (*US*); **trabalho** [tra'baʎu] *m* work; (*emprego, tarefa*) job; (*Econ*) labo(u)r; **trabalho braçal** manual work; **trabalho doméstico** housework; **trabalhoso, -a** [traba'ʎozu, ɔza] *adj* laborious, arduous

traça ['trasa] *f* moth

traçado [tra'sadu] *m* sketch, plan

tração [tra'sãw] *f* traction

traçar [tra'sa^r] *vt* to draw; (*determinar*) to set out, outline; (*planos*) to draw up; (*escrever*) to compose

traccão [tra'sãw] (*PT*) *f* = **tração**

tractor [tra'to^r] (*PT*) *m* = **trator**

tradição [tradʒi'sãw] (*pl* **-ões**) *f* tradition; **tradicional** [tradʒisjo'naw] (*pl* **-ais**) *adj* traditional

tradução [tradu'sãw] (*pl* **-ões**) *f* translation

tradutor, a [tradu'to^r, a] *m/f* translator

traduzir [tradu'zi^r] *vt* to translate

trafegar [trafe'ga^r] *vi* to move, go

tráfego ['trafegu] *m* traffic

traficante [trafi'kãtʃi] *m/f* trafficker, dealer

traficar [trafi'ka^r] *vi*: **~ (com)** to deal (in)

tráfico ['trafiku] *m* traffic

tragar [tra'ga^r] *vt* to swallow; (*fumaça*) to inhale; (*suportar*) to tolerate ▷ *vi* to inhale

tragédia [tra'ʒɛdʒja] *f* tragedy; **trágico, -a** ['traʒiku, a] *adj* tragic

trago¹ ['tragu] *m* mouthful

trago² *etc vb ver* **trazer**

traiçoeiro, -a [traj'swejru, a] *adj* treacherous; disloyal

traidor, a [traj'do^r, a] *m/f* traitor

trailer ['trejla^r] (*pl* **~s**) *m* trailer; (*tipo casa*) caravan (*BRIT*), trailer (*US*)

trair [tra'i^r] *vt* to betray; (*mulher, marido*) to be unfaithful to; (*esperanças*) not to live up to; **~-se** *vr* to give o.s. away

trajar [tra'ʒa^r] *vt* to wear

traje ['traʒi] *m* dress, clothes *pl*; **~ de banho** swimsuit

trajeto [tra'ʒetu] (*PT* **-ct-**) *m* course, path

trajetória [traʒe'tɔrja] (*PT* **-ct-**) *f* trajectory, path; (*fig*) course

tralha ['traʎa] *f* fishing net

trama ['trama] *f* (*tecido*) weft (*BRIT*), woof (*US*); (*enredo, conspiração*) plot

tramar [tra'ma^r] *vt* (*tecer*) to weave; (*maquinar*) to plot ▷ *vi*: **~ contra** to conspire against

trâmites ['tramitʃiʃ] *mpl* procedure *sg*, channels

trampolim [trãpo'lĩ] (*pl* **-ns**) *m* trampoline; (*de piscina*) diving board; (*fig*) springboard

tranca ['trãka] *f* (*de porta*) bolt; (*de carro*) lock

trança ['trãsa] *f* (*cabelo*) plait; (*galão*) braid

trancar [trã'ka^r] *vt* to lock

tranqüilidade [trãkwili'dadʒi] *f* tranquillity; (*paz*) peace

tranqüilizante [trãkwili'zãtʃi] *m* (*Med*) tranquillizer

tranqüilizar [trãkwili'za^r] *vt* to calm, quieten; (*despreocupar*): **~ alguém** to reassure sb, put sb's mind at rest; **~-se** *vr* to calm down

tranqüilo, -a [trã'kwilu, a] *adj* peaceful; (*mar, pessoa*) calm; (*criança*) quiet; (*consciência*) clear; (*seguro*) sure, certain

transação [trãza'sãw] (*PT* **-cç-**) (*pl* **-ões**) *f* transaction

transbordar [trãʒbox'da'] *vi* to overflow

transbordo [trãʒ'boxdu] *m* (*de viajantes*) change, transfer

transe ['trãzi] *m* ordeal; (*lance*) plight; (*hipnótico*) trance

transeunte [trã'zjũtʃi] *m/f* passer-by

transferência [trãʃfe'rẽsja] *f* transfer

transferir [trãʃfe'ri'] *vt* to transfer; (*adiar*) to postpone

transformação [trãʃfoxma'sãw] (*pl* **-ões**) *f* transformation

transformador [trãʃfoxma'do'] *m* (*Elet*) transformer

transformar [trãʃfox'ma'] *vt* to transform; **~-se** *vr* to turn

transfusão [trãʃfu'zãw] (*pl* **-ões**) *f* transfusion

transição [trãzi'sãw] (*pl* **-ões**) *f* transition

transitivo, -a [trãzi'tʃivu, a] *adj* (*Ling*) transitive

trânsito ['trãzitu] *m* transit, passage; (*na rua: veículos*) traffic; (: *pessoas*) flow; **transitório, -a** [trãzi'tɔrju, a] *adj* transitory; (*período*) transitional

transmissão [trãʒmi'sãw] (*pl* **-ões**) *f* transmission; (*transferência*) transfer; **~ ao vivo** live broadcast

transmissor [trãʒmi'so'] *m* transmitter

transmitir [trãʒmi'tʃi'] *vt* to transmit; (*Rádio, TV*) to broadcast; (*transferir*) to transfer; (*recado, notícia*) to pass on; **transparente** [trãʃpa'rẽtʃi] *adj* transparent; (*roupa*) see-through; (*água*) clear

transpirar [trãʃpi'ra'] *vi* to perspire; (*divulgar-se*) to become known; (*verdade*) to come out ▷ *vt* to exude

transplante [trãʃ'plãtʃi] *m* transplant

transportar [trãʃpox'ta'] *vt* to transport; (*levar*) to carry; (*enlevar*) to entrance, enrapture

transporte [trãʃ'pɔxtʃi] *m* transport; (*Com*) haulage

transtorno [trãʃ'toxnu] *m* upset, disruption

trapalhão, -lhona [trapa'ʎãw, 'ʎɔna] (*pl* **trapalhões/-s**) *m/f* bungler, blunderer

trapo ['trapu] *m* rag

trarei *etc* [tra'rej] *vb ver* **trazer**

trás [trajʃ] *prep, adv*: **para ~** backwards; **por ~ de** behind; **de ~** from behind

traseira [tra'zejra] *f* rear; (*Anat*) bottom

traste ['traʃtʃi] *m* thing; (*coisa sem valor*) piece of junk

tratado [tra'tadu] *m* treaty

tratamento [trata'mẽtu] *m* treatment

tratar [tra'ta'] *vt* to treat; (*tema*) to deal with; (*combinar*) to agree ▷ *vi*: **~ com** to deal with; (*combinar*) to agree with; **~ de** to deal with; **de que se trata?** what is it about?

trato ['tratu] *m* treatment; (*contrato*) agreement, contract; **tratos** *mpl* (*relações*) dealings

trator [tra'to'] *m* tractor

trauma ['trawma] *m* trauma

travão [tra'vãw] (*PT*): (*pl* **-ões**) *m* brake

travar [tra'va'] *vt* (*roda*) to lock; (*iniciar*) to engage in; (*conversa*) to strike up; (*luta*) to wage; (*carro*) to stop; (*passagem*) to block; (*movimentos*) to hinder ▷ *vi* (*PT*) to brake

trave ['travi] *f* beam; (*Esporte*) crossbar

través [tra'vɛʃ] *m* slant, incline; **de ~** across, sideways

travessa [tra'vesa] *f* crossbeam, crossbar; (*rua*) lane, alley; (*prato*) dish; (*para o cabelo*) comb, slide

travessão [trave'sãw] (*pl* **-ões**) *m* (*de balança*) bar, beam; (*pontuação*) dash

travesseiro [trave'sejru] *m* pillow

travessia [trave'sia] *f* (*viagem*) journey, crossing

travessões [trave'sõjʃ] *mpl de* **travessão**

travessura [trave'sura] *f* mischief, prank

travões [tra'võjʃ] *mpl de* **travão**

trazer [tra'ze'] *vt* to bring

trecho ['treʃu] *m* passage; (*de rua, caminho*) stretch; (*espaço*) space

trégua ['trɛgwa] *f* truce; (*descanso*) respite

treinador, a [trejna'do', a] *m/f* trainer

treinamento [trejna'mẽtu] *m* training

treinar [trej'na'] *vt* to train; **~-se** *vr* to train; **treino** ['trejnu] *m* training

trejeito [tre'ʒejtu] *m* gesture; (*careta*) grimace, face

trem [trẽj] (*pl* **-ns**) *m* train; **~ de aterrissagem** (*avião*) landing gear

tremendo, -a [tre'mẽdu, a] *adj* tremendous; (*terrível*) terrible, awful

tremer [tre'me'] *vi* to shudder, quake; (*terra*) to shake; (*de frio, medo*) to shiver

trêmulo, -a ['tremulu, a] *adj* shaky,
trembling
trenó [tre'nɔ] *m* sledge, sleigh (BRIT),
sled (US)
trens [trējʃ] *mpl de* **trem**
trepar [tre'paʳ] *vt* to climb ▷ *vi*: ~ **em** to
climb
trepidar [trepi'daʳ] *vi* to tremble, shake
três [treʃ] *num* three
trevas ['trevaʃ] *fpl* darkness *sg*
treze ['trezi] *num* thirteen
triângulo ['trjãgulu] *m* triangle
tribal [tri'baw] (*pl* **-ais**) *adj* tribal
tribo ['tribu] *f* tribe
tribuna [tri'buna] *f* platform, rostrum;
(*Rel*) pulpit
tribunal [tribu'naw] (*pl* **-ais**) *m* court;
(*comissão*) tribunal
tributo [tri'butu] *m* tribute; (*imposto*) tax
tricô [tri'ko] *m* knitting; **tricotar**
[triko'taʳ] *vt, vi* to knit
trigo ['trigu] *m* wheat
trilha ['triʎa] *f* (*caminho*) path; (*rasto*)
track, trail; ~ **sonora** soundtrack
trilhão [tri'ʎãw] (*pl* **-ões**) *m* billion (BRIT),
trillion (US)
trilho ['triʎu] *m* (BR: *Ferro*) rail; (*vereda*)
path, track
trilhões [tri'ʎõjʃ] *mpl de* **trilhão**
trimestral [trimeʃ'traw] (*pl* **-ais**)
adj quarterly; **trimestralmente**
[trimeʃtraw'mētʃi] *adv* quarterly
trimestre [tri'mɛʃtri] *m* (*Educ*) term;
(*Com*) quarter
trincar [trĩ'kaʳ] *vt* to crunch; (*morder*) to
bite; (*dentes*) to grit ▷ *vi* to crunch
trinco ['trĩku] *m* latch
trinta ['trĩta] *num* thirty
trio ['triu] *m* trio; ~ **elétrico** music float;
trio elétrico *see boxed note*

● **TRIO ELÉTRICO**
●
● **Trios elétricos** are lorries, carrying
● floats equipped for sound and/or live
● music, which parade through the
● streets during *carnaval*, especially in
● Bahia. Bands and popular performers
● on the floats draw crowds by giving
● frenzied performances of various
● types of music.

tripa ['tripa] *f* gut, intestine; **tripas** *fpl*
(*intestinos*) bowels; (*vísceras*) guts; (*Culin*)
tripe *sg*
tripé [tri'pɛ] *m* tripod

triplicar [tripli'kaʳ] *vt, vi* to treble; **~-se**
vr to treble
tripulação [tripula'sãw] (*pl* **-ões**) *f* crew
tripulante [tripu'lãtʃi] *m/f* crew
member
triste ['triʃtʃi] *adj* sad; (*lugar*) depressing;
tristeeza [triʃ'teza] *f* sadness;
gloominess
triturar [tritu'raʳ] *vt* to grind
triunfar [trjũ'faʳ] *vi* to triumph; **triunfo**
['trjũfu] *m* triumph
trivial [tri'vjaw] (*pl* **-ais**) *adj*
common(place), ordinary; (*insignificante*)
trivial
triz [triʃ] *m*: **por um** ~ by a hair's breadth
troca ['trɔka] *f* exchange, swap
trocadilho [troka'dʒiʎu] *m* pun, play
on words
trocado [tro'kadu] *m*: **~(s)** (small)
change
trocador, a [troka'doʳ, a] *m/f* (*em ônibus*)
conductor
trocar [tro'kaʳ] *vt* to exchange, swap;
(*mudar*) to change; (*inverter*) to change *ou*
swap round; (*confundir*) to mix up; **~-se** *vr*
to change; ~ **dinheiro** to change money
troco ['trɔku] *m* (*dinheiro*) change; (*revide*)
retort, rejoinder
troféu [tro'fɛw] *m* trophy
tromba ['trõba] *f* (*do elefante*) trunk; (*de
outro animal*) snout
trombeta [trõ'beta] *f* trumpet
trombone [trõ'bɔni] *m* trombone
trombose [trõ'bɔzi] *f* thrombosis
tronco ['trõku] *m* trunk; (*ramo*) branch;
(*de corpo*) torso, trunk
trono ['trɔnu] *m* throne
tropa ['trɔpa] *f* troop; (*exército*) army; **ir
para a** ~ (PT) to join the army
tropeçar [trope'saʳ] *vi* to stumble, trip;
(*fig*) to blunder
tropical [tropi'kaw] (*pl* **-ais**) *adj* tropical
trotar [tro'taʳ] *vi* to trot; **trote** ['trɔtʃi] *m*
trot; (*por telefone etc*) hoax call
trouxe *etc* ['trosi] *vb ver* **trazer**
trovão [tro'vãw] (*pl* **-ões**) *m* clap of
thunder; (*trovoada*) thunder; **trovejar**
[trove'ʒaʳ] *vi* to thunder; **trovoada**
[tro'vwada] *f* thunderstorm
truque ['truki] *m* trick; (*publicitário*)
gimmick
truta ['truta] *f* trout
tu [tu] (PT) *pron* you
tua ['tua] *f de* **teu**
tuba ['tuba] *f* tuba
tubarão [tuba'rãw] (*pl* **-ões**) *m* shark

tuberculose [tubexku'lɔzi] f
tuberculosis
tubo ['tubu] m tube, pipe; **~ de ensaio**
test tube
tucano [tu'kanu] m toucan
tudo ['tudu] pron everything; **~ quanto**
everything that; **antes de ~** first of all;
acima de ~ above all
tufão [tu'fãw] (pl **-ões**) m typhoon
tulipa [tu'lipa] f tulip
tumba ['tũba] f tomb; (lápide) tombstone
tumor [tu'moʳ] m tumour (BRIT), tumor
(US)
túmulo ['tumulu] m tomb; (sepultura)
burial
tumulto [tu'muwtu] m uproar, trouble;
(grande movimento) bustle; (balbúrdia)
hubbub; (motim) riot; **tumultuado, -a**
[tumuw'twadu, a] adj riotous, heated;
tumultuar [tumuw'twaʳ] vt to disrupt;
(amotinar) to rouse, incite
túnel ['tunew] (pl **-eis**) m tunnel
túnica ['tunika] f tunic
Tunísia [tu'nizja] f: **a ~** Tunisia
tupi [tu'pi] m Tupi (tribe); (Ling) Tupi
▷ m/f Tupi Indian
tupi-guarani [-gwara'ni] m (Ling) see
boxed note

> ⬡ **TUPI-GUARANI**
> ⬡
> ⬡ This is an important branch of
> ⬡ indigenous languages from the
> ⬡ tropical region of South America. It
> ⬡ takes in thirty indigenous peoples
> ⬡ and includes Tupi, Guarani, and
> ⬡ other languages. Before Brazil was
> ⬡ discovered by the Portuguese it had
> ⬡ 1,300 indigenous languages, 87%
> ⬡ of which are now extinct due to the
> ⬡ extermination of indigenous peoples
> ⬡ and the loss of territory.

tupiniquim [tupini'kĩ] (pl **-ns**) (pej) adj
Brazilian (Indian)
turbilhão [tuxbi'ʎãw] (pl **-ões**) m (de
vento) whirlwind; (de água) whirlpool
turbulência [tuxbu'lẽsja] f turbulence;
turbulento, -a [tuxbu'lẽtu, a] adj
turbulent
turco, -a ['tuxku, a] adj Turkish ▷ m/f
Turk ▷ m (Ling) Turkish
turismo [tu'riʒmu] m tourism; **turista**
[tu'riʃta] m/f tourist ▷ adj (classe)
tourist atr
turma ['tuxma] f group; (Educ) class

turquesa [tux'keza] adj inv turquoise
Turquia [tux'kia] f: **a ~** Turkey
tusso etc ['tusu] vb ver **tossir**
tutela [tu'tɛla] f protection; (Jur)
guardianship
tutor, a [tu'toʳ, a] m/f guardian
tutu [tu'tu] m (Culin) beans, bacon and
manioc flour
TV [te've] abr f (= televisão) TV

u

overtake (BRIT), pass (US); (ser superior a) to surpass ▷ vi (Auto) to overtake (BRIT), pass (US)

ultra-som m ultrasound

ultravioleta [uwtravjo'leta] adj ultraviolet

○ **PALAVRA CHAVE**

um, -a [ũ, 'uma] (pl **uns/ums**) num one; **um e outro** both; **um a um** one by one; **à uma (hora)** at one (o'clock)
▷ adj: **uns cinco** about five; **uns poucos** a few
▷ art indef **1** (sg) a; (: antes de vogal ou 'h' mudo) an; (pl) some; **ela é de uma beleza incrível** she's incredibly beautiful
2 (dando ênfase): **estou com uma fome!** I'm so hungry!
3: **um ao outro** one another; (entre dois) each other

umbigo [ũ'bigu] m navel

umbilical [ũbili'kaw] (pl **-ais**) adj: **cordão ~** umbilical cord

umedecer [umede'seʳ] vt to moisten, wet; **~-se** vr to get wet

umidade [umi'dadʒi] f dampness; (clima) humidity

úmido, -a ['umidu, a] adj wet, moist; (roupa) damp; (clima) humid

unânime [u'nanimi] adj unanimous

unha ['uɲa] f nail; (garra) claw; **unhada** [u'ɲada] f scratch

união [u'ɲjãw] (pl **-ões**) f union; (ato) joining; (unidade, solidariedade) unity; (casamento) marriage; (Tec) joint; **a U~ Européia** the European Union

unicamente [unika'mẽtʃi] adv only

único, -a ['uniku, a] adj only; (sem igual) unique; (um só) single

unidade [uni'dadʒi] f unity; (Tec, Com) unit; **~ central de processamento** (Comput) central processing unit; **~ de disco** (Comput) disk drive

unido, -a [u'nidu, a] adj joined, linked; (fig) united

unificar [unifi'kaʳ] vt to unite; **~-se** vr to join together

uniforme [uni'fɔxmi] adj uniform; (semelhante) alike, similar; (superfície) even ▷ m uniform; **uniformizado, -a** [unifoxmi'zadu, a] adj uniform, standardized; (vestido de uniforme) in uniform; **uniformizar** [unifoxmi'zaʳ] vt

---

UE abr f (= União Européia) EU

UEM abr f (= União Econômica e Monetária) EMU

Uganda [u'gãda] m Uganda

uísque ['wiʃki] m whisky (BRIT), whiskey (US)

uivar [wi'vaʳ] vi to howl; (berrar) to yell; **uivo** ['wivu] m howl; (fig) yell

úlcera ['uwsera] f ulcer

ultimamente [uwtʃima'mẽtʃi] adv lately

ultimato [uwtʃi'matu] m ultimatum

último, -a ['uwtʃimu, a] adj last; (mais recente) latest; (qualidade) lowest; (fig) final; **por ~** finally; **nos ~s anos** in recent years; **a última** (notícia) the latest (news)

ultra- [uwtra-] prefixo ultra-

ultrajar [uwtra'ʒaʳ] vt to outrage; (insultar) to insult, offend; **ultraje** [uw'traʒi] m outrage; (insulto) insult, offence (BRIT), offense (US)

ultramar [uwtra'maʳ] m overseas

ultrapassado, -a [uwtrapa'sadu, a] adj (idéias etc) outmoded

ultrapassar [uwtrapa'saʳ] vt (atravessar) to cross, go beyond; (ir além de) to exceed; (transgredir) to overstep; (Auto) to

to standardize
uniões [u'njõjʃ] *fpl de* **união**
unir [u'niʳ] *vt* to join together; *(ligar)* to
link; *(pessoas, fig)* to unite; *(misturar)* to
mix together; **~-se** *vr* to come together;
(povos etc) to unite
uníssono [u'nisonu] *m*: **em ~** in unison
universal [univex'saw] *(pl* **-ais)** *adj*
universal; *(mundial)* worldwide
universidade [univexsi'dadʒi]
f university; **universitário, -a**
[univexsi'tarju, a] *adj* university
atr ▷ *m/f (professor)* lecturer; *(aluno)*
university student
universo [uni'vexsu] *m* universe;
(mundo) world
uns [ũʃ] *mpl de* **um**
untar [ũ'taʳ] *vt (esfregar)* to rub; *(com óleo,
manteiga)* to grease
urbanismo [uxba'niʒmu] *m* town
planning
urbano, -a [ux'banu, a] *adj (da cidade)*
urban; *(fig)* urbane
urgência [ux'ʒẽsja] *f* urgency; **com
toda ~** as quickly as possible; **urgente**
[ux'ʒẽtʃi] *adj* urgent
urina [u'rina] *f* urine; **urinar** [uri'naʳ] *vi*
to urinate ▷ *vt (sangue)* to pass; *(cama)*
to wet; **urinar-se** *vr* to wet o.s.; **urinol**
[uri'nɔw] *(pl* **-óis)** *m* chamber pot
urna ['uxna] *f* urn; **~ eleitoral** ballot box
urrar [u'xaʳ] *vt, vi* to roar; *(de dor)* to yell
urso, -a ['uxsu, a] *m/f* bear
urtiga [ux'tʃiga] *f* nettle
Uruguai [uru'gwaj] *m*: **o ~** Uruguay
urze ['uxzi] *m* heather
usado, -a [u'zadu, a] *adj* used; *(comum)*
common; *(roupa)* worn; *(gasto)* worn out;
(de segunda mão) second-hand
usar [u'zaʳ] *vt (servir-se de)* to use; *(vestir)*
to wear; *(gastar com o uso)* to wear out;
(barba, cabelo curto) to have, wear ▷ *vi*: **~
de** to use; **modo de ~** directions *pl*
usina [u'zina] *f (fábrica)* factory; *(de
energia)* plant
uso ['uzu] *m* use; *(utilização)* usage;
(prática) practice
usual [u'zwaw] *(pl* **-ais)** *adj* usual;
(comum) common
usuário, -a [u'zwarju, a] *m/f* user
usufruir [uzu'frwiʳ] *vt* to enjoy ▷ *vi*: **~ de**
to enjoy
úteis ['utejʃ] *pl de* **útil**
utensílio [utẽ'silju] *m* utensil
útero ['uteru] *m* womb, uterus
útil ['utʃiw] *(pl* **-eis)** *adj* useful; *(vantajoso)*

profitable, worthwhile; **utilidade**
[utʃili'dadʒi] *f* usefulness; **utilização**
[utʃiliza'sãw] *f* use; **utilizar** [utʃili'zaʳ]
vt to use; **utilizar-se** *vr*: **utilizar-se de** to
make use of
uva ['uva] *f* grape

V

v _abr_ (= volt) v
vá _etc_ [va] _vb ver_ **ir**
vã [vã] _f de_ **vão**
vaca ['vaka] _f_ cow; **carne de ~** beef
vacina [va'sina] _f_ vaccine; **vacinar** [vasi'naʳ] _vt_ to vaccinate
vácuo ['vakwu] _m_ vacuum; (_fig_) void; (_espaço_) space
vaga ['vaga] _f_ wave; (_em hotel, trabalho_) vacancy
vagão [va'gãw] (_pl_ **-ões**) _m_ (_de passageiros_) carriage; (_de cargas_) wagon; **vagão-leito** (_pl_ **vagões-leitos** (PT)) _m_ sleeping car; **vagão-restaurante** (_pl_ **vagões-restaurantes**) _m_ buffet car
vagar [va'gaʳ] _vi_ to wander about; (_barco_) to drift; (_ficar vago_) to be vacant
vagaroso, -a [vaga'rozu, ɔza] _adj_ slow
vagina [va'ʒina] _f_ vagina
vago, -a ['vagu, a] _adj_ vague; (_desocupado_) vacant, free
vagões [va'gõjʃ] _mpl de_ **vagão**
vai _etc_ [vaj] _vb ver_ **ir**
vaia ['vaja] _f_ booing; **vaiar** [va'jaʳ] _vt, vi_ to boo, hiss
vaidade [vaj'dadʒi] _f_ vanity; (_futilidade_) futility
vaidoso, -a [vaj'dozu, ɔza] _adj_ vain

vaivém [vaj'vēj] _m_ to-ing and fro-ing
vala ['vala] _f_ ditch
vale ['vali] _m_ valley; (_escrito_) voucher; **~ postal** postal order
valer [va'leʳ] _vi_ to be worth; (_ser válido_) to be valid; (_ter influência_) to carry weight; (_servir_) to serve; (_ser proveitoso_) to be useful; **~-se** _vr_: **~-se de** to use, make use of; **~ a pena** to be worthwhile; **~ por** (_equivaler_) to be worth the same as; **para ~** (_muito_) very much, a lot; (_realmente_) for real, properly; **vale dizer** in other words; **mais vale ... (do que ...)** it would be better to ... (than ...)
valeta [va'leta] _f_ gutter
valha _etc_ ['vaʎa] _vb ver_ **valer**
validade [vali'dadʒi] _f_ validity
validar [vali'daʳ] _vt_ to validate; **válido, -a** ['validu, a] _adj_ valid
valioso, -a [va'ljozu, ɔza] _adj_ valuable
valise [va'lizi] _f_ case, grip
valor [va'loʳ] _m_ value; (_mérito_) merit; (_coragem_) courage; (_preço_) price; (_importância_) importance; **valores** _mpl_ (_morais_) values; (_num exame_) marks; (_Com_) securities; **dar ~ a** to value; **valorizar** [valori'zaʳ] _vt_ to value
valsa ['vawsa] _f_ waltz
válvula ['vawvula] _f_ valve
vampiro, -a [vã'piru, a] _m/f_ vampire
vandalismo [vãda'liʒmu] _m_ vandalism
vândalo, -a ['vãdalu, a] _m/f_ vandal
vangloriar-se [vãglo'rjaxsi] _vr_: **~ de** to boast of _ou_ about
vanguarda [vã'gwaxda] _f_ vanguard; (_arte_) avant-garde
vantagem [vã'taʒē] (_pl_ **-ns**) _f_ advantage; (_ganho_) profit, benefit; **tirar ~ de** to take advantage of; **vantajoso, -a** [vãta'ʒozu, ɔza] _adj_ advantageous; (_lucrativo_) profitable; (_proveitoso_) beneficial
vão¹, vã [vãw, vã] (_pl_ **~s/-s**) _adj_ vain; (_fútil_) futile ▷ _m_ (_intervalo_) space; (_de porta etc_) opening
vão² _vb ver_ **ir**
vaqueiro [va'kejru] _m_ cowboy
vara ['vara] _f_ stick; (_Tec_) rod; (_Jur_) jurisdiction; (_de porcos_) herd; **salto de ~** pole vault; **~ de condão** magic wand
varal [va'raw] (_pl_ **-ais**) _m_ clothes line
varanda [va'rãda] _f_ verandah; (_balcão_) balcony
varar [va'raʳ] _vt_ to pierce; (_passar_) to cross
varejista [vare'ʒiʃta] (BR) _m/f_ retailer ▷ _adj_ (_mercado_) retail
varejo [va'reʒu] (BR) _m_ (_Com_) retail trade;

a ~ retail
variação [varja'sãw] (pl **-ões**) f variation
variado, -a [va'rjadu, a] adj varied;
(sortido) assorted
variar [va'rjaʳ] vt, vi to vary; **variável**
[va'rjavew] (pl **-eis**) adj variable; (tempo,
humor) changeable
varicela [vari'sɛla] f chickenpox
variedade [varje'dadʒi] f variety
varinha [va'riɲa] f wand; **~ de condão**
magic wand
vário, -a [ˈvarju, a] adj (diverso) varied;
(pl) various, several; (Com) sundry
varizes [va'riziʃ] fpl varicose veins
varrer [va'xeʳ] vt to sweep; (fig) to sweep
away
vaselina® [vaze'lina] f vaseline®
vasilha [va'ziʎa] f (para líquidos) jug; (para
alimentos) dish; (barril) barrel
vaso [ˈvazu] m pot; (para flores) vase
vassoura [va'sora] f broom
vasto, -a [ˈvaʃtu, a] adj vast
vatapá [vata'pa] m fish or chicken with
coconut milk, shrimps, peanuts, palm oil
and spices
Vaticano [vatʃi'kanu] m: **o ~** the Vatican
vazamento [vaza'mẽtu] m leak
vazão [va'zãw] (pl **-ões**) f flow; (venda)
sale; **dar ~** (expressar) to give vent to;
(atender) to deal with; (resolver) to attend
to
vazar [va'zaʳ] vt to empty; (derramar) to
spill; (verter) to pour out ⊳ vi to leak
vazio, -a [va'ziu, a] adj empty; (pessoa)
empty-headed, frivolous; (cidade)
deserted ⊳ m emptiness; (deixado por
alguém/algo) void
vazões [va'zõjʃ] fpl de **vazão**
vê etc [ve] vb ver **ver**
veado [ˈvjadua] m deer; **carne de ~**
venison
vedado, -a [ve'dadu, a] adj (proibido)
forbidden; (fechado) enclosed
vedar [ve'daʳ] vt to ban, prohibit; (buraco)
to stop up; (entrada, passagem) to block;
(terreno) to close off
vegetação [veʒeta'sãw] f vegetation
vegetal [veʒe'taw] (pl **-ais**) adj vegetable
atr; (reino, vida) plant atr ⊳ m vegetable
vegetalista [veʒeta'liʃta] adj, m/f vegan
vegetariano, -a [veʒeta'rjanu, a] adj,
m/f vegetarian
veia [ˈveja] f vein
veículo [ve'ikulu] m vehicle; (fig: meio)
means sg; **~ com tração nas quatro
rodas**, **~ 4x4** four-wheel drive

veio [ˈveju] vb ver **vir** ⊳ m (de rocha) vein;
(na mina) seam; (de madeira) grain
vejo etc [ˈveʒu] vb ver **ver**
vela [ˈvɛla] f candle; (Auto) spark plug;
(Náut) sail; **barco à ~** sailing boat
velar [ve'laʳ] vt to veil; (ocultar) to hide;
(vigiar) to keep watch over; (um doente)
to sit up with ⊳ vi (não dormir) to stay up;
(vigiar) to keep watch; **~ por** to look after
veleiro [ve'lejru] m sailing boat (BRIT),
sailboat (US)
velejar [vele'ʒaʳ] vi to sail
velhaco, -a [ve'ʎaku, a] adj crooked
⊳ m/f crook
velhice [ve'ʎisi] f old age
velho, -a [ˈvɛʎu, a] adj old ⊳ m/f old
man/woman
velocidade [velosi'dadʒi] f speed,
velocity; (PT: Auto) gear
velório [ve'lɔrju] m wake
veloz [ve'lɔʒ] adj fast
vem [vẽj] vb ver **vir**
vêm [vẽj] vb ver **vir**
vencedor, a [vẽse'doʳ, a] adj winning
⊳ m/f winner
vencer [vẽ'seʳ] vt (num jogo) to beat;
(competição) to win; (inimigo) to defeat;
(exceder) to surpass; (obstáculos) to
overcome; (percorrer) to pass ⊳ vi (num
jogo) to win; **vencido, -a** [vẽ'sidu,
a] adj: **dar-se por vencido** to give in;
vencimento [vẽsi'mẽtu] m (Com)
expiry; (data) expiry date; (salário) salary;
(de gêneros alimentícios etc) sell-by date;
vencimentos mpl (ganhos) earnings
venda [ˈvẽda] f sale; (pano) blindfold;
(mercearia) general store; **à ~** on sale,
for sale
vendaval [vẽda'vaw] (pl **-ais**) m gale
vendedor, a [vẽde'doʳ, a] m/f seller; (em
loja) sales assistant; **~ ambulante** street
vendor
vender [vẽ'deʳ] vt, vi to sell; **~ por
atacado/a varejo** to sell wholesale/
retail
veneno [ve'nɛnu] m poison; **venenoso,
-a** [vene'nozu, ɔza] adj poisonous
venerar [vene'raʳ] vt to revere; (Rel) to
worship
venéreo, -a [ve'nɛrju, a] adj: **doença
venérea** venereal disease
Venezuela [vene'zwɛla] f: **a ~** Venezuela
venha etc [ˈveɲa] vb ver **vir**
ventania [vẽta'nia] f gale
ventar [vẽ'taʳ] vi: **está ventando** it is
windy

ventilação [vẽtʃila'sãw] f ventilation
ventilador [vẽtʃila'do^r] m ventilator;
(elétrico) fan
vento ['vẽtu] m wind; (brisa) breeze;
ventoinha [vẽ'twiɲa] f weathercock,
weather vane; (PT: Auto) fan
ventre ['vẽtri] m belly
ver [ve^r] vt to see; (olhar para, examinar) to
look at; (televisão) to watch ▷ vi to see
▷ m: **a meu ~** in my opinion; **vai ~ que ...**
maybe ...; **não tem nada a ~ (com)** it has
nothing to do (with)
veracidade [verasi'dadʒi] f truthfulness
veraneio [vera'neju] m summer
holidays pl (BRIT) ou vacation (US)
verão [ve'rãw] (pl -ões) m summer
verba ['vɛxba] f allowance; **verba(s)** f(pl)
(recursos) funds pl
verbal [vex'baw] (pl -ais) adj verbal
verbete [vex'betʃi] m (num dicionário)
entry
verbo ['vɛxbu] m verb
verdade [vex'dadʒi] f truth; **de ~** (falar)
truthfully; (ameaçar etc) really; **na ~** in
fact; **para falar a ~** to tell the truth;
verdadeiro, -a [vexda'dejru, a] adj true;
(genuíno) real; (pessoa) truthful
verde ['vexdʒi] adj green; (fruta) unripe
▷ m green; (plantas etc) greenery
verdura [vex'dura] f (hortaliça) greens pl;
(Bot) greenery; (cor verde) greenness
verdureiro, -a [vexdu'rejru, a] m/f
greengrocer (BRIT), produce dealer (US)
vereador, -a [verja'do^r, a] m/f councillor
(BRIT), councilor (US)
veredicto [vere'dʒiktu] m verdict
verga ['vexga] f (vara) stick; (de metal) rod
vergonha [vex'goɲa] f shame;
(timidez) embarrassment; (humilhação)
humiliation; (ato indecoroso) indecency;
(brio) self-respect; **ter ~** to be ashamed;
(tímido) to be shy; **vergonhoso, -a**
[vexgo'nozu, ɔza] adj shameful;
(indecoroso) disgraceful
verídico, -a [ve'ridʒiku, a] adj true,
truthful
verificar [verifi'ka^r] vt to check; (confirmar) to verify
verme ['vexmi] m worm
vermelho, -a [vex'meʎu, a] adj red ▷ m
red
verniz [vex'niʒ] m varnish; (couro) patent
leather
verões [ve'rõjʃ] mpl de **verão**
verossímil [vero'simiw] (PT -osí-) (pl
-eis) adj likely, probable; (crível) credible

verruga [ve'xuga] f wart
versão [vex'sãw] (pl -ões) f version;
(tradução) translation
versátil [vex'satʃiw] (pl -eis) adj versatile
verso ['vɛxsu] m verse; (linha) line of
poetry
versões [vex'sõjʃ] fpl de **versão**
verter [vex'te^r] vt to pour; (por acaso) to
spill; (traduzir) to translate; (lágrimas,
sangue) to shed ▷ vi: **~ de** to spring from;
~ em (rio) to flow into
vertical [vextʃi'kaw] (pl -ais) adj vertical;
(de pé) upright, standing ▷ f vertical
vespa ['veʃpa] f wasp
véspera ['vɛʃpera] f: **a ~ de** the day
before; **a ~ de Natal** Christmas Eve
vestiário [veʃ'tʃjarju] m (em casa, teatro)
cloakroom; (Esporte) changing room; (de
ator) dressing room
vestíbulo [veʃ'tʃibulu] m hall(way),
vestibule; (Teatro) foyer
vestido, -a [veʃ'tʃidu, a] adj: **~ de branco**
etc dressed in white etc ▷ m dress
vestígio [veʃ'tʃiʒju] m (rastro) track; (fig)
sign, trace
vestimenta [veʃtʃi'mẽta] f garment
vestir [veʃ'tʃi^r] vt (uma criança) to dress;
(pôr sobre si) to put on; (trajar) to wear;
(comprar, dar roupa para) to clothe; (fazer
roupa para) to make clothes for; **~-se** vr to
get dressed
vestuário [veʃ'twarju] m clothing
veterano, -a [vete'ranu, a] adj, m/f
veteran
veterinário, -a [veteri'narju, a] m/f
vet(erinary surgeon)
veto ['vɛtu] m veto
véu [vɛw] m veil
vexame [ve'ʃami] f shame, disgrace;
(tormento) affliction; (humilhação)
humiliation; (afronta) insult
vez [veʒ] f time; (turno) turn; **uma ~**
once; **algumas ~es, às ~es** sometimes;
~ por outra sometimes; **cada ~ (que)**
every time; **de ~ em quando** from time
to time; **em ~ de** instead of; **uma ~ que**
since; **3 ~es 6** 3 times 6; **de uma ~ por
todas** once and for all; **muitas ~es** many
times; (freqüentemente) often; **toda ~ que**
every time; **um de cada ~** one at a time;
uma ~ ou outra once in a while
vi [vi] vb ver **ver**
via ['via] f road, route; (meio) way;
(documento) copy; (conduto) channel
▷ prep via, by way of; **em ~s de** about to;
por ~ terrestre/marítima by land/sea

via etc vb ver **ver**

viaduto [vja'dutu] m viaduct

viagem ['vjaʒē] (pl **-ns**) f journey, trip; (o viajar) travel; (Náut) voyage; **viagens** fpl (jornadas) travels; **~ de ida e volta** return trip, round trip

viajante [vja'ʒãtʃi] adj travelling (BRIT), traveling (US) ▷ m traveller (BRIT), traveler (US)

viajar [vja'ʒaʳ] vi to travel

viável ['vjavew] (pl **-eis**) adj feasible, viable

víbora ['vibora] f viper

vibração [vibra'sãw] (pl **-ões**) f vibration; (fig) thrill

vibrante [vi'brãtʃi] adj vibrant; (discurso) stirring

vibrar [vi'braʳ] vt to brandish; (fazer estremecer) to vibrate; (cordas) to strike ▷ vi to vibrate; (som) to echo

vice ['visi] m/f deputy

vice- [visi-] prefixo vice-; **vice-presidente, -a** m/f vice president; **vice-versa** [-'vɛxsa] adv vice-versa

viciado, -a [vi'sjadu, a] adj addicted; (ar) foul ▷ m/f addict; **~ em algo** addicted to sth

viciar [vi'sjaʳ] vt (falsificar) to falsify; **~-se** vr: **~-se em algo** to become addicted to sth

vício ['visju] m vice; (defeito) failing; (costume) bad habit; (em entorpecentes) addiction

viço ['visu] m vigour (BRIT), vigor (US); (da pele) freshness

vida ['vida] f life; (duração) lifetime; (fig) vitality; **com ~** alive; **ganhar a ~** to earn one's living; **modo de ~** way of life; **dar a ~ por algo/por fazer algo** to give one's right arm for sth/to do sth; **estar bem de ~** to be well off

videira [vi'dejra] f grapevine

vidente [vi'dētʃi] m/f clairvoyant

vídeo ['vidʒu] m video; **videocassete** [vidʒuka'sɛtʃi] m video cassette ou tape; (aparelho) video (recorder); **videoteipe** [vidʒu'tejpi] m video tape

vidraça [vi'drasa] f window pane

vidrado, -a [vi'dradu, a] adj glazed; (porta) glass atr; (olhos) glassy

vidro ['vidru] m glass; (frasco) bottle; **fibra de ~** fibreglass (BRIT), fiberglass (US); **~ de aumento** magnifying glass

vier etc [vje'ʳ] vb ver **vir**

viés [vjeʃ] m slant; **ao** ou **de ~** diagonally

vieste ['vjeʃtʃi] vb ver **vir**

Vietnã [vjet'nã] m: **o ~** Vietnam; **vietnamita** [vjetna'mita] adj, m/f Vietnamese; **vigiar** [vi'ʒjaʳ] vt to watch; (ocultamente) to spy on; (presos, fronteira) to guard ▷ vi to be on the lookout

vigilância [viʒi'lãsja] f vigilance; **vigilante** [viʒi'lãtʃi] adj vigilant; (atento) alert

vigor [vi'goʳ] m energy, vigour (BRIT), vigor (US); **em ~** in force; **entrar/pôr em ~** to take effect/put into effect; **vigoroso, -a** [vigo'rozu, ɔza] adj vigorous

vil [viw] (pl **vis**) adj vile

vila ['vila] f town; (casa) villa

vilão, -lã [vi'lãw, 'lã] (pl **-s/-s**) m/f villain

vilarejo [vila'reʒu] m village

vim [vĩ] vb ver **vir**

vime ['vimi] m wicker

vinagre [vi'nagri] m vinegar

vinco ['vĩku] m crease; (sulco) furrow; (no rosto) line

vincular [vĩku'laʳ] vt to link, tie; **vínculo** ['vĩkulu] m bond, tie; (relação) link

vinda ['vĩda] f arrival; (regresso) return; **dar as boas ~s a** to welcome

vingança [vĩ'gãsa] f vengeance, revenge; **vingar** [vĩ'gaʳ] vt to avenge; **vingar-se** vr: **vingar-se de** to take revenge on; **vingativo, -a** [vĩga'tʃivu, a] adj vindictive

vinha¹ etc ['viɲa] vb ver **vir**

vinha² f vineyard; (planta) vine

vinho ['viɲu] m wine; **~ branco/rosado/tinto** white/rosé/red wine; **~ seco/doce** dry/sweet wine; **~ do Porto** port

vinte ['vĩtʃi] num twenty

viola ['vjɔla] f viola

violão [vjo'lãw] (pl **-ões**) m guitar

violar [vjo'laʳ] vt to violate; (a lei) to break

violência [vjo'lēsja] f violence; **violentar** [vjolē'taʳ] vt to force; (mulher) to rape; **violento, -a** [vjo'lētu, a] adj violent

violeta [vjo'leta] f violet

violino [vjo'linu] m violin

violões [vjo'lõjʃ] mpl de **violão**

violoncelo [vjolõ'sɛlu] m 'cello

vir [viʳ] vi to come; **~ a ser** to turn out to be; **a semana que vem** next week

vir² etc vb ver **ver**

vira-lata ['vira-] (pl **-s**) m (cão) mongrel

virar [vi'raʳ] vt to turn; (página, disco, barco) to turn over; (copo) to empty; (transformar-se em) to become ▷ vi to turn; (barco) to capsize; (mudar) to change; **~-se** vr to turn; (voltar-se) to turn round; (defender-se) to fend for o.s.

virgem ['vixʒē] (pl **-ns**) f virgin; **V~** (Astrologia) Virgo

vírgula ['vixgula] f comma; (decimal) point

viril [vi'riw] (pl **-is**) adj virile

virilha [vi'riʎa] f groin

viris [vi'riʃ] adj pl de **viril**

virtual [vix'twaw] (pl **-ais**) adj virtual; (potencial) potential

virtude [vix'tudʒi] f virtue; **em ~ de** owing to, because of; **virtuoso, -a** [vix'twozu, ɔza] adj virtuous

virulento, -a [viru'lētu, a] adj virulent

vírus ['viruʃ] m inv virus

vis [viʃ] adj pl de **vil**

visão [vi'zãw] (pl **-ões**) f vision; (Anat) eyesight; (vista) sight; (maneira de perceber) view

visar [vi'zaʳ] vt (alvo) to aim at; (ter em vista) to have in view; (ter como objetivo) to aim for

vísceras ['viseraʃ] fpl innards, bowels

visita [vi'zita] f visit, call; (pessoa) visitor; (na internet) hit; **fazer uma ~ a** to visit; **visitante** [vizi'tãtʃi] adj visiting ▷ m/f visitor; **visitar** [vizi'taʳ] vt to visit

visível [vi'zivew] (pl **-eis**) adj visible

vislumbrar [viʒlũ'braʳ] vt to glimpse, catch a glimpse of; **vislumbre** [viʒ'lũbri] m glimpse

visões [vi'zõjʃ] fpl de **visão**

visse etc ['visi] vb ver **ver**

vista ['viʃta] f sight; (Med) eyesight; (panorama) view; **à ou em ~ de** in view of; **dar na ~** to attract attention; **dar uma ~ de olhos em** to glance at; **fazer ~ grossa (a)** to turn a blind eye (to); **ter em ~** to have in mind; **à ~** visible, showing; (Com) in cash; **até a ~!** see you!

visto, -a ['viʃtu, a] pp de **ver** ▷ adj seen ▷ m (em passaporte) visa; (em documento) stamp; **pelo ~** by the looks of things

visto etc vb ver **vestir**

vistoria [viʃto'ria] f inspection

vistoso, -a [viʃ'tozu, ɔza] adj eye-catching

visual [vi'zwaw] (pl **-ais**) adj visual; **visualizar** [vizwali'zaʳ] vt to visualize

vital [vi'taw] (pl **-ais**) adj vital; **vitalício, -a** [vita'lisju, a] adj for life

vitamina [vita'mina] f vitamin; (para beber) fruit crush

vitela [vi'tela] f calf; (carne) veal

vítima ['vitʃima] f victim

vitória [vi'tɔrja] f victory; **vitorioso, -a** [vito'rjozu, ɔza] adj victorious

vitrina [vi'trina] f = **vitrine**

vitrine [vi'trini] f shop window; (armário) display case

viúvo, -a ['vjuvu, a] m/f widower/widow

viva ['viva] m cheer; **~!** hurray!

viva-voz [viva'vɔʃ] m (BR: Tel: em telefone) speakerphone; (para celular) hands-free kit

viveiro [vi'vejru] m nursery

vivência [vi'vēsja] f existence; (experiência) experience

vivenda [vi'vēda] f (casa) residence

viver [vi'veʳ] vt, vi to live ▷ m life; **~ de** to live on

vívido, -a ['vividu, a] adj vivid

vivo, -a ['vivu, a] adj living; (esperto) clever; (cor) bright; (criança, debate) lively ▷ m: **os ~s** the living

vizinhança [vizi'ɲãsa] f neighbourhood (BRIT), neighborhood (US)

vizinho, -a [vi'ziɲu, a] adj neighbouring (BRIT), neighboring (US); (perto) nearby ▷ m/f neighbour (BRIT), neighbor (US)

voar [vo'aʳ] vi to fly; (explodir) to blow up, explode

vocabulário [vokabu'larju] m vocabulary

vocábulo [vo'kabulu] m word

vocal [vo'kaw] (pl **-ais**) adj vocal

você, s [vo'se(ʃ)] pron (pl) you

vodca ['vɔdʒka] f vodka

vogal [vo'gaw] (pl **-ais**) f (Ling) vowel

vol. abr (= volume) vol.

volante [vo'lãtʃi] m steering wheel

vôlei ['volej] m volleyball

voleibol [volej'bow] m = **vôlei**

volt ['vɔwtʃi] (pl **~s**) m volt

volta ['vɔwta] f turn; (regresso) return; (curva) bend, curve; (circuito) lap; (resposta) retort; **dar uma ~** (a pé) to go for a walk; (de carro) to go for a drive; **estar de ~** to be back; **na ~ do correio** by return (post); **por ~ de** about, around; **à ou em ~ de** around; **na ~** (no caminho de volta) on the way back

voltagem [vow'taʒē] f voltage

voltar [vow'taʳ] vt to turn ▷ vi to return, go (ou come) back; **~-se** vr to turn round; **~ a fazer** to do again; **~ a si** to come to; **~-se para** to turn to; **~-se contra** to turn against

volume [vo'lumi] m volume; (pacote) package; **volumoso, -a** [volu'mozu, ɔza] adj bulky, big

voluntário, -a [volũ'tarju, a] *adj* voluntary ▷ *m/f* volunteer

volúvel [vo'luvew] (*pl* **-eis**) *adj* fickle

vomitar [vomi'ta^r] *vt, vi* to vomit; **vômito** ['vomitu] *m* (*ato*) vomiting; (*efeito*) vomit

vontade [võ'tadʒi]·*f* will; (*desejo*) wish; **com ~** (*com prazer*) with pleasure; (*com gana*) with gusto; **estar com** *ou* **ter ~ de fazer** to feel like doing

vôo ['vou] (*PT* **voo**) *m* flight; **levantar ~** to take off; **~ livre** (*Esporte*) hang-gliding

voraz [vo'rajʒ] *adj* voracious

vos [vuʃ] *pron* you; (*indireto*) to you

vós [vɔʃ] *pron* you

vosso, -a ['vɔsu, a] *adj* your ▷ *pron*: **(o) ~** yours

votação [vota'sãw] (*pl* **-ões**) *f* vote, ballot; (*ato*) voting

votar [vo'ta^r] *vt* (*eleger*) to vote for; (*aprovar*) to pass; (*submeter a votação*) to vote on ▷ *vi* to vote; **voto** ['vɔtu] *m* vote; (*promessa*) vow; **votos** *mpl* (*desejos*) wishes

vou [vo] *vb ver* **ir**

vovó [vo'vɔ] *f* grandma

vovô [vo'vo] *m* grandad

voz [vɔʒ] *f* voice; (*clamor*) cry; **a meia ~** in a whisper; **de viva ~** orally; **ter ~ ativa** to have a say; **em ~ alta/baixa** aloud/in a low voice; **~ de comando** command

vulcão [vuw'kãw] (*pl* **-s** or **-ões**) *m* volcano

vulgar [vuw'ga^r] *adj* common; (*pej: pessoa etc*) vulgar

vulnerável [vuwne'ravew] (*pl* **-eis**) *adj* vulnerable

vulto ['vuwtu] *m* figure; (*volume*) mass; (*fig*) importance; (*pessoa importante*) important person

W

walkie-talkie [wɔki'tɔki] (*pl* **-s**) *m* walkie-talkie

watt ['wɔtʃi] (*pl* **-s**) *m* watt

Web [u'ɛbi] *f* (*Comput*) web

webcam [wɛb'cã] *f* webcam

weblog [wɛb'lɔgui] *m* weblog

windsurfe [wĩd'suxfi] *m* windsurfing

X

of Mato Grosso, it aims to preserve
indigenous culture. It brings together
sixteen communities, a total of two
thousand Indians.

xadrez [ʃaˈdreʒ] *m* chess; *(tabuleiro)*
chessboard; *(tecido)* checked cloth
xampu [ʃãˈpu] *m* shampoo
xarope [ʃaˈrɔpi] *m* syrup; *(para a tosse)*
cough syrup
xeque [ˈʃɛki] *m (soberano)* sheikh; **pôr em**
~ *(fig)* to call into question
xeque-mate *(pl* **xeques-mate)** *m*
checkmate
xerocar [ʃeroˈkaʳ] *vt* to photocopy,
Xerox®
xerox® [ʃeˈrɔks] *m (copia)* photocopy;
(máquina) photocopier
xícara [ˈʃikara] *(BR)* *f* cup
xingar [ʃĩˈgaʳ] *vt* to swear at ▷ *vi* to
swear
Xingu [ʃĩˈgu] *m*: **Parque Indígena do ~**
see boxed note

✹ XINGU
✹
✹ The **Xingu** National Park was created
✹ in 1961 by the federal government and
✹ directed by the brothers Orlando and
✹ Cláudio Vilasboas, who were known
✹ internationally for their efforts to
✹ preserve Brazil's indigenous people.
✹ Situated in the north of the state

Z

light district; (: *confusão*) mess; (: *tumulto*)
free-for-all; **~ eleitoral** electoral district,
constituency
zonzo, -a ['zõzu, a] *adj* dizzy
zôo ['zou] *m* zoo
zoológico, -a [zo'lɔʒiku, a] *adj*
zoological; **jardim ~** zoo
zumbido [zũ'bidu] *m* buzz(ing); (*de
tráfego*) hum
zunzum [zũ'zũ] *m* buzz(ing)

zagueiro [za'gejru] *m* (*Futebol*) fullback
Zâmbia ['zãbja] *f* Zambia
zangado, -a [zã'gadu, a] *adj* angry;
annoyed; (*irritadiço*) bad-tempered
zangar [zã'gaʳ] *vt* to annoy, irritate ▷ *vi*
to get angry; **~-se** *vr* (*aborrecer-se*) to get
annoyed; **~-se com** to get cross with
zarpar [zax'paʳ] *vi* (*navio*) to set sail; (*ir-se*)
to set off; (*fugir*) to run away
zebra ['zebra] *f* zebra
zelador, a [zela'doʳ, a] *m/f* caretaker
zelar [ze'laʳ] *vt*, *vi*: **~ (por)** to look after
zerar [ze'raʳ] *vt* (*conta, inflação*) to reduce
to zero; (*déficit*) to pay off, wipe out
zero ['zɛru] *m* zero; (*Esporte*) nil; **zero-
quilômetro** *adj inv* brand new
ziguezague [zigi'zagi] *m* zigzag
Zimbábue [zĩ'babwi] *m*: **o ~** Zimbabwe
-zinho, -a [-'ziɲu, a] *sufixo* little;
florzinha little flower
zíper ['zipeʳ] *m* zip (BRIT), zipper (US)
zodíaco [zo'dʒiaku] *m* zodiac
zoeira ['zwejra] *f* din
zombar [zõ'baʳ] *vi* to mock; **~ de** to make
fun of; **zombaria** [zõba'ria] *f* mockery,
ridicule
zona ['zɔna] *f* area; (*de cidade*) district;
(*Geo*) zone; (*col: local de meretrício*) red-